ERISA

The Law and the Code

1995 Edition

ERISA

The Law and the Code

1995 Edition

Current Through February 1, 1995

Edited by
Michael G. Kushner
Tax Law Editor
Tax Management, Inc.

and

Dana J. Domone
Editor, BNA's Compensation and Benefits Guide
and
former staff Editor, BNA Pension Reporter

The Bureau of National Affairs, Inc., Washington, D.C.

Published by BNA Books
1250 23rd Street NW, Washington, DC 20037

International Standard Book Number: 0-87179-865-4
International Standard Serial Number: 1050-4230
Library of Congress Catalog Number: 90-644912

Printed in the United States of America

Introduction

Development of the Law

The Employee Retirement Income Security Act was signed into law by President Ford on September 2, 1974, following years of deliberation and intensive debate. The law and related tax code sections have been amended frequently since that time, as outlined below.

1980

The first major changes in the law were enacted in September 1980, when President Carter signed the Multiemployer Pension Plan Amendments Act of 1980 (P.L. 96-364).

Although ERISA itself remained virtually untouched for six years, a number of changes affecting pension and benefit plans were enacted through various tax laws that amended the qualified plan provisions of the Internal Revenue Code.

1981

In 1981, a series of savings incentive bills were introduced in Congress. Proposals were made to raise the limits on deductible contributions to individual retirement accounts and Keogh plans, encourage the adoption of employee stock ownership plans, and change the tax treatment of stock options. The retirement plan proposals and other savings incentive provisions eventually were consolidated and, in August 1981, President Reagan signed the Economic Recovery Tax Act (P.L. 97-34).

1982

In May 1982, a bill was introduced in the House to reduce the contribution and benefit limits for qualified corporate plans, modify the rules for integration with Social Security, tighten the rules for loans from plans to key employees, and limit the estate tax exclusion for retirement annuities paid to beneficiaries, among other changes. Despite opposition from the pension industry, those proposals were modified and rolled into a revenue raising package introduced in an attempt to reduce budget deficits. The revenue package became the Tax Equity and Fiscal Responsibility Act of 1982 (P.L. 97-248) and was approved by Congress in August 1982 and signed by President Reagan, only a few months after it was introduced.

1984

On July 18, 1984, the Deficit Reduction Act (P.L. 98-369) was enacted, which added and amended tax code provisions in such areas as fringe benefits, cafeteria plans, and employee welfare plans. Several weeks later, on August 23, 1984, the Retirement Equity Act (P.L. 98-397) was enacted, which amended both tax code and ERISA provisions on vesting, participation, and joint and survivor annuities. Two

ERISA provisions on vesting, participation, and joint and survivor annuities. Two other benefit laws also were enacted in 1984. P.L. 98-611 provided a two-year extension of the exclusion from gross income for educational assistance programs and P.L. 98-612 extended the exclusion for prepaid legal plans for one year.

1985

While Congress began debate on yet another tax reform law in 1985, it focused much of its attention on federal budget deficits, which resulted in passage of the Gramm-Rudman-Hollings balanced budget law (P.L. 99-177).

1986

Passage of the balanced budget law in 1985 led to some speculation during the early days of 1986 that the law could cause the death of the budget reconciliation bill then under consideration. However, the Consolidated Omnibus Budget Reconciliation Act of 1986 (P.L. 99-272) was passed by Congress and signed by President Reagan April 7 of that year. COBRA included provisions requiring the continuation of employer-sponsored group health insurance for certain individuals and their dependents. In addition, Title XI of the law amended the single-employer pension plan provisions of ERISA. Title XI is cited as the Single-Employer Pension Plan Amendments Act of 1986.

The Tax Reform Act of 1986 (P.L. 99-514) was signed by President Reagan on October 22, 1986. The 1986 Tax Reform Act made extensive changes affecting employee pension and welfare benefit plans, including amendments to the rules on non-discrimination, coverage, participation, Social Security integration, vesting, and distributions.

The 99th Congress adjourned without passing a concurrent resolution (H. Con. Res. 395) that would have made mostly technical corrections to the 1986 TRA. Most of the earlier problems with the resolution had been worked out, but it was not passed because some members of Congress wanted to include controversial, substantive provisions.

The Omnibus Budget Reconciliation Act of 1986 (P.L. 99-509) was enacted on October 21, 1986. The law requires continued benefit accruals or allocations for employees who continue to work beyond normal retirement age and requires employers to offer health insurance coverage to retirees and dependents who otherwise would lose coverage because the employer had filed for Chapter 11 bankruptcy.

1987

President Reagan signed the Omnibus Budget Reconciliation Act of 1987 (P.L. 100-203) on December 22, 1987. The law tightened the funding requirements for defined benefit pension plans and increased the premium that single employer defined benefit plans must pay to guarantee a certain level of benefits. However, provisions that would have made technical corrections were dropped before the OBRA '87 was signed into law, partly to ensure that the bill would comply with a deficit reduction agreement between the White House and Congress.

1988

President Reagan signed the Technical and Miscellaneous Revenue Act of 1988 on November 10, 1988 (P.L. 100-647). TAMRA included a number of provisions affecting employee benefits. TAMRA retained the 1989 effective date for the Code §89 non-discrimination rules, but relaxed some compliance requirements. TAMRA also amended the tax sanctions for violation of the COBRA requirements, increased the excise tax on reversions of excess plan assets, made certain clarifying amendments to pension plan rules, amended the rules of Code §457 (relating to unfunded deferred compensation arrangements for employees of governmental units and tax-exempt organizations), and extended for one year the exclusion from income of benefits from group legal service and educational assistance plans.

1989

On November 15, 1989, President Bush signed P.L. 101-140, a law that increased the public debt limit and repealed Code §89. On December 19, 1989, President Bush signed the Omnibus Budget Reconciliation Act of 1989 (P.L. 101-239). OBRA 1989 modified COBRA health care continuation coverage rules and made numerous technical corrections to prior laws. It also amended civil penalties for fiduciary violations and repealed or limited a number of provisions on employee stock ownership plans.

1990

On November 5, 1990, President Bush signed the Omnibus Budget Reconciliation Act of 1990 (P.L. 101-508). OBRA 1990 extended the sunset date for the code's tax breaks for tuition assistance and group legal service plans, increased the excise tax on reversions of excess assets to employers from plan terminations, raised plan termination insurance premiums, permitted the transfer of some excess assets to retiree health accounts, and made a number of technical changes such as eliminating obsolete provisions from the tax code.

Also in December 1990, President Bush signed P.L. 101-540, which was introduced and passed just before Congress adjourned for the November elections. The law amended Title I of ERISA to expand the definition of "employer securities" to include interests in certain publicly traded partnerships.

1991

Simplification of pension laws, expansion of retirement coverage, concern for the financial health of the Pension Benefit Guaranty Corporation, and reform of the health care system were among the topics discussed by Congress and the Bush administration throughout 1991 and 1992. However, despite the attention, only a few, minor changes to ERISA and its corresponding tax code sections were enacted during the second half of 1991.

On August 15, 1991, President Bush signed the Rural Telephone Cooperative Associations ERISA Amendments Act of 1991 (P.L. 102-89). The law removes from ERISA's definition of multiple employer welfare arrangements the welfare plans of rural telephone cooperative associations.

On December 15, 1991, President Bush signed emergency supplemental appropriations legislation (P.L. 102-229), which created a new ERISA §4001(a)(14)(C). The provision was aimed specifically at preventing Carl Icahn, chairman and chief executive officer of Trans World Airlines Inc., from escaping responsibility for TWA's pension plan underfunding.

While the Federal Deposit Insurance Corporation Improvement Act of 1991, signed by President Bush December 19, 1991 (P.L. 102-242), did not amend ERISA or its corresponding tax code sections, it did contain provisions affecting employee benefit plans. The bill allowed pass-through coverage by the Federal Deposit Insurance Corporation for benefit plan assets placed in well-capitalized financial institutions. However, pass-through coverage for bank investment contracts was eliminated. The banking bill also specified that FDIC and other successors to failed financial institutions have the same obligation under ERISA §602 to offer COBRA continuation group health coverage to former employees as the failed institution would have had if not for its failure.

On December 11, President Bush signed the Tax Extension Act of 1991 (P.L. 102-227), which extended for six months certain expiring tax provisions, including the provisions covering employer-provided educational assistance, group legal services plans, and health insurance costs of self-employed individuals. However, the six months lapsed without the provisions being extended again or made permanent; the provisions expired at the end of June 1992. (The exclusion for educational assistance was later extended through December 31, 1994).

1992

On July 3, 1992, President Bush signed unemployment benefits legislation (P.L. 102-318) that was funded, in part, by a withholding tax on certain pension plan distributions. The law, the Unemployment Compensation Amendments of 1992, allows any portion of most distributions from a qualified pension plan or annuity or a tax-sheltered annuity to be rolled over tax free into an IRA or another qualified plan or annuity. In addition, the law requires qualified plans to permit participants to elect to have any distribution eligible for rollover treatment transferred directly to an eligible transferee plan designated by the participant.

On October 24, 1992, President Bush signed the Comprehensive National Energy Policy Act of 1992 (P.L. 102-486), which includes a provision on the funding of health benefits for retired coal miners. The law requires companies who were party to labor agreements with the United Mine Workers of America as far back as 1950 to cover retiree health costs. In addition, excess union pension funds and interest on monies in the abandoned mine land reclamation fund would be transferred to the union's health benefit fund. Also, the law allows excess assets in qualified black lung benefit trusts to be used to pay accident and health premiums for retired miners. Another provision of the law expanded the exclusion from taxable income for employer-provided transit subsidies while limiting the exclusion for employer-provided parking.

1993

On August 10, 1993, President Clinton signed the Omnibus Budget Reconciliation Act of 1993 (P.L. 103-66), which lowered the amount of compensation that could be taken into account in calculating benefit accruals or allocations under qualified retirement plans. OBRA '93 extended retroactively the income tax exclusion for employer-provided educational assistance and the health insurance deduction for self-employed individuals, from June 30, 1992, through December 31, 1993. The law changed the fringe benefit treatment of moving expenses, required group health plans to honor child medical support orders, and required group health plans to continue to offer pediatric vaccines.

1994

On December 8, 1994, President Clinton signed the Retirement Protection Act, which was passed as part of the Uruguay Round Agreements Act (P.L. 103-465). That Act significantly tightened the funding rules for underfunded defined benefit pension plans that are subject to the minimum funding standard of the Code and ERISA. The Retirement Protection Act also extended the sunset date through the year 2000 for Code §420, which allows the transfer of certain excess pension assets from qualified defined benefit pension plans to individual medical accounts within such plans and required the rounding of certain annual limitations on benefits and contributions under retirement-type plans that are indexed annually for changes in the cost of living. In addition, 1994 saw the enactment of the Pension Annuitants' Protection Act (P.L. 103-401) which, by enacting ERISA §502(a)(9), clarified that individuals and the Labor Department could bring suit for a failure to provide the annuitized benefits called for under ERISA to former participants and beneficiaries of terminated defined benefit pension plans. Finally, 1994 saw the enactment of the Social Security Administrative Reform Act of 1994 (P.L. 103-296), which established the Social Security Administration as an independent federal agency and made appropriate conforming changes to the Code, and the Social Security Domestic Employment Reform Act (P.L. 103-387, also known as the "Nanny tax") which eliminated the need to withhold certain employment taxes on domestic workers who earn less than $1,000 from the employer per year.

Organization of This Book

The material that follows includes as Part 1 the text of excerpts from the committee reports on the Unemployment Compensation Amendments, the Comprehensive National Energy Policy Act, the Social Security Administrative Reform Act, the Social Security Domestic Employment Reform Act, and the Retirement Protection Act. Additional earlier legislative histories, including excerpts from conference reports on the Omnibus Budget Reconciliation Act of 1987, the Technical and Miscellaneous Revenue Act of 1988, the Section 89 Employee Benefit Plan Nondiscrimination and Qualification Rule Repeal Amendment, the Omnibus Budget Reconciliation Act of 1989, and the Omnibus Budget Reconciliation Act of 1990, are contained in a companion BNA book, *ERISA: Selected Legislative History, 1974-1991.*

Part 2 of this book includes the text of ERISA as amended.

Part 3 contains pertinent sections of the Internal Revenue Code.

Part 4 is an index to ERISA and the Internal Revenue Code. In addition, this edition is cross-indexed to regulations printed in the BNA book ERISA Regulations, 1994 Edition, edited by Michael Kushner.

Provisions of ERISA and the Internal Revenue Code that were deleted are enclosed within boldface brackets [ ]. Provisions that were added are in italics. Editor's notes appear in the text next to the subsection of the law or code to which they pertain, separated from the text by a row of diamonds.

* * *

ACKNOWLEDGEMENT

The editor wishes to express his gratitude to the following individuals for their work in the development, editing and production of this book: Roger Long, Randy Auerbach, Timothy Darby and Janet Yurkovic.

Contents

Part 1—Committee Reports

Part 2—Text of ERISA

Part 3—IRC Excerpts

Part 4—Index

ERISA Finding List

Section

U.S.C. ERISA

Part 3 — Funding

Part 4 — Fiduciary Responsibility

Section

U.S.C.   ERISA

Part 5 — Administration and Enforcement

Section
U.S.C. ERISA

Title II — Amendments to the Internal Revenue Code
Relating to Retirement Plans

Subtitle A — Participation, Vesting, Funding, Administration, etc.

Part 1 — Participation, Vesting, and Funding

* * *

* * *

* * *

Section
U.S.C.   ERISA

Subtitle B — Joint Pension, Profit-Sharing, and Employee Stock Ownership Plan Task Force; Studies

Part 1 — Joint Pension, Profit-Sharing, and Employee Stock Ownership Plan Task Force

Part 2 — Other Studies

Subtitle C — Enrollment of Actuaries

Title IV — Plan Termination Insurance

Subtitle A — Pension Benefit Guaranty Corporation

Subtitle E — Special Provisions for Multiemployer Plans

Part 1 — Employer Withdrawals

Section

U.S.C. ERISA

Part 2 — Merger or Transfer of Plan Assets or Liabilities

Part 3 — Reorganization; Minimum Contribution Requirement for Multiemployer Plans

Section

U.S.C.   ERISA

IRC Finding List

Subtitle A — Income Taxes
Chapter 1—Normal Taxes and Surtaxes
Subchapter A — Determination of Tax Liability
* * *

Subchapter B — Computation of Taxable Income
* * *

Part I — Definition of Gross Income, Adjusted Gross Income, Taxable Income, Etc.

* * *

Part II — Items Specifically Included in Gross Income
* * *

* * *

* * *

* * *

* * *

Part III — Items Specifically Excluded From Gross Income
* * *

IRC Section

IRC Section

Subchapter D — Deferred Compensation, Etc.

Part I — Pension, Profit-Sharing, Stock Bonus Plans, Etc.

Subpart A — General Rule

IRC Section

IRC Section

Part II — Certain Stock Options

* * *

Subchapter E — Accounting Periods and Methods of Accounting

* * *

Part II — Methods of Accounting

* * *

Subpart B — Taxable Year for Which Items of Gross Income Included

* * *

Subchapter F — Exempt Organizations

Part I — General Rule

* * *

* * *

* * *

Part III — Taxation of business income of certain exempt organizations

IRC Section

IRC Section

* * *

IRC Section

* * *

IRC Section

IRC Section

Subchapter B — Assessable Penalties

Chapter 76 — Judicial Proceedings

* * *

Subchapter B — Proceedings by Taxpayers and Third Parties

* * *

Subchapter C — The Tax Court

* * *

Part IV — Declaratory Judgments

IRC Section

* * *

Chapter 79 — Definitions

* * *

Chapter 80 — General Rules

Subchapter A — Application of Internal Revenue Laws

* * *

Subtitle J — Coal Industry Health Benefits

Chapter 99 — Coal Industry Health Benefits

Subchapter A — Definitions of General Applicability

IRC Section

* * *

IRC Section

Subchapter D — Other Provisions

Part 1

Committee Reports

For pre-1992 legislative history, see *ERISA: Selective Legislative History, 1974–1991* (BNA Books, 1992).

Excerpts From the Joint Explanatory Statement of the Committee of Conference on the Unemployment Compensation Amendments of 1992 (H.R. Conf. Rep. No. 102-650)

The managers on the part of the House and the Senate at the conference on the disagreeing votes of the two Houses on the amendment of the Senate to the bill (H.R. 5260) to extend the emergency unemployment compensation program, to revise the trigger provisions contained in the extended unemployment compensation program, and for other purposes, submit the following joint statement to the House and the Senate in explanation of the effect of the action agreed upon by the managers and recommended in the accompanying conference report:

* * *

V. FINANCING PROVISIONS

* * *

3. Rollover and Withholding on Nonperiodic Pension Distributions

* * *

Present Law

Distributions from tax-qualified pension plans (sec. 401(a)), qualified annuity plant (sec. 403(a)), and tax-sheltered annuities (sec. 403(b)) generally are included in gross income in the year paid or distributed under the rules relating to the taxation of annuities. A total or partial distribution of the balance to the credit of an employee may, under certain circumstances, be rolled over tax free to another plan or annuity or to an individual retirement arrangement (IRA).

For purposes of the rule denying rollover treatment in the case of certain periodic payments, payments made before, with, or after the commencement of the periodic payments are not treated as part of the series of periodic payments.

Income tax withholding on pension distributions is required unless the payee elects not to have withholding apply. If not election is made, tax is withheld from nonperiodic payments at a 10-percent rate, unless the payments are part of a qualified total distribution, in which case tables published by the Internal Revenue Service are used to determine the withholding rate. A qualified total distribution generally is a payment within one year of the entire interest in a plan.

House Bill.

No provision.

Senate Amendment.

Under the Senate amendment, any part of the taxable portion of a distribution form a qualified pension or annuity plan or a tax-sheltered annuity (other than a minimum required distribution) can be rolled over tax free to an IRA or another qualified plan or annuity, unless the distribution is one of a series of substantially equal payments made (1) over the life (or joint life expectancies) of the participant and his or her beneficiary, or (2) over a specified period of 10 years or more.

For purposes of the rule denying rollover treatment in the case of certain periodic payments, a single-sum payment that is not substantially equal to the period payments that is made before, with, or after the commencement of the periodic payments is not treated as one of the series of periodic payments. For example, if an employee receives 30 percent of his or her accrued benefit in the form of single-sum distribution upon retirement with the balance payable in annuity form, the amount of the single-sum distribution can be rolled over.

A qualified retirement or annuity plan must permit participants to elect to have any distribution that is eligible for rollover treatment transferred directly to an eligible transferee plan specified by the participant.

Withholding is imposed at a rate of 20 percent on any distribution that is eligible to be rolled over but that is not transferred directly to an eligible transferee plan. Payees cannot elect to forgo withholding with respect to such distributions.

Plan amendments required under the provision do not have to be made before the first plan year beginning on or after January 1, 1994, if the plan is operated in accordance with the provision and the amendment applies retroactively.

Effective Date

The provision is effective for distributions after December 31, 1992.

Conference Agreement

The conference agreement follows the Senate amendment, with modifications.

The conference agreement provides that the plan administrator must provide a written explanation to a recipient of his or her distribution options (including the direct trustee-to-trustee transfer option) within a reasonable period of time before making an eligible rollover distribution. The Secretary of the Treasury is directed to develop a model notice.

The administrator may require that a recipient electing a direct trustee-to-trustee transfer provide adequate information in a timely manner regarding the eligible retirement plan to which the transfer is to be made. The transferor plan and its administrator will not be subject to penalties or liability because of reasonable reliance on such information provided by a recipient, and is not required to independently verify such information. As under the Senate amendment and present law, a qualified retirement plan is not required to accept a direct trustee-to-trustee transfer.

The direct trustee-to-trustee transfer option is considered a distribution option, so that spousal consent and other similar participant and beneficiary protection rules apply. Because a direct transfer generally is considered a distribution from the transferor plan, rights and options available under the transferor plan need not be preserved under the transferee plan.

The conference agreement clarifies that the explicit exclusion from gross income of amounts transferred in a direct trustee-to-trustee transfer in accordance with the provision is not intended to affect the treatment of direct transfers under other provisions of the Code.

Under the conference agreement, in the case of section 403(b) tax-sheltered annuity plans maintained by State and local governments which are prohibited under State law from making direct trustee-to-trustee transfers, the provisions relating to trustee-to-trustee transfers and withholding do not apply to distributions before the earlier of (1) January 1, 1994, or (2) 90 days after the date on which the State law is amended to permit such transfers.

* * *

Excerpts From the Joint Explanatory Statement of the Committee of Conference on the Comprehensive National Energy Policy Act of 1992 (H.R. Conf. Rep. No. 102-1018)

The managers on the part of the House and the Senate at the conference on the disagreeing votes of the two Houses on the amendments of the Senate to the bill (H.R. 776) to provide for improved energy efficiency submit the following joint statement to the House and the Senate in explanation of the action agreed upon by the managers and recommended in the accompanying conference report.

* * *

TITLE XIX—ENERGY REVENUE PROVISIONS

A. Energy Conservation and Production Incentives

1. Employer-provided Transportation Benefits

Present Law

Under Treasury regulations, transit passes, tokens, fare cards, vouchers, and cash reimbursements provided by an employer to defray an employee's commuting costs are excludable from the employee's income (for both income and payroll tax purposes) as a de minimis fringe benefit if the total value of the benefit does not exceed $21 per month. If the total value of the benefit exceeds $21 per month, the full value of the benefit is includible in income.

Parking at or near the employer's business premises that is paid for by the employer is excludable from the income of the employee (for both income and payroll tax purposes) as a working condition fringe benefit, regardless of the value of the parking. This exclusion does not apply to any parking facility or space located on property owned or leased by the employee for residential purposes.

House Bill

Under the House bill, gross income and wages (for both income and payroll tax purposes) does not include qualified transportation fringe benefits. In general, a qualified transportation fringe is (1) transportation in a commuter highway vehicle if such transportation is in connection with travel between the employee's residence and place of employment, (2) a transit pass, or (3) qualified parking. Cash reimbursements made by the employer for such expenses under a bona fide reimbursement arrangement also qualify for the exclusion.

The maximum amount of qualified parking that is excludable from an employee's gross income is $160 per month (regardless of the total value of the parking). Other qualified transportation fringes are excludable from gross income to the extent that the aggregate value of the benefits does not exceed $60 per month (regardless of the total value of the benefits). The $60 and $160 limits are indexed for inflation, rounded down to the next whole dollar.

A commuter highway vehicle is a highway vehicle with the capacity to seat at least 6 adults (not including the driver) and at least 80 percent of the mileage use of which is for transporting employees between their residences and their place of employment using at least one-half of the adult seating capacity of the vehicle (not including the driver). Transportation furnished in a commuter highway vehicle operated by or for the employer is considered provided by the employer.

A transit pass includes any pass, token, fare-card, voucher, or similar item entitling a person to transportation on mass transit facilities (whether publicly or privately owned). Types of transit facilities that may qualify for the exclusion include, for example, rail, bus, and ferry.

Qualified parking is parking provided to an employee on or near the business premises of the employer, or on or near a location from which the employee commutes to work by mass transit, in a commuter highway vehicle, or by carpool. As under present law, the exclusion does not apply to any parking facility or space located on property owned or leased by the employee for residential purposes.

Effective Date

The provision applies to benefits provided by the employer on or after January 1, 1993.

Senate Amendment

The Senate amendment is generally the same as the House bill, except that the parking cap is $145 per month, rather than $160 per month. In addition, the $60 and $145 limits are indexed for inflation in $5 increments.

Under the Senate amendment, cash reimbursements for transit passes do not qualify for the transit exclusion if vouchers that are exchangeable only for transit passes are readily available to the employer.

Effective Date.

Same as the House bill.

Conference Agreement

The conference agreement follows the Senate amendment, except that the parking cap is $155 per month.

* * *

B. Revenue-Offset Provisions

* * *

6. Deduction For Moving Expenses

Present Law

An employee or self-employed individual may deduct from gross income certain expenses incurred as a result of moving to a new residence in connection with beginning work at a new location. For a taxpayer to claim a moving expense deduction, the new principal place of work has to be at least 35 miles farther from his or her former residence than was the former principal place of work (or his or her former residence, if he or she has no former place of work).

House Bill

No provision.

Senate Amendment

The Senate amendment increases the mileage threshold for the moving expense deduction to 55 miles.

Effective date

Taxable years beginning after December 31, 1992.

Conference Agreement

The conference agreement does not include the Senate amendment.

* * *

14. Deny Deduction for Travel Expenses Paid or Incurred in Connection with Employment Lasting One Year or More

Present Law

Unreimbursed ordinary and necessary travel expenses paid or incurred by an individual in connection with temporary employment away from home (e.g., transportation costs, and the cost of meals and lodging) are generally deductible, subject to the two-percent floor on miscellaneous itemized deductions. Travel expenses paid or incurred in connection with indefinite employment away from home, however, are not deductible.[22]

The position of the Internal Revenue Service as to whether employment is temporary or indefinite is as follows:

(1) If a taxpayer anticipates employment to last for less than one year, whether such employment is temporary or indefinite will be determined on the basis of the facts and circumstances.

(2) If a taxpayer anticipates employment to last for one year or more and that employment does, in fact, last for one year or more, there is a presumption that the employment is not temporary but rather is indefinite, and that the taxpayer is not away from home during the indefinite period of employment. However, under certain circumstances, this one-year presumption of indefiniteness may be rebutted where the employment is expected to, and does, last for one year or more, but less than two years.

(3) An expected or actual stay of two years or longer will be considered an indefinite stay, regardless of any other facts and circumstances.[23]

House Bill

No provision.

Senate Amendment

No provision. (However, H.R. 11 as amended by the Senate contains the same provision that is included in the conference report below.)

Conference Agreement

The conference agreement treats a taxpayer's employment away from home in a single location as indefinite rather than temporary if it lasts for one year or more. Thus, no deduction would be permitted for travel expenses paid or incurred in connection with such employment. As under present law, if a taxpayer's employment away from home in a single location lasts for less than one year, whether such employment is temporary or indefinite would be determined on the basis of the facts and circumstances. This change is not intended to alter present law with respect to volunteer individuals providing voluntary services to charities described in section 501(c)(3).

Effective Date

The provision is effective for costs paid or incurred after December 31, 1992.

* * *

16. Use of 501(c)(21) Black Lung Trust Assets to Fund Retiree Health Benefits

Present Law

A qualified black lung benefit trust described in section 501(c)(21) of the Internal Revenue Code is exempt from Federal income taxation. In addition, a deduction is allowed for contributions to a qualified black lung benefit trust to the extent such contributions are necessary to fund the trust.

Under present law, no assets of a qualified black lung benefit trust may be used for, or diverted to, any purpose other than (1) to satisfy liabilities, or pay insurance premiums to cover liabilities, arising under the Black Lung Acts, (2) to pay administrative costs of operating the trust, or (3) investment in U.S., State, or local securities and obligations, or in time demand deposits in a bank or insured credit union.

Under present law, excess trust assets may be paid into the national Black Lung Disability Trust Fund, or into the general fund of the U.S. Treasury.

House Bill

No provision in H.R. 776. (However, H.R. 11 as passed by the House included the provision described in the conference agreement below.)

Senate Amendment

No provision in H.R. 776. (However, H.R. 11 as passed by the Senate included the provision described in the conference agreement below.)

Conference Agreement

The conference agreement allows excess assets in qualified black lung benefit trusts to be used to pay accident and health benefits or premiums for insurance for such benefits (including administrative and other incidental expenses relating to such benefits) for retired coal miners and their spouses and dependents. The amount of assets available for such purpose is subject to a yearly limit as well as an aggregate limit. The yearly limit is to be the amount of assets in excess of 110 percent of the present value of the liability for black lung benefits determined as of the close of the preceding taxable year of the trust. The aggregate limit is the amount of assets in excess of 110 percent of the present value of the liability for black lung benefits determined as of the close of the taxable year of the trust ending prior to the effective date, plus earnings thereon. Each of these determinations is required to be made by an independent actuary.

The amounts used to pay retiree accident or health benefits are not includible in the income of the company, nor is a deduction allowed for such amounts.

Effective Date.

The provision is effective for taxable years beginning after December 31, 1991.

* * *

C. Health Benefits for Retired Coal Miners

Present Law

The United Mine Workers of America (UMWA) health and retirement funds were established in 1974 pursuant to an agreement between the UMWA and the Bituminous Coal Operator's Association (BCOA) to provide pension and health benefits to retired coal miners and their dependents. The funds have been maintained for this purpose through a series of collective bargaining agreements. The funds created in 1974 were a restructuring of the original benefit fund, which was established in 1946.

The funds consist of four different plans, each of which is funded through a separate trust. The 1950 Pension Plan provides retirement benefits to miners who retired on or before December 31, 1975, and their beneficiaries. The 1950 Benefit Plan provides health benefits for retired mine workers who receive pensions from the 1950 Pension Plan and their dependents. The 1974 Pension Plan provides retirement benefits to miners who retire after December 31, 1975, and their beneficiaries. The 1974 Benefit Plan provides health benefits to miners who retire after December 31, 1975. It also provides health benefits to miners whose last employers are no longer in business or, in some cases, no longer signatory to the applicable bargaining agreement. These miners are generally referred to as "orphan" retirees.

The Surface Mining Control and Reclamation Act of 1977, as amended, imposes a reclamation fee on coal mining operators, payable quarterly to the Secretary of the Interior for deposit in the Abandoned Mine Reclamation Fund (the AML Fund). The fee generally is the lesser of (1) 35 cents per ton of coal produced by surface coal mining and 15 cents per ton of coal produced by underground mine or (2) 10 percent of the value of the coal at the mine. The fee for lignite is the lesser of 2 percent of the value of the coal at the mine or 10 cents per ton. The reclamation fee is scheduled to expire after September 30, 1995.

House Bill

The House bill extends the abandoned mine reclamation fee through September 30, 2010.

Effective Date.

Date of enactment.

Senate Amendment

The Senate amendment provides that the 1950 Benefit Plan and the 1974 Benefit Plan are to be merged into a new UNWA Combined Benefit Fund ("Combined Fund") to provide health and death benefits for eligible retirees and their dependents. The Combined Fund is to be finances primarily by health benefit premiums, death benefit premiums, and unassigned beneficiaries premiums imposed on assigned operators. The Combined Fund will receive additional funding from transfers from the 1950 Pension Plan and the AML Fund. The amendment also creates a 1992 Benefit Fund to provide benefits for persons not eligible under the Combined Fund.

The Senate amendment extends the abandoned mine reclamation fund fee through September 30, 2004.

Conference Agreement

The Conference agreement follows the Senate amendment.

FOOTNOTES

[22] *Peurifoy v. Commissioner*, 358 U.S. 59 (1958), *aff'g* 254 F.2d 483 (4th Cir. 1957), *rev'g* 27 T.C. 149 (1957).

[23] Rev. Rul. 83-82, 1983-1 C.B. 45.

Excerpts From the Joint Explanatory Statement of the Committee of Conference on the Omnibus Budget Reconciliation Act of 1993 (H. R. Conf. Rep. No. 103-213)

The managers on the part of the House and the Senate at the conference on the disagreeing votes of the two Houses on the amendment of the Senate to the bill (H.R. 2264) to provide for reconciliation pursuant to section 7 of the concurrent resolution on the budget for fiscal year 1994, submit the following joint statement to the House and the Senate in explanation of the effect of the action agreed upon by the managers and recommended in the accompanying conference report:

The Senate amendment struck all of the House bill after the enacting clause and inserted a substitute text.

The House recedes from its disagreement to the amendment of the Senate with an amendment that is a substitute for the House bill and the Senate amendment. The differences between the House bill, the Senate amendment, and the substitute agreed to in conference are noted below, except for clerical corrections, conforming changes made necessary by agreements reached by the conferees, and minor drafting and clerical changes.

* * *

TITLE IV—STUDENT LOAN AND ERISA PROVISIONS

* * *

COORDINATION OF ERISA PREEMPTION RULES

House Bill

Section 4201 of the House bill amended section 514(b)(8) of ERISA to exempt from preemption certain additional provisions of state laws.

In 1986, ERISA was amended to add subsection (b)(8) in order to facilitate the ability of the states to assure that Medicaid was the secondary payor for all eligible individuals also covered under group health plans. Under the amendments to title XIX of the Social Security Act contained in Title V of the House bill, additional requirements relating to third-party payors are imposed on the states as a condition of receiving Federal matching Medicaid funds. The amendments to ERISA under section 4201 permit states to enforce laws enacted as a result of these additional Medicaid requirements.

Senate Amendment

Similar to House bill.

Conference Agreement

The Senate recedes with an amendment.

Under the conference agreement, group health plans are required to pay benefits in accordance with any assignments of rights on behalf of participants and beneficiaries that is required by Title XIX of the Social Security Act. In enrolling individuals under group health plans, plans are precluded from taking into account the fact that an individual is eligible for or provided assistance under Title XIX.

In addition, under the conference agreement and consistent with provisions Title V of this Act, to the extent that payment has been made under Title XIX, states would acquire the right of any other party to payment. State laws enforcing these rights must be honored by group health plans since those laws would be exempt from ERISA's preemption.

MEDICAL CHILD SUPPORT ORDERS

House Bill

No provision.

Senate Amendment

Section 12301(a) of the Senate Amendment amends section 514(b)(8) of ERISA to require group health plans to comply with state laws relating to assignment of rights of payment and child health insurance support.

Conference Agreement

The House recedes with an amendment.

Under the Conference Agreement, group health plans are required to honor "qualified medical child support orders." The term "medical child support order" means generally any judgment, decree, or order (including approval of a settlement agreement) issued by a court of competent jurisdiction providing for child support or health benefit coverage for a child of a participant. The child on whose behalf such an order is issued is an "alternative recipient" and will be treated as a participant under the plans. An order is "qualified" and must be honored by the plan if it meets certain specified requirements.

In addition, group health plans that provide for coverage for dependent children must treat dependent children placed for adoption in the home of participants under the plan the same as dependent children who are the natural children of participants, irrespective of whether that adoption has become final. For purposes of these provisions, a child is defined as an individual who has not attained age 18 as of the date of adoption or placement for adoption.

MEDICAL AND MEDICAID COVERAGE DATA BANK

House Bill

Section 5117 of the House Bill, as reported by the Committee on Energy and Commerce, established a Health Coverage Clearinghouse in order to identify third parties which may be liable for payment as primary payors for health care items and services for Medicaid beneficiaries. Under the House Bill, qualified employers are required to provide information to the clearinghouse with respect to every individual who has received wages from such employers and for whom group health plan coverage is available. The information to be provided includes the name and taxpayer identification number of the individual, the name, address, and taxpayer identification number of the employer, and whether the employer has made available group health plan coverage for the individual and his or her family.

Senate Amendment

Sections 7904 and 12101 of the Senate Amendment (as reported by the Senate Finance and Senate Labor and Human Resources Committee, respectively) establish similar clearinghouses and impose similar requirements on employers.

Conference Agreement

A full description of the Conference Agreement appears in the statement of managers describing section 13581. Conforming amendments to ERISA, ensuring that group health plans furnish required data needed for employer compliance, are adopted as part of section 4301 of the Conference Agreement.

TITLE XIII—REVENUE, HEALTH CARE, HUMAN RESOURCES, CUSTOMS AND TRADE PROVISIONS, FOOD STAMP PROGRAM, AND TIMBER SALES PROVISIONS

CHAPTER 1—REVENUE PROVISIONS

I. TRAINING AND INVESTMENT PROVISIONS

A. Education and Training Provisions

1. Extension of employer-provided educational assistance (sec. 14101 of the House Bill, sec. 8101 of the Senate Amendment, sec. 13101 of the Conference Agreement, and sec. 127 of the Code)

Present law

Prior to July 1, 1992, an employee's gross income and wages for income and employment tax purposes did not include amounts paid or incurred by the employer for educational assistance provided to the employee if such amounts were paid or incurred pursuant to an educational assistance program that met certain requirements (sec. 127). This exclusion, which expired with respect to amounts paid after June 30, 1992, was limited to $5,250 of educational assistance with respect to an individual during a calendar year. Education that did not qualify for the exclusion (e.g., because it exceeded the $5,250 limit) was excludable from income if and only if it qualified as a working condition fringe benefit (sec. 132). To be excluded as a working condition fringe, the cost of the education must have been a job-related deductible expense.

In the absence of the exclusion, for purposes of income and employment taxes, an employee generally is required to include in income and wages the value of educational assistance provided by the employer unless the cost of such assistance qualifies as a deductible job-related expense of the employee.

House Bill

The House Bill retroactively and permanently extends the exclusion for employer-provided educational assistance.

The House Bill includes a number of transition rules to deal with cases in which employers provided educational assistance to employees between July 1, 1992, and December 31, 1992. First, no interest, penalty, or addition to tax is imposed on employers or employees who continued to exclude from income educational assistance payments made after June 30, 1992. Second, if an employer included educational assistance payments made after June 30, 1992, in its employees' income and wages (for purposes of income or employment taxes) the amount included is deducted from income and wages paid in 1993 rather than requiring the taxpayers to file a request for refund for 1992.

The House Bill also clarifies the rule under which educational assistance that does not satisfy section 127 may be excluded from income if and only if it meets the requirements of a working condition fringe benefit.

Effective Date

The extension of the exclusion is effective for taxable years ending after June 30, 1992. The clarification to the working condition fringe benefit rule is effective for taxable years beginning after December 31, 1988.

Senate Amendment

The Senate Amendment is the same as the House Bill except that the exclusion is extended retroactively and through June 30, 1994, and the Senate Amendment does not contain special rules for educational assistance provided between July 1, 1992, and December 31, 1992.

Effective Date

The Senate Amendment is the same as the House Bill.

Conference Agreement

The Conference Agreement follows the Senate Amendment, except that the exclusion for employer-provided educational assistance is extended retroactively and through December 31, 1994.

The conferees intend that the Secretary will use his existing authority to the fullest extent possible to alleviate any administrative problems that may result from the expiration and retroactive extension of the exclusion and to facilitate in the simplest way possible the recoupment of excess taxes paid with respect to educational assistance provided in the last half of 1992.

Effective Date

The Conference Agreement follows the Senate Amendment.

* * *

D. Real Estate Investment Provisions

* * *

4. Changes relating to real estate investments by pension funds and others (secs. 14144-14149 of the House Bill, secs. 8144-8149 of the Senate Amendment, and secs. 13144-13149 of the Conference Agreement)

* * *

f. Relaxation of limitations on investments in real estate investment trusts by pension funds (sec. 14149 of the House Bill, sec. 8149 of the Senate Amendment, sec. 13149 of the Conference Agreement, and sec. 856(h) of the Code)

Present Law

A real estate investment trust ("REIT") is not taxed on income distributed to shareholders. A corporation does not qualify as a REIT if at any time during the last half of its taxable year more than 50 percent in value of its outstanding stock is owned, directly or indirectly, by five or fewer individuals ("the five or fewer rule"). A domestic pension trust is treated as a single individual for purposes of this rule.

Dividends paid by a REIT are not UBTI,[8] unless the stock in the REIT is debt-financed. Depending on its character, income earned by a partnership may be UBTI (sec. 512(c)). Special rules treat debt-financed income earned by a partnership as UBTI (sec. 514(c)(9)(B)(vi)).

House Bill

Qualification as a REIT

The House Bill provides that a pension trust generally is not treated as a single individual for purposes of the five-or-fewer rule. Rather, the bill treats beneficiaries of the pension trust as holding stock in the REIT in proportion to their actuarial interests in the trust. This rule does not apply if disqualified persons, within the meaning of section 4975(e)(2) (other than by reason of subparagraphs (B) and (I)), together own five percent or more of the value of the REIT stock and the REIT has earnings and profits attributable to a period during which it did not qualify as a REIT.[9]

In addition, the bill provides that a REIT cannot be a personal holding company and, therefore, is not subject to the personal holding company tax on its undistributed income.

Unrelated Business Taxable Income

Under the bill, certain pension trusts owning more than 10 percent of a REIT must treat a percentage of dividends from the REIT as UBTI. This percentage is the gross income derived from an unrelated trade or business (determined as if the REIT were a pension trust) divided by the gross income of the REIT for the year in which the dividends are paid. Dividends are not treated as UBTI, however, unless this percentage is at least five percent.

The UBTI rule applies only if the REIT qualifies as a REIT by reason of the above modification of the five or fewer rule. Moreover, the UBTI rule applies only if (1) one pension trust owns more than 25 percent of the value of the REIT, or (2) a group of pension trusts individually holding more than 10 percent of the value of the REIT collectively own more than 50 percent of the value of the REIT.

Effective Date

The provision applies to taxable years beginning on or after January 1, 1994.

Senate Amendment

The Senate Amendment is the same as the House Bill.

Conference Agreement

The Conference Agreement follows the House Bill and the Senate Amendment.

* * *

II. REVENUE-RAISING PROVISIONS

A. Individual Income and Estate and Gift Tax Provisions

* * *

3. Repeal health insurance wage base cap (sec. 14207 of the House Bill, sec. 8207 of the Senate Amendment, sec. 13207 of the Conference Agreement, and sec. 3121(x) of the Code)

Present Law

As part of the Federal Insurance Contributions Act (FICA), a tax is imposed on employees and employers up to a maximum amount of employee wages. The tax is comprised of two parts: old-age, survivor, and disability insurance (OASDI) and Medicare hospital insurance (HI). For wages paid in 1993 to covered employees, the HI tax rate is 1.45 percent on both the employer and the employee on the first $135,000 of wages and the OASDI tax rate is 6.2 percent on both the employer and the employee on the first $57,600 of wages.

Under the Self-Employment Contributions Act of 1954 (SECA), a tax is imposed on an individual's self-employment income. The self-employment tax rate is the same as the total rate for employers and employees (i.e., 2.9 percent for HI and 12.40 percent for OASDI). For 1993, the HI tax is applied to the first $135,000 of self-employment income and the OASDI tax is applied to the first $57,600 self-employment income. In general, the tax is reduced to the extent that the individual had wages for which employment taxes were withheld during the year.

The cap on wages and self-employment income subject to FICA and SECA taxes is indexed to changes in the average wages in the economy.

House Bill

The bill repeals the dollar limit on wages and self-employment income subject to HI taxes.

Effective Date

The provision is effective for wages and income received after December 31, 1993.

Senate Amendment

The Senate Amendment is the same as the House Bill. The legislative history to the Senate Amendment expresses the concern of the Senate that HI taxes paid by high-income workers under the provision would bear little relation to Medicare benefits such workers could expect to receive, and that this may make the HI program look more like welfare than social insurance. It is suggested that it may be appropriate to revisit the issue in the context of health care reform or Medicare financing improvements.

Effective Date

The Senate Amendment is the same as the House Bill.

Conference Agreement

The Conference Agreement follows the House Bill and the Senate Amendment.

* * *

7. Deny deduction for executive pay over $1 million (sec. 14211 of the House Bill, sec. 8211 of the Senate Amendment, sec. 13211 of the Conference Agreement, and sec. 162 of the Code)

Present Law

An employer is allowed a deduction for reasonable salaries and other compensation. Whether compensation is reasonable is determinèd on a case-by-case basis. However, the reasonableness standard has been used primarily to limit payments by closely-held companies where nondeductible dividends may be disguised as deductible compensation.

House Bill

In general

Under the House Bill, for purposes of the regular income tax and the alternative minimum tax, the otherwise allowable deduction for compensation paid or accrued with respect to a covered employee of a publicly held corporation is limited to no more than $1 million per year.

Certain types of compensation are not subject to the deduction limit and are not taken into account in determining whether other compensation exceeds $1 million. The following types of compensation are not taken into account: (1) remuneration payable on a commission basis; (2) remuneration payable solely on account of the attainment of one or more performance goals if certain independent director and shareholder approval requirements are met; (3) payments to a tax-qualified retirement plan (including salary reduction contributions); (4) amounts that are excludable from the executive's gross income (such as employer-provided health benefits and miscellaneous fringe benefits (sec. 132)); and (5) any remuneration payable under a written binding contract which was in effect on February 17, 1993, and all times thereafter before such remuneration was paid and which was not modified thereafter in any material respect before such remuneration was paid.

Effective Date

The House Bill applies to compensation that is otherwise deductible by the corporation in a taxable year beginning on or after January 1, 1994.

Senate Amendment

The Senate Amendment is the same as the House Bill, except that the Senate Amendment refers to "outside" directors rather than "independent" directors and there are some minor differences in the legislative history.

Effective Date

The Senate Amendment is the same as the House Bill.

Conference Agreement

In general

The Conference Agreement follows the Senate Amendment, with certain modifications and clarifications.

Under the Conference Agreement, for purposes of the regular income tax and the alternative minimum tax, the otherwise allowable deduction for compensation paid or accrued with respect to a covered employee of a publicly held corporation is limited to no more than $1 million per year.[44]

Definition of publicly held corporation

For purposes of this provision, a corporation is treated as publicly held if the corporation has a class of common equity securities that is required to be registered under section 12 of the Securities Exchange Act of 1934. In general, the Securities Exchange Act requires a corporation to register its common equity securities under section 12 if (1) the securities are listed on a national securities exchange or (2) the corporation has $5 million or more of assets and 500 or more holders of such securities. A corporation is not considered publicly held under the provision if registration of its equity securities is voluntary. Such a voluntary registration might occur, for example, if a corporation that otherwise is not required to register its equity securities does so in order to take advantage of other procedures with regard to public offerings of debt securities.

Covered Employees

Covered employees are defined by reference to the Securities and Exchange Commission (SEC) rules governing disclosure of executive compensation. Thus, with respect to a taxable year, a person is a covered employee if (1) the employee is the chief executive officer of the corporation (or an individual acting in such capacity) as of the close of the taxable year or (2) the employee's total compensation is required to be reported for the taxable year under the Securities Exchange Act of 1934 because the employee is one of the four highest compensated officers for the taxable year (other than the chief executive officer). If disclosure is required with respect to fewer than four executives (other than the chief executive officer) under the SEC rules, then only those for whom disclosure is required are covered employees.

Compensation subject to the deduction limitation

In general

Unless specifically excluded, the deduction limitation applies to all remuneration for services, including cash and the cash value of all remuneration (including benefits) paid in a medium other than cash. If an individual is a covered employee for a taxable year, the deduction limitation applies to all compensation not explicitly excluded from the deduction limitation, regardless of whether the compensation is for services as a covered employee and regardless of when the compensation was earned. The $1 million cap is reduced by excess parachute payments (as defined in sec. 280G) that are not deductible by the corporation.

The deduction limitation applies when the deduction would otherwise be taken. Thus, for example, in the case of a nonqualified stock option, the deduction is normally taken in the year the option is exercised, even though the option was granted with respect to services performed in a prior year.45

Certain types of compensation are not subject to the deduction limit and are not taken into account in determining whether other compensation exceeds $1 million. The following types of compensation are not taken into account: (1) remuneration payable on a commission basis; (2) remuneration payable solely on account of the attainment of one or more performance goals if certain outside director and shareholder approval requirements are met; (3) payments to a tax-qualified retirement plan (including salary reduction contributions); (4) amounts that are excludable from the executive's gross income (such as employer-provided health benefits and miscellaneous fringe benefits (sec. 132)); and (5) any remuneration payable under a written binding contract which was in effect on February 17, 1993, and all times thereafter before such remuneration was paid and which was not modified thereafter in any material respect before such remuneration was paid.

Commissions

In order to qualify for the exception for compensation paid in the form of commissions, the commission must be payable solely on account of income generated directly by the individual performance of the executive receiving such compensation. Thus, for example, compensation that equals a percentage of sales made by the executive qualifies for the exception. Remuneration does not fail to be attributable directly to the executive merely because the executive utilizes support services, such as secretarial or research services, in generating the income. However, if compensation is paid on account of broader performance standards, such as income produced by a business unit of the corporation, the compensation would not qualify for the exception because it is not paid with regard to income that is directly attributable to the individual executive.

Other Performance-based Compensation

In General

Compensation qualifies for the exception for performance-based compensation only if (1) it is paid solely on account of the attainment of one or more performance goals, (2) the performance goals are established by a compensation committee consisting solely of two or more outside directors, (3) the material terms under which the compensation is to be paid, including the performance goals, are disclosed to and approved by the shareholders in a separate vote prior to payment, and (4) prior to payment, the compensation committee certifies that the performance goals and any other material terms were in fact satisfied.

Definition Of Performance-based Compensation

Compensation (other than stock options or other stock appreciation rights) is not treated as paid solely on account of the attainment of one or more performance goals unless the compensation is paid to the particular executive pursuant to a preestablished objective performance formula or standard that precludes discretion.[46] In general, this means that a third party with knowledge of the relevant performance results could calculate the amount to be paid to the executive. It is intended that what constitutes a performance goal be broadly defined, and include, for example, any objective performance standard that is applied to the individual executive, a business unit (e.g., a division or a line of business), or the corporation as a whole. Performance standards could include, for example, increases in stock price, market share, sales, or earnings per share.

Stock options or other stock appreciation rights generally are treated as meeting the exception for performance-based compensation, provided that the requirements for outside director and shareholder approval are met (without the need for certification that the performance standards have been met), because the amount of compensation attributable to the options or other rights received by the executive would be based solely on an increase in the corporation's stock price. In the case of stock options, it is intended that the directors may retain discretion as to the exact number of options that are granted to an executive, provided that the maximum number of options that the individual executive may receive during a specified period is predetermined.

Stock-based compensation is not treated as performance-based if it is dependent on factors other than corporate performance. For example, if a stock option is granted to an executive with an exercise price that is less than the current fair market value of the stock at the time of grant, then the executive would have the right to receive compensation on the exercise of the option even if the stock price decreases or stays the same. Thus, stock options that are granted with an exercise price that is less than the fair market value of the stock at the time of grant do not meet the requirements for performance-based compensation. Similarly, if the executive is otherwise protected from decreases in the value of the stock (such as through automatic repricing), the compensation is not performance-based.

In contrast to options or other stock appreciation rights, grants of restricted stock are not inherently performance-based because the executive may receive compensation even if the stock price decreases or stays the same. Thus, a grant of restricted stock is treated like cash compensation and does not satisfy the definition of performance-based compensation unless the grant or vesting of the restricted stock is based upon the attainment of a performance goal and otherwise satisfies the standards for performance-based compensation under the bill.

Compensation does not qualify for the performance-based exception if the executive has a right to receive the compensation notwithstanding the failure of (1) the compensation committee to certify attainment of the performance goal (or goals) or (2) the shareholders to approve the compensation.

Definition Of Outside Directors

For purposes of the exception for perform-ance-based compensation, a director is con-sidered an outside director if he or she is not a current employee of the corporation (or re-lated entities), is not a former employee of the corporation (or related entities) who is receiv-ing compensation for prior services (other than benefits under a tax-qualified pension plan), was not an officer of the corporation (or related entities) at any time, and is not cur-rently receiving compensation for personal services in any capacity (e.g., for services as a consultant) other than as a director.

Shareholder Approval And Adequate Disclosure

In order to meet the shareholder approval requirement, the material terms under which the compensation is to be paid must be dis-closed and, after disclosure of such terms, the compensation must be approved by a majority of shares voting in a separate vote.

In the case of performance-based compen-sation paid pursuant to a plan (other than a stock option plan), the shareholder approval requirement generally is satisfied if the share-holders approve the specific terms of the plan, including the class of executives to which it applies. In the case of a stock option plan, the shareholders generally must approve the spe-cific terms of the plan, the class of executives to which it applies, the option price (or for-mula under which the price is determined), and the maximum number of shares subject to option that can be awarded under the plan to any executive.

Further shareholder approval of payments under a plan or grants of options is not re-quired after the plan has been approved. Of course, if there are material changes to the plan, shareholder approval would have to be obtained again in order for the exception to apply to payments under the modified plan.

It is intended that not all the details of a plan (or agreement) need be disclosed in all cases. In developing standards as to whether disclo-sure of the terms of a plan or agreement is adequate, the Secretary should take into ac-count the SEC rules regarding disclosure. To the extent consistent with those rules, how-ever, disclosure should be as specific as pos-sible. It is expected that shareholders will, at a minimum, be made aware of the general performance goals on which the executive's compensation is based and the maximum amount that could be paid to the executive if such performance goals were met. For exam-ple, it would not be adequate if the sharehold-ers were merely informed that an executive would be awarded $x "if the executive meets certain performance goals established by the compensation committee."

Under present law, in the case of a privately held company that becomes publicly held, the prospectus is subject to the rules similar to those applicable to publicly held companies. Thus, if there has been disclosure that would satisfy the rules described above, persons who buy stock in the publicly held company will be aware of existing compensation arrange-ments. No further shareholder approval is re-quired of compensation arrangements existing prior to the time the company became public unless there is a material modification of such arrangements. It is intended that similar rules apply in the case of other business transac-tions.

Compensation Payable Under A Written Binding Contract

Remuneration payable under a written bind-ing contract which was in effect on February 17, 1993, and at all times thereafter before such remuneration was paid is not subject to the deduction limitation.

Compensation paid pursuant to a plan quali-fies for this exception provided that the right to participate in the plan is part of a written binding contract with the covered employee in effect on February 17, 1993. For example, suppose a covered employee was hired by XYZ Corporation on January 17, 1993, and one of the terms of the written employment contract is that the executive is eligible to participate in the "XYZ Corporation Execu-tive Deferred Compensation Plan" in accord-ance with the terms of the plan. Assume further that the terms of the plan provide for participation after 6 months of employment, amounts payable under the plan are not subject to discretion, and the corporation does not have the right to amend materially the plan or terminate the plan (except on a prospective basis before any services are performed with respect to the applicable period for which such compensation is to be paid). Provided that the other conditions of the binding contract exception are met (e.g., the plan itself is in writing), payments under the plan are grandfathered, even though the employee was not actually a participant in the plan on February 17, 1993.[47]

The fact that a plan was in existence on February 17, 1993, is not by itself sufficient to qualify the plan for the exception for binding written contracts.

The exception for remuneration paid pursuant to a binding written contract ceases to apply to amounts paid after there has been a material modification to the terms of the contract.

The exception does not apply to new contracts entered into or renewed after February 17, 1993. For purposes of this rule, any contract that is entered into on or before February 17, 1993, and that is renewed after such date is treated as a new contract entered into on the day the renewal takes effect. A contract that is terminable or cancelable unconditionally at will by either party to the contract without the consent of the other, or by both parties to the contract, is treated as a new contract entered into on the date any such termination or cancellation, if made, would be effective. However, a contract is not treated as so terminable or cancelable if it can be terminated or canceled only by terminating the employment relationship of the covered employee.

Effective Date

The Conference Agreement follows the Senate Amendment.

8. Reduce compensation taken into account for qualified retirement plan purposes (sec. 14212 of the House Bill, sec. 8212 of the Senate Amendment, sec. 13212 of the Conference Agreement, and sec. 401(a)(17) of the Code)

Present Law

Under present law, the amount of a participant's compensation that can be taken into account under a tax-qualified pension plan is limited (sec. 401(a)(17)). The limit applies for determining the amount of the employer's deduction for contributions to the plan as well as for determining the amount of the participant's benefits. The limit on includible compensation is $235,840 for 1993, and is adjusted annually for inflation. The limit in effect at the beginning of a plan year applies for the entire plan year.

House Bill

Under the House Bill, the limit on compensation taken into account under a qualified plan (sec. 401(a)(17)) is reduced to $150,000. As under present law, this limit is indexed for inflation on an annual basis. Corresponding changes also are made to other provisions (secs. 404(l), 408(k)(3)(C), (6)(D)(ii), and (8), and 505(b)(7)) that take into account the section 401(a)(17) limit.

Effective Date

The provision in the House Bill applies to benefits accruing in plan years beginning after December 31, 1993. Benefits accrued prior to the Effective Date for compensation in excess of the reduced limit are grandfathered.

Senate Amendment

The Senate Amendment is the same as the House Bill, except that the limit on compensation is indexed for inflation in increments of $10,000.

Effective Date

Same as the House Bill except that special transition rules apply to governmental plans and plans maintained pursuant to a collective bargaining agreement.

In the case of an eligible participant in a plan maintained by a State or local government, the limit on compensation taken into account is the greater of the limit under the Senate Amendment and the compensation allowed to be taken into account under the plan as in effect on July 1, 1993. For purposes of this rule, an eligible participant is an individual who first became a participant in the plan during a plan year beginning before the first plan year beginning after the earlier of: (1) the plan year in which the plan is amended to reflect the proposal, or (2) December 31, 1995. This special rule does not apply unless the plan is amended to incorporate the dollar limit in effect under section 401(a)(17) by reference, effective with respect to persons other than eligible participants for benefits accruing in plan years beginning after December 31, 1995 (or earlier if the plan amendment so provides).

In the case of a plan maintained pursuant to one or more collective bargaining agreements ratified before the date of enactment, the provision does not apply to contributions or benefits accruing under such agreements in plan years beginning before the earlier of (1) the latest of (a) January 1, 1994, (b) the date on which the last of such collective bargaining agreements terminates (without regard to any extension or modification on or after the date of enactment), or (c) in the case of a plan maintained pursuant to collective bargaining under the Railway Labor Act, the date of execution of an extension or replacement of the last of such collective bargaining agreements in effect on the date of enactment, or (2) January 1, 1997.

Conference Agreement

The Conference Agreement follows the Senate Amendment.

9. Modify deduction for moving expenses (sec. 14213 of the House Bill, sec. 8213 of the Senate Amendment, sec. 13213 of the Conference Agreement, and secs. 62, 132, and 217 of the Code)

Present law

An employee or self-employed individual may claim a deduction from gross income for certain expenses incurred as a result of moving to a new residence in connection with beginning work at a new location (sec. 217). The deduction is not subject to the floor that generally limits a taxpayer's allowable miscellaneous itemized deductions to those amounts that exceed two percent of the taxpayer's adjusted gross income. Any amount received directly or indirectly by such individual as a reimbursement of moving expenses must be included in the taxpayer's gross income as compensation (sec. 82). The taxpayer may offset this income by deducting the moving expenses that are deductible items under section 217.

Deductible moving expenses are the expenses of transporting the taxpayer and members of the taxpayer's household, as well as household goods and personal effects, from the old residence to the new residence; the cost of meals and lodging enroute; the expenses for pre-move househunting trips; temporary living expenses for up to 30 days in the general location of the new job; and certain expenses related to either the sale of (or settlement of an unexpired lease) on the old residence, or the purchase of (or acquisition of a lease on) a new residence in the general location of the new job.

The moving expense deduction is subject to a number of limitations. A maximum of $1,500 can be deducted for pre-move househunting and temporary living expenses in the general location of the new job. A maximum of $3,000 (reduced by any deduction claimed for househunting or temporary living expenses) can be deducted for certain qualified expenses for the sale or purchase of a residence or settlement or acquisition of a lease.

If both a husband and wife begin new jobs in the same general location, the move is treated as a single commencement of work. If a husband and wife file separate returns, the maximum deductible amounts available to each are one-half the amounts otherwise allowed.

Also, in order for a taxpayer to claim a moving expense deduction, the taxpayer's new principal place of work must be at least 35 miles farther from the taxpayer's former residence than was the taxpayer's former principal place of work (or at least 35 miles from the taxpayer's former residence, if the taxpayer has no former place of work).

House Bill

The House Bill excludes from the definition of moving expenses: (1) the costs related to the sale of (or settlement of an unexpired lease on) the old residence, and the purchase of (or acquisition of a lease on) the new residence in the general location of the new job, and (2) the costs of meals consumed while traveling and while living in temporary quarters near the new job.

Effective Date

Generally, the provision is effective for expenses incurred after December 31, 1993.

Senate Amendment

The Senate bill is the same as the House Bill with an additional restriction. Under this restriction, an overall $10,000 cap is imposed on allowable moving expenses (including expenses subject to the limit on househunting and temporary living expenses) for each qualified move (including foreign moves). The $10,000 amount is indexed for inflation occurring after December 31, 1993.

Effective Date

Same as the House Bill.

Conference Agreement

In General

The Conference Agreement follows the House Bill with the following modifications: (1) the cost of pre-move househunting trips is excluded from the definition of moving expenses; (2) the cost of temporary living expenses for up to 30 days in the general location of the new job is excluded from the definition of moving expenses; (3) the mileage limit is increased from 35 miles to 50 miles; (4) moving expenses not paid or reimbursed by the taxpayer's employer are allowable as a deduction in calculating adjusted gross income; and (5) moving expenses paid or reimbursed by the taxpayer's employer are excludable from gross income.

Definition Of Moving Expenses

Under the Conference Agreement, moving expenses are defined as the reasonable costs of (1) moving household goods and personal effects from the former residence to the new residence and (2) traveling (including lodging during the period of travel) from the former residence to the new place of residence. Moving expenses do not include any expenses for meals.

Employer-paid moving expenses

Moving expenses are excludable from gross income and wages for income and employment tax purposes to the extent paid for by the taxpayer's employer (whether directly or through reimbursement). Moving expenses are not excludable if the taxpayer actually deducted the expenses in a prior taxable year. The conferees intend that the employer treat moving expenses as excludable unless it has actual knowledge that the employee deducted the expenses in a prior year. The employer has no obligation to determine whether the individual deducted the expenses.

The conferees intend that rules similar to the rules relating to accountable plans under section 62(c) will apply to reimbursed expenses.

Moving expenses not paid for by the employer

Moving expenses are deductible in computing adjusted gross income to the extent not paid for by the taxpayer's employer (whether directly or through reimbursement). Allowing such a deduction will treat taxpayers whose expenses are not paid for by their employer in a comparable manner to taxpayers whose moving expenses are paid for by their employer.

Effective Date

The Conference Agreement follows the House Bill and the Senate Amendment.

* * *

IV. OTHER REVENUE PROVISIONS

* * *

C. Vaccine Provisions:

Extension of the excise tax on certain vaccines for the Vaccine Injury Compensation Trust Fund; Provisions relating to the childhood vaccine immunization program (secs. 14431-14433 of the House Bill, secs. 8237 and 12203(b) of the Senate Amendment, secs. 13421-13422 of the Conference Agreement, and secs. 4131, 4980B(f), and 9510 of the Code)

* * *

House Bill

* * *

Maintenance-of-effort requirement for pediatric vaccine health care coverage

The House Bill makes the failure of health plans that provide coverage for the cost of pediatric vaccines as of May 1, 1993, to continue to provide that level of coverage subject to the excise tax penalty (under sec. 4980B(f)) applicable to plans that fail to provide COBRA health plan continuation coverage.

Effective Date

* * *

The maintenance-of-effort requirement for pediatric vaccine health care coverage applies to plan years beginning after the date of enactment.

Senate Amendment

* * *

Maintenance-of-effort requirement for pediatric vaccine health care coverage

No tax provision.

Conference Agreement

* * *

Maintenance-of-effort requirement for pediatric vaccine health care coverage

The Conference Agreement follows the House Bill.

CHAPTER 5—MEDICARE AND MEDICAID COVERAGE DATA BANK

Present Law

No Medicare and Medicaid Coverage Data Bank exists under present law. OBRA 89 authorized the establishment of a database to identify working Medicare beneficiaries and their spouses to improve identification of cases in which Medicare is secondary payer to other third party payers.

House Bill

W&M: No provision.

E&C: The House Bill directs the Secretary of Health and Human Services to establish and operate a Health Coverage Clearinghouse for the purpose of identifying indemnity insurers, service benefit plans, group health plans under the Employee Retirement Income Security Act of 1974, as amended (ERISA), health maintenance organizations, and other third parties that may be liable for payment for services provided to Medicaid, Medicare, or Indian Health Service beneficiaries (or individuals receiving services funded under the Maternal and Child Health Block Grant). The House Bill directs the Administrator of the Health Care Financing Administration and State agencies to request information from the clearinghouse concerning the employment and group health coverage of a beneficiary, the beneficiary's spouse, or, if the beneficiary is a dependent child, the beneficiary's parents. The House Bill requires IRS and the Social Security Administration to provide taxpayer identity information on these individuals. The House Bill sets forth procedures under which programs may obtain this information from the clearinghouse as well as procedures for the maintenance of a data bank by the clearinghouse. The House Bill also directs employers to provide information relating to coverage of individuals under the employer's group health plan to the clearinghouse and provides a civil monetary penalty for willful and repeated failure to comply. The provision is effective on April 1, 1995. Employers are not required to provide information to the clearinghouse after September 30, 1998.

Senate Amendment

Section 7904 of the Senate Amendment directs the Secretary of Health and Human Services to establish and operate a clearinghouse to increase information available to Medicare and Medicaid on third-party health insurance coverage available to program beneficiaries.

Section 7904 of the Senate Amendment requires employers to include limited health insurance information on each Form W-2 given to an employee, as well as on each copy that is provided to the IRS. The Senate Amendment specifically requires employers to indicate on each Form W-2 whether an employee obtained (or could have obtained) coverage under a group health plan offered by the employer, as well as the type of plan coverage (single or family) that was chosen by the employee (if any.) These requirements are made a part of the Internal Revenue Code.

The clearinghouse is given access to the following information from every Form W-2 that is filed with the IRS: the name and tax-payer identification number of every employee; the name, address, and employer identification number of every employee's employer; and the health plan information described above. In addition, the IRS is required (upon request) to disclose to the clearinghouse a taxpayer's filing status and identify information as to whether the taxpayer was married for a specified year, and, if so, the name and taxpayer identification number of the spouse.

This information is available to appropriate Federal program administrators through the clearinghouse. The clearinghouse is to maintain a data bank that matches the tax return information with the lists of health program beneficiaries. The clearinghouse also is authorized to assist these programs in collecting amounts due from insurers and is to maintain information obtained through computer matches and contacts with employers. Employers who fail to provide information on health insurance coverage are subject to civil monetary penalties. The provision is effective April 1, 1995.

Section 12101 of the Senate Amendment is generally the same as the House Bill, except that the beneficiaries affected differ and the list of agencies eligible to receive the information is expanded.

Conference Agreement

The Conference Agreement establishes a Medicare and Medicaid Coverage Data Bank within the Department of Health and Human Services. The Secretary is required to establish the Data Bank for the purposes of identifying and collecting from third parties responsible for payment of health care items and services furnished to Medicare beneficiaries, and assisting in the collection of, or collecting, amounts due from liable third parties to reimburse costs incurred by any State plan under the Medicaid program.

Employers are required to report certain information to the Data Bank concerning employee health coverage on an annual basis for years beginning with calendar year 1994 and ending in calendar year 1997. The information, reported will include: the name and taxpayer identification number (TIN) of the electing individual; the type of group health plan coverage (single or family) elected; the name, address, and identifying number of the group health plan elected by the employee; the name and TIN of each other individual (e.g., spouses and dependents) covered under the group health plan; the period during which such coverage is elected; and the name, address, and TIN of the employer.

All employers required to file a Form W-2, with employees that elect coverage under a group health plan, will report health coverage information to the Data Bank at the same time as the filing of Form W-2 required under section 6051(d) of the Internal Revenue Code of 1986. The first filing will occur on February 28, 1995. The conferees expect the Secretary to minimize the burden of this reporting requirement and coordinate, to the maximum extent possible, with the format and filing procedures established for the Form W-2.

The Data Bank will maintain health insurance information on individuals covered under employer group health plans, as required under this section, as well as certain information to verify the employment status of Medicare beneficiaries and their spouses pursuant to section 6103(l)(12) of the Internal Revenue Code of 1986.

The Secretary is authorized to disclose information provided to the Data Bank by employers to State Medicaid agencies, employers, and group health plans solely for carrying out the purposes of the Data Bank. Information that the Data Bank receives pursuant to section 6103(l)(12) can only be disclosed in the manner provided in section 6103.

The Secretary is required to maintain a system of safeguards against unauthorized disclosure of Data Bank information that are similar to those provided under sections 6103(a) and (p) of the Internal Revenue Code of 1986 regarding the confidentiality and recordkeeping procedures required with respect to tax return information, including penalties as prescribed under Section 7213(a) of such Code. The conferees intend that in establishing such procedures, the Secretary is authorized to require any party receiving Data Bank information to agree to ensure the confidentiality of this information.

Employers failing to report the required information to the Data Bank generally will be subject to penalties similar to those imposed under the Internal Revenue Code for failure to supply information returns. Such penalties may be abated if the failure to file is due to reasonable cause; penalties may be increased if the failure is willful.

The Secretary is authorized, at the request of the administrator of any State agency administering the Medicaid program, to collect or assist in the collection of amounts due from liable third parties to reimburse costs incurred by such program or plan for health care items or services. States are required to request and use information from the Data Bank, when cost effective, and to pay the required fee for the provision of information. The fee for providing collection services may be computed as a percentage of the amount collected and may be retained by the Secretary from the total amount collected.

* * *

FOOTNOTES

[8] See Rev. Rul. 66-151, 1966-1 C.B. 151.

[9] Moreover, as under present law, any investment by a pension trust must be in accordance with the fiduciary rules of the Employee Retirement Security Act ("ERISA") and the prohibited transaction rules of the Code and ERISA.

* * *

[44] The provision does not modify the present law requirement that, in order to be deductible, compensation must be reasonable. Thus, as under present law, in certain circumstances compensation less than $1 million may not be deductible.

[45] Of course, if the executive is no longer a covered employee at the time the options are exercised, then the deduction limitation would not apply.

[46] Discretion does not exist merely because the outside directors have the authority to interpret a compensation plan, agreement, or contract in accordance with its terms.

[47] Of course, as discussed below in the text, the grandfather ceases to apply if the plan is materially amended.

Excerpts from Joint Explanatory Statement of the Committee of Conference on Social Security Administrative Reform Act of 1994, H.R. Rep. 103-670

The managers on the part of the House and the Senate at the conference on the disagreeing votes of the two Houses on the amendment of the Senate to the bill (H.R. 4277) to establish the Social Security Administration as an independent agency and to make other improvements in the old-age, survivors, and disability insurance program, submit the following joint statement to the House and the Senate in explanation of the effect of the action agreed upon by the managers and recommended in the accompanying conference report: The Senate Amendment struck all of the House Bill after the enacting clause and inserted a substitute text. The House recedes from its disagreement to the amendment of the Senate with an amendment that is a substitute for the House Bill and the Senate Amendment. The differences between the House Bill, the Senate Amendment, and the substitute agreed to in conference are noted below, except for clerical corrections, conforming changes made necessary by agreements reached by the conferees, and minor drafting and clerical changes.

1. Establishment of the Social Security Administration as an Independent Agency(Sec. 101-110 of the House Bill, secs. 101-204 of the Senate Amendment, and secs. 101-110 of the Conference Agreement)

a. Status of Agency

Present law

The Social Security Administration (SSA) is a component of the Department of Health and Human Services (HHS).

House Bill

SSA would be made an independent agency in the executive branch of the Federal government, with responsibility for administration of the Old-Age, Survivors, and Disability Insurance (OASDI) and Supplemental Security Income (SSI) programs.

Senate Amendment

Same as House provision.

Conference Agreement

The Conference Agreement follows the House Bill and the Senate Amendment, with amendments providing that SSA would continue to perform its current functions in administering the Coal Industry Retirees Health Benefits Act and Part B of the Black Lung Benefits Act.

Excerpts from the Joint Explanatory Statement of the Committee of Conference on the Social Security Domestic Employment Reform Act of 1994, H.R. Rep. 103-843

The managers on the part of the House and the Senate at the conference on the disagreeing votes of the two Houses on the amendment of the Senate to the bill (H.R. 4278) to make improvements in the old-age, survivors, and disability insurance program under title II of the Social Security Act, submit the following joint statement to the House and the Senate in explanation of the effect of the action agreed upon by the managers and recommended in the accompanying conference report: The Senate Amendment struck all of the House Bill after the enacting clause and inserted a substitute text. The House recedes from its disagreement to the amendment of the Senate with an amendment that is a substitute for the House Bill and the Senate Amendment. The differences between the House Bill, the Senate Amendment, and the substitute agreed to in conference are noted below, except for clerical corrections, conforming changes made necessary by agreements reached by the conferees, and minor drafting and clerical changes.

1. Simplification of Employment Taxes on Domestic Services (Sec. 2 of House Bill and Sec. 2 of Senate Amendment)

Present Law

Individuals who hire domestic employees such as baby-sitters, housekeepers, and yard workers are required to withhold and pay employment taxes when the worker's wages exceed certain thresholds. (Individuals who hire domestic workers who are properly classified as independent contractors to provide these services are excluded from these requirements.) For Social Security, the wage threshold is reached, generally, when an employer pays $50 or more per quarter to a domestic employee. However, wages paid to domestic employees hired by farm operators are subject to the thresholds that are used for determining coverage for agricultural employees. For these employees, the wage threshold is reached if either (1) the farm operator's total farm payroll for a year is $2,500 or more, or (2) the wages paid to an employee in a year are $150 or more. (This latter test applies only if the farm operator's total payroll for a year is less than $2,500.) For Federal unemployment insurance (FUTA), the threshold is reached when an employer pays $1,000 or more in a calendar quarter to one or more domestic employees. When the $50 threshold is reached, the employer must file a quarterly report (Form 942) with the Internal Revenue Service, submitting with it the required Social Security tax for both the employer and the employee. The employer must also provide the employee and the Social Security Administration with a Wage and Tax Statement (Form W-2) at the end of the year. When the $1,000 unemployment insurance wage threshold is reached in any calendar quarter, the employer must file a report (Form 940) with the IRS at the end of the year, submitting the required tax. In addition, employers of domestic workers must: notify employees who may be eligible for the earned income tax credit of the existence of this credit; withhold income tax if the employee requests it and the employer agrees; file and pay State unemployment insurance tax in each quarter in which the State unemployment insurance wage threshold (equal to the $1,000 Federal threshold in 45 States) is reached; and, in some States, report wages paid to domestic employees to the State for purposes of State income tax.

House Bill

Reporting

The bill requires individuals who employ only domestic workers to report on a calendar-year basis any Social Security or Federal unemployment tax obligations for wages paid these workers and authorizes the Secretary of the Treasury to revise Federal Form 1040 to enable such employers to report both taxes on their own Federal income tax returns. The bill also requires the Secretary of the Treasury to provide to domestic employers a comprehensive package of informational materials, including all requirements of Federal law and a notification that they may also be subject to State unemployment insurance and workers compensation laws. Threshold

The bill changes the threshold for withholding and paying Social Security taxes on domestic workers from $50 per quarter to $1,250 annually in 1995.

Indexing

The bill indexes the threshold for increases in average wages in the economy, rounded to $50 increments.

Farm Service

The bill does not apply to domestic service on a farm.

Estimated Taxes

The bill includes domestic employers' Social Security and Federal unemployment taxes in estimated tax provisions. Employers may satisfy their tax obligations through regular estimated tax payments or increased tax withholding from their own wages.

State Unemployment

The bill authorizes the Secretary of the Treasury to enter into agreements with States to collect State unemployment taxes in the manner described above.

Age limitation

No provision.

Effective Date.

Generally applies to remuneration paid in calendar years beginning after 1994. The bill adjusts the Social Security tax threshold retroactively to $1,150 for 1993 and to $1,200 for 1994. No underpayment of taxes could be assessed (or, if assessed, could be collected), effective on or after the date of enactment. No refunds would be provided.

Senate Amendment

Reporting

Same as House Bill.

Threshold

The amendment changes the threshold from $50 per quarter to an annual threshold equal to the amount required for one quarter of Social Security coverage (estimated to be $630 in 1995).

Indexing

Same as House Bill, except the amendment would use a technically different indexing mechanism.

Farm Service

The amendment applies to domestic service on a farm.

Estimated Taxes

Same as House Bill, except no estimated tax penalty would apply to an underpayment of these taxes if they were paid on or before April 15 (or the date the return of the employer is filed, if earlier.)

State Unemployment

Same as House Bill.

Age Limitation

The amendment exempts from Social Security taxes any wages paid to a worker for domestic services performed in any year during which the worker is under the age of 18.

Effective Date

Generally applies to remuneration paid in calendar years beginning after 1994 (same as House Bill). Exemption for workers under the age of 18 applies to services performed in calendar years beginning after 1994. No provision with respect to retroactive adjustment of the threshold for 1993 and 1994.

Conference Agreement

Reporting

The Conference Agreement follows the House Bill and the Senate Amendment. The Secretary of the Treasury continues to have regulatory authority to allow States to pay the employment taxes for certain public assistance recipients who employ household workers. Several States have agreements under which the State handles the appropriate Federal employment taxes for household workers employed by public assistance recipients under State programs.

Threshold

The Conference Agreement provides that the threshold is $1,000.

Indexing

The Conference Agreement follows the House Bill and the Senate Amendment by indexing the $1,000 threshold. Indexing will occur in $100 increments, rounded down to the nearest $100.

Farm Service

The Conference Agreement follows the Senate Amendment.

Estimated Taxes

The Conference Agreement follows the House Bill, except that estimated tax penalties will not apply to amounts affected by the Conference Agreement until 1998. The conferees intend that the Internal Revenue Service disseminate the informational materials required by the statute so that taxpayers will be fully apprised of the provisions of the Conference Agreement (including the provision related to estimated taxes). Individuals not required to make estimated tax payments (including by having income taxes withheld from their wages) are not required to begin making estimated tax payments (or wage withholding) solely as a consequence of the Conference Agreement. Individuals otherwise required to make estimated tax payments (including by having income taxes withheld from their wages) are required, after 1997, to include amounts affected by the Conference Agreement in those estimated tax payment (or wage withholding).

State Unemployment

The Conference Agreement follows the House Bill and the Senate Amendment.

Age Limitation

The Conference Agreement follows the Senate Amendment, except that the exemption for workers under the age of 18 would not apply to individuals whose principal occupation is household employment. Being a student is considered to be an occupation for purposes of this test. Thus, for example, the wages of a student who is 16 years old who also babysits will be exempt from the reporting and payment requirements, regardless of whether the amount of wages paid is above or below the threshold. On the other hand, for example, the wages of a 17 year-old single mother who leaves school and goes to work as a domestic to support her family will be subject to the reporting and payment requirements; she will consequently obtain Social Security coverage with respect to those wages.

Effective Date

The $1,000 threshold is effective for calendar year 1994. The simplified reporting system, as well as the other provisions of the Conference Agreement, are effective January 1, 1995. Refunds would be given for payroll taxes on wages paid in 1994 when the total wages that an employee receives from an employer are below the $1,000 threshold. There will be no loss of Social Security wage credits with respect to amounts refunded for 1994. To provide information reporting to ensure that there is no loss of credits, an employer who would have been required to file a Form W-2 (without regard to the enactment of these provisions) will continue to be required to do so, and will be required to report wages paid for the whole year in the "social security wages" box, even though the employer will receive a refund of any Social Security taxes paid.

Example 1. Assume Employer A pays domestic employee R $500 in wages for calendar year 1994. A has been making quarterly payments of the payroll taxes due on these wages. A will not be required to make any further quarterly payments of payroll taxes with respect to 1994 that are due on or after the date of enactment of the Conference Agreement. A can obtain a refund of payroll taxes previously paid. Employee R will get Social Security credit with respect to the $500 of wages.

Example 2. Assume Employer B pays a domestic employee $1,500 in wages for calendar year 1994. B has been make quarterly payments of the payroll taxes due on these wages. B must continue to make quarterly payments of payroll taxes to the remainder of 1994.

Example 3. Assume Employer A will pay domestic employee R $500 in wages for calendar year 1995. Because the amount of these wages is below the $1,000 threshold, A is not subject to reporting.

Example 4. Assume Employer B will pay domestic employee S $1,500 in wages for calendar year 1995. Because the amount of these wages is above the $1,000 threshold, B is subject to reporting.

Excerpts from the House Report to the Retirement Protection Act of 1994, H.R. Rep. 103-826

◊ ◊ ◊

Editor's Note: The Retirement Protection Act of 1994 was enacted as part of the Uruguay Round Agreements Act (P.L. 103-465). Since identical versions of P.L. 103-465 were submitted to the House and Senate, there is no Conference Report to that act. The House Report, excerpted below, therefore, effectively constitutes the most authoritative legislative history on the statute.

◊ ◊ ◊

D. SUBTITLE D: PROVISIONS RELATING TO RETIREMENT BENEFITS

1. Treatment of Excess Pension Assets Used for Retiree Health Benefits (sec. 731 of the bill and sec. 420 of the Code)

a. Present Law

Under present law, defined benefit pension plan assets generally may not revert to an employer prior to the termination of the plan and the satisfaction of all plan liabilities. Certain procedural requirements also must be met. Any assets that revert to the employer upon such termination are includible in the gross income of the employer and subject to an excise tax. The rate of the excise tax varies depending upon whether or not the employer maintains a replacement plan or makes certain benefit increases, and can be as high as 30 percent of the amount of the reversion. Upon plan termination, the accrued benefits of all plan participants are required to be 1-percent vested.

Under present law, a pension plan may provide medical benefits to retirees through a section 401(h) account that is part of such plan. Present law permits certain qualified transfers of excess assets from the pension assets, in a defined benefit pension plan (other than a multiemployer plan) to the section 401(h) account that is a part of such plan to pay for qualified current retiree health liabilities. The assets transferred are not includible in the gross income of the employer and are not subject to the excise tax on reversions.

Assets transferred in a qualified transfer cannot exceed certain limits. The amount that can otherwise be transferred is reduced by amounts previously contributed to a health benefits account or welfare benefit fund to pay for the qualified current retiree health liabilities. The transferred assets (and any income thereon) are required to be used to pay qualified current retiree health liabilities (either directly or through reimbursement) for the taxable year of the transfer. Transferred amounts are generally required to benefit all participants in the pension plan who are entitled upon retirement to receive retiree medical benefits (other than key employees) through the section 401(h) account. Retiree health benefits of key employees may not be paid (directly or indirectly) out of transferred assets. In order for the transfer to be qualified, accrued retirement benefits under the pension plan must be nonforfeitable as if the plan terminated on the date of transfer.

Amounts not used to pay qualified current retiree health liabilities for the taxable year of the transfer are to be returned at the end of the taxable year to the general pension assets of the plan.

Under a maintenance of effort requirement, an employer that makes a transfer to a section 401(h) account from the defined benefit plan assets is required to maintain employer-provided retiree health expenditures for covered retirees at a minimum dollar level for the taxable year of the transfer and the following 4 taxable years. The minimum dollar level is the higher of the applicable employer costs for each of the 2 taxable years immediately preceding the taxable year of the transfer.

The provision permitting the transfer of excess Pension assets to pay current retiree health benefits expires for taxable years beginning after December 31, 1995.

b. Reasons for Change

It is appropriate to provide a temporary extension of the present-law rule permitting employers to transfer assets set aside for pension benefits to a section 401(h) account for retiree health benefits as long as the security of employees' pension benefits is not thereby threatened. In conjunction with the temporary extension of the provision, it is necessary to modify the maintenance of effort requirement to ensure that employers can take into account cost savings that are realized in the employer's health benefits plans.

c. Explanation of Provision

The present-law provision permitting excess defined benefit pension plan assets to be used to provide retiree health benefits under a section 401(h) account is extended for 5 years, with a modification to the maintenance of effort requirement and a clarification of the rule relating to amounts previously set aside to pay qualified retiree health liabilities.

Under the bill, the employer is required to maintain substantially the same level of employer-provided retiree health coverage for the taxable year of the transfer and the following 4 taxable years. The level of coverage that must be maintained will be based on coverage provided in the year immediately preceding the taxable year of the transfer. For purposes of determining whether there are excess assets in a defined benefit pension plan, the interest rates required to be used under the bill for purposes of minimum funding requirements would apply.

The bill clarifies how amounts that can otherwise be transferred are reduced by amounts previously set aside to pay retiree health liabilities. Under tile bill, for transfers occurring after December 31, 1995, in determining qualified retiree health liabilities with respect to a taxable year, such liabilities are reduced by the percentage that the amounts previously set aside are of total future qualified retiree health liabilities. For example, assume that on December 31, 1995, the employer has a welfare benefit fund that has $2 million in assets to pay retiree health liabilities, the present value of future qualified retiree health liabilities is $10 million, and qualified retiree health liabilities for 1996 (without regard to any offset) are $1 million. In determining the amount that can be transferred in 1996, the $1 million is reduced by 20 percent. No inference is intended as to the proper reduction in transferred amounts under present law.

d. Effective Date

The provision generally is effective with respect to taxable years beginning after December 31, 1995, and before January 1, 2001. The modification to the maintenance of effort requirement is effective for transfers occurring after the date of enactment.

2. Rounding Rule for Cost-of-Living Adjustments (sec. 732 of the bill and secs. 401(a)(17), 415, 402(g) and 408(k) of the Code)

a. Present Law

Under present law, the dollar limit on benefits under a defined benefit pension plan ($118,800 for 1994), the limit on elective deferrals under a qualified cash or deferred arrangement ($9,240 for 1994), and the minimum compensation limit for determining eligibility for participation in a simplified employee pension (SEP) ($396 for 1994) are adjusted annually for inflation. The dollar limit on annual additions to a defined contribution plan is tide greater of $30,000 or 114 of the dollar limit for benefits under defined benefit pension plans. Thus, the dollar limit will be $30,000 until the defined benefit pension plan dollar limit exceeds $120,000. The dollar limit on annual compensation that generally may be taken into account for qualified plan purposes is $150,000. The $150,000 limit is indexed in $10,000 increments.

b. Reasons for Change

In order to simplify the dollar limits applicable to qualified pension plans, it is necessary to modify the rounding rules so that the dollar limits are indexed in whole dollar increments ($5,000, $500, or $50). However, it is not appropriate to permit the modified rounding rules to reduce any dollar limit below its level under present law.

c. Explanation of Provision

The provision provides that (1) the dollar limit on benefits under a defined benefit pension plan is indexed in $5,000 increments, (2) the dollar limit on annual additions under a defined contribution plan is indexed in $5,000 increments, (3) the limit on elective deferrals is indexed in $500 increments, and (4) the minimum compensation limit for SEP participation is indexed in $50 increments.37

In addition, the provision provides that the cost-of-living adjustment with respect to any calendar year is based on the increase in the applicable index as of the close of the calendar quarter ending September 30 of the preceding calendar year so that the adjusted dollar limits would be available before the beginning of the calendar year to which they apply. No limit is reduced below the limit in effect for plan years beginning in 1994.

d. Effective Date

The provision is effective for years beginning after December 31, 1994.

* * *

F. SUBTITLE F: PENSION PLAN FUNDING AND PREMIUMS

1. Overview of Present Law

a. Defined Benefit Pension Plans

A defined benefit pension plan is a type of employer-sponsored retirement plan that provides benefits to participants based upon a formula specified in the plan. For example, a defined benefit pension plan could provide a benefit equal to a percentage of an employee's average compensation multiplied by the number of years of service with the employer. A defined benefit pension plan could also provide a flat dollar benefit based on years of service, or a specified percentage of final or average compensation. The key feature of such a plan is that the benefit promised is based on the plan formula, not on the assets or investment experience of the plan.

In order to help ensure that the promised benefits are paid to plan participants, defined benefit pension plans are subject to minimum funding requirements under both the Internal Revenue Code (the Code) and title I of the Employee Retirement Income Security Act of 1974, as amended (ERISA), which require the employer sponsoring the plan to make certain contributions to fund the plan. These requirements are discussed in detail below.

b. Pension Benefit Guaranty Corporation

As enacted in ERISA, as well as under present law, the minimum funding requirements permit an employer to fund defined benefit pension plan benefits over a period of time. Thus, it is possible that a plan may be terminated at a time when plan assets are not sufficient to provide all benefits earned by employees under the plan. In order to protect plan participants from losing retirement benefits in such circumstances, the Pension Benefit Guaranty Corporation (PBGC), a corporation within the Department of Labor, was created in 1974 by ERISA to provide an insurance program for benefits under most defined benefit pension plans maintained by private employers. According to the PBGC's annual report for fiscal year 1993, the single-employer insurance program covers more than 32 million participants in about 64,000 defined benefit pension plans.

c. Termination of Underfunded Pension Plans

Prior to 1986, an employer generally could, subject to contractual obligations, terminate a single-employer defined benefit pension plan at any time without regard to the financial health of the employer and without regard to the level of assets in the plan. If a single-employer defined benefit pension plan was terminated with assets insufficient to pay benefits at the level guaranteed by the PBGC, the employer was liable to the PBGC for the lesser of the insufficiency or an amount equal to 30 percent of the employer's net worth.

Under these rules, employers that wanted to rid themselves of unfunded liabilities could simply terminate the plan, and the PBGC would be liable for benefits. The PBGC was in some cases prevented from recouping its liability from the employer, even if the employer was financially sound. The plan termination rules were amended to prevent such transferring of liabilities to the PBGC by the Single- Employer Pension Plan Amendments Act of 1986 (SEPPAA) and were modified further by the Pension Protection Act of 1987.

Under present law, a defined benefit pension plan with assets insufficient to provide for benefit liabilities can be terminated voluntarily by the employer only if the employer and members of the controlled group of the employer are in financial distress (a distress termination). In general, benefit liabilities to plan participants and beneficiaries.

Following a distress termination, the PBGC pays out all benefits under the plan, including guaranteed benefits and those not guaranteed. The amount of benefits in excess of guaranteed benefits that are paid to plan participants depends on the level of plan funding and the amount the PBGC is able to recover from the employer. The employer is liable to the PBGC for the full amount of unfunded benefit liabilities.

d. Guaranteed Benefits

The PBGC guarantees vested retirement benefits (other than those that vest solely on account of the plan termination), up to a maximum benefit of $2,556.82 per month for plans terminating in 1994. The dollar limit is indexed annually for inflation. The guarantee is reduced for benefits starting before age 65, and does not apply to certain types of ancillary

benefits. In the case of a plan or a plan amendment that has been in effect for less than 5 years before a plan termination, the amount guaranteed is generally phased in by 20 percent a year.

e. Sources of PBGC Funding

The PBGC is funded by assets in terminated plans, amounts recovered from employers who terminate underfunded plans, premiums paid with respect to covered plans, and investment earnings. All covered plans are required to pay a flat per-participant premium and underfunded plans are subject to an additional variable premium based on the level of the underfunding.

As initially enacted in ERISA, covered plans were required to pay an annual flat premium to the PBGC of $1.00 per plan participant. The flat-rate per-participant premium has been increased several times since the enactment of ERISA, and is currently $19 per participant in 1994.

The variable rate premium was enacted by the Pension Protection Act of 1987. It was believed that underfunded plans should bear a greater share of the premium than well-funded plans because they pose a greater risk of exposure to the PBGC. The amount of the variable rate premium is $9.00 per each $1,000 of unfunded vested benefits, up to a maximum of $53 per participant. Thus, the maximum total per-participant premium for an underfunded plan is $72 per year.

2. Reasons for Change

a. Financial Status of the PBGC

As of September 30, 1993, the PBGC reported a deficit of $2.9 billion in the single-employer insurance program. This is an increase over the $2.7 billion deficit reported as of the end of the prior fiscal year. The PBGC also estimated in its 1993 annual report that approximately $53 billion in unfunded liabilities existed in single-employer defined benefit pension plans in 1993. Approximately 72 percent of this underfunding, or approximately $38 billion, is concentrated in single-employer plans sponsored by just 50 companies, primarily in the steel, automobile, tire, and airline industries.

The PBGC has estimated its future status under a variety of assumptions. The single-employer program deficit could range from $1.9 billion by the end of $2003 if losses are relatively low, to $13.8 billion by the end of 2003 if losses are high. In a study released by the U.S. General Accounting Office (GAO) in December 1992,[48] GAO reported that the 44 plans with the largest claims against the PBGC for calendar years 1986-88 had aggregate unfunded liabilities at termination of $2.7 billion. These unfunded liabilities are $990 million, or 58 percent, higher than the $1.7 billion in unfunded liabilities reported by the 44 plans on their last, pretermination annual filing with the Internal Revenue Service (IRS). GAO termed this additional unfunded liability a "hidden liability" to the PBGC because it was not reported by plans before termination.

Hidden liabilities can result from several causes. Most of the $990 million in hidden liability reported in the GAO study was due to PBGC's higher estimate of plan liabilities as a result of PBGC's use of actuarial assumptions that were different than the assumptions used by plan sponsors. Hidden liabilities also can result because of the payment of shutdown[49] or special early retirement benefits, earlier-than-anticipated retirements, and PBGC's receipt of fewer assets than reported by the plans.

b. Reasons for PBGC's Financial Status

The chronic underfunding of some defined benefit pension plans poses a significant risk to the PBGC. The PBGC's single-employer insurance program has a $2.9 billion deficit. Furthermore, the overall level of underfunding is rapidly increasing amount single employer plans and now exceeds $50 billion. Of this amount, reasonably possible future claims against the PBGC exceed $13 billion. These claims, and the continued underfunding of pension benefits threaten the future solvency

of the PBGC and may lead to a taxpayer bailout if the Federal Government is required to pay pension benefits to participants of underfunded pension plans which terminate.There is concern that the sponsors of underfunded defined benefit pension plans continue to promise additional benefit benefits without funding the plans' existing unfunded pension liabilities. Under present law, new pension liabilities can be added to an underfunded defined benefit pension plan before old liabilities are funded. Companies in financial difficulty sometimes use benefit increases as a means to increase compensation when they cannot afford to pay higher current wages. Workers may be willing to accept such unfunded future pension promises because they are at least partially insured by the PBGC and workers recognize that the immediate costs to their employers of higher wages makes such wage increases unlikely.

Under present law, sponsors of underfunded defined benefit pension plans are not required to fund their plans within a reasonable time. Under present law, plan sponsors are allowed to fund their pension liabilities over an extended period of time. Some companies have taken advantage of the flexibility under the present-law rules and have chosen to maintain their plans at significantly underfunded levels. Some companies have used this funding flexibility to maintain chronically underfunded plans whose financial condition has not improved since the passage of ERISA nearly 20 years ago. In a few cases, companies have terminated plans with no remaining assets without ever violating present-law minimum funding standards.

The PBGC lacks sufficient information from defined benefit pension plan sponsors with which to determine the risks it bears as the result of underfunded defined benefit pension plans. Under present law, the PBGC can subpoena information from plans and plan sponsors for the purpose of carrying out its responsibilities under ERISA. However, this subpoena process is rarely used because it is costly, labor intensive and time consuming. As a result, the PBGC has used this authority only in cases involving negotiations with financially plan sponsored. The PBGC has not used its subpoena authority for purposes of day-to-day policy or operational reviews of ongoing plans.

As reported by the GAO, following plan termination, plan underfunding typically is nearly 60 percent greater than previously reported by the plan sponsor on its latest Form 5500 filed with the IRS. In addition, the level of underfunding tends to rise rapidly shortly before termination of a defined benefit pension plan. In these situations, the PBGC is unable to take prompt action to protect the Government and plan participants from further loss because it lacks necessary financial information. Thus, the PBGC needs full and timely access to the records of the defined benefit pension plans that it insures, in much the same manner as the Federal Deposit Insurance Corporation (FDIC) has access to information on the financial institutions it insures.

The PBGC's deficit has increased, in part, because premiums paid to the PBGC are not sufficient to cover its operations. The PBGC's premium income continues to be insufficient to cover the costs of actual and expected plan terminations for which the PBGC is responsible. Further, the PBGC's variable rate premium does not properly reflect the risk assumed by the PBGC in providing insurance for severely underfunded defined benefit pension plans.

Under present law, plan participants are not fully aware of the extent to which their defined benefit pension plans are underfunded and that not all benefits are fully insured by the PBGC. There are certain disclosure requirements applicable to defined benefit pension plan sponsors which allow participants to monitor and understand benefits under their plan. Plans are required to provide participants with a summary plan description, which typically provides a boilerplate summary of pension benefit guarantee and melt and the extent of underfunding if a plan is less than 70 percent funded. Despite these varied reporting requirements, participants are not given clear and understandable information about (1) the extent to which their plan is underfunded and (2) which of their benefits are insured by the

PBGC, and the extent to which such benefits are insured, should their underfunded plan terminate.

c. Results Of Bill

The bill is designed to improve the funding of single-employer defined benefit pension plans and reduce the potential exposure of the PBGC. The bill also is intended to reduce or eliminate the PBGC's operating deficit and to reduce the defined benefit pension system's unfunded liabilities for which the Federal Government is potentially responsible.

Under the bill, pension plan sponsors will be required to meet their existing pension commitments in a reasonable period of time. The funding requirements will ensure that sponsors of underfunded defined benefit pension plans contribute amounts sufficient to improve the financial condition of the plans or, at a minimum, prevent plan funding from deteriorating. Further, the bill will allow employers that sponsor both underfunded defined benefit pension plans and defined contribution plans to fully fund their underfunded defined benefit plans more rapidly.

It is important to require that plan sponsors provide participants in defined benefit pension plans that are underfunded with a simple notice each year stating the extent to which the plan is underfunded, and an explanation of which benefits will or will not be guaranteed by the PBGC and the extent of the PBGC's guarantee, if the plan is terminated.

The bill provides the PBGC with better access to the records of certain troubled plans that it insures. This will allow the PBGC to take prompt action to protect participants, the PBGC, and taxpayers from any additional losses.

The bill's provision phasing out of the present-law cap on the additional premium for underfunded plans contained in the bill will require poorly funded plans, which pose the greatest risk to the PBGC, to pay their fair share of premiums. The phase out also will encourage underfunded plans to contribute more or otherwise reduce underfunding in order to avoid the payment of additional premiums.

III. RETIREMENT PROTECTION ACT OF 1994

A. PART 1—I. PENSION PLAN FUNDING

1. Minimum funding requirements (secs. 751 and 761 of the bill, secs. 412(c), 412(l), and 412(m) of the Code, and secs. 204, 302(d), and (e) of ERISA)

a. Present Law

1. In General

ERISA and the Code impose both minimum and maximum defined benefit pension plan funding requirements. The minimum funding requirements are designed to provide at least a certain level of benefit security by requiring the employer to make certain minimum contributions to the plan. The requirements recognize that, in an on-going plan, pension liabilities are generally a long-term liability. Thus, benefits are not required to be immediately funded, but can be funded over a long period of time.

The maximum funding limitations are designed to limit and allocate efficiently the loss of Federal tax revenue associated with the special tax treatment afforded qualified retirement plans. Thus, annual deductible contributions to a defined benefit pension plan are limited to an amount that is not significantly greater than the amount that would normally be necessary under the employer's long-term actuarial funding method.

The minimum and maximum funding requirements provide the employer considerable flexibility in determining the amount of the contribution that must, or can, be made in any given year. The minimum required or maximum permitted contribution that can be made depends on the funding method used by the plan and the actuarial assumptions used by the plan actuary.

In response to concerns about the financial status of underfunded pension plans, the minimum funding standards were modified, and special additional funding requirements were added for certain underfunded pension plans, by the Pension Protection Act of 1987.

The minimum and maximum funding requirements, and the special rules for underfunded pension plans, are discussed in detail below.

b. Minimum Funding Standard

1. In General

Under the Code and ERISA, certain defined benefit pension plans are required to meet a minimum funding standard for each plan year. As an administrative aid in the application of the funding standard, each defined benefit pension plan is required to maintain a special account called a "funding standard account" to which specified charges and credits (including credits for contributions to the plan) are to be made for each plan year. If, as of the close of a plan year, the account reflects credits equal to or in excess of charges, the plan is treated as meeting the minimum funding standard for the year. Thus, as a general rule, the minimum contribution for a plan year is determined as the amount by which the charges to the account would exceed credits to the account if no contribution were made to the plan.

2. Accumulated Funding Deficiencies

If, as of the close of any plan year, charges to the funding standard account exceed credits to the account, then the excess is referred to as an "accumulated funding deficiency." Unless a minimum funding waiver is obtained, an employer who is responsible for contributing to a plan with an accumulated funding deficiency is subject to a 10-percent nondeductible excise tax on the amount of the deficiency (Code sec. 4971).

If the deficiency is not corrected within the "taxable period", then an employer who is responsible for contributing to the plan is also subject to a nondeductible excise tax equally to 100 percent of the deficiency is not corrected within the "taxable period", then an employer who is responsible for contributing to the plan is also subject to a nondeductible excise tax equal to 100 percent of the deficiency. The taxable period is the period beginning with the end of the plan year in which there is a deficiency and ending on the earlier of (1) the date of a mailing of a notice of deficiency with respect to the 10-percent tax or (2) the date on which the 10-percent tax is assessed by the Internal Revenue Service (IRS). If the employer responsible for contributing to the plan is a member of a controlled group, each member of the group is jointly and severally liable for the excise tax.

For example, if the balance of charges to the funding standard account of a plan for a year would be $200,000 without any contributions, then a minimum contribution in that amount would be required to meet the minimum funding standard for the year to prevent an accumulated funding deficiency. If the total contribution is not made, then the employer would be subject to an excise tax equal to 10 percent of the deficiency for the year. if the deficiency were not corrected within the specified period, then the 100-percent excise tax would be imposed on such employer.

3. Funding Methods

In General

A defined benefit pension plan is required to use an acceptable actuarial cost method to determine the elements included in its funding standard account for a year. Generally, an actuarial cost method breaks up the cost of benefits under the plan into annual charges consisting of two elements for each plan year. These elements are referred to as (1) normal cost, and (2) supplemental cost.

Normal Cost

The normal cost for a plan for a year generally represents the cost of future benefits allocated to the year by the funding method used by the plan for current employees and, under some funding methods, for separated employees. Specifically, it is the amount actuarially determined that would be required as a contribution by the employer to maintain the plan if the plan had been in effect from the beginning of service of the included employees and if the costs for prior years had been paid, and all assumptions as to interest, mortality, time of payment, etc., had been fulfilled. The normal cost will be funded by future contributions to the plan (1) in level dollar amounts, (2) as a uniform percentage of payroll, (3) as a uniform amount per unit of service (e.g., $1 per hour), or (4) on the basis of the actuarial present value of benefits considered accruing in particular plan years. Supplemental cost

The supplemental cost for a plan year is the cost of future benefits allocated to the year that would not be met by normal costs and employee contributions. The most common supplemental cost is that attributable to past service liability, which represents the cost of future benefits under the plan (1) on the date the plan is first effective, or (2) on the date a plan amendment increasing plan benefits is first effective. Under some funding methods, there is no past service liability component.

Other supplemental costs may be attributable to net experience losses, which a waiver was obtained. Supplemental costs must be amortized over a range of years specified under the Code and ERISA.

Acceptable Methods

Normal cost and supplemental cost are key elements in computations under the minimum funding standard. Although these costs may differ substantially, depending upon the actuarial cost method used to value a plan's assets liabilities, they must be determined under an actuarial cost method permitted by ERISA.

ERISA enumerates six acceptable actuarial cost methods and provides that additional methods may be permitted under Treasury regulations. Normal costs and supplemental costs under a plan are computed on the basis of an actuarial valuation of the assets and liabilities of a plan. An actuarial valuation is required once every plan year. More frequent valuations may be required by the IRS.

4. Charges And Credits To The Funding Standard Account

In General

Under the minimum funding standard, the portion of the cost of a plan that is required to be paid for a particular year depends upon the nature of the cost. For example, the normal cost for a year is generally required to be funded currently. On the other hand, costs with respect to past service (for example, the cost of retroactive benefit increases), experience losses, and changes in actuarial assumptions, are spread over a period of years.

Normal Cost

Each plan year, a plan's funding standard account is charge with the normal cost assigned to that year under the particular acceptable actuarial cost method adopted by the plan. The charge for normal cost will require an offsetting credit in the funding standard account. Usually, an employer contribution is required to create the credit.

For example, if the normal cost for a plan year is $150,000, the funding standard account would be charge with that amount for the year. Assuming that there are no other credits in the account to offset the charge for normal cost, and employer contribution of $150,000 will be required for the year to avoid an accumulated funding deficiency.

Past Service Liability

There are 3 separate charges to the funding standard account that may arise as the result of past service liabilities. The first applies to a plan under which past service liability has increased due to a plan amendment made after January 1, 1974; the second applies only to a plan that came into existence after January 1,

1974; and the third applies only to a plan in existence on January 1, 1974. Past service liabilities result in annual charges to the funding standard account for a specified period of years. Assuming that there are no other credits in the account to offset a charge for past service liability, and employer contribution will be required for the year to avoid an accumulated funding deficiency.

In the case of a plan that was in existence on January 1, 1974, the funding standard account is charged annually with a portion of the past service liability determined as of the first day of the plan year of which the funding standard applied to the plan (generally the year beginning in 1976). In the case of a single-employer plan, the amount of the liability with which the account is charged for a year is based on amortization of the past service liability over a period of 40 plan years. The liability is required to be amortized (in much the same manner as a 40-year mortgage) in equal annual installment over the 40-year funding period unless the plan becomes fully funded.

A plan that was not in existence on January 1, 1974, is generally required to determine past service liability as of the first day of its first plan year beginning after September 2, 1974 (the date ERISA was enacted). This liability is required to be amortized by a single-employer plan in equal annual installments over a period of 30 plan years. Accordingly, if there are no other credits in the account to offset the charge for this past service liability, and if the plan does not become fully funded, annual employer contributions will be required for 30 day plan years to offset charges for this past service liability.

With respect to all plans (whether or not in existence on January 1, 1974), if a net benefit increase takes place as the result of a plan amendment, then the unfunded past service liability attributable to the net increase is determined that year and amortized over a period of 30 years.

For example, assume that a plan uses the calendar year as the plan year. Further assume that during 1987 the plan is amended to increase benefits and that the net result of plan amendments for 1987 is that the past service liability under the plan is increased by $500,000. In addition, the plan's actuary uses an interest rate of 8 percent in determining plan costs. The 30-year schedule requires that $44,414 be charged to the funding standard account each year to amortize the past service liability.

Accordingly, for each year in the 30-year period beginning with 1987, the plan's funding standard account is charged with the amount of $44,414. If there are no other credits in the account to offset the charge for past service liability, an employer contribution of $44,414 would be required for each of the 30 years to avoid an accumulated funding deficiency unless the plan becomes fully funded.

Gains And Losses From Changes In Assumptions

If the actuarial assumptions used for funding a plan are revised and, under the new assumptions, the accrued liability of a plan is less than the accrued liability computed under the previous assumptions, the decrease is a gain from changes in actuarial assumptions. If the new assumptions result in an increase in the accrued liability, the plan has a loss from changes in actuarial assumptions. The accrued liability of a plan is the actuarial present value of projected pension benefits under the plan that will not be funded by future contributions to meet normal cost. Under the funding standard, the gain or loss for a year from changes in actuarial assumptions is amortized over a period of 10 plan years, resulting in credits or charges to the funding standard account.

Experience Gains And Losses

In determining plan funding under an actuarial cost method, a plan's actuary generally makes certain assumptions regarding the future experience of a plan. These assumptions typically involve rates of interest, mortality, disability, salary increases, and other factors affecting the value of assets and liabilities. If, on the basis of these assumptions, the contributions made to the plan result in actual unfunded liabilities that are less than anticipated by the actuary, then the excess is an experi-

ence gain. If the actual unfunded liabilities are greater than those anticipated, then the difference is an experience loss. For a single-employer plan, experience gains and losses for a year are amortized over a 5-year period.

Waived Funding Deficiencies

Under the funding standard, the amount of a waived funding deficiency is amortized over a period of 5 plan years, beginning with the year following the year in which the waiver is granted. Each year, the funding standard account is charged with the amount amortized for that year unless the plan becomes fully funded. The interest rate used for purposes of determining the amortization on the waived amount is the greater of (1) the rate used in computing costs under the plan, or (2) 150 percent of the mid-term applicable Federal interest rate (AFR) in effect for the first month of the plan year.

Switchback Liability

ERISA provides that certain plans may elect to use an alternative minimum funding standard account for any year in lieu of the funding standard account. ERISA prescribed specified annual charges and credits to the alternative account. No accumulated funding deficiency is considered to exist for the year if a contribution meeting the requirements of the alternative account is made, even if a smaller contribution is required to balance charges and credits in the alternative account than would be required to balance the funding standard account for a plan year.

During years for which contributions are made under the alternative account, an employer must also maintain a record of the charges and credits to the funding standard account. If the plan later switches back from the alternative account to the funding standard account, the excess, if any, of charges over credits at the time of the change ("the switchback liability") must be amortized over a period of 5 plan years.

Reasonableness Of Actuarial Assumptions

All costs, liabilities, interest rates, and other factors are required to be determined on the basis of actuarial assumptions and methods (1) each of which is reasonable individually or (2) which result, in the aggregate, in a total plan contribution equivalent to a contribution that would be obtained if each assumption were reasonable. In addition, the assumptions are required to reflect the actuary's best estimate of experience under the plan.

5. Special Rules For Underfunded Plans

In General

A special funding rule applies to underfunded single-employer defined benefit pension plane (other than plans with no more than 100 participants on any day in the preceding plan year). This special funding rule was adopted in the Pension Protection Act of 1987 due to concerns about the solvency of the defined benefit pension plan system and because of concerns that the generally applicable funding rules were not in all cases sufficient to ensure that plans would be adequately funded.

Calculation Of Minimum Required Contribution

With respect to plans subject to the special rule, the minimum required contribution is, in general, the greater of (1) the amount determined under the normal funding rules, or (2) the sum of (a) normal cost, (b) the amount necessary to amortize experience gains and losses over 5 years and gains and losses resulting from changes in actuarial assumptions over 10 years, and (c) the deficit reduction contribution plus the amount required with respect to benefits that are contingent on unpredictable events. In no event is the amount of the contribution to exceed the amount necessary to increase the funded ratio of the plan to 100 percent.

The deficit reduction contribution is the sum of (1) the unfunded old liability amount, and (2) the unfunded new liability amount. Calculation of these amounts is based on the plan's current liability.

Current Liability

The term "current liability" generally means all liabilities to employees and their beneficiaries under the plan determined as if the plan terminated. However, the value of any "unpredictable contingent event benefit" is not taken into account in determining current liability until the event on which the benefit is contingent occurs.

The interest rate used in determining the current liability. of a plan, as well as the contribution required under the special rule, is required to be within a specified range. The permissible range is defined as a rate of interest that is not more than 10 percent above or below the weighted average of the rates of interest on 3-year Treasury securities for the 4-year period ending on the last day before the beginning of the plan year for which the interest rate is being used. The weights are established in IRS Notice 88-37. The annual rate of interest on 30-year Treasury securities is the rate published by the Board of Governors of the Federal Reserve System. The Secretary may, where appropriate, allow a lower rate of interest except that such rate may not be less than 80 percent of the average rate discussed above.

Unfunded current liability means, with respect to, any plan year, the excess of (1) the plan's current liability over (2) the value of the plan's assets reduced by any credit balance in the funding standard account. The funded current liability percentage of a plan for a plan year is the percentage that (1) the value of the plan's assets (reduced by any credit balance in the funding standard account) is of (2) the plan's current liability.

Unfunded Old Liability Amount

The unfunded old liability amount is, in general, the amount necessary to amortize the unfunded old liability under the plan in equal annual installments (until fully amortized) over a fixed period of 18 plan years (beginning with the first plan year beginning after December 31, 1988). The "funded old liability" with respect to a plan is the unfunded current liability of the plan as of the beginning of the first plan year beginning after December 31, 1987, determined without regard to any plan amendment adopted alter October 16, 1987, fiat increases plan liabilities (other than amendments adopted pursuant to certain collective bargaining agreements).

Unfunded New Liability Amount

The unfunded new liability amount for a plan year is the applicable percentage of the plan's unfunded new liability." Unfunded new liability means the unfunded current liability of the plan for the plan year, determined without regard to (1) the unamortized portion of the unfunded old liability (and the unamortized portion of the unfunded liability from certain benefit increases) and (2) the liability with respect to any unpredictable contingent event benefits, without regard to whether or not the event has occurred. Thus, in calculating the unfunded new liability, all unpredictable contingent event benefits are disregarded, even if the event on which that benefit is contingent has occurred.

If the funded current liability percentage is less than 35 percent, then the applicable percentage is 30 percent. The applicable percentage decreases by .25 of one percentage point for each 1 percentage point by which the plan's funded current liability percentage exceeds 35 percent. For example, if a plan's funded current liability percentage is 39 percent, 29 percent of the plan's unfunded new liability for the plan year must be included in the calculation of the deficit reduction contribution for the plan year.

Unpredictable Contingent Event Benefits

The value of any unpredictable contingent event benefit is not considered until the event has occurred. If the event on which an unpredictable contingent event benefit is contingent occurs during the plan year and the assets of the plan are less than current liability (calculated after the event has occurred), then an additional funding contribution (over and above the minimum funding contribution otherwise due) is required.

Unpredictable contingent event benefits include benefits that depend on contingencies that, like facility shutdowns or reductions or contractions in workforce, are not reliably. and reasonably predictable. The event on which an unpredictable contingent event benefit is contingent is generally not considered to have occurred until all events on which the benefit is contingent have occurred. The amount of the additional contribution is generally equal to the greater of (1) the unfunded portion of the benefits paid during the plan year (regardless of the form in which paid), including (except as provided by the Secretary) any payment for the purchase of an annuity contract with respect to a participant with respect to unpredictable contingent event benefits, and (2) the amount that would be determined for the year if the unpredictable contingent event benefit liabilities were amortized in equal annual installments over 7 years, beginning with the plan year in which the event occurs.

The rule relating to unpredictable contingent event benefits is phased in for plan years beginning in 1989 through 2001.

Small Plan Rule

The special rules for underfunded plans do not apply to plans with 100 or fewer employees. In the case of a plan with more than 100 but no more than 150 participants during the preceding year, the amount of the additional deficit reduction and unpredictable contingent amount benefit contribution is determined by multiplying the otherwise required additional contribution by 2 percent for each participant in excess of 100.

6. Full Funding Limit

To limit and allocate efficiently the loss of Federal tax revenue associated with the special tax treatment afforded qualified plans, ERISA and the Code limit the amount of annual contributions that can be made to a defined benefit plan.

One limitation is the full funding limit, under which no contribution is required under the minimum funding rules to the extent the plan is at the full funding limit. Before 1988, the full funding limit was 100 percent of an employer's accrued liability, as determined under the plan's funding method. However, because of concerns that employers could manipulate the limit by changing actuarial assumptions, the Pension Protection Act of 1987 amended ERISA and the Code to create a new full funding limit. The new full funding limit is equal to the lesser of the old funding limit (accrued liability) or 150 percent of the employer's current liability. Current liability is all liabilities to participants and beneficiaries under the plan determined as if the plan terminated. It represents only benefits accrued to date, and is not dependent on the actuarial funding method. As a result, the new full funding limit can be lower than the old full funding limit.

If the employer contributes an amount equal to the full funding limit, the funding standard account is credited so that the employer is not subject to the underfunding excise tax, even though the funding standard account would otherwise be left with a deficit for the year. In addition, the full funding limit affects the deductibility of employer contributions to qualified plans.[50]

7. Time For Making Contributions

Under present law, the required minimum funding contribution for a plan year must be made within 8-1/2 months after the end of the plan year.

If the contribution is made by such due date, the contribution is treated as if it were made on the last day of the plan year. In the case of single-employer defined benefit pension plans, 4 installments of estimated contributions are required for the plan year with the total 'contribution due within 8-1/2 months alter the end of the plan year. The amount of each required installment is 25 percent of the lesser of (1) 90 percent of the amount required to be contributed for the current plan year or (2) 100 percent of the amount required to be contributed for the preceding plan year. If a plan sponsor fails to make a required installment, additional interest is charged to the funding standard account.

c. Explanation of Provision

1. Special Funding Rules For Underfunded Plans

In General

The bill changes the special funding rules for underfunded single-employer defined benefit plans (other than plans with no more than 100 participants on any day in the preceding plan year) that were adopted in the Pension Protection Act of 1987.

In general, the bill (1) provides (a) a pent rule that exempts from the special funding rules applicable to underfunded plans, plans that have a funded current liability percentage of at least 90 percent and certain plans that have a funded current liability percentage between 80 percent and 90 percent, and (b) transition rules under which certain other plans are exempt, (2) modifies the calculation of the minimum required contribution applicable to underfunded plans, (3) changes the permissible range of interest rates and requires uniform mortality assumptions for the purpose of determining a plan's current liability, (4) accelerates the funding of a plan's "unfunded new liability", (5) changes the calculation of the additional funding contribution required on account of an unpredictable contingent event, (6) provides an elective transition rule for sponsors of underfunded plans to protect against possibly large increases in their minimum required contributions on account of the proposed changes in the special funding rules, and (7) changes the manner in which sponsors of defined benefit pension plans determine the full funding limit of their plans.

2. Certain Underfunded Plans Exempt From The Special Funding Rules

Permanent Rules

The bill provides two exceptions to the special funding rules for underfunded plans. First, such rules do not apply to a plan which for any plan year has a current funded liability percentage of at least 90 percent. This rule is referred to as the "90 percent exemption."

Second, the special funding rules for underfunded plans do not apply for a plan year if (1) the funded current liability percentage for the plan year is at least 80 percent and (2) the funded current liability percentage for each of the two immediately preceding plan years (or each of the second and third immediately preceding plan years) is at least 90 percent. This rule is referred to as the "volatility rule."

For purposes of these exemptions, the funded current liability percentage is determined using the highest interest rate in the permissible range and the mortality assumptions contained in the bill. In addition, assets are not reduced by credit balances in the funding standard account.

The following example illustrates the exceptions to the special funding rules for underfunded plans.

Example 1: Assume that the funded current liability percentage (determined as specified under the bill) for Plan A for each of the plan years beginning on January 1, 1996, 1997, 1998, and 1999's as follows: 95%, 95%, 75%, and 80%. For plan years 1996 and 1997, the plan is not subject to the additional funding rules for underfunded plans because the funded current liability percentage is at least 90%. The plan is subject to the additional funding rules for plan year 1998 because the funded current liability percentage is below 80%. The plan is not subject to the additional funding rules for plan year 1999, because it satisfies the volatility rule.

Transition Rules

The bill provides two transition rules under which certain plans are exempt from the new rules for underfunded pension plans.

The first rule applies for purposes of determining whether a plan is subject to the new rules in plan years beginning in 1995 and 1996. A plan is not subject to the new rules for a plan year beginning in 1995 or 1996 if (1) in that year, the plan's funded current liability percentage is at least 80 percent, and (2) the plan meets a transition test in any two of the plan years beginning in 1992, 1993, and 1994. The transition test need not be satisfied by the same method in each year. The transition test is met for a plan year if, for the plan year, the plan met one of the following requirements (under the law as then in effect):

* the plan did not have an additional charge under the special funding rules for underfunded plans (or would not have had such a charge if the plan used the highest interest rate within the permissible range[51] and assets are determined by taking into account credit balances in the funding standard account);

* the plan's full funding limit was zero; or

* the amount required to be contributed under the special rules for underfunded plans (i.e., the amount of the deficit reduction contribution) did not exceed the lesser of .5 percent of current liability or $5 million.

The second rule applies for purposes of determining whether a Alan is subject to the new rules for plan years beginning in 1996 and 1997.[52] A plan is not subject to the new rules for a plan year beginning in 1996 or 1997 if (1) in that year, the plan's funded current liability percentage is at least 80 percent, (2) the plans current liability percentage for the plan year beginning in 1995 was at least 90 percent, and (3) in the plan year beginning in 1994, the plan met one of the three transition requirements described above.

3. Calculation Of Minimum Required Contribution

The bill changes the manner in which underfunded plans calculate their minimum required contribution for a plan year. Under the bill, amounts necessary to amortize experience gains and losses and gains and losses resulting from changes of actuarial assumptions are no longer considered in the calculation of the minimum required contribution for underfunded plans.

According to the PBGC, one reason that the minim required contribution for underfunded plans adopted in the Pension Protection Act of 1987 has not been effective in increasing contributions to underfunded plans is because experience gains or gains from changes in actuarial assumptions are counted twice under present law, i.e., to reduce the minimum required contribution for underfunded plans and as a credit to the funding standard account under the normal funding rules. Thus, under the bill, the minimum required contribution for underfunded plans is, in general, the greater of (1) the amount determined under the normal funding rules, or (2) the deficit reduction contribution plus the. amount required with respect to benefits that are contingent on unpredictable events.

Further, the bill adds a third and fourth component to the calculation of the deficit reduction contribution under present law. Under the bill, the deficit reduction contribution is the sum of (1) the unfunded old liability amount, (2) the unfunded new liability amount, (3) the expected increase in current liability due to benefits accruing during the plan year, and (4) the amount needed to amortize the increase in current liability due to certain future changes in the required mortality tables. The third component replaces the normal cost component of the calculation under present law. The fourth component is discussed below.

In addition, the bill provides that the amount of the minimum required contribution for underfunded plans cannot exceed the amount necessary to increase the funded current liability percentage of the plan to 100 percent taking into account all charges and credits to the funding standard account and the expected increase in current liability attributable to benefits accruing during the plan year.

4. Changes In Interest Rates And Mortality Assumptions

In General

As under present law, the calculation of the deficit reduction contribution for underfunded plans is based on the plan's current liabilities.

Under the bill, a plan's current liability is determined as under present law, except that the bill (1) lowers the maximum interest rate that can be used to determine the current liability, and (2) requires all underfunded plans to use the same mortality table to determine current liability.

Interest Rate

For plan years beginning on or after January 1, 1999, the bill reduces the highest permissible rate that may be used to calculate current liability to 105 percent of the weighted average of the rates of interest on 30-year Treasury securities during the 4-year period ending on the last day before the beginning of the plan year. For years beginning after 1994 and before 1999, the maximum permitted interest rate is the following percentage of such 4-year weighted average rate: plan years beginning in 1995, 109 percent; plan years beginning in 1996, 108 percent; plan years beginning in 1997, 107 percent; and plan years beginning in 1998, 106 percent.

Mortality Tables

Under the bill, in the case of plan years beginning after December 31, 1994, the mortality table used to determine current liability is to be prescribed by the Secretary based upon the 1983 Group Annuity Mortality Table (GAM 83 mortality table). Such mortality table will be effective until the later of plan years beginning in 2000 or such time as the Secretary prescribes new tables by regulations. Any tables prescribed by the Secretary are to reflect the actual experience of pension plans and projected trends in such experience. In prescribing tables, the Secretary is to take into account the results of independent studies on mortality of individuals covered by pension plans. The Secretary is required to review the new tables at least every five years and update them as necessary to reflect changes in pension plan experience and trends. Increases in liability due to changes in mortality assumptions in the first year in which new mortality tables are effective are to be amortized over 10 years in equal installments.

Plans are permitted to use a different mortality table for certain participants who are entitled to benefits on account of disability ("disabled participants"). For plan years beginning in 1995, plans may use their own mortality assumptions for disabled participants (under the plan's definition of disability) provided such assumptions meet the general requirement that actuarial assumptions be reasonable. For plan years beginning on or after January 1, 1996, the Secretary is to prescribe mortality tables for disabled participants. The Secretary is to prescribe two tables: one table for persons who become entitled to disability benefits (under the plan's definition of disability) before the plan year beginning in 1995; and another table for persons who become eligible for disability benefits in a plan year beginning on or after January 1, 1995. The separate disability table may not be used with respect to persons who become entitled to disability benefits under the plan on or after January 1, 1995, unless such persons are disabled within the meaning of Title II of the Social Security Act.

Amortization Of Increase In Current Liability Under The Bill

Under the bill, increases in current liability attributable to the bill's changes in interest rates and mortality assumptions for the 1995 plan year are treated as an "additional unfunded old liability amount" and are amortized in equal annual installments over 12 years beginning with the 1995 plan year. The additional unfunded old liability amount is the difference between the current liability of the plan as of the beginning of the 1995 plan year using (1) the interest and mortality assumptions contained in the bill and (2) the mortality assumption and relative interest rate used to determine current liability for the 1993 plan year. For example, if the plan used 110 percent of the weighted average in the 1993 plan year, the relative interest rate for this calculation would be 110 percent of the weighted average in the 1995 plan year.

As an alternative to amortization of only the change in current liability due to changes in interest and mortality assumptions, an employer may make an irrevocable election to expand the 12-year amortization to the entire increase in current liability attributable to plan years beginning after December 31, 1987 and before January 1, 1995.

The increase in liability for this optional rule would be measured as the amount by which the plan's unfunded current liability as of the beginning of the 1995 plan year, valued using the new specified interest and mortality assumptions, exceeds the unamortized portion of the unfunded old liability under the plan as of the beginning of the 1995 plan year. This increase would be treated as unfunded old liability and amortized over 12 years beginning with the first plan year beginning on or after January 1, 1995. If an election is made to amortize this amount and the plan would otherwise be subject to the special rules for underfunded plans, the amount charged to the funding standard account under section 302(d) of ERISA and section 412(1) of the Code for plan years beginning after December 31, 1994 and before January 1, 2002, would not be less, for any year, than the amount that would have been required under those sections if current law had remained in effect.

5. Acceleration Of Unfunded New Liability

Under present law, if a plan's funded current liability percentage is 35 percent or less, 30 percent of the plan's unfunded new liability for the plan year must be included in the calculation of the deficit reduction contribution for the plan year. The bill increases the 35 percent threshold under present law to 60 percent. Thus, under the bill, if a plan's funded current liability percentage is 60 percent or less, 30 percent of the plan's unfunded new liability for the plan year would be included in the calculation of the deficit-reduction contribution for the plan year.

Under the bill, the 30 percent amount decreases by .40 of one percentage point for each percentage point by which the plan's funded current liability percentage exceeds 60 percent, to a minimum of 18 percent for a plan that is percent funded.

6. Unpredictable Contingent Event Benefits

The bill adds a third component to the calculation of the additional funding contribution required on account of an unpredictable contingent event. Under the bill, the amount of the additional funding contribution is equal to the greater of the amounts determined under present law or the additional contribution that would be required if the unpredictable contingent event benefit liabilities were included in the calculation of the plan's unfunded new liability for the plan year. Under present law, for purposes of calculating the unfunded new liability for a plan year, all unpredictable contingent event benefits are disregarded.

In addition, the bill limits the present value of the additional finding contribution with respect to one event to the unpredictable contingent event benefit liabilities attributable to that event.

7. Transition Rule

The bill provides an elective transition rule for sponsors of underfunded plans to protect against possibly large increases in their minimum required contributions on account of changes in the special rules. Under the transition rule, the minimum required contribution for a plan year cannot be less than the minimum required contribution determined under present law.

Relief under the transition rule depends on the plan's funded current liability percentage. This relief is based upon the amount necessary to increase the plan's funded current liability percentage by a specified percentage by the end of the plan year, including the expected increase in current liability due to benefits accruing and the expected benefit payments

during the plan year. The specified percentages and the initial funded current liability percentage are not adjusted to reflect the changes in the maximum permitted interest rate scheduled for plan years beginning before January 1, 2000.

8. Changes In Full Funding Limit

The bill changes the manner in which sponsors of defined benefit pension plans determine the full funding limit to conform to IRS practice. The bill retains the present-law rules relating to the determination of a defined benefit pension plan's full funding limit but also provides that the expected increase in current liability due to benefits accruing during the plan year be included when determining the employer's current liability. The bill allows plans to determine their 150 percent of current liability limit for full funding limit purposes without regard to the modifications of the interest rate and mortality assumptions set forth in the bill.

The bill also provides that the full funding limit is not less than 90 percent of the plan's current liability (using the modifications to the interest rate and mortality assumptions set forth in the bill). In determining whether a plan is at this 90 percent limit, plan assets are not reduced by credit balances in the funding standard account.

It is intended that reporting requirements will be revised as necessary to implement the revised funding rules, for example, to reflect the volatility rules, the liquidity requirement (discussed below), the revised full funding limitation, and the transition rules.

9. Plan Liquidity Requirement

In general, the bill requires underfunded single-employer defined benefit pension plans to make quarterly contributions sufficient to maintain liquid plan assets, i.e., cash and marketable securities, at an amount approximately equal to three times the total trust disbursements for the preceding 12-month period.

Under the bill, the plan liquidity requirement applies to underfunded single-employer defined benefit pension plans (other than small plans)[53] that (1) are required to make quarterly installments of their estimated minimum funding contribution for the plan year, and (2) have a liquidity shortfall for any quarter during the plan year. A plan has a liquidity shortfall if it is liquid assets as of the last day of the quarter are less than the base amount for the quarter. Liquid assets are cash, marketable securities and such other assets as specified by the Secretary of the Treasury. The base amount for the quarter is an amount equal to the product of three times the adjusted disbursements from the plan for the 12 months ending on the last day of the last month preceding the quarterly installment due date. If the base amount exceeds the product of two times the sum of adjusted disbursements for the 36 month ending on the last day of the last month preceding the quarterly installment due date, and an enrolled actuary certifies to the satisfaction of the Secretary of the Treasury that the excess is the result of nonrecurring circumstances, such nonrecurring circumstances are not included in the base amount. For purposes of determining the base amount, adjusted disbursements mean the amount of all disbursements from the plan's trust, including purchases of annuities, payments of single sums, other benefit payments, and administrative expenses reduced by the product of the plan's funded current liability percentage for the plan year and the sum of the purchases of annuities, payments of single sums, and such other disbursements as the Secretary of the Treasury provides in regulations.

Under the bill, the amount of the required quarterly installment for defined benefit pensions plans that have a liquidity shortfall for any quarter is the greater of the quarterly installment as determined under present law or the liquidity shortfall. The amount of the liquidity shortfall must be paid in the form of liquid assets. It may not be paid by the application of credit balances in the funding standard account. The amount of any liquidity shortfall payment when added to prior installments for the plan year cannot exceed the amount necessary to increase the funded current liability percentage of the plan to 100 percent taking into account the expected increase in current liability due to benefits accruing during the plan year.

If a liquidity shortfall payment is not made, then the plan sponsor will be subject to a nondeductible excise tax equal to 10 percent of the amount of the outstanding liquidity shortfall. A liquidity shortfall payment will no longer be considered outstanding on the earlier of (1) the last day of a later quarter for which the plan does not have a liquidity shortfall or (2) the date on which the liquidity shortfall for a later quarter is timely paid. If the liquidity shortfall remains outstanding after four quarters, the excise tax increases to 100 percent.

The bill amends ERISA to prohibit fiduciaries from making certain payments from determined benefit pension plans during the period in which the plan has a liquidity shortfall. Prohibited payments include (1) plan distributions in excess of the monthly amount paid under a single life annuity (plus any social security supplements) to plan participants or beneficiaries whose annuity starting date (as defined under present law)[54] occurs during the period in which there is a liquidity shortfall, (2) purchase of benefit annuities from insurers, or (3) other payments as provided by the Secretary of the Treasury. The bill also amends ERISA to include a civil penalty for violations of the prohibited payment rule.

Under the bill, if a fiduciary makes a prohibited distribution from the plan, he or she will be subject to a civil penalty for each prohibited distribution equal to the lesser of the amount of the distribution of $10,000. Finally, the bill amends the Code to provide that compliance with ERISA's prohibited payment rules will not result in plan disqualification for tax purposes.

d. Effective Date

The provision generally applies to plan years beginning after December 31, 1994.

2. ERISA Citations (sec. 751(a)(11) of the Bill and sec. 404(g)(4) of the Code)

a. Present Law

Under present law, contributions to tax-qualified pension plans are deductible within limits. The Code provides that amounts paid by an employer or a member of its controlled group under the following provisions of ERISA are treated as plan contributions subject to the deduction rules of the Code (Code sec. 404(g)(1)): (1) section 4041(b) of ERISA (relating to standard terminations); (2) section 4062 of ERISA (relating to liability to the PBGC in the case of a distress termination); (3) section 4603 of ERISA (relating to liability of a substantial employer for withdrawal from single-employer plans under multiple controlled groups); (4) section 4064 of ERISA (relating to liability on termination of single-employer plans under multiple controlled groups; and (5) part I of subtitle E of title IV of ERISA (relating to liability upon withdrawal from a multiemployer plan). The Code provides that the references to these sections of ERISA are to these sections as in effect on the date of enactment of the Single Employer Pension Plan Amendments Act of 1986 (SEPPAA). The amounts referred to in such sections have generally been increased since the enactment of SEPPAA.

b. Explanation of Provision

The bill provides that the references to ERISA in Code section 404(g) are to ERISA as in effect on the date of enactment of the bill.

c. Effective Date

The provision is effective on the date of enactment.

3. Contributing Sponsor (sec. 761(a)(11) of the Bill and sec. 4001(a)(13) of ERISA)

a. Present Law

Under present law, for purposes of the PBGC termination insurance program, the contributing sponsor of a plan is defined as a person (1) who is responsible, in connection with such plan, for meeting the funding requirements under section 302 of ERISA or under section 412 of the Code or (2) who is a member of the controlled group of a person described in (1), has been responsible for meeting such funding requirements, and has employed a significant number (as may be defined by the PBGC) of participants under such plan while such person was so responsible. Under the Pension Protection Act of 1987, all members of a contributing sponsor's controlled group are responsible for the minimum funding requirements.

b. Explanation of Provision

The bill defines contributing sponsor for purposes of title IV of ERISA to mean the person responsible for making minimum funding contributions to the plan under section 302 of ERISA or section 412 of the Code, without regard to the controlled group rules. All members of a contributing sponsor's controlled group remain liable for making the minimum funding contribution.

c. Effective Date

The provision is effective as if included in the Pension Protection Act of 1987.

4. Limitation on Changes In Current Liability Assumptions (secs. 752 and 762 of the Bill, sec. 412(c) of the Code, and sec. 302(c) of ERISA)

a. Present Law

Under present law, in determining plan funding under an actuarial cost method, a plan's actuary makes certain assumptions regarding the future experience of a plan.

These assumptions typically involve rates of interest, mortality, disability, salary increases, and other factors affecting the value of assets and liabilities. A plan's actuary may revise these assumptions to reflect the actual experience of the plan. Actuarial assumptions must be reasonable both individually and in the aggregate and must reflect the actuary's best estimate of experience under the plan.

b. Explanation of Provision

The bill prohibits certain underfunded plans from changing the actuarial assumptions used to determine current liability for a plan year (other than interest rate and mortality assumptions) unless the new assumptions are approved by the Secretary of the Treasury. Under the bill, approval of changes in actuarial assumptions applies to a single-employer defined benefit pension plan if: (1) the plan is subject to the termination insurance program under Title IV of ERISA; (2) the aggregated unfunded vested benefits of all underfunded plans maintained by the employer and members of the employer's controlled group exceed $50 million; and (3) the change in assumptions decreases the plan's unfunded current liability for the current plan year by (a) more than $50 million or (b) more than $5 million and at least 5 percent of the current liability.

c. Effective Date

The provision is effective with respect to changes in actuarial assumptions for plan years beginning after October 28, 1993. In addition, any changes in actuarial assumptions for plan years beginning after December 31, 1992, and before October 29, 1993, that would have been subject to the approval requirements set forth in the bill will not be effective for plan years beginning after 1994 unless approved by the Secretary of the Treasury.

5. Anticipation of Bargained Benefit Increases (secs. 753 and 763 of the Bill, sec. 412(c) of the Code, and sec. 302 of ERISA)

a. Present Law

Under final Treasury Regulations, a defined benefit plan's funding method is not considered reasonable if it anticipates changes in plan benefits that become effective, whether or not retroactively, in a future plan year or

that become effective after the first day of, but during, a current plan year. However, the regulations contain an elective exception to this general rule for collective bargained plans. Under the regulations, a collectively bargained plan's funding method is considered reasonable if the plan elects on a consistent basis to anticipate benefit increases scheduled to take effect during the term of the collective bargaining agreement applicable to the plan (Treas. Reg. 1.412(c)(3)-1(d)).

b. Explanation of Provision

The bill requires sponsors of collectively bargained plans to recognize any negotiated benefit increases scheduled to take effect in a future plan year in the plan year in which the collective bargaining agreement is entered into for purposes of the normal funding rules but not the special rules for underfunded plans.

c. Effective Date

The provision applies to plan years beginning after December 31, 1994, with respect to collective bargaining agreements in effect on or after January 1, 1995.

6. Modification of Quarterly Contribution Requirement (secs. 754 and 764 of the Bill, sec. 412(m) of the Code, and sec. 302(e) of ERISA)

a. Present Law

Under present law, the required minimum funding contribution for a plan year must be made within $8\frac{1}{2}$ months after the end of the plan year. If the contribution is made by such due date, the contribution is treated as if it were made on the last day of the plan year.

In the case of single-employer defined benefit pension plans, 4 installments of estimated contributions are required for the plan year with the total contribution due within $8\frac{1}{2}$ months after the end of the plan year. The amount of each required installment is 25 percent of the lesser of (1) 90 percent of the amount required to be contributed for the cur rent plan year or (2) 100 percent of the amount required to be contributed for the preceding plan year. If a plan sponsor fails to make a required installment, additional interest is charged to the funding standard account.

b. Explanation of Provision

Under the bill, single-employer defined benefit plans with at least a 100-percent funded current liability percentage in the proceeding plan year are not required to make quarterly estimated contributions during the current plan year.

c. Effective Date

The provision is effective for plan years beginning after the date of enactment.

7. Exceptions to Excise Tax On Nondeductible Contributions (sec. 755 of the bill and new sec. 4972(c)(6) of the Code)

a. Present Law

The Code imposes a limit on the amount of deductible contributions that can be made annually to a defined benefit pension plan. Contributions necessary to pay normal costs (as defined under the funding rules) generally are fully deductible. Contributions necessary to fund supplemental costs generally are deductible only to the extent necessary to cover such costs amortized over 10 years.

However, the amount of the deduction an employer can claim for the year cannot exceed the full funding limitation for that year, except that a special deduction rule applies to underfunded defined benefit pension plans. In the case of a single-employer defined benefit pension plan which has more than 100 participants during the plan year, the maximum amount deductible is not less than the plan's unfunded current liability as determined under the minimum funding rules. For purposes of determining whether a plan has more than 100 participants during a plan year, all defined benefit pension plans maintained by the same employer or any member of the employer's controlled group (within the meaning of secs.

414(b), (c), (m), and (o) of the Code) are treated as one plan but only employees of such member or employer are taken into account.

The Code also imposes limits on the amount of deductible contributions that can be made annually if an employer sponsors both a defined benefit pension plan and a defined contribution plan that covers some of the same employees. Under the combined plan deduction limits, the total deduction for all plans for a plan year is generally limited to the greater of (1) 25 percent of compensation or (2) the contribution necessary to meet the minimum funding requirements of the defined benefit pension plan for the year. For underfunded single-employer defined benefit pension plans with more than 100 participants for the plan year, the maximum deductible contribution for the year is not less than the plan's unfunded current liability as determined under the minimum funding rules.

There is a 10-percent nondeductible excise tax imposed on contributions in excess of the applicable deduction limit (Code sec. 4972).

b. Explanation of Provision

Under the bill, nondeductible contributions to a terminating single-employer defined benefit pension plan subject to Title IV of ERISA with less than 101 participants for the year are not subject to the excise tax on nondeductible contributions to the extent such nondeductible contributions do not exceed the plan's unfunded current liability as determined under the minimum funding rules.

In addition, employer contributions to one or more defined contribution plans that are nondeductible because they exceed the combined plan deduction limits are not subject to the 10-percent nondeductible excise tax to the extent such contributions do not exceed 6 percent of compensation in the year for which the contributions are made. The 6-percent of compensation limit is determined on an aggregate basis. For example, if an employer makes contributions to two defined contribution plans under the rule, the excise tax does not apply as long as the contributions are less than 6 percent of the aggregate compensation of participants in both plans. For purposes of this rule, the combined plan deduction limits are first applied to contributions to the defined benefit pension plan. If contributions exceed the 6-percent limit, only those in excess of 6 percent are subject to the excise tax. This provision applies only if the defined benefit pension plan is a single-employer defined benefit pension plan that has more than 100 participants. Amounts that are not subject to the excise tax in the year contributed shall not be taken into account for purposes of applying the 6-percent limit in any future year.

c. Effective Date

The provision waiving the excise tax for nondeductible contributions to a terminating single-employer defined benefit pension plan is effective for taxable years ending on or after the date of enactment. The provision waiving the excise tax for nondeductible contributions to certain defined contribution plans is effective for taxable years ending on or after December 31, 1992.

8. Prohibition on Benefit Increases Where Plan Sponsor Is In Bankruptcy (sec. 766 of the Bill, sec. 401(a) of the Code, and sec. 204 of ERISA)

a. Present Law

Under present law, there is no restriction on the adoption of plan amendments that increase benefits when a plan is underfunded.

b. Explanation of Provision

The bill amends the Code and ERISA to prohibit an employer in bankruptcy from adopting an amendment to an underfunded plan that increases benefits unless the benefit increase does not become effective until after the Effective Date of the employer's plan of reorganization. The prohibition does not apply to amendments that (1) provide reasonable, de minimis increases in liabilities for employees of the debtor, (2) repeal an amendment made within the first 2½ months of a plan year that would reduce accruals for that

plan year, as permitted under section 302(c)(8) of ERISA, or (3) are needed to meet the qualification requirements contained in the Code.

c. Effective Date

The provision is effective with respect to plan amendments adopted on or after the date of enactment.

9. Single Sum Distributions (sec. 767 of the Bill, secs. 411(a)(11), 417(e), and 415(b) of the Code, and sec. 203(e) and 205(g) of ERISA)

a. Determination of Present Value

1. Present Law

Under the Code and ERISA, if the present value of a participant's nonforfeitable accrued benefit exceeds $3,500, the benefit cannot be distributed (i.e., cashed out) without the consent of the participant.

In addition, if the present value of a joint and survivor annuity exceeds $3,500 it cannot be distributed without the consent of the participant and the participant's spouse. For purposes of these rules, present value is calculated by using an interest rate no greater than (1) the rate that would be used (as of the date of the distribution) by the PBGC for purposes of determining the present value of a lump-sum distribution on plan termination if the vested accrued benefit (using such rate) is not in excess of $25,000, or (2) 120 percent of such PBGC rate if the vested accrued benefit exceeds $25,000.

2. Explanation of Provision

Under the bill, present value for purposes of the cash-out rules must be no less than the present value determined by using the mortality table that is to be prescribed by the Secretary of the Treasury based upon the "prevailing commissioners' standard table" used to determine reserves for group annuity contracts issued on the date as of which present value is determined. The prevailing commissioners' standard table means, with respect to any contract, the most recent commissioners' standard tables prescribed by the National Association of Insurance Commissioners which are permitted to be used in computing reserves for the type of contract under the insurance laws of at least 26 States when the contract was issued (sec. 807(d)(5)(A) of the Code). Currently, the prevailing commissioners' standard table used to determine reserves for annuity contracts is the GAM 83 mortality table. Future changes in the prevailing table will only apply to the calculation of present value when the secretary of the Treasury issues guidance making such changes applicable.

In addition, present value for purposes of the cash-out rules must be no less than the present value determined by using the annual rate of interest on 30-year Treasury securities for the month before the date of distribution or such earlier time as provided in Treasury regulations. The annual rate of interest on 30-year Treasury securities is the rate published by the Board of governors of the Federal Reserve System.

A plan will not violate the prohibition on the reduction of accrued benefits merely because it calculates benefits in accordance with the provision.

3. Effective Date

The provision is generally effective for plan years beginning after December 31, 1994, except that an employer can elect to treat the provision as being effective on or after the date of enactment.

Under a transition rule for distributions from plans in effect on the date of enactment of the bill, until the earlier of the first plan year beginning after 1999 or the later of when a plan amendment applying the provision is adopted or made effective, the bill requires present value to be calculated as under present law, using the interest rate valuation methodology for lump-sum distributions under PBGC regulations in effect on September 1, 1993, the present-law Code and ERISA rules,

and the current plan provisions (provided they are consistent with present law).

b. Limitation On Maximum Benefits

1. Present Law

The Code provides limits on contributions and benefits under tax-qualified pension plans. In the case of a defined benefit pension plan, the maximum annual benefit payable is generally the lesser of (1) 100 percent of average compensation or (2) $118,800 for 1994. The dollar limit is adjusted annually for cost-of-living increases.

If the benefit under the plan is payable in a form other than a single life annuity, then the benefit must generally be converted to the actuarial equivalent of a single life annuity for purposes of applying the limit on benefits. If the benefit is payable before social security retirement age, the dollar limit on annual benefits is reduced so that the limit is actuarially equivalent to a benefit beginning at the social security retirement age. These adjustments are made using an assumed interest rate that is not less than the greater of 5 percent or the rate specified in the plan. Similarly, if the benefit is payable after social security retirement age, then the limit is actuarially increased. This adjustment is made using an assumed interest rate that is not greater than the lesser of 5 percent or the rate specified in the plan.

2. Explanation of Provision

The bill provides that the mortality table required to be used for purposes of adjusting any benefit or limitation in applying the limit on maxims benefits is to be prescribed by the Secretary of the Treasury based upon the "prevailing commissioners' standard table" used to determine reserves for group annuity contracts issued on the date as of which the adjustments described in this provision are made.

The prevailing commissioners' standard table means, with respect to any contract, the most recent commissioners' standard tables prescribed by the National Association of Insurance Commissioners which are permitted to be used in computing reserves for that type of contract under the insurance laws of at least 26 States when the contract was issued (Sec. 807(d)(5)(A) of the Code). Currently, the prevailing commissioners' standard table used to determine reserves for annuity contracts is the GAM 83 mortality table. Future changes in the prevailing table will only apply to the adjustments described in this provision when the Secretary of the Treasury issues guidance making such changes applicable. In addition, in adjusting benefits that are payable in a form other than a single life annuity, if the benefit is subject to the joint and survivor annuity rules, the interest rate is the same interest rate used to calculate benefits under those rules (as described above).

A plan will not violate the prohibition on reduction in accrued benefits merely because it calculates benefits in accordance with the provision.

3. Effective Date

The provision is effective for limitation years beginning after December 31, 1994, except that an employer can elect to treat the provision as being effective on or after the date of enactment. Benefits accrued as of the last day of the last plan year beginning before January 1, 1995, will not have to be reduced merely because of the provision. A plan does not have to be amended to comply with the provision until a date to be specified by the Secretary of the Treasury, provided the plan complies with the proposal in operation.

10. Adjustment tO Lien For Missed Minimum Funding Contributions (sec. 768 of the bill . Sec. 412(n) of the Code. and sec. 302(f) of ERISA)

a. Present Law

Under present law, in the case of a single-employer defined benefit pension plan with a funded current liability percentage of less than 100 percent, a lien arises on all controlled group property in favor of the plan 60 days after the due date of an unpaid required contribution where the cumulative missed contributions exceed $1 million. The amount of the lien is the amount of the cumulative missed contributions in excess of $1 million.

b. Explanation of Provision

The bill (1) eliminates the 60-day waiting period before the lien arises, (2) eliminates the $1 million exclusion on amounts subject to the lien, and (3) provides that the lien applies only to plans covered by the PBGC termination insurance program. Thus, for example, the lien provision does not apply to plans maintained by a professional services employer which do not have more than 25 active participants or to plans maintained exclusively for substantial owners.[55]

c. Effective Date

The provision is effective for required contributions that become due on or after the date of enactment.

11. Special Funding Rule For Certain Plans (sec. 769 of the Bill)

a. Present Law

Under certain circumstances, the PBGC may restore the operation of a plan that has terminated to the sponsor of the plan. Treasury regulations set forth rules regarding the funding of plans that have been terminated and then restored by the PBGC.

b. Explanation of Provision

The bill provides that any changes made by the bill to the funding rules of the Code or ERISA do not apply to certain plans. In particular, such changes do not apply to a plan that, on the date of enactment, is subject to a restoration payment schedule order issued by the PBGC and that meets the requirements of Treasury regulations.

Such changes do not apply to a plan maintained by an affected air carrier (as defined in section 4001(a) of ERISA) and assumed by a new plan sponsor pursuant to the terms of a written agreement with the PBGC dated January 5, 1993, and approved by the U.S. Bankruptcy Court on December 30, 1992.

The bill also provides that for the first 5 plan years beginning after December 31, 1994, certain amortization amounts are not taken into account in the calculation of offsets under section 412(1)(1)(A)(ii) of the Code (and the corresponding section of ERISA). The amortization amounts that are not taken into account are those established for plan years beginning after December 31, 1987, and before January 1, 1993, by reason of nonelective changes under the frozen entry age actuarial cost method. An example of a nonelective change is a change in the method to redetermine the unfunded liability so as to prevent the calculation of a normal cost under the method that was negative.

c. Effective Date

The provision is effective on the date of enactment.

II. AMENDMENTS RELATING TO TITLE IV OF ERISA

1. Reportable Events (Sec. 771 of the Bill and Sec. 4043 of ERISA)

a. Present Law

Under present law, the plan administrator is required to notify the PBGC of the occurrence of certain events, called reportable events, that may indicate possible risk to the financial status of the plan or the PBGC insurance program. The plan administrator is to notify the PBGC within 30 days after the plan administrator knows or has reason to know that a reportable event has occurred. If an employer making contributions under a plan knows or has reason to know that a reportable event has occurred, the employer is to notify the plan administrator of the reportable event.

b. Explanation of Provision

The bill provides that a contributing sponsor that knows or has reason to know that a reportable event has occurred (as well as the plan administrator is responsible for reporting the event to the PBGC, and repeals the requirement that an employer notify the plan administrator of reportable events.

The bill adds a number of new events to the list of reportable events. Under the bill, a reportable event occurs: (1) when a person ceases to be a member of the controlled group; (2) when a contributing sponsor or a member of a contributing sponsor's controlled group liquidates in a case under title 11, United States Code, or under any similar Federal law or law of a State or political subdivision of a State; (3) when a contributing sponsor or a member of a contributing sponsor's controlled group declares an extraordinary dividend or redeems, in any 12-month period, an aggregate of 10 percent or more of the total combined voting power of all classes of stock entitled to vote, or an aggregate of 10 percent or more of the total value of shares of all classes of stock, of a contributing sponsor and all members of its controlled group; (4) when, in any 12-month period, an aggregate of 3 percent or more of the benefit liabilities of a plan covered by the PBGC insurance program are transferred to a person that is not a member of the contributing sponsor's controlled group or to a plan maintained by a person that is not a member of the contributing sponsor's controlled group.

A contributing sponsor is required to notify the PBGC of the occurrence of one of the new reportable events at least 30 days in advance of the Effective Date of the event if (1) as of the close of the preceding plan year, aggregate unfunded vested benefits of plans maintained by the contributing sponsor (or controlled group members) exceed $50 million, and (2) the funded vested benefit percentage of the plans is less than 90 percent. This advance notice requirement does not apply to an event if the contributing sponsor or the member of the contributing sponsor's controlled group to which the event relates is a person subject to the reporting requirements of section 13 or section 15(d) of the Securities Exchange Act of 1934 or is a subsidiary (as defined for purposes of such Act) of a person subject to such reporting requirements.

Any information provided to the PBGC with respect to a reportable event generally is exempt from public disclosure.

c. Effective Date

The provision is effective for events occurring 60 days or more after the date of enactment.

2. Certain Information Required To Be Furnished to the PBGC (Sec. 772 of the Bill and new Sec. 4010 of ERISA)

a. Present Law

The PBGC receives certain financial information from plans pursuant to required filings with the Department of Labor and other Governmental agencies.

b. Explanation of Provision

The bill authorizes the PBGC to require certain contributing sponsors and controlled group members to submit to the PBGC such information as the PBGC may specify by regulation. The required information may include information that the PBGC determines is necessary to determine plan assets and liabilities and copies of audited financial statements. A contributing sponsor or controlled group member is subject to these information requirements if: (1) the total unfunded vested benefits of all underfunded plans sponsored by the controlled group exceed $50 million; (2) missed funding contributions exceed $1 million and the conditions for imposing a lien for missed contributions have been met; or (3) there are outstanding minimum finding waivers in an amount exceeding $1 million, any portion of which remains unpaid. Any information required to be provided to the PBGC under the provision would be exempt from public disclosure.

c. Effective Date

The provision is effective on the date of enactment.

3. Enforcement of Minimum Funding Requirements (sec. 773 of the Bill and sec. 4003(e) of ERISA)

a. Present Law

Under present law, the Secretary of the Treasury generally interprets and administers the minimum funding requirements. An excise tax applies with respect to the failure to satisfy the minimum funding requirements. In addition, plan participants and fiduciaries may bring suit under ERISA to enforce the minimum funding requirements. The Secretary of Labor may also bring suit to enforce the minimum funding requirements if requested to do so by a plan participant, fiduciary, or the Secretary of the Treasury. The PBGC enforces a lien that arises in favor of the plan if missed required contributions exceed $1 million.

b. Explanation of Provision

The bill gives the PBGC the authority to bring suite to enforce the minimum funding standards if the amount of missed required contributions exceeds $1 million. The bill does not change existing authority of the Department of the Treasury or the Department of Labor.

c. Effective Date

The provision is effective for minimum funding contributions that become due on or after the date of enactment.

4. Phase Out Of Variable Rate Premium Cap (sec. 774 of the Bill and sec. 4006(a)(3) of ERISA)

a. Present Law

Single-employer defined benefit pension plans covered by the termination insuranc program are required to pay a flat per-partici pant premium of $19. In addition, unde funded single-employer defined benefit pension plans are required to pay an additional premium based on the amount of underfunding for vested benefits. The additional premium is $9 per $1,000 of underfunding, and is capped at $53 per participant. Thus, the maximum per-participant premium for an underfunded plan is $72.

In determining the amount of underfunding for purposes of the additional premium, benefits are valued using an interest rate equal to 80 percent of the annual yield on 30-year Treasury securities for the month preceding the month in which the plan year begins. The value of plan assets is determined using the actuarial basis used for valuing assets for minimum funding purposes.

b. Explanation of Provision

The bill phases out the cap on the additional premium for underfunded plans over three years, beginning with plan years beginning on or after July 1, 1994. For plan years beginning on or after July 1, 1994, but before July 1, 1995, the maximum additional premium is $53 per participant, plus 20 percent of the amount of the total premium. (determined without regard to the cap) in excess of $53. For plan years beginning on or after July 1, 1995, but before July 1, 1996, the maximum additional premium is $53 per participant, plus 60 percent of the amount of the total premium (determined without regard to the cap) in excess of $53.

The bill also modifies the interest rate and asset valuation method to be used for purposes of determining the additional premium. For plan years beginning on and after July 1, 1997, the interest rate is 85 percent of the 30-year Treasury rate. For plan years beginning during or after the first year in which the successor mortality tables to GAM 83 as prescribed by the Secretary are first effective, the interest rate is 100 percent of the 30-year Treasury rate and assets are valued at market value.

c. Effective Date

The provision is generally effective as described above. In the case of regulated public utilities engaged in providing electric energy, gas, water, or sewerage disposal services (as defined in Code Sec. 7701(a)(33)(A)(i)), no premiums in excess of those under present law are payable until the first plan year beginning on or after the earlier of January 1, 1998, or the date that the regulated utility begins to collect from customers rates that reflect the cost incurred for additional premiums pursuant to a final and nonappealable determination by all public utility commissions that the increased premium costs are recoverable from customers of the utility.

5 Disclosure to Participants (sec. 775 of the Bill and new sec. 4011 of ERISA)

a. Present Law

ERISA requires that plan participants be provided with certain information. One of these requirements is that, if the plan is less than 70 percent funded, the annual deport regarding the plan must include the funded percentage of the plan. Plan administrators must also provide participants with a summary plan description (SPD) that advises participants of their rights, obligations, and eligibility for benefits under the plan.

If the benefits are guaranteed by the PBGC, the SPD must include a summary of ERISA's guarantee provisions and a statement that more information may be obtained from the PBGC or the plan administrator. Department of Labor regulations include a safe harbor statement that can be included in the SPD to satisfy the requirements regarding the PBGC guarantee.

b. Explanation of Provision

The bill amends title IV of ERISA to require that the plan administrator of a plan that must pay the additional premium applicable to underfunded plans must notify plan participants of the plan's funded status and the limits on the PBGC's guarantee should the plan terminate while underfunded, unless the plan is exempt from the special funding rules for underfunded plans (other than on account of the number of plan participants). For purposes of this exception to the disclosure requirement, a plan's funded current liability percentage is determined without subtracting any credit balance in the plan's funding standard account from assets. The notice will have to be provided in the time and manner prescribed by the PBGC.

c. Effective Date

The provision is effective for plan years beginning after the date of enactment.

6. Missing Participants (sec. 776 of the Bill and new sec. 4031 of ERISA)

a. Present Law

Under present law, one of the requirements of a standard termination is that the plan administrator distribute plan assets by purchasing irrevocable commitments from an insurer in satisfaction of all benefit liabilities that must be in annuity form and by otherwise providing all benefit liabilities that need not be provided in annuity form. Under PBGC rules, if the plan administrator has been unable to locate participants after having made a reasonable effort to do so, the administrator must either purchase irrevocable commitments to provide benefits for each participant who has not been located or, in certain circumstances, deposit the amounts in a bank.

b. Explanation of Provision

The bill provides special rules for payment of benefits in the case of participants under a plan terminating in a standard termination whom the plan administrator cannot locate after a diligent search ("missing participants").

The plan administrator is required to (1) transfer a participant's designated benefit to the PBGC or purchase an annuity from an insurer to satisfy the benefit liability to the participant and (2) provide the PBGC with such information and certifications with respect to such benefits or annuity as the PBGC may specify. Any amounts transferred to the PBGC under the provision are treated as assets under a plan trusteed by the PBGC.

After a missing participant whose benefit was transferred to the PBGC is located, if the plan could have distributed the benefit to the participant in a single sum without participant or spousal consent, the PBGC will pay the participant a single sum benefit equal to the benefit paid to the PBGC, plus interest as specified by the PBGC. In other cases (i.e., if the plan could not have distributed the benefit in a single sum without consent), the PBGC will pay a benefit based on the designated benefit and the actuarial assumptions prescribed by the PBGC at the time that the PBGC received the designated benefit. The PBGC will make such payments available in the same forms and at the same times as a guaranteed benefit would be paid, except that the PBGC can make a benefit available in the form of a single sum if the plan provided such a benefit. A designated benefit is the single sum benefit the participant would receive (1) under the plan's actuarial assumptions in the case of a distribution that can be made without participant or spousal consent, (2) under the PBGC assumptions in effect on the date that the designated benefit is transferred to the PBGC, in the case of a plan that does not pay any single sums other than those that can be made without consent, or (3) under the assumptions of the PBGC or the plan, whichever provides the higher single sum, in the case of a plan that does pay a single sum other than those that do not require consent.

The qualification requirements of the Code are amended to provide that a plan will not be treated as failing to satisfy those requirements merely because it provides for benefits to missing participants as provided in the bill.

c. Effective Date

The provision is effective with respect to distributions that occur in plan years beginning after final regulations implementing the provision are adopted by the PBGC.

7. Modification of Maximum Guarantee For Disability Benefits (sec. 777 of the Bill and sec. 4022(b) of ERISA)

a. Present Law

The PBGC guarantee generally applies to a disability benefit if the benefit is in the form of an annuity payable because of permanent and total disability and the participant became disabled before the plan termination date. As is the case with other benefits, the PBGC guarantee is reduced if the benefit begins before age 65.

b. Explanation of Provision

Disability benefits are exempted from the age reduction in the maximum PBGC insurance amount, if the participant has been determined to be entitled to social security benefits on account of disability.

c. Effective Date

The provision is effective for terminations for which a notice of intent to terminate is flied or for which the PBGC institutes termination proceedings on or after the date of enactment.

8. Procedures to Facilitate The Distribution Of Termination Benefits (sec. 778 of the Bill and secs. 4041(b) and (c) of ERISA)

a. Remedies For Noncompliance With Requirements For Standard Terminations

1. Present Law

Under present law, a single-employer defined benefit pension plan can terminate in a standard termination only after the plan administrator notifies participants of the termination, issues individual benefit notices to participants, and flies a notice with the PBGC that includes an enrolled actuary's certification of sufficiency.

The PBGC has 60 days to review the proposed termination. If the PBGC does not issue a notice of noncompliance nullifying the proposed termination, the plan administrator may distribute plan assets.

If the plan administrator fails to give all participants advance notice of how their benefits were computed or fails to fully comply with other procedural requirements designed to protect participants, the PBGC generally is required to issue a notice of noncompliance and nullify the termination.

2. Explanation of Provision

The bill provides that the PBGC is not required to issue a notice of noncompliance (and nullify a termination) in the case of failure to meet procedural requirements with respect to the termination if it determines that it would be inconsistent with the interests of participants and beneficiaries to issue the notice.

3. Effective Date

The provision applies with respect to standard terminations for which the PBGC has not, as of the date of enactment, issued a notice of noncompliance that has become final, or otherwise issued a final determination that the plan termination is nullified.

b. Distress Termination Criteria For Banking Institutions

1. Present Law

Under present law, a plan may terminate in a distress termination only if the contributing sponsor and each member of the controlled group of the contributing sponsor meet one of three financial distress standards. One of the standards of financial distress is that the entity is liquidating in bankruptcy or insolvency proceedings under title II of the United States Code or under any similar law of a State or political subdivision of a State.

2. Explanation of Provision

The bill provides that a proceeding under title II of the United States Code or any similar Federal law qualifies as a standard for distress criteria. This standard applies, for example, to bank insolvency receivership actions.

3. Effective Date

The provision is effective as if included in the SEPPAA. Thus, it is effective with respect to notices of intent to terminate filed with the PBGC on or after January 1, 1986.

FOOTNOTES

[37] The provision also applies to limits that are indexed in the same manner as these limits or are based on these limits (e.g., the compensation threshold for purposes of determining highly compensated individuals under sec. 414(q) and the excess benefit limit under the excise tax on excess distributions under sec. 4980A.

* * *

[48] U.S. General Accounting Office, Hidden Liabilities Increase Claims Against Government Insurance Program (GAO/HRD-93-7) December 30, 1992.

[49] Shutdown benefits are benefits payable only upon the closing of a facility or termination of the plan sponsor's business operations. Since plan actuaries cannot predict the probability of such occurrences, shutdown benefits are only partially funded, at best.

[50] The effect of the full funding limit on the deductibility of employer contributions is described below.

[51] For plan years beginning in 1992, 1993, and 1994, the highest rate within the permissible range is 110 percent of the 4-year weighted average of the rates on 30-year Treasury securities.

[52] For plan years beginning in 1996, a plan may satisfy either the first or the second transition rule. For plan years beginning in 1997, a plan may satisfy either the second transition rule or the permanent rule.

[53] A plan is a small plan if it had 100 or fewer participants on each day during the plan year (as determined in Code sec. 412(1)(6)).

[54] Under present law, an individual's annuity starting date is the first day of the first period for which an amount is payable as an annuity or in the case of a benefit not payable in the form of an annuity, the first day on which all events have occurred which entitle the individual to such benefit (sect. 417(f)(2) of the Code).

[55] Substantial owner is defined generally as an individual who (1) owns the entire interest in an unincorporated trade or business, (2) in the case of a partnership, is a partner.

Part 2

Text of ERISA

Employee Retirement Income Security Act, as Amended

◊ ◊ ◊

Editor's Note: This is the text of ERISA, as amended by various public laws, through and including the Retirement Protection Act of 1994 (enacted as part of the Uruguay Round Agreements Act, P.L. 103-465). In 1994, the following statutes were passed that amended ERISA or the Code sections excerpted in this volume: the Social Security Administrative Reform Act of 1994 (establishing the Social Security Administration as an independent agency); the Social Security Domestic Employment Reform Act (the so-called "Nanny tax"); the Pension Annuitants Protection Act (granting a cause of action under ERISA with respect to certain former participants and beneficiaries entitled to benefits under ERISA-covered plans); and the Retirement Protection Act (enacted as part of the Uruguay Round Agreements Act). The effective date of these changes are set forth in Editor's Notes to the affected provisions throughout this book.

Provisions of ERISA and the Code that were deleted by the changes made by the legislation described in the previous paragraph are enclosed within boldface brackets [ ]. Provisions that were added by those acts are in italics. Editor's notes appear at the beginning or end of the section or subsection of ERISA or the Code to which they pertain, separated from the text by a row of three diamonds.

◊ ◊ ◊

SHORT TITLE AND TABLE OF CONTENTS

Sec. 1. This act may be cited as the "Employee Retirement Income Security Act of 1974."

◊ ◊ ◊

Editor's Note: For table of contents, See ERISA Finding List at front of this volume

◊ ◊ ◊

Title I — Protection of Employee Benefit Rights

Subtitle A — General Provisions

FINDINGS AND DECLARATION OF POLICY

Sec. 2. (a) The Congress finds that the growth in size, scope, and numbers of employee benefit plans in recent years has been rapid and substantial; that the operational scope and economic impact of such plans is increasingly interstate; that the continued well-being and security of millions of employees and their dependents are directly affected by these plans; that they are affected with a national public interest; that they have become an important factor affecting the stability of employment and the successful development of industrial relations; that they have become an important factor in commerce because of the interstate character of their activities, and of the activities of their participants, and the employers, employee organizations, and other entities by which they are established or maintained; that a large volume of the activities of such plans is carried on by means of the mails and instrumentalities of interstate commerce; that owing to the lack of employee information and adequate safeguards concerning their operation, it is desirable in the interests of employees and their beneficiaries, and to provide for the general welfare and the free flow of commerce, that disclosure be made and safeguards be provided with respect to the establishment, operation, and administration of such plans; that they substantially affect the revenues of the United States because they are afforded preferential Federal tax treatment; that despite the enormous growth in such plans many employees with long years of employment are losing anticipated retirement benefits owing to the lack of vesting provisions in such plans; that owing to the inadequacy of current minimum standards, the soundness and stability of plans with respect to adequate funds to pay promised benefits may be endangered; that owing to the termination of plans before requisite funds have been accumulated, employees and their beneficiaries have been deprived of anticipated benefits; and that it is therefore desirable in the interests of employees and their beneficiaries, for the protection of the revenue of the United States, and to provide for the free flow of commerce, that minimum standards be provided assuring the equitable character of such plans and their financial soundness.

(b) It is hereby declared to be the policy of this Act to protect interstate commerce and the interests of participants in employee benefit plans and their beneficiaries, by requiring the disclosure and reporting to participants and beneficiaries of financial and other information with respect thereto, by establishing standards of conduct, responsibility, and obligation for fiduciaries of employee benefit plans, and by providing for appropriate remedies, sanctions, and ready access to the Federal courts.

(c) It is hereby further declared to be the policy of this Act to protect interstate commerce, the Federal taxing power, and the interests of participants in private pension plans and their beneficiaries by improving the equitable character and the soundness of such plans by requiring them to vest the accrued benefits of employees with significant periods of service, to meet minimum standards of funding, and by requiring plan termination insurance.

DEFINITIONS

Sec. 3. For purposes of this title:

(1) The terms "employee welfare benefit plan" and "welfare plan" mean any plan, fund, or program which was heretofore or is hereafter established or maintained by an employer or by an employee organization, or by both, to the extent that such plan, fund, or program was established or is maintained for the purpose of providing for its participants or their beneficiaries, through the purchase of insurance or otherwise, (A) medical, surgical, or hospital care or benefits, or benefits in the event of sickness, accident, disability, death or unemployment, or vacation benefits, apprenticeship or other training programs, or day care centers, scholarship funds, or prepaid legal services, or (B) any benefit described in section 302(c) of the Labor Management Relations Act, 1947 (other than pensions on retirement or death, and insurance to provide such pensions).

(2)(A) Except as provided in subparagraph (B), the terms "employee pension benefit plan" and "pension plan" mean any plan, fund, or program which was heretofore or is hereafter established or maintained by an employer or by an employee organization, or by both, to the extent that by its express terms or as a result of surrounding circumstances such plan, fund, or program—

(i) provides retirement income to employees, or

(ii) results in a deferral of income by employees for periods extending to the termination of covered employment or beyond, regardless of the method of calculating the contributions made to the plan, the method of calculating the benefits under the plan or the method of distributing benefits from the plan.

(B) The Secretary may by regulation prescribe rules consistent with the standards and purposes of this Act providing one or more exempt categories under which—

(i) severance pay arrangements, and

(ii) supplemental retirement income payments, under which the pension benefits of retirees or their beneficiaries are supplemented to take into account some portion or all of the increases in the cost of living (as determined by the Secretary of Labor) since retirement,

shall, for purposes of this title, be treated as welfare plans rather than pension plans. In the case of any arrangement or payment a principal effect of which is the evasion of the standards or purposes of this Act applicable to pension plans, such arrangement or payment shall be treated as a pension plan.

(3) The term "employee benefit plan" or "plan" means an employee welfare benefit plan or an employee pension benefit plan or a plan which is both an employee welfare benefit plan and an employee pension benefit plan.

(4) The term "employee organization" means any labor union or any organization of any kind, or any agency or employee representation committee, association, group, or plan, in which employees participate and which exists for the purpose, in whole or in part, of dealing with employers concerning an employee benefit plan, or other matters incidental to employment relationships; or any employees' beneficiary association organized for the purpose in whole or in part, of establishing such a plan.

(5) The term "employer" means any person acting directly as an employer, or indirectly in the interest of an employer, in relation to an employee benefit plan; and includes a group or association of employers acting for an employer in such capacity.

(6) The term "employee" means any individual employed by an employer.

(7) The term "participant" means any employee or former employee of an employer, or any member or former member of an employee organization, who is or may become eligible to receive a benefit of any type from an employee benefit plan which covers employees of such employer or members of such organization, or whose beneficiaries may be eligible to receive any such benefit.

(8) The term "beneficiary" means a person designated by a participant, or by the terms of an employee benefit plan, who is or may become entitled to a benefit thereunder.

(9) The term "person" means an individual, partnership, joint venture, corporation, mutual company, joint-stock company, trust, estate, unincorporated organization, association, or employee organization.

(10) The term "State" includes any State of the United States, the District of Columbia, Puerto Rico, the Virgin Islands, American Samoa, Guam, Wake Island, and the Canal Zone. The term "United States" when used in the geographic sense means the States and the Outer Continental Shelf lands defined in the Outer Continental Shelf Lands Act (43 U.S.C. 1331-1343).

(11) The term "commerce" means trade, traffic, commerce, transportation, or communication between any State and any place outside thereof.

(12) The term "industry or activity affecting commerce" means any activity, business, or industry in commerce or in which a labor dispute would hinder or obstruct commerce or the free flow of commerce, and includes any activity or industry "affecting commerce" within the meaning of the Labor Management Relations Act, 1947, or the Railway Labor Act.

(13) The term "Secretary" means the Secretary of Labor.

(14) The term "party in interest" means, as to an employee benefit plan—

(A) any fiduciary (including, but not limited to, any administrator, officer, trustee, or custodian), counsel, or employee of such employee benefit plan;

(B) a person providing services to such plan;

(C) an employer any of whose employees are covered by such plan;

(D) an employee organization any of whose members are covered by such plan;

(E) an owner, direct or indirect, of 50 percent or more of—

(i) the combined voting power of all classes of stock entitled to vote or the total value of shares of all classes of stock of a corporation,

(ii) the capital interest or the profits interest of a partnership, or

(iii) the beneficial interest of a trust or unincorporated enterprise, which is an employer or an employee organization described in subparagraph (C) or (D);

(F) a relative (as defined in paragraph (15) of any individual described in subparagraph (A), (B), (C), or (E);

(G) a corporation, partnership, or trust or estate of which (or in which) 50 percent or more of—

(i) the combined voting power of all classes of stock entitled to vote or the total value of shares of all classes of stock of such corporation,

(ii) the capital interest or profits interest of such partnership, or

(iii) the beneficial interest of such trust or estate,
is owned directly or indirectly, or held by persons described in subparagraph (A), (B), (C), (D), or (E);

(H) an employee, officer, director (or an individual having powers or responsibilities similar to those of officers or directors), or a 10 percent or more shareholder directly or indirectly, of a person described in subparagraph (B), (C), (D), (E), or (G), or of the employee benefit plan; or

(I) a 10 percent or more (directly or indirectly in capital or profits) partner or joint venturer of a person described in subparagraph (B), (C), (D), (E), or (G).

The Secretary, after consultation and coordination with the Secretary of the Treasury, may by regulation prescribe a percentage lower than 50 percent for subparagraph (E) and (G) and lower than 10 percent for subparagraph (H) or (I). The Secretary may prescribe regulations for determining the ownership (direct or indirect) of profits and beneficial interests, and the manner in which indirect stockholdings are taken into account. Any person who is a party in interest with respect to a plan to which a trust described in section 501 (c)(22) of the Internal Revenue Code of 1954 is permitted to make payments under section 4223 shall be treated as a party in interest with respect to such trust.

(15) The term "relative" means a spouse, ancestor, lineal descendant, or spouse of a lineal descendant.

(16)(A) The term "administrator" means—

(i) the person specifically so designated by the terms of the instrument under which the plan is operated;

(ii) if an administrator is not so designated, the plan sponsor; or

(iii) in the case of a plan for which an administrator is not designated and a plan sponsor cannot be identified, such other person as the Secretary may by regulation prescribe.

(B) The term "plan sponsor" means—

(i) the employer in the case of an employee benefit plan established or maintained by a single employer, (ii) the employee organization in the case of a plan established or maintained by an employee organization, or (iii) in the case of a plan established or maintained by two or more employers or jointly by one or more employers and one or more employee organizations, the association, committee, joint board of trustees, or other similar group of representatives of the parties who establish or maintain the plan.

(17) The term "separate account" means an account established or maintained by an insurance company under which income, gains, and losses, whether or not realized, from assets allocated to such account, are, in accordance with the applicable contract, credited to or charged against such account without regard to other income, gains, or losses of the insurance company.

(18) The term "adequate consideration" when used in part 4 of subtitle B means (A) in the case of a security for which there is a generally recognized market, either (i) the price of the security prevailing on a national securities exchange which is registered under section 6 of the Securities Exchange Act of 1934, or (ii) if the security is not traded on such a national securities exchange, a price not less favorable to the plan than the offering price for the security as established by the current bid and asked prices quoted by persons independent of the issuer and of any party in interest; and (B) in the case of an asset other than a security for which there is a generally recognized market, the fair market value of the asset as determined in good faith by the trustee or named fiduciary pursuant to the terms of the plan and in accordance with regulations promulgated by the Secretary.

(19) The term "nonforfeitable" when used with respect to a pension benefit or right means a claim obtained by a participant or his beneficiary to that part of an immediate or deferred benefit under a pension plan which arises from the participant's service, which is unconditional, and which is legally enforceable against the plan. For purposes of this paragraph, a right to an accrued benefit derived from employer contributions shall not be treated as forfeitable merely because the plan contains a provision described in section 203(a)(3).

(20) The term "security" has the same meaning as such term has under section 2(1) of the Securities Act of 1933 (15 U.S.C. 77b(1)).

(21)(A) Except as otherwise provided in subparagraph (B), a person is a fiduciary with respect to a plan to the extent (i) he exercises any discretionary authority or discretionary control respecting management of such plan or exercises any authority or control respecting management or disposition of its assets, (ii) he renders investment advice for a fee or other compensation, direct or indirect, with respect to any moneys or other property of such plan, or has any authority or responsibility to do so, or (iii) he has any discretionary authority or discretionary responsibility in the administration of such plan. Such term includes any person designated under section 405 (c)(1)(B).

(B) If any money or other property of an employee benefit plan is invested in securities issued by an investment company registered under the Investment Company Act of 1940, such investment shall not by itself cause such inves-tment company or such investment company's investment adviser or principal underwriter to be deemed to be a fiduciary or a party in interest as those terms are defined in this title, except insofar as such investment company or its investment adviser or principal underwriter acts in connection with an employee benefit plan covering employees of the investment company, the investment adviser, or its principal underwriter. Nothing contained in this subparagraph shall limit the duties imposed on such investment company, investment adviser, or principal underwriter by any other law.

(22) The term "normal retirement benefit" means the greater of the early retirement benefit under the plan, or the benefit under the plan commencing at normal retirement age. The normal retirement benefit shall be determined without regard to—

(A) medical benefits, and

(B) disability benefits not in excess of the qualified disability benefit.

For purposes of this paragraph, a qualified disability benefit is a disability benefit provided by a plan which does not exceed the benefit which would be provided for the participant if he separated from the service at normal retirement age. For purposes of this paragraph, the early retirement benefit under a plan shall be determined without regard to any benefit under the plan which the Secretary of the Treasury finds to be a benefit described in section 204(b)(1)(G).

(23) The term "accrued benefit" means—

(A) in the case of a defined benefit plan, the individual's accrued benefit determined under the plan and, except as provided in section 204(c)(3), expressed in the form of an annual benefit commencing at normal retirement age, or

(B) in the case of a plan which is an individual account plan, the balance of the individual's account.

The accrued benefit of an employee shall not be less than the amount determined under section 204(c)(2)(B) with respect to the employee's accumulated contribution.

(24) The term "normal retirement age" means the earlier of—

(A) the time a plan participant attains normal retirement age under the plan, or

(B) the later of—

(i) the time a plan participant attains age 65, or

(ii) the 5th anniversary of the time a plan participant commenced participation in the plan.

(25) The term "vested liabilities" means the present value of the immediate or deferred benefits available at normal retirement age for participants and their beneficiaries which are nonforfeitable.

(26) The term "current value" means fair market value where available and otherwise the fair value as determined in good faith by a trustee or a named fiduciary (as defined in section 402(a)(2)) pursuant to the terms of the plan and in accordance with regulations of the Secretary, assuming an orderly liquidation at the time of such determination.

(27) The term "present value", with respect to a liability, means the value adjusted to reflect anticipated events. Such adjustments shall conform to such regulations as the Secretary of the Treasury may prescribe.

(28) The term "normal service cost" or "normal cost" means the annual cost of future pension benefits and administrative expenses assigned, under an actuarial cost method, to years subsequent to a particular valuation date of a pension plan. The Secretary of the Treasury may prescribe regulations to carry out this paragraph.

(29) The term "accrued liability" means the excess of the present value, as of a particular valuation date of a pension plan, of the projected future benefits cost and administrative expenses for all plan participants and beneficiaries over the present value of future contributions for the normal cost of all applicable plan participants and beneficiaries. The Secretary of the Treasury may prescribe regulations to carry out this paragraph.

(30) The term "unfunded accrued liability" means the excess of the accrued liability, under an actuarial cost method which so provides, over the present value of the assets of a pension plan. The Secretary of the Treasury may prescribe regulations to carry out this paragraph.

(31) The term "advance funding actuarial cost method" or "actuarial cost method" means a recognized actuarial technique utilized for establishing the amount and incidence of the annual actuarial cost of pension plan benefits and expenses. Acceptable actuarial cost methods shall include the accrued benefit cost method (unit credit method), the entry age normal cost method, the individual level premium cost method, the aggregate cost method, the attained age normal cost method, and the frozen initial liability cost method. The terminal funding cost method and the current funding (pay-as-you-go) cost method are not acceptable actuarial cost methods. The Secretary of the Treasury shall issue regulations to further define acceptable actuarial cost methods.

(32) The term ''governmental plan'' means a plan established or maintained for its employees by the Government of the United States, by the government of any State or political subdivision thereof, or by any agency or instrumentality of any of the foregoing. The term ''governmental plan'' also includes any plan to which the Railroad Retirement Act of 1935 or 1937 applies, and which is financed by contributions required under that Act and any plan of an international organization which is exempt from taxation under the provisions of the International Organizations Immunities Act (59 Stat. 669).

(33)(A) The term ''church plan'' means a plan established and maintained (to the extent required in clause (ii) of subparagraph (B)) for its employees (or their beneficiaries) by a church or by a convention or association of churches which is exempt from tax under section 501 of the Internal Revenue Code of 1954.

(B) The term ''church plan'' does not include a plan—

(i) which is established and maintained primarily for the benefit of employees (or their beneficiaries) of such church or convention or association of churches who are employed in connection with one or more unrelated trades or businesses (within the meaning of section 513 of the Internal Revenue Code of 1954), or

(ii) if less than substantially all of the individuals included in the plan are individuals described in subparagraph (A) or in clause (ii) of subparagraph (C) (or their beneficiaries).

(C) For purposes of this paragraph—

(i) A plan established and maintained for its employees (or their beneficiaries) by a church or by a convention or association of churches includes a plan maintained by an organization, whether a civil law corporation or otherwise, the principal purpose or function of which is the administration or funding of a plan or program for the provision of retirement benefits or welfare benefits, or both, for the employees of a church or a convention or association of churches, if such organization is controlled by or associated with a church or a convention or association of churches.

(ii) The term employee of a church or a convention or association of churches includes—

(I) a duly ordained, commissioned, or licensed minister of a church in the exercise of his ministry, regardless of the source of his compensation;

(II) an employee of an organization, whether a civil law corporation or otherwise, which is exempt from tax under section 501 of the Internal Revenue Code of 1954 and which is controlled by or associated with a church or a convention or association of churches; and

(III) an individual described in clause (v)

(iii) A church or a convention or association of churches which is exempt from tax under section 501 of the Internal Revenue Code of 1954 shall be deemed the employer of any individual included as an employee under clause (ii).

(iv) An organization, whether a civil law corporation or otherwise, is associated with a church or a convention or association of churches if it shares common religious bonds and convictions with that church or convention or association of churches.

(v) If an employee who is included in a church plan separates from the service of a church or a convention or association of churches or an organization, whether a civil law corporation or otherwise, which is exempt from tax under section 501 of the Internal Revenue Code of 1954 and which is controlled by or associated with a church

2-10   ERISA: The Law and the Code

or a convention or association of churches, the church plan shall not fail to meet the requirements of this paragraph merely because the plan—

(I) retains the employee's accrued benefit or account for the payment of benefits to the employee or his beneficiaries pursuant to the terms of the plan; or

(II) receives contributions on the employee's behalf after the employee's separation from such service, but only for a period of 5 years after such separation, unless the employee is disabled (within the meaning of the disability provisions of the church plan or, if there are no such provisions in the church plan, within the meaning of section 72(m)(7) of the Internal Revenue Code of 1954) at the time of such separation from service.

(D)(i) If a plan established and maintained for its employees (or their beneficiaries) by a church or by a convention or association of churches which is exempt from tax under section 501 of the Internal Revenue Code of 1954 fails to meet one or more of the requirements of this paragraph and corrects its failure to meet such requirements within the correction period, the plan shall be deemed to meet the requirements of this paragraph for the year in which the correction was made and for all prior years.

(ii) If a correction is not made within the correction period, the plan shall be deemed not to meet the requirements of this paragraph beginning with the date on which the earliest failure to meet one or more of such requirements occurred.

(iii) For purposes of this subparagraph, the term "correction period" means—

(I) the period ending 270 days after the date of mailing by the Secretary of the Treasury of a notice of default with respect to the plan's failure to meet one or more of the requirements of this paragraph; or

(II) any period set by a court of competent jurisdiction after a final determination

that the plan fails to meet such requirements, or, if the court does not specify such period, any reasonable period determined by the Secretary of the Treasury on the basis of all the facts and circumstances, but in any event not less than 270 days after the determination has become final; or

(III) any additional period which the Secretary of the Treasury determines is reasonable or necessary for the correction of the default, whichever has the latest ending date.

(34) The term "individual account plan" or "defined contribution plan" means a pension plan which provides for an individual account for each participant and for benefits based solely upon the amount contributed to the participant's account, and any income, expenses, gains, and losses, and any forfeitures of accounts of other participants which may be allocated to such participant's account.

(35) The term "defined benefit plan" means a pension plan other than an individual account plan; except that a pension plan which is not an individual account plan and which provides a benefit derived from employer contributions which is based partly on the balance of the separate account of a participant—

(A) for the purposes of section 202, shall be treated as an individual account plan, and

(B) for the purposes of paragraph (23) of this section and section 204, shall be treated as an individual account plan to the extent benefits are based upon the separate account of a participant and as a defined benefit plan with respect to the remaining portion of benefits under the plan.

(36) The term "excess benefit plan" means a plan maintained by an employer solely for the purpose of providing benefits for certain employees in excess of the limitations on contributions and benefits imposed by section 415 of the Internal Revenue Code of 1954 on plans to which that section applies, without regard to whether the plan is funded. To the extent that a separable part of a plan (as determined

by the Secretary of Labor) maintained by an employer is maintained for such purpose, that part shall be treated as a separate plan which is an excess benefit plan.

(37)(A) The term "multiemployer plan" means a plan—

(i) to which more than one employer is required to contribute,

(ii) which is maintained pursuant to one or more collective bargaining agreements between one or more employee organizations and more than one employer, and

(iii) which satisfies such other requirements as the Secretary may prescribe by regulation.

(B) For purposes of this paragraph, all trades or businesses (whether or not incorporated) which are under common control within the meaning of section 4001(b)(1) are considered a single employer.

(C) Notwithstanding subparagraph (A), a plan is a multiemployer plan on and after its termination date if the plan was a multiemployer plan under this paragraph for the plan year preceding its termination date.

(D) For purposes of this title, notwithstanding the preceding provisions of this paragraph, for any plan year which began before the date of the enactment of the Multiemployer Pension Plan Amendments Act of 1980, the term "multiemployer plan" means a plan described in section 3(37) of this Act as in effect immediately before such date.

(E) Within one year after the date of the enactment of the Multiemployer Pension Plan Amendments Act of 1980, a multiemployer plan may irrevocably elect, pursuant to procedures established by the corporation and subject to the provisions of sections 4403 (b) and (c), that the plan shall not be treated as a multiemployer plan for all purposes under this Act or the Internal Revenue Code of 1954 if for each of the last 3 plan years ending prior to the effective date of the

Multiemployer Pension Plan Amendments Act of 1980—

(i) the plan was not a multiemployer plan because the plan was not a plan described in section 3(37)(A)(iii) of this Act and section 414(f)(1)(C) of the Internal Revenue Code of 1954 (as such provisions were in effect on the day before the date of the enactment of the Multiemployer Pension Plan Amendments Act of 1980); and

(ii) the plan had been identified as a plan that was not a multiemployer plan in substantially all its filings with the corporation, the Secretary of Labor and the Secretary of the Treasury.

(F)(i) For purposes of this title a qualified football coaches plan—

(I) shall be treated as a multiemployer plan to the extent not inconsistent with the purposes of this subparagraph; and

(II) notwithstanding section 401 (k)(4)(B) of the Internal Revenue Code of 1986 may include a qualified cash and deferred arrangement.

(ii) For purposes of this subparagraph, the term "qualified football coaches plan" means any defined contribution plan which is established and maintained by an organization—

(I) which is described in section 501(c) of such Code;

(II) the membership of which consists entirely of individuals who primarily coach football as full-time employees of 4-year colleges or universities described in section 170(b)(1)(A)(ii) of such Code; and

(III) which was in existence on September 18, 1986.

(38) The term "investment manager" means any fiduciary (other than a trustee or named fiduciary, as defined in section 402(a)(2))—

(A) who has the power to manage, acquire, or dispose of any asset of a plan;

(B) who is (i) registered as an investment adviser under the Investment Advisers Act of 1940; (ii) is a bank, as defined in that Act; or (iii) is an insurance company qualified to perform services described in subparagraph (A) under the laws of more than one State; and

(C) has acknowledged in writing that he is a fiduciary with respect to the plan.

(39) The terms "plan year" and "fiscal year of the plan" mean, with respect to a plan, the calendar, policy, or fiscal year on which the records of the plan are kept.

(40)(A) The term "multiple employer welfare arrangement" means an employee welfare benefit plan, or any other arrangement (other than an employee welfare benefit plan), which is established or maintained for the purpose of offering or providing any benefit described in paragraph (1) to the employees of two or more employers (including one or more self-employed individuals), or to their beneficiaries, except that such term does not include any such plan or other arrangement which is established or maintained—

(i) under or pursuant to one or more agreements which the Secretary finds to be collective bargaining agreements,

(ii) by a rural electric cooperative, or

(iii) by a rural telephone cooperative association.

(B) For purposes of this paragraph—

(i) two or more trades or businesses, whether or not incorporated, shall be deemed a single employer if such trades or businesses are within the same control group,

(ii) the term "control group" means a group of trades or businesses under common control,

(iii) the determination of whether a trade or business is under "common control" with another trade or business shall be deter-

mined under regulations of the Secretary applying principles similar to the principles applied in determining whether employees of two or more trades or businesses are treated as employed by a single employer under section 4001(b), except that, for purposes of this paragraph, common control shall not be based on an interest of less than 25 percent,

(iv) the term "rural electric cooperative" means—

(I) any organization which is exempt from tax under section 501(a) of the Internal Revenue Code of 1954 and which is engaged primarily in providing electric service on a mutual or cooperative basis, and

(II) any organization described in paragraph (4) or (6) of section 501(c) of the Internal Revenue Code of 1954 which is exempt from tax under section 501(a) of such Code and at least 80 percent of the members of which are organizations described in subclause (I), and

(v) the term "rural telephone cooperative association" means an organization described in paragraph (4) or (6) of section 501(c) of the Internal Revenue Code of 1986 which is exempt from tax under section 501(a) of such Code and at least 80 percent of the members of which are organizations engaged primarily in providing telephone service to rural areas of the United States on a mutual, cooperative, or other basis.

(41) Single-Employer Plan.—The term "single-employer plan" means an employee benefit plan other than a multiemployer plan.

◊ ◊ ◊

Editor's Note: ERISA section 3(41), below, was added by OBRA '90, section 12002(b)(2)(C) without renumbering or removing Subsection 3(41) above.

◊ ◊ ◊

(41) The term "single-employer plan" means a plan which is not a multiemployer plan.

COVERAGE

Sec. 4. (a) Except as provided in subsection (b) and in sections 201, 301, and 401, this title shall apply to any employee benefit plan if it is established or maintained—

(1) by any employer engaged in commerce or in any industry or activity affecting commerce; or

(2) by any employee organization or organizations representing employees engaged in commerce or in any industry or activity affecting commerce; or

(3) by both.

(b) The provisions of this title shall not apply to any employee benefit plan if—

(1) such plan is a governmental plan (as defined in section 3(32));

(2) such plan is a church plan (as defined in section 3(33)) with respect to which no election has been made under section 410(d) of the Internal Revenue Code of 1954;

(3) such plan is maintained solely for the purpose of complying with applicable workmen's compensation laws or unemployment compensation or disability insurance laws;

(4) such plan is maintained outside of the United States primarily for the benefit of persons substantially all of whom are nonresident aliens; or

(5) such plan is an excess benefit plan (as defined in section 3(36)) and is unfunded.

Subtitle B — Regulatory Provisions

Part 1 — Reporting and Disclosure

DUTY OF DISCLOSURE AND REPORTING

Sec. 101. (a) The administrator of each employee benefit plan shall cause to be furnished in accordance with section 104(b) to each participant covered under the plan and to each beneficiary who is receiving benefits under the plan—

(1) a summary plan description described in section 102(a)(1); and

(2) the information described in sections 104(b)(3) and 105(a) and (c).

(b) The administrator shall, in accordance with section 104(a), file with the Secretary—

(1) the summary plan description described in section 102(a)(1);

(2) a plan description containing the matter required in section 102(b);

(3) modifications and changes referred to in section 102(a)(2);

(4) the annual report containing the information required by section 103; and

(5) terminal and supplementary reports as required by subsection (c) of this section.

(c)(1) Each administrator of an employee pension benefit plan which is winding up its affairs (without regard to the number of participants remaining in the plan) shall, in accordance with regulations prescribed by the Secretary, file such terminal reports as the Secretary may consider necessary. A copy of such report shall also be filed with the Pension Benefit Guaranty Corporation.

(2) The Secretary may require terminal reports to be filed with regard to any employee welfare benefit plan which is winding up its affairs in accordance with regulations promulgated by the Secretary.

(3) The Secretary may require that a plan described in paragraph (1) or (2) file a supplementary or terminal report with the annual report in the year such plan is terminated and that a copy of such supplementary or terminal report in the case of a plan described in paragraph (1) be also filed with the Pension Benefit Guaranty Corporation.

(d) Notice of Failure To Meet Minimum Funding Standards.—

(1) In general. — If an employer maintaining a plan other than a multiemployer plan fails to make a required installment or other payment required to meet the minimum funding standard under section 302 to a plan before the 60th day following the due date for such installment or other payment, the employer shall notify each participant and beneficiary (including an alternate payee as defined in section 206(d)(3)(K)) of such plan of such failure. Such notice shall be made at such time and in such manner as the Secretary may prescribe.

(2) Subsection not to apply if waiver pending. — This subsection shall not apply to any failure if the employer has filed a waiver request under section 303 with respect to the plan year to which the required installment relates, except that if the waiver request is denied, notice under paragraph (1) shall be provided within 60 days after the date of such denial.

(3) Definitions. —For purposes of this subsection, the terms "required installment" and "due date" have the same meanings given such terms by section 302(e).

(e) Notice of Transfer of Excess Pension Assets to Health Benefits Accounts.—

(1) Notice to participants. —Not later than 60 days before the date of a qualified transfer by an employee pension benefit plan of excess pension assets to a health benefits account, the administrator of the plan shall notify (in such manner as the Secretary may prescribe) each participant and beneficiary under the plan of such transfer. Such notice shall include information with respect to the amount of excess pension assets, the portion to be transferred, the amount of health benefits liabilities expected to be provided with the assets transferred, and the amount of pension benefits of the participant which will be nonforfeitable immediately after the transfer.

(2) Notice to secretaries, administrator, and employee organizations.—

(A) In general. — Not later than 60 days before the date of any qualified transfer by an employee pension benefit plan of excess pension assets to a health benefits account, the employer maintaining the plan from which the transfer is made shall provide the Secretary, the Secretary of the Treasury, the administrator, and each employee organization representing participants in the plan a written notice of such transfer. A copy of such notice shall be available for inspection in the principal office of the administrator.

(B) Information relating to transfer. — Such notice shall identify the plan from which the transfer is made, the amount of the transfer, a detailed accounting of assets projected to be held by the plan immediately before and immediately after the transfer, and the current liabilities under the plan at the time of the transfer.

(C) Authority for additional reporting requirements. — The Secretary may prescribe such additional reporting requirements as may be necessary to carry out the purposes of this section.

(3) Definitions. — For purposes of paragraph (1), any term used in such paragraph which is also used in section 420 of the Internal Revenue Code of 1986 (as in effect on January 1, [1991] *1995*) shall have the same meaning as when used in such section.

(f) Information necessary to comply with Medicare and Medicaid coverage data bank requirements.—

(1) Provision of information by group health plan upon request of employer.—

(A) In general. — An employer shall comply with the applicable requirements of section 1144 of the Social Security Act (as added by section 13581 of the Omnibus Budget Reconciliation Act of 1993). Upon the request of an employer maintaining a group health plan, any plan sponsor, plan administrator, insurer, third-party administrator, or other person who maintains under the plan the information necessary to enable the employer to comply with the applicable requirements of section 1144 of the Social Security Act shall, in such form and manner as may be prescribed in regulations of the Secretary (in consultation with the Secretary of Health and Human Services), provide such information (not inconsistent with paragraph (2)) —

(i) in the case of a request by an employer described in subparagraph (B) and a plan that is not a multiemployer plan or a component of an arrangement described in subparagraph (C), to the Medicare and Medicaid Coverage Data Bank;

(ii) in the case of a plan that is a multiemployer plan or a component of an arrangement described in subparagraph (C), to the employer or to such Data Bank, at the option of the plan; and

(iii) in any other case, to the employer or to such Data Bank, at the option of the employer.

(B) Employer described.—An employer is described in this subparagraph for any calendar year if such employer normally employed fewer than 50 employees on a typical business day during such calendar year.

(C) Arrangement described —An arrangement described in this subparagraph is any arrangement in which two or more employers contribute for the purpose of providing group health plan coverage for employees.

(2) Information not required to be provided.—Any plan sponsor, plan administrator, insurer, third-party administrator, or other person described in paragraph (1)(A) (other than the employer) that maintains the information under the plan shall not provide to an employer in order to satisfy the requirements of section 1144 of the Social Security Act, and shall not provide to the Data Bank under such section, information that pertains in any way to—

(A) the health status of a participant, or of the participant's spouse, dependent child, or other beneficiary,

(B) the cost of coverage provided to any participant or beneficiary, or

(C) any limitations on such coverage specific to any participant or beneficiary.

(3) Regulations.—The Secretary may, in consultation with the Secretary of Health and Human Services, prescribe such regulations as are necessary to carry out this subsection.

(g) Cross References.— For regulations relating to coordination of reports to the Secretaries of Labor and the Treasury, see section 3004.

PLAN DESCRIPTION AND SUMMARY PLAN DESCRIPTION

Sec. 102. (a)(1) A summary plan description of any employee benefit plan shall be furnished to participants and beneficiaries as provided in section 104(b). The summary plan description shall include the information described in subsection (b), shall be written in a manner calculated to be understood by the average plan participant, and shall be sufficiently accurate and comprehensive to reasonably apprise such participants and beneficiaries of their rights and obligations under the plan. A summary of any material modification in the terms of the plan and any change in the information required under subsection (b) shall be written in a manner calculated to be understood by the average plan participant and shall be furnished in accordance with section 104(b)(1).

(2) A plan description (containing the information required by subsection (b)) of any employee benefit plan shall be prepared on forms prescribed by the Secretary, and shall be filed with the Secretary as required by section 104(a)(1). Any material modification in the terms of the plan and any change in the information described in subsection (b) shall be filed in accordance with section 104(a)(1)(D).

(b) The plan description and summary plan description shall contain the following information: The name and type of administration of the plan; the name and address of the person designated as agent for the service of legal process, if such person is not the administrator; the name and address of the administrator; names, titles and addresses of any trustee or trustees (if they are persons different from the administrator); a description of the relevant provisions of any applicable collective bargaining agreement; the plan's requirements respecting eligibility for participation and benefits; a description of the provisions providing for nonforfeitable pension benefits; circumstances which may result in disqualification, ineligibility, or denial or loss of benefits; the source of financing of the plan and the identity of any organization through which benefits are provided; the date of the end of the plan year and whether the records of the plan are kept on a calendar, policy, or fiscal year basis; the procedures to be followed in presenting claims for benefits under the plan and the remedies available under the plan for the redress of claims which are denied in whole or in part (including procedures required under section 503 of this Act).

ANNUAL REPORTS

Sec. 103. (a)(1)(A) An annual report shall be published with respect to every employee benefit plan to which this part applies. Such report shall be filed with the Secretary in accordance with section 104(a), and shall be

made available and furnished to participants in accordance with section 104(b).

(B) The annual report shall include the information described in subsections (b) and (c) and where applicable subsections (d) and (e) and shall also include—

(i) a financial statement and opinion, as required by paragraph (3) of this subsection, and

(ii) an actuarial statement and opinion, as required by paragraph (4) of this subsection.

(2) If some or all of the information necessary to enable the administrator to comply with the requirements of this title is maintained by—

(A) an insurance carrier or other organization which provides some or all of the benefits under the plan, or holds assets of the plan in a separate account,

(B) a bank or similar institution which holds some or all of the assets of the plan in a common or collective trust or a separate trust, or custodial account, or

(C) a plan sponsor as defined in section 3(16)(B),

such carrier, organization, bank, institution, or plan sponsor shall transmit and certify the accuracy of such information to the administrator within 120 days after the end of the plan year (or such other date as may be prescribed under regulations of the Secretary).

(3)(A) Except as provided in subparagraph (C), the administrator of an employee benefit plan shall engage, on behalf of all plan participants, an independent qualified public accountant, who shall conduct such an examination of any financial statements of the plan, and of other books and records of the plan, as the accountant may deem necessary to enable the accountant to form an opinion as to whether the financial statements and schedules required to be included in the annual report by subsection (b) of this section are presented fairly in conformity with generally accepted accounting principles applied on a basis consistent with that of the preceding year.

Such examination shall be conducted in accordance with generally accepted auditing standards, and shall involve such tests of the books and records of the plan as are considered necessary by the independent qualified public accountant. The independent qualified public accountant shall also offer his opinion as to whether the separate schedules specified in subsection (b)(3) of this section and the summary material required under section 104(b)(3) present fairly and in all material respects the information contained therein when considered in conjunction with the financial statements taken as a whole. The opinion by the independent qualified public accountant shall be made a part of the annual report. In a case where a plan is not required to file an annual report, the requirements of this paragraph shall not apply. In a case where by reason of section 104(a)(2) a plan is required only to file a simplified annual report, the Secretary may waive the requirements of this paragraph.

(B) In offering his opinion under this section the accountant may rely on the correctness of any actuarial matter certified to by an enrolled actuary, if he so states his reliance.

(C) The opinion required by subparagraph (A) need not be expressed as to any statements required by subsection (b)(3)(G) prepared by a bank or similar institution or insurance carrier regulated and supervised and subject to periodic examination by a State or Federal agency if such statements are certified by the bank, similar institution, or insurance carrier as accurate and are made a part of the annual report.

(D) For purposes of this title, the term "qualified public accountant" means—

(i) a person who is a certified public accountant, certified by a regulatory authority of a State;

(ii) a person who is a licensed public accountant, licensed by a regulatory authority of a State; or

(iii) a person certified by the Secretary as a qualified public accountant in accordance with regulations published by him for a person who practices in States where there is no certification or licensing procedure for accountants.

(4)(A) The administrator of an employee pension benefit plan subject to the reporting requirement of subsection (d) of this section shall engage, on behalf of all plan participants, an enrolled actuary who shall be responsible for the preparation of the materials comprising the actuarial statement required under subsection (d) of this section. In a case where a plan is not required to file an annual report, the requirement of this paragraph shall not apply, and, in a case where by reason of section 104(a)(2), a plan is required only to file a simplified report, the Secretary may waive the requirement of this paragraph.

(B) The enrolled actuary shall utilize such assumptions and techniques as are necessary to enable him to form an opinion as to whether the contents of the matters reported under subsection (d) of this section—

(i) are in the aggregate reasonably related to the experience of the plan and to reasonable expectations; and

(ii) represent his best estimate of anticipated experience under the plan.
The opinion by the enrolled actuary shall be made with respect to, and shall be made a part of, each annual report.

(C) For purposes of this title, the term "enrolled actuary" means an actuary enrolled under subtitle C of title III of this Act.

(D) In making a certification under this section the enrolled actuary may rely on the correctness of any accounting matter under section 103(b) as to which any qualified public accountant has expressed an opinion, if he so states his reliance.

ERISA Sec. 103 (a)(4)(D)

(b) An annual report under this section shall include a financial statement containing the following information:

(1) With respect to an employee welfare benefit plan: a statement of assets and liabilities; a statement of changes in fund balance; and a statement of changes in financial position. In the notes to financial statements, disclosures concerning the following items shall be considered by the accountant: a description of the plan including any significant changes in the plan made during the period and the impact of such changes on benefits; a description of material lease commitments, other commitments, and contingent liabilities; a description of agreements and transactions with persons known to be parties in interest; a general description of priorities upon termination of the plan; information concerning whether or not a tax ruling or determination letter has been obtained; and any other matters necessary to fully and fairly present the financial statements of the plan.

(2) With respect to an employee pension benefit plan: a statement of assets and liabilities, and a statement of changes in net assets available for plan benefits which shall include details of revenues and expenses and other changes aggregated by general source and application. In the notes to financial statements, disclosures concerning the following items shall be considered by the accountant: a description of the plan including any significant changes in the plan made during the period and the impact of such changes on benefits; the funding policy (including policy with respect to prior service cost), and any changes in such policies during the year; a description of any significant changes in plan benefits made during the period; a description of material lease commitments, other commitments, and contingent liabilities; a description of agreements and transactions with persons known to be parties in interest; a general description of priorities upon termination of the plan; information concerning whether or not a tax ruling or determination letter has been

obtained; and any other matters necessary to fully and fairly present the financial statements of such pension plan.

(3) With respect to all employee benefit plans, the statement required under paragraph (1) or (2) shall have attached the following information in separate schedules:

(A) a statement of the assets and liabilities of the plan aggregated by categories and valued at their current value, and the same data displayed in comparative form for the end of the previous fiscal year of the plan,

(B) a statement of receipts and disbursements during the preceding twelve-month period aggregated by general sources and applications;

(C) a schedule of all assets held for investment purposes aggregated and identified by issuer, borrower, or lessor, or similar party to the transaction (including a notation as to whether such party is known to be a party in interest), maturity date, rate of interest, collateral, par or maturity value, cost, and current value;

(D) a schedule of each transaction involving a person known to be party in interest, the identity of such party in interest and his relationship or that of any other party in interest to the plan, a description of each asset to which the transaction relates; the purchase or selling price in case of a sale or purchase, the rental in case of a lease, or the interest rate and maturity date in case of a loan; expenses incurred in connection with the transaction; the cost of the asset, the current value of the asset, and the net gain (or loss) on each transaction;

(E) a schedule of all loans or fixed income obligations which were in default as of the close of the plan's fiscal year or were classified during the year as uncollectable and the following information with respect to each loan on such schedule (including a notation as to whether parties involved are known to be parties in interest): the original principal amount of the loan, the amount of principal and interest received during the reporting year, the unpaid balance, the identity and address of the obligor, a detailed description of the loan (including date of making and maturity, interest rate, the type and value of collateral, and other material terms), the amount of principal and interest overdue (if any) and an explanation thereof;

(F) a list of all leases which were in default or were classified during the year as uncollectable; and the following information with respect to each lease on such schedule (including a notation as to whether parties involved are known to be parties in interest): the type of property leased (and, in the case of fixed assets such as land, buildings, leasehold, and so forth, the location of the property), the identity of the lessor or lessee from or to whom the plan is leasing, the relationship of such lessors and lessees, if any, to the plan, the employer, employee organization, or any other party in interest, the terms of the lease regarding rent, taxes, insurance, repairs, expenses, and renewal options; the date the leased property was purchased and its cost, the date the property was leased and its approximate value at such date, the gross rental receipts during the reporting period, expenses paid for the leased property during the reporting period, the net receipts from the lease, the amounts in arrears, and a statement as to what steps have been taken to collect amounts due or otherwise remedy the default;

(G) if some or all of the assets of a plan or plans are held in a common or collective trust maintained by a bank or similar institution or in a separate account maintained by an insurance carrier or a separate trust maintained by a bank as trustee, the report shall include the most recent annual statement of assets and liabilities of such common or collective trust, and in the case of a separate account or a separate trust, such other information as is required by the administrator in order to comply with this subsection; and

(H) a schedule of each reportable transaction, the name of each party to the transaction (except that, in the case of an acquisition or sale of a security on the market, the report need not identify the person from whom the security was acquired or to whom it was sold) and a description of each asset to which the transaction applies; the purchase or selling price in case of a sale or purchase, the rental in case of a lease, or the interest rate and maturity date in case of a loan; expenses incurred in connection with the transaction; the cost of the asset, the current value of the asset, and the net gain (or loss) on each transaction. For purposes of the preceding sentence, the term "reportable transaction" means a transaction to which the plan is a party if such transaction is—

(i) a transaction involving an amount in excess of 3 percent of the current value of the assets of the plan;

(ii) any transaction (other than a transaction respecting a security) which is part of a series of transactions with or in conjunction with a person in a plan year, if the aggregate amount of such transactions exceeds 3 percent of the current value of the assets of the plan;

(iii) a transaction which is part of a series of transactions respecting one or more securities of the same issuer, if the aggregate amount of such transactions in the plan year exceeds 3 percent of the current value of the assets of the plan; or

(iv) a transaction with or in conjunction with a person respecting a security, if any other transaction with or in conjunction with such person in the plan year respecting a security is required to be reported by reason of clause (i).

(4) The Secretary may, by regulation, relieve any plan from filing a copy of a statement of assets and liabilities (or other information) described in paragraph (3)(G) if such statement and other information is filed with the Secretary by the bank or insurance carrier which maintains the common or collective trust or separate account.

ERISA Sec. 103 (b)(4)

(c) The administrator shall furnish as a part of a report under this section the following information:

(1) The number of employees covered by the plan.

(2) The name and address of each fiduciary.

(3) Except in the case of a person whose compensation is minimal (determined under regulations of the Secretary) and who performs solely ministerial duties (determined under such regulations), the name of each person (including but not limited to, any consultant, broker, trustee, accountant, insurance carrier, actuary, administrator, investment manager, or custodian who rendered services to the plan or who had transactions with the plan) who received directly or indirectly compensation from the plan during the preceding year for services rendered to the plan or its participants, the amount of such compensation, the nature of his services to the plan or its participants, his relationship to the employer of the employees covered by the plan, or the employee organization, and any other office, position, or employment he holds with any party in interest.

(4) An explanation of the reason for any change in appointment of trustee, accountant, insurance carrier, enrolled actuary, administrator, investment manager, or custodian.

(5) Such financial and actuarial information including but not limited to the material described in subsections (b) and (d) of this section as the Secretary may find necessary or appropriate.

(d) With respect to an employee pension benefit plan (other than (A) a profit sharing, savings, or other plan, which is an individual account plan, (B) a plan described in section 301(b), or (C) a plan described both in section 4021(b) and in paragraph (1), (2), (3), (4), (5), (6), or (7) of section 301(a)) an annual report under this section for a plan year shall include a complete actuarial statement applicable to the plan year which shall include the following:

(1) The date of the plan year, and the date of the actuarial valuation applicable to the plan year for which the report is filed.

(2) The date and amount of the contribution (or contributions) received by the plan for the plan year for which the report is filed and contributions for prior plan years not previously reported.

(3) The following information applicable to the plan year for which the report is filed: the normal costs, the accrued liabilities, an identification of benefits not included in the calculation; a statement of the other facts and actuarial assumptions and methods used to determine costs, and a justification for any change in actuarial assumptions or cost methods; and the minimum contribution required under section 302.

(4) The number of participants and beneficiaries, both retired and nonretired, covered by the plan.

(5) The current value of the assets accumulated in the plan, and the present value of the assets of the plan used by the actuary in any computation of the amount of contributions to the plan required under section 302 and a statement explaining the basis of such valuation of present value of assets.

(6) Information required in regulations of the Pension Benefit Guaranty Corporation with respect to:

(A) the current value of the assets of the plan,

(B) the present value of all nonforfeitable benefits for participants and beneficiaries receiving payments under the plan,

(C) the present value of all nonforfeitable benefits for all other participants and beneficiaries,

(D) the present value of all accrued benefits which are not nonforfeitable (including a separate accounting of such benefits which are benefit commitments, as defined in section 4001(a)(16)), and

(E) the actuarial assumptions and techniques used in determining the values described in subparagraphs (A) through (D).

(7) A certification of the contribution necessary to reduce the accumulated funding deficiency to zero.

(8) A statement by the enrolled actuary—

(A) that to the best of his knowledge the report is complete and accurate, and

(B) the requirements of section 302 (c)(3) (relating to reasonable actuarial assumptions and methods) have been complied with.

(9) A copy of the opinion required by subsection (a)(4).

(10) A statement by the actuary which discloses—

(A) any event which the actuary has not taken into account, and

(B) any trend which, for purposes of the actuarial assumptions used, was not assumed to continue in the future,

but only if, to the best of the actuary's knowledge, such event or trend may require a material increase in plan costs or required contribution rates.

(11) If the current value of the assets of the plan is less than 70 percent of the current liability under the plan (within the meaning of section 302(d)(7)), the percentage which such value is of such liability.

(12) Such other information regarding the plan as the Secretary may by regulation require.

(13) Such other information as may be necessary to fully and fairly disclose the actuarial position of the plan.

Such actuary shall make an actuarial valuation of the plan for every third plan year, unless he determines that a more frequent valuation is necessary to support his opinion under subsection (a)(4) of this section.

(e) If some or all of the benefits under the plan are purchased from and guaranteed by an insurance company, insurance service, or other similar organization, a report under this section shall include a statement from such insurance company, service, or other similar organization covering the plan year and enumerating—

(1) the premium rate or subscription charge and the total premium or subscription charges paid to each such carrier, insurance service, or other similar organization and the approximate number of persons covered by each class of such benefits; and

(2) the total amount of premiums received, the approximate number of persons covered by each class of benefits, and the total claims paid by such company, service, or other organization; dividends or retroactive rate adjustments, commissions, and administrative service or other fees or other specific acquisition costs paid by such company, service, or other organization; any amounts held to provide benefits after retirement; the remainder of such premiums; and the names and addresses of the brokers, agents, or other persons to whom commissions or fees were paid, the amount paid to each, and for what purpose. If any such company, service, or other organization does not maintain separate experience records covering the specific groups it serves, the report shall include in lieu of the information required by the foregoing provisions of this paragraph (A) a statement as to the basis of its premium rate or subscription charge, the total amount of premiums or subscription charges received from the plan, and a copy of the financial report of the company, service, or other organization and (B) if such company, service, or organization incurs specific costs in connection with the acquisition or retention of any particular plan or plans, a detailed statement of such costs.

ERISA Sec. 103 (e)(2)

FILING WITH SECRETARY AND FURNISHING INFORMATION TO PARTICIPANTS

Sec. 104. (a)(1) The administrator of any employee benefit plan subject to this part shall file with the Secretary—

(A) the annual report for a plan year within 210 days after the close of such year (or within such time as may be required by regulations promulgated by the Secretary in order to reduce duplicative filing);

(B) the plan description within 120 days after such plan becomes subject to this part and an updated plan description, no more frequently than once every 5 years, as the Secretary may require;

(C) a copy of the summary plan description at the time such summary plan description is required to be furnished to participants and beneficiaries pursuant to subsection (b)(1)(B) of this section; and

(D) modifications and changes referred to in section 102(a)(2) within 60 days after such modification or change is adopted or occurs, as the case may be.
The Secretary shall make copies of such plan descriptions, summary plan descriptions, and annual reports available for inspection in the public document room of the Department of Labor. The administrator shall also furnish to the Secretary, upon request, any documents relating to the employee benefit plan, including but not limited to the bargaining agreement, trust agreement, contract, or other instrument under which the plan is established or operated.

(2)(A) With respect to annual reports required to be filed with the Secretary under this part, he may by regulation prescribe simplified annual reports for any pension plan which covers less than 100 participants.

(B) Nothing contained in this paragraph shall preclude the Secretary from requiring any information or data from any such plan to which this part applies where he finds such data or information is necessary to

carry out the purposes of this title nor shall the Secretary be precluded from revoking provisions for simplified reports for any such plan if he finds it necessary to do so in order to carry out the objectives of this title.

(3) The Secretary may by regulation exempt any welfare benefit plan from all or part of the reporting and disclosure requirements of this title, or may provide for simplified reporting and disclosure if he finds that such requirements are inappropriate as applied to welfare benefit plans.

(4) The Secretary may reject any filing under this section—

(A) if he determines that such filing is incomplete for purposes of this part; or

(B) if he determines that there is any material qualification by an accountant or actuary contained in an opinion submitted pursuant to section 103(a)(3)(A) or section 103(a)(4)(B).

(5) If the Secretary rejects a filing of a report under paragraph (4) and if a revised filing satisfactory to the Secretary is not submitted within 45 days after the Secretary makes his determination under paragraph (4) to reject the filing, and if the Secretary deems it in the best interest of the participants, he may take any one or more of the following actions—

(A) retain an independent qualified public accountant (as defined in section 103(a)(3)(D)) on behalf of the participants to perform an audit,

(B) retain an enrolled actuary (as defined in section 103(a)(4)(C) of this Act) on behalf of the plan participants, to prepare an actuarial statement,

(C) bring a civil action for such legal or equitable relief as may be appropriate to enforce the provisions of this part, or

(D) take any other action authorized by this title.

The administrator shall permit such account- ant or actuary to inspect whatever books and records of the plan are necessary for such audit. The plan shall be liable to the Secretary for the expenses for such audit or report, and the Secretary may bring an action against the plan in any court of competent jurisdiction to recover such expenses.

(b) Publication of the summary plan descrip- tions and annual reports shall be made to participants and beneficiaries of the particular plan as follows:

(1) The administrator shall furnish to each participant, and each beneficiary receiving benefits under the plan, a copy of the summary plan description, and all modifications and changes referred to in section 102(a)(1)—

(A) within 90 days after he becomes a par- ticipant, or (in the case of a beneficiary) within 90 days after he first receives bene- fits, or

(B) if later, within 120 days after the plan becomes subject to this part.

The administrator shall furnish to each partici- pant, and each beneficiary receiving benefits under the plan, every fifth year after the plan becomes subject to this part an updated sum- mary plan description described in section 102 which integrates all plan amendments made within such five-year period, except that in a case where no amendments have been made to a plan during such five-year period this sentence shall not apply. Notwithstanding the foregoing, the administrator shall furnish to each participant, and to each beneficiary re- ceiving benefits under the plan, the summary plan description described in section 102 every tenth year after the plan becomes subject to this part. If there is a modification or change described in section 102(a)(1), a summary description of such modification or change shall be furnished not later than 210 days after the end of the plan year in which the change is adopted to each participant, and to each beneficiary who is receiving benefits under the plan.

(2) The administrator shall make copies of the plan description and the latest annual re- port and the bargaining agreement, trust agreement, contract, or other instruments un- der which the plan was established or is oper- ated available for examination by any plan participant or beneficiary in the principal of- fice of the administrator and in such other places as may be necessary to make available all pertinent information to all participants (including such places as the Secretary may prescribe by regulations).

(3) Within 210 days after the close of the fiscal year of the plan, the administrator shall furnish to each participant, and to each bene- ficiary receiving benefits under the plan, a copy of the statements and schedules, for such fiscal year, described in subparagraphs (A) and (B) of section 103(b)(3) and such other material (including the percentage determined under section 103(d)(11)) as is necessary to fairly summarize the latest annual report.

(4) The administrator shall, upon written re- quest of any participant or beneficiary, furnish a copy of the latest updated summary plan description, plan description, and the latest annual report, any terminal report, the bar- gaining agreement, trust agreement, contract, or other instruments under which the plan is established or operated. The administrator may make a reasonable charge to cover the cost of furnishing such complete copies. The Secretary may by regulation prescribe the maximum amount which will constitute a rea- sonable charge under the preceding sentence.

(c) The Secretary may by regulation require that the administrator of any employee benefit plan furnish to each participant and to each beneficiary receiving benefits under the plan a statement of the rights of participants and beneficiaries under this title.

(d) Cross References.—For regulations re- specting coordination of reports to the Secre- taries of Labor and the Treasury, see section 3004.

ERISA Sec. 104 (d)

REPORTING OF PARTICIPANT'S BENEFIT RIGHTS

Sec. 105. (a) Each administrator of an employee pension benefit plan shall furnish to any plan participant or beneficiary who so requests in writing, a statement indicating, on the basis of the latest available information—

(1) the total benefits accrued, and

(2) the nonforfeitable pension benefits, if any, which have accrued, or the earliest date on which benefits will become nonforfeitable.

(b) In no case shall a participant or beneficiary be entitled under this section to receive more than one report described in subsection (a) during any one 12-month period.

(c) Each administrator required to register under section 6057 of the Internal Revenue Code of 1954 shall, before the expiration of the time prescribed for such registration, furnish to each participant described in subsection (a)(2)(C) of such section, an individual statement setting forth the information with respect to such participant required to be contained in the registration statement required by section 6057(a)(2) of such Code. Such statement shall also include a notice to the participant of any benefits which are forfeitable if the participant dies before a certain date.

(d) Subsection (a) of this section shall apply to a plan to which more than one unaffiliated employer is required to contribute only to the extent provided in regulations prescribed by the Secretary in coordination with the Secretary of the Treasury.

REPORTS MADE PUBLIC INFORMATION

Sec. 106. (a) Except as provided in subsection (b), the contents of the descriptions, annual reports, statements, and other documents filed with the Secretary pursuant to this part shall be public information and the Secretary shall make any such information and data available for inspection in the public document room of the Department of Labor. The Secretary may use the information and data for statistical and research purposes, and compile and publish such studies, analyses, reports, and surveys based thereon as he may deem appropriate.

(b) Information described in sections 105(a) and 105(c) with respect to a participant may be disclosed only to the extent that information respecting that participant's benefits under title II of the Social Security Act may be disclosed under such Act.

RETENTION OF RECORDS

Sec. 107. Every person subject to a requirement to file any description or report or to certify any information therefor under this title or who would be subject to such a requirement but for an exemption or simplified reporting requirement under section 104(a)(2) or (3) of this title shall maintain records on the matters of which disclosure is required which will provide in sufficient detail the necessary basic information and data from which the documents thus required may be verified, explained, or clarified, and checked for accuracy and completeness, and shall include vouchers, worksheets, receipts, and applicable resolutions, and shall keep such records available for examination for a period of not less than six years after the filing date of the documents based on the information which they contain, or six years after the date on which such documents would have been filed but for an exemption or simplified reporting requirement under section 104(a)(2) or (3).

RELIANCE ON ADMINISTRATIVE INTERPRETATIONS

Sec. 108. In any criminal proceeding under section 501 based on any act or omission in alleged violation of this part or section 412, no person shall be subject to any liability or punishment for or on account of the failure of such person to (1) comply with this part or section 412, if he pleads and proves that the act or omission complained of was in good faith, in conformity with, and in reliance on any regulation or written ruling of the Secretary, or (2) publish and file any information required by any provision of this part if he pleads and proves that he published and filed such information in good faith, and in conformity with any regulation or written ruling of the Secretary issued under this part regarding the filing of such reports. Such a defense, if established, shall be a bar to the action or proceeding, notwithstanding that (A) after such act or omission, such interpretation or opinion is modified or rescinded or is determined by judicial authority to be invalid or of no legal effect, or (B) after publishing or filing the plan description, annual reports, and other reports required by this title, such publication or filing is determined by judicial authority not to be in conformity with the requirements of this part.

FORMS

Sec. 109. (a) Except as provided in subsection (b) of this section, the Secretary may require that any information required under this title to be submitted to him, including but not limited to the information required to be filed by the administrator pursuant to section 103(b)(3) and (c), must be submitted on such forms as he may prescribe.

(b) The financial statement and opinion required to be prepared by an independent qualified public accountant pursuant to section 103(a)(3)(A), the actuarial statement required to be prepared by an enrolled actuary pursuant to section 103(a)(4)(A) and the summary plan description required by section 102(a) shall not be required to be submitted on forms.

(c) The Secretary may prescribe the format and content of the summary plan description, the summary of the annual report described in section 104(b)(3) and any other report, statements or documents (other than the bargaining agreement, trust agreement, contract, or other instrument under which the plan is established or operated), which are required to be furnished or made available to plan participants and beneficiaries receiving benefits under the plan.

ALTERNATIVE METHODS OF COMPLIANCE

Sec. 110. (a) The Secretary on his own motion or after having received the petition of an administrator may prescribe an alternative method for satisfying any requirement of this part with respect to any pension plan, or class of pension plans, to subject to such requirement if he determines—

(1) that the use of such alternative method is consistent with the purposes of this title and that it provides adequate disclosure to the participants and beneficiaries in the plan, and adequate reporting to the Secretary,

(2) that the application of such requirement of this part would—

(A) increase the costs to the plan, or—

(B) impose unreasonable administrative burdens with respect to the operation of the plan, having regard to the particular characteristics of the plan or the type of plan involved; and

(3) that the application of this part would be adverse to the interests of plan participants in the aggregate.

(b) An alternative method may be prescribed under subsection (a) by regulation or otherwise. If an alternative method is prescribed other than by regulation, the Secretary shall provide notice and an opportunity for interested persons to present their views, and shall publish in the Federal Register the provisions of such alternative method.

REPEAL AND EFFECTIVE DATE

Sec. 111. (a)(1) The Welfare and Pension Plans Disclosure Act is repealed except that such Act shall continue to apply to any conduct and events which occurred before the effective date of this part.

(2)(A) Section 664 of title 18, United States Code, is amended by striking out ''any such plan subject to the provisions of the Welfare and Pension Plans Disclosure Act'' and inserting in lieu thereof ''any employee benefit plan

ERISA Sec. 111 (a)(2)(A)

subject to any provision of title I of the Employee Retirement Income Security Act of 1974''.

(B)(i) Section 1027 of such title 18 is amended by striking out "Welfare and Pension Plans Disclosure Act" and inserting in lieu thereof "title I of the Employee Retirement Income Security Act of 1974'', and by striking out "Act" each place it appears and inserting in lieu thereof "title''.

(ii) The heading for such section is amended by striking out "WELFARE AND PENSION PLANS DISCLOSURE ACT" and inserting in lieu thereof "EMPLOYEE RETIREMENT INCOME SECURITY ACT OF 1974''.

(iii) The table of sections of chapter 47 of such title 18 is amended by striking out "Welfare and Pension Plans Disclosure Act in the item relating to section 1027 and inserting in lieu thereof "Employee Retirement Income Security Act of 1974''.

(C) Section 1954 of such title 18 is amended by striking out "any plan subject to the provisions of the Welfare and Pension Plans Disclosure Act as amended" and inserting in lieu thereof "any employee welfare benefit plan or employee pension benefit plan, respectively, subject to any provision of title I of the Employee Retirement Income Security Act of 1974''; and by striking out "sections 3(3) and 5(b)(1) and (2) of the Welfare and Pension Plans Disclosure Act, as amended" and inserting in lieu thereof "sections 3(4) and (3)(16) of the Employee Retirement Income Security Act of 1974''.

(D) Section 211 of the Labor-Management Reporting and Disclosure Act of 1959 (29 U.S.C. 441) is amended by striking out "Welfare and Pension Plans Disclosure Act" and inserting in lieu thereof "Employee Retirement Income Security Act of 1974''.

(b)(1) Except as provided in paragraph (2), this part (including the amendments and re-

peals made by subsection (a)) shall take effect on January 1, 1975.

(2) In the case of a plan which has a plan year which begins before January 1, 1975, and ends after December 31, 1974, the Secretary may postpone by regulation the effective date of the repeal of any provision of the Welfare and Pension Plans Disclosure Act (and of any amendment made by subsection (a)(2)) and the effective date of any provision of this part, until the beginning of the first plan year of such plan which begins after January 1, 1975.

(c) The provisions of this title authorizing the Secretary to promulgate regulations shall take effect on the date of enactment of this Act.

(d) Subsections (b) and (c) shall not apply with respect to amendments made to this part in provisions enacted after the date of the enactment of this Act.

Part 2 — Participation and Vesting

COVERAGE

Sec. 201. This part shall apply to any employee benefit plan described in section 4(a) (and not exempted under Section 4(b)) other than—

(1) an employee welfare benefit plan;

(2) a plan which is unfunded and is maintained by an employer primarily for the purpose of providing deferred compensation for a select group of management or highly compensated employees;

(3)(A) a plan established and maintained by a society, order, or association described in section 501(c)(8) or (9) of the Internal Revenue Code of 1954, if no part of the contributions to or under such plan are made by employers of participants in such plan, or

(B) a trust described in section 501 (c)(18) of such Code;

(4) a plan which is established and maintained by a labor organization described in section 501(c)(5) of the Internal Revenue Code of 1954 and which does not at any time after the date of enactment of this Act provide for employer contributions;

(5) any agreement providing payments to a retired partner or a deceased partner's successor in interest, as described in section 736 of the Internal Revenue Code of 1954;

(6) an individual retirement account or annuity described in section 408 of the Internal Revenue Code of 1954, or a retirement bond described in section 409 of the Internal Revenue Code of 1954 (as effective for obligations issued before January 1, 1984);

(7) an excess benefit plan; or

(8) any plan, fund or program under which an employer, all of whose stock is directly or indirectly owned by employees, former employees or their beneficiaries, proposes through an unfunded arrangement to compensate retired employees for benefits which were forfeited by such employees under a pension plan maintained by a former employer prior to the date such pension plan became subject to this Act.

MINIMUM PARTICIPATION STANDARDS

Sec. 202. (a)(1)(A) No pension plan may require, as a condition of participation in the plan, that an employee complete a period of service with the employer or employers maintaining the plan extending beyond the later of the following dates—

(i) the date on which the employee attains the age of 21; or

(ii) the date on which he completes 1 year of service.

(B)(i) In the case of any plan which provides that after not more than 3 years of service each participant has a right to 100 percent of his accrued benefit under the plan which is nonforfeitable at the time such benefit accrues, clause (ii) of subparagraph (A) shall be applied by substituting "2 years of service" for "1 year of service".

(ii) In the case of any plan maintained exclusively for employees of an educational organization (as defined in section 170(b)(1)(A)(ii) of the Internal Revenue Code of 1954) by an employer which is exempt from tax under section 501(a) of such Code, which provides that each participant having at least 1 year of service has a right to 100 percent of his accrued benefit under the plan which is nonforfeitable at the time such benefit accrues, clause (i) of subparagraph (A) shall be applied by substituting "26" for "21". This clause shall not apply to any plan to which clause (i) applies.

(2) No pension plan may exclude from participation (on the basis of age) employees who have attained a specified age,

(3)(A) For purposes of this section, the term "year of service" means a 12-month period during which the employee has not less than 1,000 hours of service. For purposes of this paragraph, computation of any 12-month period shall be made with reference to the date on which the employee's employment commenced, except that, in accordance with regulations prescribed by the Secretary, such computation may be made by reference to the first day of a plan year in the case of an employee who does not complete 1,000 hours of service during the 12-month period beginning on the date his employment commenced.

(B) In the case of any seasonal industry where the customary period of employment is less than 1,000 hours during a calendar year, the term "year of service" shall be such period as may be determined under regulations prescribed by the Secretary.

(C) For purposes of this section, the term "hour of service" means a time of service determined under regulations prescribed by the Secretary.

ERISA Sec. 202 (a)(3)(C)

(D) For purposes of this section, in the case of any maritime industry, 125 days of service shall be treated as 1,000 hours of service. The Secretary may prescribe regulations to carry out the purposes of this subparagraph.

(4) A plan shall be treated as not meeting the requirements of paragraph (1) unless it provides that any employee who has satisfied the minimum age and service requirements specified in such paragraph, and who is otherwise entitled to participate in the plan, commences participation in the plan no later than the earlier of—

(A) the first day of the first plan year beginning after the date on which such employee satisfied such requirements, or

(B) the date 6 months after the date on which he satisfied such requirements,
unless such employee was separated from the service before the date referred to in subparagraph (A) or (B), whichever is applicable.

(b)(1) Except as otherwise provided in paragraphs (2), (3), and (4), all years of service with the employer or employers maintaining the plan shall be taken into account in computing the period of service for purposes of subsection (a)(1).

(2) In the case of any employee who has any 1-year break in service (as defined in section 203(b)(3)(A)) under a plan to which the service requirements of clause (i) of subsection (a)(1)(B) apply, if such employee has not satisfied such requirements, service before such break shall not be required to be taken into account.

(3) In computing an employee's period of service for purposes of subsection (a)(1) in the case of any participant who has any 1-year break in service (as defined in section 203(b)(3)(A)), service before such break shall not be required to be taken into account under the plan until he has completed a year of service (as defined in subsection (a)(3)) after his return.

(4)(A) For purposes of paragraph (1), in the case of a nonvested participant, years of service with the employer or employers maintaining the plan before any period of consecutive 1-year breaks in service shall not be required to be taken into account in computing the period of service if the number of consecutive 1-year breaks in service within such period equals or exceeds the greater of—

(i) 5, or

(ii) the aggregate number of years of service before such period.

(B) If any years of service are not required to be taken into account by reason of a period of breaks in service to which subparagraph (A) applies, such years of service shall not be taken into account in applying subparagraph (A) to a subsequent period of breaks in service.

(C) For purposes of subparagraph (A), the term "nonvested participant" means a participant who does not have any nonforfeitable right under the plan to an accrued benefit derived from employer contributions.

(5)(A) In the case of each individual who is absent from work for any period—

(i) by reason of the pregnancy of the individual,

(ii) by reason of the birth of a child of the individual,

(iii) by reason of the placement of a child with the individual in connection with the adoption of such child by such individual, or

(iv) for purposes of caring for such child for a period beginning immediately following such birth or placement,

the plan shall treat as hours of service solely for purposes of determining under this subsection whether a 1-year break in service (as defined in section 203(b)(3)(A)) has occurred, the hours described in subparagraph (B).

(B) The hours described in this subparagraph are—

(i) the hours of service which otherwise would normally have been credited to such individual but for such absence, or

(ii) in any case in which the plan is unable to determine the hours described in clause (i), 8 hours of service per day of such absence,

except that the total number of hours treated as hours of service under this subparagraph by reason of any such pregnancy or placement shall not exceed 501 hours.

(C) The hours described in subparagraph (B) shall be treated as hours of service as provided in this paragraph—

(i) only in the year in which the absence from work begins, if a participant would be prevented from incurring a 1-year break in service in such year solely because the period of absence is treated as hours of service as provided in subparagraph (A); or

(ii) in any other case, in the immediately following year.

(D) For purposes of this paragraph, the term "year" means the period used in computations pursuant to section 202(a)(3)(A).

(E) A plan may provide that no credit will be given pursuant to this paragraph unless the individual furnishes to the plan administrator such timely information as the plan may reasonably require to establish—

(i) that the absence from work is for reasons referred to in subparagraph (A), and

(ii) the number of days for which there was such an absence.

MINIMUM VESTING STANDARDS

Sec. 203. (a) Each pension plan shall provide that an employee's right to his normal retirement benefit is nonforfeitable upon the attainment of normal retirement age and in addition shall satisfy the requirements of paragraphs (1) and (2) of this subsection.

(1) A plan satisfies the requirements of this paragraph if an employee's rights in his accrued benefit derived from his own contributions are nonforfeitable.

(2) A plan satisfies the requirements of this paragraph if it satisfies the following requirements of subparagraph (A), (B), or (C).

(A) A plan satisfies the requirements of this subparagraph if an employee who has completed at least 5 years of service has a nonforfeitable right to 100 percent of the employee's accrued benefit derived from employer contributions.

(B) A plan satisfies the requirements of this subparagraph if an employee has a nonforfeitable right to a percentage of the employee's accrued benefit derived from employer contributions determined under the table:

Years of service:	The nonforfeitable percentage is:
3	20
4	40
5	60
6	80
7 or more	100

(C) A plan satisfies the requirements of this subparagraph if—

(i) the plan is a multiemployer plan (within the meaning of section 3(37)), and

(ii) under the plan—

(I) an employee who is covered pursuant to a collective bargaining agreement described in section 3(37)(A)(ii) and who has completed at least 10 years of service has a nonforfeitable right to 100 percent of the employee's accrued benefit derived from employer contributions, and

(II) the requirements of subparagraph (A) or (B) are met with respect to employees not described in subclause (I).

(3)(A) A right to an accrued benefit derived from employer contributions shall not be treated as forfeitable solely because the plan provides that it is not payable if the participant dies (except in the case of a survivor annuity which is payable as provided in section 205).

(B) A right to an accrued benefit derived from employer contributions shall not be treated as forfeitable solely because the plan provides that the payment of benefits is suspended for such period as the employee is employed, subsequent to the commencement of payment of such benefits—

(i) in the case of a plan other than a multiemployer plan, by an employer who maintains the plan under which such benefits were being paid; and

(ii) in the case of a multiemployer plan, in the same industry, in the same trade or craft, and the same geographic area covered by the plan, as when such benefits commenced.

The Secretary shall prescribe such regulations as may be necessary to carry out the purposes of this subparagraph, including regulations with respect to the meaning of the term "employed".

(C) A right to an accrued benefit derived from employer contributions shall not be treated as forfeitable solely because plan amendments may be given retroactive application as provided in section 302(c)(8).

(D)(i) A right to an accrued benefit derived from employer contributions shall not be treated as forfeitable solely because the plan provides that, in the case of a participant who does not have a nonforfeitable right to at least 50 percent of his accrued benefit derived from employer contributions, such accrued benefit may be forfeited on account of the withdrawal by the participant of any amount attributable to the benefit derived from mandatory contributions (as defined in

the last sentence of section 204(c)(2)(C)) made by such participant.

(ii) Clause (i) shall not apply to a plan unless the plan provides that any accrued benefit forfeited under a plan provision described in such clause shall be restored upon repayment by the participant of the full amount of the withdrawal described in such clause plus, in the case of a defined benefit plan, interest.

Such interest shall be computed on such amount at the rate determined for purposes of section 204(c)(2)(C) (if such subsection applies) on the date of such repayment (computed annually from the date of such withdrawal). The plan provision required under this clause may provide that such repayment must be made (I) in the case of a withdrawal on account of separation from service, before the earlier of 5 years after the first date on which the participant is subsequently reemployed by the employer, or the close of the first period of 5 consecutive 1-year breaks in service commencing after the withdrawal; or (II) in the case of any other withdrawal, 5 years after the date of the withdrawal.

(iii) In the case of accrued benefits derived from employer contributions which accrued before the date of the enactment of this Act, a right to such accrued benefit derived from employer contributions shall not be treated as forfeitable solely because the plan provides that an amount of such accrued benefit may be forfeited on account of the withdrawal by the participant of an amount attributable to the benefit derived from mandatory contributions, made by such participant before the date of the enactment of this Act if such amount forfeited is proportional to such amount withdrawn. This clause shall not apply to any plan to which any mandatory contribution is made after the date of the enactment of this Act. The Secretary of the Treasury shall prescribe such regulations as may be necessary to carry out the purposes of this clause.

(iv) For purposes of this subparagraph, in the case of any class-year plan, a withdrawal of employee contributions shall be treated as a withdrawal of such contributions on a plan-year-by-plan-year basis in succeeding order of time.

(v) Cross Reference.—For nonforfeitability where the employee has a nonforfeitable right to Sec. 203 (a)(3)(E)(i)

(E)(i) A right to an accrued benefit derived from employer contributions under a multiemployer plan shall not be treated as forfeitable solely because the plan provides that benefits accrued as a result of service with the participant's employer before the employer had an obligation to contribute under the plan may not be payable if the employer ceases contributions to the multiemployer plan.

(ii) A participant's right to an accrued benefit derived from employer contributions under a multiemployer plan shall not be treated as forfeitable solely because—

(I) the plan is amended to reduce benefits under section 4244A or 4281, or

(II) benefit payments under the plan may be suspended under section 4245 or 4281.

(F) A matching contribution (within the meaning of section 401(m) of the Internal Revenue Code of 1986) shall not be treated as forfeitable merely because such contribution is forfeitable if the contribution to which the matching contribution relates is treated as an excess contribution under section 401(k)(8)(B) of such Code, an excess deferral under section 402(g)(2)(A) of such Code, or an excess aggregate contribution under section 401(m)(6)(B).

(b)(1) In computing the period of service under the plan for purposes of determining the nonforfeitable percentage under subsection (a)(2), all of an employee's years of service with the employer or employers maintaining the plan shall be taken into account, except that the following may be disregarded:

(A) years of service before age 18, except that in the case of a plan which does not satisfy subparagraph (A) or (B) of subsection (a)(2), the plan may not disregard any such year of service during which the employee was a participant;

(B) years of service during a period for which the employee declined to contribute to a plan requiring employee contributions;

(C) years of service with an employer during any period for which the employer did not maintain the plan or a predecessor plan, defined by the Secretary of the Treasury;

(D) service not required to be taken into account under paragraph (3);

(E) years of service before January 1, 1971, unless the employee has had at least 3 years of service after December 31, 1970;

(F) years of service before this part first applies to the plan if such service would have been disregarded under the rules of the plan with regard to breaks in service, as in effect on the applicable date; and

(G) in the case of a multiemployer plan, years of service—

(i) with an employer after—

(I) a complete withdrawal of such employer from the plan (within the meaning of section 4203), or

(II) to the extent permitted by regulations prescribed by the Secretary of the Treasury, a partial withdrawal described in section 4205(b)(2)(A)(i) in connection with the decertification of the collective bargaining representative; and

(ii) with any employer under the plan after the termination date of the plan under section 4048.

(2)(A) For purposes of this section, except as provided in subparagraph (C), the term "year of service" means a calendar year, plan year, or other 12-consecutive-month period designated by the plan (and not prohibited under regulations prescribed by the Secretary) during which the participant has completed 1,000 hours of service.

(B) For purposes of this section, the term "hour of service" has the meaning provided by section 202(a)(3)(C).

(C) In the case of any seasonal industry where the customary period of employment is less than 1,000 hours during a calendar year, the term "year of service" shall be such period as determined under regulations of the Secretary.

(D) For purposes of this section, in the case of any maritime industry, 125 days of service shall be treated as 1,000 hours of service. The Secretary may prescribe regulations to carry out the purposes of this subparagraph.

(3)(A) For purposes of this paragraph, the term "1-year break in service" means a calendar year, plan year, or other 12-consecutive-month period designated by the plan (and not prohibited under regulations prescribed by the Secretary) during which the participant has not completed more than 500 hours of service.

(B) For purposes of paragraph (1), in the case of any employee who has any 1-year break in service, years of service before such break shall not be required to be taken into account until he has completed a year of service after his return.

(C) For purposes of paragraph (1), in the case of any participant in an individual account plan or an insured defined benefit plan which satisfies the requirements of subsection 204(b)(1)(F) who has 5 consecutive 1-year breaks in service, years of service after such 5-year period shall not be required to be taken into account for purposes of determining the nonforfeitable percentage of his accrued benefit derived from employer contributions which accrued before such 5-year period.

(D)(i) For purposes of paragraph (1), in the case of a nonvested participant, years of service with the employer or employers maintaining the plan before any period of consecutive 1-year breaks in service shall not be required to be taken into account if the number of consecutive 1-year breaks in service within such period equals or exceeds the greater of—

(I) 5, or

(II) the aggregate number of years of service before such period.

(ii) If any years of service are not required to be taken into account by reason of a period of breaks in service to which clause (i) applies, such years of service shall not be taken into account in applying clause (i) to a subsequent period of breaks in service.

(iii) For purposes of clause (i), the term "nonvested participant" means a participant who does not have any nonforfeitable right under the plan to an accrued benefit derived from employer contributions.

(E)(i) In the case of each individual who is absent from work for any period—

(I) by reason of the pregnancy of the individual,

(II) by reason of the birth of a child of the individual,

(III) by reason of the placement of a child with the individual in connection with the adoption of such child by such individual, or

(IV) for purposes of caring for such child for a period beginning immediately following such birth or placement,

the plan shall treat as hours of service, solely for purposes of determining under this paragraph whether a 1-year break in service has occurred, the hours described in clause (ii)

(ii) The hours described in this clause are—

(I) the hours of service which otherwise would normally have been credited to such individual but for such absence, or

(II) in any case in which the plan is unable to determine the hours described in subclause (I), 8 hours of service per day of absence,

except that the total number of hours treated as hours of service under this clause by reason of such pregnancy or placement shall not exceed 501 hours.

(iii) The hours described in clause (ii) shall be treated as hours of service as provided in this subparagraph—

(I) only in the year in which the absence from work begins, if a participant would be prevented from incurring a 1-year break in service in such year solely because the period of absence is treated as hours of service as provided in clause (i); or

(II) in any other case, in the immediately following year.

(iv) For purposes of this subparagraph, the term "year" means the period used in computations pursuant to paragraph (2).

(v) A plan may provide that no credit will be given pursuant to this subparagraph unless the individual furnishes to the plan administrator such timely information as the plan may reasonably require to establish—

(I) that the absence from work is for reasons referred to in clause (i), and

(II) the number of days for which there was such an absence.

(4) Cross References.—

(A) For definitions of "accrued benefit" and "normal retirement age", see sections 3(23) and (24).

(B) For effect of certain cash out distributions, see section 204(d)(1).

(c)(1)(A) A plan amendment changing any vesting schedule under the plan shall be treated as not satisfying the requirements of subsection (a)(2) if the nonforfeitable percentage of the accrued benefit derived from em-

ployer contributions (determined as of the later of the date such amendment is adopted, or the date such amendment becomes effective) of any employee who is a participant in the plan is less than such nonforfeitable percentage computed under the plan without regard to such amendment.

(B) A plan amendment changing any vesting schedule under the plan shall be treated as not satisfying the requirements of subsection (a)(2) unless each participant having not less than 3 years of service is permitted to elect, within a reasonable period after adoption of such amendment, to have his nonforfeitable percentage computed under the plan without regard to such amendment.

(2) Subsection (a) shall not apply to benefits which may not be provided for designated employees in the event of early termination of the plan under provisions of the plan adopted pursuant to regulations prescribed by the Secretary of the Treasury to preclude the discrimination prohibited by section 401(a)(4) of the Internal Revenue Code of 1954.

(3) [Deleted]

(d) A pension plan may allow for nonforfeitable benefits after a lesser period and in greater amounts than are required by this part.

(e)(1) If the present value of any nonforfeitable benefit with respect to a participant in a plan exceeds $3,500, the plan shall provide that such benefit may not be immediately distributed without the consent of the participant.

[(2)(A) For purposes of paragraph (1), the present value shall be calculated—

[(i) by using an interest rate no greater than the applicable interest rate if the vested accrued benefit (using such rate) is not in excess of $25,000, and

[(ii) by using an interest rate no greater than 120 percent of the applicable interest rate if the vested accrued benefit exceeds $25,000 (as determined under clause (i)).

[In no event shall the present value determined under subclause (II) be less than $25,000.

[(B) — For purposes of subparagraph (A), the term "applicable interest rate" means the interest rate which would be used (as of the date of the distribution) by the Pension Benefit Guaranty Corporation for purposes of determining the present value of a lump sum distribution on plan termination.]

◊ ◊ ◊

Editor's Note: ERISA §203(e)(2), as set forth below, appears as amended by §767(c)(1) of the Retirement Protection Act of 1994 (enacted as part of the Uruguay Round Agreements Act, P.L. 103-465). Section 767(d)(1) of that Act provides that these amendments are effective generally with respect to plan years and limitation years beginning after December 31, 1994, except that an employer may treat the amendments as being effective on or after December 8, 1994. Section 767(d)(2) of that Act provides that a participant's accrued benefit will not be considered to be reduced in violation of the anti-cutback rule of Code §411(d)(6) or ERISA §204(g), as amended, merely because (1) the benefit is determined in accordance with Code §417(e)(3)(A) or ERISA §205(g)(3) (both as amended by the Act), or (2) the plan applies Code §415(b)(2)(E) as amended by the Act.

◊ ◊ ◊

(2) For purposes of paragraph (1), the present value shall be calculated in accordance with section 205(g)(3).

(3) This subsection shall not apply to any distribution of dividends to which section 404(k) of the Internal Revenue Code of 1954 applies.

BENEFIT ACCRUAL REQUIREMENTS

Sec. 204. (a) Each pension plan shall satisfy the requirements of subsection (b)(3), and—

(1) in the case of a defined benefit plan, shall satisfy the requirements of subsection (b)(1); and

(2) in the case of a defined contribution plan, shall satisfy the requirements of subsection (b)(2).

(b)(1)(A) A defined benefit plan satisfies the requirements of this paragraph if the accrued benefit to which each participant is entitled upon his separation from the service is not less than—

(i) 3 percent of the normal retirement benefit to which he would be entitled at the normal retirement age if he commenced participation at the earliest possible entry age under the plan and served continuously until the earlier of age 65 or the normal retirement age specified under the plan, multiplied by

(ii) the number of years (not in excess of $33\frac{1}{3}$) of his participation in the plan.
In the case of a plan providing retirement benefits based on compensation during any period, the normal retirement benefit to which a participant would be entitled shall be determined as if he continued to earn annually the average rate of compensation which he earned during consecutive years of service, not in excess of 10, for which his compensation was the highest. For purposes of this subparagraph, social security benefits and all other relevant factors used to compute benefits shall be treated as remaining constant as of the current year for all years after such current year.

(B) A defined benefit plan satisfies the requirements of this paragraph of a particular plan year if under the plan the accrued benefit payable at the normal retirement age is equal to the normal retirement benefit and the annual rate at which any individual who is or could be a participant can accrue the retirement benefits payable at normal retire ment age under the plan for any later plan year is not more than 133⅓ percent of the annual rate at which he can accrue benefits for any plan year beginning on or after such particular plan year and before such later plan year. For purposes of this subparagraph—

(i) any amendment to the plan which is in effect for the current year shall be treated as in effect for all other plan years;

(ii) any change in an accrual rate which does not apply to any individual who is or could be a participant in the current year shall be disregarded;

(iii) the fact that benefits under the plan may be payable to certain employees before normal retirement age shall be disregarded; and

(iv) social security benefits and all other relevant factors used to compute benefits shall be treated as remaining constant as of the current year for all years after the current year.

(C) A defined benefit plan satisfies the requirements of this paragraph if the accrued benefit to which any participant is entitled upon his separation from the service is not less than a fraction of the annual benefit commencing at normal retirement age to which he would be entitled under the plan as in effect on the date of his separation if he continued to earn annually until normal retirement age the same rate of compensation upon which his normal retirement benefit would be computed under the plan, determined as if he had attained normal retirement age on the date any such determination is made (but taking into account no more than the 10 years of service immediately preceding his separation from service). Such fraction shall be a fraction, not exceeding 1, the numerator of which is the total number of his years of participation in the plan (as of the date of his separation from the service) and the denominator of which is the total number of years he would have participated in the plan if he separated from the service at the normal retirement age. For purposes

of this subparagraph, social security benefits and all other relevant factors used to compute benefits shall be treated as remaining constant as of the current year for all years after such current year.

(D) Subparagraphs (A), (B), and (C) shall not apply with respect to years of participation before the first plan year to which this section applies but a defined benefit plan satisfies the requirements of this subparagraph with respect to such years of participation only if the accrued benefit of any participant with respect to such years of participation is not less than the greater of—

(i) his accrued benefit determined under the plan, as in effect from time to time prior to the date of the enactment of this Act, or

(ii) an accrued benefit which is not less than one-half of the accrued benefit to which such participant would have been entitled if subparagraph (A), (B), or (C) applied with respect to such years of participation.

(E) Notwithstanding subparagraphs (A), (B), and (C) of this paragraph, a plan shall not be treated as not satisfying the requirements of this paragraph solely because the accrual of benefits under the plan does not become effective until the employee has two continuous years of service. For purposes of this subparagraph, the term "year of service" has the meaning provided by section 202(a)(3)(A).

(F) Notwithstanding subparagraphs (A), (B), and (C), a defined benefit plan satisfies the requirements of this paragraph if such plan—

(i) is funded exclusively by the purchase of insurance contracts, and

(ii) satisfies the requirements of paragraphs (2) and (3) of section 301(b) (relating to certain insurance contract plans),

but only if an employee's accrued benefit as of any applicable date is not less than the cash surrender value his insurance contracts would have on such applicable date if the requirements of paragraphs (4), (5), and (6) of section 301(b) were satisfied.

(G) Notwithstanding the preceding subparagraphs, a defined benefit plan shall be treated as not satisfying the requirements of this paragraph if the participant's accrued benefit is reduced on account of any increase in his age or service. The preceding sentence shall not apply to benefits under the plan commencing before benefits payable under title II of the Social Security Act which benefits under the plan—

(i) do not exceed social security benefits, and

(ii) terminate when such social security benefits commence.

(H)(i) Notwithstanding the preceding subparagraphs, a defined benefit plan shall be treated as not satisfying the requirements of this paragraph if, under the plan, an employee's benefit accrual is ceased, or the rate of an employee's benefit accrual is reduced, because of the attainment of any age.

(ii) A plan shall not be treated as failing to meet the requirements of this subparagraph solely because the plan imposes (without regard to age) a limitation on the amount of benefits that the plan provides or a limitation on the number of years of service or years of participation which are taken into account for purposes of determining benefit accrual under the plan.

(iii) In the case of any employee who, as of the end of any plan year under a defined benefit plan, has attained normal retirement age under such plan—

(I) if distribution of benefits under such plan with respect to such employee has commenced as of the end of such plan year, then any requirement of this subparagraph for continued accrual of benefits under such plan with respect to such employee during such plan year shall be treated as satisfied to the extent of the actuarial equivalent of in-service distribution of benefits, and

(II) if distribution of benefits under such plan with respect to such employee has not commenced as of the end of such year in accordance with section 206(a)(3), and the payment of benefits under such plan with respect to such employee is not suspended during such plan year pursuant to section 203(a)(3)(B), then any requirement of this subparagraph for continued accrual of benefits under such plan with respect to such employee during such plan year shall be treated as satisfied to the extent of any adjustment in the benefit payable under the plan during such plan year attributable to the delay in the distribution of benefits after the attainment of normal retirement age.

The preceding provisions of this clause shall apply in accordance with regulations of the Secretary of the Treasury. Such regulations may provide for the application of the preceding provisions of this clause, in the case of any such employee, with respect to any period of time within a plan year.

(iv) Clause (i) shall not apply with respect to any employee who is a highly compensated employee (within the meaning of section 414(q) of the Internal Revenue Code of 1986) to the extent provided in regulations prescribed by the Secretary of the Treasury for purposes of precluding discrimination in favor of highly compensated employees within the meaning of subchapter D of chapter 1 of the Internal Revenue Code of 1986.

(v) A plan shall not be treated as failing to meet the requirements of clause (i) solely because the subsidized portion of any early retirement benefit is disregarded in determining benefit accruals.

(vi) Any regulations prescribed by the Secretary of the Treasury pursuant to clause (v) of section 411(b)(1)(H) of the Internal Revenue Code of 1986 shall apply with respect to the requirements of this subparagraph in the same manner and to the same extent as such regulations apply with respect to the requirements of such section 411(b)(1)(H).

(2)(A) A defined contribution plan satisfies the requirements of this paragraph if, under the plan, allocations to the employee's account are not ceased, and the rate at which amounts are allocated to the employee's account is not reduced, because of the attainment of any age.

(B) A plan shall not be treated as failing to meet the requirements of subparagraph (A) solely because the subsidized portion of any early retirement benefit is disregarded in determining benefit accruals.

(C) Any regulations prescribed by the Secretary of the Treasury pursuant to subparagraphs (C) and (D) of section 411(b)(2) of the Internal Revenue Code of 1986 shall apply with respect to the requirements of this paragraph in the same manner and to the same extent as such regulations apply with respect to the requirements of such section 411(b)(2).

(3) A plan satisfies the requirements of this paragraph if—

(A) in the case of a defined benefit plan, the plan requires separate accounting for the portion of each employee's accrued benefit derived from any voluntary employee contributions permitted under the plan; and

(B) in the case of any plan which is not a defined benefit plan, the plan requires separate accounting for each employee's accrued benefit.

(4)(A) For purposes of determining an employee's accrued benefit, the term "year of participation" means a period of service (beginning at the earliest date on which the employee is a participant in the plan and which is included in a period of service required to be taken into account under section 202(b)) as determined under regulations prescribed by the Secretary which provide for the calculation of such period on any reasonable and consistent basis.

(B) For purposes of this paragraph, except as provided in subparagraph (C), in the case of any employee whose customary employment is less than full time, the calculation of such employee's service on any basis which provides less than a ratable portion of the accrued benefit to which he would be entitled under the plan if his customary employment were full time shall not be treated as made on a reasonable and consistent basis.

(C) For purposes of this paragraph, in the case of any employee whose service is less than 1,000 hours during any calendar year, plan year or other 12-consecutive-month period designated by the plan (and not prohibited under regulations prescribed by the Secretary) the calculation of his period of service shall not be treated as not made on a reasonable and consistent basis merely because such service is not taken into account.

(D) In the case of any seasonal industry where the customary period of employment is less than 1,000 hours during a calendar year, the term "year of participation" shall be such period as determined under regulations prescribed by the Secretary.

(E) For purposes of this subsection in the case of any maritime industry, 125 days of service shall be treated as a year of participation. The Secretary may prescribe regulations to carry out the purposes of this subparagraph.

(c)(1) For purposes of this section and section 203 an employee's accrued benefit derived from employer contributions as of any applicable date is the excess (if any) of the accrued benefit for such employee as of such applicable date over the accrued benefit derived from contributions made by such employee as of such date.

(2)(A) In the case of a plan other than a defined benefit plan, the accrued benefit derived from contributions made by an employee as of any applicable date is—

(i) except as provided in clause (ii), the balance of the employee's separate account consisting only of his contributions and the income, expenses, gains, and losses attributable thereto, or

(ii) if a separate account is not maintained with respect to an employee's contributions under such a plan, the amount which bears the same ratio to his total accrued benefit as the total amount of the employee's contributions (less withdrawals) bears to the sum of such contributions and the contributions made on his behalf by the employer (less withdrawals).

(B) Defined benefit plans.—In the case of a defined benefit plan, the accrued benefit derived from the contributions made by an employee as of any applicable date is the amount equal to the employee's accumulated contributions expressed as an annual benefit commencing at normal retirement age, using an interest rate which would be used under the plan under section 205(g)(3) (as of the determination date).

(C) For purposes of this subsection, the term "accumulated contributions" means the total of—

(i) all mandatory contributions made by the employee,

(ii) interest (if any) under the plan to the end of the last plan year to which section 203(a)(2) does not apply (by reason of the applicable effective date), and

(iii) interest on the sum of the amounts determined under clauses (i) and (ii) compounded annually—

(I) at the rate of 120 percent of the Federal mid-term rate (as in effect under section 1274 of the Internal Revenue Code of 1986 for the 1st month of a plan year for the period beginning with the 1st plan year to which subsection (a)(2) applies by reason of the applicable effective date) and ending with the date on which the determination is being made and

(II) at the interest rate which would be used under the plan under section 205(g)(3) (as of the determination date)

for the period beginning with the determination date and ending on the date on which the employee attains normal retirement age.

For purposes of this subparagraph, the term "mandatory contributions" means amounts contributed to the plan by the employee which are required as a condition of employment, as a condition of participation in such plan, or as a condition of obtaining benefits under the plan attributable to employer contributions.

(D) The Secretary of the Treasury is authorized to adjust by regulation the conversion factor described in subparagraph (B) from time to time as he may deem necessary. No such adjustment shall be effective for a plan year beginning before the expiration of 1 year after such adjustment is determined and published.

(3) For purposes of this section, in the case of any defined benefit plan, if an employee's accrued benefit is to be determined as an amount other than an annual benefit commencing at normal retirement age, or if the accrued benefit derived from contributions made by an employee is to be determined with respect to a benefit other than an annual benefit in the form of a single life annuity (without ancillary benefits) commencing at normal retirement age, the employee's accrued benefit, or the accrued benefits derived from contributions made by an employee, as the case may be, shall be the actuarial equivalent of such benefit or amount determined under paragraph (1) or (2).

(4) In the case of a defined benefit plan which permits voluntary employee contributions, the portion of an employee's accrued benefit derived from such contributions shall be treated as an accrued benefit derived from employee contributions under a plan other than a defined benefit plan.

(d) Notwithstanding section 203(b)(1), for purposes of determining the employee's accrued benefit under the plan, the plan may disregard service performed by the employee with respect to which he has received—

(1) a distribution of the present value of his entire nonforfeitable benefit if such distribution was in an amount (not more than $3,500) permitted under regulations prescribed by the Secretary of the Treasury, or

(2) a distribution of the present value of his nonforfeitable benefit attributable to such service which he elected to receive.

Paragraph (1) shall apply only if such distribution was made on termination of the employee's participation in the plan. Paragraph (2) shall apply only if such distribution was made on termination of the employee's participation in the plan or under such other circumstances as may be provided under regulations prescribed by the Secretary of the Treasury.

(e) For purposes of determining the employee's accrued benefit, the plan shall not disregard service as provided in subsection (d) unless the plan provides an opportunity for the participant to repay the full amount of a distribution described in subsection (d) with, in the case of a defined benefit plan, interest at the rate determined for purposes of subsection (c)(2)(C) and provides that upon such repayment the employee's accrued benefit shall be recomputed by taking into account service so disregarded. This subsection shall apply only in the case of a participant who—

(1) received such a distribution in any plan year to which this section applies, which distribution was less than the present value of his accrued benefit,

(2) resumes employment covered under the plan, and

(3) repays the full amount of such distribution with, in the case of a defined benefit plan, interest at the rate determined for purposes of subsection (c)(2)(C).

The plan provision required under this subsection may provide that such repayment must be made (A) in the case of a withdrawal on account of separation from service, before the earlier of 5 years after the first date on which the participant is subsequently re-employed by the employer, or the close of the first period of 5 consecutive 1-year breaks in service commencing after the withdrawal; or (B) in the case of any other withdrawal, 5 years after the date of the withdrawal.

(f) For the purposes of this part, an employer shall be treated as maintaining a plan if any employee of such employer accrues benefits under such plan by reason of service with such employer.

(g)(1) The accrued benefit of a participant under a plan may not be decreased by an amendment of the plan, other than an amendment described in section 302(c)(8) or 4281.

(2) For purposes of paragraph (1), a plan amendment which has the effect of—

(A) eliminating or reducing an early retirement benefit or a retirement-type subsidy (as defined in regulations), or

(B) eliminating an optional form of benefit,

with respect to benefits attributable to service before the amendment shall be treated as reducing accrued benefits. In the case of a retirement-type subsidy, the preceding sentence shall apply only with respect to a participant who satisfies (either before or after the amendment) the preamendment conditions for the subsidy. The Secretary of the Treasury may by regulations provide that this subparagraph shall not apply to a plan amendment described in subparagraph (B) (other than a plan amendment having an effect described in subparagraph (A)).

(3) For purposes of this subsection, any—

(A) tax credit employee stock ownership plan (as defined in section 409(a) of the Internal Revenue Code of 1954), or

(B) employee stock ownership plan (as defined in section 4975(e)(7) of such Code), shall not be treated as failing to meet the

ERISA Sec. 204 (g)(3)(B)

requirements of this subsection merely because it modifies distribution options in a nondiscriminatory manner.

(h)(1) A plan described in paragraph (2) may not be amended so as to provide for a significant reduction in the rate of future benefit accrual, unless, after adoption of the plan amendment and not less than 15 days before the effective date of the plan amendment, the plan administrator provides a written notice, setting forth the plan amendment and its effective date, to—

(A) each participant in the plan,

(B) each beneficiary who is an alternate payee (within the meaning of section 206(d)(3)(K)) under an applicable qualified domestic relations order (within the meaning of section 206(d)(3)(B)(i)), and

(C) each employee organization representing participants in the plan,

except that such notice shall instead be provided to a person designated, in writing, to receive such notice on behalf of any person referred to in subparagraph (A), (B), or (C).

(2) A plan is described in this paragraph if such plan is—

(A) a defined benefit plan, or

(B) an individual account plan which is subject to the funding standards of section 302.

◊ ◊ ◊

Editor's Note: Section 766 of the Retirement Protection Act of 1994, enacted as part of the Uruguay Round Agreements Act (P. L. 103-465), redesignated former ERISA §204(i) as §204(j) and added a new ERISA §204(i) as set forth below, effective with respect to plan amendments adopted on or after December 8, 1994

◊ ◊ ◊

(i)(1) In the case of a plan described in paragraph (3) which is maintained by an employer that is a debtor in a case under title 11, United States Code, or similar Federal or State law, no amendment of the plan which increases the liabilities of the plan by reason of—

(A) any increase in benefits,

(B) any change in the accrual of benefits, or

(C) any change in the rate at which benefits become nonforfeitable under the plan,
with respect to employees of the debtor, shall be effective prior to the effective date of such employer's plan of reorganization.

(2) Paragraph (1) shall not apply to any plan amendment that—

(A) the Secretary of the Treasury determines to be reasonable and that provides for only de minimis increases in the liabilities of the plan with respect to employees of the debtor,

(B) only repeals an amendment described in section 302(c)(8),

(C) is required as a condition of qualification under part I of subchapter D of chapter 1 of the Internal Revenue Code of 1986, or

(D) was adopted prior to, or pursuant to a collective bargaining agreement entered into prior to, the date on which the employer became a debtor in a case under title 11, United States Code, or similar Federal or State law.

(3) This subsection shall apply only to plans (other than multiemployer plans) covered under section 4021 of this Act for which the funded current liability percentage (within the meaning of section 302(d)(8) of this Act) is less than 100 percent after taking into account the effect of the amendment.

(4) For purposes of this subsection, the term "employer" has the meaning set forth in section 302(c)(11)(A), without regard to section 302(c)(11)(B).

[(i)]*(j)* **Cross Reference.**—For special rules relating to plan provisions adopted to preclude discrimination, see section 203(c)(2).

REQUIREMENTS OF JOINT AND SURVIVOR ANNUITY AND PRERETIREMENT SURVIVOR ANNUITY

Sec. 205. (a) Each pension plan to which this section applies shall provide that—

(1) in the case of a vested participant who does not die before the annuity starting date, the accrued benefit payable to such participant shall be provided in the form of a qualified joint and survivor annuity, and

(2) in the case of a vested participant who dies before the annuity starting date and who has a surviving spouse, a qualified preretirement survivor annuity shall be provided to the surviving spouse of such participant.

(b)(1) This section shall apply to—

(A) any defined benefit plan,

(B) any individual account plan which is subject to the funding standards of section 302, and

(C) any participant under any other individual account plan unless—

(i) such plan provides that the participant's nonforfeitable accrued benefit (reduced by any security interest held by the plan by reason of a loan outstanding to such participant) is payable in full, on the death of the participant, to the participant's surviving spouse (or, if there is no surviving spouse or the surviving spouse consents in the manner required under subsection (c)(2), to a designated beneficiary),

(ii) such participant does not elect the payment of benefits in the form of a life annuity, and

(iii) with respect to such participant, such plan is not a direct or indirect transferee (in a transfer after December 31, 1984) of a plan which is described in subparagraph (A) or (B) or to which this clause applied with respect to the participant.

Clause (iii) of subparagraph (C) shall apply only with respect to the transferred assets (and income therefrom) if the plan separately accounts for such assets and any income therefrom.

(2)(A) In the case of—

(i) a tax credit employee stock ownership plan (as defined in section 409(a) of the Internal Revenue Code of 1954), or

(ii) an employee stock ownership plan (as defined in section 4975(e)(7) of such Code), subsection (a) shall not apply to that portion of the employee's accrued benefit to which the requirements of section 409(h) of such Code apply.

(B) Subparagraph (A) shall not apply with respect to any participant unless the requirements of clause (i), (ii), and (iii) of paragraph (1)(C) are met with respect to such participant.

◊ ◊ ◊

Editor's Note: Subsection 205(b) has two paragraphs (4). The first was added by section 1145(b) of the 1986 TRA as subsection 205(b)(3), and then changed to (4) by OBRA '89 section 7861(d)(2). The second paragraph (4) was first added as subsection 205(b)(3) by section 1898(b)(14)(B) of the 1986 TRA technical corrections to REA. It was changed to subsection 205(b)(4) by section 7862(d)(9)(B) of the OBRA '89 technical corrections.

◊ ◊ ◊

(4) This section shall not apply to a plan which the Secretary of the Treasury or his delegate has determined is a plan described in section 404(c) of the Internal Revenue Code of 1986 (or a continuation thereof) in which participation is substantially limited to individuals who, before January 1, 1976, ceased employment covered by the plan.

(4) A plan shall not be treated as failing to meet the requirements of paragraph (1)(C) or

ERISA Sec. 205 (b)(4)

(2) merely because the plan provides that benefits will not be payable to the surviving spouse of the participant unless the participant and such spouse had been married throughout the 1-year period ending on the earlier of the participant's annuity starting date or the date of the participant's death.

(c)(1) A plan meets the requirements of this section only if—

(A) under the plan, each participant—

(i) may elect at any time during the applicable election period to waive the qualified joint and survivor annuity form of benefit or the qualified preretirement survivor annuity form of benefit (or both), and

(ii) may revoke any such election at any time during the applicable election period, and

(B) the plan meets the requirements of paragraphs (2), (3), and (4).

(2) Each plan shall provide that an election under paragraph (1)(A)(i) shall not take effect unless—

(A)(i) the spouse of the participant consents in writing to such election, (ii) such election designates a beneficiary (or a form of benefits) which may not be changed without spousal consent (or the consent of the spouse expressly permits designations by the participant without any requirement of further consent by the spouse), and (iii) the spouse's consent acknowledges the effect of such election and is witnessed by a plan representative or a notary public, or

(B) it is established to the satisfaction of a plan representative that the consent required under subparagraph (A) may not be obtained because there is no spouse, because the spouse cannot be located, or because of such other circumstances as the Secretary of the Treasury may by regulations prescribe.

Any consent by a spouse (or establishment that the consent of a spouse may not be ob-

tained) under the preceding sentence shall be effective only with respect to such spouse.

(3)(A) Each plan shall provide to each participant, within a reasonable period of time before the annuity starting date (and consistent with such regulations as the Secretary of the Treasury may prescribe) a written explanation of—

(i) the terms and conditions of the qualified joint and survivor annuity,

(ii) the participant's right to make, and the effect of, an election under paragraph (1) to waive the joint and survivor annuity form of benefit,

(iii) the rights of the participant's spouse under paragraph (2), and

(iv) the right to make, and the effect of, a revocation of an election under paragraph (1).

(B)(i) Each plan shall provide to each participant, within the applicable period with respect to such participant (and consistent with such regulations as the Secretary may prescribe), a written explanation with respect to the qualified preretirement survivor annuity comparable to that required under subparagraph (A).

(ii) For purposes of clause (i), the term "applicable period" means, with respect to a participant, whichever of the following periods ends last:

(I) The period beginning with the first day of the plan year in which the participant attains age 32 and ending with the close of the plan year preceding the plan year in which the participant attains age 35.

(II) A reasonable period after the individual becomes a participant.

(III) A reasonable period ending after paragraph (5) ceases to apply to the participant.

(IV) A reasonable period ending after section 205 applies to the participant.

ERISA Sec. 205 (c)(1)

In the case of a participant who separates from service before attaining age 35, the applicable period shall be a reasonable period after separation.Sec. 205 (c)(4)

(4) Each plan shall provide that, if this section applies to a participant when part or all of the participant's accrued benefit is to be used as security for a loan, no portion of the participant's accrued benefit may be used as security for such loan unless—

(A) the spouse of the participant (if any) consents in writing to such use during the 90-day period ending on the date on which the loan is to be so secured, and

(B) requirements comparable to the requirements of paragraph (2) are met with respect to such consent.

(5)(A) The requirements of this subsection shall not apply with respect to the qualified joint and survivor annuity form of benefit or the qualified preretirement survivor annuity form of benefit, as the case may be, if such benefit may not be waived (or another beneficiary selected) and if the plan fully subsidizes the costs of such benefit.

(B) For purposes of subparagraph (A), a plan fully subsidizes the costs of a benefit if under the plan the failure to waive such benefit by a participant would not result in a decrease in any plan benefits with respect to such participant and would not result in increased contributions from such participant.

(6) If a plan fiduciary acts in accordance with part 4 of this subtitle in—

(A) relying on a consent or revocation referred to in paragraph (1)(A), or

(B) making a determination under paragraph (2),
then such consent, revocation, or determination shall be treated as valid for purposes of discharging the plan from liability to the extent of payments made pursuant to such act.

(7) For purposes of this subsection, the term "applicable election period" means—

(A) in the case of an election to waive the qualified joint survivor annuity form of benefit, the 90-day period ending on the annuity starting date, or

(B) in the case of an election to waive the qualified preretirement survivor annuity, the period which begins on the first day of the plan year in which the participant attains age 35 and ends on the date of the participant's death.

In the case of a participant who is separated from service, the applicable election period under subparagraph (B) with respect to benefits accrued before the date of such separation from service shall not begin later than such date.

(d) For purposes of this section, the term"qualified joint and survivor annuity" means an annuity—

(1) for the life of the participant with a survivor annuity for the life of the spouse which is not less than 50 percent of (and is not greater than 100 percent of) the amount of the annuity which is payable during the joint lives of the participant and the spouse, and

(2) which is the actuarial equivalent of a single annuity for the life of the participant. Such term also includes any annuity in a form having the effect of an annuity described in the preceding sentence.

(e) For purposes of this section—

(1) Except as provided in paragraph (2), the term "qualified preretirement survivor annuity" means a survivor annuity for the life of the surviving spouse of the participant if—

(A) the payments to the surviving spouse under such annuity are not less than the amounts which would be payable as a survivor annuity under the qualified joint and survivor annuity under the plan (or the actuarial equivalent thereof) if—

ERISA: The Law and the Code

(i) in the case of a participant who dies after the date on which the participant attained the earliest retirement age, such participant had retired with an immediate qualified joint and survivor annuity on the day before the participant's date of death, or

(ii) in the case of a participant who dies on or before the date on which the participant would have attained the earliest retirement age, such participant had—

(I) separated from service on the date of death,

(II) survived to the earliest retirement age,

(III) retired with an immediate qualified joint and survivor annuity at the earliest retirement age, and

(IV) died on the day after the day on which such participant would have attained the earliest retirement age, and

(B) under the plan, the earliest period for which the surviving spouse may receive a payment under such annuity is not later than the month in which the participant would have attained the earliest retirement age under the plan.

In the case of an individual who separated from service before the date of such individual's death, subparagraph (A)(ii)(I) shall not apply.

(2) In the case of any individual account plan or participant described in subparagraph (B) or (C) of subsection (b)(1), the term "qualified preretirement survivor annuity" means an annuity for the life of the surviving spouse the actuarial equivalent of which is not less than 50 percent of the portion of the account balance of the participant (as of the date of death) to which the participant had a nonforfeitable right (within the meaning of section 203).

(3) For purposes of paragraphs (1) and (2), any security interest held by the plan by reason of a loan outstanding to the participant shall be taken into account in determining the amount of the qualified preretirement survivor annuity.

(f)(1) Except as provided in paragraph (2), a plan may provide that a qualified joint and survivor annuity (or a qualified preretirement survivor annuity) will not be provided unless the participant and spouse had been married throughout the 1-year period ending on the earlier of—

(A) the participant's annuity starting date, or

(B) the date of the participant's death.

(2) For purposes of paragraph (1), if—

(A) a participant marries within 1 year before the annuity starting date, and

(B) the participant and the participant's spouse in such marriage have been married for at least a 1-year period ending on or before the date of the participant's death,

such participant and such spouse shall be treated as having been married throughout the 1-year period ending on the participant's annuity starting date.

(g)(1) A plan may provide that the present value of a qualified joint and survivor annuity or a qualified preretirement survivor annuity will be immediately distributed if such value does not exceed $3,500. No distribution may be made under the preceding sentence after the annuity starting date unless the participant and the spouse of the participant (or where the participant has died, the surviving spouse) consent in writing to such distribution.

(2) If—

(A) the present value of the qualified joint and survivor annuity or the qualified preretirement survivor annuity exceeds $3,500, and

(B) the participant and the spouse of the participant (or where the participant has died, the surviving spouse) consent in writing to the distribution,

ERISA Sec. 205 (e)(1)(A)(i)

the plan may immediately distribute the present value of such annuity.

[(3)(A) For purposes of paragraphs (1) and (2), the present value shall be calculated—

[(i) by using an interest rate no greater than the applicable interest rate if the vested accrued benefit (using such rate) is not in excess of $25,000, and

[(ii) by using an interest rate no greater than 120 percent of the applicable interest rate if the vested accrued benefit exceeds $25,000 (as determined under clause (i)).

[In no event shall the present value determined under subclause (II) be less than $25,000.

[(B) For purposes of subparagraph (A), the term "applicable interest rate" means the interest rate which would be used (as of the date of the distribution) by the Pension Benefit Guaranty Corporation for purposes of determining the present value of a lump sum distribution on plan termination.]

◊ ◊ ◊

Editor's Note: ERISA §205(g)(3) as set forth below appears as amended by §767(c)(2) of the Retirement Protection Act of 1994 (enacted as part of the Uruguay Round Agreements Act, P.L. 103-465). The amended provisions are effective generally with respect to plan years and limitation years beginning on or after December 31, 1994, except that employers may elect to treat the amendments as being effective on or after December 8, 1994. Act §767(d)(2) provides that a participant's accrued benefit shall not be considered to be reduced in violation of the anti-cutback rule of Code §411(d)(6) or ERISA §204(g) merely because the benefit is determined in accordance with Code §417(e)(3)(A) or ERISA §205(g)(3) as amended by the Act or because the plan applies Code §415(b)(2)(E) as amended by the Act.

◊ ◊ ◊

(3) Determination of present value.

(A) In general.

(i) Present value. Except as provided in subparagraph (B), for purposes of paragraphs (1) and (2), the present value shall not be less than the present value calculated by using the applicable mortality table and the applicable interest rate.

(ii) Definitions. For purposes of clause (i)

(I) Applicable mortality table. The term "applicable mortality table" means the table prescribed by the Secretary of the Treasury. Such table shall be based on the prevailing commissioners' standard table (described in section 807(d)(5)(A) of the Internal Revenue Code of 1986) used to determine reserves for group annuity contracts issued on the date as of which present value is being determined (without regard to any other subparagraph of section 807(d)(5) of such Code).

(II) Applicable interest rate. The term "applicable interest rate" means the annual rate of interest on 30-year Treasury securities for the month before the date of distribution or such other time as the Secretary of the Treasury may by regulations prescribe.

(B) Exception. In the case of a distribution from a plan that was adopted and in effect prior to the date of the enactment of the Retirement Protection Act of 1994, the present value of any distribution made before the earlier of—

(i) the later of when a plan amendment applying subparagraph (A) is adopted or made effective, or

(ii) the first day of the first plan year beginning after December 31, 1999,

shall be calculated, for purposes of paragraphs (1) and (2), using the interest rate determined under the regulations of the Pension Benefit Guaranty Corporation for determining the present value of a lump sum distribution on plan termination that were in effect on September 1, 1993, and using the provisions of the plan as in effect on the day before such date of enactment; but only if provisions of the plan met the requirements of section 205(g)(3) as in effect on the day before such date of enactment.

(h) For purposes of this section—

(1) the term "vested participant" means any participant who has a nonforfeitable right (within the meaning of section 3(19)) to any portion of such participant's accrued benefit.

(2)(A) The term "annuity starting date" means—

(i) the first day of the first period for which an amount is payable as an annuity, or

(ii) in the case of a benefit not payable in the form of an annuity, the first day on which all events have occurred which entitle the participant to such benefit.

(B) For purposes of subparagraph (A), the first day of the first period for which a benefit is to be received by reason of disability shall be treated as the annuity starting date only if such benefit is not an auxiliary benefit.

(3) The term "earliest retirement age" means the earliest date on which, under the plan, the participant could elect to receive retirement benefits.

(i) A plan may take into account in any equitable manner (as determined by the Secretary of the Treasury) any increased costs resulting from providing a qualified joint or survivor annuity or a qualified preretirement survivor annuity.

(j) If the use of any participant's accrued benefit (or any portion thereof) as security for a loan meets the requirements of subsection (c)(4), nothing in this section shall prevent any distribution required by reason of a failure to comply with the terms of such loan.

(k) No consent of a spouse shall be effective for purposes of subsection (g)(1) or (g)(2) (as the case may be) unless requirements compa-

rable to the requirements for spousal consent to an election under subsection (c)(1)(A) are met.

(l) In prescribing regulations under this section, the Secretary of the Treasury shall consult with the Secretary of Labor.

OTHER PROVISIONS RELATING TO FORM AND PAYMENT OF BENEFITS

Sec. 206. (a) Each pension plan shall provide that unless the participant otherwise elects, the payment of benefits under the plan to the participant shall begin not later than the 60th day after the latest of the close of the plan year in which—

(1) occurs the date on which the participant attains the earlier of age 65 or the normal retirement age specified under the plan,

(2) occurs the 10th anniversary of the year in which the participant commenced participation in the plan, or

(3) the participant terminates his service with the employer.

In the case of a plan which provides for the payment of an early retirement benefit, such plan shall provide that a participant who satisfied the service requirements for such early retirement benefit, but separated from the service (with any nonforfeitable right to an accrued benefit) before satisfying the age requirement for such early retirement benefit, is entitled upon satisfaction of such age requirement to receive a benefit not less than the benefit to which he would be entitled at the normal retirement age, actuarially reduced under regulations prescribed by the Secretary of the Treasury.

(b) If—

(1) a participant or beneficiary is receiving benefits under a pension plan, or

(2) a participant is separated from the service and has nonforfeitable rights to benefits, a plan may not decrease benefits of such a participant by reason of any increase in the

benefit levels payable under title II of the Social Security Act or the Railroad Retirement Act of 1937, or any increase in the wage base under such title II, if such increase takes place after the date of the enactment of this Act or (if later) the earlier of the date of first entitlement of such benefits or the date of such separation.

(c) No pension plan may provide that any part of a participant's accrued benefit derived from employer contributions (whether or not otherwise nonforfeitable) is forfeitable solely because of withdrawal by such participant of any amount attributable to the benefit derived from contributions made by such participant. The preceding sentence shall not apply (1) to the accrued benefit of any participant unless, at the time of such withdrawal, such participant has a nonforfeitable right to at least 50 percent of such accrued benefit, or (2) to the extent that an accrued benefit is permitted to be forfeited in accordance with section 203(a)(3)(D)(iii).

(d)(1) Each pension plan shall provide that benefits provided under the plan may not be assigned or alienated.

(2) For the purposes of paragraph (1) of this subsection, there shall not be taken into account any voluntary and revocable assignment of not to exceed 10 percent of any benefit payment, or of any irrevocable assignment or alienation of benefits executed before the date of enactment of this Act. The preceding sentence shall not apply to any assignment or alienation made for the purposes of defraying plan administration costs.
For purposes of this paragraph a loan made to a participant or beneficiary shall not be treated as an assignment or alienation if such loan is secured by the participant's accrued nonforfeitable benefit and is exempt from the tax imposed by section 4975 of the Internal Revenue Code of 1954 (relating to tax on prohibited transactions) by reason of section 4975(d)(1) of such code.

(3)(A) Paragraph (1) shall apply to the creation, assignment, or recognition of a right to any benefit payable with respect to a partici-pant pursuant to a domestic relations order, except that paragraph (1) shall not apply if the order is determined to be a qualified domestic relations order. Each pension plan shall provide for the payment of benefits in accordance with the applicable requirements of any qualified domestic relations order.

(B) For purposes of this paragraph—

(i) the term "qualified domestic relations order" means a domestic relations order—

(I) which creates or recognizes the existence of an alternate payee's right to, or assigns to an alternate payee the right to, receive all or a portion of the benefits payable with respect to a participant under a plan, and

(II) with respect to which the requirements of subparagraphs (C) and (D) are met, and

(ii) the term "domestic relations order" means any judgment, decree, or order (including approval of a property settlement agreement) which—

(I) relates to the provision of child support, alimony payments, or marital property rights to a spouse, former spouse, child, or other dependent of a participant, and

(II) is made pursuant to a State domestic relations law (including a community property law).

(C) A domestic relations order meets the requirements of this subparagraph only if such order clearly specifies—

(i) the name and the last known mailing address (if any) of the participant and the name and mailing address of each alternate payee covered by the order,

(ii) the amount or percentage of the participant's benefits to be paid by the plan to each such alternate payee, or the manner in which such amount or percentage is to be determined,

(iii) the number of payments or period to which such order applies, and

(iv) each plan to which such order applies.

(D) A domestic relations order meets the requirements of this subparagraph only if such order—

(i) does not require a plan to provide any type or form of benefit, or any option, not otherwise provided under the plan,

(ii) does not require the plan to provide increased benefits (determined on the basis of actuarial value), and

(iii) does not require the payment of benefits to an alternate payee which are required to be paid to another alternate payee under another order previously determined to be a qualified domestic relations order.

(E)(i) A domestic relations order shall not be treated as failing to meet the requirements of clause (i) of subparagraph (D) solely because such order requires that payment of benefits be made to an alternate payee—

(I) on or in the case of any payment before a participant has separated from service, after the date on which the participant attains (or would have attained) the earliest retirement age,

(II) as if the participant had retired on the date on which such payment is to begin under such order (but taking into account only the present value of benefits actually accrued and not taking into account the present value of any employer subsidy for early retirement), and

(III) in any form in which such benefits may be paid under the plan to the participant (other than in the form of a joint and survivor annuity with respect to the alternate payee and his or her subsequent spouse).

For purposes of subclause (II), the interest rate assumption used in determining the present value shall be the interest rate specified in the plan or, if no rate is specified, 5 percent.

(ii) For purposes of this subparagraph, the term "earliest retirement age" means the earlier of—

(I) the date on which the participant is entitled to a distribution under the plan, or

(II) the later of the date the participant attains age 50 or the earliest date on which the participant could begin receiving under the plan if the participant separated from service.

(F) To the extent provided in any qualified domestic relations order—

(i) the former spouse of a participant shall be treated as a surviving spouse of such participant for purposes of section 205 (and any spouse of the participant shall not be treated as a spouse of the participant for such purposes), and

(ii) if married for at least 1 year, the surviving former spouse shall be treated as meeting the requirements of section 205(f).

(G)(i) In the case of any domestic relations order received by a plan—

(I) the plan administrator shall promptly notify the participant and each alternate payee of the receipt of such order and the plan's procedures for determining the qualified status of domestic relations orders, and

(II) within a reasonable period after receipt of such order, the plan administrator shall determine whether such order is a qualified domestic relations order and notify the participant and each alternate payee of such determination.

(ii) Each plan shall establish reasonable procedures to determine the qualified status of domestic relations orders and to administer distributions under such qualified orders. Such procedures—

(I) shall be in writing,

(II) shall provide for the notification of each person specified in a domestic relations order as entitled to payment of benefits under the plan (at the address included in the domestic relations order) of such procedures promptly upon receipt by the plan of the domestic relations order, and

(III) shall permit an alternate payee to designate a representative for receipt of copies of notices that are sent to the alternate payee with respect to a domestic relations order.

(H)(i) During any period in which the issue of whether a domestic relations order is a qualified domestic relations order is being determined (by the plan administrator, by a court of competent jurisdiction, or otherwise), the plan administrator shall separately account for the amounts (hereinafter in this subparagraph referred to as the "segregated amounts") which would have been payable to the alternate payee during such period if the order had been determined to be a qualified domestic relations order.

(ii) If within the 18-month period described in clause (v) the order (or modification thereof) is determined to be a qualified domestic relations order, the plan administrator shall pay the segregated amounts (including any interest thereon) to the person or persons entitled thereto.

(iii) If within the 18-month period described in clause (v)—

(I) it is determined that the order is not a qualified domestic relations order, or

(II) the issue as to whether such order is a qualified domestic relations order is not resolved,

then the plan administrator shall pay the segregated amounts (including any interest thereon) to the person or persons who would have been entitled to such amounts if there had been no order.

(iv) Any determination that an order is a qualified domestic relations order which is made after the close of the 18-month period described in clause (v) shall be applied prospectively only.

(v) For purposes of this subparagraph, the 18-month period described in this clause is the 18-month period beginning with the date on which the first payment would be required to be made under the domestic relations order.

(I) If a plan fiduciary acts in accordance with part 4 of this subtitle in—

(i) treating a domestic relations order as being (or not being) a qualified domestic relations order, or

(ii) taking action under subparagraph (H), then the plan's obligation to the participant and each alternate payee shall be discharged to the extent of any payment made pursuant to such Act.

(J) A person who is an alternate payee under a qualified domestic relations order shall be considered for purposes of any provision of this Act a beneficiary under the plan. Nothing in the preceding sentence shall permit a requirement under section 4001 of the payment of more than 1 premium with respect to a participant for any period.

(K) The term "alternate payee" means any spouse, former spouse, child, or other dependent of a participant who is recognized by a domestic relations order as having a right to receive all, or a portion of, the benefits payable under a plan with respect to such participant.

(L) This paragraph shall not apply to any plan to which paragraph (1) does not apply.

(M) Payment of benefits by a pension plan in accordance with the applicable requirements of a qualified domestic relations order shall not be treated as garnishment for purposes of section 303(a) of the Consumer Credit Protection Act.

ERISA Sec. 206 (d)(3)(M)

(N) In prescribing regulations under this paragraph, the Secretary shall consult with the Secretary of the Treasury.

◊ ◊ ◊

Editor's Note: ERISA §206(e), below, was added by §761(a) of the Retirement Protection Act of 1994, enacted as part of the Uruguay Round Agreements Act (P. L. 103-465). The amendment applies to plan years beginning after December 31, 1994.

◊ ◊ ◊

(e) Limitation on Distributions Other Than Life Annuities Paid By The Plan.

(1) In general. Notwithstanding any other provision of this part, the fiduciary of a pension plan that is subject to the additional funding requirements of section 302(d) shall not permit a prohibited payment to be made from a plan during a period in which such plan has a liquidity shortfall (as defined in section 302(e)(5)).

(2) Prohibited payment. For purposes of paragraph (1), the term "prohibited payment" means—

(A) any payment, in excess of the monthly amount paid under a single life annuity (plus any social security supplements described in the last sentence of section 204(b)(1)(G)), to a participant or beneficiary whose annuity starting date (as defined in section 205(h)(2)), that occurs during the period referred to in paragraph (1),

(B) any payment for the purchase of an irrevocable commitment from an insurer to pay benefits, and

(C) any other payment specified by the Secretary of the Treasury by regulations.

(3) Period of shortfall. For purposes of this subsection, a plan has a liquidity shortfall during the period that there is an underpayment of an installment under section 302(e) by reason of paragraph (5)(A) thereof.

(4) Coordination with other provisions. Compliance with this subsection shall not constitute a violation of any other provision of this Act.

◊ ◊ ◊

Editor's Note: ERISA §206(f), as set forth below, was added by §776 of the Retirement Protection Act of 1994 (enacted as part of the Uruguay Round Agreements Act, P.L. 103-465). It applies to distributions occurring in plan years beginning after the PBGC issues final regulations implementing these provisions.

◊ ◊ ◊

(f) Missing Participants in Terminated Plans. In the case of a plan covered by title IV, the plan shall provide that, upon termination of the plan, benefits of missing participants shall be treated in accordance with section 4050.

TEMPORARY VARIANCES FROM CERTAIN VESTING REQUIREMENTS

Sec. 207. In the case of any plan maintained on January 1, 1974, if, not later than 2 years after the date of enactment of this Act, the administrator petitions the Secretary, the Secretary may prescribe an alternate method which shall be treated as satisfying the requirements of section 203(a)(2) or 204(b)(1) (other than subparagraph (D) thereof or both for a period of not more than 4 years. The Secretary may prescribe such alternate method only when he finds that—

(1) the application of such requirements would increase the costs of the plan to such an extent that there would result a substantial risk to the voluntary continuation of the plan or a substantial curtailment of benefit levels or the levels of employees' compensation,

(2) the application of such requirements or discontinuance of the plan would be adverse to the interests of plan participants in the aggregate, and

(3) a waiver or extension of time granted under section 303 or 304 of this Act would be inadequate.

In the case of any plan with respect to which an alternate method has been prescribed under the preceding provisions of this subsection for a period of not more than 4 years, if, not later than 1 year before the expiration of such period, the administrator petitions the Secretary for an extension of such alternate method, and the Secretary makes the findings required by the preceding sentence, such alternate method may be extended for not more than 3 years.

MERGERS AND CONSOLIDATIONS OF PLANS OR TRANSFERS OF PLAN ASSETS

Sec. 208. A pension plan may not merge or consolidate with, or transfer its assets or liabilities to, any other plan after the date of the enactment of this Act, unless each participant in the plan would (if the plan then terminated) receive a benefit immediately after the merger, consolidation, or transfer which is equal to or greater than the benefit he would have been entitled to receive immediately before the merger, consolidation, or transfer (if the plan had then terminated). The preceding sentence shall not apply to any transaction to the extent that participants either before or after the transaction are covered under a multiemployer plan to which title IV of this Act applies.

RECORDKEEPING AND REPORTING REQUIREMENTS

Sec. 209. (a)(1) Except as provided by paragraph (2) every employer shall, in accordance with regulations prescribed by the Secretary, maintain records with respect to each of his employees sufficient to determine the benefits due or which may become due to such employees. The plan administrator shall make a report, in such manner and at such time as may be provided in regulations prescribed by the Secretary, to each employee who is a participant under the plan and who—

(A) requests such report, in such manner and at such time as may be provided in such regulations,

(B) terminates his service with the employer, or

(C) has a 1-year break in service (as defined in section 203(b)(3)(A)). The employer shall furnish to the plan administrator the information necessary for the administrator to make the reports required by the preceding sentence. Not more than one report shall be required under subparagraph (A) in any 12-month period. Not more than one report shall be required under subparagraph (C) with respect to consecutive 1-year breaks in service. The report required under this paragraph shall be sufficient to inform the employee of his accrued benefits under the plan and the percentage of such benefits which are nonforfeitable under the plan.

(2) If more than one employer adopts a plan, each such employer shall, in accordance with regulations prescribed by the Secretary of Labor, furnish to the plan administrator the information necessary for the administrator to maintain the records and make the reports required by paragraph (1). Such administrator shall maintain the records and, to the extent provided under regulations prescribed by the Secretary, make the reports, required by paragraph (1).

(b) If any person who is required, under subsection (a), to furnish information or maintain records for any plan year fails to comply with such requirement, he shall pay to the Secretary a civil penalty of $10 for each employee with respect to whom such failure occurs, unless it is shown that such failure is due to reasonable cause.

PLANS MAINTAINED BY MORE THAN ONE EMPLOYER, PREDECESSOR PLANS, AND EMPLOYER GROUPS

Sec. 210. (a) Notwithstanding any other provision of this part or part 3, the following provisions of this subsection shall apply to a plan maintained by more than one employer:

ERISA: The Law and the Code

(1) Section 202 shall be applied as if all employees of each of the employers were employed by a single employer.

(2) Section 203 and 204 shall be applied as if all such employers constituted a single employer, except that the application of any rules with respect to breaks in service shall be made under regulations prescribed by the Secretary.

(3) The minimum funding standard provided by section 302 shall be determined as if all participants in the plan were employed by a single employer.

(b) For purposes of this part and part 3—

(1) in any case in which the employer maintains a plan of a predecessor employer, service for such predecessor shall be treated as service for the employer, and

(2) in any case in which the employer maintains a plan which is not the plan maintained by a predecessor employer, service for such predecessor shall, to the extent provided in regulations prescribed by the Secretary of the Treasury, be treated as service for the employer.

(c) For purposes of sections 202, 203, and 204, all employees of all corporations which are members of a controlled group of corporations (within the meaning of section 1563 (a) of the Internal Revenue Code of 1986, determined without regard to section 1563(a)(4) and (e)(3)(C) of such Code) shall be treated as employed by a single employer. With respect to a plan adopted by more than one such corporation, the minimum funding standard of section 302 shall be determined as if all such employers were a single employer, and allocated to each employer in accordance with regulations prescribed by the Secretary of the Treasury.

(d) For purposes of sections 202, 203, and 204, under regulations prescribed by the Secretary of the Treasury, all employees of trades or businesses (whether or not incorporated) which are under common control shall be treated as employed by a single employer. The

regulations prescribed under this subsection shall be based on principles similar to the principles which apply in the case of subsection (c).

EFFECTIVE DATES

Sec. 211. (a) Except as otherwise provided in this section, this part shall apply in the case of plan years beginning after the date of the enactment of this Act.

(b)(1) Except as otherwise provided in subsection (d), sections 205, 206(d), and 208 shall apply with respect to plan years beginning after December 31, 1975.

(2) Except as otherwise provided in subsections (c) and (d) in the case of a plan in existence on January 1, 1974, this part shall apply in the case of plan years beginning after December 31, 1975.

(c)(1) In the case of a plan maintained on January 1, 1974, pursuant to one or more agreements which the Secretary finds to be collective bargaining agreements between employee organizations and one or more employers, no plan shall be treated as not meeting the requirements of sections 204 and 205 solely by reason of a supplementary or special plan provision (within the meaning of paragraph (2)) for any plan year before the year which begins after the earlier of—

(A) the date on which the last of such agreements relating to the plan terminates (determined without regard to any extension thereof agreed to after the date of the enactment of this Act), or

(B) December 31, 1980.

For purposes of subparagraph (A) and section 307(c), any plan amendment made pursuant to a collective bargaining agreement relating to the plan which amends the plan solely to conform to any requirement contained in this Act or the Internal Revenue Code of 1954 shall not be treated as a termination of such collective bargaining agreement. This paragraph shall not apply unless the Secretary determines tha

ERISA Sec. 210 (a)(1)

the participation and vesting rules in effect on the date of enactment of this Act are not less favorable to participants, in the aggregate, than the rules provided under sections 202, 203, and 204.

(2) For purposes of paragraph (1), the term "supplementary or special plan provision" means any plan provision which—

(A) provides supplementary benefits, not in excess of one-third of the basic benefit, in the form of an annuity for the life of the participant or

(B) provides that, under a contractual agreement based on medical evidence as to the effects of working in an adverse environment for an extended period of time, a participant having 25 years of service is to be treated as having 30 years of service.

(3) This subsection shall apply with respect to a plan if (and only if) the application of this subsection results in a later effective date for this part than the effective date required by subsection (b).

(d) If the administrator of a plan elects under section 1017(d) of this Act to make applicable to a plan year and to all subsequent plan years the provisions of the Internal Revenue Code of 1954 relating to participation, vesting, funding, and form of benefit, this part shall apply to the first plan year to which such election applies and to all subsequent plan years.

(e)(1) No pension plan to which section 202 applies may make effective any plan amendment with respect to breaks in service (which amendment is made or becomes effective after January 1, 1974, and before the date on which section 202 first becomes effective with respect to such plan) which provides that any employee's participation in the plan would commence at any date later than the later of—

(A) the date on which his participation would commence under the break in service rules of section 202(b), or

(B) the date on which his participation would commence under the plan as in effect on January 1, 1974.

(2) No pension plan to which section 203 applies may make effective any plan amendment with respect to breaks in service (which amendment is made or becomes effective after January 1, 1974, and before the date on which section 203 first becomes effective with respect to such plan) if such amendment provides that the nonforfeitable benefit derived from employer contributions to which any employee would be entitled is less than the lesser of the nonforfeitable benefit derived from employer contributions to which he would be entitled under—

(A) the break in service rules of section 202(b)(3), or

(B) the plan as in effect on January 1, 1974. Subparagraph (B) shall not apply if the break in service rules under the plan would have been in violation of any law or rule of law in effect on January 1, 1974.

(f) The preceding provisions of this section shall not apply with respect to amendments made to this part in provisions enacted after the date of enactment of this Act.

Part 3—Funding

◊ ◊ ◊

Editor's Note: As indicated below, the Retirement Protection Act of 1994 (enacted as part of the Uruguay Round Agreements Act, P.L. 103-465), made significant changes to part 3 of subtitle B of ERISA. Section §769 of that Act, however, provides as follows:

SEC. 769 SPECIAL FUNDING RULES FOR CERTAIN PLANS

(a) Funding Rules Not to Apply to Certain Plans.—Any changes made by this Act to section 412 of the Internal Revenue Code of 1986 or to part 3 of subtitle B of title I of the Employee Retirement Income Security Act of 1974 shall not apply to—

(1) a plan which is, on the date of enactment of this Act, subject to a restoration payment schedule order issued by the Pension Benefit Guaranty Corporation that meets the requirements of section 1.412(e)(1)—(3) of the Treasury Regulations, or

(2) a plan established by an affected air carrier (as defined under section 4001(a)(14)(C)(ii)(I) of such Act) and assumed by a new plan sponsor pursuant to the terms of a written agreement with the Pension Benefit Guaranty Corporation dated January 5, 1993, and approved by the United States Bankruptcy Court for the District of Delaware on December 30, 1992.

(b) Change in Actuarial Method.—Any amortization installments for bases established under section 412(b) of the Internal Revenue Code of 1986 and section 302(b) of the Employee Retirement Income Security Act of 1974 for plan years beginning after December 31, 1987, and before January 1, 1993, by reason of nonelective changes under the frozen entry age actuarial cost method shall not be included in the calculation of offsets under section 412(l)(1)(A)(ii) of such Code and section 302(d)(1)(A)(ii) of such Act for the first 5 plan years beginning after December 31, 1994.

◊ ◊ ◊

COVERAGE

Sec. 301. (a) This part shall apply to any employee pension benefit plan described in section 4(a), (and not exempted under section 4(b)), other than—

(1) an employee welfare benefit plan;

(2) an insurance contract plan described in subsection (b);

(3) a plan which is unfunded and is maintained by an employer primarily for the purpose of providing deferred compensation for a select group of management or highly compensated employees;

(4)(A) a plan which is established and maintained by a society, order, or association described in section 501(c)(8) or (9) of the Internal Revenue Code of 1954, if no part of the contributions to or under such plan are

made by employers of participants in such plan; or

(B) a trust described in section 501 (c)(18) of such Code;

(5) a plan which has not at any time after the date of enactment of this Act provided for employer contributions;

(6) an agreement providing payments to a retired partner, deceased partner or a deceased partner's successor in interest as described in section 736 of the Internal Revenue Code of 1954;

(7) an individual retirement account or annuity as described in section 408(a) of the Internal Revenue Code of 1954, or a retirement bond described in section 409 of the Internal Revenue Code of 1954 (as effective for obligations issued before January 1, 1984);

(8) an individual account plan (other than a money purchase plan) and a defined benefit plan to the extent it is treated as an individual account plan (other than a money purchase plan) under section 3(35)(B) of this title;

(9) an excess benefit plan; or

(10) any plan, fund or program under which an employer, all of whose stock is directly or indirectly owned by employees, former employees or their beneficiaries, proposes through an unfunded arrangement to compensate retired employees for benefits which were forfeited by such employees under a pension plan maintained by a former employer prior to the date such pension plan became subject to this Act.

(b) For the purposes of paragraph (2) of subsection (a) a plan is an "insurance contract plan" if—

(1) the plan is funded exclusively by the purchase of individual insurance contracts,

(2) such contracts provide for level annual premium payments to be paid extending not later than the retirement age for each individual participating in the plan, and commencing

with the date the individual became a participant in the plan (or, in the case of an increase in benefits, commencing at the time such increase becomes effective),

(3) benefits provided by the plan are equal to the benefits provided under each contract at normal retirement age under the plan and are guaranteed by an insurance carrier (licensed under the laws of a State to do business with the plan) to the extent premiums have been paid,

(4) premiums payable for the plan year, and all prior plan years under such contracts have been paid before lapse or there is reinstatement of the policy,

(5) no rights under such contracts have been subject to a security interest at any time during the plan year, and

(6) no policy loans are outstanding at any time during the plan year.

A plan funded exclusively by the purchase of group insurance contracts which is determined under regulations prescribed by the Secretary of the Treasury to have the same characteristics as contracts described in the preceding sentence shall be treated as a plan described in this subsection.

(c) This part applies, with respect to a terminated multiemployer plan to which section 4021 applies, until the last day of the plan year in which the plan terminates, within the meaning of section 4041A(a)(2).

(d) Any amount of any financial assistance from the Pension Benefit Guaranty Corporation to any plan, and any repayment of such amount, shall be taken into account under this section in such manner as determined by the Secretary of the Treasury.

MINIMUM FUNDING STANDARDS

◊ ◊ ◊

Editor's Note: The changes to ERISA §302 set forth below were made by the Retirement Protection Act of 1994, which were enacted as part of the Uruguay Round Agreements Act (P. L. 103-465). Act §761(b)(1) provides that these changes apply to plan years beginning after December 31, 1994.

◊ ◊ ◊

Sec. 302. (a)(1) Every employee pension benefit plan subject to this part shall satisfy the minimum funding standard (or the alternative minimum funding standard under section 305) for any plan year to which this part applies. A plan to which this part applies shall have satisfied the minimum funding standard for such plan for a plan year if as of the end of such plan year the plan does not have an accumulated funding deficiency.

(2) For the purposes of this part, the term "accumulated funding deficiency" means for any plan the excess of the total charges to the funding standard account for all plan years (beginning with the first plan year to which this part applies) over the total credits to such account for such years or, if less, the excess of the total charges to the alternative minimum funding standard account for such plan years over the total credits to such account for such years.

(3) In any plan year in which a multiemployer plan is in reorganization, the accumulated funding deficiency of the plan shall be determined under Section 4243.

(b)(1) Each plan to which this part applies shall establish and maintain a funding standard account. Such account shall be credited and charged solely as provided in this section.

(2) For a plan year, the funding standard account shall be charged with the sum of—

(A) the normal cost of the plan for the plan year,

(B) the amounts necessary to amortize in equal annual installments (until fully amortized)—

(i) in the case of a plan in existence on January 1, 1974, the unfunded past service liability under the plan on the first day of the first plan year to which this part applies, over a period of 40 plan years,

(ii) in the case of a plan which comes into existence after January 1, 1974, the unfunded past service liability under the plan on the first day of the first plan year to which this part applies, over a period of 30 plan years,

(iii) separately, with respect to each plan year, the net increase (if any) in unfunded past service liability under the plan arising from plan amendments adopted in such year, over a period of 30 plan years,

(iv) separately, with respect to each plan year, the net experience loss (if any) under the plan, over a period of 5 plan years (15 plan years in the case of a multiemployer plan), and

(v) separately, with respect to each plan year, the net loss (if any) resulting from changes in actuarial assumptions used under the plan, over a period of 10 plan years (30 plan years in the case of a multiemployer plan),

(C) the amount necessary to amortize each waived funding deficiency (within the meaning of section 303(c)) for each prior plan year in equal annual installments (until fully amortized) over a period of 5 plan years (15 plan years in the case of a multiemployer plan), and

(D) the amount necessary to amortize in equal annual installments (until fully amortized) over a period of 5 plan years any amount credited to the funding standard account under paragraph (3)(D).

(3) For a plan year, the funding standard account shall be credited with the sum of—

(A) the amount considered contributed by the employer to or under the plan for the plan year,

(B) the amount necessary to amortize in equal annual installments (until fully amortized)—

(i) separately, with respect to each plan year, the net decrease (if any) in unfunded past service liability under the plan arising from plan amendments adopted in such year, over a period of 30 plan years (40 plan years in the case of a multiemployer plan),

(ii) separately, with respect to each plan year, the net experience gain (if any) under the plan, over a period of 5 plan years (15 plan years in the case of a multiemployer plan), and

(iii) separately, with respect to each plan year, the net gain (if any) resulting from changes in actuarial assumptions used under the plan, over a period of 10 plan years (30 plan years in the case of a multiemployer plan),

(C) the amount of the waived funding deficiency (within the meaning of section 303(c)) for the plan year, and

(D) in the case of a plan year for which the accumulated funding deficiency is determined under the funding standard account if such plan year follows a plan year for which such deficiency was determined under the alternative minimum funding standard, the excess (if any) of any debit balance in the funding standard account (determined without regard to this subparagraph) over any debit balance in the alternative minimum funding standard account.

(4) Under regulations prescribed by the Secretary of the Treasury, amounts required to be amortized under paragraph (2) or paragraph (3), as the case may be—

(A) may be combined into one amount under such paragraph to be amortized over a period determined on the basis of the re maining amortization period for all items entering into such combined amount, and

(B) may be offset against amounts required to be amortized under the other such paragraph, with the resulting amount to be amortized over a period determined on the basis of the remaining amortization periods for all items entering into whichever of the two amounts being offset is the greater.

(5) Interest.—

(A) In general.—The funding standard account (and items therein) shall be charged or credited (as determined under regulations prescribed by the Secretary of the Treasury) with interest at the appropriate rate consistent with the rate or rates of interest used under the plan to determine costs.

(B) Required change of interest rate.—For purposes of determining a plan's current liability and for purposes of determining a plan's required contribution under section 302(d) for any plan year—

(i) In general.—If any rate of interest used under the plan to determine cost is not within the permissible range, the plan shall establish a new rate of interest within the permissible range.

(ii) Permissible range.—For purposes of this subparagraph

(I) In general.—Except as provided in subclause (II), the term ''permissible range'' means a rate of interest which is not more than 10 percent above, and not more than 10 percent below the weighted average of the rates of interest on 30-year Treasury securities during the 4-year period ending on the last day before the beginning of the plan year.

(II) Secretarial authority.—If the Secretary finds that the lowest rate of interest permissible under subclause (I) is unreasonably high, the Secretary may prescribe a lower rate of interest, except that such rate may not be less than 80 percent

of the average rate determined under subclause (I).

(iii) Assumptions. — Notwithstanding subsection (c)(3)(A)(i), the interest rate used under the plan shall be—

(I) determined without taking into account the experience of the plan and reasonable expectations, but

(II) consistent with the assumptions which reflect the purchase rates which would be used by insurance companies to satisfy the liabilities under the plan.

(6) In the case of a plan which, immediately before the date of the enactment of the Multiemployer Pension Plan Amendments Act of 1980, was a multiemployer plan (within the meaning of section 3(37) as in effect immediately before such date)—

(A) any amount described in paragraph (2)(B)(ii), (2)(B)(iii), or (3)(B)(i) of this subsection which arose in a plan year beginning before such date shall be amortized in equal annual installments (until fully amortized) over 40 plan years, beginning with the plan year in which the amount arose;

(B) any amount described in paragraph (2)(B)(iv) or (3)(B)(ii) of this subsection which arose in a plan year beginning before such date shall be amortized in equal annual installments (until fully amortized) over 20 plan years, beginning with the plan year in which the amount arose;

(C) any change in past service liability which arises during the period of 3 plan years beginning on or after such date, and results from a plan amendment adopted before such date, shall be amortized in equal annual installments (until fully amortized) over 40 plan years, beginning with the plan year in which the change arises; and

(D) any change in past service liability which arises during the period of 2 plan years beginning on or after such date, and results from the changing of a group of participants from one benefit level to an-

ERISA Sec. 302 (b)(6)(D)

other benefit level under a schedule of plan benefits which—

(i) was adopted before such date, and

(ii) was effective for any plan participant before the beginning of the first plan year beginning on or after such date, shall be amortized in equal annual installments (until fully amortized) over 40 plan years, beginning with the plan year in which the increase arises.

(7) For purposes of this part—

(A) Any amount received by a multiemployer plan in payment of all or part of an employer's withdrawal liability under part 1 of subtitle E of title IV shall be considered an amount contributed by the employer to or under the plan. The Secretary of the Treasury may prescribe by regulation additional charges and credits to a multiemployer plan's funding standard account to the extent necessary to prevent withdrawal liability payments from being unduly reflected as advance funding for plan liabilities.

(B) If a plan is not in reorganization in the plan year but was in reorganization in the immediately preceding plan year, any balance in the funding standard account at the close of such immediately preceding plan year—

(i) shall be eliminated by an offsetting credit or charge (as the case may be), but

(ii) shall be taken into account in subsequent plan years by being amortized in equal annual installments (until fully amortized) over 30 plan years.

The preceding sentence shall not apply to the extent of any accumulated funding deficiency under section 418B(a) of the Internal Revenue Code of 1954 as of the end of the last plan year that the plan was in reorganization.

(C) Any amount paid by a plan during a plan year to the Pension Benefit Guaranty Corporation pursuant to section 4222 or to a fund exempt under section 501(c)(22) of such Code pursuant to section 4223 shall reduce the amount of contributions considered received by the plan for the plan year.

(D) Any amount paid by an employer pending a final determination of the employer's withdrawal liability under part 1 of subtitle E of title IV and subsequently refunded to the employer by the plan shall be charged to the funding standard account in accordance with regulations prescribed by the Secretary.

(E) For purposes of the full funding limitation under subsection (c)(7), unless otherwise provided by the plan, the accrued liability under a multiemployer plan shall not include benefits which are not nonforfeitable under the plan after the termination of the plan (taking into consideration section 411(d)(3) of the Internal Revenue Code of 1954).

(c)(1) For purposes of this part, normal costs, accrued liability, past service liabilities, and experience gains and losses shall be determined under the funding method used to determine costs under the plan.

(2)(A) For purposes of this part, the value of the plan's assets shall be determined on the basis of any reasonable actuarial method of valuation which takes into account fair market value and which is permitted under regulations prescribed by the Secretary of the Treasury.

(B) For purposes of this part, the value of a bond or other evidence of indebtedness which is not in default as to principal or interest may, at the election of the plan administrator, be determined on an amortized basis running from initial cost at purchase to par value at maturity or earliest call date. Any election under this subparagraph shall be made at such time and in such manner as the Secretary of the Treasury shall by regulations provide, shall apply to all such evidences of indebtedness, and may be revoked only with the consent of the Secretary of the Treasury.

In the case of a plan other than a multiemployer plan, this subparagraph shall not apply, but the Secretary of the Treasury may by regulations provide that the value of any dedicated bond portfolio of such plan shall be determined by using the interest rate under subsection (b)(5).

(3) For purposes of this section, all costs, liabilities, rates of interest, and other factors under the plan shall be determined on the basis of actuarial assumptions and methods—

(A) in the case of—

(i) a plan other than a multiemployer plan, each of which is reasonable (taking into account the experience of the plan and reasonable expectations) or which, in the aggregate, result in a total contribution equivalent to that which would be determined if each such assumption and method were reasonable, or

(ii) a multiemployer plan, which, in the aggregate, are reasonable (taking into account the experiences of the plan and reasonable expectations), and

(B) which, in combination, offer the actuary's best estimate of anticipated experience under the plan.

(4) For purposes of this section, if—

(A) a change in benefits under the Social Security Act or in other retirement benefits created under Federal or State law, or

(B) a change in the definition of the term "wages" under section 3121 of the Internal Revenue Code of 1954, or a change in the amount of such wages taken into account under regulations prescribed for purposes of section 401(a)(5) of the Internal Revenue Code of 1954, results in an increase or decrease in accrued liability under a plan, such increase or decrease shall be treated as an experience loss or gain.

◊ ◊ ◊

Editor's Note: The amendment to ERISA §302(c)(5) set forth below was made by §762 of the Retirement Protection Act of 1994, enacted as part of the Uruguay Round Agreements Act (P. L. 103-465). The changes are effective generally with respect to changes in assumptions for plan years beginning after October 28, 1993. However, under Act §762(b)(2), in the case of changes in assumptions for plan years beginning after December 31, 1992, and on or before October 28, 1993, such changes will cease to be effective for Plan years beginning after December 31, 1994, if (1) the change would have required the approval of the Secretary of the Treasury had the amendment applied to such change, and (2) the change is not approved.

◊ ◊ ◊

(5) [If the funding method] *(A) In general. If the funding method* for a plan is changed, the new funding method shall become the funding method used to determine costs and liabilities under the plan only if the change is approved by the Secretary of the Treasury. If the plan year for a plan is changed, the new plan year shall become the plan year for the plan only if the change is approved by the Secretary of the Treasury.

(B) Approval required for certain changes in assumptions by certain single-employer plans subject to additional funding requirement.

(i) In general. No actuarial assumption (other than the assumptions described in subsection (d)(7)(C)) used to determine the current liability for a plan to which this subparagraph applies may be changed without the approval of the Secretary of the Treasury.

(ii) Plans to which subparagraph applies. This subparagraph shall apply to a plan only if—

(I) the plan is a defined benefit plan (other than a multiemployer plan) to which title IV applies;

(II) the aggregate unfunded vested benefits as of the close of the preceding plan year (as determined under section 4006(a)(3)(E)(iii)) of such plan and all other plans maintained by the contributing sponsors (as defined in section 4001(a)(13)) and members of such sponsors' controlled groups (as defined in section 4001(a)(14)) which are covered by title IV (disregarding plans with no unfunded vested benefits) exceed $50,000,000; and

(III) the change in assumptions (determined after taking into account any changes in interest rate and mortality table) results in a decrease in the unfunded current liability of the plan for the current plan year that exceeds $50,000,000, or that exceeds $5,000,000 and that is 5 percent or more of the current liability of the plan before such change.

(6) If, as of the close of a plan year, a plan would (without regard to this paragraph) have an accumulated funding deficiency (determined without regard to the alternative minimum funding standard account permitted under section 305) in excess of the full funding limitation—

(A) the funding standard account shall be credited with the amount of such excess, and

(B) all amounts described in paragraphs (2), (B), (C), and (D) and (3)(B) of subsection (b) which are required to be amortized shall be considered fully amortized for purposes of such paragraphs.

◊ ◊ ◊

Editor's Note: ERISA §302(c)(7), as set forth below, was amended by §761(a) of the Retirement Protection Act of 1994, which was enacted as part of the Uruguay Round Agreements Act (P. L. 103-465). It applies to

plan years beginning after December 31, 1994.

◊ ◊ ◊

(7) Full-funding limitation.—

(A) In general.—For purposes of paragraph (6), the term ''full-funding limitation'' means the excess (if any) of—

(i) the lesser of—

(I) 150 percent of current liability (including the expected increase in current liability due to benefits accruing during the plan year), or

(II) the accrued liability (including normal cost) under the plan (determined under the entry age normal funding method if such accrued liability cannot be directly calculated under the funding method used for the plan), over

(ii) the lesser of—

(I) the fair market value of the plan's assets, or

(II) the value of such assets determined under paragraph (2).

[(B) Current liability.—For purposes of subparagraphs (A) and (D), the term ''current liability'' has the meaning given such term by subsection (d)(7) (without regard to subparagraph (D) thereof).]

(B) Current liability. For purposes of subparagraph (D) and subclause (I) of subparagraph (A)(i), the term "current liability" has the meaning given such term by subsection (d)(7) (without regard to subparagraphs (C) and (D) thereof) and using the rate of interest used under subsection (b)(5)(B).

(C) Special rule for paragraph (6)(B).—For purposes of paragraph (6)(B), subparagraph (A)(i) shall be applied without regard to subclause (I) thereof.

(D) Regulatory authority.—The Secretary of the Treasury may by regulations provide—

(i) for adjustments to the percentage contained in subparagraph (A)(i) to take into account the respective ages or lengths of service of the participants,

(ii) alternative methods based on factors other than current liability for the determination of the amount taken into account under subparagraph (A)(i), and

(iii) for the treatment under this section of contributions which would be required to be made under the plan but for the provisions of subparagraph (A)(i)(I).

(E) Minimum amount.

(i) In general. In no event shall the full-funding limitation determined under subparagraph (A) be less than the excess (if any) of—

(I) 90 percent of the current liability of the plan (including the expected increase in current liability due to benefits accruing during the plan year), over

(II) the value of the plan's assets determined under paragraph (2).

(ii) Current liability; assets. For purposes of clause (i)—

(I) the term "current liability" has the meaning given such term by subsection (d)(7) (without regard to subparagraph (D) thereof), and

(II) assets shall not be reduced by any credit balance in the funding standard account.

(8) For purposes of this part, any amendment applying to a plan year which—

(A) is adopted after the close of such plan year but no later than 2½ months after the close of the plan year (or, in the case of a multiemployer plan, no later than 2 years after the close of such plan year),

(B) does not reduce the accrued benefit of any participant determined as of the beginning of the first plan year to which the amendment applies, and

(C) does not reduce the accrued benefit of any participant determined as of the time of adoption except to the extent required by the circumstances,

shall, at the election of the plan administrator, be deemed to have been made on the first day of such plan year. No amendment described in this paragraph which reduces the accrued benefits of any participant shall take effect unless the plan administrator files a notice with the Secretary notifying him of such amendment and the Secretary has approved such amendment or, within 90 days after the date on which such notice was filed, failed to disapprove such amendment. No amendment described in this subsection shall be approved by the Secretary unless he determines that such amendment is necessary because of a substantial business hardship (as determined under section 303(b)) and that waiver under section 303(a) is unavailable or inadequate.

(9) For purposes of this part, a determination of experience gains and losses and a valuation of the plan's liability shall be made not less frequently than once every year, except that such determination shall be made more frequently to the extent required in particular cases under regulations prescribed by the Secretary of the Treasury.

(10) For purposes of this section—

(A) In the case of a defined benefit plan other than a multiemployer plan, any contributions for a plan year made by an employer during the period—

(i) beginning on the day after the last day of such plan year, and

(ii) ending on the date which is 8½ months after the close of the plan year, shall be deemed to have been made on such last day.

ERISA Sec. 302 (c)(10)(A)(ii)

(B) In the case of a plan not described in subparagraph (A), any contributions for a plan year made by an employer after the last day of such plan year, but not later than two and one-half months after such day, shall be deemed to have been made on such last day. For purposes of this subparagraph, such two and one-half month period may be extended for not more than six months under regulations prescribed by the Secretary of the Treasury.

(11) Liability for contributions.—

(A) In general.—Except as provided in subparagraph (B), the amount of any contribution required by this section and any required installments under subsection (e) shall be paid by the employer responsible for contributing to or under the plan the amount described in subsection (b)(3)(A).

(B) Joint and several liability where employer member of controlled group.—

(i) In general.—In the case of a plan other than a multiemployer plan, if the employer referred to in subparagraph (A) is a member of a controlled group, each member of such group shall be jointly and severally liable for payment of such contribution or required installment.

(ii) Controlled group.—For purposes of clause (i), the term "controlled group" means any group treated as a single employer under subsection (b), (c), (m), or (o) of section 414 of the Internal Revenue Code of 1986.

◊ ◊ ◊

Editor's Note: ERISA §302(c)(12), below, was added by §763 of the Retirement Protection Act of 1994, which was enacted as part of the Uruguay Round Agreements Act (P. L. 103-465). It applies to plan years beginning after December 31, 1994, with respect to collective bargaining agreements in effect on or after January 1, 1995.

◊ ◊ ◊

(12) Anticipation of benefit increases effective in the future. In determining projected benefits, the funding method of a collectively bargained plan described in section 413(a) of the Internal Revenue Code of 1986 (other than a multiemployer plan) shall anticipate benefit increases scheduled to take effect during the term of the collective bargaining agreement applicable to the plan.

◊ ◊ ◊

Editor's Note: Unless otherwise indicated, the amendments to ERISA §302(d), below, were made by §761(a) of the Retirement Protection Act of 1994, which was enacted as part of the Uruguay Round Agreements Act (P. L. 103-465) and apply to plan years beginning after December 31, 1994.

◊ ◊ ◊

(d) Additional Funding Requirements for Plans Which Are Not Multiemployer Plans.—

(1) In general. In the case of a defined benefit plan (other than a multiemployer plan) [which has an unfunded current liability] *to which this subsection applies under paragraph (9)* for any plan year, the amount charged to the funding standard account for such plan year shall be increased by the sum of—

(A) the excess (if any) of—

(i) the deficit reduction contribution determined under paragraph (2) for such plan year, over

[(ii) the sum of the charges for such plan year under subparagraphs (B) (other than clauses (iv) and (v) thereof), (C), and (D) of subsection (b)(2), reduced by the sum of the credits for such plan year under subparagraph (B)(i) of subsection (b)(3), plus]

(ii) the sum of the charges for such plan year under subsection (b)(2), reduced by the sum of the credits for such plan year under subparagraph (B) of subsection (b)(3), plu

(B) the unpredictable contingent event amount (if any) for such plan year. Such increase shall not exceed the amount necessary to increase the funded current liability percentage to 100 percent.

[Such increase shall not exceed the amount necessary to increase the funded current liability percentage to 100 percent.]

Such increase shall not exceed the amount which, after taking into account charges (other than the additional charge under this subsection) and credits under subsection (b), is necessary to increase the funded current liability percentage (taking into account the expected increase in current liability due to benefits accruing during the plan year) to 100 percent.

(2) Deficit reduction contribution. For purposes of paragraph (1), the deficit reduction contribution determined under this paragraph for any plan year is the sum of—

(A) the unfunded old liability amount, [plus]

(B) the unfunded new liability amount [.] ,

(C) the expected increase in current liability due to benefits accruing during the plan year, and

(D) the aggregate of the unfunded mortality increase amounts.

(3) Unfunded old liability amount. For purposes of this subsection—

(A) In general.—The unfunded old liability amount with respect to any plan for any plan year is the amount necessary to amortize the unfunded old liability under the plan in equal annual installments over a period of 18 plan years (beginning with the 1st plan year beginning after December 31, 1988).

(B) Unfunded old liability.—The term "unfunded old liability" means the unfunded current liability of the plan as of the beginning of the 1st plan year beginning after December 31, 1987 (determined without re-

gard to any plan amendment increasing liabilities adopted after October 28, 1987).

(C) Special rules for benefit increases under existing collective bargaining agreements.—

(i) In general.—In the case of a plan maintained pursuant to 1 or more collective bargaining agreements between employee representatives and the employer ratified before October 29, 1987, the unfunded old liability amount with respect to such plan for any plan year shall be increased by the amount necessary to amortize the unfunded existing benefit increase liability in equal annual installments over a period of 18 plan years beginning with—

(I) the plan year in which the benefit increase with respect to such liability occurs, or

(II) if the taxpayer elects, the 1st plan year beginning after December 31, 1988.

(ii) Unfunded existing benefit increase liabilities.—For purposes of clause (i), the unfunded existing benefit increase liability means, with respect to any benefit increase under the agreements described in clause (i) which takes effect during or after the 1st plan year beginning after December 31, 1987, the unfunded current liability determined—

(I) by taking into account only liabilities attributable to such benefit increase, and

(II) by reducing (but not below zero) the amount determined under paragraph (8)(A)(ii) by the current liability determined without regard to such benefit increase.

(iii) Extensions, modifications, etc. not taken into account.—For purposes of this subparagraph, any extension, amendment, or other modification of an agreement after October 28, 1987, shall not be taken into account.

(D) Special rule for required changes in actuarial assumptions.

(i) In general. The unfunded old liability amount with respect to any plan for any plan year shall be increased by the amount necessary to amortize the amount of additional unfunded old liability under the plan in equal annual installments over a period of 12 plan years (beginning with the first plan year beginning after December 31, 1994).

(ii) Additional unfunded old liability. For purposes of clause (i), the term "additional unfunded old liability" means the amount (if any) by which

(I) the current liability of the plan as of the beginning of the first plan year beginning after December 31, 1994, valued using the assumptions required by paragraph (7)(C) as in effect for plan years beginning after December 31, 1994, exceeds

(II) the current liability of the plan as of the beginning of such first plan year, valued using the same assumptions used under subclause (I) (other than the assumptions required by paragraph (7)(C)), using the prior interest rate, and using such mortality assumptions as were used to determine current liability for the first plan year beginning after December 31, 1992.

(iii) Prior interest rate. For purposes of clause (ii), the term "prior interest rate" means the rate of interest that is the same percentage of the weighted average under subsection (b)(5)(B)(ii)(I) for the first plan year beginning after December 31, 1994, as the rate of interest used by the plan to determine current liability for the first plan year beginning after December 31, 1992, is of the weighted average under subsection (b)(5)(B)(ii)(I) for such first plan year beginning after December 31, 1992.

(E) Optional rule for additional unfunded old liability.

(i) In general. If an employer makes an election under clause (ii), the additional unfunded old liability for purposes of subparagraph (D) shall be the amount (if any) by which -

(I) the unfunded current liability of the plan as of the beginning of the first plan year beginning after December 31, 1994, valued using the assumptions required by paragraph (7)(C) as in effect for plan years beginning after December 31, 1994, exceeds—

(II) the unamortized portion of the unfunded old liability under the plan as of the beginning of the first plan year beginning after December 31, 1994.

(ii) Election.

(I) An employer may irrevocably elect to apply the provisions of this subparagraph as of the beginning of the first plan year beginning after December 31, 1994.

(II) If an election is made under this clause, the increase under paragraph (1) for any plan year beginning after December 31, 1994, and before January 1, 2002, to which this subsection applies (without regard to this subclause) shall not be less than the increase that would be required under paragraph (1) if the provisions of this title as in effect for the last plan year beginning before January 1, 1995, had remained in effect.

(4) Unfunded new liability amount.—For purposes of this subsection—

(A) In general.—The unfunded new liability amount with respect to any plan for any plan year is the applicable percentage of the unfunded new liability.

(B) Unfunded new liability.— The term "unfunded new liability" means the unfunded current liability of the plan for the plan year determined without regard to—

(i) the unamortized portion of the unfunded old liability, the unamortized portion of the additional unfunded old liability, the unamortized portion of each unfunded mor *tality increase,* and the unamortized portion of the unfunded existing benefit increase liability, and

(ii) the liability with respect to any unpredictable contingent event benefits (without regard to whether the event has occurred).

(C) Applicable percentage.—The term "applicable percentage" means, with respect to any plan year, 30 percent, reduced by the product of—

(i) [.25] *.40* multiplied by

(ii) the number of percentage points (if any) by which the funded current liability percentage exceeds [35] *60* percent.

(iii) the additional amount that would be determined under paragraph (4)(A) if the unpredictable contingent event benefit liabilities were included in unfunded new liability notwithstanding paragraph (4)(B)(ii).

(5) Unpredictable contingent event amount.—

(A) In general.—The unpredictable contingent event amount with respect to a plan for any plan year is an amount equal to the [greater of] greatest of—

(i) the applicable percentage of the product of—

(I) 100 percent, reduced (but not below zero) by the funded current liability percentage for the plan year, multiplied by

(II) the amount of unpredictable contingent event benefits paid during the plan year, including (except as provided by the Secretary of the Treasury) any payment for the purchase of an annuity contract for a participant or beneficiary with respect to such benefits, [or]

(ii) the amount which would be determined for the plan year if the unpredictable contingent event benefit liabilities were amortized in equal annual installments over 7

plan years (beginning with the plan year in which such event occurs)[.] , or

(iii) the additional amount that would be determined under paragraph (4)(A) if the unpredictable contingent event benefit liabilities were included in unfunded new liability notwithstanding paragraph (4)(B)(ii).

(B) Applicable percentage.—

In the case of plan years beginning in:	The applicable percentage is:
1989 and 1990	5
1991	10
1992	15
1993	20
1994	30
1995	40
1996	50
1997	60
1998	70
1999	80
2000	90
2001 and thereafter	100

(C) Paragraph not to apply to existing benefits.—This paragraph shall not apply to unpredictable contingent event benefits (and liabilities attributable thereto) for which the event occurred before the first plan year beginning after December 31, 1988.

(D) Special rule for first year of amortization.—Unless the employer elects otherwise, the amount determined under subparagraph (A) for the plan year in which the event occurs shall be equal to 150 percent of the amount determined under subparagraph (A)(i). The amount under subparagraph (A)(ii) for subsequent plan years in the amortization period shall be adjusted in the manner provided by the Secretary of the Treasury to reflect the application of this subparagraph.

(E) Limitation. The present value of the amounts described in subparagraph (A) with respect to any one event shall not exceed the unpredictable contingent event benefit liabilities attributable to that event.

ERISA Sec. 302 (d)(5)(E)

(6) Special rules for small plans.—

(A) Plans with 100 or fewer participants.— This subsection shall not apply to any plan for any plan year if on each day during the preceding plan year such plan had no more than 100 participants.

(B) Plans with more than 100 but not more than 150 participants.—In the case of a plan to which subparagraph (A) does not apply and which on each day during the preceding plan year had no more than 150 participants, the amount of the increase under paragraph (1) for such plan year shall be equal to the product of—

(i) such increase determined without regard to this subparagraph, multiplied by

(ii) 2 percent for the highest number of participants in excess of 100 on any such day.

(C) Aggregation of plans.—For purposes of this paragraph, all defined benefit plans maintained by the same employer (or any member of such employer's controlled group) shall be treated as 1 plan, but only employees of such employer or member shall be taken into account.

(7) Current liability.—For purposes of this subsection—

(A) In general.—The term "current liability" means all liabilities to participants and their beneficiaries under the plan.

(B) Treatment of unpredictable contingent event benefits.—

(i) In general.—For purposes of subparagraph (A), any unpredictable contingent event benefit shall not be taken into account until the event on which the benefit is contingent occurs.

(ii) Unpredictable contingent event benefit.—The term "unpredictable contingent event benefit" means any benefit contingent on an event other than—

(I) age, service, compensation, death, or disability, or

(II) an event which is reasonably and reliably predictable (as determined by the Secretary of the Treasury).

[(C) Interest rates used.—The rate of interest used to determine current liability shall be the rate of interest used under subsection (b)(5).]

(C) Interest rate and mortality assumptions used. Effective for plan years beginning after December 31, 1994—

(i) Interest rate.

(I) In general. The rate of interest used to determine current liability under this subsection shall be the rate of interest used under subsection (b)(5), except that the highest rate in the permissible range under subparagraph (B)(ii) thereof shall not exceed the specified percentage under subclause (II) of the weighted average referred to in such subparagraph.

(II) Specified percentage. For purposes of subclause (I), the specified percentage shall be determined as follows:

In the case of plan years beginning in calendar year:	The specified percentage is:
1995	*109*
1996	*108*
1997	*107*
1998	*106*
1999 and thereafter	*105.*

(ii) Mortality tables.

(I) Commissioners' standard table. In the case of plan years beginning before the first plan year to which the first tables prescribed under subclause (II) apply, the mortality table used in determining current liability under this subsection shall be the table prescribed by the Secretary of the Treasury which is based on the prevailing commissioners' standard table (described in section 807(d)(5)(A) of the Internal Revenue Code of 1986) used to determine reserves for group an-

nuity contracts issued on January 1, 1993.

(II) Secretarial authority. The Secretary of the Treasury may by regulation prescribe for plan years beginning after December 31, 1999, mortality tables to be used in determining current liability under this subsection. Such tables shall be based upon the actual experience of pension plans and projected trends in such experience. In prescribing such tables, the Secretary of the Treasury shall take into account results of available independent studies of mortality of individuals covered by pension plans.

(III) Periodic review. The Secretary of the Treasury shall periodically (at least every 5 years) review any tables in effect under this subsection and shall, to the extent the Secretary determines necessary, by regulation update the tables to reflect the actual experience of pension plans and projected trends in such experience.

(iii) Separate mortality tables for the disabled. Notwithstanding clause (ii)—

(I) In general. In the case of plan years beginning after December 31, 1995, the Secretary of the Treasury shall establish mortality tables which may be used (in lieu of the tables under clause (ii)) to determine current liability under this subsection for individuals who are entitled to benefits under the plan on account of disability. Such Secretary shall establish separate tables for individuals whose disabilities occur in plan years beginning before January 1, 1995, and for individuals whose disabilities occur in plan years beginning on or after such date.

(II) Special rule for disabilities occurring after 1994. In the case of disabilities occurring in plan years beginning after December 31, 1994, the tables under subclause (I) shall apply only with respect to individuals described in such subclause who are disabled within the meaning of title II of the Social Security Act and the regulations thereunder.

(III) Plan years beginning in 1995. In the case of any plan year beginning in 1995, a plan may use its own mortality assumptions for individuals who are entitled to benefits under the plan on account of disability.

(D) Certain service disregarded.—

(i) In general.—In the case of a participant to whom this subparagraph applies, only the applicable percentage of the years of service before such individual became a participant shall be taken into account in computing the current liability of the plan.

(ii) Applicable percentage.—For purposes of this subparagraph, the applicable percentage shall be determined as follows:

If the years of participation are:	The applicable percentage is:
1	20
2	40
3	60
4	80
5 or more	100

(iii) Participants to whom subparagraph applies.—This subparagraph shall apply to any participant who, at the time of becoming a participant—

(I) has not accrued any other benefit under any defined benefit plan (whether or not terminated) maintained by the employer or a member of the same controlled group of which the employer is a member,

(II) who first becomes a participant under the plan in a plan year beginning after December 31, 1987, and

(III) has years of service greater than the minimum years of service necessary for eligibility to participate in the plan.

(iv) Election.—An employer may elect not to have this subparagraph apply. Such an election, once made, may be revoked only with the consent of the Secretary of the Treasury.

ERISA Sec. 302 (d)(7)(D)(iv)

(8) Other definitions.—For purposes of this subsection—

(A) Unfunded current liability.—The term "unfunded current liability" means, with respect to any plan year, the excess (if any) of—

(i) the current liability under the plan, over

(ii) value of the plan's assets determined under subsection (c)(2).

(B) Funded current liability percentage.— The term "funded current liability percentage" means, with respect to any plan year, the percentage which—

(i) the amount determined under subparagraph (A)(ii), is of

(ii) the current liability under the plan.

(C) Controlled group.—The term "controlled group" means any group treated as a single employer under subsections (b), (c), (m), and (o) of section 414 of the Internal Revenue Code of 1986.

(D) Adjustments to prevent omissions and duplications.— The Secretary of the Treasury shall provide such adjustments in the unfunded old liability amount, the unfunded new liability amount, the unpredictable contingent event amount, the current payment amount, and any other charges or credits under this section as are necessary to avoid duplication or omission of any factors in the determination of such amounts, charges, or credits.

(E) Deduction for credit balances.—For purposes of this subsection, the amount determined under subparagraph (A)(ii) shall be reduced by any credit balance in the funding standard account. The Secretary of the Treasury may provide for such reduction for purposes of any other provision which references this subsection.

(9) Applicability of subsection.

(A) In general. Except as provided in paragraph (6)(A), this subsection shall apply to a plan for any plan year if its funded current liability percentage for such year is less than 90 percent.

(B) Exception for certain plans at least 80 percent funded. Subparagraph (A) shall not apply to a plan for a plan year if—

(i) the funded current liability percentage for the plan year is at least 80 percent, and

(ii) such percentage for each of the 2 immediately preceding plan years (or each of the 2d and 3d immediately preceding plan years) is at least 90 percent.

(C) Funded current liability percentage. For purposes of subparagraphs (A) and (B), the term "funded current liability percentage" has the meaning given such term by paragraph (8)(B), except that such percentage shall be determined for any plan year

(i) without regard to paragraph (8)(E), and

(ii) by using the rate of interest which is the highest rate allowable for the plan year under paragraph (7)(C).

(D) Transition rules. For purposes of this paragraph:

(i) Funded percentage for years before 1995. The funded current liability percentage for any plan year beginning before January 1, 1995, shall be treated as not less than 90 percent only if for such plan year the plan met one of the following requirements (as in effect for such year):

(I) The full-funding limitation under subsection (c)(7) for the plan was zero.

(II) The plan had no additional funding requirement under this subsection (or would have had no such requirement if its funded current liability percentage had been determined under subparagraph (C)).

(III) The plan's additional funding requirement under this subsection did not exceed the lesser of 0.5 percent of current liability or $5,000,000.

(ii) Special rule for 1995 and 1996. For purposes of determining whether subparagraph (B) applies to any plan year beginning in 1995 or 1996, a plan shall be treated as meeting the requirements of subparagraph (B)(ii) if the plan met the requirements of clause (i) of this subparagraph for any two of the plan years beginning in 1992, 1993, and 1994 (whether or not consecutive).

(10) Unfunded mortality increase amount.

(A) In general. The unfunded mortality increase amount with respect to each unfunded mortality increase is the amount necessary to amortize such increase in equal annual installments over a period of 10 plan years (beginning with the first plan year for which a plan uses any new mortality table issued under paragraph (7)(C)(ii)(II) or (III)).

(B) Unfunded mortality increase. For purposes of subparagraph (A), the term "unfunded mortality increase" means an amount equal to the excess of—

(i) the current liability of the plan for the first plan year for which a plan uses any new mortality table issued under paragraph (7)(C)(ii)(II) or (III), over

(ii) the current liability of the plan for such plan year which would have been determined if the mortality table in effect for the preceding plan year had been used.

(11) Phase-in of increases in funding required by Retirement Protection Act of 1994.

(A) In general. For any applicable plan year, at the election of the employer, the increase under paragraph (1) shall not exceed the greater of

(i) the increase that would be required under paragraph (1) if the provisions of this title as in effect for plan years beginning before January 1, 1995, had remained in effect, or

(ii) the amount which, after taking into account charges (other than the additional charge under this subsection) and credits under subsection (b), is necessary to increase the funded current liability percentage (taking into account the expected increase in current liability due to benefits accruing during the plan year) for the applicable plan year to a percentage equal to the sum of the initial funded current liability percentage of the plan plus the applicable number of percentage points for such applicable plan year.

(B) Applicable number of percentage points.

(i) Initial funded current liability percentage of 75 percent or less. Except as provided in clause (ii), for plans with an initial funded current liability percentage of 75 percent or less, the applicable number of percentage points for the applicable plan year is:

In the case of plan years beginning in—	The applicable number of percentage points is—
1995	3
1996	6
1997	9
1998	12
1999	15
2000	19
2001	24

(ii) Other cases. In the case of a plan to which this clause applies, the applicable number of percentage points for any such applicable plan year is the sum of —

(I) 2 percentage points;

(II) the applicable number of percentage points (if any) under this clause for the preceding applicable plan year;

(III) the product of .10 multiplied by the excess (if any) of (a) 85 percentage points over (b) the sum of the initial funded current liability percentage and the number determined under subclause (II);

(IV) for applicable plan years beginning in 2000, 1 percentage point; and

ERISA Sec. 302 (d)(11)(B)(ii)(V)

(V) for applicable plan years beginning in 2001, 2 percentage points.

(iii) Plans to which clause (ii) applies.

(I) In general. Clause (ii) shall apply to a plan for an applicable plan year if the initial funded current liability percentage of such plan is more than 75 percent.

(II) Plans initially under clause (i). In the case of a plan which (but for this subclause) has an initial funded current liability percentage of 75 percent or less, clause (ii) (and not clause (i)) shall apply to such plan with respect to applicable plan years beginning after the first applicable plan year for which the sum of the initial funded current liability percentage and the applicable number of percentage points (determined under clause (i)) exceeds 75 percent. For purposes of applying clause (ii) to such a plan, the initial funded current liability percentage of such plan shall be treated as being the sum referred to in the preceding sentence.

(C) Definitions. For purposes of this paragraph —

(i) The term "applicable plan year" means a plan year beginning after December 31, 1994, and before January 1, 2002.

(ii) The term "initial funded current liability percentage" means the funded current liability percentage as of the first day of the first plan year beginning after December 31, 1994.

◊ ◊ ◊

Editor's Note: The amendments to ERISA §302(e)(1), set forth below, were enacted by §764 of the Retirement Protection Act of 1994, which was enacted as part of the Uruguay Round Agreements Act (P. L. 103-465). The changes apply to plan years beginning after December 8, 1994.

◊ ◊ ◊

(e) Quarterly Contributions Required.—

(1) In general.—If a defined benefit plan (other than a multiemployer plan) *which has a funded current liability percentage (as defined in subsection (d)(8)) for the preceding plan year of less than 100 percent* fails to pay the full amount of a required installment for [any plan year] *the plan year,* then the rate of interest charged to the funding standard account under subsection (b)(5) with respect to the amount of the underpayment for the period of the underpayment shall be equal to the greater of—

(A) 175 percent of the Federal mid-term rate (as in effect under section 1274 of the Internal Revenue Code of 1986 for the 1st month of such plan year), or

(B) the rate of interest used under the plan in determining costs (including adjustments under subsection (b)(5)(B)).

(2) Amount of underpayment, period of underpayment.—For purposes of paragraph (1)—

(A) Amount.—The amount of the underpayment shall be the excess of—

(i) the required installment, over

(ii) the amount (if any) of the installment contributed to or under the plan on or before the due date for the installment.

(B) Period of underpayment.—The period for which any interest is charged under this subsection with respect to any portion of the underpayment shall run from the due date for the installment to the date on which such portion is contributed to or under the plan (determined without regard to subsection (c)(10)).

(C) Order of crediting contributions.— For purposes of subparagraph (A)(ii), contributions shall be credited against unpaid required installments in the order in which such installments are required to be paid.

(3) Number of required installments; due dates. For purposes of this subsection—

(A) Payable in 4 installments.—There shall be 4 required installments for each plan year.

(B) Time for payment of installments.

In the case of the following required installments:	The due date is:
1st	April 15
2nd	July 15
3rd	October 15
4th	January 15 of the following year.

(4) Amount of required installment.— For purposes of this subsection—

(A) In general.—The amount of any required installment shall be the applicable percentage of the required annual payment.

(B) Required annual payment.—For purposes of subparagraph (A), the term "required annual payment" means the lesser of—

(i) 90 percent of the amount required to be contributed to or under the plan by the employer for the plan year under section 412 of the Internal Revenue Code of 1986 (without regard to any waiver under subsection (c) thereof), or

(ii) 100 percent of the amount so required for the preceding plan year. Clause (ii) shall not apply if the preceding plan year was not a year of 12 months.

(C) Applicable percentage.—For purposes of subparagraph (A), the applicable percentage shall be determined in accordance with the following table:

For plan years beginning in:	The applicable percentage is:
1989	6.25
1990	12.5
1991	18.75
1992 and thereafter	25

(D) Special rules for unpredictable contingent Event Benefits.—In the case of a plan to which subsection (d) applies for any calendar year and which has any unpredictable contingent event benefit liabilities—

(i) Liabilities not taken into account.— Such liabilities shall not be taken into account in computing the required annual payment under subparagraph (B).

(ii) Increase in installments.—Each required installment shall be increased by the [greater of] *greatest of*—

(I) the unfunded percentage of the amount of benefits described in subsection (d)(5)(A)(i) paid during the 3-month period preceding the month in which the due date for such installment occurs, [or]

(II) 25 percent of the amount determined under subsection (d)(5)(A)(ii) for the plan year[.] , *or*

(III) 25 percent of the amount determined under subsection (d)(5)(A)(iii) for the plan year.

(iii) Unfunded percentage.—For purposes of clause (ii)(I), the term "unfunded percentage" means the percentage determined under subsection (d)(5)(A)(i)(I) for the plan year.

(iv) Limitation on increase.—In no event shall the increases under clause (ii) exceed the amount necessary to increase the funded current liability percentage (within the meaning of subsection (d)(8)(B)) for the plan year to 100 percent.

◊ ◊ ◊

Editor's Note: ERISA §302(e)(5), set forth below, was added by §761(a) of the Retirement Protection Act of 1994, which was enacted as part of the Uruguay Round Agreements Act (P. L. 103-465). The changes apply to plan years beginning after December 31, 1994. The Act also redesignated former ERISA §302(e)(5) as §302(e)(6).

◊ ◊ ◊

(5) Liquidity requirement.

(A) In general. A plan to which this paragraph applies shall be treated as failing to pay the full amount of any required installment to the extent that the value of the liquid assets paid in such installment is less than the liquidity shortfall (whether or not such liquidity shortfall exceeds the amount of such installment required to be paid but for this paragraph).

(B) Plans to which paragraph applies. This paragraph shall apply to a defined benefit plan (other than a multiemployer plan or a plan described in subsection (d)(6)(A)) which

(i) is required to pay installments under this subsection for a plan year, and

(ii) has a liquidity shortfall for any quarter during such plan year.

(C) Period of underpayment. For purposes of paragraph (1), any portion of an installment that is treated as not paid under subparagraph (A) shall continue to be treated as unpaid until the close of the quarter in which the due date for such installment occurs.

(D) Limitation on increase. If the amount of any required installment is increased by reason of subparagraph (A), in no event shall such increase exceed the amount which, when added to prior installments for the plan year, is necessary to increase the funded current liability percentage (taking into account the expected increase in current liability due to benefits accruing during the plan year) to 100 percent.

(E) Definitions. For purposes of this paragraph

(i) Liquidity shortfall. The term "liquidity shortfall" means, with respect to any required installment, an amount equal to the excess (as of the last day of the quarter for which such installment is made) of the base amount with respect to such quarter over the value (as of such last day) of the plan's liquid assets.

(ii) Base amount.

(I) In general. The term "base amount" means, with respect to any quarter, an amount equal to 3 times the sum of the adjusted disbursements from the plan for the 12 months ending on the last day of such quarter.

(II) Special rule. If the amount determined under clause (i) exceeds an amount equal to 2 times the sum of the adjusted disbursements from the plan for the 36 months ending on the last day of the quarter and an enrolled actuary certifies to the satisfaction of the Secretary of the Treasury that such excess is the result of nonrecurring circumstances, the base amount with respect to such quarter shall be determined without regard to amounts related to those nonrecurring circumstances.

(iii) Disbursements from the plan. The term "disbursements from the plan" means all disbursements from the trust, including purchases of annuities, payments of single sums and other benefits, and administrative expenses.

(iv) Adjusted disbursements. The term "adjusted disbursements" means disbursements from the plan reduced by the product of—

(I) the plan's funded current liability percentage (as defined in subsection (d)(8)) for the plan year, and

(II) the sum of the purchases of annuities, payments of single sums, and such other disbursements as the Secretary of the Treasury shall provide in regulations.

(v) Liquid assets. The term "liquid assets" means cash, marketable securities and such other assets as specified by the Secretary of the Treasury in regulations.

(vi) Quarter. The term "quarter" means, with respect to any required installment, the 3-month period preceding the month in which the due date for such installment occurs.

(F) Regulations. The Secretary of the Treasury may prescribe such regulations as are necessary to carry out this paragraph.

[6]*(5)* Fiscal years and short years.—

(A) Fiscal years.—In applying this subsection to a plan year beginning on any date other than January 1, there shall be substituted for the months specified in this subsection, the months which correspond thereto.

(B) Short plan year.—This section shall be applied to plan years of less than 12 months in accordance with regulations prescribed by the Secretary of the Treasury.

◊ ◊ ◊

Editor's Note: The amendments to ERISA §302(f) set forth below were made by §768(b) of the Retirement Protection Act of 1994 (enacted as part of the Uruguay Round Agreements Act, P.L. 103-465). They apply generally to installments and other payments required under part 3 of subtitle B of ERISA that become due on or after December 8, 1994.

◊ ◊ ◊

(f) Imposition of Lien Where Failure To Make Required Contributions.—

(1) In general. In the case of a plan [to which this section applies] *covered under section 4021 of this Act,* if—

(A) any person fails to make a required installment under subsection (e) or any other payment required under this section before the due date for such installment or other payment, and

(B) the unpaid balance of such installment or other payment (including interest), when added to the aggregate unpaid balance of all preceding such installments or other payments for which payment was not made before the due date (including interest), exceeds $1,000,000,

then there shall be a lien in favor of the plan in the amount determined under paragraph (3) upon all property and rights to property, whether real or personal, belonging to such person and any other person who is a member of the same controlled group of which such person is a member.

(2) Plans to which subsection applies.— This subsection shall apply to a defined benefit plan (other than a multiemployer plan) for any plan year for which the funded current liability percentage (within the meaning of subsection (d)(8)(B)) of such plan is less than 100 percent.

[(3) Amount of lien.— For purposes of paragraph (1), the amount of the lien shall be equal to the lesser of—

[(A) the amount by which the unpaid balances described in paragraph (1)(B) (including interest) exceed $1,000,000, or

[(B) the aggregate unpaid balance of required installments and other payments required under this section (including interest)—

[(i) for plan years beginning after 1987, and

[(ii) for which payment has not been made before the due date]

(3) Amount of lien. For purposes of paragraph (1), the amount of the lien shall be equal to the aggregate unpaid balance of required installments and other payments required under this section (including interest)—

(A) for plan years beginning after 1987, and

(B) for which payment has not been made before the due date.

(4) Notice of failure; lien.—

(A) Notice of failure; lien.—A person committing a failure described in paragraph (1) shall notify the Pension Benefit Guaranty Corporation of such failure within 10 days of the due date for the required installment or other payment.

(B) Period of lien.—The lien imposed by paragraph (1) shall arise on the [60th day following the] due date for the required installment or other payment and shall continue until the last day of the first plan year in which the plan ceases to be described in paragraph (1)(B). Such lien shall continue to run without regard to whether such plan continues to be described in paragraph (2) during the period referred to in the preceding sentence.

(C) Certain rules to apply.—Any amount with respect to which a lien is imposed under paragraph (1) shall be treated as taxes due and owing the United States and rules similar to the rules of subsections (c), (d), and (e) of section 4068 shall apply with respect to a lien imposed by subsection (a) and the amount with respect to such lien.

(5) Enforcement.—Any lien created under paragraph (1) may be perfected and enforced only by the Pension Benefit Guaranty Corporation, or at the direction of the Pension Benefit Guaranty Corporation, by the contributing sponsor (or any member of the controlled group of the contributing sponsor).

(6) Definitions.—For purposes of this subsection—

(A) Due date; required installment.— The terms "due date," and "required installment" have the meanings given such terms by subsection (e), except that in the case of a payment other than a required installment,

the due date shall be the date such payment is required to be made under this section.

(B) Controlled group.— The term "controlled group" means any group treated as a single employer under subsections (b), (c), (m), and (o) of section 414 of the Internal Revenue Code of 1986.

(g) Qualified Transfers to Health Benefit Accounts.—For purposes of this section, in the case of a qualified transfer (as defined in section 420 of the Internal Revenue Code of 1986)—

(1) any assets transferred in a plan year on or before the valuation date for such year (and any income allocable thereto) shall, for purposes of subsection (c)(7), be treated as assets in the plan as of the valuation date for such year, and

(2) the plan shall be treated as having a net experience loss under subsection (b)(2)(B)(iv) in an amount equal to the amount of such transfer (reduced by any amounts transferred back to the plan under section 420(c)(1)(B) of such Code) and for which amortization charges begin for the first plan year after the plan year in which such transfer occurs, except that such subsection shall be applied to such amount by substituting 10 plan years for 5 plan years.

(h) Cross Reference.—For alternative amortization method for certain multiemployer plans see section 1013(d) of this Act.

VARIANCE FROM MINIMUM FUNDING STANDARD

Sec. 303. (a) If an employer, or in the case of a multiemployer plan, 10 percent or more of the number of employers contributing to or under the plan are unable to satisfy the minimum funding standard for a plan year without temporary substantial business hardship (substantial business hardship in the case of a multiemployer plan) and if application of the standard would be adverse to the interests of plan participants in the aggregate, the Secretary of the Treasury may waive the requirements of section 302(a) for such year with respect to all or any portion of the minimum funding standard other than the portion thereof determined under section 302(b)(2)(C). The Secretary of the Treasury shall not waive the minimum funding standard with respect to a plan for more than 3 of any 15 (5 of any 15 in the case of a multiemployer plan) consecutive plan years. The interest rate used for purposes of computing the amortization charge described in subsection (b)(2)(C) for any plan year shall be—

(1) in the case of a plan other than a multiemployer plan, the greater of (A) 150 percent of the Federal mid-term rate (as in effect under section 1274 of the Internal Revenue Code of 1986 for the 1st month of such plan year), or (B) the rate of interest used under the plan in determining costs (including adjustments under section 302(b)(5)(B)), and

(2) in the case of a multiemployer plan, the rate determined under section 6621 (b) of such Code.

(b) For purposes of this part, the factors taken into account in determining temporary substantial business hardship (substantial business hardship in the case of a multiemployer plan) shall include (but shall not be limited to) whether—

(1) the employer is operating at an economic loss,

(2) there is substantial unemployment or underemployment in the trade or business and in the industry concerned,

(3) the sales and profits of the industry concerned are depressed or declining, and

(4) it is reasonable to expect that the plan will be continued only if the waiver is granted.

(c) For purposes of this part, the term "waived funding deficiency" means the portion of the minimum funding standard (determined without regard to subsection (b)(3)(C) of section 302) for a plan year waived by the Secretary of the Treasury and not satisfied by employer contributions.

(d) Special Rules.—

(1) Application must be submitted before date 2½ months after close of year.— In the case of a plan other than a multiemployer plan, no waiver may be granted under this section with respect to any plan for any plan year unless an application therefor is submitted to the Secretary of the Treasury not later than the 15th day of the 3rd month beginning after the close of such plan year.

(2) Special rule if employer is member of controlled group.—

(A) In general.—In the case of a plan other than a multiemployer plan, if an employer is a member of a controlled group, the temporary substantial business hardship requirements of subsection (a) shall be treated as met only if such requirements are met—

(i) with respect to such employer, and

(ii) with respect to the controlled group of which such employer is a member (determined by treating all members of such group as a single employer). The Secretary of the Treasury may provide that an analysis of a trade or business or industry of a member need not be conducted if the Secretary of the Treasury determines such analysis is not necessary because the taking into account of such member would not significantly affect the determination under this subsection.

(B) Controlled group.—For purposes of subparagraph (A), the term "controlled group" means any group treated as a single employer under subsection (b), (c), (m), or (o) of section 414 of the Internal Revenue Code of 1986.

(e)(1) The Secretary of the Treasury shall, before granting a waiver under this section, require each applicant to provide evidence satisfactory to such Secretary that the applicant has provided notice of the filing of the application for such waiver to each employee organization representing employees covered by the affected plan, and each affected party (as defined in section 4001(a)(21)) other than the Pension Benefit Guaranty Corporation.

Such notice shall include a description of the extent to which the plan is funded for benefits which are guaranteed under title IV and for benefit liabilities.

(2) The Secretary of the Treasury shall consider any relevant information provided by a person to whom notice was given under paragraph (1).

(f) **Cross Reference.**—For corresponding duties of the Secretary of the Treasury with regard to implementation of the Internal Revenue Code of 1954, see section 412(d) of such Code.

EXTENSION OF AMORTIZATION PERIODS

Sec. 304. (a) The period of years required to amortize any unfunded liability (described in any clause of subsection (b)(2)(B) of section 302) of any plan may be extended by the Secretary for a period of time (not in excess of 10 years) if he determines that such extension would carry out the purposes of this Act and would provide adequate protection for participants under the plan and their beneficiaries and if he determines that the failure to permit such extension would—

(1) result in—

(A) a substantial risk to the voluntary continuation of the plan, or

(B) a substantial curtailment of pension benefit levels or employee compensation, and

(2) be adverse to the interests of plan participants in the aggregate.

In the case of a plan other than a multiemployer plan, the interest rate applicable for any plan year under any arrangement entered into by the Secretary in connection with an extension granted under this subsection shall be the greater of (A) 150 percent of the Federal midterm rate (as in effect under section 1274 of the Internal Revenue Code of 1986 for the 1st month of such plan year), or (B) the rate of interest used under the plan in determining

costs. In the case of a multiemployer plan, such rate shall be the rate determined under section 6621(b) of such Code.

(b)(1) No amendment of the plan which increases the liabilities of the plan by reason of any increase in benefits, any change in the accrual of benefits, or any change in the rate at which benefits become nonforfeitable under the plan shall be adopted if a waiver under section 303(a) or an extension of time under subsection (a) of this section is in effect with respect to the plan, or if a plan amendment described in section 302(c)(8) has been made at any time in the preceding 12 months (24 months in the case of a multiemployer plan). If a plan is amended in violation of the preceding sentence, any such waiver, or extension of time, shall not apply to any plan year end-ing on or after the date on which such amendment is adopted.

(2) Paragraph (1) shall not apply to any plan amendment which—

(A) the Secretary determines to be reasonable and which provides for only de minimis increases in the liabilities of the plan,

(B) only repeals an amendment described in section 302(c)(8) or

(C) is required as a condition of qualification under part I of subchapter D, of chapter 1, of the Internal Revenue Code of 1954.

(c)(1) The Secretary of the Treasury shall, before granting an extension under this section, require each applicant to provide evidence satisfactory to such Secretary that the applicant has provided notice of the filing of the application for such extension to each employee organization representing employees covered by the affected plan.

(2) The Secretary of the Treasury shall consider any relevant information provided by a person to whom notice was given under paragraph (1).

ALTERNATIVE MINIMUM FUNDING STANDARD

Sec. 305. (a) A plan which uses a funding method that requires contributions in all years not less than those required under the entry age normal funding method may maintain an alternative minimum funding standard account for any plan year. Such account shall be credited and charged solely as provided in this section.

(b) For a plan year the alternative minimum funding standard accounts shall be—

(1) charged with the sum of—

(A) the lesser of normal cost under the funding method used under the plan or normal cost determined under the unit credit method,

(B) the excess, if any, of the present value of accrued benefits under the plan over the fair market value of the assets, and

(C) an amount equal to the excess, if any, of credits to the alternative minimum funding standard account for all prior plan years over charges to such account for all such years, and

(2) credited with the amount considered contributed by the employer to or under the plan (within the meaning of section 302(c)(10)) for the plan year.

(c) The alternative minimum funding standard account (and items therein) shall be charged or credited with interest in the manner provided under section 302(b)(5) with respect to the funding standard account.

SECURITY FOR WAIVERS OF MINIMUM FUNDING STANDARD AND EXTENSIONS OF AMORTIZATION PERIOD

Sec. 306. (a) Security May Be Required.—

(1) In General.—Except as provided in subsection (c), the Secretary of the Treasury may require an employer maintaining a defined benefit plan which is a single-employer plan (within the meaning of section 4001(a)(15)) to provide security to such plan as a condition for granting or modifying a waiver under section 303 or an extension under section 304.

(2) Special Rules.—Any security provided under paragraph (1) may be perfected and enforced only by the Pension Benefit Guaranty Corporation or, at the direction of the Corporation, by a contributing sponsor (within the meaning of section 4001(a)(13)) or a member of such sponsor's controlled group (within the meaning of section 4001(a)(14)).

(b) Consultation With The Pension Benefit Guaranty Corporation.— Except as provided in subsection (c), the Secretary of the Treasury shall, before granting or modifying a waiver under section 303 or an extension under section 304 with respect to a plan described in subsection (a)(1)—

(1) provide the Pension Benefit Guaranty Corporation with—

(A) notice of the completed application for any waiver, extension, or modification, and

(B) an opportunity to comment on such application within 30 days after receipt of such notice, and

(2) consider—

(A) any comments of the Corporation under paragraph (1)(B), and

(B) any views of any employee organization representing participants in the plan which are submitted in writing to the Secretary of

ERISA Sec. 306 (b)(2)(B)

the Treasury in connection with such application.

Information provided to the Corporation under this subsection shall be considered tax return information and subject to the safeguarding and reporting requirements of section 6103(p) of the Internal Revenue Code of 1954.

(c) Exception for Certain Waivers and Extensions.—

(1) In general.—The preceding provisions of this section shall not apply to any plan with respect to which the sum of—

(A) the outstanding balance of the accumulated funding deficiencies (within the meaning of section 302(a)(2) of this Act and section 412(a) of the Internal Revenue Code of 1954) of the plan,

(B) the outstanding balance of the amount of waived funding deficiencies of the plan waived under section 303 of this Act or section 412(d) of such Code, and

(C) the outstanding balance of the amount of decreases in the minimum funding standard allowed under section 304 of this Act or section 412(e) of such Code is less than $1,000,000.

(2) Accumulated funding deficiencies.—For purposes of paragraph (1)(A), accumulated funding deficiencies shall include any increase in such amount which would result if all applications for waivers of the minimum funding standard under section 303 of this Act or section 412(d) of the Internal Revenue Code of 1954 and for extensions of the amortization period under section 304 of this Act or section 412(e) of such Code which are pending with respect to such plan were denied.

SECURITY REQUIRED UPON ADOPTION OF PLAN AMENDMENT RESULTING IN SIGNIFICANT UNDERFUNDING

Sec. 307. (a) In General.—If —

(1) a defined benefit plan (other than a multiemployer plan to which the requirements of section 302 apply) adopts an amendment an effect of which is to increase current liability under the plan for a plan year, and

(2) the funded current liability percentage of the plan for the plan year in which the amendment takes effect is less than 60 percent, including the amount of the unfunded current liability under the plan attributable to the plan amendment,
the contributing sponsor (or any member of the controlled group of the contributing sponsor) shall provide security to the plan.

(b) Form of Security.—The security required under subsection (a) shall consist of—

(1) a bond issued by a corporate surety company that is an acceptable surety for purposes of section 412,

(2) cash, or United States obligations which mature in 3 years or less, held in escrow by a bank or similar financial institution, or

(3) such other form of security as is satisfactory to the Secretary of the Treasury and the parties involved.

(c) Amount of Security.—The security shall be in an amount equal to the excess of—

(1) the lesser of—

(A) the amount of additional plan assets which would be necessary to increase the funded current liability percentage under the plan to 60 percent, including the amount of the unfunded current liability under the plan attributable to the plan amendment, or

(B) the amount of the increase in current liability under the plan attributable to the plan amendment and any other plan amend-

ERISA Sec. 306 (c)

ments adopted after December 22, 1987, and before such plan amendment, over

(2) $10,000,000.

(d) Release of Security.—The security shall be released (and any amounts thereunder shall be refunded together with any interest accrued thereon) at the end of the first plan year which ends after the provision of the security and for which the funded current liability percentage under the plan is not less than 60 percent. The Secretary of the Treasury may prescribe regulations for partial releases of the security by reason of increases in the funded current liability percentage.

(e) Notice.—A contributing sponsor which is required to provide security under subsection (a) shall notify the Pension Benefit Guaranty Corporation within 30 days after the amendment requiring such security takes effect. Such notice shall contain such information as the Corporation may require.

(f) Definitions.—For purposes of this section, the terms "current liability", "funded current liability percentage", and "unfunded current liability" shall have the meanings given such terms by section 302(d), except that in computing unfunded current liability there shall not be taken into account any unamortized portion of the unfunded old liability amount as of the close of the plan year.

EFFECTIVE DATES

Sec. 308. (a) Except as otherwise provided in this section, this part shall apply in the case of plan years beginning after the date of the enactment of this Act.

(b) Except as otherwise provided in subsections (c) and (d), in the case of a plan in existence on January 1, 1974, this part shall apply in the case of plan years beginning after December 31, 1975.

(c)(1) In the case of a plan maintained on January 1, 1974, pursuant to one or more agreements which the Secretary finds to be collective bargaining agreements between employee representatives and one or more

employers, this part shall apply only with respect to plan years beginning after the earlier of the date specified in subparagraph (A) or (B) of section 211(c)(1).

(2) This subsection shall apply with respect to a plan if (and only if) the application of this subsection results in a later effective date for this part than the effective date required by subsection (b).

(d) In the case of a plan the administrator of which elects under Section 1017(d) of this Act to have the provisions of the Internal Revenue Code of 1954 relating to participation, vesting, funding, and form of benefit to apply to a plan year and to all subsequent plan years, this part shall apply to plan years beginning on the earlier of the first plan year to which such election applies or the first plan year determined under subsections (a), (b), and (c) of this section.

(e) In the case of a plan maintained by a labor organization which is exempt from tax under section 501(c)(5) of the Internal Revenue Code of 1954 exclusively for the benefit of its employees and their beneficiaries, this part shall be applied by substituting for the term "December 31, 1975" in subsection (b), the earlier of—

(1) the date on which the second convention of such labor organization held after the date of the enactment of this Act ends, or

(2) December 31, 1980, but in no event shall a date earlier than the later of December 31, 1975, or the date determined under subsection (c) be substituted.

(f) The preceding provisions of this section shall not apply with respect to amendments made to this part in provisions enacted after the date of the enactment of this Act.

COVERAGE

Sec. 401. (a) This part shall apply to any employee benefit plan described in section 4(a) (and not exempted under section 4(b)), other than—

(1) a plan which is unfunded and is maintained by an employer primarily for the purpose of providing deferred compensation for a select group of management or highly compensated employees; or

(2) any agreement described in section 736 of the Internal Revenue Code of 1954, which provides payments to a retired partner or deceased partner or a deceased partner's successor in interest.

(b) For purposes of this part:

(1) In the case of a plan which invests in any security issued by an investment company registered under the Investment Company Act of 1940, the assets of such plan shall be deemed to include such security but shall not, solely by reason of such investment, be deemed to include any assets of such investment company.

(2) In the case of a plan to which a guaranteed benefit policy is issued by an insurer, the assets of such plan shall be deemed to include such policy, but shall not, solely by reason of the issuance of such policy, be deemed to include any assets of such insurer. For purposes of this paragraph:

(A) The term "insurer" means an insurance company, insurance service, or insurance organization, qualified to do business in a State.

(B) The term "guaranteed benefit policy" means an insurance policy or contract to the extent that such policy or contract provides for benefits the amount of which is guaranteed by the insurer. Such term includes any surplus in a separate account, but excludes any other portion of a separate account.

ESTABLISHMENT OF PLAN

Sec. 402. (a)(1) Every employee benefit plan shall be established and maintained pursuant to a written instrument. Such instrument shall provide for one or more named fiduciaries who jointly or severally shall have authority to control and manage the operation and administration of the plan.

(2) For purposes of this title, the term "named fiduciary" means a fiduciary who is named in the plan instrument, or who, pursuant to a procedure specified in the plan, is identified as a fiduciary (A) by a person who is an employer or employee organization with respect to the plan or (B) by such an employer and such an employee organization acting jointly.

(b) Every employee benefit plan shall—

(1) provide a procedure for establishing and carrying out a funding policy and method consistent with the objectives of the plan and the requirements of this title,

(2) describe any procedure under the plan for the allocation of responsibilities for the operation and administration of the plan (including any procedure described in section 405(c)(1)),

(3) provide a procedure for amending such plan, and for identifying the persons who have authority to amend the plan, and

(4) specify the basis on which payments are made to and from the plan.

(c) Any employee benefit plan may provide—

(1) that any person or group of persons may serve in more than one fiduciary capacity with respect to the plan (including service both as trustee and administrator);

(2) that a named fiduciary, or a fiduciary designated by a named fiduciary pursuant to a plan procedure described in section 405(c)(1), may employ one or more persons to render advice with regard to any responsibility such fiduciary has under the plan; or

(3) that a person who is a named fiduciary with respect to control or management of the assets of the plan may appoint an investment manager or managers to manage (including the power to acquire and dispose of) any assets of a plan.

ESTABLISHMENT OF TRUST

Sec. 403. (a) Except as provided in subsection (b), all assets of an employee benefit plan shall be held in trust by one or more trustees. Such trustee or trustees shall be either named in the trust instrument or in the plan instrument described in section 402(a) or appointed by a person who is a named fiduciary, and upon acceptance of being named or appointed, the trustee or trustees shall have exclusive authority and discretion to manage and control the assets of the plan, except to the extent that—

(1) the plan expressly provides that the trustee or trustees are subject to the direction of a named fiduciary who is not a trustee, in which case the trustees shall be subject to proper directions of such fiduciary which are made in accordance with the terms of the plan and which are not contrary to this Act, or

(2) authority to manage, acquire, or dispose of assets of the plan is delegated to one or more investment managers pursuant to section 402(c)(3).

(b) The requirements of subsection (a) of this section shall not apply—

(1) to any assets of a plan which consist of insurance contracts or policies issued by an insurance company qualified to do business in a State;

(2) to any assets of such an insurance company or any assets of a plan which are held by such an insurance company;

(3) to a plan—

(A) some or all of the participants of which are employees described in section 401(c)(1) of the Internal Revenue Code of 1986; or

(B) which consists of one or more individual retirement accounts described in section 408 of the Internal Revenue Code of 1986,

to the extent that such plan's assets are held in one or more custodial accounts which qualify under section 401(f) or 408(h) of such Code, whichever is applicable.

(4) to a plan which the Secretary exempts from the requirement of subsection (a) and which is not subject to any of the following provisions of this Act;

(A) part 2 of this subtitle,

(B) part 3 of this subtitle, or

(C) title IV of this Act; or

(5) to a contract established and maintained under section 403(b) of the Internal Revenue Code of 1954 to the extent that the assets of the contract are held in one or more custodial accounts pursuant to section 403(b)(7) of such Code.

(6) Any plan, fund or program under which an employer, all of whose stock is directly or indirectly owned by employees, former employees or their beneficiaries, proposes through an unfunded arrangement to compensate retired employees for benefits which were forfeited by such employees under a pension plan maintained by a former employer prior to the date such pension plan became subject to this Act.

(c)(1) Except as provided in paragraph (2), (3), or (4) or subsection (d), or under section 4042 and 4044 (relating to termination of insured plans) or under section 420 of the Internal Revenue Code of 1986 (as in effect on January 1, [1991] *1995*), the assets of a plan shall never inure to the benefit of any employer and shall be held for the exclusive purposes of providing benefits to participants in the plan and their beneficiaries and defraying reasonable expenses of administering the plan.

ERISA: The Law and the Code

(2)(A) In the case of a contribution, or a payment of withdrawal liability under part 1 of subtitle E of title IV—

(i) if such contribution or payment is made by an employer to a plan (other than a multiemployer plan) by a mistake of fact, paragraph (1) shall not prohibit the return of such contribution to the employer within one year after the payment of the contribution, and

(ii) if such contribution or payment is made by an employer to a multiemployer plan by a mistake of fact or law (other than a mistake relating to whether the plan is described in section 401(a) of the Internal Revenue Code of 1954 or the trust which is part of such plan is exempt from taxation under section 501(a) of such Code), paragraph (1) shall not prohibit the return of such contribution or payment to the employer within 6 months after the plan administrator determines that the contribution was made by such a mistake.

(B) If a contribution is conditioned on initial qualification of the plan under section 401 or 403(a) of the Internal Revenue Code of 1986, and if the plan receives an adverse determination with respect to its initial qualification, then paragraph (1) shall not prohibit the return of such contribution to the employer within one year after such determination, but only if the application for the determination is made by the time prescribed by law for filing the employer's return for the taxable year in which such plan was adopted, or such later date as the Secretary of the Treasury may prescribe.

(C) If a contribution is conditioned upon the deductibility of the contribution under section 404 of the Internal Revenue Code of 1954, then, to the extent the deduction is disallowed, paragraph (1) shall not prohibit the return to the employer of such contribution (to the extent disallowed) within one year after the disallowance of the deduction.

(3) In the case of a withdrawal liability payment which has been determined to be an overpayment, paragraph (1) shall not prohibit the return of such payment to the employer within 6 months after the date of such determination.

(d)(1) Upon termination of a pension plan to which section 4021 does not apply at the time of termination and to which this part applies (other than a plan to which no employer contributions have been made) the assets of the plan shall be allocated in accordance with the provisions of section 4044 of this Act, except as otherwise provided in regulations of the Secretary.

(2) The assets of a welfare plan which terminates shall be distributed in accordance with the terms of the plan, except as otherwise provided in regulations of the Secretary.

FIDUCIARY DUTIES

Sec. 404. (a)(1) Subject to sections 403(c) and (d), 4042, and 4044, a fiduciary shall discharge his duties with respect to a plan solely in the interest of the participants and beneficiaries and—

(A) for the exclusive purpose of:

(i) providing benefits to participants and their beneficiaries; and

(ii) defraying reasonable expenses of administering the plan;

(B) with the care, skill, prudence, and diligence under the circumstances then prevailing that a prudent man acting in a like capacity and familiar with such matters would use in the conduct of an enterprise of a like character and with like aims;

(C) by diversifying the investments of the plan so as to minimize the risk of large losses, unless under the circumstances it is clearly prudent not to do so; and

(D) in accordance with the documents and instruments governing the plan insofar as such documents and instruments are consistent with the provisions of this title and title IV.

ERISA Sec. 403 (c)(2)(A)

(2) In the case of an eligible individual account plan (as defined in section 407(d)(3)), the diversification requirement of paragraph (1)(C) and the prudence requirement (only to the extent that it requires diversification) of paragraph (1)(B) is not violated by acquisition or holding of qualifying employer real property or qualifying employer securities (as defined in section 407(d)(4) and (5)).

(b) Except as authorized by the Secretary by regulation, no fiduciary may maintain the indicia of ownership of any assets of a plan outside the jurisdiction of the district courts of the United States.

(c) In the case of a pension plan which provides for individual accounts and permits a participant or beneficiary to exercise control over assets in his account, if a participant or beneficiary exercises control over the assets in his account (as determined under regulations of the Secretary)—

(1) such participant or beneficiary shall not be deemed to be a fiduciary by reason of such exercise, and

(2) no person who is otherwise a fiduciary shall be liable under this part for any loss, or by reason of any breach, which results from such participant's, or beneficiary's exercise of control.

(d)(1) If, in connection with the termination of a pension plan which is a single employer plan, there is an election to establish or maintain a qualified replacement plan, or to increase benefits, as provided under section 4980(d) of the Internal Revenue Code of 1986, a fiduciary shall discharge the fiduciary's duties under this title and title IV in accordance with the following requirements:

(A) In the case of a fiduciary of the terminated plan, any requirement—

(i) under section 4980(d)(2)(B) of such Code with respect to the transfer of assets from the terminated plan to a qualified replacement plan, and

(ii) under section 4980(d)(2)(B)(ii) or 4980(d)(3) of such Code with respect to any increase in benefits under the terminated plan.

(B) In the case of a fiduciary of a qualified replacement plan, any requirement—

(i) under section 4980(d)(2)(A) of such code with respect to participation in the qualified replacement plan of active participants in the terminated plan.

(ii) under section 4980(d)(2)(B) of such Code with respect to the receipt of assets from the terminated plan, and

(iii) under section 4980(d)(2)(c) of such Code with respect to the allocation of assets to participants of the qualified replacement plan.

(2) For purposes of this subsection—

(A) any term used in this subsection which is also then used in section 4980(d) of the Internal Revenue Code of 1986 shall have the same meaning as when used in such section, and

(B) any reference to this subsection in the Internal Revenue Code of 1986 should be a reference to such Code as in effect immediately after the enactment of the Omnibus Budget Reconciliation Act of 1990.

LIABILITY FOR BREACH BY COFIDUCIARY

Sec. 405. (a) In addition to any liability which he may have under any other provision of this part, a fiduciary with respect to a plan shall be liable for a breach of fiduciary responsibility of another fiduciary with respect to the same plan in the following circumstances:

(1) if he participates knowingly in, or knowingly undertakes to conceal, an act or omission of such other fiduciary, knowing such act or omission is a breach;

(2) if, by his failure to comply with section 404(a)(1) in the administration of his specific responsibilities which give rise to his status as a fiduciary, he has enabled such other fiduciary to commit a breach; or

(3) if he has knowledge of a breach by such other fiduciary, unless he makes reasonable efforts under the circumstances to remedy the breach.

(b)(1) Except as otherwise provided in subsection (d) and in section 403(a)(1) and (2), if the assets of a plan are held by two or more trustees—

(A) each shall use reasonable care to prevent a co-trustee from committing a breach; and

(B) they shall jointly manage and control the assets of the plan, except that nothing in this subparagraph (B) shall preclude any agreement, authorized by the trust instrument, allocating specific responsibilities, obligations, or duties among trustees, in which event a trustee to whom certain responsibilities, obligations, or duties have not been allocated shall not be liable by reason of this subparagraph (B) either individually or as a trustee for any loss resulting to the plan arising from the acts or omissions on the part of another trustee to whom such responsibilities, obligations, or duties have been allocated.

(2) Nothing in this subsection shall limit any liability that a fiduciary may have under subsection (a) or any other provision of this part.

(3)(A) In the case of a plan the assets of which are held in more than one trust, a trustee shall not be liable under paragraph (1) except with respect to an act or omission of a trustee of a trust of which he is a trustee.

(B) No trustee shall be liable under this subsection for following instructions referred to in section 403(a)(1).

(c)(1) The instrument under which a plan is maintained may expressly provide for procedures (A) for allocating fiduciary responsibilities (other than trustee responsibilities) among named fiduciaries, and (B) for named fiduciaries to designate persons other than named fiduciaries to carry out fiduciary responsibilities (other than trustee responsibilities) under the plan.

(2) If a plan expressly provides for a procedure described in paragraph (1), and pursuant to such procedure any fiduciary responsibility of a named fiduciary is allocated to any person, or a person is designated to carry out any such responsibility, then such named fiduciary shall not be liable for an act or omission of such person in carrying out such responsibility except to the extent that—

(A) the named fiduciary violated section 404(a)(1)—

(i) with respect to such allocation or designation,

(ii) with respect to the establishment or implementation of the procedure under paragraph (1), or

(iii) in continuing the allocation or designation; or

(B) the named fiduciary would otherwise be liable in accordance with subsection (a).

(3) For purposes of this subsection, the term "trustee responsibility" means any responsibility provided in the plan's trust instrument (if any) to manage or control the assets of the plan, other than a power under the trust instrument of a named fiduciary to appoint an investment manager in accordance with section 402(c)(3).

(d)(1) If an investment manager or managers have been appointed under section 402(c)(3), then, notwithstanding subsections (a)(2) and (3) and subsection (b), no trustee shall be liable for the acts or omissions of such investment manager or managers, or be under an obligation to invest or otherwise manage any asset of the plan which is subject to the management of such investment manager.

(2) Nothing in this subsection shall relieve any trustee of any liability under this part for any act of such trustee.

ERISA Sec. 405 (a)(3)

PROHIBITED TRANSACTIONS

Sec. 406. (a) Except as provided in section 408:

(1) A fiduciary with respect to a plan shall not cause the plan to engage in a transaction, if he knows or should know that such transaction constitutes a direct or indirect—

(A) sale or exchange, or leasing, of any property between the plan and a party in interest;

(B) lending of money or other extension of credit between the plan and a party in interest;

(C) furnishing of goods, services, or facilities between the plan and a party in interest;

(D) transfer to, or use by or for the benefit of, a party in interest, of any assets of the plan; or

(E) acquisition, on behalf of the plan, of any employer security or employer real property in violation of section 407(a).

(2) No fiduciary who has authority or discretion to control or manage the assets of a plan shall permit the plan to hold any employer security or employer real property if he knows or should know that holding such security or real property violates section 407(a).

(b) A fiduciary with respect to a plan shall not—

(1) deal with the assets of the plan in his own interest or for his own account,

(2) in his individual or any other capacity act in any transaction involving the plan on behalf of a party (or represent a party) whose interests are adverse to the interests of the plan or the interests of its participants or beneficiaries, or

(3) receive any consideration for his own personal account from any party dealing with such plan in connection with a transaction involving the assets of the plan.

(c) A transfer of real or personal property by a party in interest to a plan shall be treated as a sale or exchange if the property is subject to a mortgage or similar lien which the plan assumes or if it is subject to a mortgage or similar lien which a party-in-interest placed on the property within the 10-year period ending on the date of the transfer.

10 PERCENT LIMITATION WITH RESPECT TO ACQUISITION AND HOLDING OF EMPLOYER SECURITIES AND EMPLOYER REAL PROPERTY BY CERTAIN PLANS

Sec. 407. (a) Except as otherwise provided in this section and section 414:

(1) A plan may not acquire or hold—

(A) any employer security which is not a qualifying employer security, or

(B) any employer real property which is not qualifying employer real property.

(2) A plan may not acquire any qualifying employer security or qualifying employer real property, if immediately after such acquisition the aggregate fair market value of employer securities and employer real property held by the plan exceeds 10 percent of the fair market value of the assets of the plan.

(3)(A) After December 31, 1984, a plan may not hold any qualifying employer securities or qualifying employer real property (or both) to the extent that the aggregate fair market value of such securities and property determined on December 31, 1984, exceeds 10 percent of the greater of—

(i) the fair market value of the assets of the plan, determined on December 31, 1984, or

(ii) the fair market value of the assets of the plan determined on January 1, 1975.

(B) Subparagraph (A) of this paragraph shall not apply to any plan which on any date after December 31, 1974, and before January 1, 1985, did not hold employer securities or employer real property (or both) the aggregate fair market value of which determined on such date exceeded 10 percent of the greater of—

(i) the fair market value of the assets of the plan, determined on such date, or

(ii) the fair market value of the assets of the plan determined on January 1, 1975.

(4)(A) After December 31, 1979, a plan may not hold any employer securities or employer real property in excess of the amount specified in regulations under subparagraph (B). This subparagraph shall not apply to a plan after the earliest date after December 31, 1974, on which it complies with such regulations.

(B) Not later than December 31, 1976, the Secretary shall prescribe regulations which shall have the effect of requiring that a plan divest itself of 50 percent of the holdings of employer securities and employer real property which the plan would be required to divest before January 1, 1985, under paragraph (2) or subsection (c) (whichever is applicable).

(b)(1) Subsection (a) of this section shall not apply to any acquisition or holding of qualifying employer securities or qualifying employer real property by an eligible individual account plan.

(2) Cross References.—

(A) For exemption from diversification requirements for holding of qualifying employer securities and qualifying employer real property by eligible individual account plans, see section 404(a)(2).

(B) For exemption from prohibited transactions for certain acquisitions of qualifying employer securities and qualifying employer real property which are not in violation of the 10 percent limitation, see section 408(e).

(C) For transitional rules respecting securities or real property subject to binding contracts in effect on June 30, 1974, see section 414(c).

(c)(1) A plan which makes the election, under paragraph (3) shall be treated as satisfying the requirement of subsection (a)(3) if and only if employer securities held on any date after December 31, 1974 and before January 1, 1985 have a fair market value, determined as of December 31, 1974, not in excess of 10 percent of the lesser of—

(A) the fair market value of the assets of the plan determined on such date (disregarding any portion of the fair market value of employer securities which is attributable to appreciation of such securities after December 31, 1974) but not less than the fair market value of plan assets on January 1, 1975, or

(B) an amount equal to the sum of (i) the total amount of the contributions to the plan received after December 31, 1974, and prior to such date, plus (ii) the fair market value of the assets of the plan, determined on January 1, 1975.

(2) For purposes of this subsection, in the case of an employer security held by a plan after January 1, 1975, the ownership of which is derived from ownership of employer securities held by the plan on January 1, 1975, or from the exercise of rights derived from such ownership, the value of such security held after January 1, 1975, shall be based on the value as of January 1, 1975, of the security from which ownership was derived. The Secretary shall prescribe regulations to carry out this paragraph.

(3) An election under this paragraph may not be made after December 31, 1975. Such an election shall be made in accordance with regulations prescribed by the Secretary, and shall be irrevocable. A plan may make an election under this paragraph only if on January 1, 1975, the plan holds no employer real property. After such election and before January 1, 1985 the plan may not acquire any employer real property.

(d) For purposes of this section—

(1) The term "employer security" means a security issued by an employer of employees

covered by the plan, or by an affiliate of such employer. A contract to which section 408(b)(5) applies shall not be treated as a security for purposes of this section.

(2) The term "employer real property" means real property (and related personal property) which is leased to an employer of employees covered by the plan, or to an affiliate of such employer. For purposes of determining the time at which a plan acquires employer real property for purposes of this section, such property shall be deemed to be acquired by the plan on the date on which the plan acquires the property or on the date on which the lease to the employer (or affiliate) is entered into, whichever is later.

(3)(A) The term "eligible individual account plan" means an individual account plan which is (i) a profit-sharing, stock bonus, thrift, or savings plan; (ii) an employee stock ownership plan; or (iii) a money purchase plan which was in existence on the date of enactment of this Act and which on such date invested primarily in qualifying employer securities. Such term excludes an individual retirement account or annuity described in section 408 of the Internal Revenue Code of 1954.

(B) Notwithstanding subparagraph (A), a plan shall be treated as an eligible individual account plan with respect to the acquisition or holding of qualifying employer real property or qualifying employer securities only if such plan explicitly provides for acquisition and holding of qualifying employer securities or qualifying employer real property (as the case may be). In the case of a plan in existence on the date of enactment of this Act, this subparagraph shall not take effect until January 1, 1976.

(C) The term "eligible individual account plan" does not include any individual account plan the benefits of which are taken into account in determining the benefits payable to a participant under any defined benefit plan.

(4) The term "qualifying employer real property" means parcels of employer real property—

(A) if a substantial number of the parcels are dispersed geographically;

(B) if each parcel of real property and the improvements thereon are suitable (or adaptable without excessive cost) for more than one use;

(C) even if all of such real property is leased to one lessee (which may be an employer, or an affiliate of an employer); and

(D) if the acquisition and retention of such property comply with the provisions of this part (other than section 404(a)(1)(B) to the extent it requires diversification, and sections 404(a)(1)(C), 406, and subsection (a) of this section).

(5) The term "qualifying employer security" means an employer security which is—

(A) stock

(B) a marketable obligation (as defined in subsection (e)), or

(C) an interest in a publicly traded partnership (as defined in section 7704(b) of the Internal Revenue Code of 1986), but only if such partnership is an existing partnership as defined in section 10211(c)(2)(A) of the Revenue Act of 1987 (Public Law 100-203). After December 17, 1987, in the case of a plan other than an eligible individual account plan, an employer security described in subparagraph (A) or (C) shall be considered a qualifying employer security only if such employer security satisfies the requirements of subsection (f)(1).

(6) The term "employee stock ownership plan" means an individual account plan—

(A) which is a stock bonus plan which is qualified, or a stock bonus plan and money purchase plan both of which are qualified, under section 401 of the Internal Revenue Code of 1954, and which is designed to invest primarily in qualifying employer securities, and

(B) which meets such other requirements as the Secretary of the Treasury may prescribe by regulation.

(7) A corporation is an affiliate of an employer if it is a member of any controlled group of corporations (as defined in section 1563(a) of the Internal Revenue Code of 1954, except that "applicable percentage" shall be substituted for "80 percent" wherever the latter percentage appears in such section) of which the employer who maintains the plan is a member. For purposes of the preceding sentence, the term "applicable percentage" means 50 percent, or such lower percentage as the Secretary may prescribe by regulation. A person other than a corporation shall be treated as an affiliate of an employer to the extent provided in regulations of the Secretary. An employer which is a person other than a corporation shall be treated as affiliated with another person to the extent provided by regulations of the Secretary. Regulations under this paragraph shall be prescribed only after consultation and coordination with the Secretary of the Treasury.

(8) The Secretary may prescribe regulations specifying the extent to which conversions, splits, the exercise of rights, and similar transactions are not treated as acquisitions.

(9) For purposes of this section, an arrangement which consists of a defined benefit plan and an individual account plan shall be treated as 1 plan if the benefits of such individual account plan are taken into account in determining the benefits payable under such defined benefit plan.

(e) For purposes of subsection (d)(5), the term "marketable obligation" means a bond, debenture, note, or certificate, or other evidence of indebtedness (hereinafter in this subsection referred to as "obligation") if—

(1) such obligation is acquired—

(A) on the market, either (i) at the price of the obligation prevailing on a national secu-

rities exchange which is registered with the Securities and Exchange Commission, or (ii) if the obligation is not traded on such a national securities exchange, at a price not less favorable to the plan than the offering price for the obligation as established by current bid and asked prices quoted by persons independent of the issuer;

(B) from an underwriter, at a price (i) not in excess of the public offering price for the obligation as set forth in a prospectus or offering circular filed with the Securities and Exchange Commission, and (ii) at which a substantial portion of the same issue is acquired by persons independent of the issuer; or

(C) directly from the issuer, at a price not less favorable to the plan than the price paid currently for a substantial portion of the same issue by persons independent of the issuer;

(2) immediately following acquisition of such obligation—

(A) not more than 25 percent of the aggregate amount of obligations issued in such issue and outstanding at the time of acquisition is held by the plan, and

(B) at least 50 percent of the aggregate amount referred to in subparagraph (A) is held by persons independent of the issuer; and

(3) immediately following acquisition of the obligation, not more than 25 percent of the assets of the plan is invested in obligations of the employer or an affiliate of the employer.

(f)(1) Stock satisfies the requirements of this paragraph if, immediately following the acquisition of such stock—

(A) no more than 25 percent of the aggregate amount of stock of the same class issued and outstanding at the time of acquisition is held by the plan, and

ERISA Sec. 407 (d)(6)(B)

(B) at least 50 percent of the aggregate amount referred to in subparagraph (A) is held by persons independent of the issuer.

(2) Until January 1, 1993, a plan shall not be treated as violating subsection (a) solely by holding stock which fails to satisfy the requirements of paragraph (1) if such stock—

(A) has been so held since December 17, 1987, or

(B) was acquired after December 17, 1987, pursuant to a legally binding contract in effect on December 17, 1987, and has been so held at all times after the acquisition.

(3) After December 17, 1987, no plan may acquire stock which does not satisfy the requirements of paragraph (1) unless the acquisition is made pursuant to a legally binding contract in effect on such date.

EXEMPTIONS FROM PROHIBITED TRANSACTIONS

Sec. 408. (a) The Secretary shall establish an exemption procedure for purposes of this subsection. Pursuant to such procedure, he may grant a conditional or unconditional exemption of any fiduciary or transaction, or class of fiduciaries or transactions, from all or part of the restrictions imposed by sections 406 and 407(a). Action under this subsection may be taken only after consultation and coordination with the Secretary of the Treasury. An exemption granted under this section shall not relieve a fiduciary from any other applicable provision of this Act. The Secretary may not grant an exemption under this subsection unless he finds that such exemption is—

(1) administratively feasible,

(2) in the interests of the plan and of its participants and beneficiaries, and

(3) protective of the rights of participants and beneficiaries of such plan.

Before granting an exemption under this subsection from section 406(a) or 407(a), the Secretary shall publish notice in the Federal Register of the pendency of the exemption, shall require that adequate notice be given to interested persons, and shall afford interested persons opportunity to present views. The Secretary may not grant an exemption under this subsection from section 406(b) unless he affords an opportunity for a hearing and makes a determination on the record with respect to the findings required by paragraphs (1), (2), and (3) of this subsection.

(b) The prohibitions provided in section 406 shall not apply to any of the following transactions:

(1) Any loans made by the plan to parties in interest who are participants or beneficiaries of the plan if such loans (A) are available to all such participants and beneficiaries on a reasonably equivalent basis, (B) are not made available to highly compensated employees (within the meaning of section 414(q) of the Internal Revenue Code of 1986) in an amount greater than the amount made available to other employees, (C) are made in accordance with specific provisions regarding such loans set forth in the plan, (D) bear a reasonable rate of interest, and (E) are adequately secured.

(2) Contracting or making reasonable arrangements with a party in interest for office space, or legal, accounting, or other services necessary for the establishment or operation of the plan, if no more than reasonable compensation is paid therefor.

(3) A loan to an employee stock ownership plan (as defined in section 407(d)(6)), if—

(A) such loan is primarily for the benefit of participants and beneficiaries of the plan, and

(B) such loan is at an interest rate which is not in excess of a reasonable rate.

If the plan gives collateral to a party in interest for such loan, such collateral may consist only of qualifying employer securities (as defined in section 407(d)(5)).

(4) The investment of all or part of a plan's assets in deposits which bear a reasonable

interest rate in a bank or similar financial institution supervised by the United States or a State, if such bank or other institution is a fiduciary of such plan and if—

(A) the plan covers only employees of such bank or other institution and employees of affiliates of such bank or other institution, or

(B) such investment is expressly authorized by a provision of the plan or by a fiduciary (other than such bank or institution or affiliate thereof) who is expressly empowered by the plan to so instruct the trustee with respect to such investment.

(5) Any contract for life insurance, health insurance, or annuities with one or more insurers which are qualified to do business in a State, if the plan pays no more than adequate consideration, and if each such insurer or insurers is—

(A) the employer maintaining the plan, or

(B) a party in interest which is wholly owned (directly or indirectly) by the employer maintaining the plan, or by any person which is a party in interest with respect to the plan, but only if the total premiums and annuity considerations written by such insurers for life insurance, health insurance, or annuities for all plans (and their employers) with respect to which such insurers are parties in interest (not including premiums or annuity considerations written by the employer maintaining the plan) do not exceed 5 percent of the total premiums and annuity considerations written for all lines of insurance in that year by such insurers (not including premiums or annuity considerations written by the employer maintaining the plan).

(6) The providing of any ancillary service by a bank or similar financial institution supervised by the United States or a State, if such bank or other institution is a fiduciary of such plan, and if—

(A) such bank or similar financial institution has adopted adequate internal safeguards which assure that the providing of such an-

cillary service is consistent with sound banking and financial practice, as determined by Federal or State supervisory authority, and

(B) the extent to which such ancillary service is provided is subject to specific guidelines issued by such bank or similar financial institution (as determined by the Secretary after consultation with Federal and State supervisory authority), and adherence to such guidelines would reasonably preclude such bank or similar financial institution from providing such ancillary service (i) in an excessive or unreasonable manner, and (ii) in a manner that would be inconsistent with the best interests of participants and beneficiaries of employee benefit plans.

Such ancillary services shall not be provided at more than reasonable compensation.

(7) The exercise of a privilege to convert securities, to the extent provided in regulations of the Secretary, but only if the plan receives no less than adequate consideration pursuant to such conversion.

(8) Any transaction between a plan and (i) a common or collective trust fund or pooled investment fund maintained by a party in interest which is a bank or trust company supervised by a State or Federal agency or (ii) a pooled investment fund of an insurance company qualified to do business in a State, if—

(A) the transaction is a sale or purchase of an interest in the fund,

(B) the bank, trust company, or insurance company receives not more than reasonable compensation, and

(C) such transaction is expressly permitted by the instrument under which the plan is maintained, or by a fiduciary (other than the bank, trust company, or insurance company, or an affiliate thereof) who has authority to manage and control the assets of the plan.

(9) The making by a fiduciary of a distribution of the assets of the plan in accordance with the terms of the plan if such assets are distributed in the same manner as provided under

section 4044 of this Act (relating to allocation of assets).

(10) Any transaction required or permitted under part 1 of subtitle E of title IV.

(11) A merger of multiemployer plans, or the transfer of assets or liabilities between multiemployer plans, determined by the Pension Benefit Guaranty Corporation to meet the requirements of section 4231.

(12) The sale by a plan to a party in interest on or after December 18, 1987, of any stock, if—

(A) the requirements of paragraphs (1) and (2) of subsection (e) are met with respect to such stock,

(B) on the later of the date on which the stock was acquired by the plan, or January 1, 1975, such stock constituted a qualifying employer security (as defined in section 407(d)(5) as then in effect), and

(C) such stock does not constitute a qualifying employer security (as defined in section 407(d)(5) as in effect at the time of the sale).

(13) Any transfer in a taxable year beginning before January 1, [1996] *2001*, of excess pension assets from a defined benefit plan to a retiree health account in a qualified transfer permitted under section 420 of the Internal Revenue Code of 1986 (as in effect on January 1, [1991] 1995.)

(c) Nothing in section 406 shall be construed to prohibit any fiduciary from—

(1) receiving any benefit to which he may be entitled as a participant or beneficiary in the plan, so long as the benefit is computed and paid on a basis which is consistent with the terms of the plan as applied to all other participants and beneficiaries;

(2) receiving any reasonable compensation for services rendered, or for the reimbursement of expenses properly and actually incurred, in the performance of his duties with the plan; except that no person so serving who already receives full-time pay from an em-

ployer or an association of employers, whose employees are participants in the plan, or from an employee organization whose members are participants in such plan shall receive compensation from such plan, except for reimbursement of expenses properly and actually incurred; or

(3) serving as a fiduciary in addition to being an officer, employee, agent, or other representative of a party in interest.

(d) Section 407(b) and subsections (b), (c), and (e) of this section shall not apply to any transaction in which a plan, directly or indirectly—

(1) lends any part of the corpus or income of the plan to;

(2) pays any compensation for personal services rendered to the plan to; or

(3) acquires for the plan any property from or sells any property to;
any person who is with respect to the plan an owner-employee (as defined in section 401(c)(3) of the Internal Revenue Code of 1954), a member of the family (as defined in section 267(c)(4) of such Code) of any such owner-employee, or a corporation controlled by any such owner-employee through the ownership, directly or indirectly, of 50 percent or more of the total combined voting power of all classes of stock entitled to vote or 50 percent or more of the total value of shares of all classes of stock of the corporation. For purposes of this subsection a shareholder employee (as defined in section 1379 of the Internal Revenue Code of 1954) as in effect on the day before the date of enactment of the Subchapter S Revision Act of 1982 and a participant or beneficiary of an individual retirement account or individual retirement annuity described in section 408 of the Internal Revenue Code of 1986 or a retirement bond described in section 409 of the Internal Revenue Code of 1954 (as effective for such obligations issued before January 1, 1984) and an employer or association of employers which establishes such an account or annuity under section 408(c) of the Internal Revenue Code

of 1986 shall be deemed to be an owner-employee.

(e) Sections 406 and 407 shall not apply to the acquisition or sale by a plan of qualifying employer securities (as defined in section 407(d)(5)) or acquisition, sale or lease by a plan of qualifying employer real property (as defined in section 407(d)(4))—

(1) if such acquisition, sale, or lease is for adequate consideration (or in the case of a marketable obligation, at a price not less favorable to the plan than the price determined under section 407(e)(1)),

(2) if no commission is charged with respect thereto, and

(3) If—

(A) the plan is an eligible individual account plan (as defined in section 407(d)(3)), or

(B) in the case of an acquisition or lease of qualifying employer real property by a plan which is not an eligible individual account plan, or of an acquisition of qualifying employer securities by such a plan, the lease or acquisition is not prohibited by section 407(a).

(f) Section 406(b)(2) shall not apply to any merger or transfer described in subsection (b)(11).

LIABILITY FOR BREACH OF FIDUCIARY DUTY

Sec. 409. (a) Any person who is a fiduciary with respect to a plan who breaches any of the responsibilities, obligations, or duties imposed upon fiduciaries by this title shall be personally liable to make good to such plan any losses to the plan resulting from each such breach, and to restore to such plan any profits of such fiduciary which have been made through use of assets of the plan by the fiduciary, and shall be subject to such other equitable or remedial relief as the court may deem appropriate, including removal of such fiduciary. A fiduciary may also be removed for a violation of section 411 of this Act.

(b) No fiduciary shall be liable with respect to a breach of fiduciary duty under this title if such breach was committed before he became a fiduciary or after he ceased to be a fiduciary.

EXCULPATORY PROVISIONS; INSURANCE

Sec. 410. (a) Except as provided in sections 405(b)(1) and 405(d), any provision in an agreement or instrument which purports to relieve a fiduciary from responsibility or liability for any responsibility, obligation, or duty under this part shall be void as against public policy.

(b) Nothing in this subpart shall preclude—

(1) a plan from purchasing insurance for its fiduciaries or for itself to cover liability or losses occurring by reason of the act or omission of a fiduciary, if such insurance permits recourse by the insurer against the fiduciary in the case of a breach of a fiduciary obligation by such fiduciary;

(2) a fiduciary from purchasing insurance to cover liability under this part from and for his own account; or

(3) an employer or an employee organization from purchasing insurance to cover potential liability of one or more persons who serve in a fiduciary capacity with regard to an employee benefit plan.

PROHIBITION AGAINST CERTAIN PERSONS HOLDING CERTAIN POSITIONS

Sec. 411. (a) No person who has been convicted of, or has been imprisoned as a result of his conviction of, robbery, bribery, extortion, embezzlement, fraud, grand larceny, burglary, arson, a felony violation of Federal or State law involving substances defined in section 102(6) of the Comprehensive Drug Abuse Prevention and Control Act of 1970, murder, rape, kidnaping, perjury, assault with intent to kill, any crime described in section 9(a)(1) of the Investment Company Act of 1940 (15 U.S.C. 80a-9(a)(1)), a violation of any provision of this Act, a violation of section 302 of the Labor-Management Relations Act, 1947 (29 U.S.C. 186), a violation of chapter 63 of title 18, United States Code, a violation of section 874, 1027, 1503, 1505, 1506, 1510, 1951, or 1954 of title 18, United States Code, a violation of the Labor-Management Reporting and Disclosure Act of 1959 (29 U.S.C. 401), any felony involving abuse or misuse of such person's position or employment in a labor organization or employee benefit plan to seek or obtain an illegal gain at the expense of the members of the labor organization or the beneficiaries of the employee benefit plan, or conspiracy to commit any such crimes or attempt to commit any such crimes, or a crime in which any of the foregoing crimes is an element, shall serve or be permitted to serve—

(1) as an administrator, fiduciary, officer, trustee, custodian, counsel, agent, employee, or representative in any capacity of any employee benefit plan,

(2) as a consultant or adviser to an employee benefit plan, including but not limited to any entity whose activities are in whole or substantial part devoted to providing goods or services to any employee benefit plan, or

(3) in any capacity that involves decision-making authority or custody or control of the moneys, funds, assets, or property of any employee benefit plan, during or for the period of thirteen years after such conviction or after the end of such imprisonment, whichever is later, unless the sentencing court on the motion of the person convicted set a lesser period of at least three years after such conviction or after the end of such imprisonment, whichever is later, or unless prior to the end of such period, in the case of a person so convicted or imprisoned (A) his citizenship rights, having been revoked as a result of such conviction, have been fully restored, or (B) if the offense is a Federal offense, the sentencing judge or, if the offense is a State or local offense, the United States district court for the district in which the offense was committed, pursuant to sentencing guidelines and policy statements under section 994(a) of title 28, United States Code,

determined that such person's service in any capacity referred to in paragraphs (1) through (3) would not be contrary to the purposes of this title.

Prior to making any such determination the court shall hold a hearing and shall give notice to such proceeding by certified mail to the Secretary of Labor and to State, county, and Federal prosecuting officials in the jurisdiction or jurisdictions in which such person was convicted. The court's determination in any such proceeding shall be final. No person shall knowingly hire, retain, employ, or otherwise place any other person to serve in any capacity in violation of this subsection. Notwithstanding the preceding provisions of this subsection, no corporation or partnership will be precluded from acting as an administrator, fiduciary, officer, trustee, custodian, counsel, agent, or employee of any employee benefit plan or as a consultant to any employee benefit plan without a notice, hearing, and determination by such court that such service would be inconsistent with the intention of this section.

(b) Any person who intentionally violates this section shall be fined not more than $10,000 or imprisoned for not more than five years, or both.

(c) For the purpose of this section:

(1) A person shall be deemed to have been "convicted" and under the disability of "conviction" from the date of the judgment of the trial court, regardless of whether that judgment remains under appeal.

(2) The term "consultant" means any person who, for compensation, advises or represents an employee benefit plan or who provides other assistance to such plan, concerning the establishment or operation of such plan.

(3) A period of parole or supervised release shall not be considered as part of a period of imprisonment.

(d) Whenever any person—

(1) by operation of this section, has been barred from office or other position in an employee benefit plan as a result of a conviction, and

(2) has filed an appeal of that conviction, any salary which would be otherwise due such person by virtue of such office or position, shall be placed in escrow by the individual or organization responsible for payment of such salary. Payment of such salary into escrow shall continue for the duration of the appeal or for the period of time during which such salary would be otherwise due, whichever is shorter.

Upon the final reversal of such person's conviction on appeal, the amounts in escrow shall be paid to such person. Upon the final sustaining of that person's conviction on appeal, the amounts in escrow shall be returned to the individual or organization responsible for payments of those amounts. Upon final reversal of such person's conviction, such person shall no longer be barred by this statute from assuming any position from which such person was previously barred.

BONDING

Sec. 412. (a) Every fiduciary of an employee benefit plan and every person who handles funds or other property of such a plan (hereafter in this section referred to as "plan official") shall be bonded as provided in this section; except that—

(1) where such plan is one under which the only assets from which benefits are paid are the general assets of a union or of an employer, the administrator, officers, and employees of such plan shall be exempt from the bonding requirements of this section, and

(2) no bond shall be required of a fiduciary (or of any director, officer, or employee of such fiduciary) if such fiduciary—

(A) is a corporation organized and doing business under the laws of the United States or of any State;

(B) is authorized under such laws to exercise trust powers or to conduct an insurance business;

(C) is subject to supervision or examination by Federal or State authority; and

(D) has at all times a combined capital and surplus in excess of such a minimum amount as may be established by regulations issued by the Secretary, which amount shall be at least $1,000,000. Paragraph (2) shall apply to a bank or other financial institution which is authorized to exercise trust powers and the deposits of which are not insured by the Federal Deposit Insurance Corporation, only if such bank or institution meets bonding or similar requirements under State law which the Secretary determines are at least equivalent to those imposed on banks by Federal law.

The amount of such bond shall be fixed at the beginning of each fiscal year of the plan. Such amount shall be not less than 10 per centum of the amount of funds handled. In no case shall such bond be less than $1,000 nor more than $500,000, except that the Secretary, after due notice and opportunity for hearing to all interested parties, and after consideration of the record, may prescribe an amount in excess of $500,000, subject to the 10 per centum limitation of the preceding sentence. For purposes of fixing the amount of such bond, the amount of funds handled shall be determined by the funds handled by the person, group, or class to be covered by such bond and by their predecessor or predecessors, if any, during the preceding reporting year, or if the plan has no preceding reporting year, the amount of funds to be handled during the current reporting year by such person, group, or class, estimated as provided in regulations of the Secretary. Such bond shall provide protection to the plan against loss by reason of acts of fraud or dishonesty on the part of the plan official, directly or through connivance with others. Any bond shall have as surety thereon a corporate surety company which is an acceptable surety on Federal bonds under authority granted by the Secretary of the Treasury pursuant to sections 6 through 13 of title 6, United States Code. Any bond shall be in a form or of a type approved by the Secretary, including individual bonds or schedule or blanket forms of bonds which cover a group or class.

(b) It shall be unlawful for any plan official to whom subsection (a) applies, to receive, handle, disburse, or otherwise exercise custody or control of any of the funds or other property of any employee benefit plan, without being bonded as required by subsection (a) and it shall be unlawful for any plan official of such plan, or any other person having authority to direct the performance of such functions, to permit such functions, or any of them, to be performed by any plan official, with respect to whom the requirements of subsection (a) have not been met.

(c) It shall be unlawful for any person to procure any bond required by subsection (a) from any surety or other company or through any agent or broker in whose business operations such plan or any party in interest in such plan has any control or significant financial interest, direct or indirect.

(d) Nothing in any other provision of law shall require any person, required to be bonded as provided in subsection (a) because he handles funds or other property of an employee benefit plan, to be bonded insofar as the handling by such person of the funds or other property of such plan is concerned.

(e) The Secretary shall prescribe such regulations as may be necessary to carry out the provisions of this section including exempting a plan from the requirements of this section where he finds that (1) other bonding arrangements or (2) the overall financial condition of the plan would be adequate to protect the interests of the beneficiaries and participants. When, in the opinion of the Secretary, the administrator of a plan offers adequate evidence of the financial responsibility of the plan, or that other bonding arrangements would provide adequate protection of the beneficiaries and participants, he may exempt such plan from the requirements of this section.

LIMITATION OF ACTIONS

Sec. 413. No action may be commenced under this title with respect to a fiduciary's breach of any responsibility, duty, or obligation under this part, or with respect to a violation of this part, after the earlier of—

(1) six years after (A) the date of the last action which constituted a part of the breach or violation, or (B) in the case of an omission, the latest date on which the fiduciary could have cured the breach or violation, or

(2) three years after the earliest date on which the plaintiff had actual knowledge of the breach or violation;

except that in the case of fraud or concealment, such action may be commenced not later than six years after the date of discovery of such breach or violation.

EFFECTIVE DATE

Sec. 414. **(a)** Except as provided in subsections (b), (c), and (d), this part shall take effect on January 1, 1975.

(b)(1) The provisions of this part authorizing the Secretary to promulgate regulations shall take effect on the date of enactment of this Act.

(2) Upon application of a plan, the Secretary may postpone until not later than January 1, 1976, the applicability of any provision of sections 402, 403 (other than 403(c)), 405 (other than 405(a) and (d)), and 410(a), as it applies to any plan in existence on the date of enactment of this Act if he determines such postponement is (A) necessary to amend the instrument establishing the plan under which the plan is maintained and (B) not adverse to the interest of participants and beneficiaries.

(3) This part shall take effect on the date of enactment of this Act with respect to a plan which terminates after June 30, 1974, and before January 1, 1975, and to which at the time of termination section 4021 applies.

ERISA Sec. 414 (b)(3)

(c) Section 406 and 407(a) (relating to prohibited transactions) shall not apply—

(1) until June 30, 1984, to a loan of money or other extension of credit between a plan and a party in interest under a binding contract in effect on July 1, 1974 (or pursuant to renewals of such a contract), if such loan or other extension of credit remains at least as favorable to the plan as an arm's-length transaction with an unrelated party would be, and if the execution of the contract, the making of the loan, or the extension of credit was not, at the time of such execution, making, or extension, a prohibited transaction (within the meaning of section 503(b) of the Internal Revenue Code of 1954 or the corresponding provisions of prior law);

(2) until June 30, 1984, to a lease or joint use of property involving the plan and a party in interest pursuant to a binding contract in effect on July 1, 1974 (or pursuant to renewals of such a contract), if such lease or joint use remains at least as favorable to the plan as an arm's-length transaction with an unrelated party would be and if the execution of the contract was not, at the time of such execution, a prohibited transaction (within the meaning of section 503(b) of the Internal Revenue Code of 1986 or the corresponding provisions of prior law);

(3) until June 30, 1984, to the sale, exchange, or other disposition of property described in paragraph (2) between a plan and a party in interest if—

(A) in the case of a sale, exchange, or other disposition of the property by the plan to the party in interest, the plan receives an amount which is not less than the fair market value of the property at the time of such disposition; and

(B) in the case of the acquisition of the property by the plan, the plan pays an amount which is not in excess of the fair market value of the property at the time of such acquisition;

(4) until June 30, 1977, to the provision of services, to which paragraphs (1), (2), and (3)

do not apply between a plan and a party in interest—

(A) under a binding contract in effect on July 1, 1974 (or pursuant to renewals of such contract), or

(B) if the party in interest ordinarily and customarily furnished such services on June 30, 1974, if such provision of services remains at least as favorable to the plan as an arm's-length transaction with an unrelated party would be and if such provision of services was not, at the time of such provision, a prohibited transaction (within the meaning of section 503(b) of the Internal Revenue Code of 1954) or the corresponding provisions of prior law; or

(5) the sale, exchange, or other disposition of property which is owned by a plan on June 30, 1974, and all times thereafter, to a party in interest, if such plan is required to dispose of such property in order to comply with the provisions of section 407(a) (relating to the prohibition against holding excess employer securities and employer real property), and if the plan receives not less than adequate consideration.

(d) Any election, or failure to elect, by a disqualified person under section 2003 (c)(1)(B) of this Act shall be treated for purposes of this part (but not for purposes of section 514) as an act or omission occurring before the effective date of this part.

(e) The preceding provisions of this section shall not apply with respect to amendments made to this part in provisions enacted after the date of the enactment of this Act.

Part 5—Administration and Enforcement

CRIMINAL PENALTIES

Sec. 501. Any person who willfully violates any provision of part 1 of this subtitle, or any regulation or order issued under any such provision, shall upon conviction be fined not more than $5,000 or imprisoned not more than one year, or both; except that in the case of such violation by a person not an individual, the fine imposed upon such person shall be a fine not exceeding $100,000.

◊ ◊ ◊

Editor's Note: Section 2 of P.L. 103-401, the Pension Annuitants Protection Act, amended ERISA §502(a) by adding a new paragraph (7), as indicated below. Note, however, that since OBRA '93 had already added ERISA §502(a)(7) and (8), the Pension Annuitants Protection Act should have designated the new provision as ERISA §502(a)(9). The new provision is set forth below as ERISA §502(a)(9), below with a "{7}" in brackets beside it to indicate its actual designation. Presumably, this will be corrected in future technical corrections legislation. Note also that §3 of P.L. 103-401 amended ERISA §502(*l*)(3)(B), as indicated below. Both provisions apply to any legal proceeding pending or brought on or after May 31, 1993. Finally, §4 of P.L. 103-401 provides that: "[n]othing in this Act shall be construed to limit the legal standing of individuals to bring a civil action as participants or beneficiaries under section 502(a) of the Employee Retirement Income Security Act of 1974 (29 U.S.C. 1132(a)), and nothing in this Act shall affect the responsibilities, obligations, or duties imposed upon fiduciaries by title I of the Employee Retirement Income Security Act of 1974."

◊ ◊ ◊

CIVIL ENFORCEMENT

Sec. 502. (a) A civil action may be brought—

(1) by a participant or beneficiary—

(A) for the relief provided for in subsection (c) of this section, or

(B) to recover benefits due to him under the terms of his plan, to enforce his rights under the terms of the plan, or to clarify his rights to future benefits under the terms of the plan;

(2) by the Secretary, or by a participant, beneficiary or fiduciary for appropriate relief under section 409;

(3) by a participant, beneficiary, or fiduciary (A) to enjoin any act or practice which violates any provision of this title or the terms of the plan, or (B) to obtain other appropriate equitable relief (i) to redress such violations or (ii) to enforce any provisions of this title or the terms of the plan;

(4) by the Secretary or by a participant, or beneficiary for appropriate relief in the case of a violation of 105(c);

(5) except as otherwise provided in subsection (b), by the Secretary (A) to enjoin any act or practice which violates any provision of this title, or (B) to obtain other appropriate equitable relief (i) to redress such violation or (ii) to enforce any provision of this title;

(6) by the Secretary to collect any civil penalty under subsection (i) or (l);

(7) by a State to enforce compliance with a qualified medical child support order (as defined in section 609(a)(2)(A)); [or]

(8) by the Secretary, or by an employer or other person referred to in section 101(f)(1),(A) to enjoin any act or practice which violates subsection (f) of section 101, or (B) to obtain appropriate equitable relief (i) to redress such violation or (ii) to enforce such subsection[.] *; or*

{(7)}(9) in the event that the purchase of an insurance contract or insurance annuity in

ERISA Sec. 502 (a){7}(9)

connection with termination of an individual's status as a participant covered under a pension plan with respect to all or any portion of the participant's pension benefit under such plan constitutes a violation of part 4 of this title or the terms of the plan, by the Secretary, by any individual who was a participant or beneficiary at the time of the alleged violation, or by a fiduciary, to obtain appropriate relief, including the posting of security if necessary, to assure receipt by the participant or beneficiary of the amounts provided or to be provided by such insurance contract or annuity, plus reasonable prejudgment interest on such amounts.

(b)(1) In the case of a plan which is qualified under section 401(a), 403(a), or 405(a) of the Internal Revenue Code of 1954 (or with respect to which an application to so qualify has been filed and has not been finally determined) the Secretary may exercise his authority under subsection (a)(5) with respect to a violation of, or the enforcement of, parts 2 and 3 of this subtitle (relating to participation, vesting, and funding) only if—

(A) requested by the Secretary of the Treasury, or

(B) one or more participants, beneficiaries, or fiduciaries, of such plan request in writing (in such manner as the Secretary shall prescribe by regulation) that he exercise such authority on their behalf. In the case of such a request under this paragraph he may exercise such authority only if he determines that such violation affects, or such enforcement is necessary to protect, claims of participants or beneficiaries to benefits under the plan.

(2) The Secretary shall not initiate an action to enforce section 515.

(c)(1) Any administrator (A) who fails to meet the requirements of paragraph (1) or (4) of section 606 or section 101(e)(1) with respect to a participant or beneficiary, or (B) who fails or refuses to comply with a request for any information which such administrator is required by this title to furnish to a participant or beneficiary (unless such failure or refusal

results from matters reasonably beyond the control of the administrator) by mailing the material requested to the last known address of the requesting participant or beneficiary within 30 days after such request may in the courts' discretion be personally liable to such participant or beneficiary in the amount of up to $100 a day from the date of such failure or refusal, and the court may in its discretion order such other relief as it deems proper.

(2) The Secretary may assess a civil penalty against any plan administrator of up to $1,000 a day from the date of such plan administrator's failure or refusal to file the annual report required to be filed with the Secretary under section 101(b)(4). For purposes of this paragraph, an annual report that has been rejected under section 104(a)(4) for failure to provide material information shall not be treated as having been filed with the Secretary.

(3) Any employer maintaining a plan who fails to meet the notice requirement of section 101(d) with respect to any participant or beneficiary or who fails to meet the requirements of section 101(e)(2) with respect to any person may in the court's discretion be liable to such participant or beneficiary or to such person in the amount of up to $100 a day from the date of such failure, and the court may in its discretion order such other relief as it deems proper.

(4) The Secretary may assess a civil penalty of not more than $1,000 for each violation by any person of section 101(f)(1).
For purposes of this paragraph, each violation described in subparagraph (A) with respect to any single participant, and each violation described in subparagraph (B) with respect to any single participant or beneficiary, shall be treated as a separate violation. The Secretary and the Secretary of Health and Human Services shall maintain such ongoing consultation as may be necessary and appropriate to coordi-nate enforcement under this subsection with enforcment under section 1144(c)(8) of the Social Security Act.

(d)(1) An employee benefit plan may sue or be sued under this title as an entity. Service of summons, subpoena, or other legal process of a court upon a trustee or an administrator of an employee benefit plan in his capacity as such shall constitute service upon the employee benefit plan. In a case where a plan has not designated in the summary plan description of the plan an individual as agent for the service of legal process, service upon the Secretary shall constitute such service. The Secretary, not later than 15 days after receipt of service under the preceding sentence, shall notify the administrator or any trustee of the plan of receipt of such service.

(2) Any money judgment under this title against an employee benefit plan shall be enforceable only against the plan as an entity and shall not be enforceable against any other person unless liability against such person is established in his individual capacity under this title.

(e)(1) Except for actions under subsection (a)(1)(B) of this section, the district courts of the United States shall have exclusive jurisdiction of civil actions under this title brought by the Secretary or by a participant, beneficiary, fiduciary, or any person referred to in section 101(f)(1). State courts of competent jurisdiction and district courts of the United States shall have concurrent jurisdiction of actions under paragraphs (1)(B) and (7) of subsection (a).

(2) Where an action under this title is brought in a district court of the United States, it may be brought in the district where the plan is administered, where the breach took place, or where a defendant resides or may be found, and process may be served in any other district where a defendant resides or may be found.

(f) The district courts of the United States shall have jurisdiction, without respect to the amount in controversy or the citizenship of the parties, to grant the relief provided for in subsection (a) of this section in any action.

(g)(1) In any action under this title (other than an action described in paragraph (2)) by a participant, beneficiary, or fiduciary, the court in its discretion may allow a reasonable attorney's fee and costs of action to either party.

(2) In any action under this title by a fiduciary for or on behalf of a plan to enforce section 515 in which a judgment in favor of the plan is awarded, the court shall award the plan—

(A) the unpaid contributions,

(B) interest on the unpaid contributions,

(C) an amount equal to the greater of—

(i) interest on the unpaid contributions, or

(ii) liquidated damages provided for under the plan in an amount not in excess of 20 percent (or such higher percentage as may be permitted under Federal or State law) of the amount determined by the court under subparagraph (A),

(D) reasonable attorney's fees and costs of the action, to be paid by the defendant, and

(E) such other legal or equitable relief as the court deems appropriate. For purposes of this paragraph, interest on unpaid contributions shall be determined by using the rate provided under the plan, or, if none, the rate prescribed under section 6621 of the Internal Revenue Code of 1954.

(h) A copy of the complaint in any action under this title by a participant, beneficiary, or fiduciary (other than an action brought by one or more participants or beneficiaries under subsection (a)(1)(B) which is solely for the purpose of recovering benefits due such participants under the terms of the plan) shall be served upon the Secretary and the Secretary of the Treasury by certified mail. Either Secretary shall have the right in his discretion to intervene in any action, except that the Secretary of the Treasury may not intervene in any action under part 4 of this subtitle. If the Secretary brings an action under subsection (a) on behalf of a participant or beneficiary, he shall notify the Secretary of the Treasury.

(i) In the case of a transaction prohibited by section 406 by a party in interest with respect to a plan to which this part applies, the Secretary may assess a civil penalty against such party in interest. The amount of such penalty

ERISA Sec. 502 (i)

may not exceed 5 percent of the amount involved in each such transaction (as defined in section 4975(f)(4) of the Internal Revenue Code of 1986) for each year or part thereof during which the prohibited transaction continues, except that, if the transaction is not corrected (in such manner as the Secretary shall prescribe in regulations which shall be consistent with section 4975(f)(5) of such Code) within 90 days after notice from the Secretary (or such longer period as the Secretary may permit), such penalty may be in an amount not more than 100 percent of the amount involved. This subsection shall not apply to a transaction with respect to a plan described in section 4975(e)(1) of such Code

(j) In all civil actions under this title, attorneys appointed by the Secretary may represent the Secretary (except as provided in section 518(a) of title 28, United States Code), but all such litigation shall be subject to the direction and control of the Attorney General.

(k) Suits by an administrator, fiduciary, participant, or beneficiary of an employee benefit plan to review a final order of the Secretary, to restrain the Secretary from taking any action contrary to the provisions of this Act, or to compel him to take action required under this title, may be brought in the district court of the United States for the district where the plan has its principal office, or in the United States District Court for the District of Columbia.

(l)(1) In the case of—

(A) any breach of fiduciary responsibility under (or other violation of) part 4 by a fiduciary, or

(B) any knowing participation in such a breach or violation by any other person, the Secretary shall assess a civil penalty against such fiduciary or other person in an amount equal to 20 percent of the applicable recovery amount.

(2) For purposes of paragraph (1), the term "applicable recovery amount" means any amount which is recovered from a fiduciary or

other person with respect to a breach or violation described in paragraph (1)—

(A) pursuant to any settlement agreement with the Secretary, or

(B) ordered by a court to be paid by such fiduciary or other person to a plan or its participants and beneficiaries in a judicial proceeding instituted by the Secretary under subsection (a)(2) or (a)(5).

(3) The Secretary may, in the Secretary's sole discretion, waive or reduce the penalty under paragraph (1) if the Secretary determines in writing that—

(A) the fiduciary or other person acted resonably and in good faith, or

(B) it is reasonable to expect that the fiduciary or other person will not be able to restore all losses to the plan (or to provide the relief ordered pursuant to subsection (a)(9)) without severe financial hardship unless such waiver or reduction is granted.

(4) The penalty imposed on a fiduciary or other person under this subsection with respect to any transaction shall be reduced by the amount of any penalty or tax imposed on such fiduciary or other person with respect to such transaction under subsection (i) of this section and section 4975 of the Internal Revenue Code of 1986.

◊ ◊ ◊

Editor's Note: ERISA §502(m), below, was added by the Retirement Protection Act of 1994 (enacted as part of the Uruguay Round Agreements Act (P. L. 103-465). Section 761(b) of that Act provides that the change applies to plan years beginning after December 31, 1994.

◊ ◊ ◊

(m) In the case of a distribution to a pension plan participant or beneficiary in violation of section 206(e) by a plan fiduciary, the Secretary shall assess a penalty against such fiduciary in an amount equal to the value of the

distribution. Such penalty shall not exceed $10,000 for each such distribution.

CLAIMS PROCEDURE

Sec. 503. In accordance with regulations of the Secretary, every employee benefit plan shall—

(1) provide adequate notice in writing to any participant or beneficiary whose claim for benefits under the plan has been denied, setting forth the specific reasons for such denial, written in a manner calculated to be understood by the participant, and

(2) afford a reasonable opportunity to any participant whose claim for benefits has been denied for a full and fair review by the appropriate named fiduciary of the decision denying the claim.

INVESTIGATIVE AUTHORITY

Sec. 504. **(a)** The Secretary shall have the power, in order to determine whether any person has violated or is about to violate any provision of this title or any regulation or order thereunder—

(1) to make an investigation, and in connection therewith to require the submission of reports, books, and records, and the filing of data in support of any information required to be filed with the Secretary under this title, and

(2) to enter such places, inspect such books and records and question such persons as he may deem necessary to enable him to determine the facts relative to such investigation, if he has reasonable cause to believe there may exist a violation of this title or any rule or regulation issued thereunder or if the entry is pursuant to an agreement with the plan.

The Secretary may make available to any person actually affected by any matter which is the subject of an investigation under this section, and to any department or agency of the United States, information concerning any matter which may be the subject of such investigation; except that any information ob-

tained by the Secretary pursuant to section 6103(g) of the Internal Revenue Code of 1954 shall be made available only in accordance with regulations prescribed by the Secretary of the Treasury.

(b) The Secretary may not under the authority of this section require any plan to submit to the Secretary any books or records of the plan more than once in any 12 month period, unless the Secretary has reasonable cause to believe there may exist a violation of this title or any regulation or order thereunder.

(c) For the purposes of any investigation provided for in this title, the provisions of sections 9 and 10 (relating to the attendance of witnesses and the production of books, records, and documents) of the Federal Trade Commission Act (15 U.S.C. 49, 50) are hereby made applicable (without regard to any limitation in such sections respecting persons, partnerships, banks, or common carriers) to the jurisdiction, powers, and duties of the Secretary or any officers designated by him. To the extent he considers appropriate, the Secretary may delegate his investigative functions under this section with respect to insured banks acting as fiduciaries of employee benefit plans to the appropriate Federal banking agency (as defined in section 3(q) of the Federal Deposit Insurance Act (12 U.S.C. 1813(q)).

REGULATIONS

Sec. 505. Subject to title III and section 109, the Secretary may prescribe such regulations as he finds necessary or appropriate to carry out the provisions of this title. Among other things, such regulations may define accounting, technical and trade terms used in such provisions; may prescribe forms; and may provide for the keeping of books and records, and for the inspection of such books and records (subject to section 504(a) and (b)).

COORDINATION AND RESPONSIBILITY OF AGENCIES ENFORCING EMPLOYEE RETIREMENT INCOME SECURITY ACT AND RELATED FEDERAL LAWS

Sec. 506. (a) Coordination With Other Agencies and Departments.—In order to avoid unnecessary expense and duplication of functions among Government agencies, the Secretary may make such arrangements or agreements for cooperation or mutual assistance in the performance of his functions under this title and the functions of any such agency as he may find to be practicable and consistent with law. The Secretary may utilize, on a reimbursable or other basis, the facilities or services of any department, agency, or establishment of the United States or of any State or political subdivision of a State, including the services of any of its employees, with the lawful consent of such department, agency, or establishment; and each department, agency, or establishment of the United States is authorized and directed to cooperate with the Secretary and, to the extent permitted by law, to provide such information and facilities as he may request for his assistance in the performance of his functions under this title. The Attorney General or his representative shall receive from the Secretary for appropriate action such evidence developed in the performance of his functions under this title as may be found to warrant consideration for criminal prosecution under the provisions of this title or other Federal law.

(b) Responsibility for Detecting and Investigating Civil and Criminal Violations of Employee Retirement Income Security Act and Related Federal Laws.—The Secretary shall have the responsibility and authority to detect and investigate and refer, where appropriate, civil and criminal violations related to the provisions of this title and other related Federal laws, including the detection, investigation, and appropriate referrals of related violations of title 18 of the United States Code. Nothing in this subsection shall be construed to preclude other appropriate Federal agencies from detecting and investigating civil and criminal violations of this title and other related Federal laws.

ADMINISTRATION

Sec. 507. (a) Subchapter II of chapter 5, and chapter 7, of title 5, United States Code (relating to administrative procedure), shall be applicable to this title.

(b) [Omitted]

(c) No employee of the Department of Labor or the Department of the Treasury shall administer or enforce this title or the Internal Revenue Code of 1954 with respect to any employee benefit plan under which he is a participant or beneficiary, any employee organization of which he is a member, or any employer organization in which he has an interest. This subsection does not apply to an employee benefit plan which covers only employees of the United States.

APPROPRIATIONS

Sec. 508. There are hereby authorized to be appropriated such sums as may be necessary to enable the Secretary to carry out his functions and duties under this Act.

SEPARABILITY OF PROVISIONS

Sec. 509. If any provision of this Act, or the application of such provision to any person or circumstances, shall be held invalid, the remainder of this Act, or the application of such provision to persons or circumstances other than those as to which it is held invalid, shall not be affected thereby.

INTERFERENCE WITH RIGHTS PROTECTED UNDER ACT

Sec. 510. It shall be unlawful for any person to discharge, fine, suspend, expel, discipline or discriminate against a participant or beneficiary for exercising any right to which he is entitled under the provisions of an employee benefit plan, this title, section 3001, or the Welfare and Pension Plans Disclosure Act, or for the purpose of interfering with the attainment of any right to which such participant may become entitled under the plan, this title, or the Welfare and Pension Plans Disclosure Act. It shall be unlawful for any person to discharge, fine, suspend, expel, or discriminate against any person because he has given information or has testified or is about to testify in any inquiry or proceeding relating to this Act or the Welfare and Pension Plans Disclosure Act. The provisions of section 502 shall be applicable in the enforcement of this section.

COERCIVE INTERFERENCE

Sec. 511. It shall be unlawful for any person through the use of fraud, force, violence, or threat of the use of force or violence, to restrain, coerce, intimidate, or attempt to restrain, coerce, or intimidate any participant or beneficiary for the purpose of interfering with or preventing the exercise of any right to which he is or may become entitled under the plan, this title, section 3001, or the Welfare and Pension Plans Disclosure Act. Any person who willfully violates this section shall be fined $10,000 or imprisoned for not more than one year, or both.

ADVISORY COUNCIL

Sec. 512. (a)(1) There is hereby established an Advisory Council on Employee Welfare and Pension Benefit Plans (hereinafter in this section referred to as the "Council") consisting of fifteen members appointed by the Secretary. Not more than eight members of the Council shall be members of the same political party.

(2) Members shall be persons qualified to appraise the programs instituted under this Act.

(3) Of the members appointed, three shall be representatives of employee organizations (at least one of whom shall be representative of any organization members of which are participants in a multiemployer plan); three shall be representatives of employers (at least one of whom shall be representative of employers maintaining or contributing to multiemployer

plans); three representatives shall be appointed from the general public, one of whom shall be a person representing those receiving benefits from a pension plan; and there shall be one representative each from the fields of insurance, corporate trust, actuarial counseling, investment counseling, investment management, and the accounting field.

(4) Members shall serve for terms of three years except that of those first appointed, five shall be appointed for terms of one year, five shall be appointed for terms of two years, and five shall be appointed for terms of three years. A member may be reappointed. A member appointed to fill a vacancy shall be appointed only for the remainder of such term. A majority of members shall constitute a quorum and action shall be taken only by a majority vote of those present and voting.

(b) It shall be the duty of the Council to advise the Secretary with respect to the carrying out of his functions under this Act and to submit to the Secretary recommendations with respect thereto. The Council shall meet at least four times each year and at such other times as the Secretary requests. In his annual report submitted pursuant to section 513(b), the Secretary shall include each recommendation which he has received from the Council during the preceding calendar year.

(c) The Secretary shall furnish to the Council an executive secretary and such secretarial, clerical, and other services as are deemed necessary to conduct its business. The Secretary may call upon other agencies of the Government for statistical data, reports, and other information which will assist the Council in the performance of its duties.

(d)(1) Members of the Council shall each be entitled to receive the daily equivalent of the annual rate of basic pay in effect for grade GS-18 of the General Schedule for each day (including travel time) during which they are engaged in the actual performance of duties vested in the Council.

(2) While away from their homes or regular places of business in the performance of services for Council, members of the Council shall be allowed travel expenses, including per diem in lieu of subsistence, in the same manner as persons employed intermittently in the Government service are allowed expenses under section 5703(b) of title 5 of the United States Code.

(e) Section 14(a) of the Federal Advisory Committee Act (relating to termination) shall not apply to the Council.

RESEARCH, STUDIES, AND ANNUAL REPORT

Sec. 513. (a)(1) The Secretary is authorized to undertake research and surveys and in connection therewith to collect, compile, analyze and publish data, information, and statistics relating to employee benefit plans, including retirement, deferred compensation, and welfare plans, and types of plans not subject to this Act.

(2) The Secretary is authorized and directed to undertake research studies relating to pension plans, including but not limited to (A) the effects of this title upon the provisions and costs of pension plans, (B) the role of private pensions in meeting the economic security needs of the Nation, and (C) the operation of private pension plans including types and levels of benefits, degree of reciprocity or portability, and financial and actuarial characteristics and practices, and methods of encouraging the growth of the private pension system.

(3) The Secretary may, as he deems appropriate or necessary, undertake other studies relating to employee benefit plans, the matters regulated by this title, and the enforcement procedures provided for under this title.

(4) The research, surveys, studies, and publications referred to in this subsection may be conducted directly, or indirectly through grant or contract arrangements.

(b) The Secretary shall submit annually a report to the Congress covering his administration of this title for the preceding year, and including (1) an explanation of any variances or extensions granted under section 110, 207, 303, or 304 and the projected date for terminating the variance; (2) the status of cases in enforcement status; (3) recommendations received from the Advisory Council during the preceding year; and (4) such information, data, research findings, studies, and recommendations for further legislation in connection with the matters covered by this title as he may find advisable.

(c) The Secretary is authorized and directed to cooperate with the Congress and its appropriate committees, subcommittees, and staff in supplying data and any other information, and personnel and services, required by the Congress in any study, examination, or report by the Congress relating to pension benefit plans established or maintained by States or their political subdivisions.

EFFECT ON OTHER LAWS

Sec. 514. (a) Except as provided in subsection (b) of this section, the provisions of this title and title IV shall supersede any and all State laws insofar as they may now or hereafter relate to any employee benefit plan described in section 4(a) and not exempt under section 4(b). This section shall take effect on January 1, 1975.

(b)(1) This section shall not apply with respect to any cause of action which arose, or any act or omission which occurred, before January 1, 1975.

(2)(A) Except as provided in subparagraph (B), nothing in this title shall be construed to exempt or relieve any person from any law of any State which regulates insurance, banking, or securities.

(B) Neither an employee benefit plan described in section 4(a), which is not exempt under section 4(b) (other than a plan established primarily for the purpose of providing death benefits), nor any trust established under such a plan, shall be deemed to be an insurance company or other insurer, bank, trust company, or investment company or to be engaged in the business of insurance or banking for purposes of any law of any State purporting to regulate insurance companies, insurance contracts, banks, trust companies, or investment companies.

(3) Nothing in this section shall be construed to prohibit use by the Secretary of services or facilities of a State agency as permitted under section 506 of this Act.

(4) Subsection (a) shall not apply to any generally applicable criminal law of a State.

(5)(A) Except as provided in subparagraph (B), subsection (a) shall not apply to the Hawaii Prepaid Health Care Act (Haw. Rev. Stat. §§ 393-1 through 393-51).

(B) Nothing in subparagraph (A) shall be construed to exempt from subsection (a)—

(i) any State tax law relating to employee benefit plans, or

(ii) any amendment of the Hawaii Prepaid Health Care Act enacted after September 2, 1974, to the extent it provides for more than the effective administration of such Act as in effect on such date.

(C) Notwithstanding subparagraph (A), parts 1 and 4 of this subtitle, and the preceding sections of this part to the extent they govern matters which are governed by the provisions of such parts 1 and 4, shall supersede the Hawaii Prepaid Health Care Act (as in effect on or after the date of the enactment of this paragraph), but the Secretary may enter into cooperative arrangements under this paragraph and section 506 with officials of the State of Hawaii to assist them in effectuating the policies of provisions of such Act which are superseded by such parts 1 and 4 and the preceding sections of this part.

(6)(A) Notwithstanding any other provision of this section—

(i) in the case of an employee welfare benefit plan which is a multiple employer welfare arrangement and is fully insured (or

which is a multiple employer welfare arrangement subject to an exemption under subparagraph (B)), any law of any State which regulates insurance may apply to such arrangement to the extent that such law provides—

(I) standards, requiring the maintenance of specified levels of reserves and specified levels of contributions, which any such plan, or any trust established under such a plan, must meet in order to be considered under such law able to pay benefits in full when due, and

(II) provisions to enforce such standards, and

(ii) in the case of any other employee welfare benefit plan which is a multiple-employer welfare arrangement, in addition to this title, any law of any State which regulates insurance may apply to the extent not inconsistent with the preceding sections of this title.

(B) The Secretary may, under regulations which may be prescribed by the Secretary, exempt from subparagraph (A)(ii), individually or by class, multiple employer welfare arrangements which are not fully insured. Any such exemption may be granted with respect to any arrangement or class of arrangements only if such arrangement or each arrangement which is a member of such class meets the requirements of section 3(1) and section 4 necessary to be considered an employee welfare benefit plan to which this title applies.

(C) Nothing in subparagraph (A) shall affect the manner or extent to which the provisions of this title apply to an employee welfare benefit plan which is not a multiple employer welfare arrangement and which is a plan, fund, or program participating in, subscribing to, or otherwise using a multiple employer welfare arrangement to fund or administer benefits to such plan's participants and beneficiaries.

(D) For purposes of this paragraph, a multiple employer welfare arrangement shall be

ERISA Sec. 514 (b)(6)(D)

considered fully insured only if the terms of the arrangement provide for benefits the amount of all of which the Secretary determines are guaranteed under a contract, or policy of insurance, issued by an insurance company, insurance service, or insurance organization, qualified to conduct business in a State.

(7) Subsection (a) shall not apply to qualified domestic relations orders (within the meaning of section 206(d)(3)(B)(i)), qualified medical child support orders (within the meaning of section 609(a)(2)(A), and the provisions of law referred to in section 609(a)(2)(B)(ii) to the extent enforced by qualified medical child support orders.

(8) Subsection (a) of this section shall not be construed to preclude any State cause of action—

(A) with respect to which the State exercises its acquired rights under section 609(b)(3) with respect to a group health plan (as defined in section 607(1)), or

(B) for recoupment of payment with respect to items or services pursuant to a State plan for medical assistance approved under title XIX of the Social Security Act which would not have been payable if such acquired rights had been executed before payment with respect to such items or services by the group health plan.

(c) For purposes of this section:

(1) The term "State law" includes all laws, decisions, rules, regulations, or other State action having the effect of law, of any State. A law of the United States applicable only to the District of Columbia shall be treated as a State law rather than a law of the United States.

(2) The term "State" includes a State, any political subdivisions thereof, or any agency or instrumentality of either, which purports to regulate, directly or indirectly, the terms and conditions of employee benefit plans covered by this title.

(d) Nothing in this title shall be construed to alter, amend, modify, invalidate, impair, or supersede any law of the United States (except as provided in sections 111 and 507(b)) or any rule or regulation issued under any such law.

DELINQUENT CONTRIBUTIONS

Sec. 515. Every employer who is obligated to make contributions to a multiemployer plan under the terms of the plan or under the terms of a collectively bargained agreement shall, to the extent not inconsistent with law, make such contributions in accordance with the terms and conditions of such plan or such agreement.

Part 6— Group Health Plans

SEC. 601. PLANS MUST PROVIDE CONTINUATION COVERAGE TO CERTAIN INDIVIDUALS.

(a) In General.—The plan sponsor of each group health plan shall provide, in accordance with this part, that each qualified beneficiary who would lose coverage under the plan as a result of a qualifying event is entitled, under the plan, to elect, within the election period, continuation coverage under the plan.

(b) Exception for Certain Plans.—Subsection (a) shall not apply to any group health plan for any calendar year if all employers maintaining such plan normally employed fewer than 20 employees on a typical business day during the preceding calendar year.

SEC. 602. CONTINUATION COVERAGE.

For purposes of section 601, the term "continuation coverage" means coverage under the plan which meets the following requirements:

(1) Type of benefit coverage.—The coverage must consist of coverage which, as of the time the coverage is being provided, is identical to the coverage provided under the plan to similarly situated beneficiaries under the plan with respect to whom a qualifying event ha not occurred. If coverage is modified under the plan for any group of similarly situated beneficiaries, such coverage shall also be modified in the same manner for all individuals who are qualified beneficiaries under the plan pursuant to this part in connection with such group.

(2) Period of coverage.—The coverage must extend for at least the period beginning on the date of the qualifying event and ending not earlier than the earliest of the following:

(A) Maximum required period.—

(i) General rule for terminations and reduced hours.—In the case of a qualifying event described in section 603(2), except as provided in clause (ii), the date which is 18 months after the date of the qualifying event.

(ii) Special rule for multiple qualifying events.—If a qualifying event (other than a qualifying event described in section 603(6)) occurs during the 18 months after the date of a qualifying event described in section 603(2), the date which is 36 months after the date of the qualifying event described in section 603(2).

(iii) Special rule for certain bankruptcy proceedings.—In the case of a qualifying event described in section 603(6) (relating to bankruptcy proceedings), the date of the death of the covered employee or qualified beneficiary (described in section 607(3)(C)(iii)), or in the case of the surviving spouse or dependent children of the covered employee, 36 months after the date of the death of the covered employee.

(iv) General rule for other qualifying events.—In the case of a qualifying event not described in section 603(2) or 603(6), the date which is 36 months after the date of the qualifying event.

(v) Qualifying event involving Medicare entitlement.—In the case of an event described in section 603(4) (without regard to whether such event is a qualifying event), the period of coverage for qualified beneficiaries other than the covered employee for

such event or any subsequent qualifying event shall not terminate before the close of the 36-month period beginning on the date the covered employee becomes entitled to benefits under title XVIII of the Social Security Act.

In the case of an individual who is determined, under title II or XVI of the Social Security Act, to have been disabled at the time of a qualifying event described in section 603(2), any reference in clause (i) or (ii) to 18 months with respect to such event is deemed a reference to 29 months, but only if the qualified beneficiary has provided notice of such determination under section 606(3) before the end of such 18 months.

(B) End of plan.—The date on which the employer ceases to provide any group health plan to any employee.

(C) Failure to pay premium.—The date on which coverage ceases under the plan by reason of a failure to make timely payment of any premium required under the plan with respect to the qualified beneficiary. The payment of any premium (other than any payment referred to in the last sentence of paragraph (3)) shall be considered to be timely if made within 30 days after the date due or within such longer period as applies to or under the plan.

(D) Group health plan coverage or Medicare entitlement.—The date on which the qualified beneficiary first becomes, after the date of the election—

(i) covered under any other group health plan (as an employee or otherwise which does not contain any exclusion, or limitation with respect to any preexisting condition of such beneficiary), or

(ii) in the case of a qualified beneficiary other than a qualified beneficiary described in section 607(3)(C), entitled to benefits under title XVIII of the Social Security Act.

(E) Termination of extended coverage for disability.—In the case of a qualified beneficiary who is disabled at the time of a qualifying event described in section 603(2), the month that begins more than 30 days after the date of the final determination under title II or XVI of the Social Security Act that the qualified beneficiary is no longer disabled.

(3) Premium requirements.—The plan may require payment of a premium for any period of continuation coverage, except that such premium—

(A) shall not exceed 102 percent of the applicable premium for such period, and

(B) may, at the election of the payor, be made in monthly installments.

In no event may the plan require the payment of any premium before the day which is 45 days after the day on which the qualified beneficiary made the initial election for continuation coverage.

In the case of an individual described in the last sentence of paragraph (2)(A), any reference in subparagraph (A) of this paragraph to "102 percent" is deemed a reference to "150 percent" for any month after the 18th month of continuation coverage described in clause (i) or (ii) of paragraph (2)(A).

(4) No requirement of insurability.—The coverage may not be conditioned upon, or discriminate on the basis of lack of, evidence of insurability.

(5) Conversion option.—In the case of a qualified beneficiary whose period of continuation coverage expires under paragraph (2)(A), the plan must, during the 180-day period ending on such expiration date, provide to the qualified beneficiary the option of enrollment under a conversion health plan otherwise generally available under the plan.

◊ ◊ ◊

Editor's Note: Section 451 of the Federal Deposit Insurance Corporation Improvement Act of 1991 covers the continuation of health plan coverage under ERISA Section 602 above in cases of failed financial institutions. Under this law, any successor to a failed financial institution has the same obligation to offer group health coverage to former employees as the failed institution would have had if not for its failure. Under the law, a successor of a failed depository institution is defined as an entity that holds all of the assets or liabilities of the failed institution and is either FDIC, a bridge bank, or an entity that acquires the failed institution's assets or liabilities from FDIC or a bridge bank. These provisions are effective for plan years beginning on or after December 19, 1991, regardless of whether the qualifying event under ERISA Section 603 below occurred before, on, or after that date.

◊ ◊ ◊

SEC. 603. QUALIFYING EVENT.

For purposes of this part, the term "qualifying event" means, with respect to any covered employee, any of the following events which, but for the continuation coverage required under this part, would result in the loss of coverage of a qualified beneficiary:

(1) The death of the covered employee.

(2) The termination (other than by reason of such employee's gross misconduct), or reduction of hours, of the covered employee's employment.

(3) The divorce or legal separation of the covered employee from the employee's spouse.

(4) The covered employee becoming entitled to benefits under title XVIII of the Social Security Act.

(5) A dependent child ceasing to be a dependent child under the generally applicable requirements of the plan.

(6) A proceeding in a case under title II, United States Code, commencing on or after July 1, 1986, with respect to the employer from whose employment the covered employee retired at any time.

In the case of an event described in paragraph (6), a loss of coverage includes a substantial elimination of coverage with respect to a qualified beneficiary described in section 607(3)(C) within one year before or after the date of commencement of the proceeding.

SEC. 604. APPLICABLE PREMIUM.

For purposes of this part—

(1) In general.—The term "applicable premium" means, with respect to any period of continuation coverage of qualified beneficiaries, the cost to the plan for such period of the coverage for similarly situated beneficiaries with respect to whom a qualifying event has not occurred (without regard to whether such cost is paid by the employer or employee).

(2) Special rule for self-insured plans.— To the extent that a plan is a self-insured plan—

(A) In general.—Except as provided in subparagraph (B), the applicable premium for any period of continuation coverage of qualified beneficiaries shall be equal to a reasonable estimate of the cost of providing coverage for such period for similarly situated beneficiaries which—

(i) is determined on an actuarial basis, and

(ii) takes into account such factors as the Secretary may prescribe in regulations.

(B) Determination on basis of past cost.—If an administrator elects to have this subparagraph apply, the applicable premium for any period of continuation coverage of qualified beneficiaries shall be equal to—

(i) the cost to the plan for similarly situated beneficiaries for the same period occurring during the preceding determination period under paragraph (3), adjusted by

(ii) the percentage increase or decrease in the implicit price deflator of the gross national product (calculated by the Department of Commerce and published in the Survey of Current Business) for the 12-month period ending on the last day of the sixth month of such preceding determination period.

(C) Subparagraph (B) not to apply where significant change.—An administrator may not elect to have subparagraph (B) apply in any case in which there is any significant difference, between the determination period and the preceding determination period, in coverage under, or in employees covered by, the plan. The determination under the preceding sentence for any determination period shall be made at the same time as the determination under paragraph (3).

(3) Determination period. —The determination of any applicable premium shall be made for a period of 12 months and shall be made before the beginning of such period.

SEC. 605. ELECTION.

For purposes of this part—

(1) Election period.—The term "election period" means the period which—

(A) begins not later than the date on which coverage terminates under the plan by reason of a qualifying event,

(B) is of at least 60 days' duration, and

(C) ends not earlier than 60 days after the later of—

(i) the date described in subparagraph (A), or

(ii) in the case of any qualified beneficiary who receives notice under section 606(4), the date of such notice.

(2) Effect of election on other beneficiaries.—Except as otherwise specified in an election, any election of continuation coverage by a qualified beneficiary described in subparagraph (A)(i) or (B) of section 607(3) shall be deemed to include an election of continuation coverage on behalf of any other qualified beneficiary who would lose coverage under the plan by reason of the qualifying event. If there is a choice among types of coverage under the plan, each qualified beneficiary is entitled to make a separate selection among such types of coverage.

SEC. 606. NOTICE REQUIREMENTS.

(a) In General.—In accordance with regulations prescribed by the Secretary—

(1) the group health plan shall provide, at the time of commencement of coverage under the plan, written notice to each covered employee and spouse of the employee (if any) of the rights provided under this subsection,

(2) the employer of an employee under a plan must notify the administrator of a qualifying event described in paragraph (1), (2), (4), or (6) of section 603 within 30 days (or, in the case of a group health plan which is a multiemployer plan, such longer period of time as may be provided in the terms of the plan) of the date of the qualifying event,

(3) each covered employee or qualified beneficiary is responsible for notifying the administrator of the occurrence of any qualifying event described in paragraph (3) or (5) of section 603 within 60 days after the date of the qualifying event and each qualified beneficiary who is determined, under title II or XVI of the Social Security Act, to have been disabled at the time of a qualifying event described in section 603(2) is responsible for notifying the plan administrator of such determination within 60 days after the date of the determination and for notifying the plan administrator within 30 days after the date of any final determination under such title or titles that the qualified beneficiary is no longer disabled, and

(4) the administrator shall notify—

(A) in the case of a qualifying event described in paragraph (1), (2), (4), or (6) of section 603, any qualified beneficiary with respect to such event, and

(B) in the case of a qualifying event described in paragraph (3) or (5) of section 603 where the covered employee notifies the administrator under paragraph (3), any qualified beneficiary with respect to such event, of such beneficiary's rights under this subsection.

(b) Alternative Means of Compliance with Requirement for Notification of Multiemployer Plans by Employers.—The requirements of subsection (a)(2) shall be considered satisfied in the case of a multiemployer plan in connection with a qualifying event described in paragraph (2) of section 603 if the plan provides that the determination of the occurrence of such qualifying event will be made by the plan administrator.

(c) Rules Relating to Notification of Qualified Beneficiaries by Plan Administrator.—For purposes of subsection (a)(4), any notification shall be made within 14 days (or, in the case of a group health plan which is a multiemployer plan, such longer period of time as may be provided in the terms of the plan) of the date on which the administrator is notified under paragraph (2) or (3), whichever is applicable, and any such notification to an individual who is a qualified beneficiary as the spouse of the covered employee shall be treated as notification to all other qualified beneficiaries residing with such spouse at the time such notification is made.

SEC. 607. DEFINITIONS AND SPECIAL RULES

For purposes of this part—

(1) Group health plan.—The term ''group health plan'' means an employee welfare benefit plan providing medical care (as defined in section 213(d) of the Internal Revenue Code of 1954) to participants or beneficiaries directly or through insurance, reimbursement or otherwise.

(2) Covered employee.—The term "covered employee" means an individual who is (or was) provided coverage under a group health plan by virtue of the performance of services by the individual for one or more persons maintaining the plan (including as an employee defined in section 401(c)(1) of the Internal Revenue Code of 1986).

(3) Qualified beneficiary.—

(A) In general.—The term "qualified beneficiary" means, with respect to a covered employee under a group health plan, any other individual who, on the day before the qualifying event for that employee, is a beneficiary under the plan—

(i) as the spouse of the covered employee, or

(ii) as the dependent child of the employee.

(B) Special rule for terminations and reduced employment.—In the case of a qualifying event described in section 603(2), the term "qualified beneficiary" includes the covered employee.

(C) Special rule for retirees and widows.— In the case of a qualifying event described in section 603(6), the term "qualified beneficiary" includes a covered employee who had retired on or before the date of substantial elimination of coverage and any other individual who, on the day before such qualifying event, is a beneficiary under the plan—

(i) as the spouse of the covered employee,

(ii) as the dependent child of the employee, or

(iii) as the surviving spouse of the covered employee.

(4) Employer.—Subsection (n) (relating to leased employees) and subsection (t) (relating to application of controlled group rules to certain employee benefits) of section 414 of the Internal Revenue Code of 1986 shall apply for purposes of this part in the same manner

and to the same extent as such subsections apply for purposes of section 106 of such Code. Any regulations prescribed by the Secretary pursuant to the preceding sentence shall be consistent and coextensive with any regulations prescribed for similar purposes by the Secretary of the Treasury (or such Secretary's delegate) under such subsections.

(5) Optional extension of required period.—A group health plan shall not be treated as failing to meet the requirements of this part solely because the plan provides both—

(A) that the period of extended coverage referred to in section 602(2) commences with the date of the loss of coverage, and

(B) that the applicable notice period provided under section 606(a)(2) commences with the date of the loss of coverage.

SEC. 608. REGULATIONS.

The Secretary may prescribe regulations to carry out the provisions of this part.

SEC. 609. ADDITIONAL STANDARDS FOR GROUP HEALTH PLANS.

(a) Group health plan coverage pursuant to medical child support orders.—

(1) In general.—Each group health plan shall provide benefits in accordance with the applicable requirements of any qualified medical child support order.

(2) Definitions.—For purposes of this subsection—

(A) Qualified medical child support order.—The term "qualified medical child support order" means a medical child support order —

(i) which creates or recognizes the existence of an alternate recipient's right to, or assigns to an alternate recipient the right to, receive benefits for which a participant or beneficiary is eligible under a group health plan, and

(ii) with respect to which the requirements of paragraphs (3) and (4) are met.

(B) Medical child support order.—The term "medical child support order" means any judgment, decree, or order (including approval of a settlement agreement) issued by a court of competent jurisdiction which —

(i) provides for child support with respect to a child of a participant under a group health plan or provides for health benefit coverage to such a child, is made pursuant to a State domestic relations law (including a community property law), and relates to benefits under such plan, or

(ii) enforces a law relating to medical child support described in section 1396g of title 42 with respect to a group health plan.

(C) Alternate recipient.—The term "alternate recipient" means any child of a participant who is recognized under a medical child support order as having a right to enrollment under a group health plan with respect to such participant.

(3) Information to be included in qualified order.—A medical child support order meets the requirements of this paragraph only if such order clearly specifies—

(A) the name and the last known mailing address (if any) of the participant and the name and mailing address of each alternate recipient covered by the order,

(B) a reasonable description of the type of coverage to be provided by the plan to each such alternate recipient, or the manner in which such type of coverage is to be determined,

(C) the period to which such order applies, and

(D) each plan to which such order applies.

(4) Restriction on new types or forms of benefits.—A medical child support order meets the requirements of this paragraph only if such order does not require a plan to provide any type or form of benefit, or any option, not otherwise provided under the plan, except to the extent necessary to meet the requirements of a law relating to medical child support described in section 1908 of the Social Security Act (as added by section 13822 of the Omnibus Budget Reconciliation Act of 1993).

(5) Procedural requirements.—

(A) Timely notifications and determinations.— In the case of any medical child support order received by a group health plan —

(i) the plan administrator shall promptly notify the participant and each alternate recipient of the receipt of such order and the plan's procedures for determining whether medical child support orders are qualified medical child support orders, and

(ii) within a reasonable period after receipt of such order, the plan administrator shall determine whether such order is a qualified medical child support order and notify the participant and each alternate recipient of such determination.

(B) Establishment of procedures for determining qualified status of orders. Each group health plan shall establish reasonable procedures to determine whether medical child support orders are qualified medical child support orders and to administer the provision of benefits under such qualified orders. Such procedures —

(i) shall be in writing,

(ii) shall provide for the notification of each person specified in a medical child support order as eligible to receive benefits under the plan (at the address included in the medical child support order) of such procedures promptly upon receipt by the plan of the medical child support order, and

(iii) shall permit an alternate recipient to designate a representative for receipt of copies of notices that are sent to the alternate recipient with respect to a medical child support order.

(6) Actions taken by fiduciaries.—If a plan fiduciary acts in accordance with part 4 of this subtitle in treating a medical child support order as being (or not being) a qualified medical child support order, then the plan's obligation to the participant and each alternate recipient shall be discharged to the extent of any payment made pursuant to such act of the fiduciary.

(7) Treatment of alternate recipients.—

(A) Treatment as beneficiary generally.—A person who is an alternate recipient under a qualified medical child support order shall be considered a beneficiary under the plan for purposes of any provision of this Act.

(B) Treatment as participant for purposes of reporting and disclosure requirements.— A person who is an alternate recipient under any medical child support order shall be considered a participant under the plan for purposes of the reporting and disclosure requirements of part 1.

(8) Direct provision of benefits provided to alternate recipients.— Any payment for benefits made by a group health plan pursuant to a medical child support order in reimbursement for expenses paid by an alternate recipient or an alternate recipient's custodial parent or legal guardian shall be made to the alternate recipient or the alternate recipient's custodial parent or legal guardian.

(b) Rights of States with respect to group health plans where participants or beneficiaries thereunder are eligible for Medicaid benefits.—

(1) Compliance by plans with assignment of rights.—A group health plan shall provide that payment for benefits with respect to a participant under the plan will be made in accordance with any assignment of rights made by or on behalf of such participant or a beneficiary of the participant as required by a State plan for medical assistance approved under title XIX of the Social Security Act pursuant to section 1912(a)(1)(A) of such Act

(as in effect on the date of the enactment of the Omnibus Budget Reconciliation Act of 1993).

(2) Enrollment and provision of benefits without regard to Medicaid eligibility.—A group health plan shall provide that, in enrolling an individual as a participant or beneficiary or in determining or making any payments for benefits of an individual as a participant or beneficiary, the fact that the individual is eligible for or is provided medical assistance under a State plan for medical assistance approved under title XIX of the Social Security Act will not be taken into account.

(3) Acquisition by States of rights of third parties.—A group health plan shall provide that, to the extent that payment has been made under a State plan for medical assistance approved under title XIX of the Social Security Act in any case in which a group health plan has a legal liability to make payment for items or services constituting such assistance, payment for benefits under the plan will be made in accordance with any State law which provides that the State has acquired the rights with respect to a participant to such payment for such items or services.

(c) Group health plan coverage of dependent children in cases of adoption.—

(1) Coverage effective upon placement for adoption.—In any case in which a group health plan provides coverage for dependent children of participants or beneficiaries, such plan shall provide benefits to dependent children placed with participants or beneficiaries for adoption under the same terms and conditions as apply in the case of dependent children who are natural children of participants or beneficiaries under the plan, irrespective of whether the adoption has become final.

(2) Restrictions based on preexisting conditions at time of placement for adoption prohibited.—A group health plan may not restrict coverage under the plan of any dependent child adopted by a participant or beneficiary, or placed with a participant or beneficiary for adoption, solely on the basis of a preexisting condition of such child at the

ERISA Sec. 609 (c)(2)

time that such child would otherwise become eligible for coverage under the plan, if the adoption or placement for adoption occurs while the participant or beneficiary is eligible for coverage under the plan.

(3) Definitions.—For purposes of this subsection —

(A) Child.—The term "child" means, in connection with any adoption, or placement for adoption, of the child, an individual who has not attained age 18 as of the date of such adoption or placement for adoption.

(B) Placement for adoption.—The term "placement", or being "placed", for adoption, in connection with any placement for adoption of a child with any person, means the assumption and retention by such person of a legal obligation for total or partial support of such child in anticipation of adoption of such child. The child's placement with such person terminates upon the termination of such legal obligation.

(d) Continued coverage of costs of a pediatric vaccine under group health plans.—A group health plan may not reduce its coverage of the costs of pediatric vaccines (as defined under section 1396s(h)(6) of title 42) below the coverage it provided as of May 1, 1993.

(e) Regulations. Any regulations prescribed under this section shall be prescribed by the Secretary of Labor, in consultation with the Secretary of Health and Human Services.

Title II—Amendments to the Internal Revenue Code Relating to Retirement Plans

◊ ◊ ◊

Editor's Note: Title II of ERISA amends the Internal Revenue Code. Text of code provisions relevant to pension and benefit plans appears in this book following the text of ERISA. Therefore, most of Title II of ERISA is not reprinted here. What follows are certain

transitional rules and effective dates as they were enacted in 1974.

◊ ◊ ◊

SEC. 1001. AMENDMENT OF INTERNAL REVENUE CODE OF 1954.

Except as otherwise expressly provided, whenever in this title an amendment or repeal is expressed in terms of an amendment to, or repeal of, a section or other provision, the reference shall be considered to be made to a section or other provision of the Internal Revenue Code of 1954.

Subtitle A—Participation, Vesting, Funding, Administration, Etc.

Part 1—Participation, Vesting, and Funding

* * *

SEC. 1012. MINIMUM VESTING STANDARDS.

* * *

(c) Variations From Certain Vesting and Accrued Benefits Requirements.—In the case of any plan maintained on January 1, 1974, if, not later than 2 years after the date of the enactment of this Act, the plan administrator petitions the Secretary of Labor, the Secretary of Labor may prescribe an alternate method which shall be treated as satisfying the requirements of subsection (a)(2) of section 411 of the Internal Revenue Code of 1954, or of subsection (b)(1) (other than subparagraph (D) thereof) of such sections 411, or of both such provisions for a period of not more than 4 years. The Secretary may prescribe such alternate method only when he finds that—

(1) the application of such requirements would increase the costs of the plan to such an extent that there would result a substantial risk to the voluntary continuation of the plan or a

substantial curtailment of benefit levels or the levels of employees' compensation,

(2) the application of such requirements or discontinuance of the plan would be adverse to the interests of plan participants in the aggregate, and

(3) a waiver or extension of time granted under section 412 (d) or (e) would be inadequate.

In the case of any plan with respect to which an alternate method has been prescribed under the preceding provisions of this subsection for a period of not more than 4 years, if, not later than 1 year before the expiration of such period, the plan administrator petitions the Secretary of Labor for an extension of such alternate method, and the Secretary makes the findings required by the preceding sentence, such alternate method may be extended for not more than 3 years.

SEC. 1013. MINIMUM FUNDING STANDARDS.

* * *

(d) Alternative Amortization Method for Certain Multiemployer Plans.—

(1) General rule.—In the case of any multiemployer plan (as defined in section 414(f) of the Internal Revenue Code of 1954) to which section 412 of such Code applies, if—

(A) on January 1, 1974, the contributions under the plan were based on a percentage of pay,

(B) the actuarial assumptions with respect to pay are reasonably related to past and projected experience, and

(C) the rates of interest under the plan are determined on the basis of reasonable actuarial assumptions, the plan may elect (in such manner and at such time as may be provided under regulations prescribed by the Secretary of the Treasury or his delegate) to fund the unfunded past service liability

under the plan existing as of the date 12 months following the first date on which such section 412 first applies to the plan by charging the funding standard account with an equal annual percentage of the aggregate pay of all participants in the plan in lieu of the level dollar charges to such account required under clauses (i), (ii), and (iii) of section 412(b)(2)(B) of such Code and section 302(b)(2)(B)(i), (ii) and (iii) of this Act.

(2) Limitation.—In the case of a plan which makes an election under paragraph (1), the aggregate of the charges required under such paragraph for a plan year shall not be less than the interest on the unfunded past service liabilities described in clauses (i), (ii), and (iii) of section 412(b)(2)(B) of the Internal Revenue Code of 1954.

* * *

Sec. 1017. EFFECTIVE DATES AND TRANSITIONAL RULES.

(a) General Rule.—Except as otherwise provided in this section, the amendments made by this part shall apply for plan years beginning after the date of the enactment of this Act.

(b) Existing Plans.—Except as otherwise provided in subsections (c) through (h), in the case of a plan in existence on January 1, 1974, the amendments made by this part shall apply for plan years beginning after December 31, 1975.

(c) Existing Plans Under Collective Bargaining Agreements.—

(1) Application of vesting rules to certain plan provisions.—

(A) Waiver of Application.—In the case of a plan maintained on January 1, 1974, pursuant to one or more agreements which the Secretary of Labor finds to be collective bargaining agreements between employee representatives and one or more employers, during the special temporary waiver period the plan shall not be treated as not meeting the requirements of section 411(b)(1) or (2) of the Internal Revenue Code of 1954 solely by reason of a supplementary or special plan provision (within the meaning of subparagraph (D)).

(B) Special temporary waiver period.—For purposes of this paragraph, the term "special temporary waiver period" means plan years beginning after December 31, 1975, and before the earlier of—

(i) the date on which the last of the collective bargaining agreements relating to the plan terminates (determined without regard to any extension thereof agreed to after the date of the enactment of this Act), or

(ii) January 1, 1981.

For purposes of clause (i), any plan amendment made pursuant to a collective bargaining agreement relating to the plan which amends the plan solely to conform to any requirement contained in this Act shall not be treated as a termination of such collective bargaining agreement.

(C) Determination by Secretary of Labor required.—Subparagraph (A) shall not apply unless the Secretary of Labor determines that the participation and vesting rules in effect on the date of the enactment of this Act are not less favorable to the employees, in the aggregate, than the rules provided under sections 410 and 411 of the Internal Revenue Code of 1954.

(D) Supplementary or special plan provisions.—For purposes of this paragraph, the term "supplementary or special plan provision" means any plan provision which—

(i) provides supplementary benefits, not in excess of one-third of the basic benefit, in the form of an annuity for the life of the participant, or

(ii) provides that, under a contractual agreement based on medical evidence as to the effects of working in an adverse environment for an extended period of time, a participant having 25 years of service is to be treated as having 30 years of service.

(2) Application of funding rules.—

(A) In general.—In the case of a plan maintained on January 1, 1974, pursuant to one or more agreements which the Secretary of Labor finds to be collective bargaining agreements between employee representatives and one or more employers, section 412 of the Internal Revenue Code of 1954, and other amendments made by this part to the extent such amendments relate to such section 412, shall not apply during the special temporary waiver period (as defined in paragraph (1)(B)).

(B) Waiver of underfunding.—In the case of a plan maintained on January 1, 1974, pursuant to one or more agreements which the Secretary of Labor finds to be collective bargaining agreements between employee representatives and one or more employers, if by reason of subparagraph (A) the requirements of section 401(a)(7) of the Internal Revenue Code of 1954 apply without regard to the amendment of such section 401(a)(7) by section 1016(a)(2)(C) of this Act, the plan shall not be treated as not meeting such requirements solely by reason of the application of the amendments made by sections 1011 and 1012 of this Act or related amendments made by this part.

(C) Labor organization conventions.—In the case of a plan maintained by a labor organization, which is exempt from tax under section 501(c)(5) of the Internal Revenue Code of 1954, exclusively for the benefit of its employees and their beneficiaries, section 412 of such Code and other amendments made by this part to the extent such amendments relate to such section 412, shall be applied by substituting for the term "December 31, 1975" in subsection (b), the earlier of—

(i) the date on which the second convention of such labor organization held after the date of the enactment of this Act ends, or

(ii) December 31, 1980, but in no even shall a date earlier than the later of Decembe

31, 1975, or the date determined under sub-paragraph (A) or (B) be substituted.

(d) Existing Plans May Elect New Provisions.—In the case of a plan in existence on January 1, 1974, the provisions of the Internal Revenue Code of 1954 relating to participation, vesting, funding, and form of benefit (as in effect from time to time) shall apply in the case of the plan year (which begins after the date of the enactment of this Act but before the applicable effective date determined under subsection (b) or (c)) selected by the plan administrator and to all subsequent plan years, if the plan administrator elects (in such manner and at such time as the Secretary of the Treasury or his delegate shall by regulations prescribe) to have such provisions so apply. Any election made under this subsection, once made, shall be irrevocable.

(e) Certain Definitions and Special Rules.—Section 414 of the Internal Revenue Code of 1954 (other than subsections (b) and (c) of such section 414), as added by section 1015(a) of this Act, shall take effect on the date of the enactment of this Act.

(f) Transitional Rules With Respect to Breaks in Service.—

(1) Participation.—In the case of a plan to which section 410 of the Internal Revenue Code of 1954 applies, if any plan amendment with respect to breaks in service (which amendment is made or becomes effective after January 1, 1974, and before the date on which such section 410 first becomes effective with respect to such plan) provides that any employee's participation in the plan would commence at any date later than the later of—

(A) the date on which his participation would commence under the break in service rules of section 410(a)(5) of such Code, or

(B) the date on which his participation would commence under the plan as in effect on January 1, 1974,

such plan shall not constitute a plan described in section 403(a) or 405(a) of such Code and a trust forming a part of such plan shall not constitute a qualified trust under section 401(a) of such Code.

(2) Vesting.—In the case of a plan to which section 411 of the Internal Revenue Code of 1954 applies, if any plan amendment with respect to breaks in service (which amendment is made or becomes effective after January 1, 1974, and before the date on which such section 411 first becomes effective with respect to such plan) provides that the nonforfeitable benefit derived from employer contributions to which any employee would be entitled is less than the lesser of the nonforfeitable benefit derived from employer contributions to which he would be entitled under—

(A) the break in service rules of section 411(a)(6) of such Code, or

(B) the plan as in effect on January 1, 1974,

such plan shall not constitute a plan described in section 403(a) or 405(a) of such Code and a trust forming a part of such plan shall not constitute a qualified trust under section 401(a) of such Code. Subparagraph (B) shall not apply if the break in service rules under the plan would have been in violation of any law or rule of law in effect on January 1, 1974.

(g) 3-Year Delay for Certain Provisions.—Subparagraphs (B) and (C) of section 404(a)(1) shall apply only in the case of plan years beginning on or after 3 years after the date of the enactment of this Act.

(h)(1) Except as provided in paragraph (2), section 413 of the Internal Revenue Code of 1954 shall apply to plan years beginning after December 31, 1953.

(2)(A) For plan years beginning before the applicable effective date of section 410 of such Code, the provisions of paragraphs (1) and (8) of subsection (b) of such section 413 shall be applied by substituting "401(a)(3)" for "410."

(B) For plan years beginning before the applicable effective date of section 411 of such Code, the provisions of subsection (b)(2) of

ERISA Sec. 1017 (h)(2)(B)

such section 413 shall be applied by substituting "401(a)(7)" for "411 (d)(3)."

(C)(i) The provisions of subsection (b)(4) of such section 413 shall not apply to plan years beginning before the applicable effective date of section 411 of such Code.

(ii) The provisions of subsection (b)(5) (other than the second sentence thereof) of such section 413 shall not apply to plan years beginning before the applicable effective date of section 412 of such Code.

* * *

Part 5—Internal Revenue Service

* * *

SEC. 1052. AUTHORIZATION OF APPROPRIATIONS.

There is authorized to be appropriated to the Department of the Treasury for the purpose of carrying out all functions of the Office of Employee Plans and Exempt Organizations for each fiscal year beginning after June 30, 1974, an amount equal to the sum of—

(1) so much of the collections from the taxes imposed under section 4940 of such Code (relating to excise tax based on investment income) as would have been collected if the rate of tax under such section was 2 percent during the second preceding fiscal year, and

(2) the greater of—

(A) an amount equal to the amount described in paragraph (1), or

(B) $30,000,000.

Subtitle B—Other Amendments To The Internal Revenue Code Relating To Retirement Plans

* * *

SEC. 2003. PROHIBITED TRANSACTIONS.

* * *

(c) **Effective Date and Savings Provisions.**—

(1)(A) The amendments made by this section shall take effect on January 1, 1975.

(B) If, before the amendments made by this section take effect, an organization described in section 401(a) of the Internal Revenue Code of 1954 is denied exemption under section 501(a) of such Code by reason of section 503 of such Code, the denial of such exemption shall not apply if the disqualified person elects (in such manner and at such time as the Secretary or his delegate shall by regulations prescribe) to pay, with respect to the prohibited transaction (within the meaning of section 503(b) or (g)) which resulted in such denial of exemption, a tax in the amount and in the manner provided with respect to the tax imposed under section 4975 of such Code. An election made under this subparagraph, once made, shall be irrevocable. The Secretary of the Treasury or his delegate shall prescribe such regulations as may be necessary to carry out the purposes of this subparagraph.

(2) Section 4975 of the Internal Revenue Code of 1954 (relating to tax on prohibited transactions) shall not apply to—

(A) a loan of money or other extension of credit between a plan and a disqualified person under a binding contract in effect or July 1, 1974 (or pursuant to renewals of such a contract), until June 30, 1984, if such loan or other extension of credit remains at least as favorable to the plan as an arm's-length transaction with an unrelated party would be, and if the execution of the contract, the making of the loan, or the extension of credit was not, at the time of such execution, making, or extension, a prohibited transaction (within the meaning of section 503(b) of such Code or the corresponding provisions of prior law);

(B) a lease or joint use of property involving the plan and a disqualified person pursuant to a binding contract in effect on July 1, 1974 (or pursuant to renewals of such a contract), until June 30, 1984, if such lease or joint use remains at least as favorable to the plan as an arm's-length transaction with an unrelated party would be and if the execution of the contract was not, at the time of such execution, a prohibited transaction (within the meaning of section 503(b) of such Code) or the corresponding provisions of prior law;

(C) the sale, exchange, or other disposition of property described in subparagraph (B) between a plan and a disqualified person before June 30, 1984, if—

(i) in the case of a sale, exchange, or other disposition of the property by the plan to the disqualified person, the plan receives an amount which is not less than the fair market value of the property at the time of such disposition; and

(ii) in the case of the acquisition of the property by the plan, the plan pays an amount which is not in excess of the fair market value of the property at the time of such acquisition;

(D) Until June 30, 1977, the provision of services to which subparagraphs (A), (B), and (C) do not apply between a plan and a disqualified person (i) under a binding contract in effect on July 1, 1974 (or pursuant to renewals of such contract), or (ii) if the disqualified person ordinarily and customarily furnished such services on June 30, 1974, if such provision of services remains at least as favorable to the plan as an arm's-length transaction with an unrelated party would be and if the provision of services was not, at the time of such provision, a prohib-

ited transaction (within the meaning of section 503(b) of such Code) or the corresponding provisions of prior law; or

(E) the sale, exchange, or other disposition of property which is owned by a plan on June 30, 1974, and all times thereafter, to a disqualified person, if such plan is required to dispose of such property in order to comply with the provisions of section 407(a)(2)(A) (relating to the prohibition against holding excess employer securities and employer real property) of the Employee Retirement Income Security Act of 1974, and if the plan receives not less than adequate consideration.

For the purposes of this paragraph, the term "disqualified person" has the meaning provided by Section 4975(e)(2) of the Internal Revenue Code of 1954.

SEC. 2004. LIMITATIONS ON BENEFITS AND CONTRIBUTIONS.

(a) Plan Requirements.—

* * *

(3) Special rule for certain plans in effect on date of enactment.—In any case in which, on the date of enactment of this Act, an individual is a participant in both a defined benefit plan and a defined contribution plan maintained by the same employer, and the sum of the defined benefit plan fraction and the defined contribution plan fraction for the year during which such date occurs exceeds 1.4, the sum of such fractions may continue to exceed 1.4 if—

(A) the defined benefit plan fraction is not increased, by amendment of the plan or otherwise, after the date of enactment of this Act, and

(B) no contributions are made under the defined contribution plan after such date. A trust which is part of a pension, profit-sharing, or stock bonus plan described in the preceding sentence shall be treated as not constituting a qualified trust under section

ERISA Sec. 2004 (a)(3)(B)

401(a) of the Internal Revenue Code of 1954 on account of the provisions of section 415(e) of such Code, as long as it is described in the preceding sentence of this subsection.

* * *

(d) Effective Date.—

(1) General rule.—The amendments made by this section shall apply to years beginning after December 31, 1975. The Secretary of the Treasury shall prescribe such regulations as may be necessary to carry out the provisions of this paragraph.

(2) Transition rule for defined benefit plans.—In the case of an individual who was an active participant in a defined benefit plan before October 3, 1973, if—

(A) the annual benefit (within the meaning of section 415(b)(2) of the Internal Revenue Code of 1954) payable to such participant on retirement does not exceed 100 percent of his annual rate of compensation on the earlier of (i) October 2, 1973, or (ii) the date on which he separated from the service of the employer,

(B) such annual benefit is no greater than the annual benefit which would have been payable to such participant on retirement if (i) all the terms and conditions of such plan in existence on such date had remained in existence until such retirement, and (ii) his compensation taken into account for any period after October 2, 1973, had not exceeded his annual rate of compensation on such date, and

(C) in the case of a participant who separated from the service of the employer prior to October 2, 1973, such annual benefit is no greater than his vested accrued benefit as of the date he separated from the service, then such annual benefit shall be treated as not exceeding the limitation of subsection (b) of section 415 of the Internal Revenue Code of 1954.

* * *

SEC. 2006. SALARY REDUCTION REGULATIONS.

(a) Inclusion of Certain Contributions in Income.—Except in the case of plans or arrangements in existence on June 27, 1974, a contribution made before January 1, 1977, to an employees' trust described in section 401(a), 403(a), or 405(a) of the Internal Revenue Code of 1954 which is exempt from tax under section 501(a) of such Code, or under an arrangement which, but for the fact that it was not in existence on June 27, 1974, would be an arrangement described in subsection (b)(2) of this section, shall be treated as a contribution made by an employee if the contribution is made under an arrangement under which the contribution will be made only if the employee elects to receive a reduction in his compensation or to forego an increase in his compensation.

(b) Administration in the Case of Certain Qualified Pension or Profit-Sharing Plans, Etc., in Existence on June 27, 1974.—No salary reduction regulations may be issued by the Secretary of the Treasury in final form before January 1, 1977, with respect to an arrangement which was in existence on June 27, 1974, and which, on that date—

(1) provided for contributions to an employees' trust described in section 401(a), 403(a), or 405(a) of the Internal Revenue Code of 1954 which is exempt from tax under section 501(a) of such Code, or

(2) was maintained as part of an arrangement under which an employee was permitted to elect to receive part of his compensation in one or more alternative forms if one of such forms results in the inclusion of amounts in income under the Internal Revenue Code of 1954.

(c) Administration of Law with Respect to Certain Plans.—

(1) Administration in the case of plans described in subsection (b).—Until salary reduction regulations have been issued in final form, the law with respect to plans or arrangements described in subsection (b) shall be administered—

(A) without regard to the proposed salary reduction regulations (37 F.R. 25938) and without regard to any other proposed salary reduction regulations, and

(B) in the manner in which such law was administered before January 1, 1972.

(2) Administration in the case of qualified profit-sharing plans.—In the case of plans or arrangements described in subsection (b), in applying this section to the tax treatment of contributions to qualified profit-sharing plans where the contributed amounts are distributable only after a period of deferral, the law shall be administered in a manner consistent with—

(A) Revenue Ruling 56-497 (1956-2 C.B. 284),

(B) Revenue Ruling 63-180 (1963-2 C.B. 189), and

(C) Revenue Ruling 68-89 (1968-1 C.B. 402).

(d) Limitation on Retroactivity of Final Regulations.—In the case of any salary reduction regulations which become final after December 31, 1976—

(1) for purposes of chapter 1 of the Internal Revenue Code of 1954 (relating to normal taxes and surtaxes), such regulations shall not apply before January 1, 1977; and

(2) for purposes of chapter 21 of such Code (relating to Federal Insurance Contributions Act) and for purposes of chapter 24 of such Code (relating to collection of income tax at source on wages), such regulations shall not apply before the day on which such regulations are issued in final form.

(e) Salary Reduction Regulations Defined.—For purposes of this section, the term "salary reduction regulations" means regulations dealing with the includibility in gross income (at the time of contribution) of amounts contributed to a plan which includes a trust that qualifies under section 401(a), or a plan described in section 403(a) or 405(a), including plans or arrangements described in subsection (b)(2), if the contribution is made under an arrangement under which the contribution will be made only if the employee elects to receive a reduction in his compensation or to forego an increase in his compensation, or under an arrangement under which the employee is permitted to elect to receive part of his compensation in one or more alternative forms (if one of such forms results in the inclusion of amounts in income under the Internal Revenue Code of 1954).

Title III—Jurisdiction, Administration, Enforcement; Joint Pension Task Force, Etc.

Subtitle A—Jurisdiction, Administration, And Enforcement

PROCEDURES IN CONNECTION WITH THE ISSUANCE OF CERTAIN DETERMINATION LETTERS BY THE SECRETARY OF THE TREASURY

Sec. 3001. (a) Before issuing an advance determination of whether a pension, profit-sharing, or stock bonus plan, a trust which is a part of such a plan, or an annuity or bond purchase plan meets the requirements of part I of subchapter D of chapter 1 of the Internal Revenue Code of 1954, the Secretary of the Treasury shall require the person applying for the determination to provide, in addition to any material and information necessary for such determination, such other material and information as may reasonably be made available at the time such application is made as the Secretary of Labor may require under title I of this Act for the administration of that title. The Secretary of the Treasury shall also require that the applicant provide evidence satisfactory to the Secretary that the applicant has notified each employee who qualifies as an interested party (within the meaning of regulations prescribed under section 7476(b)(1) of such Code (relating to declaratory judgments in connection with the qualification of certain retirement plans)) of the application for a determination.

(b)(1) Whenever an application is made to the Secretary of the Treasury for a determination of whether a pension, profit-sharing, or stock bonus plan, a trust which is a part of such a plan, or an annuity or bond purchase plan meets the requirements of part I of subchapter D of chapter 1 of the Internal Revenue Code of 1954, the Secretary shall upon request afford an opportunity to comment on the application at any time within 45 days after receipt thereof to—

(A) any employee or class of employee qualifying as an interested party within the meaning of the regulations referred to in subsection (a),

(B) the Secretary of Labor, and

(C) the Pension Benefit Guaranty Corporation.

(2) The Secretary of Labor may not request an opportunity to comment upon such an application unless he has been requested in writing to do so by the Pension Benefit Guaranty Corporation or by the lesser of—

(A) 10 employees, or

(B) 10 percent of the employees

who qualify as interested parties within the meaning of the regulations referred to in subsection (a). Upon receiving such a request, the Secretary of Labor shall furnish a copy of the request to the Secretary of the Treasury within 5 days (excluding Saturdays, Sundays, and legal public holidays (as set forth in section 6103 of title 5, United States Code)).

(3) Upon receiving such a request from the Secretary of Labor, the Secretary of the Treasury shall furnish to the Secretary of Labor such information held by the Secretary of the Treasury relating to the application as the Secretary of Labor may request.

(4) The Secretary of Labor shall, within 30 days after receiving a request from the Pension Benefit Guaranty Corporation or from the necessary number of employees who qualify as interested parties, notify the Secretary of the Treasury, the Pension Benefit Guaranty Corporation, and such employees with respect to whether he is going to comment on the application to which the request relates and with respect to any matters raised in such request on which he is not going to comment. If the Secretary of Labor indicates in the notice required under the preceding sentence that he is not going to comment on all or part of the matters raised in such request, the Secretary of the Treasury shall afford the corporation, and such employees, an opportunity to comment on the application with respect to any matter on which the Secretary of Labor has declined to comment.

(c) The Pension Benefit Guaranty Corporation and, upon petition of a group of employees referred to in subsection (b)(2), the Secretary of Labor, may intervene in any action brought for declaratory judgment under section 7476 of the Internal Revenue Code of 1954 in accordance with the provisions of such section. The Pension Benefit Guaranty Corporation is permitted to bring an action under such section 7476 under such rules as may be prescribed by the United States Tax Court.

(d) If the Secretary of the Treasury determines that a plan or trust to which this section applies meets the applicable requirements of part I of subchapter D of chapter 1 of the Internal Revenue Code of 1954 and issues a determination letter to the applicant, the Secretary shall notify the Secretary of Labor of his determination and furnish such information and material relating to the application and determination held by the Secretary of the Treasury as the

Secretary of Labor may request for the proper administration of title I of this Act. The Secretary of Labor shall accept the determination of the Secretary of the Treasury as prima facie evidence of initial compliance by the plan with the standards of parts 2, 3, and 4 of subtitle B of title I of this Act. The determination of the Secretary of the Treasury shall not be prima facie evidence on issues relating solely to part 4 of subtitle B of title I. If an application for such a determination is withdrawn, or if the Secretary of the Treasury issues a determination that the plan or trust does not meet the requirements of such part I, the Secretary shall notify the Secretary of Labor of the withdrawal or determination.

(e) This section does not apply with respect to an application for any plan received by the Secretary of the Treasury before the date on which section 410 of the Internal Revenue Code of 1954 applies to the plan, or on which such section will apply if the plan is determined by the Secretary to be a qualified plan.

PROCEDURES WITH RESPECT TO CONTINUED COMPLIANCE WITH REQUIREMENTS RELATING TO PARTICIPATION, VESTING, AND FUNDING STANDARDS

Sec. 3002. (a) In carrying out the provisions of part I of subchapter D of chapter 1 of the Internal Revenue Code of 1954 with respect to whether a plan or a trust meets the requirements of section 410(a) or 411 of such Code (relating to minimum participation standards and minimum vesting standards, respectively), the Secretary of the Treasury shall notify the Secretary of Labor when the Secretary of the Treasury issues a preliminary notice of intent to disqualify related to the plan or trust or, if earlier, at the time of commencing any proceeding to determine whether the plan or trust satisfies such requirements. Unless the Secretary of the Treasury finds that the collection of a tax imposed under the Internal Revenue Code of 1954 is in jeopardy, the Secretary of the Treasury shall not issue a determination that the plan or trust does not satisfy the requirements of such section until

the expiration of a period of 60 days after the date on which he notifies the Secretary of Labor of such review. The Secretary of the Treasury, in his discretion, may extend the 60-day period referred to in the preceding sentence if he determines that such an extension would enable the Secretary of Labor to obtain compliance with such requirements by the plan within the extension period. Except as otherwise provided in this Act, the Secretary of Labor shall not generally apply part 2 of title I of this Act to any plan or trust subject to sections 410(a) and 411 of such Code, but shall refer alleged general violations of the vesting or participation standards to the Secretary of the Treasury. (The preceding sentence shall not apply to matters relating to individuals benefits.)

(b) Unless the Secretary of the Treasury finds that the collection of a tax is in jeopardy, in carrying out the provisions of section 4971 of the Internal Revenue Code of 1954 (relating to taxes on the failure to meet minimum funding standards), the Secretary of the Treasury shall notify the Secretary of Labor before sending a notice of deficiency with respect to any tax imposed under that section on an employer, and, in accordance with the provisions of subsection (d) of that section, afford the Secretary of Labor an opportunity to comment on the imposition of the tax in the case. The Secretary of the Treasury may waive the imposition of the tax imposed under section 4971(b) of such Code in appropriate cases. Upon receiving a written request from the Secretary of Labor or from the Pension Benefit Guaranty Corporation, the Secretary of the Treasury shall cause an investigation to be commenced expeditiously with respect to whether the tax imposed under section 4971 of such Code should be applied with respect to any employer to which the request relates. The Secretary of the Treasury and the Secretary of Labor shall consult with each other from time to time with respect to the provisions of section 412 of the Internal Revenue Code of 1954 (relating to minimum funding standards) and with respect to the funding standards applicable under title I of this Act in order to coordinate the rules applicable under such standards.

(c) Regulations prescribed by the Secretary of the Treasury under sections 410(a), 411, and 412 of the Internal Revenue Code of 1954 (relating to minimum participation standards, minimum vesting standards, and minimum funding standards, respectively) shall also apply to the minimum participation, vesting, and funding standards set forth in parts 2 and 3 of subtitle B of title I of this Act. Except as otherwise expressly provided in this Act, the Secretary of Labor shall not prescribe other regulations under such parts, or apply the regulations prescribed by the Secretary of the Treasury under sections 410(a), 411, 412 of the Internal Revenue Code of 1954 and applicable to the minimum participation, vesting, and funding standards under such parts in a manner inconsistent with the way such regulations apply under sections 410(a), 411, and 412 of such Code.

(d) The Secretary of Labor and the Pension Benefit Guaranty Corporation, before filing briefs in any case involving the construction or application of minimum participation standards, minimum vesting standards, or minimum funding standards under title I of this Act, shall afford the Secretary of the Treasury a reasonable opportunity to review any such brief. The Secretary of the Treasury shall have the right to intervene in any such case.

(e) The Secretary of the Treasury shall consult with the Pension Benefit Guaranty Corporation with respect to any proposed or final regulation authorized by subpart C of part I of subchapter D of chapter 1 of the Internal Revenue Code of 1954, or by sections 4241 through 4245 of this Act, before publishing any such proposed or final regulation.

PROCEDURES IN CONNECTION WITH PROHIBITED TRANSACTIONS

Sec. 3003. (a) Unless the Secretary of the Treasury finds that the collection of a tax is in jeopardy, in carrying out the provisions of section 4975 of the Internal Revenue Code of

1954 (relating to tax on prohibited transactions) the Secretary of the Treasury shall, in accordance with the provisions of subsection (h) of such section, notify the Secretary of Labor before sending a notice of deficiency with respect to the tax imposed by subsection (a) or (b) of such section, and, in accordance with the provisions of subsection (h) of such section, afford the Secretary an opportunity to comment on the imposition of the tax in any case. The Secretary of the Treasury shall have authority to waive the imposition of the tax imposed under section 4975(b) in appropriate cases. Upon receiving a written request from the Secretary of Labor or from the Pension Benefit Guaranty Corporation, the Secretary of the Treasury shall cause an investigation to be carried out with respect to whether the tax imposed by section 4975 of such Code should be applied to any person referred to in the request.

(b) The Secretary of the Treasury and the Secretary of Labor shall consult with each other from time to time with respect to the provisions of section 4975 of the Internal Revenue Code of 1954 (relating to tax on prohibited transactions) and with respect to the provisions of title I of this Act relating to prohibited transactions and exemptions therefrom in order to coordinate the rules applicable under such standards.

(c) Whenever the Secretary of Labor obtains information indicating that a party-in-interest or disqualified person is violating section 406 of this Act, he shall transmit such information to the Secretary of the Treasury.

COORDINATION BETWEEN THE DEPARTMENT OF THE TREASURY AND THE DEPARTMENT OF LABOR

Sec. 3004. (a) Whenever in this Act or in any provision of law amended by this Act the Secretary of the Treasury and the Secretary of Labor are required to carry out provisions relating to the same subject matter (as determined by them) they shall consult with each other and shall develop rules, regulations, practices, and forms which, to the extent appropriate for the efficient administration of such provisions, are designed to reduce duplication of effort, duplication of reporting, conflicting or overlapping requirements, and the burden of compliance with such provisions by plan administrators, employers, and participants and beneficiaries.

(b) In order to avoid unnecessary expense and duplication of functions among Government agencies, the Secretary of the Treasury and the Secretary of Labor may make such arrangements or agreements for cooperation or mutual assistance in the performance of their functions under this Act, and the functions of any such agency as they find to be practicable and consistent with law. The Secretary of the Treasury and the Secretary of Labor may utilize, on a reimbursable or other basis, the facilities or services, of any department, agency, or establishment of the United States or of any State or political subdivision of a State, including the services, of any of its employees, with the lawful consent of such department, agency, or establishment; and each department, agency, or establishment of the United States is authorized and directed to cooperate with the Secretary of the Treasury and the Secretary of Labor and, to the extent permitted by law, to provide such information and facilities as they may request for their assistance in the performance of their functions under this Act. The Attorney General or his representative shall receive from the Secretary of the Treasury and the Secretary of Labor for appropriate action such evidence developed in the performance of their functions under this Act as may be found to warrant consideration for criminal prosecution under the provisions of this title or other Federal law.

Subtitle B—Joint Pension, Profit-Sharing, and Employee Stock Ownership Plan Task Force; Studies

Part 1—Joint Pension, Profit-sharing, and Employee Stock Ownership Plan Task Force

ESTABLISHMENT

Sec. 3021. The staffs of the Committee on Ways and Means and the Committee on Education and Labor of the House of Representatives, the Joint Committee on Taxation, and the Committee on Finance and the Committee on Labor and Human Resources of the Senate shall carry out the duties assigned under this title to the Joint Pension, Profit-Sharing, and Employee Stock Ownership Plan Task Force. By agreement among the chairmen of such Committees, the Joint Pension, Profit-Sharing, and Employee Stock Ownership Plan Task Force shall be furnished with office space, clerical personnel, and such supplies and equipment as may be necessary for the Joint Pension, Profit-Sharing, and Employee Stock Ownership Plan Task Force to carry out its duties under this title.

DUTIES

Sec. 3022. (a) The Joint Pension, Profit-Sharing, and Employee Stock Ownership Plan Task Force shall, within 24 months after September 2, 1974, make a full study and review of—

(1) the effect of the requirements of section 411 of title 26 and of section 203 of this Act to determine the extent of discrimination, if any, among employees in various age groups resulting from the application of such requirements;

(2) means of providing for the portability of pension rights among different pension plans;

(3) the appropriate treatment under title IV of this Act (relating to termination insurance) of plans established and maintained by small employers;

(4) the broadening of stock ownership, particularly with regard to employee stock ownership plans (as defined in section 4975(e)(7) of the title 26 and section 407(d)(6) of the Act) and all other alternative methods for broadening stock ownership to the American labor force and others;

(5) the effects and desirability of the Federal preemption of State and local law with respect to matters relating to pension and similar plans; and

(6) such other matter as any of the committees referred to in section 3021 may refer to it.

(b) The Joint Pension, Profit-Sharing, and Employee Stock Ownership Plan Task Force shall report the results of its study and review to each of the committees referred to in section 3021.

Part 2—Other Studies

CONGRESSIONAL STUDY

Sec. 3031. (a) The Committee on Education and Labor and the Committee on Ways and Means of the House of Representatives and the Committee on Finance and the Committee on Labor and Human Resources of the Senate shall study retirement plans established and maintained or financed (directly and indirectly) by the Government of the United States, by any State (including the District of Columbia) or political subdivision thereof, or by any agency or instrumentality of any of the foregoing. Such study shall include an analysis of—

(1) the adequacy of existing levels of participation, vesting, and financing arrangements,

(2) existing fiduciary standards, and

(3) the necessity for Federal legislation and standards with respect to such plans.

In determining whether any such plan is adequately financed, each committee shall consider the necessity for minimum funding standards, as well as the taxing power of the government maintaining the plan.

(b) Not later than December 31, 1976, the Committee on Education and Labor and the Committee on Ways and Means shall each submit to the House of Representatives the results of the studies conducted under this section, together with such recommendations as they deem appropriate. The Committee on Finance and the Committee on Labor and Human Resources shall each submit to the Senate the results of the studies conducted under this section together with such recommendations as they deem appropriate not later than such date.

PROTECTION FOR EMPLOYEES UNDER FEDERAL PROCUREMENT, CONSTRUCTION, AND RESEARCH CONTRACTS AND GRANTS

Sec. 3032. (a) The Secretary of Labor shall, during the 2-year period beginning on September 2, 1974, conduct a full and complete study and investigation of the steps necessary to be taken to insure that professional, scientific, and technical personnel and others working in associated occupations employed under Federal procurement, construction, or research contracts or grants will, to the extent feasible, be protected against forfeitures of pension or retirement rights or benefits, otherwise provided, as a consequence of job transfers or loss of employment resulting from terminations or modifications of Federal contracts, grants, or procurement policies. The Secretary of Labor shall report the results of his study and investigation to the Congress within 2 years after September 2, 1974. The Secretary of Labor is authorized, to the extent provided by law, to obtain the services of private research institutions and such other persons by contract or other arrangement as he determines necessary in carrying out the provisions of this section.

(b) In the course of conducting the study and investigation described in subsection (a) of this section, and in developing the regulations referred to in subsection (c) of this section, the Secretary of Labor shall consult—

(1) with appropriate professional societies, business organizations, and labor organizations, and

(2) with the heads of interested Federal departments and agencies.

(c) Within 1 year after the date on which he submits his report to the Congress under subsection (a) of this section, the Secretary of Labor shall, if he determines it to be feasible, develop regulations which will provide the protection of pension and retirement rights and benefits referred to in subsection (a) of this section.

(d)(1) Any regulations developed pursuant to subsection (c) of this section shall take effect if, and only if—

(A) the Secretary of Labor, not later than the day which is 3 years after September 2, 1974, delivers a copy of such regulations to the House of Representatives and a copy to the Senate, and

(B) before the close of the 120-day period which begins on the day on which the copies of such regulations are delivered to the House of Representatives and to the Senate, neither the House of Representatives nor the Senate adopts, by an affirmative vote of a majority of those present and voting in that House, a resolution of disapproval.

(2) For purposes of this subsection, the term "resolution of disapproval" means only a resolution of either House of Congress, the matter after the resolving clause of which is as follows: "That the ____ does not favor the taking effect of the regulations transmitted to the Congress by the Secretary of Labor on ____", the first blank space therein being filled with the name of the resolving House and the second blank space therein being filled with the day and year.

(3) A resolution of disapproval in the House of Representatives shall be referred to the Committee on Education and Labor. A reso-

lution of disapproval in the Senate shall be referred to the Committee on Labor and Human Resources.

(4)(A) If the committee to which a resolution of disapproval has been referred has not reported it at the end of 7 calendar days after its introduction, it is in order to move either to discharge the committee from further consideration of the resolution or to discharge the committee from further consideration of any other resolution of disapproval which has been referred to the committee.

(B) A motion to discharge may be made only by an individual favoring the resolution, is highly privileged (except that it may not be made after the committee has reported a resolution of disapproval), and debate thereon shall be limited to not more than 1 hour, to be divided equally between those favoring and those opposing the resolution. An amendment to the motion is not in order, and it is not in order to move to reconsider the vote by which the motion is agreed to or disagreed to.

(C) If the motion to discharge is agreed to or disagreed to, the motion may not be renewed, nor may another motion to discharge the committee be made with respect to any other resolution of disapproval.

(5)(A) When the committee has reported, or has been discharged from further consideration of, a resolution of disapproval, it is at any time thereafter in order (even though a previous motion to the same effect has been disagreed to) to move to proceed to the consideration of the resolution. The motion is highly privileged and is not debatable. An amendment to the motion is not in order, and it is not in order to move to reconsider the vote by which the motion is agreed to or disagreed to.

(B) Debate on the resolution of disapproval shall be limited to not more than 10 hours, which shall be divided equally between those favoring and those opposing the resolution. A motion further to limit debate is not debatable. An amendment to, or motion to

ERISA Sec. 3032 (d)(5)(B)

recommit, the resolution is not in order, and it is not in order to move to reconsider the vote by which the resolution is agreed to or disagreed to.

(6)(A) Motions to postpone, made with respect to the discharge from committee or the consideration of a resolution of disapproval, and motions to proceed to the consideration of other business, shall be decided without debate.

(B) Appeals from the decisions of the Chair relating to the application of the rules of the House of Representatives or the Senate, as the case may be, to the procedure relating to any resolution of disapproval shall be decided without debate.

(7) Whenever the Secretary of Labor transmits copies of the regulations to the Congress, a copy of such regulations shall be delivered to each House of Congress on the same day and shall be delivered to the Clerk of the House of Representatives if the House is not in session and to the Secretary of the Senate if the Senate is not in session.

(8) The 120 day period referred to in paragraph (1) shall be computed by excluding—

(A) the days on which either House is not in session because of an adjournment of more than 3 days to a day certain or an adjournment of the Congress sine die, and

(B) any Saturday and Sunday, not excluded under subparagraph (A), when either House is not in session.

(9) This subsection is enacted by the Congress—

(A) as an exercise of the rulemaking power of the House of Representatives and the Senate, respectively, and as such they are deemed a part of the rules of each House, respectively, but applicable only with respect to the procedure to be followed in that House in the case of resolutions of disapproval described in paragraph (2); and they supersede other rules only to the extent that they are inconsistent therewith; and

(B) with full recognition of the constitutional right of either House to change the rules (so far as relating to the procedure of that House) at any time, in the same manner and to the same extent as in the case of any other rule of that House.

Subtitle C—Enrollment Of Actuaries

ESTABLISHMENT OF JOINT BOARD FOR THE ENROLLMENT OF ACTUARIES

Sec. 3041. The Secretary of Labor and the Secretary of the Treasury shall, not later than the last day of the first calendar month beginning after the date of the enactment of this Act, establish a Joint Board for the Enrollment of Actuaries (hereinafter in this part referred to as the ''Joint Board'').

ENROLLMENT BY JOINT BOARD

Sec. 3042. (a) The Joint Board shall, by regulations, establish reasonable standards and qualifications for persons performing actuarial services with respect to plans to which this Act applies and, upon application by any individual, shall enroll such individual if the Joint Board finds that such individual satisfies such standards and qualifications. With respect to individuals applying for enrollment before January 1, 1976, such standards and qualifications shall include a requirement for an appropriate period of responsible actuarial experience relating to pension plans. With respect to individuals applying for enrollment on or after January 1, 1976, such standards and qualifications shall include—

(1) education and training in actuarial mathematics and methodology, as evidenced by—

(A) a degree in actuarial mathematics or its equivalent from an accredited college or university,

ERISA Sec. 3032 (d)(6)(A)

(B) successful completion of an examination in actuarial mathematics and methodology to be given by the Joint Board, or

(C) successful completion of other actuarial examinations deemed adequate by the Joint Board, and

(2) an appropriate period of responsible actuarial experience. Notwithstanding the preceding provisions of this subsection, the Joint Board may provide for the temporary enrollment for the period ending on January 1, 1976, of actuaries under such interim standards as it deems adequate.

(b) The Joint Board may, after notice and an opportunity for a hearing, suspend or terminate the enrollment of an individual under this section if the Joint Board finds that such individual—

(1) has failed to discharge his duties under this Act, or

(2) does not satisfy the requirements for enrollment as in effect at the time of his enrollment.

The Joint Board may also, after notice and opportunity for hearing, suspend or terminate the temporary enrollment of an individual who fails to discharge his duties under this Act or who does not satisfy the interim enrollment standards.

AMENDMENT OF INTERNAL REVENUE CODE

Sec. 3043. Section 7701(a) of the Internal Revenue Code of 1954 (relating to definitions) is amended by adding at the end thereof the following new paragraph:

"**(35) Enrolled actuary.**—The term enrolled actuary' means a person who is enrolled by the Joint Board for the Enrollment of Actuaries established under subtitle C of the title III of the Employee Retirement Income Security Act of 1974."

Title IV—Plan Termination Insurance

Subtitle A—Pension Benefit Guaranty Corporation

DEFINITIONS

Sec. 4001. (a) For purposes of this title, the term—

(1) "administrator" means the person or persons described in paragraph (16) of section 3 of this Act;

(2) "substantial employer", for any plan year of a single-employer plan, means one or more persons—

(A) who are contributing sponsors of the plan in such plan year,

(B) who, at any time during such plan year, are members of the same controlled group, and

(C) whose required contributions to the plan for each plan year constituting one of—

(i) the two immediately preceding plan years, or

(ii) the first two of the three immediately preceding plan years,

total an amount greater than or equal to 10 percent of all contributions required to be paid to or under the plan for such plan year;

(3) "multiemployer plan" means a plan—

(A) to which more than one employer is required to contribute,

(B) which is maintained pursuant to one or more collective bargaining agreements between one or more employee organizations and more than one employer, and

(C) which satisfies such other requirements as the Secretary of Labor may prescribe by regulation, except that, in applying this paragraph—

(i) a plan shall be considered a multiemployer plan on and after its termination date if the plan was a multiemployer plan under this paragraph for the plan year preceding such termination, and

(ii) for any plan year which began before the date of the enactment of the Multiemployer Pension Plan Amendments Act of 1980, the term "multiemployer plan" means a plan described in section 414(f) of the Internal Revenue Code of 1954 as in effect immediately before such date;

(4) "corporation", except where the context clearly requires otherwise, means the Pension Benefit Guaranty Corporation established under section 4002;

(5) "fund" means the appropriate fund established under section 4005;

(6) "basic benefits" means benefits guaranteed under section 4022 (other than under section 4022(c)), or under section 4022A (other than under section 4022A(g));

(7) "non-basic benefits" means benefits guaranteed under section 4022(c) or 4022A(g);

(8) "nonforfeitable benefit" means, with respect to a plan, a benefit for which a participant has satisfied the conditions for entitlement under the plan or the requirements of this Act (other than submission of a formal application, retirement, completion of a required waiting period, or death in the case of a benefit which returns all or a portion of a participant's accumulated mandatory employee contributions upon the participant's death), whether or not the benefit may subsequently be reduced or suspended by a plan amendment, an occurrence of any condition, or operation of this Act or the Internal Revenue Code of 1954;

(9) "reorganization index" means the amount determined under section 4241(b);

(10) "plan sponsor" means, with respect to a multiemployer plan—

(A) the plan's joint board of trustees, or

(B) if the plan has no joint board of trustees, the plan administrator;

(11) "contribution base unit" means a unit with respect to which an employer has an obligation to contribute under a multiemployer plan, as defined in regulations prescribed by the Secretary of the Treasury;

(12) "outstanding claim for withdrawal liability" means a plan's claim for the unpaid balance of the liability determined under part 1 of subtitle E for which demand has been made, valued in accordance with regulations prescribed by the corporation;

◊ ◊ ◊

Editor's Note: ERISA §4001(a)(13), as set forth below, appears as amended by §761(a)(11) of the Retirement Protection Act of 1994 (enacted as part of the Uruguay Round Agreements Act, P.L. 103-465). The changes are effective as if included in the Pension Protection Act (OBRA '87).

◊ ◊ ◊

[**(13)** "contributing sponsor" of a single employer plan, means a person—

[(A) who is responsible, in connection with such plan, for meeting the funding requirements under section 302 of this Act or section 412 of the Internal Revenue Code of 1954, or]

[(B) who is a member of the controlled group of a person described in subparagraph (A), has been responsible for meeting such funding requirements, and has employed a significant number (as may be defined in regulations of the corporation) of participants under such plan while such person was so responsible;]

(13) "contributing sponsor", of a single-employer plan, means a person described in section 302(c)(11)(A) of this Act (without regard to section 302(c)(11)(B) of this Act) or section 412(c)(11)(A) of the Internal Revenue

Code of 1986 (without regard to section 412(c)(11)(B) of such Code).

(14) in the case of a single-employer plan—

(A) "controlled group" means, in connection with any person, a group consisting of such person and all other persons under common control with such person;

(B) the determination of whether two or more persons are under "common control" shall be made under regulations of the corporation which are consistent and coextensive with regulations prescribed by the Secretary of the Treasury under subsections (b) and (c) of section 414 of the Internal Revenue Code of 1954; and

(C)(i) notwithstanding any other provision of this title, during any period in which an individual possesses, directly or indirectly, the power to direct or cause the direction of the management and policies of an affected air carrier of which he is accountable owner, whether through the ownership of voting securities, by contract, or otherwise, the affected air carrier shall be considered to be under common control not only with those persons described in subparagraph (B), but also with all related persons; and

(ii) for purposes of this subparagraph, the term—

(I) "affected air carrier" means an air carrier, as defined in Section 101(3) of the Federal Aviation Act of 1958, that holds a certificate of public convenience and necessity under section 401 of such Act for route number 147, as of November 12, 1991;

(II) "related person" means any person which has under common control (as determined under subparagraph (B)) with an affected air carrier on October 10, 1991, or any successor to such related person;

(III) "accountable owner" means any individual who on October 10, 1991, owned directly or indirectly through the application of section 318 of the Internal

Revenue Code of 1986 more than 50 percent of the total voting power of the stock of an affected air carrier;

(IV) "successor" means any person that acquires, directly or indirectly through the application of section 318 of the Internal Revenue Code of 1986, more than 50 percent of the total voting power of the stock of a related person, more than 50 percent of the total value of securities (as defined in section 3(20) of this Act) of the related person, more than 50 percent of the total value of the assets of the related person, or any person into which such related person shall be merged or consolidated; and

(V) "individual" means a living human being.

(15) "single-employer plan" means any defined benefit plan (as defined in section 3(35)) which is not a multiemployer plan;

(16) "benefit liabilities" means the benefits of employees and their beneficiaries under the plan (within the meaning of section 401(a)(2) of the Internal Revenue Code of 1986);

(17) "amount of unfunded guaranteed benefits", of a participant or beneficiary as of any date under a single-employer plan, means an amount equal to the excess of—

(A) the actuarial present value (determined as of such date on the basis of assumptions prescribed by the corporation for purposes of section 4044) of the benefits of the participant or beneficiary under the plan which are guaranteed under section 4022, over

(B) the current value (as of such date) of the assets of the plan which are required to be allocated to those benefits under section 4044;

(18) "amount of unfunded benefit liabilities" means, as of any date, the excess (if any) of—

(A) the value of the benefit liabilities under the plan (determined as of such date on the basis of assumptions prescribed by the corporation for purposes of section 4044), over

(B) the current value (as of such date) of the assets of the plan;

(19) "outstanding amount of benefit liabilities" means, with respect to any plan, the excess (if any) of—

(A) the value of the benefit liabilities under the plan (determined as of the termination date on the basis of assumptions prescribed by the corporation for purposes of section 4044), over

(B) the value of the benefit liabilities which would be so determined by only taking into account benefits which are guaranteed under section 4022 or to which assets of the plan are allocated under section 4044;

(20) "person" has the meaning set forth in section 3(9);

(21) "affected party" means, with respect to a plan—

(A) each participant in the plan,

(B) each beneficiary under the plan who is a beneficiary of a deceased participant or who is an alternate payee (within the meaning of section 206(d)(3)(K)) under an applicable qualified domestic relations order (within the meaning of section 206(d)(3)(B)(i)),

(C) each employee organization representing participants in the plan, and

(D) the corporation,

except that, in connection with any notice required to be provided to the affected party, if an affected party has designated, in writing, a person to receive such notice on behalf of the affected party, any reference to the affected party shall be construed to refer to such person.

(b)(1) An individual who owns the entire interest in an unincorporated trade or business is treated as his own employer, and a partnership is treated as the employer of each partner who

is an employee within the meaning of Section 401(c)(1) of the Internal Revenue Code of 1954. For purposes of this title, under regulations prescribed by the corporation, all employees of trades or businesses (whether or not incorporated) which are under common control shall be treated as employed by a single employer and all such trades and businesses as a single employer. The regulations prescribed under the preceding sentence shall be consistent and coextensive with regulations prescribed for similar purposes by the Secretary of the Treasury under section 414(c) of the Internal Revenue Code of 1954.

(2) For purposes of subtitle E—

(A) except as otherwise provided in subtitle E, contributions or other payments shall be considered made under a plan for a plan year if they are made within the period prescribed under section 412(c)(10) of the Internal Revenue Code of 1954 (determined, in the case of a terminated plan, as if the plan had continued beyond the termination date), and

(B) the term "Secretary of the Treasury" means the Secretary of the Treasury or such Secretary's delegate.

PENSION BENEFIT GUARANTY CORPORATION

Sec. 4002. (a) There is established within the Department of Labor a body corporate to be known as the Pension Benefit Guaranty Corporation. In carrying out its functions under this title, the corporation shall be administered by the chairman of the board of directors in accordance with policies established by the board. The purposes of this title, which are to be carried out by the corporation, are—

(1) to encourage the continuation and maintenance of voluntary private pension plans for the benefit of their participants,

(2) to provide for the timely and uninterrupted payment of pension benefits to participants and beneficiaries under plans to which this title applies, and

ERISA Sec. 4001 (a)(18)(B)

(3) to maintain premiums established by the corporation under section 4006 at the lowest level consistent with carrying out its obligations under this title.

(b) To carry out the purposes of this title, the corporation has the powers conferred on a nonprofit corporation under the District of Columbia Nonprofit Corporation Act and, in addition to any specific power granted to the corporation elsewhere in this title or under that Act, the corporation has the power—

(1) to sue and be sued, complain and defend, in its corporate name and through its own counsel, in any court, State or Federal;

(2) to adopt, alter, and use a corporate seal, which shall be judicially noticed;

(3) to adopt, amend, and repeal, by the board of directors, bylaws, rules, and regulations relating to the conduct of its business and the exercise of all other rights and powers granted to it by this Act and such other bylaws, rules and regulations as may be necessary to carry out the purposes of this title;

(4) to conduct its business (including the carrying on of operations and the maintenance of offices) and to exercise all other rights and powers granted to it by this Act in any State or other jurisdiction without regard to qualification, licensing, or other requirements imposed by law in such State or other jurisdiction;

(5) to lease, purchase, accept gifts or donations of, or otherwise to acquire, to own, hold, improve, use, or otherwise deal in or with, and to sell, convey, mortgage, pledge, lease, exchange, or otherwise dispose of, any property, real, personal, or mixed, or any interest therein wherever situated;

(6) to appoint and fix the compensation of such officers, attorneys, employees, and agents as may be required, to determine their qualifications, to define their duties, and, to the extent desired by the corporation, require bonds for them and fix the penalty thereof, and to appoint and fix the compensation of experts and consultants in accordance with the provi-

sions of section 3109 of title 5, United States Code;

(7) to utilize the personnel and facilities of any other agency or department of the United States Government, with or without reimbursement, with the consent of the head of such agency or department; and

(8) to enter into contracts, to execute instruments, to incur liabilities, and to do any and all other acts and things as may be necessary or incidental to the conduct of its business and the exercise of all other rights and powers granted to the corporation by this Act.

(c) [Deleted]

(d) The board of directors of the corporation consists of the Secretary of the Treasury, the Secretary of Labor, and the Secretary of Commerce. Members of the board shall serve without compensation, but shall be reimbursed for travel, subsistence, and other necessary expenses incurred in the performance of their duties as members of the board. The Secretary of Labor is the chairman of the board of directors.

(e) The board of directors shall meet at the call of its chairman, or as otherwise provided by the bylaws of the corporation.

(f) As soon as practicable, but not later than 180 days after the date of enactment of this Act, the board of directors shall adopt initial bylaws and rules relating to the conduct of the business of the corporation. Thereafter, the board of directors may alter, supplement, or repeal any existing bylaw or rule, and may adopt additional bylaws and rules from time to time as may be necessary. The chairman of the board shall cause a copy of the bylaws of the corporation to be published in the Federal Register not less often than once each year.

(g)(1) The corporation, its property, its franchise, capital, reserves, surplus, and its income (including, but not limited to, any income of any fund established under section 4005), shall be exempt from all taxation now or hereafter imposed by the United States (other than taxes imposed under chapter 21 of Title 26,

ERISA Sec. 4002 (g)(1)

relating to Federal Insurance Contributions Act and chapter 23 of Title 26, relating to Federal Unemployment Tax Act) or by any State or local taxing authority, except that any real property and any tangible personal property (other than cash and securities) of the corporation shall be subject to State and local taxation to the same extent according to its value as other real and tangible personal property is taxed. Sec. 4002 (g)(2)

(2) The receipts and disbursements of the corporation in the discharge of its functions shall be included in the totals of the budget of the United States Government. The United States is not liable for any obligation or liability incurred by the corporation.

(h)(1) There is established an advisory committee to the corporation, for the purpose of advising the corporation as to its policies and procedures relating to (A) the appointment of trustees in termination proceedings, (B) investment of moneys, (C) whether plans being terminated should be liquidated immediately or continued in operation under a trustee, and (D) such other issues as the corporation may request from time to time. The advisory committee may also recommend persons for appointment as trustees in termination proceedings, make recommendations with respect to the investment of moneys in the funds, and advise the corporation as to whether a plan subject to being terminated should be liquidated immediately or continued in operation under a trustee.

(2) The advisory committee consists of seven members appointed, from among individuals recommended by the board of directors, by the President. Of the seven members, two shall represent the interests of employee organizations, two shall represent the interests of employers who maintain pension plans, and three shall represent the interests of the general public. The President shall designate one member as chairman at the time of the appointment of that member.

(3) Members shall serve for terms of 3 years each, except that, of the members first appointed, one of the members representing the interests of employee organizations, one of the members representing the interests of employers, and one of the members representing the interests of the general public shall be appointed for terms of 2 years each, one of the members representing the interests of the general public shall be appointed for a term of 1 year, and the other members shall be appointed to full 3-year terms. The advisory committee shall meet at least six times each year and at such other times as may be determined by the chairman or requested by any three members of the advisory committee.

(4) Members shall be chosen on the basis of their experience with employee organizations, with employers who maintain pension plans, with the administration of pension plans, or otherwise on account of outstanding demonstrated ability in related fields. Of the members serving on the advisory committee at any time, no more than four shall be affiliated with the same political party.

(5) An individual appointed to fill a vacancy occurring other than by the expiration of a term of office shall be appointed only for the unexpired term of the member he succeeds. Any vacancy occurring in the office of a member of the advisory committee shall be filled in the manner in which that office was originally filled.

(6) The advisory committee shall appoint and fix the compensation of such employees as it determines necessary to discharge its duties, including experts and consultants in accordance with the provisions of section 3109 of title 5, United States Code. The corporation shall furnish to the advisory committee such professional, secretarial, and other services as the committee may request.

(7) Members of the advisory committee shall, for each day (including travel time) during which they are attending meetings or conferences of the committee or otherwise engaged in the business of the committee, be compensated at a rate fixed by the corporation which is not in excess of the daily equivalent of the annual rate of basic pay in effect for grade GS-18 of the General Schedule, and

while away from their homes or regular places of business they may be allowed travel expenses, including per diem in lieu of subsistence, as authorized by section 5703 of title 5, United States Code.

(8) The Federal Advisory Committee Act does not apply to the advisory committee established by this subsection.

◊ ◊ ◊

Editor's Note: ERISA §4003(a), as set forth below, appears as amended by §776(b)(1) of the Retirement Protection Act of 1994 (enacted as part of the Uruguay Round Agreements Act, P.L. 103-465). The changes are effective with respect to distributions that occur in plan years commencing after final regulations are prescribed by the Pension Benefit Guaranty Corporation.

◊ ◊ ◊

INVESTIGATORY AUTHORITY; COOPERATION WITH OTHER AGENCIES; CIVIL ACTIONS

Sec. 4003. **(a)** The corporation may make such investigations as it deems necessary to enforce any provision of this title or any rule or regulation thereunder, and may require or permit any person to file with it a statement in writing, under oath or otherwise as the corporation shall determine, as to all the facts and circumstances concerning the matter to be investigated. The corporation shall annually audit a statistically significant number of plans terminating under section 4041(b) to determine whether participants and beneficiaries have received their benefit commitments *and whether section 4050(a) has been satisfied.* Each audit shall include a statistically significant number of participants and beneficiaries.

(b) For the purpose of any such investigation, or any other proceeding under this title, any member of the board of directors of the corporation, or any officer designated by the chairman, may administer oaths and affirmations, subpena witnesses, compel their attendance, take evidence, and require the production of any books, papers, correspondence, memoranda, or other records which the corporation deems relevant or material to the inquiry.

(c) In case of contumacy by, or refusal to obey a subpena issued to, any person, the corporation may invoke the aid of any court of the United States within the jurisdiction of which such investigation or proceeding is carried on, or where such person resides or carries on business, in requiring the attendance and testimony of witnesses and the production of books, papers, correspondence, memoranda, and other records. The court may issue an order requiring such person to appear before the corporation, or member or officer designated by the corporation, and to produce records or to give testimony related to the matter under investigation or in question. Any failure to obey such order of the court may be punished by the court as a contempt thereof. All process in any such case may be served in the judicial district in which such person is an inhabitant or may be found.

(d) In order to avoid unnecessary expense and duplication of functions among government agencies, the corporation may make such arrangements or agreements for cooperation or mutual assistance in the performance of its functions under this title as is practicable and consistent with law. The corporation may utilize the facilities or services any department, agency, or establishment of the United States or of any State or political subdivision of a State, including the services of any of its employees, with the lawful consent of such department, agency, or establishment. The head of each department, agency, or establishment of the United States shall cooperate with the corporation and, to the extent permitted by law, provide such information and facilities as it may request for its assistance in the performance of its functions under this title. The Attorney General or his representative shall receive from the corporation for appropriate action such evidence developed in the performance of its functions under this title as may be found to warrant consideration for criminal prosecution under the provisions of this or any other Federal law.

◊ ◊ ◊

Editor's Note: ERISA §4003(e), below, appears as amended by §773 of the Retirement Protection Act of 1994 (enacted as part of the Uruguay Round Agreements Act, P.L. 103-465). The changes made by Act §773 apply to installments and other payments required under ERISA §302 (or Code §412) that become due on or after December 8, 1994.

◊ ◊ ◊

(e)(1) Civil actions may be brought by the corporation for appropriate relief, legal or equitable or both, to enforce *(A)* the provisions of this title[.] , *and (B) in the case of a plan which is covered under this title (other than a multiemployer plan) and for which the conditions for imposition of a lien described in section 302(f)(1)(A) and (B) of this Act or section 412(n)(1)(A) and (B) of the Internal Revenue Code of 1986 have been met, section 302 of this Act and section 412 of such Code.*

(2) Except as otherwise provided in this title, where such an action is brought in a district court of the United States, it may be brought in the district where the plan is administered, where the violation took place, or where a defendant resides or may be found, and process may be served in any other district where a defendant resides or may be found.

(3) The district courts of the United States shall have jurisdiction of actions brought by the corporation under this title without regard to the amount in controversy in any such action.

(4) [Repealed].

(5) In any action brought under this title, whether to collect premiums, penalties, and interest under section 4007 or for any other purpose, the court may award to the corporation all or a portion of the costs of litigation incurred by the corporation in connection with such action.

(6)(A) Except as provided in subparagraph (C), an action under this subsection may not be brought after the later of—

(i) 6 years after the date on which the cause of action arose, or

(ii) 3 years after the applicable date specified in subparagraph (B).

(B)(i) Except as provided in clause (ii), the applicable date specified in this subparagraph is the earliest date on which the corporation acquired or should have acquired actual knowledge of the existence of such cause of action.

(ii) If the corporation brings the action as a trustee, the applicable date specified in this subparagraph is the date on which the corporation became a trustee with respect to the plan if such date is later than the date described in clause (i).

(C) In the case of fraud or concealment, the period described in subparagraph (A)(ii) shall be extended to 6 years after the applicable date specified in subparagraph (B).

(f)(1) Except with respect to withdrawal liability disputes under part 1 of subtitle E, any person who is a fiduciary, employer, contributing sponsor, member of a contributing sponsor's controlled group, participant, or beneficiary, and is adversely affected by any action of the corporation with respect to a plan in which such person has an interest, or who is an employee organization representing such a participant or beneficiary so adversely affected for purposes of collective bargaining with respect to such plan, may bring an action against the corporation for appropriate equitable relief in the appropriate court.

(2) For purposes of this subsection, the term "appropriate court" means—

(A) the United States district court before which proceedings under section 4041 or 4042 are being conducted,

(B) if no such proceedings are being conducted, the United States district court for the judicial district in which the plan has its principal office, or

(C) the United States District Court for the District of Columbia.

(3) In any action brought under this subsection, the court may award all or a portion of the costs and expenses incurred in connection with such action to any party who prevails or substantially prevails in such action.

(4) This subsection shall be the exclusive means for bringing actions against the corporation under this title, including actions against the corporation in its capacity as a trustee under section 4042 or 4049.

(5)(A) Except as provided in subparagraph (C), an action under this subsection may not be brought after the later of—

(i) 6 years after the date on which the cause of action arose, or

(ii) 3 years after the applicable date specified in subparagraph (B).

(B)(i) Except as provided in clause (ii), the applicable date specified in this subparagraph is the earliest date on which the plaintiff acquired or should have acquired actual knowledge of the existence of such cause of action.

(ii) In the case of a plaintiff who is a fiduciary bringing the action in the exercise of fiduciary duties, the applicable date specified in this subparagraph is the date on which the plaintiff became a fiduciary with respect to the plan if such date is later than the date specified in clause (i).

(C) In the case of fraud or concealment, the period described in subparagraph (A)(ii) shall be extended to 6 years after the applicable date specified in subparagraph (B).

(6) The district courts of the United States have jurisdiction of actions brought under this subsection without regard to the amount in controversy.

(7) In any suit, action, or proceeding in which the corporation is a party, or intervenes under section 4301, in any State court, the corporation may, without bond or security, remove such suit, action, or proceeding from the State court to the United States district court for the district or division in which such suit, action, or proceeding is pending by following any procedure for removal now or hereafter in effect.

TEMPORARY AUTHORITY FOR INITIAL PERIOD [Repealed]

SEC. 4005. ESTABLISHMENT OF PENSION BENEFIT GUARANTY FUNDS

Sec. 4005. (a) There are established on the books of the Treasury of the United States four revolving funds to be used by the corporation in carrying out its duties under this title. One of the funds shall be used with respect to basic benefits guaranteed under section 4022, one of the funds shall be used with respect to basic benefits guaranteed under section 4022A, one of the funds shall be used with respect to nonbasic benefits guaranteed under section 4022 (if any), and the remaining fund shall be used with respect to nonbasic benefits guaranteed under section 4022A (if any), other than subsection (g)(2) thereof (if any). Whenever in this title reference is made to the term "fund" the reference shall be considered to refer to the appropriate fund established under this subsection.

(b)(1) Each fund established under this section shall be credited with the appropriate portion of—

(A) funds borrowed under subsection (c),

(B) premiums, penalties, interest, and charges collected under this title,

(C) the value of the assets of a plan administered under section 4042 by a trustee to the extent that they exceed the liabilities of such plan,

(D) the amount of any employer liability payments collected under subtitle D, to the extent that such payments exceed liabilities of the plan (taking into account all other plan assets),

(E) earnings on investments of the fund or on assets credited to the fund under this subsection,

(F) attorney's fees awarded to the corporation, and

(G) receipts from any other operations under this title.

(2) Subject to the provisions of subsection (a), each fund shall be available—

(A) for making such payments as the corporation determines are necessary to pay benefits guaranteed under section 4022 or 4022A *or benefits payable under section 4050*,

(B) to purchase assets from a plan being terminated by the corporation when the corporation determines such purchase will best protect the interests of the corporation, participants in the plan being terminated, and other insured plans,

(C) to repay to the Secretary of the Treasury such sums as may be borrowed (together with interest thereon) under subsection (c),

(D) to pay the operational and administrative expenses of the corporation, including reimbursement of the expenses incurred by the Department of the Treasury in maintaining the funds, and the Comptroller General in auditing the corporation, and

(E) to pay to participants and beneficiaries the estimated amount of benefits which are guaranteed by the corporation under this title and the estimated amount of other benefits to which plan assets are allocated under section 4044, under single-employer plans which are unable to pay benefits when due or which are abandoned.

(3) Whenever the corporation determines that the moneys of any fund are in excess of current needs, it may request the investment of such amounts as it determines advisable by the Secretary of the Treasury in obligations issued or guaranteed by the United States but, until all borrowings under subsection (c) have been repaid, the obligations in which such excess moneys are invested may not yield a rate of return in excess of the rate of interest payable on such borrowings.

(c) The corporation is authorized to issue to the Secretary of the Treasury notes or other obligations in an aggregate amount of not to exceed $100,000,000, in such forms and denominations, bearing such maturities, and subject to such terms and conditions as may be prescribed by the Secretary of the Treasury. Such notes or other obligations shall bear interest at a rate determined by the Secretary of the Treasury, taking into consideration current average market yield on outstanding marketable obligations of the United States of comparable maturities during the month preceding the issuance of such notes or other obligations of the corporation. The Secretary of the Treasury is authorized and directed to purchase any notes or other obligations issued by the corporation under this subsection, and for that purpose he is authorized to use as a public debt transaction the proceeds from the sale of any securities issued under the Second Liberty Bond Act, as amended, and the purposes for which securities may be issued under that Act, as amended, are extended to include any purchase of such notes and obligations. The Secretary of the Treasury may at any time sell any of the notes or other obligations acquired by him under this subsection. All redemptions, purchases, and sales by the Secretary of the Treasury of such notes or other obligations shall be treated as public debt transactions of the United States.

(d)(1) A fifth fund shall be established for the reimbursement of uncollectible withdrawal liability under section 4222, and shall be credited with the appropriate—

(A) premiums, penalties, and interest charges collected under this title, and

(B) earnings on investments of the fund or on assets credited to the fund.

ERISA Sec. 4005 (b)(1)(E)

The fund shall be available to make payments pursuant to the supplemental program established under section 4222, including those expenses and other charges determined to be appropriate by the corporation.

(2) The corporation may invest amounts of the fund in such obligations as the corporation considers appropriate.

(e)(1) A sixth fund shall be established for the supplemental benefit guarantee program provided under section 4022A(g)(2).

(2) Such fund shall be credited with the appropriate—

(A) premiums, penalties, and interest charges collected under section 4022A (g)(2), and

(B) earnings on investments of the fund or on assets credited to the fund.

The fund shall be available for making payments pursuant to the supplemental benefit guarantee program established under section 4022A(g)(2) including those expenses and other charges determined to be appropriate by the corporation.

(3) The corporation may invest amounts of the fund in such obligations as the corporation considers appropriate.

(f)(1) A seventh fund shall be established and credited with—

(A) premiums, penalties, and interest charges collected under section 4006(a) (3)(A)(i) (not described in subparagraph (B)) to the extent attributable to the amount of the premium in excess of $8.50,

(B) premiums, penalties, and interest charges collected under section 4006(a)(3)(E), and

(C) earnings on investments of the fund or on assets credited to the fund.

(2) Amounts in the fund shall be available for transfer to other funds established under this section with respect to a single-employer plan but shall not be available to pay—

(A) administrative costs of the corporation, or

(B) benefits under any plan which was terminated before October 1, 1988, unless no other amounts are available for such payment.

(3) The corporation may invest amounts of the fund in such obligations as the corporation considers appropriate.

(g)(1) Amounts in any fund established under this section may be used only for the purposes for which such fund was established and may not be used to make loans to (or on behalf of) any other fund or to finance any other activity of the corporation.

(2) None of the funds borrowed under subsection (c) may be used to make loans to (or on behalf of) any fund other than a fund described in the second sentence of subsection (a).

(3) Any repayment to the corporation of any amount paid out of any fund in connection with a multiemployer plan shall be deposited in such fund.

(h) Any stock in a person liable to the corporation under this title which is paid to the corporation by such person or a member of such person's controlled group in satisfaction of such person's liability under this title may be voted only by the custodial trustees or outside money managers of the corporation.

PREMIUM RATES

Sec. 4006. **(a)(1)** The corporation shall prescribe such schedules of premium rates and bases for the application of those rates as may be necessary to provide sufficient revenue to the fund for the corporation to carry out its functions under this title. The premium rates charged by the corporation for any period shall be uniform for all plans, other than multiemployer plans, insured by the corporation with respect to basic benefits guaranteed by it under section 4022, and shall be uniform for all multiemployer plans with respect to basic benefits guaranteed by it under section 4022A.

(2) The corporation shall maintain separate schedules of premium rates, and bases for the application of those rates, for—

(A) basic benefits guaranteed by it under section 4022 for single-employer plans,

(B) basic benefits guaranteed by it under section 4022A for multiemployer plans,

(C) nonbasic benefits guaranteed by it under section 4022 for single-employer plans,

(D) nonbasic benefits guaranteed by it under section 4022A for multiemployer plans, and

(E) reimbursements of uncollectible withdrawal liability under section 4222.

The corporation may revise such schedules whenever it determines that revised schedules are necessary. Except as provided in section 4022A(f), in order to place a revised schedule described in subparagraph (A) or (B) in effect, the corporation shall proceed in accordance with subsection (b)(1), and such schedule shall apply only to plan years beginning more than 30 days after the date on which a joint resolution approving such revised schedule is enacted.

(3)(A) Except as provided in subparagraph (C), the annual premium rate payable to the corporation by all plans for basic benefits guaranteed under this title is—

(i) in the case of a single-employer plan, for plan years beginning after December 31, 1990, an amount equal to the sum of $19 plus the additional premium (if any) determined under subparagraph (E) for each individual who is a participant in such plan during the plan year;

(ii) in the case of a multiemployer plan, for the plan year within which the date of enactment of the Multiemployer Pension Plan Amendments Act of 1980 falls, an amount for each individual who is a participant in

such plan for such plan year equal to the sum of—

(I) 50 cents, multiplied by a fraction the numerator of which is the number of months in such year ending on or before such date and the denominator of which is 12, and

(II) $1.00, multiplied by a fraction equal to 1 minus the fraction determined under clause (i),

(iii) in the case of a multiemployer plan for plan years after the date of enactment of the Multiemployer Pension Plan Amendments Act of 1980, an amount equal to—

(I) $1.40 for each participant, for the first, second, third, and fourth plan years,

(II) $1.80 for each participant, for the fifth and sixth plan years,

(III) $2.20 for each participant, for the seventh and eighth plan years, and

(IV) $2.60 for each participant, for the ninth plan year, and for each succeeding plan year.

(B) The corporation may prescribe by regulation the extent to which the rate described in subparagraph (A)(i) applies more than once for any plan year to an individual participating in more than one plan maintained by the same employer, and the corporation may prescribe regulations under which the rate described in subparagraph (A)(iii) will not apply to the same participant in any multiemployer plan more than once for any plan year.

(C)(i) If the sum of—

(I) the amounts in any fund for basic benefits guaranteed for multiemployer plans, and

(II) the value of any assets held by the corporation for payment of basic benefits guaranteed for multiemployer plans, is for any calendar year less than 2 times the amount of basic benefits guaranteed by the corporation under this title for multiemployer plans which were paid out of any such fund or assets during the preceding calendar year, the annual premium rates under subparagraph (A) shall be increased to the next highest premium level necessary to insure that such sum will be at least 2 times greater than such amount during the following calendar year.

(ii) If the board of directors of the corporation determines that an increase in the premium rates under subparagraph (A) is necessary to provide assistance to plans which are receiving assistance under section 4261 and to plans the board finds are reasonably likely to require such assistance, the board may order such increase in the premium rates.

(iii) The maximum annual premium rate which may be established under this subparagraph is $2.60 for each participant.

(iv) The provisions of this subparagraph shall not apply if the annual premium rate is increased to a level in excess of $2.60 per participant under any other provisions of this title.

(D)(i) Not later than 120 days before the date on which an increase under subparagraph (C)(ii) is to become effective, the corporation shall publish in the Federal Register a notice of the determination described in subparagraph (C)(ii), the basis for the determination, the amount of the increase in the premium, and the anticipated increase in premium income that would result from the increase in the premium rate. The notice shall invite public comment, and shall provide for a public hearing if one is requested. Any such hearing shall be commenced not later than 60 days before the date on which the increase is to become effective.

(ii) The board of directors shall review the hearing record established under clause (i) and shall, not later than 30 days before the date on which the increase is to become effective, determine (after consideration of the comments received) whether the amount

of the increase should be changed and shall publish its determination in the Federal Register.

◊ ◊ ◊

Editor's Note: ERISA §4006(a)(3)(E), below, appears as amended by §774(b) of the Retirement Protection Act of 1994 (enacted as part of the Uruguay Round Agreements Act, P.L. 103-465). The amendments apply to plan years beginning after December 8, 1994. Note also that §774(c) of that Act provides as follows:

(c) Transition Rule for Certain Public Utilities.—In the case of a regulated public utility described in section 7701(a)(33)(A)(i) of the Internal Revenue Code of 1986, the amendments made by this section shall not apply to plan years beginning before the earlier of—

(1) January 1, 1998, or

(2) the date the registered public utility begins to collect from utility customers rates that reflect the costs incurred or projected to be incurred for additional premiums under section 4006(a)(3)(E) of the Employee Retirement Income Security Act of 1974 pursuant to final and nonappealable determinations by all public utility commissions (or other authorities having jurisdiction over the rates and terms of service by the regulated public utility) that the costs are just and reasonable and recoverable from customers of the regulated public utility.

◊ ◊ ◊

(E)(i) The additional premium determined under this subparagraph with respect to any plan for any plan year shall be an amount equal to the amount determined under clause (ii) divided by the number of participants in such plan as of the close of the preceding plan year.

(ii) The amount determined under this clause for any plan year shall be an amount equal to $9.00 for each $1,000 (or fraction thereof) of unfunded vested benefits under the plan as of the close of the preceding plan year.

ERISA Sec. 4006 (a)(3)(E)(ii)

(iii) For purposes of clause (ii)—

(I) Except as provided in subclause (II) *or (III)*, the term "unfunded vested benefits" means the amount which would be the unfunded current liability (within the meaning of section 302(d)(8)(A)) if only vested benefits were taken into account

(II) The interest rate used in valuing vested benefits for purposes of subclause (I) shall be equal to [80 percent] *the applicable percentage* of the annual yield on 30-year Treasury securities for the month preceding the month in which the plan year begins. *For purposes of this subclause, the applicable percentage is 80 percent for plan years beginning before July 1, 1997, 85 percent for plan years beginning after June 30, 1997, and before the 1st plan year to which the first tables prescribed under section 302(d)(7)(C)(ii)(II) apply, and 100 percent for such 1st plan year and subsequent plan years.*

(III) In the case of any plan year for which the applicable percentage under subclause (II) is 100 percent, the value of the plan's assets used in determining unfunded current liability under subclause (I) shall be their fair market value.

◊ ◊ ◊

Editor's Note: Former §4006(a)(3)(E)(iv) of ERISA, containing the $53 cap on the variable rate premium, was stricken by §774(a) of the Retirement Protection Act of 1994 (enacted as part of the Uruguay Round Agreements Act (P.L. 103-465). The amendment generally applies to plan years beginning on or after July 1, 1994. However, under a transitional rule provided by Act §774(a)(2)(B), the cap is phased out in stages for plan years beginning on or after July 1, 1994, and before July 1, 1996.

Thus, for plan years beginning on or after July 1, 1994, but before July 1, 1995, plans must pay 20% of the additional premium that had previously been limited by the cap. For plan years beginning on or after July 1, 1995,

and before July 1, 1996, the percentage rises to 60%. Finally, with respect to plan years beginning on or after July 1, 1996, the cap is fully phased out. For a special effective date for regulated public utilities, see the Editor's Note at the beginning of ERISA §4006(a)(3)(E).

◊ ◊ ◊

[(iv)(I) Except as provided in this clause, the aggregate increase in the premium payable with respect to any participant by reason of this subparagraph shall not exceed $53.

[(II) If an employer made contributions to a plan during 1 or more of the 5 plan years preceding the 1st plan year to which this subparagraph applies in an amount not less than the maximum amount allowable as a deduction with respect to such contributions under section 404 of such Code, the dollar amount in effect under subclause (I) for the 1st 5 plan years to which this subparagraph applies shall be reduced by $3 for each plan year for which such contributions were made in such amount.]

[(v)] *(iv)* No premium shall be determined under this subparagraph for any plan year if, as of the close of the preceding plan year, contributions to the plan for the preceding plan year were not less than the full funding limitation for the preceding plan year under section 412(c)(7) of the Internal Revenue Code of 1986.

(4) The corporation may prescribe, subject to the enactment of a joint resolution in accordance with this section or section 4022A(f), alternative schedules of premium rates, and bases for the application of those rates, for basic benefits guaranteed by it under sections 4022 and 4022A based, in whole or in part, on the risks insured by the corporation in each plan.

(5)(A) In carrying out its authority under paragraph (1) to establish schedules of premium rates, and bases for the application of those rates, for nonbasic benefits guaranteed under sections 4022 and 4022A, the premium rates charged by the corporation for any period for nonbasic benefits guaranteed shall—

(i) be uniform by category of nonbasic benefits guaranteed,

(ii) be based on the risks insured in each category, and

(iii) reflect the experience of the corporation (including experience which may be reasonably anticipated) in guaranteeing such benefits.

(B) Notwithstanding subparagraph (A), premium rates charged to any multiemployer plan by the corporation for any period for supplemental guarantees under section 4022A(g)(2) may reflect any reasonable considerations which the corporation determines to be appropriate.

(6)(A) In carrying out its authority under paragraph (1) to establish premium rates and bases for basic benefits guaranteed under section 4022 with respect to single-employer plans, the corporation shall establish such rates and bases in coverage schedules in accordance with the provisions of this paragraph.

(B) The corporation may establish annual premiums for single-employer plans composed of the sum of—

(i) a charge based on a rate applicable to the excess, if any, of the present value of the basic benefits of the plan which are guaranteed over the value of the assets of the plan, not in excess of 0.1 percent, and

(ii) an additional charge based on a rate applicable to the present value of the basic benefits of the plan which are guaranteed.

The rate for the additional charge referred to in clause (ii) shall be set by the corporation for every year at a level which the corporation estimates will yield total revenue approximately equal to the total revenue to be

derived by the corporation from the charges referred to in clause (i) of this subparagraph.

(C) The corporation may establish annual premiums for single-employer plans based on—

(i) the number of participants in a plan, but such premium rates shall not exceed the rates described in paragraph (3),

(ii) unfunded basic benefits guaranteed under this title, but such premium rates shall not exceed the limitations applicable to charges referred to in subparagraph (B)(i), or

(iii) total guaranteed basic benefits, but such premium rates shall not exceed the rates for additional charges referred to in subparagraph (B)(ii).

If the corporation uses two or more of the rate bases described in this subparagraph, the premium rates shall be designed to produce approximately equal amounts of aggregate premium revenue from each of the rate bases used.

(D) For purposes of this paragraph, the corporation shall by regulation define the terms "value of assets" and "present value of the benefits of the plan which are guaranteed" in a manner consistent with the purposes of this title and the provisions of this section.

(b)(1) In order to place a revised schedule (other than a schedule described in subsection (a)(2)(C), (D), or (E) in effect, the corporation shall transmit the proposed schedule, its proposed effective date, and the reasons for its proposal to the Committee on Ways and Means and the Committee on Education and Labor of the House of Representatives and to the Committee on Finance and the Committee on Labor and Human Resources of the Senate.

(2) The succeeding paragraphs of this subsection are enacted by Congress as an exercise of the rulemaking power of the Senate and the House of Representatives, respectively, and as such they shall be deemed a part of the rules of each House, respectively, but applicable

ERISA Sec. 4006 (b)(2)

only with respect to the procedure to be followed in that House in the case of resolutions described in paragraph (3). They shall supersede other rules only to the extent that they are inconsistent therewith. They are enacted with full recognition of the constitutional right of either House to change the rules (so far as relating to the procedure of that House) at any time, in the same manner and to the same extent as in the case of any rule of that House.

(3) For the purpose of the succeeding paragraphs of this subsection, "resolution" means only a joint resolution, the matter after the resolving clause of which is as follows: "The proposed revised schedule transmitted to Congress by the Pension Benefit Guaranty Corporation on _____ is hereby approved.", the blank space therein being filled with the date on which the corporation's message proposing the rate was delivered.

(4) A resolution shall be referred to the Committee on Ways and Means and the Committee on Education and Labor of the House of Representatives and to the Committee on Finance and the Committee on Labor and Human Resources of the Senate.

(5) If a committee to which has been referred a resolution has not reported it before the expiration of 10 calendar days after its introduction, it shall then (but not before) be in order to move to discharge the committee from further consideration of that resolution, or to discharge the committee from further consideration of any other resolution with respect to the proposed adjustment which has been referred to the committee. The motion to discharge may be made only by a person favoring the resolution, shall be highly privileged (except that it may not be made after the committee has reported a resolution with respect to the same proposed rate), and debate thereon shall be limited to not more than 1 hour, to be divided equally between those favoring and those opposing the resolution. An amendment to the motion is not in order, and it is not in order to move to reconsider the vote by which the motion is agreed to or disagreed to. If the motion to discharge is agreed to or disagreed

to, the motion may not be renewed, nor may another motion to discharge the committee be made with respect to any other resolution with respect to the same proposed rate.

(6) When a committee has reported, or has been discharged from further consideration of a resolution, it is at any time thereafter in order (even though a previous motion to the same effect has been disagreed to) to move to proceed to the consideration of the resolution. The motion is highly privileged and is not debatable. An amendment to the motion is not in order, and it is not in order to move to reconsider the vote by which the motion is agreed to or disagreed to. Debate on the resolution shall be limited to not more than 10 hours, which shall be divided equally between those favoring and those opposing the resolution. A motion further to limit debate is not debatable. An amendment to, or motion to recommit, the resolution is not in order, and it is not in order to move to reconsider the vote by which the resolution is agreed to or disagreed to.

(7) Motions to postpone, made with respect to the discharge from committee, or the consideration of, a resolution and motions to proceed to the consideration of other business shall be decided without debate. Appeals from the decisions of the Chair relating to the application of the rules of the Senate or the House of Representatives, as the case may be, to the procedure relating to a resolution shall be decided without debate.

(c)(1) Except as provided in subsection (a)(3), and subject to paragraph (2), the rate for all plans for basic benefits guaranteed under this title with respect to plan years ending after September 2, 1974, is—

(A) in the case of a plan which was not a multiemployer plan in a plan year—

(i) with respect to each plan year beginning before January 1, 1978, an amount equal to $1 for each individual who was a participant in such plan during the plan year.

(ii) with respect to each plan year beginning after December 31, 1977, and before

January 1, 1986, an amount equal to $2.60 for each individual who was a participant in such plan during the plan year, and

(iii) with respect to each plan year beginning after December 31, 1985, and before January 1, 1988, an amount equal to $8.50 for each individual who was a participant in such plan during the plan year, and

(iv) with respect to each plan year beginning after December 31, 1987, and before January 1, 1991, an amount equal to $16 for each individual who was a participant in such plan during the plan year, and

(B) in the case of each plan which was a multiemployer plan in a plan year, an amount equal to 50 cents for each individual who was a participant in such plan during the plan year.

(2) The rate applicable under this subsection for the plan year preceding September 1, 1975, is the product of—

(A) the rate described in the preceding sentence; and

(B) a fraction—

(i) the numerator of which is the number of calendar months in the plan year which ends after September 2, 1974, and before the date on which the new plan year commences, and

(ii) the denominator of which is 12.

PAYMENT OF PREMIUMS

Sec. 4007. (a) The designated payor of each plan shall pay the premiums imposed by the corporation under this title with respect to that plan when they are due. Premiums under this title are payable at the time, and on an estimated, advance, or other basis, as determined by the corporation. Premiums imposed by this title on the date of enactment (applicable to that portion of any plan year during which such date occurs) are due within 30 days after such date. Premiums imposed by this title on the first plan year commencing after the date

of enactment of this Act are due within 30 days after such plan year commences. Premiums shall continue to accrue until a plan's assets are distributed pursuant to a termination procedure, or until a trustee is appointed pursuant to section 4042, whichever is earlier. The corporation may waive or reduce premiums for a multiemployer plan for any plan year during which such plan receives financial assistance from the corporation under section 4261, except that any amount so waived or reduced shall be treated as financial assistance under such section.

(b) If any basic benefit premium is not paid when it is due the corporation is authorized to assess a late payment charge of not more than 100 percent of the premium payment which was not timely paid. The preceding sentence shall not apply to any payment of premium made within 60 days after the date on which payment is due, if before such date, the designated payor obtains a waiver from the corporation based upon a showing of substantial hardship arising from the timely payment of the premium. The corporation is authorized to grant a waiver under this subsection upon application made by the designated payor, but the corporation may not grant a waiver if it appears that the plan administrator will be unable to pay the premium within 60 days after the date on which it is due. If any premium is not paid by the last date prescribed for a payment, interest on the amount of such premium at the rate imposed under section 6601(a) of the Internal Revenue Code of 1954 (relating to interest on underpayment, nonpayment, or extensions of time for payment of tax) shall be paid for the period from such last date to the date paid.

(c) If any designated payor fails to pay a premium when due, the corporation is authorized to bring a civil action in any district court of the United States within the jurisdiction of which the plan assets are located, the plan is administered, or in which a defendant resides or is found for the recovery of the amount of the premium penalty, and interest, and process may be served in any other district. The district courts of the United States shall have jurisdiction over actions brought under this subsection by the corporation without regard to the amount in controversy.

(d) The corporation shall not cease to guarantee basic benefits on account of the failure of a designated payor to pay any premium when due.

(e)(1) For purposes of this section, the term "designated payor" means—

(A) the contributing sponsor or plan administrator in the case of a single-employer plan, and

(B) the plan administrator in the case of a multiemployer plan.

(2) If the contributing sponsor of any single-employer plan is a member of a controlled group, each member of such group shall be jointly and severally liable for any premiums required to be paid by such contributing sponsor. For purposes of the preceding sentence, the term "controlled group" means any group treated as a single employer under subsection (b), (c), (m), or (o) of section 414 of the Internal Revenue Code of 1986.

REPORT BY THE CORPORATION

Sec. 4008. As soon as practicable after the close of each fiscal year the corporation shall transmit to the President and the Congress a report relative to the conduct of its business under this title for that fiscal year. The report shall include financial statements setting forth the finances of the corporation at the end of such fiscal year and the result of its operations (including the source and application of its funds) for the fiscal year and shall include an actuarial evaluation of the expected operations and status of the funds established under section 4005 for the next five years (including a detailed statement of the actuarial assumptions and methods used in making such evaluation).

PORTABILITY ASSISTANCE

Sec. 4009. The corporation shall provide advice and assistance to individuals with respect to evaluating the economic desirability of establishing individual retirement accounts or other forms of individual retirement savings for which a deduction is allowable under section 219 of the Internal Revenue Code of 1986 and with respect to evaluating the desirability, in particular cases, of transferring amounts representing an employee's interest in a qualified plan to such an account upon the employee's separation from service with an employer.

◊ ◊ ◊

Editor's Note: Section 4010 of ERISA, below, was added by §772 of the Retirement Protection Act of 1994, which was enacted as part of the Uruguay Round Agreements Act (P. L. 103-465). It is effective beginning on December 8, 1994.

◊ ◊ ◊

SEC. 4010. AUTHORITY TO REQUIRE CERTAIN INFORMATION.

(a) Information Required. Each person described in subsection (b) shall provide the corporation annually, on or before a date specified by the corporation in regulations, with—

(1) such records, documents, or other information that the corporation specifies in regulations as necessary to determine the liabilities and assets of plans covered by this title; and

(2) copies of such person's audited (or, if unavailable, unaudited) financial statements, and such other financial information as the corporation may prescribe in regulations.

(b) Persons Required To Provide Information. The persons covered by subsection (a) are each contributing sponsor, and each member of a contributing sponsor's controlled group, of a single-employer plan covered by this title, if—

(1) the aggregate unfunded vested benefits at the end of the preceding plan year (as determined under section 4006(a)(3)(E)(iii)) of plans maintained by the contributing sponsor and the members of its controlled group exceed $50,000,000 (disregarding plans with no unfunded vested benefits);

(2) the conditions for imposition of a lien described in section 302(f)(1)(A) and (B) of this Act or section 412(n)(1)(A) and (B) of the Internal Revenue Code of 1986 have been met with respect to any plan maintained by the contributing sponsor or any member of its controlled group; or

(3) minimum funding waivers in excess of $1,000,000 have been granted with respect to any plan maintained by the contributing sponsor or any member of its controlled group, and any portion thereof is still outstanding.

(c) Information Exempt From Disclosure Requirements. Any information or documentary material submitted to the corporation pursuant to this section shall be exempt from disclosure under section 552 of title 5, United States Code, and no such information or documentary material may be made public, except as may be relevant to any administrative or judicial action or proceeding. Nothing in this section is intended to prevent disclosure to either body of Congress or to any duly authorized committee or subcommittee of the Congress.

◊ ◊ ◊

Editor's Note: ERISA §4011 was added by §775 of the Retirement Protection Act of 1994 (enacted as part of the Uruguay Round Agreements Act, P.L. 103-465). It applies to plan years beginning after December 8, 1994.

◊ ◊ ◊

SEC. 4011. NOTICE TO PARTICIPANTS.

(a) In General. The plan administrator of a plan subject to the additional premium under section 4006(a)(3)(E) shall provide, in a form and manner and at such time as prescribed in regulations of the corporation, notice to plan participants and beneficiaries of the plan's funding status and the limits on the corporation's guaranty should the plan terminate while underfunded. Such notice shall be written in a manner so as to be understood by the average plan participant.

(b) Exception. Subsection (a) shall not apply to any plan to which section 302(d) does not apply for the plan year by reason of paragraph (9) thereof.

Subtitle B—Coverage

PLANS COVERED

Sec. 4021. (a) Except as provided in subsection (b), this title applies to any plan (including a successor plan) which, for a plan year—

(1) is an employee pension benefit plan (as defined in paragraph (2) of section 3 of this Act) established or maintained—

(A) by an employer engaged in commerce or in any industry or activity affecting commerce, or

(B) by any employee organization, or organization representing employees, engaged in commerce or in any industry or activity affecting commerce, or

(C) by both,

which has, in practice, met the requirements of part I of subchapter D of chapter 1 of the Internal Revenue Code of 1954 (as in effect for the preceding 5 plan years of the plan) applicable to plans described in paragraph (2) for the preceding 5 plan years; or

(2) is, or has been determined by the Secretary of the Treasury to be, a plan described in section 401(a) of the Internal Revenue Code of 1954, or which meets, or has been determined by the Secretary of the Treasury to meet, the requirements of section 404(a)(2) of such Code.

For purposes of this title, a successor plan is considered to be a continuation of a predecessor plan. For this purpose, unless otherwise specifically indicated in this title, a successor plan is a plan which covers a group of employees which includes substantially the same employees as a previously established plan, and provides substantially the same benefits as that plan provided.

(b) This section does not apply to any plan—

(1) which is an individual account plan, as defined in paragraph (34) of section 3 of this Act,

(2) established and maintained for its employees by the Government of the United States, by the government of any State or political subdivision thereof, or by any agency or instrumentality of any of the foregoing, or to which the Railroad Retirement Act of 1935 or 1937 applies and which is financed by contributions required under that Act,

(3) which is a church plan as defined in section 414(e) of the Internal Revenue Code of 1954, unless that plan has made an election under section 410(d) of such Code, and has notified the corporation in accordance with procedures prescribed by the corporation, that it wishes to have the provisions of this part apply to it,

(4)(A) established and maintained by a society, order, or association described in section 501(c)(8) or (9) of the Internal Revenue Code of 1954, if no part of the contributions to or under the plan is made by employers of participants in the plan, or

(B) of which a trust described in section 501(c)(18) of such Code is a part;

(5) which has not at any time after the date of enactment of this Act provided for employer contributions;

(6) which is unfunded and which is maintained by an employer primarily for the purpose of providing deferred compensation for a select group of management or highly compensated employees;

(7) which is established and maintained outside of the United States primarily for the benefit of individuals substantially all of whom are nonresident aliens;

(8) which is maintained by an employer solely for the purpose of providing benefits for certain employees in excess of the limitations on contributions and benefits imposed by section 415 of the Internal Revenue Code of 1954 on plans to which that section applies, without regard to whether the plan is funded, and, to the extent that a separable part of a plan (as determined by the corporation) maintained by an employer is maintained for such purpose, that part shall be treated for purposes of this title, as a separate plan which is an excess benefit plan;

(9) which is established and maintained exclusively for substantial owners as defined in section 4022(b)(6);

(10) of an international organization which is exempt from taxation under the International Organizations Immunities Act;

(11) maintained solely for the purpose of complying with applicable workmen's compensation laws or unemployment compensation or disability insurance laws;

(12) which is a defined benefit plan, to the extent that it is treated as an individual account plan under paragraph (35)(B) of section 3 of this Act; or

(13) established and maintained by a professional service employer which does not at any time after the date of enactment of this Act have more than 25 active participants in the plan.

(c)(1) For purposes of subsection (b)(1), the term "individual account plan" does not include a plan under which a fixed benefit is promised if the employer or his representative participated in the determination of that benefit.

(2) For purposes of this paragraph and for purposes of subsection (b)(13)—

(A) the term "professional service employer" means any proprietorship, partnership, corporation, or other association or organization (i) owned or controlled by professional individuals or by executors or administrators of professional individuals, (ii) the principal business of which is the performance of professional services, and

(B) the term "professional individuals" includes but is not limited to, physicians, dentists, chiropractors, osteopaths, optometrists, other licensed practitioners of the healing arts, attorneys at law, public accountants, public engineers, architects, draftsmen, actuaries, psychologists, social or physical scientists, and performing artists.

(3) In the case of a plan established and maintained by more than one professional service employer, the plan shall not be treated as a plan described in subsection (b)(13) if, at any time after the date of enactment of this Act the plan has more than 25 active participants.

SINGLE EMPLOYER PLAN BENEFITS GUARANTEED

Sec. 4022. (a) Subject to the limitations contained in subsection (b), the corporation shall guarantee in accordance with this section the payment of all nonforfeitable benefits (other than benefits becoming nonforfeitable solely on account of the termination of a plan) under a single employer plan which terminates at a time when this title applies to it.

(b)(1) Except to the extent provided in paragraph (7)—

(A) no benefits provided by a plan which has been in effect for less than 60 months at the time the plan terminates shall be guaranteed under this section, and

(B) any increase in the amount of benefits under a plan resulting from a plan amendment which was made, or became effective, whichever is later, within 60 months before the date on which the plan terminates shall be disregarded.

(2) For purposes of this subsection, the time a successor plan (within the meaning of section 4021(a)) has been in effect includes the time a previously established plan (within the meaning of section 4021(a)) was in effect. For purposes of determining what benefits are guaranteed under this section in the case of a plan to which section 4021 does not apply on the day after the date of enactment of this Act, the 60-month period referred to in paragraph (1) shall be computed beginning on the first date on which such section does apply to the plan.

◊ ◊ ◊

Editor's Note: ERISA §4022(b)(3), as set forth below, appears as amended by §777 of the Retirement Protection Act of 1994 (enacted as part of the Uruguay Round Agreements Act, P.L. 103-465). The amendment apples to plan terminations under ERISA §4041(c) with respect to which notices of intent to terminate are provided under ERISA §4041(a)(2), or under ERISA §4042 with respect to which proceedings are instituted by the PBGC on or after December 8, 1994.

◊ ◊ ◊

(3) The amount of monthly benefits described in subsection (a) provided by a plan, which are guaranteed under this section with respect to a participant, shall not have an actuarial value which exceeds the actuarial value of a monthly benefit in the form of a life annuity commencing at age 65 equal to the lesser of—

(A) his average monthly gross income from his employer during the 5 consecutive calendar year period (or, if less, during the number of calendar years in such period in which he actively participates in the plan) during which his gross income from that employer was greater than during any other such period with that employer determined by dividing $\frac{1}{12}$ of the sum of all such gross income by the number of such calendar years in which he had such gross income, or

ERISA Sec. 4022 (b)(3)(A)

(B) $750 multiplied by a fraction, the numerator of which is the contribution and benefit base (determined under section 230 of the Social Security Act) in effect at the time the plan terminates and the denominator of which is such contribution and benefit base in effect in calendar year 1974.

The provisions of this paragraph do not apply to nonbasic benefits. *The maximum guaranteed monthly benefit shall not be reduced solely on account of the age of a participant in the case of a benefit payable by reason of disability that occurred on or before the termination date, if the participant demonstrates to the satisfaction of the corporation that the Social Security Administration has determined that the participant satisfies the definition of disability under title II or XVI of the Social Security Act, and the regulations thereunder. If a benefit payable by reason of disability is converted to an early or normal retirement benefit for reasons other than a change in the health of the participant, such early or normal retirement benefit shall be treated as a continuation of the benefit payable by reason of disability and this subparagraph shall continue to apply.*

(4)(A) The actuarial value of a benefit, for purposes of this subsection, shall be determined in accordance with regulations prescribed by the corporation.

(B) For purposes of paragraph (3)—

(i) the term ''gross income'' means ''earned income'' within the meaning of section 911(b) of the Internal Revenue Code of 1954 (determined without regard to any community property laws),

(ii) in the case of a participant in a plan under which contributions are made by more than one employer, amounts received as gross income from any employer under that plan shall be aggregated with amounts received from any other employer under that plan during the same period, and

(iii) any non-basic benefit shall be disregarded.

(5)(A) For purposes of this title, the term ''substantial owner'' means an individual who—

(i) owns the entire interest in an unincorporated trade or business,

(ii) in the case of a partnership, is a partner who owns, directly or indirectly, more than 10 percent of either the capital interest or the profits interests in such partnership, or

(iii) in the case of a corporation, owns, directly or indirectly, more than 10 percent in value of either the voting stock of that corporation or all the stock of that corporation.

For purposes of clause (iii) the constructive ownership rules of section 1563(e) of the Internal Revenue Code of 1954 shall apply (determined without regard to section 1563(e)(3)(C)). For purposes of this title an individual is also treated as a substantial owner with respect to a plan if, at any time within the 60 months preceding the date on which the determination is made, he was a substantial owner under the plan.

(B) In the case of a participant in a plan under which benefits have not been increased by reason of any plan amendments and who is covered by the plan as a substantial owner, the amount of benefits guaranteed under this section shall not exceed the product of—

(i) a fraction (not to exceed 1) the numerator of which is the number of years the substantial owner was an active participant in the plan, and the denominator of which is 30, and

(ii) the amount of the substantial owner's monthly benefits guaranteed under subsection (a) (as limited under paragraph (3) of this subsection).

(C) In the case of a participant in a plan other than a plan described in subparagraph

(B), who is covered by the plan as a substantial owner, the amount of the benefit guaranteed under this section shall, under regulations prescribed by the corporation, treat each benefit increase attributable to a plan amendment as if it were provided under a new plan. The benefits guaranteed under this section with respect to all such amendments shall not exceed the amount which would be determined under subparagraph (B) if subparagraph (B) applied.

(6)(A) No benefits accrued under a plan after the date on which the Secretary of the Treasury issues notice that he has determined that any trust which is a part of a plan does not meet the requirements of section 401(a) of the Internal Revenue Code of 1954, or that the plan does not meet the requirements of section 404(a)(2) of such Code, are guaranteed under this section unless such determination is erroneous. This subparagraph does not apply if the Secretary subsequently issues a notice that such trust meets the requirements of section 401(a) of such Code or that the plan meets the requirements of section 404(a)(2) of such Code and if the Secretary determines that the trust or plan has taken action necessary to meet such requirements during the period between the issuance of the notice referred to in the preceding sentence and the issuance of the notice referred to in this sentence.

(B) No benefits accrued under a plan after the date on which an amendment of the plan is adopted which causes the Secretary of the Treasury to determine that any trust under the plan has ceased to meet the requirements of section 401(a) of the Internal Revenue Code of 1954 or that the plan has ceased to meet the requirements of section 404(a)(2) of such Code, are guaranteed under this section unless such determination is erroneous. This subparagraph shall not apply if the amendment is revoked as of the date it was first effective or amended to comply with such requirements.

(7) Benefits described in paragraph (1) are guaranteed only to the extent of the greater of—

(A) 20 percent of the amount which, but for the fact that the plan or amendment has not been in effect for 60 months or more, would be guaranteed under this section, or

(B) $20 per month,

multiplied by the number of years (but not more than 5) the plan or amendment, as the case may be, has been in effect. In determining how many years a plan or amendment has been in effect for purposes of this paragraph, the first 12 months beginning with the date on which the plan or amendment is made or first becomes effective (whichever is later) constitutes one year, and each consecutive period of 12 months thereafter constitutes an additional year. This paragraph does not apply to benefits payable under a plan unless the corporation finds substantial evidence that the plan was terminated for a reasonable business purpose and not for the purpose of obtaining the payment of benefits by the corporation under this title.

(c)(1) In addition to benefits paid under the preceding provisions of this section with respect to a terminated plan, the corporation shall pay the portion of the amount determined under paragraph (2) which is allocated with respect to each participant under section 4044(a). Such payment shall be made to such participant or to such participant's beneficiaries (including alternate payees, within the meaning of section 206(d)(3)(K)).

(2) The amount determined under this paragraph is an amount equal to the product derived by multiplying—

(A) the outstanding amount of benefit liabilities under the plan (including interest calculated from the termination date), by

(B) the applicable recovery ratio.

(3)(A) Except as provided in subparagraph (C), for purposes of this subsection, the term "recovery ratio" means the average ratio, with respect to prior plan terminations described in subparagraph (B), of—

(i) the value of the recovery of the corporation under section 4062, 4063, or 4064 in connection with such prior terminations, to

(ii) the amount of unfunded benefit liabilities under such plans as of the termination date in connection with such prior terminations.

(B) A plan termination described in this subparagraph is a termination with respect to which—

(i) the corporation has determined the value of recoveries under section 4062, 4063, or 4064 and

(ii) notices of intent to terminate were provided after December 17, 1987, and during the 5-Federal fiscal year period ending with the fiscal year preceding the fiscal year in which occurs the date of the notice of intent to terminate with respect to the plan termination for which the recovery ratio is being determined.

(C) In the case of a terminated plan with respect to which the outstanding amount of benefit liabilities exceeds $20,000,000, for purposes of this section, the term "recovery ratio" means, with respect to the termination of such plan, the ratio of—

(i) the value of the recoveries of the corporation under section 4062, 4063, or 4064 in connection with such plan, to

(ii) the amount of unfunded benefit liabilities under such plan as of the termination date.

(4) Determinations under this subsection shall be made by the corporation. Such determinations shall be binding unless shown by clear and convincing evidence to be unreasonable.

(d) The corporation is authorized to guarantee the payment of such other classes of benefits and to establish the terms and conditions under

which such other classes of benefits are guaranteed as it determines to be appropriate.

(e) For purposes of subsection (a), a qualified preretirement survivor annuity (as defined in section 205(e)(1)) with respect to a participant under a terminated single-employer plan shall not be treated as forfeitable solely because the participant has not died as of the termination date.

◊ ◊ ◊

Editor's Note: ERISA §4022(f), below, was added by §766 of the Retirement Protection Act of 1994, enacted as part of the Uruguay Round Agreements Act (P. L. 103-465). It applies to plan amendments adopted on or after December 8, 1994.

◊ ◊ ◊

(f) For purposes of this section, the effective date of a plan amendment described in section 204(i)(1) shall be the effective date of the plan of reorganization of the employer described in section 204(i)(1) or, if later, the effective date stated in such amendment.

MULTIEMPLOYER PLAN BENEFITS GUARANTEED

Sec. 4022A. (a) The corporation shall guarantee, in accordance with this section, the payment of all nonforfeitable benefits (other than benefits becoming nonforfeitable solely on account of the termination of a plan) under a multiemployer plan—

(1) to which this title applies, and

(2) which is insolvent under section 4245(b) or 4281(d)(2).

(b)(1)(A) For purposes of this section, a benefit or benefit increase which has been in effect under a plan for less than 60 months is not eligible for the corporation's guarantee. For purposes of this paragraph, any month of any plan year during which the plan was insolvent or terminated (within the meaning of section 4041A(a)(2)) shall not be taken into account.

(B) For purposes of this section, a benefit or benefit increase which has been in effect under a plan for less than 60 months before the first day of the plan year for which an amendment reducing the benefit or the benefit increase is taken into account under section 4244A(a)(2) in determining the minimum contribution requirement for the plan year under section 4243(b) is not eligible for the corporation's guarantee.

(2) For purposes of this section—

(A) the date on which a benefit or a benefit increase under a plan is first in effect is the later of—

(i) the date on which the documents establishing or increasing the benefit were executed, or

(ii) the effective date of the benefit or benefit increase;

(B) the period of time for which a benefit or a benefit increase has been in effect under a successor plan includes the period of time for which the benefit or benefit increase was in effect under a previously established plan; and

(C) in the case of a plan to which section 4021 did not apply on September 3, 1974, the time periods referred to in this section are computed beginning on the date on which section 4021 first applies to the plan.

(c)(1) Except as provided in subsection (g), the monthly benefit of a participant or a beneficiary which is guaranteed under this section by the corporation with respect to a plan is the product of—

(A) 100 percent of the accrual rate up to $5, plus 75 percent of the lesser of—

(i) $15, or

(ii) the accrual rate, if any, in excess of $5, and

(B) the number of the participant's years of credited service.

(2) Except as provided in paragraph (6) of this subsection and in subsection (g), in applying paragraph (1) with respect to a plan described in paragraph (5)(A), the term "65 percent" shall be substituted in paragraph (1)(A) for the term "75 percent".

(3) For purposes of this section, the accrual rate is—

(A) the monthly benefit of the participant or beneficiary which is described in subsection (a) and which is eligible for the corporation's guarantee under subsection (b), except that such benefit shall be—

(i) no greater than the monthly benefit which would be payable under the plan at normal retirement age in the form of a single life annuity, and

(ii) determined without regard to any reduction under section 411(a)(3)(E) of the Internal Revenue Code of 1954; divided by

(B) the participant's years of credited service.

(4) For purposes of this subsection—

(A) a year of credited service is a year in which the participant completed—

(i) a full year of participation in the plan, or

(ii) any period of service before participation which is credited for purposes of benefit accrual as the equivalent of a full year of participation;

(B) any year for which the participant is credited for purposes of benefit accrual with a fraction of the equivalent of a full year of participation shall be counted as such a fraction of a year of credited service; and

(C) years of credited service shall be determined by including service which may otherwise be disregarded by the plan under section 411(a)(3)(E) of the Internal Revenue Code of 1954.

ERISA Sec. 4022A (c)(4)(C)

(5)(A) A plan is described in this subparagraph if—

(i) the first plan year—

(I) in which the plan is insolvent under section 4245(b) or 4281(d)(2), and

(II) for which benefits are required to be suspended under section 4245, or reduced or suspended under section 4281, until they do not exceed the levels provided in this subsection,

begins before the year 2000; and

(ii) the plan sponsor has not established to the satisfaction of the corporation that, during the period of 10 consecutive plan years (or of such lesser number of plan years for which the plan was maintained) immediately preceding the first plan year to which the minimum funding standards of section 412 of the Internal Revenue Code of 1954 apply, the total amount of the contributions required under the plan for each plan year was at least equal to the sum of—

(I) the normal cost for that plan year, and

(II) the interest for the plan year (determined under the plan) on the unfunded past service liability for that plan year, determined as of the beginning of that plan year.

(B) A plan shall not be considered to be described in subparagraph (A) if—

(i) it is established to the satisfaction of the corporation that—

(I) the total amount of the contributions received under the plan for the plan years for which the actuarial valuations (performed during the period described in subparagraph (A)(ii)) were performed was at least equal to the sum described in subparagraph (A)(ii); or

(II) the rates of contribution to the plan under the collective bargaining agreements negotiated when the findings of such valuations were available were reasonably expected to provide such contributions;

(ii) the number of actuarial valuations performed during the period described in subparagraph (A)(ii) is—

(I) at least 2, in any case in which such period consists of more than 6 plan years, and

(II) at least 1, in any case in which such period consists of 6 or fewer plan years; and

(iii) if the proposition described in clause (i)(I) is to be established, the plan sponsor certifies that to the best of the plan sponsor's knowledge there is no information available which establishes that the total amount of the contributions received under the plan for any plan year during the period described in subparagraph (A)(ii) for which no valuation was performed is less than the sum described in subparagraph (A)(ii).

(6) Notwithstanding paragraph (2), in the case of a plan described in paragraph (5)(A), if for any period of 3 consecutive plan years beginning with the first plan year to which the minimum funding standards of section 412 of the Internal Revenue Code of 1954 apply, the value of the assets of the plan for each such plan year is an amount equal to at least 8 times the benefit payments for such plan year—

(A) paragraph (2) shall not apply to such plan; and

(B) the benefit of a participant or beneficiary guaranteed by the corporation with respect to the plan shall be an amount determined under paragraph (1).

(d) In the case of a benefit which has been reduced under section 411(a)(3)(E) of the Internal Revenue Code of 1954, the corporation shall guarantee the lesser of—

(1) the reduced benefit, or

(2) the amount determined under subsection (c).

(e) The corporation shall not guarantee benefits under a multiemployer plan which, under section 4022(b)(6), would not be guaranteed under a single-employer plan.

(f)(1) No later than 5 years after the date of the enactment of the Multiemployer Pension Plan Amendments Act of 1980, and at least every fifth year thereafter, the corporation shall—

(A) conduct a study to determine—

(i) the premiums needed to maintain the basic-benefit guarantee levels for multiemployer plans described in subsection (c), and

(ii) whether the basic-benefit guarantee levels for multiemployer plans may be increased without increasing the basic-benefit premiums for multiemployer plans under this title; and

(B) report such determinations to the Committee on Ways and Means and the Committee on Education and Labor of the House of Representatives and to the Committee on Finance and the Committee on Labor and Human Resources of the Senate.

(2)(A) If the last report described in paragraph (1) indicates that a premium increase is necessary to support the existing basic-benefit guarantee levels for multiemployer plans, the corporation shall transmit to the Committee on Ways and Means and the Committee on Education and Labor of the House of Representatives and to the Committee on Finance and the Committee on Labor and Human Resources of the Senate by March 31 of any calendar year in which congressional action under this subsection is requested—

(i) a revised schedule of basic-benefit guarantees for multiemployer plans which would be necessary in the absence of an increase in premiums approved in accordance with section 4006(b),

(ii) a revised schedule of basic-benefit premiums for multiemployer plans which is necessary to support the existing basic-benefit guarantees for such plans, and

(iii) a revised schedule of basic-benefit guarantees for multiemployer plans for which the schedule of premiums necessary is higher than the existing premium schedule for such plans but lower than the revised schedule of premiums for such plans specified in clause (ii), together with such schedule of premiums.

(B) The revised schedule of increased premiums referred to in subparagraph (A)(ii) or (A)(iii) shall go into effect as approved by the enactment of a joint resolution.

(C) If an increase in premiums is not so enacted, the revised guarantee schedule described in subparagraph (A)(i) shall go into effect on the first day of the second calendar year following the year in which such revised guarantee schedule was submitted to the Congress.

(3)(A) If the last report described in paragraph (1) indicates that basic-benefit guarantees for multiemployer plans can be increased without increasing the basic-benefit premiums for multiemployer plans under this title, the corporation shall submit to the Committee on Ways and Means and the Committee on Education and Labor of the House of Representatives and to the Committee on Finance and the Committee on Labor and Human Resources of the Senate by March 31 of the calendar year in which congressional action under this paragraph is requested—

(i) a revised schedule of increases in the basic-benefit guarantees which can be supported by the existing schedule of basic-benefit premiums for multiemployer plans, and

(ii) a revised schedule of basic-benefit premiums sufficient to support the existing basic-benefit guarantees.

(B) The revised schedules referred to in subparagraph (A)(1) or subparagraph (A)(ii) shall go into effect as approved by the enactment of a joint resolution.

(4)(A) The succeeding subparagraphs of this paragraph are enacted by the Congress as an exercise of the rulemaking power of the Senate and the House of Representatives, respectively, and as such they shall be deemed a part of the rules of each House, respectively, but applicable only with respect to the procedure to be followed in that House in the case of joint resolutions (as defined in subparagraph (B)). Such subparagraphs shall supersede other rules only to the extent that they are inconsistent therewith. They are enacted with full recognition of the constitutional right of either House to change the rules (so far as relating to the procedure of that House) at any time, in the same manner, and to the same extent as in the case of any rule of that House.

(B) For purposes of this subsection, "joint resolution" means only a joint resolution, the matter after the resolving clause of which is as follows: "The proposed schedule described in _____ transmitted to the Congress by the Pension Benefit Guaranty Corporation on _____ is hereby approved.", the first blank space therein being filled with "section 4022A(f)(2)(A)(ii) of the Employee Retirement Income Security Act of 1974", "section 4022A(f)(2)(A)(iii) of the Employee Retirement Income Security Act of 1974", "section 4022A(f)(3)(A)(i) of the Employee Retirement Income Security Act of 1974", or "section 4022A(f)(3)(A)(ii) of the Employee Retirement Income Security Act of 1974" (whichever is applicable), and the second blank space therein being filled with the date on which the corporation's message proposing the revision was submitted.

(C) The procedure for disposition of a joint resolution shall be the procedure described in section 4006(b)(4) through (7).

(g)(1) The corporation may guarantee the payment of such other classes of benefits under multiemployer plans, and establish the terms and conditions under which those other classes of benefits are guaranteed, as it determines to be appropriate.

(2)(A) The corporation shall prescribe regulations to establish a supplemental program to guarantee benefits under multiemployer plans which would be guaranteed under this section but for the limitations in subsection (c). Such regulations shall be proposed by the corporation no later than the end of the 18th calendar month following the date of the enactment of the Multiemployer Pension Plan Amendments Act of 1980. The regulations shall make coverage under the supplemental program available no later than January 1, 1983. Any election to participate in the supplemental program shall be on a voluntary basis, and a plan electing such coverage shall continue to pay the premiums required under section 4006(a)(2)(B) to the revolving fund used pursuant to section 4005 in connection with benefits otherwise guaranteed under this section. Any such election shall be irrevocable, except to the extent otherwise provided by regulations prescribed by the corporation.

(B) The regulations prescribed under this paragraph shall provide—

(i) that a plan must elect coverage under the supplemental program within the time permitted by the regulations;

(ii) unless the corporation determines otherwise, that a plan may not elect supplemental coverage unless the value of the assets of the plan as of the end of the plan year preceding the plan year in which the election must be made is an amount equal to 15 times the total amount of the benefit payments made under the plan for that year; and

(iii) such other reasonable terms and conditions for supplemental coverage, including funding standards and any other reasonable limitations with respect to plans or benefits covered or to means of program financing, as the corporation determines are necessary and appropriate for a feasible supplemental program consistent with the purposes of this title.

(3) Any benefits guaranteed under this sub section shall be considered nonbasic benefit for purposes of this title.

(4)(A) No revised schedule of premiums under this subsection, after the initial schedule, shall go into effect unless—

(i) the revised schedule is submitted to the Congress, and

(ii) a joint resolution described in subparagraph (B) is not enacted before the close of the 60th legislative day after such schedule is submitted to the Congress.

(B) For purposes of subparagraph (A), a joint resolution described in this subparagraph is a joint resolution the matter after the resolving clause of which is as follows: "The revised premium schedule transmitted to the Congress by the Pension Benefit Guaranty Corporation under section 4022A(g)(4) of the Employee Retirement Income Security Act of 1974 on _____ is hereby disapproved.", the blank space therein being filled with the date on which the revised schedule was submitted.

(C) For purposes of subparagraph (A), the term "legislative day" means any calendar day other than a day on which either House is not in session because of a sine die adjournment or an adjournment of more than 3 days to a day certain.

(D) The procedure for disposition of a joint resolution described in subparagraph (B) shall be the procedure described in paragraphs (4) through (7) of section 4006(b).

(5) Regulations prescribed by the corporation to carry out the provisions of this subsection, may, to the extent provided therein, supersede the requirements of sections 4245, 4261, and 4281, and the requirements of section 418E of the Internal Revenue Code of 1954, but only with respect to benefits guaranteed under this subsection.

(h)(1) Except as provided in paragraph (3), subsections (b) and (c) shall not apply with respect to the nonforfeitable benefits accrued as of July 29, 1980, with respect to a participant or beneficiary under a multiemployer plan—

(1) who is in pay status on July 29, 1980, or

(2) who is within 36 months of the normal retirement age and has a nonforfeitable right to a pension as of that date.

(2) The benefits described in paragraph (1) shall be guaranteed by the corporation in the same manner and to the same extent as benefits are guaranteed by the corporation under section 4022 (without regard to this section).

(3) This subsection does not apply with respect to a plan for plan years following a plan year—

(A) in which the plan has terminated within the meaning of section 4041A(a)(2), or

(B) in which it is determined by the corporation that substantially all the employers have withdrawn from the plan pursuant to an agreement or arrangement to withdraw.

AGGREGATE LIMIT ON BENEFITS GUARANTEED

Sec. 4022B. **(a)** Notwithstanding sections 4022 and 4022A, no person shall receive from the corporation pursuant to a guarantee by the corporation of basic benefits with respect to a participant under all multiemployer and single employer plans an amount, or amounts, with an actuarial value which exceeds the actuarial value of a monthly benefit in the form of a life annuity commencing at age 65 equal to the amount determined under section 4022(b)(3)(B) as of the date of the last plan termination.

(b) For purposes of this section—

(1) the receipt of benefits under a multiemployer plan receiving financial assistance from the corporation shall be considered the receipt of amounts from the corporation pursuant to a guarantee by the corporation of basic benefits except to the extent provided in regulations prescribed by the corporation, and

(2) the date on which a multiemployer plan, whether or not terminated, begins receiving financial assistance from the corporation shall be considered a date of plan termination.

PLAN FIDUCIARIES

Sec. 4023. Notwithstanding any other provision of this Act, a fiduciary of a plan to which section 4021 applies is not in violation of the fiduciary's duties as a result of any act or of any withholding of action required by this title.

Subtitle C—Terminations

Termination Of Single Employer Plans

Sec. 4041. (a) General Rules Governing Single-Employer Plan Terminations.—

(1) Exclusive means of plan termination.—Except in the case of a termination for which proceedings are otherwise instituted by the corporation as provided in section 4042, a single-employer plan may be terminated only in a standard termination under subsection (b) or a distress termination under subsection (c).

(2) 60-day notice of intent to terminate.— Not less than 60 days before the proposed termination date of a standard termination under subsection (b) or a distress termination under subsection (c), the plan administrator shall provide to each affected party (other than the corporation in the case of a standard termination) a written notice of intent to terminate stating that such termination is intended and the proposed termination date. The written notice shall include any related additional information required by regulations of the corporation.

(3) Adherence to collective bargaining agreements.—The corporation shall not proceed with a termination of a plan under this section if the termination would violate the terms and conditions of an existing collective bargaining agreement. Nothing in the preceding sentence shall be construed as limiting the authority of the corporation to institute proceedings to involuntarily terminate a plan under section 4042.

(b) Standard Termination of Single-Employer Plans.—

(1) General requirements.—A single employer plan may terminate under a standard termination only if—

(A) the plan administrator provides the 60-day advance notice of intent to terminate to affected parties required under subsection (a)(2),

(B) the requirements of subparagraphs (A) and (B) of paragraph (2) are met,

(C) the corporation does not issue a notice of noncompliance under subparagraph (C) of paragraph (2), and

(D) when the final distribution of assets occurs, the plan is sufficient for benefit liabilities (determined as of the termination date).

(2) Termination procedure.—

(A) Notice to the corporation.—As soon as practicable after the date on which the notice of intent to terminate is provided pursuant to subsection (a)(2), the plan administrator shall send a notice to the corporation setting forth—

(i) certification by an enrolled actuary—

(I) of the projected amount of the assets of the plan (as of the proposed date of final distribution of assets),

(II) of the actuarial present value (as of such date) of the benefit liabilities (determined as of the proposed termination date) under the plan, and

(III) that the plan is projected to be sufficient (as of such proposed date of final distribution) for such benefit liabilities,

(ii) such information as the corporation may prescribe in regulations as necessary to enable the corporation to make determinations under subparagraph (C), and

(iii) certification by the plan administrator that—

(I) the information on which the enrolled actuary based the certification under clause (i) is accurate and complete, and

(II) the information provided to the corporation under clause (ii) is accurate and complete.

Clause (i) and clause (iii)(I) shall not apply to a plan described in section 412(i) of the Internal Revenue Code of 1986.

(B) Notice to participants and beneficiaries of benefit commitments.—No later than the date on which a notice is sent by the plan administrator under subparagraph (A), the plan administrator shall send a notice to each person who is a participant or beneficiary under the plan—

(i) specifying the amount of the benefit liabilities (if any) attributable to such person as of the proposed termination date, and the benefit form on the basis of which such amount is determined, and

(ii) including the following information used in determining such benefit liabilities:

(I) the length of service,

(II) the age of the participant or beneficiary,

(III) wages,

(IV) the assumptions, including the interest rate, and

(V) such other information as the corporation may require.

Such notice shall be written in such manner as is likely to be understood by the participant or beneficiary and as may be prescribed in regulations of the corporation.

◊ ◊ ◊

Editor's Note: ERISA §4041(b)(2)(C), as set forth below, appears as amended by §778(a) of the Retirement Protection Act of 1994 (enacted as part of the Uruguay Round Agreements Act, P.L. 103-465). The amendments apply to plan terminations under ERISA §4041(b) with respect to which the PBGC had not, as of December 8, 1994, issued a notice of noncompliance that has become final, or otherwise issued a final determination that the plan termination is nullified.

◊ ◊ ◊

(C) Notice from the corporation of noncompliance.—

(i) In general.—Within 60 days after receipt of the notice under subparagraph (A), the corporation shall issue a notice of noncompliance to the plan administrator if—

[(I) it has reason to believe that any requirement of subsection (a)(2) or subparagraph (A) or (B) has not been met, or]

(I) it determines, based on the notice sent under paragraph (2)(A) of subsection (b), that there is reason to believe that the plan is not sufficient for benefit liabilities,

(II) it otherwise determines, on the basis of information provided by affected parties or otherwise obtained by the corporation, that there is reason to believe that the plan is not sufficient for benefit liabilities[.] *, or*

(III) it determines that any other requirement of subparagraph (A) or (B) of this paragraph or of subsection (a)(2) has not been met, unless it further determines that the issuance of such notice would be inconsistent with the interests of participants and beneficiaries.

(ii) Extension.—The corporation and the plan administrator may agree to extend the 60-day period referred to in clause (i) by a written agreement signed by the corporation

ERISA Sec. 4041 (b)(2)(C)(ii)

and the plan administrator before the expiration of the 60-day period. The 60-day period shall be extended as provided in the agreement and may be further extended by subsequent written agreements signed by the corporation and the plan administrator made before the expiration of a previously agreed-upon extension of the 60-day period. Any extension may be made upon such terms and conditions (including the payment of benefits) as are agreed upon by the corporation and the plan administrator.

(D) Final distribution of assets in absence of notice of noncompliance.—The plan administrator shall commence the final distribution of assets pursuant to the standard termination of the plan as soon as practicable after the expiration of the 60-day (or extended) period referred to in subparagraph (C), but such final distributions may occur only if—

(i) the plan administrator has not received during such period a notice of noncompliance from the corporation under subparagraph (C), and

(ii) when such final distribution occurs, the plan is sufficient for benefit liabilities (determined as of the termination date).

(3) Methods of final distribution of assets.—

(A) In general.—In connection with any final distribution of assets pursuant to the standard termination of the plan under this subsection, the plan administrator shall distribute the assets in accordance with section 4044. In distributing such assets, the plan administrator shall—

(i) purchase irrevocable commitments from an insurer to provide all benefit liabilities under the plan, or

◊◊◊

Editor's Note: ERISA §4041(b)(3)(A)(ii), as set forth below, appears as amended by §776(c) of the Retirement Protection Act of 1994 (enacted as part of the Uruguay Round Agreements Act, P.L. 103-465). The amendment applies to distributions that occur in plan years commencing after final regulations implementing the provisions of Act §776 (relating to missing participants) are implemented by the PBGC.

◊◊◊

(ii) in accordance with the provisions of the plan and any applicable regulations, otherwise fully provide all benefit liabilities under the plan. *A transfer of assets to the corporation in accordance with section 4050 on behalf of a missing participant shall satisfy this subparagraph with respect to such participant.*

(B) Certification to the corporation of final distribution of assets.—Within 30 days after the final distribution of assets is completed pursuant to the standard termination of the plan under this subsection, the plan administrator shall send a notice to the corporation certifying that the assets of the plan have been distributed in accordance with the provisions of subparagraph (A) so as to pay all benefit liabilities under the plan.

(4) Continuing authority.—Nothing in this section shall be construed to preclude the continued exercise by the corporation, after the termination date of a plan terminated in a standard termination under this subsection, of its authority under section 4003 with respect to matters relating to the termination. A certification under paragraph (3)(B) shall not affect the corporation's obligations under section 4022.

(c) Distress Termination of Single-Employer Plans.—

(1) In general.—A single-employer plan may terminate under a distress termination only if—

(A) the plan administrator provides the 60-day advance notice of intent to terminate to affected parties required under subsection (a)(2),

(B) the requirements of subparagraph (A) of paragraph (2) are met, and

(C) the corporation determines that the requirements of subparagraph (B) of paragraph (2) are met.

(2) Termination requirements.—

(A) Information submitted to the corporation.—As soon as practicable after the date on which the notice of intent to terminate is provided pursuant to subsection (a)(2), the plan administrator shall provide the corporation, in such form as may be prescribed by the corporation in regulations, the following information:

(i) such information as the corporation may prescribe by regulation as necessary to make determinations under subparagraph (B) and paragraph (3);

(ii) unless the corporation determines the information is not necessary for purposes of paragraph (3)(A) or section 4062, certification by an enrolled actuary of—

(I) the amount (as of the proposed termination date and, if applicable, the proposed distribution date) of the current value of the assets of the plan,

(II) the actuarial present value (as of such dates) of the benefit liabilities under the plan,

(III) whether the plan is sufficient for benefit liabilities as of such dates,

(IV) the actuarial present value (as of such dates) of benefits under the plan guaranteed under section 4022, and

(V) whether the plan is sufficient for guaranteed benefits as of such dates;

(iii) in any case in which the plan is not sufficient for benefit liabilities as of such date—

(I) the name and address of each participant and beneficiary under the plan as of such date, and

(II) such other information as shall be prescribed by the corporation by regulation as necessary to enable the corporation to be able to make payments to participants and beneficiaries as required under section 4022(c); and

(iv) certification by the plan administrator that—

(I) the information on which the enrolled actuary based the certifications under clause (ii) is accurate and complete, and

(II) the information provided to the corporation under clauses (i) and (iii) is accurate and complete.

Clause (ii) and clause (iv)(I) shall not apply to a plan described in section 412(i) of the Internal Revenue Code of 1986.

(B) Determination by the corporation of necessary distress criteria.—Upon receipt of the notice of intent to terminate required under subsection (a)(2) and the information required under subparagraph (A), the corporation shall determine whether the requirements of this subparagraph are met as provided in clause (i), (ii), or (iii). The requirements of this subparagraph are met if each person who is (as of the proposed termination date) a contributing sponsor of such plan or a member of such sponsor's controlled group meets the requirements of any of the following clauses:

(i) Liquidation in bankruptcy or insolvency proceedings.—The requirements of this clause are met by a person if—

ERISA Sec. 4041 (c)(2)(B)(i)

◊ ◊ ◊

Editor's Note: ERISA §4041(c)(2) (B)(i)(I), as set forth below, appears as amended by §778(b) of the Retirement Protection Act of 1994 (enacted as part of the Uruguay Round Agreements Act, P.L. 103-465). The amendments apply as if included in the Single-Employer Pension Plan Amendments Act of 1986.

◊ ◊ ◊

(I) such person has filed or has had filed against such person, as of the proposed termination date, a petition seeking liquidation in a case under title 11, United States Code, or under any similar *Federal law* or law of a State or political subdivision of a State (or a case described in clause (ii) filed by or against such person has been converted, as of such date, to a case in which liquidation is sought), and

(II) such case has not, as of the termination date, been dismissed.

(ii) Reorganization in bankruptcy or insolvency proceedings.—The requirements of this clause are met by a person if—

(I) such person has filed, or has had filed against such person, as of the proposed termination date, a petition seeking reorganization in a case under title 11, United States Code, or under any similar law of a State or political subdivision of a State (or a case described in clause (i) filed by or against such person has been converted, as of such date, to such a case in which reorganization is sought),

(II) such case has not, as of the proposed termination date, been dismissed, and

(III) such person timely submits to the corporation any request for the approval of the bankruptcy court (or other appropriate court in a case under such similar law of a State or political subdivision) of the plan termination, and

(IV) the bankruptcy court (or such other appropriate court) determines that, unless

the plan is terminated, such person will be unable to pay all its debts pursuant to a plan of reorganization and will be unable to continue in business outside the chapter 11 reorganization process and approves the termination.

(iii) Termination required to enable payment of debts while staying in business or to avoid unreasonably burdensome pension costs caused by declining workforce. The requirements of this clause are met by a person if such person demonstrates to the satisfaction of the corporation that—

(I) unless a distress termination occurs, such person will be unable to pay such person's debts when due and will be unable to continue in business, or

(II) the costs of providing pension coverage have become unreasonably burdensome to such persons, solely as a result of a decline of such person's workforce covered as participants under all single-employer pension plans of which such person is a contributing sponsor.

(C) Notification of determinations by the corporation.—The corporation shall notify the plan administrator as soon as practicable of its determinations made pursuant to subparagraph (B).

(3) Termination procedure.—

(A) Determinations by the corporation relating to plan sufficiency for guaranteed benefits and for benefit liabilities. If the corporation determines that the requirements for a distress termination set forth in paragraphs (1) and (2) are met, the corporation shall—

(i) determine that the plan is sufficient for guaranteed benefits (as of the termination date) or that the corporation is unable to make such determination on the basis of information made available to the corporation,

(ii) determine that the plan is sufficient for benefit liabilities (as of the termination date) or that the corporation is unable to make such determination on the basis of information made available to the corporation, and

(iii) notify the plan administrator of the determinations made pursuant to this subparagraph as soon as practicable.

(B) Implementation of termination.—After the corporation notifies the plan administrator of its determinations under subparagraph (A), the termination of the plan shall be carried out as soon as practicable, as provided in clause (i), (ii), or (iii).

(i) Cases of sufficiency for benefit liabilities.—In any case in which the corporation determines that the plan is sufficient for benefit liabilities, the plan administrator shall proceed to distribute the plan's assets and make certification to the corporation with respect to such distribution, in the manner described in subsection (b)(3), and shall take such other actions as may be appropriate to carry out the termination of the plan.

(ii) Cases of sufficiency for guaranteed benefits without a finding of sufficiency for benefit liabilities.—In any case in which the corporation determines that the plan is sufficient for guaranteed benefits, but further determines that it is unable to determine that the plan is sufficient for benefit liabilities on the basis of the information made available to it, the plan administrator shall proceed to distribute the plan's assets in the manner described in subsection (b)(3), make certification to the corporation that the distribution has occurred, and take such actions as may be appropriate to carry out the termination of the plan.

(iii) Cases without any finding of sufficiency.—In any case in which the corporation determines that it is unable to determine that the plan is sufficient for guaranteed benefits on the basis of the information made available to it, the corporation shall commence proceedings in accordance with section 4042.

(C) Finding after authorized commencement of termination that plan is unable to pay benefits.—

(i) Findings with respect to benefit liabilities which are not guaranteed benefits.—If, after the plan administrator has begun to terminate the plan as authorized under subparagraph (B)(i), the plan administrator finds that the plan is unable, or will be unable, to pay benefit liabilities which are not benefits guaranteed by the corporation under section 4022, the plan administrator shall notify the corporation of such finding as soon as practicable thereafter.

(ii) Finding with respect to guaranteed benefits.—If, after the plan administrator has begun to terminate the plan as authorized by subparagraph (B)(i) or (ii), the plan administrator finds that the plan is unable, or will be unable, to pay all benefits under the plan which are guaranteed by the corporation under section 4022, the plan administrator shall notify the corporation of such finding as soon as practicable thereafter. If the corporation concurs in the finding of the plan administrator (or the corporation itself makes such a finding), the corporation shall institute appropriate proceedings under section 4042.

(D) Administration of the plan during interim period.—

(i) In general.—The plan admin-istrator shall—

(I) meet the requirements of clause (ii) for the period commencing on the date on which the plan administrator provides a notice of distress termination to the corporation under subsection (a)(2) and ending on the date on which the plan administrator receives notification from the corporation of its determinations under subparagraph (A), and

(II) meet the requirements of clause (ii) commencing on the date on which the plan administrator or the corporation makes a finding under subparagraph (C)(ii).

ERISA Sec. 4041 (c)(3)(D)(i)(II)

(ii) Requirements.—The requirements of this clause are met by the plan administrator if the plan administrator—

(I) refrains from distributing assets or taking any other actions to carry out the proposed termination under this subsection,

(II) pays benefits attributable to employer contributions, other than death benefits, only in the form of an annuity,

(III) does not use plan assets to purchase irrevocable commitments to provide benefits from an insurer, and

(IV) continues to pay all benefit liabilities under the plan, but, commencing on the proposed termination date, limits the payment of benefits under the plan to those benefits which are guaranteed by the corporation under section 4022 or to which assets are required to be allocated under section 4044.

In the event the plan administrator is later determined not to have met the requirements for distress termination, any benefits which are not paid solely by reason of compliance with subclause (IV) shall be due and payable immediately (together with interest, at a reasonable rate, in accordance with regulations of the corporation).

(d) Sufficiency.—For purposes of this section—

(1) Sufficiency for benefit liabilities.—A single employer plan is sufficient for benefit liabilities if there is no amount of unfunded benefit liabilities under the plan.

(2) Sufficiency for guaranteed benefits.—A single-employer plan is sufficient for guaranteed benefits if there is no amount of unfunded guaranteed benefits under the plan.

(e) Limitation on the Conversion of a Defined Benefit Plan to a Defined Contribution Plan.—The adoption of an amendment to a plan which causes the plan to become a plan described in section 4021(b)(1) consti-

tutes a termination of the plan. Such an amendment may take effect only after the plan satisfies the requirements for standard termination under subsection (b) or distress termination under subsection (c).

TERMINATION OF MULTI-EMPLOYER PLANS

Sec. 4041A. (a) Termination of a multiemployer plan under this section occurs as a result of—

(1) the adoption after the date of enactment of the Multiemployer Pension Plan Amendments Act of 1980 of a plan amendment which provides that participants will receive no credit for any purpose under the plan for service with any employer after the date specified by such amendment;

(2) the withdrawal of every employer from the plan, within the meaning of section 4203 or the cessation of the obligation of all employers to contribute under the plan; or

(3) the adoption of an amendment to the plan which causes the plan to become a plan described in section 4021(b)(1).

(b)(1) The date on which a plan terminates under paragraph (1) or (3) of subsection (a) is the later of—

(A) the date on which the amendment is adopted, or

(B) the date on which the amendment takes effect.

(2) The date on which a plan terminates under paragraph (2) of subsection (a) is the earlier of—

(A) the date on which the last employer withdraws, or

(B) the first day of the first plan year for which no employer contributions were required under the plan.

(c) Except as provided in subsection (f)(1), the plan sponsor of a plan which terminates under paragraph (2) of subsection (a) shall—

(1) limit the payment of benefits to benefits which are nonforfeitable under the plan as of the date of the termination, and

(2) pay benefits attributable to employer contributions, other than death benefits, only in the form of an annuity, unless the plan assets are distributed in full satisfaction of all nonforfeitable benefits under the plan.

(d) The plan sponsor of a plan which terminates under paragraph (2) of subsection (a) shall reduce benefits and suspend benefit payments in accordance with section 4281.

(e) In the case of a plan which terminates under paragraph (1) or (3) of subsection (a), the rate of an employer's contributions under the plan for each plan year beginning on or after the plan termination date shall equal or exceed the highest rate of employer contributions at which the employer had an obligation to contribute under the plan in the 5 preceding plan years ending on or before the plan termination date, unless the corporation approves a reduction in the rate based on a finding that the plan is or soon will be fully funded.

(f)(1) The plan sponsor of a terminated plan may authorize the payment other than in the form of an annuity of a participant's entire nonforfeitable benefit attributable to employer contributions, other than a death benefit, if the value of the entire nonforfeitable benefit does not exceed $1,750. The corporation may authorize the payment of benefits under the terms of a terminated plan other than nonforfeitable benefits, or the payment other than in the form of an annuity of benefits having a value greater than $1,750, if the corporation determines that such payment is not adverse to the interest of the plan's participants and beneficiaries generally and does not unreasonably increase the corporation's risk of loss with respect to the plan.

(2) The corporation may prescribe reporting requirements for terminated plans, and rules and standards for the administration of such plans, which the corporation considers appropriate to protect the interests of plan partici-

pants and beneficiaries or to prevent unreasonable loss to the corporation.

INSTITUTION OF TERMINATION PROCEEDINGS BY THE CORPORATION

Sec. 4042. (a) The corporation may institute proceedings under this section to terminate a plan whenever it determines that—

(1) the plan has not met the minimum funding standard required under section 412 of the Internal Revenue Code of 1954, or has been notified by the Secretary of the Treasury that a notice of deficiency under section 6212 of such Code has been mailed with respect to the tax imposed under section 4971(a) of such Code,

(2) the plan will be unable to pay benefits when due,

◊ ◊ ◊

Editor's Note: ERISA §4042(a)(3), as set forth below, appears as amended by §771(e)(2) of the Retirement Protection Act of 1994 (enacted as part of the Uruguay Round Agreements Act, P.L. 103-465). The amendments applies to events occurring more than 60 days after December 8, 1994.

◊ ◊ ◊

(3) the reportable event described in section [4043(b)(7)] *4043(c)(7)* has occurred, or

(4) the possible long-run loss of the corporation with respect to the plan may reasonably be expected to increase unreasonably if the plan is not terminated.
The corporation shall as soon as practicable institute proceedings under this section to terminate a single-employer plan whenever the corporation determines that the plan does not have assets available to pay benefits which are currently due under the terms of the plan. The corporation may prescribe a simplified procedure to follow in terminating small plans as long as that procedure includes substantial

safeguards for the rights of the participants and beneficiaries under the plans, and for the employers who maintain such plans (including the requirement for a court decree under subsection (c)). Notwithstanding any other provision of this title, the corporation is authorized to pool assets of terminated plans for purposes of administration, investment, payment of liabilities of all such terminated plans, and such other purposes as it determines to be appropriate in the administration of this title.

(b)(1) Whenever the corporation makes a determination under subsection (a) with respect to a plan or is required under subsection (a) to institute proceedings under this section, it may, upon notice to the plan, apply to the appropriate United States district court for the appointment of a trustee to administer the plan with respect to which the determination is made pending the issuance of a decree under subsection (c) ordering the termination of the plan. If within 3 business days after the filing of an application under this subsection, or such other period as the court may order, the administrator of the plan consents to the appointment of a trustee, or fails to show why a trustee should not be appointed, the court may grant the application and appoint a trustee to administer the plan in accordance with its terms until the corporation determines that the plan should be terminated or that termination is unnecessary. The corporation may request that it be appointed as trustee of a plan in any case.

(2) Notwithstanding any other provision of this title—

(A) upon the petition of a plan administrator or the corporation, the appropriate United States district court may appoint a trustee in accordance with the provisions of this section if the interests of the plan participants would be better served by the appointment of the trustee, and

(B) upon the petition of the corporation, the appropriate United States district court shall appoint a trustee proposed by the corporation for a multiemployer plan which is in reorganization or to which section 4041A(d)

applies, unless such appointment would be adverse to the interests of the plan participants and beneficiaries in the aggregate.

(3) The corporation and plan administrator may agree to the appointment of a trustee without proceeding in accordance with the requirements of paragraphs (1) and (2).

(c) If the corporation is required under subsection (a) of this section to commence proceedings under this section with respect to a plan or, after issuing a notice under this section to a plan administrator, has determined that the plan should be terminated, it may, upon notice to the plan administrator, apply to the appropriate United States district court for a decree adjudicating that the plan must be terminated in order to protect the interests of the participants or to avoid any unreasonable deterioration of the financial condition of the plan or any unreasonable increase in the liability of the fund. If the trustee appointed under subsection (b) disagrees with the determination of the corporation under the preceding sentence he may intervene in the proceeding relating to the application for the decree, or make application for such decree himself. Upon granting a decree for which the corporation or trustee has applied under this subsection the court shall authorize the trustee appointed under subsection (b) (or appoint a trustee if one has not been appointed under such subsection and authorize him) to terminate the plan in accordance with the provisions of this subtitle. If the corporation and the plan administrator agree that a plan should be terminated and agree to the appointment of a trustee without proceeding in accordance with the requirements of this subsection (other than this sentence) the trustee shall have the power described in subsection (d)(1) and, in addition to any other duties imposed on the trustee under law or by agreement between the corporation and the plan administrator, the trustee is subject to the duties described in subsection (d)(3). Whenever a trustee appointed under this title is operating a plan with discretion as to the date upon which final distribution of the assets is to be commenced, the trustee shall notify the corporation at least 10 days before the date on which he proposes to commence such distribution.

(3) In the case of a proceeding initiated under this section, the plan administrator shall provide the corporation, upon the request of the corporation, the information described in clauses (ii), (iii), and (iv) of section 4041(c)(2)(A).

(d)(1)(A) A trustee appointed under subsection (b) shall have the power—

(i) to do any act authorized by the plan or this title to be done by the plan administrator or any trustee of the plan;

(ii) to require the transfer of all (or any part) of the assets and records of the plan to himself as trustee;

(iii) to invest any assets of the plan which he holds in accordance with the provisions of the plan, regulations of the corporation, and applicable rules of law;

(iv) to limit payment of benefits under the plan to basic benefits or to continue payment of some or all of the benefits which were being paid prior to his appointment;

(v) in the case of a multiemployer plan, to reduce benefits or suspend benefit payments under the plan, give appropriate notices, amend the plan, and perform other acts required or authorized by subtitle (E) to be performed by the plan sponsor or administrator;

(vi) to do such other acts as he deems necessary to continue operation of the plan without increasing the potential liability of the corporation, if such acts may be done under the provisions of the plan; and

(vii) to require the plan sponsor, the plan administrator, any contributing or withdrawn employer, and any employee organization representing plan participants to furnish any information with respect to the plan which the trustee may reasonably need in order to administer the plan.

If the court to which application is made under subsection (c) dismisses the application with prejudice, or if the corporation fails to apply for a decree under subsection (c) within 30 days after the date on which the trustee is appointed under subsection (b), the trustee shall transfer all assets and records of the plan held by him to the plan administrator within 3 business days after such dismissal or the expiration of such 30-day period, and shall not be liable to the plan or any other person for his acts as trustee except for willful misconduct, or for conduct in violation of the provisions of part 4 of subtitle B of title I of this Act (except as provided in subsection (d)(1)(A)(v)). The 30-day period referred to in this subparagraph may be extended as provided by agreement between the plan administrator and the corporation or by court order obtained by the corporation.

(B) If the court to which an application is made under subsection (c) issues the decree requested in such application, in addition to the powers described in subparagraph (A), the trustee shall have the power—

(i) to pay benefits under the plan in accordance with the requirements of this title;

(ii) to collect for the plan any amounts due the plan, including but not limited to the power to collect from the persons obligated to meet the requirements of section 302 or the terms of the plan;

(iii) to receive any payment made by the corporation to the plan under this title;

(iv) to commence, prosecute, or defend on behalf of the plan any suit or proceeding involving the plan;

(v) to issue, publish, or file such notices, statements, and reports as may be required by the corporation or any order of the court;

(vi) to liquidate the plan assets;

(vii) to recover payments under section 4045(a); and

(viii) to do such other acts as may be necessary to comply with this title or any order of the court and to protect the interests of plan participants and beneficiaries.

(2) As soon as practicable after his appointment, the trustee shall give notice to interested parties of the institution of proceedings under this title to determine whether the plan should be terminated or to terminate the plan, whichever is applicable. For purposes of this paragraph, the term "interested party" means—

(A) the plan administrator,

(B) each participant in the plan and each beneficiary of a deceased participant,

(C) each employer who may be subject to liability under section 4062, 4063, or 4064,

(D) each employer who is or may be liable to the plan under section part 1 of subtitle E,

(E) each employer who has an obligation to contribute, within the meaning of section 4212(a), under a multiemployer plan, and

(F) each employee organization which, for purposes of collective bargaining, represents plan participants employed by an employer described in subparagraph (C), (D), or (E).

(3) Except to the extent inconsistent with the provisions of this Act, or as may be otherwise ordered by the court, a trustee appointed under this section shall be subject to the same duties as those of a trustee under section 704 of title 11, United States Code, and shall be, with respect to the plan, a fiduciary within the meaning of paragraph (21) of section 3 of this Act and under section 4975(e) of the Internal Revenue Code of 1954 (except to the extent that the provisions of this title are inconsistent with the requirements applicable under part 4 of subtitle B of title I of this Act and of such section 4975).

(e) An application by the corporation under this section may be filed notwithstanding the pendency in the same or any other court of any bankruptcy, mortgage foreclosure, or equity receivership proceeding, or any proceeding to reorganize, conserve, or liquidate such plan or its property, or any proceeding to enforce a lien against property of the plan.

(f) Upon the filing of an application for the appointment of a trustee or the issuance of a decree under this section, the court to which an application is made shall have exclusive jurisdiction of the plan involved and its property wherever located with the powers, to the extent consistent with the purposes of this section, of a court of the United States having jurisdiction over cases under chapter 11 of title 11. Pending an adjudication under subsection (c) of this section such court shall stay, and upon appointment by it of a trustee, as provided in this section such court shall continue the stay of, any pending mortgage foreclosure, equity receivership, or other proceeding to reorganize, conserve, or liquidate the plan or its property and any other suit against any receiver, conservator, or trustee of the plan or its property. Pending such adjudication and upon the appointment by it of such trustee, the court may stay any proceeding to enforce a lien against property of the plan or any other suit against the plan.

(g) An action under this subsection may be brought in the judicial district where the plan administrator resides or does business or where any asset of the plan is situated. A district court in which such action is brought may issue process with respect to such action in any other judicial district.

(h)(1) The amount of compensation paid to each trustee appointed under the provisions of this title shall require the prior approval of the corporation, and, in the case of a trustee appointed by a court, the consent of that court.

(2) Trustees shall appoint, retain, and compensate accountants, actuaries, and other professional service personnel in accordance with regulations prescribed by the corporation.

REPORTABLE EVENTS

◊ ◊ ◊

Editor's Note: ERISA §4043, below, appears as amended by §771 of the Retirement Protection Act of 1994 (enacted as part of the Uruguay Round Agreements Act, P.L. 103-465). The changes made by Act §771 apply to events occurring 60 days or more after the Act's enactment date. That enactment date is December 8, 1994.

◊ ◊ ◊

Sec. 4043. (a) Within 30 days after the plan administrator *or the contributing sponsor* knows or has reason to know that a reportable event described in subsection [(b)]*(c)* has occurred, he shall notify the corporation that such event has occurred, *unless a notice otherwise required under this subsection has already been provided with respect to such event.* The corporation is authorized to waive the requirement of the preceding sentence with respect to any or all reportable events with respect to any plan, and to require the notification to be made by including the event in the annual report made by the plan. [Whenever an employer making contributions under a plan to which section 4021 applies knows or has reason to know that a reportable event has occurred he shall notify the plan administrator immediately.]

(b)(1) The requirements of this subsection shall be applicable to a contributing sponsorif, as of the close of the preceding plan year—

(A) the aggregate unfunded vested benefits (as determined under section 4006(a)(3)(E)(iii)) of plans subject to this title which are maintained by such sponsor and members of such sponsor's controlled groups (disregarding plans with no unfunded vested benefits) exceed $50,000,000, and

(B) the funded vested benefit percentage for such plans is less than 90 percent.

For purposes of subparagraph (B), the funded vested benefit percentage means the percentage which the aggregate value of the assets of such plans bears to the aggregate vested benefits of such plans (determined in accordance with section 4006(a)(3)(E)(iii)).

(2) This subsection shall not apply to an event if the contributing sponsor, or the member of the contributing sponsor's controlled group to which the event relates, is

(A) a person subject to the reporting requirements of section 13 or 15(d) of the Securities Exchange Act of 1934, or

(B) a subsidiary (as defined for purposes of such Act) of a person subject to such reporting requirements.

(3) No later than 30 days prior to the effective date of an event described in paragraph (9), (10), (11), (12), or (13) of subsection (c), a contributing sponsor to which the requirements of this subsection apply shall notify the corporation that the event is about to occur.

(4) The corporation may waive the requirement of this subsection with respect to any or all reportable events with respect to any contributing sponsor.

[(b)]*(c)* For purposes of this section a reportable event occurs—

(1) when the Secretary of the Treasury issues notice that a plan has ceased to be a plan described in section 4021(a)(2), or when the Secretary of Labor determines the plan is not in compliance with title I of this Act;

(2) when an amendment of the plan is adopted if, under the amendment, the benefit payable with respect to any participant may be decreased;

(3) when the number of active participants is less than 80 percent of the number of such participants at the beginning of the plan year, or is less than 75 percent of the number of such participants at the beginning of the previous plan year;

ERISA Sec. 4043 [(b)]*(c)*(3)

(4) when the Secretary of the Treasury determines that there has been a termination or partial termination of the plan within the meaning of section 411(d)(3) of the Internal Revenue Code of 1954, but the occurrence of such a termination or partial termination does not, by itself, constitute or require a termination of a plan under this title;

(5) when the plan fails to meet the minimum funding standards under section 412 of such Code (without regard to whether the plan is a plan described in section 4021(a)(2) of this Act) or under section 302 of this Act;

(6) when the plan is unable to pay benefits thereunder when due;

(7) when there is a distribution under the plan to a participant who is a substantial owner as defined in section 4022(b)(6) if—

(A) such distribution has a value of $10,000 or more;

(B) such distribution is not made by reason of the death of the participant; and

(C) immediately after the distribution, the plan has nonforfeitable benefits which are not funded;

(8) when a plan merges, consolidates, or transfers its assets under section 208 of this Act, or when an alternative method of compliance is prescribed by the Secretary of Labor under section 110 of this Act; [or]

[**(9)** when any other event occurs which the corporation determines may be indicative of a need to terminate the plan.]

(9) when, as a result of an event, a person ceases to be a member of the controlled group;

(10) when a contributing sponsor or a member of a contributing sponsor's controlled group liquidates in a case under title 11, United States Code, or under any similar Federal law or law of a State or political subdivision of a State;

(11) when a contributing sponsor or a member of a contributing sponsor's controlled

group declares an extraordinary dividend (as defined in section 1059(c) of the Internal Revenue Code of 1986) or redeems, in any 12-month period, an aggregate of 10 percent or more of the total combined voting power of all classes of stock entitled to vote, or an aggregate of 10 percent of more of the total value of shares of all classes of stock, of a contributing sponsor and all members of its controlled group;

(12) when, in any 12-month period, an aggregate of 3 percent or more of the benefit liabilities of a plan covered by this title and maintained by a contributing sponsor or a member of its controlled group are transferred to a person that is not a member of the controlled group or to a plan or plans maintained by a person or persons that are not such a contributing sponsor or a member of its controlled group; or

(13) when any other event occurs that may be indicative of a need to terminate the plan and that is prescribed by the corporation in regulations.

For purposes of paragraph (7), all distributions to a participant within any 24-month period are treated as a single distribution.

[(c)]*(d)* The Secretary of the Treasury shall notify the corporation—

(1) whenever a reportable event described in paragraph (1), (4), or (5) of subsection [(b)]*(c)* occurs, or

(2) whenever any other event occurs which the Secretary of the Treasury believes indicates that the plan may not be sound.

[(d)]*(e)* The Secretary of Labor shall notify the corporation—

(1) whenever a reportable event described in paragraph (1), (5), or (8) of subsection [(b)]*(c)* occurs, or

(2) whenever any other event occurs which the Secretary of Labor believes indicates that the plan may not be sound.

ERISA Sec. 4043 [(b)]*(c)*(4)

(f) Any information or documentary material submitted to the corporation pursuant to this section shall be exempt from disclosure under section 552 of title 5, United States Code, and no such information or documentary material may be made public, except as may be relevant to any administrative or judicial action or proceeding. Nothing in this section is intended to prevent disclosure to either body of Congress or to any duly authorized committee or subcommittee of the Congress.

ALLOCATION OF ASSETS

Sec. 4044. (a) In the case of the termination of a single-employer plan, the plan administrator shall allocate the assets of the plan (available to provide benefits) among the participants and beneficiaries of the plan in the following order:

(1) First, to that portion of each individual's accrued benefit which is derived from the participant's contributions to the plan which were not mandatory contributions.

(2) Second, to that portion of each individual's accrued benefit which is derived from the participant's mandatory contributions.

(3) Third, in the case of benefits payable as an annuity—

(A) in the case of the benefit of a participant or beneficiary which was in pay status as of the beginning of the 3-year period ending on the termination date of the plan, to each such benefit, based on the provisions of the plan (as in effect during the 5-year period ending on such date) under which such benefit would be the least,

(B) in the case of a participant's or beneficiary's benefit (other than a benefit described in subparagraph (A)) which would have been in pay status as of the beginning of such 3-year period if the participant had retired prior to the beginning of the 3-year period and if his benefits had commenced (in the normal form of annuity under the plan) as of the beginning of such period, to each such benefit based on the provisions of the plan

(as in effect during the 5-year period ending on such date) under which such benefit would be the least.

For purposes of subparagraph (A), the lowest benefit in pay status during a 3-year period shall be considered the benefit in pay status for such period.

(4) Fourth—

(A) to all other benefits (if any) of individuals under the plan guaranteed under this title (determined without regard to section 4022B(a)), and

(B) to the additional benefits (if any) which would be determined under subparagraph (A) if section 4022(b)(5) did not apply.

For purposes of this paragraph, section 4021 shall be applied without regard to subsection (c) thereof.

(5) Fifth, to all other nonforfeitable benefits under the plan.

(6) Sixth, to all other benefits under the plan.

(b) For purposes of subsection (a)—

(1) The amount allocated under any paragraph of subsection (a) with respect to any benefit shall be properly adjusted for any allocation of assets with respect to that benefit under a prior paragraph of subsection (a).

(2) If the assets available for allocation under any paragraph of subsection (a) (other than paragraphs (5) and (6)) are insufficient to satisfy in full the benefits of all individuals which are described in that paragraph, the assets shall be allocated pro rata among such individuals on the basis of the present value (as of the termination date) of their respective benefits described in that paragraph.

(3) This paragraph applies if the assets available for allocation under paragraph (5) of subsection (a) are not sufficient to satisfy in full the benefits of individuals described in that paragraph.

(A) If this paragraph applies, except as provided in subparagraph (B), the assets shall be allocated to the benefits of individuals described in such paragraph (5) on the basis of the benefits of individuals which would have been described in such paragraph (5) under the plan as in effect at the beginning of the 5-year period ending on the date of plan termination.

(B) If the assets available for allocation under subparagraph (A) are sufficient to satisfy in full the benefits described in such subparagraph (without regard to this subparagraph), then for purposes of subparagraph (A), benefits of individuals described in such subparagraph shall be determined on the basis of the plan as amended by the most recent plan amendment effective during such 5-year period under which the assets available for allocation are sufficient to satisfy in full the benefits of individuals described in subparagraph (A) and any assets remaining to be allocated under such subparagraph shall be allocated under subparagraph (A) on the basis of the plan as amended by the next succeeding plan amendment effective during such period.

(4) If the Secretary of Treasury determines that the allocation made pursuant to this section (without regard to this paragraph) results in discrimination prohibited by section 401(a)(4) of the Internal Revenue Code of 1954 then, if required to prevent the disqualification of the plan (or any trust under the plan) under section 401(a) or 403(a) of such Code, the assets allocated under subsection (a)(4)(B), (a)(5), and (a)(6) shall be reallocated to the extent necessary to avoid such discrimination.

(5) The term ''mandatory contributions'' means amounts contributed to the plan by a participant which are required as a condition of employment, as a condition of participation in such plan, or as a condition of obtaining benefits under the plan attributable to employer contributions. For this purpose, the total amount of mandatory contributions of a participant is the amount of such contributions reduced (but not below zero) by the sum of the amounts paid or distributed to him under the plan before its termination.

(6) A plan may establish subclasses and categories within the classes described in paragraphs (1) through (6) of subsection (a) in accordance with regulations prescribed by the corporation.

(c) Any increase or decrease in the value of the assets of a single employer plan occurring during the period beginning on the later of (1) the date a trustee is appointed under section 4042(b) or (2) the date on which the plan is terminated is to be allocated between the plan and the corporation in the manner determined by the court (in the case of a court-appointed trustee) or as agreed upon by the corporation and the plan administrator in any other case. Any increase or decrease in the value of the assets of a single-employer plan occurring after the date on which the plan is terminated shall be credited to, or suffered by, the corporation.

(d)(1) Subject to paragraph (3), any residual assets of a single-employer plan may be distributed to the employer if—

(A) all liabilities of the plan to participants and their beneficiaries have been satisfied,

(B) the distribution does not contravene any provision of law, and

(C) the plan provides for such a distribution in these circumstances.

(2)(A) In determining the extent to which a plan provides for the distribution of plan assets to the employer for purposes of paragraph (1)(C), any such provision, and any amendment increasing the amount which may be distributed to the employer, shall not be treated as effective before the end of the fifth calendar year following the date of the adoption of such provision or amendment.

(B) A distribution to the employer from a plan shall not be treated as failing to satisfy the requirements of this paragraph if the plan has been in effect for fewer than 5 years and the plan has provided for such a distribution since the effective date of the plan.

(C) Except as otherwise provided in regulations of the Secretary of the Treasury, in any case in which a transaction described in section 208 occurs, subparagraph (A) shall continue to apply separately with respect to the amount of any assets transferred in such transaction.

(D) For purposes of this subsection, the term "employer" includes any member of the controlled group of which the employer is a member. For purposes of the preceding sentence, the term "controlled group" means any group treated as a single employer under subsection (b), (c), (m) or (o) of section 414 of the Internal Revenue Code of 1986.

(3)(A) Before any distribution from a plan pursuant to paragraph (1), if any assets of the plan attributable to employee contributions remain after satisfaction of all liabilities described in subsection (a), such remaining assets shall be equitably distributed to the participants who made such contributions or their beneficiaries (including alternate payees, within the meaning of section 206(d)(3)(K)).

(B) For purposes of subparagraph (A), the portion of the remaining assets which are attributable to employee contributions shall be an amount equal to the product derived by multiplying—

(i) the market value of the total remaining assets, by

(ii) a fraction—

(I) the numerator of which is the present value of all portions of the accrued benefits with respect to participants which are derived from participants' mandatory contributions (referred to in subsection (a)(2)), and

(II) the denominator of which is the present value of all benefits with respect to which assets are allocated under paragraphs (2) through (6) of subsection (a).

(C) For purposes of this paragraph, each person who is, as of the termination date—

(i) a participant under the plan, or

(ii) an individual who has received, during the 3-year period ending with the termination date, a distribution from the plan of such individual's entire nonforfeitable benefit in the form of a single sum distribution in accordance with section 203(e) or in the form of irrevocable commitments purchased by the plan from an insurer to provide such nonforfeitable benefit,
shall be treated as a participant with respect to the termination, if all or part of the nonforfeitable benefit with respect to such person is or was attributable to participants' mandatory contributions (referred to in subsection (a)(2)).

(4) Nothing in this subsection shall be construed to limit the requirements of section 4980(d) of the Internal Revenue Code of 1986 (as in effect immediately after the enactment of the Omnibus Budget Reconciliation Act of 1990) or section 404(d) of this Act with respect to any distribution of residual assets of a single-employer plan to the employer.

RECAPTURE OF CERTAIN PAYMENTS

Sec. 4045. (a) Except as provided in subsection (c), the trustee is authorized to recover for the benefit of a plan from a participant the recoverable amount (as defined in subsection (b)) of all payments from the plan to him which commenced within the 3-year period immediately preceding the time the plan is terminated.

(b) For purposes of subsection (a) the recoverable amount is the excess of the amount determined under paragraph (1) over the amount determined under paragraph (2).

(1) The amount determined under this paragraph is the sum of the amount of the actual payments received by the participant within the 3-year period.

(2) The amount determined under this paragraph is the sum of—

(A) the sum of the amount such participant would have received during each consecutive 12-month period within the 3 years if the participant received the benefit in the form described in paragraph (3),

(B) the sum for each of the consecutive 12-month periods of the lesser of—

(i) the excess, if any, of $10,000 over the benefit in the form described in paragraph (3), or

(ii) the excess of the actual payment, if any, over the benefit in the form described in paragraph (3), and

(C) the present value at the time of termination of the participant's future benefits guaranteed under this title as if the benefits commenced in the form described in paragraph (3).

(3) The form of benefit for purposes of this subsection shall be the monthly benefit the participant would have received during the consecutive 12-month period, if he had elected at the time of the first payment made during the 3-year period, to receive his interest in the plan as a monthly benefit in the form of a life annuity commencing at the time of such first payment.

(c)(1) In the event of a distribution described in section 4043(b)(7) the 3-year period referred to in subsection (b) shall not end sooner than the date on which the corporation is notified of the distribution.

(2) The trustee shall not recover any payment made from a plan after or on account of the death of a participant, or to a participant who is disabled (within the meaning of section 72(m)(7) of the Internal Revenue Code of 1954).

(3) The corporation is authorized to waive, in whole or in part, the recovery of any amount which the trustee is authorized to recover for the benefit of a plan under this section in any

case in which it determines that substantial economic hardship would result to the participant or his beneficiaries from whom such amount is recoverable.

REPORTS TO TRUSTEE

Sec. 4046. The corporation and the plan administrator of any plan to be terminated under this subtitle shall furnish to the trustee such information as the corporation or the plan administrator has and, to the extent practicable, can obtain regarding—

(1) the amount of benefits payable with respect to each participant under a plan to be terminated,

(2) the amount of basic benefits guaranteed under section 4022 or 4022A which are payable with respect to each participant in the plan,

(3) the present value, as of the time of termination, of the aggregate amount of basic benefits payable under section 4022 or 4022A (determined without regard to section 4022B),

(4) the fair market value of the assets of the plan at the time of termination,

(5) the computations under section 4044, and all actuarial assumptions under which the items described in paragraphs (1) through (4) were computed, and

(6) any other information with respect to the plan the trustee may require in order to terminate the plan.

RESTORATION OF PLANS

Sec. 4047. Whenever the corporation determines that a plan which is to be terminated under section 4041 or 4042, or which is in the process of being terminated under section 4041 or 4042, should not be terminated under section 4041 or 4042 as a result of such circumstances as the corporation determines to be relevant, the corporation is authorized to cease any activities undertaken to terminate the plan, and to take whatever action is necessary and within its power to restore the plan to its status prior to the determination that the plan was to be terminated under section 4041 or 4042. In the case of a plan which has been terminated under section 4041 or 4042 the corporation is authorized in any such case in which the corporation determines such action to be appropriate and consistent with its duties under this title, to take such action as may be necessary to restore the plan to its pretermination status, including, but not limited to, the transfer to the employer or a plan administrator of control of part or all of the remaining assets and liabilities of the plan.

DATE OF TERMINATION

Sec. 4048. (a) For purposes of this title the termination date of a single-employer plan is—

(1) in the case of a plan terminated in a standard termination in accordance with the provisions of section 4041(b), the termination date proposed in the notice provided under section 4041(a)(2),

(2) in the case of a plan terminated in a distress termination in accordance with the provisions of section 4041(c), the date established by the plan administrator and agreed to by the corporation,

(3) in the case of a plan terminated in accordance with the provisions of section 4042, the date established by the corporation and agreed to by the plan administrator, or

(4) in the case of a plan terminated under section 4041(c) or 4042 in any case in which no agreement is reached between the plan administrator and the corporation (or the trustee), the date established by the court.

(b) For purposes of this title, the date of termination of a multiemployer plan is—

(1) in the case of a plan terminated in accordance with the provisions of section 4041A, the date determined under subsection (b) of that section; or

(2) in the case of a plan terminated in accordance with the provisions of section 4042,

the date agreed to between the plan administrator and the corporation (or the trustee appointed under section 4042(b)(2), if any), or, if no agreement is reached, the date established by the court.

DISTRIBUTION TO PARTICIPANTS AND BENEFICIARIES OF LIABILITY PAYMENTS TO SECTION 4049 TRUST [Repealed]

◊ ◊ ◊

Editor's Note: ERISA §4050, set forth below, was added by §776 of the Retirement Protection Act of 1994 (enacted as part of the Uruguay Round Agreements Act, P.L. 103-465). It applies to distributions that occur in plan years beginning after final regulations implementing these provisions are prescribed by the PBGC.

◊ ◊ ◊

SEC. 4050. MISSING PARTICIPANTS.

(a) General Rule.

(1) Payment to the corporation. A plan administrator satisfies section 4041(b)(3)(A) in the case of a missing participant only if the plan administrator

(A) transfers the participant's designated benefit to the corporation or purchases an irrevocable commitment from an insurer in accordance with clause (i) of section 4041(b)(3)(A), and

(B) provides the corporation such information and certifications with respect to such designated benefits or irrevocable commitments as the corporation shall specify.

(2) Treatment of transferred assets. A transfer to the corporation under this section shall be treated as a transfer of assets from a terminated plan to the corporation as trustee, and shall be held with assets of terminated plans for which the corporation is trustee under section 4042, subject to the rules set forth in that section.

(3) Payment by the corporation. After a missing participant whose designated benefit was transferred to the corporation is located—

(A) in any case in which the plan could have distributed the benefit of the missing participant in a single sum without participant or spousal consent under section 205(g), the corporation shall pay the participant or beneficiary a single sum benefit equal to the designated benefit paid the corporation plus interest as specified by the corporation, and

(B) in any other case, the corporation shall pay a benefit based on the designated benefit and the assumptions prescribed by the corporation at the time that the corporation received the designated benefit.

The corporation shall make payments under subparagraph (B) available in the same forms and at the same times as a guaranteed benefit under section 4022 would be available to be paid, except that the corporation may make a benefit available in the form of a single sum if the plan provided a single sum benefit (other than a single sum described in subsection (b)(2)(A)).

(b) Definitions. For purposes of this section

(1) Missing participant. The term "missing participant" means a participant or beneficiary under a terminating plan whom the plan administrator cannot locate after a diligent search.

(2) Designated benefit. The term "designated benefit" means the single sum benefit the participant would receive

(A) under the plan's assumptions, in the case of a distribution that can be made without participant or spousal consent under section 205(g);

(B) under the assumptions of the corporation in effect on the date that the designated benefit is transferred to the corporation, in the case of a plan that does not pay any single sums other than those described in subparagraph (A); or

(C) under the assumptions of the corporation or of the plan, whichever provides the higher single sum, in the case of a plan that pays a single sum other than those described in subparagraph (A).

(c) Regulatory Authority. The corporation shall prescribe such regulations as are necessary to carry out the purposes of this section, including rules relating to what will be considered a diligent search, the amount payable to the corporation, and the amount to be paid by the corporation.

Subtitle D—Liability Amounts Payable By The Corporation

Sec. 4061. The corporation shall pay benefits under a single-employer plan terminated under this title subject to the limitations and requirements of subtitle B of this title. The corporation shall provide financial assistance to pay benefits under a multiemployer plan which is insolvent under section 4245 or 4281(d)(2)(A), subject to the limitations and requirements of subtitles B, C, and E of this title. Amounts guaranteed by the corporation under sections 4022 and 4022A shall be paid by the corporation only out of the appropriate fund. The corporation shall make payments under the supplemental program to reimburse multiemployer plans for uncollectible withdrawal liability only out of the fund established under section 4005(e).

LIABILITY FOR TERMINATION OF SINGLE-EMPLOYER PLANS UNDER A DISTRESS TERMINATION OR A TERMINATION BY THE CORPORATION

Sec. 4062. (a) In General.—In any case in which a single-employer plan is terminated in a distress termination under section 4041(c) or a termination otherwise instituted by the corporation under section 4042, any person who is, on the termination date, a contributing sponsor of the plan or a member of such a contributing sponsor's controlled group shall incur liability under this section. The liability under this section of all such persons shall be joint and several. The liability under this section consists of—

(1) liability to the corporation, to the extent provided in subsection (b), and

(2) liability to the trustee appointed under subsection (b) or (c) of section 4042 to the extent provided in subsection (c).

(b) Liability to the Corporation.

(1) Amount of liability.—

(A) In general.—Except as provided in subparagraph (B), the liability to the corporation of a person described in subsection (a) shall be the total amount of the unfunded benefit liabilities (as of the termination date) to all participants and beneficiaries under the plan, together with interest (at a reasonable rate) calculated from the termination date in accordance with regulations prescribed by the corporation.

(B) Special rule in case of subsequent insufficiency.—For purposes of subparagraph (A), in any case described in section 4041(c)(3)(C)(ii), actuarial present values shall be determined as of the date of the notice to the corporation (or the finding by the corporation) described in such section.

(2) Payment of liability.—

(A) In general.—Except as provided in subparagraph (B), the liability to the corporation under this subsection shall be due and payable to the corporation as of the termination date, in cash or securities acceptable to the corporation.

(B) Special rule.—Payment of so much of the liability under paragraph (i)(A) as exceeds 30 percent of the collective net worth of all persons described in subsection (a) (including interest) shall be made under commercially reasonable terms prescribed by the corporation. The parties involved shall make a reasonable effort to reach agreement on such commercially reasonable terms. Any such terms prescribed by the corporation shall provide for deferral of 50 percent of any amount of liability otherwise payable for any year under this subparagraph if a person subject to such liability demonstrates to the satisfaction of the corporation that no person subject to such liability has any individual pre-tax profits for such person's fiscal year ending during such year.

(3) Alternative arrangements.—The corporation and any person liable under this section may agree to alternative arrangements for the satisfaction of liability to the corporation under this subsection.

(c) Liability to Section 4042 Trustee.—A person described in subsection (a) shall be subject to liability under this subsection to the trustee appointed under subsection (b) or (c) of section 4042. The liability of such person under this subsection shall consist of—

(1) the outstanding balance of the accumulated funding deficiencies (within the meaning of section 302(a)(2) of this Act and section 412(a) of the Internal Revenue Code of 1954) of the plan (if any) (which, for purposes of this subparagraph, shall include the amount of any increase in such accumulated funding deficiencies of the plan which would result if all pending applications for waivers of the minimum funding standard under section 303 of this Act or section 412(d) of such Code and for extensions of the amortization period under section 304 of this Act or section 412(e) of such Code with respect to such plan were denied and if no additional contributions (other than those already made by the termination date) were made for the plan year in which the termination date occurs or for any previous plan year),

(2) the outstanding balance of the amount of waived funding deficiencies of the plan waived before such date under section 303 of this Act or section 412(d) of such Code (if any), and

(3) the outstanding balance of the amount of decreases in the minimum funding standard allowed before such date under section 304 of this Act or section 412(e) of such Code (if any),

together with interest (at a reasonable rate) calculated from the termination date in accordance with regulations prescribed by the corporation. The liability under this subsection shall be due and payable to such trustee as of the termination date, in cash or securities acceptable to such trustee.

(d) Definitions.

(1) Collective net worth of persons subject to liability.—

(A) In general.—The collective net worth of persons subject to liability in connection with a plan termination consists of the sum of the individual net worths of all persons who—

(i) have individual net worths which are greater than zero, and

(ii) are (as of the termination date) contributing sponsors of the terminated plan or members of their controlled groups.

(B) Determination of net worth.—For purposes of this paragraph, the net worth of a person is—

(i) determined on whatever basis best reflects, in the determination of the corporation, the current status of the person's operations and prospects at the time chosen for determining the net worth of the person, and

(ii) increased by the amount of any transfers of assets made by the person which are determined by the corporation to be improper under the circumstances, including any such transfers which would be inappropriate under title 11, United States Code, if the person were a debtor in a case under chapter 7 of such title.

(C) Timing of determination.—For purposes of this paragraph, determinations of net worth shall be made as of a day chosen by the corporation (during the 120-day period ending with the termination date) and

shall be computed without regard to any liability under this section.

(2) Pre-tax profits.—The term "pre-tax profits" means—

(A) except as provided in subparagraph (B), for any fiscal year of any person, such person's consolidated net income (excluding any extraordinary charges to income and including any extraordinary credits to income) for such fiscal year, as shown on audited financial statements prepared in accordance with generally accepted accounting principles, or

(B) for any fiscal year of an organization described in section 501(c) of the Internal Revenue Code of 1954, the excess of income over expenses (as such terms are defined for such organizations under generally accepted accounting principles),

before provision for or deduction of Federal or other income tax, any contribution to any single-employer plan of which such person is a contributing sponsor at any time during the period beginning on the termination date and ending with the end of such fiscal year, and any amounts required to be paid for such fiscal year under this section. The corporation may by regulation require such information to be filed on such forms as may be necessary to determine the existence and amount of such pre-tax profits.

(3) Liability payment years.—The liability payment years in connection with a terminated plan consist of the consecutive one-year periods following the last plan year preceding the termination date, excluding the first such year in any case in which the first such year ends less than 180 days after the termination date.

(e) Treatment of Substantial Cessation of Operations.—If an employer ceases operations at a facility in any location and, as a result of such cessation of operations, more than 20 percent of the total number of his employees who are participants under a plan established and maintained by him are separated from employment, the employer shall be treated with respect to that plan as if he were a substantial employer under a plan under which more than one employer makes contributions and the provisions of sections 4063, 4064, and 4065 shall apply.

LIABILITY OF SUBSTANTIAL EMPLOYER FOR WITHDRAWAL FROM SINGLE-EMPLOYER PLANS UNDER MULTIPLE CONTROLLED GROUPS

Sec. 4063. (a) Except as provided in subsection (d), the plan administrator of a single-employer plan which has two or more contributing sponsors at least two of whom are not under common control—

(1) shall notify the corporation of the withdrawal during a plan year of a substantial employer for such plan year from the plan, within 60 days after such withdrawal, and

(2) request that the corporation determine the liability of all persons with respect to the withdrawal of the substantial employer.
The corporation shall, as soon as practicable thereafter, determine whether there is liability resulting from the withdrawal of the substantial employer and notify the liable persons of such liability.

(b) Except as provided in subsection (c), any one or more contributing sponsors who withdraw, during a plan year for which they constitute a substantial employer, from a single-employer plan which has two or more contributing sponsors at least two of whom are not under common control, shall, upon notification of such contributing sponsors by the corporation as provided by subsection (a), be liable, together with the members of their controlled groups, to the corporation in accordance with the provisions of section 4062 and this section. The amount of liability shall be computed on the basis of an amount determined by the corporation to be the amount described in section 4062 for the entire plan, as if the plan had been terminated by the corporation on the date of the withdrawal referred to in subsection (a)(1), multiplied by a fraction—

(1) the numerator of which is the total amount required to be contributed to the plan by such contributing sponsors for the last 5 years ending prior to the withdrawal, and

(2) the denominator of which is the total amount required to be contributed to the plan by all contributing sponsors for such last 5 years.
In addition to and in lieu of the manner prescribed in the preceding sentence, the corporation may also determine such liability on any other equitable basis prescribed by the corporation in regulations. Any amount collected by the corporation under this subsection shall be held in escrow subject to disposition in accordance with the provisions of paragraphs (2) and (3) of subsection (c).

(c)(1) In lieu of payment of a contributing sponsor's liability under this section, the contributing sponsor may be required to furnish a bond to the corporation in an amount not exceeding 150 percent of his liability to insure payment of his liability under this section. The bond shall have as surety thereon a corporate surety company which is an acceptable surety on Federal bonds under authority granted by the Secretary of the Treasury under sections 6 through 13 of title 6, United States Code. Any such bond shall be in a form or of a type approved by the Secretary including individual bonds or schedule or blanket forms of bonds which cover a group or class.

(2) If the plan is not terminated under section 4041(c) or 4042 within the 5-year period commencing on the day of withdrawal, the liability is abated and any payment held in escrow shall be refunded without interest (or the bond cancelled) in accordance with by-laws or rules prescribed by the corporation.

(3) If the plan terminates under section 4041(c) or 4042 within the 5-year period commencing on the day of withdrawal, the corporation shall—

(A) demand payment or realize on the bond and hold such amount in escrow for the benefit of the plan;

(B) treat any escrowed payments under this section as if they were plan assets and apply them in a manner consistent with this subtitle; and

(C) refund any amount to the contributing sponsor which is not required to meet any obligation of the corporation with respect to the plan.

(d) The provisions of this subsection apply in the case of a withdrawal described in subsection (a), and the provisions of subsections (b) and (c) shall not apply, if the corporation determines that the procedure provided for under this subsection is consistent with the purposes of this section and section 4064 and is more appropriate in the particular case. Upon a showing by the plan administrator of the plan that the withdrawal from the plan by one or more contributing sponsors has resulted, or will result, in a significant reduction in the amount of aggregate contributions to or under the plan, the corporation may—

(1) require the plan fund to be equitably allocated between those participants no longer working in covered service under the plan as a result of the withdrawal, and those participants who remain in covered service under the plan;

(2) treat that portion of the plan funds allocable under paragraph (1) to participants no longer in covered service as a plan termination under section 4042; and

(3) treat that portion of the plan fund allocable to participants remaining in covered service as a separate plan.

(e) The corporation is authorized to waive the application of the provisions of subsections (b), (c), and (d) of this section whenever it determines that there is an indemnity agreement in effect among contributing sponsors under the plan which is adequate to satisfy the purposes of this section and of section 4064.

LIABILITY ON TERMINATION OF SINGLE-EMPLOYER PLANS UNDER MULTIPLE CONTROLLED GROUPS

Sec. 4064. (a) This section applies to all contributing sponsors of a single-employer plan which has two or more contributing sponsors at least two of whom are not under common control at the time such plan is terminated under section 4041(c) or 4042, or who, at any time within the 5 plan years preceding the date of termination, made contributions under the plan.

(b) The corporation shall determine the liability with respect to each contributing sponsor and each member of its controlled group in a manner consistent with section 4062, except that the amount of liability determined under section 4062(b)(1) with respect to the entire plan shall be allocated to each controlled group by multiplying such amount by a fraction—

(1) the numerator of which is the amount required to be contributed to the plan for the last 5 plan years ending prior to the termination date by persons in such controlled group as contributing sponsors, and

(2) the denominator of which is the total amount required to be contributed to the plan for such last 5 plan years by all persons as contributing sponsors,
and section 4068(a) shall be applied separately with respect to each controlled group. The corporation may also determine the liability of each such contributing sponsor and member of its controlled group on any other equitable basis prescribed by the corporation in regulations.

ANNUAL REPORT OF PLAN ADMINISTRATOR

Sec. 4065. For each plan year for which section 4021 applies to a plan, the plan administrator shall file with the corporation, on a form prescribed by the corporation, an annual report which identifies the plan and plan administrator and which includes—

(1) a copy of each notification required under section 4063 with respect to such year,

(2) a statement disclosing whether any reportable event (described in section 4043(b)) occurred during the plan year except to the extent the corporation waives such requirement, and

(3) in the case of a multiemployer plan, information with respect to such plan which the corporation determines is necessary for the enforcement of subtitle E and requires by regulation, which may include—

(A) a statement certified by the plan's enrolled actuary of—

(i) the value of all vested benefits under the plan as of the end of the plan year, and

(ii) the value of the plan's assets as of the end of the plan year;

(B) a statement certified by the plan sponsor of each claim for outstanding withdrawal liability (within the meaning of section 4001(a)(12)) and its value as of the end of that plan year and as of the end of the preceding plan year; and

(C) the number of employers having an obligation to contribute to the plan and the number of employers required to make withdrawal liability payments.

The report shall be filed within 6 months after the close of the plan year to which it relates. The corporation shall cooperate with the Secretary of the Treasury and the Secretary of Labor in an endeavor to coordinate the timing and content, and possibly obtain the combination, of reports under this section with reports required to be made by plan administrators to such Secretaries.

ANNUAL NOTIFICATION TO SUBSTANTIAL EMPLOYERS

Sec. 4066. The plan administrator of each single-employer plan which has at least two contributing sponsors at least two of whom are not under common control shall notify, within 6 months after the close of each plan year, any contributing sponsor of the plan who is described in section 4001(a)(2) that such contributing sponsor (along or together with members of such contributing sponsor's controlled group) constitutes a substantial employer for that year.

RECOVERY OF LIABILITY FOR PLAN TERMINATION

Sec. 4067. The corporation is authorized to make arrangements with any contributing sponsors and members of their controlled groups who are or may become liable under section 4062, 4063, or 4064 for payment of their liability, including arrangements for deferred payment of amounts of liability to the corporation accruing as of the termination date on such terms and for such periods as the corporation deems equitable and appropriate.

LIEN FOR LIABILITY

Sec. 4068. (a) If any person liable to the corporation under section 4062, 4063, or 4064 neglects or refuses to pay, after demand, the amount of such liability (including interest), there shall be a lien in favor of the corporation in the amount of such liability (including interest) upon all property and rights to property, whether real or personal, belonging to such person, except that such lien may not be in an amount in excess of 30 percent of the collective net worth of all persons described in section 4062(a).

(b) The lien imposed by subsection (a) arises on the date of termination of a plan, and continues until the liability imposed under section 4062, 4063, or 4064 is satisfied or becomes unenforceable by reason of lapse of time.

(c)(1) Except as otherwise provided under this section, the priority of a lien imposed under subsection (a) shall be determined in the same manner as under section 6323 of the Internal Revenue Code of 1954 (as in effect on the date of the enactment of the Single-Employer Pension Plan Amendments Act of 1986). Such section 6323 shall be applied for purposes of this section by disregarding subsection (g)(4) and by substituting—

(A) "lien imposed by section 4068 of the Employee Retirement Income Security Act of 1974" for "lien imposed by section 6321" each place it appears in subsections (a), (b), (c)(1), (c)(4)(B), (d), (e), and (h)(5);

(B) "the corporation" for "the Secretary" in subsections (a) and (b)(9)(C);

(C) "the payment of the amount on which the section 4068(a) lien is based" for "the collection of any tax under this title" in subsection (b)(3);

(D) "a person whose property is subject to the lien" for "the taxpayer" in subsections (b)(8), (c)(2)(A)(i) (the first place it appears), (c)(2)(A)(ii), (c)(2)(B), (c)(4)(B), and (c)(4)(C) (in the matter preceding clause (i));

(E) "such person" for "the taxpayer" in subsections (c)(2)(A)(i) (the second place it appears) and (c)(4)(C)(ii);

(F) "payment of the loan value of the amount on which the lien is based is made to the corporation" for "satisfaction of a levy pursuant to section 6332(b)" in subsection (b)(9)(C);

(G) "section 4068(a) lien" for "tax lien" each place it appears in subsections (c)(1), (c)(2)(A), (c)(2)(B), (c)(3)(B)(iii), (c)(4)(B), (d), and (h)(5); and

(H) "the date on which the lien is first filed" for the "date of the assessment of the tax" in subsection (g)(3)(A).

(2) In a case under title 11 of the United States Code or in insolvency proceedings, the lien imposed under subsection (a) shall be treated in the same manner as a tax due and owing to the United States for purposes of title 11 of section 3713 of title 31 of the United States Code.

(3) For purposes of applying section 6323(a) of the Internal Revenue Code of 1954 to determine the priority between the lien imposed under subsection (a) and a Federal tax lien, each lien shall be treated as a judgment lien arising as of the time notice of such lien is filed.

(4) For purposes of this subsection, notice of the lien imposed by subsection (a) shall be filed in the same manner as under section 6323(f) and (g) of the Internal Revenue Code of 1954.

(d)(1) In any case where there has been a refusal or neglect to pay the liability imposed under section 4062, 4063, or 4064, the corporation may bring civil action in a district court of the United States to enforce the lien of the corporation under this section with respect to such liability or to subject any property, of whatever nature, of the liable person, or in which he has any right, title, or interest to the payment of such liability.

(2) The liability imposed by section 4062, 4063, or 4064 may be collected by a proceeding in court if the proceeding is commenced within 6 years after the date upon which the plan was terminated or prior to the expiration of any period for collection agreed upon in writing by the corporation and the liable person before the expiration of such 6-year period.

The period of limitations provided under this paragraph shall be suspended for the period the assets of the liable person are in the control or custody of any court of the United States, or of any State, or of the District of Columbia, and for 6 months thereafter, and for any period during which the liable person is outside the United States if such period of absence is for a continuous period of at least 6 months.

(e) If the corporation determines that release of the lien or subordination of the lien to any other creditor of the liable person would not adversely affect the collection of the liability imposed under section 4062, 4063, or 4064, or that the amount realizable by the corporation from the property to which the lien attaches will ultimately be increased by such release or subordination, and that the ultimate collection of the liability will be facilitated by such release or subordination, the corporation may issue a certificate of release or subordination of the lien with respect to such property, or any part thereof.

(f) Definitions. For purposes of this section—

(1) The collective net worth of persons subject to liability in connection with a plan termination shall be determined as provided in section 4062(d)(1).

(2) The term ''pre-tax profits'' has the meaning provided in section 4062(d)(2).

TREATMENT OF TRANSACTIONS TO EVADE LIABILITY; EFFECT OF CORPORATE REORGANIZATION

Sec. 4069. (a) Treatment of Transactions to Evade Liability.—If a principal purpose of any person in entering into any transaction is to evade liability to which such person would be subject under this subtitle and the transaction becomes effective within five years before the termination date of the termination on which such liability would be based, then such person and the members of such person's controlled group (determined as of the termination date) shall be subject to liability under this subtitle in connection with such termination as if such person were a contributing sponsor of the terminated plan as of the termination date. This subsection shall not cause any person to be liable under this subtitle in connection with such plan termination for any increases or improvements in the benefits provided under the plan which are adopted after the date on which the transaction referred to in the preceding sentence becomes effective.

(b) Effect of Corporate Reorganization.— For purposes of this subtitle, the following rules apply in the case of certain corporate reorganizations:

(1) **Change of identity, form, etc.**—If a person ceases to exist by reason of a reorganization which involves a mere change in identity, form, or place of organization, however effected, a successor corporation resulting from such reorganization shall be treated as the person to whom this subtitle applies.

(2) **Liquidation into parent corporation.**—If a person ceases to exist by reason of liquidation into a parent corporation, the parent corporation shall be treated as the person to whom this subtitle applies.

(3) **Merger, consolidation, or division.** — If a person ceases to exist by reason of a merger, consolidation, or division, the successor corporation or corporations shall be treated as the person to whom this subtitle applies.

ENFORCEMENT AUTHORITY RELATING TO TERMINATIONS OF SINGLE-EMPLOYER PLANS

Sec. 4070. (a) In General.—Any person who is with respect to a single-employer plan a fiduciary, contributing sponsor, member of a contributing sponsor's controlled group, participant, or beneficiary, and is adversely affected by an act or practice of any party (other than the corporation) in violation of any provision of section 4041, 4042, 4062, 4063, 4064, or 4069, or who is an employee organization representing such a participant or beneficiary so adversely affected for purposes of collective bargaining with respect to such plan, may bring an action—

(1) to enjoin such act or practice, or

(2) to obtain other appropriate equitable relief (A) to redress such violation or (B) to enforce such provision.

(b) Status of Plan as Party to Action and with Respect to Legal Process.—A single-employer plan may be sued under this section as an entity. Service of summons, subpoena, or other legal process of a court upon a trustee or an administrator of a single-employer plan in such trustee's or administrator's capacity as such shall constitute service upon the plan. If a plan has not designated in the summary plan description of the plan an individual as agent for the service of legal process, service upon any contributing sponsor of the plan shall constitute such service. Any money judgment

ERISA Sec. 4070 (b)

under this section against a single-employer plan shall be enforceable only against the plan as an entity and shall not be enforceable against any other person unless liability against such person is established in such person's individual capacity.

(c) Jurisdiction and Venue.—The district courts of the United States shall have exclusive jurisdiction of civil actions under this section. Such actions may be brought in the district where the plan is administered, where the violation took place, or where a defendant resides or may be found, and process may be served in any other district where a defendant resides or may be found. The district courts of the United States shall have jurisdiction, without regard to the amount in controversy or the citizenship of the parties, to grant the relief provided for in subsection (a) in any action.

(d) Right of Corporation to Intervene.—A copy of the complaint or notice of appeal in any action under this section shall be served upon the corporation by certified mail. The corporation shall have the right in its discretion to intervene in any action.

(e) Awards of Costs and Expenses.—

(1) General rule.—In any action brought under this section, the court in its discretion may award all or a portion of the costs and expenses incurred in connection with such action, including reasonable attorney's fees, to any party who prevails or substantially prevails in such action.

(2) Exemption for plans.—Notwithstanding the preceding provisions of this subsection, no plan shall be required in any action to pay any costs and expenses (including attorney's fees).

(f) Limitation on Actions.—

(1) In general.—Except as provided in paragraph (3), an action under this section may not be brought after the later of—

(A) 6 years after the date on which the cause of action arose, or

(B) 3 years after the applicable date specified in paragraph (2).

(2) Applicable date.—

(A) General rule.—Except as provided in subparagraph (B), the applicable date specified in this paragraph is the earliest date on which the plaintiff acquired or should have acquired actual knowledge of the existence of such cause of action.

(B) Special rule for plaintiffs who are fiduciaries.—In the case of a plaintiff who is a fiduciary bringing the action in the exercise of fiduciary duties, the applicable date specified in this paragraph is the date on which the plaintiff became a fiduciary with respect to the plan if such date is later than the date described in subparagraph (A).

(3) Cases of fraud or concealment.—In the case of fraud or concealment, the period described in paragraph (1)(B) shall be extended to 6 years after the applicable date specified in paragraph (2).

PENALTY FOR FAILURE TO TIMELY PROVIDE REQUIRED INFORMATION

Sec. 4071. The corporation may assess a penalty, payable to the corporation, against any person who fails to provide any notice or other material information required under this subtitle or subtitle A, B, or C, as section 302(f)(4) or 307(e) or any regulations prescribed under any such subtitle or such section, within the applicable time limit specified therein. Such penalty shall not exceed $1,000 for each day for which such failure continues.

Subtitle E—Special Provisions For Multiemployer Plans

Part 1—Employer Withdrawals

WITHDRAWAL LIABILITY ESTABLISHED

Sec. 4201. (a) If an employer withdraws from a multiemployer plan in a complete withdrawal or a partial withdrawal, then the employer is liable to the plan in the amount determined under this part to be the withdrawal liability.

(b) For purposes of subsection (a)—

(1) The withdrawal liability of an employer to a plan is the amount determined under section 4211 to be the allocable amount of unfunded vested benefits, adjusted—

(A) first, by any de minimis reduction applicable under section 4209,

(B) next, in the case of a partial withdrawal, in accordance with section 4206,

(C) then, to the extent necessary to reflect the limitation on annual payments under section 4219(c)(1)(B), and

(D) finally, in accordance with section 4225.

(2) The term ''complete withdrawal'' means a complete withdrawal described in section 4203.

(3) The term ''partial withdrawal'' means a partial withdrawal described in section 4205.

DETERMINATION AND COLLECTION OF LIABILITY; NOTIFICATION OF EMPLOYER

Sec. 4202. When an employer withdraws from a multiemployer plan, the plan sponsor, in accordance with this part, shall—

(1) determine the amount of the employer's withdrawal liability,

(2) notify the employer of the amount of the withdrawal liability, and

(3) collect the amount of the withdrawal liability from the employer.

COMPLETE WITHDRAWAL

Sec. 4203. (a) For purposes of this part, a complete withdrawal from a multiemployer plan occurs when an employer—

(1) permanently ceases to have an obligation to contribute under the plan, or

(2) permanently ceases all covered operations under the plan.

(b)(1) Notwithstanding subsection (a), in the case of an employer that has an obligation to contribute under a plan for work performed in the building and construction industry, a complete withdrawal occurs only as described in paragraph (2), if—

(A) substantially all the employees with respect to whom the employer has an obligation to contribute under the plan perform work in the building and construction industry, and

(B) the plan—

(i) primarily covers employees in the building and construction industry, or

(ii) is amended to provide that this subsection applies to employers described in this paragraph.

(2) A withdrawal occurs under this paragraph if—

(A) an employer ceases to have an obligation to contribute under the plan, and

(B) the employer—

(i) continues to perform work in the jurisdiction of the collective bargaining agreement of the type for which contributions were previously required, or

(ii) resumes such work within 5 years after the date on which the obligation to contribute under the plan ceases, and does not renew the obligation at the time of the resumption.

(3) In the case of a plan terminated by mass withdrawal (within the meaning of section 4041A(a)(2)), paragraph (2) shall be applied by substituting "3 years" for "5 years" in subparagraph (B)(ii).

(c)(1) Notwithstanding subsection (a), in the case of an employer that has an obligation to contribute under a plan for work performed in the entertainment industry, primarily on a temporary or project-by-project basis, if the plan primarily covers employees in the entertainment industry, a complete withdrawal occurs only as described in subsection (b)(2) applied by substituting "plan" for "collective bargaining agreement" in subparagraph (B)(i) thereof.

(2) For purposes of this subsection, the term "entertainment industry" means—

(A) theater, motion picture (except to the extent provided in regulations prescribed by the corporation), radio, television, sound or visual recording, music, and dance, and

(B) such other entertainment activities as the corporation may determine to be appropriate.

(3) The corporation may by regulation exclude a group or class of employers described in the preceding sentence from the application of this subsection if the corporation determines that such exclusion is necessary—

(A) to protect the interest of the plan's participants and beneficiaries, or

(B) to prevent a significant risk of loss to the corporation with respect to the plan.

(4) A plan may be amended to provide that this subsection shall not apply to a group or class of employers under the plan.

(d)(1) Notwithstanding subsection (a), in the case of an employer who—

(A) has an obligation to contribute under a plan described in paragraph (2) primarily for work described in such paragraph, and

(B) does not continue to perform work within the jurisdiction of the plan,
a complete withdrawal occurs only as described in paragraph (3).

(2) A plan is described in this paragraph if substantially all of the contributions required under the plan are made by employers primarily engaged in the long and short haul trucking industry, the household goods moving industry, or the public warehousing industry.

(3) A withdrawal occurs under this paragraph if—

(A) an employer permanently ceases to have an obligation to contribute under the plan or permanently ceases all covered operations under the plan, and

(B) either—

(i) the corporation determines that the plan has suffered substantial damage to its contribution base as a result of such cessation, or

(ii) the employer fails to furnish a bond issued by a corporate surety company that is an acceptable surety for purposes of section 412, or an amount held in escrow by a bank or similar financial institution satisfactory to the plan, in an amount equal to 50 percent of the withdrawal liability of the employer.

(4) If, after an employer furnishes a bond or escrow to a plan under paragraph (3)(B)(ii), the corporation determines that the cessation of the employer's obligation to contribute under the plan (considered together with any cessations by other employers), or cessation of covered operations under the plan, has resulted in substantial damage to the contribution base of the plan, the employer shall be treated as having withdrawn from the plan on the date on which the obligation to contribute or covered operations ceased, and such bond or escrow shall be paid to the plan. The corporation shall not make a determination under this paragraph more than 60 months after the date on which such obligation to contribute or covered operations ceased.

(5) If the corporation determines that the employer has no further liability under the plan either—

(A) because it determines that the contribution base of the plan has not suffered substantial damage as a result of the cessation of the employer's obligation to contribute or cessation of covered operations (considered together with any cessation of contribution obligation, or of covered operations, with respect to other employers), or

(B) because it may not make a determination under paragraph (4) because of the last sentence thereof,

then the bond shall be cancelled or the escrow refunded.

(6) Nothing in this subsection shall be construed as a limitation on the amount of the withdrawal liability of any employer.

(e) For purposes of this part, the date of a complete withdrawal is the date of the cessation of the obligation to contribute or the cessation of covered operations.

(f)(1) The corporation may prescribe regulations under which plans in industries other than the construction or entertainment industries may be amended to provide for special withdrawal liability rules similar to the rules described in subsections (b) and (c).

(2) Regulations under paragraph (1) shall permit use of special withdrawal liability rules—

(A) only in industries (or portions thereof) in which, as determined by the corporation, the characteristics that would make use of such rules appropriate are clearly shown, and

(B) only if the corporation determines, in each instance in which special withdrawal liability rules are permitted, that use of such

rules will not pose a significant risk to the corporation under this title.

SALE OF ASSETS

Sec. 4204. (a)(1) A complete or partial withdrawal of an employer (hereinafter in this section referred to as the "seller") under this section does not occur solely because, as a result of a bona fide, arm's-length sale of assets to an unrelated party (hereinafter in this section referred to as the "purchaser"), the seller ceases covered operations or ceases to have an obligation to contribute for such operations, if—

(A) the purchaser has an obligation to contribute to the plan with respect to the operations for substantially the same number of contribution base units for which the seller had an obligation to contribute to the plan;

(B) the purchaser provides to the plan for a period of 5 plan years commencing with the first plan year beginning after the sale of assets, a bond issued by a corporate surety company that is an acceptable surety for purposes of section 412 of this Act, or an amount held in escrow by a bank or similar financial institution satisfactory to the plan, in an amount equal to the greater of—

(i) the average annual contribution required to be made by the seller with respect to the operations under the plan for the 3 plan years preceding the plan year in which the sale of the employer's assets occurs, or

(ii) the annual contribution that the seller was required to make with respect to the operations under the plan for the last plan year before the plan year in which the sale of the assets occurs,
which bond or escrow shall be paid to the plan if the purchaser withdraws from the plan, or fails to make a contribution to the plan when due, at any time during the first 5 plan years beginning after the sale; and

(C) the contract for sale provides that, if the purchaser withdraws in a complete withdrawal, or a partial withdrawal with respect

ERISA Sec. 4204 (a)(1)(C)

to operations, during such first 5 plan years, the seller is secondarily liable for any withdrawal liability it would have had to the plan with respect to the operations (but for this section) if the liability of the purchaser with respect to the plan is not paid.

(2) If the purchaser—

(A) withdraws before the last day of the fifth plan year beginning after the sale, and

(B) fails to make any withdrawal liability payment when due,

then the seller shall pay to the plan an amount equal to the payment that would have been due from the seller but for this section.

(3)(A) If all, or substantially all, of the seller's assets are distributed, or if the seller is liquidated before the end of the 5 plan year period described in paragraph (1)(C), then the seller shall provide a bond or amount in escrow equal to the present value of the withdrawal liability the seller would have had but for this subsection.

(B) If only a portion of the seller's assets are distributed during such period, then a bond or escrow shall be required, in accordance with regulations prescribed by the corporation, in a manner consistent with subparagraph (A).

(4) The liability of the party furnishing a bond or escrow under this subsection shall be reduced, upon payment of the bond or escrow to the plan, by the amount thereof.

(b)(1) For the purposes of this part, the liability of the purchaser shall be determined as if the purchaser had been required to contribute to the plan in the year of the sale and the 4 plan years preceding the sale the amount the seller was required to contribute for such operations for such 5 plan years.

(2) If the plan is in reorganization in the plan year in which the sale of assets occurs, the purchaser shall furnish a bond or escrow in an amount equal to 200 percent of the amount described in subsection (a)(1)(B).

(c) The corporation may by regulation vary the standards in subparagraphs (B) and (C) of subsection (a)(1) if the variance would more effectively or equitably carry out the purposes of this title. Before it promulgates such regulations, the corporation may grant individual or class variances or exemptions from the requirements of such subparagraphs if the particular case warrants it. Before granting such an individual or class variance or exemption, the corporation—

(1) shall publish notice in the Federal Register of the pendency of the variance or exemption,

(2) shall require that adequate notice be given to interested persons, and

(3) shall afford interested persons an opportunity to present their views.

(d) For purposes of this section, the term "unrelated party" means a purchaser or seller who does not bear a relationship to the seller or purchaser, as the case may be, that is described in section 267(b) of the Internal Revenue Code of 1954, or that is described in regulations prescribed by the corporation applying principles similar to the principles of such section.

PARTIAL WITHDRAWALS

Sec. 4205. (a) Except as otherwise provided in this section, there is a partial withdrawal by an employer from a plan on the last day of a plan year if for such plan year—

(1) there is a 70-percent contribution decline, or

(2) there is a partial cessation of the employer's contribution obligation.

(b) For purposes of subsection (a)—

(1)(A) There is a 70-percent contribution decline for any plan year if during each plan year in the 3-year testing period the employer's contribution base units do not exceed 30 percent of the employer's contribution base units for the high base year.

(B) For purposes of subparagraph (A)—

(i) The term "3-year testing period" means the period consisting of the plan year and the immediately preceding 2 plan years.

(ii) The number of contribution base units for the high base year is the average number of such units for the 2 plan years for which the employer's contribution base units were the highest within the 5 plan years immediately preceding the beginning of the 3-year testing period.

(2)(A) There is a partial cessation of the employer's contribution obligation for the plan year if, during such year—

(i) the employer permanently ceases to have an obligation to contribute under one or more but fewer than all collective bargaining agreements under which the employer has been obligated to contribute under the plan but continues to perform work in the jurisdiction of the collective bargaining agreement of the type for which contributions were previously required or transfers such work to another location, or

(ii) an employer permanently ceases to have an obligation to contribute under the plan with respect to work performed at one or more but fewer than all of its facilities, but continues to perform work at the facility of the type for which the obligation to contribute ceased.

(B) For purposes of subparagraph (A), a cessation of obligations under a collective bargaining agreement shall not be considered to have occurred solely because, with respect to the same plan, one agreement that requires contributions to the plan has been substituted for another agreement.

(c)(1) In the case of a plan in which a majority of the covered employees are employed in the retail food industry, the plan may be amended to provide that this section shall be applied with respect to such plan—

(A) by substituting "35 percent" for "70 percent" in subsections (a) and (b), and

(B) by substituting "65 percent" for "30 percent" in subsection (b).

(2) Any amendment adopted under paragraph (1) shall provide rules for the equitable reduction of withdrawal liability in any case in which the number of the plan's contribution base units, in the 2 plan years following the plan year of withdrawal of the employer, is higher than such number immediately after the withdrawal.

(3) Section 4208 shall not apply to a plan which has been amended under paragraph (1).

(d) In the case of a plan described in section 404(c) of the Internal Revenue Code of 1954, or a continuation thereof, the plan may be amended to provide rules setting forth other conditions consistent with the purposes of this Act under which an employer has liability for partial withdrawal.

◊ ◊ ◊

Editor's Note: The following special provisions of §108(c) MPPAA (P.L. 96-364) are exceptions to Section 4205:

(2)(A) For the purpose of applying section 4205 of the Employee Retirement Income Security Act of 1974 in the case of an employer described in subparagraph (B)—

(i) "more than 75 percent" shall be substituted for "70 percent" in subsections (a) and (b) of such section,

(ii) "25 percent or less" shall be substituted for "30 percent" in subsection (b) of such section, and

(iii) the number of contribution units for the high base year shall be the average annual number of such units for calendar years 1970 and 1971.

(B) An employer is described in this subparagraph if—

(i) the employer is engaged in the trade or business of shipping bulk cargoes in the Great Lakes Maritime Industry, and whose fleet consists of vessels the gross registered tonnage of which was at least 7,800, as stated in the American Bureau of Shipping Record, and

(ii) whose fleet during any 5 years from the period 1970 through and including 1979 has experienced a 33 percent or more increase in the contribution units as measured from the average annual contribution units for the calendar years 1970 and 1971.

(3)(A) For the purpose of determining the withdrawal liability of an employer under title IV of the Employee Retirement Income Security Act of 1974 from a plan that terminates while the plan is insolvent (within the meaning of section 4245 of such Act), the plan's unfunded vested benefits shall be reduced by an amount equal to the sum of all overburden credits that were applied in determining the plan's accumulated funding deficiency for all plan years preceding the first plan year in which the plan is insolvent, plus interest thereon.

(B) The provisions of subparagraph (A) apply only if—

(i) the plan would have been eligible for the overburden credit in the last plan year beginning before the date of the enactment of this Act, if section 4243 of the Employee Retirement Income Security Act of 1974 had been in effect for that plan year, and

(ii) the Pension Benefit Guaranty Corporation determines that the reduction of unfunded vested benefits under subparagraph (A) would not significantly increase the risk of loss to the corporation.

(4) In the case of an employer who withdrew before the date of enactment of this Act from a multiemployer plan covering employees in the seagoing industry (as determined by the corporation), sections 4201 through 4219 of the Employee Retirement Income Security Act of 1974, as added by this Act, are effective as of May 3, 1979. For the purpose of applying section 4217 for purposes of the preceding sentence, the date "May 2, 1979," shall be substituted for "April 28, 1980," and the date "May 3, 1979" shall be substituted for "April 29, 1980". For purposes of this paragraph, terms which are used in title IV of the Employee Retirement Income Security Act of 1974, or in regulations prescribed under that title, and which are used in the preceding sentence have the same meaning as when used in that Act or those regulations. For purposes of this paragraph, the

term "employer" includes only a substantial employer covering employees in the seagoing industry (as so determined) in connection with ports on the West Coast of the United States, but does not include an employer who withdrew from a plan because of a change in the collective bargaining representative.

(d) For purposes of section 4205 of the Employee Retirement Income Security Act of 1974—

(1) subsection (a)(1) of such section shall not apply to any plan year beginning before April 29, 1982,

(2) subsection (a)(2) of such section shall not apply with respect to any cessation of contribution obligations occurring before April 29, 1980, and

(3) in applying subsection (b) of such section, the employer's contribution base units for any plan year ending before April 29, 1980, shall be deemed to be equal to the employer's contribution base units for the last plan year ending before such date.

(e)(1) In the case of a partial withdrawal under section 4205 of the Employee Retirement Income Security Act of 1974, an employer who—

(A) before December 13, 1979, had publicly announced the total cessation of covered operations at a facility in a State (and such cessation occurred within 12 months after the announcement),

(B) had not been obligated to make contributions to the plan on behalf of the employees at such facility for more than 8 years before the discontinuance of contributions, and

(C) after the discontinuance of contributions does not within 1 year after the date of the partial withdrawal perform work in the same State of the type for which contributions were previously required,

shall be liable under such section with respect to such partial withdrawal in an amount not greater than the amount determined under paragraph (2).

(2) The amount determined under this paragraph is the excess (if any) of—

(A) the present value (on the withdrawal date) of the benefits under the plan which—

(i) were vested on the withdrawal date (or, if earlier, at the time of separation from service with the employer at the facility),

(ii) were accrued by employees who on December 13, 1979 (or, if earlier, at the time of separation from service with the employer at the facility), were employed at the facility, and

(iii) are attributable to service with the withdrawing employer, over

(B)(i) the sum of—

(I) all employer contributions to the plan on behalf of employees at the facility before the withdrawal date,

(II) interest (to the withdrawal date) on amounts described in subclause (I), and

(III) $100,000, reduced by

(ii) the sum of—

(I) the benefits paid under the plan on or before the withdrawal date with respect to former employees who separated from employment at the facility, and

(II) interest (to the withdrawal date) on amounts described in subclause (I).

(3) For purposes of paragraph (2)—

(A) actuarial assumptions shall be those used in the last actuarial report completed before December 13, 1979,

(B) the term "withdrawal date" means the date on which the employee ceased work at the facility of the type for which contributions were previously required, and

(C) the term "facility" means the facility referred to in paragraph (1).

◊ ◊ ◊

ADJUSTMENT FOR PARTIAL WITHDRAWAL

Sec. 4206. (a) The amount of an employer's liability for a partial withdrawal, before the application of sections 4219(c)(1) and 4225, is equal to the product of—

(1) the amount determined under section 4211, and adjusted under section 4209 if appropriate, determined as if the employer had withdrawn from the plan in a complete withdrawal—

(A) on the date of the partial withdrawal, or

(B) in the case of a partial withdrawal described in section 4205(a)(1) (relating to 70-percent contribution decline), on the last day of the first plan year in the 3-year testing period, multiplied by

(2) a fraction which is 1 minus a fraction—

(A) the numerator of which is the employer's contribution base units for the plan year following the plan year in which the partial withdrawal occurs, and

(B) the denominator of which is the average of the employer's contribution base units for—

(i) except as provided in clause (ii), the 5 plan years immediately preceding the plan year in which the partial withdrawal occurs, or

(ii) in the case of a partial withdrawal described in section 4205(a)(1) (relating to 70-percent contribution decline), the 5 plan years immediately preceding the beginning of the 3-year testing period.

(b)(1) In the case of an employer that has withdrawal liability for a partial withdrawal from a plan, any withdrawal liability of that employer for a partial or complete withdrawal from that plan in a subsequent plan year shall be reduced by the amount of any partial withdrawal liability (reduced by any abatement or reduction of such liability) of the employer with respect to the plan for a previous plan year.

(2) The corporation shall prescribe such regulations as may be necessary to provide for proper adjustments in the reduction provided by paragraph (1) for—

(A) changes in unfunded vested benefits arising after the close of the prior year for which partial withdrawal liability was determined,

(B) changes in contribution base units occurring after the close of the prior year for which partial withdrawal liability was determined, and

(C) any other factors for which it determines adjustment to be appropriate,

so that the liability for any complete or partial withdrawal in any subsequent year (after the

ERISA Sec. 4206 (b)(2)(C)

application of the reduction) properly reflects the employer's share of liability with respect to the plan.

REDUCTION OR WAIVER OF COMPLETE WITHDRAWAL LIABILITY

Sec. 4207. (a) The corporation shall provide by regulation for the reduction or waiver of liability for a complete withdrawal in the event that an employer who was withdrawn from a plan subsequently resumes covered operations under the plan or renews an obligation to contribute under the plan, to the extent that the corporation determines that reduction or waiver of withdrawal liability is consistent with the purposes of this Act.

(b) The corporation shall prescribe by regulation a procedure and standards for the amendment of plans to provide alternative rules for the reduction or waiver of liability for a complete withdrawal in the event that an employer who has withdrawn from the plan subsequently resumes covered operations or renews an obligation to contribute under the plan. The rules may apply only to the extent that the rules are consistent with the purposes of this Act.

REDUCTION OF PARTIAL WITHDRAWAL LIABILITY

Sec. 4208. (a)(1) If, for any 2 consecutive plan years following the plan year in which an employer has partially withdrawn from a plan under section 4205(a)(1) (referred to elsewhere in this section as the "partial withdrawal year"), the number of contribution base units with respect to which the employer has an obligation to contribute under the plan for each such year is not less than 90 percent of the total number of contribution base units with respect to which the employer had an obligation to contribute under the plan for the high base year (within the meaning of section 4205(b)(1)(B)(ii)), then the employer shall have no obligation to make payments with respect to such partial withdrawal (other than delinquent payments) for plan years beginning after the second consecutive plan year following the partial withdrawal year.

(2)(A) For any plan year for which the number of contribution base units with respect to which an employer who has partially withdrawn under section 4205(a)(1) has an obligation to contribute under the plan equals or exceeds the number of units for the highest year determined under paragraph (1) without regard to "90 percent of", the employer may furnish (in lieu of payment of the partial withdrawal liability determined under section 4206) a bond to plan in the amount determined by the plan sponsor (not exceeding 50 percent of the annual payment otherwise required).

(B) If the plan sponsor determines under paragraph (1) that the employer has no further liability to the plan for the partial withdrawal, then the bond shall be cancelled.

(C) If the plan sponsor determines under paragraph (1) that the employer continues to have liability to the plan for the partial withdrawal, then—

(i) the bond shall be paid to the plan,

(ii) the employer shall immediately be liable for the outstanding amount of liability due with respect to the plan year for which the bond was posted, and

(iii) the employer shall continue to make the partial withdrawal liability payments as they are due.

(b) If—

(1) for any 2 consecutive plan years following a partial withdrawal under section 4205(a)(1), the number of contribution base units with respect to which the employer has an obligation to contribute for each such year exceeds 30 percent of the total number of contribution base units with respect to which the employer has an obligation to contribute for the high base year (within the meaning of section 4205(b)(1) (B)(ii), and

(2) the total number of contribution base units with respect to which all employers un der the plan have obligations to contribute in each of such 2 consecutive years is not less than 90 percent of the total number of contribution base units for which all employers had obligations to contribute in the partial withdrawal plan year;

then, the employer shall have no obligation to make payments with respect to such partial withdrawal (other than delinquent payments) for plan years beginning after the second such consecutive plan year.

(c) In any case in which, in any plan year following a partial withdrawal under section 4205(a)(1), the number of contribution base units with respect to which the employer has an obligation to contribute for such year equals or exceeds 110 percent (or such other percentage as the plan may provide by amendment and which is not prohibited under regulations prescribed by the corporation) of the number of contribution base units with respect to which the employer has an obligation to contribute in the partial withdrawal year, then the amount of the employer's partial withdrawal liability payment for such year shall be reduced pro rata, in accordance with regulations prescribed by the corporation.

(d)(1) An employer to whom section 4202(b) (relating to the building and construction industry) applies is liable for a partial withdrawal only if the employer's obligation to contribute under the plan is continued for no more than an insubstantial portion of its work in the craft and area jurisdiction of the collective bargaining agreement of the type for which contributions are required.

(2) An employer to whom section 4202(c) (relating to the entertainment industry) applies shall have no liability for a partial withdrawal except under the conditions and to the extent prescribed by the corporation by regulation.

(e)(1) The corporation may prescribe regulations providing for the reduction or elimination of partial withdrawal liability under any conditions with respect to which the corporation determines that reduction or elimination of partial withdrawal liability is consistent with the purposes of this Act.

(2) Under such regulations, reduction of withdrawal liability shall be provided only with respect to subsequent changes in the employer's contributions for the same operations, or under the same collective bargaining agreement, that gave rise to the partial withdrawal, and changes in the employer's contribution base units with respect to other facilities or other collective bargaining agreements shall not be taken into account.

(3) The corporation shall prescribe by regulation a procedure by which a plan may by amendment adopt rules for the reduction or elimination of partial withdrawal liability under any other conditions, subject to the approval of the corporation based on its determination that adoption of such rules by the plan is consistent with the purposes of this Act.

DE MINIMIS RULE

Sec. 4209. (a) Except in the case of a plan amended under subsection (b), the amount of the unfunded vested benefits allocable under section 4211 to an employer who withdraws from a plan shall be reduced by the smaller of—

(1) 3/4 of 1 percent of the plan's unfunded vested obligations (determined as of the end of the plan year ending before the date of withdrawal), or

(2) $50,000,

reduced by the amount, if any, by which the unfunded vested benefits allowable to the employer, determined without regard to this subsection, exceeds $100,000.

(b) A plan may be amended to provide for the reduction of the amount determined under section 4211 by not more than the greater of—

(1) the amount determined under subsection (a), or

(2) the lesser of—

(A) the amount determined under subsection (a)(1), or

(B) $100,000,

reduced by the amount, if any, by which the amount determined under section 4211 for the employer, determined without regard to this subsection, exceeds $150,000.

(c) This section does not apply—

(1) to an employer who withdraws in a plan year in which substantially all employers withdraw from the plan, or

(2) in any case in which substantially all employers withdraw from the plan during a period of one or more plan years pursuant to an agreement or arrangement to withdraw, to an employer who withdraws pursuant to such agreement or arrangement.

(d) In any action or proceeding to determine or collect withdrawal liability, if substantially all employers have withdrawn from a plan within a period of 3 plan years, an employer who has withdrawn from such plan during such period shall be presumed to have withdrawn from the plan pursuant to an agreement or arrangement, unless the employer proves otherwise by a preponderance of the evidence.

NO WITHDRAWAL LIABILITY FOR CERTAIN TEMPORARY CONTRIBUTION OBLIGATION PERIODS

Sec. 4210. (a) An employer who withdraws from a plan in complete or partial withdrawal is not liable to the plan if the employer—

(1) first had an obligation to contribute to the plan after the date of the enactment of the Multiemployer Pension Plan Amendments Act of 1980,

(2) had an obligation to contribute to the plan for no more than the lesser of—

(A) 6 consecutive plan years preceding the date on which the employer withdraws, or

(B) the number of years required for vesting under the plan,

(3) was required to make contributions to the plan for each such plan year in an amount equal to less than 2 percent of the sum of all employer contributions made to the plan for each such year, and

(4) has never avoided withdrawal liability because of the application of this section with respect to the plan.

(b) Subsection (a) shall apply to an employer with respect to a plan only if—

(1) the plan is not a plan which primarily covers employees in the building and construction industry;

(2) the plan is amended to provide that subsection (a) applies;

(3) the plan provides, or is amended to provide, that the reduction under section 411(a)(3)(E) of the Internal Revenue Code of 1954 applies with respect to the employees of the employer; and

(4) the ratio of the assets of the plan for the plan year preceding the first plan year for which the employer was required to contribute to the plan to the benefit payments made during that plan year was at least 8 to 1.

METHODS FOR COMPUTING WITHDRAWAL LIABILITY

Sec. 4211. (a) The amount of the unfunded vested benefits allocable to an employer that withdraws from a plan shall be determined in accordance with subsection (b), (c), or (d) of this section.

(b)(1) Except as provided in subsections (c) and (d), the amount of unfunded vested benefits allocable to an employer that withdraws is the sum of—

(A) the employer's proportional share of the unamortized amount of the change in the plan's unfunded vested benefits for plan years ending after September 25, 1980, as determined under paragraph (2),

(B) the employer's proportional share, if any, of the unamortized amount of the plan's unfunded vested benefits at the end of the plan year ending before September 26, 1980, as determined under paragraph (3); and

(C) the employer's proportional share of the unamortized amounts of the reallocated unfunded vested benefits (if any) as determined under paragraph (4).

If the sum of the amounts determined with respect to an employer under paragraphs (2), (3), and (4) is negative, the unfunded vested benefits allocable to the employer shall be zero.

(2)(A) An employer's proportional share of the unamortized amount of the change in the plan's unfunded vested benefits for plan years ending after September 25, 1980, is the sum of the employer's proportional shares of the unamortized amount of the change in unfunded vested benefits for each plan year in which the employer has an obligation to contribute under the plan ending—

(i) after such date, and

(ii) before the plan year in which the withdrawal of the employer occurs.

(B) The change in a plan's unfunded vested benefits for a plan year is the amount by which—

(i) the unfunded vested benefits at the end of the plan year; exceeds

(ii) the sum of—

(I) the unamortized amount of the unfunded vested benefits for the last plan year ending before September 26, 1980, and

(II) the sum of the unamortized amounts of the change in unfunded vested benefits for each plan year ending after September 25, 1980, and preceding the plan year for which the change is determined.

(C) The unamortized amount of the change in a plan's unfunded vested benefits with respect to a plan year is the change in unfunded vested benefits for the plan year, reduced by 5 percent of such change for each succeeding plan year.

(D) The unamortized amount of the unfunded vested benefits for the last plan year ending before September 26, 1980, is the amount of the unfunded vested benefits as of the end of that plan year reduced by 5 percent of such amount for each succeeding plan year.

(E) An employer's proportional share of the unamortized amount of a change in unfunded vested benefits is the product of—

(i) the unamortized amount of such change (as of the end of the plan year preceding the plan year in which the employer withdraws); multiplied by

(ii) a fraction—

(I) the numerator of which is the sum of the contributions required to be made under the plan by the employer for the year in which such change arose and for the 4 preceding plan years, and

(II) the denominator of which is the sum for the plan year in which such change arose and the 4 preceding plan years of all contributions made by employers who had an obligation to contribute under the plan for the plan year in which such change arose reduced by the contributions made in such years by employers who had withdrawn from the plan in the year in which the change arose.

(3) An employer's proportional share of the unamortized amount of the plan's unfunded vested benefits for the last plan year ending before September 26, 1980, is the product of—

(A) such unamortized amount; multiplied by—

(B) a fraction—

ERISA Sec. 4211 (b)(3)(B)

ERISA: The Law and the Code

(i) the numerator of which is the sum of all contributions required to be made by the employer under the plan for the most recent 5 plan years ending before September 26, 1980, and

(ii) the denominator of which is the sum of all contributions made for the most recent 5 plan years ending before September 26, 1980, by all employers—

(I) who had an obligation to contribute under the plan for the first plan year ending on or after such date, and

(II) who had not withdrawn from the plan before such date.

(4)(A) An employer's proportional share of the unamortized amount of the reallocated unfunded vested benefits is the sum of the employer's proportional shares of the unamortized amount of the reallocated unfunded vested benefits for each plan year ending before the plan year in which the employer withdrew from the plan.

(B) Except as otherwise provided in regulations prescribed by the corporation, the reallocated unfunded vested benefits for a plan year is the sum of—

(i) any amount which the plan sponsor determines in that plan year to be uncollectible for reasons arising out of cases or proceedings under title 11, United States Code, or similar proceedings,

(ii) any amount which the plan sponsor determines in that plan year will not be assessed as a result of the operation of section 4209, 4219(c)(1)(B), or section 4225 against an employer to whom a notice described in section 4219 has been sent, and

(iii) any amount which the plan sponsor determines to be uncollectible or unassessable in that plan year for other reasons under standards not inconsistent with regulations prescribed by the corporation.

(C) The unamortized amount of the reallocated unfunded vested benefits with respect to a plan year is the reallocated unfunded

vested benefits for the plan year, reduced by 5 percent of such reallocated unfunded vested benefits for each succeeding plan year.

(D) An employer's proportional share of the unamortized amount of the reallocated unfunded vested benefits with respect to a plan year is the product of—

(i) the unamortized amount of the reallocated unfunded vested benefits (as of the end of the plan year preceding the plan year in which the employer withdraws); multiplied by

(ii) the fraction defined in paragraph (2)(E)(ii).

(c)(1) A multiemployer plan, other than a plan which primarily covers employees in the building and construction industry, may be amended to provide that the amount of unfunded vested benefits allocable to an employer that withdraws from the plan is an amount determined under paragraph (2), (3), (4), or (5) of this subsection, rather than under subsection (b) or (d). A plan prescribed in section 4203(b)(1)(B)(i) (relating to the building and construction industry) may be amended, to the extent provided in regulations prescribed by the corporation, to provide that the amount of the unfunded vested benefits allocable to an employer not described in section 4203(b)(1)(A) shall be determined in a manner different from that provided in subsection (b).

(2)(A) The amount of the unfunded vested benefits allocable to any employer under this paragraph is the sum of the amounts determined under subparagraphs (B) and (C).

(B) The amount determined under this subparagraph is the product of—

(i) the plan's unfunded vested benefits as of the end of the last plan year ending before September 26, 1980, reduced as if those obligations were being fully amortized in level annual installments over 15 years beginning with the first plan year ending on or after such date; multiplied by

ERISA Sec. 4211 (b)(3)(B)(i)

(ii) a fraction—

(I) the numerator of which is the sum of all contributions required to be made by the employer under the plan for the last 5 plan years ending before September 26, 1980, and

(II) the denominator of which is the sum of all contributions made for the last 5 plan years ending before September 26, 1980, by all employers who had an obligation to contribute under the plan for the first plan year ending after September 25, 1980, and who had not withdrawn from the plan before such date.

(C) The amount determined under this subparagraph is the product of—

(i) an amount equal to—

(I) the plan's unfunded vested benefits as of the end of the plan year preceding the plan year in which the employer withdraws, less

(II) the sum of the value as of such date of all outstanding claims for withdrawal liability which can reasonably be expected to be collected, with respect to employers withdrawing before such plan year, and that portion of the amount determined under subparagraph (B)(i) which is allocable to employers who have an obligation to contribute under the plan in the plan year preceding the plan year in which the employer withdraws and who also had an obligation to contribute under the plan for the first plan year ending after September 25, 1980, multiplied by

(ii) a fraction—

(I) the numerator of which is the total amount required to be contributed under the plan by the employer for the last 5 plan years ending before the date on which the employer withdraws, and

(II) the denominator of which is the total amount contributed under the plan by all employers for the last 5 plan years ending before the date on which the employer

withdraws, increased by the amount of any employer contributions owed with respect to earlier periods which were collected in those plan years, and decreased by any amount contributed by an employer who withdrew from the plan under this part during those plan years.

(D) The corporation may by regulation permit adjustments in any denominator under this section, consistent with the purposes of this title, where such adjustment would be appropriate to ease administrative burdens of plan sponsors in calculating such denominators.

(3) The amount of the unfunded vested benefits allocable to an employer under this paragraph is the product of—

(A) the plan's unfunded vested benefits as of the end of the plan year preceding the plan year in which the employer withdraws, less the value as of the end of such year of all outstanding claims for withdrawal liability which can reasonably be expected to be collected from employers withdrawing before such year; multiplied by

(B) a fraction—

(i) the numerator of which is the total amount required to be contributed by the employer under the plan for the last 5 plan years ending before the withdrawal, and

(ii) the denominator of which is the total amount contributed under the plan by all employers for the last 5 plan years ending before the withdrawal, increased by any employer contributions owed with respect to earlier periods which were collected in those plan years, and decreased by any amount contributed to the plan during those plan years by employers who withdrew from the plan under this section during those plan years.

(4)(A) The amount of the unfunded vested benefits allocable to an employer under this paragraph is equal to the sum of—

ERISA Sec. 4211 (c)(4)(A)

(i) the plan's unfunded vested benefits which are attributable to participants' service with the employer (determined as of the end of the plan year preceding the plan year in which the employer withdraws), and

(ii) the employer's proportional share of any unfunded vested benefits which are not attributable to service with the employer or other employers who are obligated to contribute under the plan in the plan year preceding the plan year in which the employer withdraws (determined as of the end of the plan year preceding the plan year in which the employer withdraws).

(B) The plan's unfunded vested benefits which are attributable to participants' service with the employer is the amount equal to the value of nonforfeitable benefits under the plan which are attributable to participants' service with such employer (determined under plan rules not inconsistent with regulations of the corporation) decreased by the share of plan assets determined under subparagraph (C) which is allocated to the employer as provided under subparagraph (D).

(C) The value of plan assets determined under this subparagraph is the value of plan assets allocated to nonforfeitable benefits which are attributable to service with the employers who have an obligation to contribute under the plan in the plan year preceding the plan year in which the employer withdraws, which is determined by multiplying —

(i) the value of the plan assets as of the end of the plan year preceding the plan year in which the employer withdraws, by

(ii) a fraction—

(I) the numerator of which is the value of nonforfeitable benefits which are attributable to service with such employers, and

(II) the denominator of which is the value of all nonforfeitable benefits under the plan as of the end of the plan year.

(D) The share of plan assets, determined under subparagraph (C), which is allocated to the employer shall be determined in accordance with one of the following methods which shall be adopted by the plan by amendment:

(i) by multiplying the value of plan assets determined under subparagraph (C) by a fraction—

(I) the numerator of which is the value of the nonforfeitable benefits which are attributable to service with the employer, and

(II) the denominator of which is the value of the nonforfeitable benefits which are attributable to service with all employers who have an obligation to contribute under the plan in the plan year preceding the plan year in which the employer withdraws;

(ii) by multiplying the value of plan assets determined under subparagraph (C) by a fraction—

(I) the numerator of which is the sum of all contributions (accumulated with interest) which have been made to the plan by the employer for the plan year preceding the plan year in which the employer withdraws and all preceding plan years; and

(II) the denominator of which is the sum of all contributions (accumulated with interest) which have been made to the plan (for the plan year preceding the plan year in which the employer withdraws and all preceding plan years) by all employers who have an obligation to contribute to the plan for the plan year preceding the plan year in which the employer withdraws; or

(iii) by multiplying the value of plan assets under subparagraph (C) by a fraction—

(I) the numerator of which is the amount determined under clause (ii)(I) of this subparagraph, less the sum of benefit payments (accumulated with interest) made to participants (and their benefici

ERISA Sec. 4211 (c)(4)(A)(i)

aries) for the plan years described in such clause (ii)(I) which are attributable to service with the employer; and

(II) the denominator of which is the amount determined under clause (ii)(II) of this subparagraph, reduced by the sum of benefit payments (accumulated with interest) made to participants (and their beneficiaries) for the plan years described in such clause (ii)(II) which are attributable to service with respect to the employers described in such clause (ii)(II).

(E) The amount of the plan's unfunded vested benefits for a plan year preceding the plan year in which an employer withdraws, which is not attributable to service with employers who have an obligation to contribute under the plan in the plan year preceding the plan year in which such employer withdraws, is equal to—

(i) an amount equal to—

(I) the value of all nonforfeitable benefits under the plan at the end of such plan year, reduced by

(II) the value of nonforfeitable benefits under the plan at the end of such plan year which are attributable to participants' service with employers who have an obligation to contribute under the plan for such plan year; reduced by

(ii) an amount equal to—

(I) the value of the plan assets as of the end of such plan year, reduced by

(II) the value of plan assets as of the end of such plan year as determined under subparagraph (C); reduced by

(iii) the value of all outstanding claims for withdrawal liability which can reasonably be expected to be collected with respect to employers withdrawing before the year preceding the plan year in which the employer withdraws.

(F) The employer's proportional share described in subparagraph (A)(ii) for a plan year is the amount determined under sub-

paragraph (E) for the employer, but not in excess of an amount which bears the same ratio to the sum of the amounts determined under subparagraph (E) for all employers under the plan as the amount determined under subparagraph (C) for the employer bears to the sum of the amounts determined under subparagraph (C) for all employers under the plan.

(G) The corporation may prescribe by regulation other methods which a plan may adopt for allocating assets to determine the amount of the unfunded vested benefits attributable to service with the employer and to determine the employer's share of unfunded vested benefits not attributable to service with employers who have an obligation to contribute under the plan in the plan year in which the employer withdraws.

(5)(A) The corporation shall prescribe by regulation a procedure by which a plan may, by amendment, adopt any other alternative method for determining an employer's allocable share of unfunded vested benefits under this section, subject to the approval of the corporation based on its determination that adoption of the method by the plan would not significantly increase the risk of loss to plan participants and beneficiaries or to the corporation.

(B) The corporation may prescribe by regulation standard approaches for alternative methods, other than those set forth in the preceding paragraphs of this subsection, which a plan may adopt under subparagraph (A), for which the corporation may waive or modify the approval requirements of subparagraph (A). Any alternative method shall provide for the allocation of substantially all of a plan's unfunded vested benefits among employers who have an obligation to contribute under the plan.

(C) Unless the corporation by regulation provides otherwise, a plan may be amended to provide that a period of more than 5 but not more than 10 plan years may be used for determining the numerator and denominator of any fraction which is used under any

ERISA Sec. 4211 (c)(5)(C)

method authorized under this section for determining an employer's allocable share of unfunded vested benefits under this section.

(D) The corporation may by regulation permit adjustments in any denominator under this section, consistent with the purposes of this title, where such adjustment would be appropriate to ease administrative burdens of plan sponsors in calculating such denominators.

(d)(1) The method of calculating an employer's allocable share of unfunded vested benefits set forth in subsection (c)(3) shall be the method for calculating an employer's allocable share of unfunded vested benefits under a plan to which section 404(c) of the Internal Revenue Code of 1954, or a continuation of such a plan, applies, unless the plan is amended to adopt another method authorized under subsection (b) or (c).

(2) Sections 4204, 4209, 4219(c)(1)(B), and 4225 shall not apply with respect to the withdrawal of an employer from a plan described in paragraph (1) unless the plan is amended to provide that any of such sections apply.

(e) In the case of a transfer of liabilities to another plan incident to an employer's withdrawal or partial withdrawal, the withdrawn employer's liability under this part shall be reduced in an amount equal to the value, as of the end of the last plan year ending on or before the date of the withdrawal, of the transferred unfunded vested benefits.

(f) In the case of a withdrawal following a merger of multiemployer plans, subsection (b), (c) or (d) shall be applied in accordance with regulations prescribed by the corporation; except that, if a withdrawal occurs in the first plan year beginning after a merger of multiemployer plans, the determination under this section shall be made as if each of the multiemployer plans had remained separate plans.

OBLIGATION TO CONTRIBUTE; SPECIAL RULES

Sec. 4212. (a) For purposes of this part, the term "obligation to contribute" means an obligation to contribute arising—

(1) under one or more collective bargaining (or related) agreements, or

(2) as a result of a duty under applicable labor-management relations law, but does not include an obligation to pay withdrawal liability under this section or to pay delinquent contributions.

(b) Payments of withdrawal liability under this part shall not be considered contributions for purposes of this part.

(c) If a principal purpose of any transaction is to evade or avoid liability under this part, this part shall be applied (and liability shall be determined and collected) without regard to such transaction.

ACTUARIAL ASSUMPTIONS, ETC.

Sec. 4213. (a) The corporation may prescribe by regulation actuarial assumptions which may be used by a plan actuary in determining the unfunded vested benefits of a plan for purposes of determining an employer's withdrawal liability under this part. Withdrawal liability under this part shall be determined by each plan on the basis of—

(1) actuarial assumptions and methods which, in the aggregate, are reasonable (taking into account the experience of the plan and reasonable expectations) and which, in combination, offer the actuary's best estimate of anticipated experience under the plan, or

(2) actuarial assumptions and methods set forth in the corporation's regulations for purposes of determining an employer's withdrawal liability.

(b) In determining the unfunded vested benefits of a plan for purposes of determining an employer's withdrawal liability under this part, the plan actuary may—

(1) rely on the most recent complete actuarial valuation used for purposes of section 412 of the Internal Revenue Code of 1954 and reasonable estimates for the interim years of the unfunded vested benefits, and

(2) in the absence of complete data, rely on the data available or on data secured by a sampling which can reasonably be expected to be representative of the status of the entire plan.

(c) For purposes of this part, the term "unfunded vested benefits" means with respect to a plan, an amount equal to—

(A) the value of nonforfeitable benefits under the plan, less

(B) the value of the assets of the plan.

APPLICATION OF PLAN AMENDMENTS

Sec. 4214. (a) No plan rule or amendment adopted after January 31, 1981, under section 4209 or 4211(c) may be applied without the employer's consent with respect to liability for a withdrawal or partial withdrawal which occurred before the date on which the rule or amendment was adopted.

(b) All plan rules and amendments authorized under this part shall operate and be applied uniformly with respect to each employer, except that special provisions may be made to take into account the creditworthiness of an employer. The plan sponsor shall give notice to all employers who have an obligation to contribute under the plan and to all employee organizations representing employees covered under the plan of any plan rules or amendments adopted pursuant to this section.

PLAN NOTIFICATION TO CORPORATION OF POTENTIALLY SIGNIFICANT WITHDRAWALS

Sec. 4215. The corporation may, by regulation, require the plan sponsor of a multiemployer plan to provide notice to the corporation when the withdrawal from the plan by any employer has resulted, or will

result, in a significant reduction in the amount of aggregate contributions under the plan made by employers.

SPECIAL RULES FOR SECTION 404(c) PLANS

Sec. 4216. (a) In the case of a plan described in subsection (b)—

(1) if an employer withdraws prior to a termination described in section 4041A(a)(2), the amount of withdrawal liability to be paid in any year by such employer shall be an amount equal to the greater of—

(A) the amount determined under section 4219(c)(1)(C)(i), or

(B) the product of—

(i) the number of contribution base units for which the employer would have been required to make contributions for the prior plan year if the employer had not withdrawn, multiplied by

(ii) the contribution rate for the plan year which would be required to meet the amortization schedules contained in section 4243(d)(3)(B)(ii) (determined without regard to any limitation on such rate otherwise provided by this title)

except that an employer shall not be required to pay an amount in excess of the withdrawal liability computed with interest; and

(2) the withdrawal liability of an employer who withdraws after December 31, 1983, as a result of a termination described in section 4041A(a)(2) which is agreed to by the labor organization that appoints the employee representative on the joint board of trustees which sponsors the plan, shall be determined under subsection (c) if—

(A) as a result of prior employer withdrawals in any plan year commencing after January 1, 1980, the number of contribution base units is reduced to less than 67 percent of the average number of such units for the calendar years 1974 through 1979; and

(B) at least 50 percent of the withdrawal liability attributable to the first 33 percent decline described in subparagraph (A) has been determined by the plan sponsor to be uncollectible within the meaning of regulations of the corporation of general applicability; and

(C) the rate of employer contributions under the plan for each plan year following the first plan year beginning after the date of enactment of the Multiemployer Pension Plan Amendments Act of 1980 and preceding the termination date equals or exceeds the rate described in section 4243(d)(3).

(b) A plan is described in this subsection if—

(1) it is a plan described in section 404(c) of the Internal Revenue Code of 1954 or a continuation thereof; and

(2) participation in the plan is substantially limited to individuals who retired prior to January 1, 1976.

(c)(1) The amount of an employer's liability under this paragraph is the product of—

(A) the amount of the employer's withdrawal liability determined without regard to this section, and

(B) the greater of 90 percent, or a fraction—

(i) the numerator of which is an amount equal to the portion of the plan's unfunded vested benefits that is attributable to plan participants who have a total of 10 or more years of signatory service, and

(ii) the denominator of which is an amount equal to the total unfunded vested benefits of the plan.

(2) For purposes of paragraph (1), the term "a year of signatory service" means a year during any portion of which a participant was employed for an employer who was obligated to contribute in that year, or who was subsequently obligated to contribute.

APPLICATION OF PART IN CASE OF CERTAIN PRE-1980 WITHDRAWALS

Sec. 4217. (a) For the purpose of determining the amount of unfunded vested benefits allocable to an employer for a partial or complete withdrawal from a plan which occurs after September 25, 1980, and for the purpose of determining whether there has been a partial withdrawal after such date, the amount of contributions, and the number of contribution base units, of such employer properly allocable—

(1) to work performed under a collective bargaining agreement for which there was a permanent cessation of the obligation to contribute before September 26, 1980, or

(2) to work performed at a facility at which all covered operations permanently ceased before September 26, 1980, or for which there was a permanent cessation of the obligation to contribute before that date,
shall not be taken into account.

(b) A plan may, in a manner not inconsistent with regulations, which shall be prescribed by the corporation, adjust the amount of unfunded vested benefits allocable to other employers under a plan maintained by an employer described in subsection (a).

WITHDRAWAL NOT TO OCCUR MERELY BECAUSE OF CHANGE IN BUSINESS FORM OR SUSPENSION OF CONTRIBUTIONS DURING LABOR DISPUTE

Sec. 4218. Notwithstanding any other provision of this part, an employer shall not be considered to have withdrawn from a plan solely because—

(1) an employer ceases to exist by reason of—

(A) a change in corporate structure described in section 4069(b), or

(B) a change to an unincorporated form of business enterprise, if the change causes n interruption in employer contributions or obligations to contribute under the plan, or

(2) an employer suspends contributions under the plan during a labor dispute involving its employees.

For purposes of this part, a successor or parent corporation or other entity resulting from any such change shall be considered the original employer.

NOTICE, COLLECTION, ETC., OF WITHDRAWAL LIABILITY

Sec. 4219. (a) An employer shall, within 30 days after a written request from the plan sponsor, furnish such information as the plan sponsor reasonably determines to be necessary to enable the plan sponsor to comply with the requirements of this part.

(b)(1) As soon as practicable after an employer's complete or partial withdrawal, the plan sponsor shall—

(A) notify the employer of—

(i) the amount of the liability, and

(ii) the schedule for liability payments, and

(B) demand payment in accordance with the schedule.

(2)(A) No later than 90 days after the employer receives the notice described in paragraph (1), the employer—

(i) may ask the plan sponsor to review any specific matter relating to the determination of the employer's liability and the schedule of payments,

(ii) may identify any inaccuracy in the determination of the amount of the unfunded vested benefits allocable to the employer, and

(iii) may furnish any additional relevant information to the plan sponsor.

(B) After a reasonable review of any matter raised, the plan sponsor shall notify the employer of—

(i) the plan sponsor's decision,

(ii) the basis for the decision, and

(iii) the reason for any change in the determination of the employer's liability or schedule of liability payments.

(c)(1)(A)(i) Except as provided in subparagraphs (B) and (D) of this paragraph and in paragraphs (4) and (5), an employer shall pay the amount determined under section 4211, adjusted if appropriate first under section 4209 and then under section 4206 over the period of years necessary to amortize the amount in level annual payments determined under subparagraph (C), calculated as if the first payment were made on the first day of the plan year following the plan year in which the withdrawal occurs and as if each subsequent payment were made on the first day of each subsequent plan year. Actual payment shall commence in accordance with paragraph (2).

(ii) The determination of the amortization period described in clause (i) shall be based on the assumptions used for the most recent actuarial valuation for the plan.

(B) In any case in which the amortization period described in subparagraph (A) exceeds 20 years, the employer's liability shall be limited to the first 20 annual payments determined under subparagraph (C).

(C)(i) Except as provided in subparagraph (E), the amount of each annual payment shall be the product of—

(I) the average annual number of contribution base units for the period of 3 consecutive plan years, during the period of 10 consecutive plan years ending before the plan year in which the withdrawal occurs, in which the number of contribution base units for which the employer had an obligation to contribute under the plan is the highest, and

ERISA Sec. 4219 (c)(1)(C)(i)(I)

(II) the highest contribution rate at which the employer had an obligation to contribute under the plan during the 10 plan years ending with the plan year in which the withdrawal occurs.

For purposes of the preceding sentence, a partial withdrawal described in section 4205 (a)(1) shall be deemed to occur on the last day of the first year of the 3-year testing period described in section 4205(b)(1) (B)(i).

(ii)(I) A plan may be amended to provide that for any plan year ending before 1986 the amount of each annual payment shall be (in lieu of the amount determined under clause (i)) the average of the required employer contributions under the plan for the period of 3 consecutive plan years (during the period of 10 consecutive plan years ending with the plan year preceding the plan year in which the withdrawal occurs) for which such required contributions were the highest.

(II) Subparagraph (B) shall not apply to any plan year to which this clause applies.

(III) This clause shall not apply in the case of any withdrawal described in subparagraph (D).

(IV) If under a plan this clause applies to any plan year but does not apply to the next plan year, this clause shall not apply to any plan year after such next plan year.

(V) For purposes of this clause, the term "required contributions" means, for any period, the amounts which the employer was obligated to contribute for such period (not taking into account any delinquent contribution for any other period).

(iii) A plan may be amended to provide that for the first plan year ending on or after September 26, 1980, the number "5" shall be substituted for the number "10" each place it appears in clause (i) or clause (ii) (whichever is appropriate). If the plan is so amended, the number "5" shall be in-

creased by one for each succeeding plan year until the number "10" is reached.

(D) In any case in which a multiemployer plan terminates by the withdrawal of every employer from the plan, or in which substantially all the employers withdraw from a plan pursuant to an agreement or arrangement to withdraw from the plan—

(i) the liability of each such employer who has withdrawn shall be determined (or redetermined) under this paragraph without regard to subparagraph (B), and

(ii) notwithstanding any other provision of this part, the total unfunded vested benefits of the plan shall be fully allocated among all such employers in a manner not inconsistent with regulations which shall be prescribed by the corporation.

Withdrawal by an employer from a plan, during a period of 3 consecutive plan years within which substantially all the employers who have an obligation to contribute under the plan withdraw, shall be presumed to be a withdrawal pursuant to an agreement or arrangement, unless the employer proves otherwise by a preponderance of the evidence.

(E) In the case of a partial withdrawal described in section 4205(a), the amount of each annual payment shall be the product of—

(i) the amount determined under subparagraph (C) (determined without regard to this subparagraph), multiplied by

(ii) the fraction determined under section 4206(a)(2).

(2) Withdrawal liability shall be payable in accordance with the schedule set forth by the plan sponsor under subsection (b)(1) beginning no later than 60 days after the date of the demand notwithstanding any request for review or appeal of determinations of the amount of such liability or of the schedule.

(3) Each annual payment determined under paragraph (1)(C) shall be payable in 4 equal installments due quarterly, or at other intervals specified by plan rules. If a payment is not made when due, interest on the payment shall accrue from the due date until the date on which the payment is made.

(4) The employer shall be entitled to prepay the outstanding amount of the unpaid annual withdrawal liability payments determined under paragraph (1)(C), plus accrued interest, if any, in whole or in part, without penalty. If the prepayment is made pursuant to a withdrawal which is later determined to be part of a withdrawal described in paragraph (1)(D), the withdrawal liability of the employer shall not be limited to the amount of the prepayment.

(5) In the event of a default, a plan sponsor may require immediate payment of the outstanding amount of an employer's withdrawal liability, plus accrued interest on the total outstanding liability from the due date of the first payment which was not timely made. For purposes of this section, the term "default" means—

(A) the failure of an employer to make, when due, any payment under this section, if the failure is not cured within 60 days after the employer receives written notification from the plan sponsor of such failure, and

(B) any other event defined in rules adopted by the plan which indicates a substantial likelihood that an employer will be unable to pay its withdrawal liability.

(6) Except as provided in paragraph (1)(A)(ii), interest under this subsection shall be charged at rates based on prevailing market rates for comparable obligations, in accordance with regulations prescribed by the corporation.

(7) A multiemployer plan may adopt rules for other terms and conditions for the satisfaction of an employer's withdrawal liability if such rules—

(A) are consistent with this Act, and

(B) are not inconsistent with regulations of the corporation.

(8) In the case of a terminated multiemployer plan, an employer's obligation to make payments under this section ceases at the end of the plan year in which the assets of the plan (exclusive of withdrawal liability claims) are sufficient to meet all obligations of the plan, as determined by the corporation.

(d) The prohibitions provided in section 406(a) do not apply to any action required or permitted under this part.

APPROVAL OF AMENDMENTS

Sec. 4220. (a) Except as provided in subsection (b), if an amendment to a multiemployer plan authorized by any preceding section of this part is adopted more than 36 months after the effective date of this section, the amendment shall be effective only if the corporation approves the amendment, or, within 90 days after the corporation receives notice and a copy of the amendment from the plan sponsor, fails to disapprove the amendment.

(b) An amendment permitted by section 4211(c)(5) may be adopted only in accordance with that section.

(c) The corporation shall disapprove an amendment referred to in subsection (a) or (b) only if the corporation determines that the amendment creates an unreasonable risk of loss to plan participants and beneficiaries or to the corporation.

RESOLUTION OF DISPUTES

Sec. 4221. (a)(1) Any dispute between an employer and the plan sponsor of a multiemployer plan concerning a determination made under sections 4201 through 4219 shall be resolved through arbitration. Either party may initiate the arbitration proceeding within a 60-day period after the earlier of—

(A) the date of notification to the employer under section 4219(b)(2)(B), or

(B) 120 days after the date of the employer's request under section 4219(b)(2)(A).

The parties may jointly initiate arbitration within the 180-day period after the date of the plan sponsor's demand under section 4219(b)(1).

(2) An arbitration proceeding under this section shall be conducted in accordance with fair and equitable procedures to be promulgated by the corporation. The plan sponsor may purchase insurance to cover potential liability of the arbitrator. If the parties have not provided for the costs of the arbitration, including arbitrator's fees, by agreement, the arbitrator shall assess such fees. The arbitrator may also award reasonable attorney's fees.

(3)(A) For purposes of any proceeding under this section, any determination made by a plan sponsor under sections 4201 through 4219 and section 4225 is presumed correct unless the party contesting the determination shows by a preponderance of the evidence that the determination was unreasonable or clearly erroneous.

(B) In the case of the determination of a plan's unfunded vested benefits for a plan year, the determination is presumed correct unless a party contesting the determination shows by a preponderance of evidence that—

(i) the actuarial assumptions and methods used in the determination were, in the aggregate, unreasonable (taking into account the experience of the plan and reasonable expectations), or

(ii) the plan's actuary made a significant error in applying the actuarial assumptions or methods.

(b)(1) If no arbitration proceeding has been initiated pursuant to subsection (a), the amounts demanded by the plan sponsor under section 4219(b)(1) shall be due and owing on the schedule set forth by the plan sponsor. The plan sponsor may bring an action in a State or

Federal court of competent jurisdiction for collection.

(2) Upon completion of the arbitration proceedings in favor of one of the parties, any party thereto may bring an action, no later than 30 days after the issuance of an arbitrator's award, in an appropriate United States district court in accordance with section 4301 to enforce, vacate, or modify the arbitrator's award.

(3) Any arbitration proceedings under this section shall, to the extent consistent with this title, be conducted in the same manner, subject to the same limitations, carried out with the same powers (including subpena power), and enforced in United States courts as an arbitration proceeding carried out under title 9, United States Code.

(c) In any proceeding under subsection (b), there shall be a presumption, rebuttable only by a clear preponderance of the evidence, that the findings of fact made by the arbitrator were correct.

(d) Payments shall be made by an employer in accordance with the determinations made under this part until the arbitrator issues a final decision with respect to the determination submitted for arbitration, with any necessary adjustments in subsequent payments for overpayments or underpayments arising out of the decision of the arbitrator with respect to the determination. If the employer fails to make timely payment in accordance with such final decision, the employer shall be treated as being delinquent in the making of a contribution required under the plan (within the meaning of section 515).

(e) If any employer requests in writing that the plan sponsor make available to the employer general information necessary for the employer to compute its withdrawal liability with respect to the plan (other than information which is unique to that employer), the plan sponsor shall furnish the information to the employer without charge. If any employer requests in writing that the plan sponsor make an estimate of such employer's potential withdrawal liability with respect to the plan or t provide information unique to that employer, the plan sponsor may require the employer to pay the reasonable cost of making such estimate or providing such information.

REIMBURSEMENTS FOR UNCOLLECTIBLE WITHDRAWAL LIABILITY

Sec. 4222. (a) By May 1, 1982, the corporation shall establish by regulation a supplemental program to reimburse multiemployer plans for withdrawal liability payments which are due from employers and which are determined to be uncollectible for reasons arising out of cases or proceedings involving the employers under title 11, United States Code, or similar cases or proceedings. Participation in the supplemental program shall be on a voluntary basis, and a plan which elects coverage under the program shall pay premiums to the corporation in accordance with a premium schedule which shall be prescribed from time to time by the corporation. The premium schedule shall contain such rates and bases for the application of such rates as the corporation considers to be appropriate.

(b) The corporation may provide under the program for reimbursement of amounts of withdrawal liability determined to be uncollectible for any other reasons the corporation considers appropriate.

(c) The cost of the program (including such administrative and legal costs as the corporation considers appropriate) may be paid only out of premiums collected under such program.

(d) The supplemental program may be offered to eligible plans on such terms and conditions, and with such limitations with respect to the payment of reimbursements (including the exclusion of de minimis amounts of uncollectible employer liability, and the reduction or elimination of reimbursements which cannot be paid from collected premiums) and such restrictions on withdrawal from the program, as the corporation considers necessary and appropriate.

(e) The corporation may enter into arrangements with private insurers to carry out in whole or in part the program authorized by this section and may require plans which elect coverage under the program to elect coverage by those private insurers.

WITHDRAWAL LIABILITY PAYMENT FUND

Sec. 4223. (a) The plan sponsors of multiemployer plans may establish or participate in a withdrawal liability payment fund.

(b) For purposes of this section, the term "withdrawal liability payment fund", and the term "fund", mean a trust which—

(1) is established and maintained under section 501(c)(22) of the Internal Revenue Code of 1954,

(2) maintains agreements which cover a substantial portion of the participants who are in multiemployer plans which (under the rules of the trust instrument) are eligible to participate in the fund,

(3) is funded by amounts paid by the plans which participate in the fund, and

(4) is administered by a Board of Trustees, and in the administration of the fund there is equal representation of—

(A) trustees representing employers who are obligated to contribute to the plans participating in the fund, and

(B) trustees representing employees who are participants in plans which participate in the fund.

(c)(1) If an employer withdraws from a plan which participates in a withdrawal liability payment fund, then, to the extent provided in the trust, the fund shall pay to that plan—

(A) the employer's unattributable liability,

(B) the employer's withdrawal liability payments which would have been due but for section 4208, 4209, 4219, or 4225,

(C) the employer's withdrawal liability payments to the extent they are uncollectible.

(2) The fund may provide for the payment of the employer's attributable liability if the fund—

(A) provides for the payment of both the attributable and the unattributable liability of the employer in a single payment, and

(B) is subrogated to all rights of the plan against the employer.

(3) For purposes of this section, the term—

(A) "attributable liability" means the excess, if any, determined under the provisions of a plan not inconsistent with regulations of the corporation, of—

(i) the value of vested benefits accrued as a result of service with the employer, over

(ii) the value of plan assets attributed to the employer, and

(B) "unattributable liability" means the excess of withdrawal liability over attributable liability.

Such terms may be further defined, and the manner in which they shall be applied may be prescribed, by the corporation by regulation.

(4)(A) The trust of a fund shall be maintained for the exclusive purpose of paying—

(i) any amount described in paragraph (1) and paragraph (2), and

(ii) reasonable and necessary administrative expenses in connection with the establishment and operation of the trust and the processing of claims against the fund.

(B) The amounts paid by a plan to a fund shall be deemed a reasonable expense of administering the plan under sections 403(c)(1) and 404(a)(1)(A)(ii), and the payments made by a fund to a participating plan shall be deemed services necessary for the operation of the plan within the meaning of section 408(b)(2) or within the meaning of

section 4975(d)(2) of the Internal Revenue Code of 1954.

(d)(1) For purposes of this part—

(A) only amounts paid by the fund to a plan under subsection (c)(1)(A) shall be credited to withdrawal liability otherwise payable by the employer, unless the plan otherwise provides, and

(B) any amounts paid by the fund under subsection (c) to a plan shall be treated by the plan as a payment of withdrawal liability to such plan.

(2) For purposes of applying provisions relating to the funding standard accounts (and minimum contribution requirements), amounts paid from the plan to the fund shall be applied to reduce the amount treated as contributed to the plan.

(e) The fund shall be subrogated to the rights of the plan against the employer that has withdrawn from the plan for amounts paid by a fund to a plan under—

(1) subsection (c)(1)(A), to the extent not credited under subsection (d)(1)(A), and

(2) subsection (c)(1)(C).

(f) Notwithstanding any other provision of this Act, a fiduciary of the fund shall discharge the fiduciary's duties with respect to the fund in accordance with the standards for fiduciaries prescribed by this Act (to the extent not inconsistent with the purposes of this section), and in accordance with the documents and instruments governing the fund insofar as such documents and instruments are consistent with the provisions of this Act (to the extent not inconsistent with the purposes of this section). The provisions of the preceding sentence shall supersede any and all State laws relating to fiduciaries insofar as they may now or hereafter relate to a fund to which this section applies.

(g) No payments shall be made from a fund to a plan on the occasion of a withdrawal o partial withdrawal of an employer from suc!

ERISA Sec. 4223 (c)(1)(C)

plan if the employees representing the withdrawn contribution base units continue, after such withdrawal, to be represented under section 9 of the National Labor Relations Act (or other applicable labor laws) in negotiations with such employer by the labor organization which represented such employees immediately preceding such withdrawal.

(h) Nothing in this section shall be construed to prohibit the purchase of insurance by an employer from any other person, to limit the circumstances under which such insurance would be payable, or to limit in any way the terms and conditions of such insurance.

(i) The corporation may provide by regulation rules not inconsistent with this section governing the establishment and maintenance of funds, but only to the extent necessary to carry out the purposes of this part (other than section 4222).

ALTERNATIVE METHOD OF WITHDRAWAL LIABILITY PAYMENTS

Sec. 4224. A multiemployer plan may adopt rules providing for other terms and conditions for the satisfaction of an employer's withdrawal liability if such rules are consistent with this Act and with such regulations as may be prescribed by the corporation.

LIMITATION ON WITHDRAWAL LIABILITY

Sec. 4225. (a)(1) In the case of bona fide sale of all or substantially all of the employer's assets in an arm's-length transaction to an unrelated party (within the meaning of section 4204(d)), the unfunded vested benefits allocable to an employer (after the application of all sections of this part having a lower number designation than this section), other than an employer undergoing reorganization under title 11, United States Code, or similar provisions of State law, shall not exceed the greater of—

(A) a portion (determined under paragraph (2)) of the liquidation or dissolution value of the employer (determined after the sale or exchange of such assets), or

(B) the unfunded vested benefits attributable to employees of the employer.

(2) For purposes of paragraph (1), the portion shall be determined in accordance with the following table:

If the liquidation or distribution value of the employer after the sale or exchange is—	The portion is—
Not more than $2,000,000	30 percent of the amount
More than $2,000,000, but not more than $4,000,000	$600,000, plus 35 percent of the amount in excess of $2,000,000
More than $4,000,000, but not more than $6,000,000	$1,300,000, plus 40 percent of the amount in excess of $4,000,000
More than $6,000,000, but not more than $7,000,000	$2,100,000, plus 45 percent of the amount in excess of $6,000,000
More than $7,000,000, but not more than $8,000,000	$2,550,000, plus 50 percent of the amount in excess of $7,000,000
More than $8,000,000, but not more than $9,000,000	$3,050,000, plus 60 percent of the amount in excess of $8,000,000
More than $9,000,000, but not more than $10,000,000	$3,650,000, plus 70 percent of the amount in excess of $9,000,000
More than $10,000,000	$4,350,000, plus 80 percent of the amount in excess of $10,000,000

(b) In the case of an insolvent employer undergoing liquidation or dissolution, the unfunded vested benefits allocable to that employer shall not exceed an amount equal to the sum of—

(1) 50 percent of the unfunded vested benefits allocable to the employer (determined without regard to this section), and

(2) that portion of 50 percent of the unfunded vested benefits allocable to the employer (as determined under paragraph (1))

ERISA Sec. 4225 (b)(2)

which does not exceed the liquidation or dissolution value of the employer determined —

(A) as of the commencement of liquidation or dissolution, and

(B) after reducing the liquidation or dissolution value of the employer by the amount determined under paragraph (1).

(c) To the extent that the withdrawal liability of an employer is attributable to his obligation to contribute to or under a plan as an individual (whether as a sole proprietor or as a member of a partnership), property which may be exempt from the estate under section 522 of title 11, United States Code, or under similar provisions of law, shall not be subject to enforcement of such liability.

(d) For purposes of this section—

(1) an employer is insolvent if the liabilities of the employer, including withdrawal liability under the plan (determined without regard to subsection (b)), exceed the assets of the employer (determined as of the commencement of the liquidation or dissolution), and

(2) the liquidation or dissolution value of the employer shall be determined without regard to such withdrawal liability.

(e) In the case of one or more withdrawals of an employer attributable to the same sale, liquidation, or dissolution, under regulations prescribed by the corporation—

(1) all such withdrawals shall be treated as a single withdrawal for the purpose of applying this section, and

(2) the withdrawal liability of the employer to each plan shall be an amount which bears the same ratio to the present value of the withdrawal liability payments to all plans (after the application of the preceding provisions of this section) as the withdrawal liability of the employer to such plan (determined without regard to this section) bears to the withdrawal liability of the employer to all such plans (determined without regard to this section).

Part 2— Merger or Transfer of Plan Assets or Liabilities

MERGERS AND TRANSFERS BETWEEN MULTIEMPLOYER PLANS

Sec. 4231. (a) Unless otherwise provided in regulations prescribed by the corporation, a plan sponsor may not cause a multiemployer plan to merge with one or more multiemployer plans, or engage in a transfer of assets and liabilities to or from another multiemployer plan, unless such merger or transfer satisfies the requirements of subsection (b).

(b) A merger or transfer satisfies the requirements of this section if—

(1) in accordance with regulations of the corporation, the plan sponsor of a multiemployer plan notifies the corporation of a merger with or transfer of plan assets or liabilities to another multiemployer plan at least 120 days before the effective date of the merger or transfer;

(2) no participant's or beneficiary's accrued benefit will be lower immediately after the effective date of the merger or transfer than the benefit immediately before that date;

(3) the benefits of participants and beneficiaries are not reasonably expected to be subject to suspension under section 4245; and

(4) an actuarial valuation of the assets and liabilities of each of the affected plans has been performed during the plan year preceding the effective date of the merger or transfer, based upon the most recent data available as of the day before the start of that plan year, or other valuation of such assets and liabilities performed under such standards and procedures as the corporation may prescribe by regulation.

(c) The merger of multiemployer plans or the transfer of assets or liabilities between multiemployer plans, shall be deemed not to constitute a violation of the provisions of section 406(a) or section 406(b)(2) if the corporation determines that the merger or transfer otherwise satisfies the requirements of this section.

(d) A plan to which liabilities are transferred under this section is a successor plan for purposes of section 4022A(b)(2)(B).

TRANSFERS BETWEEN A MULTIEMPLOYER PLAN AND A SINGLE EMPLOYER PLAN

Sec. 4232. (a) A transfer of assets or liabilities between, or a merger of, a multiemployer plan and a single-employer plan shall satisfy the requirements of this section.

(b) No accrued benefit of a participant or beneficiary may be lower immediately after the effective date of a transfer or merger described in subsection (a) than the benefit immediately before that date.

(c)(1) Except as provided in paragraphs (2) and (3), a multiemployer plan which transfers liabilities to a single-employer plan shall be liable to the corporation if the single-employer plan terminates within 60 months after the effective date of the transfer. The amount of liability shall be the lesser of—

(A) the amount of the plan asset insufficiency of the terminated single-employer plan, less 30 percent of the net worth of the employer who maintained the single-employer plan, determined in accordance with section 4062 or 4064, or

(B) the value, on the effective date of the transfer, of the unfunded benefits transferred to the single-employer plan which are guaranteed under section 4022.

(2) A multiemployer plan shall be liable to the corporation as provided in paragraph (1) unless, within 180 days after the corporation receives an application (together with such information as the corporation may reasonably require for purposes of such application) from the multiemployer plan sponsor for a determination under this paragraph—

(A) the corporation determines that the interests of the plan participants and beneficiaries and of the corporation are adequately protected, or

(B) fails to make any determination regarding the adequacy with which such interests are protected with respect to such transfer of liabilities.

If, after the receipt of such application, the corporation requests from the plan sponsor additional information necessary for the determination, the running of the 180-day period shall be suspended from the date of such request until the receipt by the corporation of the additional information requested. The corporation may by regulation prescribe procedures and standards for the issuance of determinations under this paragraph. This paragraph shall not apply to any application submitted less than 180 days after the date of enactment of the Multiemployer Pension Plan Amendments Act of 1980.

(3) A multiemployer plan shall not be liable to the corporation as provided in paragraph (1) in the case of a transfer from the multiemployer plan to a single-employer plan of liabilities which accrued under a single-employer plan which merged with the multiemployer plan, if, the value of liabilities transferred to the single-employer plan does not exceed the value of the liabilities for benefits which accrued before the merger, and the value of the assets transferred to the single-employer plan is substantially equal to the value of the assets which would have been in the single-employer plan if the employer had maintained and funded it as a separate plan under which no benefits accrued after the date of the merger.

(4) The corporation may make equitable arrangements with multiemployer plans which are liable under this subsection for satisfaction of their liability.

(d) Benefits under a single-employer plan to which liabilities are transferred in accordance with this section are guaranteed under section 4022 to the extent provided in that section as of the effective date of the transfer and the plan is a successor plan.

ERISA Sec. 4232 (d)

(e)(1) Except as provided in paragraph (2), a multiemployer plan may not transfer liabilities to a single-employer plan unless the plan sponsor of the plan to which the liabilities would be transferred agrees to the transfer.

(2) In the case of a transfer described in subsection (c)(3), paragraph (1) of this subsection is satisfied by the advance agreement to the transfer by the employer who will be obligated to contribute to the single-employer plan.

(f)(1) The corporation may prescribe by regulation such additional requirements with respect to the transfer of assets or liabilities as may be necessary to protect the interests of plan participants and beneficiaries and the corporation.

(2) Except as otherwise determined by the corporation, a transfer of assets or liabilities to a single-employer plan from a plan in reorganization under section 4241 is not effective unless the corporation approves such transfer.

(3) No transfer to which this section applies, in connection with a termination described in section 4041A(a)(2) shall be effective unless the transfer meets such requirements as may be established by the corporation to prevent an increase in the risk of loss to the corporation.

PARTITION

Sec. 4233. (a) The corporation may order the partition of a multiemployer plan in accordance with this section.

(b) A plan sponsor may apply to the corporation for an order partitioning a plan. The corporation may not order the partition of a plan except upon notice to the plan sponsor and the participants and beneficiaries whose vested benefits will be affected by the partition of the plan, and upon finding that—

(1) a substantial reduction in the amount of aggregate contributions under the plan has resulted or will result from a case or proceeding under title 11, United States Code, with respect to an employer;

(2) the plan is likely to become insolvent;

(3) contributions will have to be increased significantly in reorganization to meet the minimum contribution requirement and prevent insolvency; and

(4) partition would significantly reduce the likelihood that the plan will become insolvent.

(c) The corporation may order the partition of a plan notwithstanding the pendency of a proceeding described in subsection (b)(1).

(d) The corporation's partition order shall provide for a transfer of no more than the nonforfeitable benefits directly attributable to service with the employer referred to in subsection (b)(1) and an equitable share of assets.

(e) The plan created by the partition is—

(1) a successor plan to which section 4022A applies, and

(2) a terminated multiemployer plan to which section 4041A(d) applies, with respect to which only the employer described in subsection (b)(1) has withdrawal liability, and to which section 4068 applies.

(f) The corporation may proceed under section 4042(c) through (h) for a decree partitioning a plan and appointing a trustee for the terminated portion of a partitioned plan. The court may order the partition of a plan upon making the findings described in subsection (b)(1) through (4), and subject to the conditions set forth in subsections (c) through (e).

ASSET TRANSFER RULES

Sec. 4234. (a) A transfer of assets from a multiemployer plan to another plan shall comply with asset-transfer rules which shall be adopted by the multiemployer plan and which—

(1) do not unreasonably restrict the transfer of plan assets in connection with the transfer of plan liabilities, and

(2) operate and are applied uniformly with respect to each proposed transfer, except that the rules may provide for reasonable variations taking into account the potential financial impact of a proposed transfer on the multiemployer plan.

Plan rules authorizing asset transfers consistent with the requirements of section 4232(c)(3) shall be considered to satisfy the requirements of this subsection.

(b) The corporation shall prescribe regulations which exempt de minimis transfers of assets from the requirements of this part.

(c) This part shall not apply to transfers of assets pursuant written reciprocity agreements, except to the extent provided in regulations prescribed by the corporation.

TRANSFERS PURSUANT TO CHANGE IN BARGAINING REPRESENTATIVE

Sec. 4235. (a) In any case in which an employer has completely or partially withdrawn from a multiemployer plan (hereafter in this section referred to as the "old plan") as a result of a certified change of collective bargaining representative occurring after September 25, 1980, if participants of the old plan who are employed by the employer will, as a result of that change, participate in another multiemployer plan (hereafter in this section referred to as the "new plan"), the old plan shall transfer assets and liabilities to the new plan in accordance with this section.

(b)(1) The employer shall notify the plan sponsor of the old plan of a change in multiemployer plan participation described in subsection (a) no later than 30 days after the employer determines that the change will occur.

(2) The plan sponsor of the old plan shall—

(A) notify the employer of—

(i) the amount of the employer's withdrawal liability determined under part 1 with respect to the withdrawal,

(ii) the old plan's intent to transfer to the new plan the nonforfeitable benefits of the employees who are no longer working in covered service under the old plan as a result of the change of bargaining representative, and

(iii) the amount of assets and liabilities which are to be transferred to the new plan, and

(B) notify the plan sponsor of the new plan of the benefits, assets, and liabilities which will be transferred to the new plan.

(3) Within 60 days after receipt of the notice described in paragraph (2)(B), the new plan may file an appeal with the corporation to prevent the transfer. The transfer shall not be made if the corporation determines that the new plan would suffer substantial financial harm as a result of the transfer. Upon notification described in paragraph (2), if—

(A) the employer fails to object to the transfer within 60 days after receipt of the notice described in paragraph (2)(A), or

(B) the new plan either—

(i) fails to file such an appeal, or

(ii) the corporation, pursuant to such an appeal, fails to find that the new plan would suffer substantial financial harm as a result of the transfer described in the notice under paragraph (2)(B) within 180 days after the date on which the appeal is filed,

then the plan sponsor of the old plan shall transfer the appropriate amount of assets and liabilities to the new plan.

(c) If the plan sponsor of the old plan transfers the appropriate amount of assets and liabilities under this section to the new plan, then the amount of the employer's withdrawal liability (as determined under section 4201(b) without regard to such transfer and this section) with respect to the old plan shall be reduced by the amount by which—

(1) the value of the unfunded vested benefits allocable to the employer which were transferred by the plan sponsor of the old plan to the new plan, exceeds

(2) the value of the assets transferred.

(d) In any case in which there is a complete or partial withdrawal described in subsection (a), if—

(1) the new plan files an appeal with the corporation under subsection (b)(3), and

(2) the employer is required by section 4219 to begin making payments of withdrawal liability before the earlier of—

(A) the date on which the corporation finds that the new plan would not suffer substantial financial harm as a result of the transfer, or

(B) the last day of the 180-day period beginning on the date on which the new plan files its appeal,

then the employer shall make such payments into an escrow held by a bank or similar financial institution satisfactory to the old plan. If the transfer is made, the amounts paid into the escrow shall be returned to the employer. If the transfer is not made, the amounts paid into the escrow shall be paid to the old plan and credited against the employer's withdrawal liability.

(e)(1) Notwithstanding subsection (b), the plan sponsor shall not transfer any assets to the new plan if—

(A) the old plan is in reorganization (within the meaning of section 4241(a)), or

(B) the transfer of assets would cause the old plan to go into reorganization (within the meaning of section 4241(a)).

(2) In any case in which a transfer of assets from the old plan to the new plan is prohibited by paragraph (1), the plan sponsor of the old plan shall transfer—

(A) all nonforfeitable benefits described in subsection (b)(2), if the value of such benefits does not exceed the withdrawal liability of the employer with respect to such withdrawal, or

(B) such nonforfeitable benefits having a value equal to the withdrawal liability of the employer, if the value of such benefits exceeds the withdrawal liability of the employer.

(f)(1) Notwithstanding subsections (b) and (e), the plan sponsors of the old plan and the new plan may agree to a transfer of assets and liabilities that complies with sections 4231 and 4234, rather than this section, except that the employer's liability with respect to the withdrawal from the old plan shall be reduced under subsection (c) as if assets and liabilities had been transferred in accordance with this section.

(2) If the employer withdraws from the new plan within 240 months after the effective date of a transfer of assets and liabilities described in this section, the amount of the employer's withdrawal liability to the new plan shall be the greater of—

(A) the employer's withdrawal liability determined under part 1 with respect to the new plan, or

(B) the amount by which the employer's withdrawal liability to the old plan was reduced under subsection (c), reduced by 5 percent for each 12-month period following the effective date of the transfer and ending before the date of the withdrawal from the new plan.

(g) For purposes of this section—

(1) "appropriate amount of assets" means the amount by which the value of the nonforfeitable benefits to be transferred exceeds the amount of the employer's withdrawal liability to the old plan (determined under part 1 without regard to section 4211(e)), and

(2) "certified change of collective bargaining representative" means a change of collec tive bargaining representative certified under the Labor-Management Relations Act, 1947, or the Railway Labor Act.

Part 3— Reorganization; Minimum Contribution Requirement for Multiemployer Plans

REORGANIZATION STATUS

Sec. 4241. (a) A multiemployer plan is in reorganization for a plan year if the plan's reorganization index for that year is greater than zero.

(b)(1) A plan's reorganization index for any plan year is the excess of—

(A) the vested benefits charge for such year, over

(B) the net charge to the funding standard account for such year.

(2) For purposes of this part, the net charge to the funding standard account for any plan year is the excess (if any) of—

(A) the charges to the funding standard account for such year under section 412(b)(2) of the Internal Revenue Code of 1954, over

(B) the credits to the funding standard account under Section 412(b)(3)(B) of such Code.

(3) For purposes of this part, the vested benefits charge for any plan year is the amount which would be necessary to amortize the plan's unfunded vested benefits as of the end of the base plan year in equal annual installments—

(A) over 10 years, to the extent such benefits are attributable to persons in pay status, and

(B) over 25 years, to the extent such benefits are attributable to other participants.

(4)(A) The vested benefits charge for a plan year shall be based on an actuarial valuation of the plan as of the end of the base plan year, adjusted to reflect—

(i) any—

(I) decrease of 5 percent or more in the value of plan assets, or increase of 5 percent or more in the number of persons in pay status, during the period beginning on the first day of the plan year following the base plan year and ending on the adjustment date, or

(II) at the election of the plan sponsor, actuarial valuation of the plan as of the adjustment date or any later date not later than the last day of the plan year for which the determination is being made,

(ii) any change in benefits under the plan which is not otherwise taken into account under this subparagraph and which is pursuant to any amendment—

(I) adopted before the end of the plan year for which the determination is being made, and

(II) effective after the end of the base plan year and on or before the end of the plan year referred to in subclause (I), and

(iii) any other event (including an event described in subparagraph (B)(i)(I)) which, as determined in accordance with regulations prescribed by the Secretary, would substantially increase the plan's vested benefit charge.

(B)(i) In determining the vested benefits charge for a plan year following a plan year in which the plan was not in reorganization, any change in benefits which—

(I) results from the changing of a group of participants from one benefit level to another benefit level under a schedule of plan benefits as a result of changes in a collective bargaining agreement, or

(II) results from any other change in a collective bargaining agreement,

shall not be taken into account except to the extent provided in regulations prescribed by the Secretary of the Treasury.

ERISA Sec. 4241 (b)(4)(B)(i)(II)

(ii) Except as otherwise determined by the Secretary of the Treasury, in determining the vested benefits charge for any plan year following any plan year in which the plan was in reorganization, any change in benefits—

(I) described in clause (i)(I), or

(II) described in clause (i)(II) as determined under regulations prescribed by the Secretary of the Treasury,

shall, for purposes of subparagraph (A)(ii), be treated as a change in benefits pursuant to an amendment to a plan.

(5)(A) For purposes of this part, the base plan year for any plan year is—

(i) if there is a relevant collective bargaining agreement, the last plan year ending at least 6 months before the relevant effective date, or

(ii) if there is no relevant collective bargaining agreement, the last plan year ending at least 12 months before the beginning of the plan year.

(B) For purposes of this part, a relevant collective bargaining agreement is a collective bargaining agreement—

(i) which is in effect for at least 6 months during the plan year, and

(ii) which has not been in effect for more than 36 months as of the end of the plan year.

(C) For purposes of this part, the relevant effective date is the earliest of the effective dates for the relevant collective bargaining agreements.

(D) For purposes of this part, the adjustment date is the date which is—

(i) 90 days before the relevant effective date, or

(ii) if there is no relevant effective date, 90 days before the beginning of the plan year.

(6) For purposes of this part, the term "person in pay status" means—

(A) a participant or beneficiary on the last day of the base plan year who, at any time during such year, was paid an early, late, normal, or disability retirement benefit (or a death benefit related to a retirement benefit), and

(B) to the extent provided in regulations prescribed by the Secretary of the Treasury, any other person who is entitled to such a benefit under the plan.

(7) For purposes of paragraph (3)—

(A) in determining the plan's unfunded vested benefits, plan assets shall first be allocated to the vested benefits attributable to persons in pay status, and

(B) the vested benefits charge shall be determined without regard to reductions in accrued benefits under section 4244A which are first effective in the plan year.

(8) For purposes of this part, any outstanding claim for withdrawal liability shall not be considered a plan asset, except as otherwise provided in regulations prescribed by the Secretary of the Treasury.

(9) For purposes of this part, the term "unfunded vested benefits" means with respect to a plan, an amount (determined in accordance with regulations prescribed by the Secretary of the Treasury) equal to—

(A) the value of nonforfeitable benefits under the plan, less

(B) the value of assets of the plan.

(c) Except as provided in regulations prescribed by the corporation, while a plan is in reorganization a benefit with respect to a participant (other than a death benefit) which is attributable to employer contributions and which has a value of more than $1,750 may not be paid in a form other than an annuity which (by itself or in combination with social security, railroad retirement, or workers' com-

ERISA Sec. 4241 (b)(4)(B)(ii)

pensation benefits) provides substantially level payments over the life of the participant.

(d) Any multiemployer plan which terminates under section 4041A(a)(2) shall not be considered in reorganization after the last day of the plan year in which the plan is treated as having terminated.

NOTICE OF REORGANIZATION AND FUNDING REQUIREMENTS

Sec. 4242. (a)(1) If—

(A) a multiemployer plan is in reorganization for a plan year, and

(B) section 4243 would require an increase in contributions for such plan year,

the plan sponsor shall notify the persons described in paragraph (2) that the plan is in reorganization and that, if contributions to the plan are not increased, accrued benefits under the plan may be reduced or an excise tax may be imposed (or both such reduction and imposition may occur).

(2) The persons described in this paragraph are—

(A) each employer who has an obligation to contribute under the plan (within the meaning of section 4201(h)(5)), and

(B) each employee organization which, for purposes of collective bargaining, represents plan participants employed by such an employer.

(3) The determination under paragraph (1)(B) shall be made without regard to the overburden credit provided by section 4244.

(b) The corporation may prescribe additional or alternative requirements for assuring, in the case of a plan with respect to which notice is required by subsection (a)(1), that the persons described in subsection (a)(2) —

(1) receive appropriate notice that the plan is in reorganization,

(2) are adequately informed of the implications of reorganization status, and

(3) have reasonable access to information relevant to the plan's reorganization status.

MINIMUM CONTRIBUTION REQUIREMENT

Sec. 4243. (a)(1) For any plan year for which a plan is in reorganization—

(A) the plan shall continue to maintain its funding standard account while it is in reorganization, and

(B) the plan's accumulated funding deficiency under section 302(a) for such plan year shall be equal to the excess (if any) of—

(i) the sum of the minimum contribution requirement for such plan year (taking into account any overburden credit under section 4244(a)) plus the plan's accumulated funding deficiency for the preceding plan year (determined under this section if the plan was in reorganization during such year or under section 302(a) if the plan was not in reorganization), over

(ii) amounts considered contributed by employers to or under the plan for the plan year (increased by any amount waived under subsection (f) for the plan year).

(2) For purposes of paragraph (1), withdrawal liability payments (whether or not received) which are due with respect to withdrawals before the end of the base plan year shall be considered amounts contributed by the employer to or under the plan if, as of the adjustment date, it was reasonable for the plan sponsor to anticipate that such payments would be made during the plan year.

(b)(1) Except as otherwise provided in this section, for purposes of this part the minimum contribution requirement for a plan year in which a plan is in reorganization is an amount equal to the excess of—

(A) the sum of—

(i) the plan's vested benefits charge for the plan year, and

(ii) the increase in normal cost for the plan year determined under the entry age normal funding method which is attributable to plan amendments adopted while the plan was in reorganization, over

(B) the amount of the overburden credit (if any) determined under section 4244 for the plan year.

(2) If the plan's current contribution base for the plan year is less than the plan's valuation contribution base for the plan year, the minimum contribution require- ment for such plan year shall be equal to the product of the amount determined under paragraph (1) (after any adjustment re- quired by this part other than this paragraph) and a fraction—

(A) the numerator of which is the plan's current contribution base for the plan year, and

(B) the denominator of which is the plan's valuation contribution base for the plan year.

(3)(A) If the vested benefits charge for a plan year of a plan in reorganization is less than the plan's cash-flow amount for the plan year, the plan's minimum contribution re- quirement for the plan year is the amount determined under paragraph (1) (determined before the application of paragraph (2)) after substituting the term "cash-flow amount" for the term "vested benefits charge" in para- graph (1)(A).

(B) For purposes of subparagraph (A), a plan's cash-flow amount for a plan year is an amount equal to—

(i) the amount of the benefits payable un- der the plan for the base plan year, plus the amount of the plan's administrative ex- penses for the base plan year, reduced by

(ii) the value of the available plan assets for the base plan year determined under regulations prescribed by the Secretary of the Treasury,

adjusted in a manner consistent with section 4241(b)(4).

(c)(1) For purposes of this part, a plan's cur- rent contribution base for a plan year is the number of contribution base units with respect to which   contributions are required to be made under the plan for that plan year, deter- mined in accordance with regulations pre- scribed by the Secretary of the Treasury.

(2)(A) Except as provided in subparagraph (B), for purposes of this part a plan's valuation contribution base is the number of contribu- tion base units for which contributions were received for the base plan year—

(i) adjusted to reflect declines in the con- tribution base which have occurred (or could reasonably be anticipated) as of the adjust- ment date for the plan year referred to in paragraph (1),

(ii) adjusted upward (in accordance with regulations prescribed by the Secretary of the Treasury) for any contribution base re- duction in the base plan year caused by a strike or lockout or by unusual events, such as fire, earthquake, or severe weather condi- tions, and

(iii) adjusted (in accordance with regula- tions prescribed by the Secretary of the Treasury) for reductions in the contribution base resulting from transfers of liabilities.

(B) For any plan year—

(i) in which the plan is insolvent (within the meaning of section 4245(b)(1), and

(ii) beginning with the first plan year be- ginning after the expiration of all relevant collective bargaining agreements which were in effect in the plan year in which the plan became insolvent,
the plan's valuation contribution base is the greater of the number of contribution base units for which contributions were received for the first or second plan year preceding the first plan year in which the plan is insol vent, adjusted as provided in clause (ii) o: (iii) of subparagraph (A).

(d)(1) Under regulations prescribed by the Secretary of the Treasury, the minimum contribution requirement applicable to any plan for any plan year which is determined under subsection (b) (without regard to subsection (b)(2)) shall not exceed an amount which is equal to the sum of—

(A) the greater of—

(i) the funding standard requirement for such plan year, or

(ii) 107 percent of—

(I) if the plan was not in reorganization in the preceding plan year, the funding standard requirement for such preceding plan year, or

(II) if the plan was in reorganization in the preceding plan year, the sum of the amount determined under this subparagraph for the preceding plan year and the amount (if any) determined under subparagraph (B) for the preceding plan year, plus

(B) if for the plan year a change in benefits is first required to be considered in computing the charges under section 412(b)(2)(A) or (B) of the Internal Revenue Code of 1954, the sum of—

(i) the increase in normal cost for a plan year determined under the entry age normal funding method due to increases in benefits described in section 4241(b)(4)(A) (ii) (determined without regard to section 4241(b)(4)(B)(i)), and

(ii) the amount necessary to amortize in equal annual installments the increase in the value of vested benefits under the plan due to increases in benefits described in clause (i) over—

(I) 10 years, to the extent such increase in value is attributable to persons in pay status, or

(II) 25 years, to the extent such increase in value is attributable to other participants.

(2) For purposes of paragraph (1), the funding standard requirement for any plan year is an amount equal to the net charge to the funding standard account for such plan year (as defined in section 4241(b)(2)).

(3)(A) In the case of a plan described in section 4216(b), if a plan amendment which increases benefits is adopted after January 1, 1980—

(i) paragraph (1) shall apply only if the plan is a plan described in subparagraph (B), and

(ii) the amount under paragraph (1) shall be determined without regard to paragraph (1)(B).

(B) A plan is described in this subparagraph if—

(i) the rate of employer contributions under the plan for the first plan year beginning on or after the date on which an amendment increasing benefits is adopted, multiplied by the valuation contribution base for that plan year, equals or exceeds the sum of—

(I) the amount that would be necessary to amortize fully, in equal annual installments, by July 1, 1986, the unfunded vested benefits attributable to plan provisions in effect on July 1, 1977 (determined as of the last day of the base plan year); and

(II) the amount that would be necessary to amortize fully, in equal annual installments, over the period described in subparagraph (C), beginning with the first day of the first plan year beginning on or after the date on which the amendment is adopted, the unfunded vested benefits (determined as of the last day of the base plan year) attributable to each plan amendment after July 1, 1977; and

(ii) the rate of employer contributions for each subsequent plan year is not less than the lesser of—

(I) the rate which when multiplied by the valuation contribution base for that sub-

ERISA Sec. 4243 (d)(3)(B)(ii)(I)

sequent plan year produces the annual amount that would be necessary to complete the amortization schedule described in clause (i), or

(II) the rate for the plan year immediately preceding such subsequent plan year, plus 5 percent of such rate.

(C) The period determined under this subparagraph is the lesser of—

(i) 12 years, or

(ii) a period equal in length to the average of the remaining expected lives of all persons receiving benefits under the plan.

(4) Paragraph (1) shall not apply with respect to a plan, other than a plan described in paragraph (3), for the period of consecutive plan years in each of which the plan is in reorganization, beginning with a plan year in which occurs the earlier of the date of the adoption or the effective date of any amendment of the plan which increases benefits with respect to service performed before the plan year in which the adoption of the amendment occurred.

(e) In determining the minimum contribution requirement with respect to a plan for a plan year under subsection (b), the vested benefits charge may be adjusted to reflect a plan amendment reducing benefits under section 412(c)(8) of the Internal Revenue Code of 1954.

(f)(1) The Secretary of the Treasury may waive any accumulated funding deficiency under this section in accordance with the provisions of section 303(a).

(2) Any waiver under paragraph (1) shall not be treated as a waived funding deficiency (within the meaning of section 303(c)).

(g) For purposes of making any determination under this part, the requirements of section 302(c)(3) shall apply.

OVERBURDEN CREDIT AGAINST MINIMUM CONTRIBUTION REQUIREMENT

Sec. 4244. (a) For purposes of determining the minimum contribution requirement under section 4243 (before the application of section 4243(b)(2) or (d)) the plan sponsor of a plan which is overburdened for the plan year shall apply an overburden credit against the plan's minimum contribution requirement for the plan year (determined without regard to section 4243(b)(2) or (d) and without regard to this section).

(b) A plan is overburdened for a plan year if—

(1) the average number of pay status participants under the plan in the base plan year exceeds the average of the number of active participants in the base plan year and the 2 plan years preceding the base plan year, and

(2) the rate of employer contributions under the plan equals or exceeds the greater of—

(A) such rate for the preceding plan year, or

(B) such rate for the plan year preceding the first year in which the plan is in reorganization.

(c) The amount of the overburden credit for a plan year is the product of—

(1) one-half of the average guaranteed benefit paid for the base plan year, and

(2) the overburden factor for the plan year. The amount of the overburden credit for a plan year shall not exceed the amount of the minimum contribution requirement for such year (determined without regard to this section).

(d) For purposes of this section, the overburden factor of a plan for the plan year is an amount equal to—

(1) the average number of pay status participants for the base plan year, reduced by

(2) the average of the number of active participants for the base plan year and for each of the 2 plan years preceding the base plan year

(e) For purposes of this section—

(1) The term "pay status participant" means, with respect to a plan, a participant receiving retirement benefits under the plan.

(2) The number of active participants for a plan year shall be the sum of—

(A) the number of active employees who are participants in the plan and on whose behalf contributions are required to be made during the plan year;

(B) the number of active employees who are not participants in the plan but who are in an employment unit covered by a collective bargaining agreement which requires the employees' employer to contribute to the plan, unless service in such employment unit was never covered under the plan or a predecessor thereof, and

(C) the total number of active employees attributed to employers who made payments to the plan for the plan year of withdrawal liability pursuant to part 1, determined by dividing—

(i) the total amount of such payments, by

(ii) the amount equal to the total contributions received by the plan during the plan year divided by the average number of active employees who were participants in the plan during the plan year.

The Secretary of the Treasury shall by regulation provide alternative methods of determining active participants where (by reason of irregular employment, contributions on a unit basis, or otherwise) this paragraph does not yield a representative basis for determining the credit.

(3) The term "average number" means, with respect to pay status participants for a plan year, a number equal to one-half the sum of—

(A) the number with respect to the plan as of the beginning of the plan year, and

(B) the number with respect to the plan as of the end of the plan year.

(4) The average guaranteed benefit paid is 12 times the average monthly pension payment guaranteed under section 4022A(c)(1) determined under the provisions of the plan in effect at the beginning of the first plan year in which the plan is in reorganization and without regard to section 4022A(c)(2).

(5) The first year in which the plan is in reorganization is the first of a period of 1 or more consecutive plan years in which the plan has been in reorganization not taking into account any plan years the plan was in reorganization prior to any period of 3 or more consecutive plan years in which the plan was not in reorganization.

(f)(1) Notwithstanding any other provision of this section, a plan is not eligible for an overburden credit for a plan year if the Secretary of the Treasury finds that the plan's current contribution base for the plan year was reduced, without a corresponding reduction in the plan's unfunded vested benefits attributable to pay status participants, as a result of a change in an agreement providing for employer contributions under the plan.

(2) For purposes of paragraph (1), a complete or partial withdrawal of an employer (within the meaning of part 1) does not impair a plan's eligibility for an overburden credit, unless the Secretary of the Treasury finds that a contribution base reduction described in paragraph (1) resulted from a transfer of liabilities to another plan in connection with the withdrawal.

(g) Notwithstanding any other provision of this section, if 2 or more multiemployer plans merge, the amount of the overburden credit which may be applied under this section with respect to the plan resulting from the merger for any of the 3 plan years ending after the effective date of the merger shall not exceed the sum of the used overburden credit for each of the merging plans for its last plan year ending before the effective date of the merger. For purposes of the preceding sentence, the used overburden credit is that portion of the credit which does not exceed the excess of the minimum contribution requirement (determined without regard to any overburden requirement under this section) over the employer contributions required under the plan.

ADJUSTMENTS IN ACCRUED BENEFITS

Sec. 4244A. (a)(1) Notwithstanding sections 203 and 204, a multiemployer plan in reorganization may be amended in accordance with this section, to reduce or eliminate accrued benefits attributable to employer contributions which, under section 4022A(b), are not eligible for the corporation's guarantee. The preceding sentence shall only apply to accrued benefits under plan amendments (or plans) adopted after March 26, 1980, or under collective bargaining agreements entered into after March 26, 1980.

(2) In determining the minimum contribution requirement with respect to a plan for a plan year under section 4243(b), the vested benefits charge may be adjusted to reflect a plan amendment reducing benefits under this section or section 412(c)(8) of the Internal Revenue Code of 1954, but only if the amendment is adopted and effective no later than 2 1/2 months after the end of the plan year, or within such extended period as the Secretary of the Treasury may prescribe by regulation under section 412(c)(10) of such Code.

(b)(1) Accrued benefits may not be reduced under this section unless—

(A) notice has been given, at least 6 months before the first day of the plan year in which the amendment reducing benefits is adopted, to—

(i) plan participants and beneficiaries,

(ii) each employer who has an obligation to contribute (within the meaning of section 4212(a)) under the plan, and

(iii) each employee organization which, for purposes of collective bargaining, represents plan participants employed by such an employer,

that the plan is in reorganization and that, if contributions under the plan are not increased, accrued benefits under the plan will be reduced or an excise tax will be imposed on employers;

(B) in accordance with regulations prescribed by the Secretary of the Treasury—

(i) any category of accrued benefits is not reduced with respect to inactive participants to a greater extent proportionally than such category of accrued benefits is reduced with respect to active participants,

(ii) benefits attributable to employer contributions other than accrued benefits and the rate of future benefit accruals are reduced at least to an extent equal to the reduction in accrued benefits of inactive participants, and

(iii) in any case in which the accrued benefit of a participant or beneficiary is reduced by changing the benefit form or the requirements which the participant or beneficiary must satisfy to be entitled to the benefit, such reduction is not applicable to—

(I) any participant or beneficiary in pay status on the effective date of the amendment, or the beneficiary of such a participant, or

(II) any participant who has attained normal retirement age, or who is within 5 years of attaining normal retirement age, on the effective date of the amendment, or the beneficiary of any such participant; and

(C) the rate of employer contributions for the plan year in which the amendment becomes effective and for all succeeding plan years in which the plan is in reorganization equals or exceeds the greater of—

(i) the rate of employer contributions, calculated without regard to the amendment, for the plan year in which the amendment becomes effective, or

(ii) the rate of employer contributions for the plan year preceding the plan year in which the amendment becomes effective.

(2) The plan sponsors shall include in any notice required to be sent to plan participants and beneficiaries under paragraph (1) information as to the rights and remedies of plan participants and beneficiaries as well as how to contact the Department of Labor for further information and assistance where appropriate.

(c) A plan may not recoup a benefit payment which is in excess of the amount payable under the plan because of an amendment retroactively reducing accrued benefits under this section.

(d)(1)(A) A plan which has been amended to reduce accrued benefits under this section may be amended to increase or restore accrued benefits, or the rate of future benefit accruals, only if the plan is amended to restore levels of previously reduced accrued benefits of inactive participants and of participants who are within 5 years of attaining normal retirement age to at least the same extent as any such increase in accrued benefits or in the rate of future benefit accruals.

(B) For purposes of this subsection, in the case of a plan which has been amended under this section to reduce accrued benefits—

(i) an increase in a benefit, or in the rate of future benefit accruals, shall be considered a benefit increase to the extent that the benefit, or the accrual rate, is thereby increased above the highest benefit level, or accrual rate, which was in effect under the terms of the plan before the effective date of the amendment reducing accrued benefits, and

(ii) an increase in a benefit, or in the rate of future benefit accruals, shall be considered a benefit restoration to the extent that the benefit, or the accrual rate, is not thereby increased above the highest benefit level, or accrual rate, which was in effect under the

terms of the plan immediately before the effective date of the amendment reducing accrued benefits.

(2) If a plan is amended to partially restore previously reduced accrued benefit levels, or the rate of future benefit accruals, the benefits of inactive participants shall be restored in at least the same proportions as other accrued benefits which are restored.

(3) No benefit increase under a plan may take effect in a plan year in which an amendment reducing accrued benefits under the plan, in accordance with this section, is adopted or first becomes effective.

(4) A plan is not required to make retroactive benefit payments with respect to that portion of an accrued benefit which was reduced and subsequently restored under this section.

(e) For purposes of this section, "inactive participant" means a person not in covered service under the plan who is in pay status under the plan or who has a nonforfeitable benefit under the plan.

(f) The Secretary of the Treasury may prescribe rules under which, notwithstanding any other provision of this section, accrued benefit reductions or benefit increases for different participant groups may be varied equitably to reflect variations in contribution rates and other relevant factors reflecting differences in negotiated levels of financial support for plan benefit obligations.

INSOLVENT PLANS

Sec. 4245. (a) Notwithstanding sections 203 and 204, in any case in which benefit payments under an insolvent multiemployer plan exceed the resource benefit level, any such payments of benefits which are not basic benefits shall be suspended, in accordance with this section, to the extent necessary to reduce the sum of such payments and the payments of such basic benefits to the greater of the resource benefit level or the level of basic benefits, unless an alternative procedure is

ERISA Sec. 4245 (a)

prescribed by the corporation under section 4022A(g)(5).

(b) For purposes of this section, for a plan year—

(1) a multiemployer plan is insolvent if the plan's available resources are not sufficient to pay benefits under the plan when due for the plan year, or if the plan is determined to be insolvent under subsection (d);

(2) "resource benefit level" means the level of monthly benefits determined under subsections (c)(1) and (3) and (d)(3) to be the highest level which can be paid out of the plan's available resources;

(3) "available resources" means the plan's cash, marketable assets, contributions, withdrawal liability payments, and earnings, less reasonable administrative expenses and amounts owed for such plan year to the corporation under section 4261(b)(2); and

(4) "insolvency year" means a plan year in which a plan is insolvent.

(c)(1) The plan sponsor of a plan in reorganization shall determine in writing the plan's resource benefit level for each insolvency year, based on the plan sponsor's reasonable projection of the plan's available resources and the benefits payable under the plan.

(2) The suspension of benefit payments under this section shall, in accordance with regulations prescribed by the Secretary of the Treasury, apply in substantially uniform proportions to the benefits of all persons in pay status (within the meaning of section 4241(b)(6)) under the plan, except that the Secretary of the Treasury may prescribe rules under which benefit suspensions for different participant groups may be varied equitably to reflect variations in contribution rates and other relevant factors including differences in negotiated levels of financial support for plan benefit obligations.

(3) Notwithstanding paragraph (2), if a plan sponsor determines in writing a resource benefit level for a plan year which is below the

level of basic benefits, the payment of all benefits other than basic benefits must be suspended for that plan year.

(4)(A) If, by the end of an insolvency year, the plan sponsor determines in writing that the plan's available resources in that insolvency year could have supported benefit payments above the resource benefit level for that insolvency year, the plan sponsor shall distribute the excess resources to the participants and beneficiaries who received benefit payments from the plan in that insolvency year, in accordance with regulations prescribed by the Secretary of the Treasury.

(B) For purposes of this paragraph, the term "excess resources" means available resources above the amount necessary to support the resource benefit level, but no greater than the amount necessary to pay benefits for the plan year at the benefit levels under the plan.

(5) If, by the end of an insolvency year, any benefit has not been paid at the resource benefit level, amounts up to the resource benefit level which were unpaid shall be distributed to the participants and beneficiaries, in accordance with regulations prescribed by the Secretary of the Treasury, to the extent possible taking into account the plan's total available resources in that insolvency year.

(6) Except as provided in paragraph (4) or (5), a plan is not required to make retroactive benefit payments with respect to that portion of a benefit which was suspended under this section.

(d)(1) As of the end of the first plan year in which a plan is in reorganization, and at least every 3 plan years thereafter (unless the plan is no longer in reorganization), the plan sponsor shall compare the value of plan assets (determined in accordance with section 4243(b)(3)(B)(ii)) for that plan year with the total amount of benefit payments made under the plan for that plan year. Unless the plan sponsor determines that the value of plan assets exceeds 3 times the total amount of benefit payments, the plan sponsor shall determine whether the plan will be insolvent in any of the next 3 plan years.

(2) If, at any time, the plan sponsor of a plan in reorganization reasonably determines, taking into account the plan's recent and anticipated financial experience, that the plan's available resources are not sufficient to pay benefits under the plan when due for the next plan year, the plan sponsor shall make such determination available to interested parties.

(3) The plan sponsor of a plan in reorganization shall determine in writing for each insolvency year the resource benefit level and the level of basic benefits no later than 3 months before the insolvency year.

(e)(1) If the plan sponsor of a plan in reorganization determines under subsection (d)(1) or (2) that the plan may become insolvent (within the meaning of subsection (b)(1)), the plan sponsor shall—

(A) notify the Secretary of the Treasury, the corporation, the parties described in section 4242(a)(2), and the plan participants and beneficiaries of that determination, and

(B) inform the parties described in section 4242(a)(2) and the plan participants and beneficiaries that if insolvency occurs certain benefit payments will be suspended, but that basic benefits will continue to be paid.

(2) No later than 2 months before the first day of each insolvency year, the plan sponsor of a plan in reorganization shall notify the Secretary of the Treasury, the corporation, and the parties described in paragraph (1)(B) of the resource benefit level determined in writing for that insolvency year.

(3) In any case in which the plan sponsor anticipates that the resource benefit level for an insolvency year may not exceed the level of basic benefits, the plan sponsor shall notify the corporation.

(4) Notice required by this subsection shall be given in accordance with regulations prescribed by the corporation, except that notice

to the Secretary of the Treasury shall be given in accordance with regulations prescribed by the Secretary of the Treasury.

(5) The corporation may prescribe a time other than the time prescribed by this section for the making of a determination or the filing of a notice under this section.

(f)(1) If the plan sponsor of an insolvent plan, for which the resource benefit level is above the level of basic benefits, anticipates that, for any month in an insolvency year, the plan will not have funds sufficient to pay basic benefits, the plan sponsor may apply for financial assistance from the corporation under section 4261.

(2) A plan sponsor who has determined a resource benefit level for an insolvency year which is below the level of basic benefits shall apply for financial assistance from the corporation under section 4261.

Part 4— Financial Assistance

FINANCIAL ASSISTANCE

Sec. 4261. (a) If, upon receipt of an application for financial assistance under section 4245(f) or section 4281(d), the corporation verifies that the plan is or will be insolvent and unable to pay basic benefits when due, the corporation shall provide the plan financial assistance in an amount sufficient to enable the plan to pay basic benefits under the plan.

(b)(1) Financial assistance shall be provided under such conditions as the corporation determines are equitable and are appropriate to prevent unreasonable loss to the corporation with respect to the plan.

(2) A plan which has received financial assistance shall repay the amount of such assistance to the corporation on reasonable terms consistent with regulations prescribed by the corporation.

(c) Pending determination of the amount described in subsection (a), the corporation may provide financial assistance in such amounts as it considers appropriate in order to avoid undue hardship to plan participants and beneficiaries.

Part 5— Benefits After Termination

BENEFITS UNDER CERTAIN TERMINATED PLANS

Sec. 4281. (a) Notwithstanding sections 203 and 204, the plan sponsor of a terminated multiemployer plan to which section 4041A(d) applies shall amend the plan to reduce benefits, and shall suspend benefit payments, as required by this section.

(b)(1) The value of nonforfeitable benefits under a terminated plan referred to in subsection (a), and the value of the plan's assets, shall be determined in writing, in accordance with regulations prescribed by the corporation, as of the end of the plan year during which section 4041A(d) becomes applicable to the plan, and each plan year thereafter.

(2) For purposes of this section, plan assets include outstanding claims for withdrawal liability (within the meaning of section 4001(a)(12)).

(c)(1) If, according to the determination made under subsection (b), the value of nonforfeitable benefits exceeds the value of the plan's assets, the plan sponsor shall amend the plan to reduce benefits under the plan to the extent necessary to ensure that the plan's assets are sufficient, as determined and certified in accordance with regulations prescribed by the corporation, to discharge when due all of the plan's obligations with respect to nonforfeitable benefits.

(2) Any plan amendment required by this subsection shall, in accordance with regulations prescribed by the Secretary of the Treasury—

(A) reduce benefits only to the extent necessary to comply with paragraph (1);

(B) reduce accrued benefits only to the extent that those benefits are not eligible for the corporation's guarantee under section 4022A(b);

(C) comply with the rules for and limitations on benefit reductions under a plan in reorganization, as prescribed in section 4244A, except to the extent that the corporation prescribes other rules and limitations in regulations under this section; and

(D) take effect no later than 6 months after the end of the plan year for which it is determined that the value of nonforfeitable benefits exceeds the value of the plan's assets.

(d)(1) In any case in which benefit payments under a plan which is insolvent under paragraph (2)(A) exceed the resource benefit level, any such payments which are not basic benefits shall be suspended, in accordance with this subsection, to the extent necessary to reduce the sum of such payments and such basic benefits to the greater of the resource benefit level or the level of basic benefits, unless an alternative procedure is prescribed by the corporation in connection with a supplemental guarantee program established under section 4022A(g)(2).

(2) For the purposes of this subsection, for a plan year—

(A) a plan is insolvent if—

(i) the plan has been amended to reduce benefits to the extent permitted by subsection (c), and

(ii) the plan's available resources are not sufficient to pay benefits under the plan when due for the plan year; and

(B) "resource benefit level" and "available resources" have the meanings set forth in paragraphs (2) and (3), respectively, of section 4245(b).

(3) The plan sponsor of a plan which is insolvent (within the meaning of paragraph

(2)(A)) shall have the powers and duties of the plan sponsor of a plan in reorganization which is insolvent (within the meaning of section 4245(b)(1)), except that regulations governing the plan sponsor's exercise of those powers and duties under this section shall be prescribed by the corporation, and the corporation shall prescribe by regulation notice requirements which assure that plan participants and beneficiaries receive adequate notice of benefit suspensions.

(4) A plan is not required to make retroactive benefit payments with respect to that portion of a benefit which was suspended under this subsection, except that the provisions of section 4245(c)(4) and (5) shall apply in the case of plans which are insolvent under paragraph (2)(A), in connection with the plan year during which such section 4041A(d) first became applicable to the plan and every year thereafter, in the same manner and to the same extent as such provisions apply to insolvent plans in reorganization under section 4245, in connection with insolvency years under such section 4245.

Part 6—Enforcement

CIVIL ACTIONS

Sec. 4301. (a)(1) A plan fiduciary, employer, plan participant, or beneficiary, who is adversely affected by the act or omission of any party under this subtitle with respect to a multiemployer plan, or an employee organization which represents such a plan participant or beneficiary for purposes of collective bargaining, may bring an action for appropriate legal or equitable relief, or both.

(2) Notwithstanding paragraph (1), this section does not authorize an action against the Secretary of the Treasury, the Secretary of Labor, or the corporation.

(b) In any action under this section to compel an employer to pay withdrawal liability, any failure of the employer to make any withdrawal liability payment within the time prescribed shall be treated in the same manner as a delinquent contribution (within the meaning of section 515).

(c) The district courts of the United States shall have exclusive jurisdiction of an action under this section without regard to the amount in controversy, except that State courts of competent jurisdiction shall have concurrent jurisdiction over an action brought by a plan fiduciary to collect withdrawal liability.

(d) An action under this section may be brought in the district where the plan is administered or where a defendant resides or does business, and process may be served in any district where a defendant resides, does business, or may be found.

(e) In any action under this section, the court may award all or a portion of the costs and expenses incurred in connection with such action, including reasonable attorney's fees, to the prevailing party.

(f) An action under this section may not be brought after the later of—

(1) 6 years after the date on which the cause of action arose, or

(2) 3 years after the earliest date on which the plaintiff acquired or should have acquired actual knowledge of the existence of such cause of action; except that in the case of fraud or concealment, such action may be brought not later than 6 years after the date of discovery of the existence of such cause of action.

(g) A copy of the complaint in any action under this section or section 4221 shall be served upon the corporation by certified mail. The corporation may intervene in any such action.

PENALTY FOR FAILURE TO PROVIDE NOTICE

Sec. 4302. Any person who fails, without reasonable cause, to provide a notice required under this subtitle or any implementing regulations shall be liable to the corporation in an amount up to $100 for each day for which such failure continues. The corporation may bring a civil action against any such person in the United States District Court for the District of Columbia or in any district court of the United States within the jurisdiction of which the plan assets are located, the plan is administered, or a defendant resides or does business, and process may be served in any district where a defendant resides, does business, or may be found.

ELECTION OF PLAN STATUS

Sec. 4303. (a) Within one year after the date of the enactment of the Multiemployer Pension Plan Amendments Act of 1980, a multiemployer plan may irrevocably elect, pursuant to procedures established by the corporation, that the plan shall not be treated as a multiemployer plan for any purpose under this Act or the Internal Revenue Code of 1954 if for each of the last 3 plan years ending prior to the effective date of the Multiemployer Pension Plan Amendments Act of 1980—

(1) the plan was not a multiemployer plan because the plan was not a plan described in section 3(37)(A)(iii) of this Act and section 414(f)(1)(C) of the Internal Revenue Code of 1954 (as such provisions were in effect on the day before the date of the enactment of the Multiemployer Pension Plan Amendments Act of 1980); and

(2) the plan had been identified as a plan that was not a multiemployer plan in substantially all its filings with the corporation, the Secretary of Labor and the Secretary of the Treasury.

(b) An election described in subsection (a) shall be effective only if—

(1) the plan is amended to provide that it shall not be treated as a multiemployer plan for all purposes under this Act and the Internal Revenue Code of 1954, and

(2) written notice of the amendment is provided to the corporation within 60 days after the amendment is adopted.

(c) An election described in subsection (a) shall be treated as being effective as of the date of the enactment of the Multiemployer Pension Plan Amendments Act of 1980.

Subtitle F—Transition Rules And Effective Dates

AMENDMENTS TO INTERNAL REVENUE CODE OF 1954

Sec. 4401. (a) Section 404 of the Internal Revenue Code of 1954 (relating to deduction for contributions of an employer to employees' trust or annuity plan in compensation under a deferred-payment plan) is amended by adding at the end thereof the following new subsection:

(g) Certain Employer Liability Payments Considered as Contributions.— For purposes of this section any amount paid by an employer under section 4062, 4063, or 4064 or part 1 of subtitle E of title IV of the Employee Retirement Income Security Act of 1974 shall be treated as a contribution to which this section applies by such employer to or under a stock bonus, pension, profit-sharing, or annuity plan.

(b) Section 6511(d) of the Internal Revenue Code of 1954 (relating to special rules applicable to income taxes) is amended by adding at the end thereof the following new paragraph:

(6) Special period of limitation with respect to amounts included in income subsequently recaptured under qualified plan termination.— If the claim for credit or refund relates to an overpayment of tax imposed by subtitle A on account of the recapture, under section 4045 of the Employee Retirement Income Security Act of 1974, of amounts included in income for a prior taxable year, the 3-year period of limitation prescribed in subsection (a) shall be extended, for purposes of permitting a credit or refund of the amount of the recapture, until the date which occurs one year after the date on which such recaptured amount is paid by the taxpayer.

EFFECTIVE DATE; SPECIAL RULES

Sec. 4402. (a) The provisions of this title take effect on September 2, 1974.

(b) Notwithstanding the provisions of subsection (a), the corporation shall pay benefits guaranteed under this title with respect to any plan—

(1) which is not a multiemployer plan,

(2) which terminates after June 30, 1974, and before the date of enactment of this Act,

(3) to which section 4021 would apply if that section were effective beginning on July 1, 1974, and

(4) with respect to which a notice is filed with the Secretary of Labor and received by him not later than 10 days after the date of enactment of this Act, except that, for reasonable cause shown, such notice may be filed with the Secretary of Labor and received by him not later than October 31, 1974, stating that the plan is a plan described in paragraphs (1), (2), and (3).

The corporation shall not pay benefits guaranteed under this title with respect to a plan described in the preceding sentence unless the corporation finds substantial evidence that the plan was terminated for a reasonable business purpose and not for the purpose of obtaining the payment of benefits by the corporation under this title or for the purpose of avoiding the liability which might be imposed under subtitle D if the plan terminated on or after September 2, 1974. The provisions of subtitle D do not apply in the case of such plan which terminates before September 2, 1974. For purposes of determining whether a plan is a plan described in paragraph (2), the provisions of section 4048 shall not apply, but the corporation shall make the determination on the basis of the date on which benefits ceased to accrue or on any other reasonable basis consistent with the purposes of this subsection.

(c)(1) Except as provided in paragraphs (2), (3), and (4), the corporation shall not pay benefits guaranteed under this title with re-

spect to a multiemployer plan which terminates before August 1, 1980. Whenever the corporation exercises the authority granted under paragraph (2) or (3), the corporation shall notify the Committee on Education and Labor and the Committee on Ways and Means of the House of Representatives, and the Committee on Labor and Human Resources and the Committee on Finance of the Senate.

(2) The corporation may, in its discretion, pay benefits guaranteed under this title with respect to a multiemployer plan which terminates after the date of enactment of this Act and before August 1, 1980, if—

(A) the plan was maintained during the 60 months immediately preceding the date on which the plan terminates, and

(B) the corporation determines that the payment by the corporation of benefits guaranteed under this title with respect to that plan will not jeopardize the payments the corporation anticipates it may be required to make in connection with benefits guaranteed under this title with respect to multiemployer plans which terminate after July 31, 1980.

(3) Notwithstanding any provision of section 4021 or 4022 which would prevent such payments, the corporation, in carrying out its authority under paragraph (2), may pay benefits guaranteed under this title with respect to a multiemployer plan described in paragraph (2) in any case in which those benefits would otherwise not be payable if—

(A) the plan has been in effect for at least 5 years,

(B) the plan has been in substantial compliance with the funding requirements for a qualified plan with respect to the employees and former employees in those employment units on the basis of which the participating employers have contributed to the plan for the preceding 5 years, and

(C) the participating employers and employee organization or organizations had no reasonable recourse other than termination.

ERISA Sec. 4402 (c)(3)(C)

(4) If the corporation determines, under paragraph (2) or (3), that it will pay benefits guaranteed under this title with respect to a multiemployer plan which terminates before August 1, 1980, the corporation—

(A) may establish requirements for the continuation of payments which commenced before January 2, 1974, with respect to retired participants under the plan,

(B) may not, notwithstanding any other provision of this title, make payments with respect to any participant under such a plan who, on January 1, 1974, was receiving payment of retirement benefits, in excess of the amounts and rates payable with respect to such participant on that date,

(C) may not make any payments with respect to benefits guaranteed under this title in connection with such a plan which are derived, directly or indirectly, from amounts borrowed under section 4005(c), and

(D) shall review from time to time payments made under the authority granted to it by paragraphs (2) and (3), and reduce or terminate such payments to the extent necessary to avoid jeopardizing the ability of the corporation to make payments of benefits guaranteed under this title in connection with multiemployer plans which terminate after July 31, 1980, without increasing premium rates for such plans.

(d) Notwithstanding any other provision of this title, guaranteed benefits payable by the corporation pursuant to its discretionary authority under this section shall continue to be paid at the level guaranteed under section 4022, without regard to any limitation on payment under subparagraph (C) or (D) of subsection (c)(4).

(e)(1) Except as provided in paragraphs (2), (3), and (4), the amendments to this Act made by the Multiemployer Pension Plan Amendments Act of 1980 shall take effect on the date of the enactment of that Act.

(2)(A) Except as provided in this paragraph, part 1 of subtitle E, relating to withdrawal liability, takes effect on September 26, 1980.

(B) For purposes of determining withdrawal liability under part 1 of subtitle E, an employer who has withdrawn from a plan shall be considered to have withdrawn from a multiemployer plan if, at the time of the withdrawal, the plan was a multiemployer plan as defined in section 4001(a)(3) as in effect at the time of the withdrawal.

(3) Sections 4241 through 4245, relating to multiemployer plan reorganization, shall take effect, with respect to each plan, on the first day of the first plan year beginning on or after the earlier of—

(A) the date on which the last collective bargaining agreement providing for employer contributions under the plan, which was in effect on the date of the enactment of the Multiemployer Pension Plan Amendments Act of 1980, expires, without regard to extensions agreed to on or after the date of the enactment of that Act, or

(B) 3 years after the date of the enactment of the Multiemployer Pension Plan Amendments Act of 1980.

(4) Section 4235 shall take effect on September 26, 1980.

(f)(1) In the event that before the date of enactment of the Multiemployer Pension Plan Amendments Act of 1980, the corporation has determined that—

(A) an employer has withdrawn from a multiemployer plan under section 4063, and

(B) the employer is liable to the corporation under such section,

the corporation shall retain the amount of liability paid to it or furnished in the form of a bond and shall pay such liability to the plan in the event the plan terminates in accordance with section 4041A(a)(2) before the earlier of September 26, 1985, or the day after the 5-year period commencing on the date of such withdrawal.

(2) In any case in which the plan is not so terminated within the period described in paragraph (1), the liability of the employer is abated and any payment held in escrow shall be refunded without interest to the employer or the employer's bond shall be cancelled.

(g)(1) In any case in which an employer or employers withdrew from a multiemployer plan before the effective date of part 1 of subtitle E, the corporation may—

(A) apply section 4063(d), as in effect before the amendments made by the Multiemployer Pension Plan Amendments Act of 1980, to such plan,

(B) assess liability against the withdrawn employer with respect to the resulting terminated plan,

(C) guarantee benefits under the terminated plan under section 4022, as in effect before such amendments, and

(D) if necessary, enforce such action through suit brought under section 4003.

(2) The corporation shall use the revolving fund used by the corporation with respect to basic benefits guaranteed under section 4022A in guaranteeing benefits under a terminated plan described in this subsection.

(h)(1) In the case of an employer who entered into a collective bargaining agreement—

(A) which was effective on January 12, 1979, and which remained in effect through May 15, 1982, and

(B) under which contributions to a multiemployer plan were to cease on January 12, 1982,

any withdrawal liability incurred by the employer pursuant to part 1 of subtitle E as a result of the complete or partial withdrawal of the employer from the multiemployer plan before January 16, 1982, shall be void.

(2) In any case in which—

(A) an employer engaged in the grocery wholesaling business—

(i) had ceased all covered operations under a multiemployer plan before June 30, 1981, and had relocated its operations to a new facility in another State, and

(ii) had notified a local union representative on May 14, 1980, that the employer had tentatively decided to discontinue operations and relocate to a new facility in another State, and

(B) all State and local approvals with respect to construction of and commencement of operations at the new facility had been obtained, a contract for construction had been entered into, and construction of the new facility had begun before September 26, 1980, any withdrawal liability incurred by the employer pursuant to part 1 of subtitle E as a result of the complete or partial withdrawal of the employer from the multiemployer plan before June 30, 1981, shall be void.

Speaker of the
House of Representatives.

Vice President of the
United States and
President of the Senate.

(i) The preceding provisions of this section shall not apply with respect to amendments made to this title in provisions enacted after the date of the enactment of the Tax Reform Act of 1986.

Part 3

IRC Excerpts

Selected Sections of the Internal Revenue Code

Subtitle A— Income Taxes

Chapter 1— Normal Taxes And Surtaxes

Subchapter A— Determination Of Tax Liability

* * *

Part IV— Credits Against Tax

* * *

SEC. 41. EMPLOYEE STOCK OWNERSHIP CREDIT. [Repealed]

* * *

Subchapter B— Computation of Taxable Income

* * *

Part I— Definition of Gross Income, Adjusted Gross Income, Taxable Income, Etc.

SEC. 61. GROSS INCOME DEFINED.

(a) General Definition.— Except as otherwise provided in this subtitle, gross income means all income from whatever source derived, including (but not limited to) the following items:

(1) Compensation for services, including fees, commissions, fringe benefits, and similar items;

(2) Gross income derived from business;

(3) Gains derived from dealings in property;

(4) Interest;

(5) Rents;

(6) Royalties;

(7) Dividends;

(8) Alimony and separate maintenance payments;

(9) Annuities;

(10) Income from life insurance and endowment contracts;

(11) Pensions;

(12) Income from discharge of indebtedness;

(13) Distributive share of partnership gross income;

(14) Income in respect of a decedent; and

(15) Income from an interest in an estate or trust.

(b) Cross References.— For items specifically included in gross income, see part II (sec. 71 and following). For items specifically excluded from gross income, see part III (sec. 101 and following).

SEC. 62. ADJUSTED GROSS INCOME DEFINED

(a) General Rule.— For purposes of this subtitle, the term ''adjusted gross income'' means, in the case of an individual, gross income minus the following deductions:

* * *

(6) Pension, profit-sharing and annuity plans of self-employed individuals.— In the case of an individual who is an employee within the meaning of section 401(c)(1), the deduction allowed by section 404.

(7) Retirement savings.— The deduction allowed by section 219 (relating to deduction for certain retirement savings).

(8) Certain portion of lump-sum distributions from pension plans taxed under section 402(d).— The deduction allowed by section 402(d).

* * *

Part II— Items Specifically Included in Gross Income

SEC. 72. ANNUITIES; CERTAIN PROCEEDS OF ENDOWMENT AND LIFE INSURANCE CONTRACTS.

(a) General Rule for Annuities.—Except as otherwise provided in this chapter, gross income includes any amount received as an annuity (whether for a period certain or during one or more lives) under an annuity, endowment, or life insurance contract.

(b) Exclusion Ratio.—

(1) In general.— Gross income does not include that part of any amount received as an annuity under an annuity, endowment, or life insurance contract which bears the same ratio to such amount as the investment in the contract (as of the annuity starting date) bears to the expected return under the contract (as of such date).

(2) Exclusion limited to investment. The portion of any amount received as an annuity which is excluded from gross income under paragraph (1) shall not exceed the unrecovered investment in the contract immediately before the receipt of such amount.

(3) Deduction where annuity payments cease before entire investment recovered.—

(A) In general.— If—

(i) after the annuity starting date, payments as an annuity under the contract cease by reason of the death of an annuitant, and

(ii) as of the date of such cessation, there is unrecovered investment in the contract,

the amount of such unrecovered investment (in excess of any amount specified in sub-

section (e)(5) which was not included in gross income) shall be allowed as a deduction to the annuitant for his last taxable year.

(B) Payments to other persons.—In the case of any contract which provides for payments meeting the requirements of subparagraphs (B) and (C) of subsection (c)(2), the deduction under subparagraph (A) shall be allowed to the person entitled to such payments for the taxable year in which such payments are received.

(C) Net operating loss deductions provided.— For purposes of section 172, a deduction allowed under this paragraph shall be treated as if it were attributable to a trade or business of the taxpayer.

(4) Unrecovered investment.— For purposes of this subsection, the unrecovered investment in the contract as of any date is—

(A) the investment in the contract as of the annuity starting date, reduced by

(B) the aggregate amount received under the contract on or after such annuity starting date and before the date as of which the determination is being made, to the extent such amount was excludable from gross income under this subtitle.

(c) Definitions.—

(1) Investment in the contract.— For purposes of subsection (b), the investment in the contract as of the annuity starting date is—

(A) the aggregate amount of premiums or other consideration paid for the contract, minus

(B) the aggregate amount received under the contract before such date, to the extent that such amount was excludable from gross income under this subtitle or prior income tax laws.

(2) Adjustment in investment where there is refund feature.— If—

(A) the expected return under the contract depends in whole or in part on the life expectancy of one or more individuals;

(B) the contract provides for payments to be made to a beneficiary (or to the estate of an annuitant) on or after the death of the annuitant or annuitants; and

(C) such payments are in the nature of a refund of the consideration paid, then the value (computed without discount for interest) of such payments on the annuity starting date shall be subtracted from the amount determined under paragraph (1). Such value shall be computed in accordance with actuarial tables prescribed by the Secretary. For purposes of this paragraph and of subsection (e)(2)(A), the term "refund of the consideration paid" includes amounts payable after the death of an annuitant by reason of a provision in the contract for a life annuity with minimum period of payments certain, but (if part of the consideration was contributed by an employer) does not include that part of any payment to a beneficiary (or to the estate of the annuitant) which is not attributable to the consideration paid by the employee for the contract as determined under paragraph (1)(A).

(3) Expected return.— For purposes of subsection (b), the expected return under the contract shall be determined as follows:

(A) Life expectancy.— If the expected return under the contract, for the period on and after the annuity starting date, depends in whole or in part on the life expectancy of one or more individuals, the expected return shall be computed with reference to actuarial tables prescribed by the Secretary.

(B) Installment payments.— If subparagraph (A) does not apply, the expected return is the aggregate of the amounts receivable under the contract as an annuity.

(4) Annuity starting date.— For purposes of this section, the annuity starting date in the case of any contract is the first day of the first period for which an amount is received as an

annuity under the contract; except that if such date was before January 1, 1954, then the annuity starting date is January 1, 1954.

(d) Treatment of Employee Contributions Under Defined Contribution Plans as Separate Contracts.— For purposes of this section, employee contributions (and any income allocable thereto) under a defined contribution plan may be treated as a separate contract.

(e) Amounts Not Received as Annuities.—

(1) Application of subsection.—

(A) In general.— This subsection shall apply to any amount which—

(i) is received under an annuity, endowment, or life insurance contract, and

(ii) is not received as an annuity,

if no provision of this subtitle (other than this subsection) applies with respect to such amount.

(B) Dividends.— For purposes of this section, any amount received which is in the nature of a dividend or similar distribution shall be treated as an amount not received as an annuity.

(2) General rule.— Any amount to which this subsection applies—

(A) if received on or after the annuity starting date, shall be included in gross income, or

(B) if received before the annuity starting date—

(i) shall be included in gross income to the extent allocable to income on the contract, and

(ii) shall not be included in gross income to the extent allocable to the investment in the contract.

(3) Allocation of amounts to income and investment.— For purposes of paragraph (2)(B)—

(A) Allocation to income.— Any amount to which this subsection applies shall be treated as allocable to income on the contract to the extent that such amount does not exceed the excess (if any) of—

(i) the cash value of the contract (determined without regard to any surrender charge) immediately before the amount is received, over

(ii) the investment in the contract at such time.

(B) Allocation to investment.— Any amount to which this subsection applies shall be treated as allocable to investment in the contract to the extent that such amount is not allocated to income under subparagraph (A).

(4) Special rules for application of paragraph (2)(B).— For purposes of paragraph (2)(B)—

(A) Loans treated as distributions.—If, during any taxable year, an individual—

(i) receives (directly or indirectly) any amount as a loan under any contract to which this subsection applies, or

(ii) assigns or pledges (or agrees to assign or pledge) any portion of the value of any such contract,

such amount or portion shall be treated as received under the contract as an amount not received as an annuity. The preceding sentence shall not apply for purposes of determining investment in the contract, except that the investment in the contract shall be increased by any amount included in gross income by reason of the amount treated as received under the preceding sentence.

(B) Treatment of policyholder dividends.— Any amount described in paragraph (1)(B) shall not be included in gross income under paragraph (2)(B)(i) to the extent such amount is retained by the insurer as a premium or other consideration paid for the contract.

(C) Treatment of transfers without adequate consideration.—

(i) In general.— If an individual who holds an annuity contract transfers it without full and adequate consideration, such individual shall be treated as receiving an amount equal to the excess of—

(I) the cash surrender value of such contract at the time of transfer, over

(II) the investment in such contract at such time,

under the contract as an amount not received as an annuity.

(ii) Exception for certain transfers between spouses or former spouses.— Clause (i) shall not apply to any transfer to which section 1041(a) (relating to transfers of property between spouses or incident to divorce) applies.

(iii) Adjustment to investment in contract of transferee.— If under clause (i) an amount is included in the gross income of the transferor of an annuity contract, the investment in the contract of the transferee in such contract shall be increased by the amount so included.

(5) Retention of existing rules in certain cases.—

(A) In general.— In any case to which this paragraph applies—

(i) paragraphs (2)(B) and (4)(A) shall not apply, and

(ii) if paragraph (2)(A) does not apply,

the amount shall be included in gross income, but only to the extent it exceeds the investment in the contract.

(B) Existing contracts.— This paragraph shall apply to contracts entered into before August 14, 1982. Any amount allocable to investment in the contract after August 13,

IRC Sec. 72 (e)(3)(A)

1982, shall be treated as from a contract entered into after such date.

(C) Certain life insurance and endowment contracts.— Except as provided in paragraph (10) and except to the extent prescribed by the Secretary by regulations, this paragraph shall apply to any amount not received as an annuity which is received under a life insurance or endowment contract.

(D) Contacts under qualified plans.— Except as provided in paragraph (8), this paragraph shall apply to any amount received—

(i) from a trust described in section 401(a) which is exempt from tax under section 501(a),

(ii) from a contract—

(I) purchased by a trust described in clause (i),

(II) purchased as part of a plan described in section 403(a),

(III) described in section 403(b), or

(IV) provided for employees of a life insurance company under a plan described in section 818(a)(3), or

(iii) from an individual retirement account or an individual retirement annuity.

Any dividend described in section 404(k) which is received by a participant or beneficiary shall, for purposes of this subparagraph, be treated as paid under a separate contract to which clause (ii)(I) applies.

(E) Full refunds, surrenders, redemptions, and maturities.— This paragraph shall apply to—

(i) any amount received, whether in a single sum or otherwise, under a contract in full discharge of the obligation under the contract which is in the nature of a refund of the consideration paid for the contract, and

(ii) any amount received under a contract on its complete surrender, redemption, or maturity.

In the case of any amount to which the preceding sentence applies, the rule of paragraph (2)(A) shall not apply.

(6) Investment in the contract.— For purposes of this subsection, the investment in the contract as of any date is—

(A) the aggregate amount of premiums or other consideration paid for the contract before such date, minus

(B) the aggregate amount received under the contract before such date, to the extent that such amount was excludable from gross income under this subtitle or prior income tax laws.

(7) Special rules for plans where substantially all contributions are employee contributions.— [Repealed]

(8) Extension of paragraph (2)(B) to qualified plans.—

(A) In general.— Notwithstanding any other provision of this subsection, in the case of any amount received before the annuity starting date from a trust or contract described in paragraph (5)(D), paragraph (2)(B) shall apply to such amounts.

(B) Allocation of amount received.— For purposes of paragraph (2)(B), the amount allocated to the investment in the contract shall be the portion of the amount described in subparagraph (A) which bears the same ratio to such amount as the investment in the contract bears to the account balance. The determination under the preceding sentence shall be made as of the time of the distribution or at such other time as the Secretary may prescribe.

(C) Treatment of forfeitable rights.— If an employee does not have a nonforfeitable right to any amount under any trust or contract to which subparagraph (A) applies, such amount shall not be treated as part of the account balance.

IRC Sec. 72 (e)(8)(C)

(D) Investment in the contract before 1987.— In the case of a plan which on May 5, 1986, permitted withdrawal of any employee contributions before separation from service, subparagraph (A) shall apply only to the extent that amounts received before the annuity starting date (when increased by amounts previously received under the contract after December 31, 1986) exceed the investment in the contract as of December 31, 1986.

(9) [Deleted.]

(10) Treatment of modified endowment contracts.—

(A) In general.— Notwithstanding paragraph (5)(C), in the case of any modified endowment contract (as defined in section 7702A)—

(i) paragraphs (2)(B) and (4)(A) shall apply, and

(ii) in applying paragraph (4)(A), "any person" shall be substituted for "an individual".

(B) Treatment of certain burial contracts.— Notwithstanding subparagraph (A), paragraph (4)(A) shall not apply to any assignment (or pledge) of a modified endowment contract if such assignment (or pledge) is solely to cover the payment of expenses referred to in section 7702(e)(2)(C)(iii) and if the maximum death benefit under such contract does not exceed $25,000.

(11) Anti-abuse rules.—

(A) In general.— For purposes of determining the amount includible in gross income under this subsection

(i) all modified endowment contracts issued by the same company to the same policyholder during any calendar year shall be treated as 1 modified endowment contract, and

(ii) all annuity contracts issued by the same company to the same policyholder

during any calendar year shall be treated as 1 annuity contract.

The preceding sentence shall not apply to any contract described in paragraph (5)(D).

(B) Regulatory authority.— The Secretary may by regulations prescribe such additional rules as may be necessary or appropriate to prevent avoidance of the purposes of this subsection through serial purchases of contracts or otherwise.

(f) Special Rules for Computing Employees' Contributions.— In computing, for purposes of subsection (c)(1)(A), the aggregate amount of premiums or other consideration paid for the contract, and for purposes of subsection (e)(6), the aggregate premiums or other consideration paid, amounts contributed by the employer shall be included, but only to the extent that—

(1) such amounts were includible in the gross income of the employee under this subtitle or prior income tax laws; or

(2) if such amounts had been paid directly to the employee at the time they were contributed, they would not have been includible in the gross income of the employee under the law applicable at the time of such contribution.

Paragraph (2) shall apply to amounts which were contributed by the employer after December 31, 1962, and which would not have been includible in the gross income of the employee by reason of the application of section 911 if such amounts had been paid directly to the employee at the time of contribution. The preceding sentence shall not apply to amounts which were contributed by the employer, as determined under regulations prescribed by the Secretary, to provide pension or annuity credits, to the extent such credits are attributable to services performed before January 1, 1963, and are provided pursuant to pension or annuity plan provisions in existence on March 12, 1962, and on that date applicable to such services.

(g) Rules for Transferee Where Transfer Was for Value.— Where any contract (or any interest therein) is transferred (by assignment or otherwise) for a valuable consideration, to the extent that the contract (or interest therein) does not, in the hands of the transferee, have a basis which is determined by reference to the basis in the hands of the transferor, then—

(1) for purposes of this section, only the actual value of such consideration, plus the amount of the premiums and other consideration paid by the transferee after the transfer, shall be taken into account in computing the aggregate amount of the premiums or other consideration paid for the contract;

(2) for purposes of subsection (c)(1)(B), there shall be taken into account only the aggregate amount received under the contract by the transferee before the annuity starting date, to the extent that such amount was excludable from gross income under this subtitle or prior income tax laws; and

(3) the annuity starting date is January 1, 1954, or the first day of the first period for which the transferee received an amount under the contract as an annuity, whichever is the later.

For purposes of this subsection, the term "transferee" includes a beneficiary of, or the estate of, the transferee.

(h) Option to Receive Annuity in Lieu of Lump Sum.— If—

(1) a contract provides for payment of a lump sum in full discharge of an obligation under the contract, subject to an option to receive an annuity in lieu of such lump sum;

(2) the option is exercised within 60 days after the day on which such lump sum first became payable; and

(3) part or all of such lump sum would (but for this subsection) be includible in gross income by reason of subsection (e)(1),

then, for purposes of this subtitle, no part of such lump sum shall be considered as includible in gross income at the time such lump sum first became payable.

(i) [Repealed.]

(j) Interest.— Notwithstanding any other provision of this section, if any amount is held under an agreement to pay interest thereon, the interest payments shall be included in gross income.

(k) [Repealed.]

(*l*) Face-Amount Certificates.— For purposes of this section, the term "endowment contract" includes a face-amount certificate, as defined in section 2(a)(15) of the Investment Company Act of 1940 (15 U.S.C., sec. 80a-2), issued after December 31, 1954.

(m) Special Rules Applicable to Employee Annuities and Distributions Under Employee Plans.—

(1) [Repealed.]

(2) Computation of consideration paid by the employee.— In computing—

(A) the aggregate amount of premiums or other consideration paid for the contract for purposes of subsection (c)(1)(A) (relating to the investment in the contract),

(B) the consideration for the contract contributed by the employee for purposes of subsection (d)(1) (relating to employee's contributions recoverable in 3 years) and subsection (e)(7) (relating to plans where substantially all contributions are employee contributions), and

(C) the aggregate premiums or other consideration paid for purposes of subsection (e)(6) (relating to certain amounts not received as an annuity), any amount allowed as a deduction with respect to the contract under section 404 which was paid while the employee was an employee within the meaning of section 401(c)(1) shall be treated as consideration contributed by the employer, and there shall not be taken into account any portion of the premiums or other consideration for the contract paid while the employee was an owner-employee which is properly allocable (as determined under regulations prescribed by the Secretary) to the cost of life, accident, health, or other insurance.

(3) Life insurance contracts.—

(A) This paragraph shall apply to any life insurance contract— Sec. 72 (m)(3)(A)(i)

(i) purchased as a part of a plan described in section 403(a), or

(ii) purchased by a trust described in section 401(a) which is exempt from tax under section 501(a) if the proceeds of such contract are payable directly or indirectly to a participant in such trust or to a beneficiary of such participant.

(B) Any contribution to a plan described in subparagraph (A)(i) or a trust described in subparagraph (A)(ii) which is allowed as a deduction under section 404, and any income of a trust described in subparagraph (A)(ii), which is determined in accordance with regulations prescribed by the Secretary to have been applied to purchase the life insurance protection under a contract described in subparagraph (A), is includible in the gross income of the participant for the taxable year when so applied.

(C) In the case of the death of an individual insured under a contract described in subparagraph (A), an amount equal to the cash surrender value of the contract immediately before the death of the insured shall be treated as a payment under such plan or a distribution by such trust, and the excess of the amount payable by reason of the death of the insured over such cash surrender value shall not be includible in gross income under this section and shall be treated as provided in section 101.

(4) Amounts constructively received.— [Repealed.]

(5) Penalties applicable to certain amounts received by 5-percent owners.—

(A) This paragraph applies to amounts which are received from a qualified trust described in section 401(a) or under a plan described in section 403(a) at any time by an individual who is, or has been, a 5-percent owner, or by a successor of such an individual, but only to the extent such amounts are determined, under regulations prescribed by the Secretary, to exceed the benefits provided for such individual under the plan formula.

(B) If a person receives an amount to which this paragraph applies, his tax under this chapter for the taxable year in which such amount is received shall be increased by an amount equal to 10 percent of the portion of the amount so received which is includible in his gross income for such taxable year.

(C) For purposes of this paragraph, the term "5-percent owner" means any individual who, at any time during the 5 plan years preceding the plan year ending in the taxable year in which the amount is received, is a 5-percent owner (as defined in section 416(i) (1)(B)).

(6) Owner-employee defined.— For purposes of this subsection, the term "owner-employee" has the meaning assigned to it by section 401(c)(3) and includes an individual for whose benefit an individual retirement account or annuity described in section 408(a) or (b) is maintained. For purposes of the preceding sentence, the term "owner-employee" shall include an employee within the meaning of section 401(c)(1).

(7) Meaning of disabled.— For purposes of this section, an individual shall be considered to be disabled if he is unable to engage in any substantial gainful activity by reason of any medically determinable physical or mental impairment which can be expected to result in death or to be of long continued and indefinite duration. An individual shall not be considered to be disabled unless he furnishes

IRC Sec. 72 (m)(3)

proof of the existence thereof in such form and manner as the Secretary may require.

(8) [Repealed.]

(9) [Repealed.]

(10) Determination of investment in the contract in the case of qualified domestic relations orders.— Under regulations prescribed by the Secretary, in the case of a distribution or payment made to an alternate payee who is the spouse or former spouse of the participant pursuant to a qualified domestic relations order (as defined in section 414(p)), the investment in the contract as of the date prescribed in such regulations shall be allocated on a pro rata basis between the present value of such distribution or payment and the present value of all other benefits payable with respect to the participant to which such order relates.

(n) Annuities Under Retired Service-man's Family Protection Plan or Survivor Benefit Plan.— Subsection b shall not apply in the case of amounts received after December 31, 1965, as an annuity under chapter 73 of title 10 of the United States Code, but all such amounts shall be excluded from gross income until there has been so excluded (under section 122(b)(1) or this section, including amounts excluded before January 1, 1966) an amount equal to the consideration for the contract (as defined by section 122(b)(2)), plus any amount treated pursuant to section 101(b)(2)(D) as additional consideration paid by the employee. Thereafter all amounts so received shall be included in gross income.

(o) Special Rules for Distributions From Qualified Plans to Which Employee Made Deductible Contributions.—

(1) Treatment of contributions.— For purposes of this section and sections 402 and 403, notwithstanding section 414(h), any deductible employee contribution made to a qualified employer plan or government plan shall be treated as an amount contributed by the employer which is not includible in the gross income of the employee.

(2) Additional tax if amount received before age 59½.— [Repealed.]

(3) Amounts constructively received.—

(A) In general.— For purposes of this subsection, rules similar to the rules provided by subsection (p) (other than the exception contained in paragraph (2) thereof) shall apply.

(B) Purchase of life insurance.— To the extent any amount of accumulated deductible employee contributions of an employee are applied to the purchase of life insurance contracts, such amount shall be treated as distributed to the employee in the year so applied.

(4) Special rule for treatment of roll-over amounts.— For purposes of sections 402(c), 403(a)(4), and 408(d)(3), the Secretary shall prescribe regulations providing for such allocations of amounts attributable to accumulated deductible employee contributions, and for such other rules, as may be necessary to ensure that such accumulated deductible employee contributions do not become eligible for additional tax benefits (or freed from limitations) through the use of rollovers.

(5) Definitions and special rules.— For purposes of this subsection—

(A) Deductible employee contributions.— The term "deductible employee contributions" means any qualified voluntary employee contribution (as defined in section 219(e)(2)) made after December 31, 1981, in a taxable year beginning after such date and made for a taxable year beginning before January 1, 1987, and allowable as a deduction under section 219(a) for such taxable year.

(B) Accumulated deductible employee contributions.— The term "accumulated deductible employee contributions" means the deductible employee contributions—

(i) increased by the amount of income and gain allocable to such contributions, and

(ii) reduced by the sum of the amount of loss and expense allocable to such contributions and the amounts distributed with respect to the employee which are attributable to such contributions (or income or gain allocable to such contributions).

(C) Qualified employer plan.— The term "qualified employer plan" has the meaning given to such term by subsection (p)(3)(A)(i).

(D) Government plan.— The term "government plan" has the meaning given such term by subsection (p)(3)(B).

(6) Ordering rules.— Unless the plan specifies otherwise, any distribution from such plan shall not be treated as being made from the accumulated deductible employee contributions until all other amounts to the credit of the employee have been distributed.

(p) Loans Treated as Distributions.— For purposes of this section—

(1) Treatment as distributions.—

(A) Loans.— If during any taxable year a participant or beneficiary receives (directly or indirectly) any amount as a loan from a qualified employer plan, such amount shall be treated as having been received by such individual as a distribution under such plan.

(B) Assignments or pledges.— If during any taxable year a participant or beneficiary assigns (or agrees to assign) or pledges (or agrees to pledge) any portion of his interest in a qualified employer plan, such portion shall be treated as having been received by such individual as a loan from such plan.

(2) Exception for certain loans.—

(A) General rule.— Paragraph (1) shall not apply to any loan to the extent that such loan (when added to the outstanding balance of all other loans from such plan whether made on, before, or after August 13, 1982), does not exceed the lesser of—

(i) $50,000, reduced by the excess (if any) of—

(I) the highest outstanding balance of loans from the plan during the 1-year period ending on the day before the date on which such loan was made, over

(II) the outstanding balance of loans from the plan on the date on which such loan was made, or

(ii) the greater of (I) one-half of the present value of the nonforfeitable accrued benefit of the employee under the plan, or (II) $10,000.

For purposes of clause (ii), the present value of the nonforfeitable accrued benefit shall be determined without regard to any accumulated deductible employee contributions (as defined in subsection (o)(5)(B)).

(B) Requirement that loan be repayable within 5 years.—

(i) In general.— Subparagraph (A) shall not apply to any loan unless such loan, by its terms, is required to be repaid within 5 years.

(ii) Exception for home loans.— Clause (i) shall not apply to any loan used to acquire any dwelling unit which within a reasonable time is to be used (determined at the time the loan is made) as the principal residence of the participant.

(C) Requirement of level amortization.— Except as provided in regulations, this paragraph shall not apply to any loan unless substantially level amortization of such loan (with payments not less frequently than quarterly) is required over the term of the loan.

(D) Related employers and related plans.— For purposes of this paragraph—

(i) the rules of subsections (b), (c), and (m) of section 414 shall apply, and

(ii) all plans of an employer (determined after the application of such subsections) shall be treated as 1 plan.

IRC Sec. 72 (o)(5)(B)(ii)

(3) Denial of interest deductions in certain cases.—

(A) In general.— No deduction otherwise allowable under this chapter shall be allowed under this chapter for any interest paid or accrued on any loan to which paragraph (1) does not apply by reason of paragraph (2) during the period.

(B) Period to which subparagraph (A) applies.— For purposes of subparagraph (A), the period described in this subparagraph is the period—

(i) on or after the 1st day on which the individual to whom the loan is made is a key employee (as defined in section 416(i)), or

(ii) such loan is secured by amounts attributable to elective deferrals described in subparagraph (A) or (C) of section 402(g)(3).

(4) Qualified employer plan, etc.— For purposes of this subsection—

(A) Qualified employer plan.—

(i) In general.— The term "qualified employer plan" means—

(I) a plan described in section 401(a) which includes a trust exempt from tax under section 501(a),

(II) an annuity plan described in section 403(a), and

(III) a plan under which amounts are contributed by an individual's employer for an annuity contract described in section 403(b).

(ii) Special rules.— The term "qualified employer plan"—

(I) shall include any plan which was (or was determined to be) a qualified employer plan or a government plan, but

(II) shall not include a plan described in subsection (e)(7).

(B) Government plan.— The term "government plan" means any plan, whether or not qualified, established and maintained for its employees by the United States, by a State or political subdivision thereof, or by an agency or instrumentality of any of the foregoing.

(5) Special rules for loans, etc., from certain contracts.— For purposes of this subsection, any amount received as a loan under a contract purchased under a qualified employer plan (and any assignment or pledge with respect to such a contract) shall be treated as a loan under such employer plan.

(q) 10-percent Penalty for Premature Distribution From Annuity Contracts.—

(1) Imposition of penalty.— If any taxpayer receives any amount under an annuity contract, the taxpayer's tax under this chapter for the taxable year in which such amount is received shall be increased by an amount equal to 10 percent of the portion of such amount which is includible in gross income.

(2) Subsection not to apply to certain distributions.— Paragraph (1) shall not apply to any distribution—

(A) made on or after the date on which the taxpayer attains age 59½,

(B) commencing on or after the death of the holder (or, where the holder is not an individual, the death of the primary annuitant (as defined in subsection (s)(6)(B))),

(C) attributable to the taxpayer's becoming disabled within the meaning of subsection (m)(7),

(D) which is a part of a series of substantially equal periodic payments (not less frequently than annually) made for the life (or life expectancy) of the taxpayer or the joint lives (or joint life expectancies) of such taxpayer and his designated beneficiary,

(E) from a plan, contract, account, trust, or annuity described in subsection (e)(5)(D),

IRC Sec. 72 (q)(2)(E)

(F) allocable to investment in the contract before August 14, 1982,

(G) under a qualified funding asset (within the meaning of section 130(d), but without regard to whether there is a qualified assignment,

(H) to which subsection (t) applies (without regard to paragraph (2) thereof),

(I) under an immediate annuity contract (within the meaning of section 72(u)(4)), or

(J) which is purchased by an employer upon the termination of a plan described in section 401(a) or 403(a) and which is held by the employer until such time as the employee separates from service.

(3) Change in substantially equal payments.— If—

(A) paragraph (1) does not apply to a distribution by reason of paragraph (2)(D), and

(B) the series of payments under such paragraph are subsequently modified (other than by reason of death or disability—

(i) before the close of the 5-year period beginning on the date of the first payment and after the taxpayer attains age 59½, or

(ii) before the taxpayer attains age 59½, the taxpayer's tax for the 1st taxable year in which such modification occurs shall be increased by an amount, determined under regulations, equal to the tax which (but for paragraph (2)(D)) would have been imposed, plus interest for the deferral period (within the meaning of subsection (t)(4)(B)).

(r) Certain Railroad Retirement Benefits Treated as Received Under Employer Plans.—

(1) In general.— Notwithstanding any other provision of law, any benefit provided under the Railroad Retirement Act of 1974 (other than a tier 1 railroad retirement benefit)

shall be treated for purposes of this title as a benefit provided under an employer plan which meets the requirements of section 401(a).

(2) Tier 2 taxes treated as contributions.—

(A) In general.— For purposes of paragraph (1)—

(i) the tier 2 portion of the tax imposed by section 3201 (relating to tax on employees) shall be treated as an employee contribution,

(ii) the tier 2 portion of the tax imposed by section 3211 (relating to tax on employee representatives) shall be treated as an employee contribution, and

(iii) the tier 2 portion of the tax imposed by section 3221 (relating to tax on employers) shall be treated as an employer contribution.

(B) Tier 2 portion.— For purposes of subparagraph (A)—

(i) After 1984.— With respect to compensation paid after 1984, the tier 2 portion shall be the taxes imposed by sections 3201(b), 3211(a)(2), and 3221(b).

(ii) After September 30, 1981, and before 1985.— With respect to compensation paid before 1985 for services rendered after September 30, 1981, the tier 2 portion shall be— Sec. 72 (r)(2)(B)(ii)(I)

(I) so much of the tax imposed by section 3201 as is determined at the 2 percent rate, and

(II) so much of the taxes imposed by sections 3211 and 3221 as is determined at the 11.75 percent rate.

With respect to compensation paid for services rendered after December 31, 1983 and before 1985, subclause (I) shall be applied by substituting "2.75 percent" for "2 percent", and subclause (II) shall be applied by substituting "12.75 percent" for "11.75 percent".

(iii) Before October 1, 1981.— With respect to compensation paid for services rendered during any period before October 1, 1981, the tier 2 portion shall be the excess (if any) of—

(I) the tax imposed for such period by section 3201, 3211, or 3221, as the case may be (other than any tax imposed with respect to man-hours), over

(II) the tax which would have been imposed by such section for such period had the rates of the comparable taxes imposed by chapter 21 for such period applied under such section.

(C) Contributions not allocable to supplemental annuity or windfall benefits.— For purposes of paragraph (1), no amount treated as an employee contribution under this paragraph shall be allocated to—

(i) any supplemental annuity paid under section 2(b) of the Railroad Retirement Act of 1974, or

(ii) any benefit paid under section 3(h), 4(e), or 4(h) of such Act.

(3) Tier 1 railroad retirement benefit.— For purposes of paragraph (1), the term "tier 1 railroad retirement benefit" has the meaning given such term by section 86(d)(4).

(s) Required distributions where holder dies before entire interest is distributed.—

(1) In general.— A contract shall not be treated as an annuity contract for purposes of this title unless it provides that—

(A) if any holder of such contract dies on or after the annuity starting date and before the entire interest in such contract has been distributed, the remaining portion of such interest will be distributed at least as rapidly as under the method of distributions being used as of the date of his death, and

(B) if any holder of such contract dies before the annuity starting date, the entire interest in such contract will be distributed within 5 years after the death of such holder.

(2) Exception for certain amounts payable over life of beneficiary.— If—

(A) any portion of the holder's interest is payable to (or for the benefit of) a designated beneficiary,

(B) such portion will be distributed (in accordance with regulations) over the life of such designated beneficiary (or over a period not extending beyond the life expectancy of such beneficiary), and

(C) such distributions begin not later than 1 year after the date of the holder's death or such later date as the Secretary may by regulations prescribe,

then for purposes of paragraph (1), the portion referred to in subparagraph (A) shall be treated as distributed on the day on which such distributions begin.

(3) Special rule where surviving spouse beneficiary.— If the designated beneficiary referred to in paragraph (2)(A) is the surviving spouse of the holder of the contract, paragraphs (1) and (2) shall be applied by treating such spouse as the holder of such contract.

(4) Designated beneficiary.— For purposes of this subsection, the term "designated beneficiary" means any individual designated a beneficiary by the holder of the contract.

(5) Exception for certain annuity contracts.— This subsection shall not apply to any annuity contract—

(A) which is provided—

(i) under a plan described in section 401(a) which includes a trust exempt from tax under section 501, or

(ii) under a plan described in section 403(a),

(B) which is described in section 403(b),

(C) which is an individual retirement annuity or provided under an individual retirement account or annuity, or

(D) which is a qualified funding asset (as defined in section 130(d), but without regard to whether there is a qualified assignment).

(6) Special rule where holder is corporation or other non-individual.—

(A) In general.— For purposes of this subsection, if the holder of the contract is not an individual, the primary annuitant shall be treated as the holder of the contract.

(B) Primary annuitant.— For purposes of subparagraph (A), the term "primary annuitant" means the individual, the events in the life of whom are of primary importance in affecting the timing or amount of the payout under the contract.

(7) Treatment of changes in primary annuitant where holder of contract is not an individual.—For purposes of this subsection, in the case of a holder of an annuity contract which is not an individual, if there is a change in a primary annuitant (as defined in paragraph (6)(B)), such change shall be treated as the death of the holder.

(t) 10-Percent Additional Tax on Early Distributions From Qualified Retirement Plans.—

(1) Imposition of additional tax.— If any taxpayer receives any amount from a qualified retirement plan (as defined in section 4974(c)), the taxpayer's tax under this chapter for the taxable year in which such amount is received shall be increased by an amount equal to 10 percent of the portion of such amount which is includible in gross income.

(2) Subsection not to apply to certain distributions.— Except as provided in paragraphs (3) and (4), paragraph (1) shall not apply to any of the following distributions:

(A) In general.— Distributions which are—

(i) made on or after the date on which the employee attains age 59½,

(ii) made to a designated beneficiary (or to the estate of the employee) on or after the death of the employee,

(iii) attributable to the employee's being disabled within the meaning of subsection (m)(7),

(iv) part of a series of substantially equal periodic payments (not less frequently than annually) made for the life (or life expectancy) of the employee or the joint lives (or joint life expectancies) of such employee and his designated beneficiary,

(v) made to an employee after separation from service after attainment of age 55, or

(vi) dividends paid with respect to stock of a corporation which are described in section 404(k).

(B) Medical expenses.— Distributions made to the employee (other than distributions described in subparagraph (A) or (C)) to the extent such distributions do not exceed the amount allowable as a deduction under section 213 to the employee for amounts paid during the taxable year for medical care (determined without regard to whether the employee itemizes deductions for such taxable year).

(C) Payments to alternate payees pursuant to qualified domestic relations orders.— Any distribution to an alternate payee pursuant to a qualified domestic relations order (within the meaning of section 414(p)(1)).

(3) Limitations.—

(A) Certain exceptions not to apply to individual retirement plans.— Subparagraphs (A)(v), (B), and (C) of paragraph (2) shall not apply to distributions from an individual retirement plan.

(B) Periodic payments under qualified plans must begin after separation.— Paragraph (2)(A)(iv) shall not apply to any amount paid from a trust described in section 401(a) which is exempt from tax under section 501(a) or from a contract described in section 72(e)(5)(D)(ii) unless the series of payments begins after the employee separates from service.

(4) Change in substantially equal payments.—

(A) In general.— If—

(i) paragraph (1) does not apply to a distribution by reason of paragraph (2)(A)(iv), and

(ii) the series of payments under such paragraph are subsequently modified (other than by reason of death or disability)

(I) before the close of the 5-year period beginning with the date of the first payment and after the employee attains age 59½, or

(II) before the employee attains age 59½,

the taxpayer's tax for the 1st taxable year in which such modification occurs shall be increased by an amount, determined under regulations, equal to the tax which (but for paragraph (2)(A)(iv)) would have been imposed, plus interest for the deferral period.

(B) Deferral period.— For purposes of this paragraph, the term "deferral period" means the period beginning with the taxable year in which (without regard to paragraph (2)(A)(iv)) the distribution would have been includible in gross income and ending with the taxable year in which the modification described in subparagraph (A) occurs.

(5) Employee.— For purposes of this subsection, the term "employee" includes any participant, and in the case of an individual retirement plan, the individual for whose benefit such plan was established.

(u) Treatment of Annuity Contracts Not Held by Natural Persons.—

(1) In general.— If any annuity contract is held by a person who is not a natural person—

(A) such contract shall not be treated as an annuity contract for purposes of this subtitle (other than subchapter L), and

(B) the income on the contract for any taxable year of the policyholder shall be treated as ordinary income received or accrued by the owner during such taxable year.

For purposes of this paragraph, holding by a trust or other entity as an agent for a natural person shall not be taken into account.

(2) Income on the contract.—

(A) In general.— For purposes of paragraph (1), the term "income on the con-tract" means, with respect to any taxable year of the policyholder, the excess of—

(i) the sum of the net surrender value of the contract as of the close of the taxable year plus all distributions under the contract received during the taxable year or any prior taxable year, reduced by

(ii) the sum of the amount of net premiums under the contract for the taxable year and prior taxable years and amounts includible in gross income for prior taxable years with respect to such contract under this subsection.

Where necessary to prevent the avoidance of this subsection, the Secretary may substitute "fair market value of the contract" for "net surrender value of the contract" each place it appears in the preceding sentence.

(B) Net premiums.— For purposes of this paragraph, the term "net premiums" means the amount of premiums paid under the contract reduced by any policyholder dividends.

(3) Exceptions.— This subsection shall not apply to any annuity contract which—

(A) is acquired by the estate of a decedent by reason of the death of the decedent,

(B) is held under a plan described in section 401(a) or 403(a), under a program described

IRC Sec. 72 (u)(3)(B)

in section 403(b), or under an individual retirement plan,

(C) is a qualified funding asset (as defined in section 130(d), but without regard to whether there is a qualified assignment),

(D) is purchased by an employer upon the termination of a plan described in section 401(a) or 403(a) and is held by the employer until all amounts under such contract are distributed to the employee for whom such contract was purchased or the employee's beneficiary, or

(E) is an immediate annuity.

(4) Immediate annuity.— For purposes of this subsection, the term "immediate annuity" means an annuity—

(A) which is purchased with a single premium or annuity consideration,

(B) the annuity starting date (as defined in subsection (c)(4)) of which commences no later than 1 year from the date of the purchase of the annuity, and

(C) which provides for a series of substantially equal periodic payments (to be made not less frequently than annually) during the annuity period.

(v) 10-Percent Additional Tax for Taxable Distributions From Modified Endowment Contracts.—

(1) Imposition of additional tax.— If any taxpayer receives any amount under a modified endowment contract (as defined in section 7702A), the taxpayer's tax under this chapter for the taxable year in which such amount is received shall be increased by an amount equal to 10 percent of the portion of such amount which is includible in gross income.

(2) Subsection not to apply to certain distributions.— Paragraph (1) shall not apply to any distribution—

(A) made on or after the date on which the taxpayer attains age 59½,

(B) which is attributable to the taxpayer's becoming disabled (within the meaning of subsection (m)(7)), or

(C) which is part of a series of substantially equal periodic payments (not less frequently than annually) made for the life (or life expectancy) of the taxpayer or the joint lives (or joint life expectancies) of such taxpayer and his beneficiary.

(w) Cross Reference.—For limitation on adjustments to basis of annuity contracts sold, see section 1021.

* * *

SEC. 79. GROUP-TERM LIFE INSURANCE PURCHASED FOR EMPLOYEES.

(a) General Rule.— There shall be included in the gross income of an employee for the taxable year an amount equal to the cost of group-term life insurance on his life provided for part or all of such year under a policy (or policies) carried directly or indirectly by his employer (or employers); but only to the extent that such cost exceeds the sum of—

(1) the cost of $50,000 of such insurance, and

(2) the amount (if any) paid by the employee toward the purchase of such insurance.

(b) Exceptions.—Subsection (a) shall not apply to—

(1) the cost of group-term life insurance on the life of an individual which is provided under a policy carried directly or indirectly by an employer after such individual has terminated his employment with such employer and is disabled (within the meaning of section 72(m)(7)),

(2) the cost of any portion of the group-term life insurance on the life of an employee provided during part or all of the taxable year to the employee under which—

IRC Sec. 72 (u)(3)(C)

(A) the employer is directly or indirectly the beneficiary, or

(B) a person described in section 170(c) is the sole beneficiary,

for the entire period during such taxable year for which the employee receives such insurance, and

(3) the cost of any group-term life insurance which is provided under a contract to which section 72(m)(3) applies.

(c) Determination of Cost of Insurance.— For purposes of this section and section 6052, the cost of group-term insurance on the life of an employee provided during any period shall be determined on the basis of uniformprmums (computed on the basis of 5-year age brackets) prescribed by regulations by the Secretary.

(d) Nondiscrimination Requirements.—

(1) In general.— In the case of a discriminatory group-term life insurance plan—

(A) subsection (a)(1) shall not apply with respect to any key employee, and

(B) the cost of group term life insurance on the life of any key employee shall be the greater of—

(i) such cost determined without regard to subsection (c), or

(ii) such cost determined with regard to subsection (c).

(2) Discriminatory group-term life insurance plan.— For purposes of this subsection, the term "discriminatory group-term life insurance plan" means any plan of an employer for providing group-term life insurance unless—

(A) the plan does not discriminate in favor of key employees as to eligibility to participate, and

(B) the type and amount of benefits available under the plan do not discriminate in favor of participants who are key employees.

(3) Nondiscriminatory eligibility classification.—

(A) In general.— A plan does not meet requirements of subparagraph (A) of paragraph (2) unless—

(i) such plan benefits 70 percent or more of all employees of the employer,

(ii) at least 85 percent of all employees who are participants under the plan are not key employees,

(iii) such plan benefits such employees as qualify under a classification set up by the employer and found by the Secretary not to be discriminatory in favor of key employees, or

(iv) in the case of a plan which is part of a cafeteria plan, the requirements of section 125 are met.

(B) Exclusion of certain employees.— For purposes of subparagraph (A), there may be excluded from consideration—

(i) employees who have not completed 3 years of service;

(ii) part-time or seasonal employees;

(iii) employees not included in the plan who are included in a unit of employees covered by an agreement between employee representatives and one or more employers which the Secretary finds to be a collective bargaining agreement, if the benefits provided under the plan were the subject of good faith bargaining between such employee representatives and such employer or employers; and

(iv) employees who are nonresident aliens and who receive no earned income (within the meaning of section 911(d)(2)) from the employer which constitutes income from sources within the United States (within the meaning of section 861(a)(3)).

IRC Sec. 79 (d)(3)(B)(iv)

(4) Nondiscriminatory benefits. — A plan does not meet the requirements of paragraph (2)(B) unless all benefits available to participants who are key employees are available to all other participants.

(5) Special rule. — A plan shall not fail to meet the requirements of paragraph (2)(B) merely because the amount of life insurance on behalf of the employees under the plan bears a uniform relationship to the total compensation or basic or regular rate of compensation of such employees.

(6) Key employee defined. — For purposes of this subsection, the term "key employee" has the meaning given to such term by paragraph (1) of section 416(i). Such term also includes any former employee if such employee when he retired or separated from service was a key employee.

(7) Exemption for church plans. —

(A) In general. — This subsection shall not apply to a church plan maintained for church employees.

(B) Definitions. — For purposes of subparagraph (A), the terms "church plan" and "church employee" have the meaning given such terms by paragraphs (1) and (3)(B) of section 414(e), respectively, except that—

(i) section 414(e) shall be applied by substituting "section 501(c)(3)" for "section 501" each place it appears, and

(ii) the term "church employee" shall not include an employee of—

(I) an organization described in section 170(b)(1)(A)(ii) above the secondary school level (other than a school for religious training),

(II) an organization described in section 170(b)(1)(A)(iii), and

(III) an organization decribed in section 501(c)(3), the basis of the exemption for which is substantially similar to the basis

for exemption of an organization described in subclause (II).

(e) Employee Includes Former Employee. — For purposes of this section, the term "employee" includes a former employee.

* * *

SEC. 83. PROPERTY TRANSFERRED IN CONNECTION WITH PERFORMANCE OF SERVICES.

(a) General rule. — If, in connection with the performance of services, property is transferred to any person other than the person for whom such services are performed, the excess of—

(1) the fair market value of such property (determined without regard to any restriction other than a restriction which by its terms will never lapse) at the first time the rights of the person having the beneficial interest in such property are transferable or are not subject to a substantial risk of forfeiture, whichever occurs earlier, over

(2) the amount (if any) paid for such property,

shall be included in the gross income of the person who performed such services in the first taxable year in which the rights of the person having the beneficial interest in such property are transferable or are not subject to a substantial risk of forfeiture, whichever is applicable. The preceding sentence shall not apply if such person sells or otherwise disposes of such property in an arm's length transaction before his rights in such property become transferable or not subject to a substantial risk of forfeiture.

(b) Election to include in gross income in year of transfer. —

(1) In general. — Any person who performs services in connection with which property is transferred to any person may elect to include in his gross income for the taxable year which such property is transferred, the excess of—

(A) the fair market value of such property at the time of transfer (determined without regard to any restriction other than a restriction which by its terms will never lapse), over

(B) the amount (if any) paid for such property.

If such election is made, subsection (a) shall not apply with respect to the transfer of such property, and if such property is subsequently forfeited, no deduction shall be allowed in respect of such forfeiture.

(2) Election.— An election under paragraph (1) with respect to any transfer of property shall be made in such manner as the Secretary prescribes and shall be made not later than 30 days after the date of such transfer. Such election may not be revoked except with the consent of the Secretary.

(c) Special rules.— For purposes of this section—

(1) Substantial risk of forfeiture.— The rights of a person in property are subject to a substantial risk of forfeiture if such person's rights to full enjoyment of such property are conditioned upon the future performance of substantial services by any individual.

(2) Transferability of property.— The rights of a person in property are transferable only if the rights in such property of any transferee are not subject to a substantial risk of forfeiture.

(3) Sales which may give rise to suit under section 16(b) of the Securities Exchange Act of 1934.— So long as the sale of property at a profit could subject a person to suit under section 16(b) of the Securities Exchange Act of 1934, such person's rights in such property are—

(A) subject to a substantial risk of forfeiture, and

(B) not transferable.

(d) Certain restrictions which will never lapse.—

(1) Valuation.— In the case of property subject to a restriction which by its terms will never lapse, and which allows the transferee to sell such property only at a price determined under a formula, the price so determined shall be deemed to be the fair market value of the property unless established to the contrary by the Secretary, and the burden of proof shall be on the Secretary with respect to such value.

(2) Cancellation.— If, in the case of property subject to a restriction which by its terms will never lapse, the restriction is canceled, then, unless the taxpayer establishes—

(A) that such cancellation was not compensatory, and

(B) that the person, if any, who would be allowed a deduction if the cancellation were treated as compensatory, will treat the transaction as not compensatory, as evidenced in such manner as the Secretary shall prescribe by regulations,

the excess of the fair market value of the property (computed without regard to the restrictions) at the time of cancellation over the sum of—

(C) the fair market value of such property (computed by taking the restriction into account) immediately before the cancellation, and

(D) the amount, if any, paid for the cancellation,

shall be treated as compensation for the taxable year in which such cancellation occurs.

(e) Applicability of section.— This section shall not apply to—

(1) a transaction to which section 421 applies,

(2) a transfer to or from a trust described in section 401(a) or a transfer under an annuity plan which meets the requirements of section 404(a)(2),

(3) the transfer of an option without a readily ascertainable fair market value,

(4) the transfer of property pursuant to the exercise of an option with a readily ascertainable fair market value at the date of grant, or

(5) group-term life insurance to which section 79 applies.

(f) Holding period.— In determining the period for which the taxpayer has held property to which subsection (a) applies, there shall be included only the period beginning at the first time his rights in such property are transferable or are not subject to a substantial risk of forfeiture, whichever occurs earlier.

(g) Certain exchanges.— If property to which subsection (a) applies is exchanged for property subject to restrictions and conditions substantially similar to those to which the property given in such exchange was subject, and if section 354, 355, 356, or 1036 (or so much of section 1031 as relates to section 1036) applied to such exchange, or if such exchange was pursuant to the exercise of a conversion privilege—

(1) such exchange shall be disregarded for purposes of subsection (a), and

(2) the property received shall be treated as property to which subsection (a) applies.

(h) Deduction by employer.— In the case of a transfer of property to which this section applies or a cancellation of a restriction described in subsection (d), there shall be allowed as a deduction under section 162, to the person for whom were performed the services in connection with which such property was transferred, an amount equal to the amount included under subsection (a), (b), or (d)(2) in the gross income of the person who performed such services. Such deduction shall be allowed for the taxable year of such person in which or with which ends the taxable year in which such amount is included in the gross

income of the person who performed such services.

$$* * *$$

SEC. 86. SOCIAL SECURITY AND TIER 1 RAILROAD RETIREMENT BENEFITS

(a) In general—

(1) In general. Except as provided in paragraph (2), gross income for the taxable year of any taxpayer described in subsection (b) (notwithstanding section 207 of the Social Security Act) includes social security benefits in an amount equal to the lesser of

(A) one-half of the social security benefits received during the taxable year, or

(B) one-half of the excess described in subsection (b)(1).

(2) Additional amount. In the case of a taxpayer with respect to whom the amount determined under subsection (b)(1)(A) exceeds the adjusted base amount included in gross income under this section shall be equal to the lesser of—

(A) the sum of—

(i) 85 percent of such excess, plus

(ii) the lesser of the amount determined under paragraph (1) or an amount equal to one-half of the difference between the adjusted base amount and the base amount of the taxpayer, or

(B) 85 percent of the social security benefit received during the taxable year.

(b) Taxpayers to whom subsection (a) applies.

(1) In general. A taxpayer is described in this subsection if

(A) the sum of

(i) the modified adjusted gross income of the taxpayer for the taxable year, plus

(ii) one-half of the social security benefits received during the taxable year, exceeds

(B) the base amount.

(2) Modified adjusted gross income. For purposes of this subsection, the term "modified adjusted gross income" means adusted gross income

(A) determined without regard to this section and sections 135, 911, 931, and 933, and

(B) increased by the amount of interest received or accrued by the taxpayer during the taxable year which is exempt from tax.

(c) Base amount and adjusted base amount. For purposes of this section

(1) Base amount. The term "base amount" means—

(A) except as otherwise provided in this paragraph, $25,000,

(B) $32,000 in the case of a joint return, and

(C) zero in the case of a taxpayer who—

(i) is married as of the close of the taxable year (within the meaning of section 7703) but does not file a joint return for such year, and

(ii) does not live apart from his spouse at all times during the taxable year.

(2) Adjusted base amount. The term "adjusted base amount" means—

(A) except as otherwise provided in this paragraph, $34,000,

(B) $44,000 in the case of a joint return, and

(C) zero in the case of a taxpayer described in paragraph (1)(C).

◊ ◊ ◊

Editor's Note: The last sentence of §86(d)(1), as indicated below was stricken by §309(d) of P.L. 103-296, effective with respect to benefits received after December 31, 1995, in taxable years ending after that date. This change was a conforming change necessitated by that act's repeal of §203(i) of the Social Security Act.

◊ ◊ ◊

(d) Social security benefit.

(1) In general. For purposes of this section, the term "social security benefit" means any amount received by the taxpayer by reason of entitlement to—

(A) a monthly benefit under title II of the Social Security Act, or

(B) a tier 1 railroad retirement benefit.

[For purposes of the preceding sentence, the amount received by any taxpayer shall be determined as if the Social Security Act did not contain §203(i) thereof.]

(2) Adjustment for repayments during year.

(A) In general. For purposes of this section, the amount of social security benefits received during any taxable year shall be reduced by any repayment made by the taxpayer during the taxable year of a social security benefit previously received by the taxpayer (whether or not such benefit was received during the taxable year).

(B) Denial of deduction. If (but for this subparagraph) any portion of the repayments referred to in subparagraph (A) would have been allowable as a deduction for the taxable year under section 165, such portion shall be allowable as a deduction only to the extent it exceeds the social security benefits received by the taxpayer during the taxable year (and not repaid during such taxable year).

IRC Sec. 86 (d)(2)(B)

(3) Workmen's compensation benefits substituted for social security benefits. For purposes of this section, if, by reason of section 224 of the Social Security Act (or by reason of section 3(a)(1) of the Railroad Retirement Act of 1974), any social security benefit is reduced by reason of the receipt of a benefit under a workmen's compensation act, the term "social security benefit" includes that portion of such benefit received under the workmen's compensation act which equals such reduction.

(4) Tier 1 railroad retirement benefit. For purposes of paragraph (1), the term "tier 1 railroad retirement benefit" means—

(A) the amount of the annuity under the Railroad Retirement Act of 1974 equal to the amount of the benefit to which the taxpayer would have been entitled under the Social Security Act if all of the service after December 31, 1936, of the employee (on whose employment record the annuity is being paid) had been included in the term "employment" as defined in the Social Security Act, and

(B) a monthly annuity amount under section 3(f)(3) of the Railroad Retirement Act of 1974.

(5) Effect of early delivery of benefit checks. For purposes of subsection (a), in any case where section 708 of the Social Security Act causes social security benefit checks to be delivered before the end of the calendar month for which they are issued, the benefits involved shall be deemed to have been received in the succeeding calendar month.

(e) Limitation on amount included where taxpayer receives lump-sum payment.

(1) Limitation. If—

(A) any portion of a lump-sum payment of social security benefits received during the taxable year is attributable to prior taxable years, and

(B) the taxpayer makes an election under this subsection for the taxable year,

then the amount included in gross income under this section for the taxable year by reason of the receipt of such portion shall not exceed the sum of the increases in gross income under this chapter for prior taxable years which would result solely from taking into account such portion in the taxable years to which it is attributable.

(2) Special rules.

(A) Year to which benefit attributable. For purposes of this subsection, a social security benefit is attributable to a taxable year if the generally applicable payment date for such benefit occurred during such taxable year.

(B) Election. An election under this subsection shall be made at such time and in such manner as the Secretary shall by regulations prescribe. Such election, once made, may be revoked only with the consent of the Secretary.

(f) Treatment as pension or annuity for certain purposes. For purposes of—

(1) section 22(c)(3)(A) (relating to reduction for amounts received as pension or annuity),

(2) section 32(c)(2) (defining earned income),

(3) section 219(f)(1) (defining compensation), and

(4) section 911(b)(1) (defining foreign earned income),

any social security benefit shall be treated as an amount received as a pension or annuity.

* * *

Part III— Items Specifically Excluded From Gross Income

* * *

SEC. 101. CERTAIN DEATH BENEFITS

(a) Proceeds of life insurance contracts payable by reason of death.—

(1) General rule.— Except as otherwise provided in paragraph (2), subsection (d), and subsection (f), gross income does not include amounts received (whether in a single sum or otherwise) under a life insurance contract, if such amounts are paid by reason of the death of the insured.

(2) Transfer for valuable consideration.— In the case of a transfer for a valuable consideration, by assignment or otherwise, of a life insurance contract or any interest therein, the amount excluded from gross income by paragraph (1) shall not exceed an amount equal to the sum of the actual value of such consideration and the premiums and other amounts subsequently paid by the transferee. The preceding sentence shall not apply in the case of such a transfer—

(A) if such contract or interest therein has a basis for determining gain or loss in the hands of a transferee determined in whole or in part by reference to such basis of such contract or interest therein in the hands of the transferor, or

(B) if such transfer is to the insured, to a partner of the insured, to a partnership in which the insured is a partner, or to a corporation in which the insured is a shareholder or officer.

(b) Employees' death benefits.—

(1) General rule.— Gross income does not include amounts received (whether in a single sum or otherwise) by the beneficiaries or the estate of an employee, if such amounts are paid by or on behalf of an employer and are paid by reason of the death of the employee.

(2) Special rules for paragraph (1).—

(A) $5,000 limitation.— The aggregate amounts excludable under paragraph (1) with respect to the death of any employee shall not exceed $5,000.

(B) Nonforfeitable rights.— Paragraph (1) shall not apply to amounts with respect to which the employee possessed, immediately before his death, a nonforfeitable right to receive the amounts while living. This subparagraph shall not apply to a lump sum distribution (as defined in section 402(e)(4))—

(i) by a stock bonus, pension, or profit-sharing trust described in section 401(a) which is exempt from tax under section 501(a),

(ii) under an annuity contract under a plan described in section 403(a), or

(iii) under an annuity contract purchased by an employer which is an organization referred to in section 170(b)(1)(A) (ii) or (vi) or which is a religious organization (other than a trust) and which is exempt from tax under section 501(a), but only with respect to the portion of such total distributions payable which bears the same ratio to the amount of such total distributions payable which is (without regard to this subsection) includible in gross income, as the amounts contributed by the employer for such annuity contract which are excludable from gross income under section 403(b) bear to the total amounts contributed by the employer for such annuity contract.

(C) Joint and survivor annuities.— Paragraph (1) shall not apply to amounts received by a surviving annuitant under a joint and survivor's annuity contract after the first day of the first period for which an amount was received as an annuity by the employee (or would have been received if the employee had lived).

(D) Other annuities.— In the case of any amount to which section 72 (relating to annuities, etc.) applies, the amount which is excludable under paragraph (1) (as modified by the preceding subparagraphs of this paragraph) shall be determined by reference to the value of such amount as of the day on which the employee died. Any amount so excludable under paragraph (1) shall, for purposes of section 72, be treated as additional consideration paid by the employee. Paragraph (1) shall not apply in the case of an annuity under chapter 73 of title 10 of the United States Code if the member or former member of the uniformed services by reason of whose death such annuity is payable died after attaining retirement age.

(3) Treatment of self-employed individuals.— For purposes of this subsection—

(A) Self-employed individual not considered employee.— Except as provided in subparagraph (B), the term "employee" does not include a self-employed individual described in section 401(c)(1).

(B) Special rule for certain distributions.— In the case of any amount paid or distributed—

(i) by a trust described in section 401(a) which is exempt from tax under section 501(a), or

(ii) under a plan described in section 403(a),

the term "employee" includes a self-employed individual described in section 401(c)(1).

(c) Interest.— If any amount excluded from gross income by subsection (a) or (b) is held under an agreement to pay interest thereon, the interest payments shall be included in gross income.

(d) Payment of life insurance proceeds at a date later than death.—

(1) General rule.— The amounts held by an insurer with respect to any beneficiary shall be prorated (in accordance with such regulations as may be prescribed by the Secretary) over the period or periods with respect to which such payments are to be made. There shall be excluded from the gross income of such beneficiary in the taxable year received any amount determined by such proration. Gross income includes, to the extent not excluded by the preceding sentence, amounts received under agreements to which this subsection applies.

(2) Amount held by an insurer.— An amount held by an insurer with respect to any beneficiary shall mean an amount to which subsection (a) applies which is—

(A) held by any insurer under an agreement provided for in the life insurance contract, whether as an option or otherwise, to pay such amount on a date or dates later than the death of the insured, and

(B) equal to the value of such agreement to such beneficiary—

(i) as of the date of death of the insured (as if any option exercised under the life insurance contract were exercised at such time), and

(ii) as discounted on the basis of the interest rate used by the insurer in calculating payments under the agreement and mortality tables prescribed by the Secretary.

(3) Application of subsection.— This subsection shall not apply to any amount to which subsection (c) is applicable.

(e) [Repealed.]

(f) Proceeds of flexible premium contracts issued before January 1, 1985 payable by reason of death.—

(1) In general.— Any amount paid by reason of the death of the insured under a flexible premium life insurance contract issued before January 1, 1985 shall be excluded from gross income only if—

(A) under such contract—

(i) the sum of the premiums paid under such contract does not at any time exceed the guideline premium limitation as of such time, and

(ii) any amount payable by reason of the death of the insured (determined without regard to any qualified additional benefit) is not at any time less than the applicable percentage of the cash value of such contract at such time, or

(B) by the terms of such contract, the cash value of such contract may not at any time exceed the net single premium with respect to the amount payable by reason of the death of the insured (determined without regard to any qualified additional benefit) at such time.

(2) Guideline premium limitation.— For purposes of this subsection—

(A) Guideline premium limitation.— The term ''guideline premium limitation'' means, as of any date, the greater of—

(i) the guideline single premium, or

(ii) the sum of the guideline level premiums to such date.

(B) Guideline single premium.— The term ''guideline single premium'' means the premium at issue with respect to future benefits under the contract (without regard to any qualified additional benefit), and with respect to any charges for qualified additional benefits, at the time of a determination under subparagraph (A) or (E) and which is based on—

(i) the mortality and other charges guaranteed under the contract, and

(ii) interest at the greater of an annual effective rate of 6 percent or the minimum rate or rates guaranteed upon issue of the contract.

(C) Guideline level premium.— The term

''guideline level premium'' means the level annual amount, payable over the longest period permitted under the contract (but ending not less than 20 years from date of issue or not later than age 95, if earlier), computed on the same basis as the guideline single premium, except that subparagraph (B)(ii) shall be applied by substituting ''4 percent'' for ''6 percent''.

(D) Computational rules.— In computing the guideline single premium or guideline level premium under subparagraph (B) or (C)—

(i) the excess of the amount payable by reason of the death of the insured (determined without regard to any qualified additional benefit) over the cash value of the contract shall be deemed to be not greater than such excess at the time the contract was issued,

(ii) the maturity date shall be the latest maturity date permitted under the contract, but not less than 20 years after the date of issue or (if earlier) age 95, and

(iii) the amount of any endowment benefit (or sum of endowment benefits) shall be deemed not to exceed the least amount payable by reason of the death of the insured (determined without regard to any qualified additional benefit) at any time under the contract.

(E) Adjustments.— The guideline single premium and guideline level premium shall be adjusted in the event of a change in the future benefits or any qualified additional benefit under the contract which was not reflected in any guideline single premiums or guideline level premium previously determined.

(3) Other definitions and special rules.— For purposes of this subsection—

(A) Flexible premium life insurance contract.— The terms ''flexible premium life insurance contract'' and ''contract'' mean a life insurance contract (including any qualified additional benefits) which provides for

IRC Sec. 101 (f)(3)(A)

the payment of one or more premiums which are not fixed by the insurer as to both timing and amount. Such terms do not include that portion of any contract which is treated under State law as providing any annuity benefits other than as a settlement option.

(B) Premiums paid.— The term "premiums paid" means the premiums paid under the contract less any amounts (other than amounts includible in gross income) to which section 72(e) applies. If, in order to comply with the requirements of paragraph (1)(A), any portion of any premium paid during any contract year is returned by the insurance company (with interest) within 60 days after the end of a contract year—

(i) the amount so returned (excluding interest) shall be deemed to reduce the sum of the premiums paid under the contract during such year, and

(ii) notwithstanding the provisions of section 72(e), the amount of any interest so returned shall be includible in the gross income of the recipient.

(C) Applicable percentage.— The term "applicable percentage" means—

(i) 140 percent in the case of an insured with an attained age at the beginning of the contract year of 40 or less, and

(ii) in the case of an insured with an attained age of more than 40 as of the beginning of the contract year, 140 percent reduced (but not below 105 percent) by one percent for each year in excess of 40.

(D) Cash value.— The cash value of any contract shall be determined without regard to any deduction for any surrender charge or policy loan.

(E) Qualified additional benefits.— The term "qualified additional benefits" means any—

(i) guaranteed insurability,

(ii) accidental death benefit,

(iii) family term coverage, or

(iv) waiver of premium.

(F) Premium payments not disqualifying contract.— The payment of a premium which would result in the sum of the premiums paid exceeding the guideline premium limitation shall be disregarded for purposes of paragraph (1)(A)(i) if the amount of such premium does not exceed the amount necessary to prevent the termination of the contract without cash value on or before the end of the contract year.

(G) Net single premium.— In computing the net single premium under paragraph (1)(B)—

(i) the mortality basis shall be that guaranteed under the contract (determined by reference to the most recent mortality table allowed under all State laws on the date of issuance),

(ii) interest shall be based on the greater of—

(I) an annual effective rate of 4 percent (3 percent for contracts issued before July 1, 1983), or

(II) the minimum rate or rates guaranteed upon issue of the contract, and

(iii) the computational rules of paragraph (2)(D) shall apply, except that the maturity date referred to in clause (ii) thereof shall not be earlier than age 95.

(H) Correction of errors.— If the taxpayer establishes to the satisfaction of the Secretary that—

(i) the requirements described in paragraph (1) for any contract year was not satisfied due to reasonable error, and

(ii) reasonable steps are being taken to remedy the error,

the Secretary may waive the failure to satisfy such requirements.

(I) Regulations.— The Secretary shall prescribe such regulations as may be necessary or appropriate to carry out the purposes of this subsection.

* * *

SEC. 104. COMPENSATION FOR INJURIES OR SICKNESS.

(a) In general.— Except in the case of amounts attributable to (and not in excess of) deductions allowed under section 213 (relating to medical, etc., expenses) for any prior taxable year, gross income does not include—

(1) amounts received under workmen's compensation acts as compensation for personal injuries or sickness;

(2) the amount of any damages received (whether by suit or agreement and whether as lump sums or as periodic payments) on account of personal injuries or sickness;

(3) amounts received through accident or health insurance for personal injuries or sickness (other than amounts received by an employee, to the extent such amounts (A) are attributable to contributions by the employer which were not includible in the gross income of the employee, or (B) are paid by the employer);

(4) amounts received as a pension, annuity, or similar allowance for personal injuries or sickness resulting from active service in the armed forces of any country or in the Coast and Geodetic Survey or the Public Health Service, or as a disability annuity payable under the provisions of section 808 of the Foreign Service Act of 1980; and

(5) amounts received by an individual as disability income attributable to injuries incurred as a direct result of a violent attack which the Secretary of State determines to be a terrorist attack and which occurred while such individual was an employee of the United States engaged in the performance of his official duties outside the United States.

For purposes of paragraph (3), in the case of an individual who is, or has been, an employee within the meaning of section 401(c)(1) (relating to self-employed individuals), contributions made on behalf of such individual while he was such an employee to a trust described in section 401(a) which is exempt from tax under section 501(a), or under a plan described in section 403(a), shall, to the extent allowed as deductions under section 404, be treated as contributions by the employer which were not includible in the gross income of the employee. Paragraph (2) shall not apply to any punitive damages in connection with a case not involving physical injury or physical sickness.

(b) Termination of application of subsection (a)(4) in certain cases.—

(1) In general.— Subsection (a)(4) shall not apply in the case of any individual who is not described in paragraph (2).

(2) Individuals to whom subsection (a)(4) continues to apply.— An individual is described in this paragraph if—

(A) on or before September 24, 1975, he was entitled to receive any amount described in subsection (a)(4),

(B) on September 24, 1975, he was a member of any organization (or reserve component thereof) referred to in subsection (a)(4) or under a binding written commitment to become such a member,

(C) he receives an amount described in subsection (a)(4) by reason of a combat-related injury, or

(D) on application therefor, he would be entitled to receive disability compensation from the Veterans' Administration.

(3) Special rules for combat-related injuries.— For purposes of this subsection, the term "combat-related injury" means personal injury or sickness—

(A) which is incurred—

(i) as a direct result of armed conflict,

(ii) while engaged in extrahazardous service, or

(iii) under conditions simulating war; or

(B) which is caused by an instrumentality of war.

In the case of an individual who is not described in subparagraph (A) or (B) of paragraph (2), except as provided in paragraph (4), the only amounts taken into account under subsection (a)(4) shall be the amounts which he receives by reason of a combat-related injury.

(4) Amount excluded to be not less than veterans' disability compensation.— In the case of any individual described in paragraph (2), the amounts excludable under subsection (a)(4) for any period with respect to any individual shall not be less than the maximum amount which such individual, on application therefor, would be entitled to receive as disability compensation from the Veterans' Administration.

(c) Cross references.—

(1) For exclusion from employee's gross income of employer contributions to accident and health plans, see section 106.

(2) For exclusion of part of disability retirement pay from the application of subsection (a)(4) of this section, see section 1403 of title 10, United States Code (relating to career compensation laws).

SEC. 105. AMOUNTS RECEIVED UNDER ACCIDENT AND HEALTH PLANS.

(a) Amounts Attributable to Employer Contributions.— Except as otherwise provided in this section, amounts received by an employee through accident or health insurance for personal injuries or sickness shall be included in gross income to the extent such amounts (1) are attributable to contributions by the employer which were not includible in the gross income of the employee, or (2) are paid by the employer.

(b) Amounts Expended for Medical Care.— Except in the case of amounts attributable to (and not in excess of) deductions allowed under section 213 (relating to medical, etc., expenses) for any prior taxable year, gross income does not include amounts referred to in subsection (a) if such amounts are paid, directly or indirectly, to the taxpayer to reimburse the taxpayer for expenses incurred by him for the medical care (as defined in section 213(d)) of the taxpayer, his spouse, and his dependents (as defined in section 152). Any child to whom section 152(e) applies shall be treated as a dependent of both parents for purposes of this subsection.

(c) Payments Unrelated to Absence from Work.— Gross income does not include amounts referred to in subsection (a) to the extent such amounts—

(1) constitute payment for the permanent loss of use of a member or function of the body, or the permanent disfigurement, of the taxpayer, his spouse, or a dependent (as defined in section 152), and

(2) are computed with reference to the nature of the injury without regard to the period the employee is absent from work.

(d) [Repealed.]

(e) Accident and Health Plans.— For purposes of this section and section 104—

(1) amounts received under an accident or health plan for employees, and

(2) amounts received from a sickness and disability fund for employees maintained under the law of a State, or the District of Columbia,

shall be treated as amounts received through accident or health insurance.

(f) Rules for Application of Section 213.— For purposes of section 213(a) (relating to medical, dental, etc., expenses) amounts excluded from gross income under subsection (c) or (d) shall not be considered as compensation (by insurance or otherwise) for expenses paid for medical care.

(g) Self-Employed Individual Not Considered an Employee.— For purposes of this section, the term "employee" does not include an individual who is an employee within the meaning of section 401(c)(1) (relating to self-employed individuals).

(h) Amount Paid to Highly Compensated Individual Under a Discriminatory Self-Insured Medical Expense Reimbursement Plan.—

(1) In general.— In the case of amounts paid to a highly compensated individual under a self-insured medical reimbursement plan which does not satisfy the requirements of paragraph (2) for a plan year, subsection (b) shall not apply to such amounts to the extent they constitute an excess reimbursement of such highly compensated individual.

(2) Prohibition of discrimination.— A self-insured medical reimbursement plan satisfies the requirements of this paragraph only if—

(A) the plan does not discriminate in favor of highly compensated individuals as to eligibility to participate; and

(B) the benefits provided under the plan do not discriminate in favor of participants who are highly compensated individuals.

(3) Nondiscriminatory eligibility classification.—

(A) In general.— A self-insured medical reimbursement plan does not satisfy the requirements of subparagraph (A) of paragraph (2) unless such plan benefits—

(i) 70 percent or more of all employees, or 80 percent or more of all the employees who are eligible to benefit under the plan if 70 percent or more of all employees are eligible to benefit under the plan; or

(ii) such employees as qualify under a classification set up by the employer and found by the Secretary not to be discriminatory in favor of highly compensated individuals.

(B) Exclusion of certain employees.— For purposes of subparagraph (A), there may be excluded from consideration—

(i) employees who have not completed 3 years of service;

(ii) employees who have not attained age 25;

(iii) part-time or seasonal employees;

(iv) employees not included in the plan who are included in a unit of employees covered by an agreement between employee representatives and one or more employers which the Secretary finds to be a collective bargaining agreement, if accident and health benefits were the subject of good faith bargaining between such employee representatives and such employer or employers; and

(v) employees who are nonresident aliens and who receive no earned income (within the meaning of section 911(d)(2)) from the employer which constitutes income from sources within the United States (within the meaning of section 861(a)(3)).

(4) Nondiscriminatory benefits.— A self-insured medical reimbursement plan does not meet the requirements of subparagraph (B) of paragraph (2) unless all benefits provided for participants who are highly compensated individuals are provided for all other participants.

(5) Highly compensated individual defined.— For purposes of this subsection, the term "highly compensated individual" means an individual who is—

IRC Sec. 105 (h)(5)

(A) one of the 5 highest paid officers,

(B) a shareholder who owns (with the application of section 318) more than 10 percent in value of the stock of the employer, or

(C) among the highest paid 25 percent of all employees (other than employees described in paragraph (3)(B) who are not participants).

(6) Self-insured medical reimbursement plan.— The term ''self-insured medical reimbursement plan'' means a plan of an employer to reimburse employees for expenses referred to in subsection (b) for which reimbursement is not provided under a policy of accident or health insurance.

(7) Excess reimbursement of a highly compensated individual.— For purposes of this section, the excess reimbursement of a highly compensated individual which is attributable to a self-insured medical reimbursement plan is—

(A) in the case of a benefit available to highly compensated individuals but not to all other participants (or which otherwise fails to satisfy the requirements of paragraph (2)(B)), the amount reimbursed under the plan to the employee with respect to such benefit, and

(B) in the case of benefits (other than benefits described in subparagraph (A)) paid to a highly compensated individual by a plan which fails to satisfy the requirements of paragraph (2), the total amount reimbursed to the highly compensated individual for the plan year, multiplied by fraction—

(i) the numerator of which is the total amount reimbursed to all participants who are highly compensated individuals under the plan for the plan year, and

(ii) the denominator of which is the total amount reimbursed to all employees under the plan for such plan year.

(8) Certain controlled groups, etc.— All employees who are treated as employed by a

single employer under subsection (b), (c), or (m) of section 414 shall be treated as employed by a single employer for purposes of this section.

(9) Regulation.— The Secretary shall prescribe such regulations as may be necessary to carry out the provisions of this section.

(10) Time of inclusion.— Any amount paid for a plan year that is included in income by reason of this subsection shall be treated as received or accrued in the taxable year of the participant in which the plan year ends.

(i) Sick Pay Under Railroad Unemployment Insurance Act.—Notwithstanding any other provision of law, gross income includes benefits paid under section 2(a) of the Railroad Unemployment Insurance Act for days of sickness; except to the extent such sickness (as determined in accordance with standards prescribed by the Railroad Retirement Board) is the result of on-the-job injury.

SEC. 106. CONTRIBUTIONS BY EMPLOYER TO ACCIDENT AND HEALTH PLANS.

Gross income of an employee does not include employer-provided coverage under an accident or health plan.

* * *

SEC. 117. QUALIFIED SCHOLARSHIPS.

(a) General rule.— Gross income does not include any amount received as a qualified scholarship by an individual who is a candidate for a degree at an educational organization described in section 170(b)(1)(A)(ii).

(b) Qualified scholarship.—For purposes of this section—

(1) In general.— The term ''qualified scholarship'' means any amount received by an individual as a scholarship or fellowship grant to the extent the individual establishes that, in accordance with the conditions of the grant, such amount was used for qualified tuition and related expenses.

(2) Qualified tuition and related expenses.— For purposes of paragraph (1), the term "qualified tuition and related expenses" means—

(A) tuition and fees required for the enrollment or attendance of a student at an educational organization described in section 170(b)(1)(A)(ii), and

(B) fees, books, supplies, and equipment required for courses of instruction at such an educational organization.

(c) Limitation.— Subsections (a) and (d) shall not apply to that portion of any amount received which represents payment for teaching, research, or other services by the student required as a condition for receiving the qualified scholarship or qualified tuition reduction.

(d) Qualified tuition reduction.—

(1) In general.— Gross income shall not include any qualified tuition reduction.

(2) Qualified tuition reduction.— For purposes of this subsection, the term "qualified tuition reduction" means the amount of any reduction in tuition provided to an employee of an organization described in section 170(b)(1)(A)(ii) for the education (below the graduate level) at such organization (or another organization described in section 170(b)(1)(A)(ii)) of—

(A) such employee, or

(B) any person treated as an employee (or whose use is treated as an employee use) under the rules of section 132(f).

(3) Reduction must not discriminate in favor of highly compensated, etc.— Paragraph (1) shall apply with respect to any qualified tuition reduction provided with respect to any highly compensated employee only if such reduction is available on substantially the same terms to each member of a group of employees which is defined under a reasonable classification set up by the employer which does not discriminate in favor of highly compensated employees (within the meaning of section 414(q)). For purposes of this paragraph, the term "highly compensated employee" has the meaning given such term by section 414(q).

◊ ◊ ◊

Editor's Note: Paragraph (5) of Subsection 117(d), below, appears as such in the original. However, it probably should have been renumbered paragraph (4).

◊ ◊ ◊

(5) Special rules for teaching and research assistants.— In the case of the education of an individual who is a graduate student at an educational organization described in section 170(b)(1)(A)(ii) and who is engaged in teaching or research activities for such organization, paragraph (2) shall be applied as if it did not contain the phrase "(below the graduate level)".

* * *

SEC. 119. MEALS OR LODGING FURNISHED FOR THE CONVENIENCE OF THE EMPLOYER.

(a) Meals and lodging furnished to employee, his spouse, and his dependents pursuant to employment.— There shall be excluded from gross income of an employee the value of any meals or lodging furnished to him, his spouse, or any of his dependents by or on behalf of his employer for the convenience of the employer, but only if—

(1) in the case of meals, the meals are furnished on the business premises of the employer, or

(2) in the case of lodging, the employee is required to accept such lodging on the business premises of his employer as a condition of his employment.

(b) Special rules.— For purposes of subsection (a)—

(1) Provisions of employment contract or State statute not to be determinative.— In determining whether meals or lodging are furnished for the convenience of the employer, the provisions of an employment contract or of a State statute fixing terms of employment shall not be determinative of whether the meals or lodging are intended as compensation.

(2) Certain factors not taken into account with respect to meals.— In determining whether meals are furnished for the convenience of the employer, the fact that a charge is made for such meals, and the fact that the employee may accept or decline such meals, shall not be taken into account.

(3) Certain fixed charges for meals.—

(A) In general.— If—

(i) an employee is required to pay on a periodic basis a fixed charge for his meals, and

(ii) such meals are furnished by the employer for the convenience of the employer,

there shall be excluded from the employee's gross income an amount equal to such fixed charge.

(B) Application of subparagraph (A).— Subparagraph (A) shall apply—

(i) whether the employee pays the fixed charge out of his stated compensation or out of his own funds, and

(ii) only if the employee is required to make the payment whether he accepts or declines the meals.

(c) Employees living in certain camps.—

(1) In general.— In the case of an individual who is furnished lodging in a camp located in a foreign country by or on behalf of his employer, such camp shall be considered to be part of the business premises of the employer.

(2) Camp.— For purposes of this section, a camp constitutes lodging which is—

(A) provided by or on behalf of the employer for the convenience of the employer because the place at which such individual renders services is in a remote area where satisfactory housing is not available on the open market,

(B) located, as near as practicable, in the vicinity of the place at which such individual renders services, and

(C) furnished in a common area (or enclave) which is not available to the public and which normally accommodates 10 or more employees.

(d) Lodging furnished by certain educational institutions to employees.—

(1) In general.— In the case of an employee of an educational institution, gross income shall not include the value of qualified campus lodging furnished to such employee during the taxable year.

(2) Exception in cases of inadequate rent.— Paragraph (1) shall not apply to the extent of the excess of—

(A) the lesser of—

(i) 5 percent of the appraised value of the qualified campus lodging, or

(ii) the average of the rentals paid by individuals (other than employees or students of the educational institution) during such calendar year for lodging provided by the educational institution which is comparable to the qualified campus lodging provided to the employee, over

(B) the rent paid by the employee for the qualified campus lodging during such calendar year.

The appraised value under subparagraph (A)(i) shall be determined as of the close of the calendar year in which the taxable year begins, or, in the case of a rental period not greater than 1 year, at any time during the calendar year in which such period begins.

(3) Qualified campus lodging.— For purposes of this subsection, the term "qualified campus lodging" means lodging to which subsection (a) does not apply and which is—

(A) located on, or in the proximity of, a campus of the educational institution, and

(B) furnished to the employee, his spouse, and any of his dependents by or on behalf of such institution for use as a residence.

(4) Educational institution.— For purposes of this paragraph, the term "educational institution" means an institution described in section 170(b)(1)(A)(ii).

SEC. 120. AMOUNTS RECEIVED UNDER QUALIFIED GROUP LEGAL SERVICES PLANS.

(a) Exclusion by Employee for Contributions and Legal Services Provided by Employer.— Gross income of an employee, his spouse, or his dependents, does not include

(1) amounts contributed by an employer on behalf of an employee, his spouse, or his dependent under a qualified group legal services plan (as defined in subsection (b)); or

(2) the value of legal service provided, or amounts paid for legal services, under a qualified group legal services plan (as defined in subsection (b)) to, or with respect to, an employee, his spouse, or his dependents.

No exclusion shall be allowed under this section with respect to an individual for any taxable year to the extent that the value of insurance (whether through an insurer or self-insurance) against legal costs incurred by the individual (or his spouse or dependents) provided under a qualified group legal services plan exceeds $70.

(b) Qualified Group Legal Services Plan.— For purposes of this section, a qualified group legal services plan is a separate written plan of an employer for the exclusive benefit of his employees or their spouses or dependents to provide such employees, spouse, or dependents with specified benefits consisting of personal legal services through prepayment of, or provision in advance for, legal fees in whole or in part by the employer, if the plan meets the requirements of subsection (c).

(c) Requirements.—

(1) Discrimination.— The contributions or benefits provided under the plan shall not discriminate in favor of employees who are highly compensated employees (within the meaning of section 414(q)).

(2) Eligibility.— The plan shall benefit employees who qualify under a classification set up by the employer and found by the Secretary not to be discriminatory in favor of employees who are described in paragraph (1). For purposes of this paragraph, there shall be excluded from consideration employees not included in the plan who are included in a unit of employees covered by an agreement which the Secretary of Labor finds to be a collective bargaining agreement between employee representatives and one or more employers, if there is evidence that group legal services plan benefits were the subject of good faith bargaining between such employee representatives and such employer or employers.

(3) Contribution Limitation.— Not more than 25 percent of the amounts contributed under the plan during the year may be provided for the class of individuals who are shareholders or owners (or their spouses or dependents), each of whom (on any day of the year) owns more than 5 percent of the stock or of the capital or profits interest in the employer.

(4) Notification.— The plan shall give notice to the Secretary, in such manner as the Secretary may by regulations prescribe, that it is applying for recognition of the status of a qualified group legal services plan.

(5) Contributions.— Amounts contributed under the plan shall be paid only (A) to insurance companies, or to organizations or persons that provide personal legal services, or indemnification against the cost of personal legal services, in exchange for a prepayment or a payment of a premium, (B) to organizations or trusts described in section 501(c)(20), (C) to organizations described in section 501(c) which are permitted by that section to receive payments from an employer for support of one or more qualified group legal services plan or plans, except that such organizations shall pay or credit the contribution to an organization or trust described in section 501(c)(20), (D) as prepayments to providers of legal services under the plan, or (E) a combination of the above.

(d) Other Definitions and Special Rules.— For purposes of this section

(1) Employee.— The term "employee" includes, for any year, an individual who is an employee within the meaning of section 401(c)(1) (relating to self-employed individuals).

(2) Employer.— An individual who owns the entire interest in an unincorporated trade or business shall be treated as his own employer. A parnership shall be treated as the employer of each partner who is an employee within the meaning of paragraph (1).

(3) Allocations.— Allocations of amounts contributed under the plan shall be made in accordance with regulations prescribed by the Secretary and shall take into account the expected relative utilization of benefits to be provided from such contributions or plan assets and the manner in which any premium or other charge was developed.

(4) Dependent.— The term "dependent" has the meaning given to it by section 152.

(5) Exclusive benefit.— In the case of a plan to which contributions are made by more than one employer, in determining whether the plan is for the exclusive benefit of an employer's employees or their spouses or dependents, the employees of any empoyer who maintains the plan shall be considered to be

the employees of each employer who maintains the plan.

(6) Attribution rules.— For purposes of this section—

(A) ownership of stock in a corporation shall be determined in accordance with the rules and provided under subsections (d) and (e) of section 1563 (without regard to section 1563(e)(3)(C)), and

(B) the interest of an employee in a trade or business which is not incorporated shall be determined in accordance with regulations prescribed by the Secretary, which shall be based on principles similar to the principles which apply in the case of subparagraph (A).

(7) Time of notice to secretary.— A plan shall not be a qualified group legal services plan for any period prior to the time notification was provided to the Secretary in accordance with subsection (c)(4), if such notice is given after the time prescribed by the Secretary by regulations for giving such notice.

(e) Termination.— This section and section 501(c)(20) shall not apply to taxable years beginning after June 30, 1992.

* * *

SEC. 122. CERTAIN REDUCED UNIFORMED SERVICES RETIREMENT PAY.

(a) General rule.— In the case of a member or former member of the uniformed services of the United States, gross income does not include the amount of any reduction in his retired or retainer pay pursuant to the provisions of chapter 73 of title 10, United States Code.

(b) Special rule.—

(1) Amount excluded from gross income.— In the case of any individual referred to in subsection (a), all amounts received after December 31, 1965, as retired or retainer pay shall be excluded from gross income until there has been so excluded an amount equal to the consideration for the contract. The preceding sentence shall apply only to the extent that the amounts received would, but for such sentence, be includible in gross income.

(2) Consideration for the contract.— For purposes of paragraph (1) and section 72(n), the term "consideration for the contract" means, in respect of any individual, the sum of—

(A) the total amount of the reductions before January 1, 1966, in his retired or retainer pay by reason of an election under chapter 73 of title 10 of the United States Code, and

(B) any amounts deposited at any time by him pursuant to section 1438 or 1452(d) of such title 10.

* * *

SEC. 125. CAFETERIA PLANS.

(a) In General.— Except as provided in subsection (b), no amount shall be included in the gross income of a participant in a cafeteria plan solely because, under the plan, the participant may choose among the benefits of the plan.

(b) Exception for Highly Compensated Participants and Key Employees.—

(1) Highly compensated participants.— In the case of a highly compensated participant, subsection (a) shall not apply to any benefit attributable to a plan year for which the plan discriminates in favor of—

(A) highly compensated individuals as to eligibility to participate, or

(B) highly compensated participants as to contributions and benefits.

(2) Key employees.— In the case of a key employee (within the meaning of section 416(i)(1)), subsection (a) shall not apply to any benefit attributable to a plan for which the statutory nontaxable benefits provided to key employees exceed 25 percent of the aggregate of such benefits provided for all employees under the plan.

For purposes of the preceding sentence, statutory nontaxable benefits shall be determined without regard to the last sentence of subsection (f).

(3) Years of inclusion.— For purposes of determining the taxable year of inclusion, any benefit described in paragraph (1) or (2) shall be treated as received or accrued in the taxable year of the participant or key employee in which the plan year ends.

(c) Discrimination as to Benefits or Contributions.— For purposes of subparagraph (B) of subsection (b)(1), a cafeteria plan does not discriminate where qualified benefits and total benefits (or employer contributions allocable to qualified benefits and employer contributions for total benefits) do not discriminate in favor of highly compensated participants.

(d) Cafeteria Plan Defined.— For purposes of this section.—

(1) In general.— The term "cafeteria plan" means a written plan under which—

(A) all participants are employees, and

(B) the participants may choose among 2 or more benefits consisting of cash and qualified benefits.

(2) Deferred compensation plans excluded.—

(A) In general.—The term "cafeteria plan" does not include any plan which provides for deferred compensation.

(B) Exception for cash and deferred arrangements.— Subparagraph (A) shall not apply to a profit-sharing or stock bonus plan or rural cooperative plan (within the meaning of section 401(k)(7)) which includes a qualified cash or deferred arrangement (as defined in section 401(k)(2)) to the extent of amounts which a covered employee may elect to have the employer pay as contributions to a trust under such plan on behalf of the employee.

(C) Exception for certain plans maintained by educational institutions.—Subparagraph (A) shall not apply to a plan maintained by an educational organization described in section 170(b)(1)(A)(ii) to the extent of amounts which a covered employee may elect to have the employer pay as contributions for post-retirement group life insurance if—

(i) all contributions for such insurance must be made before retirement, and

(ii) such life insurance does not have a cash surrender value at any time. For purposes of section 79, any life insurance described in the preceding sentence shall be treated as group-term life insurance.

(e) Highly Compensated Participant and Individual Defined.— For purposes of this section—

(1) Highly compensated participant.— The term "highly compensated participant" means a participant who is—

(A) an officer,

(B) a shareholder owning more than 5 percent of the voting power or value of all classes of stock of the employer,

(C) highly compensated, or

(D) a spouse or dependent (within the meaning of section 152) of an individual described in subparagraph (A), (B), or (C).

(2) Highly compensated individual.— The term "highly compensated individual" means an individual who is described in subparagraph (A), (B), (C), or (D) or paragraph (1).

(f) Qualified Benefits Defined.— For purposes of this section, the term "qualified benefit" means any benefit which, with the application of subsection (a), is not includible in the gross income of the employee by reason of an express provision of this chapter (other than section 117, 127, or 132). Such term includes any group term life insurance which

is includible in gross income only because it exceeds the dollar limitation of section 79 and such term includes any other benefit permitted under regulations.

(g) Special Rules.—

(1) Collectively bargained plans not considered discriminatory.— For purposes of this section, a plan shall not be treated as discriminatory if the plan is maintained under an agreement which the Secretary finds to be a collective bargaining agreement between employee representatives and one or more employers.

(2) Health benefits.—For purposes of subparagraph (B) of subsection (b)(1), a cafeteria plan which provides health benefits shall not be treated as discriminatory if—

(A) contributions under the plan on behalf of each participant include an amount which—

(i) equals 100 percent of the cost of the health benefit coverage under the plan of the majority of the highly compensated participants similarly situated, or

(ii) equals or exceeds 75 percent of the cost of the health benefit coverage of the participant (similarly situated) having the highest cost health benefit coverage under the plan, and

(B) contributions or benefits under the plan in excess of those described in subparagraph (A) bear a uniform relationship to compensation.

(3) Certain participation eligibility rules not treated as discriminatory.— For purposes of subparagraph (A) of subsection (b)(1), a classification shall not be treated as discriminatory if the plan—

(A) benefits a group of employees described in section 410(b)(2)(A)(i), and

(B) meets the requirements of clauses (i) and (ii):

(i) No employee is required to complete more than 3 years of employment with the employer or employers maintaining the plan as a condition of participation in the plan, and the employment requirements for each employee is the same.

(ii) Any employee who has satisfied the employment requirements of clause (i) and who is otherwise entitled to participate in the plan commences participation no later than the first day of the first plan year beginning after the date the employment requirement was satisfied unless the employee was separated from service before the first day of that plan year.

(4) Certain controlled groups, etc.— All employees who are treated as employed by a single employer under subsection (b), (c), or (m) of section 414 shall be treated as employed by a single employer for purposes of this section.

(h) Cross Reference.— For reporting and recordkeeping requirements, see section 6039D.

* * *

SEC. 127. EDUCATIONAL ASSISTANCE PROGRAMS.

(a) Exclusion From Gross Income.—

(1) In general.— Gross income of an employee does not include amounts paid or expenses incurred by the employer for educational assistance to the employee if the assistance is furnished pursuant to a program which is described in subsection (b).

(2) $5,250 maximum exclusion.— If, but for this paragraph, this section would exclude from gross income more than $5,250 of educational assistance furnished to an individual during a calendar year, this section shall apply only to the first $5,250 of such assistance so furnished.

(b) Educational Assistance Program.—

(1) In general.— For purposes of this seciton, an educational assistance program is a separate written plan of an employer for the exclusive benefit of his employees to provide such employees with educational assistance. The program must meet the requirements of paragraphs (2) through (6) of this subsection.

(2) Eligibility.— The program shall benefit employees who qualify under a classification set up by the employer and found by the Secretary not to be discriminatory in favor of employees who are highly compensated employees (within the meaning of section 414(q)) or their dependents. For purposes of this paragraph, there shall be excluded from consideration employees not included in the program who are included in a unit of employees covered by an agreement which the Secretary of Labor finds to be a collective bargaining agreement between employee representatives and one or more employers, if there is evidence that educational assistance benefits were the subject of good faith bargaining between such employee reprsentatives and such employer or employers.

(3) Principal shareholders or owners.— Not more than 5 percent of the amounts paid or incurred by the employer for educational assistance during the year may be provided for the class of individuals who are shareholders or owners (or their spouses or dependents), each of whom (on any day of the year) owns more than 5 percent of the stock or of the capital or profits interest in the employer.

(4) Other benefits as an alternative.— A program must not provide eligible employees with a choice between educational assistance and other remuneration includible in gross income. For purposes of this section, the business practices of the employer (as well as the written program) will be taken into account.

(5) No funding required.— A program referred to in paragraph (1) is not required to be funded.

(6) Notification of employees.— Reasonable notification of the availability and terms of the program must be provided to eligible employees.

(c) Definitions, Special Rules.— For purposes of this section

(1) Educational assistance.— The term "educational assistance" means—

(A) the payment, by an employer, of expenses incurred by or on behalf of an employee for education of the employee (including, but not limited to, tuition, fees, and similar payments, books, supplies, and equipment), and

(B) the provision, by an employer, of courses of instruction for such employee (including books, supplies, and equipment),but does not include payment for, or the provision of, tools or supplies which may be retained by the employee after completion of a course of instruction, or meals, lodging, or transportation. The term "educational assistance" also does not include any payment for, or the provisions of any benefits with respect to any course or other education involving sports, games, or hobbies.

(2) Employee.— The term "employee" includes, for any year, an individual who is an employee within the meaning of section 401(c)(1) (relating to self-employed individuals).

(3) Employer.— An individual who owns the entire interest in an unincorporated trade or business shall be treated as his own employer. A partnership shall be treated as the employer of each partner who is an employee within the meaning of paragraph (2).

(4) Attribution rules.—

(A) Ownership of stock.— Ownership of stock in a corporation shall be determined in accordance with the rules provided under subsections (d) and (e) of section 1563 (without regard to section 1563(e)(3)(C)).

(B) Interest in unincorporated trade or business.— The interest of an employee in a trade or business which is not incorporated shall be determined in accordance with

regulations prescribed by the Secretary, which shall be based on principles similar to principles which apply in the case of subparagraph (A).

(5) Certain tests not applicable.— An educational assistance program shall not be held or considered to fail to meet any requirements of subsection (b) merely because—

(A) of utilization rates for the different types of educational assistance made available under the program; or

(B) successful completion, or attaining a particular course grade, is required for or considered in determining reimbursement under the program.

(6) Relationship to current law.— This section shall not be construed to affect the deduction or inclusion in income of amounts (not within the exclusion under this section) which are paid or incurred, or received as reimbursement, for educational expenses under section 117, 162, or 212.

(7) Disallowance of excluded amounts as credit or deduction.— No deduction or credit shall be allowed to the employee under any other section of this chapter for any amount excluded from income by reason of this section.

(d) Termination.— This section shall not apply to taxable years beginning after December 31, 1994.

(e) Cross Reference.— For reporting and recordkeeping requirements, see section 6039D.

* * *

SEC. 129. DEPENDENT CARE ASSISTANCE PROGRAMS.

(a) Exclusion.—

(1) In general.— Gross income of an employee does not include amounts paid or incurred by the employer for dependent care assistance provided to such employee if the assistance is furnished pursuant to a program which is described in subsection (d).

(2) Limitation of exclusion.—

(A) In general.— The amount which may be excluded under paragraph (1) for dependent care assistance with respect to dependent care services provided during a taxable year shall not exceed $5,000 ($2,500 in the case of a separate return by a married individual).

(B) Year of inclusion.— The amount of any excess under subparagraph (A) shall be included in gross income in the taxable year in which the dependent care services were provided (even if payment of dependent care assistance for such services occurs in a subsequent taxable year).

(C) Marital status.— For purposes of this paragraph, marital status shall be determined under the rules of paragraphs (3) and (4) of section 21(e).

(b) Earned Income Limitation.—

(1) In general.— The amount excluded from the income of an employee under subsection (a) for any taxable year shall not exceed—

(A) in the case of an employee who is not married at the close of such taxable year, the earned income of such employee for such taxable year, or

(B) in the case of an employee who is married at the close of such taxable year, the lesser of—

(i) the earned income of such employee for such taxable year, or

(ii) the earned income of the spouse of such employee for such taxable year.

(2) Special rule for certain spouses.— For purposes of paragraph (1), the provisions of section 21(d)(2) shall apply in determining the earned income of a spouse who is a student or incapable of caring for himself.

(c) Payments to Related Individuals.— No amount paid or incurred during the taxable year of an employee by an employer in providing dependent care assistance to such employee shall be excluded under subsection (a) if such amount was paid or incurred to an individual—

(1) with respect to whom, for such taxable year, a deduction is allowable under section 151(c) (relating to personal exemptions for dependents) to such employee or the spouse of such employee, or

(2) who is a child of such employee (within the meaning of section 151(c)(3)) under the age of 19 at the close of such taxable year.

(d) Dependent Care Assistance Program.—

(1) In general.— For purposes of this section a dependent care assistance program is a separate written plan of an employer for the exclusive benefit of his employees to provide such employees with dependent care assistance which meets the requirements of paragraphs (2) through (8) of this subsection. If any plan would qualify as a dependent care assistance program but for a failure to meet the requirements of this subsection, then, notwithstanding such failure, such plan shall be treated as a dependent care assistance program in the case of employees who are not highly compensated employees.

(2) Discrimination.— The contributions or benefits provided under the plan shall not discriminate in favor of employees who are highly compensated employees (within the meaning of section 414(q) or their dependents.

(3) Eligibility.— The program shall benefit employees who qualify under a classification system set up by the employer and found by the Secretary not to be discriminatory in favor of employees described in paragraph (2), or their dependents.

(4) Principal shareholders or owners.— Not more than 25 percent of the amounts paid or incurred by the employer for dependent care assistance during the year may be pro-

IRC Sec. 129 (d)(4)

vided for the class of individuals who are shareholders or owners (or their spouses or dependents), each of whom (on any day of the year) owns more than 5 percent of the stock or of the capital or profits interest in the employer.

(5) No funding required.— A program referred to in paragraph (1) is not required to be funded.

(6) Notification of eligible employees.— Reasonable notification of the availability and terms of the program shall be provided to eligible employees.

(7) Statement of expenses.— The plan shall furnish to an employee, on or before January 31, a written statement showing the amounts paid or expenses incurred by the employer in providing dependent care assistance to such employee during the previous calendar year.

(8) Benefits.—

(A) In general.— A plan meets the requirements of this paragraph if the average benefits provided to employees who are not highly compensated is at least 55 percent of the average benefits provided to highly compensated employees.

(B) Salary reduction agreements.— For purposes of subparagraph (A), in the case of any benefits provided through a salary reduction agreement, there shall be disregarded any employees whose compensation (within the meaning of section 415(q)(7) is less than $25,000.

(9) Excluded employees.— For purposes of paragraphs (3) and (8), there shall be excluded from consideration—

(A) subject to rules similar to the rules of section 410(b)(4), employees who have not attained the age of 21 and completed 1 year of service (as defined in section 410(a)(3)), and

(B) employees not included in a dependent care assistance program who are included in

a unit of employees covered by an agreement which the Secretary finds to be a collective bargaining agreeement between employee representatives and 1 or more employers, if there is evidence that dependent care benefits were the subject of good faith bargaining between such employee representatives and such employer or employers.

(e) Definitions and Special Rules.— For purposes of this section—

(1) Dependent care assistance.— The term ''dependent care assistance'' means the payment of, or provision of, those services which if paid for by the employee would be considered employment-related expenses under section 21(b)(2) (relating to expenses for household and dependent care services necessary for gainful employment).

(2) Earned income.— The term ''earned income'' shall have the meaning given such term in section 32(c)(2), but such term shall not include any amounts paid or incurred by an employer for dependent care assistance to an employee.

(3) Employee.— The term ''employee'' includes, for any year, an individual who is an employee within the meaning of section 401(c)(1) (relating to self-employed individuals).

(4) Employer.— An individual who owns the entire interest in an unincorporated trade or business shall be treated as his own employer. A partnership shall be treated as the employer of each partner who is an employee within the meaning of paragraph (3).

(5) Attribution rules.—

(A) Ownership of stock.— Ownership of stock in a corporation shall be determined in accordance with the rules provided under subsections (d) and (e) of section 1563 (without regard to section 1563(e)(3)(C)).

(B) Interest in unincorporated trade or business.— The interest of an employee in a trade or business which is not incorporated shall be determined in accordance with regulations prescribed by the Secretary, which shall be based on principles similar to the principles which apply in the case of subparagraph (A).

(6) Utilization test not applicable.— A dependent care assistance program shall not be held or considered to fail to meet any requirements of subsection (d) (other than paragraphs (4) and (8) thereof) merely because of utilization rates for the different types of assistance made available under the program.

(7) Disallowance of excluded amounts as credit or deduction.— No deduction or credit shall be allowed to the employee under any other section of this chapter for any amount excluded from the gross income of the employee by reason of this section.

(8) Treatment of onsite facilities.— In the case of an onsite facility maintained by an employer, except to the extent provided in regulations, the amount of dependent care assistance provided to an employee excluded with respect to any dependent shall be based on—

(A) utilization of the facility by a dependent of the employee, and

(B) the value of the services provided with respect to such dependent.

* * *

SEC. 132. CERTAIN FRINGE BENEFITS.

(a) Exclusion from Gross Income.— Gross income shall not include any fringe benefit which qualifies as a—

(1) no-additional-cost service,

(2) qualified employee discount,

(3) working condition fringe,

(4) de minimis fringe,

(5) qualified transportation fringe or

(6) qualified moving expense reimbursement.

(b) No-Additional-Cost Service Defined.— For purposes of this section, the term "no-additional-cost service" means any service provided by an employer to an employee for use by such employee if—

(1) such service is offered for sale to customers in the ordinary course of the line of business by the employer in which the employee is performing services, and

(2) the employer incurs no substantial additional cost (including forgone revenue) in providing such service to the employee (determined without regard to any amount paid by the employee for such service).

(c) Qualified Employee Discount Defined.— For purposes of this section—

(1) Qualified employee discount.— The term "qualified employee discount" means any employee discount with respect to qualified property or services to the extent such discount does not exceed—

(A) in the case of property, the gross profit percentage of the price at which the property is being offered by the employer to customers, or

(B) in the case of services, 20 percent of the price at which the services are being offered by the employer to customers.

(2) Gross profit percentage.—

(A) In general.— The term "gross profit percentage" means the percent which—

(i) the excess of the aggregate sales price of property sold by the employer to customers over the aggregate cost of such property to the employer, is of—

(ii) the aggregate sale price of such property.

(B) Determination of gross profit percentage.— Gross profit percentage shall be determined on the basis of—

(i) all property offered to customers in the ordinary course of the line of business of the

IRC Sec. 132 (c)(2)(B)(i)

employer in which the employee is performing services (or a reasonable classification of property selected by the employer), and

(ii) the employer's experience during a representative period.

(3) Employee discount defined.— The term "employee discount" means the amount by which—

(A) the price at which the property or services are provided to an employee by the employer for use by such employee, is less than

(B) the price at which such property or services are being offered by the employer to customers.

(4) Qualified property or services.— The term "qualified property or services" means any property (other than real property and other than personal property of a kind held for investment) or services which are offered for sale to customers in the ordinary course of the line of business of the employer in which the employee is performing services.

(d) Working Condition Fringe Defined.— For purposes of this section, the term "working condition fringe" means any property or services provided to an employee of the employer to the extent that, if the employee paid for such property or services, such payment would be allowable as a deduction under section 162 or 167.

(e) De Minimis Fringe Defined.— For purposes of this section—

(1) In general.— The term "de minimis fringe" means any property or service the value of which is (after taking into account the frequency with which similar fringes are provided by the employer to the employer's employees) so small as to make accounting for it unreasonable or administratively impracticable.

(2) Treatment of certain eating facilities.— The operation by an employer of any eating facility for employees shall be treated as a de minimis fringe if—

(A) such facility is located on or near the business premises of the employer, and

(B) revenue derived from such facility normally equals or exceeds the direct operating costs of such facility.

The preceding sentence shall apply with respect to any highly compensated employee only if access to the facility is available on substantially the same terms to each member of a group of employees which is defined under a reasonable classification set up by the employer which does not discriminate in favor of highly compensated employees.

(f) Qualified Transportation Fringe.—

(1) In general.— For purposes of this section, the term "qualified transportation fringe" means any of the following provided by an employer to an employee:

(A) Transportation in a commuter highway vehicle if such transportation is in connection with travel between the employee's residence and place of employment.

(B) Any transit pass.

(C) Qualified parking.

(2) Limitation on exclusion.— The amount of the fringe benefits which are provided by an employer to any employee and which may be excluded from gross income under subsection (a)(5) shall not exceed—

(A) $60 per month in the case of the aggregate of the benefits described in subparagraphs (A) and (B) of paragraph (1), and

(B) $155 per month in the case of qualified parking.

(3) Cash reimbursements.— For purposes of this subsection, the term "qualified transportation fringe" includes a cash reimbursement by an employer to an employee for a benefit described in paragraph (1). The preceding sentence shall apply to a cash reimbursement for any transit pass only if a voucher or similar item which may be exchanged only for a transit pass is not readily available for direct distribution by the employer to the employee.

(4) Benefit not in lieu of compensation.— Subsection (a)(5) shall not apply to any qualified transportation fringe unless such benefit is provided in addition to (and not in lieu of) any compensation otherwise payable to the employee.

(5) Definitions.— For purposes of this subsection—

(A) Transit pass.— The term ''transit pass'' means any pass, token, farecard, voucher, or similar item entitling a person to transportation (or transportation at a reduced price) if such transportation is—

(i) on mass transit facilities (whether or not publicly owned), or

(ii) provided by any person in the business of transporting persons for compensation or hire if such transportation is provided in a vehicle meeting the requirements of subparagraph (B)(i).

(B) Commuter highway vehicle.— The term ''commuter highway vehicle'' means any highway vehicle—

(i) the seating capacity of which is at least 6 adults (not including the driver), and

(ii) at least 80 percent of the mileage use of which can reasonably be expected to be—

(I) for purposes of transporting employees in connection with travel between their residences and their place of employment, and

(II) on trips during which the number of employees transported for such purposes is at least 1/2 of the adult seating capacity of such vehicle (not including the driver).

(C) Qualified parking.— The term ''qualified parking'' means parking provided to an employee on or near the business premises of the employer or on or near a location from which the employee commutes to work by transportation described in subparagraph (A), in a commuter highway vehicle, or by carpool. Such term shall not include any parking on or near property used by the employee for residential purposes.

(D) Transportation provided by employer.— Transportation referred to in paragraph (1)(A) shall be considered to be provided by an employer if such transportation is furnished in a commuter highway vehicle operated by or for the employer.

(E) Employee.— For purposes of this subsection, the term ''employee'' does not include an individual who is an employee within the meaning of section 401(c)(1).

(6) Inflation adjustment.— In the case of any taxable year beginning in a calendar year after 1993, the dollar amounts contained in paragraph (2) (A) and (B) shall be increased by an amount equal to—

(A) such dollar amount, multiplied by

(B) the cost-of-living adjustment determined under section 1(f)(3) for the calendar year in which the taxable year begins, determined by substituting ''calendar year 1992'' for ''calendar year 1989'' in subparagraph (B) thereof.

If any increase determined under the preceding sentence is not a multiple of $5, such increase shall be rounded to the next lowest multiple of $5.

(7) Coordination with other pro-visions.— For purposes of this section, the terms ''working condition fringe'' and ''de minimis fringe'' shall not include any qualified transportation fringe (determined without regard to paragraph (2)).

(g) Qualified Moving Expense Reimbursement.— For purposes of this section, the term ''qualified moving expense reimbursement'' means any amount received (directly or indirectly) by an individual from an employer as

IRC Sec. 132 (g)

a payment for (or a reimbursement of) expenses which would be deductible as moving expenses under section 217 if directly paid or incurred by the individual. Such term shall not include any payment for (or reimbursement of) an expense actually deducted by the individual in a prior taxable year.

(h) Certain Individuals Treated as Employees for Purposes of Subsections (a)(1) and (2).—For purposes of paragraphs (1) and (2) of subsection (a)—

(1) Retired and disabled employees and surviving spouse of employee treated as employee.—With respect to a line of business of an employer, the term "employee" includes—

(A) any individual who was formerly employed by such employer in such line of business and who separated from service with such employer in such line of business by reason of retirement or disability, and

(B) any widow or widower of any individual who died while employed by such employer in such line of business or while an employee within the meaning of subparagraph (A).

(2) Spouse and dependent children.—

(A) In general.— Any use by the spouse or a dependent child of the employee shall be treated as use by the employee.

(B) Dependent child.— For purposes of subparagraph (A), the term "dependent child" means any child (as defined in section 151(e)(3)) of the employee—

(i) who is a dependent of the employee, or

(ii) both of whose parents are deceased and who has not attained age 25.

For purposes of the preceding sentence, any child to whom section 152(e) applies shall be treated as the dependent of both parents.

(i) Reciprocal Agreements.— For purposes of paragraph (1) of subsection (a), any service provided by an employer to an employee of another employer shall be treated as provided by the employer of such employee if—

(1) such service is provided pursuant to a written agreement between such employers, and

(2) neither of such employers incurs any substantial additional costs (including foregone revenue) in providing such service or pursuant to such agreement.

(j) Special Rules.—

(1) Exclusions under subsection (a)(1) and (2) apply to highly compensated employees only if no discrimination.— Paragraphs (1) and (2) of subsection (a) shall apply with respect to any fringe benefit described therein provided with respect to any highly compensated employee only if such fringe benefit is available on substantially the same terms to each member of a group of employees which is defined under a reasonable classification set up by the employer which does not discriminate in favor of highly compensated employees. For purposes of this paragraph and subsection (e), there may be excluded from consideration employees who may be excluded from consideration under section 89(h).

(2) Special rule for leased sections of department stores.—

(A) In general.—For purposes of paragraph (2) of subsection (a), in the case of a leased section of a department store—

(i) such section shall be treated as part of the line of business of the person operating the department store, and

(ii) employees in the leased section shall be treated as employees of the person operating the department store.

(B) Leased section of department store.— For purposes of subparagraph (A), a leased section of a department store is any part of the department store where over-the-counter sales of property are made under a lease or similar arrangement where it appears to the general public that individuals making such sales are employed by the person operating the department store.

(3) Auto salesmen.—

(A) In general.— For purposes of subsection (a)(3), qualified automobile demonstration use shall be treated as a working condition fringe.

(B) Qualified automobile demonstration use.— For purposes of subparagraph (A), the term "qualified demonstration use" means any use of an automobile by a full-time automobile salesman in the sales area in which the automobile dealer's sales office is located if—

(i) such use is provided primarily to facilitate the salesman's performance of services for the employer, and

(ii) there are substantial restrictions on the personal use of such automobile by such salesman.

(4) On-premises gyms and other athletic facilities.—

(A) In general.— Gross income shall not include the value of any on-premises athletic facility provided by an employer to his employees.

(B) On-premises athletic facility. For purposes of this paragraph, the term "on-premises athletic facility" means any gym or other athletic facility—

(i) which is located on the premises of the employer,

(ii) which is operated by the employer, and

(iii) substantially all the use of which is by employees of the employer, their spouses, and their dependent children (within the meaning of subsection (h)).

(5) Special rule for affiliates of airlines.—

(A) In general.— If—

(i) a qualified affiliate is a member of an affiliated group another member of which operates an airline, and

(ii) employees of the qualified affiliate who are directly engaged in providing airline-related services are entitled to no-additional-cost service with respect to air transportation provided by such other member,

then for purposes of applying paragraph (1) of subsection (a) to such no-additional-cost service provided to such employees, such qualified affiliate shall be treated as engaged in the same line of business as such other member.

(B) Qualified affiliate.— For purposes of this paragraph, the term "qualified affiliate" means any corporation which is predominantly engaged in airline-related services.

(C) Airline-related services.— For purposes of this paragraph, the term "airline-related services" means any of the following services provided in connection with air transportation:

(i) Catering.

(ii) Baggage handling.

(iii) Ticketing and reservations.

(iv) Flight planning and weather analysis.

(v) Restaurants and gift shops located at an airport.

(vi) Such other similar services provided to the airline as the Secretary may prescribe.

(D) Affiliated group.— For purposes of this section, the term "affiliated group" has the meaning given such term by section 1504(a).

IRC Sec. 132 (j)(5)(D)

(6) Highly compensated employee.— For purposes of this section, the term "highly compensated employee" has the meaning given such term by section 414(q).

(7) Air cargo.— For purposes of subsection (b), the transportation of cargo by air and the transportation of passengers by air shall be treated as the same service.

(8) Application of section to otherwise taxable educational or training benefits.— Amounts paid or expenses incurred by the employer for education or training provided to the employee which are not excludable from gross income under section 127 shall be excluded from gross income under this section if (and only if) such amounts or expenses are a working condition fringe.

(k) Customers Not to Include Employees.— For purposes of this section (other than subsection (c)(2)), the term "customers" shall only include customers who are not employees.

(l) Section Not to Apply to Fringe Benefits Expressly Provided for Elsewhere. This section shall not apply to any fringe benefits of a type the tax treatment of which is provided for in any other section of this chapter.

(m) Regulations.— The Secretary shall prescribe such regulations as may be necessary or appropriate to carry out the purposes of this section.

SEC. 133. INTEREST ON CERTAIN LOANS USED TO ACQUIRE EMPLOYER SECURITIES.

(a) In general.— Gross income does not include 50 percent of the interest received by—

(1) a bank (within the meaning of section 581),

(2) an insurance company to which subchapter L applies,

(3) a corporation actively engaged in the business of lending money, or

(4) a regulated investment company (as defined in section 851),with respect to a securities acquisition loan.

(b) Securities Acquisition Loan.—

(1) In general.— For purposes of this section, the term "securities acquisition loan" means—

(A) any loan to a corporation or to an employee stock ownership plan to the extent that the proceeds are used to acquire employer securities for the plan, or

(B) any loan to a corporation to the extent that, within 30 days, employer securities are transferred to the plan in an amount equal to the proceeds of such loan and such securities are allocable to accounts of plan participants within 1 year of the date of such loan.

For purposes of this paragraph, the term "employer securities" has the meaning given such term by section 409(l). The term "securities acquisition loan" shall not include a loan with a term greater than 15 years.

(2) Loans between related persons.— The term "securities acquisition loan" shall not include—

(A) any loan made between corporations which are members of the same controlled group of corporations, or

(B) any loan made between an employee stock ownership plan and any person that is—

(i) the employer of any employees who are covered by the plan; or

(ii) a member of a controlled group of corporations which includes such employer.

For purposes of this paragraph, subparagraphs (A) and (B) shall not apply to any loan which, but for such subparagraphs, would be a securities acquisition loan if such loan was not originated by the employer of any employees who are covered by the plan or by any member of the controlled group of corporations which includes such employer, except that this section shall not apply to any interest received on such loan during such time as such loan is held by such employer (or any member of such controlled group).

(3) Terms applicable to certain securities acquisition loans.— A loan to a corporation shall not fail to be treated as a securities acquisition loan merely because the proceeds of such loan are lent to any employee stock ownership plan sponsored by such corporation (or by any member of the controlled group of corporations which includes such corporation) if such loan includes—

(A) repayment terms which are substantially similar to the terms of the loan of such corporation from a lender described in subsection (a), or

(B) repayment terms providing for more rapid repayment of principal or interest on such loan, but only if allocations under the plan attributable to such repayment do not discriminate in favor of highly compensated employees (within the meaning of section 414(q)).

(4) Controlled group of corporations.— For purposes of this paragraph, the term ''controlled group of corporations'' has the meaning given such term by section 409(*l*)(4).

(5) Treatment of refinancings.—The term ''securities acquisition loan'' shall include any loan which—

(A) is (or is part of a series of loans) used to refinance a loan described in subparagraph (A) or (B) or paragraph (1), and

(B) meets the requirements of paragraphs (2) and (3).

(6) Plan must hold more than 50 percent of stock after acquisition or transfer.—

(A) In general.— A loan shall not be treated as a securities acquisition loan for purposes of this section unless, immediately after the acquisition or transfer referred to in subparagraph (A) or (B) of paragraph (1), respectively, the employee stock ownership plan owns more than 50 percent of—

(i) each class of outstanding stock of the corporation issuing the employer securities, or

(ii) the total value of all outstanding stock of the corporation.

(B) Failure to retain minimum stock interest.—

(i) In general.— Subsection (a) shall not apply to any interest received with respect to a securities acquisition loan which is allocable to any period during which the employee stock ownership plan does not own stock meeting the requirements of subparagraph (A).

(ii) Exception.— To the extent provided by the Secretary, clause (i) shall not apply to any period if, within 90 days of the first date on which the failure occurred (or such longer period not in excess of 180 days as the Secretary may prescribe), the plan acquires stock which results in its meeting the requirement of subparagraph (A).

(C) Stock.— For purposes of subparagraph (A)

(i) In general.—The term ''stock'' means stock other than stock described in section 1504(a)(4).

(ii) Treatment of certain rights.— The Secretary may provide that warrants, options, contracts to acquire stock, convertible debt interests and other similar interests be treated as stock for 1 or more purposes under subparagraph (A).

(D) Aggregation rule.— For purposes of determining whether the requirements of subparagraph (A) are met, an employee stock ownership plan shall be treated as owning stock in the corporation issuing the employer securities which is held by any other employee stock ownership plan which is maintained by—

(i) the employer maintaining the plan, or

(ii) any member of a controlled group of corporations (within the meaning of section

IRC Sec. 133 (b)(6)(D)(ii)

409(*l*)(4)) of which the employer described in clause (i) is a member.

(7) Voting rights of employer securities.— A loan shall not be treated as a securities acquisition loan for purposes of this section unless—

(A) the employee stock ownership plan meets the requirements of section 409(e)(2) with respect to all employer securities acquired by, or transferred to, the plan in connection with such loan (without regard to whether or not the employer has a registration-type class of securities), and

(B) no stock described in section 409(*l*)(3) is acquired by, or transferred to, the plan in connection with such loan unless—

(i) such stock has voting rights equivalent to the stock to which it may be converted, and

(ii) the requirements of subparagraph (A) are met with respect to such voting rights.

(c) Employee Stock Ownership Plan.—For purposes of this section, the term ''employee stock ownership plan'' has the meaning given to such term by section 4975(e)(7).

(d) Application With Section 483 and Original Issue Discount Rules.— In applying section 483 and subpart A of part V of subchapter P to any obligation to which this section applies, appropriate adjustments shall be made to the applicable Federal rate to take into account the exclusion under subsection (a).

(e) Period to Which Interest Exclusion Applies.—

(1) In general.— In the case of—

(A) an original securities acquisition loan, and

(B) any securities acquisition loan (or series of such loans) used to refinance the original securities acquisition loan,

subsection (A) shall apply only to interest accruing during the exludable period with respect to the original securities acquisition loan.

(2) Excludable period.— For purposes of this subsection, the term ''excludable period'' means, with respect to any original securities acquisition loan—

(A) In general.— The 7-year period beginning on the date of such loan.

(B) Loans described in subsection (b)(1)(A).— If the term of an original securities acquisition loan described in subsection (b)(1)(A) is greater than 7 years, the term of such loan. This subparagraph shall not apply to a loan described in subsection (b)(3)(B).

(3) Original securities acquisition loan.— For the purposes of this subsection, the term ''original securities acquisition loan'' means a securities acquisition loan described in subparagraph (A) or (B) of subsection (b)(1).

* * *

Part V— Deductions For Personal Exemptions

* * *

SEC. 152. DEPENDENT DEFINED.

(a) General definition.— For purposes of this subtitle, the term ''dependent'' means any of the following individuals over half of whose support, for the calendar year in which the taxable year of the taxpayer begins, was received from the taxpayer (or is treated under subsection (c) or (e) as received from the taxpayer):

(1) A son or daughter of the taxpayer, or a descendant of either,

(2) A stepson or stepdaughter of the taxpayer,

(3) A brother, sister, stepbrother, or stepsister of the taxpayer,

(4) The father or mother of the taxpayer, or an ancestor of either,

(5) A stepfather or stepmother of the taxpayer,

(6) A son or daughter of a brother or sister of the taxpayer,

(7) A brother or sister of the father or mother of the taxpayer,

(8) A son-in-law, daughter-in-law, father-in-law, mother-in-law, brother-in-law, or sister-in-law of the taxpayer, or

(9) An individual (other than an individual who at any time during the taxable year was the spouse, determined without regard to section 7703, of the taxpayer) who, for the taxable year of the taxpayer, has as his principal place of abode the home of the taxpayer and is a member of the taxpayer's household.

(b) Rules relating to general definition.— For purposes of this section—

(1) The terms "brother" and "sister" include a brother or sister by the halfblood.

(2) In determining whether any of the relationships specified in subsection (a) or paragraph (1) of this subsection exists, a legally adopted child of an individual (and a child who is a member of an individual's household, if placed with such individual by an authorized placement agency for legal adoption by such individual), or a foster child of an individual (if such child satisfies the requirements of subsection (a)(9) with respect to such individual), shall be treated as a child of such individual by blood.

(3) The term "dependent" does not include any individual who is not a citizen or national of the United States unless such individual is a resident of the United States or of a country contiguous to the United States. The preceding sentence shall not exclude from the definition of "dependent" any child of the taxpayer legally adopted by him, if, for the taxable year of the taxpayer, the child has as his principal place of abode the home of the

taxpayer and is a member of the taxpayer's household, and if the taxpayer is a citizen or national of the United States.

(4) A payment to a wife which is includible in the gross income of the wife under section 71 or 682 shall not be treated as a payment by her husband for the support of any dependent.

(5) An individual is not a member of the taxpayer's household if at any time during the taxable year of the taxpayer the relationship between such individual and the taxpayer is in violation of local law.

(c) Multiple support agreements.— For purposes of subsection (a), over half of the support of an individual for a calendar year shall be treated as received from the taxpayer if—

(1) no one person contributed over half of such support;

(2) over half of such support was received from persons each of whom, but for the fact that he did not contribute over half of such support, would have been entitled to claim such individual as a dependent for a taxable year beginning in such calendar year;

(3) the taxpayer contributed over 10 percent of such support; and

(4) each person described in paragraph (2) (other than the taxpayer) who contributed over 10 percent of such support files a written declaration (in such manner and form as the Secretary may by regulations prescribe) that he will not claim such individual as a dependent for any taxable year beginning in such calendar year.

(d) Special support test in case of students.— For purposes of subsection (a), in the case of any individual who is—

(1) a son, stepson, daughter, or stepdaughter of the taxpayer (within the meaning of this section), and

(2) a student (within the meaning of section 151(c)(4)),

IRC Sec. 152 (d)(2)

amounts received as scholarships for study at an educational organization described in section 170(b)(1)(A)(ii) shall not be taken into account in determining whether such individual received more than half of his support from the taxpayer.

(e) Support test in case of child of divorced parents, etc.—

(1) Custodial parent gets exemption.— Except as otherwise provided in this subsection, if—

(A) a child (as defined in section 151(c)(3)) receives over half of his support during the calendar year from his parents—

(i) who are divorced or legally separated under a decree of divorce or separate maintenance,

(ii) who are separated under a written separation agreement, or

(iii) who live apart at all times during the last 6 months of the calendar year, and

(B) such child is in the custody of one or both of his parents for more than one-half of the calendar year,

such child shall be treated, for purposes of subsection (a), as receiving over half of his support during the calendar year from the parent having custody for a greater portion of the calendar year (hereinafter in this subsection referred to as the "custodial parent").

(2) Exception where custodial parent releases claim to exemption for the year.— A child of parents described in paragraph (1) shall be treated as having received over half of his support during a calendar year from the noncustodial parent if—

(A) the custodial parent signs a written declaration (in such manner and form as the Secretary may by regulations prescribe) that such custodial parent will not claim such child as a dependent for any taxable year beginning in such calendar year, and

(B) the noncustodial parent attaches such written declaration to the noncustodial parent's return for the taxable year beginning during such calendar year.

For purposes of this subsection, the term "noncustodial parent" means the parent who is not the custodial parent.

(3) Exception for multiple-support agreement.— This subsection shall not apply in any case where over half of the support of the child is treated as having been received from a taxpayer under the provisions of subsection (c).

(4) Exception for certain pre-1985 instruments.—

(A) In general.— A child of parents described in paragraph (1) shall be treated as having received over half his support during a calendar year from the noncustodial parent if—

(i) a qualified pre-1985 instrument between the parents applicable to the taxable year beginning in such calendar year provides that the noncustodial parent shall be entitled to any deduction allowable under section 151 for such child, and

(ii) the noncustodial parent provides at least $600 for the support of such child during such calendar year.

For purposes of this subparagraph, amounts expended for the support of a child or children shall be treated as received from the noncustodial parent to the extent that such parent provided amounts for such support.

(B) Qualified pre-1985 instrument.— For purposes of this paragraph, the term "qualified pre-1985 instrument" means any decree of divorce or separate maintenance or written agreement—

(i) which is executed before January 1, 1985,

IRC Sec. 152 (e)

(ii) which on such date contains the provision described in subparagraph (A)(i), and

(iii) which is not modified on or after such date in a modification which expressly provides that this paragraph shall not apply to such decree or agreement.

(5) Special rule for support received from new spouse of parent.— For purposes of this subsection, in the case of the remarriage of a parent, support of a child received from the parent's spouse shall be treated as received from the parent.

(6) Cross reference.— For provision treating child as dependent of both parents for purposes of medical expense deduction, see section 213(d)(5).

* * *

Part VI— Itemized Deductions for Individuals and Corporations

SEC. 162. TRADE OR BUSINESS EXPENSES.

(a) In general.— There shall be allowed as a deduction all the ordinary and necessary expenses paid or incurred during the taxable year in carrying on any trade or business, including—

(1) a reasonable allowance for salaries or other compensation for personal services actually rendered;

(2) traveling expenses (including amounts expended for meals and lodging other than amounts which are lavish or extravagant under the circumstances) while away from home in the pursuit of a trade or business; and

(3) rentals or other payments required to be made as a condition to the continued use or possession, for purposes of the trade or business, of property to which the taxpayer has not taken or is not taking title or in which he has no equity.

For purposes of the preceding sentence, the place of residence of a Member of Congress (including any Delegate and Resident Commissioner) within the State, congressional district, or possession which he represents in Congress shall be considered his home, but amounts expended by such Members within each taxable year for living expenses shall not be deductible for income tax purposes in excess of $3,000. For purposes of paragraph (2), the taxpayer shall not be treated as being temporarily away from home during any period of employment if such period exceeds 1 year.

* * *

(*l*) Special Rules for Health Insurance Costs of Self-Employed Individuals.—

(1) In general.— In the case of an individual who is an employee within the meaning of section 401(c)(1), there shall be allowed as a deduction under this section an amount equal to 25 percent of the amount paid during the taxable year for insurance which constitutes medical care for the taxpayer, his spouse, and dependents.

(2) Limitations.—

(A) Dollar amount.— No deduction shall be allowed under paragraph (1) to the extent that the amount of such deduction exceeds the taxpayer's earned income (within the meaning of section 401(c) derived by the taxpayer from the trade or business with respect to which the plan providing the medical care coverage is established).

(B) Other coverage.— Paragraph (1) shall not apply to any taxpayer for any calendar month for which the taxpayer is eligible to participate in any subsidized health plan maintained by any employer of the taxpayer or of the spouse of the taxpayer.

(3) Health insurance credit.— The amount otherwise taken into account under paragraph (1) as paid for insurance which constitutes medical care shall be reduced by the amount (if any) of the health insurance

IRC Sec. 162 (l)(3)

credit allowable to the taxpayer for the taxable year under section 32.

(4) Deduction not allowed for self-employment tax purposes.— The deduction allowable by reason of this subsection shall not be taken into account in determining an individual's net earnings from self-employment (within the meaning of section 1402(a)) for purposes of chapter 2.

(5) Treatment of certain S corporation shareholders.— This subsection shall apply in the case of any individual treated as a partner under section 1372(a), except that—

(A) for purposes of this subsection, such individual's wages (as defined in section 3121) from the S corporation shall be treated as such individual's earned income (within the meaning of section 401(c)(1), and

(B) there shall be such adjustments in the application of this subsection as the Secretary may by regulations prescribe.

(6) Termination.— This subsection shall not apply to any taxable year beginning after December 31, 1993.

(m) Certain excessive employee remuneration.—

(1) In general.— In the case of any publicly held corporation, no deduction shall be allowed under this chapter for applicable employee remuneration with respect to any covered employee to the extent that the amount of such remuneration for the taxable year with respect to such employee exceeds $1,000,000.

(2) Publicly held corporation.— For purposes of this subsection, the term "publicly held corporation" means any corporation issuing any class of common equity securities required to be registered under section 12 of the Securities Exchange Act of 1934.

(3) Covered employee.— For purposes of this subsection, the term "covered employee" means any employee of the taxpayer if—

(A) as of the close of the taxable year, such employee is the chief executive officer of the taxpayer or is an individual acting in such a capacity, or

(B) the total compensation of such employee for the taxable year is required to be reported to shareholders under the Securities Exchange Act of 1934 by reason of such employee being among the 4 highest compensated officers for the taxable year (other than the chief executive officer).

(4) Applicable employee remuneration.— For purposes of this subsection—

(A) In general.— Except as otherwise provided in this paragraph, the term "applicable employee remuneration" means, with respect to any covered employee for any taxable year, the aggregate amount allowable as a deduction under this chapter for such taxable year (determined without regard to this subsection) for remuneration for services performed by such employee (whether or not during the taxable year).

(B) Exception for remuneration payable on commission basis.— The term "applicable employee remuneration" shall not include any remuneration payable on a commission basis solely on account of income generated directly by the individual performance of the individual to whom such remuneration is payable.

(C) Other performance-based compensation.— The term "applicable employee remuneration" shall not include any remuneration payable solely on account of the attainment of one or more performance goals, but only if—

(i) the performance goals are determined by a compensation commitee of the board of directors of the taxpayer which is comprised solely of 2 or more outside directors,

(ii) the material terms under which the remuneration is to be paid, including the performance goals, are disclosed to shareholders and approved by a majority of the vote in a separate shareholder vote before the payment of such remuneration, and

(iii) before any payment of such remuneration, the compensation committee referred to in clause (i) certifies that the performance goals and any other material terms were in fact satisfied.

(D) Exception for existing binding contracts.— The term "applicable employee remuneration" shall not include any remuneration payable under a written binding contract which was in effect on February 17, 1993, and which was not modified thereafter in any material respect before such remuneration is paid.

(E) Remuneration.— For purposes of this paragraph,the term "remuneration" includes any remuneration (including benefits) in any medium other than cash, but shall not include—

(i) any payment referred to in so much of section 3121(a)(5) as precedes subparagraph (E) thereof, and

(ii) any benefit provided to or on behalf of an employee if at the time such benefit is provided it is reasonable to believe that the employee will be able to exclude such benefit from gross income under this chapter.

For purposes of clause (i), section 3121(a)(5) shall be applied without regard to section 3121(v)(1).

(F) Coordination with disalllowed golden parachute payments.— The dollar limitation contained in paragraph (1) shall be reduced (but not below zero) by the amount (if any) which would have been included in the applicable employee remuneration of the covered employee for the taxable year but for being disallowed under section 280G.

(n) Special rule for certain group health plans.—

(1) In general.— No deduction shall be allowed under this chapter to an employer for any amount paid or incurred in connection with a group health plan if the plan does not reimburse for inpatient hospital care services provided in the State of New York—

(A) except as provided in subparagraphs (B) and (C), at the same rate as licensed commercial insurers are required to reimburse hospitals for such services when such reimbursement is not through such a plan.

(B) in the case of any reimbursement through a health maintenance organization, at the same rate as health maintenance organizations are required to reimburse hospitals for such services for individuals not covered by such a plan (determined without regard to any government-supported individuals exempt from such rate), or

(C) in the case of any reimbursement through any corporation organized under Article 43 of the New York State Insurance Law, at the same rate as any such corporation is required to reimburse hospitals for such services for individuals not covered by such a plan.

(2) State law exception.— Paragraph (1) shall not apply to any group health plan which is not required under the laws of the State of New York (determined without regard to this subsection or other provisions of Federal law) to reimburse at the rates provided in paragraph (1).

(3) Group health plan.— For purposes of this subsection, the term "group health plan" means a plan of, or contributed to by, an employer or employee organization (including a self-insured plan) to provide health care (directly or otherwise) to any employee, any former employee, the employer, or any other individual associated or formerly associated with the employer in a business relationship, or any member of their family.

* * *

(o) Cross Reference.—

* * *

(3) For special rules relating to—

(A) funded welfare benefit plans, see section 419, and

(B) deferred compensation plans and other deferred benefits, see section 404.

* * *

SEC. 194A. CONTRIBUTIONS TO EMPLOYER LIABILITY TRUSTS.

(a) Allowance of Deduction.— There shall be allowed as a deduction for the taxable year an amount equal to the amount—

(1) which is contributed by an employer to a trust described in section 501(c)(22) (relating to withdrawal liability payment fund) which meets the requirements of section 4223(h) of the Employee Retirement Income Security Act of 1974, and

(2) which is properly allocable to such taxable year.

(b) Allocation to Taxable Year.— In the case of a contribution described in subsection (a) which relates to any specified period of time which includes more than one taxable year, the amount properly allocable to any taxable year in such period shall be determined by prorating such amounts to such taxable years under regulations prescribed by the Secretary.

(c) Disallowance of Deduction.— No deduction shall be allowed under subsection (a) with respect to any contribution described in subsection (a) which does not relate to any specified period of time.

* * *

Part VII— Additional Itemized Deductions for Individuals

* * *

SEC. 219. RETIREMENT SAVINGS.

(a) Allowance of Deduction.— In the case of an individual, there shall be allowed as a de-

duction an amount equal to the qualified retirement contributions of the individual for the taxable year.

(b) Maximum Amount of Deduction.—

(1) In general.— The amount allowable as a deduction under subsection (a) to any individual for any taxable year shall not exceed the lesser of—

(A) $2,000, or

(B) an amount equal to the compensation includible in the individual's gross income for such taxable year.

(2) Special rule for employer contributions under simplified employee pensions.— This section shall not apply with respect to an employer contribution to a simplified employee pension.

(3) Plans under section 501(c)(18).— Notwithstanding paragraph (1), the amount allowable as a deduction under subsection (a) with respect to any contributions on behalf of an employee to a plan described in section 501(c)(18) shall not exceed the lesser of—

(A) $7,000, or

(B) an amount equal to 25 percent of the compensation (as defined in section 415(c)(3)) includible in the individual's gross income for such taxable year.

(c) Special Rules for Certain Married Individuals.—

(1) In general.— In the case of any individual with respect to whom a deduction is otherwise allowable under subsection (a)—

(A) who files a joint return under section 6013 for a taxable year, and

(B) whose spouse—

(i) has no compensation (determined without regard to section 911) for the taxable year, or

(ii) elects to be treated for purposes of subsection (b)(1)(B) as having no compensation for the taxable year,

there shall be allowed as a deduction any amount paid in cash for the taxable year by or on behalf of the individual to an individual retirement plan established for the benefit of his spouse.

(2) Limitation.— The amount allowable as a deduction under paragraph (1) shall not exceed the excess of—

(A) the lesser of—

(i) $2,250, or

(ii) an amount equal to the compensation includable in the individual's gross income for the taxable year, over

(B) the amount allowable as a deduction under subsection (a) for the taxable year.

In no event shall the amount allowable as a deduction under paragraph (1) exceed $2,000.

(d) Other Limitations and Restrictions.—

(1) Beneficiary must be under age 70½.— No deduction shall be allowed under this section with respect to any qualified retirement contribution for the benefit of an individual if such individual has attained age 70½ before the close of such individual's taxable year for which the contribution was made.

(2) Recontributed amounts.— No deduction shall be allowed under this section with respect to a rollover contribution described in section 402(c), 403(a)(4), 403(b)(8), or 408(d)(3).

(3) Amounts contributed under endowment contract.— In the case of an endowment contract described in section 408(b), no deduction shall be allowed under this section for that portion of the amounts paid under the contract for the taxable year which is properly

allocable, under regulations prescribed by the Secretary, to the cost of life insurance.

(4) Denial of deduction for amount contributed to inherited annuities or accounts.— No deduction shall be allowed under this section with respect to any amount paid to an inherited individual retirement account or individual retirement annuity (within the meaning of section 408(d)(3)(C)(ii)).

(e) Qualified Retirement Contribution.— For purposes of this section, the term "qualified retirement contribution" means—

(1) any amount paid in cash for the taxable year by or on behalf of an individual to an individual retirement plan for such individual's benefit, and

(2) any amount contributed on behalf of any individual to a plan described in section 501(c)(18).

(f) Other Definitions and Special Rules.—

(1) Compensation.— For purposes of this section, the term "compensation" includes earned income (as defined in section 401(c)(2)). The term "compensation" does not include any amount received as a pension or annuity and does not include any amount received as deferred compensation. The term "compensation" shall include any amount includible in the individual's gross income under section 71 with respect to a divorce or separation instrument described in subparagraph (A) of section 71(b)(2). For purposes of this paragraph, section 401(c)(2) shall be applied as if the term trade or business for purposes of section 1402 included service described in subsection (c)(6).

(2) Married individuals.— The maximum deduction under subsections (b) and (c) shall be computed separately for each individual, and this section shall be applied without regard to any community property laws.

(3) Time when contributions deemed made.— For purposes of this section, a taxpayer shall be deemed to have made a contribution to an individual retirement plan on the last day of the preceding taxable year if the contribution is made on account of such taxable year and is made not later than the time prescribed by law for filing the return for such taxable year (not including extensions thereof).

(4) Reports.— The Secretary shall prescribe regulations which prescribe the time and the manner in which reports to the Secretary and plan participants shall be made by the plan administrator of a qualified employer or government plan receiving qualified voluntary employee contributions.

(5) Employer payments.— For purposes of this title, any amount paid by an employer to an individual retirement plan shall be treated as payment of compensation to the employee (other than a self-employed individual who is an employee within the meaning of section 401(c)(1)) includible in his gross income in the taxable year for which the amount was contributed, whether or not a deduction for such payment is allowable under this section to the employee.

(6) Excess contributions treated as contribution made during subsequent year for which there is an unused limitation.—

(A) In general.— If for the taxable year the maximum amount allowable as a deduction under this section for contributions to an individual retirement plan exceeds the amount contributed, then the taxpayer shall be treated as having made an additional contribution for the taxable year in an amount equal to the lesser of—

(i) the amount of such excess, or

(ii) the amount of the excess contributions for such taxable year (determined under section 4973(b)(2) without regard to subparagraph (C) thereof).

(B) Amount contributed.— For purposes of this paragraph, the amount contributed—

(i) shall be determined without regard to this paragraph, and

(ii) shall not include any rollover contribution.

(C) Special rule where excess deduction was allowed for closed year.— Proper reduction shall be made in the amount allowable as a deduction by reason of this paragraph for any amount allowed as a deduction under this section for a prior taxable year for which the period for assessing deficiency has expired if the amount so allowed exceeds the amount which should have been allowed for such prior taxable year.

(7) Election not to deduct contributions.— For election not to deduct contributions to individual retirement plans, see section 408(o)(2)(B)(ii).

(g) Limitation on Deduction for Active Participants in Certain Pension Plans.—

(1) In general.— If (for any part of any plan year ending with or within a taxable year) an individual or the individual's spouse is an active participant, each of the dollar limitations contained in subsections (b)(1)(A) and (c)(2) for such taxable year shall be reduced (but not below zero) by the amount determined under paragraph (2).

(2) Amount of reduction.—

(A) In general.— The amount determined under this paragraph with respect to any dollar limitation shall be the amount which bears the same ratio to such limitation as— Sec. 219 (g)(2)(A)(i)

(i) the excess of—

(I) the taxpayer's adjusted gross income for such taxable year, over

(II) the applicable dollar amount, bears to (ii) $10,000.

(B) No reduction below $200 until complete phase-out.— No dollar limitation shall be reduced below $200 under paragraph (1) unless (without regard to this subparagraph) such limitation is reduced to zero.

IRC Sec. 219 (f)(4)

(C) Rounding.— Any amount determined under this paragraph which is not a multiple of $10 shall be rounded to the next lowest $10.

(3) **Adjusted gross income; applicable dollar amount.**— For purposes of this subsection—

(A) Adjusted gross income.— Adjusted gross income of any taxpayer shall be determined—

(i) after application of sections 86 and 469, and

(ii) without regard to sections 135 and 911 or the deduction allowable under this section.

(B) Applicable dollar amount.— The term "applicable dollar amount" means—

(i) in the case of a taxpayer filing a joint return, $40,000,

(ii) in the case of any other taxpayer (other than a married individual filing a separate return), $25,000, and

(iii) in the case of a married individual filing a separate return, zero.

(4) **Special rule for married individuals filing separately and living apart.**— A husband and wife who—

(A) file separate returns for any taxable year, and

(B) live apart at all times during such taxable year,

shall not be treated as married individuals for purposes of this subsection.

(5) **Active participant.**— For purposes of this subsection, the term "active participant" means, with respect to any plan year, an individual—

(A) who is an active participant in—

(i) a plan described in section 401(a) which includes a trust exempt from tax under section 501(a),

(ii) an annuity plan described in section 403(a),

(iii) a plan established for its employees by the United States, by a State or political subdivision thereof, or by an agency or instrumentality of any of the foregoing,

(iv) an annuity contract described in section 403(b), or

(v) a simplified employee pension (within the meaning of section 408(k)), or

(B) who makes deductible contributions to a trust described in section 501(c)(18).

The determination of whether an individual is an active participant shall be made without regard to whether or not such individual's rights under a plan, trust, or contract are nonforfeitable. An eligible deferred compensation plan (within the meaning of section 457(b)) shall not be treated as a plan described in subparagraph (A)(iii).

(6) **Certain individuals not treated as active participants.**— For purposes of this subsection, any individual described in any of the following subparagraphs shall not be treated as an active participant for any taxable year solely because of any participation so described:

(A) Members of reserve components.— Participation in a plan described in subparagraph (A)(iii) of paragraph (5) by reason of service as a member of a reserve component of the Armed Forces (as defined in section 261(a) of title 10), unless such individual has served in excess of 90 days on active duty (other than active duty for training) during the year.

(B) Volunteer firefighters.— A volunteer firefighter—

(i) who is a participant in a plan described in subparagraph (A)(iii) of paragraph (5)

IRC Sec. 219 (g)(6)(B)(i)

based on his activity as a volunteer fire-fighter, and

(ii) whose accrued benefit as of the beginning of the taxable year is not more than an annual benefit of $1,800 (when expressed as a single life annuity commencing at age 65).

(h) Cross Reference.— For failure to provide required reports, see section 6652(h).

* * *

Part IX— Items Not Deductible

SEC. 267. LOSSES, EXPENSES, AND INTEREST WITH RESPECT TO TRANSACTIONS BETWEEN RELATED TAXPAYERS

(a) In general.—

(1) Deduction for losses disallowed.— No deduction shall be allowed in respect of any loss from the sale or exchange of property, directly or indirectly, between persons specified in any of the paragraphs of subsection (b). The preceding sentence shall not apply to any loss of the distributing corporation (or the distributee) in the case of a distribution in complete liquidation.

(2) Matching of deduction and payee income item in the case of expenses and interest.— If—

(A) by reason of the method of accounting of the person to whom the payment is to be made, the amount thereof is not (unless paid) includible in the gross income of such person, and

(B) at the close of the taxable year of the taxpayer for which (but for this paragraph) the amount would be deductible under this chapter, both the taxpayer and the person to whom the payment is to be made are persons specified in any of the paragraphs of subsection (b),

then any deduction allowable under this chapter in respect of such amount shall be allowable as of the day as of which such amount is includible in the gross income of the person to whom the payment is made (or, if later, as of the day on which it would be so allowable but for this paragraph). For purposes of this paragraph, in the case of a personal service corporation (within the meaning of section 441(i)(2)), such corporation and any employee-owner (within the meaning of section 269A(b)(2), as modified by section 441(i)(2)) shall be treated as persons specified in subsection (b).

(3) Payments to foreign persons.— The Secretary shall by regulations apply the matching principle of paragraph (2) in cases in which the person to whom the payment is to be made is not a United States person.

(b) Relationships.— The persons referred to in subsection (a) are:

(1) Members of a family, as defined in subsection (c)(4);

(2) An individual and a corporation more than 50 percent in value of the outstanding stock of which is owned, directly or indirectly, by or for such individual;

(3) Two corporations which are members of the same controlled group (as defined in subsection (f));

(4) A grantor and a fiduciary of any trust;

(5) A fiduciary of a trust and a fiduciary of another trust, if the same person is a grantor of both trusts;

(6) A fiduciary of a trust and a bene-ficiary of such trust;

(7) A fiduciary of a trust and a bene-ficiary of another trust, if the same person is a grantor of both trusts;

(8) A fiduciary of a trust and a corporation more than 50 percent in value of the outstanding stock of which is owned, directly or indirectly, by or for the trust or by or for a person who is a grantor of the trust;

(9) A person and an organization to which section 501 (relating to certain educational and charitable organizations which are exempt from tax) applies and which is controlled directly or indirectly by such person or (if such person is an individual) by members of the family of such individual;

(10) A corporation and a partnership if the same persons own—

(A) more than 50 percent in value of the outstanding stock of the corporation, and

(B) more than 50 percent of the capital interest, or the profits interest, in the partnership;

(11) An S corporation and another S corporation if the same persons own more than 50 percent in value of the outstanding stock of each corporation; or

(12) An S corporation and a C corporation, if the same persons own more than 50 percent in value of the outstanding stock of each corporation.

(c) Constructive ownership of stock.— For purposes of determining, in applying subsection (b), the ownership of stock—

(1) Stock owned, directly or indirectly, by or for a corporation, partnership, estate, or trust shall be considered as being owned proportionately by or for its shareholders, partners, or beneficiaries;

(2) An individual shall be considered as owning the stock owned, directly or indirectly, by or for his family;

(3) An individual owning (otherwise than by the application of paragraph (2)) any stock in a corporation shall be considered as owning the stock owned, directly or indirectly, by or for his partner;

(4) The family of an individual shall include only his brothers and sisters (whether by the whole or half blood), spouse, ancestors, and lineal descendants; and

(5) Stock constructively owned by a person by reason of the application of paragraph (1) shall, for the purpose of applying paragraph (1), (2), or (3), be treated as actually owned by

such person, but stock constructively owned by an individual by reason of the application of paragraph (2) or (3) shall not be treated as owned by him for the purpose of again applying either of such paragraphs in order to make another the constructive owner of such stock.

(d) Amount of gain where loss previously disallowed.— If—

(1) in the case of a sale or exchange of property to the taxpayer a loss sustained by the transferor is not allowable to the transferor as a deduction by reason of subsection (a)(1) (or by reason of section 24(b) of the Internal Revenue Code of 1939); and

(2) after December 31, 1953, the taxpayer sells or otherwise disposes of such property (or of other property the basis of which in his hands is determined directly or indirectly by reference to such property) at a gain,

then such gain shall be recognized only to the extent that it exceeds so much of such loss as is properly allocable to the property sold or otherwise disposed of by the taxpayer. This subsection applies with respect to taxable years ending after December 31, 1953. This subsection shall not apply if the loss sustained by the transferor is not allowable to the transferor as a deduction by reason of section 1091 (relating to wash sales) or by reason of section 118 of the Internal Revenue Code of 1939.

(e) Special rules for pass-thru entities.—

(1) In general.— In the case of any amount paid or incurred by, to, or on behalf of, a pass-thru entity, for purposes of applying subsection (a)(2)—

(A) such entity,

(B) in the case of—

(i) a partnership, any person who owns (directly or indirectly) any capital interest or profits interest of such partnership, or (ii) an S corporation, any person who owns (directly or indirectly) any of the stock of such corporation,

IRC Sec. 267 (e)(1)(B)(i)

(C) any person who owns (directly or indirectly) any capital interest or profits interest of a partnership in which such entity owns (directly or indirectly) any capital interest or profits interest, and

(D) any person related (within the meaning of subsection (b) of this section or section 707(b)(1)) to a person described in subparagraph (B) or (C),

shall be treated as persons specified in a paragraph of subsection (b). Subparagraph (C) shall apply to a transaction only if such transaction is related either to the operations of the partnership described in such subparagraph or to an interest in such partnership.

(2) Pass-thru entity.— For purposes of this section, the term "pass-thru entity" means—

(A) a partnership, and

(B) an S corporation.

(3) Constructive ownership in the case of partnerships.— For purposes of determining ownership of a capital interest or profits interest of a partnership, the principles of subsection (c) shall apply, except that—

(A) paragraph (3) of subsection (c) shall not apply, and

(B) interests owned (directly or indirectly) by or for a C corporation shall be considered as owned by or for any shareholder only if such shareholder owns (directly or indirectly) 5 percent or more in value of the stock of such corporation.

(4) Subsection (a)(2) not to apply to certain guaranteed payments of partnerships.— In the case of any amount paid or incurred by a partnership, subsection (a)(2) shall not apply to the extent that section 707(c) applies to such amount.

(5) Exception for certain expenses and interest of partnerships owning low-income housing.—

(A) In general.— This subsection shall not apply with respect to qualified expenses and interest paid or incurred by a partnership owning low-income housing to—

(i) any qualified 5-percent or less partner of such partnership, or

(ii) any person related (within the meaning of subsection (b) of this section or section 707(b)(1)) to any qualified 5-percent or less partner of such partnership.

(B) Qualified 5-percent or less partner.— For purposes of this paragraph, the term "qualified 5-percent or less partner" means any partner who has (directly or indirectly) an interest of 5 percent or less in the aggregate capital and profits interests of the partnership but only if—

(i) such partner owned the low-income housing at all times during the 2-year period ending on the date such housing was transferred to the partnership, or

(ii) such partnership acquired the low-income housing pursuant to a purchase, assignment, or other transfer from the Department of Housing and Urban Development or any State or local housing authority.

For purposes of the preceding sentence, a partner shall be treated as holding any interest in the partnership which is held (directly or indirectly) by any person related (within the meaning of subsection (b) of this section or section 707(b)(1)) to such partner.

(C) Qualified expenses and interest.— For purpose of this paragraph, the term "qualified expenses and interest" means any expense or interest incurred by the partnership with respect to low-income housing held by the partnership but—

(i) only if the amount of such expense or interest (as the case may be) is unconditionally required to be paid by the partnership not later than 10 years after the date such amount was incurred, and

(ii) in the case of such interest, only if such interest is incurred at an annual rate not in excess of 12 percent.

(D) Low-income housing.— For purposes of this paragraph, the term "low-income housing" means—

(i) any interest in property described in clause (i), (ii), (iii), or (iv) of section 1250(a)(1)(B), and

(ii) any interest in a partnership owning such property.

(6) Cross reference.— For additional rules relating to partnerships, see section 707(b).

(f) Controlled group defined; special rules applicable to controlled groups.—

(1) Controlled group defined.— For purposes of this section, the term "controlled group" has the meaning given to such term by section 1563(a), except that—

(A) "more than 50 percent" shall be substituted for "at least 80 percent" each place it appears in section 1563(a), and

(B) the determination shall be made without regard to subsections (a)(4) and (e)(3)(C) of section 1563.

(2) Deferral (rather than denial) of loss from sale or exchange between members.— In the case of any loss from the sale or exchange of property which is between members of the same controlled group and to which subsection (a)(1) applies (determined without regard to this paragraph but with regard to paragraph (3))—

(A) subsections (a)(1) and (d) shall not apply to such loss, but

(B) such loss shall be deferred until the property is transferred outside such controlled group and there would be recognition of loss under consolidated return principles or

until such other time as may be prescribed in regulations.

(3) Loss deferral rules not to apply in certain cases.—

(A) Transfer to DISC.— For purposes of applying subsection (a)(1), the term "controlled group" shall not include a DISC.

(B) Certain sales of inventory.— Except to the extent provided in regulations prescribed by the Secretary, subsection (a)(1) shall not apply to the sale or exchange of property between members of the same controlled group (or persons described in subsection (b)(10)) if—

(i) such property in the hands of the transferor is property described in section 1221(1),

(ii) such sale or exchange is in the ordinary course of the transferor's trade or business,

(iii) such property in the hands of the transferee is property described in section 1221(1), and

(iv) the transferee or the transferor is a foreign corporation.

(C) Certain foreign currency losses.— To the extent provided in regulations, subsection (a)(1) shall not apply to any loss sustained by a member of a controlled group on the repayment of a loan made to another member of such group if such loan is payable in a foreign currency or is denominated in such a currency and such loss is attributable to a reduction in value of such foreign currency.

(g) Coordination with section 1041.— Subsection (a)(1) shall not apply to any transfer described in section 1041(a) (relating to transfers of property between spouses or incident to divorce).

* * *

IRC Sec. 267 (g)

SEC. 280G. GOLDEN PARACHUTE PAYMENTS.

(a) General rule.— No deduction shall be allowed under this chapter for any excess parachute payment.

(b) Excess parachute payment.— For purposes of this section—

(1) In general.— The term "excess parachute payment" means an amount equal to the excess of any parachute payment over the portion of the base amount allocated to such payment.

(2) Parachute payment defined.—

(A) In general.— The term "parachute payment" means any payment in the nature of compensation to (or for the benefit of) a disqualified individual if—

(i) such payment is contingent on a change—

(I) in the ownership or effective control of the corporation, or

(II) in the ownership of a substantial portion of the assets of the corporation, and

(ii) the aggregate present value of the payments in the nature of compensation to (or for the benefit of) such individual which are contingent on such change equals or exceeds an amount equal to 3 times the base amount.

For purposes of clause (ii), payments not treated as parachute payments under paragraph (4)(A), (5), or (6) shall not be taken into account.

(B) Agreements.— The term "parachute payment" shall also include any payment in the nature of compensation to (or for the benefit of) a disqualified individual if such payment is made pursuant to an agreement which violates any generally enforced securities laws or regulations. In any proceeding involving the issue of whether any payment made to a disqualified individual is a para-

chute payment on account of a violation of any generally enforced securities laws or regulations, the burden of proof with respect to establishing the occurrence of a violation of such a law or regulation shall be upon the Secretary.

(C) Treatment of certain agreements entered into within 1 year before change of ownership.— For purposes of subparagraph (A)(i), any payment pursuant to—

(i) an agreement entered into within 1 year before the change described in subparagraph (A)(i), or

(ii) an amendment made within such 1-year period of a previous agreement,

shall be presumed to be contingent on such change unless the contrary is established by clear and convincing evidence.

(3) Base amount.—

(A) In general.— The term "base amount" means the individual's annualized includible compensation for the base period.

(B) Allocation.— The portion of the base amount allocated to any parachute payment shall be an amount which bears the same ratio to the base amount as—

(i) the present value of such payment, bears to

(ii) the aggregate present value of all such payments.

(4) Treatment of amounts which taxpayer establishes as reasonable compensation.— In the case of any payment described in paragraph (2)(A)—

(A) the amount treated as a parachute payment shall not include the portion of such payment which the taxpayer establishes by clear and convincing evidence is reasonable compensation for personal services to be rendered on or after the date of the change described in paragraph (2)(A)(i), and

(B) the amount treated as an excess parachute payment shall be reduced by the portion of such payment which the taxpayer establishes by clear and convincing evidence is reasonable compensation for personal services actually rendered before the date of the change described in paragraph (2)(A)(i).

For purposes of subparagraph (B), reasonable compensation for services actually rendered before the date of the change described in paragraph (2)(A)(i) shall be first offset against the base amount.

(5) Exemption for small business corporations, etc.—

(A) In general.— Notwithstanding paragraph (2), the term "parachute payment" does not include—

(i) any payment to a disqualified individual with respect to a corporation which (immediately before the change described in paragraph (2)(A)(i)) was a small business corporation (as defined in section 1361(b) but without regard to paragraph (1)(C) thereof), and

(ii) any payment to a disqualified individual with respect to a corporation (other than a corporation described in clause (i)) if—

(I) immediately before the change described in paragraph (2)(A)(i), no stock in such corporation was readily tradeable on an established securities market or otherwise, and

(II) the shareholder approval requirements of subparagraph (B) are met with respect to such payment.

The Secretary may, by regulations, prescribe that the requirements of subclause (I) of clause (ii) are not met where a substantial portion of the assets of any entity consists (directly or indirectly) of stock in such corporation and interests in such other entity are readily tradeable on an established securities market, or otherwise. Stock described in section 1504(a)(4) shall not be taken into account under clause (ii)(I) if the payment

does not adversely affect the shareholder's redemption and liquidation rights.

(B) Shareholder approval requirements.— The shareholder approval requirements of this subparagraph are met with respect to any payment if—

(i) such payment was approved by a vote of the persons who owned, immediately before the change described in paragraph (2)(A)(i), more than 75 percent of the voting power of all outstanding stock of the corporation, and

(ii) there was adequate disclosure to shareholders of all material facts concerning all payments which (but for this paragraph) would be parachute payments with respect to a disqualified individual.

The regulations prescribed under subsection (a) shall include regulations providing for the application of this subparagraph in the case of shareholders which are not individuals (including the treatment of nonvoting interests in an entity which is a shareholder) and where an entity holds a de minimis amount of stock in the corporation.

(6) Exemption for payments under qualified plans.— Notwithstanding paragraph (2), the term "parachute payment" shall not include any payment to or from—

(A) a plan described in section 401(a) which includes a trust exempt from tax under section 501(a),

(B) an annuity plan described in section 403(a), or

(C) a simplified employee pension (as defined in section 408(k)).

(c) Disqualified individuals.— For purposes of this section, the term "disqualified individual" means any individual who is—

(1) an employee, independent contractor, or other person specified in regulations by the Secretary who performs personal services for any corporation, and

IRC Sec. 280G (c)(1)

(2) is an officer, shareholder, or highly-compensated individual.

For purposes of this section, a personal service corporation (or similar entity) shall be treated as an individual. For purposes of paragraph (2), the term "highly-compensated individual" only includes an individual who is (or would be if the individual were an employee) a member of the group consisting of the highest paid 1 percent of the employees of the corporation or, if less, the highest paid 250 employees of the corporation.

(d) Other definitions and special rules.— For purposes of this section—

(1) Annualized includible compensation for base period.— The term "annualized includible compensation for the base period" means the average annual compensation which—

(A) was payable by the corporation with respect to which the change in ownership or control described in paragraph (2)(A) of subsection (b) occurs, and

(B) was includible in the gross income of the disqualified individual for taxable years in the base period.

(2) Base period.— The term "base period" means the period consisting of the most recent 5 taxable years ending before the date on which the change in ownership or control described in paragraph (2)(A) of subsection (b) occurs (or such portion of such period during which the disqualified individual performed personal services for the corporation).

(3) Property transfers.— Any transfer of property—

(A) shall be treated as a payment, and

(B) shall be taken into account as its fair market value.

(4) Present value.— Present value shall be determined by using a discount rate equal to 120 percent of the applicable Federal rate (determined under section 1274(d)), compounded semiannually.

(5) Treatment of affiliated groups.— Except as otherwise provided in regulations, all members of the same affiliated group (as defined in section 1504, determined without regard to section 1504(b)) shall be treated as 1 corporation for purposes of this section. Any person who is an officer of any member of such group shall be treated as an officer of such 1 corporation.

(e) Regulations.— The Secretary shall prescribe such regulations as may be necessary or appropriate to carry out the purposes of this section (including regulations for the application of this section in the case of related corporations and in the case of personal service corporations).

* * *

Subchapter D— Deferred Compensation, Etc.

Part I. Pension, profit-sharing, stock bonus plans, etc.

SEC. 401. QUALIFIED PENSION, PROFIT-SHARING, AND STOCK BONUS PLANS.

(a) Requirements for Qualification.— A trust created or organized in the United States and forming part of a stock bonus, pension, or profit-sharing plan of an employer for the exclusive benefit of his employees or their beneficiaries shall constitute a qualified trust under this section—

(1) If contributions are made to the trust by such employer, or employees, or both, or by another employer who is entitled to deduct his contributions under section 404(a)(3)(B) (relating to deduction for contributions to profit sharing and stock bonus plans), for the purpose of distributing to such employees or their beneficiaries the corpus and income of the fund accumulated by the trust in accordance with such plan;

(2) If under the trust instrument it is impossible, at any time prior to the satisfaction of all liabilities with respect to employees and their beneficiaries under the trust, for any part of the corpus or income to be (within the taxable year or thereafter) used for, or diverted to, purposes other than for the exclusive benefit of his employees or their beneficiaries but this paragraph shall not be construed, in the case of a multiemployer plan, to prohibit the return of a contribution within 6 months after the plan administrator determines that the contribution was made by a mistake of fact or law (other than a mistake relating to whether the plan is described in section 401(a) or the trust which is part of such plan is exempt from taxation under section 501(a), or the return of any withdrawal liability payment determined to be an overpayment within 6 months of such determination);

(3) If the plan of which such trust is a part satisfies the requirements of section 410 (relating to minimum participation standards); and

(4) If the contributions or benefits provided under the plan do not discriminate in favor of highly compensated employees (within the meaning of section 414(q)). For purposes of this paragraph, there shall be excluded from consideration employees described in section 410(b)(3)(A) and (C).

(5) Special rules relating to nondiscrimination requirements.—

(A) Salaried or clerical employees.— A classification shall not be considered discriminatory within the meaning of paragraph (4) or section 410(b)(2)(A)(i) merely because it is limited to salaried or clerical employees.

(B) Contributions and benefits may bear uniform relationship to compensation.— A plan shall not be considered discriminatory within the meaning of paragraph (4) merely because the contributions or benefits of, or on behalf of, the employees under the plan bear a uniform relationship to the compensation (within the meaning of section 414(s)) of such employees.

(C) Certain disparity permitted.— A plan shall not be considered discriminatory within the meaning of paragraph (4) merely because the contributions or benefits of, or on behalf of, the employees under the plan favor highly compensated employees (as defined in section 414(q)) in the manner permitted under subsection (*l*).

(D) Integrated defined benefit plan.—

(i) In general.— A defined benefit plan shall not be considered discriminatory within the meaning of paragraph (4) merely because the plan provides that the employer-derived accrued retirement benefit for any participant under the plan may not exceed the excess (if any) of—

(I) the participant's final pay with the employer, over

(II) the employer-derived retirement benefit created under Federal law attributable to service by the participant with the employer.

For purposes of this clause, the employer-derived retirement benefit created under Federal law shall be treated as accruing ratably over 35 years.

(ii) Final pay.— For purposes of this subparagraph, the participant's final pay is the compensation (as defined in section 414(q)(7)) paid to the participant by the employer for any year—

(I) which ends during the 5-year period ending with the year in which the participant separated from service for the employer, and

(II) for which the participant's total compensation from the employer was highest.

(E) 2 or more plans treated as single plan.— For purposes of determining whether 2 or more plans of an employer satisfy the requirements of paragraph (4) when considered as a single plan—

IRC Sec. 401 (a)(5)(E)

(i) Contributions.— If the amount of contributions on behalf of the employees allowed as a deduction under section 404 for the taxable year with respect to such plans, taken together, bears a uniform relationship to the compensation (within the meaning of section 414(s)) of such employees, the plans shall not be considered discriminatory merely because the rights of employees to, or derived from, the employer contributions under the separate plans do not become nonforfeitable at the same rate.

(ii) Benefits.— If the employees' rights to benefits under the separate plans do not become nonforfeitable at the same rate, but the levels of benefits provided by the separate plans satisfy the requirements of regulations prescribed by the Secretary to take account of the differences in such rates, the plans shall not be considered discriminatory merely because of the difference in such rates.

(6) A plan shall be considered as meeting the requirements of paragraph (3) during the whole of any taxable year of the plan if on one day in each quarter it satisfied such requirements.

(7) A trust shall not constitute a qualified trust under this section unless the plan of which such trust is a part satisfies the requirements of section 411 (relating to minimum vesting standards).

(8) A trust forming part of a defined benefit plan shall not constitute a qualified trust under this section unless the plan provides that forfeitures must not be applied to increase the benefits any employee would otherwise receive under the plan.

(9) Required Distributions.—

(A) In general.— A trust shall not constitute a qualified trust under this subsection unless the plan provides that the entire interest of each employee—

(i) will be distributed to such employee not later than the required beginning date, or

(ii) will be distributed, beginning not later than the required beginning date, in accordance with regulations, over the life of such employee or over the lives of such employee and designated beneficiary (or over a period not extending beyond the life expectancy of such employee or the life expectancy of such employee and a designated beneficiary.

(B) Required distribution where employee dies before entire interest is distributed.—

(i) where distributions have begun under subparagraph (A)(ii).— A trust shall not constitute a qualified trust under this section unless the plan provides that if—

(I) the distribution of the employee's interest has begun in accordance with subparagraph (A)(ii), and

(II) the employee dies before his entire interest has been distributed to him,

the remaining portion of such interest will be distributed at least as rapidly as under the method of distribution being used under subparagraph (A)(ii) as of the date of his death.

(ii) 5-year rule for other cases. A trust shall not constitute a qualified trust under this section unless the plan provides that, if an employee dies before the distribution of the employee's interest has begun in accordance with subparagraph (A)(ii), the entire interest of the employee will be distributed within 5 years after the death of such employee.

(iii) Exception to the 5-year rule for certain amounts payable over life of beneficiary.— If—

(I) any portion of the employee's interest is payable to (or for the benefit of) a designated beneficiary,

(II) such portion will be distributed (in accordance with regulations) over the life of such designated beneficiary (or over a period not extending beyond the life expectancy of such beneficiary), and

IRC Sec. 401 (a)(5)(E)(i)

(III) such distributions begin not later than 1 year after the date of the employee's death or such later date as the Secretary may by regulations prescribe,

for purposes of clause (ii), the portion referred to in subclause (I) shall be treated as distributed on the date on which such distribution began.

(iv) Special rules for surviving spouse of employee.— If the designated beneficiary referred to in clause (iii)(I) is the surviving spouse of the employee—

(I) the date on which the distributions are required to begin under clause (iii)(III) shall not be earlier than the date on which the employee would have attained age 70½, and

(II) if the surviving spouse dies before the distributions to such spouse begin, this subparagraph shall be applied as if the surviving spouse were the employee.

(C) Required beginning date.— For purposes of this paragraph, the term "required beginning date" means April 1 of the calendar year following the calendar year in which the employee attains age 70½. In the case of a governmental plan or church plan, the required beginning date shall be the later of the date determined under the preceding sentence or April 1 of the calendar year following the calendar year in which the employee retires. For the purposes of the subparagraph, the term "church plan" means a plan maintained by a church for church employees, and the term "church" means any church (as defined in section 3121(w)(3)(A)) or qualified church-controlled organization (as defined in section 3121(w)(3)(B)).

(D) Life expectancy.— For purposes of this paragraph, the life expectancy of an employee and the employee's spouse (other than in the case of a life annuity) may be redetermined but not more frequently than annually.

(E) Designated beneficiary.— For purposes of this paragraph, the term "designated beneficiary" means any individual designated as a beneficiary by the employee.

(F) Treatment of payments to children.— Under regulations prescribed by the Secretary, for purposes of this paragraph, any amount paid to a child shall be treated as if it had been paid to the surviving spouse if such amount will become payable to the surviving spouse upon such child reaching majority (or other designated event permitted under regulations.)

(G) Treatment of incidental death benefit distributions.— For purposes of this title, any distribution required under the incidental death benefit requirements of this subsection shall be treated as a distribution required under this subparagraph.

(10) Other requirements.—

(A) Plans benefiting owner-employees.— In the case of any plan which provides contributions or benefits for employees some or all of whom are owner-employees (as defined in subsection (c)(3)), a trust forming part of such plan shall constitute a qualified trust under this section only if the requirements of subsection (d) are also met.

(B) Top-heavy plans.—

(i) In general.— In the case of any top-heavy plan, a trust forming part of such plan shall constitute a qualified trust under this section only if the requirements of section 416 are met.

(ii) Plans which may become top-heavy.— Except to the extent provided in regulations, a trust forming part of a plan (whether or not a top-heavy plan) shall constitute a qualified trust under this section only if such plan contains provisions—

(I) which will take effect if such plan becomes a top-heavy plan, and

(II) which meet the requirements of section 416.

IRC Sec. 401 (a)(10)(B)(ii)(II)

(iii) Exemption for governmental plans.— This subparagraph shall not apply to any governmental plan.

(11) Requirement of joint and survivor annuity and preretirement survivor annuity.—

(A) In general.— In the case of any plan to which this paragraph applies, except as provided in section 417, a trust forming part of such plan shall not constitute a qualified trust under this section unless—

(i) in the case of a vested participant who does not die before the annuity starting date, the accrued benefit payable to such participant is provided in the form of a qualified joint and survivor annuity, and

(ii) in the case of a vested participant who dies before the annuity starting date and who has a surviving spouse, a qualified preretirement survivor annuity is provided to the surviving spouse of such participant.

(B) Plans to which paragraph applies.— This paragraph shall apply to—

(i) any defined benefit plan,

(ii) any defined contribution plan which is subject to the funding standards of section 412, and

(iii) any participant under any other defined contribution plan unless—

(I) such plan provides that the participant's nonforfeitable accrued benefit (reduced by any security interest held by the plan by reason of a loan outstanding to such participant) is payable in full, on the death of the participant, to the participant's surviving spouse (or, if there is no surviving spouse or the surviving spouse consents in the manner required under section 417(a)(2), to a designated beneficiary),

(II) such participant does not elect a payment of benefits in the form of a life annuity, and

(III) with respect to such participant, such plan is not a direct or indirect transferee (in a transfer after December 31, 1984) of a plan which is described in clause (i) or (ii) or to which this clause applied with respect to the participant.

Clause (iii)(III) shall apply only with respect to the transferred assets (and income therefrom) if the plan separately accounts for such assets and any income therefrom.

(C) Exception for certain ESOP benefits.

(i) In general.— In the case of—

(I) a tax credit employee stock ownership plan (as defined in section 409(a)), or

(II) an employee stock ownership plan (as defined in section 4975(e)(7)),

subparagraph (A) shall apply to that portion of the employee's accrued benefit to which the requirements of section 409(h) apply.

(ii) Nonforfeitable benefit must be paid in full, etc. In the case of any participant, clause (i) shall apply only if the requirements of subclauses (I), (II), and (III) of subparagraph (B)(iii) are met with respect to such participant.

(D) Special rule where participant and spouse married less than 1 year— A plan shall not be treated as failing to meet the requirements of subparagraphs (B)(iii) or (C) merely because the plan provides that benefits will not be payable to the surviving spouse of the participant unless the participant and such spouse had been married throughout the 1-year period ending on the earlier of the participant's annuity starting date or the date of the participant's death.

(E) Exception for plans described in section 404(c).— This paragraph shall not apply to a plan which the Secretary has determined is a plan described in section 404(c) (or continuation thereof) in which participation is substantially limited to individuals who before January 1, 1976, ceased employment covered by the plan.

(F) Cross reference.— For—

(i) provisions under which participants may elect to waive the requirements of this paragraph, and

(ii) other definitions and special rules for purposes of this paragraph,

see section 417.

(12) A trust shall not constitute a qualified trust under this section unless the plan of which such trust is a part provides that in the case of any merger or consolidation with, or transfer of assets or liabilities to, any other plan after September 2, 1974, each participant in the plan would (if the plan then terminated) receive a benefit immediately after the merger, consolidation, or transfer which is equal to or greater than the benefit he would have been entitled to receive immediately before the merger, consolidation, or transfer (if the plan had then terminated). The preceding sentence does not apply to any multiemployer plan with respect to any transaction to the extent that participants either before or after the transaction are covered under a multiemployer plan to which title IV of the Employee Retirement Income Security Act of 1974 applies.

(13) Assignment and alienation.—

(A) In general.— A trust shall not constitute a qualified trust under this section unless the plan of which such trust is a part provides that benefits provided under the plan may not be assigned or alienated. For purposes of the preceding sentence, there shall not be taken into account any voluntary and revocable assignment of not to exceed 10 percent of any benefit payment made by any participant who is receiving benefits under the plan unless the assignment or alienation is made for purposes of defraying plan administration costs. For purposes of this paragraph a loan made to a participant or beneficiary shall not be treated as an assignment or alienation if such loan is secured by the

participant's accrued nonforfeitable benefit and is exempt from the tax imposed by section 4975 (relating to tax on prohibited transactions) by reason of section 4975(d)(1). This paragraph shall take effect on January 1, 1976, and shall not apply to assignments which were irrevocable on September 2, 1974.

(B) Special rules for domestic relations orders.— Subparagraph (A) shall apply to the creation, assignment, or recognition of a right to any benefit payable with respect to a participant pursuant to a domestic relations order, except that subparagraph (A) shall not apply if the order is determined to be a qualified domestic relations order.

(14) A trust shall not constitute a qualified trust under this section unless the plan of which such trust is a part provides that, unless the participant otherwise elects, the payment of benefits under the plan to the participant will begin not later than the 60th day after the latest of the close of the plan year in which—

(A) the date on which the participant attains the earlier of age 65 or the normal retirement age specified under the plan,

(B) occurs the 10th anniversary of the year in which the participant commenced participation in the plan, or

(C) the participant terminates his service with the employer.

In the case of a plan which provides for the payment of an early retirement benefit, a trust forming a part of such plan shall not constitute a qualified trust under this section unless a participant who satisfied the service requirements for such early retirement benefit, but separated from the service (with any nonforfeitable right to an accrued benefit) before satisfying the age requirement for such early retirement benefit, is entitled upon satisfaction of such age requirement to receive a benefit not less than the benefit to which he would be entitled at the normal retirement age, actuari-

IRC Sec. 401 (a)(14)(C)

ally reduced under regulations prescribed by the Secretary.

(15) A trust shall not constitute a qualified trust under this section unless under the plan of which such trust is a part—

(A) in the case of a participant or beneficiary who is receiving benefits under such plan, or

(B) in the case of a participant who is separated from the service and who has nonforfeitable rights to benefits,

such benefits are not decreased by reason of any increase in the benefit levels payable under title II of the Social Security Act or any increase in the wage base under such title II, if such increase takes place after September 2, 1974, or (if later) the earlier of the date of first receipt of such benefits or the date of such separation, as the case may be.

(16) A trust shall not constitute a qualified trust under this section if the plan of which such trust is a part provides for benefits or contributions which exceed the limitations of section 415.

◊ ◊ ◊

Editor's Note: Code §401(a)(17)(B) as set forth below appears as amended by §732 of the Retirement Protection Act of 1994 (enacted as part of the Uruguay Round Agreements Act, P.L. 103-465). The amendments apply generally to years beginning after December 31, 1994. However, the amendment providing for rounding of indexed amounts does not apply to any year to the extent that the rounding would require the indexed amount to be reduced below the amount in effect for years beginning in 1994. Previously, §401(a)(17) had been amended by OBRA '93. For the effective date of the OBRA changes, see Editor's Note at the end of §401(a)(17), below.

◊ ◊ ◊

(17) Compensation limit.—

(A) In general.—A trust shall not constitute a qualified trust under this section unless, under the plan of which the trust is a part, the annual compensation of each employee taken into account under the plan for any year does not exceed $150,000. In determining the compensation of an employee, the rules of section 414(q)(6) shall apply, except that in applying such rules, the term "family" shall include only the spouse of the employee and any lineal descendants of the employee who have not attained age 19 before the close of the year.

[(B) Cost-of-living adjustment.—

[(i) In general.— If, for any calendar year after 1994, the excess (if any) of—

[(I) $150,000, increased by the cost-of-living adjustment for the calendar year, over

[(II) the dollar amount in effect under subparagraph (A) for taxable years beginning in the calendar year,

is equal to or greater than $10,000, then the $150,000 amount under subparagraph (A) (as previously adjusted under this subparagraph) for any taxable year beginning in any subsequent calendar year shall be increased by the amount of such excess, rounded to the next lowest multiple of $10,000.

[(ii) Cost-of-living adjustment.— The cost-of-living adjustment for any calendar year shall be the adjustment made under section 415(d) for such calendar year, except that the base period for purposes of section 415(d)(1)(A) shall be the calendar quarter beginning October 1, 1993.]

(B) Cost-of-living adjustment. The Secretary shall adjust annually the $150,000 amount in subparagraph (A) for increase in the cost-of-living at the same time and in the same manner as adjustments under section 415(d); except that the base period sha be the calendar quarter beginning Octobe

1, 1993, and any increase which is not a multiple of $10,000 shall be rounded to the next lowest multiple of $10,000.

◊ ◊ ◊

Editor's Note: Section 401(a)(17) was amended by §13212 of OBRA '93. Section 13212(d) of OBRA '93 contained the effective dates, below.

◊ ◊ ◊

(d) Effective Dates.—

(1) In general.— Except as provided in this subsection, the amendments made by this section shall apply to benefits accruing in plan years beginning after December 31, 1993.

(2) Collectively Bargained Plans.— In the case of a plan maintained pursuant to 1 or more collective bargaining agreements between employee representatives and 1 or more employers ratified before the date of the enactment of this Act, the amendments made by this section shall not apply to contributions or benefits pursuant to such agreements for plan years beginning before the earlier of—

(A) the latest of—

(i) January 1, 1994,

(ii) the date on which the last of such collective bargaining agreements terminates (without regard to any extension, amendment, or modification of such agreements on or after such date of enactment), or

(iii) in the case of a plan maintained pursuant to collective bargaining under the Railway Labor Act, the date of execution of an extension or replacement of the last of such collective bargining agreements in effect on such date of enactment, or

(B) January 1, 1997.

(3) Transition rule for state and local plans.—

(A) In general.— In the case of an eligible participant in a government plan (within the meaning of section 414(d) of the Internal Revenue Code of 1986), the dollar limitation under section 401(a)(17) of such Code shall not apply to the extent the amount of compensation which is allowed to be taken into account under the plan would be reduced below the amount which was allowed to be taken into account under the plan as in effect on July 1, 1993.

(B) Eligible participant.— For purposes of subparagraph (A), an eligible participant is an individual who first became a participant in the plan during a plan year beginning before the 1st plan year beginning after the earlier of—

(i) the plan year in which the plan is amended to reflect the amendments made by this section, or

(ii) December 31, 1995.

(C) Plan must be amended to incorporate limits— This paragraph shall not apply to any eligible participant of a plan unless the plan is amended so that the plan incorporates by reference the dollar limitation under section 401(a)(17) of the Internal Revenue Code of 1986, effective with respect to noneligible participants for plan years beginning after December 31, 1995 (or earlier if the plan amendment so provides).

◊ ◊ ◊

(18) [Repealed.]

(19) A trust shall not constitute a qualified trust under this section if under the plan of which such trust is a part any part of a participant's accrued benefit derived from employer contributions (whether or not otherwise nonforfeitable) is forfeitable solely because of withdrawal by such participant of any amount attributable to the benefit derived from contributions made by such participant. The preceding sentence shall not apply to the accrued benefit of any participant unless, at the time of such withdrawal, such participant has a nonforfeitable right to at least 50 percent of such accrued benefit (as determined under section 411). The first sentence of this paragraph shall not apply to the extent that an accrued benefit is permitted to be forfeited in accordance with section 411(a)(3)(D)(iii) (relating to proportional forfeitures of benefits accrued before September 2, 1974, in the event of withdrawal of certain mandatory contributions).

IRC Sec. 401 (a)(19)

(20) A trust forming part of a pension plan shall not be treated as failing to constitute a qualified trust under this section merely because the pension plan of which such trust is a part makes 1 or more distributions within 1 taxable year to a distributee on account of a termination of the plan of which the trust is a part, or in the case of a profit-sharing or stock bonus plan, a complete discontinuance of contributions under such plan. This paragraph shall not apply to a defined benefit plan unless the employer maintaining such plan files a notice with the Pension Benefit Guaranty Corporation (at the time and in the manner prescribed by the Pension Benefit Guaranty Corporation) notifying the Corporation of such payment or distribution and the Corporation has approved such payment or distribution or, within 90 days after the date on which such notice was filed, has failed to disapprove such payment or distribution. For purposes of this paragraph, rules similar to the rules of section 402(a)(6)(B) (as in effect before its repeal by section 211 of the Unemployment Compensation Amendments of 1992) shall apply.

(21) [Repealed.]

(22) If a defined contribution plan (other than a profit sharing plan)—

(A) is established by an employer whose stock is not readily tradable on an established market, and

(B) after acquiring securities of the employer, more than 10 percent of the total assets of the plan are securities of the employer,

any trust forming part of such plan shall not constitute a qualified trust under this section unless the plan meets the requirements of subsection (e) of section 409. The requirements of subsection (e) of section 409 shall not apply to any employees of an employer who are participants in any defined contribution plan established and maintained by such employer if the stock of such employer is not readily tradable on an established market and the trade or business of such employer consists of publishing on a regular basis a newspaper for general circulation. For purposes of the preceding sentence, subsections (b), (c), (m), and (o) of section 414 shall not apply except for determining whether stock of the employer is not readily tradable on an established market.

(23) A stock bonus plan shall not be treated as meeting the requirements of this section unless such plan meets the requirements of subsections (h) and (o) of section 409, except that in applying section 409(h) for purposes of this paragraph, the term "employer securities" shall include any securities of the employer held by the plan.

(24) Any group trust which otherwise meets the requirements of this section shall not be treated as not meeting such requirements on account of the participation or inclusion in such trust of the moneys of any plan or governmental unit described in section 818(a)(6).

(25) Requirement that actuarial assumptions be specified.— A defined benefit plan shall not be treated as providing definitely determinable benefits unless, whenever the amount of any benefit is to be determined on the basis of actuarial assumptions, such assumptions are specified in the plan in a way which precludes employer discretion.

(26) Additional participation requirements.—

(A) In general.—A trust shall not constitute a qualified trust under this subsection unless such trust is part of a plan which on each day of the plan year benefits the lesser of—

(i) 50 employees of the employer, or

(ii) 40 percent or more of all employees of the employer.

(B) Treatment of excludable employees.—

(i) In general.—A plan may exclude from consideration under this paragraph employees described in paragraphs (3) and (4)(A) of section 410(b).

(ii) Separate application for certain excludable employees.— If employees described in section 410(b)(4)(B) are covered under a plan which meets the requirements of subparagraph (A) separately with respect to such employees, such employees may be excluded from consideration in determining whether any plan of the employer meets such requirements if—

(I) the benefits for such employees are provided under the same plan as benefits for other employees,

(II) the benefits provided to such employees are not greater than comparable benefits provided to other employees under the plan, and

(III) no highly compensated employee (within the meaning of section 414(q)) is included in the group of such employees for more than 1 year.

(C) Eligibility to participate.— In the case of contributions under section 401(k) or 401(m), employees who are eligible to contribute (or may elect to have contributions made on their behalf) shall be treated as benefiting under the plan.

(D) Special rule for collective bargaining units.— Except to the extent provided in regulations, a plan covering only employees described in section 410(b)(3)(A) may exclude from consideration any employees who are not included in the unit or units in which the covered employees are included.

(E) Paragraph not to apply to multiemployer plans.— Except to the extent provided in regulations, this paragraph shall not apply to employees in a multiemployer plan (within the meaning of section 414(f)) who are covered by collective bargaining agreements.

(F) Special rule for certain dispositions for acquisitions.— Rules similar to the rules of section 410(b)(6)(C) shall apply for purposes of this paragraph.

(G) Separate lines of business.— At the election of the employer and with the consent of the Secretary, this paragraph may be applied separately with respect to each separate line of business of the employer. For purposes of this paragraph, the term "separate line of business" has the meaning given such term by section 414(r) (without regard to paragraph (7) thereof).

(H) Special rule for certain police or firefighters.—

(i) In general.— An employer may elect to have this paragraph applied separately with respect to any classification of qualified public safety employees for whom a separate plan is maintained.

(ii) Qualified public safety employee.— For purposes of this subparagraph, the term "qualified public safety employee" means any employee of any police department or fire department organized and operated by a State or political subdivision if the employee provides police protection, firefighting services, or emergency medical services for any area within the jurisdiction of such State or political subdivision.

(I) Regulations.— The Secretary may by regulation provide that any separate benefit structure, any separate trust, or any other separate arrangement is to be treated as a separate plan for purposes of applying this paragraph.

(27) Determinations as to profit-sharing plans.—

(A) Contributions need not be based on profits.— The determination of whether the plan under which any contributions are made is a profit-sharing plan shall be made without regard to current or accumulated profits of the employer and without regard to whether the employer is a tax-exempt organization.

(B) Plan must designate type.— In the case of a plan which is intended to be a money purchase pension plan or a profit-sharing plan, a trust forming part of such plan shall not constitute a qualified trust under this subsection unless the plan designates such

IRC Sec. 401 (a)(27)(B)

intent at such time and in such manner as the Secretary may prescribe.

(28) Additional requirements relating to employee stock ownership plans.—

(A) In general.— In the case of a trust which is part of an employee stock ownership plan (within the meaning of section 4975(e)(7)) or a plan which meets the requirements of section 409(a), such trust shall not constitute a qualified trust under this section unless such plan meets the requirements of subparagraphs (B) and (C).

(B) Diversification of investments.—

(i) In general.— A plan meets the requirements of this subparagraph if each qualified participant in the plan may elect within 90 days after the close of each plan year in the qualified election period to direct the plan as to the investment of at least 25 percent of the participant's account in the plan (to the extent such portion exceeds the amount to which a prior election under this subparagraph applies). In the case of the election year in which the participant can make his last election, the preceding sentence shall be applied by substituting "50 percent" for "25 percent".

(ii) Method of meeting requirements. A plan shall be treated as meeting the requirements of clause (i) if—

(I) the portion of the participant's account covered by the election under clause (i) is distributed within 90 days after the period during which the election may be made, or

(II) the plan offers at least 3 investment options (not inconsistent with regulations prescribed by the Secretary) to each participant making an election under clause (i) and within 90 days after the period during which the election may be made, the plan invests the portion of the participant's account covered by the election in accordance with such election.

(iii) Qualified participant.— For purposes of this subparagraph, the term "qualified participant" means any employee who has completed at least 10 years of participation under the plan and has attained age 55.

(iv) Qualified election period.— For purposes of this subparagraph, the term "qualified election period" means the 6-plan-year period beginning with the later of—

(I) the 1st plan year in which the individual first became a qualified participant, or

(II) the 1st plan year beginning after December 31, 1986.

For purposes of the preceding sentence, an employer may elect to treat an individual first becoming a qualified participant in the 1st plan year beginning in 1987 as having become a participant in the 1st plan year beginning in 1988.

(v) Coordination with distribution rules.— Any distribution required by this subparagraph shall not be taken into account in determining whether a subsequent distribution is a lump sum distribution under section 402(d)(4)(A) or in determining whether section 402(c)(10) applies.

(C) Use of independent appraiser.— A plan meets the requirements of this subparagraph if all valuations of employer securities which are not readily tradable on an established securities market with respect to activities carried on by the plan are by an independent appraiser. For purposes of the preceding sentence, the term "independent appraiser" means any appraiser meeting requirements similar to the requirements of the regulations prescribed under section 170(a)(1).

(29) Security required upon adoption of plan amendment resulting in significant underfunding.—

(A) In general.— If—

(i) a defined benefit plan (other than a multiemployer plan to which the requirements of section 412 apply) adopts a amendment an effect of which is to increase current liability under the plan for a plan year, and

(ii) the funded current liability percentage of the plan for the plan year in which the amendment takes effect is less than 60 percent, including the amount of the unfunded current liability under the plan attributable to the plan amendment,

the trust of which such plan is a part shall not constitute a qualified trust under this subsection unless such amendment does not take effect until the contributing sponsor (or any member of the controlled group of the contributing sponsor) provides security to the plan.

(B) Form of security.— The security required under subparagraph (A) shall consist of—

(i) a bond issued by a corporate surety company that is an acceptable surety for purposes of section 412 of the Employee Retirement Income Security Act of 1974,

(ii) cash, or United States obligations which mature in 3 years or less, held in escrow by a bank or similar financial institution, or

(iii) such other form of security as is satisfactory to the Secretary and the parties involved.

(C) Amount of security.— The security shall be in an amount equal to the excess of—

(i) the lesser of—

(I) the amount of additional plan assets which would be necessary to increase the funded current liability percentage under the plan to 60 percent, including the amount of the unfunded current liability under the plan attributable to the plan amendment, or

(II) the amount of the increase in current liability under the plan attributable to the

plan amendment and any other plan amendments adopted after December 22, 1987, and such plan amendment, over

(ii) $10,000,000.

(D) Release of security.— The security shall be released (and any amounts thereunder shall be refunded together with any interest accrued thereon) at the end of the first plan year which ends after the provision of the security and for which the funded current liability percentage under the plan is not less than 60 percent. The Secretary may prescribe regulations for partial releases of the security by reason of increases in the funded current liability percentage.

(E) Definitions.—For purposes of this paragraph, the terms ''current liability'', ''funded current liability percentage'', and ''unfunded current liability'' shall have the meanings given such terms by section 412(l), except that in computing unfunded current liability there shall not be taken into account any unamortized portion of the unfunded old liability amount as of the close of the plan year.

(30) Limitations on elective deferrals.— In the case of a trust which is part of a plan under which elective deferrals (within the meaning of section 402(g)(3)) may be made with respect to any individual during a calendar year, such trust shall not constitute a qualified trust under this subsection unless the plan provides that the amount of such deferrals under such plan and all other plans, contracts, or arrangements of an employer maintaining such plan may not exceed the amount of the limitation in effect under section 402(g)(1) for taxable years beginning in such calendar year.

(31) Optional direct transfer of eligible rollover distributions.—

(A) In general.— A trust shall not constitute a qualified trust under this section unless the plan of which such trust is a part provides that if the distributee of any eligible rollover distribution—

IRC Sec. 401 (a)(31)(A)

(i) elects to have such distribution paid directly to an eligible retirement plan, and

(ii) specifies the eligible retirement plan to which such distribution is to be paid (in such form and at such time as the plan administrator may prescribe), such distribution shall be made in the form of a direct trustee-to-trustee transfer to the eligible retirement plan so specified.

(B) Limitation.— Subparagraph (A) shall apply only to the extent that the eligible rollover distribution would be includible in gross income if not transferred as provided in subparagraph (A) (determined without regard to sections 402(c) and 403(a)(4)).

(C) Eligible rollover distribution.— For purposes of this paragraph, the term "eligible rollover distribution" has the meaning given such term by section 402(f)(2)(A).

(D) Eligible retirement plan.— For purposes of this paragraph, the term "eligible retirement plan" has the meaning given such term by section 402(c)(8)(B), except that a qualified trust shall be considered an eligible retirement plan only if it is a defined contribution plan, the terms of which permit the acceptance of rollover distributions.

◊ ◊ ◊

Editor's Note: Code §401(a)(32), below, was added by §751(a) of the Retirement Protection Act of 1994, which was enacted as part of the Uruguay Round Agreements Act (P.L. 103-465). The change applies to plan years beginning after December 31, 1994.

◊ ◊ ◊

(32) Treatment of failure to make certain payments if plan has liquidity shortfall.

(A) In general. A trust forming part of a pension plan to which section 412(m)(5) applies shall not be treated as failing to constitute a qualified trust under this section

merely because such plan ceases to make any payment described in subparagraph (B) during any period that such plan has a liquidity shortfall (as defined in section 412(m)(5)).

(B) Payments described. A payment is described in this subparagraph if such payment is

(i) any payment, in excess of the monthly amount paid under a single life annuity (plus any social security supplements described in the last sentence of section 411(a)(9)), to a participant or beneficiary whose annuity starting date (as defined in section 417(f)(2)) occurs during the period referred to in subparagraph (A),

(ii) any payment for the purchase of an irrevocable commitment from an insurer to pay benefits, and

(iii) any other payment specified by the Secretary by regulations.

(C) Period of shortfall. For purposes of this paragraph, a plan has a liquidity shortfall during the period that there is an underpayment of an installment under section 412(m) by reason of paragraph (5)(A) thereof.

◊ ◊ ◊

Editor's Note: Code §401(a)(33), below, was added by §766 of the Retirement Protection Act of 1994, enacted as part of the Uruguay Round Agreements Act (P.L. 103-465). It applies to plan amendments adopted on or after December 8, 1994.

◊ ◊ ◊

(33) Prohibition on benefit increases while sponsor is in bankruptcy.

(A) In general. A trust which is part of a plan to which this paragraph applies shall not constitute a qualified trust under this sec tion if amendment to such plan is adopted while the employer is a debtor in a case under title 11, United States Code, or simi

IRC Sec. 401 (a)(31)(A)(i)

lar Federal or State law, if such amendment increases liabilities of the plan by reason of

(i) any increase in benefits,

(ii) any change in the accrual of benefits, or

(iii) any change in the rate at which benefits become nonforfeitable under the plan,

with respect to employees of the debtor, and such amendment is effective prior to the effective date of such employer's plan of reorganization.

(B) Exceptions. This paragraph shall not apply to any plan amendment if—

(i) the plan, were such amendment to take effect, would have a funded current liability percentage (as defined in section 412(l)(8)) of 100 percent or more,

(ii) the Secretary determines that such amendment is reasonable and provides for only de minimis increases in the liabilities of the plan with respect to employees of the debtor,

(iii) such amendment only repeals an amendment described in subsection 412(c)(8), or

(iv) such amendment is required as a condition of qualification under this part.

(C) Plans to which this paragraph applies. This paragraph shall apply only to plans (other than multiemployer plans) covered under section 4021 of the Employee Retirement Income Security Act of 1974.

(D) Employer. For purposes of this paragraph, the term "employer" means the employer referred to in section 412(c)(11) (without regard to subparagraph (B) thereof).

◊ ◊ ◊

Editor's Note: Code §401(a)(34), as set forth below, was added by §776(d) of the Retirement Protection Act of 1994 (enacted as part of the Uruguay Round Agreements Act, P.L. 103-465). It applies to distributions occurring in plan years beginning after the PBGC issues final regulations implementing these provisions.

◊ ◊ ◊

(34) Benefits of missing participants on plan termination. In the case of a plan covered by title IV of the Employee Retirement Income Security Act of 1974, a trust forming part of such plan shall not be treated as failing to constitute a qualified trust under this section merely because the pension plan of which such trust is a part, upon its termination, transfers benefits of missing participants to the Pension Benefit Guaranty Corporation in accordance with section 4050 of such Act.

Paragraphs (11), (12), (13), (14), (15), (19), and (20) shall only apply in the case of a plan to which section 411 (relating to minimum vesting standards) applies without regard to subsection (e)(2) of such section.

(b) Certain Retroactive Changes in Plan.— A stock bonus, pension, profit-sharing, or annuity plan shall be considered as satisfying the requirements of subsection (a) for the period beginning with the date on which it was put into effect, or for the period beginning with the earlier of the date on which there was adopted or put into effect any amendment which caused the plan to fail to satisfy such requirements, and ending with the time prescribed by law for filing the return of the employer for his taxable year in which such plan or amendment was adopted (including extensions thereof) or such later time as the Secretary may designate, if all provisions of the plan which are necessary to satisfy such requirements are in effect by the end of such period and have been made effective for all purposes for the whole of such period.

IRC Sec. 401 (b)

(c) Definitions and Rules Relating to Self-Employed Individuals and Owner-Employees.— For purposes of this section—

(1) Self-employed individual treated as employee.—

(A) In general.— The term "employee" includes, for any taxable year, an individual who is a self-employed individual for such taxable year.

(B) Self-employed individual.— The term "self-employed individual" means, with respect to any taxable year, an individual who has earned income (as defined in paragraph (2)) for such taxable year. To the extent provided in regulations prescribed by the Secretary, such term also includes, for any taxable year—

(i) an individual who would be a self-employed individual within the meaning of the preceding sentence but for the fact that the trade or business carried on by such individual did not have net profits for the taxable year, and

(ii) an individual who has been a self-employed individual within the meaning of the preceding sentence for any prior taxable year.

(2) Earned income.—

(A) In general.— The term "earned income" means the net earnings from self-employment (as defined in section 1402(a)), but such net earnings shall be determined—

(i) only with respect to a trade or business in which personal services of the taxpayer are a material income-producing factor,

(ii) without regard to paragraphs (4) and (5) of section 1402(c),

(iii) in the case of any individual who is treated as an employee under sections 3121(d)(3)(A), (C), or (D), without regard to paragraph (2) of section 1402(c),

(iv) without regard to items which are not included in gross income for purposes of this chapter, and the deductions properly allocable to or chargeable against such items,

(v) with regard to the deductions allowed by section 404 to the taxpayer, and

(vi) with regard to the deduction allowed to the taxpayer by section 164(f).

For purposes of this subparagraph, section 1402, as in effect for a taxable year ending on December 31, 1962, shall be treated as having been in effect for all taxable years ending before such date.

(B) [Repealed.]

(C) Income from disposition of certain property.— For purposes of this section, the term "earned income" includes gains (other than any gain which is treated under any provision of this chapter as gain from the sale or exchange of a capital asset) and net earnings derived from the sale or other disposition of, the transfer of any interest in, or the licensing of the use of property (other than good will) by an individual whose personal efforts created such property.

(3) Owner-employee.—The term "owner-employee" means an employee who—

(A) owns the entire interest in an unincorporated trade or business, or

(B) in the case of a partnership, is a partner who owns more than 10 percent of either the capital interest or the profits interest in such partnership.

To the extent provided in regulations prescribed by the Secretary, such term also means an individual who has been an owner-employee within the meaning of the preceding sentence.

(4) Employer.— An individual who owns the entire interest in an unincorporated trade or business shall be treated as his own employer. A partnership shall be treated as the employer of each partner who is an employee within the meaning of paragraph (1).

(5) Contributions on behalf of owner-employees.— The term "contribution on behalf of an owner-employee" includes, except as the context otherwise requires, a contribution under a plan—

(A) by the employer for an owner-employee, and

(B) by an owner-employee as an employee.

(6) Special rule for certain fishermen.— For purposes of this subsection, the term "self-employed individual" includes an individual described in section 3121(b)(20) (related to certain fishermen).

(d) Additional requirements for qualification of trusts and plans benefiting owner-employees.— A trust forming part of a pension or profit-sharing plan which provides contributions or benefits for employees some or all of whom are owner-employees shall constitute a qualified trust under this section only if, in addition to meeting the requirements of subsection (a), the following requirements of this subsection are met by the trust and by the plan of which such trust is a part:

(1)(A) If the plan provides contributions or benefits for an owner-employee who controls, or for two or more owner-employees who together control, the trade or business with respect to which the plan is established, and who also control as an owner-employee or as owner-employees one or more other trades or businesses, such plan and the plans established with respect to such other trades or businesses, when coalesced, constitute a single plan which meets the requirements of subsection (a) (including paragraph (10) thereof) and of this subsection with respect to the employees of all such trades or businesses (including the trade or business with respect to which the plan intended to qualify under this section is established).

(B) For purposes of subparagraph (A), an owner-employee, or two or more owner-employees, shall be considered to control a trade or business if such owner-employee,

or such two or more owner-employees together—

(i) own the entire interest in an unincorporated trade or business, or

(ii) in the case of a partnership, own more than 50 percent of either the capital interest or the profits interest in such partnership.

For purposes of the preceding sentence, an owner-employee, or two or more owner-employees, shall be treated as owning any interest in a partnership which is owned, directly or indirectly, by a partnership which such owner-employee, or such two or more owner-employees, are considered to control within the meaning of the preceding sentence.

(2) The plan does not provide contributions or benefits for any owner-employee who controls (within the meaning of paragraph (1)(B)), or for two or more owner-employees who together control, as an owner-employee or as owner-employees, any other trade or business, unless the employees of each trade or business which such owner-employee or such owner-employees control are included under a plan which meets the requirements of subsection (a) (including paragraph (10) thereof) and of this subsection, and provides contributions and benefits for employees which are not less favorable than contributions and benefits provided for owner-employees under the plan.

(3) Under the plan, contributions on behalf of any owner-employee may be made only with respect to the earned income of such owner-employee which is derived from the trade or business with respect to which such plan is established.

(e) Contributions for Premiums on Annuity, Etc., Contracts.— [Repealed.]

(f) Certain Custodial Accounts and Contracts.— For purposes of this title, a custodial account, an annuity contract, or a contract (other than a life, health or accident, property, casualty, or liability insurance contract) issued

IRC Sec. 401 (f)

by an insurance company qualified to do business in a State shall be treated as a qualified trust under this section if—

(1) the custodial account or contract would, except for the fact that it is not a trust, constitute a qualified trust under this section, and

(2) in the case of a custodial account the assets thereof are held by a bank (as defined in section 408(n)) or another person who demonstrates, to the satisfaction of the Secretary, that the manner in which he will hold the assets will be consistent with the requirements of this section.

For purposes of this title, in the case of a custodial account or contract treated as a qualified trust under this section by reason of this subsection, the person holding the assets of such account or holding such contract shall be treated as the trustee thereof.

(g) Annuity Defined.— For purposes of this section and sections 402, 403, and 404, the term "annuity" includes a face-amount certificate, as defined in section 2(a)(15) of the Investment Company Act of 1940 (15 U.S.C., sec. 80a-2); but does not include any contract or certificate issued after December 31, 1962, which is transferable, if any person other than the trustee of a trust described in section 401(a) which is exempt from tax under section 501(a) is the owner of such contract or certificate.

(h) Medical, etc., Benefits for Retired Employees and Their Spouses and Dependents.— Under regulations prescribed by the Secretary, and subject to the provisions of section 420, a pension or annuity plan may provide for the payment of benefits for sickness, accident hospitalization, and medical expenses of retired employees, their spouses and their dependents, but only if—

(1) such benefits are subordinate to the retirement benefits provided by the plan,

(2) a separate account is established and maintained for such benefit,

(3) the employer's contributions to such separate account are reasonable and ascertainable,

(4) it is impossible, at any time prior to the satisfaction of all liabilities under the plan to provide such benefits, for any part of the corpus or income of such separate account to be (within the taxable year or thereafter) used for, or diverted to, any purposes other than the providing of such benefits,

(5) not withstanding the provisions of subsection (a)(2), upon the satisfaction of all liabilities under the plan to provide such benefits, any amount remaining in such separate account must, under the terms of the plan, be returned to the employer, and

(6) in the case of an employee who is a key employee, a separate account is established and maintained for such benefits payable to such employee (and his spouse and dependents) and such benefits (to the extent attributable to plan years beginning after March 31, 1984, for which the employee is a key employee) are only payable to such employee (and his spouse and dependents) from such separate account.

For purposes of paragraph (6), the term "key employee" means any employee, who at any time during the plan year or any preceding plan year during which contributions were made on behalf of such employee, is or was a key employee as defined in section 416(i). In no event shall the requirements of paragraph (1) be treated as met if the aggregate actual contributions for medical benefits, when added to actual contributions for life insurance protection under the plan, exceed 25 percent of the total actual contributions to the plan (other than contributions to fund past service credits) after the date on which the account is established.

(i) Certain Union-Negotiated Pension Plans.— In the case of a trust forming part of a pension plan which has been determined by the Secretary to constitute a qualified trust under subsection (a) and to be exempt from taxation under section 501(a) for a period beginning after contributions were first made to or for such trust, if it is shown to the satisfaction of the Secretary that—

(1) such trust was created pursuant to a collective bargaining agreement between employee representatives and one or more employers,

(2) any disbursements of contributions, made to or for such trust before the time as of which the Secretary determined that the trust constituted a qualified trust, substantially complied with the terms of the trust, and the plan of which the trust is a part, as subsequently qualified, and

(3) before the time as of which the Secretary determined that the trust constitutes a qualified trust, the contributions to or for such trust were not used in a manner which would jeopardize the interests of its beneficiaries,

then such trust shall be considered as having constituted a qualified trust under subsection (a) and as having been exempt from taxation under section 501(a) for the period beginning on the date on which contributions were first made to or for such trust and ending on the date such trust first constituted (without regard to this subsection) a qualified trust under subsection (a).

(j) Defined Benefit Plans Providing Benefits for Self-Employed Individuals nd Shareholder-Employees.— [Repealed.]

(k) Cash or Deferred Arrangements.—

(1) General rule.—A profit-sharing or stock bonus plan, a pre-ERISA money purchase plan, or a rural cooperative plan shall not be considered as not satisfying the requirements of subsection (a) merely because the plan includes a qualified cash or deferred arrangement.

(2) Qualified cash or deferred arrangement.—A qualified cash or deferred arrangement is any arrangement which is part of a profit-sharing or stock bonus plan, a pre-

ERISA money purchase plan, or a rural cooperative plan which meets the requirements of subsection (a)—

(A) under which a covered employee may elect to have the employer make payments as contributions to a trust under the plan on behalf of the employee, or to the employee directly in cash;

(B) under which amounts held by the trust which are attributable to employer contributions made pursuant to the employee's election—

(i) may not be distributable to participants or other beneficiaries earlier than—

(I) separation from service, death, or disability,

(II) an event described in paragraph (10),

(III) in the case of a profit-sharing or stock bonus plan, the attainment of age 59½, or

(IV) in the case of contributions to a profit-sharing or stock bonus plan to which section 402(e)(3) applies, upon hardship of the employee, and

(ii) will not be distributable merely by reason of the completion of a stated period of participation or the lapse of a fixed number of years;

(C) which provides that an employee's right to his accrued benefit derived from employer contributions made to the trust pursuant to his election is nonforfeitable, and

(D) which does not require, as a condition of participation in the arrangement, that an employee complete a period of service with the employer (or employers) maintaining the plan extending beyond the period permitted under section 410(a)(1) (determined without regard to subparagraph (B)(i) thereof).

IRC Sec. 401 (k)(2)(D)

(3) Application of participation and discrimination standards.—

(A) A cash or deferred arrangement shall not be treated as a qualified cash or deferred arrangement unless—

(i) those employees eligible to benefit under the arrangement satisfy the provisions of section 410(b)(1), and

(ii) the actual deferral percentage for eligible highly compensated employees (as defined in paragraph (5)) for such year bears a relationship to the actual deferral percentage for all other eligible employees for such plan year which meets either of the following tests:

(I) The actual deferral percentage for the group of eligible highly compensated employees is not more than the actual deferral percentage of all other eligible employees multiplied by 1.25.

(II) The excess of the actual deferral percentage for the group of eligible highly compensated employees over that of all other eligible employees is not more than 2 percentage points, and the actual deferral percentage for the group of eligible highly compensated employees is not more than the actual deferral percentage of all other eligible employees multiplied by 2.

If 2 or more plans which include cash or deferred arrangements are considered as 1 plan for purposes of section 401(a)(4) or 410(b), the cash or deferred arrangements included in such plans shall be treated as 1 arrangement for purposes of this subparagraph.

If an eligible highly compensated employee is a participant under 2 or more cash or deferred arrangements of the employer, for purposes of determining the deferral percentage with respect to such employee, all such cash or deferred arrangements shall be treated as 1 cash or deferred arrangement.

(B) For purposes of subparagraph (A), the actual deferral percentage for a specified group of employees for a plan year shall be the average of the ratios (calculated separately for each employee in such group) of—

(i) the amount of employer contributions actually paid over to the trust on behalf of each such employee for such plan year to

(ii) the employee's compensation for such plan year.

(C) A cash or deferred arrangement shall be treated as meeting the requirements of subsection (a)(4) with respect to contributions if the requirements of subparagraph (A)(ii) are met.

(D) For purposes of subparagraph (B), the employer contributions on behalf of any employee—

(i) shall include any employer contributions made pursuant to the employee's election under paragraph (2), and

(ii) under such rules as the Secretary may prescribe, may, at the election of the employer, include—

(I) matching contributions (as defined in 401(m)(4)(A)) which meet the requirements of paragraph (2) (B) and (C), and

(II) qualified nonelective contributions (within the meaning of section 401(m)(4)(C)).

(4) Other requirements.—

(A) Benefits (other than matching contributions) must not be contingent on election to defer.— A cash or deferred arrangement of any employer shall not be treated as a qualified cash or deferred arrangement if any other benefit is conditioned (directly or indirectly) on the employee electing to have the employer make or not make contributions under the arrangement in lieu of receiving cash. The preceding sentence shall not apply to any matching contribution (as defined in section 401(m)) made by reason of such an election.

(B) State and local governments and tax-exempt organizations not eligible.— A cash or deferred arrangement shall not be treated as a qualified cash or deferred arrangement if it is part of a plan maintained by—

(i) a State or local government or political subdivision thereof, or any agency or instrumentality thereof, or

(ii) any organization exempt from tax under this subtitle. This subparagraph shall not apply to a rural cooperative plan.

(C) Coordination with other plans.— Except as provided in section 401(m), any employer contribution made pursuant to an employee's election under a qualified cash or deferred arrangement shall not be taken into account for purposes of determining whether any other plan meets the requirements of section 401(a) or 410(b). This subparagraph shall not apply for purposes of determining whether a plan meets the average benefit requirement of section 410(b)(2)(A)(ii).

(5) Highly compensated employee.— For purposes of this subsection, the term "highly compensated employee" has the meaning given such term by section 414(q).

(6) Pre-ERISA money purchase plan.— For purposes of this subsection, the term "pre-ERISA money purchase plan" means a pension plan—

(A) which is a defined contribution plan (as defined in section 414(i)),

(B) which was in existence on June 27, 1974, and which, on such date, included a salary reduction arrangement, and

(C) under which neither the employee contributions nor the employer contributions may exceed the levels provided for by the contribution formula in effect under the plan on such date.

(7) Rural cooperative plan.— For purposes of this subsection—

(A) In general.— The term "rural cooperative plan" means any pension plan—

(i) which is a defined contribution plan (as defined in section 414(i)), and

(ii) which is established and maintained by a rural cooperative.

(B) Rural cooperative defined.— For purposes of subparagraph (A), the term "rural cooperative" means—

(i) any organization which—

(I) is exempt from tax under this subtitle or which is a State or local government or political subdivision thereof (or agency or instrumentality thereof), and

(II) is engaged primarily in providing electric service on a mutual or cooperative basis,

(ii) any organization described in paragraph (4) or (6) of section 501(c) and at least 80 percent of the members of which are organizations described in clause (i),

(iii) a cooperative telephone company described in section 501(c)(12), and

(iv) an organization which is a national association of organizations described in clause (i), (ii), or (iii).

(8) Arrangement not disqualified if excess contributions distributed.—

(A) In general.— A cash or deferred arrangement shall not be treated as failing to meet the requirements of clause (ii) of paragraph (3)(A) for any plan year if, before the close of the following plan year—

(i) the amount of the excess contributions for such plan year (and any income allocable to such contributions) is distributed, or

(ii) to the extent provided in regulations, the employee elects to treat the amount of the excess contributions as an amount distributed to the employee and then contributed by the employee to the plan.

IRC Sec. 401 (k)(8)(A)(ii)

Any distribution of excess contributions (and income) may be made without regard to any other provision of law.

(B) Excess contributions.—For purposes of subparagraph (A), the term "excess contributions" means, with respect to any plan year, the excess of—

(i) the aggregate amount of employer contributions actually paid over to the trust on behalf of highly compensated employees for such plan year, over

(ii) the maximum amount of such contributions permitted under the limitations of clause (ii) of paragraph (3)(A) (determined by reducing contributions made on behalf of highly compensated employees in order of the actual deferral percentages beginning with the highest of such percentages).

(C) Method of distributing excess contributions.— Any distribution of the excess contributions for any plan year shall be made to highly compensated employees on the basis of the respective portions of the excess contributions attributable to each of such employees.

(D) Additional tax under section 72(t) not to apply.— No tax shall be imposed under section 72(t) on any amount required to be distributed under this paragraph.

(E) Treatment of matching contributions forfeited by reason of excess deferral or contribution.— For purposes of paragraph (2)(C), a matching contribution (within the meaning of subsection (m)) shall not be treated as forfeitable merely because such contribution is forfeitable if the contribution to which the matching contribution relates is treated as an excess contribution under subparagraph (B), an excess deferral under section 402(g)(2)(A), or an excess aggregate contribution under section 401(m)(6)(B).

(F) Cross reference.— For excise tax on certain excess contributions, see section 4979.

(9) Compensation.— For purposes of this subsection, the term "compensation" has the meaning given such term by section 414(s).

(10) Distributions upon termination of plan or disposition of assets or subsidiary.—

(A) In general.— The following events are described in this paragraph:

(i) Termination.— The termination of the plan without establishment or maintenance of another defined contribution plan (other than an employee stock ownership plan as defined in section 4975(e)(7)).

(ii) Disposition of assets.— The disposition by a corporation of substantially all of the assets (within the meaning of section 409(d)(2)) used by such corporation in a trade or business of such corporation, but only with respect to an employee who continues employment with the corporation acquiring such assets.

(iii) Disposition of subsidiary.— The disposition by a corporation of such corporation's interest in a subsidiary (within the meaning of section 409(d)(3)), but only with respect to an employee who continues employment with such subsidiary.

(B) Distributions must be lump sum distributions.—

(i) In general.— An event shall not be treated as described in subparagraph (A) with respect to any employee unless the employee receives a lump sum distribution by reason of the event.

(ii) Lump sum distribution.— For purposes of this subparagraph, the term "lump sum distribution" has the meaning given such term by section 402(d)(4), without regard to clauses (i), (ii), (iii), and (iv) of subparagraph (A), subparagraph (B), or subparagraph (F) thereof.

(C) Transferor corporation must maintain plan.— An event shall not be treated as described in clause (ii) or (iii) of subparagraph (A) unless the transferor corporation continues to maintain the plan after the disposition.

(*l*) Permitted Disparity in Plan Contributions or Benefits.—

(1) In general.— The requirements of this subsection are met with respect to a plan if—

(A) in the case of a defined contribution plan, the requirements of paragraph (2) are met, and

(B) in the case of a defined benefit plan, the requirements of paragraph (3) are met.

(2) Defined contribution plan.—

(A) In general.— A defined contribution plan meets the requirements of this paragraph if the excess contribution percentage does not exceed the base contribution percentage by more than the lesser of—

(i) the base contribution percentage, or

(ii) the greater of—

(I) 5.7 percentage points, or

(II) the percentage equal to the portion of the rate of tax under section 3111(a) (in effect as of the beginning of the year) which is attributable to old-age insurance.

(B) Contribution percentages.— For purposes of this paragraph—

(i) Excess contribution percentage.— The term ''excess contribution percentage'' means the percentage of compensation which is contributed by the employer under the plan with respect to that portion of each participant's compensation in excess of the integration level.

(ii) Base contribution percentage.— The term ''base contribution percentage'' means the percentage of compensation contributed by the employer under the plan with respect to that portion of each participant's compensation not in excess of the integration level.

(3) Defined benefit plan.— A defined benefit plan meets the requirements of this paragraph if—

(A) Excess plans.—

(i) In general.— In the case of a plan other than an offset plan—

(I) the excess benefit percentage does not exceed the base benefit percentage by more than the maximum excess allowance,

(II) any optional form of benefit, preretirement benefit, actuarial factor, or other benefit or feature provided with respect to compensation in excess of the integration level is provided with respect to compensation not in excess of such level, and

(III) benefits are based on average annual compensation.

(ii) Benefit percentages.— For purposes of this subparagraph, the excess and base benefit percentages shall be computed in the same manner as the excess and base contribution percentages under paragraph (2)(B), except that such determination shall be made on the basis of benefits attributable to employer contributions rather than contributions.

(B) Offset plans.— In the case of an offset plan, the plan provides that—

(i) a participant's accrued benefit attributable to employer contributions (within the meaning of section 411(c)(1)) may not be reduced (by reason of the offset) by more than the maximum offset allowance, and

(ii) benefits are based on average annual compensation.

(4) Definitions relating to paragraph (3).— For purposes of paragraph (3)—

(A) Maximum excess allowance.— The maximum excess allowance is equal to—

(i) in the case of benefits attributable to any year of service with the employer taken

IRC Sec. 401 (*l*)(4)(A)(i)

into account under the plan, ¾ of a percentage point, and

(ii) in the case of total benefits, ¾ of a percentage point, multiplied by the participant's years of service (not in excess of 35) with the employer taken into account under the plan.

In no event shall the maximum excess allowance exceed the base benefit percentage.

(B) Maximum offset allowance.— The maximum offset allowance is equal to—

(i) in the case of benefits attributable to any year of service with the employer taken into account under the plan, ¾ percent of the participant's final average compensation, and

(ii) in the case of total benefits, ¾ percent of the participant's final average compensation, multiplied by the participant's years of service (not in excess of 35) with the employer taken into account under the plan.

In no event shall the maximum offset allowance exceed 50 percent of the benefit which would have accrued without regard to the offset reduction.

(C) Reductions.—

(i) In general.— The Secretary shall prescribe regulations requiring the reduction of the ¾ percentage factor under subparagraph (A) or (B)—

(I) in the case of a plan other than an offset plan which has an integration level in excess of covered compensation, or

(II) with respect to any participant in an offset plan who has final average compensation in excess of covered compensation.

(ii) Basis of reductions.— Any reductions under clause (i) shall be based on the percentages of compensation replaced by the employer-derived portions of primary insurance amounts under the Social Security Act for participants with compensation in excess of covered compensation.

(D) Offset plan.— The term "offset plan" means any plan with respect to which the benefit attributable to employer contributions for each participant is reduced by an amount specified in the plan.

(5) Other definitions and special rules.— For purposes of this subsection—

(A) Integration level.—

(i) In general.— The term "integration level" means the amount of compensation specified under the plan (by dollar amount or formula) at or below which the rate at which contributions or benefits are provided (expressed as a percentage) is less than such rate above such amount.

(ii) Limitation.— The integration level for any year may not exceed the contribution and benefit base in effect under section 230 of the Social Security Act for such year.

(iii) Level to apply to all participants.— A plan's integration level shall apply with respect to all participants in the plan.

(iv) Multiple integration levels.— Under rules prescribed by the Secretary, a defined benefit plan may specify multiple integration levels.

(B) Compensation.— The term "compensation" has the meaning given such term by section 414(s).

(C) Average annual compensation.— The term "average annual compensation" means the participant's highest average annual compensation for—

(i) any period of at least 3 consecutive years, or

(ii) if shorter, the participant's full period of service.

(D) Final average compensation.—

(i) In general.— The term "final average compensation" means the participant's average annual compensation for—

(I) the 3-consecutive year period ending with the current year, or

(II) if shorter, the participant's full period of service.

(ii) Limitation.— A participant's final average compensation shall be determined by not taking into account in any year compensation in excess of the contribution and benefit base in effect under section 230 of the Social Security Act for such year.

(E) Covered compensation.—

(i) In general.— The term "covered compensation" means, with respect to an employee, the average of the contribution and benefit bases in effect under section 230 of the Social Security Act for each year in the 35-year period ending with the year in which the employee attains the social security retirement age.

(ii) Computation for any year.— For purposes of clause (i), the determination for any year preceding the year in which the employee attains the social security retirement age shall be made by assuming that there is no increase in the bases described in clause (i) after the determination year and before the employee attains the social security retirement age.

(iii) Social security retirement age.— For purposes of this subparagraph, the term "social security retirement age" has the meaning given such term by section 415(b)(8).

(F) Regulations.— The Secretary shall prescribe such regulations as are necessary or appropriate to carry out the purposes of this subsection, including—

(i) in the case of a defined benefit plan which provides for unreduced benefits commencing before the social security retirement age (as defined in section 415(b)(8)), rules providing for the reduction of the maximum excess allowance and the maximum offset allowance, and

(ii) in the case of an employee covered by 2 or more plans of the employer which fail to meet the requirements of subsection (a)(4) (without regard to this subsection), rules preventing the multiple use of the disparity permitted under this subsection with respect to any employee.

For purposes of clause (i), unreduced benefits shall not include benefits for disability (within the meaning of section 223(d) of the Social Security Act).

(6) Special rule for plan maintained by railroads.— In determining whether a plan which includes employees of a railroad employer who are entitled to benefits under the Railroad Retirement Act of 1974 meets the requirements of this subsection, rules similar to the rules set forth in this subsection shall apply. Such rules shall take into account the employer-derived portion of the employees' tier 2 railroad retirement benefits and any supplemental annuity under the Railroad Retirement Act of 1974.

(m) Nondiscrimination Test for Matching Contributions and Employee Contributions.—

(1) In general.— A defined contribution plan shall be treated as meeting the requirements of subsection (a)(4) with respect to the amount of any matching contribution or employee contribution for any plan year only if the contribution percentage requirement of paragraph (2) of this subsection is met for such plan year.

(2) Requirements.—

(A) Contribution percentage requirement.— A plan meets the contribution percentage requirement of this paragraph for any plan year only if the contribution percentage for eligible highly compensated employees does not exceed the greater of—

(i) 125 percent of such percentage for all other eligible employees, or

IRC Sec. 401 (m)(2)(A)(i)

(ii) the lesser of 200 percent of such percentage for all other eligible employees, or such percentage for all other eligible employees plus 2 percentage points.

(B) Multiple plans treated as a single plan.— If two or more plans of an employer to which matching contributions, employee contributions, or elective deferrals are made are treated as one plan for purposes of section 410(b), such plans shall be treated as one plan for purposes of this subsection. If a highly compensated employee participates in two or more plans of an employer to which contributions to which this subsection applies are made, all such contributions shall be aggregated for purposes of this subsection.

(3) Contribution percentage.— For purposes of paragraph (2), the contribution percentage for a specified group of employees for a plan year shall be the average of the ratios (calculated separately for each employee in such group) of—

(A) the sum of the matching contributions and employee contributions paid under the plan on behalf of each such employee for such plan year, to—

(B) the employee's compensation (within the meaning of section 414(s)) for such plan year.

Under regulations, an employer may elect to take into account (in computing the contribution percentage) elective deferrals and qualified nonelective contributions under the plan or any other plan of the employer. If matching contributions are taken into account for purposes of subsection (k)(3)(A)(ii) for any plan year, such contributions shall not be taken into account under subparagraph (A) for such year.

(4) Definitions.— For purposes of this subsection—

(A) Matching contribution.— The term "matching contribution" means—

(i) any employer contribution made to a defined contribution plan on behalf of an employee on account of an employee contribution made by such employee, and

(ii) any employer contribution made to a defined contribution plan on behalf of an employee on account of an employee's elective deferral.

(B) Elective deferral.— The term "elective deferral" means any employer contribution described in section 402(g)(3).

(C) Qualified nonelective contributions.— The term "qualified nonelective contribution" means any employer contribution (other than a matching contribution) with respect to which—

(i) the employee may not elect to have the contribution paid to the employee in cash instead of being contributed to the plan, and

(ii) the requirements of subparagraphs (B) and (C) of subsection (k)(2) are met.

(5) Employees taken into consideration.—

(A) In general.— Any employee who is eligible to make an employee contribution (or, if the employer takes elective contributions into account, elective contributions) or to receive a matching contribution under the plan being tested under paragraph (1) shall be considered an eligible employee for purposes of this subsection.

(B) Certain nonparticipants.— If an employee contribution is required as a condition of participation in the plan, any employee who would be a participant in the plan if such employee made such a contribution shall be treated as an eligible employee on behalf of whom no employer contributions are made.

(6) Plan not disqualified if excess aggregate contributions distributed before end of following plan year.—

(A) In general.— A plan shall not be treated as failing to meet the requirements of para-

IRC Sec. 401 (m)(2)(A)(ii)

graph (1) for any plan year if, before the close of the following plan year, the amount of the excess aggregate contributions for such plan year (and any income allocable to such contributions) is distributed (or, if forfeitable, is forfeited). Such contributions (and such income) may be distributed without regard to any other provision of law.

(B) Excess aggregate contributions.— For purposes of subparagraph (A), the term ''excess aggregate contributions'' means, with respect to any plan year, the excess of—

(i) the aggregate amount of the matching contributions and employee contributions (and any qualified nonelective contribution or elective contribution taken into account in computing the contribution percentage) actually made on behalf of highly compensated employees for such plan year, over

(ii) the maximum amount of such contributions permitted under the limitations of paragraph (2)(A) (determined by reducing contributions made on behalf of highly compensated employees in order of their contribution percentages beginning with the highest of such percentages).

(C) Method of distributing excess aggregate contributions.— Any distribution of the excess aggregate contributions for any plan year shall be made to highly compensated employees on the basis of the respective portions of such amounts attributable to each of such employees. Forfeitures of excess aggregate contributions may not be allocated to participants whose contributions are reduced under this paragraph.

(D) Coordination with subsection (k) and 402(g).— The determination of the amount of excess aggregate contributions with respect to a plan shall be made after—

(i) first determining the excess deferrals (within the meaning of section 402(g)), and

(ii) then determining the excess contributions under subsection (k).

(7) Treatment of distributions.—

(A) Additional tax of section 72(t) not applicable.— No tax shall be imposed under section 72(t) on any amount required to be distributed under paragraph (6).

(B) Exclusion of employee contributions.— Any distribution attributable to employee contributions shall not be included in gross income except to the extent attributable to income on such contributions.

(8) Highly compensated employee.— For purposes of this subsection, the term ''highly compensated employee'' has the meaning given to such term by section 414(q).

(9) Regulations.— The Secretary shall prescribe such regulations as may be necessary to carry out the purposes of this subsection and subsection (k) including—

(A) such regulations as may be necessary to prevent the multiple use of the alternative limitation with respect to any highly compensated employee, and

(B) regulations permitting appropriate aggregation of plans and contributions.

For purposes of the preceding sentence, the term ''alternative limitation'' means the limitation of section 401(k)(3)(A)(ii)(II) and the limitation of paragraph (2)(A)(ii) of this subsection.

(10) Cross reference.— For excise tax on certain excess contributions, see section 4979.

(n) Coordination with qualified domestic relations orders.— The Secretary shall prescribe such rules or regulations as may be necessary to coordinate the requirements of subsection (a)(13)(B) and section 414(p) (and the regulations issued by the Secretary of Labor thereunder) with the other provisions of this chapter.

(o) Cross Reference.— For exemption from tax of a trust qualified under this section, see Section 501(a).

IRC Sec. 401 (o)

SEC. 402. TAXABILITY OF BENEFICI-ARY OF EMPLOYEES' TRUST.

(a) Taxability of Beneficiary of Exempt Trust.— Except as otherwise provided in this section, any amount actually distributed to any distributee by any employees' trust described in section 401(a) which is exempt from tax under section 501(a) shall be taxable to the distributee, in the taxable year of the distributee in which distributed, under section 72 (relating to annuities).

(b) Taxability of Beneficiary of Nonexempt Trust.—

(1) Contributions.— Contributions to an employees' trust made by an employer during a taxable year of the employer which ends with or within a taxable year of the trust for which the trust is not exempt from tax under section 501(a) shall be included in the gross income of the employee in accordance with section 83 (relating to property transferred in connection with performance of services), except that the value of the employee's interest in the trust shall be substituted for the fair market value of the property for purposes of applying such section.

(2) Distributions.— The amount actually distributed or made available to any distributee by any trust described in paragraph (1) shall be taxable to the distributee, in the taxable year in which so distributed or made available, under section 72 (relating to annuities), except that distributions of income of such trust before the annuity starting date (as defined in section 72(c)(4)) shall be included in the gross income of the employee without regard to section 72(e)(5) (relating to amounts not received as annuities).

(3) Grantor Trusts.— A beneficiary of any trust described in paragraph (1) shall not be considered the owner of any portion of such trust under subpart E of part I of subchapter J (relating to grantors and others treated as substantial owners).

(4) Failure to meet requirements of section 410(b).—

(A) Highly compensated employees.— If 1 of the reasons a trust is not exempt from tax under section 501(a) is the failure of the plan of which it is a part to meet the requirements of section 401(a)(26) or 410(b), then a highly compensated employee shall, in lieu of the amount determined under paragraph (1) or (2) include in gross income for the taxable year with or within which the taxable year of the trust ends an amount equal to the vested accrued benefit of such employee (other than the employee's investment in the contract) as of the close of such taxable year of the trust.

(B) Failure to meet coverage tests.— If a trust is not exempt from tax under section 501(a) for any taxable year solely because such trust is part of a plan which fails to meet the requirements of section 401(a)(26) or 410(b), paragraphs (1) and (2) shall not apply by reason of such failure to any employee who was not a highly compensated employee during—

(i) such taxable year, or

(ii) any preceding period for which service was creditable to such employee under the plan.

(C) highly compensated employee.— For purposes of this paragraph, the term "highly compensated employee" has the meaning given such term by section 414(q).

(c) Rules Applicable to Rollovers from Exempt Trusts.—

(1) Exclusion from income.— If—

(A) any portion of the balance to the credit of an employee in a qualified trust is paid to the employee in an eligible rollover distribution,

(B) the distributee transfers any portion of the property received in such distribution to an eligible retirement plan, and

(C) in the case of a distribution of property other than money, the amount so transferred consists of the property distributed,

then such distribution (to the extent so transferred) shall not be includible in gross income for the taxable year in which paid.

(2) Maximum amount which may be rolled over.— In the case of any eligible rollover distribution, the maximum amount transferred to which paragraph (1) applies shall not exceed the portion of such distribution which is includible in gross income (determined without regard to paragraph (1)).

(3) Transfer must be made within 60 days of receipt.— Paragraph (1) shall not apply to any transfer of a distribution made after the 60th day following the day on which the distributee received the property distributed.

(4) Eligible rollover distribution.— For purposes of this subsection, the term "eligible rollover distribution" means any distribution to an employee of all or any portion of the balance to the credit of the employee in a qualified trust; except that such term shall not include—

(A) any distribution which is one of a series of substantially equal periodic payments (not less frequently than annually) made—

(i) for the life (or life expectancy) of the employee or the joint lives (or joint life expectancies) of the employee and the employee's designated beneficiary, or

(ii) for a specified period of 10 years or more, and

(B) any distribution to the extent such distribution is required under section 401(a)(9).

(5) Transfer treated as rollover contribution under section 408.— For purposes of this title, a transfer to an eligible retirement plan described in clause (i) or (ii) of paragraph (8)(B) resulting in any portion of a distribution being excluded from gross income under paragraph (1) shall be treated as a rollover contribution described in section 408(d)(3).

(6) Sales of distributed property.— For purposes of this subsection—

(A) Transfer of proceeds from sale of distributed property treated as transfer of distributed property.— The transfer of an amount equal to any portion of the proceeds from the sale of property received in the distribution shall be treated as the transfer of property received in the distribution.

(B) Proceeds attributable to increase in value.— The excess of fair market value of property on sale over its fair market value on distribution shall be treated as property received in the distribution.

(C) Designation where amount of distribution exceeds rollover contribution.— In any case where part or all of the distribution consists of property other than money—

(i) the portion of the money or other property which is to be treated as attributable to amounts not included in gross income, and

(ii) the portion of the money or other property which is to be treated as included in the rollover contribution,

shall be determined on a ratable basis unless the taxpayer designates otherwise. Any designation under this subparagraph for a taxable year shall be made not later than the time prescribed by law for filing the return for such taxable year (including extensions thereof). Any such designation, once made, shall be irrevocable.

(D) Nonrecognition of gain or loss.— No gain or loss shall be recognized on any sale described in subparagraph (A) to the extent that an amount equal to the proceeds is transferred pursuant to paragraph (1).

(7) Special rule for frozen deposits.—

(A) In general.— The 60-day period described in paragraph (3) shall not—

(i) include any period during which the amount transferred to the employee is a frozen deposit, or

(ii) end earlier than 10 days after such amount ceases to be a frozen deposit.

(B) Frozen deposits.— For purposes of this subparagraph, the term "frozen deposit" means any deposit which may not be withdrawn because of—

(i) the bankruptcy or insolvency of any financial institution, or

(ii) any requirement imposed by the State in which such institution is located by reason of the bankruptcy or insolvency (or threat thereof) of 1 or more financial institutions in such State.

A deposit shall not be treated as a frozen deposit unless on at least 1 day during the 60-day period described in paragraph (3) (without regard to this paragraph) such deposit is described in the preceding sentence.

(8) Definitions.— For purposes of this subsection—

(A) Qualified trust.— The term "qualified trust" means an employees' trust described in section 401(a) which is exempt from tax under section 501(a).

(B) Eligible retirement plan.— The term "eligible retirement plan" means—

(i) an individual retirement account described in section 408(a),

(ii) an individual retirement annuity described in section 408(b) (other than an endowment contract),

(iii) a qualified trust, and

(iv) an annuity plan described in section 403(a).

(9) Rollover where spouse receives distribution after death of employee.— If any distribution attributable to an employee is

paid to the spouse of the employee after the employee's death, the preceding provisions of this subsection shall apply to such distribution in the same manner as if the spouse were the employee; except that a trust or plan described in clause (iii) or (iv) of paragraph (8)(B) shall not be treated as an eligible retirement plan with respect to such distribution.

(10) Denial of averaging for subsequent distributions.— If paragraph (1) applies to any distribution paid to any employee, paragraphs (1) and (3) of subsection (d) shall not apply to any distribution (paid after such distribution) of the balance to the credit of the employee under the plan under which the preceding distribution was made (or under any other plan which, under subsection (d)(4)(C), would be aggregated with such plan).

(d) Tax on Lump Sum Distributions.—

(1) Imposition of separate tax on lump sum distributions.—

(A) Separate tax.— There is hereby imposed a tax (in the amount determined under subparagraph (B)) on a lump sum distribution.

(B) Amount of tax.— The amount of tax imposed by subparagraph (A) for any taxable year is an amount equal to 5 times the tax which would be imposed by subsection (c) of section 1 if the recipient were an individual referred to in such subsection and the taxable income were an amount equal to 1/5 of the excess of—

(i) the total taxable amount of the lump sum distribution for the taxable year, over

(ii) the minimum distribution allowance.

(C) Minimum distribution allowance.— For purposes of this paragraph, the minimum distribution allowance for any taxable year is an amount equal to—

(i) the lesser of $10,000 or one-half of the total taxable amount of the lump sum distribution for the taxable year, reduced (but not below zero) by

(ii) 20 percent of the amount (if any) by which such total taxable amount exceeds $20,000.

(D) Liability for tax.— The recipient shall be liable for the tax imposed by this paragraph.

(2) Distributions of annuity contracts.—

(A) In general.— In the case of any recipient of a lump sum distribution for any taxable year, if the distribution (or any part thereof) is an annuity contract, the total taxable amount of the distribution shall be aggregated for purposes of computing the tax imposed by paragraph (1)(A), except that the amount of tax so computed shall be reduced (but not below zero) by that portion of the tax on the aggregate total taxable amount which is attributable to annuity contracts.

(B) Beneficiaries.— For purposes of this paragraph, a beneficiary of a trust to which a lump sum distribution is made shall be treated as the recipient of such distribution if the beneficiary is an employee (including an employee within the meaning of section 401(c)(1)) with respect to the plan under which the distribution is made or if the beneficiary is treated as the owner of such trust for purposes of subpart E of part I of subchapter J.

(C) Annuity contracts.— For purposes of this paragraph, in the case of the distribution of an annuity contract, the taxable amount of such distribution shall be deemed to be the current actuarial value of the contract, determined on the date of such distribution.

(D) Trusts.— In the case of a lump sum distribution with respect to any individual which is made only to 2 or more trusts, the tax imposed by paragraph (1)(A) shall be computed as if such distribution was made to a single trust,   but the liability for such tax shall be apportioned among such trusts according to the relative amounts received by each.

(E) Regulations.— The Secretary shall prescribe such regulations as may be necessary to carry out the purposes of this paragraph.

(3) Allowance of deduction.— The total taxable amount of a lump sum distribution for any taxable year shall be allowed as a deduction from gross income for such taxable year, but only to the extent included in the taxpayer's gross income for such taxable year.

(4) Definitions and special rules.—

(A) Lump sum distribution.— For purposes of this section and section 403, the term "lump sum distribution" means the distribution or payment within 1 taxable year of the recipient of the balance to the credit of an employee which becomes payable to the recipient—

(i) on account of the employee's death,

(ii) after the employee attains age $59\frac{1}{2}$,

(iii) on account of the employee's separation from the service, or

(iv) after the employee has become disabled (within the meaning of section 72(m)(7)),

from a trust which forms a part of a plan described in section 401(a) and which is exempt from tax under section 501 or from a plan described in section 403(a). Clause (iii) of this subparagraph shall be applied only with respect to an individual who is an employee without regard to section 401(c)(1), and clause (iv) shall be applied only with respect to an employee within the meaning of section 401(c)(1). A distribution of an annuity contract from a trust or annuity plan referred to in the first sentence of this subparagraph shall be treated as a lump sum distribution. For purposes of this subparagraph, a distribution to 2 or more trusts shall be treated as a distribution to 1 recipient. For purposes of this subsection, the balance to the credit of the employee does not include the accumulated deductible employee con-

IRC Sec. 402 (d)(4)(A)(iv)

tributions under the plan (within the meaning of section 72(o)(5)).

(B) Averaging to apply to 1 lump sum distribution after age 59 ½.— Paragraph (1) shall apply to a lump sum distribution with respect to an employee under subparagraph (A) only if—

(i) such amount is received on or after the date on which the employee has attained age 59½, and

(ii) the taxpayer elects for the taxable year to have all such amounts received during such taxable year so treated.

Not more than 1 election may be made under this subparagraph by any taxpayer with respect to any employee. No election may be made under this subparagraph by any taxpayer other than an individual, an estate, or a trust. In the case of a lump sum distribution made with respect to an employee to 2 or more trusts, the election under this subparagraph shall be made by the personal representative of the taxpayer.

(C) Aggregation of certain trusts and plans.— For purposes of determining the balance to the credit of an employee under subparagraph (A)—

(i) all trusts which are part of a plan shall be treated as a single trust, all pension plans maintained by the employer shall be treated as a single plan, all profit-sharing plans maintained by the employer shall be treated as a single plan, and all stock bonus plans maintained by the employer shall be treated as a single plan, and

(ii) trusts which are not qualified trusts under section 401(a) and annuity contracts which do not satisfy the requirements of section 404(a)(2) shall not be taken into account.

(D) Total taxable amount.— For purposes of this section and section 403, the term "total taxable amount" means, with respect to a lump sum distribution, the amount of such distribution which exceeds the sum of—

(i) the amounts considered contributed by the employee (determined by applying section 72(f)), reduced by any amounts previously distributed which were not includible in gross income, and

(ii) the net unrealized appreciation attributable to that part of the distribution which consists of the securities of the employer corporation so distributed.

(E) Community property laws.— The provisions of this subsection, other than paragraph (3), shall be applied without regard to community property laws.

(F) Minimum period of service.— For purposes of this subsection, no amount distributed to an employee from or under a plan may be treated as a lump sum distribution under subparagraph (A) unless the employee has been a participant in the plan for 5 or more taxable years before the taxable year in which such amounts are distributed.

(G) Amounts subject to penalty.— This subsection shall not apply to amounts described in subparagraph (A) of section 72(m)(5) to the extent that section 72(m)(5) applies to such amounts.

(H) Balance to credit of employee not to include amounts payable under qualified domestic relations order.— For purposes of this subsection, the balance to the credit of an employee shall not include any amount payable to an alternate payee under a qualified domestic relations order (within the meaning of section 414(p)).

(I) Transfers to cost-of-living arrangement not treated as distribution.— For purposes of this subsection, the balance to the credit of an employee under a defined contribution plan shall not include any amount transferred from such defined contribution plan to a qualified cost-of-living arrangement (within the meaning of section 415(k)(2)) under a defined benefit plan.

(J) Lump sum distributions of alternate payees.— If any distribution or payment of the balance to the credit of an employee would be treated as a lump sum distribution, then, for purposes of this subsection, the payment under a qualified domestic relations order (within the meaning of section 414(p)) of the balance to the credit of an alternate payee who is the spouse or former spouse of the employee shall be treated as a lump sum distribution. For purposes of this subparagraph, the balance to the credit of the alternate payee shall not include any amount payable to the employee.

(K) Treatment of portion not rolled over.— If any portion of a lump sum distribution is transferred in a transfer to which subsection (c) applies, paragraphs (1) and (3) shall not apply with respect to the distribution.

(L) Securities.— For purposes of this subsection, the terms "securities" and "securities of the employer corporation" have the respective meanings provided by subsection (e)(4)(E).

(5) Special rule where portions of lump sum distribution attributable to rollover of bond purchased under qualified bond purchase plan.— If any portion of a lump sum distribution is attributable to a transfer described in section 405(d)(3)(A)(ii) (as in effect before its repeal by the Tax Reform Act of 1984), paragraphs (1) and (3) of this subsection shall not apply to such portion.

(6) Treatment of potential future vesting.—

(A) In general.— For purposes of determining whether any distribution which becomes payable to the recipient on account of the employee's separation from service is a lump sum distribution, the balance to the credit of the employee shall be determined without regard to any increase in vesting which may occur if the employee is reemployed by the employer.

(B) Recapture in certain cases.— If—

(i) an amount is treated as a lump sum distribution by reason of subparagraph (A),

(ii) special lump sum treatment applies to such distribution,

(iii) the employee is subsequently reemployed by the employer, and

(iv) as a result of services performed after being so reemployed, there is an increase in the employee's vesting for benefits accrued before the separation referred to in subparagraph (A),

under regulations prescribed by the Secretary, the tax imposed by this chapter for the taxable year (in which the increase in vesting first occurs) shall be increased by the reduction in tax which resulted from the special lump sum treatment (and any election under paragraph (4)(B) shall not be taken into account for purposes of determining whether the employee may make another election under paragraph (4)(B)).

(C) Special lump sum treatment.—For purposes of this paragraph, special lump sum treatment applies to any distribution if any portion of such distribution is taxed under the subsection by reason of an election under paragraph (4)(B).

(D) Vesting.— For purposes of this paragraph, the term "vesting" means the portion of the accrued benefits derived from employer contributions to which the participant has a nonforfeitable right.

(7) Coordination with foreign tax credit limitations.— Subsections (a), (b), and (c) of section 904 shall be applied separately with respect to any lump sum distribution on which tax is imposed under paragraph (1), and the amount of such distribution shall be treated as the taxable income for purposes of such separate application.

IRC Sec. 402 (d)(7)

(e) Other Rules Applicable to Exempt Trusts.—

(1) Alternate payees.—

(A) Alternate payee treated as distributee.— For purposes of subsection (a) and section 72, an alternate payee who is the spouse or former spouse of the participant shall be treated as the distributee of any distribution or payment made to the alternate payee under a qualified domestic relations order (as defined in section 414(p)).

(B) Rollovers.— If any amount is paid or distributed to an alternate payee who is the spouse or former spouse of the participant by reason of any qualified domestic relations order (within the meaning of section 414(p)), subsection (c) shall apply to such distribution in the same manner as if such alternate payee were the employee.

(2) Distributions by United States to nonresident aliens.— The amount includible under subsection (a) in the gross income of a nonresident alien with respect to a distribution made by the United States in respect of services performed by an employee of the United States shall not exceed an amount which bears the same ratio to the amount includible in gross income without regard to this paragraph as—

(A) the aggregate basic pay paid by the United States to such employee for such services, reduced by the amount of such basic pay which was not includible in gross income by reason of being from sources without the United States, bears to

(B) the aggregate basic pay paid by the United States to such employee for such services.

In the case of distributions under the civil service retirement laws, the term "basic pay" shall have the meaning provided in section 8331(3) of title 5, United States Code.

(3) Cash or deferred arrangements.— For purposes of this title, contributions made by an employer on behalf of an employee to a trust which is a part of a qualified cash or deferred arrangement (as defined in section 401(k)(2)) shall not be treated as distributed or made available to the employee nor as contributions made to the trust by the employee merely because the arrangement includes provisions under which the employee has an election whether the contribution will be made to the trust or received by the employee in cash.

(4) Net unrealized appreciation.—

(A) Amounts attributable to employee contributions.— For purposes of subsection (a) and section 72, in the case of a distribution other than a lump sum distribution, the amount actually distributed to any distributee from a trust described in subsection (a) shall not include any net unrealized appreciation in securities of the employer corporation attributable to amounts contributed by the employee (other than deductible employee contributions within the meaning of section 72(o)(5)). This subparagraph shall not apply to a distribution to which subsection (c) applies.

(B) Amounts attributable to employer contributions.— For purposes of subsection (a) and section 72, in the case of any lump sum distribution which includes securities of the employer corporation, there shall be excluded from gross income the net unrealized appreciation attributable to that part of the distribution which consists of securities of the employer corporation. In accordance with rules prescribed by the Secretary, a taxpayer may elect, on the return of tax on which a lump sum distribution is required to be included, not to have this subparagraph apply to such distribution.

(C) Determination of amounts and adjustments.— For purposes of subparagraphs (A) and (B), net unrealized appreciation and the resulting adjustments to basis shall be determined in accordance with regulations prescribed by the Secretary.

(D) Lump sum distribution.—For purposes of this paragraph, the term "lump sum distribution" has the meaning given such term by subsection (d)(4)(A) (without regard to subsection (d)(4)(F)).

(E) Definitions relating to securities.—For purposes of this paragraph—

(i) Securities.— The term "securities" means only shares of stock and bonds or debentures issued by a corporation with interest coupons or in registered form.

(ii) Securities of the employer.—The term "securities of the employer corporation" includes securities of a parent or subsidiary corporation (as defined in subsections (e) and (f) of section 424) of the employer corporation.

(5) Taxability of beneficiary of certain foreign situs trusts.— For purposes of subsections (a), (b), and (c), a stock bonus, pension, or profit-sharing trust which would qualify for exemption from tax under section 501(a) except for the fact that it is a trust created or organized outside the United States shall be treated as if it were a trust exempt from tax under section 501(a).

(6) Direct trustee-to-trustee transfers.— Any amount transferred in a direct trustee-to-trustee transfer in accordance with section 401(a)(31) shall not be includible in gross income for the taxable year of such transfer.

(f) Written Explanation to Recipients of Distributions Eligible for Rollover Treatment.—

(1) In general.— The plan administrator of any plan shall, within a reasonable period of time before making an eligible rollover distribution from an eligible retirement plan, provide a written explanation to the recipient—

(A) of the provisions under which the recipient may have the distribution directly transferred to another eligible retirement plan,

(B) of the provision which requires the withholding of tax on the distribution if it is not directly transferred to another eligible retirement plan,

(C) of the provisions under which the distribution will not be subject to tax if transferred to an eligible retirement plan within 60 days after the date on which the recipient received the distribution, and

(D) if applicable, of the provisions of subsections (d) and (e) of this section.

(2) Definitions.— For purposes of this subsection—

(A) Eligible rollover distribution.— The term "eligible rollover distribution" has the same meaning as when used in subsection (c) of this section or paragraph (4) of section 403(a).

(B) Eligible retirement plan.— The term "eligible retirement plan" has the meaning given such term by subsection (c)(8)(B).

◊ ◊ ◊

Editor's Note: Code §402(g)(5) as set forth below appears as amended by §732(c) of the Retirement Protection Act of 1994 (enacted as part of the Uruguay Round Agreements Act, P.L. 103-465). The amendments apply generally to years beginning after December 31, 1994. However, §732(e)(2) of the 1994 Act provides that the amendment does not apply to any year to the extent that the rounding of dollar amounts would require the indexed amount to be reduced below the amount in effect for years beginning in 1994.

◊ ◊ ◊

(g) Limitation on Exclusion for Elective Deferrals.—

(1) In general.— Notwithstanding subsections (e)(3) and (h)(1)(B), the elective deferrals of any individual for any taxable year shall be included in such individual's gross

income to the extent the amount of such deferrals for the taxable year exceeds $7,000.

(2) Distribution of excess deferrals.—

(A) In general.— If any amount (hereinafter in this paragraph referred to as "excess deferrals") is included in the gross income of an individual under paragraph (1) for any taxable year—

(i) not later than the 1st March 1 following the close of the taxable year, the individual may allocate the amount of such excess deferrals among the plans under which the deferrals were made and may notify each such plan of the portion allocated to it, and

(ii) not later than the 1st April 15 following the close of the taxable year, each such plan may distribute to the individual the amount allocated to it under clause (i) (and any income allocable to such amount).

The distribution described in clause (ii) may be made notwithstanding any other provision of law.

(B) Treatment of distribution under section 401(k).— Except to the extent provided under rules prescribed by the Secretary, notwithstanding the distribution of any portion of an excess deferral from a plan under subparagraph (A)(ii), such portion shall, for purposes of applying section 401(k)(3)(A)(ii), be treated as an employer contribution.

(C) Taxation of distribution.— In the case of a distribution to which subparagraph (A) applies—

(i) except as provided in clause (ii), such distribution shall not be included in gross income, and

(ii) any income on the excess deferral shall, for purposes of this chapter, be treated as earned and received in the taxable year in which such income is distributed.

No tax shall be imposed under section 72(t) on any distribution described in the preceding sentence.

(D) Partial distributions.— If a plan distributes only a portion of any excess deferral and income allocable thereto, such portion shall be treated as having been distributed ratably from the excess deferral and the income.

(3) Elective deferrals.— For purposes of this subsection, the term "elective deferrals means, with respect to any taxable year, the sum of—

(A) any employer contribution under a qualified cash or deferred arrangement (as defined in section 401(k)) to the extent not includible in gross income for the taxable year under subsection (a)(8) (determined without regard to this subsection),

(B) any employer contribution to the extent not includible in gross income for the taxable year under subsection (h)(1)(B) (determined without regard to this subsection), and

(C) any employer contribution to purchase an annuity contract under section 403(b) under a salary reduction agreement (within the meaning of section 3121(a)(5)(D)). An employer contribution shall not be treated as an elective deferral described in subparagraph (C) if under the salary reduction agreement such contribution is made pursuant to a one-time irrevocable election made by the employee at the time of initial eligibility to participate in the agreement or is made pursuant to a similar arrangement involving a one-time irrevocable election specified in regulations.

(4) Increase in limit for amounts contributed under section 403(b) contracts.— The limitation under paragraph (1) shall be increased (but not to an amount in excess of $9,500) by the amount of any employer contributions for the taxable year described in paragraph (3)(C).

(5) Cost-of-living adjustment.— The Secretary shall adjust the $7,000 amount under paragraph (1) at the same time and in the same manner as under section 415(d); *except that any increase under this paragraph which is not a multiple of $500 shall be rounded to the next lowest multiple of $500.*

(6) Disregard of community property laws.— This subsection shall be applied without regard to community property laws.

(7) Coordination with section 72.— For purposes of applying section 72, any amount includible in gross income for any taxable year under this subsection but which is not distributed from the plan during such taxable year shall not be treated as investment in the contract.

(8) Special rule for certain organizations.—

(A) In general.— In the case of a qualified employee of a qualified organization, with respect to employer contributions described in paragraph (3)(C) made by such organization, the limitation of paragraph (1) for any taxable year shall be increased by whichever of the following is the least:

(i) $3,000,

(ii) $15,000 reduced by amounts not included in gross income for prior taxable years by reason of this paragraph, or

(iii) the excess of $5,000 multiplied by the number of years of service of the employee with the qualified organization over the employer contributions described in paragraph (3) made by the organization on behalf of such employee for prior taxable years (determined in the manner prescribed by the Secretary).

(B) Qualified organization.— For purposes of this paragraph, the term "qualified organization" means any educational organization, hospital, home health service agency, health and welfare service agency, church, or convention or association of churches. Such term includes any organiza-

tion described in section 414(e)(3)(B)(ii). Terms used in this subparagraph shall have the same meaning as when used in section 415(c)(4).

(C) Qualified employee.— For purposes of this paragraph, the term "qualified employee" means any employee who has completed 15 years of service with the qualified organization.

(D) Years of service.— For purposes of this paragraph, the term "years of service" has the meaning given such term by section 403(b).

(h) Special Rules for Simplified Employee Pensions.— For purposes of this chapter—

(1) In general.— Except as provided in paragraph (2), contributions made by an employer on behalf of an employee to an individual retirement plan pursuant to a simplified employee pension (as defined in section 408(k))—

(A) shall not be treated as distributed or made available to the employee or as contributions made by the employee, and

(B) if such contributions are made pursuant to an arrangement under section 408(k)(6) under which an employee may elect to have the employer make contributions to the simplified employee pension on behalf of the employee, shall not be treated as distributed or made available or as contributions made by the employee merely because the simplified employee pension includes provisions for such election.

(2) Limitations on employer contributions.— Contributions made by an employer to a simplified employee pension with respect to an employee for any year shall be treated as distributed or made available to such employee and as contributions made by the employee to the extent such contributions exceed the lesser of—

(A) 15 percent of the compensation (within the meaning of section 414(s)) from such employer includible in the employee's gross income for the year (determined without regard to the employer contributions to the simplified employee pension), or

(B) the limitation in effect under section 415(c)(1)(A), reduced in the case of any highly compensated employee (within the meaning of section 414(q)) by the amount taken into account with respect to such employee under section 408(k)(3)(D).

(3) Distributions.— Any amount paid or distributed out of an individual retirement plan pursuant to a simplified employee pension shall be included in gross income by the payee or distributee, as the case may be, in accordance with the provisions of section 408(d).

(i) Treatment of Self-Employed Individuals.— For purposes of this section, except as otherwise provided in subparagraph (A) of subsection (d)(4), the term "employee" includes a self-employed individual (as defined in section 401(c)(1)(B)) and the employer of such individual shall be the person treated as his employer under section 401(c)(4).

(j) Effect of Disposition of Stock by Plan on Net Unrealized Appreciation.—

(1) In general.— For purposes of subsection (e)(4), in the case of any transaction to which this subsection applies, the determination of net unrealized appreciation shall be made without regard to such transaction.

(2) Transaction to which subsection applies.— This subsection shall apply to any transaction in which—

(A) the plan trustee exchanges the plan's securities of the employer corporation for other such securities, or

(B) the plan trustee disposes of securities of the employer corporation and uses the proceeds of such disposition to acquire securities of the employer corporation within 90 days (or such longer period as the Secretary may prescribe), except that this subparagraph shall not apply to any employee with respect to whom a distribution of money was

made during the period after such disposition and before such acquisition.

SEC. 403. TAXATION OF EMPLOYEE ANNUITIES.

(a) Taxability of Beneficiary Under a Qualified Annuity Plan.—

(1) Distributee taxable under section 72.— If an annuity contract is purchased by an employer for an employee under a plan which meets the requirements of section 404(a)(2) (whether or not the employer deducts the amounts paid for the contract under such section), the amount actually distributed to any distributee under the contract shall be taxable to the distributee (in the year in which so distributed) under section 72 (relating to annuities).

(2) Capital gains treatment for certain distributions. [Repealed.]

(3) Self-employed individuals.— For purposes of this subsection, the term, "employee" includes an individual who is an employee within the meaning of section 401(c)(1), and the employer of such individual is the person treated as his employer under section 401(c)(4).

(4) Rollover amounts.—

(A) General rule.— If—

(i) any portion of the balance to the credit of an employee in an employee annuity described in paragraph (1) is paid to him in an eligible rollover distribution (within the meaning of section 402(c)(4)),

(ii) the employee transfers any portion of the property he receives in such distribution to an eligible retirement plan, and

(iii) in the case of a distribution of property other than money, the amount so transferred consists of the property distributed,

then such distribution (to the extent so transferred) shall not be includible in gross income for the taxable year in which paid.

(B) Certain rules made applicable.— Rules similar to the rules of paragraphs (2) through (7) of section 402(c) shall apply for purposes of subparagraph (A).

(5) Direct trustee-to-trustee transfer.— Any amount transferred in a direct trustee-to-trustee transfer in accordance with section 401(a)(31) shall not be includible in gross income for the taxable year of such transfer.

(b) Taxability of Beneficiary Under Annuity Purchased by Section 501(c)(3) Organization or Public School.—

(1) General rule.— If—

(A) an annuity contract is purchased—

(i) for an employee by an employer described in section 501(c)(3) which is exempt from tax under section 501(a), or

(ii) for an employee (other than an employee described in clause (i)), who performs services for an educational organization described in section 170(b)(1)(A)(ii), by an employer which is a State, a political subdivision of a State, or an agency or instrumentality of any one or more of the foregoing,

(B) such annuity contract is not subject to subsection (a),

(C) the employee's rights under the contract are nonforfeitable, except for failure to pay future premiums,

(D) except in the case of a contract purchased by a church, such contract is purchased under a plan which meets the nondiscrimination requirements of (paragraph 12), and

(E) in the case of a contract purchased under a plan which provides a salary reduction agreement, the plan meets the requirements of section 401(a)(30),

then amounts contributed by such employer for such annuity contract on or after such rights become nonforfeitable shall be ex-

cluded from the gross income of the employee for the taxable year to the extent that the aggregate of such amounts does not exceed the exclusion allowance for such taxable year. The amount actually distributed to any distributee under such contract shall be taxable to the distributee (in the year in which so distributed) under section 72 (relating to annuities). For purposes of applying the rules of this subsection to amounts contributed by an employer for a taxable year, amounts transferred to a contract described in this paragraph by reason of a rollover contribution described in paragraph (8) of this subsection or section 408(d)(3)(A)(iii) shall not be considered contributed by such employer.

(2) Exclusion allowance.—

(A) In general.— For purposes of this subsection, the exclusion allowance for any employee for the taxable year is an amount equal to the excess, if any, of—

(i) the amount determined by multiplying 20 percent of his includible compensation by the number of years of service over

(ii) the aggregate of amounts contributed by the employer for annuity contracts and excludable from the gross income of the employee for any prior taxable year.

(B) Election to have allowance determined under section 415 rule.— In the case of an employee who makes an election under section 415(c)(4)(D) to have the provisions of section 415(c)(4)(C) (relating to special rule for section 403(b) contracts purchased by educational institutions, hospitals, home health service agencies, and certain churches, etc.) apply, the exclusion allowance for any such employee for the taxable year is the amount which could be contributed (under section 415 without regard to section 415(c)(8)) by his employer under a plan described in section 403(a) if the annuity contract for the benefit of such employee were treated as a defined contribution plan maintained by the employer.

IRC Sec. 403 (b)(2)(B)

sters or lay employees.—For purposes of this subsection and section 415(c)(4)(A)—

(i) all years of service by—

(I) a duly ordained, commissioned, or licensed minister of a church, or

(II) a lay person,

as an employee of a church, a convention or association of churches, including an organization described in section 414(e)(3)(B)(ii), shall be considered as years of service for 1 employer, and

(ii) all amounts contributed for annuity contracts by each such church (or convention or association of churches) or such organization during such years for such minister or lay person shall be considered to have been contributed by 1 employer. For purposes of the preceding sentence, the terms "church" and "convention or association of churches" have the same meaning as when used in section 414(e).

(D) Alternative exclusion allowance.—

(i) In general.—In the case of any individual described in subparagraph (C), the amount determined under subparagraph (A) shall not be less than the lesser of—

(I) $3,000, or

(II) the includible compensation of such individual.

(ii) Subparagraph not to apply to individuals with adjusted gross income over $17,000.— This subparagraph shall not apply with respect to any taxable year to any individual whose adjusted gross income for such taxable year (determined separately and without regard to any community property laws) exceeds $17,000.

(iii) Special rule for foreign missionaries.— In the case of an individual described in subparagraph (C)(i) performing services outside the United States, there shall be included as includable compensation for any

year under clause (i)(II) any amount contributed during such year by a church (or convention or association of churches) for an annuity contract with respect to such individual.

(3) Includable compensation.— For purposes of this subsection, the term "includable compensation" means, in the case of any employee, the amount of compensation which is received from the employer described in paragraph (1)(A), and which is includable in gross income (computed without regard to section 911) for the most recent period (ending not later than the close of the taxable year) which under paragraph (4) may be counted as one year of service. Such term does not include any amount contributed by the employer for any annuity contract to which this subsection applies.

(4) Years of service.— In determining the number of years of service for purposes of this subsection, there shall be included—

(A) one year for each full year during which the individual was a full-time employee of the organization purchasing the annuity for him, and

(B) a fraction of a year (determined in accordance with regulations prescribed by the Secretary) for each full year during which such individual was a part-time employee of such organization and for each part of a year during which such individual was a full-time or part-time employee of such organization.

In no case shall the number of years of service be less than one.

(5) Application to more than one annuity contract.— If for any taxable year of the employee this subsection applies to 2 or more annuity contracts purchased by the employer, such contracts shall be treated as one contract.

(6) Forfeitable rights which become nonforfeitable.—For purposes of this subsection and section 72(f) (relating to special rules for computing employees' contributions to annuity contracts), if rights of the employee under

IRC Sec. 403 (b)(2)(C)(i)

an annuity contract described in subparagraphs (A) and (B) of paragraph (1) change from forfeitable to nonforfeitable rights, then the amount (determined without regard to this subsection) includible in gross income by reason of such change shall be treated as an amount contributed by the employer for such annuity contract as of the time such rights become nonforfeitable.

(7) Custodial accounts for regulated investment company stock.—

(A) Amounts paid treated as contributions.— For purposes of this title, amounts paid by an employer described in paragraph (1)(A) to a custodial account which satisfies the requirements of section 401(f)(2) shall be treated as amounts contributed by him for an annuity contract for his employee if—

(i) the amounts are to be invested in regulated investment company stock to be held in that custodial account, and

(ii) under the custodial account no such amounts may be paid or made available to any distributee before the employee dies, attains age 59½, separates from service, becomes disabled (within the meaning of section 72(m)(7)), or in the case of contributions made pursuant to a salary reduction agreement (within the meaning of section 3121(a)(1)(D)), encounters financial hardship.

(B) Account treated as plan.— For purposes of this title, a custodial account which satisfies the requirements of section 401(f)(2) shall be treated as an organization described in section 401(a) solely for purposes of subchapter F and subtitle F with respect to amounts received by it (and income from investment thereof).

(C) Regulated investment company.— For purposes of this paragraph, the term "regulated investment company" means a domestic corporation which is a regulated investment company within the meaning of section 851(a).

(8) Rollover Amounts.—

(A) General Rule.— If—

(i) any portion of the balance to the credit of an employee in an annuity contract described in paragraph (1) is paid to him in an eligible rollover distribution (within the meaning of section 402(c)(4)),

(ii) the employee transfers any portion of the property he receives in such distribution to an individual retirement plan or to an annuity contract described in paragraph (1), and

(iii) in the case of a distribution of property other than money, the property so transferred consists of the property distributed,

then such distribution (to the extent so transferred) shall not be includible in gross income for the taxable year in which paid.

(B) Certain rules made applicable.— Rules similar to the rules of paragraphs (2) through (7) of section 402(c) shall apply for purposes of subparagraph (A).

(9) Retirement income accounts provided by churches, etc.—

(A) Amounts paid treated as contributions.For purposes of this title—

(i) a retirement income account shall be treated as an annuity contract described in this subsection, and

(ii) amounts paid by an employer described in paragraph (1)(A) to a retirement income account shall be treated as amounts contributed by the employer for an annuity contract for the employee on whose behalf such account is maintained.

(B) Retirement income account.— For purposes of this paragraph, the term "retirement income account" means a defined contribution program established or maintained by a church, a convention or association of churches, including an organization described in section 414(e)(3)(A), to provide benefits under section 403(b) for an

IRC Sec. 403 (b)(9)(B)

employee described in paragraph (1) or his beneficiaries.

(10) Distribution requirements.— Under regulations prescribed by the Secretary, this subsection shall not apply to any annuity contract (or to any custodial account described in paragraph (7) or retirement income account described in paragraph (9)) unless requirements similar to the requirements of sections 401(a)(9) and 401(a)(31) are met (and requirements similar to the incidental death benefit requirements of section 401(a) are met) with respect to such annuity contract (or custodial account or retirement income account). Any amount transferred in an direct trustee-to-trustee transfer in accordance with section 401(a)(31) shall not be includible in gross income for the taxable year of the transfer.

(11) Requirement that distributions not begin before age 59½, separation from service, death, or disability.— This subsection shall not apply to any annuity contract unless under such contract distributions attributable to contributions made pursuant to a salary reduction agreement (within the meaning of section 402(g)(3)(C)) may be paid only—

(A) when the employee attains age 59½, separates from service, dies, or becomes disabled (within the meaning of section 72(m)(7)), or

(B) in the case of hardship.

Such contract may not provide for the distribution of any income attributable to such contributions in the case of hardship.

(12) Nondiscrimination requirements.—

(A) In general.— For purposes of paragraph (1)(D), a plan meets the nondiscrimination requirements of this paragraph if—

(i) with respect to contributions not made pursuant to a salary reduction agreement, such plan meets the requirements of paragraphs (4), (5), (17), and (26) of section 401(a), section 401(m), and section 410(b)

in the same manner as if such plan were described in section 401(a), and

(ii) all employees of the organization may elect to have the employer make contributions of more than $200 pursuant to a salary reduction agreement if any employee of the organization may elect to have the organization make contributions for such contracts pursuant to such agreement.

For purposes of clause (i), a contribution shall be treated as not made pursuant to a salary reduction agreement if under the agreement it is made pursuant to a 1-time irrevocable election made by the employee at the time of initial eligibility to participate in the agreement or is made pursuant to a similar arrangement involving a one-time irrevocable election specified in regulations.

For purposes of clause (ii), there may be excluded any employee who is a participant in an eligible deferred compensation plan (within the meaning of section 457) or a qualified cash or deferred arrangement of the organization or another annuity contract described in this subsection. Any nonresident alien described in section 410(b)(3)(C) may also be excluded. Subject to the conditions applicable under section 410(b)(4), there may be excluded for purposes of this subparagraph employees who are students performing services described in section 3121(b)(10) and employees who normally work less than 20 hours per week.

(B) Church.— For purposes of paragraph (1)(D), the term "church" has the meaning given to such term by section 3121(w)(3)(A). Such term shall include any qualified church-controlled organization (as defined in section 3121(w)(3)(B)).

(c) Taxability of Beneficiary Under Nonqualified Annuities or Under Annuities Purchased by Exempt Organizations.— Premiums paid by an employer for an annuity contract which is not subject to subsection (a) shall be included in the gross income of the employee in accordance with section 83 (relating to property transferred in connection with performance of services), except that the value of such contract shall be substituted for the fair market value of the property for purposes of applying such section. The preceding sentence shall not apply to that portion of the premiums paid which is excluded from gross income under subsection (b). In the case of any portion of any contract which is attributable to premiums to which this subsection applies, the amount actually paid or made available under such contract to any beneficiary which is attributable to such premiums shall be taxable to the beneficiary (in the year in which so paid or made available) under section 72 (relating to annuities).

SEC. 404. DEDUCTION FOR CONTRIBUTIONS OF AN EMPLOYER TO AN EMPLOYEES' TRUST OR ANNUITY PLAN AND COMPENSATION UNDER A DEFERRED-PAYMENT PLAN.

(a) General Rule.— If contributions are paid by an employer to or under a stock bonus, pension, profit-sharing, or annuity plan, or if compensation is paid or accrued on account of any employee under a plan deferring the receipt of such compensation, such contributions or compensation shall not be deductible under this chapter; but, if they would otherwise be deductible, they shall be deductible under this section, subject, however, to the following limitations as to the amounts deductible in any year:

(1) Pension trusts.—

(A) In general.— In the taxable year when paid, if the contributions are paid into a pension trust, and if such taxable year ends within or with a taxable year of the trust for which the trust is exempt under section 501(a), in an amount determined as follows:

(i) the amount necessary to satisfy the minimum funding standard provided by section 412(a) for plan years ending within or with such taxable year (or for any prior plan year), if such amount is greater than the amount determined under clause (ii) or (iii)

(whichever is applicable with respect to the plan),

(ii) the amount necessary to provide with respect to all of the employees under the trust the remaining unfunded cost of their past and current service credits distributed as a level amount, or a level percentage of compensation, over the remaining future service of each such employee, as determined under regulations prescribed by the Secretary, but if such remaining unfunded cost with respect to any 3 individuals is more than 50 percent of such remaining unfunded cost, the amount of such unfunded cost attributable to such individuals shall be distributed over a period of at least 5 taxable years,

(iii) an amount equal to the normal cost of the plan, as determined under regulations prescribed by the Secretary, plus, if past service or other supplementary pension or annuity credits are provided by the plan, an amount necessary to amortize the unfunded costs attributable to such credits in equal annual payments (until fully amortized) over 10 years, as determined under regulations prescribed by the Secretary.

In determining the amount deductible in such year under the foregoing limitations the funding method and the actuarial assumptions used shall be those used for such year under section 412, and the maximum amount deductible for such year shall be an amount equal to the full funding limitation for such year determined under section 412.

(B) Special rule in case of certain amendments.— In the case of a plan which the Secretary of Labor finds to be collectively bargained which makes an election under this subparagraph (in such manner and at such time as may be provided under the regulations prescribed by the Secretary), if the full funding limitation determined under section 412(c)(7) for such year is zero, if as a result of any plan amendment applying to such plan year, the amount determined under section 412(c)(7)(B) exceeds the amount determined under section 412(c)(7)(A), and if the funding method and the actuarial assumptions used are those used for such year under section 412, the maximum amount deductible in such year under the limitations of this paragraph shall be an amount equal to the lesser of—

(i) the full funding limitation for such year determined by applying section 412(c)(7) but increasing the amount referred to in subparagraph (A) thereof by the decrease in the present value of all unamortized liabilities resulting from such amendment, or

(ii) the normal cost under the plan reduced by the amount necessary to amortize in equal annual installments over 10 years (until fully amortized) the decrease described in clause (i).

In the case of any election under this subparagraph, the amount deductible under the limitations of this paragraph with respect to any of the plan years following the plan year for which such election was made shall be determined as provided under such regulations as may be prescribed by the Secretary to carry out the purposes of this subparagraph.

(C) Certain collectively bargained plans.— In the case of a plan which the Secretary of Labor finds to be collectively bargained, established or maintained by an employer doing business in not less than 40 States and engaged in the trade or business of furnishing or selling services described in section 168(i)(10)(C), with respect to which the rates have been established or approved by a State or political subdivision thereof, by any agency or instrumentality of the United States, or by a public service or public utility commission or other similar body of any State or political subdivision thereof, and in the case of any employer which is a member of a controlled group with such employer, subparagraph (B) shall be applied by substituting for the words "plan amendment" the words "plan amendment or increase in benefits payable under title II of the Social Security Act". For purposes of this subpara-

graph, the term "controlled group" has the meaning provided by section 1563(a), determined without regard to section 1563(a)(4) and (e)(3)(C).

(D) Special rule in case of certain plans.— In the case of any defined benefit plan (other than a multiemployer plan) which has more than 100 participants for the plan year, except as provided in regulations, the maximum amount deductible under the limitations of this paragraph shall not be less than the unfunded current liability determined under section 412(l). For purposes of determining whether a plan has more than 100 participants, all defined benefit plans maintained by the same employer (or any member of such employer's controlled group (within the meaning of section 412(l)(8)(c))) shall be treated as 1 plan, but only employees of such member or employer shall be taken into account.

(E) Carryover.— Any amount paid in a taxable year in excess of the amount deductible in such year under the foregoing limitations shall be deductible in the succeeding taxable years in order of time to the extent of the difference between the amount paid and deductible in each such succeeding year and the maximum amount deductible for such year under the foregoing limitations.

(2) Employees' annuities.— In the taxable year when paid, in an amount determined in accordance with paragraph (l), if the contributions are paid toward the purchase of retirement annuities, or retirement annuities and medical benefits as described in Sec. 401(h), and such purchase is a part of a plan which meets the requirements of section 401(a)(3), (4), (5), (6), (7), (8), (9), (11), (12), (13), (14), (15), (16), (17), (18), (19), (20), (22), (26), (27), and (31) and, if applicable, the requirements of section 401(a)(10) and of section 401(d), and if refunds of premiums, if any, are applied within the current taxable year or next succeeding taxable year towards the purchase of such retirement annuities, or such retirement annuities and medical benefits.

(3) Stock bonus and profit-sharing trusts.—

(A) Limits on deductible contributions.—

(i) In general.— In the taxable year when paid, if the contributions are paid into a stock bonus or profit-sharing trust, and if such taxable year ends within or with a taxable year of the trust with respect to which the trust is exempt under section 501(a), in an amount not in excess of 15 percent of the compensation otherwise paid or accrued during the taxable year to the beneficiaries under the stock bonus or profit-sharing plan.

(ii) Carryover of excess contributions.— Any amount paid into the trust in any taxable year in excess of the limitation of clause (i) (or the corresponding provision of prior law) shall be deductible in the succeeding taxable years in order of time, but the amount so deductible under this clause in any 1 such succeeding taxable year together with the amount allowable under clause (i) shall not exceed 15 percent of the compensation otherwise paid or accrued during such taxable year to the beneficiaries under the plan.

(iii) Certain retirement plans excluded.— For purposes of this subparagraph, the term "stock bonus or profit-sharing trust" shall not include any trust designed to provide benefits upon retirement and covering a period of years, if under the plan the amounts to be contributed by the employer can be determined actuarially as provided in paragraph (1).

(iv) 2 or more trusts treated as 1 trust.— If the contributions are made to 2 or more stock bonus or profit-sharing trusts, such trusts shall be considered a single trust for purposes of applying the limitations in this subparagraph.

(v) Pre-87 limitation carryforwards.—

(I) In general.— The limitation of clause (i) for any taxable year shall be increased by the unused pre-87 limitation carryforwards (but not to an amount in excess of 25 percent of the compensation described in clause (i)).

(II) Unused pre-87 limitation carryforwards.— For purposes of subclause (I), the term "unused pre-87 limitation carryforwards" means the amount by which the limitation of the first sentence of this subparagraph (as in effect on the day before the date of the enactment of the Tax Reform Act of 1986) for any taxable year beginning before January 1, 1987, exceeded the amount paid to the trust for such taxable year (to the extent such excess was not taken into account in prior taxable years).

(B) Profit-sharing plan of affiliated group.— In the case of a profit-sharing plan, or a stock bonus plan in which contributions are determined with reference to profits, of a group of corporations which is an affiliated group within the meaning of section 1504, if any member of such affiliated group is prevented from making a contribution which it would otherwise have made under the plan, by reason of having no current or accumulated earnings or profits or because such earnings or profits are less than the contributions which it would otherwise have made, then so much of the contribution which such member was so prevented from making may be made, for the benefit of the employees of such member, by the other members of the group, to the extent of current or accumulated earnings or profits, except that such contribution by each such other member shall be limited, where the group does not file a consolidated return, to that proportion of its total current and accumulated earnings or profits remaining after adjustment for its contribution deductible without regard to this subparagraph which the total prevented contribution bears to the total current and accumulated earnings or profits of all the members of the group remaining after adjustment for all contributions deductible without regard to this subparagraph. Contributions made under the preceding sentence shall be deductible under subparagraph (A) of this paragraph by

IRC Sec. 404 (a)(3)(B)

the employer making such contribution, and, for the purpose of determining amounts which may be carried forward and deducted under the second sentence of subparagraph (A) of this paragraph in succeeding taxable years, shall be deemed to have been made by the employer on behalf of whose employees such contributions were made. The term "compensation otherwise paid or accrued during the taxable year to all employees" shall include any amount with respect to which an election under section 415(c)(3)(C) is in effect, but only to the extent that any contribution with respect to such amount is nonforfeitable.

(4) Trusts created or organized outside the United States.— If a stock bonus, pension, or profit-sharing trust would qualify for exemption under section 501(a) except for the fact that it is a trust created or organized outside the United States, contributions to such a trust by an employer which is a resident, or corporation, or other entity of the United States, shall be deductible under the preceding paragraphs.

(5) Other plans.— If the plan is not one included in paragraph (1), (2), or (3), in the taxable year in which an amount attributable to the contribution is includible in the gross income of employees participating in the plan, but, in the case of a plan in which more than one employee participates only if separate accounts are maintained for each employee. For purposes of this section, any vacation pay which is treated as deferred compensation shall be deductible for the taxable year of the employer in which paid to the employee.

(6) Time when contributions deemed made.— For purposes of paragraphs (1), (2), and (3), a taxpayer shall be deemed to have made a payment on the last day of the preceding taxable year if the payment is on account of such taxable year and is made not later than the time prescribed by law for filing the return for such taxable year (including extensions thereof).

(7) Limitation on deductions where combination of defined contribution plan and defined benefit plan.—

(A) In general.— If amounts are deductible under the foregoing paragraphs of this subsection (other than paragraph (5)) in connection with 1 or more defined contribution plans and 1 or more defined benefit plans or in connection with trusts or plans described in 2 or more of such paragraphs, the total amount deductible in a taxable year under such plans shall not exceed the greater of—

(i) 25 percent of the compensation otherwise paid or accrued during the taxable year to the beneficiaries under such plans, or

(ii) the amount of contributions made to or under the defined benefit plans to the extent such contributions do not exceed the amount of employer contributions necessary to satisfy the minimum funding standard provided by section 412 with respect to any such defined benefit plans for the plan year which ends with or within such taxable year (or for any prior plan year).

A defined contribution plan which is a pension plan shall not be treated as failing to provide definitely determinable benefits merely by limiting employer contributions to amounts deductible under this section. For purposes of clause (ii), if paragraph (1)(D) applies to a defined benefit plan for any plan year, the amount necessary to satisfy the minimum funding standard provided by section 412 with respect to such plan for such plan year shall not be less than the unfunded current liability of such plan under section 412(l).

(B) Carryover of contributions in excess of the deductible limit.— Any amount paid under the plans in any taxable year in excess of the limitation of subparagraph (A) shall be deductible in the succeeding taxable years in order of time, but the amount so deductible under this subparagraph in any 1 such succeeding taxable year together with the amount allowable under subparagraph

IRC Sec. 404 (a)(4)

(A) shall not exceed 25 percent of the compensation otherwise paid or accrued during such taxable year to the beneficiaries under the plans.

(C) Paragraph not to apply in certain cases.— This paragraph shall not have the effect of reducing the amount otherwise deductible under paragraphs (1), (2), and (3), if no employee is a beneficiary under more than 1 trust or under a trust and an annuity plan.

(D) Section 412(i) plans.— For purposes of this paragraph, any plan described in section 412(i) shall be treated as a defined benefit plan.

(8) Self-employed individuals.— In the case of a plan included in paragraph (1), (2), or (3) which provides contributions or benefits for employees some or all of whom are employees within the meaning of section 401(c)(1), for purposes of this section—

(A) the term "employee" includes an individual who is an employee within the meaning of section 401(c)(1), and the employer of such individual is the person treated as his employer under section 401(c)(4);

(B) the term "earned income" has the meaning assigned to it by section 401(c)(2);

(C) the contributions to such plan on behalf of an individual who is an employee within the meaning of section 401(c)(1) shall be considered to satisfy the conditions of section 162 or 212 to the extent that such contributions do not exceed the earned income of such individual (determined without regard to the deductions allowed by this section) derived from the trade or business with respect to which such plan is established, and to the extent that such contributions are not allocable (determined in accordance with regulations prescribed by the Secretary) to the purchase of life, accident, health or other insurance; and

(D) any reference to compensation shall, in the case of an individual who is an employee within the meaning of section 401(c)(1), be considered to be a reference to the earned income of such individual derived from the trade or business with respect to which the plan is established.

(9) Certain contributions to employee stock ownership plans.—

(A) Principal payments.— Notwith-standing the provisions of paragraphs (3) and (7), if contributions are paid into a trust which forms a part of an employee stock ownership plan (as described in section 4957(e)(7)), and such contributions are, on or before the time prescribed in paragraph (6), applied by the plan to the repayment of the principal of a loan incurred for the purpose of acquiring qualifying employer securities (as described in section 4975(e)(8)), such contributions shall be deductible under this paragraph for the taxable year determined under paragraph (6). The amount deductible under this paragraph shall not, however, exceed 25 percent of the compensation otherwise paid or accrued during the taxable year to the employees under such employee stock ownership plan. Any amount paid into such trust in any taxable year in excess of the amount deductible under this paragraph shall be deductible in the succeeding taxable years in order of time to the extent of the difference between the amount paid and deductible in each such succeeding year and the maximum amount deductible for such year under the preceding sentence.

(B) Interest payment.— Notwithstanding the provisions of paragraphs (3) and (7), if contributions are made to an employee stock ownership plan (described in subparagraph (A)) and such contributions are applied by the plan to the repayment of interest on a loan incurred for the purpose of acquiring qualifying employer securities (as described in subparagraph (A)), such contributions shall be deductible for the taxable year with respect to which such contributions are made as determined under paragraph (6).

IRC Sec. 404 (a)(9)(B)

(b) Method of Contributions, etc., Having the Effect of a Plan; Certain Deferred Benefits.—

(1) Methods of contributions, etc., having the effect of a plan.— If—

(A) there is no plan, but

(B) there is a method or arrangement of employer contributions of compensation which has the effect of a stock bonus, pension, profit-sharing, or annuity plan, or other plan deferring the receipt of compensation (including a plan described in paragraph (2)),

subsection (a) shall apply as if there were such a plan.

(2) Plans providing certain deferred benefits.—

(A) In general.— For purposes of this section, any plan providing for deferred benefits (other than compensation) for employees, their spouses, or their dependents shall be treated as a plan deferring the receipt of compensation. In the case of such a plan, for purposes of this section, the determination of when an amount is includible in gross income shall be made without regard to any provisions of this chapter excluding such benefits from gross income.

(B) Exception.— Subparagraph (A) shall not apply to any benefit provided through a welfare benefit fund (as defined in section 419(e)).

(c) Certain Negotiated Plans.— If contributions are paid by an employer—

(1) under a plan under which such contributions are held in trust for the purpose of paying (either from principal or income or both) for the benefit of employees and their families and dependents at least medical or hospital care, or pensions on retirement or death of employees; and

(2) such plan was established prior to January 1, 1954, as a result of an agreement between employee representatives and the Government of the United States during a period of Government operation, under seizure powers, of a major part of the productive facilities of the industry in which such employer is engaged,

such contributions shall not be deductible under this section nor be made nondeductible by this section, but the deductibility thereof shall be governed solely by section 162 (relating to trade or business expenses). For purposes of this chapter and subtitle B, in the case of any individual who before July 1, 1974, was a participant in a plan described in the preceding sentence

(A) such individual, if he is or was an employee within the meaning of section 401(c)(1), shall be treated (with respect to service covered by the plan) as being an employee other than an employee within the meaning of section 401(c)(1) and as being an employee of a participating employer under the plan,

(B) earnings derived from service covered by the plan shall be treated as not being earned income within the meaning of section 401(c)(2), and

(C) such individual shall be treated as an employee of a participating employer under the plan with respect to service before July 1, 1975, covered by the plan.

Section 277 (relating to deductions incurred by certain membership organizations in transactions with members) does not apply to any trust described in this subsection. The first and third sentences of this subsection shall have no application with respect to amounts contributed to a trust on or after any date on which such trust is qualified for exemption from tax under section 501(a).

(d) Deductibility of Payments of Deferred Compensation, Etc., to Independent Contractors.— If a plan would be described in so much of subsection (a) as precedes paragraph (1) thereof (as modified by subsection (b)) but for the fact that there is no employer-employee relationship, the contributions or compensation—

(1) shall not be deductible by the payor thereof under this chapter, but

(2) shall (if they would be deductible under this chapter but for paragraph (1)) be deductible under this subsection for the taxable year in which an amount attributable to the contribution or compensation is includible in the gross income of the persons participating in the plan.

(e) Contributions Allocable to Life Insurance Protection for Self-Employed Individuals.— In the case of a self-employed individual described in section 401(c)(1), contributions which are allocable (determined under regulations prescribed by the Secretary) to the purchase of life, accident, health, or other insurance shall not be taken into account under paragraph (1), (2), or (3) of subsection (a).

(f) Certain Loan Repayments Considered as Contributions.— [Repealed.]

(g) Certain Employer Liability Payments Considered as Contributions.—

(1) In general.— For purposes of this section, any amount paid by an employer under section 4041(b), 4062, 4063, or 4064, or part 1 of subtitle E of title IV of the Employee Retirement Income Security Act of 1974 shall be treated as a contribution to which this section applies by such employer to or under a stock bonus, pension, profit-sharing, or annuity plan.

(2) Controlled group deductions.— In the case of a payment described in paragraph (1) made by an entity which is liable because it is a member of a commonly controlled group of corporations, trades, or businesses, within the meaning of subsection (b) or (c) of section 414, the fact that the entity did not directly employ participants of the plan with respect to which the liability payment was made shall not affect the deductibility of a payment which otherwise satisfies the conditions of section 162 (relating to trade or business expenses) or section 212 (relating to expenses for the production of income).

(3) Timing of deduction of contributions.—

(A) In general.— Except as otherwise provided in this paragraph, any payment described in paragraph (1) shall (subject to the last sentence of subsection (a)(1)(A)) be deductible under this section when paid.

(B) Contributions under standard terminations.— Subparagraph (A) shall not apply (and subsection (a)(1)(A) shall apply) to any payments described in paragraph (1) which are paid to terminate a plan under section 4041(b) of the Employee Retirement Income Security Act of 1974 to the extent such payments result in the assets of the plan being in excess of the total amount of benefits under such plan which are guaranteed by the Pension Benefit Guaranty Corporation under section 4022 of such Act.

(C) Contributions to certain trusts.— Subparagraph (A) shall not apply to any payment described in paragraph (1) which is made under section 4062(c) of such Act and such payment shall be deductible at such time as may be prescribed in regulations which are based on principles similar to the principles of subsection (a)(1)(A).

IRC Sec. 404 (g)(3)(C)

◊ ◊ ◊

Editor's Note: The changes to Code §404(g)(4) set forth below were enacted by §751(a)(11) of the Retirement Protection Act of 1994 (enacted as part of the Uruguay Round Agreements Act (P.L. 103-465). The amendment is effective as of December 8, 1994.

◊ ◊ ◊

(4) References to Employee Retirement Income Security Act of 1974.— For purposes of this section, any reference to a section of the Employee Retirement Income Security Act of 1974 shall be treated as a reference to such section as in effect on the date of the enactment of [the Single-Employer Pension Plan Amendments Act of 1986] *the Retirement Protection Act of 1994.*

(h) Special Rules for Simplified Employee Pensions.—

(1) In General.— Employee contributions to a simplified employee pension shall be treated as if they are made to a plan subject to the requirements of this section. Employer contributions to a simplified employee pension are subject to the following limitations:

(A) Contributions made for a year are deductible—

(i) in the case of a simplified employee pension maintained on a calendar year basis, for the taxable year with or within which the calendar year ends, or

(ii) in the case of a simplified employee pension which is maintained on the basis of the taxable year of the employer, for such taxable year.

(B) Contributions shall be treated for purposes of this subsection as if they were made for a taxable year if such contributions are made on account of such taxable year and are made not later than the time prescribed by law for filing the return for such taxable year (including extensions thereof).

(C) The amount deductible in a taxable year for a simplified employee pension shall not exceed 15 percent of the compensation paid to the employees during the calendar year ending with or within the taxable year (or during the taxable year in the case of a taxable year described in subparagraph (A)(ii)). The excess of the amount contributed over the amount deductible for a taxable year shall be deductible in the succeeding taxable years in order of time, subject to the 15 percent limit of the preceding sentence.

(2) Effect on stock bonus and profit-sharing trust.— For any taxable year for which the employer has a deduction under paragraph (1), the otherwise applicable limitations in subsection (a)(3)(A) shall be reduced by the amount of the allowable deductions under paragraph (1) with respect to participants in the stock bonus or profit-sharing trust.

(3) Coordination with subsection (a)(7).— For purposes of subsection (a)(7), a simplified employee pension shall be treated as if it were a separate stock bonus or profit-sharing trust.

(i) [Repealed.]

(j) Special Rules Relating to Application With Section 415.—

(1) No deduction in excess of section 415 limitation.— In computing the amount of any deduction allowable under paragraph (1), (2) (3), (4), (7), or (10) of subsection (a) for any year—

(A) in the case of a defined benefit plan there shall not be taken into account any benefits for any year in excess of any limitation on such benefits under section 415 for such year, or

(B) in the case of a defined contribution plan, the amount of any contributions otherwise taken into account shall be reduced by any annual additions in excess of the limitation under section 415 for such year.

(2) No advance funding of cost-of-living adjustments.—For purposes of clause (i), (ii) or (iii) of subsection (a)(1)(A), and in computing the full funding limitation, there shall not be taken into account any adjustments under section 415(d)(1) for any year before the year for which such adjustment first takes effect.

(k) Deduction for Dividends Paid on Certain Employer Securities.—

(1) General rule.— In the case of a corporation, there shall be allowed as a deduction for a taxable year the amount of any applicable dividend paid in cash by such corporation during the taxable year with respect to applicable employer securities. Such deduction shall be in addition to the deductions allowed under subsection (a).

(2) Applicable dividend.— For purposes of this subsection—

(A) In general.— The term ''applicable dividend'' means any dividend which, in accordance with plan provisions—

(i) is paid in cash to the participants in the plan or their beneficiaries,

(ii) is paid to the plan and is distributed in cash to participants in the plan or their beneficiaries not later that 90 days after the close of the plan year in which paid, or

(iii) is used to make payments on a loan described in subsection (a)(9) the proceeds of which were used to acquire the employer securities (whether or not allocated to participants) with respect to which the dividend is paid.

(B) Limitation on certain dividends.— A dividend described in subparagraph (A)(iii) which is paid with respect to any employer security which is allocated to a participant shall not be treated as an applicable dividend unless the plan provides that employer securities with a fair market value of not less than the amount of such dividend are allocated to such participant for the year which (but for subparagraph (A)) such dividend would have been allocated to such participant.

(3) Applicable employer securities.—For purposes of this subsection, the term ''applicable employer securities'' means, with respect to any dividend, employer securities which are held on the record date for such dividend by an employee stock ownership plan which is maintained by—

(A) the corporation paying such dividend, or

(B) any other corporation which is a member of a controlled group of corporations (within the meaning of section 409(1)(4)) which includes such corporation.

(4) Time for deduction.—

(A) In general.— The deduction under paragraph (1) shall be allowable in the taxable year of the corporation to which the dividend is paid or distributed to a participant or his beneficiary.

(B) Repayment of loans.— In the case of an applicable dividend described in clause (iii) of paragraph (2)(A), the deduction under paragraph (1) shall be allowable in the taxable year of the corporation in which such dividend is used to repay the loan described in such clause.

(5) Other rules.— For purposes of this subsection—

(A) Disallowance of deduction.— The Secretary may disallow the deduction under paragraph (1) for any dividend if the Secretary determines that such dividend constitutes, in substance, an evasion of taxation.

(B) Plan qualification.— A plan shall not be treated as violating the requirements of section 401, 409, or 4975(e)(7), or as engaging in a prohibited transaction for purposes of section 4975(d)(3), merely by reason of any payment or distribution described in paragraph (2)(A).

IRC Sec. 404 (k)(5)(B)

(6) Definitions.— For purposes of this subsection—

(A) Employer securities.— The term "employer securities" has the meaning given such term by section 409(l).

(B) Employee stock ownership plan.— The term "employee stock ownership plan" has the meaning given such term by section 4975(e)(7). Such term includes a tax credit employee stock ownership plan (as defined in section 409).

◊ ◊ ◊

Editor's Note: Section 404(*l*), below, was amended by OBRA '93 §13212. For the effective date of this provision, set forth in §13212(d) of OBRA '93, see the Editor's Note at the end of Code §401(a)(17), above.

◊ ◊ ◊

(*l*) Limitation on Amount of Annual Compensation Taken Into Account.— For purposes of applying the limitations of this section, the amount of annual compensation of each employee taken into account under the plan for any year shall not exceed $150,000. The Secretary shall adjust the $150,000 amount at the same time, and by the same amount, as any adjustment under section 401(a)(17)(B). For purposes of clause (i), (ii), or (iii) of subsection (a)(1)(A), and in computing the full funding limitation, any adjustment under the preceding sentence shall not be taken into account for any year before the year for which such adjustment first takes effect. In determining the compensation of an employee, the rules of section 414(q)(6) shall apply, except that in applying such rules, the term "family" shall include only the spouse of the employee and any lineal descendants of the employee who have not attained age 19 before the close of the year.

SEC. 404A. DEDUCTION FOR CERTAIN FOREIGN DEFERRED COMPENSATION PLANS.

(a) General Rule.— Amounts paid or accrued by an employer under a qualified foreign plan—

(1) shall not be allowable as a deduction under this chapter, but

(2) if they would otherwise be deductible, shall be allowed as a deduction under this section for the taxable year for which such amounts are properly taken into account under this section.

(b) Rules for Qualified Funded Plans.— For purposes of this section—

(1) In general.— Except as otherwise provided in this section, in the case of a qualified funded plan contributions are properly taken into account for the taxable year in which paid.

(2) Payment after close of taxable year.— For purposes of paragraph (1), a payment made after the close of a taxable year shall be treated as made on the last day of such year if the payment is made—

(A) on account of such year, and

(B) not later than the time prescribed by law for filing the return for such year (including extensions thereof).

(3) Limitations.— In the case of a qualified funded plan, the amount allowable as a deduction for the taxable year shall be subject to— Sec. 404A (b)(3)(A)

(A) in the case of—

(i) a plan under which the benefits are fixed or determinable, limitations similar to those contained in clauses (ii) and (iii) of subparagraph (A) of section 404(a)(1) (determined without regard to the last sentence of such subparagraph (A)), or

(ii) any other plan, limitations similar to the limitations contained in paragraph (3) of section 404(a), and

(B) limitations similar to those contained in paragraph (7) of section 404(a).

(4) Carryover.— If—

(A) the aggregate of the contributions paid during the taxable year reduced by any contributions not allowable as a deduction under paragraphs (1) and (2) of subsection (g), exceeds

(B) the amount allowable as a deduction under subsection (a) (determined without regard to subsection (d)),

such excess shall be treated as an amount paid in the succeeding taxable year.

(5) Amounts must be paid to qualified trust, etc.— In the case of a qualified funded plan, a contribution shall be taken into account only if it is paid—

(A) to a trust (or the equivalent of a trust) which meets the requirements of section 401(a)(2),

(B) for a retirement annuity, or

(C) to a participant or beneficiary.

(c) Rules Relating to Qualified Reserve Plans.— For purposes of this section—

(1) In general.— In the case of a qualified reserve plan, the amount properly taken into account for the taxable year is the reasonable addition for such year to a reserve for the taxpayer's liability under the plan. Unless otherwise required or permitted in regulations prescribed by the Secretary, the reserve for the taxpayer's liability shall be determined under the unit credit method modified to reflect the requirements of paragraphs (3) and (4). All benefits paid under the plan shall be charged to the reserve.

(2) Income item.— In the case of a plan which is or has been a qualified reserve plan, an amount equal to that portion of any decrease for the taxable year in the reserve which is not attributable to the payment of benefits shall be included in gross income.

(3) Rights must be nonforfeitable, etc.— In the case of a qualified reserve plan, an item shall be taken into account for a taxable year only if—

(A) there is no substantial risk that the rights of the employee will be forfeited, and

(B) such item meets such additional requirements as the Secretary may by regulations prescribe as necessary or appropriate to ensure that the liability will be satisfied.

(4) Spreading of certain increases and decreases in reserves.— There shall be amortized over a 10-year period any increase or decrease to the reserve on account of—

(A) the adoption of the plan or a plan amendment,

(B) experience gains and losses, and

(C) any change in actuarial assumptions,

(D) changes in the interest rate under subsection (g)(3)(B), and

(E) such other factors as may be prescribed by regulations.

(d) Amounts Taken Into Account Must Be Consistent With Amounts Allowed Under Foreign Law.—

(1) General rule.— In the case of any plan, the amount allowed as a deduction under subsection (a) for any taxable year shall equal— Sec. 404A (d)(1)(A)

(A) the lesser of—

(i) the cumulative United States amount, or

(ii) the cumulative foreign amount, reduced by

(B) the aggregate amount determined under this section for all prior taxable years.

(2) Cumulative amounts defined.— For purposes of paragraph (1)—

(A) Cumulative United States amount.— The term "cumulative United States

IRC Sec. 404A (d)(2)(A)

amount'' means the aggregate amount determined with respect to the plan under this section for the taxable year and for all prior taxable years to which this section applies. Such determination shall be made for each taxable year without regard to the application of paragraph (1).

(B) Cumulative foreign amount.— The term ''cumulative foreign amount'' means the aggregate amount allowed as a deduction under the appropriate foreign tax laws for the taxable year and all prior taxable years to which this section applies.

(3) Effect on earnings and profits, etc.— In determining the earnings and profits and accumulated profits of any foreign corporation with respect to a qualified foreign plan, except as provided in regulations, the amount determined under paragraph (1) with respect to any plan for any taxable year shall in no event exceed the amount allowed as a deduction under the appropriate foreign tax laws for such taxable year.

(e) Qualified Foreign Plan.— For purposes of this section, the term ''qualified foreign plan'' means any written plan of an employer for deferring the receipt of compensation but only if—

(1) such plan is for the exclusive benefit of the employer's employees or their beneficiaries,

(2) 90 percent or more of the amounts taken into account for the taxable year under the plan are attributable to services—

(A) performed by nonresident aliens, and

(B) the compensation for which is not subject to tax under this chapter, and

(3) the employer elects (at such time and in such manner as the Secretary shall by regulations prescribe) to have this section apply to such plan.

(f) Funded and Reserve Plans.— For purposes of this section—

(1) Qualified funded plan.— The term ''qualified funded plan'' means a qualified foreign plan which is not a qualified reserve plan.

(2) Qualified reserve plan.— The term ''qualified reserve plan'' means a qualified foreign plan with respect to which an election made by the taxpayer is in effect for the taxable year. An election under the preceding sentence shall be made in such manner and form as the Secretary may by regulations prescribe and, once made, may be revoked only with the consent of the Secretary.

(g) Other Special Rules.—

(1) No deduction for certain amounts.— Except as provided in section 404(a)(5), no deduction shall be allowed under this section for any item to the extent such item is attributable to services—

(A) performed by a citizen or resident of the United States who is a highly compensated employee (within the meaning of section 414(q)), or

(B) performed in the United States the compensation for which is subject to tax under this chapter.

(2) Taxpayer must furnish information.—

(A) In general.— No deduction shall be allowed under this section with respect to any plan for any taxable year unless the taxpayer furnishes to the Secretary with respect to such plan (at such time as the Secretary may by regulations prescribe)—

(i) a statement from the foreign tax authorities specifying the amount of the deduction allowed in computing taxable income under foreign law for such year with respect to such plan,

(ii) if the return under foreign tax law shows the deduction for plan contribution

IRC Sec. 404A (d)(2)(B)

or reserves as a separate, identifiable item, a copy of the foreign tax return for the taxable year, or

(iii) such other statement, return, or other evidence as the Secretary prescribes by regulation as being sufficient to establish the amount of the deduction under foreign law.

(B) Redetermination where foreign tax deduction is adjusted.—If the deduction under foreign tax law is adjusted, the taxpayers shall notify the Secretary of such adjustment on or before the date prescribed by regulations, and the Secretary shall redetermine the amount of the tax year or years affected. In any case described in the preceding sentence, rules similar to the rules of subsection (c) of section 905 shall apply.

(3) Actuarial assumptions must be reasonable; full funding.—

(A) In general.—Except as provided in subparagraph (B), principles similar to those set forth in paragraphs (3) and (7) of section 412(c) shall apply for purposes of this section.

(B) Interest rate for reserve plan.—

(i) In general.— In the case of a qualified reserve plan, in lieu of taking rates of interest into account under subparagraph (A), the rate of interest for the plan shall be the rate selected by the taxpayer which is within the permissible range.

(ii) Rate remains in effect so long as it falls within permissible range.— Any rate selected by the taxpayer for the plan under this subparagraph shall remain in effect for such plan until the first taxable year for which such rate is no longer within the permissible range. At such time, the taxpayer shall select a new rate of interest which is within the permissible range applicable at such time.

(iii) Permissible range.—For purposes of this subparagraph, the term "permissible range" means a rate of interest which is not more than 20 percent above, and not more than 20 percent below, the average rate of interest for long-term corporate bonds in the appropriate country for the 15-year period ending on the last day before the beginning of the taxable year.

(4) Accounting method.— Any change in the method (but not the actuarial assumptions) used to determine the amount allowed as a deduction under subsection (a) shall be treated as a change in accounting method under section 446(e).

(5) Section 481 applies to election.— For purposes of section 481, any election under this section shall be treated as a change in the taxpayer's method of accounting. In applying section 481 with respect to any such election, the period for taking into account any increase or decrease in accumulated profits, earnings and profits or taxable income resulting from the application of section 481(a)(2) shall be the year for which the election is made and the fourteen succeeding years.

(h) Regulations.— The Secretary shall prescribe such regulations as may be necessary to carry out the purposes of this section (including regulations providing for the coordination of the provisions of this section with section 404 in the case of a plan which has been subject to both of such sections).

SEC. 405. QUALIFIED BOND PURCHASE PLANS. [REPEALED.]

SEC. 406. EMPLOYEES OF FOREIGN AFFILIATES COVERED BY SECTION 3121(*l*) AGREEMENTS.

(a) Treatment as Employees of American Employer.— For purposes of applying this part with respect to a pension, profit-sharing, or stock bonus plan described in section 401(a) or an annuity plan described in section 403(a) of an American employer (as defined in section 3121(h)), an individual who is a citizen or resident of the United States and who is an employee of a foreign affiliate (as defined in section 3121(*l*)(8)) of such American employer shall be treated as an employee of such an American employer, if—

(1) such American employer has entered into an agreement under section 3121(*l*) which applies to the foreign affiliate of which such individual is an employee;

(2) the plan of such American employer expressly provides for contributions or benefits for individuals who are citizens or residents of the United States and who are employees of its foreign affiliates to which an agreement entered into by such American employer under section 3121(*l*) applies; and

(3) contributions under a funded plan of deferred compensation (whether or not a plan described in section 401(a) or 403(a)) are not provided by any other person with respect to the remuneration paid to such individual by the foreign affiliate.

(b) Special Rules for Application of Section 401(a).—

(1) Nondiscrimination requirements.— For purposes of applying section 401(a)(4) and section 410(b) with respect to an individual who is treated as an employee of an American employer under subsection (a)—

(A) if such individual is a highly compensated employee (within the meaning of section 414(q)), he shall be treated as having such capacity with respect to such American employer; and

(B) the determination of whether such individual is a highly compensated employee (as so defined) shall be made by treating such individual's total compensation (determined with the application of paragraph (2) of this subsection) as compensation paid by such American employer and by determining such individual's status with regard to such American employer.

(2) Determination of compensation.— For purposes of applying paragraph (5) of section 401(a) with respect to an individual who is treated as an employee of an American employer under subsection (a)—

(A) the total compensation of such individual shall be the remuneration paid to such individual by the foreign affiliate which would constitute his total compensation if his services had been performed for such American employer, and the basic or regular rate of compensation of such individual shall be determined under regulations prescribed by the Secretary; and

(B) such individual shall be treated as having paid the amount paid by such American employer which is equivalent to the tax imposed by section 3101.

(c) Termination of Status as Deemed Employee Not to be Treated as Separation from Service for Purposes of Limitation of Tax.— For purposes of applying section 402(d) with respect to an individual who is treated as an employee of an American employer under subsection (a), such individual shall not be considered as separated from the service of such American employer solely by reason of the fact that—

(1) the agreement entered into by such American employer under section 3121(*l*) which covers the employment of such individual is terminated under the provisions of such section,

(2) such individual becomes an employee of a foreign affiliate with respect to which such agreement does not apply,

(3) such individual ceases to be an employee of the foreign affiliate by reason of which he is treated as an employee of such American employer, if he becomes an employee of another entity in which such American employer has not less than a 10-percent interest (within the meaning of section 3121(1)(6)), or

(4) the provision of the plan described in subsection (a)(2) is terminated.

(d) Deductibility of Contributions.— For purposes of applying section 404 with respect to contributions made to or under a pension, profit-sharing, stock bonus, or annuity plan by an American employer, or by another taxpayer which is entitled to deduct its contributions under section 404(a)(3)(B), on behalf of an individual who is treated as an employee of such American employer under subsection (a)—

(1) except as provided in paragraph (2), no deduction shall be allowed to such American employer or to any other taxpayer which is entitled to deduct its contributions under such sections,

(2) there shall be allowed as a deduction to the foreign affiliate of which such individual is an employee an amount equal to the amount which (but for paragraph (1)) would be deductible under section 404 by the American employer if he were an employee of the American employer, and

(3) any reference to compensation shall be considered to be a reference to the total compensation of such individual (determined with the application of subsection (b)(2)).

Any amount deductible by a foreign affiliate under this subsection shall be deductible for its taxable year with or within which the taxable year of such American employer ends.

(e) Treatment as Employee Under Related Provisions.— An individual who is treated as an employee of an American employer under subsection (a) shall also be treated as an employee of such American employer, with respect to the plan described in subsection (a)(2), for purposes of applying the following provisions of this title:

(1) Section 72(f) (relating to special rules for computing employees' contributions).

(2) Section 101(b) (relating to employees' death benefits).

(3) Section 2039 (relating to annuities).

SEC. 407. CERTAIN EMPLOYEES OF DOMESTIC SUBSIDIARIES ENGAGED IN BUSINESS OUTSIDE THE UNITED STATES.

(a) Treatment as Employees of Domestic Parent Corporation.—

(1) In general.— For purpose of applying this part with respect to a pension, profitsharing, or stock bonus plan described in section 401(a) or an annuity plan described in section 403(a) of a domestic parent corporation, an individual who is a citizen or resident of the United States and who is an employee of a domestic subsidiary (within the meaning of paragraph (2)) of such domestic parent corporation shall be treated as an employee of such domestic parent corporation, if—

(A) the plan of such domestic parent corporation expressly provides for contributions or benefits for individuals who are citizens or residents of the United States and who are employees of its domestic subsidiaries; and

(B) contributions under a funded plan of deferred compensation (whether or not a plan described in section 401(a) or 403(a)) are not provided by any other person with respect to the remuneration paid to such individual by the domestic subsidiary.

(2) Definitions.— For purposes of this section—

(A) Domestic subsidiary.— A corporation shall be treated as a domestic subsidiary for any taxable year only if—

(i) such corporation is a domestic corporation 80 percent or more of the outstanding voting stock of which is owned by another domestic corporation;

(ii) 95 percent or more of its gross income for the three-year period immediately preceding the close of its taxable year which ends on or before the close of the taxable year of such other domestic corporation (or for such part of such period during which the corporation was in existence) was derived from sources without the United States; and

IRC Sec. 407 (a)(2)(A)(ii)

(iii) 90 percent or more of its gross income for such period (or such part) was derived from the active conduct of a trade or business.

If for the period (or part thereof) referred to in clauses (ii) and (iii) such corporation has no gross income, the provisions of clauses (ii) and (iii) shall be treated as satisfied if it is reasonable to anticipate that, with respect to the first taxable year thereafter for which such corporation has gross income, the provisions of such clauses will be satisfied.

(B) Domestic parent corporation.— The domestic parent corporation of any domestic subsidiary is the domestic corporation which owns 80 percent or more of the outstanding voting stock of such domestic subsidiary.

(b) Special Rules for Application of Section 401(a).—

(1) Nondiscrimination requirements.— For purposes of applying section 401(a)(4) and section 410(b) with respect to an individual who is treated as an employee of a domestic parent corporation under subsection (a)— Sec. 407 (b)(1)(A)

(A) if such individual is a highly compensated employee (within the meaning of section 414(q)), he shall be treated as having such capacity with respect to such domestic parent corporation; and

(B) the determination of whether such individual is a highly compensated employee (as so defined) shall be made by treating such individual's total compensation (determined with the application of paragraph (2) of this subsection) as compensation paid by such domestic parent corporation and by determining such individual's status with regard to such domestic parent corporation.

(2) Determination of compensation.— For purposes of applying paragraph (5) of section 401(a) with respect to an individual who is treated as an employee of a domestic parent corporation under subsection (a), the total compensation of such individual shall be the remuneration paid to such individual by the domestic subsidiary which would constitute his total compensation if his services had been performed for such domestic parent corporation, and the basic or regular rate of compensation of such individual shall be determined under regulations prescribed by the Secretary.

(c) Termination of Status as Deemed Employee Not To Be Treated as Separation From Service for Purposes of Limitation of Tax.— For purposes of applying section 402(d) with respect to an individual who is treated as an employee of a domestic parent corporation under subsection (a), such individual shall not be considered as separated from the service of such domestic parent corporation solely by reason of the fact that—

(1) the corporation of which such individual is an employee ceases, for any taxable year, to be a domestic subsidiary within the meaning of subsection (a)(2)(A),

(2) such individual ceases to be an employee of a domestic subsidiary of such domestic parent corporation, if he becomes an employee of another corporation controlled by such domestic parent corporation, or

(3) the provision of the plan described in subsection (a)(1)(A) is terminated.

(d) Deductibility of Contributions.— For purposes of applying section 404 with respect to contributions made to or under a pension, profit-sharing, stock bonus, or annuity plan by a domestic parent corporation, or by another corporation which is entitled to deduct its contributions under section 404(a)(3)(B), or behalf of an individual who is treated as an employee of such domestic corporation under subsection (a)—

(1) except as provided in paragraph (2), no deduction shall be allowed to such domestic parent corporation or to any other corporation which is entitled to deduct its contributions under such sections,

(2) there shall be allowed as a deduction to the domestic subsidiary of which such individual is an employee an amount equal to the amount which (but for paragraph (1)) would be deductible under section 404 by the domestic parent corporation if he were an employee of the domestic parent corporation, and

(3) any reference to compensation shall be considered to be a reference to the total compensation of such individual (determined with the application of subsection (b)(2)).

Any amount deductible by a domestic subsidiary under this subsection shall be deductible for its taxable year with or within which the taxable year of such domestic parent corporation ends.

(e) Treatment as Employee Under Related Provisions.— An individual who is treated as an employee of a domestic parent corporation under subsection (a) shall also be treated as an employee of such domestic parent corporation, with respect to the plan described in subsection (a)(1)(A), for purposes of applying the following provisions of this title:

(1) Section 72(f) (relating to special rules for computing employees' contributions).

(2) Section 101(b) (relating to employees' death benefits).

(3) Section 2039 (relating to annuities).

SEC. 408. INDIVIDUAL RETIREMENT ACCOUNTS.

(a) Individual Retirement Account.— For purposes of this section, the term "individual retirement account" means a trust created or organized in the United States for the exclusive benefit of an individual or his beneficiaries, but only if the written governing instrument creating the trust meets the following requirements:

(1) Except in the case of a rollover contribution described in subsection (d)(3), in section 402(c), 403(a)(4), or 403(b)(8), no contribution will be accepted unless it is in cash, and

contributions will not be accepted for the taxable year in excess of $2,000 on behalf of any individual.

(2) The trustee is a bank (as defined in subsection (n)) or such other person who demonstrates to the satisfaction of the Secretary that the manner in which such other person will administer the trust will be consistent with the requirements of this section.

(3) No part of the trust funds will be invested in life insurance contracts.

(4) The interest of an individual in the balance in his account is nonforfeitable.

(5) The assets of the trust will not be commingled with other property except in a common trust fund or common investment fund.

(6) Under regulations prescribed by the Secretary, rules similar to the rules of section 401(a)(9) and the incidental death benefit requirements of section 401(a) shall apply to the distribution of the entire interest of an individual for whose benefit the trust is maintained.

(b) Individual Retirement Annuity.— For purposes of this section, the term "individual retirement annuity" means an annuity contract, or an endowment contract (as determined under regulations prescribed by the Secretary), issued by an insurance company which meets the following requirements:

(1) The contract is not transferable by the owner.

(2) Under the contract—

(A) the premiums are not fixed,

(B) the annual premium on behalf of any individual will not exceed $2,000, and

(C) any refund of premiums will be applied before the close of the calendar year following the year of the refund toward the payment of future premiums or the purchase of additional benefits.

(3) Under regulations prescribed by the Secretary, rules similar to the rules of section

IRC Sec. 408 (b)(3)

401(a)(9) and the incidental death benefit requirements of section 401(a) shall apply to the distribution of the entire interest of the owner.

(4) The entire interest of the owner is nonforfeitable.

Such term does not include such an annuity contract for any taxable year of the owner in which it is disqualified on the application of subsection (e) or for any subsequent taxable year. For purposes of this subsection, no contract shall be treated as an endowment contract if it matures later than the taxable year in which the individual in whose name such contract is purchased attains age 70½; if it is not for the exclusive benefit of the individual in whose name it is purchased or his beneficiaries; or if the aggregate annual premiums under all such contracts purchased in the name of such individual for any taxable year exceed $2,000.

(c) Accounts Established by Employers and Certain Associations of Employees.— A trust created or organized in the United States by an employer for the exclusive benefit of his employees or their beneficiaries, or by an association of employees (which may include employees within the meaning of section 401(c)(1)) for the exclusive benefit of its members or their beneficiaries, shall be treated as an individual retirement account (described in subsection (a)), but only if the written governing instrument creating the trust meets the following requirements:

(1) The trust satisfies the requirements of paragraphs (1) through (6) of subsection (a).

(2) There is a separate accounting for the interest of each employee or member (or spouse of an employee or member).

The assets of the trust may be held in a common fund for the account of all individuals who have an interest in the trust.

(d) Tax Treatment of Distributions.—

(1) In general.— Except as otherwise provided in this subsection, any amount paid or distributed out of an individual retirement plan shall be included in gross income by the payee or distributee, as the case may be, in the manner provided under section 72.

(2) Special rules for applying section 72.— For purposes of applying section 72 to any amount described in paragraph (1)—

(A) all individual retirement plans shall be treated as 1 contract,

(B) all distributions during any taxable year shall be treated as 1 distribution, and

(C) the value of the contract, income on the contract, and investment in the contract shall be computed as of the close of the calendar year in which the taxable year begins.

For purposes of subparagraph (C), the value of the contract shall be increased by the amount of any distributions during the calendar year.

(3) Rollover contribution.— An amount is described in this paragraph as a rollover contribution if it meets the requirements of subparagraphs (A) and (B).

(A) In general.— Paragraph (1) does not apply to any amount paid or distributed out of an individual retirement account or individual retirement annuity to the individual for whose benefit the account or annuity is maintained if—

(i) the entire amount received (including money and any other property) is paid into an individual retirement account or individual retirement annuity (other than an endowment contract) for the benefit of such individual not later than the 60th day after the day on which he receives the payment or distribution;

(ii) no amount in the account and no part of the value of the annuity is attributable to any source other than a rollover contribution

IRC Sec. 408 (b)(4)

(as defined in section 402) from an employee's trust described in section 401(a) which is exempt from tax under section 501(a) or from an annuity plan described in section 403(a) (and any earnings on such contribution), and the entire amount received (including property and other money) is paid (for the benefit of such individual) into another such trust or annuity plan not later than the 60th day on which the individual receives the payment or the distribution; or

(iii)(I) the entire amount received (including the money and other property) represents the entire interest in the account or the entire value of the annuity,

(II) no amount in the account and no part of the value of the annuity is attributable to any source other than a rollover contribution from an annuity contract described in section 403(b) and any earnings on such rollover, and

(III) the entire amount thereof is paid into another annuity contract described in section 403(b) (for the benefit of such individual) not later than the 60th day after he receives the payment or distribution.

(B) Limitation.— This paragraph does not apply to any amount described in subparagraph (A)(i) received by an individual from an individual retirement account or individual retirement annuity if at any time during the 1-year period ending on the day of such receipt such individual received any other amount described in that subparagraph from an individual retirement account or an individual retirement annuity which was not includible in his gross income because of the application of this paragraph.

(C) Denial of rollover treatment for inherited accounts, etc.—

(i) In general.— In the case of an inherited individual retirement account or individual retirement annuity—

(I) this paragraph shall not apply to any amount received by an individual from such an account or annuity (and no amount transferred from such account or annuity to another individual retirement account or annuity shall be excluded from gross income by reason of such transfer), and

(II) such inherited account or annuity shall not be treated as an individual retirement account or annuity for purposes of determining whether any other amount is a rollover contribution.

(ii) Inherited individual retirement account or annuity.— An individual retirement account or individual retirement annuity shall be treated as inherited if—

(I) the individual for whose benefit the account or annuity is maintained acquired such account by reason of the death of another individual, and

(II) such individual was not the surviving spouse of such other individual.

(D) Partial rollovers permitted.—

(i) In general.— If any amount paid or distributed out of an individual retirement account or individual retirement annuity would meet the requirements of subparagraph (A) but for the fact that the entire amount was not paid into an eligible plan as required by clause (i), (ii), or (iii) of subparagraph (A), such amount shall be treated as meeting the requirements of subparagraph (A) to the extent it is paid into an eligible plan referred to in such clause not later than the 60th day referred to in such clause.

(ii) Eligible plan.— For purposes of clause (i), the term ''eligible plan'' means any account, annuity, contract, or plan referred to in subparagraph (A).

(E) Denial of rollover treatment for required distributions.— This paragraph shall not apply to any amount to the extent such amount is required to be distributed under subsection (a)(6) or (b)(3).

IRC Sec. 408 (d)(3)(E)

(F) Frozen deposits.— For purposes of this paragraph, rules similar to the rules of section 402(c)(7) (relating to frozen deposits) shall apply.

(4) Contributions returned before due date of return.— Paragraph (1) does not apply to the distribution of any contribution paid during a taxable year to an individual retirement account or for an individual retirement annuity if—

(A) such distribution is received on or before the day prescribed by law (including extensions of time) for filing such individual's return for such taxable year,

(B) no deduction is allowed under section 219 with respect to such contribution, and

(C) such distribution is accompanied by the amount of net income attributable to such contribution.

In the case of such a distribution, for purposes of section 61, any net income described in subparagraph (C) shall be deemed to have been earned and receivable in the taxable year in which such contribution is made.

(5) Certain distributions of excess contributions after due date for taxable year.—

(A) In general.— In the case of any individual, if the aggregate contributions (other than rollover contributions) paid for any taxable year to an individual retirement account or for an individual retirement annuity do not exceed $2,250, paragraph (1) shall not apply to the distribution of any such contribution to the extent that such contribution exceeds the amount allowable as a deduction under section 219 for the taxable year for which the contribution was paid—

(i) if such distribution is received after the date described in paragraph (4),

(ii) but only to the extent that no deduction has been allowed under section 219 with respect to such excess contribution.

If employer contributions on behalf of the individual are paid for the taxable year to a simplified employee pension, the dollar limitation of the preceding sentence shall be increased by the lesser of the amount of such contributions or the dollar limitation in effect under section 415(c)(1)(A) for such taxable year.

(B) Excess rollover contributions attributable to erroneous information.— If—

(i) the taxpayer reasonably relies on information supplied pursuant to subtitle F for determining the amount of a rollover contribution, but

(ii) the information was erroneous,

subparagraph (A) shall be applied by increasing the dollar limit set forth therein by that portion of the excess contribution which was attributable to such information.

For purposes of this paragraph, the amount allowable as a deduction under section 219 shall be computed without regard to section 219(g).

(6) Transfer of account incident to divorce.— The transfer of an individual's interest in an individual retirement account or an individual retirement annuity to his spouse or former spouse under a divorce or separation instrument described in subparagraph (A) of section 71(b)(2) is not to be considered a taxable transfer made by such individual notwithstanding any other provision of this subtitle, and such interest at the time of the transfer is to be treated as an individual retirement account of such spouse, and not of such individual. Thereafter such account or annuity for purposes of this subtitle is to be treated as maintained for the benefit of such spouse.

(7) Special rules for simplified employee pensions.—

(A) Transfer or rollover of contribution prohibited until deferral test met.— Notwithstanding any other provision of this subsection or section 72(t), paragraph (1) and section 72(t)(1) shall apply to the transfer c distribution from a simplified employee pension of any contribution under a salary reduction arrangement described in subsection (k)(6) (or any income allocable thereto) before a determination as to whether the requirements of subsection (k)(6)(A)(iii) are met with respect to such contribution.

(B) Certain exclusions treated as deductions.— For purposes of paragraphs (4) and (5) and section 4973, any amount excludable or excluded from gross income under section 402(h) shall be treated as an amount allowable or allowed as a deduction under section 219.

(e) Tax Treatment of Accounts and Annuities.—

(1) Exemption from tax.— Any individual retirement account is exempt from taxation under this subtitle unless such account has ceased to be an individual retirement account by reason of paragraph (2) or (3). Notwithstanding the preceding sentence, any such account is subject to the taxes imposed by section 511 (relating to imposition of tax on unrelated business income of charitable, etc. organizations).

(2) Loss of exemption of account where employee engages in prohibited transaction.—

(A) In general.— If, during any taxable year of the individual for whose benefit any individual retirement account is established, that individual or his beneficiary engages in any transaction prohibited by section 4975 with respect to such account, such account ceases to be an individual retirement account as of the first day of such taxable year. For purposes of this paragraph—

(i) the individual for whose benefit any account was established is treated as the creator of such account, and

(ii) the separate account for any individual within an individual retirement account maintained by an employer or association of employees is treated as a separate individual retirement account.

(B) Account treated as distributing all its assets.— In any case in which any account ceases to be an individual retirement account by reason of subparagraph (A) as of the first day of any taxable year, paragraph (1) of subsection (d) applies as if there were a distribution on such first day in an amount equal to the fair market value (on such first day) of all assets in the account (on such first day).

(3) Effect of borrowing on annuity contract.— If during any taxable year the owner of an individual retirement annuity borrows any money under or by use of such contract, the contract ceases to be an individual retirement annuity as of the first day of such taxable year. Such owner shall include in gross income for such year an amount equal to the fair market value of such contract as of such first day.

(4) Effect of pledging account as security.— If, during any taxable year of the individual for whose benefit an individual retirement account is established, that individual uses the account or any portion thereof as security for a loan, the portion so used is treated as distributed to that individual.

(5) Purchase of endowment contract by individual retirement account.— If the assets of an individual retirement account or any part of such assets are used to purchase an endowment contract for the benefit of the individual for whose benefit the account is established—

(A) to the extent that the amount of the assets involved in the purchase are not attributable to the purchase of life insurance, the purchase is treated as a rollover contribution described in subsection (d)(3), and

(B) to the extent that the amount of the assets involved in the purchase are attributable to the purchase of life, health, accident, or other insurance, such amounts are treated as distributed to that individual (but the provisions of subsection (f) do not apply).

(6) Commingling individual retirement account amounts in certain common trust funds and common investment funds.— Any common trust fund or common investment fund of individual retirement account assets which is exempt from taxation under this subtitle does not cease to be exempt on account of the participation or inclusion of assets of a trust exempt from taxation under section 501(a) which is described in section 401(a).

(f) [Repealed.]

(g) Community Property Laws.— This section shall be applied without regard to any community property laws.

(h) Custodial Accounts.— For purposes of this section, a custodial account shall be treated as a trust if the assets of such account are held by a bank (as defined in subsection (n)) or another person who demonstrates, to the satisfaction of the Secretary, that the manner in which he will administer the account will be consistent with the requirements of this section, and if the custodial account would, except for the fact that it is not a trust, constitute an individual retirement account described in subsection (a). For purposes of this title, in the case of a custodial account treated as a trust by reason of the preceding sentence, the custodian of such account shall be treated as the trustee thereof.

(i) Reports.— The trustee of an individual retirement account and the issuer of an endowment contract described in subsection (b) or an individual retirement annuity shall make such reports regarding such account, contract, or annuity to the Secretary and to the individual for whom the account, contract, or annuity is, or is to be, maintained with respect to the contributions (and the years to which they relate), distributions, and such other matters as the Secretary may require under regulations. The reports required by this subsection—

(1) shall be filed at such time and in such manner as the Secretary prescribes in such regulations, and

(2) shall be furnished to individuals—

(A) not later than January 31 of the calendar year following the calendar year to which such reports relate, and

(B) in such manner as the Secretary prescribes in such regulations.

(j) Increase in Maximum Limitations for Simplified Employee Pensions.— In the case of any simplified employee pension, subsections (a)(1) and (b)(2) of this section shall be applied by increasing the $2,000 amounts contained therein by the amount of the limitation in effect under section 415(c)(1)(A).

(k) Simplified Employee Pension Defined.—

(1) In general.— For purposes of this title, the term "simplified employee pension" means an individual retirement account or individual retirement annuity—

(A) with respect to which the requirements of paragraphs (2), (3), (4), and (5) of this subsection are met, and

(B) if such account or annuity is part of a top-heavy plan (as defined in section 416), with respect to which the requirements of section 416(c)(2) are met.

(2) Participation requirements.— This paragraph is satisfied with respect to a simplified employee pension for a year only if for such year the employer contributes to the simplified employee pension of each employee who—

(A) has attained age 21,

(B) has performed service for the employer during at least 3 of the immediately preceding 5 years, and

(C) received at least $300 in compensation (within the meaning of section 414(q)(7)) from the employer for the year. For purposes of this paragraph, there shall be excluded from consideration employees described in subparagraph (A) or (C) of section 410(b)(3). For purposes of any arrangemen described in subsection (k)(6), any employee who is eligible to have employer contributions made on the employee's behalf under such arrangement shall be treated as if such a contribution was made.

(3) Contributions may not discriminate in favor of the highly compensated, etc.—

(A) In general.— The requirements of this paragraph are met with respect to a simplified employee pension for a year if for such year the contributions made by the employer to simplified employee pensions for his employees do not discriminate in favor of any highly compensated employee (within the meaning of section 414(q)).

(B) Special rules.— For purposes of subparagraph (A), there shall be excluded from consideration employees described in subparagraph (A) or (C) of section 410(b)(3).

◊ ◊ ◊

Editor's Note: Section 404(k)(3)(C), below, was amended by OBRA '93 §13212. For the effective date of this provision, set forth in 13212(d) of OBRA '93, see the Editor's Note at the end of Code §401(a)(17), above.

◊ ◊ ◊

(C) Contributions must bear uniform relationship to compensation.— For purposes of subparagraph (A) and except as provided in subparagraph (D), employer contributions to simplified employee pensions (other than contributions under an arrangement described in paragraph (6)) shall be considered discriminatory unless contributions thereto bear a uniform relationship to the compensation (not in excess of the first $150,000) of each employee maintaining a simplified employee pension.

(D) Permitted disparity.— For purposes of subparagraph (C), the rules of section 401(*l*)(2) shall apply to contributions to simplified employee pensions (other than con-

tributions under an arrangement described in paragraph (6)).

(4) Withdrawals must be permitted.— A simplified employee pension meets the requirements of this paragraph only if—

(A) employer contributions thereto are not conditioned on the retention in such pension of any portion of the amount contributed, and

(B) there is no prohibition imposed by the employer on withdrawals from the simplified employee pension.

(5) Contributions must be made under written allocation formula.— The requirements of this paragraph are met with respect to a simplified employee pension only if employer contributions to such pension are determined under a definite written allocation formula which specifies—

(A) the requirements which an employee must satisfy to share in an allocation, and

(B) the manner in which the amount allocated is computed.

(6) Employee may elect salary reduction arrangement.—

(A) Arrangements which qualify.—

(i) In general.— A simplified employee pension shall not fail to meet the requirements of this subsection for a year merely because, under the terms of the pension, an employee may elect to have the employer make payments—

(I) as elective employer contributions to the simplified employee pension on behalf of the employee, or

(II) to the employee directly in cash.

(ii) 50 percent of eligible employees must elect.— Clause (i) shall not apply to a simplified employee pension unless an election described in clause (i)(I) is made or is in effect with respect to not less than 50 percent of the employees of the employer eligible to participate.

(iii) Requirements relating to deferral percentage.— Clause (i) shall not apply to a simplified employee pension for any year unless the deferral percentage for such year of each highly compensated employee eligible to participate is not more than the product of—

(I) the average of the deferral percentages for such year of all employees (other than highly compensated employees) eligible to participate, multiplied by

(II) 1.25.

(iv) Limitations on elective deferrals.— Clause (i) shall not apply to a simplified employee pension unless the requirements of section 401(a)(30) are met.

(B) Exception where more than 25 employees.— This paragraph shall not apply with respect to any year in the case of a simplified employee pension maintained by an employer with more than 25 employees who were eligible to participate (or would have been required to be eligible to participate if a pension was maintained) at any time during the preceding year.

(C) Distributions of excess contributions.—

(i) In general.— Rules similar to the rules of section 401(k)(8) shall apply to any excess contribution under this paragraph. Any excess contribution under a simplified employee pension shall be treated as an excess contribution for purposes of section 4979.

(ii) Excess contribution.— For purposes of clause (i), the term "excess contribution" means, with respect to a highly compensated employee, the excess of elective employer contributions under this paragraph over the maximum amount of such contributions allowable under subparagraph (A)(iii).

(D) Deferral percentage.— For purposes of this paragraph, the deferral percentage for an employee for a year shall be the ratio of—

(i) the amount of elective employer contributions actually paid over to the simplified employee pension on behalf of the employee for the year, to

(ii) the employee's compensation (not in excess of the first $150,000) for the year.

(E) Exception for state and local and tax-exempt pensions.— This paragraph shall not apply to a simplified employee pension maintained by—

(i) a State or local government or political subdivision thereof, or any agency or instrumentality thereof, or

(ii) an organization exempt from tax under this title.

(F) Exception where pension does not meet requirements necessary to insure distribution of excess contributions.— This paragraph shall not apply with respect to any year for which the simplified employee pension does not meet such requirements as the Secretary may prescribe as are necessary to insure that excess contributions are distributed in accordance with subparagraph (C), including—

(i) reporting requirements, and

(ii) requirements which, notwithstanding paragraph (4), provide that contributions (and any income allocable thereto) may not be withdrawn from a simplified employee pension until a determination has been made that the requirements of subparagraph (A)(iii) have been met with respect to such contributions.

(G) Highly compensated employee.— For purposes of this paragraph, the term "highly compensated employee" has the meaning given such term by section 414(q).

(7) Definitions.— For purposes of this subsection and subsection (l)—

(A) Employee, employer, or owner-employee.— The terms "employee", "employer", and "owner-employee" shall have the respective meanings given such terms by section 401(c).

(B) Compensation.— Except as pro-vided in paragraph (2)(C), the term "compensation" has the meaning given such term by section 414(s).

(C) Year.— The term "year" means—

(i) the calendar year, or

(ii) if the employer elects, subject to such terms and conditions as the Secretary may prescribe, to maintain the simplified employee pension on the basis of the employer's taxable year.

◊ ◊ ◊

Editor's Note: Code §408(k)(8) as set forth below appears as amended by §732 of the Retirement Protection Act of 1994 (enacted as part of the Uruguay Round Agreements Act, P.L. 103-465). The amendments apply generally to years beginning after December 31, 1994. However, the amendment providing for rounding of indexed amounts shall not apply to any year to the extent that the rounding would require the indexed amount to be reduced below the amount in effect for years beginning in 1994. Section 404(k)(8) also was amended by OBRA '93. For the effective date of this provision, set forth in §13212(d) of OBRA '93, see the Editor's Note at the end of Code §401(a)(17), above.

◊ ◊ ◊

(8) Cost-of-living adjustment.— The Secretary shall adjust the $300 amount in paragraph (2)(C) at the same time and in the same manner as under section 415(d) and shall adjust the $150,000 amount in paragraphs (3)(C) and (6)(D)(ii) at the same time, and by the same amount, as any adjustment under section 401(a)(17)(B); *except that any increase in the $300 amount which is not a multiple of $50 shall be rounded to the next lowest multiple of $50.*

(9) Cross reference.— For excise tax on certain excess contributions, see section 4979.

(*l*) Simplified Employer Reports.— An employer who makes a contribution on behalf of an employee to a simplified employee pension shall provide such simplified reports with respect to such contributions as the Secretary may require by regulations. The reports required by this subsection shall be filed at such time and in such manner, and information with respect to such contributions shall be furnished to the employee at such time and in such manner, as may be required by regulations.

(m) Investment in Collectibles Treated as Distributions.—

(1) In general.— The acquisition by an individual retirement account or by an individually-directed account under a plan described in section 401(a) of any collectible shall be treated (for purposes of this section and section 402) as a distribution from such account in an amount equal to the cost to such account of such collectible.

(2) Collectible defined.— For purposes of this subsection, the term "collectible" means—

(A) any work of art,

(B) any rug or antique,

(C) any metal or gem,

(D) any stamp or coin,

(E) any alcoholic beverage, or

IRC Sec. 408 (m)(2)(E)

(F) any other tangible personal property specified by the Secretary for purposes of this subsection.

(3) Exception for certain coins.— In the case of an individual retirement account, paragraph (2) shall not apply to—

(A) any gold coin described in paragraph (7), (8), (9), or (10) of section 5112(a) of title 31,

(B) any silver coin described in section 5112(e) of title 31, or

(C) any coin issued under the laws of any State.

(n) Bank.— For purposes of subsection (a)(2), the term "bank" means—

(1) any bank (as defined in section 581),

(2) an insured credit union (within the meaning of section 101(6) of the Federal Credit Union Act), and

(3) a corporation which, under the laws of the State of its incorporation, is subject to supervision and examination by the Commissioner of Banking or other officer of such State in charge of the administration of the banking laws of such State.

(o) Definitions and Rules Relating to Nondeductible Contributions to Individual Retirement Plans.—

(1) In general.— Subject to the provisions of this subsection, designated nondeductible contributions may be made on behalf of an individual to an individual retirement plan.

(2) Limits on amounts which may be contributed.—

(A) In general.— The amount of the designated nondeductible contributions made on behalf of any individual for any taxable year shall not exceed the nondeductible limit for such taxable year.

(B) Nondeductible limit.— For purposes of this paragraph

(i) In general.—The term "nondeductible limit" means the excess of—

(I) the amount allowable as a deduction under section 219 (determined without regard to section 219(g)), over

(II) the amount allowable as a deduction under section 219 (determined with regard to section 219(g)).

(ii) Taxpayer may elect to treat deductible contributions as nondeductible.— If a taxpayer elects not to deduct an amount which (without regard to this clause) is allowable as a deduction under section 219 for any taxable year, the nondeductible limit for such taxable year shall be increased by such amount.

(C) Designated nondeductible contributions.—

(i) In general.— For purposes of this paragraph, the term "designated nondeductible contribution" means any contribution to an individual retirement plan for the taxable year which is designated (in such manner as the Secretary may prescribe) as a contribution for which a deduction is not allowable under section 219.

(ii) Designation.— Any designation under clause (i) shall be made on the return of tax imposed by chapter 1 for the taxable year.

(3) Time when contributions made.— In determining for which taxable year a designated nondeductible contribution is made, the rule of section 219(f)(3) shall apply.

(4) Individual required to report amount of designated nondeductible contributions.—

(A) In general.— Any individual who—

(i) makes a designated nondeductible contribution to any individual retirement plan for any taxable year, or

IRC Sec. 408 (m)(2)(F)

(ii) receives any amount from any individual retirement plan for any taxable year,

shall include on his return of the tax imposed by chapter 1 for such taxable year and any succeeding taxable year (or on such other form as the Secretary may prescribe for any such taxable year) information described in subparagraph (B).

(B) Information required to be supplied.— The following information is described in this subparagraph:

(i) The amount of designated nondeductible contributions for the taxable year.

(ii) The amount of distributions from individual retirement plans for the taxable year.

(iii) The excess (if any) of—

(I) the aggregate amount of designated nondeductible contributions for all preceding taxable years, over

(II) the aggregate amount of distributions from individual retirement plans which was excludable from gross income for such taxable years.

(iv) The aggregate balance of all individual retirement plans of the individual as of the close of the calendar year in which the taxable year begins.

(v) Such other information as the Secretary may prescribe.

(C) Penalty for reporting contributions not made.— For penalty where individual reports designated nondeductible contributions not made, see section 6693(b).

(p) Cross References.—

(1) For tax on excess contributions in individual retirement accounts or annuities, see section 4973.

(2) For tax on certain accumulations in individual retirement accounts or annuities, see section 4974.

SEC. 409. QUALIFICATIONS FOR TAX CREDIT EMPLOYEE STOCK OWNERSHIP PLANS.

(a) Tax Credit Employee Stock Ownership Plan Defined.— Except as otherwise provided in this title, for purposes of this title, the term "tax credit employee stock ownership plan" means a defined contribution plan which—

(1) meets the requirements of section 401(a),

(2) is designed to invest primarily in employer securities, and

(3) meets the requirements of subsections (b), (c), (d), (e), (f), (g), (h), and (o) of this section.

(b) Required Allocation of Employee Securities.—

(1) In general.— A plan meets the requirements of this subsection if—

(A) the plan provides for the allocation for the plan year of all employer securities transferred to it or purchased by it (because of the requirements of section 41(c)(1)(B)) to the accounts of all participants who are entitled to share in such allocation, and

(B) for the plan year the allocation to each participant so entitled is an amount which bears substantially the same proportion to the amount of all such securities allocated to all such participants in the plan for that year as the amount of compensation paid to such participant during that year bears to the compensation paid to all such participants during that year.

(2) Compensation in excess of $100,000 disregarded.— For purposes of paragraph (1), compensation of any participant in excess of the first $100,000 per year shall be disregarded.

(3) Determination of compensation.— For purposes of this subsection, the amount of compensation paid to a participant for any period is the amount of such participant's compensation (within the meaning of section 415(c)(3)) for such period.

(4) Suspension of allocation in certain cases.— Notwithstanding paragraph (1), the allocation to the account of any participant which is attributable to the basic employee plan credit or the credit allowed under section 41 (relating to the employee stock ownership credit) may be extended over whatever period may be necessary to comply with the requirements of section 415.

(c) Participants Must Have Nonforfeitable Rights.— A plan meets the requirements of this subsection only if it provides that each participant has a nonforfeitable right to any employer security allocated to his account.

(d) Employer Securities Must Stay in the Plan.— A plan meets the requirements of this subsection only if it provides that no employer security allocated to a participant's account under subsection (b) (or allocated to a participant's account in connection with matched employer and employee contributions) may be distributed from that account before the end of the 84th month beginning after the month in which the security is allocated to the account. To the extent provided in the plan, the preceding sentence shall not apply in the case of—

(1) death, disability, separation from service, or termination of the plan;

(2) a transfer of a participant to the employment of an acquiring employer from the employment of the selling corporation in the case of a sale to the acquiring corporation of substantially all of the assets used by the selling corporation in a trade or business conducted by the selling corporation, or

(3) with respect to the stock of a selling corporation, a disposition of such selling corporation's interest in a subsidiary when the participant continues employment with such subsidiary.

This subsection shall not apply to any distribution required under section 401(a)(9) or to

any distribution or reinvestment required under section 401(a)(28).

(e) Voting Rights.—

(1) In general.— A plan meets the requirements of this subsection if it meets the requirements of paragraph (2) or (3), whichever is applicable.

(2) Requirements where employer has a registration-type class of securities.— If the employer has a registration-type class of securities, the plan meets the requirements of this paragraph only if each participant or beneficiary in the plan is entitled to direct the plan as to the manner in which securities of the employer which are entitled to vote and are allocated to the account of such participant or beneficiary are to be voted.

(3) Requirement for other employers.— If the employer does not have a registration-type class of securities, the plan meets the requirements of this paragraph only if each participant or beneficiary in the plan is entitled to direct the plan as to the manner in which voting rights under securities of the employer which are allocated to the account of such participant or beneficiary are to be exercised with respect to any corporate matter which involves the voting of such shares with respect to the approval or disapproval of any corporate merger or consolidation, recapitalization, reclassification, liquidation, dissolution, sale of substantially all assets of a trade or business, or such similar transaction as the Secretary may prescribe in regulations.

(4) Registration-type class of securities defined.— For purposes of this subsection, the term "registration-type class of securities" means—

(A) a class of securities required to be registered under section 12 of the Securities Exchange Act of 1934, and

(B) a class of securities which would be required to be so registered except for the exemption from registration provided in subsection (g)(2)(H) of such section 12.

IRC Sec. 409 (b)(4)

(5) 1 vote per participant.— A plan meets the requirements of paragraph (3) with respect to an issue if—

(A) the plan permits each participant 1 vote with respect to such issue, and

(B) the trustee votes the shares held by the plan in the proportion determined after application of subparagraph (A).

(f) Plan Must Be Established Before Employer's Due Date.—

(1) In general.— A plan meets the requirements of this subsection only if it is established on or before the due date (including any extension of such date) for the filing of the employer's tax return for the first taxable year of the employer for which an employee plan credit is claimed by the employer with respect to the plan.

(2) Special rule for first year.— A plan which otherwise meets the requirements of this section shall not be considered to have failed to meet the requirements of section 401(a) merely because it was not established by the close of the first taxable year of the employer for which an employee plan credit is claimed by the employer with respect to the plan.

(g) Transferred Amounts Must Stay in Plan Even Though Investment Credit is Redetermined or Recaptured.— A plan meets the requirement of this subsection only if it provides that amounts which are transferred to the plan (because of the requirements of section 48(n)(1) or 41(c)(1)(B)) shall remain in the plan (and, if allocated under the plan, shall remain so allocated) even though part or all of the employee plan credit or the credit allowed under section 41 (relating to employee stock ownership credit) is recaptured or redetermined. For purposes of the preceding sentence, the references to section 48(n)(1) and the employee plan credit shall refer to such section and credit as in effect before the enactment of the Tax Reform Act of 1984.

(h) Right to Demand Employer Securities; Put Option.—

(1) In general.— A plan meets the requirements of this subsection if a participant who is entitled to a distribution from the plan—

(A) has a right to demand that his benefits be distributed in the form of employer securities, and

(B) if the employer securities are not readily tradable on an established market, has a right to require that the employer repurchase employer securities under a fair valuation formula.

(2) Plan may distribute cash in certain cases.— A plan which otherwise meets the requirements of this subsection or of section 4975(e)(7) shall not be considered to have failed to meet the requirements of section 401(a) merely because under the plan the benefits may be distributed in cash or in the form of employer securities. In the case of an employer whose charter or bylaws restrict the ownership of substantially all outstanding employer securities to employees or to a trust described in section 401(a), a plan which otherwise meets the requirements of this subsection or section 4975(e)(7) shall not be considered to have failed to meet the requirements of this subsection or of section 401(a) merely because it does not permit a participant to exercise the right described in paragraph (1)(A) if such plan provides that participants entitled to a distribution from the plan shall have a right to receive such distribution in cash, except that such plan may distribute employer securities subject to a requirement that such securities may be resold to the employer under the terms which meet the requirements of paragraph (1)(B).

(3) Special rule for banks.— In the case of a plan established and maintained by a bank (as defined in section 581) which is prohibited by law from redeeming or purchasing its own securities, the requirements of paragraph (1)(B) shall not apply if the plan provides that participants entitled to a distribution from the plan shall have a right to receive a distribution in cash.

(4) Put option period.—An employer shall be deemed to satisfy the requirements of paragraph (1)(B) if it provides a put option for a period of at least 60 days following the date of distribution of stock of the employer and, if the put option is not exercised within such 60-day period, for an additional period of at least 60 days in the following plan year (as provided in regulations promulgated by the Secretary).

(5) Payment requirement for total distribution.—If an employer is required to repurchase employer securities which are distributed to the employee as part of a total distribution, the requirements of paragraph (1)(B) shall be treated as met if—

(A) the amount to be paid for the employer securities is paid in substantially equal periodic payments (not less frequently than annually) over a period beginning not later than 30 days after the exercise of the put option described in paragraph (4) and not exceeding 5 years, and

(B) there is adequate security provided and reasonable interest paid on the unpaid amounts referred to in subparagraph (A).

For purposes of this paragraph, the term "total distribution" means the distribution within 1 taxable year to the recipient of the balance to the credit of the recipient's account.

(6) Payment requirement for installment distributions.— If an employer is required to repurchase employer securities as part of an installment distribution, the requirements of paragraph (1)(B) shall be treated as met if the amount to be paid for the employer securities is paid not later than 30 days after the exercise of the put option described in paragraph (4).

(7) Exception where employee elected diversification.— Paragraph (1)(A) shall not apply with respect to the portion of the participant's account which the employee elected to have reinvested under section 401(a)(28)(B).

(i) Reimbursement for Expenses of Establishing and Administering Plan.— A plan which otherwise meets the requirements of this section shall not be treated as failing to meet such requirements merely because it provides that—

(1) Expenses of establishing plan.— As reimbursement for the expenses of establishing the plan, the employer may withhold from amounts due the plan for the taxable year for which the plan is established (or the plan may pay) so much of the amounts paid or incurred in connection with the establishment of the plan as does not exceed the sum of—

(A) 10 percent of the first $100,000 which the employer is required to transfer to the plan for that taxable year under section 41(c)(1)(B), and

(B) 5 percent of any amount so required to be transferred in excess of the first $100,000; and

(2) Administrative expenses.— As reimbursement for the expenses of administering the plan, the employer may withhold from amounts due the plan (or the plan may pay) so much of the amounts paid or incurred during the taxable year as expenses of administering the plan as does not exceed the lesser of—

(A) the sum of—

(i) 10 percent of the first $100,000 of the dividends paid to the plan with respect to stock of the employer during the plan year ending with or within the employer's taxable year, and

(ii) 5 percent of the amount of such dividends in excess of $100,000, or

(B) $100,000.

(j) Conditional Contributions to the Plan.— A plan which otherwise meets the requirements of this section shall not be treated as failing to satisfy such requirements (or as failing to satisfy the requirements of section 401(a) of this title or of section 403(c)(1) of the Employee Retirement Income Security Act of 1974) merely because of the return of a contribution (or a provision permitting such a return) if—

(1) the contribution to the plan is conditioned on a determination by the Secretary that such plan meets the requirements of this section,

(2) the application for a determination described in paragraph (1) is filed with the Secretary not later than 90 days after the date on which an employee plan credit is claimed, and

(3) the contribution is returned within 1 year after the date on which the Secretary issues notice to the employer that such plan does not satisfy the requirements of this section.

(k) Requirements Relating to Certain Withdrawals.— Notwithstanding any other law or rule of law—

(1) the withdrawal from a plan which otherwise meets with requirements of this section by the employer of an amount contributed for purposes of the matching employee plan credit shall not be considered to make the benefits forfeitable, and

(2) the plan shall not, by reason of such withdrawal, fail to be for the exclusive benefit of participants or their beneficiaries, if the withdrawn amounts were not matched by employee contributions or were in excess of the limitations of section 415. Any withdrawal described in the preceding sentence shall not be considered to violate the provisions of section 403(c)(1) of the Employee Retirement Income Security Act of 1974. For purposes of this subsection, the reference to the matching employee plan credit shall refer to such credit as in effect before the enactment of the Tax Reform Act of 1984.

(*l*) Employer Securities Defined.— For purposes of this section—

(1) In General.— The term "employer securities" means common stock issued by the employer (or by a corporation which is a member of the same controlled group) which is readily tradable on an established securities market.

(2) Special rule where there is no readily tradable common stock.— If there is no common stock which meets the requirements of paragraph (1), the term "employer securities" means common stock issued by the employer (or by a corporation which is a member of the same controlled group) having a combination of voting power and dividend rights equal to or in excess of—

(A) that class of common stock of the employer (or of any other such corporation) having the greatest voting power, and

(B) that class of common stock of the employer (or of any other such corporation) having the greatest dividend rights.

(3) Preferred stock may be issued in certain cases.— Noncallable preferred stock shall be treated as employer securities if such stock is convertible at any time into stock which meets the requirements of paragraph (1) or (2) (whichever is applicable) and if such conversion is at a conversion price which (as of the date of the acquisition by the tax credit employee stock ownership plan) is reasonable. For purposes of the preceding sentence, under regulations prescribed by the Secretary, preferred stock shall be treated as noncallable if after the call there will be a reasonable opportunity for a conversion which meets the requirements of the preceding sentence.

(4) Application to controlled group of corporations.—

(A) In general.— For purposes of this subsection, the term "controlled group of corporations" has the meaning given to such term by section 1563(a) (determined without regard to subsections (a)(4) and (e)(3)(C) of section 1563).

(B) Where common parent owns at least 50 percent of first-tier subsidiary.— For purposes of subparagraph (A), if the common parent owns directly stock possessing at least 50 percent of the voting power of all

IRC Sec. 409 (*l*)(4)(B)

classes of stock and at least 50 percent of each class of nonvoting stock in a first tier subsidiary, such subsidiary (and all other corporations below it in the chain which would meet the 80 percent test of section 1563(a) if the first tier subsidiary were the common parent) shall be treated as includible corporations.

(C) Where common parent owns 100 percent of first-tier subsidiary.— For purposes of subparagraph (A), if the common parent owns directly stock possessing all of the voting power of all classes of stock and all of the nonvoting stock, in a first-tier subsidiary, and if the first-tier subsidiary owns directly stock possessing at least 50 percent of the voting power of all classes of stock, and at least 50 percent of each class of nonvoting stock, in a second-tier subsidiary of the common parent, such second-tier subsidiary (and all other corporations below it in the chain which would meet the 80 percent test of section 1563(a) if the second-tier subsidiary were the common parent) shall be treated as includible corporations.

(5) Nonvoting common stock may be acquired in certain cases.— Nonvoting common stock of an employer described in the second sentence of section 401(a)(22) shall be treated as employer securities if an employer has a class of nonvoting common stock outstanding and the specific shares that the plan acquires have been issued and outstanding for at least 24 months.

(m) Nonrecognition of Gain or Loss on Contribution of Employer Securities to Tax Credit Employee Stock Ownership Plan.—No gain or loss shall be recognized to the taxpayer with respect to the transfer of employer securities to a tax credit employee stock ownership plan maintained by the taxpayer to the extent that such transfer is required under section 41(c)(1)(B), or subparagraph (A) or (B) of section 48(n)(1).

(n) Securities Received in Certain Transactions.—

(1) In general.— A plan to which section 1042 applies and an eligible worker-owned cooperative (within the meaning of section 1042(c)) shall provide that no portion of the assets of the plan or cooperative attributable to (or allocable in lieu of) employer securities acquired by the plan or cooperative in a sale to which section 1042 applies may accrue (or be allocated directly or indirectly under any plan of the employer meeting the requirements of section 401(a))—

(A) during the nonallocation period, for the benefit of—

(i) any taxpayer who makes an election under section 1042(a) with respect to employer securities,

(ii) any individual who is related to the taxpayer (within the meaning of section 267(b)), or

(B) for the benefit of any other person who owns (after application of section 318(a)) more than 25 percent of—

(i) any class of outstanding stock of the corporation which issued such employer securities or of any corporation which is a member of the same controlled group of corporations (within the meaning of subsection (*l*)(4)) as such corporation, or

(ii) the total value of any class of outstanding stock of any such corporation.

For purposes of subparagraph (B), section 318(a) shall be applied without regard to the employee trust exception in paragraph (2)(B)(i).

(2) Failure to meet requirements.— If a plan fails to meet the requirements of paragraph (1)—

(A) the plan shall be treated as having distributed to the person described in paragraph (1) the amount allocated to the account of such person in violation of paragraph (1) at the time of such allocation,

(B) the provisions of section 4979A shall apply, and

(C) the statutory period for the assessment of any tax imposed by section 4979A shall not expire before the date which is 3 years from the later of—

(i) the 1st allocation of employer securities in connection with a sale to the plan to which section 1042 applies, or

(ii) the date on which the Secretary is notified of such failure.

(3) Definitions and special rules.— For purposes of this subsection—

(A) Lineal descendants.— Paragraph (1)(A)(ii) shall not apply to any individual if—

(i) such individual is a lineal descendant of the taxpayer, and

(ii) the aggregate amount allocated to the benefit of all such lineal descendants during the nonallocation period does not exceed more than 5 percent of the employer securities (or amounts allocated in lieu thereof) held by the plan which are attributable to a sale to the plan by any person related to such descendants (within the meaning of section 267(c)(4)) in a transaction to which section 1042 applied.

(B) 25-percent shareholders.— A person shall be treated as failing to meet the stock ownership limitation under paragraph (1)(B) if such person fails such limitation—

(i) at any time during the 1-year period ending on the date of sale of qualified securities to the plan or cooperative, or

(ii) on the date as of which qualified securities are allocated to participants in the plan or cooperative.

(C) Nonallocation period.— The term "nonallocation period" means the period beginning on the date of the sale of the qualified securities and ending on the later of—

(i) the date which is 10 years after the date of sale, or

(ii) the date of the plan allocation attributable to the final payment of acquisition indebtedness incurred in connection with such sale.

(o) Distribution and Payment Requirements.— A plan meets the requirements of this subsection if—

(1) Distribution requirement.—

(A) In general.— The plan provides that, if the participant and, if applicable pursuant to sections 401(a)(11) and 417, with the consent of the participant's spouse elects, the distribution of the participant's account balance in the plan will commence not later than 1 year after the close of the plan year—

(i) in which the participant separates from service by reason of the attainment of normal retirement age under the plan, disability, or death, or

(ii) which is the 5th plan year following the plan year in which the participant otherwise separates from service, except that this clause shall not apply if the participant is reemployed by the employer before distribution is required to begin under this clause.

(B) Exception for certain financed securities.— For purposes of this subsection, the account balance of a participant shall not include any employer securities acquired with the proceeds of the loan described in section 404(a)(9) until the close of the plan year in which such loan is repaid in full.

(C) Limited distribution period.— The plan provides that, unless the participant elects otherwise, the distribution of the participant's account balance will be in substantially equal periodic payments (not less frequently than annually) over a period not longer than the greater of—

IRC Sec. 409 (o)(1)(C)

(i) 5 years, or

(ii) in the case of a participant with an account balance in excess of $500,000, 5 years plus 1 additional year (but not more than 5 additional years) for each $100,000 or fraction thereof by which such balance exceeds $500,000.

(2) Cost-of-living adjustment.— The Secretary shall adjust the dollar amounts under paragraph (1)(C) at the same time and in the same manner as under section 415(d).

(p) Cross References.—

(1) For requirements of allowance of employee plan credit, see section 48(n).

(2) For assessable penalties for failure to meet requirements of this section, or for failure to make contributions required with respect to the allowance of an employee plan credit or employee stock ownership credit, see section 6699.

(3) For requirements for allowance of an employee stock ownership credit, see section 41.

SEC. 410. MINIMUM PARTICIPATION STANDARDS.

(a) Participation.—

(1) Minimum age and service conditions.—

(A) General rule.— A trust shall not constitute a qualified trust under section 401(a) if the plan of which it is a part requires, as a condition of participation in the plan, that an employee complete a period of service with employer or employers maintaining the plan extending beyond the later of the following dates—

(i) the date on which the employee attains the age of 21, or

(ii) the date on which he completes 1 year of service.

(B) Special rules for certain plans.—

(i) In the case of any plan which provides that after not more than 2 years of service each participant has a right to 100 percent of his accrued benefit under the plan which is nonforfeitable (within the meaning of section 411) at the time such benefit accrues, clause (ii) of subparagraph (A) shall be applied by substituting "2 years of service" for "1 year of service".

(ii) In the case of any plan maintained exclusively for employees of an educational institution (as defined in section 170(b)(1)(A)(ii)) by an employer which is exempt from tax under section 501(a) which provides that each participant having at least 1 year of service has a right to 100 percent of his accrued benefit under the plan which is nonforfeitable (within the meaning of section 411) at the time such benefit accrues, clause (i) of subparagraph (A) shall be applied by substituting "26" for "21". This clause shall not apply to any plan to which clause (i) applies.

(2) Maximum age conditions.— A trust shall not constitute a qualified trust under section 401(a) if the plan of which it is a part excludes from participation (on the basis of age) employees who have attained a specified age.

(3) Definition of year of service.—

(A) General rule.— For purposes of this subsection, the term "year of service" means a 12-month period during which the employee has not less than 1,000 hours of service. For purposes of this paragraph, computation of any 12-month period shall be made with reference to the date on which the employee's employment commenced, except that, under regulations prescribed by the Secretary of Labor, such computation may be made by reference to the first day of a plan year in the case of an employee who does not complete 1,000 hours of service during the 12-month period beginning on the date his employment commenced.

(B) Seasonal industries.— In the case of any seasonal industry where the customary period of employment is less than 1,000 hours during a calendar year, the term "year of service" shall be such period as may be determined under regulations prescribed by the Secretary of Labor.

(C) Hours of service.— For purposes of this subsection the term "hours of service" means a time of service determined under regulations prescribed by the Secretary of Labor.

(D) Maritime industries.— For purposes of this subsection, in the case of any maritime industry, 125 days of service shall be treated as 1,000 hours of service. The Secretary of Labor may prescribe regulations to carry out this subparagraph.

(4) Time of participation.— A plan shall be treated as not meeting the requirements of paragraph (1) unless it provides that any employee who has satisfied the minimum age and service requirements specified in such paragraph, and who is otherwise entitled to participate in the plan, commences participation in the plan no later than the earlier of—

(A) the first day of the first plan year beginning after the date on which such employee satisfied such requirements, or

(B) the date 6 months after the date on which he satisfied such requirements,

unless such employee was separated from the service before the date referred to in subparagraph (A) or (B), whichever is applicable.

(5) Breaks in service.—

(A) General rule.— Except as otherwise provided in subparagraphs (B), (C), and (D), all years of service with the employer or employers maintaining the plan shall be taken into account in computing the period of service for purposes of paragraph (1).

(B) Employees under 2-year 100 percent vesting.— In the case of any employee who has any 1-year break in service (as defined

in section 411(a)(6)(A)) under a plan to which the service requirements of clause (i) of paragraph (1)(B) apply, if such employee has not satisfied such requirements, service before such break shall not be required to be taken into account.

(C) 1-year break in service.— In computing an employee's period of service for purposes of paragraph (1) in the case of any participant who has any 1-year break in service (as defined in section 411(a)(6)(A)), service before such break shall not be required to be taken into account under the plan until he has completed a year of service (as defined in paragraph (3)) after his return.

(D) Nonvested participants.—

(i) In general.— For purposes of paragraph (1), in the case of a nonvested participant, years of service with the employer or employers maintaining the plan before any period of consecutive 1-year breaks in service shall not be required to be taken into account in computing the period of service if the number of consecutive 1-year breaks in service within such period equals or exceeds the greater of—

(I) 5, or

(II) the aggregate number of years of service before such period.

(ii) Years of service not taken into account.— If any years of service are not required to be taken into account by reason of a period of breaks in service to which clause (i) applies, such years of service shall not be taken into account in applying clause (i) to a subsequent period of breaks in service.

(iii) Nonvested participant defined.— For purposes of clause (i), the term "nonvested participant" means a participant who does not have any nonforfeitable right under the plan to an accrued benefit derived from employer contributions.

(E) Special rule for maternity or paternity absences.—

IRC Sec. 410 (a)(5)(E)

(i) General rule.— In the case of each individual who is absent from work for any period—

(I) by reason of the pregnancy of the individual,

(II) by reason of the birth of a child of the individual,

(III) by reason of the placement of a child with the individual in connection with the adoption of such child by such individual, or

(IV) for purposes of caring for such child for a period beginning immediately following such birth or placement,

the plan shall treat as hours of service, solely for purposes of determining under this paragraph whether a 1-year break in service (as defined in section 411(a)(6)(A)) has occurred, the hours described in clause (ii).

(ii) Hours treated as hours of service.— The hours described in this clause are—

(I) the hours of service which otherwise would normally have been credited to such individual but for such absence, or

(II) in any case in which the plan is unable to determine the hours described in subclause (I), 8 hours of service per day of such absence,

except that the total number of hours treated as hours of service under this clause by reason of any such pregnancy or placement shall not exceed 501 hours.

(iii) Year to which hours are credited.The hours described in clause (ii) shall be treated as hours of service as provided in this subparagraph—

(I) only in the year in which the absence from work begins, if a participant would be prevented from incurring a 1-year break in service in such year solely because the period of absence is treated as

hours of service as provided in clause (i), or

(II) in any other case, in the immediately following year.

(iv) Year defined.— For purposes of this subparagraph, the term "year" means the period used in computations pursuant to paragraph (3).

(v) Information required to be filed.— A plan shall not fail to satisfy the requirements of this subparagraph solely because it provides that no credit will be given pursuant to this subparagraph unless the individual furnishes to the plan administrator such timely information as the plan may reasonably require to establish—

(I) that the absence from work is for reasons referred to in clause (i), and

(II) the number of days for which there was such an absence.

(b) Minimum Coverage Requirements.—

(1) In general.—A trust shall not constitute a qualified trust under section 401(a) unless such trust is designated by the employer as part of a plan which meets 1 of the following requirements:

(A) The plan benefits at least 70 percent of employees who are not highly compensated employees.

(B) The plan benefits—

(i) a percentage of employees who are not highly compensated employees which is at least 70 percent of

(ii) the percentage of highly compensated employees benefiting under the plan.

(C) The plan meets the requirements of paragraph (2).

IRC Sec. 410 (a)(5)(E)(i)

(2) Average benefit percentage test.—

(A) In general.— A plan shall be treated as meeting the requirements of this paragraph if—

(i) the plan benefits such employees as qualify under a classification set up by the employer and found by the Secretary not to be discriminatory in favor of highly compensated employees, and

(ii) the average benefit percentage for employees who are not highly compensated employees is at least 70 percent of the average benefit percentage for highly compensated employees.

(B) Average benefit percentage.— For purposes of this paragraph, the term ''average benefit percentage'' means, with respect to any group, the average of the benefit percentages calculated separately with respect to each employee in such group (whether or not a participant in any plan).

(C) Benefit percentage.— For purposes of this paragraph

(i) In general.— The term ''benefit percentage'' means the employer-provided contribution or benefit of an employee under all qualified plans maintained by the employer, expressed as a percentage of such employee's compensation (within the meaning of section 414(s)).

(ii) Period for computing percentage.— At the election of an employer, the benefit percentage for any plan year shall be computed on the basis of contributions or benefits for—

(I) such plan year, or

(II) any consecutive plan year period (not greater than 3 years) which ends with such plan year and which is specified in such election.

An election under this clause, once made, may be revoked or modified only with the consent of the Secretary.

(D) Employees taken into account.— For purposes of determining who is an employee for purposes of determining the average benefit percentage under subparagraph (B)—

(i) except as provided in clause (ii), paragraph (4)(A) shall not apply, or

(ii) if the employer elects, paragraph (4)(A) shall be applied by using the lowest age and service requirements of all qualified plans maintained by the employer.

(E) Qualified plan.— For purposes of this paragraph, the term ''qualified plan'' means any plan which (without regard to this subsection) meets the requirements of section 401(a).

(3) Exclusion of certain employees.— For purposes of this subsection, there shall be excluded from consideration—

(A) employees who are included in a unit of employees covered by an agreement which the Secretary of Labor finds to be a collective bargaining agreement between employee representatives and one or more employers, if there is evidence that retirement benefits were the subject of good faith bargaining between such employee representatives and such employer or employers,

(B) in the case of a trust established or maintained pursuant to an agreement which the Secretary of Labor finds to be a collective bargaining agreement between air pilots represented in accordance with title II of the Railway Labor Act and one or more employers, all employees not covered by such agreement, and

(C) employees who are nonresident aliens and who receive no earned income (within the meaning of section 911(d)(2)) from the employer which constitutes income from sources within the United States (within the meaning of section 861(a)(3)). Subparagraph (A) shall not apply with respect to coverage of employees under a plan pursuant to an agreement under such subparagraph. Subparagraph (B) shall not apply in the case of a plan which provides contributions or benefits for employees whose principal duties are not customarily performed aboard aircraft in flight.

(4) Exclusion of employees not meeting age and service requirements.—

(A) In general.— If a plan—

(i) prescribes minimum age and service requirements as a condition of participation, and

(ii) excludes all employees not meeting such requirements from participation,

then such employees shall be excluded from consideration for purposes of this subsection.

(B) Requirements may be met separately with respect to excluded group.— If employees not meeting the minimum age or service requirements of subsection (a)(1) (without regard to subparagraph (B) thereof) are covered under a plan of the employer which meets the requirements of paragraph (1) separately with respect to such employees, such employees may be excluded from consideration in determining whether any plan of the employer meets the requirements of paragraph (1).

(C) Requirements not treated as being met before entry date.— An employee shall not be treated as meeting the age and service requirements described in this paragraph until the first date on which, under the plan, any employee with the same age and service would be eligible to commence participation in the plan.

(5) Line of business exception.—

(A) In general.—If, under section 414(r), an employer is treated as operating separate lines of business for a year, the employer may apply the requirements of this subsection for such year separately with respect to employees in each separate line of business.

(B) Plan must be nondiscriminatory.—Subparagraph (A) shall not apply with respect

to any plan maintained by an employer unless such plan benefits such employees as qualify under a classification set up by the employer and found by the Secretary not to be discriminatory in favor of highly compensated employees.

(6) Definitions and special rules.— For purposes of this subsection—

(A) Highly compensated employee.— The term "highly compensated employee" has the meaning given such term by section 414(q).

(B) Aggregation rules.— An employer may elect to designate—

(i) 2 or more trusts,

(ii) 1 or more trusts and 1 or more annuity plans, or

(iii) 2 or more annuity plans,

as part of 1 plan intended to qualify under section 401(a) to determine whether the requirements of this subsection are met with respect to such trusts or annuity plans. If an employer elects to treat any trusts or annuity plans as 1 plan under this subparagraph, such trusts or annuity plans shall be treated as 1 plan for purposes of section 401(a)(4).

(C) Special rules for certain dispositions or acquisitions.—

(i) In general.— If a person becomes, or ceases to be, a member of a group described in subsection (b), (c), (m), or (o) of section 414, then the requirements of this subsection shall be treated as having been met during the transition period with respect to any plan covering employees of such person or any other member of such group if—

(I) such requirements were met immediately before each such change, and

(II) the coverage under such plan is not significantly changed during the transition period (other than by reason of the change in members of a group) or such plan meets such other requirements as the Secretary may prescribe by regulation.

(ii) Transition period.— For purposes of clause (i), the term "transition period" means the period—

(I) beginning on the date of the change in members of a group, and

(II) ending on the last day of the 1st plan year beginning after the date of such change.

(D) Special rule for certain employee stock ownership plans.— A trust which is part of a tax credit employee stock ownership plan which is the only plan of an employer intended to qualify under section 401(a) shall not be treated as not a qualified trust under section 401(a) solely because it fails to meet the requirements of this subsection if—

(i) such plan benefits 50 percent or more of all the employees who are eligible under a nondiscriminatory classification under the plan, and

(ii) the sum of the amounts allocated to each participant's account for the year does not exceed 2 percent of the compensation of that participant for the year.

(E) Eligibility to contribute.— In the case of contributions which are subject to section 401(k) or 401(m), employees who are eligible to contribute (or elect to have contributions made on their behalf) shall be treated as benefiting under the plan (other than for purposes of paragraph (2)(A)(ii)).

(F) Employers with only highly compensated employees.— A plan maintained by an employer which has no employees other than highly compensated employees for any year shall be treated as meeting the requirements of this subsection for such year.

(G) Regulations.— The Secretary shall prescribe such regulations as may be necessary or appropriate to carry out the purposes of this subsection.

(c) Application of Participation Standards to Certain Plans.—

(1) The provisions of this section (other than paragraph (2) of this subsection) shall not apply to—

(A) a governmental plan (within the meaning of section 414(d)),

(B) a church plan (within the meaning of section 414(e)) with respect to which the election provided by subsection (d) of this section has not been made,

(C) a plan which has not at any time after September 2, 1974, provided for employer contributions, and

(D) a plan established and maintained by a society, order, or association described in section 501(c)(8) or (9) if no part of the contributions to or under such plan are made by employers of participants in such plan.

(2) A plan described in paragraph (1) shall be treated as meeting the requirements of this section, for purposes of section 401(a), if such plan meets the requirements of section 401(a)(3) as in effect on September 1, 1974.

(d) Election by Church to Have Participation, Vesting, Funding, etc., Provisions Apply.—

(1) In general.— If the church or convention or association of churches which maintains any church plan makes an election under this subsection (in such form and manner as the Secretary may by regulations prescribe), then the provisions of this title relating to participation, vesting, funding, etc. (as in effect from time to time) shall apply to such church plan as if such provisions did not contain an exclusion for church plans.

(2) Election irrevocable.— An election under this subsection with respect to any church plan shall be binding with respect to such plan, and, once made, shall be irrevocable.

IRC Sec. 410 (d)(2)

SEC. 411. MINIMUM VESTING STANDARDS.

(a) General Rule.— A trust shall not constitute a qualified trust under section 401(a) unless the plan of which such trust is a part provides that an employee's right to his normal retirement benefit is nonforfeitable upon the attainment of normal retirement age (as defined in paragraph (8)) and in addition satisfies the requirements of paragraphs (1), (2), and (11) of this subsection and the requirements of subsection (b)(3), and also satisfied, in the case of a defined benefit plan, the requirements of subsection (b)(1) and, in the case of a defined contribution plan, the requirements of subsection (b)(2).

(1) Employee contributions.— A plan satisfies the requirements of this paragraph if an employee's rights in his accrued benefit derived from his own contributions are nonforfeitable.

(2) Employer contributions.— A plan satisfies the requirements of this paragraph if it satisfies the requirements of subparagraph (A), (B), or (C).

(A) 5-year vesting.— A plan satisfies the requirements of this subparagraph if an employee who has completed at least 5 years of service has a nonforfeitable right to 100 percent of the employee's accrued benefit derived from employer contributions.

(B) 3 to 7 year vesting.— A plan satisfies the requirements of this subparagraph if an employee has a nonforfeitable right to a percentage of the employee's accrued benefit derived from employer contributions determined under the following table:

Years of service	The nonforfeitable percentage is:
3	20
4	40
5	60
6	80
7 or more	100

(C) Multiemployer plans.— A plan satisfies the requirements of this subparagraph if—

(i) the plan is a multiemployer plan (within the meaning of section 414(f)), and

(ii) under the plan—

(I) an employee who is covered pursuant to a collective bargaining agreement described in section 414(f)(1)(B) and who has completed at least 10 years of service has a nonforfeitable right to 100 percent of the employee's accrued benefit derived from employer contributions, and

(II) the requirements of subparagraph (A) or (B) are met with respect to employees not described in subclause (I).

(3) Certain permitted forfeitures, suspensions, etc.— For purposes of this subsection—

(A) Forfeiture on account of death.— A right to an accrued benefit derived fromemployer contributions shall not be treated as forfeitable solely because the plan provides that it is not payable if the participant dies (except in the case of a survivor annuity which is payable as provided in section 401(a)(11)).

(B) Suspension of benefits from reemployment of retiree.— A right to an accrued benefit derived from employer contributions shall not be treated as forfeitable solely because the plan provides that the payment of benefits is suspended for such period as the employee is employed, subsequent to the commencement of payment of such benefits—

(i) in the case of a plan other than a multiemployer plan, by the employer who maintains the plan under which such benefits were being paid; and

(ii) in the case of a multiemployer plan, in the same industry, the same trade or craft, and the same geographic area covered by the plan as when such benefits commenced.

The Secretary of Labor shall prescribe such regulations as may be necessary to carry out the purposes of this subparagraph, including regulations with respect to the meaning of the term "employed".

(C) Effect of retroactive plan amendments.— A right to an accrued benefit derived from employer contributions shall not be treated as forfeitable solely because plan amendments may be given retroactive application as provided in section 412(c)(8).

(D) Withdrawal of mandatory contribution.—

(i) A right to an accrued benefit derived from employer contributions shall not be treated as forfeitable solely because the plan provides that, in the case of a participant who does not have a nonforfeitable right to at least 50 percent of his accrued benefit derived from employer contributions, such accrued benefit may be forfeited on account of the withdrawal by the participant of any amount attributable to the benefit derived from mandatory contributions (as defined in subsection (c)(2)(C)) made by such participant.

(ii) Clause (i) shall not apply to a plan unless the plan provides that any accrued benefit forfeited under a plan provision described in such clause shall be restored upon repayment by the participant of the full amount of the withdrawal described in such clause plus, in the case of a defined benefit plan, interest. Such interest shall be computed on such amount at the rate determined for purposes of subsection (c)(2)(C) on the date of such repayment (computed annually from the date of such withdrawal).

The plan provision required under this clause may provide that such repayment must be made (I) in the case of a withdrawal on account of separation from service, before the earlier of 5 years after the first date on which the participant is subsequently reemployed by the employer, or the close of the first period of 5 consecutive 1-year breaks in service commencing after the withdrawal; or (II) in the case of any other withdrawal, 5 years after the date of the withdrawal.

(iii) In the case of accrued benefits derived from employer contributions which accrued before September 2, 1974, a right to such accrued benefit derived from employer contributions shall not be treated as forfeitable solely because the plan provides that an amount of such accrued benefit may be forfeited on account of the withdrawal by the participant of an amount attributable to the benefit derived from mandatory contributions (as defined in subsection (c)(2)(C)) made by such participant before September 2, 1974, if such amount forfeited is proportional to such amount withdrawn. This clause shall not apply to any plan to which any mandatory contribution is made after September 2, 1974. The Secretary shall prescribe such regulations as may be necessary to carry out the purposes of this clause.

(iv) For purposes of this subparagraph, in the case of any class-year plan, a withdrawal of employee contributions shall be treated as a withdrawal of employee contributions on a plan year by plan year basis in succeeding order of time.

(v) For nonforfeitability where the employee has a nonforfeitable right to at least 50 percent of his accrued benefit, see section 401(a)(19).

(E) Cessation of contributions under a multiemployer plan.— A right to an accrued benefit derived from employer contributions under a multiemployer plan shall not be treated as forfeitable solely because the plan provides that benefits accrued as a result of service with the participant's employer before the employer had an obligation to contribute under the plan may not be payable if the employer ceases contributions to the multiemployer plan.

(F) Reduction and suspension of benefits by a multiemployer plan.— A participant's right to an accrued benefit derived from employer contributions under a multiem-

IRC Sec. 411 (a)(3)(F)

ployer plan shall not be treated as forfeitable solely because—

(i) the plan is amended to reduce benefits under section 418D or under section 4281 of the Employee Retirement Income Security Act of 1974, or

(ii) benefit payments under the plan may be suspended under section 418E or under section 4281 of the Employee Retirement Income Security Act of 1974.

(G) Treatment of matching contributions forfeited by reason of excess deferral.— A matching contribution (within the meaning of section 401(m)) shall not be treated as forfeitable merely because such contribution is forfeitable if the contribution to which the matching contribution relates is treated as an excess contribution under section 401(k) (8)(B), an excess deferral under section 402(g)(2)(A), or an excess aggregate contribution under section 401(m)(6)(B).

(4) Service included in determination of nonforfeitable percentage.— In computing the period of service under the plan for purposes of determining the nonforfeitable percentage under paragraph (2), all of an employee's years of service with the employer or employers maintaining the plan shall be taken into account, except that the following may be disregarded:

(A) years of service before age 18, except that in the case of a plan which does not satisfy subparagraph (A) or (B) of paragraph (2), the plan may not disregard any such year of service during which the employee was a participant;

(B) years of service during a period for which the employee declined to contribute to a plan requiring employee contributions;

(C) years of service with an employer during any period for which the employer did not maintain the plan or a predecessor plan (as defined under regulations prescribed by the Secretary);

(D) service not required to be taken into account under paragraph (6);

(E) years of service before January 1, 1971, unless the employee has had at least 3 years of service after December 3, 1970;

(F) years of service before the first plan year to which this section applies, if such service would have been disregarded under the rules of the plan with regard to breaks in service as in effect on the applicable date; and

(G) in the case of a multiemployer plan, years of service—

(i) with an employer after—

(I) a complete withdrawal of that employer from the plan (within the meaning of section 4203 of the Employee Retirement Income Security Act of 1974), or

(II) to the extent permitted in regulations prescribed by the Secretary, a partial withdrawal described in section 4205 (b)(2)(A)(i) of such Act in conjunction with the decertification of the collective bargaining representative, and

(ii) with any employer under the plan after the termination date of the plan under section 4048 of such Act.

(5) Year of service.—

(A) General rule.— For purposes of this subsection, except as provided in sub-paragraph (C), the term "year of service" means a calendar year, plan year, or other 12-consecutive month period designated by the plan (and not prohibited under regulations prescribed by the Secretary of Labor) during which the participant has completed 1,000 hours of service.

(B) Hours of service.— For purposes of this subsection, the term "hour of service" has the meaning provided by section 410(a)(3)(C).

(C) Seasonal industries.— In the case of any seasonable industry where the customary period of employment is less than 1,000 hours during a calendar year, the term "year of service" shall be such period as may be determined under regulations prescribed by the Secretary of Labor.

(D) Maritime industries.— For purposes of this subsection, in the case of any maritime industry, 125 days of service shall be treated as 1,000 hours of service. The Secretary of Labor may prescribe regulations to carry out the purposes of this subparagraph.

(6) Breaks in service.—

(A) Definition of 1-year break in service.— For purposes of this paragraph, the term "1-year break in service" means a calendar year, plan year, or other 12-consecutive month period designated by the plan (and not prohibited under regulations prescribed by the Secretary of Labor) during which the participant has not completed more than 500 hours of service.

(B) 1 year of service after 1-year break in service.— For purposes of paragraph (4), in the case of any employee who has any 1-year break in service, years of service before such break shall not be required to be taken into account until he has completed a year of service after his return.

(C) 5 consecutive 1-year breaks in service under defined contribution plan.— For purposes of paragraph (4), in the case of any participant in a defined contribution plan, or an insured defined benefit plan which satisfies the requirements of subsection (b)(1)(F), who has 5 consecutive 1-year breaks in service, years of service after such 5-year period shall not be required to be taken into account for purposes of determining the nonforfeitable percentage of his accrued benefit derived from employer contributions which accrued before such 5-year period.

(D) Nonvested participants.—

(i) In general.— For purposes of paragraph (4), in the case of a nonvested participant, years of service with the employer or employers maintaining the plan before any

period of consecutive 1-year breaks in service shall not be required to be taken into account if the number of consecutive 1-year breaks in service within such period equals or exceeds the greater of—

(I) 5, or

(II) the aggregate number of years of service before such period.

(ii) Years of service not taken into account.— If any years of service are not taken into account by reason of a period of breaks in service to which clause (i) applies, such years of service shall not be taken into account in applying clause (i) to a subsequent period of breaks in service.

(iii) Nonvested participant defined.— For purposes of clause (i), the term "nonvested participant" means a participant who does not have any nonforfeitable right under the plan to an accrued benefit derived from employer contributions.

(E) Special rule for maternity or paternity absences.—

(i) General rule.— In the case of each individual who is absent from work for any period—

(I) by reason of the pregnancy of the individual,

(II) by reason of the birth of a child of the individual,

(III) by reason of the placement of a child with the individual in connection with the adoption of such child by such individual, or

(IV) for purposes of caring for such child for a period beginning immediately following such birth or placement,

the plan shall treat as hours of service, solely for purposes of determining under this paragraph whether a 1-year break in service has occurred, the hours described in clause (ii),

IRC Sec. 411 (a)(6)(E)(i)(IV)

(ii) Hours treated as hours of service.— The hours described in this clause are—

(I) the hours of service which otherwise would normally have been credited to such individual but for such absence, or

(II) in any case in which the plan is unable to determine the hours described in sub-clause (I), 8 hours of service per day of absence,

except that the total number of hours treated as hours of service under this clause by reason of any such pregnancy or placement shall not exceed 501 hours.

(iii) Year to which hours are credited.The hours described in clause (ii) shall be treated as hours of service as provided in this sub-paragraph—

(I) only in the year in which the absence from work begins, if a participant would be prevented from incurring a 1-year break in service in such year solely because the period of absence is treated as hours of service as provided in clause (i); or

(II) in any other case, in the immediately following year.

(iv) Year defined.— For purposes of this subparagraph, the term "year" means the period used in computations pursuant to paragraph (5).

(v) Information required to be filed.— A plan shall not fail to satisfy the requirements of this subparagraph solely because it provides that no credit will be given pursuant to this subparagraph unless the individual furnishes the plan administrator such timely information as the plan may reasonably require to establish—

(I) that the absence from work is for reasons referred to in clause (i), and

(II) the number of days for which there was an absence.

(7) Accrued benefit.—

(A) In general.— For purposes of this section, the term "accrued benefit" means—

(i) in the case of a defined benefit plan, the employee's accrued benefit determined under the plan and, except as provided in subsection (c)(3), expressed in the form of an annual benefit commencing at normal retirement age, or

(ii) in the case of a plan which is not a defined benefit plan, the balance of the employee's account.

(B) Effect of certain distributions.— Notwithstanding paragraph (4), for purposes of determining the employee's accrued benefit under the plan, the plan may disregard servce performed by the employee with respect to which he has received—

(i) a distribution of the present value of his entire nonforfeitable benefit if such distribution was in an amount (not more than $3,500) permitted under regulations prescribed by the Secretary, or

(ii) a distribution of the present value of his nonforfeitable benefit attributable to such service which he elected to receive. Clause (i) of this subparagraph shall apply only if such distribution was made on termination of the employee's participation in the plan. Clause (ii) of this subparagraph shall apply only if such distribution was made on termination of the employee's participation in the plan or under such other circumstances as may be provided under regulations prescribed by the Secretary.

(C) Repayment of subparagraph (B) distributions.— For purposes of determining the employee's accrued benefit under a plan, the plan may not disregard service as provided in subparagraph (B) unless the plan provides an opportunity for the participant to repay the full amount of the distribution described in such subparagraph (B) with, in the case of a defined benefit plan, interest at the rate determined for purposes of subsection (c)(2)(C) and provides that upon such repayment the employee's accrued benefit shall be recomputed by taking into account service so disregarded. This subparagraph shall apply only in the case of a participant who—

(i) received such a distribution in any plan year to which this section applies, which distribution was less than the present value of his accrued benefit,

(ii) resumes employment covered under the plan, and

(iii) repays the full amount of such distribution with, in the case of a defined benefit plan, interest at the rate determined for purposes of subsection (c)(2)(C).

The plan provision required under this subparagraph may provide that such repayment must be made (I) in the case of a withdrawal on account of separation from service, before the earlier of 5 years after the first date on which the participant is subsequently reemployed by the employer, or the close of the first period of 5 consecutive 1-year breaks in service commencing after the withdrawal; or (II) in the case of any other withdrawal, 5 years after the date of the withdrawal.

(D) Accrued benefit attributable to employee contributions.— The accrued benefit of an employee shall not be less than the amount determined under subsection (c)(2)(B) with respect to the employee's accumulated contributions.

(8) Normal retirement age.— For purposes of this section, the term "normal retirement age" means the earlier of—

(A) the time a plan participant attains normal retirement age under the plan, or

(B) The later of—

(i) the time a plan participant attains age 65, or

(ii) the 5th anniversary of the time a plan participant commenced participation in the plan.

(9) Normal retirement benefit.— For purposes of this section, the term "normal retirement benefit" means the greater of the early retirement benefit under the plan, or the benefit under the plan commencing at normal retirement age. The normal retirement benefit shall be determined without regard to—

(A) medical benefits, and

(B) disability benefits not in excess of the qualified disability benefit.

For purposes of this paragraph, a qualified disability benefit is a disability benefit provided by a plan which does not exceed the benefit which would be provided for the participant if he separated from the service at normal retirement age. For purposes of this paragraph, the early retirement benefit under a plan shall be determined without regard to any benefits commencing before benefits payable under title II of the Social Security Act become payable which—

(i) do not exceed such social security benefits, and

(ii) terminate when such social security benefits commence.

(10) Changes in vesting schedule.

(A) General rule.— A plan amendment changing any vesting schedule under the plan shall be treated as not satisfying the requirements of paragraph (2) if the nonforfeitable percentage of the accrued benefit derived from employer contributions (determined as of the later of the date such amendment is adopted, or the date such amendment becomes effective) of any employee who is a participant in the plan is less than such nonforfeitable percentage computed under the plan without regard to such amendment.

(B) Election of former schedule.— A plan amendment changing any vesting schedule

under the plan shall be treated as not satisfying the requirements of paragraph (2) unless each participant having not less than 3
years of service is permitted to elect, within
a reasonable period after the adoption of
such amendment, to have his nonforfeitable
percentage computed under the plan without
regard to such amendment.

◊ ◊ ◊

Editor's Note: Code §411(a)(11)(B), as set
forth below, appears as amended by
§767(a)(1) of the Retirement Protection Act
of 1994 (enacted as part of the Uruguay Round
Agreements Act, P.L. 103-465). The change
generally applies to plan years and limitation
years beginning after December 31, 1994, except that an employer may elect to treat the
amendment as being effective on or after December 8, 1994. Note that §767(d)(2) of the
1994 Act provides that a participant's accrued
benefit will not be considered to have been
reduced in violation of the anti-cutback rule of
Code §411(d)(6) or ERISA §204(g) merely
because the benefit is determined in accordance with amended Code §417(e)(3)(A) or
amended ERISA §205(g)(3), or because the
plan applies amended Code §415(b)(2)(E).

◊ ◊ ◊

**(11) Restrictions on certain mandatory
distributions.—**

(A) In general.— If the present value of any
nonforfeitable accrued benefit exceeds
$3,500, a plan meets the requirements of this
paragraph only if such plan provides that
such benefit may not be immediately distributed without the consent of the participant.

[(B) Determination of present value.—

[(i) In general.— For purposes of subparagraph (A), the present value shall be calculated—

[(I) by using an interest rate no greater
than the applicable interest rate if the

vested accrued benefit (using such rate)
is not in excess of $25,000, and

[(II) by using an interest rate no greater
than 120 percent of the applicable interest
rate if the vested accrued benefit exceeds
$25,000 (as determined under subclause
(I)).

[In no event shall the present value determined under subclause (II) be less than
$25,000.

[(ii) Applicable interest rate.— For purposes of clause (i), the term "applicable
interest rate" means the interest rate which
would be used (as of the date of the distribution) by the Pension Benefit Guaranty Corporation for purposes of determining the
present value of a lump sum distribution on
plan termination.]

*(B) Determination of present value. For
purposes of subparagraph (A), the present
value shall be calculated in accordance with
section 417(e)(3).*

(C) Dividend distributions of ESOPs arrangement.— This paragraph shall not apply to any distribution of dividends to which
section 404(k) applies.

(b) Accrued Benefit Requirements.—

(1) Defined Benefit Plans.—

(A) 3-percent method.— A defined benefit
plan satisfies the requirements of this paragraph if the accrued benefit to which each
participant is entitled upon his separation
from the service is not less than—

(i) 3 percent of the normal retirement
benefit to which he would be entitled if he
commenced participation at the earliest possible entry age under the plan and served
continuously until the earlier of age 65 or the
normal retirement age specified under the
plan, multiplied by

(ii) the number of years (not in excess of
33⅓) of his participation in the plan.

In the case of a plan providing retirement
benefits based on compensation during any

period, the normal retirement benefit to which a participant would be entitled shall be determined as if he continued to earn annually the average rate of compensation which he earned during consecutive years of service, not in excess of 10, for which his compensation was the highest. For purposes of this subparagraph, social security benefits and all other relevant factors used to compute benefits shall be treated as remaining constant as of the current year for all years after such current year.

(B) 133⅓ percent rule.— A defined benefit plan satisfies the requirements of this paragraph for a particular plan year if under the plan the accrued benefit payable at the normal retirement age is equal to the normal retirement benefit and the annual rate at which any individual who is or could be a participant can accrue the retirement benefits payable at normal retirement age under the plan for any later plan year is not more than 133⅓ percent of the annual rate at which he can accrue benefits for any plan year beginning on or after such particular plan year and before such later plan year. For purposes of this subparagraph—

(i) any amendment to the plan which is in effect for the current year shall be treated as in effect for all other plan years;

(ii) any change in an accrual rate which does not apply to any individual who is or could be a participant in the current year shall be disregarded;

(iii) the fact that benefits under the plan may be payable to certain employees before normal retirement age shall be disregarded; and

(iv) social security benefits and all other relevant factors used to compute benefits shall be treated as remaining constant as of the current year for all years after the current year.

(C) Fractional rule.— A defined benefit plan satisfies the requirements of this paragraph if the accrued benefit to which any participant is entitled upon his separation from the service is not less than a fraction of the annual benefit commencing at normal retirement age to which he would be entitled under the plan as in effect on the date of his separation if he continued to earn annually until normal retirement age the same rate of compensation upon which his normal retirement benefit would be computed under the plan, determined as if he had attained normal retirement age on the date on which any such determination is made (but taking into account no more than the 10 years of service immediately preceding his separation from service). Such fraction shall be a fraction, not exceeding 1, the numerator of which is the total number of his years of participation in the plan (as of the date of his separation from the service) and the denominator of which is the total number of years he would have participated in the plan if he separated from the service at the normal retirement age. For purposes of this subparagraph, social security benefits and all other relevant factors used to compute benefits shall be treated as remaining constant as of the current year for all years after such current year.

(D) Accrual for service before effective date.— Subparagraphs (A), (B), and (C) shall not apply with respect to years of participation before the first plan year to which this section applies, but a defined benefit plan satisfies the requirements of this subparagraph with respect to such years of participation only if the accrued benefit of any participant with respect to such years of participation is not less than the greater of—

(i) his accrued benefit determined under the plan, as in effect from time to time prior to September 2, 1974, or

(ii) an accrued benefit which is not less than one-half of the accrued benefit to which such participant would have been entitled if subparagraph (A), (B), or (C) applied with respect to such years of participation.

IRC Sec. 411 (b)(1)(D)(ii)

(E) First two years of service.— Notwithstanding subparagraphs (A), (B), and (C) of this paragraph, a plan shall not be treated as not satisfying the requirements of this paragraph solely because the accrual of benefits under the plan does not become effective until the employee has two continuous years of service. For purposes of this subparagraph, the term "years of service" has the meaning provided by section 410(a)(3)(A).

(F) Certain insured defined benefit plans.— Notwithstanding subparagraphs (A), (B), and (C), a defined benefit plan satisfies the requirements of this paragraph if such plan—

(i) is funded exclusively by the purchase of insurance contracts, and

(ii) satisfies the requirements of paragraphs (2) and (3) of section 412(i) (relating to certain insurance contract plans),

but only if an employee's accrued benefit as of any applicable date is not less than the cash surrender value his insurance contracts would have on such applicable date if the requirements of paragraphs (4), (5), and (6) of section 412(i) were satisfied.

(G) Accrued benefit may not decrease on account of increasing age or service.— Notwithstanding the preceding subparagraphs, a defined benefit plan shall be treated as not satisfying the requirements of this paragraph if the participant's accrued benefit is reduced on account of any increase in his age or service. The preceding sentence shall not apply to benefits under the plan commencing before entitlement to benefits payable under title II of the Social Security Act which benefits under the plan—

(i) do not exceed such social security benefits, and

(ii) terminate when such social security benefits commence.

(H) Continued accrual beyond normal retirement age.—

(i) In general.—Notwithstanding the preceding subparagraphs, a defined benefit plan shall be treated as not satisfying the requirements of this paragraph if, under the plan, an employee's benefit accrual is ceased, or the rate of an employee's benefit accrual is reduced, because of the attainment of any age.

(ii) Certain limitations permitted.— A plan shall not be treated as failing to meet the requirements of this subparagraph solely because the plan imposes (without regard to age) a limitation on the amount of benefits that the plan provides or a limitation on the number of years of service or years of participation which are taken into account for purposes of determining benefit accrual under the plan.

(iii) Adjustments under plan for delayed retirement taken into account.In the case of any employee who, as of the end of any plan year under a defined benefit plan, has attained normal retirement age under such plan—

(I) if distribution of benefits under such plan with respect to such employee has commenced as of the end of such plan year, then any requirement of this subparagraph for continued accrual of benefits under such plan with respect to such employee during such plan year shall be treated as satisfied to the extent of the actuarial equivalent of in-service distribution of benefits, and

(II) if distribution of benefits under such plan with respect to such employee has not commenced as of the end of such year in accordance with section 401(a)(14)(C), and the payment of benefits under such plan with respect to such employee is not suspended during such plan year pursuant to subsection (a)(3)(B), then any requirement of this subparagraph for continued accrual of benefits under such plan with respect to such employee during such plan year shall be treated as satisfied to the extent of any adjustment in the benefit payable under the plan during such plan year attributable to the delay in the distribution of benefits after the attainment of normal retirement age.

The preceding provisions of this clause shall apply in accordance with regulations of the Secretary. Such regulations may provide for the application of the preceding provisions of this clause, in the case of any such employee, with respect to any period of time within a plan year.

(iv) Disregard of subsidized portion of early retirement benefit.— A plan shall not be treated as failing to meet the requirements of clause (i) solely because the subsidized portion of any early retirement benefit is disregarded in determining benefit accruals.

(v) Coordination with other requirements.— The Secretary shall provide by regulation for the coordination of the requirements of this subparagraph with the requirements of subsection (a), sections 404, 410, and 415, and the provisions of this subchapter precluding discrimination in favor of highly compensated employees.

(2) Defined contribution plans.—

(A) In general.— A defined contribution plan satisfies the requirements of this paragraph if, under the plan, allocations to the employee's account are not ceased, and the rate at which amounts are allocated to the employee's account is not reduced, because of the attainment of any age.

(B) Application to target benefit plans.— The Secretary shall provide by regulation for the application of the requirements of this paragraph to target benefit plans.

(C) Coordination with other requirements.— The Secretary may provide by regulation for the coordination of the requirements of this paragraph with the requirements of subsection (a), sections 404, 410, and 415, and the provisions of this subchapter precluding discrimination in favor of highly compensated employees.

(3) Separate accounting required in certain cases.— A plan satisfies the requirements of this paragraph if—

(A) in the case of a defined benefit plan, the plan requires separate accounting for the portion of each employee's accrued benefit derived from any voluntary employee contributions permitted under the plan; and

(B) in the case of any plan which is not a defined benefit plan, the plan requires separate accounting for each employee's accrued benefit.

(4) Year of participation.—

(A) Definition.— For purposes of determining an employee's accrued benefit, the term ''year of participation'' means a period of service (beginning at the earliest date on which the employee is a participant in the plan and which is included in a period of service required to be taken into account under section 410(a)(5) determined without regard to section 410(a)(5)(E)) as determined under regulations prescribed by the Secretary of Labor which provide for the calculation of such period on any reasonable and consistent basis.

(B) Less than full time service.— For purposes of this paragraph, except as provided in subparagraph (C), in the case of any employee whose customary employment is less than full time, the calculation of such employee's service on any basis which provides less than a ratable portion of the accrued benefit to which he would be entitled under the plan if his customary employment were full time shall not be treated as made on a reasonable and consistent basis.

(C) Less than 1,000 hours of service during year.— For purposes of this paragraph, in the case of any employee whose service is less than 1,000 hours during any calendar year, plan year or other 12-consecutive month period designated by the plan (and not prohibited under regulations prescribed by the Secretary of Labor) the calculation of his period of service shall not be treated as

IRC Sec. 411 (b)(4)(C)

not made on a reasonable and consistent basis solely because such service is not taken into account.

(D) Seasonal industries.— In the case of any seasonal industry where the customary period of employment is less than 1,000 hours during a calendar year, the term "year of participation" shall be such period as determined under regulations prescribed by the Secretary of Labor.

(E) Maritime industries.— For purposes of this subsection, in the case of any maritime industry, 125 days of service shall be treated as a year of participation. The Secretary of Labor may prescribe regulations to carry out the purposes of this subparagraph.

(c) Allocation of Accrued Benefits Between Employer and Employee Contributions.—

(1) Accrued benefit derived from employer contributions.— For purposes of this section, an employee's accrued benefit derived from employer contributions as of any applicable date is the excess, if any, of the accrued benefit for such employee as of such applicable date over the accrued benefit derived from contributions made by such employee as of such date.

(2) Accrued benefit derived from employee contributions.—

(A) Plans other than defined benefit plans.— In the case of a plan other than a defined benefit plan, the accrued benefit derived from contributions made by an employee as of any applicable date is—

(i) except as provided in clause (ii), the balance of the employee's separate account consisting only of his contributions and the income, expenses, gains, and losses attributable thereto, or

(ii) if a separate account is not maintained with respect to an employee's contributions under such a plan, the amount which bears the same ratio to his total accrued benefit as the total amount of the employee's contributions (less withdrawals) bears to the sum of

such contributions and the contributions made on his behalf by the employer (less withdrawals).

(B) Defined Benefit Plans.— In the case of a defined benefit plan, the accrued benefit derived from contributions made by an employee as of any applicable date is the amount equal to the employee's accumulated contributions expressed as an annual benefit commencing at normal retirement age, using an interest rate which would be used under the plan under section 417(e)(3) (as of the determination date).

(C) Definition of accumulated contributions.— For purposes of this subsection, the term "accumulated contributions" means the total of—

(i) all mandatory contributions made by the employee,

(ii) interest (if any) under the plan to the end of the last plan year to which subsection (a)(2) does not apply (by reason of the applicable effective date), and

(iii) interest on the sum of the amounts determined under clauses (i) and (ii) compounded annually—

(I) at the rate of 120 percent of the Federal mid-term rate (as in effect under section 1274 for the 1st month of a plan year) for the period beginning with the 1st plan year to which subsection (a)(2) applies (by reason of the applicable effective date) and ending with the date on which the determination is being made, and

(II) at the interest rate which would be used under the plan under section 417(e)(3) (as of the determination date) for the period beginning with the determination date and ending on the date on which the employee attains normal retirement age.

(D) Adjustments.— The Secretary is authorized to adjust by regulation the conversion factor described in subparagraph (B) from time to time as he may deem necessary. No such adjustment shall be effective for a plan year beginning before the expiration of 1 year after such adjustment is determined and published.

(E) Limitation.— [Deleted]

(3) Actuarial adjustment.— For purposes of this section, in the case of any defined benefit plan, if an employee's accrued benefit is to be determined as an amount other than an annual benefit commencing at normal retirement age, or if the accrued benefit derived from contributions made by an employee is to be determined with respect to a benefit other than an annual benefit in the form of a single life annuity (without ancillary benefits) commencing at normal retirement age, the employee's accrued benefit, or the accrued benefits derived from contributions made by an employee, as the case may be, shall be the actuarial equivalent of such benefit or amount determined under paragraph (1) or (2).

(d) Special Rules.—

(1) Coordination with section 401(a)(4).— A plan which satisfies the requirements of this section shall be treated as satisfying any vesting requirements resulting from the application of section 401(a)(4) unless—

(A) there has been a pattern of abuse under the plan (such as dismissal of employees before their accrued benefits become nonforfeitable) tending to discriminate in favor of employees who are highly compensated employees (within the meaning of section 414(q)), or

(B) there have been, or there is reason to believe there will be, an accrual of benefits or forfeitures tending to discriminate in favor of employees who are highly compensated employees (within the meaning of section 414(q)).

(2) Prohibited discrimination.— Subsection (a) shall not apply to benefits which may not be provided for designated employees in the event of early termination of the plan under provisions of the plan adopted pursuant

to regulations prescribed by the Secretary to preclude the discrimination prohibited by section 401(a)(4).

(3) Termination or partial termination; discontinuance of contributions.— Notwithstanding the provisions of subsection (a), a trust shall not constitute a qualified trust under section 401(a) unless the plan of which such trust is a part provides that—

(A) upon its termination or partial termination, or

(B) in the case of a plan to which section 412 does not apply, upon complete discontinuance of contributions under the plan,

the rights of all affected employees to benefits accrued to the date of such termination, partial termination, or discontinuance, to the extent funded as of such date, or the amounts credited to the employees' accounts, are nonforfeitable. This paragraph shall not apply to benefits or contributions which, under provisions of the plan adopted pursuant to regulations prescribed by the Secretary to preclude the discrimination prohibited by section 401(a)(4), may not be used for designated employees in the event of early termination of the plan. For purposes of this paragraph, in the case of the complete discontinuance of contributions under a profit-sharing or stock bonus plan, such plan shall be treated as having terminated on the day on which the plan administrator notifies the Secretary (in accordance with regulations) of the discontinuance.

(4) Class year plans.— [Deleted.]

(5) Treatment of voluntary employee contributions.— In the case of a defined benefit plan which permits voluntary employee contributions, the portion of an employee's accrued benefit derived from such contributions shall be treated as an accrued benefit derived from employee contributions under a plan other than a defined benefit plan.

(6) Accrued benefit not to be decreased by amendment.—

(A) In general.— A plan shall be treated as not satisfying the requirements of this section if the accrued benefit of a participant is decreased by an amendment of the plan, other than an amendment described in section 412(c)(8), or section 4281 of the Employee Retirement Income Security Act of 1974.

(B) Treatment of certain plan amendments.— For purposes of subparagraph (A), a plan amendment which has the effect of—

(i) eliminating or reducing an early retirement benefit or a retirement-type subsidy (as defined in regulations), or

(ii) eliminating an optional form of benefit,

with respect to benefits attributable to service before the amendment shall be treated as reducing accrued benefits. In the case of a retirement-type subsidy, the preceding sentence shall apply only with respect to a participant who satisfies (either before or after the amendment) the preamendment conditions for the subsidy. The Secretary may by regulations provide that this subparagraph shall not apply to a plan amendment described in clause (ii) (other than a plan amendment having an effect described in clause (i)).

(C) Special Rule for ESOPs.— For purposes of this paragraph, any—

(i) tax credit employee stock ownership plan (as defined in section 409(a)), or

(ii) employee stock ownership plan (as defined in section 4975(e)(7)),

shall not be treated as failing to meet the requirements of this paragraph merely because it modifies distribution options in a nondiscriminatory manner.

(e) Application of Vesting Standards to Certain Plans.—

(1) The provisions of this section (other than paragraph (2)) shall not apply to—

(A) a governmental plan (within the meaning of section 414(d)),

(B) a church plan (within the meaning of section 414(e)) with respect to which the election provided by section 410(d) has not been made,

(C) a plan which has not, at any time after September 2, 1974, provided for employer contributions, and

(D) a plan established and maintained by a society, order, or association described in section 501(c)(8) or (9), if no part of the contributions to or under such plan are made by employers of participants in such plan.

(2) A plan described in paragraph (1) shall be treated as meeting the requirements of this section, for purposes of section 401(a), if such plan meets the vesting requirements resulting from the application of section 401(a)(4) and 401(a)(7) as in effect on September 1, 1974.

◊ ◊ ◊

Editor's Note: Unless otherwise indicated, Code §412, as set forth below, appears as amended by §751(a) of the Retirement Protection Act of 1994 (enacted as part of the Uruguay Round Agreements Act, P.L. 103-465). Under §751(b)(1) of the 1994 Act, changes made by Act §751(a) are effective generally for plan years beginning after December 31, 1994. Section §769 of the 1994 Act, however, exempts certain plans from *all* changes made to Code §412 by the Act. Plans that qualify for this exemption are certain plans that, after December 8, 1994, are subject to a PBGC restoration schedule order and certain plans established by air carriers. For text of §769 of the 1994 Act, see the Editor's Note to ERISA §302 in Chapter 2 of this book.

◊ ◊ ◊

SEC. 412. MINIMUM FUNDING STANDARDS.

(a) General Rule. Except as provided in subsection (h), this section applies to a plan if, for any plan year beginning on or after the effective date of this section for such plan

(1) such plan included a trust which qualified (or was determined by the Secretary to have qualified) under section 401(a), or

(2) such plan satisfied (or was determined by the Secretary to have satisfied) the requirements of section 403(a).

A plan to which this section applies shall have satisfied the minimum funding standard for such plan for a plan year if as of the end of such plan year, the plan does not have an accumulated funding deficiency. For purposes of this section and section 4971, the term "accumulated funding deficiency" means for any plan the excess of the total charges to the funding standard account for all plan years (beginning with the first plan year to which this section applies) over the total credits to such account for such years or, if less, the excess of the total charges to the alternative minimum funding standard account for such plan years over the total credits to such account for such years. In any plan year in which a multiemployer plan is in reorganization, the accumulated funding deficiency of the plan shall be determined under section 418B.

(b) Funding Standard Account.

(1) Account required. Each plan to which this section applies shall establish and maintain a funding standard account. Such account shall be credited and charged solely as provided in this section.

(2) Charges to account. For a plan year, the funding standard account shall be charged with the sum of

(A) the normal cost of the plan for the plan year.

(B) the amounts necessary to amortize in equal annual installments (until fully amortized)

(i) in the case of a plan in existence on January 1, 1974, the unfunded past service liability under the plan on the first day of the first plan year to which this section applies, over a period of 40 plan years,

(ii) in the case of a plan which comes into existence after January 1, 1974, the unfunded past service liability under the plan on the first day of the first plan year to which this section applies, over a period of 30 plan years,

(iii) separately, with respect to each plan year, the net increase (if any) in unfunded past service liability under the plan arising from plan amendments adopted in such year, over a period of 30 plan years,

(iv) separately, with respect to each plan year, the net experience loss (if any) under the plan, over a period of 5 plan years (15 plan years in the case of a multiemployer plan), and

(v) separately, with respect to each plan year, the net loss (if any) resulting from changes in actuarial assumptions used under

IRC Sec. 412 (b)(2)(B)(v)

the plan, over a period of 10 plan years (30 plan years in the case of a multiemployer plan),

(C) the amount necessary to amortize each waived funding deficiency (within the meaning of subsection (d)(3)) for each prior plan year in equal annual installments (until fully amortized) over a period of 5 plan years (15 plan years in the case of a multiemployer plan), and

(D) the amount necessary to amortize in equal annual installments (until fully amortized) over a period of 5 plan years any amount credited to the funding standard account under paragraph (3)(D).

For additional requirements in the case of plans other than multiemployer plans, see subsection (*l*).

(3) **Credits to account.**For a plan year, the funding standard account shall be credited with the sum of

(A) the amount considered contributed by the employer to or under the plan for the plan year,

(B) the amount necessary to amortize in equal annual installments (until fully amortized)

(i) separately, with respect to each plan year, the net decrease (if any) in unfunded past service liability under the plan arising from plan amendments adopted in such year, over a period of 30 plan years,

(ii) separately, with respect to each plan year, the net experience gain (if any) under the plan, over a period of 5 plan years (15 plan years in the case of a multiemployer plan), and

(iii) separately, with respect to each plan year, the net gain (if any) resulting from changes in actuarial assumptions used under the plan, over a period of 10 plan years (30 plan years in the case of a multiemployer plan),

(C) the amount of the waived funding deficiency (within the meaning of subsection (d)(3)) for the plan year, and

(D) in the case of a plan year for which the accumulated funding deficiency is determined under the funding standard account if such plan year follows a plan year for which such deficiency was determined under the alternative minimum funding standard, the excess (if any) of any debit balance in the funding standard account (determined without regard to this subparagraph) over any debit balance in the alternative minimum funding standard account.

(4) **Combining and offsetting amounts to be amortized.** Under regulations prescribed by the Secretary, amounts required to be amortized under paragraph (2) or paragraph (3), as the case may be

(A) may be combined into one amount under such paragraph to be amortized over a period determined on the basis of the remaining amortization period for all items entering into such combined amount, and

(B) may be offset against amounts required to be amortized under the other such paragraph, with the resulting amount to be amortized over a period determined on the basis of the remaining amortization periods for all items entering into whichever of the two amounts being offset is the greater.

(5) **Interest.**

(A) In general. The funding standard account (and items therein) shall be charged or credited (as determined under regulations prescribed by the Secretary) with interest at the appropriate rate consistent with the rate or rates of interest used under the plan to determine costs.

(B) Required change of interest rate. For purposes of determining a plan's current liability and for purposes of determining a plan's required contribution under section 412(*l*) for any plan year

IRC Sec. 412 (b)(2)(C)

(i) In general. If any rate of interest used under the plan to determine cost is not within the permissible range, the plan shall establish a new rate of interest within the permissible range.

(ii) Permissible range. For purposes of this subparagraph

(I) In general.Except as provided in subclause (II), the term "permissible range" means a rate of interest which is not more than 10 percent above, and not more than 10 percent below, the weighted average of the rates of interest on 30-year Treasury securities during the 4-year period ending on the last day before the beginning of the plan year.

(II) Secretarial authority. If the Secretary finds that the lowest rate of interest permissible under subclause (I) is unreasonably high, the Secretary may prescribe a lower rate of interest, except that such rate may not be less than 80 percent of the average rate determined under subclause (I).

(iii) Assumptions. Notwithstanding subsection (c)(3)(A)(i), the interest rate used under the plan shall be

(I) determined without taking into account the experience of the plan and reasonable expectations, but

(II) consistent with the assumptions which reflect the purchase rates which would be used by insurance companies to satisfy the liabilities under the plan.

(6) Certain amortization charges and credits. In the case of a plan which, immediately before the date of the enactment of the Multiemployer Pension Plan Amendments Act of 1980, was a multiemployer plan (within the meaning of section 414(f) as in effect immediately before such date)

(A) any amount described in paragraph (2)(B)(ii), (2)(B)(iii), or (3)(B)(i) of this subsection which arose in a plan year beginning before such date shall be amortized in equal annual installments (until fully amortized) over 40 plan years, beginning with the plan year in which the amount arose;

(B) any amount described in paragraph (2)(B)(iv) or (3)(B)(ii) of this subsection which arose in a plan year beginning before such date shall be amortized in equal annual installments (until fully amortized) over 20 plan years, beginning with the plan year in which the amount arose;

(C) any change in past service liability which arises during the period of 3 plan years beginning on or after such date, and results from a plan amendment adopted before such date, shall be amortized in equal annual installments (until fully amortized) over 40 plan years, beginning with the plan year in which the change arises; and

(D) any change in past service liability which arises during the period of 2 plan years beginning on or after such date, and results from the changing of a group of participants from one benefit level to another benefit level under a schedule of plan benefits which

(i) was adopted before such date, and

(ii) was effective for any plan participant before the beginning of the first plan year beginning on or after such date,

shall be amortized in equal annual installments (until fully amortized) over 40 plan years, beginning with the plan year in which the change arises.

(7) Special rules for multiemployer plans. For purposes of this section

(A) Withdrawal liability.Any amount received by a multiemployer plan in payment of all or part of an employer's withdrawal liability under part 1 of subtitle E of title IV of the Employee Retirement Income Security Act of 1974 shall be considered an amount contributed by the employer to or under the plan. The Secretary may prescribe by regulation additional charges and credits

IRC Sec. 412 (b)(7)(A)

to a multiemployer plan's funding standard account to the extent necessary to prevent withdrawal liability payments from being unduly reflected as advance funding for plan liabilities.

(B) Adjustments when a multiemployer plan leaves reorganization.If a multiemployer plan is not in reorganization in the plan year but was in reorganization in the immediately preceding plan year, any balance in the funding standard account at the close of such immediately preceding plan year

(i) shall be eliminated by an offsetting credit or charge (as the case may be), but

(ii) shall be taken into account in subsequent plan years by being amortized in equal annual installments (until fully amortized) over 30 plan years.
The preceding sentence shall not apply to the extent of any accumulated funding deficiency under section 418B(a) as of the end of the last plan year that the plan was in reorganization.

(C) Plan payments to supplemental program or withdrawal liability payment fund.Any amount paid by a plan during a plan year to the Pension Benefit Guaranty Corporation pursuant to section 4222 of such Act or to a fund exempt under section 501(c)(22) pursuant to section 4223 of such Act shall reduce the amount of contributions considered received by the plan for the plan year.

(D) Interim withdrawal liability payments. Any amount paid by an employer pending a final determination of the employer's withdrawal liability under part 1 of subtitle E of title IV of such Act and subsequently refunded to the employer by the plan shall be charged to the funding standard account in accordance with regulations prescribed by the Secretary.

(E) For purposes of the full funding limitation under subsection (c)(7), unless otherwise provided by the plan, the accrued liability under a multiemployer plan shall not include benefits which are not nonforfeitable under the plan after the termination of the plan (taking into consideration section 411(d)(3)).

(c) Special Rules.

(1) Determinations to be made under funding method. For purposes of this section, normal costs, accrued liability, past service liabilities, and experience gains and losses shall be determined under the funding method used to determine costs under the plan.

(2) Valuation of assets.

(A) In general. For purposes of this section, the value of the plan's assets shall be determined on the basis of any reasonable actuarial method of valuation which takes into account fair market value and which is permitted under regulations prescribed by the Secretary.

(B) Election with respect to bonds. The value of a bond or other evidence of indebtedness which is not in default as to principal or interest may, at the election of the plan administrator, be determined on an amortized basis running from initial cost at purchase to par value at maturity or earliest call date. Any election under this subparagraph shall be made at such time and in such manner as the Secretary shall by regulations provide, shall apply to all such evidences of indebtedness, and may be revoked only with the consent of the Secretary. In the case of a plan other than a multiemployer plan, this subparagraph shall not apply, but the Secretary may by regulations provide that the value of any dedicated bond portfolio of such plan shall be determined by using the interest rate under subsection (b)(5).

(3) Actuarial assumptions must be reasonable. For purposes of this section, all costs, liabilities, rates of interest, and other factors under the plan shall be determined on the basis of actuarial assumptions and methods

(A) in the case of—

(i) a plan other than a multiemployer plan, each of which is reasonable (taking into account the experience of the plan and reasonable expectations) or which, in the aggregate, result in a total contribution equivalent to that which would be determined if each such assumption and method were reasonable, or

(ii) a multiemployer plan, which, in the aggregate, are reasonable (taking into account the experiences of the plan and reasonable expectations), and

(B) which, in combination, offer the actuary's best estimate of anticipated experience under the plan.

(4) Treatment of certain changes as experience gain or loss. For purposes of this section, if

(A) a change in benefits under the Social Security Act or in other retirement benefits created under Federal or State law, or

(B) a change in the definition of the term ''wages'' under section 3121, or a change in the amount of such wages taken into account under regulations prescribed for purposes of section 401(a)(5),results in an increase or decrease in accrued liability under a plan, such increase or decrease shall be treated as an experience loss or gain.

◊ ◊ ◊

Editor's Note: The amendment set forth below to §412(c)(5) applies to changes in assumptions for plan years beginning after October 28, 1993. In the case of changes in assumptions for plan years beginning after December 31, 1992, and on or before October 28, 1993, such changes shall cease to be effective for plan years beginning after December 1, 1994, if the change would have required the approval of the Secretary of the Treasury ad the amendment applied to such change, nd the change is not so approved.

◊ ◊ ◊

(5) Change in funding method or in plan year requires approval. [If the funding method]

(A) In general. If the funding method for a plan is changed, the new funding method shall become the funding method used to determine costs and liabilities under the plan only if the change is approved by the Secretary. If the plan year for a plan is changed, the new plan year shall become the plan year for the plan only if the change is approved by the Secretary.

(B) Approval required for certain changes in assumptions by certain single-employer plans subject to additional funding requirement.

(i) In general. No actuarial assumption (other than the assumptions described in subsection (l)(7)(C)) used to determine the current liability for a plan to which this subparagraph applies may be changed without the approval of the Secretary.

(ii) Plans to which subparagraph applies. This subparagraph shall apply to a plan only if—

(I) the plan is a defined benefit plan (other than a multiemployer plan) to which title IV of the Employee Retirement Income Security Act of 1974 applies;

(II) the aggregate unfunded vested benefits as of the close of the preceding plan year (as determined under section 4006(a)(3)(E)(iii) of the Employee Retirement Income Security Act of 1974) of such plan and all other plans maintained by the contributing sponsors (as defined in section 4001(a)(13) of such Act) and members of such sponsors' controlled groups (as defined in section 4001(a)(14) of such Act) which are covered by title IV of such Act (disregarding plans with no unfunded vested benefits) exceed $50,000,000; and

(III) the change in assumptions (determined after taking into account any

IRC Sec. 412 (c)(5)(B)(i)(III)

changes in interest rate and mortality table) results in a decrease in the unfunded current liability of the plan for the current plan year that exceeds $50,000,000, or that exceeds $5,000,000 and that is 5 percent or more of the current liability of the plan before such change."

(6) Full funding. If, as of the close of a plan year, a plan would (without regard to this paragraph) have an accumulated funding deficiency (determined without regard to the alternative minimum funding standard account permitted under subsection (g)) in excess of the full funding limitation

(A) the funding standard account shall be credited with the amount of such excess, and

(B) all amounts described in paragraphs (2)(B), (C), and (D) and (3)(B) of subsection (b) which are required to be amortized shall be considered fully amortized for purposes of such paragraphs.

(7) Full-funding limitation.

(A) In general. For purposes of paragraph (6), the term "full-funding limitation" means the excess (if any) of

(i) the lesser of (I) 150 percent of current liability *(including the expected increase in current liability due to benefits accruing during the plan year)*, or (II) the accrued liability (including normal cost) under the plan (determined under the entry age normal funding method if such accrued liability cannot be directly calculated under the funding method used for the plan), over

(ii) the lesser of

(I) the fair market value of the plan's assets, or

(II) the value of such assets determined under paragraph (2).

[(B) Current liability. For purposes of subparagraphs (A) and (D), the term "current liability" has the meaning given such term

by subsection (*l*)(7) (without regard to subparagraph (D) thereof).]

(B) Current liability.For purposes of subparagraph (D) and subclause (I) of subparagraph (A)(i), the term "current liability" has the meaning given such term by subsection (*l*)(7) (without regard to subparagraphs (C) and (D) thereof) and using the rate of interest used under subsection (b)(5)(B).

(C) Special rule for paragraph (6)(B). For purposes of paragraph (6)(B), subparagraph (A)(i) shall be applied without regard to subclause (I) thereof.

(D) Regulatory authority. The Secretary may by regulations provide

(i) for adjustments to the percentage contained in subparagraph (A)(i) to take into account the respective ages or lengths of service of the participants,

(ii) alternative methods based on factors other than current liability for the determination of the amount taken into account under subparagraph (A)(i), and

(iii) for the treatment under this section of contributions which would be required to be made under the plan but for the provisions of subparagraph (A)(i)(I).

(E) Minimum amount.

(i) In general. In no event shall the full-funding limitation determined under subparagraph (A) be less than the excess (if any) of

(I) 90 percent of the current liability of the plan (including the expected increase in current liability due to benefits accruing during the plan year), over

(II) the value of the plan's assets determined under paragraph (2).

(ii) Current liability; assets.For purposes of clause (i)

(I) the term "current liability" has the meaning given such term by subsection

(I)(7) (without regard to subparagraph (D) thereof), and

(II) assets shall not be reduced by any credit balance in the funding standard account.

(8) Certain retroactive plan amendments. For purposes of this section, any amendment applying to a plan year which

(A) is adopted after the close of such plan year but no later than 2 and one-half months after the close of the plan year (or, in the case of a multiemployer plan, no later than 2 years after the close of such plan year),

(B) does not reduce the accrued benefit of any participant determined as of the beginning of the first plan year to which the amendment applies, and

(C) does not reduce the accrued benefit of any participant determined as of the time of adoption except to the extent required by the circumstances, shall, at the election of the plan administrator, be deemed to have been made on the first day of such plan year. No amendment described in this paragraph which reduces the accrued benefit of any participant shall take effect unless the plan administrator files a notice with the Secretary of Labor notifying him of such amendment and the Secretary of Labor has approved such amendment, or within 90 days after the date on which such notice was filed, failed to disapprove such amendment. No amendment described in this subsection shall be approved by the Secretary of Labor unless he determines that such amendment is necessary because of a substantial business hardship (as determined under subsection (d)(2)) and that a waiver under subsection (d)(1) is unavailable or inadequate.

(9) Annual valuation. For purposes of this section, a determination of experience gains and losses and a valuation of the plan's liability shall be made not less frequently than once every year, except that such determination shall be made more frequently to the extent required in particular cases under regulations prescribed by the Secretary.

(10) Time when certain contributions deemed made. For purposes of this section

(A) Defined Benefit Plans other than multiemployer plans. In the case of a defined benefit plan other than a multiemployer plan, any contributions for a plan year made by an employer during the period

(i) beginning on the day after the last day of such plan year, and

(ii) ending on the day which is $8\frac{1}{2}$ months after the close of the plan year,

shall be deemed to have been made on such last day.

(B) Other plans. In the case of a plan not described in subparagraph (A), any contributions for a plan year made by an employer after the last day of such plan year, but not later than two and one-half months after such day, shall be deemed to have been made on such last day. For purposes of this subparagraph, such two and one-half month period may be extended for not more than six months under regulations prescribed by the Secretary.

(11) Liability for contributions.

(A) In general. Except as provided in subparagraph (B), the amount of any contribution required by this section and any required installments under subsection (m) shall be paid by the employer responsible for contributing to or under the plan the amount described in subsection (b)(3)(A).

(B) Joint and several liability where employer member of controlled group.

(i) In general. In the case of a plan other than a multiemployer plan, if the employer referred to in subparagraph (A) is a member of a controlled group, each member of such group shall be jointly and severally liable for payment of such contribution or required installment.

IRC Sec. 412 (c)(11)(B)(i)

(ii) Controlled group. For purposes of clause (i), the term "controlled group" means any group treated as a single employer under subsection (b), (c), (m), or (o) of section 414.

◊ ◊ ◊

Editor's Note: Section 412(c)(12), below, as added by §753(a) of the Retirement Protection Act of 1994 (adopted as part of Uruguay Round Agreements Act, P.L. 103-465) is effective generally for plan years beginning after December 31, 1994, with respect to collective bargaining agreements in effect on or after January 1, 1995. But see Editor's Note at the beginning of Code §412, for special effective date rules under Act §769 for certain plans subject to a PBGC restoration schedule order and the plans of certain air carriers.

◊ ◊ ◊

(12) Anticipation of benefit increases effective in the future. In determining projected benefits, the funding method of a collectively bargained plan described in section 413(a) (other than a multiemployer plan) shall anticipate benefit increases scheduled to take effect during the term of the collective bargaining agreement applicable to the plan.

(d) Variance from Minimum Funding Standard.

(1) Waiver in case of business hardship. If an employer, or in the case of a multiemployer plan, 10 percent or more of the number of employers contributing to or under the plan, are unable to satisfy the minimum funding standard for a plan year without temporary substantial business hardship (substantial business hardship in the case of a multiemployer plan) and if application of the standard would be adverse to the interests of plan participants in the aggregate, the Secretary may waive the requirements of subsection (a) for such year with respect to all or any portion of the minimum funding standard other than the portion thereof determined under subsection (b)(2)(C).

The Secretary shall not waive the minimum funding standards with respect to a plan for more than 3 of any 15 (5 of any 15 in the case of a multiemployer plan) consecutive plan years. The interest rate used for purposes of computing the amortization charge described in subsection (b)(2)(C) for any plan year shall be

(A) in the case of a plan other than a multiemployer plan, the greater of (i) 150 percent of the Federal mid-term rate (as in effect under section 1274 for the 1st month of such plan year), or (ii) the rate of interest used under the plan in determining costs (including adjustments under subsection (b)(5)(B)), and

(B) in the case of a multiemployer plan, the rate determined under section 6621(b).

(2) Determination of business hardship. For purposes of this section, the factors taken into account in determining temporary substantial business hardship (substantial business hardship in the case of a multiemployer plan) shall include (but shall not be limited to) whether or not—

(A) the employer is operating at an economic loss,

(B) there is substantial unemployment or underemployment in the trade or business and in the industry concerned,

(C) the sales and profits of the industry concerned are depressed or declining, and

(D) it is reasonable to expect that the plan will be continued only if the waiver is granted.

(3) Waived funding deficiency. For purposes of this section, the term "waived funding deficiency" means the portion of the minimum funding standard (determined without regard to subsection (b)(3)(C)) for a plan year waived by the Secretary and not satisfied by employer contributions.

IRC Sec. 412 (c)(11)(B)(ii)

(4) Application must be submitted before date 2½ months after close of year. In the case of a plan other than a multiemployer plan, no waiver may be granted under this subsection with respect to any plan for any plan year unless an application therefor is submitted to the Secretary not later than the 15th day of the 3rd month beginning after the close of such plan year.

(5) Special rule if employer is member of controlled group.

(A) In general. In the case of a plan other than a multiemployer plan, if an employer is a member of a controlled group, the temporary substantial business hardship requirements of paragraph (1) shall be treated as met only if such requirements are met

(i) with respect to such employer, and

(ii) with respect to the controlled group of which such employer is a member (determined by treating all members of such group as a single employer).

The Secretary may provide that an analysis of a trade or business or industry of a member need not be conducted if the Secretary determines such analysis is not necessary because the taking into account of such member would not significantly affect the determination under this subsection.

(B) Controlled group. For purposes of subparagraph (A), the term ''controlled group'' means any group treated as a single employer under subsection (b), (c), (m), or (o) of section 414.

(e) Extension of Amortization Periods. The period of years required to amortize any unfunded liability (described in any clause of subsection (b)(2)(B)) of any plan may be extended by the Secretary of Labor for a period of time (not in excess of 10 years) if he determines that such extension would carry out the purposes of the Employee Retirement Income Security Act of 1974 and would provide adequate protection for participants under the plan and their beneficiaries and if he determines that the failure to permit such extension would—

(1) result in—

(A) a substantial risk to the voluntary continuation of the plan, or

(B) a substantial curtailment of pension benefit levels or employee compensation, and

(2) be adverse to the interests of plan participants in the aggregate.

In the case of a plan other than a multiemployer plan, the interest rate applicable for any plan year under any arrangement entered into by the Secretary in connection with an extension granted under this subsection shall be the greater of (A) 150 percent of the Federal mid-term rate (as in effect under section 1274 for the 1st month of such plan year), or (B) the rate of interest used under the plan in determining costs. In the case of a multiemployer plan, such rate shall be the rate determined under section 6621(b).

(f) Requirements Relating to Waivers and Extensions.

(1) Benefits may not be increased during waiver or extension period. No amendment of the plan which increases the liabilities of the plan by reason of any increase in benefits, any change in the accrual of benefits, or any change in the rate at which benefits become nonforfeitable under the plan shall be adopted if a waiver under subsection (d)(1) or an extension of time under subsection (e) is in effect with respect to the plan, or if a plan amendment described in subsection (c)(8) has been made at any time in the preceding 12 months (24 months for multiemployer plans). If a plan is amended in violation of the preceding sentence, any such waiver or extension of time shall not apply to any plan year ending on or after the date on which such amendment is adopted.

IRC Sec. 412 (f)(1)

(2) Exception. Paragraph (1) shall not apply to any plan amendment which

(A) the Secretary of Labor determines to be reasonable and which provides for only de minimis increases in the liabilities of the plan,

(B) only repeals an amendment described in subsection (c)(8), or

(C) is required as a condition of qualification under this part.

(3) Security for waivers and extensions; consultations.

(A) Security may be required.

(i) In general. Except as provided in subparagraph (C), the Secretary may require an employer maintaining a defined benefit plan which is a single-employer plan (within the meaning of section 4001(a)(15) of the Employee Retirement Income Security Act of 1974) to provide security to such plan as a condition for granting or modifying a waiver under subsection (d) or an extension under subsection (e).

(ii) Special rules. Any security provided under clause (i) may be perfected and enforced only by the Pension Benefit Guaranty Corporation, or at the direction of the Corporation, by a contributing sponsor (within the meaning of section 4001(a)(13) of such Act), or a member of such sponsor's controlled group (within the meaning of section 4001(a)(14) of such Act).

(B) Consultation with the Pension Benefit Guaranty Corporation.Except as provided in subparagraph (C), the Secretary shall, before granting or modifying a waiver under subsection (d) or an extension under subsection (e) with respect to a plan described in subparagraph (A)(i)

(i) provide the Pension Benefit Guaranty Corporation with—

(I) notice of the completed application for any waiver, extension, or modification, and

(II) an opportunity to comment on such application within 30 days after receipt of such notice, and

(ii) consider—

(I) any comments of the Corporation under clause (i)(II), and

(II) any views of any employee organization (within the meaning of section 3(4) of the Employee Retirement Income Security Act of 1974) representing participants in the plan which are submitted in writing to the Secretary in connection with such application.

Information provided to the corporation under this subparagraph shall be considered tax return information and subject to the safeguarding and reporting requirements of section 6103(p).

(C) Exceptions for certain waivers and extensions.

(i) In general. The preceding provisions of this paragraph shall not apply to any plan with respect to which the sum of

(I) the outstanding balance of the accumulated funding deficiencies (within the meaning of subsection (a) and section 302(a) of such Act) of the plan,

(II) the outstanding balance of the amount of the waived funding deficiencies of the plan waived under subsection (d) or section 303 of such Act, and

(III) the outstanding balance of the amount of decreases in the minimum funding standard allowed under subsection (e) or section 304 of such Act,

is less than $1,000,000.

(ii) Accumulated funding deficiencies For purposes of clause (i)(I), accumulated funding deficiencies shall include any in crease in such amount which would result if all applications for waivers of the minimum funding standard under subsection (d) or section 303 of such Act and for extensions of the amortization period under subsection (e) or section 304 of such Act which are pending with respect to such plan were denied.

(4) Additional requirements.

(A) Advance notice. The Secretary shall, before granting a waiver under subsection (d) or an extension under subsection (e), require each applicant to provide evidence satisfactory to the Secretary that the applicant has provided notice of the filing of the application for such waiver or extension to each employee organization representing employees covered by the affected plan, and each participant, beneficiary, and alternate payee (within the meaning of section 414(p)(8)). Such notice shall include a description of the extent to which the plan is funded for benefits which are guaranteed under title IV of such Act and for benefit liabilities.

(B) Consideration of relevant information. The Secretary shall consider any relevant information provided by a person to whom notice was given under subparagraph (A).

(g) Alternative Minimum Funding Standard.

(1) In general. A plan which uses a funding method that requires contributions in all years not less than those required under the entry age normal funding method may maintain an alternative minimum funding standard account for any plan year. Such account shall be credited and charged solely as provided in this subsection.

(2) Charges and credits to account. For a plan year the alternative minimum funding standard account shall be

(A) charged with the sum of

(i) the lesser of normal cost under the funding method used under the plan or nor-

mal cost determined under the unit credit method,

(ii) the excess, if any, of the present value of accrued benefits under the plan over the fair market value of the assets, and

(iii) an amount equal to the excess (if any) of credits to the alternative minimum standard account for all prior plan years over charges to such account for all such years, and

(B) credited with the amount considered contributed by the employer to or under the plan for the plan year.

(3) Special rules. The alternative minimum funding standard account (and items therein) shall be charged or credited with interest in the manner provided under subsection (b)(5) with respect to the funding standard account.

(h) Exceptions. This section shall not apply to

(1) any profit-sharing or stock bonus plan,

(2) any insurance contract plan described in subsection (i),

(3) any governmental plan (within the meaning of section 414(d)),

(4) any church plan (within the meaning of section 414(e)) with respect to which the election provided by section 410(d) has not been made,

(5) any plan which has not, at any time after September 2, 1974, provided for employer contributions, or

(6) any plan established and maintained by a society, order, or association described in section 501(c)(8) or (9), if no part of the contributions to or under such plan are made by employers of participants in such plan.

No plan described in paragraph (3), (4), or (6) shall be treated as a qualified plan for purposes of section 401(a) unless such plan meets the requirements of section 401(a)(7) as in effect on September 1, 1974.

IRC Sec. 412 (h)(6)

(i) Certain Insurance Contract Plans. A plan is described in this subsection if

(1) the plan is funded exclusively by the purchase of individual insurance contracts,

(2) such contracts provided for level annual premium payments to be paid extending not later than the retirement age for each individual participating in the plan, and commencing with the date the individual became a participant in the plan (or, in the case of an increase in benefits, commencing at the time such increase becomes effective),

(3) benefits provided by the plan are equal to the benefits provided under each contract at normal retirement age under the plan and are guaranteed by an insurance carrier (licensed under the laws of a State to do business with the plan) to the extent premiums have been paid,

(4) premiums payable for the plan year, and all prior plan years, under such contracts have been paid before lapse or there is reinstatement of the policy,

(5) no rights under such contracts have been subject to a security interest at any time during the plan year, and

(6) no policy loans are outstanding at any time during the plan year.

A plan funded exclusively by the purchase of group insurance contracts which is determined under regulations prescribed by the Secretary to have the same characteristics as contracts described in the preceding sentence shall be treated as a plan described in this subsection.

(j) Certain Terminated Multiemployer Plans. This section applies with respect to a terminated multiemployer plan to which section 4021 of the Employee Retirement Income Security Act of 1974 applies, until the last day of the plan year in which the plan terminates, within the meaning of section 4041A(a)(2) of that Act.

(k) Financial Assistance. Any amount of any financial assistance from the Pension Benefit Guaranty Corporation to any plan, and any repayment of such amount, shall be taken into account under this section in such manner as determined by the Secretary.

(l) Additional Funding Requirements for Plans Which Are Not Multiemployer Plans.

(1) In general. In the case of a defined benefit plan (other than a multiemployer plan) [which has an unfunded current liability] *to which this subsection applies under paragraph (9)* for any plan year, the amount charged to the funding standard account for such plan year shall be increased by the sum of

(A) the excess (if any) of

(i) the deficit reduction contribution determined under paragraph (2) for such plan year, over

[(ii) the sum of the charges for such plan year under subparagraphs (B) (other than clauses (iv) and (v) thereof), (C), and (D) of subsection (b)(2), reduced by the sum of the credits for such plan year under subparagraph (B)(i) of subsection (b)(3), plus]

(ii) the sum of the charges for such plan year under subsection (b)(2), reduced by the sum of the credits for such plan year under subparagraph (B) of subsection (b)(3), plus

(B) the unpredictable contingent event amount (if any) for such plan year.

[Such increase shall not exceed the amount necessary to increase the funded current liability percentage to 100 percent.] *Such increase shall not exceed the amount which, after taking into account charges (other than the additional charge under this subsection) and credits under subsection (b), is necessary to increase the funded current liability percentage (taking into account the expected increase in current liability due t benefits accruing during the plan year) to 100 percent.*

(2) Deficit reduction contribution. For purposes of paragraph (1), the deficit reduction contribution determined under this paragraph for any plan year is the sum of—

(A) the unfunded old liability amount, [plus]

(B) the unfunded new liability amount.

(C) the expected increase in current liability due to benefits accruing during the plan year, and

(D) the aggregate of the unfunded mortality increase amounts.

(3) Unfunded old liability amount. For purposes of this subsection

(A) In general. The unfunded old liability amount with respect to any plan for any plan year is the amount necessary to amortize the unfunded old liability under the plan in equal annual installments over a period of 18 plan years (beginning with the 1st plan year beginning after December 31, 1988).

(B) Unfunded old liability. The term "unfunded old liability" means the unfunded current liability of the plan as of the beginning of the 1st plan year beginning after December 31, 1987 (determined without regard to any plan amendment increasing liabilities adopted after October 16, 1987).

(C) Special rules for benefit increases under existing collective bargaining agreements.

(i) In general. In the case of a plan maintained pursuant to 1 or more collective bargaining agreements between employee representatives and the employer ratified before October 29, 1987, the unfunded old liability amount with respect to such plan for any plan year shall be increased by the amount necessary to amortize the unfunded existing benefit increase liability in equal annual installments over a period of 18 plan years beginning with

(I) the plan year in which the benefit increase with respect to such liability occurs, or

(II) if the taxpayer elects, the 1st plan year beginning after December 31, 1988.

(ii) Unfunded existing benefit increase liabilities. For purposes of clause (i), the unfunded existing benefit increase liability means, with respect to any benefit increase under the agreements described in clause (i) which takes effect during or after the 1st plan year beginning after December 31, 1987, the unfunded current liability determined

(I) by taking into account only liabilities attributable to such benefit increase, and

(II) by reducing (but not below zero) the amount determined under paragraph (8)(A)(ii) by the current liability determined without regard to such benefit increase.

(iii) Extensions, modifications, etc. not taken into account. For purposes of this subparagraph, any extension, amendment, or other modification of an agreement after October 28, 1987, shall not be taken into account.

(D) Special rule for required changes in actuarial assumptions.

(i) In general.The unfunded old liability amount with respect to any plan for any plan year shall be increased by the amount necessary to amortize the amount of additional unfunded old liability under the plan in equal annual installments over a period of 12 plan years (beginning with the first plan year beginning after December 31, 1994).

(ii) Additional unfunded old liability.For purposes of clause (i), the term 'additional unfunded old liability' means the amount (if any) by which—

(I) the current liability of the plan as of the beginning of the first plan year beginning after December 31, 1994, valued using the assumptions required by para-

IRC Sec. 412 (l)(3)(D)(ii)(I)

graph (7)(C) as in effect for plan years beginning after December 31, 1994, exceeds

(II) the current liability of the plan as of the beginning of such first plan year, valued using the same assumptions used under subclause (I) (other than the assumptions required by paragraph (7)(C)), using the prior interest rate, and using such mortality assumptions as were used to determine current liability for the first plan year beginning after December 31, 1992.

(iii) Prior interest rate.For purposes of clause (ii), the term 'prior interest rate' means the rate of interest that is the same percentage of the weighted average under subsection (b)(5)(B)(ii)(I) for the first plan year beginning after December 31, 1994, as the rate of interest used by the plan to determine current liability for the first plan year beginning after December 31, 1992, is of the weighted average under subsection (b)(5)(B)(ii)(I) for such first plan year beginning after December 31, 1992.

(E) Optional rule for additional unfunded old liability.

(i) In general.If an employer makes an election under clause (ii), the additional unfunded old liability for purposes of subparagraph (D) shall be the amount (if any) by which—

(I) the unfunded current liability of the plan as of the beginning of the first plan year beginning after December 31, 1994, valued using the assumptions required by paragraph (7)(C) as in effect for plan years beginning after December 31, 1994, exceeds

(II) the unamortized portion of the unfunded old liability under the plan as of the beginning of the first plan year beginning after December 31, 1994.

(ii) Election..

(I) An employer may irrevocably elect to apply the provisions of this subparagraph as of the beginning of the first plan year beginning after December 31, 1994.

(II) If an election is made under this clause, the increase under paragraph (1) for any plan year beginning after December 31, 1994, and before January 1, 2002, to which this subsection applies (without regard to this subclause) shall not be less than the increase that would be required under paragraph (1) if the provisions of this title as in effect for the last plan year beginning before January 1, 1995, had remained in effect.

(4) Unfunded new liability amount. For purposes of this subsection

(A) In general. The unfunded new liability amount with respect to any plan for any plan year is the applicable percentage of the unfunded new liability.

(B) Unfunded new liability. The term "unfunded new liability" means the unfunded current liability of the plan for the plan year determined without regard to

(i) the unamortized portion of the unfunded old liability, *the unamortized portion of the additional unfunded old liability, the unamortized portion of each unfunded mortality increase,* and the unamortized portion of the unfunded existing benefit increase liability, and

(ii) the liability with respect to any unpredictable contingent event benefits (without regard to whether the event has occurred).

(C) Applicable percentage. The term "applicable percentage" means, with respect to any plan year, 30 percent, reduced by the product of

(i) [.25] .40 multiplied by

(ii) the number of percentage points (if any) by which the funded current liability percentage exceeds [35] 60 percent.

(5) Unpredictable contingent event amount.

(A) In general. The unpredictable contingent event amount with respect to a plan for any plan year is an amount equal to the [greater of] *greatest of*—

(i) the applicable percentage of the product of—

(I) 100 percent, reduced (but not below zero) by the funded current liability percentage for the plan year, multiplied by

(II) the amount of unpredictable contingent event benefits paid during the plan year, including (except as provided by the Secretary) any payment for the purchase of an annuity contract for a participant or beneficiary with respect to such benefits, [or]

(ii) the amount which would be determined for the plan year if the unpredictable contingent event benefit liabilities were amortized in equal annual installments over 7 plan years (beginning with the plan year in which such event occurs)[.] *or*

(iii) the additional amount that would be determined under paragraph (4)(A) if the unpredictable contingent event benefit liabilities were included in unfunded new liability notwithstanding paragraph (4)(B)(ii).

(B) Applicable percentage.

In the case of plan years beginning in:	The applicable percentage is:
1989 and 1990	5
1991	10
1992	15
1993	20
1994	30
1995	40
1996	50
1997	60
1998	70
1999	80
2000	90
2001 and thereafter	100

(C) Paragraph not to apply to existing benefits. This paragraph shall not apply to un-predictable contingent event benefits (and liabilities attributable thereto) for which the event occurred before the first plan year beginning after December 31, 1988.

(D) Special rule for first year of amortization. Unless the employer elects otherwise, the amount determined under subparagraph (A) for the plan year in which the event occurs shall be equal to 150 percent of the amount determined under subparagraph (A)(i). The amount under subparagraph (A)(ii) for subsequent plan years in the am-ortization period shall be adjusted in the manner provided by the Secretary to reflect the application of this subparagraph.

(E) Limitation. The present value of the amounts described in subparagraph (A) with respect to any one event shall not exceed the unpredictable contingent event benefit liabilities attributable to that event.

(6) Special rules for small plans.

(A) Plans with 100 or fewer participants. This subsection shall not apply to any plan for any plan year if on each day during the preceding plan year such plan had no more than 100 participants.

(B) Plans with more than 100 but not more than 150 participants. In the case of a plan to which subparagraph (A) does not apply and which on each day during the preceding plan year had no more than 150 participants, the amount of the increase under paragraph (1) for such plan year shall be equal to the product of

(i) such increase determined without regard to this subparagraph, multiplied by

(ii) 2 percent for the highest number of participants in excess of 100 on any such day.

(C) Aggregation of plans. For purposes of this paragraph, all defined benefit plans maintained by the same employer (or any member of such employer's controlled group) shall be treated as 1 plan, but only

IRC Sec. 412 (*l*)(6)(C)

employees of such employer or member shall be taken into account.

(7) Current liability. For purposes of this subsection

(A) In general. The term "current liability" means all liabilities to employees and their beneficiaries under the plan.

(B) Treatment of unpredictable contingent event benefits.

(i) In general. For purposes of subparagraph (A), any unpredictable contingent event benefit shall not be taken into account until the event on which the benefit is contingent occurs.

(ii) Unpredictable contingent event benefit. The term "unpredictable contingent event benefit" means any benefit contingent on an event other than

(I) age, service, compensation, death, or disability, or

(II) an event which is reasonably and reliably predictable (as determined by the Secretary).

[(C) Interest rates used. The rate of interest used to determine current liability shall be the rate of interest used under subsection (b)(5).]

(C) Interest rate and mortality assumptions used. Effective for plan years beginning after December 31, 1994—

(i) Interest rate.

(I) In general.The rate of interest used to determine current liability under this subsection shall be the rate of interest used under subsection (b)(5), except that the highest rate in the permissible range under subparagraph (B)(ii) thereof shall not exceed the specified percentage under subclause (II) of the weighted average referred to in such subparagraph.

(II) Specified percentage. For purposes of subclause (I), the specified percentage shall be determined as follows:

In the case of plan years beginning in calendar year:	The specified percentage is:
1995	109
1996	108
1997	107
1998	106
1999 and thereafter	105.

(ii) Mortality tables.

(I) Commissioners' standard table.In the case of plan years beginning before the first plan year to which the first tables prescribed under subclause (II) apply, the mortality table used in determining current liability under this subsection shall be the table prescribed by the Secretary which is based on the prevailing commissioners' standard table (described in section 807(d)(5)(A)) used to determine reserves for group annuity contracts issued on January 1, 1993.

(II) Secretarial authority. The Secretary may by regulation prescribe for plan years beginning after December 31, 1999, mortality tables to be used in determining current liability under this subsection. Such tables shall be based upon the actual experience of pension plans and projected trends in such experience. In prescribing such tables, the Secretary shall take into account results of available independent studies of mortality of individuals covered by pension plans.

(III) Periodic review.The Secretary shall periodically (at least every 5 years) review any tables in effect under this subsection and shall, to the extent the Secretary determines necessary, by regulation update the tables to reflect the actual experience of pension plans and projected trends in such experience.

(iii) Separate mortality tables for the disabled—Notwithstanding clause (ii)

(I) In general.In the case of plan years beginning after December 31, 1995, the Secretary shall establish mortality tables which may be used (in lieu of the tables under clause (ii)) to determine current liability under this subsection for individuals who are entitled to benefits under the plan on account of disability. The Secretary shall establish separate tables for individuals whose disabilities occur in plan years beginning before January 1, 1995, and for individuals whose disabilities occur in plan years beginning on or after such date.

(II) Special rule for disabilities occurring after 1994. In the case of disabilities occurring in plan years beginning after December 31, 1994, the tables under subclause (I) shall apply only with respect to individuals described in such subclause who are disabled within the meaning of title II of the Social Security Act and the regulations thereunder.

(III) Plan years beginning in 1995.In the case of any plan year beginning in 1995, a plan may use its own mortality assumptions for individuals who are entitled to benefits under the plan on account of disability.

(D) Certain service disregarded.

(i) In general. In the case of a participant to whom this subparagraph applies, only the applicable percentage of the years of service before such individual became a participant shall be taken into account in computing the current liability of the plan.

(ii) Applicable percentage. For purposes of this subparagraph, the applicable percentage shall be determined as follows:

If the years of participation are:	The applicable percentage is:
1	20
2	40
3	60
4	80
5 or more	100

(iii) Participants to whom subparagraph applies. This subparagraph shall apply to any participant who, at the time of becoming a participant

(I) has not accrued any other benefit under any defined benefit plan (whether or not terminated) maintained by the employer or a member of the same controlled group of which the employer is a member,

(II) who first becomes a participant under the plan in a plan year beginning after December 31, 1987 and

(III) has years of service greater than the minimum years of service necessary for eligibility to participate in the plan.

(iv) Election. An employer may elect not to have this subparagraph apply. Such an election, once made, may be revoked only with the consent of the Secretary.

(8) Other definitions. For purposes of this subsection

(A) Unfunded current liability. The term "unfunded current liability" means, with respect to any plan year, the excess (if any) of

(i) the current liability under the plan, over

(ii) value of the plan's assets determined under subsection (c)(2).

(B) Funded current liability percentage. The term "funded current liability percentage" means, with respect to any plan year, the percentage which

(i) the amount determined under subparagraph (A)(ii), is of

(ii) the current liability under the plan.

which a plan uses any new mortality table issued under paragraph (7)(C)(ii)(II) or (III)).

(B) Unfunded mortality increase.For purposes of subparagraph (A), the term "unfunded mortality increase" means an amount equal to the excess of

(i) the current liability of the plan for the first plan year for which a plan uses any new mortality table issued under paragraph (7)(C)(ii)(II) or (III), over

(ii) the current liability of the plan for such plan year which would have been determined if the mortality table in effect for the preceding plan year had been used.

(11) Phase-in of increases in funding required by retirement protection act of 1994.

(A) In general.For any applicable plan year, at the election of the employer, the increase under paragraph (1) shall not exceed the greater of

(i) the increase that would be required under paragraph (1) if the provisions of this title as in effect for plan years beginning before January 1, 1995, had remained in effect, or

(ii) the amount which, after taking into account charges (other than the additional charge under this subsection) and credits under subsection (b), is necessary to increase the funded current liability percentage (taking into account the expected increase in current liability due to benefits accruing during the plan year) for the applicable plan year to a percentage equal to the sum of the initial funded current liability percentage of the plan plus the applicable number of percentage points for such applicable plan year.

(B) Applicable number of percentage points.

(i) Initial funded current liability percentage of 75 percent or less.Except as provided in clause (ii), for plans with an initial funded current liability percentage of 75 percent or

less, the applicable number of percentage points for the applicable plan year is:

In the case of applicable plan years beginning in:	The applicable number of percentage points is:
1995	3
1996	6
1997	9
1998	12
1999	15
2000	19
2001	24

(ii) Other cases.In the case of a plan to which this clause applies, the applicable number of percentage points for any such applicable plan year is the sum of

(I) 2 percentage points;

(II) the applicable number of percentage points (if any) under this clause for the preceding applicable plan year;

(III) the product of .10 multiplied by the excess (if any) of (a) 85 percentage points over (b) the sum of the initial funded current liability percentage and the number determined under subclause (II);

(IV) for applicable plan years beginning in 2000, 1 percentage point; and

(V) for applicable plan years beginning in 2001, 2 percentage points.

(iii) Plans to which clause (ii) applies.

(I) In general. Clause (ii) shall apply to a plan for an applicable plan year if the initial funded current liability percentage of such plan is more than 75 percent.

(II) Plans initially under clause (i). In the case of a plan which (but for this subclause) has an initial funded current liability percentage of 75 percent or less clause (ii) (and not clause (i)) shall apply to such plan with respect to applicable plan years beginning after the first applicable plan year for which the sum of the

(C) Controlled group. The term "controlled group" means any group treated as a single employer under subsection (b), (c), (m), and (o) of section 414.

(D) Adjustments to prevent omissions and duplications. The Secretary shall provide such adjustments in the unfunded old liability amount, the unfunded new liability amount, the unpredictable contingent event amount, the current payment amount, and any other charges or credits under this section as are necessary to avoid duplication or omission of any factors in the determination of such amounts, charges, or credits.

(E) Deduction for credit balances. For purposes of this subsection, the amount determined under subparagraph (A)(ii) shall be reduced by any credit balance in the funding standard account. The Secretary may provide for such reduction for purposes of any other provision which references this subsection.

(9) Applicability of subsection.

(A) In general. Except as provided in paragraph (6)(A), this subsection shall apply to a plan for any plan year if its funded current liability percentage for such year is less than 90 percent.

(B) Exception for certain plans at least 80 percent funded. Subparagraph (A) shall not apply to a plan for a plan year if —

(i) the funded current liability percentage for the plan year is at least 80 percent, and

(ii) such percentage for each of the 2 immediately preceding plan years (or each of the 2d and 3d immediately preceding plan years) is at least 90 percent.

(C) Funded current liability percentage. For purposes of subparagraphs (A) and (B), the term 'funded current liability percentage' has the meaning given such term by paragraph (8)(B), except that such percentage shall be determined for any plan year

(i) without regard to paragraph (8)(E), and

(ii) by using the rate of interest which is the highest rate allowable for the plan year under paragraph (7)(C).

(D) Transition rules. For purposes of this paragraph:

(i) Funded percentage for years before 1995. The funded current liability percentage for any plan year beginning before January 1, 1995, shall be treated as not less than 90 percent only if for such plan year the plan met one of the following requirements (as in effect for such year):

(I) The full-funding limitation under subsection (c)(7) for the plan was zero.

(II) The plan had no additional funding requirement under this subsection (or would have had no such requirement if its funded current liability percentage had been determined under subparagraph (C)).

(III) The plan's additional funding requirement under this subsection did not exceed the lesser of 0.5 percent of current liability or $5,000,000.

(ii) Special rule for 1995 and 1996. For purposes of determining whether subparagraph (B) applies to any plan year beginning in 1995 or 1996, a plan shall be treated as meeting the requirements of subparagraph (B)(ii) if the plan met the requirements of clause (i) of this subparagraph for any two of the plan years beginning in 1992, 1993, and 1994 (whether or not consecutive).

(10) Unfunded mortality increase amount.

(A) In general. The unfunded mortality increase amount with respect to each unfunded mortality increase is the amount necessary to amortize such increase in equal annual installments over a period of 10 plan years (beginning with the first plan year for

*initial funded current liability percentage
and the applicable number of percentage
points (determined under clause (i)) exceeds 75 percent. For purposes of applying clause (ii) to such a plan, the initial
funded current liability percentage of
such plan shall be treated as being the
sum referred to in the preceding sentence.*

*(C) Definitions.For purposes of this para-
graph:*

*(i) The term 'applicable plan year' means
a plan year beginning after December 31,
1994, and before January 1, 2002.*

*(ii) The term 'initial funded current liabil-
ity percentage' means the funded current
liability percentage as of the first day of the
first plan year beginning after December 31,
1994.*

◊ ◊ ◊

Editor's Note: Code §412(m)(1) as set forth
below appears as amended by §754(a) of the
Retirement Protection Act of 1994 (enacted as
part of the Uruguay Round Agreements Act,
P.L. 103-465). Under §754(b) of the 1994 Act,
the change is effective generally for plan
years beginning after December 8, 1994. But
see Editor's Note at the beginning of Code
§412 for special effective date rules for certain
plans subject to a PBGC restoration schedule
order and the plans of certain air carriers.

◊ ◊ ◊

(m) Quarterly Contributions Required.

(1) In general. If a defined benefit plan
(other than a multiemployer plan) *which has
a funded current liability percentage (as defined in subsection (l)(8)) for the preceding
plan year of less than 100 percent* fails to pay
the full amount of a required installment for
[any plan year] *the plan year*, then the rate of
interest charged to the funding standard account under subsection (b)(5) with respect to
the amount of the underpayment for the period

of the underpayment shall be equal to the
greater of

(A) 175 percent of the Federal mid-term rate
(as in effect under section 1274 for the 1st
month of such plan year), or

(B) the rate of interest used under the plan
in determining costs (including adjustments
under subsection (b)(5)(B)).

**(2) Amount of underpayment, period of
underpayment.** For purposes of paragraph
(1)

(A) Amount. The amount of the underpayment shall be the excess of

(i) the required installment, over

(ii) the amount (if any) of the installment
contributed to or under the plan on or before
the due date for the installment.

(B) Period of underpayment. The period for
which interest is charged under this subsection with regard to any portion of the underpayment shall run from the due date for the
installment to the date on which such portion
is contributed to or under the plan (determined without regard to subsection (c)(10)).

(C) Order of crediting contributions. For
purposes of subparagraph (A)(ii), contributions shall be credited against unpaid required installments in the order in which
such installments are required to be paid.

**(3) Number of required installments; due
dates.** For purposes of this subsection

(A) Payable in 4 installments. There shall
be 4 required installments for each plan year.

(B) Time for payment of installments.

In the case of the following required installments:	The due date is:
1st	April 15
2nd	July 15
3rd	October 15
4th	January 15 of the fol- lowing year

IRC Sec. 412 (l)(11)(C)

(4) Amount of required installment. For purposes of this subsection—

(A) In general.The amount of any required installment shall be the applicable percentage of the required annual payment.

(B) Required annual payment. For purposes of subparagraph (A), the term "required annual payment" means the lesser of

(i) 90 percent of the amount required to be contributed to or under the plan by the employer for the plan year under section 412 (without regard to any waiver under subsection (c) thereof), or

(ii) 100 percent of the amount so required for the preceding plan year. Clause (ii) shall not apply if the preceding plan year was not a year of 12 months.

(C) Applicable percentage. For purposes of subparagraph (A), the applicable percentage shall be determined in accordance with the following table:

For plan years beginning in:	The applicable percentage is:
1989	6.25
1990	12.5
1991	18.75
1992 and thereafter	25

(D) Special rules for unpredictable contingent event benefits.In the case of a plan to which subsection (1) applies for any calendar year and which has any unpredictable contingent event benefit liabilities

(i) Liabilities not taken into account. Such liabilities shall not be taken into account in computing the required annual payment under subparagraph (B).

(ii) Increase in installments. Each required installment shall be increased by the [greater of] *greatest of—*

(I) the unfunded percentage of the amount of benefits described in subsection (1)(5)(A)(i) paid during the 3-month

period preceding the month in which the due date for such installment occurs, [or]

(II) 25 percent of the amount determined under subsection (1)(5)(A)(ii) for the plan year[.] , *or*

(III) 25 percent of the amount determined under subsection (1)(5)(A)(iii) for the plan year.

(iii) Unfunded percentage. For purposes of clause (ii)(I), the term "unfunded percentage" means the percentage determined under subsection (1)(5)(A)(i)(I) for the plan year.

(iv) Limitation on increase.In no event shall the increases under clause (ii) exceed the amount necessary to increase the funded current liability percentage (within the meaning of subsection (1)(8)(B)) for the plan year to 100 percent.

(5) Liquidity requirement.

(A) In general. A plan to which this paragraph applies shall be treated as failing to pay the full amount of any required installment to the extent that the value of the liquid assets paid in such installment is less than the liquidity shortfall (whether or not such liquidity shortfall exceeds the amount of such installment required to be paid but for this paragraph).

(B) Plans to which paragraph applies.This paragraph shall apply to a defined benefit plan (other than a multiemployer plan or a plan described in subsection (1)(6)(A)) which

(i) is required to pay installments under this subsection for a plan year, and

(ii) has a liquidity shortfall for any quarter during such plan year.

(C) Period of underpayment.For purposes of paragraph (1), any portion of an installment that is treated as not paid under subparagraph (A) shall continue to be treated as unpaid until the close of the quarter in

IRC Sec. 412 (m)(5)(C)

which the due date for such installment occurs.

(D) Limitation on increase. If the amount of any required installment is increased by reason of subparagraph (A), in no event shall such increase exceed the amount which, when added to prior installments for the plan year, is necessary to increase the funded current liability percentage (taking into account the expected increase in current liability due to benefits accruing during the plan year) to 100 percent.

(E) Definitions. For purposes of this paragraph:

(i) Liquidity shortfall. The term "liquidity shortfall" means, with respect to any required installment, an amount equal to the excess (as of the last day of the quarter for which such installment is made) of the base amount with respect to such quarter over the value (as of such last day) of the plan's liquid assets.

(ii) Base amount.

(I) In general. The term "base amount" means, with respect to any quarter, an amount equal to 3 times the sum of the adjusted disbursements from the plan for the 12 months ending on the last day of such quarter.

(II) Special rule. If the amount determined under clause (i) exceeds an amount equal to 2 times the sum of the adjusted disbursements from the plan for the 36 months ending on the last day of the quarter and an enrolled actuary certifies to the satisfaction of the Secretary that such excess is the result of nonrecurring circumstances, the base amount with respect to such quarter shall be determined without regard to amounts related to those nonrecurring circumstances.

(iii) Disbursements from the plan. The term "disbursements from the plan" means all disbursements from the trust, including purchases of annuities, payments of single sums and other benefits, and administrative expenses.

(iv) Adjusted disbursements. The term "adjusted disbursements" means disbursements from the plan reduced by the product of—

(I) the plan's funded current liability percentage (as defined in subsection (l)(8)) for the plan year, and

(II) the sum of the purchases of annuities, payments of single sums, and such other disbursements as the Secretary shall provide in regulations.

(v) Liquid assets. The term "liquid assets" means cash, marketable securities and such other assets as specified by the Secretary in regulations.

(vi) Quarter. The term "quarter" means, with respect to any required installment, the 3-month period preceding the month in which the due date for such installment occurs.

(F) Regulations. The Secretary may prescribe such regulations as are necessary to carry out this paragraph.

[(5)](6) Fiscal years and short years.

(A) Fiscal years. In applying this subsection to a plan year beginning on any date other than January 1, there shall be substituted for the months specified in this subsection, the months which correspond thereto.

(B) Short plan year. This subsection shall be applied to plan years of less than 12 months in accordance with regulations prescribed by the Secretary.

◊ ◊ ◊

Editor's Note: The amendments to Code §412(n)(2), (3) and (4), as set forth below, were made by §768(a) of the Retirement Protection Act of 1994 (enacted as part of the Uruguay Round Agreements Act, P.L. 103-465). The amendments apply to installments and other payments due under Code §412 that become due on or after December 8, 1994.

◊ ◊ ◊

(n) Imposition of Lien Where Failure To Make Required Contributions.

(1) In general. In the case of a plan to which this section applies, if—

(A) any person fails to make a required installment under subsection (m) or any other payment required under this section before the due date for such installment or other payment, and

(B) the unpaid balance of such installment or other payment (including interest), when added to the aggregate unpaid balance of all preceding such installments or other payments for which payment was not made before the due date (including interest), exceeds $1,000,000,

then there shall be a lien in favor of the plan in the amount determined under paragraph (3) upon all property and rights to property, whether real or personal, belonging to such person and any other person who is a member of the same controlled group of which such person is a member.

(2) Plans to which subsection applies. This subsection shall apply to a defined benefit plan (other than a multiemployer plan) for any plan year for which the funded current liability percentage (within the meaning of subsection (*l*)(8)(B)) of such plan is less than 100 percent. *This subsection shall not apply to any plan to which section 4021 of the Employee Retirement Income Security Act of 1974 does not apply (as such section is in*

effect on the date of the enactment of the Retirement Protection Act of 1994).

[(3) **Amount of lien.** For purposes of paragraph (i), the amount of the lien shall be equal to the lesser of—

[(A) the amount by which the unpaid balances described in paragraph (1)(B) (including interest) exceed $1,000,000, of—

[(B) the aggregate unpaid balance of required installments and other payments required under this section (including interest)—

[(i) for plan years beginning after 1987, and

[(ii) for which payment has not been made before the due date.]

(3) Amount of lien. For purposes of paragraph (1), the amount of the lien shall be equal to the aggregate unpaid balance of required installments and other payments required under this section (including interest)

(A) for plan years beginning after 1987, and

(B) for which payment has not been made before the due date.

(4) Notice of failure; lien.

(A) Notice of failure. A person committing a failure described in paragraph (1) shall notify the Pension Benefit Guaranty Corporation of such failure within 10 days of the due date for the required installment or other payment.

(B) Period of lien. The lien imposed by paragraph (1) shall arise on the [60th day following the] due date for the required installment or other payment and shall continue until the last day of the first plan year in which the plan ceases to be described in paragraph (1)(B). Such lien shall continue to run without regard to whether such plan continues to be described in paragraph (2) during the period referred to in the preceding sentence.

IRC Sec. 412 (n)(4)(B)

(C) Certain rules to apply. Any amount with respect to which a lien is imposed under paragraph (1) shall be treated as taxes due and owing the United States and rules similar to the rules of subsections (c), (d), and (e) of section 4068 of the Employee Retirement Income Security Act of 1974 shall apply with respect to a lien imposed by subsection (a) and the amount with respect to such lien.

(5) Enforcement. Any lien created under paragraph (1) may be perfected and enforced only by the Pension Benefit Guaranty Corporation, or at the direction of the Pension Benefit Guaranty Corporation, by the contributing sponsor (or any member of the controlled group of the contributing sponsor).

(6) Definitions. For purposes of this subsection

(A) Due date; required installment. The terms "due date" and "required installment" have the meanings given such terms by subsection (m), except that in the case of a payment other than a required installment, the due date shall be the date such payment is required to be made under this section.

(B) Controlled group. The term "controlled group" means any group treated as a single employer under subsections (b), (c), (m), and (o) of section 414.

SEC. 413. COLLECTIVELY BARGAINED PLANS, ETC.

(a) Application of Subsection (b).— Subsection (b) applies to—

(1) a plan maintained pursuant to an agreement which the Secretary of Labor finds to be a collective-bargaining agreement between employee representatives and one or more employers, and

(2) each trust which is a part of such plan.

(b) General Rule.— If this subsection applies to a plan, notwithstanding any other provision of this title—

(1) Participation.— Section 410 shall be applied as if all employees of each of the employers who are parties to the collective-bargaining agreement and who are subject to the same benefit computation formula under the plan were employed by a single employer.

(2) Discrimination, etc.— Sections 401(a)(4) and 411(d)(3) shall be applied as if all participants who are subject to the same benefit computation formula and who are employed by employers who are parties to the collective-bargaining agreement were employed by a single employer.

(3) Exclusive benefit.— For purposes of section 401(a), in determining whether the plan of an employer is for the exclusive benefit of his employees and their beneficiaries, all plan participants shall be considered to be his employees.

(4) Vesting.— Section 411 (other than subsection (d)(3)) shall be applied as if all employers who have been parties to the collective-bargaining agreement constituted a single employer, except that the application of any rules with respect to breaks in service shall be made under regulations prescribed by the Secretary of Labor.

(5) Funding.— The minimum funding standard provided by section 412 shall be determined as if all participants in the plan were employed by a single employer.

(6) Liability for funding tax.— For a plan year the liability under section 4971 of each employer who is a party to the collective-bargaining agreement shall be determined in a reasonable manner not inconsistent with regulations prescribed by the Secretary—

(A) first on the basis of their respective delinquencies in meeting required employer contributions under the plan, and

(B) then on the basis of their respective liabilities for contributions under the plan.

For purposes of this subsection and the last sentence of section 4971(a), an employer's withdrawal liability under part 1 of subtitle

E of title IV of the Employee Retirement Income Security Act of 1974 shall not be treated as a liability for contributions under the plan.

(7) Deduction limitations.—Each applicable limitation provided by section 404(a) shall be determined as if all participants in the plan were employed by a single employer.

The amounts contributed to or under the plan by each employer who is a party to the agreement, for the portion of his taxable year which is included within such a plan year, shall be considered not to exceed such a limitation if the anticipated employer contributions for such plan year (determined in a manner consistent with the manner in which actual employer contributions for such plan year are determined) do not exceed such limitation. If such anticipated contributions exceed such a limitation, the portion of each such employer's contributions which is not deductible under section 404 shall be determined in accordance with regulations prescribed by the Secretary.

(8) Employees of labor unions.—For purposes of this subsection, employees of employee representatives shall be treated as employees of an employer described in subsection (a)(1) if such representatives meet the requirements of sections 401(a)(4) and 410 with respect to such employees.

(9) Plans covering a professional employee.—Notwithstanding subsection (a), in the case of a plan (and trust forming part thereof) which covers any professional employee, paragraph (1) shall be applied by substituting "section 410(a)" for "section 410", and paragraph (2) shall not apply.

(c) Plans Maintained by More Than One Employer.—In the case of a plan maintained by more than one employer—

(1) Participation.—Section 410(a) shall be applied as if all employees of each of the employers who maintain the plan were employed by a single employer.

(2) Exclusive benefit.—For purposes of section 401(a), in determining whether the plan of an employer is for the exclusive benefit of his employees and their beneficiaries all plan participants shall be considered to be his employees.

(3) Vesting.—Section 411 shall be applied as if all employers who maintain the plan constituted a single employer, except that the application of any rules with respect to breaks in service shall be made under regulations prescribed by the Secretary of Labor.

(4) Funding.—

(A) In general.—In the case of a plan established after December 31, 1988, each employer shall be treated as maintaining a separate plan for purposes of section 412 unless such plan uses a method for determining required contributions which provides that any employer contributes not less than the amount which would be required if such employer maintained a separate plan.

(B) Other plans.—In the case of a plan not described in subparagraph (A), the requirements of section 412 shall be determined as if all participants in the plan were employed by a single employer unless the plan administrator elects not later than the close of the first plan year of the plan beginning after the date of enactment of the Technical and Miscellaneous Revenue Act of 1988 to have the provisions of subparagraph (A) apply. An election under the preceding sentence shall take effect for the plan year in which made and, once made, may be revoked only with the consent of the Secretary.

(5) Liability for funding tax.—For a plan year the liability under section 4971 of each employer who maintains the plan shall be determined in a reasonable manner not inconsistent with regulations prescribed by the Secretary—

(A) first on the basis of their respective delinquencies in meeting required employer contributions under the plan, and

IRC Sec. 413 (c)(5)(A)

(B) then on the basis of their respective liabilities for contributions under the plan.

(6) Deduction limitations.—

(A) In general.—In the case of a plan established after December 31, 1988, each applicable limitation provided by section 404(a) shall be determined as if each employer were maintaining a separate plan.

(B) Other plans.—

(i) In general.— In the case of a plan not described in subparagraph (A), each applicable limitation provided by section 404(a) shall be determined as if all participants in the plan were employed by a single employer, except that if an election is made under paragraph (4)(B), subparagraph (A) shall apply to such plan.

(ii) Special rule.— If this subparagraph applies, the amounts contributed to or under the plan by each employer who maintains the plan (for the portion of the taxable year included within a plan year) shall be considered not to exceed any such limitation if the anticipated employer contributions for such plan year (determined in a reasonable manner not inconsistent with regulations prescribed by the Secretary) do not exceed such limitation. If such anticipated contributions exceed such a limitation, the portion of each such employer's contributions which is not deductible under section 404 shall be determined in accordance with regulations prescribed by the Secretary.

(7) Allocations.—

(A) In general.—Except as provided in subparagraph (B), allocations of amounts under paragraphs (4), (5), and (6) among the employers maintaining the plan shall not be inconsistent with regulations prescribed for this purpose by the Secretary.

(B) Assets and liabilities of plan.—For purposes of applying paragraphs (4)(A) and (6)(A), the assets and liabilities of each plan shall be treated as the assets and liabilities

which would be allocated to a plan maintained by the employer if the employer withdrew from the multiple employer plan.

SEC. 414. DEFINITIONS AND SPECIAL RULES.

(a) Service for Predecessor Employer.— For purposes of this part—

(1) in any case in which the employer maintains a plan of a predecessor employer, service for such predecessor shall be treated as service for the employer, and

(2) in any case in which the employer maintains a plan which is not the plan maintained by a predecessor employer, service for such predecessor shall, to the extent provided in regulations prescribed by the Secretary, be treated as service for the employer.

(b) Employees of Controlled Group of Corporations.— For purposes of sections 401, 408(k), 410, 411, 415, and 416, all employees of all corporations which are members of a controlled group of corporations (within the meaning of section 1563(a), determined without regard to section 1563(a)(4) and (e)(3)(C)) shall be treated as employed by a single employer. With respect to a plan adopted by more than one such corporation, the applicable limitations provided by section 404(a) shall be determined as if all such employers were a single employer, and allocated to each employer in accordance with regulations prescribed by the Secretary.

(c) Employees of Partnerships, Proprietorships, etc., Which Are Under Common Control.— For purposes of sections 401, 408(k), 410, 411, 415, and 416, under regulations prescribed by the Secretary, all employees of trades or businesses (whether or not incorporated) which are under common control shall be treated as employed by a single employer. The regulations prescribed under this subsection shall be based on principles similar to the principles which apply in the case of subsection (b).

IRC Sec. 413 (c)(5)(B)

(d) Governmental Plan.— For purposes of this part, the term ''governmental plan'' means a plan established and maintained for its employees by the Government of the United States, by the government of any State or political subdivision thereof, or by any agency or instrumentality of any of the foregoing. The term ''governmental plan'' also includes any plan to which the Railroad Retirement Act of 1935 or 1937 applies and which is financed by contributions required under that Act and any plan of an international organization which is exempt from taxation by reason of the International Organizations Immunities Act (59 Stat. 669).

(e) Church Plan.—

(1) In general.— For purposes of this part, the term ''church plan'' means a plan established and maintained (to the extent required in paragraph (2)(B)) for its employees (or their beneficiaries) by a church or by a convention or association of churches which is exempt from tax under section 501.

(2) Certain plans excluded.— The term ''church plan'' does not include a plan—

(A) which is established and maintained primarily for the benefit of employees (or their beneficiaries) of such church or convention or association of churches who are employed in connection with one or more unrelated trades or businesses (within the meaning of section 513); or

(B) if less than substantially all of the individuals included in the plan are individuals described in paragraph (1) or (3)(B) (or their beneficiaries).

(3) Definitions and other provisions.— For purposes of this subsection—

(A) Treatment as church plan.— A plan established and maintained for its employees (or their beneficiaries) by a church or by a convention or association of churches includes a plan maintained by an organization, whether a civil law corporation or otherwise, the principal purpose or function of which is the administration or funding of a plan or program for the provision of retirement benefits or welfare benefits, or both, for the employees of a church or a convention or association of churches, if such organization is controlled by or associated with a church or a convention or association of churches.

(B) Employee defined.— The term employee of a church or a convention or association of churches shall include—

(i) a duly ordained, commissioned, or licensed minister of a church in the exercise of his ministry, regardless of the source of his compensation;

(ii) an employee of an organization, whether a civil law corporation or otherwise, which is exempt from tax under section 501 and which is controlled by or associated with a church or a convention or association of churches; and

(iii) an individual described in subparagraph (E).

(C) Church treated as employer.— A church or a convention or association of churches which is exempt from tax under section 501 shall be deemed the employer of any individual included as an employee under subparagraph (B).

(D) Association with church.— An organization, whether a civil law corporation or otherwise, is associated with a church or a convention or association of churches if it shares common religious bonds and convictions with that church or convention or association of churches.

(E) Special rule in case of separation from plan.— If an employee who is included in a church plan separates from the service of a church or a convention or association of churches or an organization described in clause (ii) of paragraph (3)(B), the church plan shall not fail to meet the requirements of this subsection merely because the plan—

(i) retains the employee's accrued benefit or account for the payment of benefits to the

IRC Sec. 414 (e)(3)(E)(i)

employee or his beneficiaries pursuant to the terms of the plan; or

(ii) receives contributions on the employee's behalf after the employee's separation from such service, but only for a period of 5 years after such separation, unless the employee is disabled (within the meaning of the disability provisions of the church plan or, if there are no such provisions in the church plan, within the meaning of section 72(m)(7)) at the time of such separation from service.

(4) Correction of failure to meet church plan requirements.—

(A) In general.— If a plan established and maintained for its employees (or their beneficiaries) by a church or by a convention or association of churches which is exempt from tax under section 501 fails to meet one or more of the requirements of this subsection and corrects its failure to meet such requirements within the correction period, the plan shall be deemed to meet the requirements of this subsection for the year in which the correction was made and for all prior years.

(B) Failure to correct.— If a correction is not made within the correction period, the plan shall be deemed not to meet the requirements of this subsection beginning with the date on which the earliest failure to meet one or more of such requirements occurred.

(C) Correction period defined.— The term "correction period" means—

(i) the period ending 270 days after the date of mailing by the Secretary of a notice of default with respect to the plan's failure to meet one or more of the requirements of this subsection;

(ii) any period set by a court of competent jurisdiction after a final determination that the plan fails to meet such requirements, or, if the court does not specify such period, any reasonable period determined by the Secretary on the basis of all the facts and circumstances, but in any event not less than 270

days after the determination has become final; or

(iii) any additional period which the Secretary determines is reasonable or necessary for the correction of the default,

whichever has the latest ending date.

(f) Multiemployer Plan.—

(1) Definition.— For purposes of this part, the term "multiemployer plan" means a plan—

(A) to which more than one employer is required to contribute,

(B) which is maintained pursuant to one or more collective bargaining agreements between one or more employee organizations and more than one employer, and

(C) which satisfies such other requirements as the Secretary of Labor may prescribe by regulation.

(2) Cases of common control.— For purposes of this subsection, all trades or businesses (whether or not incorporated) which are under common control within the meaning of subsection (c) are considered a single employer.

(3) Continuation of status after termination.— Notwithstanding paragraph (1), a plan is a multiemployer plan on and after its termination date under title IV of the Employee Retirement Income Security Act of 1974 if the plan was a multiemployer plan under this subsection for the plan year preceding its termination date.

(4) Transitional rule.— For any plan year which began before the date of the enactment of the Multiemployer Pension Plan Amendments Act of 1980, the term "multiemployer plan" means a plan described in this subsection as in effect immediately before that date.

(5) Special election.— Within one year after the date of the enactment of the Multiemployer Pension Plan Amendments Act of

1980, a multiemployer plan may irrevocably elect, pursuant to procedures established by the Pension Benefit Guaranty Corporation and subject to the provisions of section 4403(b) and (c) of the Employee Retirement Income Security Act of 1974, that the plan shall not be treated as a multiemployer plan for any purpose under such Act or this title, if for each of the last 3 plan years ending prior to the effective date of the Multiemployer Pension Plan Amendments Act of 1980—

(A) the plan was not a multiemployer plan because the plan was not a plan described in section 3(37)(A)(iii) of the Employee Retirement Income Security Act of 1974 and section 414(f)(1)(C) (as such provisions were in effect on the day before the date of the enactment of the Multiemployer Pension Plan Amendments Act of 1980); and

(B) the plan had been identified as a plan that was not a multiemployer plan in substantially all its filings with the Pension Benefit Guaranty Corporation, the Secretary of Labor and the Secretary.

(g) Plan Administrator.— For purposes of this part, the term ''plan administrator'' means—

(1) the person specifically so designated by the terms of the instrument under which the plan is operated;

(2) in the absence of a designation referred to in paragraph (1)—

(A) in the case of a plan maintained by a single employer, such employer,

(B) in the case of a plan maintained by two or more employers or jointly by one or more employers and one or more employee organizations, the association, committee, joint board of trustees, or other similar group of representatives of the parties who maintained the plan, or

(C) in any case to which subparagraph (A) or (B) does not apply, such other person as the Secretary may by regulation, prescribe.

(h) Tax Treatment of Certain Contributions.—

(1) In general.— Effective with respect to taxable years beginning after December 31, 1973, for purposes of this title, any amount contributed—

(A) to an employees' trust described in section 401(a), or

(B) under a plan described in section 403(a),

shall not be treated as having been made by the employer if it is designated as an employee contribution.

(2) Designation by units of government.— For purposes of paragraph (1), in the case of any plan established by the government of any State or political subdivision thereof, or by any agency or instrumentality of any of the foregoing, where the contributions of employing units are designated as employee contributions but where any employing unit picks up the contributions, the contributions so picked up shall be treated as employer contributions.

(i) Defined Contribution Plan.— For purposes of this part, the term ''defined contribution plan'' means a plan which provides for an individual account for each participant and for benefits based solely on the amount contributed to the participant's account, and any income, expenses, gains and losses, and any forfeitures of accounts of other participants which may be allocated to such participant's account.

(j) Defined Benefit Plan.— For purposes of this part, the term ''defined benefit plan'' means any plan which is not a defined contribution plan.

(k) Certain Plans.— A defined benefit plan which provides a benefit derived from employer contributions which is based partly on the balance of the separate account of a participant shall—

IRC Sec. 414 (k)

(1) for purposes of section 410 (relating to minimum participation standards), be treated as a defined contribution plan,

(2) for purposes of sections 72(d) (relating to treatment of employee contributions as separate contract), 411(a)(7)(A) (relating to minimum vesting standards) 415 (relating to limitations on benefits and contributions under qualified plans), and 401(m) (relating to nondiscrimination tests for matching requirements and employee contributions), be treated as consisting of a defined contribution plan to the extent benefits are based on the separate account of a participant and as a defined benefit plan with respect to the remaining portion of benefits under the plan, and

(3) for purposes of section 4975 (relating to tax on prohibited transactions), be treated as a defined benefit plan.

(*l*) Merger and Consolidations of Plans or Transfers of Plan Assets.—

(1) In general.— A trust which forms a part of a plan shall not constitute a qualified trust under section 401 and a plan shall be treated as not described in section 403(a) unless in the case of any merger or consolidation of the plan with, or in the case of any transfer of assets or liabilities of such plan to, any other trust plan after September 2, 1974, each participant in the plan would (if the plan then terminated) receive a benefit immediately after the merger, consolidation, or transfer which is equal to or greater than the benefit he would have been entitled to receive immediately before the merger, consolidation, or transfer (if the plan had then terminated). The preceding sentence does not apply to any multiemployer plan with respect to any transaction to the extent that participants either before or after the transaction are covered under a multiemployer plan to which title IV of the Employee Retirement Income Security Act of 1974 applies.

(2) Allocation of assets in plan spin-offs, etc.—

(A) In general.— In the case of a plan spin-off of a defined benefit plan, a trust which forms part of—

  (i) the original plan, or

  (ii) any plan spun off from such plan, shall not constitute a qualified trust under this section unless the applicable percentage of excess assets are allocated to each of such plans.

(B) Applicable percentage.— For purposes of subparagraph (A), the term "applicable percentage" means, with respect to each of the plans described in clauses (i) and (ii) of subparagraph (A), the percentage determined by dividing—

  (i) the excess (if any) of—

    (I) the amount determined under section 412(c)(7)(A)(i) with respect to the plan, over

    (II) the amount of the assets required to be allocated to the plan after the spin-off (without regard to this paragraph), by—

  (ii) the sum of the excess amounts determined separately under clause (i) for all such plans.

(C) Excess assets.— For purposes of subparagraph (A), the term "excess assets" means an amount equal to the excess (if any) of—

  (i) the fair market value of the assets of the original plan immediately before the spin-off, over

  (ii) the amount of assets required to be allocated after the spin-off to all plans (determined without regard to this paragraph).

(D) Certain spun-off plans not taken into account.—

  (i) In general.— A plan involved in a spin-off which is described in clause (ii), (iii), or (iv) shall not be taken into account for purposes of this paragraph, except that the amount determined under subparagraph (C)(ii) shall be increased by the amount of assets allocated to such plan.

(ii) Plans transferred out of controlled groups.— A plan is described in this clause if, after such spin-off, such plan is maintained by an employer who is not a member of the same controlled group as the employer maintaining the original plan.

(iii) Plans transferred out of multiple employer plans.— A plan as described in this clause if, after the spin-off, any employer maintaining such plan (and any member of the same controlled group as such employer) does not maintain any other plan remaining after the spin-off which is also maintained by another employer (or member of the same controlled group as such other employer) which maintained the plan in existence before the spin-off.

(iv) Terminated plans.— A plan is described in this clause if, pursuant to the transaction involving the spin-off, the plan is terminated.

(v) Controlled group.— For purposes of this subparagraph, the term "controlled group" means any group treated as a single employer under subsection (b), (c), (m), or (o).

(E) Paragraph not to apply to multiemployer plans.— This paragraph does not apply to any multiemployer plan with respect to any spin-off to the extent that participants either before or after the spin-off are covered under a multiemployer plan to which title IV of the Employee Retirement Income Security Act of 1974 applies.

(F) Application to similar transaction.— Except as provided by the Secretary, rules similar to the rules of this paragraph shall apply to transactions similar to spin-offs.

(G) Special rules for bridge banks.— For purposes of this paragraph, in the case of a bridge bank established under section 11(i)

of the Federal Deposit Insurance Act (12 U.S.C. 1821(i))—

(i) such bank shall be treated as a member of any controlled group which includes any insured bank (as defined in section 3(h) of such Act (12 U.S.C. 1813(h)))—

(I) which maintains a defined benefit plan,

(II) which is closed by the appropriate bank regulatory authorities, and

(III) any asset and liabilities of which are received by the bridge bank, and

(ii) the requirements of this paragraph shall not be treated as met with respect to such plan unless during the 180-day period beginning on the date such insured bank is closed—

(I) the bridge bank has the right to require the plan to transfer (subject to the provisions of this paragraph) not more than 50 percent of the excess assets (as defined in subparagraph (C)) to a defined benefit plan maintained by the bridge bank with respect to participants or former participants (including retirees and beneficiaries) in the original plan employed by the bridge bank or formerly employed by the closed bank, and

(II) no other merger, spin-off, termination, or similar transaction involving the portion of the excess assets described in subclause (I) may occur without the prior written consent of the bridge bank.

(m) Employees of an Affiliated Service Group.—

(1) In general.— For purposes of the employee benefit requirements listed in paragraph (4), except to the extent otherwise provided in regulations, all employees of the members of an affiliated service group shall be treated as employed by a single employer.

(2) Affiliated service group.— For purposes of this subsection, the term "affiliated service group" means a group consisting of a

service organization (hereinafter in this paragraph referred to as the "first organization") and one or more of the following:

(A) any service organization which—

(i) is a shareholder or partner in the first organization, and

(ii) regularly performs services for the first organization or is regularly associated with the first organization in performing services for third persons, and

(B) any other organization if—

(i) a significant portion of the business of such organization is the performance of services (for the first organization, for organizations described in subparagraph (A), or for both) of a type historically performed in such service field by employees, and

(ii) 10 percent or more of the interests in such organization is held by persons who are highly compensated employees (within the meaning of section 414(q)) of the first organization or an organization described in subparagraph (A).

(3) Service organizations.— For purposes of this subsection, the term "service organization" means an organization the principal business of which is the performance of services.

(4) Employee benefit requirements.— For purposes of this subsection, the employee benefit requirements listed in this paragraph are—

(A) paragraphs (3), (4), (7), (16), (17), and (26) of section 401(a), and

(B) sections 408(k), 410, 411, 415, and 416.

(5) Certain organizations performing management functions.— For purposes of this subsection, the term "affiliated service group" also includes a group consisting of—

(A) an organization the principal business of which is performing, on a regular and continuing basis, management functions for 1

organization (or for 1 organization and other organizations related to such 1 organization), and

(B) the organization (and related organizations) for which such functions are so performed by the organization described in subparagraph (A).

For purposes of this paragraph, the term "related organizations" has the same meaning as the term "related persons" when used in section 144(a)(3).

(6) Other Definitions.— For purposes of this subsection—

(A) Organization defined.— The term "organization" means a corporation, partnership, or other organization.

(B) Ownership.— In determining ownership, the principles of section 318(a) shall apply.

(7) Prevention of avoidance.— The Secretary shall prescribe such regulations as may be necessary to prevent the avoidance with respect to service organizations, through the use of separate organizations, of any employee benefit requirement listed in paragraph (4).

(n) Employee Leasing.—

(1) In general.— For purposes of the requirements listed in paragraph (3), with respect to any person (hereinafter in this subsection referred to as the "recipient") for whom a leased employee performs services—

(A) the leased employee shall be treated as an employee of the recipient, but

(B) contributions or benefits provided by the leasing organization which are attributable to services performed for the recipient shall be treated as provided by the recipient.

(2) Leased employee.— For purposes of paragraph (1), the term "leased employee" means any person who is not an employee of the recipient and who provides services to the recipient if—

(A) such services are provided pursuant to an agreement between the recipient and any other person (in this subsection referred to as the "leasing organiza-tion"),

(B) such person has performed such services for the recipient (or for the recipient and related persons) on a substantially full-time basis for a period of at least 1 year, and

(C) such services are of a type historically performed, in the business field of the recipient, by employees.

(3) Requirements.— For purposes of this subsection, the requirements listed in this paragraph are—

(A) paragraphs (3), (4), (7), (16), (17), and (26) of section 401(a),

(B) sections 408(k), 410, 411, 415, and 416, and

(C) sections 79, 106, 117(d), 120, 125, 127, 129, 132, 274(j), 505, and 4980B.

(4) Time when first considered as employee.—

(A) In general.— In the case of any leased employee, paragraph (1) shall apply only for purposes of determining whether the requirements listed in paragraph (3) are met for periods after the close of the period referred to in paragraph (2)(B).

(B) Years of service.— In the case of a person who is an employee of the recipient (whether by reason of this subsection or otherwise), for purposes of the requirements listed in paragraph (3), years of service for the recipient shall be determined by taking into account any period for which such employee would have been a leased employee but for the requirements of paragraph (2)(B).

(5) Safe harbor.—

(A) In general.— In the case of requirements described in subparagraphs (A) and (B) of paragraph (3), this subsection shall not apply to any leased employee with respect to services performed for a recipient if—

(i) such employee is covered by a plan which is maintained by the leasing organization and meets the requirements of subparagraph (B), and

(ii) leased employees (determined without regard to this paragraph) do not constitute more than 20 percent of the recipient's nonhighly compensated work force.

(B) Plan requirements.— A plan meets the requirements of this subparagraph if—

(i) such plan is a money purchase pension plan with a nonintegrated employer contribution rate for each participant of at least 10 percent of compensation,

(ii) such plan provides for full and immediate vesting, and

(iii) each employee of the leasing organization (other than employees who perform substantially all of their services for the leasing organization) immediately participates in such plan.

Clause (iii) shall not apply to any individual whose compensation from the leasing organization in each plan year during the 4-year period ending with the plan year is less than $1,000.

(C) Definitions.— For purposes of this paragraph—

(i) Highly compensated employee.— The term "highly compensated employee" has the meaning given such term by section 414(q).

(ii) Nonhighly compensated work force.— The term "nonhighly compensated work force" means the aggregate number of individuals (other than highly compensated employees)—

(I) who are employees of the recipient (without regard to this subsection) and have performed services for the recipient (or for the recipient and related persons) on a substantially full-time basis for a period of at least 1 year, or

(II) who are leased employees with respect to the recipient (determined without regard to this paragraph).

(iii) Compensation.— The term "compensation" has the same meaning as when used in section 415; except that such term shall include—

(I) any employer contribution under a qualified cash or deferred arrangement to the extent not included in gross income under section 402(e)(3) or 402(h)(1)(B),

(II) any amount which the employee would have received in cash but for an election under a cafeteria plan (within the meaning of section 125), and

(III) any amount contributed to an annuity contract described in section 403(b) pursuant to a salary reduction agreement (within the meaning of section 3121(a)(5)(D)).

(6) Other rules.— For purposes of this subsection

(A) Related persons.— The term "related persons" has the same meaning as when used in section 144(a)(3).

(B) Employees of entities under common control.— The rules of subsections (b), (c), (m), and (o) shall apply.

(o) Regulations.— The Secretary shall prescribe regulations (which may provide rules in addition to the rules contained in subsections (m) and (n)) as may be necessary to prevent the avoidance of any employee benefit requirement listed in subsection (m)(4) or (n)(3) or any requirement under section 457 through the use of—

(1) separate organizations,

(2) employee leasing, or

(3) other arrangements.

The regulations prescribed under subsection (n) shall include provisions to minimize the recordkeeping requirements of subsection (n) in the case of an employer which has no top-heavy plans (within the meaning of section 416(g)) and which uses the services of persons (other than employees) for an insignificant percentage of the employer's total workload.

(p) Qualified Domestic Relations Order Defined.— For purposes of this subsection and section 401(a)(13)—

(1) In general.—

(A) Qualified domestic relations order.— The term "qualified domestic relations order" means a domestic relations order—

(i) which creates or recognizes the existence of an alternate payee's right to, or assigns to an alternate payee the right to, receive all or a portion of the benefits payable with respect to a participant under a plan, and

(ii) with respect to which the requirements of paragraphs (2) and (3) are met.

(B) Domestic relations order.— The term "domestic relations order" means any judgment, decree, or order (including approval of a property settlement agreement) which—

(i) relates to the provision of child support, alimony payments, or marital property rights to a spouse, former spouse, child, or other dependent of a participant, and

(ii) is made pursuant to a State domestic relations law (including a community property law).

(2) Order must clearly specify certain facts.— A domestic relations order meets the requirements of this paragraph only if such order clearly specifies—

IRC Sec. 414 (n)(5)(C)(ii)(I)

(A) the name and last known mailing address (if any) of the participant and the name and mailing address of each alternate payee covered by the order,

(B) the amount or percentage of the participant's benefits to be paid by the plan to each such alternate payee, or the manner in which such amount or percentage is to be determined,

(C) the number of payments or period to which such order applies, and

(D) each plan to which such order applies.

(3) Order may not alter amount, form, etc., of benefits. — A domestic relations order meets the requirements of this paragraph only if such order—

(A) does not require a plan to provide any type or form of benefit, or any option not otherwise provided under the plan,

(B) does not require the plan to provide increased benefits (determined on the basis of actuarial value), and

(C) does not require the payment of benefits to an alternate payee which are required to be paid to another alternate payee under another order previously determined to be a qualified domestic relations order.

(4) Exception for certain payments made after earliest retirement age. —

(A) In general.— A domestic relations order shall not be treated as failing to meet the requirements of subparagraph (A) of paragraph (3) solely because such order requires that payment of benefits be made to an alternate payee—

(i) in the case of any payment before a participant has separated from service, on or after the date on which the participant attains (or would have attained) the earliest retirement age,

(ii) as if the participant had retired on the date on which such payment is to begin

under such order (but taking into account only the present value of the benefits actually accrued and not taking into account the present value of any employer subsidy for early retirement), and

(iii) in any form in which such benefits may be paid under the plan to the participant (other than in the form of a joint and survivor annuity with respect to the alternate payee and his or her subsequent spouse).

For purposes of clause (ii), the interest rate assumption used in determining the present value shall be the interest rate specified in the plan or, if no rate is specified, 5 percent.

(B) Earliest retirement age.— For purposes of this paragraph, the term "earliest retirement age" means the earlier of—

(i) the date on which the participant is entitled to a distribution under the plan, or

(ii) the later of—

(I) the date the participant attains age 50, or

(II) the earliest date on which the participant could begin receiving benefits under the plan if the participant separated from service.

(5) Treatment of former spouse as surviving spouse for purposes of determining survivor benefits. — To the extent provided in any qualified domestic relations order—

(A) the former spouse of a participant shall be treated as a surviving spouse of such participant for purposes of sections 401(a)(11) and 417 (and any spouse of the participant shall not be treated as a spouse of the participant for such purposes), and

(B) if married for at least 1 year, the surviving former spouse shall be treated as meeting the requirements of section 417(d).

IRC Sec. 414 (p)(5)(B)

(6) Plan procedures with respect to orders.—

(A) Notice and determination by administrator.— In the case of any domestic relations order received by a plan—

(i) the plan administrator shall promptly notify the participant and each alternate payee of the receipt of such order and the plan's procedures for determining the qualified status of domestic relations orders, and

(ii) within a reasonable period after receipt of such order, the plan administrator shall determine whether such order is a qualified domestic relations order and notify the participant of such determination.

(B) Plan to establish reasonable procedures.— Each plan shall establish reasonable procedures to determine the qualified status of domestic relations orders and to administer distributions under such qualified orders.

(7) Procedures for period during which determination is being made.—

(A) In general.— During any period in which the issue of whether a domestic relations order is a qualified domestic relations order is being determined (by the plan administrator, by a court of competent jurisdiction, or otherwise), the plan administrator shall separately account for the amounts (hereinafter in this paragraph referred to as the "segregated amounts") which would have been payable to the alternate payee during such period if the order had been determined to be a qualified domestic relations order.

(B) Payment to alternate payee if order determined to be qualified domestic relations order.— If within the 18-month period described in subparagraph (E) the order (or modification thereof) is determined to be a qualified domestic relations order, the plan administrator shall pay the segregated amounts (including any interest thereon) to the person or persons entitled thereto.

(C) Payment to plan participant in certain cases.— If within the 18-month period described in subparagraph (E)—

(i) it is determined that the order is not a qualified domestic relations order, or

(ii) the issue as to whether such order is a qualified domestic relations order is not resolved,

then the plan administrator shall pay the segregated amounts (including any interest thereon) to the person or persons who would have been entitled to such amounts if there had been no order.

(D) Subsequent determination or order to be applied prospectively only.— Any determination that an order is a qualified domestic relations order which is made after the close of the 18-month period described in subparagraph (E) shall be applied prospectively only.

(E) Determination of 18-month period.— For purposes of this paragraph, the 18-month period described in this subparagraph is the 18-month period beginning with the date on which the first payment would be required to be made under the domestic relations order.

(8) Alternate payee defined.— The term "alternate payee" means any spouse, former spouse, child, or other dependent of a participant who is recognized by a domestic relations order as having a right to receive all, or a portion of, the benefits payable under a plan with respect to such participant.

(9) Subsection not to apply to plans to which section 401(a)(13) does not apply.— This subsection shall not apply to any plan to which section 401(a)(13) does not apply. For purposes of this title, except as provided in regulations, any distribution from an annuity contract under section 403(b) pursuant to a qualified domestic relations order shall be treated in the same manner as a distrbution from a plan to which section 401(a)(13) applies.

IRC Sec. 414 (p)(6)

(10) Waiver of certain distribution requirements. — With respect to the requirements of subsections (a) and (k) of section 401, section 403(b), and section 409(d), a plan shall not be treated as failing to meet such requirements solely by reason of payments to an alternative payee pursuant to a qualified domestic relations order.

(11) Application of rules to governmental and church plans. — For purposes of this title, a distribution or payment from a governmental plan (as defined in subsection (d)) or a church plan (as described in subsection (e)) shall be treated as made pursuant to a qualified domestic relations order if it is made pursuant to a domestic relations order which meets the requirement of clause (i) of paragraph (1)(A).

(12) Consultation with the Secretary. — In prescribing regulations under this subsection and section 401(a)(13), the Secretary of Labor shall consult with the Secretary.

(q) Highly Compensated Employee. —

(1) In general. — The term "highly compensated employee" means any employee who, during the year or the preceding year—

(A) was at any time a 5-percent owner,

(B) received compensation from the employer in excess of $75,000,

(C) received compensation from the employer in excess of $50,000 and was in the top-paid group of employees for such year, or

(D) was at any time an officer and received compensation greater than 50 percent of the amount in effect under section 415(b)(1)(A) for such year.

The Secretary shall adjust the $75,000 and $50,000 amounts under this pargaraph at the same time and in the same manner as under section 415(d).

(2) Special rule for current year. — In the case of the year for which the relevant determination is being made, an employee not described in subparagraph (B), (C), or (D) of paragraph (1) for the preceding year (without regard to this paragraph) shall not be treated as described in subparagraph (B), (C), or (D) of paragraph (1) unless such employee is a member of the group consisting of the 100 employees paid the greatest compensation during the year for which such determination is being made.

(3) 5-percent owner. — An employee shall be treated as a 5-percent owner for any year if at any time during such year such employee was a 5-percent owner (as defined in section 416(i)(1)) of the employer.

(4) Top-paid group. — An employee is in the top-paid group of employees for any year if such employee is in the group consisting of the top 20 percent of the employees when ranked on the basis of compensation paid during such year.

(5) Special rules for treatment of officers. —

(A) Not more than 50 officers taken into account. For purposes of paragraph (1)(D), no more than 50 employees (or, if lesser, the greater of 3 employees or 10 percent of the employees) shall be treated as officers.

(B) At least 1 officer taken into account. — If for any year no officer of the employer is described in paragraph (1)(D), the highest paid officer of the employer for such year shall be treated as described in such paragraph.

(6) Treatment of certain family members. —

(A) In general. — If any individual is a member of the family of a 5-percent owner or of a highly compensated employee in the group consisting of the 10 highly compensated employees paid the greatest compensation during the year, then—

(i) such individual shall not be considered a separate employee, and

IRC Sec. 414 (q)(6)(A)(i)

(ii) any compensation paid to such individual (and any applicable contribution or benefit on behalf of such individual) shall be treated as if it were paid to (or on behalf of) the 5-percent owner or highly compensated employee.

(B) Family.— For purposes of subparagraph (A), the term "family" means, with respect to any employee, such employee's spouse and lineal ascendants or descendants and the spouses of such lineal ascendants or descendants.

(C) Rules to apply to other provisions.—

(i) In general.— Except as provided in regulations and in clause (ii), the rules of subparagraph (A) shall be applied in determining the compensation of (or any contributions or benefits on behalf of) any employee for purposes of any section with respect to which a highly compensated employee is defined by reference to this subsection.

(ii) Exception for determining integration levels.— Clause (i) shall not apply in determining the portion of the compensation of a participant which is under the integration level for purposes of section 401(l).

(7) Compensation.— For purposes of this subsection—

(A) In general.— The term "compensation" means compensation within the meaning of section 415(c)(3).

(B) Certain provisions not taken into account.— The determination under subparagraph (A) shall be made—

(i) without regard to sections 125, 402(e)(3), and 402(h)(1)(B), and

(ii) in the case of employer contributions made pursuant to a salary reduction agreement, without regard to section 403(b).

(8) Excluded employees.— For purposes of subsection (r) and for purposes of determining the number of employees in the top-paid

group under paragraph (4) or the number of officers taken into account under paragraph (5), the following employees shall be excluded—

(A) employees who have not completed 6 months of service,

(B) employees who normally work less than 17½ hours per week,

(C) employees who normally work during not more than 6 months during any year,

(D) employees who have not attained age 21, and

(E) except to the extent provided in regulations, employees who are included in a unit of employees covered by an agreement which the Secretary of Labor finds to be a collective bargaining agreement between employee representatives and the employer.

Except as provided by the Secretary, the employer may elect to apply subparagraph (A), (B), (C), or (D) by substituting a shorter period of service, smaller number of hours or months, or lower age for the period of service, number of hours or months, or age (as the case may be) than that specified in such subparagraph.

(9) Former employees.— A former employee shall be treated as a highly compensated employee if—

(A) such employee was a highly compensated employee when such employee separated from service, or

(B) such employee was a highly compensated employee at any time after attaining age 55.

(10) Coordination with other provisions.— Subsections (b), (c), (m), (n), and (o) shall be applied before the application of this section.

(11) Special rule for nonresident aliens.— For purposes of this subsection and subsection (r), employees who are nonresident aliens and who receive no earned income (within the meaning of section 911(d)(2)) from the employer which constitutes income from sources within the United States (within the meaning of section 861(a)(3)) shall not be treated as employees.

(12) Simplified method for determining highly compensated employees.—

(A) In general.— If an election by the employer under this paragraph applies to any year, in determining whether an employee is a highly compensated employee for such year—

(i) subparagraph (B) of paragraph (1) shall be applied by substituting ''$50,000'' for ''$75,000'', and

(ii) subparagraph (C) of paragraph (1) shall not apply.

(B) Requirement for election.— An election under this paragraph shall not apply to any year unless—

(i) at all times during such year, the employer maintained significant business activities (and employed employees) in at least 2 significantly separate geographic areas, and

(ii) the employer satisfies such other conditions as the Secretary may prescribe.

(r) Special Rules for Separate Line of Business.—

(1) In general.— For purposes of sections 129(d)(8) and 410(b), an employer shall be treated as operating separate lines of business during any year if the employer for bona fide business reasons operates separate lines of business.

(2) Line of business must have 50 employees, etc.— A line of business shall not be treated as separate under paragraph (1) unless—

(A) such line of business has at least 50 employees who are not excluded under subsection (q)(8),

(B) the employer notifies the Secretary that such line of business is being treated as separate for purposes of paragraph (1), and

(C) such line of business meets guidelines prescribed by the Secretary or the employer receives a determination from the Secretary that such line of business may be treated as separate for purposes of paragraph (1).

(3) Safe harbor rule.—

(A) In general.— The requirements of subparagraph (C) of paragraph (2) shall not apply to any line of business if the highly compensated employee percentage with respect to such line of business is—

(i) not less than one-half, and

(ii) not more than twice,

the percentage which highly compensated employees are of all employees of the employer. An employer shall be treated as meeting the requirements of clause (i) if at least 10 percent of all highly compensated employees of the employer perform services solely for such line of business.

(B) Determination may be based on preceding year.— The requirements of subparagraph (A) shall be treated as met with respect to any line of business if such requirements were met with respect to such line of business for the preceding year and if—

(i) no more than a de minimis number of employees were shifted to or from the line of business after the close of the preceding year, or

(ii) the employees shifted to or from the line of business after the close of the preceding year contained a substantially proportional number of highly compensated employees.

(4) Highly compensated employee percentage defined.— For purposes of this subsection, the term ''highly compensated employee percentage'' means the percentage which highly compensated employees performing services for the line of business are of all employees performing services for the line of business.

(5) Allocation of benefits to line of business. — For purposes of this subsection, benefits which are attributable to services provided to a line of business shall be treated as provided by such line of business.

(6) Headquarters personnel, etc. — The Secretary shall prescribe rules providing for—

(A) the allocation of headquarters personnel among the lines of business of the employer, and

(B) the treatment of other employees providing services for more than 1 line of business of the employer or not in lines of business meeting the requirements of paragraph (2).

(7) Separate operating units. — For purposes of this subsection, the term "separate line of business" includes an operating unit in a separate geographic area separately operated for a bona fide business reason.

(8) Affiliated service groups. — This subsection shall not apply in the case of any affiliated service group (within the meaning of section 414(m)).

(s) Compensation. — For purposes of any applicable provision—

(1) In general. — Except as provided in this subsection, the term "compensation" has the meaning given such term by section 415(c)(3)

(2) Employer may elect to treat certain deferrals as compensation. — An employer may elect to include as compensation any amount which is contributed by the employer pursuant to a salary reduction agreement and which is not includible in the gross income of an employee under section 125, 402(e)(3), 402(h), or 403(b).

(3) Alternative determination of compensation. — The Secretary shall by regulation provide for alternative methods of determining compensation which may be used by an employer, except that such regulations shall provide that an employer may not use an alternative method if the use of such method discriminates in favor of highly compensated employees (within the meaning of subsection (q)).

(4) Applicable provision. — For purposes of this subsection, the term "applicable provision" means any provision which specifically refers to this subsection.

(t) Application of Controlled Group Rules to Certain Employee Benefits.—

(1) In general. — All employees who are treated as employed by a single employer under subsection (b), (c), or (m) shall be treated as employed by a single employer for purposes of an applicable section. The provisions of subsection (o) shall apply with respect to the requirements of an applicable section.

(2) Applicable section. — For purposes of this subsection, the term "applicable section" means section 79, 106, 117(d), 120, 125, 127, 129, 132, 274(j), 505, or 4980B.

SEC. 415. LIMITATIONS ON BENEFITS AND CONTRIBUTIONS UNDER QUALIFIED PLANS.

(a) General Rule.—

(1) Trusts. — A trust which is a part of a pension, profit-sharing, or stock bonus plan shall not constitute a qualified trust under section 401(a) if—

(A) in the case of a defined benefit plan, the plan provides for the payment of benefits with respect to a participant which exceeds the limitation of subsection (b),

(B) in the case of a defined contribution plan, contributions and other additions under the plan with respect to any participant for any taxable year exceeds the limitation of subsection (c), or

(C) in any case in which an individual is a participant in both a defined benefit plan and a defined contribution plan maintained by the employer, the trust has been disqualified under subsection (g),

(2) Section applies to certain annuities and accounts. — In the case of—

(A) an employee annuity plan described in section 403(a), or

(B) an annuity contract described in section 403(b), or

(C) a simplified employee pension described in section 408(k),

such a contract, plan, or pension shall not be considered to be described in section 403(a), 403(b), or 408(k), as the case may be, unless it satisfies the requirements of subparagraph (A) or subparagraph (B) of paragraph (1), whichever is appropriate, and has not been disqualified under subsection (g). In the case of an annuity contract described in section 403(b), the preceding sentence shall apply only to the portion of the annuity contract which exceeds the limitation of subsection (b) or the limitation of subsection (c), whichever is appropriate, and the amount of the contribution for such portion shall reduce the exclusion allowance as provided in section 403(b)(2).

(b) Limitation for Defined Benefit Plans. —

(1) In general. — Benefits with respect to a participant exceed the limitation of this subsection if, when expressed as an annual benefit (within the meaning of paragraph (2)), such annual benefit is greater than the lesser of—

(A) $90,000, or

(B) 100 percent of the participant's average compensation for his high 3 years.

(2) Annual Benefit. —

(A) In general. — For purposes of paragraph (1), the term "annual benefit" means a benefit payable annually in the form of a straight life annuity (with no ancillary benefits) under a plan to which employees do not contribute and under which no rollover con-

tributions (as defined in sections 402(c), 403(a)(4), and 408(d)(3)) are made.

(B) Adjustment for certain other forms of benefit. — If the benefit under the plan is payable in any form other than the form described in subparagraph (A), or if the employees contribute to the plan or make rollover contributions (as defined in section 402(c), 403(a)(4), and 408(d)(3)), the determinations as to whether the limitation described in paragraph (1) has been satisfied shall be made, in accordance with regulations prescribed by the Secretary, by adjusting such benefit so that it is equivalent to the benefit described in subparagraph (A). For purposes of this subparagraph, any ancillary benefit which is not directly related to retirement income benefits shall not be taken into account; and that portion of any joint and survivor annuity which constitutes a qualified joint and survivor annuity (as defined in section 417) shall not be taken into account.

(C) Adjustment to $90,000 limit where benefit begins before the social security retirement age. — If the retirement income benefit under the plan begins before the social security retirement age, the determination as to whether the $90,000 limitation set forth in paragraph (1)(A) has been satisfied shall be made, in accordance with regulations prescribed by the Secretary, by reducing the limitation of paragraph (1)(A) so that such limitation (as so reduced) equals an annual benefit (beginning when such retirement income benefit begins) which is equivalent to a $90,000 annual benefit beginning at the social security retirement age. The reduction under this subparagraph shall be made in such manner as the Secretary may prescribe which is consistent with the reduction for old-age insurance benefits commencing before the social security retirement age under the Social Security Act.

(D) Adjustment to $90,000 limit where benefit begins after the social security retirement age. — If the retirement income benefit under the plan begins after the social security retirement age, the determination as to

IRC Sec. 415 (b)(2)(D)

whether the $90,000 limitation set forth in paragraph (1)(A) has been satisfied shall be made, in accordance with regulations prescribed by the Secretary, by increasing the limitation of paragraph (1)(A) so that such limitation (as so increased) equals an annual benefit (beginning when such retirement income benefit begins) which is equivalent to a $90,000 annual benefit beginning at the social security retirement age.

◊ ◊ ◊

Editor's Note: Code §415(b)(2)(E), below, appears as amended by §767(b) of the Retirement Protection Act of 1994 (enacted as part of the Uruguay Round Agreements Act, P.L. 103-465). That Act redesignated §415(b)(2)(E)(ii) and (iii) as §415(b)(2)(E)(iii) and (iv), respectively, struck §415(b)(2)(E)(i), and added new §415(b)(2)(E)(i), (ii), and (v), all as set forth below. The changes are effective generally with respect to plan years and limitation years beginning after December 31, 1994, except that employers may elect to treat the changes as being effective on or after December 8, 1994. Note, however, that §767(d)(2) of the 1994 Act provides that a participant's accrued benefit will not be considered to be reduced in violation of the anti-cutback rule of Code §411(d)(6) or ERISA §204(g) merely because the benefit is determined in accordance with Code §417(e)(3)(A) or ERISA §205(g)(3), as amended by that Act, or because the plan applies Code §415(b)(2)(E), as amended by the Act. Also, §767(d)(3) of the 1994 Act provides that an accrued benefit will not be required to be reduced below the accrued benefit as of the last day of the last plan year beginning before January 1, 1995, merely because of the changes in these provisions made by the Act. Act §767(d)(3) further provides that a plan that operates in accordance with the amendments made by Act §767(b) will not be disqualified under Code §401 or be treated as not being operated in accordance with its plan document until such date as the Secretary of the Treasury provides merely becasue the plan

has not been amended to include the amendments made by Act §767(b).

◊ ◊ ◊

(E) Limitation on certain assumptions.—

[(i) For purposes of adjusting any benefit or limitation under subparagraph (B) or (C), the interest rate assumption shall not be less than the greater of 5 percent or the rate specified in the plan.]

(i) Except as provided in clause (ii), for purposes of adjusting any benefit or limitation under subparagraph (B) or (C), the interest rate assumption shall not be less than the greater of 5 percent or the rate specified in the plan.

(ii) For purposes of adjusting the benefit or limitation of any form of benefit subject to section 417(e)(3), the applicable interest rate (as defined in section 417(e)(3)) shall be substituted for "5 percent" in clause (i).

[(ii)]*(iii)* For purposes of adjusting any limitation under subparagraph (D), the interest rate assumption shall not be greater than the lesser of 5 percent or the rate specified in the plan.

[(iii)]*(iv)* For purposes of this subsection, no adjustments under subsection (d)(1) shall be taken into account before the year for which such adjustment first takes effect.

(v) For purposes of adjusting any benefit or limitation under subparagraph (B), (C), or (D), the mortality table used shall be the table prescribed by the Secretary. Such table shall be based on the prevailing commissioners' standard table (described in section 807(d)(5)(A)) used to determine reserves for group annuity contracts issued on the date the adjustment is being made (without regard to any other subparagraph of section 807(d)(5)).

(F) Plans maintained by governments and tax-exempt organizations.— In the case of a governmental plan (within the meaning of section 414(d)), a plan maintained by an organization (other than a governmental unit) exempt from tax under this subtitle, or a qualified merchant marine plan—

(i) subparagraph (C) shall be applied—

(I) by substituting "age 62" for "social security retirement age" each place it appears, and

(II) as if the last sentence thereof read as follows: "The reduction under this subparagraph shall not reduce the limitation of paragraph (1)(A) below (i) $75,000 if the benefit begins at or after age 55, or (ii) if the benefit begins before age 55, the equivalent of the $75,000 limitation for age 55.", and

(ii) subparagraph (D) shall be applied by substituting "age 65" for "social security retirement age" each place it appears.

For purposes of this subparagraph, the term "qualified merchant marine plan" means a plan in existence on January 1, 1986, the participants in which are merchant marine officers holding licenses issued by the Secretary of Transportation under title 46, United State Code.

(G) Special limitation for qualified police or firefighters.— In the case of a qualified participant—

(i) subparagraph (C) shall not reduce the limitation of paragraph (1)(A) to an amount less than $50,000, and

(ii) the rules of subparagraph (F) shall apply.

The Secretary shall adjust the $50,000 amount in clause (i) at the same time and in the same manner as under section 415(d).

(H) Qualified participant defined.— For purposes of subparagraph (G), the term "qualified participant" means a participant—

(i) in a defined benefit plan which is maintained by a State or political subdivision thereof,

(ii) with respect to whom the period of service taken into account in determining the amount of the benefit under such defined benefit plan includes at least 15 years of service of the participant—

(I) as a full-time employee of any police department or fire department which is organized and operated by the State or political subdivision maintaining such defined benefit plan to provide police protection, firefighting services, or emergency medical services for any area within the jurisdiction of such State or political subdivision, or

(II) as a member of the Armed Forces of the United States.

(3) Average compensation for high 3 years.— For purposes of paragraph (1), a participant's high 3 years shall be the period of consecutive calendar years (not more than 3) during which the participant both was an active participant in the plan and had the greatest aggregate compensation from the employer. In the case of an employee within the meaning of section 401(c)(1), the preceding sentence shall be applied by substituting for "compensation from the employer" the following "the participant's earned income (within the meaning of section 401(c)(2) but determined without regard to any exclusion under section 911)".

(4) Total annual benefit not in excess of $10,000.— Notwithstanding the preceding provisions of this subsection, the benefits payable with respect to a participant under any defined benefit plan shall be deemed not to exceed the limitation of this subsection if—

(A) the retirement benefits payable with respect to such participant under such plan and under all other defined benefit plans of the employer do not exceed $10,000 for the plan year, or for any prior plan year, and

(B) the employer has not at any time maintained a defined contribution plan in which the participant participated.

(5) Reduction for participation or service of less than 10 years.—

(A) Dollar limitation.— In the case of an employee who has less than 10 years of participation in a defined benefit plan, the limitation referred to in paragraph (1)(A) shall be the limitation determined under such paragraph (without regard to this paragraph) multiplied by a fraction—

(i) the numerator of which is the number of years (or part thereof) of participation in the defined benefit plan of the employer, and

(ii) the denominator of which is 10.

(B) Compensation and benefits limitations.—The provisions of subparagraph (A) shall apply to the limitation under paragraphs (1)(B) and (4) and subsection (e), except that such subparagraph shall be applied with respect to years of service with an employer rather than years of participation in a plan.

(C) Limitation on reduction.— In no event shall subparagraph (A) or (B) reduce the limitations referred to in paragraphs (1) and (4) to an amount less than 1/10 of such limitation (determined without regard to this paragraph).

(D) Application to changes in benefit structure.— To the extent provided in regulations, subparagraph (A) shall be applied separately with respect to each change in the benefit structure of a plan.

(6) Computation of benefits and contributions.— The computation of—

(A) benefits under a defined contribution plan, for purposes of section 401(a)(4),

(B) contributions made on behalf of a paricipant in a defined benefit plan, for purposes of section 401(a)(4), and

(C) contributions and benefits provided for a participant in a plan described in section 414(k), for purposes of this section

shall not be made on a basis inconsistent with regulations prescribed by the Secretary.

(7) Benefits under certain collectively bargained plans.—For a year, the limitation referred to in paragraph (i)(B) shall not apply to benefits with respect to a participant under a defined benefit plan—

(A) which is maintained for such year pursuant to a collective bargaining agreement between employee representatives and one or more employers,

(B) which, at all times during such year, has at least 100 participants,

(C) under which benefits are determined solely by reference to length of service, the particular years during which service was rendered, age at retirement, and date of retirement,

(D) which provide that an employee who has at least 4 years of service has a nonforfeitable right to 100 percent of his accrued benefit derived from employer contributions, and

(E) which requires, as a condition of participation in the plan, that an employee complete a period of not more than 60 consecutive days of service with the employer or employers maintaining the plan.

This paragraph shall not apply to a participant whose compensation for any 3 years during the 10-year period immediately preceding the year in which he separates from service exceeded the average compensation for such 3 years of all participants in such plan. This paragraph shall not apply to a participant for any period for which he is a participant under another plan to which this section applies which is maintained by an employer maintaining this plan. For any year for which the paragraph applies to benefits with respect to a participant, paragraph (1)(A) and subsection (d)(1)(A) shall be applied with respect to such participant by substituting the greater of $68,212 or one-half of the amount otherwise

IRC Sec. 415 (b)(5)

applicable for such year under paragraph (1)(A) for $90,000.

(8) Social Security retirement age defined.— For purposes of this subsection, the term "social security retirement age" means the age used as the retirement age under section 216(l)(2) of the Social Security Act, except that such section shall be applied—

(A) without regard to the age increase factor, and

(B) as if the early retirement age under section 216(l)(2) of such Act were 62.

(9) Special rule for commercial airline pilots.—

(A) In general.— Except as provided in subparagraph (B), in the case of any participant who is a commercial airline pilot—

(i) the rule of paragraph (2)(F)(i)(II) shall apply, and

(ii) if, as of the time the participant's retirement, regulations prescribed by the Federal Aviation Administration require an individual to separate from service as a commercial airline pilot after attaining any age occurring on or after age 60 and before the social security retirement age, paragraph (2)(C) (after application of clause (i) shall be applied by substituting such age for the social security retirement age.

(B) Individuals who separate from service before age 60.— If a participant, rules of paragraph (2)(F) shall apply.

(10) Special rule for state and local government plans.—

(A) Limitation to equal accrued benefit.— In the case of a plan maintained for its employees by any State or political subdivision thereof, or by any agency or instrumentality of the foregoing, the limitation with respect to a qualified participant under this subsection shall not be less than the accrued benefit of the participant under the plan (determined

without regard to any amendment of the plan made after October 14, 1987)

(B) Qualified participant.— For purposes of this paragraph, the term "qualified participant" means a participant who first became a participant in the plan maintained by the employer before January 1, 1990.

(C) Election.— This paragraph shall not apply to any plan unless each employer maintaining the plan elects before the close of the 1st plan year beginning after December 31, 1989, to have this subsection (other than paragraph (2)(G) applied without regard to paragraph (2)(F).

◊ ◊ ◊

Editor's Note: Code §415(c)(1)(A) and 415(d) as set forth below appear as amended by §732(b) of the Retirement Protection Act of 1994 (enacted as part of the Uruguay Round Agreements Act, P.L. 103-465). The amendments apply generally to years beginning after December 31, 1994. However, §732(e)(2) of the 1994 Act provides that the amendment providing for rounding of indexed amounts will not apply to any year to the extent that the rounding would require the indexed amount to be reduced below the amount in effect for years beginning in 1994. Further, §767(d)(3) of the 1994 Act provides that a plan that operates in accordance with the amendments made by Act §767(b) will not be disqualified under Code §401 or be treated as not being operated in accordance with its plan document until such date as the Secretary of the Treasury provides merely becasue the plan has not been amended to include the amendments made by Act §767(b).

◊ ◊ ◊

(c) Limitation for Defined Contribution Plans.—

(1) In general.— Contributions and other additions with respect to a participant exceed the limitation of this subsection if, when expressed as an annual addition (within the meaning of paragraph (2)) to the participant's account, such annual addition is greater than the lesser of—

(A) $30,000 [(or, if greater, ¼ of the dollar limitation in effect under subsection (b)(1)(A))], or,

(B) 25 percent of the participant's compensation.

(2) Annual addition.— For purposes of paragraph (1), the term "annual addition" means the sum for any year of—

(A) employer contributions,

(B) the employee contributions, and

(C) forfeitures.

For the purposes of this paragraph, employee contributions under subparagraph (B) are determined without regard to any rollover contributions (as defined in sections 402(c), 403(a)(4), 403(b)(8), and 408(d)(3)) without regard to employee contributions to a simplified employee pension which are excludable from gross income under section 408(k)(6). Subparagraph (B) of paragraph (1) shall not apply to any contribution for medical benefits (within the meaning of section 419A(f)(2)) after separation from service which is treated as an annual addition.

(3) Participant's compensation.— For purposes of paragraph (1)—

(A) In general.— The term "participant's compensation" means the compensation of the participant from the employer for the year.

(B) Special rule for self-employed individuals.— In the case of an employee within the meaning of section 401(c)(1), subparagraph (A) shall be applied by substituting "the participant's earned income (within the meaning of section 401(c)(2) but determined without regard to any exclusion under section 911)" for "compensation of the participant from the employer".

(C) Special rules for permanent and total disability.— In the case of a participant in any defined contribution plan—

(i) who is permanently and totally disabled (as defined in section 22(e)(3)).

(ii) who is not a highly compensated employee (within the meaning of section 414(q)), and

(iii) with respect to whom the employer elects, at such time and in such manner as the Secretary may prescribe, to have this subparagraph apply,

the term "participant's compensation" means the compensation the participant would have received for the year if the participant was paid at the rate of compensation paid immediately before becoming permanently and totally disabled. This subparagraph shall apply only if contributions made with respect to amounts treated as compensation under this subparagraph are nonforfeitable when made.

(4) Special election for section 403(b) contracts purchased by educational organizations, hospitals, home health service agencies and certain churches, etc.—

(A) In the case of amounts contributed for an annuity contract described in section 403(b) for the year in which occurs a participant's separation from the service with an educational organization, a hospital, a home health service agency, a health and welfare service agency, or a church, convention or association of churches, or an organization described in section 414(e)(3)(B)(ii), at the election of the participant there is substituted for the amount specified in paragraph (1)(B) the amount of the exclusion allowance which would be determined under section 403(b)(2) (without regard to this section) for the participant's taxable year in which such separation occurs if the participant's years of service were computed only by taking into account his service for the employer (as determined for purposes of section 403(b)(2)) during the period of year

IRC Sec. 415 (c)(1)(A)

(not exceeding ten) ending on the date of such separation.

(B) In the case of amounts contributed for an annuity contract described in section 403(b) for any year in the case of a participant who is an employee of an educational organization, a hospital, a home health service agency, a health and welfare service agency, or a church, convention or association of churches, or an organization described in section 414(e)(3)(B)(ii), at the election of the participant there is substituted for the amount specified in paragraph (1)(B) the least of—

(i) 25 percent of the participant's includible compensation (as defined in section 403(b)(3)) plus $4,000,

(ii) the amount of the exclusion allowance determined for the year under section 403(b)(2), or

(iii) $15,000.

(C) In the case of amounts contributed for an annuity contract described in section 403(b) for any year for a participant who is an employee of an educational organization, a hospital, a home health service agency, a health and welfare service agency, or a church, convention or association of churches, or an organization described in section 414(e)(3)(B)(ii), at the election of the participant the provisions of section 403(b)(2)(A) shall not apply.

(D)(i) The provisions of this paragraph apply only if the participant elects its application at the time and in the manner provided under regulations prescribed by the Secretary. Not more than one election may be made under subparagraph (A) by any participant. A participant who elects to have the provisions of subparagraph (A), (B), or (C) of this paragraph apply to him may not elect to have any other subparagraph of this paragraph apply to him. Any election made under this paragraph is irrevocable.

(ii) For purposes of this paragraph the term "educational organization" means an educational organization as described in section 170(b)(1)(A)(ii).

(iii) For purposes of this paragraph the term "home health service agency" means an organization described in subsection 501(c)(3) which is exempt from tax under section 501(a) and which has been determined by the Secretary of Health and Human Services to be a home health agency (as defined in section 1861(o) of the Social Security Act).

(iv) For purposes of this paragraph, the terms "church" and "convention or association of churches" have the same meaning as when used in section 414(e).

(5) [Repealed.]

(6) **Special rule for employee stock ownership plans.**— If no more than one-third of the employer contributions to an employee stock ownership plan (as described in section 4975(e)(7)) for a year which are deductible under paragraph (3) of section 404(a) are allocated to highly compensated employees (within the meaning of section 414(q)), the limitations imposed by this section shall not apply to—

(A) forfeitures of employer securities (within the meaning of section 409) under such an employee stock ownership plan if such securities were acquired with the proceeds of a loan (as described in section 404(a)(9)(A)), or

(B) employer contribtuions to such an employee stock ownership plan which are deductible under section 404(a)(9)(B) and charged against the participant's account.

(7) **Certain contributions by church plans not treated as exceeding limits.**—

(A) Alternative exclusion allowance.— Any contribution or addition with respect to any participant, when expressed as an annual addition, which is allocable to the application of section 403(b)(2)(D) to such participant for such year, shall be treated as not exceeding the limitations of paragraph (1).

(B) Contributions not in excess of $40,000 ($10,000 per year).—

(i) In general.— Notwithstanding any other provision of this subsection, at the election of a participant who is an employee of a church, a convention or association of churches, including an organization described in section 414(e)(3)(B)(ii), contributions and other additions for an annuity contract or retirement income account described in section 403(b) with respect to such participant, when expressed as an annual addition to such participant's account, shall be treated as not exceeding the limitation of paragraph (1) if such annual addition is not in excess of $10,000.

(ii) $40,000 aggregate limitation.— The total amount of additions with respect to any participant which may be taken into account for purposes of this subparagraph for all years may not exceed $40,000.

(iii) No election if paragraph (4)(A) election made.— No election may be made under this subparagraph for any year if an election is made under paragraph (4)(A) for such year.

(C) Annual addition.— For purposes of this paragraph, the term "annual addition" has the meaning given such term by paragraph (2).

[(d) Cost-of-Living Adjustments.—

[(1) In general.— The Secretary shall adjust annually—

[(A) the $90,000 amount in subsection (b)(1)(A), and

[(B) in the case of a participant who is separated from service, the amount taken into account under subsection (b)(1)(B),

for increases in the cost of living in accordance with regulations prescribed by the Secretary. Such regulations shall provide for adjustment procedures which are similar to

the procedures used to adjust benefit amounts under section 215(i)(2)(A) of the Social Security Act.

[(2) Base periods.— The base period taken into account—

[(A) for purposes of subparagraph (A) of paragraph (1) is the calendar quarter beginning October 1, 1986, and

[(B) for purposes of subparagraph (B) of paragraph (1) is the last calendar quarter of the calendar year before the calendar year in which the participant is separated from service.

[(3) Freeze on adjustment to defined contribution and benefit limits.— The Secretary shall not make any adjustment under subparagraph (A) of paragraph (1) with respect to any year beginning after December 31, 1982, and before January 1, 1988.]

(d) Cost-of-Living Adjustments.

(1) In general. The Secretary shall adjust annually

(A) the $90,000 amount in subsection (b)(1)(A),

(B) in the case of a participant who separated from service, the amount taken into account under subsection (b)(1)(B), and

(C) the $30,000 amount in subsection (c)(1)(A),

for increases in the cost-of-living in accordance with regulations prescribed by the Secretary.

(2) Method. The regulations prescribed under paragraph (1) shall provide for—

(A) an adjustment with respect to any calendar year based on the increase in the applicable index for the calendar quarter ending September 30 of the preceding calendar year over such index for the base period, and

(B) adjustment procedures which are similar to the procedures used to adjust benefit

amounts under section 215(i)(2)(A) of the Social Security Act.

(3) Base period. For purposes of paragraph (2)

(A) $90,000 amount. The base period taken into account for purposes of paragraph (1)(A) is the calendar quarter beginning October 1, 1986.

(B) Separations after December 31, 1994. The base period taken into account for purposes of paragraph (1)(B) with respect to individuals separating from service with the employer after December 31, 1994, is the calendar quarter beginning July 1 of the calendar year preceding the calendar year in which such separation occurs.

(C) Separations before January 1, 1995. The base period taken into account for purposes of paragraph (1)(B) with respect to individuals separating from service with the employer before January 1, 1995, is the calendar quarter beginning October 1 of the calendar year preceding the calendar year in which such separation occurs.

(D) $30,000 amount. The base period taken into account for purposes of paragraph (1)(C) is the calendar quarter beginning October 1, 1993.

(4) Rounding. Any increase under subparagraph (A) or (C) of paragraph (1) which is not a multiple of $5,000 shall be rounded to the next lowest multiple of $5,000.

(e) Limitation in Case of Defined Benefit Plan and Defined Contribution Plan for Same Employee.—

(1) In general.— In any case in which an individual is a participant in both a defined benefit plan and a defined contribution plan maintained by the same employer, the sum of the defined benefit plan fraction and the defined contribution benefit plan fraction and the defined contribution plan fraction for any year may not exceed 1.0.

(2) Defined benefit plan fraction.— For purposes of this subsection, the defined benefit plan fraction for any year is a fraction—

(A) the numerator of which is the projected annual benefit of the participant under the plan (determined as of the close of the year), and

(B) the denominator of which is the lesser of—

(i) the product of 1.25, multiplied by the dollar limitation in effect under subsection (b)(1)(A) for such year, or

(ii) the product of—

(I) 1.4, multiplied by

(II) the amount which may be taken into account under subsection (b)(1)(B) with respect to such individual under the plan for such year.

(3) Defined contribution plan fraction.— For purposes of this subsection, the defined contribution plan fraction for any year is a fraction—

(A) the numerator of which is the sum of the annual additions to the participant's account as of the close of the year, and

(B) the denominator of which is the sum of the lesser of the following amounts determined for such year and for each prior year of service with the employer:

(i) the product of 1.25, multiplied by the dollar limitation in effect under subsection (c)(1)(A) for such year (determined without regard to subsection (c)(6)), or

(ii) the product of—

(I) 1.4, multiplied by

(II) the amount which may be taken into account under subsection (c)(1)(B) (or subsection (c)(7), if applicable) with respect to such individual under such plan for such year.

(4) Special transition rules for defined contribution fraction.— In applying paragraph (3) with respect to years beginning before January 1, 1976—

(A) the aggregate amount taken into account under paragraph (3)(A) may not exceed the aggregate amount taken into account under paragraph (3)(B), and

(B) the amount taken into account under subsection (c)(2)(B)(i) for any year concerned is an amount equal to—

(i) the excess of the aggregate amount of employee contributions for all years beginning before January 1, 1976, during which the employee was an active participant of the plan, over 10 percent of the employee's aggregate compensation for all such years, multiplied by

(ii) a fraction the numerator of which is 1 and the denominator of which is the number of years beginning before January 1, 1976, during which the employee was an active participant in the plan.

Employee contributions made on or after October 2, 1973, shall be taken into account under subparagraph (B) of the preceding sentence only to the extent that the amount of such contributions does not exceed the maximum amount of contributions permissible under the plan as in effect on October 2, 1973.

(5) Special rules for sections 403(b) and 408.— For purposes of this section, any annuity contract described in section 403(b) (except in the case of a participant who has elected under subsection (c)(4)(D) to have the provisions of subsection (c)(4)(C) apply) for the benefit of a participant shall be treated as a defined contribution plan maintained by each employer with respect to which the participant has the control required under subsection (b) or (c) of section 414 (as modified by subsection (h)). For purposes of this section, any contribution by an employer to a simplified employee pension for an individual for a taxable year shall be treated as an employer contribution to a defined contribution plan for such individual for such year. In the case of any annuity contract described in section 403(b), the amount of the contribution disqualified by reason of subsection (g) shall reduce the exclusion allowance as provided in section 403(b)(2).

(6) Special transition rule for defined contribution fraction for years ending after December 31, 1982.—

(A) In general.— At the election of the plan administrator, in applying paragraph (3) with respect to any year ending after December 31, 1982, the amount taken into account under paragraph (3)(B) with respect to each participant for all years ending before January 1, 1983, shall be an amount equal to the product of—

(i) the amount determined under paragraph (3)(B) (as in effect for the year ending in 1982) for the year ending in 1982, multiplied by

(ii) the transition fraction.

(B) Transition fraction.— The term "transition fraction" means a fraction—

(i) the numerator of which is the lesser of—

(I) $51,875, or

(II) 1.4, multiplied by 25 percent of the compensation of the participant for the year ending in 1981, and

(ii) the denominator of which is the lesser of—

(I) $41,500, or

(II) 25 percent of the compensation of the participant for the year ending in 1981.

(C) Plan must have been in existence on or before July 1, 1982. This paragraph shall apply only to plans which were in existence on or before July 1, 1982.

IRC Sec. 415 (e)(4)

(f) Combining of Plans.—

(1) In general.— For purposes of applying the limitations of subsections (b), (c), and (e)—

(A) all defined benefit plans (whether or not terminated) of an employer are to be treated as one defined benefit plan, and

(B) all defined contribution plans (whether or not terminated) of an employer are to be treated as one defined contribution plan.

(2) Annual compensation taken into account for defined benefit plans.— If the employer has more than one defined benefit plan—

(A) subsection (b)(1)(B) shall be applied separately with respect to each such plan, but

(B) in applying subsection (b)(1)(B) to the aggregate of such defined benefit plans for purposes of this subsection, the high 3 years of compensation taken into account shall be the period of consecutive calendar years (not more than 3) during which the individual had the greatest aggregate compensation from the employer.

(g) Aggregation of Plans.— The Secretary, in applying the provisions of this section to benefits or contributions under more than one plan maintained by the same employer, and to any trust, contracts, accounts, or bonds referred to in subsection (a)(2), with respect to which the participant has the control required under section 414(b) or (c), as modified by subsection (h), shall, under regulations prescribed by the Secretary, disqualify one or more trusts, plans, contracts, accounts, or bonds, or any combination thereof until such benefits or contributions do not exceed the limitations contained in this section. In addition to taking into account such other factors as may be necessary to carry out the purposes of subsections (e) and (f), the regulations prescribed under this paragraph shall provide that no plan which has been terminated shall be disqualified until all other trusts, plans, contracts, accounts, or bonds have been disqualified.

(h) 50 Percent Control.— For purposes of applying subsections (b) and (c) of section 414 to this section, the phrase "more than 50 percent" shall be substituted for the phrase "at least 80 percent" each place it appears in section 1563(a)(1).

(i) Records Not Available For Past Periods.— Where for the period before January 1, 1976, or (if later) the first day of the first plan year of the plan, the records necessary for the application of this section are not available, the Secretary may by regulations prescribe alternative methods for determining the amounts to be taken into account for such period.

(j) Regulations; Definition of Year.— The Secretary shall prescribe such regulations as may be necessary to carry out the purposes of this section, including, but not limited to, regulations defining the term "year" for purposes of any provision of this section.

(k) Special Rules.—

(1) Defined benefit plan and defined contribution plan.— For purposes of this title, the term "defined contribution plan" or "defined benefit plan" means a defined contribution plan (within the meaning of section 414(i)) or a defined benefit plan (within the meaning of section 414(j)), whichever applies, which is—

(A) a plan described in section 401(a) which includes a trust which is exempt from tax under section 501(a),

(B) an annuity plan described in section 403(a),

(C) an annuity contract described in section 403(b),

(D) an individual retirement account described in section 408(a),

(E) an individual retirement annuity described in section 408(b), or

IRC Sec. 415 (k)(1)(E)

(F) a simplified employee pension.

(2) Contributions to provide cost-of-living protection under defined benefit plans.—

(A) In general.— In the case of a defined benefit plan which maintains a qualified cost-of-living arrangement—

(i) any contribution made directly by an employee under such arrangement—

(I) shall not be treated as an annual addition for purposes of subsection (c), but

(II) shall be so treated for purposes of subsection (e), and

(ii) any benefit under such arrangement which is allocable to an employer contribution which was transferred from a defined contribution plan and to which the requirements of subsection (c) were applied shall, for purposes of subsection (b), be treated as a benefit derived from an employee contribution (and subsections (c) and (e) shall not again apply to such contribution by reason of such transfer).

(B) Qualified cost-of-living arrangement defined.— For purposes of this paragraph, the term "qualified cost-of-living arrangement" means an arrangement under a defined benefit plan which—

(i) provides a cost-of-living adjustment to a benefit provided under such plan or a separate plan subject to the requirements of section 412, and

(ii) meets the requirements of subparagraphs (C), (D), (E), and (F) and such other requirements as the Secretary may prescribe.

(C) Determination of amount of benefit.— An arrangement meets the requirement of this subparagraph only if the cost-of-living adjustment of participants is based—

(i) on increases in the cost-of-living after the annuity starting date, and

(ii) on average cost-of-living increases determined by reference to 1 or more indexes prescribed by the Secretary, except that the arrangement may provide that the increase for any year will not be less than 3 percent of the retirement benefit (determined without regard to such increase).

(D) Arrangement elective; time for election.— An arrangement meets the requirements of this subparagraph only if it is elective, it is available under the same terms to all participants, and it provides that such election may at least be made in the year in which the participant—

(i) attains the earliest retirement age under the defined benefit plan (determined without regard to any requirement of separation from service), or

(ii) separates from service.

(E) Nondiscrimination requirements.— An arrangement shall not meet the requirements of this subparagraph if the Secretary finds that a pattern of discrimination exists with respect to participation.

(F) Special rules for key employees.—

(i) In general.— An arrangement shall not meet the requirements of this paragraph if any key employee is eligible to participate.

(ii) Key employee.— For purposes of this subparagraph, the term "key employee" has the meaning given such term by section 416(i)(1), except that in the case of a plan other than a top-heavy plan (within the meaning of section 416(g)), such term shall not include an individual who is a key employee solely by reason of section 416(i)(1)(A)(i).

(l) Treatment of Certain Medical Benefits.—

(1) In general.— For purposes of this section contributions allocated to any individual medical account which is part of a pension or annuity plan shall be treated as an annual addition to a defined contribution plan for purposes of subsection (c). Subparagraph (B) of subsection (c)(1) shall not apply to any amount treated as an annual addition under the preceding sentence.

(2) Individual Medical Benefit Account.— For purposes of paragraph (1), the term ''individual medical account'' means any separate account—

(A) which is established for a participant under a pension or annuity plan, and

(B) from which benefits described in section 401(h) are payable solely to such participant, his spouse, or his dependents.

SEC. 416. SPECIAL RULES FOR TOP-HEAVY PLANS.

(a) General Rule.— A trust shall not constitute a qualified trust under section 401(a) for any plan year if the plan of which it is a part is a top-heavy plan for such plan year unless such plan meets—

(1) the vesting requirements of subsection (b), and

(2) the minimum benefit requirements of subsection (c).

(b) Vesting Requirements.—

(1) In general.— A plan satisfies the requirements of this subsection if it satisfies the requirements of either of the following subparagraphs:

(A) 3-year vesting.— A plan satisfies the requirements of this subparagraph if an employee who has completed at least 3 years of service with the employer or employers maintaining the plan has a nonforfeitable right to 100 percent of his accrued benefit derived from employer contributions.

(B) 6-year graded vesting.— A plan satisfies the requirements of this subparagraph if an employee has a nonforfeitable right to a percentage of his accrued benefit derived from employer contributions determined under the following table:

Years of Service	The nonforfeitable percentage is:
2	20
3	40
4	60
5	80
6 or more	100

(2) Certain rules made applicable.— Except to the extent inconsistent with the provisions of this subsection, the rules of section 411 shall apply for purposes of this subsection.

(c) Plan Must Provide Minimum Benefits.—

(1) Defined benefit plans.—

(A) In general.— A defined benefit plan meets the requirements of this subsection if the accrued benefit derived from employer contributions of each participant who is a non-key employee, when expressed as an annual retirement benefit, is not less than the applicable percentage of the participant's average compensation for years in the testing period.

(B) Applicable percentage.— For purposes of subparagraph (A), the term "applicable percentage" means the lesser of—

(i) 2 percent multiplied by the number of years of service with the employer, or

(ii) 20 percent.

(C) Years of service.— For purposes of this paragraph—

(i) In general.—Except as provided in clause (ii), years of service shall be determined under the rules of paragraphs (4), (5), and (6) of section 411(a).

(ii) Exception for years during which plan was not top-heavy.—A year of service with the employer shall not be taken into account under this paragraph if—

(I) the plan was not a top-heavy plan for any plan year ending during such year of service, or

(II) such year of service was completed in a plan year beginning before January 1, 1984.

(D) Average compensation for high years.—For purposes of this paragraph—

(i) In general.—A participant's testing period shall be the period of consecutive years (not exceeding 5) during which the participant had the greatest aggregate compensation from the employer.

(ii) Year must be included in year of service.— The years taken into account under clause (i) shall be properly adjusted for years not included in a year of service.

(iii) Certain years not taken into account.— Except to the extent provided in the plan, a year shall not be taken into account under clause (i) if—

(I) such year ends in a plan year beginning before January 1, 1984, or

(II) such year begins after the close of the last year in which the plan was a top-heavy plan.

(E) Annual retirement benefit.— For purposes of this paragraph, the term "annual retirement benefit" means a benefit payable annually in the form of a single life annuity (with no ancillary benefits) beginning at the normal retirement age under the plan.

(2) Defined contribution plans.—

(A) In general.— A defined contribution plan meets the requirements of the subsection if the employer contribution for the year for each participant who is a non-key employee is not less than 3 percent of such participant's compensation (within the meaning of section 415).

(B) Special rule where maximum contribution less than 3 percent.—

(i) In general.— The percentage referred to in subparagraph (A) for any year shall not exceed the percentage at which contributions are made (or required to be made) under the plan for the year for the key employee for whom such percentage is the highest for the year.

(ii) Treatment of aggregation groups.—

(I) For purposes of this subparagraph, all defined contribtuion plans required to be included in an aggregation group under subsection (g)(2)(A)(i) shall be treated as one plan.

(II) This subparagraph shall not apply to any plan required to be included in an aggregation group if such plan enables a defined benefit plan required to be included in such group to meet the requirements of section 401(a)(4) or 410.

(d) Not More Than $200,000 in Annual Compensation Taken Into Account. [Repealed.]

(e) Plan Must Meet Requirements Without Taking Into Account Social Security and Similar Contributions and Benefits.— A top-heavy plan shall not be treated as meeting the requirement of subsection (b) or (c) unless such plan meets such requirement without taking into account contributions or benefits under chapter 2 (relating to tax on self-employment income), chapter 21 (relating to Federal Insurance Contributions Act), title II of the Social Security Act, or any other Federal or State law.

(f) Coordination Where Employer Has 2 or More Plans.— The Secretary shall prescribe such regulations as may be necessary or appropriate to carry out the purposes of this section where the employer has 2 or more plans including (but not limited to) regulations to prevent inappropriate omissions or required duplication of minimum benefits or contributions.

(g) Top-Heavy Plan Defined.— For purposes of this section—

(1) In general.—

(A) Plans not required to be aggregated.— Except as provided in subparagraphs (B), the term "top-heavy plan" means, with respect to any plan year—

(i) any defined benefit plan if, as of the determination date, the present value of the cumulative accrued benefits under the plan for key employees exceeds 60 percent of the present value of the cumulative accrued benefits under the plan for all employees, and

(ii) any defined contribution plan if, as of the determination date, the aggregate of the accounts of key employees under the plan exceeds 60 percent of the aggregate of the accounts of all employees under such plan.

(B) Aggregated plans.— Each plan of an employer required to be included in an aggregation group shall be treated as a top-heavy plan if such group is a top-heavy group.

(2) Aggregation.— For purposes of this subsection—

(A) Aggregation group.—

(i) Required aggregation.— The term "aggregation group" means—

(I) each plan of the employer in which a key employee is a participant, and

(II) each other plan of the employer which enables any plan described in subclause (I) to meet the requirements of section 401(a)(4) or 410.

(ii) Permissive aggregation.— The employer may treat any plan not required to be included in an aggregation group under clause (i) as being part of such group if such group would continue to meet the requirements of sections 401(a)(4) and 410 with such plan being taken into account.

(B) Top-heavy group.— The term "top-heavy group" means any aggregation group if—

(i) the sum (as of the determination date) of—

(I) the present value of the cumulative accrued benefits for key employees under all defined benefit plans included in such group, and

(II) the aggregate of the accounts of key employees under all defined contribution plans included in such group,

(ii) exceeds 60 percent of a similar sum determined for all employees.

(3) Distributions during last 5 years taken into account.— For purposes of determining—

(A) the present value of the cumulative accrued benefit for any employee, or

(B) the amount of the account of any employee,

such present value or amount shall be increased by the aggregate distributions made with respect to such employee under the plan during the 5-year period ending on the determination date. The proceeding sentence shall also apply to distributions under a terminated plan which if it had not been terminated would have been required to be included in an aggregation group.

(4) Other special rules.—For purposes of this subsection—

(A) Rollover contributions to plan not taken into account.— Except to the extent provided in regulations, any rollover contribution (or similar transfer) initiated by the employee and made after December 31, 1983, to a plan shall not be taken into account with respect to the transferee plan for purposes of determining whether such plan is a top-heavy plan (or whether any aggregation group which includes such plan is a top-heavy group).

(B) Benefits not taken into account if employee ceases to be key employee.— If any individual is a non-key employee with respect to any plan for any plan year, but such individual was a key employee with respect to such plan for any prior plan year, any accrued benefit for such employee (and the account of such employee) shall not be taken into account.

(C) Determination date.— The term "determination date" means, with respect to an plan year—

(i) the last day of the preceding plan year or

(ii) in the case of the first plan year of any plan, the last day of such plan year.

(D) Years.—To the extent provided in regulations, this section shall be applied on the basis of any year specified in such regulations in lieu of plan years.

(E) Benefits not taken into account if employee not employed for last 5 years.—If any individual has not performed services for the employer maintaining the plan at any time during the 5-year period ending on the determination date, any accrued benefit for such individual (and account of such individual) shall not be taken into account.

(F) Accrued benefits treated as accruing ratably.— The accrued benefit of any employee (other than a key employee) shall be determined—

(i) under the method which is used for accrual purposes for all plans of the employer, or

(ii) if there is no method described in clause (i), as if such benefit accrued not more rapidly than the slowest accrual rate permitted under section 411(b)(1)(C).

(h) Adjustments in Section 415 Limits for Top-Heavy Plans.—

(1) In general.— In the case of any top-heavy plan, paragraphs (2)(B) and (3)(B) of section 415(e) shall be applied by substituting "1.0" for "1.25".

(2) Exception where benefits for key employees do not exceed 90 percent of total benefits and additional contributions are made for non-key employees.— Paragraph (1) shall not apply with respect to any top-heavy plan if the requirements of subparagraphs (A) and (B) of this paragraph are met with respect to such plan.

(A) Minimum benefit requirements.—

(i) In general.— The requirements of this subparagraph are met with respect to any top-heavy plan if such plan (and any plan required to be included in an aggregation group with such plan) meets the requirements of subsection (c) as modified by clause (ii).

(ii) Modifications.— For purposes of clause (i)—

(I) paragraph (1)(B) of subsection (c) shall be applied by substituting "3 percent" for "2 percent", and by increasing (but not by more than 10 percentage points) 20 percent by 1 percentage point for each year for which such plan was taken into account under this subsection, and

(II) paragraph (2)(A) shall be applied by substituting "4 percent" for "3 percent".

(B) Benefits for key employees cannot exceed 90 percent of total benefits.— A plan meets the requirements of this subparagraph if such plan would not be a top-heavy plan if "90 percent" were substituted for "60 percent" each place it appears in paragraphs (1)(A) and (2)(B) of subsection (g).

(3) Transition rule.— If, but for this paragraph, paragraph (1) would begin to apply with respect to any top-heavy plan, the application of paragraph (1) shall be suspended with respect to any individual so long as there are no—

(A) employer contributions, forfeitures, or voluntary nondeductible contributions allocated to such individual, or

(B) accruals for such individual under the defined benefit plan.

(4) Coordination with transitional rule under section 415.— In the case of any top-heavy plan to which paragraph (1) applies, section 415(e)(6)(B)(i) shall be applied by substituting "$41,500" for "$51,875".

(i) Definitions.— For purposes of this section—

(1) Key employee.—

(A) In general.— The term "key employee" means an employee who, at any time during the plan year or any of the 4 preceding plan years, is—

(i) an officer of the employer having an annual compensation greater than 50 percent of the amount in effect under section 415(b)(1)(A) for any such plan year,

(ii) 1 of the 10 employees having annual compensation from the employer of more than the limitation in effect under section 415(c)(1)(A) and owning (or considered as owning within the meaning of section 318) the largest interests in the employer,

(iii) a 5-percent owner of the employer, or

(iv) a 1-percent owner of the employer having an annual compensation from the employer of more than $150,000.
For purposes of clause (i), no more than 50 employees (or, if lesser, the greater of 3 or 10 percent of the employees) shall be treated as officers. For purposes of clause (ii), if 2 employees have the same interest in the employer, the employee having greater annual compensation from the employer shall be treated as having a larger interest.

Such term shall not include any officer or employee of any entity referred to in section 414(d) (relating to governmental plans). For purposes of determining the number of officers taken into account under clause (i), employees described in section 414(q)(8) shall be excluded.

(B) Percentage owners.—

(i) 5-percent owner.—For purposes of this paragraph, the term "5-percent owner" means—

(I) if the employer is a corporation, any person who owns (or is considered as owning within the meaning of section 318) more than 5 percent of the outstanding stock of the corporation or stock possessing more than 5 percent of the total

combined voting power of all stock of the corporation, or

(II) if the employer is not a corporation, any person who owns more than 5 percent of the capital or profits interest in the employer.

(ii) 1-percent owner.—For purposes of this paragraph, the term "1-percent owner" means any person who would be described in clause (i) if "1 percent" were substituted for "5 percent" each place it appears in clause (i).

(iii) Constructive ownership rules.— For purposes of this subparagraph and subparagraph (A) (ii)—

(I) subparagraph (C) of section 318 (a)(2) shall be applied by substituting "5 percent for "50 percent" and

(II) in the case of any employer which is not a corporation, ownership in such employer shall be determined in accordance with regulations prescribed by the Secretary which shall be based on principles similar to the principles of section 318 (as modified by subclause (I)).

(C) Aggregation rules do not apply for purposes of determining ownership in the employer.—The rules of subsections (b), (c), and (m) of section 414 shall not apply for purposes of determining ownership in the employer.

(D) Compensation.—For purposes of this paragraph, the term "compen-sation" has the meaning given such term by section 414(q)(7).

(2) Non-key employee.— The term "non-key employee" means any employee who is not a key employee.

(3) Self-employed individuals.—In the case of a self-employed individual described in section 401(c)(1)—

(A) such individual shall be treated as an employee, and

(B) such individual's earned income (within the meaning of section 401(c)(2)) shall be treated as compensation.

(4) Treatment of employees covered by collective bargaining agreements.— The requirements of subsections (b), (c), and (d) shall not apply with respect to any employee included in a unit of employees covered by an agreement which the Secretary of Labor finds to be a collective bargaining agreement between employee representatives and 1 or more employers if there is evidence that retirement benefits were the subject of good faith bargaining between such employee representatives and such employer or employers.

(5) Treatment of beneficiaries.—The terms "employee" and "key employee" include their beneficiaries.

(6) Treatment of simplified employee pensions.—

(A) Treatment as defined contribution plans.— A simplified employee pension shall be treated as a defined contribution plan.

(B) Election to have determinations based on employer contributions.— In the case of a simplified employee pension, at the election of the employer, paragraphs (1)(A)(ii) and (2)(B) of subsection (g) shall be applied by taking into account aggregate employer contributions in lieu of the aggregate of the accounts of employees.

SEC. 417. DEFINITIONS AND SPECIAL RULES FOR PURPOSES OF MINIMUM SURVIVOR ANNUITY REQUIREMENTS.

(a) Election to Waive Qualified Joint and Survivor Annuity or Qualified Preretirement Annuity.—

(1) In general.— A plan meets the requirements of section 401(a)(11) only if—

(A) under the plan, each participant—

(i) may elect at any time during the applicable election period to waive the qualified joint and survivor annuity form of benefit or the qualified preretirement survivor annuity form of benefit (or both), and

(ii) may revoke any such election at any time during the applicable election period, and

(B) the plan meets the requirements of paragraphs (2), (3), and (4) of this subsection.

(2) Spouse must consent to election.— Each plan shall provide that an election under paragraph (1)(A)(i) shall not take effect unless—

(A)(i) the spouse of the participant consents in writing to such election, (ii) such election designates a beneficiary (or a form of benefits) which may not be changed without spousal consent (or the consent of the spouse expressly permits designations by the participant without any requirement of further consent by the spouse), and (iii) the spouse's consent acknowledges the effect of such election and is witnessed by a plan representative or a notary public, or

(B) it is established to the satisfaction of a plan representative that the consent required under subparagraph (A) may not be obtained because there is no spouse, because the spouse cannot be located, or because of such other circumstances as the Secretary may by regulations prescribe.

Any consent by a spouse (or establishment that the consent of a spouse may not be obtained) under the preceding sentence shall be effective only with respect to such spouse.

(3) Plan to provide written explanations.—

(A) Explanation of joint and survivor annuity.— Each plan shall provide to each participant, within a reasonable period of time before the annuity starting date (and consistent with such regulations as the Secretary may prescribe), a written explanation of—

(i) the terms and conditions of the qualified joint and survivor annuity,

(ii) the participant's right to make, and the effect of, an election under paragraph (1) to waive the joint and survivor annuity form of benefit,

(iii) the rights of the participant's spouse under paragraph (2), and

(iv) the right to make, and the effect of, a revocation of an election under paragraph (1).

(B) Explanation of qualified preretirement survivor annuity.—

(i) In general.— Each plan shall provide to each participant, within the applicable period with respect to such participant (and consistent with such regulations as the Secretary may prescribe), a written explanation with respect to the qualified preretirement survivor annuity comparable to that required under subparagraph (A).

(ii) Applicable period.— For purposes of clause (i), the term "applicable period" means, with respect to a participant, whichever of the following periods ends last:

(I) The period beginning with the first day of the plan year in which the participant attains age 32 and ending with the close of the plan year preceding the plan year in which the participant attains age 35.

(II) A reasonable period after the individual becomes a participant.

(III) A reasonable period ending after paragraph (5) ceases to apply to the participant.

(IV) A reasonable period ending after section 401(a)(11) applies to the participant.

In the case of a participant who separates from service before attaining age 35, the applicable period shall be a reasonable period after separation.

(4) Requirement of spousal consent for using plan assets as security for loans.— Each plan shall provide that, if section 401(a)(11) applies to a participant when part or all of the participant's accrued benefit is to be used as security for a loan, no portion of the participant's accrued benefit may be used as security for such loan unless—

(A) the spouse of the participant (if any) consents in writing to such use during the 90-day period ending on the date on which the loan is to be so secured, and

(B) requirements comparable to the requirements of paragraph (2) are met with respect to such consent.

(5) Special rule where plan fully subsidizes costs.—

(A) In general.— The requirements of this subsection shall not apply with respect to the qualified joint and survivor annuity form of benefit or the qualified preretirement survivor annuity form of benefit, as the case may be, if such benefit may not be waived (or another beneficiary selected) and if the plan fully subsidizes the costs of such benefit.

(B) Definition.— For purposes of subparagraph (A), a plan fully subsidizes the costs of a benefit if under the plan the failure to waive such benefit by a participant would not result in a decrease in any plan benefit with respect to such participant and would not result in increased contributions from such participant.

(6) Applicable election period.— For purposes of this subsection, the term "applicable election period" means—

(A) in the case of an election to waive the qualified joint and survivor annuity form of benefit, the 90-day period ending on the annuity starting date, or

(B) in the case of an election to waive the qualified preretirement survivor annuity, the period which begins on the first day of the plan year in which the participant attains age 35 and ends on the date of the participant's death.

In the case of a participant who is separated from service, the applicable election period under subparagraph (B) with respect to benefits accrued before the date of such separation from service shall not begin later than such date.

(b) Definition of Qualified Joint and Survivor Annuity.— For purposes of this section and section 401(a)(11), the term "qualified joint and survivor annuity" means an annuity—

(1) for the life of the participant with a survivor annuity for the life of the spouse which is not less than 50 percent of (and is not greater than 100 percent of) the amount of the annuity which is payable during the joint lives of the participant and the spouse, and

(2) which is the actuarial equivalent of a single annuity for the life of the participant.

Such term also includes any annuity in a form having the effect of an annuity described in the preceding sentence.

(c) Definition of Qualified Preretirement Survivor Annuity.— For purposes of this section and section 401(a)(11)—

(1) **In general.**— Except as provided in paragraph (2), the term "qualified preretirement survivor annuity" means a survivor annuity for the life of the surviving spouse of the participant if—

(A) the payments to the surviving spouse under such an annuity are not less than the amount which would be payable as a survivor annuity under the qualified joint and survivor annuity under the plan (or the actuarial equivalent thereof)—

(i) in the case of a participant who dies after the date on which the participant attained the earliest retirement age, such participant had retired with an immediate qualified joint and survivor annuity on the day before the participant's date of death, or

(ii) in the case of a participant who dies on or before the date on which the participant would have attained the earliest retirement age, such participant had—

(I) separated from service on the date of death,

(II) survived to the earliest retirement age,

(III) retired with an immediate qualified joint and survivor annuity at the earliest retirement age, and

(IV) died on the day after the day on which such participant would have attained the earliest retirement age, and

(B) under the plan, the earliest period for which the surviving spouse may receive a payment under such annuity is not later than the month in which the participant would have attained the earliest retirement age under the plan.

In the case of an individual who separated from service before the date of such individual's death, subparagraph (A)(ii)(I) shall not apply.

(2) **Special rule for defined contribution plans.**— In the case of any defined contribution plan or participant described in clause (ii) or (iii) of section 401(a)(11)(B), the term "qualified preretirement survivor annuity" means an annuity for the life of the surviving spouse the actuarial equivalent of which is not

IRC Sec. 417 (c)(2)

less than 50 percent of the portion of the account balance of the participant (as of the date of death) to which the participant had a nonforfeitable right (within the meaning of section 411(a)).

(3) Security interests taken into account.— For purposes of paragraphs (1) and (2), any security interest held by the plan by reason of a loan outstanding to the participant shall be taken into account in determining the amount of the qualified preretirement survivor annuity.

(d) Survivor Annuities Need Not Be Provided if Participant and Spouse Married Less Than 1 Year.—

(1) In general.— Except as provided in paragraph (2), a plan shall not be treated as failing to meet the requirements of section 401(a)(11) merely because the plan provides that a qualified joint and survivor annuity (or a qualified preretirement survivor annuity) will not be provided unless the participant and spouse had been married throughout the 1-year period ending on the earlier of—

(A) the participant's annuity starting date, or

(B) the date of the participant's death.

(2) Treatment of certain marriages within 1 year of annuity starting date for purposes of qualified joint and survivor annuities.— For purposes of paragraph (1), if—

(A) a participant marries within 1 year before the annuity starting date, and

(B) the participant and the participant's spouse in such marriage have been married for at least a 1-year period ending on or before the date of the participant's death,

such participant and such spouse shall be treated as having been married throughout the 1-year period ending on the participant's annuity starting date.

(e) Restrictions on Cash-Outs.—

(1) Plan may require distribution if present value not in excess of $3,500.— A plan may provide that the present value of a qualified joint and survivor annuity or a qualified preretirement survivor annuity will be immediately distributed if such value does not exceed $3,500. No distribution may be made under the preceding sentence after the annuity starting date unless the participant and the spouse of the participant (or where the participant has died, the surviving spouse) consents in writing to such distribution.

(2) Plan may distribute benefit in excess of $3,500 only with consent.—If—

(A) the present value of the qualified joint and survivor annuity or the qualified preretirement survivor annuity exceeds $3,500, and

(B) the participant and the spouse of the participant (or where the participant has died, the surviving spouse) consent in writing to the distribution,

the plan may immediately distribute the present value of such annuity.

[(3) Determination of present value.—

[(A) In general.— For purposes of paragraphs (1) and (2), the present value shall be calculated—

[(i) by using an interest rate no greater than the applicable interest rate if the vested accrued benefit (using such rate) is not in excess of $25,000, and

[(ii) by using an interest rate no greater than 120 percent of the applicable interest rate if the vested accrued benefit exceeds $25,000 (as determined under clause (i)).

[In no event shall the present value determined under clause (ii) be less than $25,000.

[(B) Applicable interest rate.— For purposes of subparagraph (A), the term "applicable interest rate" means the interest rate which would be used (as of the date of the distribution) by the Pension Benefit Guaranty Corporation for purposes of determining the present value of a lump sum distribution on plan termination.]

◊ ◊ ◊

Editor's Note: Code §417(e)(3), below, appears as amended by §767(a)(2) of the Retirement Protection Act of 1994 (enacted as part of the Uruguay Round Agreements Act, P.L. 103-465). It is effective generally with respect to plan years beginning after December 31, 1994, except that an employer may elect to treat the amended provision as being effective on or after December 8, 1994. Note, however, that §767(d)(2) of the 1994 Act provides that a participant's accrued benefit shall not be considered to be reduced in violation of the anti-cutback rule of Code §411(d)(6) or ERISA §204(g) merely because the benefit is determined in accordance with Code §417(e)(3)(A) or ERISA §205(g)(3) as amended by the Act or because the plan applies Code §415(b)(2)(E) as amended by the 1994 Act.

◊ ◊ ◊

(3) Determination of present value.

(A) In general.

(i) Present value. Except as provided in subparagraph (B), for purposes of paragraphs (1) and (2), the present value shall not be less than the present value calculated by using the applicable mortality table and the applicable interest rate.

(ii) Definitions. For purposes of clause (i)

(I) Applicable mortality table. The term 'applicable mortality table' means the table prescribed by the Secretary. Such table shall be based on the prevailing commissioners' standard table (described in section 807(d)(5)(A)) used to determine reserves for group annuity contracts issued on the date as of which present value is being determined (with-

out regard to any other subparagraph of section 807(d)(5)).

(II) Applicable interest rate. The term 'applicable interest rate' means the annual rate of interest on 30-year Treasury securities for the month before the date of distribution or such other time as the Secretary may by regulations prescribe.

(B) Exception. In the case of a distribution from a plan that was adopted and in effect before the date of the enactment of the Retirement Protection Act of 1994, the present value of any distribution made before the earlier of

(i) the later of the date a plan amendment applying subparagraph (A) is adopted or made effective, or

(ii) the first day of the first plan year beginning after December 31, 1999,

shall be calculated, for purposes of paragraphs (1) and (2), using the interest rate determined under the regulations of the Pension Benefit Guaranty Corporation for determining the present value of a lump sum distribution on plan termination that were in effect on September 1, 1993, and using the provisions of the plan as in effect on the day before such date of enactment; but only if such provisions of the plan met the requirements of section 417(e)(3) as in effect on the day before such date of enactment.

(f) Other Definitions and Special Rules.— For purposes of this section and section 401(a)(11)—

(1) Vested participant.— The term "vested participant" means any participant who has a nonforfeitable right (within the meaning of section 411(a)) to any portion of such participant's accrued benefit.

(2) Annuity starting date.—

(A) In general.— The term "annuity starting date" means—

(i) the first day of the first period for which an amount is payable as an annuity, or

(ii) in the case of a benefit not payable in the form of an annuity, the first day on which all events have occurred which entitle the participant to such benefit.

(B) Special rule for disability benefits.— For purposes of subparagraph (A), the first day of the first period for which a benefit is to be received by reason of disability shall be treated as the annuity starting date only if such benefit is not an auxiliary benefit.

(3) Earliest retirement age.— The term "earliest retirement age" means the earliest date on which, under the plan, the participant could elect to receive retirement benefits.

(4) Plan may take into account increased costs.—A plan may take into account in any equitable manner (as determined by the Secretary) any increased costs resulting from providing a qualified joint or survivor annuity or a qualified preretirement survivor annuity.

(5) Distributions by reason of security interests.— If the use of any participant's accrued benefit (or any portion thereof) as security for a loan meets the requirements of subsection (a)(4), nothing in this section or section 411(a)(11) shall prevent any distribution required by reason of a failure to comply with the terms of such loan.

(6) Requirements for certain spousal consents.— No consent of a spouse shall be effective for purposes of subsection (e)(1) or (e)(2) (as the case may be) unless requirements comparable to the requirements for spousal consent to an election under subsection (a)(1)(A) are met.

(7) Consultation with the Secretary of Labor.— In prescribing regulations under this section and section 401(a)(11), the Secretary shall consult with the Secretary of Labor.

Subpart C— Special Rules for Multiemployer Plans

SEC. 418. REORGANIZATION STATUS.

(a) General Rule.— A multiemployer plan is in reorganization for a plan year if the plan's reorganization index for that year is greater than zero.

(b) Reorganization Index.— For purposes of this subpart

(1) In general.— A plan's reorganization index for any plan year is the excess of—

(A) the vested benefits charge for such year, over

(B) the net charge to the funding standard account for such year.

(2) Net charge to funding standard account.— The net charge to the funding standard account for any plan year is the excess (if any) of—

(A) the charges to the funding standard account for such year under section 412(b)(2), over

(B) the credits to the funding standard account under section 412(b)(3)(B).

(3) Vested benefits charge.— The vested benefits charge for any plan year is the amount which would be necessary to amortize the plan's unfunded vested benefits as of the end of the base plan year in equal annual installments—

(A) over 10 years, to the extent such benefits are attributable to persons in pay status, and

(B) over 25 years, to the extent such benefits are attributable to other participants.

(4) Determination of vested benefits charge.—

(A) In general.— The vested benefits charge for a plan year shall be based on a actuarial valuation of the plan as of the end of the base plan year, adjusted to reflect—

(i) any—

(I) decrease of 5 percent or more in the value of plan assets, or increase of 5 percent or more in the number of persons in pay status, during the period beginning on the first day of the plan year following the base plan year and ending on the adjustment date, or

(II) at the election of the plan sponsor, actuarial valuation of the plan as of the adjustment date or any later date not later than the last day of the plan year for which the determination is being made,

(ii) any change in benefits under the plan which is not otherwise taken into account under this subparagraph and which is pursuant to any amendment—

(I) adopted before the end of the plan year for which the determination is being made, and

(II) effective after the end of the base plan year and on or before the end of the plan year referred to in subclause (I), and

(iii) any other event (including an event described in subparagraph (B)(i)(I)) which, as determined in accordance with regulations prescribed by the Secretary, would substantially increase the plan's vested benefit charge.

(B) Certain changes in benefit levels.—

(i) In general.— In determining the vested benefits charge for a plan year following a plan year in which the plan was not in reorganization, any change in benefits which—

(I) results from the changing of a group of participants from one benefit level to another benefit level under a schedule of plan benefits as a result of changes in a collective bargaining agreement, or

(II) results from any change in a collective bargaining agreement,

shall not be taken into account except to the extent provided in regulations prescribed by the Secretary.

(ii) Plan in reorganization.—Except as otherwise determined by the Secretary, in determining the vested benefits charge for any plan year following any plan year in which the plan was in reorganization, any change in benefits—

(I) described in clause (i)(I), or

(II) described in clause (i)(II) as determined under regulations prescribed by the Secretary,

shall, for purposes of subparagraph (A)(ii), be treated as a change in benefits pursuant to an amendment to a plan.

(5) Base plan year.—

(A) In general.—The base plan year for any plan year is—

(i) if there is a relevant collective bargaining agreement, the last plan year ending at least 6 months before the relevant effective date, or

(ii) if there is no relevant collective bargaining agreement, the last plan year ending at least 12 months before the beginning of the plan year.

(B) Relevant collective bargaining agreement.— A relevant collective bargaining agreement is a collective bargaining agreement—

(i) which is in effect for at least 6 months during the plan year, and

(ii) which has not been in effect for more than 36 months as of the end of the plan year.

(C) Relevant effective date.— The relevant effective date is the earliest of the effective dates for the relevant collective bargaining agreements.

(D) Adjustment date.— The adjustment date is the date which is—

(i) 90 days before the relevant effective date, or

(ii) if there is no relevant effective date, 90 days before the beginning of the plan year.

(6) Person in pay status.— The term "person in pay status" means—

(A) a participant or beneficiary on the last day of the base plan year who, at any time during such year, was paid an early, late, normal, or disability retirement benefit (or a death benefit related to a retirement benefit), and

(B) to the extent provided in regulations prescribed by the Secretary, any other person who is entitled to such a benefit under the plan.

(7) Other definitions and special rules.—

(A) Unfunded vested benefits.— The term "unfunded vested benefits" means, in connection with a plan, an amount (determined in accordance with regulations prescribed by the Secretary) equal to—

(i) the value of vested benefits under the plan, less

(ii) the value of the assets of the plan.

(B) Vested benefits.— The term "vested benefits" means any nonforfeitable benefit (within the meaning of section 4001(a)(8) of the Employee Retirement Income Security Act of 1974).

(C) Allocation of assets.— In determining the plan's unfunded vested benefits, plan assets shall first be allocated to the vested benefits attributable to persons in pay status.

(D) Treatment of certain benefit reductions.— The vested benefits charge shall be determined without regard to reductions in accrued benefits under section 418D which are first effective in the plan year.

(E) Withdrawal liability.— For purposes of this part, any outstanding claim for withdrawal liability shall not be considered a plan asset, except as otherwise provided in regulations prescribed by the Secretary.

(c) Prohibition of Nonannuity Payments.— Except as provided in regulations prescribed by the Pension Benefit Guaranty Corporation, while a plan is in reorganization a benefit with respect to a participant (other than a death benefit) which is attributable to employer contributions and which has a value of more than $1,750 may not be paid in a form other than an annuity which (by itself or in combination with social security, railroad retirement, or workers' compensation benefits) provides substantially level payments over the life of the participant.

(d) Terminated Plans.— Any multiemployer plan which terminates under section 4041A(a)(2) of the Employee Retirement Income Security Act of 1974 shall not be considered in reorganization after the last day of the plan year in which the plan is treated as having terminated.

SEC. 418A. NOTICE OF REORGANIZATION AND FUNDING REQUIREMENTS.

(a) Notice Requirement.—

(1) In general.—If—

(A) a multiemployer plan is in reorganization for a plan year, and

(B) section 418B would require an increase in contributions for such plan year, the plan sponsor shall notify the persons described in paragraph (2) that the plan is in reorganization and that, if contributions to the plan are not increased, accrued benefits under the plan may be reduced or an excise tax may be imposed (or both such reduction and imposition may occur).

(2) Persons to whom notice is to be given.— The persons described in this paragraph are—

(A) each employer who has an obligation to contribute under the plan (within the meaning of section 4212(a) of the Employee Retirement Income Security Act of 1974), and

(B) each employee organization which, for purposes of collective bargaining, represents plan participants employed by such an employer.

(3) Overburden credit not taken into account. — The determination under paragraph (1)(B) shall be made without regard to the overburden credit provided by section 418C.

(b) Additional Requirements. — The Pension Benefit Guaranty Corporation may prescribe additional or alternative requirements for assuring, in the case of a plan with respect to which notice is required by subsection (a)(1), that the persons described in subsection (a)(2)—

(1) receive appropriate notice that the plan is in reorganization,

(2) are adequately informed of the implications of reorganization status, and

(3) have reasonable access to information relevant to the plan's reorganization status.

SEC. 418B. MINIMUM CONTRIBUTION REQUIREMENT.

(a) Accumulated Funding Deficiency in Reorganization. —

(1) In general. — For any plan year in which a multiemployer plan is in reorganization—

(A) the plan shall continue to maintain its funding standard account, and

(B) the plan's accumulated funding deficiency under section 412(a) for such plan year shall be equal to the excess (if any) of—

(i) the sum of the minimum contribution requirement for such plan year (taking into account any overburden credit under section 418C(a)) plus the plan's accumulated funding deficiency for the preceding plan year (determined under this section if the plan was in reorganization during such plan year

or under section 412(a) if the plan was not in reorganization), over

(ii) amounts considered contributed by employers to or under the plan for the plan year (increased by any amount waived under subsection (f) for the plan year).

(2) Treatment of withdrawal liability payments. — For purposes of paragraph (1), withdrawal liability payments (whether or not received) which are due with respect to withdrawals before the end of the base plan year shall be considered amounts contributed by the employer to or under the plan if, as of the adjustment date, it was reasonable for the plan sponsor to anticipate that such payments would be made during the plan year.

(b) Minimum Contribution Requirement. —

(1) In general. — Except as otherwise provided in this section for purposes of this subpart the minimum contribution requirement for a plan year in which a plan is in reorganization is an amount equal to the excess of—

(A) the sum of—

(i) the plan's vested benefits charge for the plan year; and

(ii) the increase in normal cost for the plan year determined under the entry age normal funding method which is attributable to plan amendments adopted while the plan was in reorganization, over

(B) the amount of the overburden credit (if any) determined under section 418C for the plan year.

(2) Adjustment for reductions in contribution base units. — If the plan's current contribution base for the plan year is less than the plan's valuation contribution base for the plan year, the minimum contribution requirement for such plan year shall be equal to the product of the amount determined under paragraph (1) (after any adjustment required by this subpart other than this paragraph) multiplied by a fraction—

(A) the numerator of which is the plan's current contribution base for the plan year, and

(B) the denominator of which is the plan's valuation contribution base for the plan year.

(3) Special rule where cash-flow amount exceeds vested benefits charge.—

(A) In general.— If the vested benefits charge for a plan year of a plan in reorganization is less than the plan's cash-flow amount for the plan year, the plan's minimum contribution requirement for the plan year is the amount determined under paragraph (1) (determined before the application of paragraph (2)) after substituting the term "cash-flow amount" for the term "vested benefits charge" in paragraph (1)(A).

(B) Cash-flow amount.— For purposes of subparagraph (A), a plan's cash-flow amount for a plan year is an amount equal to—

(i) the amount of the benefits payable under the plan for the base plan year, plus the amount of the plan's administrative expenses for the base plan year, reduced by

(ii) the value of the available plan assets for the base plan year determined under regulations prescribed by the Secretary, adjusted in a manner consistent with section 418(b)(4).

(c) Current Contribution Base; Valuation Contribution Base.—

(1) Current contribution base.— For purposes of this subpart, a plan's current contribution base for a plan year is the number of contribution base units with respect to which contributions are required to be made under the plan for that plan year determined in accordance with regulations prescribed by the Secretary.

(2) Valuation contribution base.—

(A) In general.— Except as provided in subparagraph (B), for purposes of this subpart a plan's valuation contribution base is the number of contribution base units for which contributions were received for the base plan year—

(i) adjusted to reflect declines in the contribution base which have occurred (or could reasonably be anticipated) as of the adjustment date for the plan year referred to in paragraph (1),

(ii) adjusted upward (in accordance with regulations prescribed by the Secretary) for any contribution base reduction in the base plan year caused by a strike or lockout or by unusual events, such as fire, earthquake, or severe weather conditions, and

(iii) adjusted (in accordance with regulations prescribed by the Secretary) for reductions in the contribution base resulting from transfers of liabilities.

(B) Insolvent plans.— For any plan year—

(i) in which the plan is insolvent (within the meaning of section 418E(b)(1)), and

(ii) beginning with the first plan year beginning after the expiration of all relevant collective bargaining agreements which were in effect in the plan year in which the plan became insolvent,

the plan's valuation contribution base is the greater of the number of contribution base units for which contributions were received for the first or second plan year preceding the first plan year in which the plan is insolvent, adjusted as provided in clause (ii) or (iii) of subparagraph (A).

(3) Contribution base unit.— For purposes of this subpart, the term "contribution base unit" means a unit with respect to which an employer has an obligation to contribute under a multiemployer plan (as defined in regulations prescribed by the Secretary).

(d) Limitation on Required Increases in Rate of Employer Contributions.—

(1) In general.— Under regulations prescribed by the Secretary, the minimum contribution requirement applicable to any plan for any plan year which is determined under subsection (b) (without regard to subsection (b)(2)) shall not exceed an amount which is equal to the sum of—

(A) the greater of—

(i) the funding standard requirement for such plan year, or

(ii) 107 percent of—

(I) if the plan was not in reorganization in the preceding plan year, the funding standard requirement for such preceding plan year, or

(II) if the plan was in reorganization in the preceding plan year, the sum of the amount determined under this subparagraph for the preceding plan year and the amount (if any) determined under subparagraph (B) for the preceding plan year, plus

(B) if for the plan year a change in benefits is first required to be considered in computing the charges under section 412(b)(2)(A) or (B), the sum of—

(i) the increase in normal cost for a plan year determined under the entry age normal funding method due to increases in benefits described in section 418(b)(4)(A)(ii) (determined without regard to section 418(b)(4)(b)(ii)), and

(ii) the amount necessary to amortize in equal annual installments the increase in the value of vested benefits under the plan due to increases in benefits described in clause (i) over—

(I) 10 years, to the extent such increase in value is attributable to persons in pay status, or

(II) 25 years, to the extent such increase in value is attributable to other participants.

(2) Funding standard requirement.— For purposes of paragraph (1), the funding standard requirement for any plan year is an amount equal to the net charge to the funding standard account for such plan year (as defined in section 418(b)(2)).

(3) Special rule for certain plans.—

(A) In general.— In the case of a plan described in section 4216(b) of the Employee Retirement Income Security Act of 1974, if a plan amendment which increases benefits is adopted after January 1, 1980—

(i) paragraph (1) shall apply only if the plan is a plan described in subparagraph (B), and

(ii) the amount under paragraph (1) shall be determined without regard to subparagraph (1)(B).

(B) Eligible plans.— A plan is described in this subparagraph if—

(i) the rate of employer contributions under the plan for the first plan year beginning on or after the date on which an amendment increasing benefits is adopted, multiplied by the valuation contribution base for that plan year, equals or exceeds the sum of—

(I) the amount that would be necessary to amortize fully, in equal annual installments, by July 1, 1986, the unfunded vested benefits attributable to plan provisions in effect on July 1, 1977 (determined as of the last day of the base plan year); and

(II) the amount that would be necessary to amortize fully, in equal annual installments, over the period described in subparagraph (C), beginning with the first day of the first plan year beginning on or after the date on which the amendment is adopted, the unfunded vested benefits (determined as of the last day of the base plan year) attributable to each plan amendment after July 1, 1977; and

(ii) the rate of employer contributions for each subsequent plan year is not less than the lesser of—

(I) the rate which when multiplied by the valuation contribution base for that subsequent plan year produces the annual amount that would be necessary to complete the amortization schedule described in clause (i), or

(II) the rate for the plan year immediately preceding such subsequent plan year, plus 5 percent of such rate.

(C) Period.— The period determined under this subparagraph is the lesser of—

(i) 12 years, or

(ii) a period equal in length to the average of the remaining expected lives of all persons receiving benefits under the plan.

(4) Exception in case of certain benefit increases.— Paragraph (1) shall not apply with respect to a plan, other than a plan described in paragraph (3), for the period of consecutive plan years in each of which the plan is in reorganization, beginning with a plan year in which occurs the earlier of the date of the adoption or the effective date of any amendment of the plan which increases benefits with respect to service performed before the plan year in which the adoption of the amendment occurred.

(e) Certain Retroactive Plan Amendments.— In determining the minimum contribution requirement with respect to a plan for a plan year under subsection (b), the vested benefits charge may be adjusted to reflect a plan amendment reducing benefits under section 412(c)(8).

(f) Waiver of Accumulated Funding Deficiency.—

(1) In general.— The Secretary may waive any accumulated funding deficiency under

this section in accordance with the provisions of section 412(d)(1).

(2) Treatment of waiver.— Any waiver under paragraph (1) shall not be treated as a waived funding deficiency (within the meaning of section 412(d)(3)).

(g) Actuarial Assumptions Must Be Reasonable.— For purposes of making any determination under this subpart, the requirements of section 412(c)(3) shall apply.

SEC. 418C. OVERBURDEN CREDIT AGAINST MINIMUM CONTRIBUTION REQUIREMENT.

(a) General Rule.— For purposes of determining the contribution under section 418B (before the application of section 418B(2) or (d)), the plan sponsor of a plan which is overburdened for the plan year shall apply an overburden credit against the plan's minimum contribution requirement for the plan year (determined without regard to section 418B(b)(2) or (d) and without regard to this section).

(b) Definition of Overburdened Plan.— A plan is overburdened for a plan year if—

(1) the average number of pay status participants under the plan in the base plan year exceeds the average of the number of active participants in the base plan year and the 2 plan years preceding the base plan year, and

(2) the rate of employer contributions under the plan equals or exceeds the greater of—

(A) such rate for the preceding plan year, or

(B) such rate for the plan year preceding the first year in which the plan is in reorganization.

(c) Amount of Overburden Credit.— The amount of the overburden credit for a plan year is the product of—

(1) one-half of the average guaranteed benefit paid for the base plan year, and

(2) the overburden factor for the plan year.

The amount of the overburden credit for a plan year shall not exceed the amount of the minimum contribution requirement for such year (determined without regard to this section).

(d) Overburden Factor.— For purposes of this section, the overburden factor of a plan for the plan year is an amount equal to—

(1) the average number of pay status participants for the base plan year, reduced by

(2) the average of the number of active participants for the base plan year and for each of the 2 plan years preceding the base plan year.

(e) Definitions.— For purposes of this section—

(1) Pay status participant.— The term "pay status participant" means, with respect to a plan, a participant receiving retirement benefits under the plan.

(2) Number of active participants.— The number of active participants for a plan year shall be the sum of—

(A) the number of active employees who are participants in the plan and on whose behalf contributions are required to be made during the plan year;

(B) the number of active employees who are not participants in the plan but who are in an employment unit covered by a collective bargaining agreement which requires the employees' employer to contribute to the plan unless service in such employment unit was never covered under the plan or a predecessor thereof, and

(C) the total number of active employees attributed to employers who made payments to the plan for the plan year of withdrawal liability pursuant to part 1 of subtitle E of title IV of the Employee Retirement Income Security Act of 1974, determined by dividing—

(i) the total amount of such payments, by

(ii) the amount equal to the total contributions received by the plan during the plan year divided by the average number of active employees who were participants in the plan during the plan year.

The Secretary shall by regulations provide alternative methods of determining active participants where (by reason of irregular employment, contributions on a unit basis, or otherwise) this paragraph does not yield a representative basis for determining the credit.

(3) Average number.— The term "average number" means, with respect to pay status participants for a plan year, a number equal to one-half the sum of—

(A) the number with respect to the plan as of the beginning of the plan year, and

(B) the number with respect to the plan as of the end of the plan year.

(4) Average guaranteed benefit.—The average guaranteed benefit paid is 12 times the average monthly pension payment guaranteed under section 4022A(c)(1) of the Employee Retirement Income Security Act of 1974 determined under the provisions of the plan in effect at the beginning of the first plan year in which the plan is in reorganization and without regard to section 4022A(c)(2).

(5) First year in reorganization.—The first year in which the plan is in reorganization is the first of a period of 1 or more consecutive plan years in which the plan has been in reorganization not taking into account any plan years the plan was in reorganization prior to any period of 3 or more consecutive plan years in which the plan was not in reorganization.

(f) No Overburden Credit in Case of Certain Reductions in Contributions.—

(1) In general.—Notwithstanding any other provision of this section, a plan is not eligible for an overburden credit for a plan year if the Secretary finds that the plan's current contribution base for any plan year was reduced, without a corresponding reduction in the plan's unfunded vested benefits attributable to pay status participants, as a result of a change in an agreement providing for employer contributions under the plan.

(2) Treatment of certain withdrawals.— For purposes of paragraph (1), a complete or partial withdrawal of an employer (within the meaning of part 1 of subtitle E of title IV of the Employee Retirement Income Security Act of 1974) does not impair a plan's eligibility for an overburden credit, unless the Secretary finds that a contribution base reduction described in paragraph (1) resulted from a transfer of liabilities to another plan in connection with the withdrawal.

(g) Mergers.— Notwithstanding any other provision of this section, if 2 or more multiemployer plans merge, the amount of the overburden credit which may be applied under this section with respect to the plan resulting from the merger for any of the 3 plan years ending after the effective date of the merger shall not exceed the sum of the used overburden credit for each of the merging plans for its last plan year ending before the effective date of the merger. For purposes of the preceding sentence, the used overburden credit is that portion of the credit which does not exceed the excess of the minimum contribution requirement determined without regard to any overburden credit under this section over the employer contributions required under the plan.

SEC. 418D. ADJUSTMENTS IN ACCRUED BENEFITS.

(a) Adjustments in Accrued Benefits.—

(1) In general.— Notwithstanding section 411, a multiemployer plan in reorganization may be amended, in accordance with this section, to reduce or eliminate accrued benefits attributable to employer contributions which, under section 4022A(b) of the Employee Retirement Income Security Act of 1974, are not eligible for the Pension Benefit Guaranty Corporation's guarantee. The preceding sentence shall only apply to accrued benefits under plan amendments (or plans) adopted after March 26, 1980, or under collective bargaining agreement[s] entered into after March 26, 1980.

(2) Adjustment of vested benefits charge.— In determining the minimum contribution requirement with respect to a plan for a plan year under section 418B(b), the vested benefits charge may be adjusted to reflect a plan amendment reducing benefits under this section or section 412(c)(8), but only if the amendment is adopted and effective no later than 2 1/2 months after the end of the plan year, or within such extended period as the Secretary may prescribe by regulations under section 412(c)(10).

(b) Limitation on Reduction.—

(1) In general.— Accrued benefits may not be reduced under this section unless—

(A) notice has been given, at least 6 months before the first day of the plan year in which the amendment reducing benefits is adopted, to—

(i) plan participants and beneficiaries.

(ii) each employer who has an obligation to contribute (within the meaning of section 4212(a) of the Employee Retirement Income Security Act of 1974) under the plan, and

(iii) each employee organization which, for purposes of collective bargaining, represents plan participants employed by such an employer,

that the plan is in reorganization and that, if contributions under the plan are not increased, accrued benefits under the plan will be reduced or an excise tax will be imposed on employers;

(B) in accordance with regulations prescribed by the Secretary—

(i) any category of accrued benefits is not reduced with respect to inactive participants to a greater extent proportionally that such category of accrued benefits is reduced with respect to active participants,

(ii) benefits attributable to employer contributions other than accrued benefits and the rate of future benefit accruals are reduced at least to an extent equal to the reduction in accrued benefits of inactive participants, and

(iii) in any case in which the accrued benefit of a participant or beneficiary is reduced by changing the benefit form or the requirements which the participant or beneficiary must satisfy to be entitled to the benefit, such reduction is not applicable to—

(I) any participant or beneficiary in pay status on the effective date of the amendment, or the beneficiary of such a participant, or

(II) any participant who has attained normal retirement age, or who is within 5 years of attaining normal retirement age, on the effective date of the amendment, or the beneficiary of any such participant; and

(C) the rate of employer contributions for the plan year in which the amendment becomes effective and for all succeeding plan years in which the plan is in reorganization equals or exceeds the greater of—

(i) the rate of employer contributions, calculated without regard to the amendment, for the plan year in which the amendment becomes effective, or

(ii) the rate of employer contributions for the plan year preceding the plan year in which the amendment becomes effective.

(2) Information required to be included in notice.—The plan sponsors shall include in any notice required to be sent to plan participants and beneficiaries under paragraph (1) information as to the rights and remedies of plan participants and beneficiaries as well as how to contact the Department of Labor for further information and assistance where appropriate.

(c) No Recoupment.— A plan may not recoup a benefit payment which is in excess of the amount payable under the plan because of an amendment retroactively reducing accrued benefits under this section.

(d) Benefit Increases Under Multiemployer Plan in Reorganization.—

(1) Restoration of previously reduced benefits.—

(A) In general.— A plan which has been amended to reduce accrued benefits under this section may be amended to increase or restore accrued benefits, or the rate of future benefit accruals, only if the plan is amended to restore levels of previously reduced accrued benefits of inactive participants and of participants who are within 5 years of attaining normal retirement age to at least the same extent as any such increase in accrued benefits or in the rate of future benefit accruals.

(B) Benefit increases and benefit restorations.— For purposes of this subsection, in the case of a plan which has been amended under this section to reduce accrued benefits—

(i) an increase in a benefit, or in the rate of future benefit accruals, shall be considered a benefit increase to the extent that the benefit, or the accrual rate, is thereby increased above the highest benefit level, or accrual rate, which was in effect under the terms of the plan before the effective date of the amendment reducing accrued benefits, and

(ii) an increase in a benefit, or in the rate of future benefit accruals, shall be considered a benefit restoration to the extent that the benefit, or the accrual rate, is not thereby increased above the highest benefit level, or accrual rate, which was in effect under the terms of the plan immediately before the effective date of the amendment reducing accrued benefits.

(2) Uniformity in benefit restoration.—If a plan is amended to partially restore previously reduced accrued benefit levels, or the rate of future benefit accruals, the benefits of inactive participants shall be restored in at least the same proportions as other accrued benefits which are restored.

(3) No benefit increases in year of benefit reduction.— No benefit increase under a plan may take effect in a plan year in which an amendment reducing accrued benefits under the plan, in accordance with this section, is adopted or first becomes effective.

(4) Retroactive payments.— A plan is not required to make retroactive benefit payments with respect to that portion of an accrued benefit which was reduced and subsequently restored under this section.

(e) Inactive Participant.— For purposes of this section, the term "inactive participant" means a person not in covered service under the plan who is in pay status under the plan or who has a nonforfeitable benefit under the plan.

(f) Regulations.— The Secretary may prescribe rules under which, notwithstanding any other provision of this section, accrued benefit reductions or benefit increases for different participant groups may be varied equitably to reflect variations in contribution rates and other relevant factors reflecting differences in negotiated levels of financial support for plan benefit obligations.

SEC. 418E. INSOLVENT PLANS.

(a) Suspension of Certain Benefit Payments.—Notwithstanding section 411, in any case in which benefit payments under an insolvent multiemployer plan exceed the resource benefit level, any such payments of benefits which are not basic benefits shall be suspended, in accordance with this section, to the extent necessary to reduce the sum of such payments and the payments of such basic benefits to the greater of the resource benefit level or the level of basic benefits, unless an alternative procedure is prescribed by the Pension Benefit Guaranty Corporation under sec-

tion 4022A(g)(5) of the Employee Retirement Income Security Act of 1974.

(b) Definitions.— For purposes of this section, for a plan year—

(1) Insolvency.—A multiemployer plan is insolvent if the plan's available resources are not sufficient to pay benefits under the plan when due for the plan year, or if the plan is determined to be insolvent under subsection (d).

(2) Resource benefit level.— The term "resource benefit level" means the level of monthly benefits determined under subsections (c)(1) and (3) and (d)(3) to be the highest level which can be paid out of the plan's available resources.

(3) Available resources.— The term "available resources" means the plan's cash, marketable assets, contributions, withdrawal liability payments, and earnings, less reasonable administrative expenses and amounts owed for such plan year to the Pension Benefit Guaranty Corporation under section 4261(b)(2) of the Employee Retirement Income Security Act of 1974.

(4) Insolvency year.— The term "insolvency year" means a plan year in which a plan is insolvent.

(c) Benefit Payments Under Insolvent Plans.—

(1) Determination of resource benefit level.—The plan sponsor of a plan in reorganization shall determine in writing the plan's resource benefit level for each insolvency year, based on the plan sponsor's reasonable projection of the plan's available resources and the benefits payable under the plan.

(2) Uniformity of the benefit suspension.—The suspension of benefit payments under this section shall, in accordance with regulations prescribed by the Secretary, apply in substantially uniform proportions to the benefits of all persons in pay status (within the meaning of section 418(b)(6)) under the plan, except that the Secretary may prescribe rules under which benefit suspensions for different participant groups may be varied equitably to reflect variations in contribution rates and other relevant factors including differences in negotiated levels of financial support for plan benefit obligations.

(3) Resource benefit level below level of basic benefits.—Notwithstanding paragraph (2), if a plan sponsor determines in writing a resource benefit level for a plan year which is below the level of basic benefits, the payment of all benefits other than basic benefits shall be suspended for that plan year.

(4) Excess resources.—

(A) In general.—If, by the end of an insolvency year, the plan sponsor determines in writing that the plan's available resources in that insolvency year could have supported benefit payments above the resource benefit level for that insolvency year, the plan sponsor shall distribute the excess resources to the participants and beneficiaries who received benefit payments from the plan in that insolvency year, in accordance with regulations prescribed by the Secretary.

(B) Excess resources.— For purposes of this paragraph, the term "excess resources" means available resources above the amount necessary to support the resource benefit level, but no greater than the amount necessary to pay benefits for the plan year at the benefit levels under the plan.

(5) Unpaid benefits.— If, by the end of an insolvency year, any benefit has not been paid at the resource benefit level, amounts up to the resource benefit level which were unpaid shall be distributed to the participants and beneficiaries, in accordance with regulations prescribed by the Secretary, to the extent possible taking into account the plan's total available resources in that insolvency year.

(6) Retroactive payments.— Except as provided in paragraph (4) or (5), a plan is not required to make retroactive benefit payments with respect to that portion of a benefit which was suspended under this section.

(d) Plan Sponsor Determination.—

(1) Triennial test.— As of the end of the first plan year in which a plan is in reorganization, and at least every 3 plan years thereafter (unless the plan is no longer in reorganization), the plan sponsor shall compare the value of plan assets (determined in accordance with section 418B(b)(3)(B)(ii)) for that plan year with the total amount of benefit payments made under the plan for that plan year. Unless the plan sponsor determines that the value of plan assets exceeds 3 times the total amount of benefit payments, the plan sponsor shall determine whether the plan will be insolvent in any of the next 3 plan years.

(2) Determination of insolvency.—If, at any time, the plan sponsor of a plan in reorganization reasonably determines, taking into account the plan's recent and anticipated financial experience, that the plan's available resources are not sufficient to pay benefits under the plan when due for the next plan year, the plan sponsor shall make such determination available to interested parties.

(3) Determination of resource benefit level.—The plan sponsor of a plan in reorganization shall determine in writing for each insolvency year the resource benefit level and the level of basic benefits no later than 3 months before the insolvency year.

(e) Notice Requirements.—

(1) Impending insolvency.— If the plan sponsor of a plan in reorganization determines under subsection (d)(1) or (2) that the plan may become insolvent (within the meaning of subsection (b)(1)), the plan sponsor shall—

(A) notify the Secretary, the Pension Benefit Guaranty Corporation, the parties described in section 418A(a)(2), and the plan participants and beneficiaries of that determination, and

(B) inform the parties described in section 418A(a)(2) and the plan participants and beneficiaries that if insolvency occurs certain benefit payments will be suspended, but that basic benefits will continue to be paid.

(2) Resource benefit level.— No later than 2 months before the first day of each insolvency year, the plan sponsor of a plan in reorganization shall notify the Secretary, the Pension Benefit Guaranty Corporation, the parties described in section 418A(a)(2), and the plan participants and beneficiaries of the resource benefit level determined in writing for that insolvency year.

(3) Potential need for financial assistance.— In any case in which the plan sponsor anticipates that the resource benefit level for an insolvency year may not exceed the level of basic benefits, the plan sponsor shall notify the Pension Benefit Guaranty Corporation.

(4) Regulations.— Notice required by this subsection shall be given in accordance with regulations prescribed by the Pension Benefit Guaranty Corporation, except that notice to the Secretary shall be given in accordance with regulations prescribed by the Secretary.

(5) Corporation may prescribe time.— The Pension Benefit Guaranty Corporation may prescribe a time other than the time prescribed by this section for the making of a determination or the filing of a notice under this section.

(f) Financial Assistance.—

(1) Permissive application.—If the plan sponsor of an insolvent plan for which the resource benefit level is above the level of basic benefits anticipates that, for any month in an insolvency year, the plan will not have funds sufficient to pay basic benefits, the plan sponsor may apply for financial assistance from the Pension Benefit Guaranty Corporation under section 4261 of the Employee Retirement Income Security Act of 1974.

(2) Mandatory application.— A plan sponsor who has determined a resource benefit level for an insolvency year which is below the level of basic benefits shall apply for financial assistance from the Pension Benefit Guaranty Corporation under section 4261 of the Employee Retirement Income Security Act of 1974.

(g) Financial Assistance.—Any amount of any financial assistance from the Pension Benefit Guaranty Corporation to any plan, and any repayment of such amount, shall be taken into account under this subpart in such manner as determined by the Secretary.

Subpart D— Treatment of Welfare Benefit Funds

SEC. 419. TREATMENT OF FUNDED WELFARE BENEFIT PLANS

(a) General Rule.— Contributions paid or accrued by an employer to a welfare benefit fund—

(1) shall not be deductible under this chapter, but,

(2) if they would otherwise be deductible, shall (subject to the limitation of subsection (b)) be deductible under this section for the taxable year in which paid.

(b) Limitation.—The amount of the deduction allowable under subsection (a)(2) for any taxable year shall not exceed the welfare benefit fund's qualified cost for the taxable year.

(c) Qualified Cost.— For purposes of this section—

(1) In general.— Except as otherwise provided in this subsection, the term ''qualified cost'' means, with respect to any taxable year, the sum of—

(A) the qualified direct cost for such taxable year, and

(B) subject to the limitation of section 419A(b), any addition to a qualified asset account for the taxable year.

(2) Reduction for fund's after-tax income.— In the case of any welfare benefit fund, the qualified cost for any taxable year shall be reduced by such fund's after-tax income for such taxable year.

(3) Qualified direct cost.—

(A) In general.—The term "qualified direct cost" means, with respect to any taxable year, the aggregate amount (including administrative expenses) which would have been allowable as a deduction to the employer with respect to the benefits provided during the taxable year, if—

(i) such benefits were provided directly by the employer, and

(ii) the employer used the cash receipts and disbursements method of accounting.

(B) Time when benefits provided.—For purposes of subparagraph (A), a benefit shall be treated as provided when such benefit would be includible in the gross income of the employee if provided directly by the employer (or would be so includible but for any provision of this chapter excluding such benefit from gross income).

(C) 60-month amortization of child care facilities.—

(i) In general.— In determining qualified direct costs with respect to any child care facility for purposes of subparagraph (A), in lieu or depreciation the adjusted basis of such facility shall be allowable as a deduction ratably over a period of 60 months beginning with the month in which the facility is placed in service.

(ii) Child care facility.— The term "child care facility" means any tangible property which qualifies under regulations prescribed by the Secretary as a child care center primarily for children of employees of the employer; except that such term shall not include any property—

(I) not of a character subject to depreciation; or

(II) located outside the United States.

(4) After-tax income.—

(A) In general.— The term "after-tax income" means, with respect to any taxable year, the gross income of the welfare benefit fund reduced by the sum of—

(i) the deductions allowed by this chapter which are directly connected with the production of such gross income, and

(ii) the tax imposed by this chapter on the fund for the taxable year.

(B) Treatment of certain amounts.In determining the gross income of any welfare benefit fund—

(i) contributions and other amounts received from employees shall be taken into account, but

(ii) contributions from the employer shall not be taken into account.

(5) Item only taken into account once.— No item may be taken into account more than once in determining the qualified cost of any welfare benefit fund.

(d) Carryover of Excess Contributions.— If—

(1) the amount of the contributions paid (or deemed paid under this subsection) by the employer during any taxable year to a welfare benefit fund exceeds

(2) the limitation of subsection (b),

such excess shall be treated as an amount paid by the employer to such fund during the succeeding year.

(e) Welfare Benefit Fund.— For purposes of this section—

(1) In general.— The term "welfare benefit fund" means any fund—

(A) which is part of a plan of an employer, and

(B) through which the employer provides welfare benefits to employees or their beneficiaries.

(2) Welfare benefit.— The term "welfare benefit" means any benefit other than a benefit with respect to which—

(A) section 83(h) applies,

(B) section 404 applies (determined without regard to section 404(b)(2)), or

(C) section 404A applies.

(3) Fund.—The term "fund" means—

(A) any organization described in paragraph (7), (9), (17), or (20) of section 501(c),

(B) any trust, corporation, or other organization not exempt from the tax imposed by this chapter, and

(C) to the extent provided in regulations, any account held for an employer by any person.

(4) Treatment of amounts held pursuant to certain insurance contracts.—

(A) In general.—Notwithstanding paragraph (3)(C), the term "fund" shall not include amounts held by an insurance company pursuant to an insurance contract if—

(i) such contract is a life insurance contract described in section 264(a)(1), or

(ii) such contract is a qualified nonguaranteed contract.

(B) Qualified nonguaranteed contract.—

(i) In general.— For purposes of this paragraph, the term "qualified nonguaranteed contract" means any insurance contract (including a reasonable premium stabilization reserve held thereunder) if—

(I) there is no guarantee of a renewal of such contract, and

(II) other than insurance protection, the only payments to which the employer or

employees are entitled are experience rated refunds or policy dividends which are not guaranteed and which are determined by factors other than the amount of welfare benefits paid to (or on behalf of) the employees of the employer or their beneficiaries.

(ii) Limitation.— In the case of any qualified nonguaranteed contracts, subparagraph (A) shall not apply unless the amount of any experience rated refund or policy dividend payable to an employer with respect to a policy year is treated by the employer as received or accrued in the taxable year in which the policy year ends.

(f) Method of Contributions, Etc., Having the Effect of a Plan.— If—

(1) there is no plan, but

(2) there is a method or arrangement of employer contributions or benefits which has the effect of a plan,

this section shall apply as if there were a plan.

(g) Extension to Plans for Independent Contractors.—If any fund would be a welfare benefit fund (as modified by subsection (f)) but for the fact that there is no employer-employee relationship—

(1) this section shall apply as if there were such a relationship, and

(2) any reference in this section to the employer shall be treated as a reference to the person for whom services are provided, and any reference in this section to an employee shall be treated as a reference to the person providing the services.

SEC 419A. QUALIFIED ASSET ACCOUNT; LIMITATION ON ADDITIONS TO ACCOUNT

(a) General rule. For purposes of this subpart and section 512, the term "qualified asset account" means any account consisting of assets set aside to provide for the payment of—

(1) disability benefits,

(2) medical benefits,

(3) SUB or severance pay benefits, or

(4) life insurance benefits.

(b) Limitation on additions to account. No addition to any qualified asset account may be taken into account under section 419(c)(1)(B) to the extent such addition results in the amount in such account exceeding the account limit.

(c) Account limit. For purposes of this section—

(1) In general. Except as otherwise provided in this subsection, the account limit for any qualified asset account for any taxable year is the amount reasonably and actuarially necessary to fund—

(A) claims incurred but unpaid (as of the close of such taxable year) for benefits referred to in subsection (a), and

(B) administrative costs with respect to such claims.

(2) Additional reserve for post-retirement medical and life insurance benefits. The account limit for any taxable year may include a reserve funded over the working lives of the covered employees and actuarially determined on a level basis (using assumptions that are reasonable in the aggregate) as necessary for—

(A) post-retirement medical benefits to be provided to covered employees (determined on the basis of current medical costs), or

(B) post-retirement life insurance benefits to be provided to covered employees.

(3) Amount taken into account for SUB or severance pay benefits.

(A) In general. The account limit for any taxable year with respect to SUB or severance pay benefits is 75 percent of the average annual qualified direct costs for SUB or severance pay benefits for any 2 of the im-

mediately preceding 7 taxable years (as selected by the fund).

(B) Special rule for certain new plans. In the case of any new plan for which SUB or severance pay benefits are not available to any key employee, the Secretary shall, by regulations, provide for an interim amount to be taken into account under paragraph (1).

(4) Limitation on amounts to be taken into account.

(A) Disability benefits. For purposes of paragraph (1), disability benefits payable to any individual shall not be taken into account to the extent such benefits are payable at an annual rate in excess of the lower of—

(i) 75 percent of such individual's average compensation for his high 3 years (within the meaning of section 415(b)(3)), or

(ii) the limitation in effect under section 415(b)(1)(A).

(B) Limitation on SUB or severance pay benefits. For purposes of paragraph (3), any SUB or severance pay benefit payable to any individual shall not be taken into account to the extent such benefit is payable at an annual rate in excess of 150 percent of the limitation in effect under section 415(c)(1)(A).

(5) Special limitation where no actuarial certification.

(A) In general. Unless there is an actuarial certification of the account limit determined under this subsection for any taxable year, the account limit for such taxable year shall not exceed the sum of the safe harbor limits for such taxable year.

(B) Safe harbor limits.

(i) Short-term disability benefits. In the case of short-term disability benefits, the safe harbor limit for any taxable year is 17.5 percent of the qualified direct costs (other than insurance premiums) for the immediately preceding taxable year with respect to such benefits.

IRC Sec. 419A (c)(5)(B)(i)

(ii) Medical benefits. In the case of medical benefits, the safe harbor limit for any taxable year is 35 percent of the qualified direct costs (other than insurance premiums) for the immediately preceding taxable year with respect to medical benefits.

(iii) SUB or severance pay benefits. In the case of SUB or severance pay benefits, the safe harbor limit for any taxable year is the amount determined under paragraph (3).

(iv) Long-term disability or life insurance benefits. In the case of any long-term disability benefit or life insurance benefit, the safe harbor limit for any taxable year shall be the amount prescribed by regulations.

(d) Requirement of separate accounts for post-retirement medical or life insurance benefits provided to key employees.

(1) In general. In the case of any employee who is a key employee—

(A) a separate account shall be established for any medical benefits or life insurance benefits provided with respect to such employee after retirement, and

(B) medical benefits and life insurance benefits provided with respect to such employee after retirement may only be paid from such separate account.

The requirements of this paragraph shall apply to the first taxable year for which a reserve is taken into account under subsection (c)(2) and to all subsequent taxable years.

(2) Coordination with section 415. For purposes of section 415, any amount attributable to medical benefits allocated to an account established under paragraph (1) shall be treated as an annual addition to a defined contribution plan for purposes of section 415(c). Subparagraph (B) of section 415(c)(1) shall not apply to any amount treated as an annual addition under the preceding sentence.

(3) Key employee. For purposes of this section, the term "key employee" means any employee who, at any time during the plan year or any preceding plan year, is or was a key employee as defined in section 416(i).

(e) Special limitations on reserves for medical benefits or life insurance benefits provided to retired employees.

(1) Reserve must be nondiscriminatory. No reserve may be taken into account under subsection (c)(2) for post-retirement medical benefits or life insurance benefits to be provided to covered employees unless the plan meets the requirements of section 505(b) with respect to such benefits (whether or not such requirements apply to such plan). The preceding sentence shall not apply to any plan maintained pursuant to an agreement between employee representatives and 1 or more employers if the Secretary finds that such agreement is a collective bargaining agreement and that post-retirement medical benefits or life insurance benefits were the subject of good faith bargaining between such employee representatives and such employer or employers.

(2) Limitation on amount of life insurance benefits. Life insurance benefits shall not be taken into account under subsection (c)(2) to the extent the aggregate amount of such benefits to be provided with respect to the employee exceeds $50,000.

(f) Definitions and other special rules. For purposes of this section—

(1) SUB or severance pay benefit. The term "SUB or severance pay benefit" means—

(A) any supplemental unemployment compensation benefit (as defined in section 501(c)(17)(D)), and

(B) any severance pay benefit.

(2) Medical benefit. The term "medical benefit" means a benefit which consists of the providing (directly or through insurance) of medical care (as defined in section 213(d)).

(3) Life insurance benefit. The term "life insurance benefit" includes any other death benefit.

(4) Valuation. For purposes of this section, the amount of the qualified asset account shall be the value of the assets in such account (as determined under regulations).

(5) Special rule for collective bargained and employee pay-all plans. No account limits shall apply in the case of any qualified asset account under a separate welfare benefit fund—

(A) under a collective bargaining agreement, or

(B) an employee pay-all plan under section 501(c)(9) if—

(i) such plan has at least 50 employees (determined without regard to subsection (h)(1)), and

(ii) no employee is entitled to a refund with respect to amounts in the fund, other than a refund based on the experience of the entire fund.

(6) Exception for 10-or-more employer plans.

(A) In general. This subpart shall not apply in the case of any welfare benefit fund which is part of a 10 or more employer plan. The preceding sentence shall not apply to any plan which maintains experience-rating arrangements with respect to individual employers.

(B) 10 or more employer plan. For purposes of subparagraph (A), the term "10 or more employer plan" means a plan—

(i) to which more than 1 employer contributes, and

(ii) to which no employer normally contributes more than 10 percent of the total contributions contributed under the plan by all employers.

(7) Adjustments for existing excess reserves.

(A) Increase in account limit. The account limit for any of the first 4 taxable years to which this section applies shall be increased by the applicable percentage of any existing excess reserves.

(B) Applicable percentage. For purposes of subparagraph (A)—

In the case of—	The applicable percentage is—
The first taxabale year to which this section applies	80
The second taxable year to which this section applies	60
The third taxable year to which this section applies	40
The fourth taxable year to which this section aplies	20

(C) Existing excess reserve. For purposes of computing the increase under subparagraph (A) for any taxable year, the term "existing excess reserve" means the excess (if any) of—

(i) the amount of assets set aside at the close of the first taxable year ending after July 18, 1984, for purposes described in subsection (a), over

(ii) the account limit determined under this section (without regard to this paragraph) for the taxable year for which such increase is being computed.

(D) Funds to which paragraph applies. This paragraph shall apply only to a welfare benefit fund which, as of July 18, 1984, had assets set aside for purposes described in subsection (a).

(g) Employer taxed on income of welfare benefit fund in certain cases.

(1) In general. In the case of any welfare benefit fund which is not an organization described in paragraph (7), (9), (17), or (20) of section 501(c), the employer shall include in gross income for any taxable year an amount

IRC Sec. 419A (g)(1)

equal to such fund's deemed unrelated income for the fund's taxable year ending within the employer's taxable year.

(2) Deemed unrelated income. For purposes of paragraph (1), the deemed unrelated income of any welfare benefit fund shall be the amount which would have been its unrelated business taxable income under section 512(a)(3) if such fund were an organization described in paragraph (7), (9), (17), or (20) of section 501(c).

(3) Coordination with section 419. If any amount is included in the gross income of an employer for any taxable year under paragraph (1) with respect to any welfare benefit fund—

(A) the amount of the tax imposed by this chapter which is attributable to the amount so included shall be treated as a contribution paid to such welfare benefit fund on the last day of such taxable year, and

(B) the tax so attributable shall be treated as imposed on the fund for purposes of section 419(c)(4)(A).

(h) Aggregation rules. For purposes of this subpart—

(1) Aggregation of funds.

(A) Mandatory aggregation. For purposes of subsections (c)(4), (d)(2), and (e)(2), all welfare benefit funds of an employer shall be treated as 1 fund.

(B) Permissive aggregation for purposes not specified in subparagraph (A). For purposes of this section (other than the provisions specified in subparagraph (A)), at the election of the employer, 2 or more welfare benefit funds of such employer may (to the extent not inconsistent with the purposes of this subpart and section 512) be treated as 1 fund.

(2) Treatment of related employers. Rules similar to the rules of subsections (b), (c), (m), and (n) of section 414 shall apply.

(i) Regulations. The Secretary shall prescribe such regulations as may be appropriate to carry out the purposes of this subpart. Such regulations may provide that the plan administrator of any welfare benefit fund which is part of a plan to which more than 1 employer contributes shall submit such information to the employers contributing to the fund as may be necessary to enable the employers to comply with the provisions of this section.

◊ ◊ ◊

Editor's Note: Code §420, as set forth below, appears as amended by §731(a) of the Retirement Protection Act of 1994 (enacted as part of the Uruguay Round Agreements Act, P.L. 103-465). The changes are effective generally as of December 8, 1994. However, the amendments to Code §420(c)(3) and 420(e)(1) apply to taxable years beginning after December 31, 1995.

◊ ◊ ◊

SEC. 420. TRANSFERS OF EXCESS PENSION ASSETS TO RETIREE HEALTH ACCOUNTS

(a) General Rule. If there is a qualified transfer of any excess pension assets of a defined benefit plan (other than a multiemployer plan) to a health benefits account which is part of such plan

(1) a trust which is part of such plan shall not be treated as failing to meet the requirements of subsection (a) or (h) of section 401 solely by reason of such transfer (or any other action authorized under this section),

(2) no amount shall be includible in the gross income of the employer maintaining the plan solely by reason of such transfer,

(3) such transfer shall not be treated

(A) as an employer reversion for purposes of section 4980, or

(B) as a prohibited transaction for purposes of section 4975, and

(4) the limitations of subsection (d) shall apply to such employer.

(b) Qualified Transfer. - For purposes of this section

(1) In general. The term "qualified transfer" means a transfer

(A) of excess pension assets of a defined benefit plan to a health benefits account which is part of such plan in a taxable year beginning after December 31, 1990,

(B) which does not contravene any other provision of law, and

(C) with respect to which the following requirements are met in connection with the plan

(i) the requirements of subsection (c)(1),

(ii) the vesting requirements of subsection (c)(2), and

(iii) the minimum [cost] *benefits* requirements of subsection (c)(3).

(2) Only 1 transfer per year.

(A) In general. No more than 1 transfer with respect to any plan during a taxable year may be treated as a qualified transfer for purposes of this section.

(B) Exception. A transfer described in paragraph (4) shall not be taken into account for purposes of subparagraph (A).

(3) Limitation on amount transferred. The amount of excess pension assets which may be transferred in a qualified transfer shall not exceed the amount which is reasonably estimated to be the amount the employer maintaining the plan will pay (whether directly or through reimbursement) out of such account during the taxable year of the transfer for qualified current retiree health liabilities.

(4) Special rule for 1990.

(A) In general. Subject to the provisions of subsection (c), a transfer shall be treated as a qualified transfer if such transfer

(i) is made after the close of the taxable year preceding the employer's first taxable year beginning after December 31, 1990, and before the earlier of

(I) the due date (including extensions) for the filing of the return of tax for such preceding taxable year, or

(II) the date such return is filed, and

(ii) does not exceed the expenditures of the employer for qualified current retiree health liabilities for such preceding taxable year.

(B) Deduction reduced. The amount of the deductions otherwise allowable under this chapter to an employer for the taxable year preceding the employer's first taxable year beginning after December 31, 1990, shall be reduced by the amount of any qualified transfer to which this paragraph applies.

(C) Coordination with reduction rule. Subsection (e)(1)(B) shall not apply to a transfer described in subparagraph (A).

(5) Expiration. No transfer in a taxable year beginning after December 31, [1995] *2000*, shall be treated as a qualified transfer.

(c) Requirements of Plans Transferring Assets.

(1) Use of transferred assets.

(a) In general. Any assets transferred to a health benefits account in a qualified transfer (and any income allocable thereto) shall be used only to pay qualified current retiree health liabilities (other than liabilities of key employees not taken into account under subsection (e)(1)(D)) for the taxable year of the transfer (whether directly or through reimbursement)).

(B) Amounts not used to pay for health benefits.

(i) In general. Any assets transferred to a health benefits account in a qualified transfer (and any income allocable thereto) which are not used as provided in subparagraph (A)

IRC Sec. 420 (c)(1)(B)(i)

shall be transferred out of the account to the transferror plan.

(ii) Tax treatment of amounts. Any amount transferred out of an account under clause (i)

(I) shall not be includible in the gross income of the employer for such taxable year, but

(II) shall be treated as an employer reversion for purposes of section 4980 (without regard to subsection (d) thereof).

(C) Ordering rule. For purposes of this section, any amount paid out of a health benefits account shall be treated as paid first out of the assets and income described in subparagraph (A).

(2) Requirements relating to pension benefits accruing before transfer.

(A) In general. The requirements of this paragraph are met if the plan provides that the accrued pension benefits of any participant or beneficiary under the plan become nonforfeitable in the same manner which would be required if the plan had terminated immediately before the qualified transfer (or in the case of a participant who separated during the 1-year period ending on the date of the transfer, immediately before such separation).

(B) Special rule for 1990. In the case of a qualified transfer described in subsection (b)(4), the requirements of this paragraph are met with respect to any participant who separated from service during the taxable year to which such transfer relates by recomputing such participant's benefits as if subparagraph (A) had applied immediately before such separation.

[(3) Minimum cost requirements.

[(A) In general. The requirements of this paragraph are met if each group health plan or arrangement under which applicable health benefits are provided provides that the applicable employer cost for each tax-

able year during the cost maintenance period shall not be less than the higher of the applicable employer costs for each of the 2 taxable years immediately preceding the taxable year of the qualified transfer.

[(B) Applicable employer cost. For purposes of this paragraph, the term "applicable employer cost" means, with respect to any taxable year, the amount determined by dividing

[(i) the qualified current retiree health liabilities of the employer for such taxable year, determined

[(I) without regard to any reduction under subsection (e)(1)(B), and

[(II) in the case of a taxable year in which there was no qualified transfer, in the same manner as if there had been such a transfer at the end of the taxable year, by

[(ii) the number of individuals to whom coverage for applicable health benefits was provided during such taxable year.

[(C) Election to compute cost separately. An employer may elect to have this paragraph applied separately with respect to individuals eligible for benefits under title XVIII of the Social Security Act at any time during the taxable year and with respect to individuals not so eligible.

[(D) Cost maintenance period. For purposes of this paragraph, the term "cost maintenance period" means the period of 5 taxable years beginning with the taxable year in which the qualified transfer occurs. If the taxable year is in 2 or more overlapping cost maintenance periods, this paragraph shall be applied by taking into account the highest applicable employer cost required to be provided under subparagraph (A) for such taxable year.]

(3) Maintenance of benefit requirements.

(A) In general. The requirements of this paragraph are met if each group health plan or arrangement under which applicable

health benefits are provided provides that the applicable health benefits provided by the employer during each taxable year during the benefit maintenance period are substantially the same as the applicable health benefits provided by the employer during the taxable year immediately preceding the taxable year of the qualified transfer.

(B) Election to apply separately. An employer may elect to have this paragraph applied separately with respect to individuals eligible for benefits under title XVIII of the Social Security Act at any time during the taxable year and with respect to individuals not so eligible.

(C) Benefit maintenance period. For purposes of this paragraph, the term "benefit maintenance period" means the period of 5 taxable years beginning with the taxable year in which the qualified transfer occurs. If a taxable year is in 2 or more benefit maintenance periods, this paragraph shall be applied by taking into account the highest level of benefits required to be provided under subparagraph (A) for such taxable year.

(d) Limitations on Employer. For purposes of this title

(1) Deduction limitations. No deduction shall be allowed—

(A) for the transfer of any amount to a health benefits account in a qualified transfer (or any retransfer to the plan under subsection (c)(1)(B)),

(B) for qualified current retiree health liabilities paid out of the assets (and income) described in subsection (c)(1), or

(C) for any amounts to which subparagraph (B) does not apply and which are paid for qualified current retiree health liabilities for the taxable year to the extent such amounts are not greater than the excess (if any) of

(i) the amount determined under subparagraph (A) (and income allocable thereto), over

(ii) the amount determined under subparagraph (B).

(e) Definition and special rules. For purposes of this section

(1) Qualified current retiree health liabilities. For purposes of this section—

(A) In general. The term "qualified current retiree health liabilities" means, with respect to any taxable year, the aggregate amounts (including administrative expenses) which would have been allowable as a deduction to the employer for such taxable year with respect to applicable health benefits provided during such taxable year if

(i) such benefits were provided directly by the employer, and

(ii) the employer used the cash receipts and disbursements method of accounting.

For purposes of the preceding sentence, the rule of section 419(c)(3)(B) shall apply.

[(B) Reduction for amounts previously set aside. The amount determined under subparagraph (A) shall be reduced by any amount previously contributed to a health benefits account or welfare benefit fund (as defined in section 419(e)(1)) to pay for the qualified current retiree health liabilities. The portion of any reserves remaining as of the close of December 31, 1990, shall be allocated on a pro rata basis to qualified current retiree health liabilities.]

(B) Reductions for amounts previously set aside. The amount determined under subparagraph (A) shall be reduced by the amount which bears the same ratio to such amount as

(i) the value (as of the close of the plan year preceding the year of the qualified transfer) of the assets in all health benefits accounts or welfare benefit funds (as defined in section 419(e)(1)) set aside to pay for the qualified current retiree health liability, bears to

IRC *Sec. 420 (e)(1)(B)(i)*

(ii) the present value of the qualified current retiree health liabilities for all plan years (determined without regard to this subparagraph).

(C) Applicable health benefits. The term "applicable health benefits" mean health benefits or coverage which are provided to

(i) retired employees who, immediately before the qualified transfer, are entitled to receive such benefits upon retirement and who are entitled to pension benefits under the plan, and

(ii) their spouses and dependents.

(D) Key employees excluded. If an employee is a key employee (within the meaning of section 416(i)(1)) with respect to any plan year ending in a taxable year, such employee shall not be taken into account in computing qualified current retiree health liabilities for such taxable year [or in calculating applicable employer cost under subsection (c)(3)(B)] *and shall not be subject to the minimum benefit requirement of subsection (c)(3).*

(2) Excess pension assets. The term "excess pension assets" means the excess (if any) of

(A) the amount determined under section 412(c)(7)(A)(ii), over

(B) the greater of

(i) the amount determined under section 412(c)(7)(A)(i), or

(ii) 125 percent of current liability (as defined in section 412(c)(7)(B)).

The determination under this paragraph shall be made as of the most recent valuation date of the plan preceding the qualified transfer.

(3) Health benefits account.— The term "health benefits account" means an account established and maintained under section 401(h).

(4) Coordination with section 412. In the case of a qualified transfer to a health benefits account

(A) any assets transferred in a plan year on or before the valuation date for such year (and any income allocable thereto) shall, for purposes of section 412, be treated as assets in the plan as of the valuation date for such year, and

(B) the plan shall be treated as having a net experience loss under section 412(b)(2)(B)(iv) in an amount equal to the amount of such transfer (reduced by the amounts transferred back to the pension plan under subsection (c)(1)(B)) and for which amortization charges begin for the first plan year after the plan year in which such transfer occurs, except that such section shall be applied to such amount by substituting "10 plan years" for "5 plan years."

SEC. 421. GENERAL RULES

(a) Effect of qualifying transfer. If a share of stock is transferred to an individual in a transfer in respect of which the requirements of section 422(a) or 423(a) are met—

(1) no income shall result at the time of the transfer of such share to the individual upon his exercise of the option with respect to such share;

(2) no deduction under section 162 (relating to trade or business expenses) shall be allowable at any time to the employer corporation, a parent or subsidiary corporation of such corporation, or a corporation issuing or assuming a stock option in a transaction to which section 424(a) applies, with respect to the share so transferred; and

(3) no amount other than the price paid under the option shall be considered as received by any of such corporations for the share so transferred.

(b) Effect of disqualifying disposition. If the transfer of a share of stock to an individual pursuant to his exercise of an option would otherwise meet the requirements of 422(a) or 423(a) except that there is a failure to meet any of the holding period requirements of section 422(a)(1) or 423(a)(1), then any increase in the income of such individual or deduction from the income of his employer corporation for the taxable year in which such exercise occurred attributable to such disposition, shall be treated as an increase in income or a deduction from income in the taxable year of such individual or of such employer corporation in which such disposition occurred.

(c) Exercise by estate.

(1) In general. If an option to which this part applies is exercised after the death of the employee by the estate of the decedent, or by a person who acquired the right to exercise such option by bequest or inheritance or by reason of the death of the decedent, the provisions of subsection (a) shall apply to the same extent as if the option had been exercised by the decedent, except that—

(A) the holding period and employment requirements of 422(a) and 423(a) shall not apply, and

(B) any transfer by the estate of stock acquired shall be considered a disposition of such stock for purposes of section 423(c).

(2) Deduction for estate tax. If an amount is required to be included under section 423(c) in gross income of the estate of the deceased employee or of a person described in paragraph (1), there shall be allowed to the estate or such person a deduction with respect to the estate tax attributable to the inclusion in the taxable estate of the deceased employee of the net value for estate tax purposes of the option. For this purpose, the deduction shall be determined under section 691(c) as if the option acquired from the deceased employee were an item of gross income in respect of the decedent under section 691 and as if the amount includible in gross income under section 423(c) were an amount included in gross income under section 691 in respect of such item of gross income.

(3) Basis of shares acquired. In the case of a share of stock acquired by the exercise of an option to which paragraph (1) applies—

(A) the basis of such share shall include so much of the basis of the option as is attributable to such share; except that the basis of such share shall be reduced by the excess (if any) of (i) the amount which would have been includible in gross income under section 423(c) if the employee had exercised the option on the date of his death and had held the share acquired pursuant to such exercise at the time of his death, over (ii) the amount which is includible in gross income under such section; and

(B) the last sentence of section 423(c) shall apply only to the extent that the amount includible in gross income under such section exceeds so much of the basis of the option as is attributable to such share.

SEC. 422. INCENTIVE STOCK OPTIONS

(a) In general. Section 421(a) shall apply with respect to the transfer of a share of stock to an individual pursuant to his exercise of an incentive stock option if—

(1) no disposition of such share is made by him within 2 years from the date of the granting of the option nor within 1 year after the transfer of such share to him, and

(2) at all times during the period beginning on the date of the granting of the option and ending on the day 3 months before the date of such exercise, such individual was an employee of either the corporation granting such option, a parent or subsidiary corporation of such corporation, or a corporation or a parent or subsidiary corporation of such corporation issuing or assuming a stock option in a transaction to which section 424(a) applies.

(b) Incentive stock option. For purposes of this part, the term "incentive stock option" means an option granted to an individual for any reason connected with his employment by a corporation, if granted by the employer corporation or its parent or subsidiary corporation, to purchase stock of any of such corporations, but only if—

(1) the option is granted pursuant to a plan which includes the aggregate number of shares which may be issued under options and the employees (or class of employees) eligible to receive options, and which is approved by the stockholders of the granting corporation within 12 months before or after the date such plan is adopted;

(2) such option is granted within 10 years from the date such plan is adopted, or the date such plan is approved by the stockholders, whichever is earlier;

(3) such option by its terms is not exercisable after the expiration of 10 years from the date such option is granted;

(4) the option price is not less than the fair market value of the stock at the time such option is granted;

(5) such option by its terms is not transferable by such individual otherwise than by will or the laws of descent and distribution, and is exercisable, during his lifetime, only by him; and

(6) such individual, at the time the option is granted, does not own stock possessing more than 10 percent of the total combined voting power of all classes of stock of the employer corporation or of its parent or subsidiary corporation.

Such term shall not include any option if (as of the time the option is granted) the terms of such option provide that it will not be treated as an incentive stock option.

(c) Special rules.

(1) Good faith efforts to value of stock. If a share of stock is transferred pursuant to the exercise by an individual of an option which would fail to qualify as an incentive stock option under subsection (b) because there was a failure in an attempt, made in good faith, to meet the requirement of subsection (b)(4), the

requirement of subsection (b)(4) shall be considered to have been met. To the extent provided in regulations by the Secretary, a similar rule shall apply for purposes of subsection (d).

(2) Certain disqualifying dispositions where amount realized is less than value at exercise. If—

(A) an individual who has acquired a share of stock by the exercise of an incentive stock option makes a disposition of such share within either of the periods described in subsection (a)(1), and

(B) such disposition is a sale or exchange with respect to which a loss (if sustained) would be recognized to such individual,

then the amount which is includible in the gross income of such individual, and the amount which is deductible from the income of his employer corporation, as compensation attributable to the exercise of such option shall not exceed the excess (if any) of the amount realized on such sale or exchange over the adjusted basis of such share.

(3) Certain transfers by insolvent individuals. If an insolvent individual holds a share of stock acquired pursuant to his exercise of an incentive stock option, and if such share is transferred to a trustee, receiver, or other similar fiduciary in any proceeding under title 11 or any other similar insolvency proceeding, neither such transfer, nor any other transfer of such share for the benefit of his creditors in such proceeding, shall constitute a disposition of such share for purposes of subsection (a)(1).

(4) Permissible provisions. An option which meets the requirements of subsection (b) shall be treated as an incentive stock option even if—

(A) the employee may pay for the stock with stock of the corporation granting the option,

(B) the employee has a right to receive property at the time of exercise of the option, or

(C) the option is subject to any condition not inconsistent with the provisions of subsection (b).

Subparagraph (B) shall apply to a transfer of property (other than cash) only if section 83 applies to the property so transferred.

(5) 10-percent shareholder rule. Subsection (b)(6) shall not apply if at the time such option is granted the option price is at least 110 percent of the fair market value of the stock subject to the option and such option by its terms is not exercisable after the expiration of 5 years from the date such option is granted.

(6) Special rule when disabled. For purposes of subsection (a)(2), in the case of an employee who is disabled (within the meaning of section 22(e)(3)), the 3-month period of subsection (a)(2) shall be 1 year.

(7) Fair market value. For purposes of this section, the fair market value of stock shall be determined without regard to any restriction other than a restriction which, by its terms, will never lapse.

(d) $100,000 per year limitation.

(1) In general. To the extent that the aggregate fair market value of stock with respect to which incentive stock options (determined without regard to this subsection) are exercisable for the 1st time by any individual during any calendar year (under all plans of the individual's employer corporation and its parent and subsidiary corporations) exceeds $100,000, such options shall be treated as options which are not incentive stock options.

(2) Ordering rule. Paragraph (1) shall be applied by taking options into account in the order in which they were granted.

(3) Determination of fair market value. For purposes of paragraph (1), the fair market value of any stock shall be determined as of the time the option with respect to such stock is granted.

SEC. 423. EMPLOYEE STOCK PURCHASE PLANS.

(a) General rule.— Section 421(a) shall apply with respect to the transfer of a share of stock to an individual pursuant to his exercise of an option granted after December 31, 1963, under an employee stock purchase plan (as defined in subsection (b)) if—

(1) no disposition of such share is made by him within 2 years after the date of the granting of the option nor within 1 year after the transfer of such share to him; and

(2) at all times during the period beginning with the date of the granting of the option and ending on the day 3 months before the date of such exercise, he is an employee of the corporation granting such option, a parent or subsidiary corporation of such corporation, or a corporation or a parent or subsidiary corporation of such corporation issuing or assuming a stock option in a transaction to which section 424(a) applies.

(b) Employee Stock Purchase Plan.— For purposes of this part, the term "employee stock purchase plan" means a plan which meets the following requirements:

(1) the plan provides that options are to be granted only to employees of the employer corporation or of its parent or subsidiary corporation to purchase stock in any such corporation;

(2) such plan is approved by the stockholders of the granting corporation within 12 months before or after the date such plan is adopted;

(3) under the terms of the plan, no employee can be granted an option if such employee, immediately after the option is granted, owns stock possessing 5 percent or more of the total combined voting power or value of all classes of stock of the employer corporation or of its parent or subsidiary corporation. For purposes of this paragraph, the rules of section 424(d) shall apply in determining the stock ownership of an individual, and stock which the employee may purchase under outstanding options shall be treated as stock owned by the employee;

(4) under the terms of the plan, options are to be granted to all employees of any corporation whose employees are granted any of such options by reason of their employment by such corporation, except that there may be excluded—

(A) employees who have been employed less than 2 years,

(B) employees whose customary employment is 20 hours or less per week,

(C) employees whose customary employment is for not more than 5 months in any calendar year, and

(D) highly compensated employees (within the meaning of section 414(q));

(5) under the terms of the plan, all employees granted such options shall have the same rights and privileges, except that the amount of stock which may be purchased by any employee under such option may bear a uniform relationship to the total compensation, or the basic or regular rate of compensation, of employees, and the plan may provide that no employee may purchase more than a maximum amount of stock fixed under the plan;

(6) under the terms of the plan, the option price is not less than the lesser of—

(A) an amount equal to 85 percent of the fair market value of the stock at the time such option is granted, or

(B) an amount which under the terms of the option may not be less than 85 percent of the fair market value of the stock at the time such option is exercised;

(7) under the terms of the plan, such option cannot be exercised after the expiration of—

(A) 5 years from the date such option is granted, if, under the terms of such plan, the option price is to be not less than 85 percent

of the fair market value of such stock at the time of the exercise of the option, or

(B) 27 months from the date such option is granted, if the option price is not determinable in the manner described in subparagraph (A);

(8) under the terms of the plan, no employee may be granted an option which permits his rights to purchase stock under all such plans of his employer corporation and its parent and subsidiary corporations to accrue at a rate which exceeds $25,000 of fair market value of such stock (determined at the time such option is granted) for each calendar year in which such option is outstanding at any time. For purposes of this paragraph—

(A) the right to purchase stock under an option accrues when the option (or any portion thereof) first becomes exercisable during the calendar year;

(B) the right to purchase stock under an option accrues at the rate provided in the option, but in no case may such rate exceed $25,000 of fair market value of such stock (determined at the time such option is granted) for any one calendar year; and

(C) a right to purchase stock which has accrued under one option granted pursuant to the plan may not be carried over to any other option; and

(9) under the terms of the plan, such option is not transferable by such individual otherwise than by will or the laws of descent and distribution, and is exercisable, during his lifetime, only by him.

For purposes of paragraphs (3) to (9) inclusive, where additional terms are contained in an offering made under a plan, such additional terms shall, with respect to options exercised under such offering, be treated as a part of the terms of such plan.

(c) Special Rule Where Option Price Is Between 85 Percent and 100 Percent of Value of Stock.— If the option price of a share of stock acquired by an individual pursuant to a transfer to which subsection (a) applies was less than 100 percent of the fair market value of such share at the time such option was granted, then, in the event of any disposition of such share by him which meets the holding period requirements of subsection (a), or in the event of his death (whenever occurring) while owning such share, there shall be included as compensation (and not as gain upon the sale or exchange of a capital asset) in his gross income, for the taxable year in which falls the date of such disposition or for the taxable year closing with his death, whichever applies, an amount equal to the lesser of—

(1) the excess of the fair market value of the share at the time of such disposition or death over the amount paid for the share under the option, or

(2) the excess of the fair market value of the share at the time the option was granted over the option price.

If the option price is not fixed or determinable at the time the option is granted, then for purposes of this subsection, the option price shall be determined as if the option were exercised at such time. In the case of the disposition of such share by the individual, the basis of the share in his hands at the time of such disposition shall be increased by an amount equal to the amount so includible in his gross income.

SEC. 424. DEFINITIONS AND SPECIAL RULES.

(a) **Corporate Reorganizations, Liquidations, Etc.**— For purposes of this part, the term "issuing or assuming a stock option in a transaction to which section 424 applies" means a substitution of a new option for the old option, or an assumption of the old option, by an employer corporation, or a parent or subsidiary of such corporation, by reason of a corporate merger, consolidation, acquisition of property or stock, separation, reorganization, or liquidation, if—

(1) the excess of the aggregate fair market value of the shares subject to the option immediately after the substitution or assumption over the aggregate option price of such shares is not more than the excess of the aggregate fair market value of all shares subject to the option immediately before such substitution or assumption over the aggregate option price of such shares, and

(2) the new option or the assumption of the old option does not give the employee additional benefits which he did not have under the old option.

For purposes of this subsection, the parent-subsidiary relationship shall be determined at the time of any such transaction under this subsection.

(b) **Acquisition of New Stock.**— For purposes of this part, if stock is received by an individual in a distribution to which section 305, 354, 355, 356, or 1036 (or so much of section 1031 as relates to section 1036) applies, and such distribution was made with respect to stock transferred to him upon his exercise of the option, such stock shall be considered as having been transferred to him on his exercise of such option. A similar rule shall be applied in the case of a series of such distributions.

(c) **Disposition.**—

(1) **In general.**— Except as provided in paragraphs (2), (3), and (4), for purposes of this part, the term "disposition" includes a sale, exchange, gift, or a transfer of legal title, but does not include—

(A) a transfer from a decedent to an estate or a transfer by bequest or inheritance;

(B) an exchange to which section 354, 355, 356, or 1036 (or so much of section 1031 as relates to section 1036) applies; or

(C) a mere pledge or hypothecation.

(2) **Joint tenancy.**— The acquisition of a share of stock in the name of the employee and

another jointly with the right of survivorship or a subsequent transfer of a share of stock into such joint ownership shall not be deemed a disposition, but a termination of such joint tenancy (except to the extent such employee acquires ownership of such stock) shall be treated as a disposition by him occurring at the time such joint tenancy is terminated.

(3) Special rule where incentive stock is acquired through use of other statutory option stock.—

(A) Nonrecognition sections not to apply.— If—

(i) there is a transfer of statutory option stock in connection with the exercise of any incentive stock option, and

(ii) the applicable holding period requirements (under section 422(a)(1) or 423(a)(1)) are not met before such transfer,

then no section referred to in subparagraph (B) of paragraph (1) shall apply to such transfer.

(B) Statutory option stock.—For purpose of subparagraph (A), the term "statutory option stock" means any stock acquired through the exercise of a qualified stock option, an incentive stock option, an option granted under an employee stock purchase plan, or a restricted stock option.

(4) Transfers between spouses or incident to divorce.— In the case of any transfer described in subsection (a) of section 1041—

(A) such transfer shall not be treated as a disposition for purposes of this part, and

(B) the same tax treatment under this part with respect to the transferred property shall apply to the transferee as would have applied to the transferor.

(d) Attribution of Stock Ownership.— For purposes of this part, in applying the percentage limitations of sections 422(b)(6) and 423(b)(3)—

(1) the individual with respect to whom such limitation is being determined shall be considered as owning the stock owned, directly or indirectly, by or for his brothers and sisters (whether by the whole or half blood), spouse, ancestors, and lineal descendants, and

(2) stock owned, directly or indirectly, by or for a corporation, partnership, estate, or trust, shall be considered as being owned proportionately by or for its shareholders, partners, or beneficiaries.

(e) Parent Corporation.— For purposes of this part, the term "parent corporation" means any corporation (other than the employer corporation) in an unbroken chain of corporations ending with the employer corporation if, at the time of the granting of the option, each of the corporations other than the employer corporation owns stock possessing 50 percent or more of the total combined voting power of all classes of stock in one of the other corporations in such chain.

(f) Subsidiary Corporation.— For purposes of this part, the term "subsidiary corporation" means any corporation (other than the employer corporation) in an unbroken chain of corporations beginning with the employer corporation if, at the time of the granting of the option, each of the corporations other than the last corporation in the unbroken chain owns stock possessing 50 percent or more of the total combined voting power of all classes of stock in one of the other corporations in such chain.

(g) Special Rule for Applying Subsections (e) and (f).— In applying subsections (e) and (f) for purposes of section 422(a)(2) and 423(a)(2), there shall be substituted for the term "employer corporation" wherever it appears in subsections (e) and (f) the term "grantor corporation", or the term "corporation issuing or assuming a stock option in a transaction to which section 424(a) applies", as the case may be.

(h) Modification, Extension, or Renewal of Option.—

(1) In general.—For purposes of this part, if the terms of any option to purchase stock are modified, extended, or renewed, such modification, extension, or renewal shall be considered as the granting of a new option.

(2) Special rule for section 423 options.— In the case of the transfer of stock pursuant to the exercise of an option to which section 423 applies and which has been so modified, extended, or renewed, the fair market value of such stock at the time of the granting of the option shall be considered as whichever of the following is the highest—

(A) the fair market value of such stock on the date of the original granting of the option,

(B) the fair market value of such stock on the date of the making of such modification, extension, or renewal, or

(C) the fair market value of such stock at the time of the making of any intervening modification, extension, or renewal.

(3) Definition of modification.— The term "modification" means any change in the terms of the option which gives the employee additional benefits under the option, but such term shall not include a change in the terms of the option—

(A) attributable to the issuance or assumption of an option under subsection (a);

(B) to permit the option to qualify under section 423(b)(9); or

(C) in the case of an option not immediately exercisable in full, to accelerate the time at which the option may be exercised.

(i) Stockholder Approval.—For purposes of this part, if the grant of an option is subject to approval by stockholders, the date of grant of the option shall be determined as if the option had not been subject to such approval.

(j) Cross References.—For provisions requiring the reporting of certain acts with respect to a qualified stock option, an incentive stock option, options granted under employer stock purchase plans, or a restricted stock option, see section 6039.

* * *

Subchapter E—Accounting Periods and Methods of Accounting

* * *

Part II—Methods of Accounting

Subpart B—Taxable Year for Which Items of Gross Income Included

* * *

SEC. 457. DEFERRED COMPENSATION PLANS OF STATE AND LOCAL GOVERNMENTS AND TAX-EXEMPT ORGANIZATIONS.

(a) Year of Inclusion in Gross Income.—In the case of a participant in an eligible deferred compensation plan, any amount of compensation deferred under the plan, and any income attributable to the amounts so deferred, shall be includible in gross income only for the taxable year in which such compensation or other income is paid or otherwise made available to the participant or other beneficiary.

(b) Eligible Deferred Compensation Plan Defined.—For purposes of this section, the term "eligible deferred compensation plan" means a plan established and maintained by an eligible employer—

(1) in which only individuals who perform service for the employer may be participants,

(2) which provides that (except as provided in paragraph (3)) the maximum amount which may be deferred under the plan for the taxable year shall not exceed the lesser of—

(A) $7,500, or

(B) 33⅓ percent of the participant's includible compensation,

(3) which may provide that, for 1 or more of the participant's last 3 taxable years ending before he attains normal retirement age under the plan, the ceiling set forth in paragraph (2) shall be the lesser of—

(A) $15,000, or

(B) the sum of—

(i) the plan ceiling established for purposes of paragraph (2) for the taxable year (determined without regard to this paragraph), plus

(ii) so much of the plan ceiling established for purposes of paragraph (2) for taxable years before the taxable year as has not previously been used under paragraph (2) or this paragraph,

(4) which provides that compensation will be deferred for any calendar month only if an agreement providing for such deferral has been entered into before the beginning of such month,

(5) which meets the distribution requirements of subsection (d), and

(6) which provides that—

(A) all amounts of compensation deferred under the plan,

(B) all property and rights purchased with such amounts, and

(C) all income attributable to such amounts, property, or rights,

shall remain (until made available to the participant or other beneficiary) solely the property and rights of the employer (without being restricted to the provision of benefits under the plan), subject only to the claims of the employer's general creditors.

A plan which is established and maintained by an employer which is described in subsection (e)(1)(A) and which is administered in a manner which is inconsistent with the requirements of any of the preceding paragraphs shall be treated as not meeting the requirements of such paragraph as of the 1st plan year beginning more than 180 days after the date of notification by the Secretary of the inconsistency unless the employer corrects the inconsistency before the 1st day of such plan year.

(c) Individuals Who Are Participants in More Than 1 Plan.—

(1) In general.—The maximum amount of the compensation of any one individual which may be deferred under subsection (a) during any taxable year shall not exceed $7,500 (as modified by any adjustment provided under subsection (b)(3)).

(2) Coordination with certain other deferrals.—In applying paragraph (1) of this subsection—

(A) any amount excluded from gross income under section 403(b) for the taxable year, and

(B) any amount—

(i) excluded from gross income under section 402(e)(3) or section 402(h)(1)(B) for the taxable year, or

(ii) with respect to which a deduction is allowable by reason of a contribution to an organization described in section 501(c)(18) for the taxable year,

shall be treated as an amount deferred under subsection (a). In applying section 402(g)(8)(A)(iii) or 403(b)(2)(A)(ii), an amount deferred under subsection (a) for any year of service shall be taken into account as if described in section 402(g)(3)(C) or 403(b)(2)(A)(ii), respectively. Subparagraph (B) shall not apply in the case of a participant in a rural cooperative plan (as defined in section 401(k)(7)).

IRC Sec. 457 (b)(2)(B)

(d) Distribution Requirements.—

(1) In general.—For purposes of subsection (b)(5), a plan meets the distribution requirements of this subsection if—

(A) under the plan amounts will not be made available to participants or beneficiaries earlier than—

(i) the calendar year in which the participant attains age 70½,

(ii) when the participant is separated from service with the employer, or

(iii) when the participant is faced with an unforeseeable emergency (determined in the manner prescribed by the Secretary in regulations), and

(B) the plan meets the minimum distribution requirements of paragraph (2).

(2) Minimum distribution requirements.—A plan meets the minimum distribution requirements of this paragraph if such plan meets the requirements of subparagraphs (A), (B), and (C):

(A) Application of section 401(a)(9).— A plan meets the requirements of this subparagraph if the plan meets the requirements of section 401(a)(9).

(B) Additional distribution requirements.— A plan meets the requirements of this subparagraph if—

(i) in the case of a distribution beginning before the death of the participant, such distribution will be made in a form under which—

(I) the amounts payable with respect to the participant will be paid at times specified by the Secretary which are not later than the time determined under section 401(a)(9)(G) (relating to incidental death benefits), and

(II) any amount not distributed to the participant during his life will be distributed after the death of the participant at least

as rapidly as under the method of distributions being used under subclause (I) as of the date of his death, or

(ii) in the case of a distribution which does not begin before the death of the participant, the entire amount payable with respect to the participant will be paid during a period not to exceed 15 years (or the life expectancy of the surviving spouse if such spouse is the beneficiary).

(C) Nonincreasing benefits.—A plan meets the requirements of this subparagraph if any distribution payable over a period of more than 1 year can only be made in substantially nonincreasing amounts (paid not less frequently than annually).

(e) Other Definitions and Special Rules.— For purposes of this section—

(1) Eligible employer.— The term "eligible employer" means—

(A) a State, political subdivision of a State, and any agency or instrumentality of a State or political subdivision of a State, and

(B) any other organization (other than a governmental unit) exempt from tax under this subtitle.

(2) Performance of service.— The performance of service includes performance of service as an independent contractor and the person (or governmental unit) for whom such services are performed shall be treated as the employer.

(3) Participant.— The term "participant means an individual who is eligible to defer compensation under the plan.

(4) Beneficiary.— The term "beneficiary" means a beneficiary of the participant, his estate, or any other person whose interest in the plan is derived from the participant.

(5) Includible compensation.— The term "includible compensation" means compensation for service performed for the employer which (taking into account the provisions of this section and other provisions of this chapter) is currently includible in gross income.

(6) Compensation taken into account at present value.— Compensation shall be taken into account at its present value.

(7) Community property laws.— The amount of includible compensation shall be determined without regard to any community property laws.

(8) Income attributable.— Gains from the disposition of property shall be treated as income attributable to such property.

(9) Benefits not treated as made available by reason of certain elections.—If—

(A) the total amount payable to a participant under the plan does not exceed $3,500, and

(B) no additional amounts may be deferred under the plan with respect to the participant,

the amount payable to the participant under the plan shall not be treated as made available merely because such participant may elect to receive a lump sum payable after separation from service and within 60 days of the election.

(10) Transfers between plans.— A participant shall not be required to include in gross income any portion of the entire amount payable to such participant solely by reason of the transfer of such portion from 1 eligible deferred compensation plan to another eligible deferred compensation plan.

(11) Certain plans excepted.— Any bona fide vacation leave, sick leave, compensatory time, severance pay, disability pay, or death benefit plan shall be treated as a plan not providing for the deferral of compensation.

(12) Exception for nonelective deferred compensation of nonemployees.—

(A) In general.— This section shall not apply to nonelective deferred compensation

attributable to services not performed as an employee.

(B) Nonelective deferred compensation.— For purposes of subparagraph (A), deferred compensation shall be treated as nonelective only if all individuals (other than those who have not satisfied any applicable initial service requirement) with the same relationship to the payor are covered under the same plan with no individual variations or options under the plan.

(13) Special rule for churches.— The term "eligible employer" shall not include a church (as defined in section 3121(w)(3)(A)) or qualified church-controlled organization (as defined in section 3121(w)(3)(B)).

(f) Tax Treatment of Participants Where Plan or Arrangement of Employer Is Not Eligible.—

(1) In general.— In the case of a plan of an eligible employer providing for a deferral of compensation, if such plan is not an eligible deferred compensation plan, then—

(A) the compensation shall be included in the gross income of the participant or beneficiary for the 1st taxable year in which there is no substantial risk of forfeiture of the rights to such compensation, and

(B) the tax treatment of any amount made available under the plan to a participant or beneficiary shall be determined under section 72 (relating to annuities, etc.).

(2) Exceptions.— Paragraph (1) shall not apply to—

(A) a plan described in section 401(a) which includes a trust exempt from tax under section 501(a),

(B) an annuity plan or contract described in section 403,

(C) that portion of any plan which consists of a transfer of property described in section 83, and

(D) that portion of any plan which consists of a trust to which section 402(b) applies.

(3) Definitions.—For purposes of this subsection—

(A) Plan includes arrangements, etc. The term "plan" includes any agreement or arrangement.

(B) Substantial risk of forfeiture. The rights of a person to compensation are subject to a substantial risk of forfeiture if such person's rights to such compensation are conditioned upon the future performance of substantial services by any individual.

* * *

Subchapter F— Exempt Organizations

Part I— General rule

SEC. 501. EXEMPTION FROM TAX ON CORPORATIONS, CERTAIN TRUSTS, ETC.

(a) Exemption From Taxation.— An organization described in subsection (c) or (d) or section 401(a) shall be exempt from taxation under this subtitle unless such exemption is denied under section 502 or 503.

(b) Tax on Unrelated Business Income and Certain Other Activities.— An organization exempt from taxation under subsection (a) shall be subject to tax to the extent provided in parts II, III, and VI of this subchapter, but (notwithstanding parts II, III, and VI of this subchapter) shall be considered an organization exempt from income taxes for the purpose of any law which refers to organizations exempt from income taxes.

(c) List of Exempt Organizations.— The following organizations are referred to in subsection (a):

(1) Any corporation organized under Act of Congress which is an instrumentality of the United States but only if such corporation—

(A) is exempt from federal income taxes—

(i) under such Act as amended and supplemented before July 18, 1984, or

(ii) under this title without regard to any provision of law which is not contained in this title and which is not contained in a revenue Act, or

(B) is described in subsection (*l*).

(2) Corporations organized for the exclusive purpose of holding title to property, collecting income therefrom, and turning over the entire amount thereof, less expenses, to an organization which itself is exempt under this section. Rules similar to the rules of subparagraph (G) of paragraph (25) shall apply for purposes of this paragraph.

(3) Corporations, and any community chest, fund, or foundation, organized and operated exclusively for religious, charitable, scientific, testing for public safety, literary, or educational purposes, or to foster national or international amateur sports competition (but only if no part of its activities involve the provision of athletic facilities or equipment), or for the prevention of cruelty to children or animals, no part of the net earnings of which inures to the benefit of any private shareholder or individual, no substantial part of the activities of which is carrying on propaganda, or otherwise attempting to influence legislation, (except as otherwise provided in subsection (h)), and which does not participate in, or intervene in (including the publishing or distributing of statements), any political campaign on behalf of (or in opposition to) any candidate for public office.

(4) Civic leagues or organizations not organized for profit but operated exclusively for the promotion of social welfare, or local associations of employees, the membership of which is limited to the employees of a designated person or persons in a particular municipality, and the net earnings of which are devoted exclusively to charitable, educational, or recreational purposes.

(5) Labor, agricultural, or horticultural organizations.

(6) Business leagues, chambers of commerce, real-estate boards, boards of trade, or professional football leagues (whether or not administering a pension fund for football players), not organized for profit and no part of the net earnings of which inures to the benefit of any private shareholder or individual.

(7) Clubs organized for pleasure, recreation, and other nonprofitable purposes, substantially all of the activities of which are for such purposes and no part of the net earnings of which inures to the benefit of any private shareholder.

(8) Fraternal beneficiary societies, orders, or associations—

(A) operating under the lodge system or for the exclusive benefit of the members of a fraternity itself operating under the lodge system, and

(B) providing for the payment of life, sick, accident, or other benefits to the members of such society, order, or association or their dependents.

(9) Voluntary employees' beneficiary associations providing for the payment of life, sick, accident, or other benefits to the members of such association or their dependents or designated beneficiaries, if no part of the net earnings of such association inures (other than through such payments) to the benefit of any private shareholder or individual.

(10) Domestic fraternal societies, orders, or associations, operating under the lodge system—

(A) the net earnings of which are devoted exclusively to religious, charitable, scientific, literary, educational, and fraternal purposes, and

(B) which do not provide for the payment of life, sick, accident, or other benefits.

(11) Teachers' retirement fund associations of a purely local character, if—

(A) no part of their net earnings inures (other than through payment of retirement benefits) to the benefit of any private shareholder or individual, and

(B) the income consists solely of amounts received from public taxation, amounts received from the assessments on the teaching salaries of members, and income in respect of investments.

(12)(A) Benevolent life insurance associations of a purely local character, mutual ditch or irrigation companies, mutual or cooperative telephone companies, or like organizations; but only if 85 percent or more of the income consists of amounts collected from members for the sole purpose of meeting losses and expenses.

(B) In the case of a mutual or cooperative telephone company, subparagraph (A) shall be applied without taking into account any income received or accrued—

(i) from a nonmember telephone company for the performance of communication services which involve members of the mutual or cooperative telephone company,

(ii) from qualified pole rentals,

(iii) from the sale of display listings in a directory furnished to the members of the mutual or cooperative telephone company, or

(iv) from the prepayment of a loan under Section 306A, 306B, or 311 of the Rural Electrification Act of 1936 (as in effect on January 1, 1987).

(C) In the case of a mutual or cooperative electric company, subparagraph (A) shall be applied without taking into account any income received or accrued—

(i) from qualified pole rentals, or

(ii) from the prepayment of a loan under section 306A, 306B, or 311 of the Rural Electrification Act of 1936 (as in effect on January 1, 1987).

(D) For purposes of this paragraph, the term "qualified pole rental" means any rental of a pole (or other structure used to support wires) if such pole (or other structure)—

(i) is used by the telephone or electric company to support one or more wires which are used by such company in providing telephone or electric services to its members, and

(ii) is used pursuant to the rental to support one or more wires (in addition to the wires described in clause (i)) for use in connection with the transmission by wire of electricity or of telephone or other communications.

For purposes of the preceding sentence, the term "rental" includes any sale of the right to use the pole (or other structure).

(13) Cemetery companies owned and operated exclusively for the benefit of their members or which are not operated for profit; and any corporation chartered solely for the purpose of the disposal of bodies by burial or cremation which is not permitted by its charter to engage in any business not necessarily incident to that purpose, no part of the net earnings of which inures to the benefit of any private shareholder or individual.

(14)(A) Credit unions without capital stock organized and operated for mutual purposes and without profit.

(B) Corporations or associations without capital stock organized before September 1, 1957, and operated for mutual purposes and without profit for the purpose of providing reserve funds for, and insurance of, shares or deposits in—

(i) domestic building and loan associations,

(ii) cooperative banks without capital stock organized and operated for mutual purposes and without profit,

(iii) mutual savings banks not having capital stock represented by shares, or

(iv) mutual savings banks described in section 591(b).

(C) Corporations or associations organized before September 1, 1957, and operated for mutual purposes and without profit for the purpose of providing reserve funds for associations or banks described in clause (i), (ii), or (iii) of subparagraph (B); but only if 85 percent or more of the income is attributable to providing such reserve funds and to investments. This subparagraph shall not apply to any corporation or association entitled to exemption under subparagraph (B).

(15)(A) Insurance companies or associations other than life (including interinsurers and reciprocal underwriters) if the net written premiums (or, if greater, direct written premiums) for the taxable year do not exceed $350,000.

(B) For purposes of subparagraph (A), in determining whether any company or association is described in subparagraph (A), such company or association shall be treated as receiving during the taxable year amounts described in subparagraph (A) which are received during such year by all other companies or associations which are members of the same controlled group as the insurance company or association for which the determination is being made.

(C) For purposes of subparagraph (B), the term "controlled group" has the meaning given such term by section 831(b)(2)(B)(ii).

(16) Corporations organized by an association subject to part IV of this subchapter or members thereof, for the purpose of financing the ordinary crop operations of such members or other producers, and operated in conjunction with such association. Exemption shall not be denied any such corporation because it has capital stock, if the dividend rate of such

stock is fixed at not to exceed the legal rate of interest in the State of incorporation or 8 percent per annum, whichever is greater, on the value of the consideration for which the stock was issued, and if substantially all such stock (other than nonvoting preferred stock, the owners of which are not entitled or permitted to participate, directly or indirectly, in the profits of the corporation, on dissolution or otherwise, beyond the fixed dividends) is owned by such association, or members thereof; nor shall exemption be denied any such corporation because there is accumulated and maintained by it a reserve required by State law or a reasonable reserve for any necessary purpose.

(17)(A) A trust or trusts forming part of a plan providing for the payment of supplemental unemployment compensation benefits, if—

(i) under the plan, it is impossible, at any time prior to the satisfaction of all liabilities with respect to employees under the plan, for any part of the corpus or income to be (within the taxable year or thereafter) used for, or diverted to, any purpose other than the providing of supplemental unemployment compensation benefits,

(ii) such benefits are payable to employees under a classification which is set forth in the plan and which is found by the Secretary not to be discriminatory in favor of employees who are highly compensated employees (within the meaning of section 414(q)), and

(iii) such benefits do not discriminate in favor of employees who are highly compensated employees (within the meaning of section 414(q)). A plan shall not be considered discriminatory within the meaning of this clause merely because the benefits received under the plan bear a uniform relationship to the total compensation, or the basic or regular rate of compensation, of the employees covered by the plan.

(B) In determining whether a plan meets the requirements of subparagraph (A), any benefits provided under any other plan shall

not be taken into consideration, except that a plan shall not be considered discriminatory—

(i) merely because the benefits under the plan which are first determined in a nondiscriminatory manner within the meaning of subparagraph (A) are then reduced by any sick, accident, or unemployment compensation benefits received under State or Federal law (or reduced by a portion of such benefits if determined in a nondiscriminatory manner), or

(ii) merely because the plan provides only for employees who are not eligible to receive sick, accident, or unemployment compensation benefits under State or Federal law the same benefits (or a portion of such benefits if determined in a nondiscriminatory manner) which such employees would receive under such laws if such employees were eligible for such benefits, or

(iii) merely because the plan provides only for employees who are not eligible under another plan (which meets the requirements of subparagraph (A)) of supplemental unemployment compensation benefits provided wholly by the employer the same benefits (or a portion of such benefits if determined in a nondiscriminatory manner) which such employees would receive under such other plan if such employees were eligible under such other plan, but only if the employees eligible under both plans would make a classification which would be nondiscriminatory within the meaning of subparagraph (A).

(C) A plan shall be considered to meet the requirements of subparagraph (A) during the whole of any year of the plan if on one day in each quarter it satisfies such requirements.

(D) The term "supplemental unemployment compensation benefits" means only—

(i) benefits which are paid to an employee because of his involuntary separation from the employment of the employer (whether or not such separation is temporary) resulting directly from a reduction in force, the discontinuance of a plant or operation, or other similar conditions, and

(ii) sick and accident benefits subordinate to the benefits described in clause (i).

(E) Exemption shall not be denied under subsection (a) to any organization entitled to such exemption as an association described in paragraph (9) of this subsection merely because such organization provides for the payment of supplemental unemployment benefits (as defined in subparagraph (D)(i)).

(18) A trust or trusts created before June 25, 1959, forming part of a plan providing for the payment of benefits under a pension plan funded only by contributions of employees, if—

(A) under the plan, it is impossible, at any time prior to the satisfaction of all liabilities with respect to employees under the plan, for any part of the corpus or income to be (within the taxable year or thereafter) used for, or diverted to, any purpose other than the providing of benefits under the plan,

(B) such benefits are payable to employees under a classification which is set forth in the plan and which is found by the Secretary not to be discriminatory in favor of employees who are highly compensated employees (within the meaning of section 414(q)),

(C) such benefits do not discriminate in favor of employees who are highly compensated employees (within the meaning of section 414(q)). A plan shall not be considered discriminatory within the meaning of this subparagraph merely because the benefits received under the plan bear a uniform relationship to the total compensation, or the basic or regular rate of compensation, of the employees covered by the plan and

(D) in the case of a plan under which an employee may designate certain contributions as deductible—

(i) such contributions do not exceed the amount with respect to which a deduction is allowable under section 219(b)(3).

(ii) requirements similar to the requirements of section 401(k)(3)(A)(ii) are met with respect to such elective contributions,

(iii) such contributions are treated as elective deferrals for purposes of section 402(g) (other than paragraph (4) thereof), and

(iv) the requirements of section 401(a)(30) are met.

For purposes of subparagraph (D)(ii), rules similar to the rules of section 401(k)(8) shall apply. For purposes of section 4979, any excess contribution under clause (ii) shall be treated as an excess contribution under a cash or deferred arrangement.

(19) A post or organization of past or present members of the Armed Forces of the United States, or an auxiliary unit or society of, or a trust or foundation for, any such post or organization—

(A) organized in the United States or any of its possessions,

(B) at least 75 percent of the members of which are past or present members of the Armed Forces of the United States and substantially all of the other members of which are individuals who are cadets or are spouses, widows, or widowers of past or present members of the Armed Forces of the United States or of cadets, and

(C) no part of the net earnings of which inures to the benefit of any private shareholder or individual.

(20) An organization or trust created or organized in the United States, the exclusive function of which is to form part of a qualified group legal services plan or plans, within the meaning of section 120. An organization or trust which receives contributions because of section 120(c)(5)(C) shall not be prevented from qualifying as an organization described

IRC Sec. 501 (c)(20)

in this paragraph merely because it provides legal services or indemnification against the cost of legal services unassociated with a qualified group legal services plan.

(21)(A) A trust or trusts established in writing, created or organized in the United States, and contributed to by any person (except an insurance company) if—

(i) the purpose of such trust or trusts is exclusively—

(I) to satisfy, in whole or in part, the liability of such person for, or with respect to, claims for compensation for disability or death due to pneumoconiosis under Black Lung Acts,

(II) to pay premiums for insurance exclusively covering such liability,

(III) to pay administrative and other incidental expenses of such trust in connection with the operation of the trust and the processing of claims against such person under Black Lung Acts, and

(IV) to pay accident or health benefits for retired miners and their spouses and dependents (including administrative and other incidental expenses of such trust in connection therewith) or premiums for insurance exclusively covering such benefits; and

(ii) no part of the assets of the trust may be used for, or diverted to, any purpose other than—

(I) the purposes described in clause (i),

(II) investment (but only to the extent that the trustee determines that a portion of the assets is not currently needed for the purposes described in clause (i)) in qualified investments, or

(III) payment into the Black Lung Disability Trust Fund established under section 9501, or into the general fund of the United States Treasury (other than in satisfaction of any tax or other civil or criminal liability of the person who established or contributed to the trust).

(B) No deduction shall be allowed under this chapter for any payment described in subparagraph (A)(i)(IV) from such trust.

(C) Payments described in subparagraph (A)(i)(IV) may be made from such trust during a taxable year only to the extent that the aggregate amount of such payments during such taxable year does not exceed the lesser of—

(i) the excess (if any) (as of the close of the preceding taxable year) of—

(I) the fair market value of the assets of the trust, over

(II) 110 percent of the present value of the liability described in subparagraph (A)(i)(I) of such person, or

(ii) the excess (if any) of—

(I) the sum of a similar excess determined as of the close of the last taxable year ending before the date of the enactment of this subparagraph plus earnings thereon as of the close of the taxable year preceding the taxable year involved, over

(II) the aggregate payments described in subparagraph (A)(i)(IV) made from the trust during all taxable years beginning after the date of the enactment of this subparagraph.

The determinations under the preceding sentence shall be made by an independent actuary using actuarial methods and assumptions (not inconsistent with the regulations prescribed under section 192(c)(1)(A), each of which is reasonable and which are reasonable in the aggregate.

(D) For purposes of this paragraph:

(i) The term "Black Lung Acts" means part C of title IV of the Federal Mine Safety and Health Act of 1977, and any State law providing compensation for disability or death due to that pneumoconiosis.

(ii) The term ''qualified investments'' means—

(I) public debt securities of the United States,

(II) obligations of a State or local government which are not in default as to principal or interest, and

(III) time or demand deposits in a bank (as defined in section 581) or an insured credit union (within the meaning of section 101(6) of the Federal Credit Union Act, 12 U.S.C. 1752(6)) located in the United States.

(iii) The term ''miner'' has the same meaning as such term has when used in section 402(d) of the Black Lung Benefits Act (30 U.S.C. 902(d)).

(iv) The term ''incidental expenses'' includes legal, accounting, actuarial, and trustee expenses.

(22) A trust created or organized in the United States and established in writing by the plan sponsors of multiemployer plans if—

(A) the purpose of such trust is exclusively—

(i) to pay any amount described in section 4223(c) or (h) of the Employee Retirement Income Security Act of 1974, and

(ii) to pay reasonable and necessary administrative expenses in connection with the establishment and operation of the trust and the processing of claims against the trust,

(B) no part of the assets of the trust may be used for, or diverted to, any purpose other than—

(i) the purposes described in subparagraph (A), or

(ii) the investment in securities, obligations, or time or demand deposits described in clause (ii) of paragraph (21)(B),

(C) such trust meets the requirements of paragraphs (2), (3), and (4) of section 4223(b), 4223(h), or, if applicable, section 4223(c) of the Employee Retirement Income Security Act of 1974, and

(D) the trust instrument provides that, on dissolution of the trust, assets of the trust may not be paid other than to plans which have participated in the plan or, in the case of a trust established under section 4223(h) of such Act, to plans with respect to which employers have participated in the fund.

(23) Any association organized before 1880 where more than 75 percent of the members of which are present or past members of the Armed Forces and a principal purpose of which is to provide insurance and other benefits to veterans or their dependents.

(24) A trust described in section 4049 of the Employee Retirement Income Security Act of 1974 (as in effect on the date of the enactment of the Single-Employer Pension Plan Amendments Act of 1986).

(25)(A) Any corporation or trust which—

(i) has no more than 35 shareholders or beneficiaries,

(ii) has only 1 class of stock or beneficial interest, and

(iii) is organized for the exclusive purposes of—

(I) acquiring real property and holding title to, and collecting income from, such property, and

(II) remitting the entire amount of income from such property (less expenses) to 1 or more organizations described in subparagraph (C) which are shareholders of such corporation or beneficiaries of such trust.

For purposes of clause (iii), the term ''real property'' shall not include any interest as a tenant in common (or similar interest) and shall not include any indirect interest.

(B) A corporation or trust shall be described in subparagraph (A) without regard to whether the corporation or trust is organized by 1 or more organizations described in subparagraph (C).

(C) An organization is described in this subparagraph if such organization is—

(i) a qualified pension, profit sharing, or stock bonus plan that meets the requirements of section 401(a),

(ii) a governmental plan (within the meaning of section 414(d)),

(iii) the United States, any State or political subdivision thereof, or any agency or instrumentality of any of the foregoing, or

(iv) any organization described in paragraph (3).

(D) A corporation or trust shall in no event be treated as described in subparagraph (A) unless such corporation or trust permits its shareholders or beneficiaries—

(i) to dismiss the corporation's or trust's investment adviser, following reasonable notice, upon a vote of the shareholders or beneficiaries holding a majority of interest in the corporation or trust, and

(ii) to terminate their interest in the corporation or trust by either, or both, of the following alternatives, as determined by the corporation or trust:

(I) by selling or exchanging their stock in the corporation or interest in the trust (subject to any Federal or State securities law) to any organization described in subparagraph (C) so long as the sale or exchange does not increase the number of shareholders or beneficiaries in such corporation or trust above 35, or

(II) by having their stock or interest redeemed by the corporation or trust after the shareholder or beneficiary has pro-

vided 90 days notice to such corporation or trust.

(E)(i) For purposes of this title—

(I) a corporation which is a qualified subsidiary shall not be treated as a separate corporation, and

(II) all assets, liabilities, and items of income, deduction, and credit of a qualified subsidiary shall be treated as assets, liabilities, and such items (as the case may be) of the corporation or trust described in subparagraph (A).

(ii) For purposes of this subparagraph, the term "qualified subsidiary" means any corporation if, at all times during the period such corporation was in existence, 100 percent of the stock of such corporation is held by the corporation or trust described in subparagraph (A).

(iii) For purposes of this subtitle, if any corporation which was a qualified subsidiary ceases to meet the requirements of clause (ii), such corporation shall be treated as a new corporation acquiring all of its assets (and assuming all of its liabilities) immediately before such cessation from the corporation or trust described in subparagraph (A) in exchange for its stock.

(F) For purposes of subparagraph (A), the term "real property" includes any personal property which is leased under, or in connection with, a lease of real property, but only if the rent attributable to such personal property (determined under the rules of section 856(d)(1)) for the taxable year does not exceed 15 percent of the total rent for the taxable year attributable to both the real and personal property leased under, or in connection with, such lease.

(G)(i) An organization shall not be treated as failing to be described in this paragraph merely by reason of the receipt of any otherwise disqualifying income which is incidentally derived from the holding of real property.

(ii) Clause (i) shall not apply if the amount of gross income described in such clause exceeds 10 percent of the organization's gross income for the taxable year unless the organization establishes to the satisfaction of the Secretary that the receipt of gross income described in clause (i) in excess of such limitation was inadvertent and reasonable steps are being taken to correct the circumstances giving rise to such income.

(d) Religious and Apostolic Organizations.— The following organizations are referred to in subsection (a): Religious or apostolic associations or corporations, if such associations or corporations have a common treasury or community treasury, even if such associations or corporations engage in business for the common benefit of the members, but only if the members thereof include (at the time of filing their returns) in their gross income their entire pro rata shares, whether distributed or not, of the taxable income of the association or corporation for such year. Any amount so included in the gross income of a member shall be treated as a dividend received.

(e) Cooperative Hospital Service Organizations.—For purposes of this title, an organization shall be treated as an organization organized and operated exclusively for charitable purposes, if—

(1) such organization is organized and operated solely—

(A) to perform, on a centralized basis, one or more of the following services which, if performed on its own behalf by a hospital which is an organization described in subsection (c)(3) and exempt from taxation under subsection (a), would constitute activities in exercising or performing the purpose or function constituting the basis for its exemption: data processing, purchasing (including the purchasing of insurance on a group basis), warehousing, billing and collection, food, clinical, industrial engineering, laboratory, printing, communications, record center, and personnel (including selection, testing, training, and education of personnel) services; and

(B) to perform such services solely for two or more hospitals each of which is—

(i) an organization described in subsection (c)(3) which is exempt from taxation under subsection (a),

(ii) a constituent part of an organization described in subsection (c)(3) which is exempt from taxation under subsection (a) and which, if organized and operated as a separate entity, would constitute an organization described in subsection (c)(3), or

(iii) owned and operated by the United States, a State, the District of Columbia, or a possession of the United States, or a political subdivision or an agency or instrumentality of any of the foregoing;

(2) such organization is organized and operated on a cooperative basis and allocates or pays, within $8\frac{1}{2}$ months after the close of its taxable year, all net earnings to patrons on the basis of services performed for them; and

(3) if such organization has capital stock, all of such stock outstanding is owned by its patrons.

For purposes of this title, any organization which, by reason of the preceding sentence, is an organization described in subsection (c)(3) and exempt from taxation under subsection (a), shall be treated as a hospital and as an organization referred to in section 170(b)(1)(A)(iii).

(f) Cooperative Service Organizations of Operating Educational Organizations.— For purposes of this title, if an organization is—

(1) organized and operated solely to hold, commingle, and collectively invest and reinvest (including arranging for and supervising the performance by independent contractors of investment services related thereto) in stocks and securities, the moneys contributed

IRC Sec. 501 (f)(1)

thereto by each of the members of such organization, and to collect income therefrom and turn over the entire amount thereof, less expenses, to such members,

(2) organized and controlled by one or more such members, and

(3) comprised solely of members that are organizations described in clause (ii) or (iv) of section 170(b)(1)(A)—

(A) which are exempt from taxation under subsection (a), or

(B) the income of which is excluded from taxation under section 115(a),

then such organization shall be treated as an organization organized and operated exclusively for charitable purposes.

(g) Definition of Agricultural.— For purposes of subsection (c)(5), the term "agricultural" includes the art or science of cultivating land, harvesting crops or aquatic resources, or raising livestock.

(h) Expenditures by Public Charities to Influence Legislation.—

(1) General rule.—In the case of an organization to which this subsection applies, exemption from taxation under subsection (a) shall be denied because a substantial part of the activities of such organization consists of carrying on propaganda, or otherwise attempting, to influence legislation, but only if such organization normally—

(A) makes lobbying expenditures in excess of the lobbying ceiling amount for such organization for each taxable year, or

(B) makes grass roots expenditures in excess of the grass roots ceiling amount for such organization for each taxable year.

(2) Definitions.—For purposes of this subsection—

(A) Lobbying expenditures.The term "lobbying expenditures" means expenditures for the purpose of influencing legislation (as defined in section 4911(d)).

(B) Lobbying ceiling amount.—The lobbying ceiling amount for any organization for any taxable year is 150 percent of the lobbying nontaxable amount for such organization for such taxable year, determined under section 4911.

(C) Grass roots expenditures.— The term "grass roots expenditures" means expenditures for the purpose of influencing legislation (as defined in section 4911(d) without regard to paragraph (1)(B) thereof).

(D) Grass roots ceiling amount.—The grass roots ceiling amount for any organization for any taxable year is 150 percent of the grass roots nontaxable amount for such organization for such taxable year, determined under section 4911.

(3) Organizations to which this subsection applies.—This subsection shall apply to any organization which has elected (in such manner and at such time as the Secretary may prescribe) to have the provisions of this subsection apply to such organization and which, for the taxable year which includes the date the election is made, is described in subsection (c)(3) and—

(A) is described in paragraph (4), and

(B) is not a disqualified organization under paragraph (5).

(4) Organizations permitted to elect to have this subsection apply.—An organization is described in this paragraph if it is described in—

(A) section 170(b)(1)(A)(ii) (relating to educational institutions),

(B) section 170(b)(1)(A)(iii) (relating to hospitals and medical research organizations),

(C) section 170(b)(1)(A)(iv) (relating to organizations supporting government schools),

(D) section 170(b)(1)(A)(vi) (relating to organizations publicly supported by charitable contributions),

(E) section 509(a)(2) (relating to organizations publicly supported by admissions, sales, etc.), or

(F) section 509(a)(3) (relating to organizations supporting certain types of public charities) except that for purposes of this subparagraph, section 509(a)(3) shall be applied without regard to the last sentence of section 509(a).

(5) Disqualified organizations.— For purposes of paragraph (3) an organization is a disqualified organization if it is—

(A) described in section 170(b)(1)(A)(i) (relating to churches),

(B) an integrated auxiliary of a church or of a convention or association of churches, or

(C) a member of an affiliated group of organizations (within the meaning of section 4911(f)(2)) if one or more members of such group is described in subparagraph (A) or (B).

(6) Years for which election is effective.— An election by an organization under this subsection shall be effective for all taxable years of such organization which—

(A) end after the date the election is made, and

(B) begin before the date the election is revoked by such organization (under regulations prescribed by the Secretary).

(7) No effect on certain organizations.— With respect to any organization for a taxable year for which—

(A) such organization is a disqualified organization (within the meaning of paragraph (5)), or

(B) an election under this subsection is not in effect for such organization,

nothing in this subsection or in section 4911 shall be construed to affect the interpretation of the phrase, "no substantial part of the activities of which is carrying on propaganda, or otherwise attempting, to influence legislation," under subsection (c)(3).

(8) Affiliated organizations.—For rules regarding affiliated organizations, see section 4911(f).

(i) Prohibition of Discrimination by Certain Social Clubs.—Notwithstanding subsection (a), an organization which is described in subsection (c)(7) shall not be exempt from taxation under subsection (a) for any taxable year if, at any time during such taxable year, the charter, bylaws, or other governing instrument, of such organization or any written policy statement of such organization contains a provision which provides for discrimination against any person on the basis of race, color, or religion. The preceding sentence to the extent it relates to discrimination on the basis of religion shall not apply to—

(1) an auxiliary of a fraternal beneficiary society if such society—

(A) is described in subsection (c)(8) and exempt from tax under subsection (a), and

(B) limits its membership to the members of a particular religion, or

(2) a club which in good faith limits its membership to the members of a particular religion in order to further the teachings or principles of that religion, and not to exclude individuals of a particular race or color.

(j) Special Rules for Certain Amateur Sports Organizations.—

(1) In general.— In the case of a qualified amateur sports organization—

(A) the requirement of subsection (c)(3) that no part of its activities involve the provision of athletic facilities or equipment shall not apply, and

(B) such organization shall not fail to meet the requirements of subsection (c)(3) merely

IRC Sec. 501 (j)(1)(B)

because its membership is local or regional in nature.

(2) Qualified amateur sports organization defined.— For purposes of this subsection, the term "qualified amateur sports organization" means any organization organized and operated exclusively to foster national or international amateur sports competition if such organization is also organized and operated primarily to conduct national or international competition in sports or to support and develop amateur athletes for national or international competition in sports.

(k) Treatment of Certain Organizations Providing Child Care.— For purposes of subsection (c)(3) of this section and sections 170(c)(2), 2055(a)(2), and 2522(a)(2), the term "educational purposes" includes the providing care of children away from their homes if—

(1) substantially all of the care provided by the organization is for purposes of enabling individuals to be gainfully employed, and

(2) the services provided by the organization are available to the general public.

(l) Government Corporations Exempt Under Subsection (c)(1).—The organization described in this subsection is the Central Liquidity Facility established under title III of the Federal Credit Union Act (12 U.S.C. 1795 et seq.).

(m) Certain Organizations Providing Commercial-Type Insurance Not Exempt From Tax.—

(1) Denial of tax exemption where providing commercial-type insurance is substantial part of activities.—An organiza tion described in paragraphs (3) or (4) of subsection (c) shall be exempt from tax under subsection (a) only if no substantial part of its activities consists of providing commercial-type insurance.

(2) Other organizations taxed as insurance companies on insurance business.— In the case of an organization described in para-

graph (3) or (4) of subsection (c) which is exempt from tax under subsection (a) after the application of paragraph (1) of this subsection—

(A) the activity of providing commercial-type insurance shall be treated as an unrelated trade or business (as defined in section 513), and

(B) in lieu of the tax imposed by section 511 with respect to such activity, such organization shall be treated as an insurance company for purposes of applying subchapter L with respect to such activity.

(3) Commercial-type insurance.— For purposes of this subsection, the term "commercial-type insurance" shall not include—

(A) insurance provided at substantially below cost to a class of charitable recipients,

(B) incidental health insurance provided by a health maintenance organization of a kind customarily provided by such organization, and

(C) property or casualty insurance provided (directly or through an organization described in section 414(e)(3)(B)(ii)) by a church or convention or association of churches for such church or convention or association of churches,

(D) providing retirement or welfare benefits (or both) by a church or a convention or association of churches (directly or through an organization described in section 414(e)(3)(A) or 414(e)(3)(B)(ii)) for the employees (including employees described in section 414(e)(3)(B)) of such church or convention or association of churches or the beneficiaries of such employees, and

(E) charitable gift annuities.

(4) Insurance includes annuities.— For purposes of this subsection, the issuance of annuity contracts shall be treated as providing insurance.

(5) Charitable gift annuity.— For purposes of paragraph (3)(E), the term "charitable gift annuity" means an annuity if—

(A) a portion of the amount paid in connection with the issuance of the annuity is allowable as a deduction under section 170 or 2055, and

(B) the annuity is described in section 514(c)(5) (determined as if any amount paid in cash in connection with such issuance were property).

(n) Cross Reference.—For nonexemption of Communist-controlled organizations, see section 11(b) of the Internal Security Act of 1950 (64 Stat. 997; 40 U.S.C. 790(b)).

SEC. 503. REQUIREMENTS FOR EXEMPTION.

(a) Denial of Exemption to Organizations Engaged in Prohibited Transactions.—

(1) General rule.—

(A) An organization described in section 501(c)(17) shall not be exempt from taxation under section 501(a) if it has engaged in a prohibited transaction after December 31, 1959.

(B) An organization described in section 401(a) which is referred to in section 4975(g)(2) or (3) shall not be exempt from taxation under section 501(a) if it has engaged in a prohibited transaction after March 1, 1954.

(C) An organization described in section 501(c)(18) shall not be exempt from taxation under section 501(a) if it has engaged in a prohibited transaction after December 31, 1969.

(2) Taxable years affected.— An organization described in section 501(c)(17) or (18) or paragraph (a)(1)(B) shall be denied exemption from taxation under section 501(a) by reason of paragraph (1) only for taxable years after the taxable year during which it is notified by the Secretary that it has engaged in a prohibited transaction, unless such organization entered into such prohibited transaction with the purpose of diverting corpus or income of the organization from its exempt purposes, and such transaction involved a substantial part of the corpus or income of such organization.

(b) Prohibited Transactions.— For purposes of this section, the term "prohibited transaction" means any transaction in which an organization subject to the provisions of this section—

(1) lends any part of its income or corpus, without the receipt of adequate security and a reasonable rate of interest, to;

(2) pay any compensation, in excess of a reasonable allowance for salaries or other compensation for personal services actually rendered, to;

(3) makes any part of its services available on a preferential basis to;

(4) makes any substantial purchase of securities or any other property, for more than adequate consideration in money or money's worth, from;

(5) sells any substantial part of its securities or other property, for less than an adequate consideration in money or money's worth, to; or

(6) engages in any other transaction which results in a substantial diversion of its income or corpus to;

the creator of such organization (if a trust); a person who has made a substantial contribution to such organization; a member of the family (as defined in section 267(c)(4)) of an individual who is the creator of such trust or who has made a substantial contribution to such organization; or a corporation controlled by such creator or person through the ownership, directly or indirectly, of 50 percent or more of the total combined voting power of all classes of stock entitled to vote or 50 percent or more of the total value of shares of all classes of stock of the corporation.

(c) Future Status of Organizations Denied Exemption.— Any organization described in section 501(c)(17) or (18) or subsection (a)(1)(B) which is denied exemption under section 501(a) by reason of subsection (a) of this section, with respect to any taxable year following the taxable year in which notice of denial of exemption was received, may under regulations prescribed by the Secretary, file claim for exemption, and if the Secretary, pursuant to such regulations, is satisfied that such organization will not knowingly again engage in a prohibited transaction, such organization shall be exempt with respect to taxable years after the year in which such claim is filed.

(d) [Repealed]

(e) Special Rules.— For purposes of subsection (b)(1), a bond, debenture, note, or certificate or other evidence of indebtedness (hereinafter in this subsection referred to as "obligation") shall not be treated as a loan made without the receipt of adequate security if—

(1) such obligation is acquired—

(A) on the market, either (i) at the price of the obligation prevailing on a national securities exchange which is registered with the Securities and Exchange Commission, or (ii) if the obligation is not traded on such a national securities exchange, at a price not less favorable to the trust than the offering price for the obligation as established by current bid and asked prices quoted by persons independent of the issuer;

(B) from an underwriter, at a price (i) not in excess of the public offering price for the obligation as set forth in a prospectus or offering circular filed with the Securities and Exchange Commission, and (ii) at which a substantial portion of the same issue is acquired by persons independent of the issuer; or

(C) directly from the issuer, at a price not less favorable to the trust than the price paid currently for a substantial portion of the same issue by persons independent of the issuer;

(2) immediately following acquisition of such obligation—

(A) not more than 25 percent of the aggregate amount of obligations issued in such issue and outstanding at the time of acquisition is held by the trust, and

(B) at least 50 percent of the aggregate amount referred to in subparagraph (A) is held by persons independent of the issuer; and

(3) immediately following acquisition of the obligation, not more than 25 percent of the assets of the trust is invested in obligations of persons described in subsection (b).

(f) Loans With Respect to Which Employers Are Prohibited From Pledging Certain Assets.— Subsection (b)(1) shall not apply to a loan made by a trust described in section 401(a) to the employer (or to a renewal of such a loan or, if the loan is repayable upon demand, to a continuation of such a loan) if the loan bears a reasonable rate of interest, and if (in the case of a making or renewal)—

(1) the employer is prohibited (at the time of such making or renewal) by any law of the United States or regulation thereunder from directly or indirectly pledging, as a security for such a loan, a particular class or classes of his assets the value of which (at such time) represents more than one-half of the value of all his assets;

(2) the making or renewal, as the case may be, is approved in writing as an investment which is consistent with the exempt purpose of the trust by a trustee who is independent of the employer, and no other such trustee has previously refused to give such written approval; and

(3) immediately following the making or renewal, as the case may be, the aggregate amount loaned by the trust to the employer, without the receipt of adequate security, does not exceed 25 percent of the value of all the assets of the trust.

For purposes of paragraph (2), the term "trustee" means, with respect to any trust for which there is more than one trustee who is independent of the employer, a majority of such independent trustees. For purposes of paragraph (3), the determination as to whether any amount loaned by the trust to the employer is loaned without the receipt of adequate security shall be made without regard to subsection (e).

SEC. 505. ADDITIONAL REQUIREMENTS FOR ORGANIZATIONS DESCRIBED IN PARAGRAPH (9), (17), OR (20) OF SECTION 501(c).

(a) Certain Requirements Must Be Met in the Case of Organizations Described in Paragraph (9) or (20) of Section 501(c).—

(1) Voluntary employees' beneficiary associations, etc.— An organization described in paragraph (9) or (20) of subsection (c) of section 501 which is part of a plan shall not be exempt from tax under section 501(a) unless such plan meets the requirements of subsection (b) of this section.

(2) Exception for collective bargaining agreements.— Paragraph (1) shall not apply to any organization which is part of a plan maintained pursuant to an agreement between employee representatives and 1 or more employers if the Secretary finds that such agreement is a collective bargaining agreement and that such plan was the subject of good faith bargaining between such employee representatives and such employer or employers.

(b) Nondiscrimination Requirements.—

(1) In general.— Except as otherwise provided in this subsection, a plan meets the requirements of this subsection only if—

(A) each class of benefits under the plan is provided under a classification of employ-

ees which is set forth in the plan and which is found by the Secretary not to be discriminatory in favor of employees who are highly compensated individuals, and

(B) in the case of each class of benefits, such benefits do not discriminate in favor of employees who are highly compensated individuals.

A life insurance, disability, severance pay, or supplemental unemployment compensation benefit shall not be considered to fail to meet the requirements of subparagraph (B) merely because the benefits available bear a uniform relationship to the total compensation, or the basic or regular rate of compensation, of employees covered by the plan.

(2) Exclusion of certain employees.— For purposes of paragraph (1), there may be excluded from consideration—

(A) employees who have not completed 3 years of service,

(B) employees who have not attained age 21,

(C) seasonal employees or less than half-time employees,

(D) employees not included in the plan who are included in a unit of employees covered by an agreement between employee representatives and 1 or more employers which the Secretary finds to be a collective bargaining agreement if the class of benefits involved was the subject of good faith bargaining between such employee representatives and such employer or employers, and

(E) employees who are nonresident aliens and who receive no earned income (within the meaning of section 911(d)(2)) from the employer which constitutes income from sources within the United States (within the meaning of section 861(a)(3)).

(3) Application of subsection where other nondiscrimination rules provided.— In the case of any benefit for which a provision of this chapter other than this subsection provides nondiscrimination rules, paragraph (1) shall not apply but the requirements of this subsection shall be met only if the nondiscrimination rules so provided are satisfied with respect to such benefit.

(4) Aggregation rules.— At the election of the employer, 2 or more plans of such employer may be treated as 1 plan.

(5) Highly compensated individual.—For purposes of this subsection, the determination as to whether an individual is a highly compensated individual shall be made under rules similar to the rules for determining whether an individual is a highly compensated employee (within the meaning of section 414(q)).

(6) Compensation.— For purposes of this subsection, the term "compensation" has the meaning given such term by section 414(s).

◊ ◊ ◊

Editor's Note: Section 505(b)(7), below, was amended by §13212(c) of OBRA '93. The OBRA '93 changes were effective generally for benefits accruing in plan years beginning after December 31, 1993, but transition rules were provided for collectively bargained and state and local government plans. For those transition rules, see §13212(d) of OBRA '93.

◊ ◊ ◊

(7) Compensation limit.— A plan shall not be treated as meeting the requirements of this subsection unless under the plan the annual compensation of each employee taken into account for any year does not exceed $150,000. The Secretary shall adjust the $150,000 amount at the same time, and by the same amount, as any adjustment under Section 401(a)(17)(B). This paragraph shall not apply in determining whether the requirements of section 79(d) are met.

(c) Requirement That Organization Notify Secretary That It Is Applying For Tax-Exempt Status.—

(1) In general.—An organization shall not be treated as an organization described in paragraph (9), (17), or (20) of section 501(c)—

(A) unless it has given notice to the Secretary, in such manner as the Secretary may by regulation prescribe, that it is applying for recognition of such status, or

(B) for any period before the giving of such notice, if such notice is given after the time prescribed by the Secretary by regulations for giving notice under this subsection.

(2) Special rule for existing organizations.— In the case of any organization in existence on July 18, 1984, the time for giving notice under paragraph (1) shall not expire before the date 1 year after such date of the enactment.

Part III— Taxation of Business Income of Certain Exempt Organization

* * *

SEC. 511. IMPOSITION OF TAX ON UNRELATED BUSINESS INCOME OF CHARITABLE, ETC., ORGANIZATIONS.

(a) Charitable, Etc., Organizations Taxable at Corporation Rates.—

(1) Imposition of tax.— There is hereby imposed for each taxable year on the unrelated business taxable income (as defined in section 512) of every organization described in paragraph (2) a tax computed as provided in section 11. In making such computation for purposes of this section, the term "taxable income" as used in section 11 shall be read as "unrelated business taxable income".

(2) Organization subject to tax.—

(A) Organizations described in sections 401(a) and 501(c).The tax imposed by paragraph (1) shall apply in the case of any organization (other than a trust described in subsection (b) or an organization described in section 501(c)(1)) which is exempt, except as provided in this part or part II (relating to private foundations), from taxation under this subtitle by reason of section 501(a).

(B) State colleges and universities.The tax imposed by paragraph (1) shall apply in the case of any college or university which is an agency or instrumentality of any government or any political subdivision thereof, or which is owned or operated by a government or any political subdivision thereof, or by any agency or instrumentality of one or more governments or political subdivisions. Such tax shall also apply in the case of any corporation wholly owed by one or more such colleges or universities.

(b) Tax on Charitable, Etc., Trusts.—

(1) Imposition of tax.— There is hereby imposed for each taxable year on the unrelated business taxable income of every trust described in paragraph (2) a tax computed as provided in section 1(e). In making such computation for purposes of this section, the term "taxable income" as used in section 1 shall be read as "unrelated business taxable income" as defined in section 512.

(2) Charitable, etc., trusts subject to tax.—The tax imposed by paragraph (1) shall apply in the case of any trust which is exempt, except as provided in this part of part II (relating to private foundations), from taxtion under this subtitle by reason of section 501(a) and which, if it were not for such exemption, would be subject to subchapter J (sec. 641 and following, relating to estates, trusts, beneficiaries, and decedents).

(c) Special Rule for Section 501(c)(2) Corporations.— If a corporation described in section 501(c)(2)—

(1) pays any amount of its net income for a taxable year to an organization exempt from taxation under section 501(a) (or which would pay such an amount but for the fact that the expenses of collecting its income exceed its income), and

(2) such corporation and such organization file a consolidated return for the taxable year,

such corporation shall be treated, for purposes of the tax imposed by subsection (a), as being organized and operated for the same purposes as such organization, in addition to the purposes described in section 501(c)(2).

(d) Tax Preferences.—[Repealed.]

SEC. 512. UNRELATED BUSINESS TAXABLE INCOME.

(a) Definition.—For purposes of this title—

(1) General rule.— Except as otherwise provided in this subsection, the term "unrelated business taxable income" means the gross income derived by any organization from any unrelated trade or business (as defined in section 513) regularly carried on by it, less the deductions allowed by this chapter which are directly connected with the carrying on of such trade or business, both computed with the modifications provided in subsection (b).

(2) Special rule for foreign organizations.— In the case of an organization described in section 511 which is a foreign organization, the unrelated business taxable income shall be—

(A) its unrelated business taxable income which is derived from sources within the United States and which is not effectively connected with the conduct of a trade or business within the United States, plus

(B) its unrelated business taxable income which is effectively connected with the conduct of a trade or business within the United States.

(3) Special rules applicable to organizations described in paragraph (7), (9), (17), or (20) of section 501(c).—

(A) General rule.—In the case of an organization described in paragraph (7), (9), (17), or (20) of section 501(c), the term "unrelated business taxable income" means the gross income (excluding any exempt function income), less the deductions allowed by this chapter which are directly connected with the production of the gross income (excluding exempt function income), both computed with the modifications provide in paragraph (6), (10), (11), and (12) of subsection (b). For purposes of the preceding sentence, the deductions provided by section 243, 244, and 245 (relating to dividends received by corporations) shall be treated as not directly connected with the production of gross income.

(B) Exempt function income.—For purposes of subparagraph (A), the term "exempt function income" means the gross income from dues, fees, charges, or similar amounts paid by members of the organization as consideration for providing such members or their dependents or guests goods, facilities, or services in furtherance of the purposes constituting the basis for the exemption of the organization to which such income is paid. Such term also means all income (other than an amount equal to the gross income derived from any unrelated trade or business regularly carried on by such organization computed as if the organization were subject to paragraph (1)), which is set aside—

(i) for a purpose specified in section 170(c)(4), or

(ii) in the case of an organization described in paragraph (9), (17), or (20) of section 501(c), to provide for the payment of life, sick, accident, or other benefits,

including reasonable costs of administration directly connected with a purpose described in clause (i) or (ii). If during the taxable year, an amount which is attributable to income so set aside is used for a purpose other than that described in clause (i) or (ii), such amount shall be included, under subparagraph (A), in unrelated business taxable income for the taxable year.

(C) Applicability to certain corporations described in section 501(c)(2).— In the case of a corporation described in section 501(c)(2), the income of which is payable to an organization described in paragraph (7), (9), (17), or (20) of section 501(c), subparagraph (A) shall apply as if such corporation were the organization to which the income is payable. For purposes of the preceding sentence, such corporation shall be treated as having exempt function income for a taxable year only if it files a consolidated return with such organization for such year.

(D) Nonrecognition of gain.—If property used directly in the performance of the exempt function of an organization described in paragraph (7), (9), (17), or (20) of section 501(c) is sold by such organization, and within a period beginning 1 year before the date of such sale, and ending 3 years after such date, other property is purchased and used by such organization directly in the performance of its exempt function, gain (if any) from such sale shall be recognized only to the extent that such organization's sales price of the old property exceeds the organization's cost of purchasing the other property.

For purposes of this subparagraph, the destruction in whole or in part, theft, seizure, requisition, or condemnation of property, shall be treated as the sale of such property, and rules similar to the rules provided by subsections (b), (c), (e), and (j) of section 1034 shall apply.

(E) Limitation on amount of set aside in the case of organizations described in paragraph (9), (17), or (20) of section 501(c).—

(i) In general.—In the case of any organization described in paragraph (9), (17), or (20) of section 501(c), a set-aside for any purpose specified in clause (ii) of subparagraph (B) may be taken into account under subparagraph (B) only to the extent that such set-aside does not result in an amount of assets set aside for such purpose in excess of the account limit determined under section 419A (without regard to subsection (f)(6) thereof) for the taxable year (not taking into account any reserve described in section 419A(c)(2)(A) for post-retirement medical benefits).

(ii) Treatment of existing reserves for post-retirement medical or life insurance benefits.—

(I) Clause (i) shall not apply to any income attributable to an existing reserve for post-retirement medical or life insurance benefits.

(II) For purposes of subclause (I), the term "reserve for post-retirement medical or life insurance benefits" means the greater of the amount of assets set aside for purposes of post-retirement medical or life insurance benefits to be provided to covered employees as of the close of the last plan year ending before the date of the enactment of the Tax Reform Act of 1984 or on July 18, 1984.

(III) All payments during plan years ending on or after the date of enactment of the Tax Reform Act of 1984 of post-retirement medical benefits or life insurance benefits shall be charged against the reserve referred to in subclause (II). Except to the extent provided in regulations prescribed by the Secretary, all plans of an employer shall be treated as 1 plan for purposes of the preceding sentence.

(iii) Treatment of tax exempt organizations.— This subparagraph shall not apply to any organization if substantially all of the contributions to such organization are made by employers who were exempt from tax under this chapter throughout the 5-taxable year period ending with the taxable year in which the contributions are made.

(4) Special rule applicable to organizations described in section 501(c)(19).— In the case of an organization described in section 501(c)(19), the term "unrelated business taxable income" does not include any amount attributable to payments for life, sick, accident, or health insurance with respect to members of such organizations or their dependents which is set aside for the purpose of providing for the payment of insurance benefits or for a purpose specified in section 170(c)(4). If an amount set aside under the preceding sentence is used during the taxable year for a purpose other than a purpose described in the preceding sentence, such amount shall be included, under paragraph (1), in unrelated business taxable income for the taxable year.

(5) Definition of payments with respect to securities loans.—

(A) The term "payments with respect to securities loans" includes all amounts received in respect of a security (as defined in section 1236(c)) transferred by the owner to another person in a transaction to which section 1058 applies (whether or not title to the security remains in the name of the lender) including—

(i) amounts in respect of dividends, interest, or other distributions,

(ii) fees computed by reference to the period beginning with the transfer of securities by the owner and ending with the transfer of identical securities back to the transferor by the transferee and the fair market value of the security during such period,

(iii) income from collateral security for such loan, and

(iv) income from the investment of collateral security.

(B) Subparagraph (A) shall apply only with respect to securities transferred pursuant to an agreement between the transferor and the transferee which provides for—

(i) reasonable procedures to implement the obligation of the transferee to furnish to the transferor, for each business day during such period, collateral with a fair market value not less than the fair market value of the security at the close of business on the preceding business day,

(ii) termination of the loan by the transferor upon notice of not more than 5 business days, and

(iii) return to the transferor of securities identical to the transferred securities upon termination of the loan.

(b) Modifications.— The modifications referred to in subsection (a) are the following:

(1) There shall be excluded all dividends, interest, payments with respect to securities loans (as defined in section 512(a)(5)), amounts received or accrued as consideration for entering into agreements to make loans, and annuities, and all deductions directly connected with such income.

(2) There shall be excluded all royalties (including overriding royalties) whether measured by production or by gross or taxable income from the property, and all deductions directly connected with such income.

(3) In the case of rents—

(A) Except as provided in subparagraph (B), there shall be excluded—

(i) all rents from real property (including property described in section 1245(a)(3)(C)), and

(ii) all rents from personal property (including for purposes of this paragraph as personal property any property described in section 1245(a)(3)(B)) leased with such real property, if the rents attributable to such personal property are an incidental amount of the total rents received or accrued under the lease, determined at the time the personal property is placed in service.

(B) Subparagraph (A) shall not apply—

(i) if more than 50 percent of the total rent received or accrued under the lease is attrib-

utable to personal property described in Subparagraph (A)(ii), or

(ii) if the determination of the amount of such rent depends in whole or in part on the income or profits derived by any person from the property leased (other than an amount based on a fixed percentage or percentages of receipts or sales).

(C) There shall be excluded all deductions directly connected with rents excluded under subparagraph (A).

(4) Notwithstanding paragraph (1), (2), (3), or (5), in the case of debt-financed property (as defined in section 514) there shall be included, as an item of gross income derived from an unrelated trade or business, the amount ascertained under section 514(a)(1), and there shall be allowed, as a deduction, the amount ascertained under section 514(a)(2).

(5) There shall be excluded all gains or losses from the sale, exchange, or other disposition of property other than—

(A) stock in trade or other property of a kind which would properly be includible in inventory if on hand at the close of the taxable year, or

(B) property held primarily for sale to customers in the ordinary course of the trade or business.

There shall also be excluded all gains or losses recognized, in connection with the organization's investment activities, from the lapse or termination of options, to buy or sell securities (as defined in section 1236(c)). This paragraph shall not apply with respect to the cutting of timber which is considered, on the application of section 631, as a sale or exchange of such timber or real property and all gains or losses from the forfeiture of good-faith deposits (that are consistent with established business practice) for the purchase, sale or lease of real property in connection with the organization's investment activities.

(6) The net operating loss deduction provided in section 172 shall be allowed, except that—

(A) the net operating loss for any taxable year, the amount of the net operating loss carryback or carryover to any taxable year, and the net operating loss deduction for any taxable year shall be determined under section 172 without taking into account any amount of income or deduction which is excluded under this part in computing the unrelated business taxable income; and

(B) the terms "preceding taxable year" and "preceding taxable years" as used in section 172 shall not include any taxable year for which the organization was not subject to the provisions of this part.

(7) There shall be excluded all income derived from research for (A) the United States, or any of its agencies or instrumentalities, or (B) any State or political subdivision thereof; and there shall be excluded all deductions directly connected with such income.

(8) In the case of a college, university, or hospital, there shall be excluded all income derived from research performed for any person, and all deductions directly connected with such income.

(9) In the case of an organization operated primarily for purposes of carrying on fundamental research the results of which are freely available to the general public, there shall be excluded all income derived from research performed for any person, and all deductions directly connected with such income.

(10) In the case of any organization described in section 511(a), the deduction allowed by section 170 (relating to charitable etc. contributions and gifts) shall be allowed (whether or not directly connected with the carrying on of the trade or business), but shall not exceed 10 percent of the unrelated business taxable income computed without the benefit of this paragraph.

(11) In the case of any trust described in section 511(b), the deduction allowed by section 170 (relating to charitable etc. contributions and gifts) shall be allowed (whether or not directly connected with the carring on of the trade or business), and for such purpose a distribution made by the trust to a beneficiary described in section 170 shall be considered as a gift or contribution. The deduction allowed by this paragraph shall be allowed with the limitations prescribed in section 170(b)(1)(A) and (B) determined with reference to the unrelated business taxable income computed without the benefit of this paragraph (in lieu of with reference to adjusted gross income).

(12) Except for purposes of computing the net operating loss under section 172 and paragraph (6), there shall be allowed a specific deduction of $1,000. In the case of a diocese, province of a religious order, or a convention or association of churches, there shall also be allowed, with respect to each parish, individual church, district, or other local unit, a specific deduction equal to the lower of—

(A) $1,000, or

(B) the gross income derived from any unrelated trade or business regularly carried on by such local unit.

(13) Notwithstanding paragraphs (1), (2), or (3), amounts of interest, annuities, royalties, and rents derived from any organization (in this paragraph called the "controlled organization") of which the organization deriving such amounts (in this paragraph called the "controlling organization") has control (as defined in section 368(c)) shall be included as an item of gross income (whether or not the activity from which such amounts are derived represents a trade or business or is regularly carried on) in an amount which bears the same ratio as—

(A)(i) in the case of a controlled organization which is not exempt from taxtion under section 501(a), the excess of the amount of taxable income of the controlled organization over the amount of such organization's taxable income which if derived directly by the controlling organization would not be unrelated business taxable income, or

(ii) in the case of a controlled organization which is exempt from taxation under section 501(a), the amount of unrelated business taxable income of the controlled organization, bears to

(B) the taxable income of the controlled organization (determined in the case of a controlled organization to which subparagraph (A)(ii) applies as if it were not an organization exempt from taxation under section 501(a)), but not less than the amount determined in clause (i) or (ii), as the case may be, of subparagraph (A),

both amounts computed without regard to amounts paid directly or indirectly to the controlling organization. There shall be allowed all deductions directly connected with amounts included in gross income under the preceding sentence.

(14) [Repealed]

(15) Except as provided in paragraph (4), in the case of a trade or business—

(A) which consists of providing services under license issued by a Federal regulatory agency,

(B) which is carried on by a religious order or by an educational organization described in section 170(b)(1)(A)(ii) maintained by such religious order, and which was so carried on before May 27, 1959, and

(C) less than 10 percent of the net income of which for each taxable year is used for activities which are not related to the purpose constituting the basis for the religious order's exemption,

there shall be excluded all gross income derived from such trade or business and all deductions directly connected with the carrying on of such trade or business, so long as it is established to the satisfaction of the Secretary that the rates or other charges for such services

are competitive with rates or other charges charged for similar services by persons not exempt from taxation.

(16)(A) Notwithstanding paragraph (5)(B), there shall be excluded all gains or losses from the sale, exchange, or other disposition of any real property described in subparagraph (B) if—

(i) such property was acquired by the organization from—

(I) a financial institution described in section 581 or 591(a) which is in conservatorship or receivership, or

(II) the conservator or receiver of such an institution (or any government agency or corporation succeeding to the rights or interests of the conservator or receiver),

(ii) such property is designated by the organization within the 9-month period beginning on the date of its acquisition as property held for sale, except that not more than one-half (by value determined as of such date) of property acquired in a single transaction may be so designated,

(iii) such sale, exchange, or disposition occurs before the later of—

(I) the date which is 80 months after the date of the acquisition of such property, or

(II) the date specified by the Secretary in order to assure an orderly disposition of property held by persons described in subparagraph (A), and

(iv) while such property was held by the organization, the aggregate expenditures on improvements and development activities included in the basis of the property are (or were) not in excess of 20 percent of the net selling price of such property.

(B) Property is described in this subparagraph if it is real property which—

(i) was held by the financial institution at the time it entered into conservatorship or receivership, or

(ii) was foreclosure property (as defined in section 514(c)(9)(H)(v)) which secured indebtedness held by the financial institution at such time.

For purposes of this subparagraph, real property includes an interest in a mortgage.

(c) Special Rules for Partnerships.—

(1) In general.— If a trade or business regularly carried on by a partnership of which an organization is a member is an unrelated trade or business with respect to such organization, such organization in computing its unrelated business taxable income shall, subject to the exceptions, additions, and limitations contained in subsection (b), include its share (whether or not distributed) of the gross income of the partnership from such unrelated trade or business and its share of the partnership deductions directly connected with such gross income.

(2) Special rule where partnership year is different from organization's year.— If the taxable year of the organization is different from that of the partnership, the amounts to be included or deducted in computing the unrelated business taxable income under paragraph (1) shall be based upon the income and deductions of the partnership for any taxable year of the partnership ending within or with the taxable year of the organization.

SEC. 513. UNRELATED TRADE OR BUSINESS.

(a) General Rule.— The term "unrelated trade or business" means, in the case of any organization subject to the tax imposed by section 511, any trade or business the conduct of which is not substantially related (aside from the need of such organization for income or funds or the use it makes of the profits derived) to the exercise or performance by such organization of its charitable, educational, or other purpose or function constitut-

ing the basis for its exemption under section 501 (or, in the case of an organization described in section 511(a)(2)(B), to the exercise or performance of any purpose or function described in section 501(c)(3)), except that such term does not include any trade or business—

(1) in which substantially all the work in carrying on such trade or business is performed for the organization without compensation; or

(2) which is carried on, in the case of an organization described in section 501(c)(3) or in the case of a college or university described in section 511(a)(2)(B), by the organization primarily for the convenience of its members, students, patients, officers, or employees, or, in the case of a local association of employees described in section 501(c)(4) organized before May 27, 1969, which is the selling by the organization of items of work-related clothes and equipment and items normally sold through vending machines, through food dispensing facilities, or by snack bars, for the convenience of its members at their usual places of employment; or

(3) which is the selling of merchandise, substantially all of which has been received by the organization as gifts or contributions.

(b) Special Rules for Trusts.— The term "unrelated trade or business" means, in the case of—

(1) a trust computing its unrelated business taxable income under section 512 for purposes of section 681; or

(2) a trust described in section 401(a), or section 501(c)(17), which is exempt from tax under section 501(a);

any trade or business regularly carried on by such trust or by a partnership of which it is a member.

(c) Advertising, Etc., Activities.— For purposes of this section, the term "trade or business" includes any activity which is carried

IRC Sec. 513 (c)

on for the production of income from the sale of goods or the performance of services. For purposes of the preceding sentence, an activity does not lose identity as a trade or business merely because it is carried on within a larger aggregate of similar activities or within a larger complex of other endeavors which may, or may not, be related to the exempt purposes of the organization. Where an activity carried on for profit constitutes an unrelated trade or business, no part of such trade or business shall be excluded from such classification merely because it does not result in profit.

(d) Certain Activities of Trade Shows, State Fairs, Etc.—

(1) General rule.— The term "unrelated trade or business" does not include qualified public entertainment activities of an organization described in paragraph (2)(C), or qualified convention and trade show activities of an organization described in paragraph (3)(C).

(2) Qualified public entertainment activities.—For purposes of this subsection—

(A) Public entertainment activity.— The term "public entertainment activity" means any entertainment or recreational activity of a kind traditionally conducted at fairs or expositions promoting agricultural and educational purposes, including, but not limited to, any activity one of the purposes of which is to attract the public to fairs or expositions or to promoted the breeding of animals or the development of products or equipment.

(B) Qualified public entertainment activity.— The term "qualified public entertainment activity" means a public entertainment activity which is conducted by a qualifying organization described in subparagraph (C) in—

(i) conjunction with an international, national, State, regional, or local fair or exposition,

(ii) accordance with the provisions of State law which permit the activity to be operated or conducted solely by such an organization, or by an agency, instrumentality, or political subdivision of such State, or

(iii) accordance with the provisions of State law which permit such an organization to be granted a license to conduct not more than 20 days of such activity on payment to the State of a lower percentage of the revenue from such licensed activity than the State requires from organizations not described in section 501(c)(3), (4), or (5).

(C) Qualifying organization.— For purposes of this paragraph, the term "qualifying organization" means an organization which is described in section 501(c)(3), (4), or (5) which regularly conducts, as one of its substantial exempt purposes, an agricultural and educational fair or exposition.

(3) Qualified convention and trade show activities.—

(A) Convention and trade show activity.— The term "convention and trade show activity" means any activity of a kind traditionally conducted at conventions, annual meetings, or trade shows, including, but not limited to, any activity one of the purposes of which is to attract persons in an industry generally (without regard to membership in the sponsoring organization) as well as members of the public to the show for the purpose of displaying industry products or to stimulate interest in, and demand for, industry products or services, or the educate persons engaged in the industry in the development of new products and services or new rules and regulations affecting the industry.

(B) Qualified convention and trade show activity.— The term "qualified convention and trade show activity" means a convention and trade show activity carried out by a qualifying organization described in subparagraph (C) in conjunction with an international, national, State, regional, or local convention, annual meeting, or show conducted by an organization described in subparagraph (C) if one of the purposes of such organization in sponsoring the activity is the promotion and stimulation of interest in, and demand for, the products and services of that industry in general or to educate persons in attendance regarding new developments or products and services related to the exempt activities of the organization, and the show is designed to achieve such purpose through the character of the exhibits and the extent of the industry products displayed.

(C) Qualifying organization.— For purposes of this paragraph, the term "qualifying organization" means an organization described in section 501(c)(3), (4), (5), or (6) which regularly conducts as one of its substantial exempt purposes a show which stimulates interest in, and demand for, the products of a particular industry or segment of such industry or which educates persons in attendance regarding new developments or products and services related to the exempt activities of the organizations.

(4) Such activities not to affect exempt status.—An organization described in section 501(c)(3), (4), or (5) shall not be considered as not entitled to the exemption allowed under section 501(a) solely because of qualified public entertainment activities conducted by it.

(e) Certain Hospital Services.—In the case of a hospital described in section 170(b)(1)(A)(iii), the term "unrelated trade or business" does not include the furnishing of one or more of the services described in section 501(e)(1)(A) to one or more hospitals described in section 170(b)(1)(A)(iii) if—

(1) such services are furnished solely to such hospitals which have facilities to serve not more than 100 inpatients;

(2) such services, if performed on its own behalf by the recipient hospital, would constitute activities in exercising or performing the purpose or function constituting the basis for its exemption; and

(3) such services are provided at a fee or cost which does not exceed the actual cost of providing such services, such cost including straight line depreciation and a reasonable amount for return on capital goods used to provide such services.

(f) Certain Bingo Games.—

(1) In general.— The term "unrelated trade or business" does not include any trade or business which consists of conducting bingo games.

(2) Bingo game defined.—For purposes of paragraph (1), the term "bingo game" means any game of bingo—

(A) of a type in which usually—

(i) the wages are placed,

(ii) the winners are determined, and

(iii) the distribution of prizes or other property is made,

in the presence of all persons placing wagers in such game,

(B) the conducting of which is not an activity ordinarily carried out on a commercial basis, and

(C) the conducting of which does not violate any State or local law.

(g) Certain Pole Rentals.— In the case of a mutual or cooperative telephone or electric company, the term "unrelated trade or business" does not include engaging in qualified pole rentals (as defined in section 501(c)(12)(D)).

(h) Certain Distributions of Low Cost Articles Without Obligation to Purchase and Exchanges and Rentals of Member Lists.—

(1) In general.— In the case of an organization which is described in section 501 and contributions to which are deductible under paragraph (2) or (3) of section 170(c), the term "unrelated trade or business" does not include—

(A) activities relating to the distribution of low cost articles if the distribution of such articles is incidental to the solicitation of charitable contributions, or

(B) any trade or business which consists of—

(i) exchanging with another such organization, names and addresses of donors to (or members of) such organization, or

(ii) renting such names and addresses to another such organization.

(2) Low cost article defined.— For purposes of this subsection—

(A) In general.— The term "low cost article" means any article which has a cost not in excess of $5 to the organization which distributes such item (or on whose behalf such item is distributed).

(B) Aggregation rule.— If more than 1 item is distributed by or on behalf of an organization to a single distributee in any calendar year, the aggregate of the items so distributed in such calendar year to such distributee shall be treated as 1 article for purposes of subparagraph (A).

(C) Indexation of $5 amount.— In the case of any taxable year beginning in a calendar year after 1987, the $5 amount in subparagraph (A) shall be increased by an amount equal to—

(i) $5, multiplied by

(ii) the cost-of-living adjustment determined under section 1(f)(3) for the calendar year in which the taxable year begins, by substituting "calendar year 1987" for "calendar year 1989" in subparagraph (B) thereof.

(3) Distribution which is incidental to the solicitation of charitable contributions described.— For purposes of this subsection, any distribution of low cost articles by an organization shall be treated as a distribution incidental to the solicitation of charitable contributions only if—

(A) such distribution is not made at the request of the distributee,

(B) such distribution is made without the express consent of the distributee, and

(C) the articles so distributed are accompanied by—

(i) a request for a charitable contribution (as defined in section 170(c)) by the distributee to such organization, and

(ii) a statement that the distributee may retain the low cost article regardless of whether such distributee makes a charitable contribution to such organization.

SEC. 514. UNRELATED DEBT-FINANCED INCOME.

(a) Unrelated Debt-Financed Income and Deductions.—In computing under section 512 the unrelated business taxable income for any taxable year—

(1) Percentage of income taken into account.— There shall be included with respect to each debt-financed property as an item of gross income derived from an unrelated trade or business an amount which is the same percentage (but not in excess of 100 percent) of the total gross income derived during the taxable year from or on account of such property as (A) the average acquisition indebtedness (as defined in subsection (c)(7)) for the taxable year with respect to the property is of (B) the average amount (determined under regulations prescribed by the Secretary) of the adjusted basis of such property during the period it is held by the organization during such taxable year.

(2) Percentage of deductions taken into account.— There shall be allowed as a deduction with respect to each debt-financed property an amount determined by applying (except as provided in the last sentence of this paragraph) the percentage derived under this paragraph (1) to the sum determined under paragraph (3). The percentage derived under this paragraph shall not be applied with respect to the deduction of any capital loss resulting from the carryback or carryover of net capital losses under section 1212.

(3) Deductions allowable.— The sum referred to in paragraph (2) is the sum of the deductions under this chapter which are directly connected with the debt-financed property or the income therefrom, except that if the debt-financed property is of a character which is subject to the allowance for depreciation provided in section 167, the allowance shall be computed only by use of the straight-line method.

(b) Definition of Debt-Financed Property.—

(1) In general.— For purposes of this section, the term "debt-financed property" means any property which is held to produce income and with respect to which there is an acquisition indebtedness (as defined in subsection (c)) at any time during the taxable year (or, if the property was disposed of during the taxable year, with respect to which there was an acquisition indebtedness at any time during the 12-month period ending with the date of such disposition), except that such term does not include—

(A)(i) any property substantially all the use of which is substantially related (aside from the need of the organization for income or funds) to the exercise or performance by such organization of its charitable, educational, or other purpose or function constituting the basis for its exemption under section 501 (or, in the case of an organization described in section 511(a)(2)(B), to the exercise or performance of any purpose or function designated in section 501(c)(3)), or (ii) any property to which clause (i) does not apply, to the extent that its use is so substantially related;

(B) except in the case of income excluded under section 512(b)(5), any property to the extent that income from such property is taken into account in computing the gross income of any unrelated trade or business;

(C) any property to the extent that the income from such property is excluded by reason of the provisions of paragraph (7), (8), or (9) of section 512(b) in computing the gross income of any unrelated trade or business; or

(D) any property to the extent that it is used in any trade or business described in paragraph (1), (2), or (3) of section 513(a).

For purposes of subparagraph (A), substantially all the use of a property shall be considered to be substantially related to the exercise or performance by an organization of its charitable, educational, or other purpose or function constitution the basis for its exemption under section 501 if such property is real property subject to a lease to a medical clinic entered into primarily for purposes which are substantially related (aside from the need of such organization for income or funds or the use it makes of the rents derived) to the exercise or performance by such organization of its charitable, educational, or other purpose or function constituting the basis for its exemption under section 501.

(2) Special rule for related uses.— For purposes of applying paragraphs (1)(A), (C), and (D), the use of any property by an exempt organization which is related to an organization shall be treated as use by such organization.

(3) Special rules when land is acquired for exempt use within 10 years.—

(A) Neighborhood land.— If an organization acquires real property for the principal purpose of using the land (commencing within 10 years of the time of acquisition) in the manner described in paragraph (1)(A) and at the time of acquisition the property is in the neighborhood of other property owned by the organization which is used in such manner, the real property acquired for such future use shall not be treated as debt-financed property so long as the organization does not abandon its intent to so use the land within the 10-year period. The preced-

IRC Sec. 514 (b)(3)(A)

ing sentence shall not apply for any period after the expiration of the 10-year period, and shall apply after the first 5 years of the 10-year period only if the organization establishes to the satisfaction of the Secretary that it is reasonably certain that the land will be used in the described manner before the expiration of the 10-year period.

(B) Other cases.— If the first sentence of subparagraph (A) is inapplicable only because—

(i) the acquired land is not in the neighborhood referred to in subparagraph (A), or

(ii) the organization (for the period after the first 5 years of the 10-year period) is unable to establish to the satisfaction of the Secretary that it is reasonably certain that the land will be used in the manner described in paragraph (1)(A) before the expiration of the 10-year period,

but the land is converted to such use by the organization within the 10-year period, the real property (subject to the provisions of subparagraph (D)) shall not be treated as debt-financed property for any period before such conversion. For purposes of this subparagraph, land shall not be treated as used in the manner described in paragraph (1)(A) by reason of the use made of any structure which was on the land when acquired by the organization.

(C) Limitations.— Subparagraphs (A) and (B)—

(i) shall apply with respect to any structure on the land when acquired by the organization, or to the land occupied by the structure, only if (and so long as) the intended future use of the land in the manner described in paragraph (1)(A) requires that the structure be demolished or removed in order to use the land in such manner;

(ii) shall not apply to structures erected on the land after the acquisition of the land; and

(iii) shall not apply to property subject to a lease which is a business lease (as defined in this section immediately before the enactment of the Tax Reform Act of 1976).

(D) Refund of taxes when subparagraph (B) applies.— If an organization for any taxable year has not used land in the manner to satisfy the actual use condition of subparagraph (B) before the time prescribed by law (including extensions thereof) for filing the return for such taxable year, the tax for such year shall be computed without regard to the application of subparagraph (B), but if and when such use condition is satisfied, the provisions of subparagraph (B) shall then be applied to such taxable year. If the actual use condition of subparagraph (B) is satisfied for any taxable year after such time for filing the return, and if credit or refund of any overpayment for the taxable year resulting from the satisfaction of such use condition is prevented at the close of the taxable year in which the use condition is satisfied, by the operation of any law or rule of law (other than chapter 74, relating to closing agreements and compromises), credit or refund of such overpayment may nevertheless be allowed or made if claim therefor is filed before the expiration of 1 year after the close of the taxable year in which the use condition is satisfied.

(E) Special rule for churches.—In applying this paragraph to a church or convention or association of churches, in lieu of the 10-year period referred to in subparagraphs (A) and (B) a 15-year period shall be applied, and subparagraphs (A) and (B)(ii) shall apply whether or not the acquired land meets the neighborhood test.

(c) Acquisition Indebtedness.—

(1) General rule.— For purposes of this section, the term "acquisition indebt-edness" means, with respect to any debt-financed property, the unpaid amount of—

(A) the indebtedness incurred by the organization in acquiring or improving such property;

(B) the indebtedness incurred before the acquisition or improvement of such property if such indebtedness would not have been incurred but for such acquisition or improvement; and

(C) the indebtedness incurred after the acquisition or improvement of such property if such indebtedness would not have been incurred but for such acquisition or improvement and the incurrence of such indebtedness was reasonably foreseeable at the time of such acquisition or improvement.

(2) Property acquired subject to mortgage, etc.— For purposes of this subsection—

(A) General rule.— Where property (no matter how acquired) is acquired subject to a mortgage or other similar lien, the amount of indebtedness secured by such mortgage or lien shall be considered as an indebtedness of the organization incurred in acquiring such property even though the organization did not assume or agree to pay such indebtedness.

(B) Exceptions.—Where property subject to a mortgage is acquired by an organization by bequest or devise, the indebtedness secured by the mortgage shall not be treated as acquisition indebtedness during a period of 10 years following the date of the acquisition. If an organization acquires property by gift subject to a mortgage which was placed on the property more than 5 years before the gift, which property was held by the donor more than 5 years before the gift, the indebtedness secured by such mortgage shall not be treated as acquisition indebtedness during a period of 10 years following the date of such gift. This subparagraph shall not apply if the organization, in order to acquire the equity in the property by bequest, devise, or gift, assumes and agrees to pay the indebtedness secured by the mortgage, or if the organization makes any payment for the equity in the property owned by the decedent or the donor.

(C) Liens for taxes or assessments.— Where State law provides that—

(i) a lien for taxes, or

(ii) a lien for assessments,

made by a State or a political subdivision thereof attaches to property prior to the time when such taxes or assessments become due and payable, then such lien shall be treated as similar to a mortgage (within the meaning of subparagraph (A)) but only after such taxes or assessments become due and payable and the organization has had an opportunity to pay such taxes or assessments in accordance with State law.

(3) Extension of obligations.—For purposes of this section, an extension, renewal, or refinancing of an obligation evidencing a preexisting indebtedness shall not be treated as the creation of a new indebtedness.

(4) Indebtedness incurred in performing exempt purpose.—For purposes of this section the term ''acquisition indebted-ness'' does not include indebtedness the incurrence of which is inherent in the performance of exercise of the purpose or function constituting the basis of the organization's exemption, such as the indebtedness incurred by a credit union described in section 501(c)(14) in accepting deposits from its members.

(5) Annuities.— For purposes of this section, the term ''acquisition indebted-ness'' does not include an obligation to pay an annuity which—

(A) is the sole consideration (other than a mortgage to which paragraph (2)(B) applies) issued in exchange for property if, at the time of the exchange, the value of the annuity is less than 90 percent of the value of the property received in the exchange,

(B) is payable over the life of one individual in being at the time the annuity is issued, or over the lives of two individuals in being at such time, and

(C) is payable under a contract which—

IRC Sec. 514 (c)(5)(C)

(i) does not guarantee a minimum amount of payments or specify a maximum amount of payments, and

(ii) does not provide for any adjustment of the amount of the annuity payments by reference to the income received from the transferred property or any other property.

(6) Certain federal financing.— For purposes of this section, the term "acquisition indebtedness" does not include and obligation, to the extent that it is insured by the Federal Housing Administration, to finance the purchase, rehabilitation, or construction of housing for low and moderate income persons.

(7) Average acquistion indebtedness.— For purposes of this section, the term "average acquisition indebtedness" for any taxable year with respect to a debt-financed property means the average amount, determined under regulations prescribed by the Secretary, of the acquisition indebtedness during the period the property is held by the organization during the taxable year, except that for the purpose of computing the percentage of any gain or loss to be taken into account on a sale or other disposition of debt-financed property, such term means the highest amount of the acquisition indebtedness with respect to such property during the 12-month period ending with the date of the sale or other disposition.

(8) Securities to loans.—For purposes of this section—

(A) payments with respect to securities loans (as defined in section 512(a)(5)) shall be deemed to be derived from the securities loaned and not from collateral security or the investment of collateral security from such loans,

(B) any deductions which are directly connected with collateral security for such loan, or with the investment of collateral security, shall be deemed to be deductions which are directly connected with the securities loaned, and

(C) an obligation to return collateral security shall not be treated as acquisition indebtedness (as defined in paragraph (1)).

(9) Real property acquired by a qualified organization.—

(A) In general.— Except as provided in subparagraph (B), the term "acquisition indebtedness" does not, for purposes of this section, include indebtedness incurred by a qualified organization in acquiring or improving any real property. For purposes of this paragraph, an interest in a mortgage shall in no event be treated as real property.

(B) Exceptions.—The provisions of subparagraph (A) shall not apply in any case in which—

(i) the price for the acquisition or improvement is not a fixed amount determined as of the date of the acquisition or the completion of the improvement;

(ii) the amount of any indebtedness or any other amount payable with respect to such indebtedness, or the time for making any payment of any such amount, is dependent, in whole or in part, upon any revenue, income, or profits derived from such real property;

(iii) the real property is at any time after the acquisition leased by the qualified organization to the person selling such property to such organization or to any person who bears a relationship described in section 267(b) or 707(b) to such person;

(iv) the real property is acquired by a qualified trust from, or is at any time after the acquisition leased by such trust to, any person who—

(I) bears a relationship which is described in subparagraph (C), (E), or (G) of section 4975(e)(2) to any plan with respect to which such trust was formed, or

(II) bears a relationship which is described in subparagraph (F) or (H) of section 4975(e)(2) to any person described in subclause (I);

(v) any person described in clause (iii) or (iv) provides the qualified organization with financing in connection with the acquisition or improvement; or

(vi) the real property is held by a partnership unless the partnership meets the requirements of clauses (i) through (v) and unless—

(I) all of the partners of the partnership are qualified organizations,

(II) each allocation to a partner of the partnership which is a qualified organization is a qualified allocation (within the meaning of section 168(h)(6)), or

(III) such partnership meets the requirements of subparagraph (E).

For purposes of subclause (I) of clause (vi), an organization shall not be treated as a qualified organization if any income of such organization is unrelated business income. For purposes of this paragraph, an interest in a mortgage shall in no event be treated as real property.

(C) Qualified organization.For purposes of this paragraph, the term "qualified organization" means—

(i) an organization described in section 170(b)(1)(A)(ii) and it affiliated support organizations described in section 509(a)(3);

(ii) any trust which constitutes a qualified trust under section 401; or

(iii) an organization described in section 501(c)(25).

(D) Other pass-thru entities; tiered entities.—Rules similar to the rules of subparagraph (B)(vi) shall also apply in the case of any pass-thru entity other than a partnership and in the case of tiered partnerships and other entities.

(E) Certain allocations permitted.—

(i) In general.— A partnership meets the requirements of this subparagraph if—

(I) the allocation of items to any partner which is a qualified organization cannot result in such partner having a share of the overall partnership income for any taxable year greater than such partner's share of the overall partnership loss for the taxable year for which such partner's loss share will be the smallest, and

(II) each allocation with respect to the partnership has substantial economic effect within the meaning of section 704(b)(2).

For purposes of this clause, items allocated under section 704(c) shall not be taken into account.

(ii) Special rules.—

(I) Chargebacks.—Except as pro-vided in regulations, a partnership may without violating the requirements of this subparagraph provide for chargebacks with respect to disproportionate losses previously allocated to qualified organizations and disproportionate income previously allocated to other partners. Any chargeback referred to in the preceding sentence shall not be at a ratio in excess of the ratio under which the loss or income (as the case may be) was allocated.

(II) Preferred rates of return, etc. To the extent provided in regulations, a partnership may without violating the requirements of this subparagraph provide for reasonable preferred returns or reasonable guaranteed payments.

(iii) Regulations.— The Secretary shall prescribe such regulations as may be necessary to carry out the purposes of this subparagraph, including regulations which may provide for exclusion or segregation of items.

(F) Special rules for organizations described in section 501(c)(25).—

(i) In general.— In computing under section 512 the unrelated business taxable income of a disqualified holder of an interest in an organization described in section 501(c)(25), there shall be taken into account—

(I) as gross income derived from an unrelated trade or business, such holder's pro rata share of the items of income described in clause (ii)(I) of such organization, and

(II) as deductions allowable in computing unrelated business taxable income, such holder's pro rata share of the items of deduction described in clause (ii)(II) of such organization.

Such amounts shall be taken into account for the taxable year of the holder in which (or with which) the taxable year of such organization ends.

(ii) Description of amounts.— For purposes of clause (i)—

(I) gross income is described in this clause to the extent such income would (but for this paragraph) be treated under subsection (a) as derived from an unrelated trade or business, and

(II) any deduction is described in this clause to the extent it would (but for this paragraph) be allowable under subsection (a)(2) in computing unrelated business taxable income.

(iii) Disqualified holder.— For purposes of this subparagraph, the term "disqualified holder" means any shareholder (or beneficiary) which is not described in clause (i) or (ii) of subparagraph (C).

(G) Special rules for purposes of the exceptions.—Except as otherwise provided by regulations—

(i) Small leases disregarded—For purposes of clauses (iii) and (iv) of subparagraph (B), a lease to a person described in such clause (iii) or (iv) shall be disregarded if no more than 25 percent of the leasable floor space in a building (or complex of buildings) is covered by the lease and if the lease is on commercially reasonable terms.

(ii) Commercially reasonable financing.—Clause (v) of subparagraph (B) shall not apply if the financing is on commercially reasonable terms.

(H) Qualifying sales by financial institutions—

(i) In general— In the case of a qualifying sale by a financial institution, except as provided in regulations, clauses (i) and (ii) of subparagraph (B) shall not apply with respect to financing provided by such institution for such sale.

(ii) Qualifying sale—For purposes of this clause, there is a qualifying sale by a financial institution if—

(I) a qualified organization acquires property described in clause (iii) from a financial institution and any gain recognized by the financial institution with respect to the property is ordinary income,

(II) the stated principal amount of the financing provided by the financial institution does not exceed the amount of the outstanding indebtedness (including accrued but unpaid interest) of the financial institution with respect to the property described in clause (iii) immediately before the acquisition referred to in clause (iii) or (v), whichever is applicable, and

(III) the present value (determined as of the time of the sale and by using the applicable Federal rate determined under section 1274(d)) of the maximum amount payable pursuant to the financing that is determined by reference to the revenue, income, or profits derived from the property cannot exceed 30 percent of the total purchase price of the property (including the contingent payments).

(iii) Property to which subparagraph applies.— Property is described in this clause if such property is foreclosure property, or is real property which—

(I) was acquired by the qualified organization from a financial institution which is in conservatorship or receivership, or from the conservator or receiver of such an institution, and

(II) was held by the financial institution at the time it entered into conservatorship or receivership.

(iv) Financial institution.—For purposes of this subparagraph, the term "financial institution" means—

(I) any financial institution described in section 581 or 591(a)

(II) any other corporation which is a direct or indirect subsidiary of an institution referred to in subclause (I) but only if, by virtue of being affiliated with such institution, such other corporation is subject to supervision and examination by a Federal or State agency which regulates institutions referred to in subclause (I), and

(III) any person acting as a conservator or receiver of an entity referred to in subclause (I) or (II) (or any government agency or corporation succeeding to the rights or interest of such person).

(v) Foreclosure property.— For purposes of this subparagraph, the term "foreclosure property" means any real property acquired by the financial institution as the result of having bid on such property at foreclosure, or by operation of an agreement or process of law, after there was a default (or a default was imminent) on indebtedness which such property secured.

◊ ◊ ◊

(d) Basis of Debt-Financed Property Acquired in Corporate Liquidation.— For purposes of this subtitle, if the property was acquired in a complete or partial liquidation of a corporation in exchange for its stock, the basis of the property shall be the same as it would be in the hands of the transferor corporation, increased by the amount of gain recognized to the transferor corporation upon such distribution and by the amount of any gain to the organization which was included, on account of such distribution, in unrelated business taxable income under subsection (a).

(e) Allocation Rules.— Where debt-financed property is held for purposes described in subsection (b)(1)(A), (B), (C), or (D) as well as for other purposes, proper allocation shall be made with respect to basis, indebtedness, and income and deductions. The allocations required by this section shall be made in accordance with regulations prescribed by the Secretary to the extent proper to carry out the purpose of this section.

(f) Personal Property Leased With Real Property.— For purposes of this section, the term "real property" includes personal property of the lessor leased by it to a lessee of its real estate if the lease of such personal property is made under, or in connection with, the lease of such real estate.

(g) Regulations.— The Secretary shall prescribe such regulations as may be necessary or appropriate to carry out the purposes of this section, including regulations to prevent the circumvention of any provision of this section through the use of segregated asset accounts.

* * *

IRC Sec. 514 (g)

Subchapter J— Estates, Trusts, Beneficiaries, and Decedents

* * *

Part II— Income in respect of decedents

* * *

SEC. 691. RECIPIENTS OF INCOME IN RESPECT OF DECEDENTS

(a) Inclusion in gross income.—

(1) General rule.—The amount of all items of gross income in respect of a decedent which are not properly includible in respect of the taxable period in which falls the date of his death or a prior period (including the amount of all items of gross income in respect of a prior decedent, if the right to receive such amount was acquired by reason of the death of the prior decedent or by bequest, devise, or inheritance from the prior decedent) shall be included in the gross income, for the taxable year when received, of:

(A) the estate of the decedent, if the right to receive the amount is acquired by the decedent's estate from the decedent;

(B) the person who, by reason of the death of the decedent, acquires the right to receive the amount, if the right to receive the amount is not acquired by the decedent's estate from the decedent; or

(C) the person who acquires from the decedent the right to receive the amount by bequest, devise, or inheritance, if the amount is received after a distribution by the decedent's estate of such right.

(2) Income in case of sale, etc.—If a right, described in paragraph (1), to receive an amount is transferred by the estate of the decedent or a person who received such right by reason of the death of the decedent or by bequest, devise, or inheritance from the decedent, there shall be included in the gross income of the estate or such person, as the case may be, for the taxable period in which the transfer occurs, the fair market value of such

right at the time of such transfer plus the amount by which any consideration for the transfer exceeds such fair market value. For purposes of this paragraph, the term "transfer" includes sale, exchange, or other disposition, or the satisfaction of an installment obligation at other than face value, but does not include transmission at death to the estate of the decedent or a transfer to a person pursuant to the right of such person to receive such amount by reason of the death of the decedent or by bequest, devise, or inheritance from the decedent.

(3) Character of income determined by reference to decedent.— The right, described in paragraph (1), to receive an amount shall be treated, in the hands of the estate of the decedent or any person who acquired such right by reason of the death of the decedent, or by bequest, devise, or inheritance from the decedent, as if it had been acquired by the estate or such person in the transaction in which the right to receive the income was originally derived and the amount includible in gross income under paragraph (1) or (2) shall be considered in the hands of the estate or such person to have the character which it would have had in the hands of the decedent if the decedent had lived and received such amount.

(4) Installment obligations acquired from decedent.—In the case of an installment obligation reportable by the decedent on the installment method under section 453, if such obligation is acquired by the decedent's estate from the decedent or by any person by reason of the death of the decedent or by bequest, devise, or inheritance from the decedent—

(A) an amount equal to the excess of the face amount of such obligation over the basis of the obligation in the hands of the decedent (determined under section 453B) shall, for the purpose of paragraph (1), be considered as an item of gross income in respect of the decedent; and

(B) such obligation shall, for purposes of paragraphs (2) and (3), be considered a right to receive an item of gross income in respect of the decedent, but the amount includible in gross income under paragraph (2) shall be reduced by an amount equal to the basis of the obligation in the hands of the decedent (determined under section 453B).

(5) Other rules relating to installment obligations.—

(A) In general.— In the case of an installment obligation reportable by the decedent on the installment method under section 453, for purposes of paragraph (2)—

(i) the second sentence of paragraph (2) shall be applied by inserting "(other than the obligor)" after "or a transfer to a person",

(ii) any cancellation of such an obligation shall be treated as a transfer, and

(iii) any cancellation of such an obligation occurring at the death of the decedent shall be treated as a transfer by the estate of the decedent (or, if held by a person other than the decedent before the death of the decedent, by such person).

(B) Face amount treated as fair market value in certain cases.— In any case to which the first sentence of paragraph (2) applies by reason of subparagraph (A), if the decedent and the obligor were related persons (within the meaning of section 453(f)(1)), the fair market value of the installment obligation shall be treated as not less than its face amount.

(C) Cancellation includes becoming unenforceable.— For purposes of subparagraph (A), an installment obligation which becomes unenforceable shall be treated as if it were canceled.

(b) Allowance of deductions and credit.— The amount of any deduction specified in section 162, 163, 164, 212, or 611 (relating to deductions for expenses, interest, taxes, and depletion) or credit specified in section 27 (relating to foreign tax credit), in respect of a decedent which is not properly allowable to the decedent in respect of the taxable period in which falls the date of his death, or a prior period, shall be allowed:

(1) Expenses, interest, and taxes.— In the case of a deduction specified in sections 162, 163, 164, or 212 and a credit specified in section 27, in the taxable year when paid—

(A) to the estate of the decedent; except that

(B) if the estate of the decedent is not liable to discharge the obligation to which the deduction or credit relates, to the person who, by reason of the death of the decedent or by bequest, devise, or inheritance acquires, subject to such obligation, from the decedent an interest in property of the decedent.

(2) Depletion.—In the case of the deduction specified in section 611, to the person described in subsection (a)(1)(A), (B), or (C) who, in the manner described therein, receives the income to which the deduction relates, in the taxable year when such income is received.

(c) Deduction for estate tax.—

(1) Allowance of deduction.—

(A) General rule.— A person who includes an amount in gross income under subsection (a) shall be allowed, for the same taxable year, as a deduction an amount which bears the same ratio to the estate tax attributable to the net value for estate tax purposes of all the items described in subsection (a)(1) as the value for estate tax purposes of the items of gross income or portions thereof in respect of which such person included the amount in gross income (or the amount included in gross income, whichever is lower) bears to the value for estate tax purposes of all the items described in subsection (a)(1).

(B) Estates and trusts.—In the case of an estate or trust, the amount allowed as a deduction under subparagraph (A) shall be computed by excluding from the gross income of the estate or trust the portion (if any) of the items described in subsection (a)(1) which is properly paid, credited, or to be

IRC Sec. 691 (c)(1)(B)

distributed to the beneficiaries during the taxable year.

(C) Excess retirement accumulation tax.— For purposes of this subsection, no deduction shall be allowed for the portion of the estate tax attributable to the increase in such tax under section 4980A(d).

(2) Method of computing deduction.— For purposes of paragraph (1)—

(A) The term "estate tax" means the tax imposed on the estate of the decedent or any prior decedent under section 2001 or 2101, reduced by the credits against such tax.

(B) The net value for estate tax purposes of all the items described in subsection (a)(1) shall be the excess of the value for estate tax purposes of all the items described in subsection (a)(1) over the deductions from the gross estate in respect of claims which represent the deductions and credit described in subsection (b). Such net value shall be determined with respect to the provisions of section 421(c)(2), relating to the deduction for estate tax with respect to stock options to which part II of subchapter D applies.

(C) The estate tax attributable to such net value shall be an amount equal to the excess of the estate tax over the estate tax computed without including in the gross estate such net value.

(3) Special rule for generation-skipping transfers.—In the case of any tax imposed by chapter 13 on a taxable termination or a direct skip occurring as a result of the death of the transferor, there shall be allowed a deduction (under principles similar to the principles of this subsection) for the portion of such tax attributable to items of gross income of the trust which were not properly includible in the gross income of the trust for periods before the date of such termination.

(4) Coordination with capital gain provisions.— For purposes of sections 1(h), 1201, and 1211, the amount of any gain taken into account with respect to any item described in subsection (a)(1) shall be reduced (but not below zero) by the amount of the deduction allowable under paragraph (1) of this subsection with respect to such item.

(5) Coordination with section 402(d).— For purposes of section 402(d) (other than paragraph (1)(C) thereof), the total taxable amount of any lump sum distribution shall be reduced by the amount of the deduction allowable under paragraph (1) of this subsection which is attributable to the total taxable amount (determined without regard to this paragraph).

(d) Amounts received by surviving annuitant under joint and survivor annuity contract.—

(1) Deduction for estate tax.—For purposes of computing the deduction under subsection (c)(1)(A), amounts received by a surviving annuitant—

(A) as an annuity under a joint and survivor annuity contract where the decedent annuitant died after December 31, 1953, and after the annuity starting date (as defined in section 72(c)(4)), and

(B) during the surviving annuitant's life expectancy period,

shall, to the extent included in gross income under section 72, be considered as amounts included in gross income under subsection (a).

(2) Net value for estate tax purposes.— In determining the net value for estate tax purposes under subsection (c)(2)(B) for purposes of this subsection, the value for estate tax purposes of the items described in paragraph (1) of this subsection shall be computed—

(A) by determining the excess of the value of the annuity at the date of the death of the deceased annuitant over the total amount excludable from the gross income of the surviving annuitant under section 72 during the surviving annuitant's life expectancy period, and

(B) by multiplying the figure so obtained by the ratio which the value of the annuity for estate tax purposes bears to the value of the annuity at the date of the death of the deceased.

(3) Definitions.—For purposes of this subsection—

(A) The term "life expectancy period" means the period beginning with the first day of the first period for which an amount is received by the surviving annuitant under the contract and ending with the close of the taxable year with or in which falls the termination of the life expectancy of the surviving annuitant. For purposes of this subparagraph, the life expectancy of the surviving annuitant shall be determined, as of the date of the death of the deceased annuitant, with reference to actuarial tables prescribed by the Secretary.

(B) The surviving annuitant's expected return under the contract shall be computed, as of the death of the deceased annuitant, with reference to actuarial tables prescribed by the Secretary.

(e) Cross reference.—For application of this section to income in respect of a deceased partner, see section 753.

* * *

Subchapter O— Gain or Loss on Disposition of Property
* * *

Part III— Common Nontaxable Exchanges
* * *

SEC. 1042. SALES OF STOCK TO EMPLOYEE STOCK OWNERSHIP PLANS OR CERTAIN COOPERATIVES.

(a) Nonrecognition of Gain.—If—

(1) the taxpayer or executor elects in such form as the Secretary may prescribe the application of this section with respect to any sale of qualified securities,

(2) the taxpayer purchases qualified replacement property within the replacement period, and

(3) the requirements of subsection (b) are met with respect to such sale,

then the gain (if any) on such sale which would be recognized as long-term capital gain shall be recognized only to the extent that the amount realized on such sale exceeds the cost to the taxpayer of such qualified replacement property.

(b) Requirements to Qualify for Nonrecognition.— A sale of qualified securities meets the requirements of this subsection if—

(1) Sale to employee organizations.—The qualified securities are sold to—

(A) an employee stock ownership plan (as defined in section 4975(e)(7)), or

(B) an eligible worker-owned cooperative.

(2) Plan must hold 30 percent of stock after sale.— The plan or cooperative referred to in paragraph (1) owns (after application of section 318(a)(4)), immediately after the sale, at least 30 percent of—

(A) each class of outstanding stock of the corporation (other than stock described in section 1504(a)(4)) which issued the qualified securities, or

(B) the total value of all outstanding stock of the corporation (other than stock described in section 1504(a)(4)).

(3) Written statement required.—

(A) In general.—The taxpayer files with the Secretary the written statement described in subparagraph (B).

(B) Statement.— A statement is described in this subparagraph if it is a verified written statement of—

(i) the employer whose employees are covered by the plan described in paragraph (1), or

(ii) any authorized officer of the cooperative described in paragraph (1),

consenting to the application of sections 4978 and 4979A with respect to such employer or cooperative.

(4) 3-Year holding period.— The taxpayer's holding period with respect to the qualified securities is at least 3 years (determined as of the time of the sale).

(c) Definitions; Special Rules.— For purposes of this section—

(1) Qualified securities.— The term "qualified securities" means employer securities (as defined in section 409(*l*)) which—

(A) are issued by a domestic corporation that has no stock outstanding that are readily tradable on an established securities market, and

(B) were not received by the taxpayer in—

(i) a distribution from a plan described in section 401(a), or

(ii) a transfer pursuant to an option or other right to acquire stock to which Section 83, 422, or 423 applied (or to which section 422 or 424 (as in effect on the day before the date of the enactment of the Revenue Reconciliation Act of 1990)) applied.

(2) Eligible worker-owned cooperative.— The term "eligible worker-owned cooperative" means any organization—

(A) to which part I of subchapter T applies,

(B) a majority of the membership of which is comprised of employees of such organization,

(C) a majority of the voting stock of which is owned by members,

(D) a majority of the board of directors of which is elected by the members on the basis of 1 person 1 vote, and

(E) a majority of the allocated earnings and losses of which are allocated to members on the basis of—

(i) patronage,

(ii) capital contributions, or

(iii) some combination of clauses (i) and (ii).

(3) Replacement period.— The term "replacement period" means the period which begins 3 months before the date on which the sale of qualified securities occurs and which ends 12 months after the date of such sale.

(4) Qualified replacement property.—

(A) In general.— The term "qualified replacement property" means any security issued by a domestic operating corporation which—

(i) did not, for the taxable year preceding the taxable year in which such security was purchased, have passive investment income (as defined in section 1362(d)(3)(D)) in excess of 25 percent of the gross receipts of such corporation for such preceding taxable year, and

(ii) is not the corporation which issued the qualified securities which such security is replacing or a member of the same controlled group of corporations (within the meaning of section 1563(a)(1)) as such corporation.

For purposes of clause (i), income which is described in section 954(c)(3) (as in effect immediately before the Tax Reform Act of 1986) shall not be treated as passive investment income.

(B) Operating corporation.— For purposes of this paragraph—

(i) In general.— The term "operating corporation" means a corporation more than 50 percent of the assets of which were, at the time the security was purchased or before the close of the replacement period, used in the active conduct of the trade or business.

(ii) Financial institutions and insurance companies.— The term "operating corporation" shall include—

(I) any financial institution described in section 581 or 593, and

(II) an insurance company subject to tax under subchapter L.

(C) Controlling and controlled corporations treated as 1 corporation.—

(i) In general.— For purposes of applying this paragraph, if—

(I) the corporation issuing the security owns stock representing control of 1 or more other corporations,

(II) 1 or more other corporations own stock representing control of the corporation issuing the security, or

(III) both,

then all such corporations shall be treated as 1 corporation.

(ii) Control.— For purposes of clause (i), the term "control" has the meaning given such term by section 304(c). In determining control, there shall be disregarded any qualified replacement property of the taxpayer with respect to the section 1042 sale being tested.

(D) Security defined.— For purposes of this paragraph the term "security" has the meaning given such term by section 165(g)(2), except that such term shall not include any security issued by a government or political subdivision thereof.

(5) Securities sold by underwriter.— No sale of securities by an underwriter to an employee stock ownership plan or eligible worker-owned cooperative in the ordinary course of his trade or business as an underwriter, whether or not guaranteed, shall be treated as a sale for purposes of subsection (a).

(6) Time for filing election.— An election under subsection (a) shall be filed not later than the last day prescribed by law (including extensions thereof) for filing the return of tax imposed by this chapter for the taxable year in which the sale occurs.

(7) Section not to apply to gain of C corporation.— Subsection (a) shall not apply to any gain on the sale of any qualified securities which is includible in the gross income of any C corporation.

(d) Basis of Qualified Replacement Property.— The basis of the taxpayer in qualified replacement property purchased by the taxpayer during the replacement period shall be reduced by the amount of gain not recognized by reason of such purchase and the application of subsection (a). If more than one item of qualified replacement property is purchased, the basis of each of such items shall be reduced by an amount determined by multiplying the total gain not recognized by reason of such purchase and the application of subsection (a) by a fraction—

(1) the numerator of which is the cost of such item of property, and

(2) the denominator of which is the total cost of all such items of property.

Any reduction in basis under this subsection shall not be taken into account for purposes of section 1278(a)(2)(A)(ii) (relating to definition of market discount).

(e) Recapture of Gain on Disposition of Qualified Replacement Property.—

(1) In general.— If a taxpayer disposes of any qualified replacement property, then, notwithstanding any other provision of this title, gain (if any) shall be recognized to the extent of the gain which was not recognized under subsection (a) by reason of the acquisition by such taxpayer of such qualified replacement property.

(2) Special rule for corporations controlled by the taxpayer.—If—

(A) a corporation issuing qualified replacement property disposes of a substantial portion of its assets other than in the ordinary course of its trade or business, and

(B) any taxpayer owning stock representing control (within the meaning of section 304(c)) of such corporation at the time of such disposition holds any qualified replacement property of such corporation at such time,

then the taxpayer shall be treated as having disposed of such qualified replacement property at such time.

(3) Recapture not to apply in certain cases.— Paragraph (1) shall not apply to any transfer of qualified replacement property—

(A) in any reorganization (within the meaning of section 368) unless the person making the election under subsection (a)(1) owns stock representing control in the acquiring or acquired corporation and such property is substituted basis property in the hands of the transferee,

(B) by reason of the death of the person making such election,

(C) by gift, or

(D) in any transaction to which section 1042(a) applies.

(f) Statute of Limitations.— If any gain is realized by the taxpayer on the sale or exchange of any qualified securities and there is in effect an election under subsection (a) with respect to such gain, then—

(1) the statutory period for the assessment of any deficiency with respect to such gain shall not expire before the expiration of 3 years from the date the Secretary is notified by the taxpayer (in such manner as the Secretary may by regulations prescribe) of—

(A) the taxpayer's cost of purchasing qualified replacement property which the taxpayer claims results in nonrecognition of any part of such gain,

(B) the taxpayer's intention not to purchase qualified replacement property within the replacement period, or

(C) a failure to make such purchase within the replacement period, and

(2) such deficiency may be assessed before the expiration of such 3-year period notwithstanding the provisions of any other law or rule of law which would otherwise prevent such assessment.

* * *

Subchapter S—Tax Treatment of S Corporations and Their Shareholders

* * *

Part III— Special Rules

* * *

SEC. 1372. PARTNERSHIP RULES TO APPLY FOR FRINGE BENEFIT PURPOSES.

(a) General Rule.—For purposes of applying the provisions of this subtitle which relate to employee fringe benefits

(1) the S corporation shall be treated as a partnership, and

(2) any 2-percent shareholder of the S corporation shall be treated as a partner of such partnership.

(b) 2-Percent Shareholder Defined.— For purposes of this section, the term "2-percent shareholder" means any person who owns (or is considered as owning within the meaning of section 318) on any day during the taxable year of the S corporation more than 2 percent of the outstanding stock of such corporation or stock possessing more than 2 percent of the total combined voting power of all stock of such corporation.

* * *

Chapter 6— Consolidated Returns

* * *

Subchapter B— Related Rules

* * *

Part II— Certain Controlled Corporations

* * *

SEC. 1563. DEFINITIONS AND SPECIAL RULES.

(a) Controlled Group of Corporations.— For purposes of this part, the term ''controlled group of corporations'' means any group of—

(1) Parent-subsidiary controlled group.— One or more chains of corporations connected through stock ownership with a common parent corporation if—

(A) stock possessing at least 80 percent of the total combined voting power of all classes of stock entitled to vote or at least 80 percent of the total value of shares of all classes of stock of each of the corporations, except the common parent corporation, is owned (within the meaning of subsection (d)(1)) by one or more of the other corporations; and

(B) the common parent corporation owns (within the meaning of subsection (d)(1)) stock possessing at least 80 percent of the total combined voting power of all classes of stock entitled to vote or at least 80 percent of the total value of shares of all classes of stock of at least one of the other corporations, excluding, in computing such voting power or value, stock owned directly by such other corporations.

(2) Brother-sister controlled group.— Two or more corporations if 5 or fewer persons who are individuals, estates, or trusts own (within the meaning of subsection (d)(2)) stock possessing—

(A) at least 80 percent of the total combined voting power of all classes of stock entitled to vote or at least 80 percent of the total value of shares of all classes of the stock of each corporation, and

(B) more than 50 percent of the total combined voting power of all classes of stock entitled to vote or more than 50 percent of the total value of shares of all classes of stock of each corporation, taking into account the stock ownership of each such person only to the extent such stock ownership is identical with respect to each such corporation.

(3) Combined group.— Three or more corporations each of which is a member of a group of corporations described in paragraph (1) or (2), and one of which—

(A) is a common parent corporation included in a group of corporations described in paragraph (1), and also

(B) is included in a group of corporations described in paragraph (2).

(4) Certain insurance companies.— Two or more insurance companies subject to taxation under section 801 which are members of a controlled group of corporations described in paragraph (1), (2), or (3). Such insurance companies shall be treated as a controlled group of corporations separate from any other corporations which are members of the controlled group of corporations described in paragraph (1), (2), or (3).

(b) Component Member.—

(1) General rule.— For purposes of this part, a corporation is a component member of a controlled group of corporations on a December 31 of any taxable year (and with respect to the taxable year which includes such December 31) if such corporation—

(A) is a member of such controlled group of corporations on the December 31 included in such year and is not treated as an excluded member under paragraph (2), or

(B) is not a member of such controlled group of corporations on the December 31 included in such year but is treated as an additional member under paragraph (3).

(2) Excluded members.—A corporation which is a member of a controlled group of corporations on December 31 of any taxable year shall be treated as an excluded member of such group for the taxable year including such December 31 if such corporation—

(A) is a member of such group for less than one-half the number of days in such taxable year which precede such December 31,

(B) is exempt from taxation under section 501(a) (except a corporation which is subject to tax on its unrelated business taxable income under section 511) for such taxable year,

(C) is a foreign corporation subject to tax under section 881 for such taxable year,

(D) is an insurance company subject to taxation under section 801 (other than an insurance company which is a member of a controlled group described in subsection (a)(4)), or

(E) is a franchised corporation, as defined in subsection (f)(4).

(3) Additional members.— A corporation which—

(A) was a member of a controlled group of corporations at any time during a calendar year,

(B) is not a member of such group on December 31 of such calendar year, and

(C) is not described, with respect to such group, in subparagraph (B), (C), (D), or (E) of paragraph (2),

shall be treated as an additional member of such group on December 31 for its taxable year including such December 31 if it was a member of such group for one-half (or more)

of the number of days in such taxable year which precede such December 31.

(4) Overlapping groups.—If a corporation is a component member of more than one controlled group of corporations with respect to any taxable year, such corporation shall be treated as a component member of only one controlled group. The determination as to the group of which such corporation is a component member shall be made under regulations prescribed by the Secretary which are consistent with the purposes of this part.

(c) Certain Stock Excluded.—

(1) General rule.— For purposes of this part, the term "stock" does not include—

(A) nonvoting stock which is limited and preferred as to dividends,

(B) treasury stock, and

(C) stock which is treated as "excluded stock" under paragraph (2).

(2) Stock treated as "excluded stock."—

(A) Parent-subsidiary controlled group.— For purposes of subsection (a)(1), if a corporation (referred to in this paragraph as "parent corporation") owns (within the meaning of subsections (d)(1) and (e)(4)), 50 percent or more of the total combined voting power of all classes of stock entitled to vote or 50 percent or more of the total value of shares of all classes of stock in another corporation (referred to in this paragraph as "subsidiary corporation"), the following stock of the subsidiary corporation shall be treated as excluded stock—

(i) stock in the subsidiary corporation held by a trust which is part of a plan of deferred compensation for the benefit of the employees of the parent corporation or the subsidiary corporation,

(ii) stock in the subsidiary corporation owned by an individual (within the meaning of subsection (d)(2)) who is a principal stockholder or officer of the parent corporation. For purposes of this clause, the term "principal stockholder" of a corporation means an individual who owns (within the meaning of subsection (d)(2)) 5 percent or more of the total combined voting power of all classes of stock entitled to vote or 5 percent or more of the total value of shares of all classes of stock in such corporation,

(iii) stock in the subsidiary corporation owned (within the meaning of subsection (d)(2)) by an employee of the subsidiary corporation if such stock is subject to conditions which run in favor of such parent (or subsidiary) corporation and which substantially restrict or limit the employee's right (or if the employee constructively owns such stock, the direct owner's right) to dispose of such stock, or

(iv) stock in the subsidiary corporation owned (within the meaning of subsection (d)(2)) by an organization (other than the parent corporation) to which section 501 (relating to certain educational and charitable organizations which are exempt from tax) applies and which is controlled directly or indirectly by the parent corporation or subsidiary corporation, by an individual, estate, or trust that is a principal stockholder (within the meaning of clause (ii)) of the parent corporation, or by an officer of the parent corporation, or by any combination thereof.

(B) Brother-sister controlled group.— For purposes of subsection (a)(2), if 5 or fewer persons who are individuals, estates, or trusts (referred to in this subparagraph as "common owners") own (within the meaning of subsection (d)(2), 50 percent or more of the total combined voting power of all classes of stock entitled to vote or 50 percent or more of the total value of shares of all classes of stock in a corporation, the following stock of such corporation shall be treated as excluded stock—

(i) stock in such corporation held by an employees' trust described in section 401(a) which is exempt from tax under section 501(a), if such trust is for the benefit of the employees of such corporation,

(ii) stock in such corporation owned (within the meaning of subsection (d)(2)) by an employee of the corporation if such stock is subject to conditions which run in favor of any of such common owners (or such corporation) and which substantially restrict or limit the employee's right (or if the employee constructively owns such stock, the direct owner's right) to dispose of such stock. If a condition which limits or restricts the employee's right (or the direct owner's right) to dispose of such stock also applies to the stock held by any of the common owners pursuant to a bona fide reciprocal stock purchase arrangement, such condition shall not be treated as one which restricts or limits the employee's right to dispose of such stock, or

(iii) stock in such corporation owned (within the meaning of subsection (d)(2)) by an organization to which section 501 (relating to certain educational and charitable organizations which are exempt from tax) applies and which is controlled directly or indirectly by such corporation, by an individual, estate, or trust that is a principal stockholder (within the meaning of subparagraph (A)(ii)) of such corporation, by an officer of such corporation, or by any combination thereof.

(d) Rules for Determining Stock Ownership.—

(1) Parent-subsidiary controlled group.— For purposes of determining whether a corporation is a member of a parent-subsidiary controlled group of corporations (within the meaning of subsection (a)(1)), stock owned by a corporation means—

(A) stock owned directly by such corporation, and

(B) stock owned with the application of paragraphs (1), (2), and (3) of subsection (e).

IRC Sec. 1563 (d)(1)(B)

(2) Brother-sister controlled group.— For purposes of determining whether a corporation is a member of a brother-sister controlled group of corporations (within the meaning of subsection (a)(2)), stock owned by a person who is an individual, estate, or trust means—

(A) stock owned directly by such person, and

(B) stock owned with the application of subsection (e).

(e) Constructive Ownership.—

(1) Options.—If any person has an option to acquire stock, such stock shall be considered as owned by such person. For purposes of this paragraph, an option to acquire such an option, and each one of a series of such options, shall be considered as an option to acquire such stock.

(2) Attribution from partnerships.— Stock owned, directly or indirectly, by or for a partnership shall be considered as owned by any partner having an interest of 5 percent or more in either the capital or profits of the partnership in proportion to his interest in capital or profits, whichever such proportion is the greater.

(3) Attribution from estates or trusts.—

(A) Stock owned, directly or indirectly, by or for an estate or trust shall be considered as owned by any beneficiary who has an actuarial interest of 5 percent or more in such stock, to the extent of such actuarial interest. For purposes of this subparagraph, the actuarial interest of each beneficiary shall be determined by assuming the maximum exercise of discretion by the fiduciary in favor of such beneficiary and the maximum use of such stock to satisfy his rights as a beneficiary.

(B) Stock owned, directly or indirectly, by or for any portion of a trust of which a person is considered the owner under subpart E of part I of subchapter J (relating to grantors and others treated as substantial owners) shall be considered as owned by such person.

(C) This paragraph shall not apply to stock owned by any employees' trust described in section 401(a) which is exempt from tax under section 501(a).

(4) Attribution from corporations.— Stock owned, directly or indirectly, by or for a corporation shall be considered as owned by any person who owns (within the meaning of subsection (d)) 5 percent or more in value of its stock in that proportion which the value of the stock which such person so owns bears to the value of all the stock in such corporation.

(5) Spouse.— An individual shall be considered as owning stock in a corporation owned, directly or indirectly, by or for his spouse (other than a spouse who is legally separated from the individual under a decree of divorce whether interlocutory or final, or a decree of separate maintenance), except in the case of a corporation with respect to which each of the following conditions is satisfied for its taxable year—

(A) The individual does not, at any time during such taxable year, own directly any stock in such corporation;

(B) The individual is not a director or employee and does not participate in the management of such corporation at any time during such taxable year;

(C) Not more than 50 percent of such corporation's gross income for such taxable year was derived from royalties, rents, dividends, interest, and annuities; and

(D) Such stock in such corporation is not, at any time during such taxable year, subject to conditions which substantially restrict or limit the spouse's right to dispose of such stock and which run in favor of the individual or his children who have not attained the age of 21 years.

(6) Children, grandchildren, parents, and grandparents.—

(A) Minor children.— An individual shall be considered as owning stock owned, directly or indirectly, by or for his children who have not attained the age of 21 years, and, if the individual has not attained the age of 21 years, the stock owned, directly or indirectly, by or for his parents.

(B) Adult children and grandchildren.—An individual who owns (within the meaning of subsection (d)(2), but without regard to this subparagraph) more than 50 percent of the total combined voting power of all classes of stock entitled to vote or more than 50 percent of the total value of shares of all classes of stock in a corporation shall be considered as owning the stock in such corporation owned, directly or indirectly, by or for his parents, grandparents, grandchildren, and children who have attained the age of 21 years.

(C) Adopted child.— For purposes of this section, a legally adopted child of an individual shall be treated as a child of such individual by blood.

(f) Other Definitions and Rules.—

(1) Employee defined.— For purposes of this section the term ''employee'' has the same meaning such term is given by paragraphs (1) and (2) of section 3121(d).

(2) Operating rules.—

(A) In general.—Except as provided in subparagraph (B), stock constructively owned by a person by reason of the application of paragraph (1), (2), (3), (4), (5), or (6) of subsection (e) shall, for purposes of applying such paragraphs, be treated as actually owned by such person.

(B) Members of family.— Stock constructively owned by an individual by reason of the application of paragraph (5) or (6) of subsection (e) shall not be treated as owned by him for purposes of again applying such paragraphs in order to make another the constructive owner of such stock.

(3) Special rules.— For purposes of this section—

(A) If stock may be considered as owned by a person under subsection (e)(1) and under any other paragraph of subsection (e), it shall be considered as owned by him under subsection (e)(1).

(B) If stock is owned (within the meaning of subsection (d)) by two or more persons, such stock shall be considered as owned by the person whose ownership of such stock results in the corporation being a component member of a controlled group. If by reason of the preceding sentence, a corporation would (but for this sentence) become a component member of two controlled groups, it shall be treated as a component member of one controlled group. The determination as to the group of which such corporation is a component member shall be made under regulations prescribed by the Secretary which are consistent with the purposes of this part.

(C) If stock is owned by a person within the meaning of subsection (d) and such ownership results in the corporation being a component member of a controlled group, such stock shall not be treated as excluded stock under subsection (c)(2), if by reason of treating such stock as excluded stock the result is that such corporation is not a component member of a controlled group of corporations.

(4) Franchised corporation.—If—

(A) a parent corporation (as defined in subsection (c)(2)(A)), or a common owner (as defined in subsection (c)(2)(B)), of a corporation which is a member of a controlled group of corporations is under a duty (arising out of a written agreement) to sell stock of such corporation (referred to in this paragraph as ''franchised corporation'') which is franchised to sell the products of another member, or the common owner, of such controlled group;

(B) such stock is to be sold to an employee (or employees) of such franchised corporation pursuant to a bona fide plan designated to eliminate the stock ownership of the parent corporation or of the common owner in the franchised corporation;

(C) such plan—

(i) provides a reasonable selling price for such stock, and

(ii) requires that a portion of the employee's share of the profits of such corporation (whether received as compensation or as a dividend) be applied to the purchase of such stock (or the purchase of notes, bonds, debentures, or other similar evidence of indebtedness of such franchised corporation held by such parent corporation or common owner);

(D) such employee (or employees) owns directly more than 20 percent of the total value of shares of all classes of stock in such franchised corporation;

(E) more than 50 percent of the inventory of such franchised corporation is acquired from members of the controlled group, the common owner, or both; and

(F) all of the conditions contained in subparagraphs (A), (B), (C), (D), and (E) have been met for one-half (or more) of the number of days preceding the December 31 included within the taxable year (or if the taxable year does not include December 31, the last day of such year) of the franchised corporation,

then such franchised corporation shall be treated as an excluded member of such group, under subsection (b)(2), for such taxable year.

* * *

Subtitle B— Estate And Gift Taxes

Chapter 11— Estate Tax
Subchapter A— Estate Of Citizens Or Residents

* * *

Part III— Gross Estate

* * *

SEC. 2039. ANNUITIES.

(a) In General.— The gross estate shall include the value of an annuity or other payment receivable by any beneficiary by reason of surviving the decedent under any form of contract or agreement entered into after March 3, 1931 (other than as insurance under policies on the life of the decedent), if, under such contract or agreement, an annuity or other payment was payable to the decedent, or the decedent possessed the right to receive such annuity or payment, either alone or in conjunction with another for his life or for any period not ascertainable without reference to his death or for any period which does not in fact end before his death.

(b) Amount Includible.— Subsection (a) shall apply to only such part of the value of the annuity or other payment receivable under such contract or agreement as is proportionate to that part of the purchase price therefor contributed by the decedent. For purposes of this section, any contribution by the decedent's employer or former employer to the purchase price of such contract or agreement (whether or not to an employee's trust or fund forming part of a pension, annuity, retirement, bonus or profit-sharing plan) shall be considered to be contributed by the decedent if made by reason of his employment.

* * *

Subtitle C— Employment Taxes

Chapter 21— Federal Insurance Contributions Act

Subchapter C— General Provisions
* * *

SEC. 3121. DEFINITIONS.

(a) **Wages.**—For purposes of this chapter, the term "wages" means all remuneration for employment, including the cash value of all remuneration (including benefits) paid in any medium other than cash; except that such term shall not include—

(1) in the case of the taxes imposed by sections 3101(a) and 3111(a), that part of the remuneration which, after remuneration (other than remuneration referred to in the succeeding paragraphs of this subsection) equal to the contribution and benefit base (as determined under section 230 of the Social Security Act) with respect to employment has been paid to an individual by an employer during a calendar year with respect to which such contribution and benefit base is effective, is paid to such individual by such employer during such calendar year.

If an employer (hereinafter referred to as successor employer) during any calendar year acquires substantially all the property used in the trade or business of another employer (herinafter referred to as a predecessor), or used in a separate unit of a trade or business of a predecessor, and immediately after the acquisition employs in his trade or business an individual who immediately prior to the acquisition was employed in a trade or business of such predecessor, then, for the purpose of determining whether the successor employer has paid remuneration (other than remuneration referred to in the succeeding paragraphs of this subsection) with respect to employment equal to the Contribution and benefit base (as determined under Section 230 of the Social Security Act) to such individual during such calendar year, any remuneration (other than remuneration referred to in the succeeding paragraphs of this subsection) with respect to employment paid (or considered under this paragraph as having been paid) to such individual by such predecessor during such calendar year and prior to such acquisition shall be considered as having been paid by such successor employer;

(2) the amount of any payment (including any amount paid by an employer for insurance or annuities, or into a fund, to provide for any such payment) made to, or on behalf of, an employee or any of his dependents under a plan or system established by an employer which makes provision for his employees generally (or for his employees generally and their dependents) or for a class or classes of his employees (or for a class or classes of his employees and their dependents), on account of—

(A) sickness or accident disability (but, in the case of payments made to an employee or any of his dependents, this subparagraph shall exclude from the term "wages" only payments which are received under a workmen's compensation law), or

(B) medical or hospitalization expenses in connections with sickness or accident disability, or

(C) death, except that this paragraph does not apply to a payment for group-term life insurance to the extent that such payment is includible in the gross income of the employee;

(3) [Stricken.]

(4) any payment on account of sickness or accident disability, or medical or hospitalization expenses in connection with sickness or accident disability, made by an employer to, or on behalf of, an employee after the expiration of 6 calendar months following the last calendar month in which the employee worked for such employer;

(5) any payment made to, or on behalf of, an employee or his beneficiary—

(A) from or to a trust described in section 401(a) which is exempt from tax under section 501(a) at the time of such payment unless such payment is made to an employee of the trust as remuneration for services rendered as such employee and not as a beneficiary of the trust,

(B) under or to an annuity plan which, at the time of such payment, is a plan described in section 403(a),

(C) under a simplified employee pension plan (as defined in section 408(k)(1)), other than any contributions described in section 408(k)(6),

(D) under or to an annuity contract described in section 403(b), other than a payment for the purchase of such contract which is made by reason of a salary reduction agreement (whether evidenced by a written instrument or otherwise),

(E) under or to an exempt governmental deferred compensation plan (as defined in subsection (v)(3)),

(F) to supplement pension benefits under a plan or trust described in any of the foregoing provisions of this paragraph to take into account some portion or all of the increase in the cost of living (as determined by the Secretary of Labor) since retirement but only if such supplemental payments are under a plan which is treated as a welfare plan under section 3(2)(B)(ii) of the Employee Retirement Income Security Act of 1974; or

(G) under a cafeteria plan (within the meaning of section 125) if such payment would not be treated as wages without regard to such plan and it is reasonable to believe that (if section 125 applied for purposes of this section) section 125 would not treat any wages as constructively received,

(6) the payment by an employer (without deduction from the remuneration of the employee)—

(A) of the tax imposed upon an employee under section 3101, or

(B) of any payment required from an employee under a State unemployment compensation law,

with respect to remuneration paid to an employee for domestic service in a private home of the employer or for agricultural labor;

(7)(A) remuneration paid in any medium other than cash to an employee for service not in the course of the employer's trade or business or for domestic service in a private home of the employer;

[(B) cash remuneration paid by an employer in any calendar quarter to an employee for domestic service in a private home of the employer, if the cash remuneration paid in such quarter by the employer to the employee for such service is less than $50. As used in this subparagraph, the term "domestic service in a private home of the employer" does not include service described in subsection (g)(5);]

◊ ◊ ◊

Editor's Note: Code §3121(a)(7)(B) was amended to read as set forth below by §2 of P.L. 103-387, the Social Security Domestic Employment Reform Act of 1994 (the "Nanny tax."), effective with respect to remuneration paid after December 31, 1993.

◊ ◊ ◊

(B) cash remuneration paid by an employer in any calendar year to an employee for domestic service in a private home of the employer (including domestic service described in subsection (g)(5)), if the cash remuneration paid in such year by the employer to the employee for such service is less than the applicable dollar threshold (as defined in subsection (x)) for such year;

(C) cash remuneration paid by an employer in any calendar year to an employee for service not in the course of the employer's trade or business, if the cash remuneration paid in such year by the employer to the employee for such service is less than $100. As used in this subparagraph, the term "service not in the course of the employer's trade or business" does not include domestic service in a private home of the employer and does not include service described in subsection (g)(5);

(8)(A) remuneration paid in any medium other than cash for agricultural labor;

(B) cash remuneration paid by an employer in any calendar year to an employee for agricultural labor unless—

(i) the cash remuneration paid in such year by the employer to the employee for such labor is $150 or more, or

(ii) the employer's expenditures for agricultural labor in such year equal or exceed $2,500,

except that clause (ii) shall not apply in determining whether remuneration paid to an employee constitutes "wages" under this section if such employee (I) is employed as a hand harvest laborer and is paid on a piece rate basis in an operation which has been, and is customarily and generally recognized as having been, paid on a piece rate basis in the region of employment, (II) commutes daily from his permanent residence to the farm on which he is so employed, and (III) has been employed in agriculture less than 13 weeks during the preceding calendar year;

(9) [Stricken.]

* * *

(10) remuneration paid by an employer in any calendar year to an employee for service described in subsection (d)(3)(C) (relating to home workers), if the cash remuneration paid

in such year by the employer to the employee for such service is less than $100;

(11) remuneration paid to or on behalf of an employee if (and to the extent that) at the time of the payment of such remuneration it is reasonable to believe that a corresponding deduction is allowable under section 217 (determined without regard to section 274(n));

(12) (A) tips paid in any medium other than cash;

(B) cash tips received by an employee in any calendar month in the course of his employment by an employer unless the amount of such cash tips is $20 or more;

(13) any payment or series of payments by an employer to an employee or any of his dependents which is paid—

(A) upon or after the termination of an employee's employment relationship because of (i) death, or (ii) retirement for disability, and

(B) under a plan established by the employer which makes provision for his employees generally or a class or classes of his employees (or for such employees or class or classes of employees and their dependents),

other than such payment or series of payments which would have been paid if the employee's employment relationship had not been so terminated;

(14) any payment made by an employer to a survivor or the estate of a former employee after the calendar year in which such employee died;

(15) any payment made by an employer to an employee, if at the time such payment is made such employee is entitled to disability insurance benefits under section 223(a) of the Social Security Act and such entitlement commenced prior to the calendar year in which such payment is made, and if such employee did not perform any services for such em-

ployer during the period for which such payment is made;

(16) remuneration is paid by an organization exempt from income tax under section 501(a) (other than an organization described in section 401(a)) or under section 521 in any calendar year to an employee for service rendered in the employ of such organization, if the remuneration paid in such year by the organization to the employee for such service is less than $100;

(17) any contribution, payment, or service provided by an employer which may be excluded from the gross income of an employee, his spouse, or his dependents, under the provisions of section 120 (relating to amounts received under qualified group legal services plans);

(18) any payment made, or benefit furnished, to or for the benefit of an employee if at the time of such payment or such furnishing it is reasonable to believe that the employee will be able to exclude such payment or benefit from income under section 127 or 129;

(19) the value of any meals or lodging furnished by or on behalf of the employer if at the time of such furnishing it is reasonable to believe that the employee will be able to exclude such items from income under section 119;

(20) any benefit provided to or on behalf of an employee if at the time such benefit is provided it is reasonable to believe that the employee will be able to exclude such benefit from income under section 74(c), 117, or 132; or

(21) in the case of a member of an Indian tribe, any remuneration on which no tax is imposed by this chapter by reason of section 7873 (relating to income derived by Indians from exercise of fishing rights).

Nothing in the regulations prescribed for purposes of chapter 24 (relating to income tax withholding) which provides an exclusion from "wages" as used in such chapter shall be construed to require a similar exclusion from

"wages" in the regulations prescribed for purposes of this chapter. Except as otherwise provided in regulations prescribed by the Secretary, any third party which makes a payment included in wages solely by reason of the parenthetical matter contained in subparagraph (A) of paragraph (2) shall be treated for purposes of this chapter and chapter 22 as the employer with respect to such wages.

* * *

(v) Treatment of certain deferred compensation and salary reduction arrangements.—

(1) Certain employer contributions treated as wages.— Nothing in any paragraph of subsection (a) (other than paragraph (1)) shall exclude from the term "wages"—

(A) any employer contribution under a qualified cash or deferred arrangement (as defined in section 401(k)) to the extent not included in gross income by reason of section 402(e)(3), or

(B) any amount treated as an employer contribution under section 414(h)(2) where the pickup referred to in such section is pursuant to a salary reduction agreement (whether evidenced by a written instrument or otherwise).

(2) Treatment of certain nonqualified deferred compensation plans.—

(A) In general.— Any amount deferred under a nonqualified deferred compensation plan shall be taken into account for purposes of this chapter as of the later of—

(i) when services are performed, or

(ii) when there is no substantial risk of forfeiture of the rights to such amount.

The preceding sentence shall not apply to any excess parachute payment (as defined in section 280(G)(b)).

(B) Taxed only once.— Any amount taken into account as wages by reason of subparagraph (A) (and the income attributable thereto) shall not thereafter be treated as wages for purposes of this chapter.

(C) Nonqualified deferred compensation plan.— For purposes of this paragraph, the term "nonqualified deferred compensation plan" means any plan or other arrangement for deferral of compensation other than a plan described in subsection (a)(5).

(3) Exempt governmental deferred compensation plan.—For purposes of subsection (a)(5), the term "exempt governmental deferred compensation plan" means any plan providing for deferral of compensation established and maintained for its employees by the United States, by a State or political subdivision thereof, or by an agency or instrumentality of any of the foregoing. Such term shall not include—

(A) any plan to which section 83, 402(b), 403(c), 457(a), or 457(f)(1) applies,

(B) any annuity contract described in section 403(b), and

(C) the Thrift Savings Fund (within the meaning of subchapter III of chapter 84 of title 5, United States Code).

* * *

◊ ◊ ◊

Editor's Note: Section 3121 (x), below, was added to the Code by §2 of P.L. 103-387, the Social Security Domestic Employment Reform Act of 1994 (the "Nanny tax"), effective with respect to remuneration paid after December 31, 1994. Note also that the predecessor version of §3121(x), relating to applicable contribution base, was stricken by OBRA '93.

◊ ◊ ◊

(x) Applicable Dollar Threshold. For purposes of subsection (a)(7)(B), the term 'applicable dollar threshold' means $1,000. In the case of calendar years after 1995, the Commissioner of Social Security shall adjust such $1,000 amount at the same time and in the

same manner as under section 215(a)(1)(B)(ii) of the Social Security Act with respect to the amounts referred to in section 215(a)(1)(B)(i) of such Act, except that, for purposes of this paragraph, 1993 shall be substituted for the calendar year referred to in section 215(a)(1)(B)(ii)(II) of such Act. If any amount as adjusted under the preceding sentence is not a multiple of $100, such amount shall be rounded to the next lowest multiple of $100.

Chapter 23— Federal Unemployment Tax Act

* * *

SEC. 3304. APPROVAL OF STATE LAWS.

(a) Requirements.— The Secretary of Labor shall approve any State law submitted to him, within 30 days of such submission, which he finds provides that—

(1) all compensation is to be paid through public employment offices or such other agencies as the Secretary of Labor may approve;

(2) no compensation shall be payable with respect to any day of unemployment occurring within 2 years after the first day of the first period with respect to which contributions are required;

(3) all money received in the unemployment fund shall (except for refunds of sums erroneously paid into such fund and except for refunds paid in accordance with the provisions of section 3305(b)) immediately upon such receipt be paid over to the Secretary of the Treasury to the credit of the Unemployment Trust Fund established by section 904 of the Social Security Act (42 U.S.C. 1104);

(4) all money withdrawn from the unemployment fund of the State shall be used solely in the payment of unemployment compensation, exclusive of expenses of administration, and for refunds of sums erroneously paid into such fund and refunds paid in accordance with the provisions of section 3305(b); except that—

(A) an amount equal to the amount of employee payments into the unemployment fund of a State may be used in the payment of cash benefits to individuals with respect to their disability, exclusive of expenses of administration;

(B) the amounts specified by section 903(c)(2) of the Social Security Act may, subject to the conditions prescribed in such section, be used for expenses incurred by the State for administration of its unemployment compensation law and public employment offices;

(C) nothing in this paragraph shall be construed to prohibit deducting an amount from unemployment compensation otherwise payable to an individual and using the amount so deducted to pay for health insurance, *or the withholding of federal, state, or local individual income tax,* if the individual elected to have such deduction made and such deduction was made under a program approved by the Secretary of Labor; and

(D) amounts may be deducted from unemployment benefits and used to repay overpayments as provided in section 303(g) of the Social Security Act;

(5) compensation shall not be denied in such State to any otherwise eligible individual for refusing to accept new work under any of the following conditions:

(A) if the position offered is vacant due directly to a strike, lockout, or other labor dispute;

(B) if the wages, hours, or other conditions of the work offered are substantially less favorable to the individual than those prevailing for similar work in the locality;

(C) if as a condition of being employed the individual would be required to join a company union or to resign from or refrain from joining any bona fide labor organization;

(6)(A) compensation is payable on the basis of service to which section 3309(a)(1) applies, in the same amount, on the same terms, and subject to the same conditions as compensation payable on the basis of other service subject to such law except that—

(i) with respect to services in an instructional research, or principal administrative capacity for an educational institution to which section 3309(a)(1) applies, compensation shall not be payable based on such services for any week commencing during the period between two successive academic years or terms (or, when an agreement provides instead for a similar period between two regular but not successive terms, during such period) to any individual if such individual performs such services in the first of such academic years (or terms) and if there is a contract or reasonable assurance that such individual will perform services in any such capacity for any educational institution in the second of such academic years or terms.

(ii) with respect to services in any other capacity for an educational institution to which section 3309(a)(1) applies—

(I) compensation payable on the basis of such services shall be denied to any individual for any week which commences during a period between two successive academic years or terms if such individual performs such services in the first of such academic years or terms and there is a reasonable assurance that such individual will perform such services in the second of such academic years or terms, except that

(II) if compensation is denied to any individual for any week under subclause (I) and such individual was not offered an opportunity to perform such services for the educational institution for the second of such academic years or terms, such individual shall be entitled to a retroactive payment of the compensation for each week for which the individual filed a timely claim for compensation and for which compensation was denied solely by reason of subclause (I),

(iii) with respect to any services described in clause (i) or (ii), compensation payable on the basis of such services shall be denied to any individual for any week which commences during an established and customary vacation period or holiday recess if such individual performs such services in the period immediately before such vacation period or holiday recess, and there is a reasonable assurance that such individual will perform such services in the period immediately following such vacation period or holiday recess, and

(iv) with respect to any services described in clause (i) or (ii), compensation payable on the basis of services in any such capacity shall be denied as specified in clauses (i), (ii), and (iii) to any individual who performed such services in an educational institution while in the employ of an educational service agency, and for this purpose the term "educational service agency" means a governmental agency or governmental entity which is established and operated exclusively for the purpose of providing such services to one or more educational institutions, and

(v) with respect to services to which section 3309(a)(I) applies, if such services are provided to or on behalf of an educational institution, compensation may be denied under the same circumstances as described in clause (i) through (iv), and

(B) payments (in lieu of contributions) with respect to service to which section 3309(a)(1) applies may be made into the State unemployment fund on the basis set forth in section 3309(a)(2);

(7) an individual who has received compensation during his benefit year is required to have had work since the beginning of such year in order to qualify for compensation in his next benefit year;

(8) compensation shall not be denied to an individual for any week because he is in training with the approval of the State agency (or because of the application, to any such week in training, of State law provisions relating to availability for work, active search for work, or refusal to accept work);

(9)(A) compensation shall not be denied or reduced to an individual solely because he files a claim in another State (or a contiguous country with which the United States has an agreement with respect to unemployment compensation) or because he resides in another State (or such a contiguous country) at the time he files a claim for unemployment compensation;

(B) the State shall participate in any arrangements for the payment of compensation on the basis of combining an individual's wages and employment covered under the State law with his wages and employment covered under the unemployment compensation law of other States which are approved by the Secretary of Labor in consultation with the State unemployment compensation agencies as reasonably calculated to assure the prompt and full payment of compensation in such situations. Any such arrangement shall include provisions for (i) applying the base period of a single State law to a claim involving the combining of an individual's wages and employment covered under two or more State laws, and (ii) avoiding duplicate use of wages and employment by reason of such combining;

(10) compensation shall not be denied to any individual by reason of cancellation of wage credits or total reduction of his benefit rights for any cause other than discharge for misconduct connected with his work, fraud in connection with a claim for compensation, or receipt of disqualifying income;

(11) extended compensation shall be payable as provided by the Federal-State Extended Unemployment Compensation Act of 1970;

(12) no person shall be denied compensation under such State law solely on the basis of pregnancy or termination of pregnancy;

IRC Sec. 3304 (a)(12)

(13) compensation shall not be payable to any individual on the basis of any services, substantially all of which consist of participating in sports or athletic events or training or preparing to so participate, for any week which commences during the period between two successive sport seasons (or similar periods) if such individual performed such services in the first of such seasons (or similar periods) and there is a reasonable assurance that such individual will perform such services in the later of such seasons (or similar periods);

(14)(A) compensation shall not be payable on the basis of services performed by an alien unless such alien is an individual who was lawfully admitted for permanent residence at the time such services were performed, was lawfully present for purposes of performing such services, or was permanently residing in the United States under color of law at the time such services were performed (including an alien who was lawfully present in the United States as a result of the application of the provisions of section 203(a)(7) or section 212(d)(5) of the Immigration and Nationality Act),

(B) any data or information required of individuals applying for compensation to determine whether compensation is not payable to them because of their alien status shall be uniformly required from all applicants for compensation, and

(C) in the case of an individual whose application for compensation would otherwise be approved, no determination by the State agency that compensation to such individual is not payable because of his alien status shall be made except upon a preponderance of the evidence;

(15) the amount of compensation payable to an individual for any week which begins after March 31, 1980, and which begins in a period with respect to which such individual is receiving a governmental or other pension, retirement or retired pay, annuity, or any other similar periodic payment which is based on

the previous work of such individual shall be reduced (but not below zero) by an amount equal to the amount of such pension, retirement or retired pay, annuity, or other payment, which is reasonably attributable to such week except that—

(A) the requirements of this paragraph shall apply to any pension, retirement or retired pay, annuity, or other similar periodic payment only if—

(i) such pension, retirement or retired pay, annuity, or similar payment is under a plan maintained (or contributed to) by a base period employer or chargeable employer (as determined under applicable law), and

(ii) in the case of such a payment not made under the Social Security Act or the Railroad Retirement Act of 1974 (or the corresponding provisions of prior law), services performed for such employer by the individual after the beginning of the base period (or remuneration for such services) affect eligibility for, or increase the amount of, such pension, retirement or retired pay, annuity, or similar payment, and

(B) the State law may provide for limitations on the amount of any such a reduction to take into account contributions made by the individual for the pension, retirement or retired pay, annuity, or other similar periodic payment;

(16)(A) wage information contained in the records of the agency administering the State law which is necessary (as determined by the Secretary of Health and Human Services in regulations) for purposes of determining an individual's eligibility for aid or services, or the amount of such aid or services, under a State plan for aid and services to needy families with children approved under part A of title IV of the Social Security Act, shall be made available to a State or political subdivision thereof when such information is specifically requested by such State or political subdivision for such purposes, and

(B) such safeguards are established as are necessary (as determined by the Secretary of Health and Human Services in regulations) to insure that such information is used only for the purposes authorized under subparagraph (A);

(17) any interest required to be paid on advances under title XII of the Social Security Act shall be paid in a timely manner and shall not be paid, directly or indirectly (by an equivalent reduction in State unemployment taxes or otherwise) by such State from amounts in such State's unemployment fund; and

(18) all the rights, privileges, or immunities conferred by such law or by acts done pursuant thereto shall exist subject to the power of the legislature to amend or repeal such law at any time.

◊ ◊ ◊

Editor's Note: The version of Code §3304(a)(17)-(19) set forth below, appear as amended by §702(b) of the Retirement Protection Act of 1994 (enacted as part of the Uruguay Round Agreements Act, P.L. 103-465). The provisions apply to payments made after December 31, 1996.

◊ ◊ ◊

(17) any interest required to be paid on advances under title XII of the Social Security Act shall be paid in a timely manner and shall not be paid, directly or indirectly (by an equivalent reduction in State unemployment taxes or otherwise) by such State from amounts in such State's unemployment fund;

(18) Federal individual income tax from unemployment compensation is to be deducted and withheld if an individual receiving such compensation voluntarily requests such deduction and withholding; and

(19) all the rights, privileges, or immunities conferred by such law or by acts done pursuant thereto shall exist subject to the power of the legislature to amend or repeal such law at any time.

* * *

Chapter 24— Collection Of Income Tax At Source On Wages

* * *

SEC. 3405. SPECIAL RULES FOR PENSIONS, ANNUITIES, AND CERTAIN OTHER DEFERRED INCOME.

(a) Periodic Payments.—

(1) **Withholding as if payment were wages.**—The payor of any periodic payment (as defined in subsection (e)(2)) shall withhold from such payment the amount which would be required to be withheld from such payment if such payment were a payment of wages by an employer to an employee for the appropriate payroll period.

(2) **Election of no withholding.**— An individual may elect to have paragraph (1) not apply with respect to periodic payments made to such individual. Such an election shall remain in effect until revoked by such individual.

(3) **When election takes effect.**— Any election under this subsection (and any revocation of such an election) shall take effect as provided by subsection (f)(3) of section 3402 for withholding exemption certificates.

(4) **Amount withheld where no withholding exemption certificate in effect.**— In the case of any payment with respect to which a withholding exemption certificate is not in effect, the amount withheld under paragraph (1) shall be determined by treating the payee as a married individual claiming 3 withholding exemptions.

(b) Nonperiodic Distribution.—

(1) **Withholding.**— The payor of any nonperiodic distribution (as defined in subsection (e)(3)) shall withhold from such distribution

an amount equal to 10 percent of such distribution.

(2) Election of no withholding.—

(A) In general.— An individual may elect not to have paragraph (1) apply with respect to any nonperiodic distribution.

(B) Scope of election.— An election under subparagraph (A)

(i) except as provided in clause (ii), shall be on a distribution-by-distribution basis, or

(ii) to the extent provided in regulations, may apply to subsequent nonperiodic distributions made by the payor to the payee under the same arrangement.

(c) Eligible Rollover Distributions.—

(1) In general.— In the case of any designated distribution which is an eligible rollover distribution—

(A) subsections (a) and (b) shall not apply, and

(B) the payor of such distribution shall withhold from such distribution an amount equal to 20 percent of such distribution.

(2) Exception.—Paragraph (1)(B) shall not apply to any distribution if the distributee elects under section 401(a)(31)(A) to have such distribution paid directly to an eligible retirement plan.

(3) Eligible rollover distribution.— For purposes of this subsection, the term "eligible rollover distribution" has the meaning given such term by section 402(f)(2)(A) (or in the case of an annuity contract under section 403(b), a distribution from such contract described in section 402(f)(2)(A)).

(d) Liability for Withholding.—

(1) In general.— Except as provided in paragraph (2), the payor of a designated distribution (as defined in subsection (e)(1)) shall withhold, and be liable for, payment of the tax required to be withheld under this section.

(2) Plan administrator liable in certain cases.—

(A) In general.—In the case of any plan to which this paragraph applies, paragraph (1) shall not apply and the plan administrator shall withhold, and be liable for, payment of the tax unless the plan administrator—

(i) directs the payor to withhold such tax, and

(ii) provides the payor with such information as the Secretary may require by regulations.

(B) Plans to which paragraph applies.— This paragraph applies to any plan described in, or which at any time has been determined to be described in—

(i) section 401(a),

(ii) section 403(a), or

(iii) section 301(d) of the Tax Reduction Act of 1975.

(e) Definitions and Special Rules.— For purposes of this section—

(1) Designated distribution.—

(A) In general.— Except as provided in subparagraph (B), the term 'designated distribution' means any distribution or payment from or under—

(i) an employer deferred compensation plan,

(ii) an individual retirement plan (as defined in section 7701(a)(37)), or

(iii) a commercial annuity.

(B) Exceptions.— The term 'designated distribution' shall not include—

(i) any amount which is wages without regard to this section,

(ii) the portion of a distribution or payment which it is reasonable to believe is not includible in gross income,

(iii) any amount which is subject to withholding under subchapter A of chapter 3 (relating to withholding of tax on nonresident aliens and foreign corporations) by the person paying such amount or which would be so subject but for a tax treaty, or

(iv) any distribution described in section 404(k)(2).

For purposes of clause (ii), any distribution or payment from or under an individual retirement plan shall be treated as includible in gross income.

(2) Periodic payment.— The term 'periodic payment' means a designated distribution which is an annuity or similar periodic payment.

(3) Nonperiodic distribution.— The term 'nonperiodic distribution' means any designated distribution which is not a periodic payment.

(4) [Repealed]

(5) Employer deferred compensation plan.— The term 'employer deferred compensation plan' means any pension, annuity, profit-sharing, or stock bonus plan or other plan deferring the receipt of compensation.

(6) Commercial annuity.— The term 'commercial annuity' means an annuity, endowment, or life insurance contract issued by an insurance company licensed to do business under the laws of any State.

(7) Plan administrator.— The term 'plan administrator' has the meaning given such term by section 414(g).

(8) Maximum amount withheld.— The maximum amount to be withheld under this section on any designated distribution shall not exceed the sum of the amount of money and the fair market value of other property (other than securities of the employer corporation) received in the distribution. No amount shall be required to be withheld under this section in the case of any designated distribu-

tion which consists only of securities of the employer corporation and cash (not in excess of $200) in lieu of financial shares. For purposes of this paragraph, the term "securities of the employer corporation" has the meaning given such term by section 402(e)(4)(E).

(9) Separate arrangements to be treated separately.— If the payor has more than 1 arrangement under which designated distributions may be made to any individual, each such arrangement shall be treated separately.

(10) Time and manner of election.—

(A) In general.— Any election and any revocation under this section shall be made at such time and in such manner as the Secretary shall prescribe.

(B) Payor required to notify payee of rights to elect.—

(i) Periodic payments.—The payor of any periodic payment—

(I) shall transmit to the payee notice of the right to make an election under subsection (a) not earlier than 6 months before the first of such payments and not later than when making the first of such payments,

(II) if such a notice is not transmitted under subclause (I) when making such first payment, shall transmit such a notice when making such first payment, and

(III) shall transmit to payees, not less frequently than once each calendar year, notice of their rights to make elections under subsection (a) and to revoke such elections.

(ii) Nonperiodic distributions.— The payor of any nonperiodic distribution shall transmit to the payee notice of the right to make any election provided in subsection (b) at the time of the distribution (or at such earlier time as may be provided in regulations).

(iii) Notice.—Any notice transmitted pursuant to this subparagraph shall be in such

IRC Sec. 3405 (e)(10)(B)(iii)

form and contain such information as the Secretary shall prescribe.

(11) Withholding includes deduction.— The terms "withholding", "withhold", and "withheld" include "deducting", "deduct", and "deducted".

(12) Failure to provide correct TIN.— If—

(A) a payee fails to furnish his TIN to the payor in the manner required by the Secretary, or

(B) the Secretary notifies the payor before any payment or distribution that the TIN furnished by the payee is incorrect,

no election under section (a)(2) or (b)(3) shall be treated as in effect and subsection (a)(4) shall not apply to such payee.

(13) Election may not be made with respect to certain payments outside of the United States or its possessions.—

(A) In general.— Except as provided in subparagraph (B), in the case of any periodic payment or nonperiodic distributions which is to be delivered outside of the United States and any possession of the United States, no election may be made under subsection (a)(2) or (b)(2) with respect to such payment.

(B) Exception.— Subparagraph (A) shall not apply if the recipient certifies to the payor, in such manner as the Secretary may prescribe, that such person is not—

(i) a United States citizen or a resident alien of the United States, or

(ii) an individual to whom section 877 applies.

(f) Withholding To Be Treated as Wage Withholding Under Section 3402 for Other Purposes.—For purposes of this chapter (and so much of subtitle F as relates to this chapter)

(1) any designated distribution (whether or not an election under this section applies to

such distribution) shall be treated as if it were wages paid by an employer to an employee with respect to which there has been withholding under section 3402, and

(2) in the case of any designated distribution not subject to withholding under this section by reason of an election under this section, the amount withheld shall be treated as zero.

* * *

Subtitle D— Miscellaneous Excise Taxes

* * *

Chapter 43— Qualified Pension, Etc., Plans

SEC. 4971. TAXES ON FAILURE TO MEET MINIMUM FUNDING STANDARDS.

(a) Initial Tax.— For each taxable year of an employer who maintains a plan to which section 412 applies, there is hereby imposed a tax of 10 percent (5 percent in the case of a multiemployer plan) on the amount of the accumulated funding deficiency under the plan, determined as of the end of the plan year ending with or within such taxable year.

(b) Additional Tax.— In any case in which an initial tax is imposed by subsection (a) on an accumulated funding deficiency and such accumulated funding deficiency is not corrected within the taxable period, there is hereby imposed a tax equal to 100 percent of such accumulated funding deficiency to the extent not corrected.

(c) Definitions.— For purposes of this section—

(1) Accumulated funding deficiency.— The term "accumulated funding deficiency" has the meaning given to such term by the last two sentences of section 412(a).

(2) Correct.— The term "correct" means with respect to an accumulated funding deficiency, the contribution, to or under the plan of the amount necessary to reduce such accumulated funding deficiency as of the end of a plan year in which such deficiency arose to zero.

(3) Taxable period.— The term "taxable period" means, with respect to an accumulated funding deficiency, the period beginning with the end of a plan year in which there is an accumulated funding deficiency and ending on the earlier of—

(A) the date of mailing of a notice of deficiency with respect to the tax imposed by subsection (a), or

(B) the date on which the tax imposed by subsection (a) is assessed.

(d) Notification of the Secretary of Labor.— Before issuing a notice of deficiency with respect to the tax imposed by subsection (a) or (b), the Secretary shall notify the Secretary of Labor and provide him a reasonable opportunity (but not more than 60 days)—

(1) to require the employer responsible for contributing to or under the plan to eliminate the accumulated funding deficiency, or

(2) to comment on the imposition of such tax.

In the case of a multiemployer plan which is in reorganization under section 418, the same notice and opportunity shall be provided to the Pension Benefit Guaranty Corporation.

◊ ◊ ◊

Editor's Note: Code §4971(e), (f), and (g), as set forth below, appear as amended by §751(a) of the Retirement Protection Act of 1994, enacted as part of the Uruguay Round Agreements Act (P.L. 103-465). The changes apply to plan years beginning after December 31, 1994.

◊ ◊ ◊

(e) Liability for Tax.—

(1) In general.— Except as provided in paragraph (2), the tax imposed by subsection [(a) or (b)] *(a), (b), or (f)* shall be paid by the employer responsible for contributing to or under the plan the amount described in section 412(b)(3)(A).

(2) Joint and several liability where employer member of controlled group.—

(A) In general.— In the case of a plan other than a multiemployer plan, if the employer referred to in paragraph (1) is a member of a controlled group, each member of such group shall be jointly and severally liable for the tax imposed by subsection [**(a) or (b)**] *(a), (b), or (f)*.

(B) Controlled group.— For purposes of subparagraph (A), the term "controlled group" means any group treated as a single employer under subsection (b), (c), (m), or (o) of section 414.

(f) Failure To Pay Liquidity Shortfall.

(1) In general. In the case of a plan to which section 412(m)(5) applies, there is hereby imposed a tax of 10 percent of the excess (if any) of—

(A) the amount of the liquidity shortfall for any quarter, over

(B) the amount of such shortfall which is paid by the required installment under section 412(m) for such quarter (but only if such installment is paid on or before the due date for such installment).

(2) Additional tax. If the plan has a liquidity shortfall as of the close of any quarter and as of the close of each of the following 4 quarters, there is hereby imposed a tax equal to 100 percent of the amount on which tax was imposed by paragraph (1) for such first quarter.

(3) Definitions and special rule.

(A) Liquidity shortfall; quarter. For purposes of this subsection, the terms "liquidity shortfall" and "quarter" have the respective

meanings given such terms by section 412(m)(5).

(B) Special rule. If the tax imposed by paragraph (2) is paid with respect to any liquidity shortfall for any quarter, no further tax shall be imposed by this subsection on such shortfall for such quarter.

[(f)]*(g)* **Cross References.**—For disallowance of deductions for taxes paid under this section, see section 275.

For liability for tax in case of an employer party to collective bargaining agreement, see section 413(b)(6).

For provisions concerning notification of Secretary of Labor of imposition of tax under this section, waiver of the tax imposed by subsection (b), and other coordination between Secretary of the Treasury and Secretary of Labor with respect to compliance with this section, see section 3002(b) of title III of the Employee Retirement Income Security Act of 1974.

SEC. 4972. TAX ON NONDE-DUCTIBLE CONTRIBUTIONS TO QUALIFIED EMPLOYER PLANS.

(a) Tax Imposed.— In the case of any qualified employer plan, there is hereby imposed a tax equal to 10 percent of the nondeductible contributions under the plan (determined as of the close of the taxable year of the employer).

(b) Employer Liable for Tax.— The tax imposed by this section shall be paid by the employer making the contributions.

(c) Nondeductible contributions.—For purposes of this section—

(1) In general.— The term ''nondeductible contributions'' means, with respect to any qualified employer plan, the sum of—

(A) the excess (if any) of—

(i) the amount contributed for the taxable year by the employer to or under such plan, over

(ii) the amount allowable as a deduction under section 404 for such contributions, (determined without regard to subsection (e) thereof), and

(B) the amount determined under this subsection for the preceding taxable year reduced by the sum of—

(i) the portion of the amount so determined returned to the employer during the taxable year, and

(ii) the portion of the amount so determined deductible under section 404 for the taxable year (determined without regard to subsection (e) thereof).

(2) Ordering rule for section 404.— For purposes of paragraph (1), the amount allowable as a deduction under section 404 for any taxable year shall be treated as—

(A) first from carryforwards to such taxable year from preceding taxable years (in order of time), and

(B) then from contributions made during such taxable year.

(3) Contributions which may be returned to employer.— In determining the amount of nondeductible contributions for any taxable year, there shall not be taken into account any contribution for such taxable year which is distributed to the employer in a distribution described in section 4980(c)(2)(B)(ii) if such distribution is made on or before the last day on which a contribution may be made for such taxable year under section 404(a)(6).

(4) Special rule for self-employed individuals.—For purposes of paragraph (1), if—

(A) the amount which is required to be contributed to a plan under section 412 on behalf of an individual who is an employee (within the meaning of section 401(c)(1)), exceeds

(B) the earned income (within the meaning of section 404(a)(8)) of such individual derived from the trade or business with respect to which such plan is established,

such excess shall be treated as an amount allowable as a deduction under section 404.

(5) Pre-1987 contributions.— The term "nondeductible contribution" shall not include any contribution made for a taxable year beginning before January 1, 1987.

◊ ◊ ◊

Editor's Note: Code §4972(c)(6), below, was added by §755(a) of the Retirement Protection Act of 1994, which was enacted as part of the Uruguay Round Agreements Act (P.L. 103-465). Section 755(b) of that Act provides that Code §4972(c)(6)(A) applies to taxable years ending on or after December 8, 1994, whereas Code §4972(c)(6)(B) applies to taxable years ending on or after December 31, 1992.

◊ ◊ ◊

(6) Exceptions. In determining the amount of nondeductible contributions for any taxable year, there shall not be taken into account

(A) contributions that would be deductible under section 404(a)(1)(D) if the plan had more than 100 participants if

(i) the plan is covered under section 4021 of the Employee Retirement Income Security Act of 1974, and

(ii) the plan is terminated under section 4041(b) of such Act on or before the last day of the taxable year, and

(B) contributions to 1 or more defined contribution plans which are not deductible when contributed solely because of section 404(a)(7), but only to the extent such contributions do not exceed 6 percent of compensation (within the meaning of section 404(a)) paid or accrued (during the taxable year for which the contributions were made) to beneficiaries under the plans.

If 1 or more defined benefit plans were taken into account in determining the amount allowable as a deduction under section 404 for contributions to any defined contribution plan, subparagraph (B) shall apply only if such defined benefit plans are described in section 404(a)(1)(D). For purposes of subparagraph (B), the deductible limits under section 404(a)(7) shall first be applied to amounts contributed to a defined benefit plan and then to amounts described in subparagraph (B).

(d) Definitions.— For purposes of this section—

(1) Qualified employer plan.—

(A) In general.— The term "qualified employer plan" means—

(i) any plan meeting the requirements of section 401(a) which includes a trust exempt from tax under section 501(a),

(ii) an annuity plan described in section 403(a), and

(iii) any simplified employee pension (within the meaning of section 408(k)).

(B) Exemption for governmental and tax exempt plans.— The term "qualified employer plan" does not include a plan described in subparagraph (A) or (B) of section 4980(c)(1).

(2) Employer.— In the case of a plan which provides contributions or benefits for employees some or all of whom are self-employed individuals within the meaning of section 401(c)(1), the term "employer" means the person treated as the employer under section 401(c)(4).

SEC. 4973. TAX ON EXCESS CONTRIBUTIONS TO INDIVIDUAL RETIREMENT ACCOUNTS, CERTAIN SECTION 403(b) CONTRACTS, AND CERTAIN INDIVIDUAL RETIREMENT ANNUITIES.

(a) Tax Imposed.—In the case of—

(1) an individual retirement account (within the meaning of section 408(a)), or

(2) an individual retirement annuity (within the meaning of section 408(b)), a custodial account treated as an annuity contract under section 403(b)(7)(A) (relating to custodial accounts for regulated investment company stock),

there is imposed for each taxable year a tax in an amount equal to 6 percent of the amount of the excess contributions to such individual's accounts or annuities (determined as of the close of the taxable year). The amount of such tax for any taxable year shall not exceed 6 percent of the value of the account or annuity (determined as of the close of the taxable year). In the case of an endowment contract described in section 408(b), the tax imposed by this section does not apply to any amount allocable to life, health, accident, or other insurance under such contract. The tax imposed by this subsection shall be paid by such individual.

(b) Excess Contributions.—For purposes of this section, in the case of individual retirement accounts or individual retirement annuities, the term "excess contributions" means the sum of—

(1) the excess (if any) of—

(A) the amount contributed for the taxable year to the accounts or for the annuities (other than a rollover contribution described in sections 402(c), 403(a)(4), 403(b)(8), or 408(d)(3)), over

(B) the amount allowable as a deduction under section 219 for such contributions, and

(2) the amount determined under this subsection for the preceding taxable year, reduced by the sum of—

(A) the distributions out of the account for the taxable year which were included in the gross income of the payee under section 408(d)(1),

(B) the distributions out of the account for the taxable year to which section 408(d)(5) applies, and

(C) the excess (if any) of the maximum amount allowable as a deduction under section 219 for the taxable year over the amount contributed (determined without regard to section 219(f)(6)) to the accounts or for the annuities for the taxable year.

For purposes of this subsection, any contribution which is distributed from the individual retirement account or the individual retirement annuity in a distribution to which section 408(d)(4) applies shall be treated as an amount not contributed. For purposes of paragraphs (1)(B) and (2)(C), the amount allowable as a deduction under section 219 shall be computed without regard to section 219(g).

(c) Section 403(b) Contracts.— For purposes of this section, in the case of a custodial account referred to in subsection (a)(2), the term "excess contributions" means the sum of—

(1) the excess (if any) of the amount contributed for the taxable year to such account (other than a rollover contribution described in section 403(b)(8) or 408 (d)(3)(A)(iii)), over the lesser of the amount excludable from gross income under section 403(b) or the amount permitted to be contributed under the limitations contained in section 415 (or under whichever such section is applicable, if only one is applicable), and

(2) the amount determined under this subsection for the preceding taxable year, reduced by—

(A) the excess (if any) of the lesser of (i) the amount excludable from gross income under section 403(b) or (ii) the amount permitted to be contributed under the limitations contained in section 415 over the amount contributed to the account for the taxable year (or under whichever such section is applicable, if only one is applicable), and

(B) the sum of the distributions out of the account (for all prior taxable years) which are included in gross income under section 72(e).

SEC. 4974. EXCISE TAX ON CERTAIN ACCUMULATIONS IN QUALIFIED RETIREMENT PLANS.

(a) General Rule.— If the amount distributed during the taxable year of the payee under any qualified retirement plan or any eligible deferred compensation plan (as defined in section 457(b)) is less than the minimum required distribution for such taxable year, there is hereby imposed a tax equal to 50 percent of the amount by which such minimum required distribution exceeds the actual amount distributed during the taxable year. The tax imposed by this section shall be paid by the payee.

(b) Minimum Required Distribution.— For purposes of this section, the term "minimum required distribution" means the minimum amount required to be distributed during a taxable year under section 401(a)(9), 403(b)(10), 408(a)(6), 408(b)(3), or 457(d)(2), as the case may be, as determined under regulations prescribed by the Secretary.

(c) Qualified Retirement Plan.—For purposes of this section, the term "qualified retirement plan" means—

(1) a plan described in section 401(a) which includes a trust exempt from tax under section 501(a),

(2) an annuity plan described in section 403(a),

(3) an annuity contract described in section 403(b),

(4) an individual retirement account described in section 408(a), or

(5) an individual retirement annuity described in section 408(b).

Such term includes any plan, contract, account, or annuity which, at any time, has been determined by the Secretary to be such a plan, contract, account, or annuity.

(d) Waiver of Tax in Certain Cases.— If the taxpayer establishes to the satisfaction of the Secretary that—

(1) the shortfall described in subsection (a) in the amount distributed during any taxable year was due to reasonable error, and

(2) reasonable steps are being taken to remedy the shortfall,

the Secretary may waive the tax imposed by subsection (a) for the taxable year.

SEC. 4975. TAX ON PROHIBITED TRANSACTIONS.

(a) Initial Taxes on Disqualified Person.— There is hereby imposed a tax on each prohibited transaction. The rate of tax shall be equal to 5 percent of the amount involved with respect to the prohibited transaction for each year (or part thereof) in the taxable period. The tax imposed by this subsection shall be paid by any disqualified person who participates in the prohibited transaction (other than a fiduciary acting only as such).

(b) Additional Taxes on Disqualified Person.— In any case in which an initial tax is imposed by subsection (a) on a prohibited transaction and the transaction is not corrected within the taxable period, there is hereby imposed a tax equal to 100 percent of the amount involved. The tax imposed by this subsection shall be paid by any disqualified person who participated in the prohibited transaction (other than a fiduciary acting only as such).

(c) Prohibited Transaction.—

(1) General Rule.—For purposes of this section, the term "prohibited transaction" means any direct or indirect—

(A) sale or exchange, or leasing, of any property between a plan and a disqualified person;

(B) lending of money or other extension of credit between a plan and a disqualified person;

(C) furnishing of goods, services, or facilities between a plan and a disqualified person;

(D) transfer to, or use by or for the benefit of, a disqualified person of the income or assets of a plan;

(E) act by a disqualified person who is a fiduciary whereby he deals with the income or assets of a plan in his own interest or for his own account; or

(F) receipt of any consideration for his own personal account by any disqualified person who is a fiduciary from any party dealing with the plan in connection with a transaction involving the income or assets of the plan.

(2) Special exemption.— The Secretary shall establish an exemption procedure for purposes of this subsection. Pursuant to such procedure, he may grant a conditional or unconditional exemption of any disqualified person or transaction or class of disqualified persons or transactions, from all or part of the restrictions imposed by paragraph (1) of this subsection. Action under this subparagraph may be taken only after consultation and coordination with the Secretary of Labor. The Secretary may not grant an exemption under this paragraph unless he finds that such exemption is—

(A) administratively feasible,

(B) in the interests of the plan and of its participants and beneficiaries, and

(C) protective of the rights of participants and beneficiaries of the plan.

Before granting an exemption under this paragraph, the Secretary shall require adequate notice to be given to interested persons and shall publish notice in the Federal Register of the pendency of such exemption and shall afford interested persons an opportunity to present views. No exemption may be granted under this paragraph with respect to a transaction described in subparagraph (E) or (F) of paragraph (1) unless the Secretary affords an opportunity for hearing and makes a determination on the record with respect to the findings required under subparagraphs (A), (B), and (C) of this paragraph, except that in lieu of such hearing the Secretary may accept any record made by the Secretary of Labor with respect to an application for exemption under section 408(a) of title I of the Employee Retirement Income Security Act of 1974.

(3) Special rule for individual retirement accounts.— An individual for whose benefit an individual retirement account is established and his beneficiaries shall be exempt [from] the tax imposed by this section with respect to any transaction concerning such account (which would otherwise be taxable under this section) if, with respect to such transaction, the account ceases to be an individual retirement account by reason of the application of section 408(e)(2)(A) or if section 408(e)(4) applies to such account.

(d) Exemptions.—The prohibitions provided in subsection (c) shall not apply to—

(1) any loan made by the plan to a disqualified person who is a participant or beneficiary of the plan if such loan—

(A) is available to all such participants or beneficiaries on a reasonably equivalent basis,

(B) is not made available to highly compensated employees (within the meaning of section 414(q) of the Internal Revenue Code of

IRC Sec. 4975 (c)

1986) in an amount greater than the amount made available to other employees,

(C) is made in accordance with specific provisions regarding such loans set forth in the plan,

(D) bears a reasonable rate of interest, and

(E) is adequately secured;

(2) any contract, or reasonable arrangement, made with a disqualified person for office space, or legal, accounting, or other services necessary for the establishment or operation of the plan, if no more than reasonable compensation is paid therefor;

(3) any loan to a leveraged employee stock ownership plan (as defined in subsection (e)(7)), if—

(A) such loan is primarily for the benefit of participants and beneficiaries of the plan, and

(B) such loan is at a reasonable rate of interest, and any collateral which is given to a disqualified person by the plan consists only of qualifying employer securities (as defined in subsection (e)(8));

(4) the investment of all or part of a plan's assets in deposits which bear a reasonable interest rate in a bank or similar financial institution supervised by the United States or a State, if such bank or other institution is a fiduciary of such plan and if—

(A) the plan covers only employees of such bank or other institution and employees of affiliates of such bank or other institution, or

(B) such investment is expressly authorized by a provision of the plan or by a fiduciary (other than such bank or institution or affiliates thereof) who is expressly empowered by the plan to so instruct the trustee with respect to such investment;

(5) any contract for life insurance, health insurance, or annuities with one or more insurers which are qualified to do business in a State if the plan pays no more than adequate consideration, and if each such insurer or insurers is—

(A) the employer maintaining the plan, or

(B) a disqualified person which is wholly owned (directly or indirectly) by the employer establishing the plan, or by any person which is a disqualified person with respect to the plan, but only if the total premiums and annuity considerations written by such insurers for life insurance, health insurance, or annuities for all plans (and their employers) with respect to which such insurers are disqualified persons (not including premiums or annuity considerations written by the employer maintaining the plan) do not exceed 5 percent of the total premiums and annuity considerations written for all lines of insurance in that year by such insurers (not including premiums or annuity considerations written by the employer maintaining the plan);

(6) the provision of any ancillary service by a bank or similar financial institution supervised by the United States or a State, if such service is provided at not more than reasonable compensation, if such bank or other institution is a fiduciary of such plan, and if—

(A) such bank or similar financial institution has adopted adequate internal safeguards which assure that the provision of such ancillary service is consistent with sound banking and financial practice, as determined by Federal or State supervisory authority, and

(B) the extent to which such ancillary service is provided is subject to specific guidelines issued by such bank or similar financial institution (as determined by the Secretary after consultation with Federal and State supervisory authority), and under such guidelines the bank or similar financial institution does not provide such ancillary service—

(i) in an excessive or unreasonable manner, and

(ii) in a manner that would be inconsistent with the best interests of participants and beneficiaries of employee benefit plans;

(7) the exercise of a privilege to convert securities, to the extent provided in regulations of the Secretary, but only if the plan receives no less than adequate consideration pursuant to such conversion;

(8) any transaction between a plan and a common or collective trust fund or pooled investment fund maintained by a disqualified person which is a bank or trust company supervised by a State or Federal agency or between a plan and a pooled investment fund of an insurance company qualified to do business in a State if—

(A) the transaction is a sale or purchase of an interest in the fund,

(B) the bank, trust company, or insurance company receives not more than reasonable compensation, and

(C) such transaction is expressly permitted by the instrument under which the plan is maintained, or by a fiduciary (other than the bank, trust company, or insurance company, or an affiliate thereof) who has authority to manage and control the assets of the plan;

(9) receipt by a disqualified person of any benefit to which he may be entitled as a participant or beneficiary in the plan, so long as the benefit is computed and paid on a basis which is consistent with the terms of the plan as applied to all other participants and beneficiaries;

(10) receipt by a disqualified person of any reasonable compensation for services rendered, or for the reimbursement of expenses properly and actually incurred, in the performance of his duties with the plan, but no person so serving who already receives full-time pay from an employer or an association of employers, whose employees are participants in the

plan, or from an employee organization whose members are participants in such plan shall receive compensation from such fund, except for reimbursement of expenses properly and actually incurred;

(11) service by a disqualified person as a fiduciary in addition to being an officer, employee, agent, or other representative of a disqualified person;

(12) the making by a fiduciary of a distribution of the assets of the trust in accordance with the terms of the plan if such assets are distributed in the same manner as provided under section 4044 of title IV of the Employee Retirement Income Security Act of 1974 (relating to allocation of assets);

(13) any transaction which is exempt from section 406 of such Act by reason of section 408(e) of such Act (or which would be so exempt if such section 406 applied to such transaction) or which is exempt from section 406 of such Act by reason of section 408(b) of such Act;

(14) any transaction required or permitted under part 1 of subtitle E of title IV or section 4223 of the Employee Retirement Income Security Act of 1974, but this paragraph shall not apply with respect to the application of subsection (c)(1)(E) or (F); or

(15) a merger of multiemployer plans, or the transfer of assets or liabilities between multiemployer plans, determined by the Pension Benefit Guaranty Corporation to meet the requirements of section 4231 of such Act, but this paragraph shall not apply with respect to the application of subsection (c)(1)(E) or (F).

The exemptions provided by this subsection (other than paragraphs (9) and (12)) shall not apply to any transaction with respect to a trust described in section 401(a) which is part of a plan providing contributions or benefits for employees some or all of whom are owner-employees (as defined in section 401(c)(3)) in which a plan directly or indirectly lends any part of the corpus or income of the plan to, pays any compensation for personal services rendered to the plan to, or acquires for the plan any property from or sells any property to, any such owner-employee, a member of the family (as defined in section 267(c)(4)) of any such owner-employee, or a corporation controlled by any such owner-employee through the ownership, directly or indirectly, of 50 percent or more of the total combined voting power of all classes of stock entitled to vote or 50 percent or more of the total value of shares of all classes of stock of the corporation. For purposes of the preceding sentence, a shareholder-employee (as defined in section 1379, as in effect on the day before the date of the enactment of the Subchapters Revision Act of 1982), a participant or beneficiary of an individual retirement account or an individual retirement annuity as defined in section 408, and an employer or association of employees which establishes such an account or annuity under section 408(c) shall be deemed to be an owner-employee.

(e) Definitions.—

(1) Plan.— For purposes of this section, the term "plan" means a trust described in section 401(a), which forms a part of a plan, or a plan described in section 403(a) which trust or plan is exempt from tax under section 501(a), an individual retirement account described in section 408(a) or an individual retirement annuity described in section 408(b) (or a trust, plan, account, or annuity which, at any time, has been determined by the Secretary to be such a trust, plan, or account).

(2) Disqualified person.— For purposes of this section, the term "disqualified person" means a person who is—

(A) a fiduciary;

(B) a person providing services to the plan;

(C) an employer any of whose employees are covered by the plan;

(D) an employee organization any of whose members are covered by the plan;

(E) an owner, direct or indirect, of 50 percent or more of—

(i) the combined voting power of all classes of stock entitled to vote or the total value of shares of all classes of stock of a corporation,

(ii) the capital interest or the profits interest of a partnership, or

(iii) the beneficial interest of a trust or unincorporated enterprise,

which is an employer or an employee organization described in subparagraph (C) or (D);

(F) a member of the family (as defined in paragraph (6)) of any individual described in subparagraph (A), (B), (C), or (E);

(G) a corporation, partnership, or trust or estate of which (or in which) 50 percent or more of—

(i) the combined voting power of all classes of stock entitled to vote or the total value of shares of all classes of stock of such corporation,

(ii) the capital interest or profits interest of such partnership, or

(iii) the beneficial interest of such trust or estate, is owned directly or indirectly, or held by persons described in subparagraph (A), (B), (C), (D), or (E);

(H) an officer, director (or an individual having powers or responsibilities similar to those of officers or directors), a 10 percent or more shareholder, or a highly compensated employee (earning 10 percent or more of the yearly wages of an employer) of a person described in subparagraph (C), (D), (E), or (G); or

(I) a 10 percent or more (in capital or profits) partner or joint venturer of a person described in subparagraph (C), (D), (E), or (G).

The Secretary, after consultation and coordination with the Secretary of Labor or his delegate, may by regulation prescribe a percentage lower than 50 percent for subparagraphs (E) and (G) and lower than 10 percent for subparagraphs (H) and (I).

(3) Fiduciary.— For purposes of this section, the term "fiduciary" means any person who—

(A) exercises any discretionary authority or discretionary control respecting management of such plan or exercises any authority or control respecting management or disposition of its assets,

(B) renders investment advice for a fee or other compensation, direct or indirect, with respect to any moneys or other property of such plan, or has any authority or responsibility to do so, or

(C) has any discretionary authority or discretionary responsibility in the administration of such plan.

Such term includes any person designated under section 405(c)(1)(B) of the Employee Retirement Income Security Act of 1974.

(4) Stockholdings.— For purposes of paragraphs (2)(E)(i), and (G)(i) there shall be taken into account indirect stockholdings which would be taken into account under section 267(c), except that, for purposes of this paragraph, section 267(c)(4) shall be treated as providing that the members of the family of an individual are the members within the meaning of paragraph (6).

(5) Partnerships; trusts.— For purposes of paragraphs (2)(E)(ii) and (iii), (G)(ii) and (iii), and (I) the ownership of profits or beneficial interests shall be determined in accordance with the rules for constructive ownership of stock provided in section 267(c) (other than paragraph (3) thereof), except that section 267(c)(4) shall be treated as providing that the members of the family of an individual are the members within the meaning of paragraph (6).

(6) Members of family.—For purposes of paragraph (2)(F), the family of any individual shall include his spouse, ancestor, lineal descendant, and any spouse of a lineal descendant.

(7) Employee stock ownership plan.— The term "employee stock ownership plan" means a defined contribution plan—

(A) which is a stock bonus plan which is qualified, or a stock bonus and a money purchase plan both of which are qualified under section 401(a) and which are designed to invest primarily in qualifying employer securities; and

(B) which is otherwise defined in regulations prescribed by the Secretary.

A plan shall not be treated as an employee stock ownership plan unless it meets the requirements of section 409(h), section 409(o), and, if applicable, section 409(n) and, if the employer has a registration-type class of securities (as defined in section 409(e)(4)), it meets the requirements of section 409(e).

(8) Qualifying employer security.— The term "qualifying employer security" means an employer security within the meaning of section 409(l).

If any moneys or other property of a plan are invested in shares of an investment company registered under the Investment Company Act of 1940, the investment shall not cause that investment company or that investment company's investment adviser or principal underwriter to be treated as a fiduciary or a disqualified person for purposes of this section, except when an investment company or its investment adviser or principal underwriter acts in connection with a plan covering employees of the investment company, its investment adviser, or its principal underwriter.

(9) Section made applicable to withdrawal liability payment funds.—

(A) In general.—The term "plan" includes a trust described in section 501(c)(22).

(B) Disqualified person.— In the case of any trust to which this section applies by reason of subparagraph (A), the term "disqualified person" includes any person who is a disqualified person with respect to any plan to which such trust is permitted to make payments under section 4223 of the Employee Retirement Income Security Act of 1974.

(f) Other Definitions and Special Rules.— For purposes of this section—

(1) Joint and several liability.— If more than one person is liable under subsection (a) or (b) with respect to any one prohibited transaction, all such persons shall be jointly and severally liable under such subsection with respect to such transaction.

(2) Taxable period.— The term "taxable period" means, with respect to any prohibited transaction, the period beginning with the date on which the prohibited transaction occurs and ending on the earliest of—

(A) the date of mailing of a notice of deficiency with respect to the tax imposed by subsection (a) under section 6212,

(B) the date on which the tax imposed by subsection (a) is assessed, or

(C) the date on which correction of the prohibited transaction is completed.

(3) Sale or exchange; encumbered property.— A transfer of real or personal property by a disqualified person to a plan shall be treated as a sale or exchange if the property is subject to a mortgage or similar lien which the plan assumes or if it is subject to a mortgage or similar lien which a disqualified person placed on the property within the 10-year period ending on the date of the transfer.

(4) Amount involved.— The term "amount involved" means, with respect to a prohibited transaction, the greater of the amount of money and the fair market value of the other property given or the amount of money and the fair market value of the other property received; except that, in the case of services described in paragraphs (2) and (10) of subsection (d) the amount involved shall be only the excess compensation. For purposes

of the preceding sentence, the fair market value—

(A) in the case of the tax imposed by subsection (a), shall be determined as of the date on which the prohibited transaction occurs; and

(B) in the case of the tax imposed by subsection (b), shall be the highest fair market value during the taxable period.

(5) Correction.—The terms "correcti-on" and "correct" mean, with respect to a prohibited transaction, undoing the transaction to the extent possible, but in any case placing the plan in a financial position not worse than that in which it would be if the disqualified person were acting under the highest fiduciary standards.

(g) Application of Section.— This section shall not apply—

(1) in the case of a plan to which a guaranteed benefit policy (as defined in section 401(b)(2)(B) of the Employee Retirement Income Security Act of 1974) is issued, to any assets of the insurance company, insurance service, or insurance organization merely because of its issuance of such policy;

(2) to a governmental plan (within the meaning of section 414(d)); or

(3) to a church plan (within the meaning of section 414(e)) with respect to which the election provided by section 410(d) has not been made.

In the case of a plan which invests in any security issued by an investment company registered under the Investment Company Act of 1940, the assets of such plan shall be deemed to include such security but shall not, by reason of such investment, be deemed to include any assets of such company.

(h) Notification of Secretary of Labor.— Before sending a notice of deficiency with respect to the tax imposed by subsection (a) or (b), the Secretary shall notify the Secretary of Labor and provide him a reasonable opportunity to obtain a correction of the prohibited transaction or to comment on the imposition of such tax.

(i) Cross Reference.— For provisions concerning coordination procedures between Secretary of Labor and Secretary of Treasury with respect to application of tax imposed by this section and for authority to waive imposition of the tax imposed by subsection (b), see section 3003 of the Employee Retirement Income Security Act of 1974.

SEC. 4976. TAXES WITH RESPECT TO FUNDED WELFARE BENEFIT PLANS.

(a) General Rule.—If—

(1) an employer maintains a welfare benefit fund, and

(2) there is a disqualified benefit provided during any taxable year,

there is hereby imposed on such employer a tax equal to 100 percent of such disqualified benefit.

(b) Disqualified Benefit.—For purposes of subsection (a)—

(1) In general.— The term "disqualified benefit" means—

(A) any post-retirement medical benefit or life insurance benefit provided with respect to a key employee if a separate account is required to be established for such employee under section 419A(d) and such payment is not from such account,

(B) any post-retirement medical benefit or life insurance benefit provided with respect to an individual in whose favor discrimination is prohibited unless the plan meets the requirements of section 505(b) with respect to such benefit (whether or not such requirements apply to such plan), and

(C) any portion of a welfare benefit fund reverting to the benefit of the employer.

(2) Exception for collective bargaining plans.— Paragraph (1)(B) shall not apply to any plan maintained pursuant to an agreement between employee representatives and 1 or more employers if the Secretary finds that such agreement is a collective bargaining agreement and that the benefits referred to in paragraph (1)(B) were the subject of good faith bargaining between such employee representatives and such employer or employers.

(3) Exception for nondeductible contributions.— Paragraph (1)(C) shall not apply to any amount attributable to a contribution to the fund which is not allowable as a deduction under section 419 for the taxable year or any prior taxable year (and such contribution shall not be included in any carryover under section 419(d)),

(4) Exception for certain amounts charged against existing reserve.—Subparagraphs (A) and (B) of paragraph (1) shall not apply to post-retirement benefits charged against an existing reserve for post-retirement medical or life insurance benefits (as defined in section 512(a)(3)(E)) or charged against the income on such reserve.

(c) Definitions.— For purposes of this section, the terms used in this section shall have the same respective meanings as when used in subpart D of part I of subchapter D of chapter 1.

SEC. 4977. TAX ON CERTAIN FRINGE BENEFITS PROVIDED BY AN EMPLOYER.

(a) Imposition of Tax.— In the case of an employer to whom an election under this section applies for any calendar year, there is hereby imposed a tax for such calendar year equal to 30 percent of the excess fringe benefits.

(b) Excess Fringe Benefits.— For purposes of subsection (a), the term "excess fringe benefits" means, with respect to any calendar year—

(1) the aggregate value of the fringe benefits provided by the employer during the calendar year which were not includible in gross income under paragraphs (1) and (2) of section 132(a), over

(2) 1 percent of the aggregate amount of compensation—

(A) which was paid by the employer during such calendar year to employees, and

(B) was includible in gross income for purposes of chapter 1.

◊ ◊ ◊

Editor's Note: Section 4977(c)(2), below, was amended by OBRA '93 Section 13213(d)(3)(B), effective for expenses incurred after December 31, 1994.

◊ ◊ ◊

(c) Effect of Election on Section 132(a).— If—

(1) an election under this section is in effect with respect to an employer for any calendar year, and

(2) at all times on or after January 1, 1984, and before the close of the calendar year involved, substantially all of the employees of the employer were entitled to employee discounts on goods or services provided by the employer in 1 line of business, for purposes of paragraphs (1) and (2) of section 132(a) (but not for purposes of section 132(i)(2) all employees of any line of business of the employer which was in existence on January 1, 1984, shall be treated as employees of the line of business referred to in paragraph (2).

(d) Period of Election.— An election under this section shall apply to the calendar year for which made and all subsequent calendar years unless revoked by the employer.

(e) Treatment of Controlled Groups.— All employees treated as employed by a single employer under subsection (b), (c), or (m) of section 414 shall be treated as employed by a single employer for purposes of this section.

(f) Section To Apply Only To Employment Within The United States.— Except as otherwise provided in regulations, this section shall apply only with respect to employment within the United States.

SEC. 4978. TAX ON CERTAIN DISPOSITIONS BY EMPLOYEE STOCK OWNERSHIP PLANS AND CERTAIN COOPERATIVES.

(a) Tax on Dispositions of Securities to Which Section 1042 Applies Before Close of Minimum Holding Period.— If, during the 3-year period after the date on which the employee stock ownership plan or eligible worker-owned cooperative acquired any qualified securities in a sale to which section 1042 applied, such plan or cooperative disposes of any qualified securities and—

(1) the total number of shares held by such plan or cooperative after such disposition is less than the total number of employer securities held immediately after such sale, or

(2) except to the extent provided in regulations, the value of qualified securities held by such plan or cooperative after such disposition is less than 30 percent of the total value of all employer securities as of such disposition,

there is hereby imposed a tax on the disposition equal to the amount determined under subsection(b).

(b) Amount of Tax.—

(1) In general.— the amount of tax imposed by subsection (a) shall be equal to 10 percent of the amount realized on the disposition.

(2) Limitation.— The amount realized taken into account under paragraph (1) shall not exceed that portion allocable to qualified securities acquired in the sale to which section 1042 applied determined as if such securities were disposed of—

(A) first, from section 133 securities (as defined in section 4978B(e)(2)) acquired during the 3-year period ending on the date of such disposition, beginning with the securities first so acquired.

(B) second, from section 133 securities (as so defined) acquired before such 3-year period unless such securities (or proceeds from the disposition) have been allocated to accounts of participants or beneficiaries.

(C) third, from qualified securities to which section 1042 applied acquired during the 3-year period ending on the date of the disposition, beginning with the securities first so acquired, and

(D) then from any other employer securities.
If subsection (d) or section 4978B(d) applies to a disposition, the disposition shall be treated as made from employer securities in the opposite order of the preceding sentence.

(3) Distributions to employees.— The amount realized on any distribution to an employee for less than fair market value shall be determined as if the qualified security had been sold to the employee at fair market value.

(c) Liability for Payment of Taxes.— The tax imposed by this subsection shall be paid by—

(1) the employer, or

(2) the eligible worker-owned cooperative,

that made the written statement described in section 1042(b)(3).

(d) Section Not To Apply to Certain Dispositions.—

(1) Certain distributions to employees.— This section shall not apply with respect to any distribution of qualified securities (or sale of such securities) which is made by reason of—

(A) the death of the employee,

(B) the retirement of the employee after the employee has attained 59½ years of age,

(C) the disability of the employee (within the meaning of section 72(m)(7)), or

(D) the separation of the employee from service for any period which results in a 1-year break in service (within the meaning of section 411(a)(6)(A)).

(2) Certain reorganizations.— In the case of any exchange of qualified securities in any reorganization described in section 368(a)(1) for stock of another corporation, such exchange shall not be treated as a disposition for purposes of this section.

(3) Liquidation of corporation into cooperative.— In the case of any exchange of qualified securities pursuant to the liquidation of the corporation issuing qualified securities into the eligible worker-owned cooperative in a transaction which meets the requirements of section 332 (determined by substituting "100 percent" "80 percent" each place it appears in section 332(b)(1)), such exchange shall not be treated as a disposition for purposes of this section.

(4) Dispositions to meet diversification requirements.— This section shall not apply to any disposition of qualified securities which is required under section 401(a)(28).

(e) Definitions and Special Rules.— For purposes of this section—

(1) Employee stock ownership plan.— The term "employee stock ownership plan" has the meaning given such term by section 4975(e)(7).

(2) Qualified securities.— The term "qualified securities" has the meaning given such term by section 1042(c)(1).

(3) Eligible worker-owned cooperative.— The term "eligible worker-owned cooperative" has the meaning given such term by section 1042(c)(1).

(4) Disposition.— The term "dis-position" includes any distribution.

(5) Employer securities.—The term "employer securities" has the meaning given to such term by section 409(2).

SECTION 4978A. TAX ON CERTAION DISPOSITIONS OF EMPLOYER SECURITIES TO WHICH SECTION 2057 APPLIED [REPEALED]

SEC. 4978B. TAX ON DISPOSITION OF EMPLOYER SECURITIES TO WHICH SECTION 133 APPLIED.

(a) Imposition of Tax.— In the case of an employee stock ownership plan which has acquired section 133 securities, there is hereby imposed a tax on each taxable event in an amount equal to the amount determined under subsection (b).

(b) Amount of Tax.—

(1) In general.— The amount of the tax imposed by subsection (a) shall be equal to 10 percent of the amount realized on the disposition to the extent allocable to section 133 securities under section 4978(b)(2).

(2) Dispositions other than sales or exchanges.— For purposes of paragraph (1), in the case of a disposition of employer securities which is not a sale or exchange, the amount realized on such disposition shall be the fair market value of such securities at the time of disposition.

(c) Taxable Event.—For the purposes of this section, the term "taxable event" means any of the following dispositions:

(1) Dispositions within 3 years.—Any disposition of any employer securities by an employee stock ownership plan within 3 years after such plan acquired section 133 securities if—

(A) the total number of employer securities held by such plan after disposition is less than the total number of employer securities held after such acquisition, or

(B) except to the extent provided in regulations, the value of employer securities held by such plan after the disposition is 50 percent or less of the total value of all employer securities as of the time of the disposition.

For purposes of subparagraph (B), the aggregation rule of section 133(b)(6)(D) shall apply.

(2) Stock disposed of before allocation.— Any disposition of section 133 securities to which paragraph (1) does not apply if—

(A) such disposition occurs before such securities are allocated to accounts of participants or their beneficiaries, and

(B) the proceeds from such disposition are not so allocated.

(d) Section Not to Apply to Certain Dispositions.—

(1) In general.— This section shall not apply to any dispositions described in paragraph (1), (3), or (4) of section 4978(d).

(2) Certain reorganizations.— For purposes of this section, any exchange of section 133 securities for employer securities of another corporation in any reorganization described in section 368(a)(1) shall not be treated as a disposition, but the employer securities received shall be treated as section 133 securities and as having been held by the plan during the period the securities which were exchanged were held.

(3) Forced disposition occurring by operation of state law.— Any forced disposition of section 133 securities by an employee stock ownership plan occurring by operation of a state law shall not be treated as a disposition. This paragraph shall only apply to securities which, at the time the securities were acquired by the plan, were regularly traded on an established securities market.

(4) Coordination with other taxes.— This section shall not apply to any disposition which is subject to tax under section 4978 or section 4978A (as in effect on the day before the date of enactment of this section).

(e) Definitions and Special Rules.— For purposes of this section—

(1) Liability for payment of taxes.— The tax imposed by this section shall be paid by the employer.

(2) Section 133 securities.— The term "section 133 securities" means employer securities acquired by an employee stock ownership plan in a transaction to which section 133 applied.

(3) Disposition.—The term "dis-position" includes any distribution.

(4) Ordering rules.— For ordering rules for dispositions of employer securities, see section 4978(b)(2).

SEC. 4979. TAX ON CERTAIN EXCESS CONTRIBUTIONS.

(a) General Rule.— In the case of any plan, there is hereby imposed a tax for the taxable year equal to 10 percent of the sum of—

(1) any excess contributions under such plan for the plan year ending in such taxable year, and

(2) any excess aggregate contributions under the plan for the plan year ending in such taxable year.

(b) Liability for Tax.— The tax imposed by subsection (a) shall be paid by the employer.

(c) Excess Contributions.—For purposes of this section, the term "excess contributions" has the meaning given such term by sections 401(k)(8)(B), 408(k)(6)(C), and 501(c)(18).

(d) Excess Aggregate Contribution.— For purposes of this section, the term "excess aggregate contribution" has the meaning given to such term by section 401(m)(6)(B). For purposes of determining excess aggregate contributions under an annuity contract described in section 403(b), such contract shall be treated as a plan described in subsection (e)(1).

(e) Plan.— For purposes of this section, the term "plan" means—

(1) a plan described in section 401(a) which includes a trust exempt from tax under section 501(a),

(2) any annuity plan described in section 403(a),

(3) any annuity contract described in section 403(b),

(4) a simplified employee pension of an employer which satisfies the requirements of section 408(k), and

(5) a plan described in section 501(c)(18). Such term includes any plan which, at any time, has been determined by the Secretary to be such a plan.

(f) No Tax Where Excess Distributed Within 2½ Months of Close of Year.—

(1) In general.— No tax shall be imposed under this section on any excess contribution or excess aggregate contribution, as the case may be, to the extent such contribution (together with any income allocable thereto) is distributed (or, if forfeitable, is forfeited) before the close of the first 2½ months of the following plan year.

(2) Year of inclusion.—

(A) In general.—Except as provided in subparagraph (B), any amount distributed as provided in paragraph (1) shall be treated as received and earned by the recipient in his taxable year for which such contribution was made.

(B) De minimis distributions.— If the total excess contributions and excess aggregate contributions distributed to a recipient under a plan for any plan year are less than $100, such distributions (and any income allocable thereto) shall be treated as earned and reeived by the recipient in his taxable year in which such distributions were made.

SEC. 4980. TAX ON REVERSION OF QUALIFIED PLAN ASSETS TO EMPLOYER.

(a) Imposition of Tax.— There is hereby imposed a tax of 20 percent of the amount of any employer reversion from a qualified plan.

(b) Liability for Tax.— The tax imposed by subsection (a) shall be paid by the employer maintaining the plan.

(c) Definitions and Special Rules.— For purposes of this section—

(1) Qualified plan.—The term "quali-fied plan" means any plan meeting the requirements of section 401(a) or 403(a), other than—

(A) a plan maintained by an employer if such employer has, at all times, been exempt from tax under subtitle A, or

(B) a governmental plan (within the meaning of section 414(d)).

Such term shall include any plan which, at any time, has been determined by the Secretary to be a qualified plan.

(2) Employer reversion.—

(A) In general.—The term "employer reversion" means the amount of cash and the fair market value of other property received (directly or indirectly) by an employer from the qualified plan.

(B) Exceptions.— The term "employer reversion" shall not include—

(i) except as provided in regulations, any amount distributed to or on behalf of any employee (or his beneficiaries) if such amount could have been so distributed before termination of such plan without violating any provision of section 401, or

(ii) any distribution to the employer which is allowable under section 401(a)(2)—

(I) in the case of a multiemployer plan, by reason of mistakes of law or fact or the return of any withdrawal liability payment,

(II) in the case of a plan other than a multiemployer plan, by reason of mistake of fact, or

(III) in the case of any plan, by reason of the failure of the plan to initially qualify or the failure of contributions to be deductible.

(3) Exception for employee stock ownership plans.—

(A) In general.— If, upon an employer reversion from a qualified plan, any applicable amount is transferred from such plan to an employee stock ownership plan described in section 4975(e)(7) or a tax credit employee stock ownership plan (as described in section 409), such amount shall not be treated as an employer reversion for purposes of this section (or includible in the gross income of the employer) if—

(i) the requirements of subparagraphs (B), (C), and (D) are met, and

(ii) under the plan, employer securities to which subparagraph (B) applies must, except to the extent necessary to meet the requirements of section 401(a)(28), remain in the plan until distribution to participants in accordance with the provisions of such plan.

(B) Investment in employer securities.— The requirements of this subparagraph are met if, within 90 days after the transfer (or such longer period as the Secretary may prescribe), the amount transferred is invested in employer securities (as defined in section 409(*l*)) or used to repay loans used to purchase such securities.

(C) Allocation requirements.—The requirements of this subparagraph are met if the portion of the amount transferred which is not allocated under the plan to accounts of participants in the plan year in which the transfer occurs—

(i) is credited to a suspense account and allocated from such account to accounts of participants no less rapidly than ratably over a period not to exceed 7 years, and

(ii) when allocated to accounts of participants under the plan, is treated as an employer contribution for purposes of section 415(c), except that—

(I) the annual addition (as determined under section 415(c)) attributable to each such allocation shall not exceed the value of such securities as of the time such securities were credited to such suspense account, and

(II) no additional employer contributions shall be permitted to an employee stock ownership plan described in subparagraph (A) of the employer before the allocation of such amount.

The amount allocated in the year of transfer shall not be less than the lesser of the maximum amount allowable under section 415 or $\frac{1}{8}$ of the amount attributable to the securities acquired. In the case of dividends on securities held in the suspense account, the requirements of this subparagraph are met only if the dividends are allocated to accounts of participants or paid to participants in proportion to their accounts, or used to repay loans used to purchase employer securities.

(D) Participants.— The requirements of this subparagraph are met if at least half of the participants in the qualified plan are participants in the employee stock ownership plan (as of the close of the 1st plan year for which an allocation of the securities is required).

(E) Applicable amount.— For purposes of this paragraph, the term "applicable amount" means any amount which—

(i) is transferred after March 31, 1985, and before January 1, 1989, or

(ii) is transferred after December 31, 1988, pursuant to a termination which occurs after March 31, 1985, and before January 1, 1989.

(F) No credit or deduction allowed.— No credit or deduction shall be allowed under chapter 1 for any amount transferred to an employee stock ownership plan in a transfer to which this paragraph applies.

(G) Amount transferred to include income thereon, etc.— The amount transferred shall not be treated as meeting the requirements of subparagraphs (B) and (C) unless amounts attributable to such amount also meet such requirements.

(4) Time for payment of tax.— For purposes of subtitle F, the time for payment of the tax imposed by subsection (a) shall be the last day of the month following the month in which the employer reversion occurs.

(d) Increase in Tax for Failure to Establish Replacement Plan or Increase Benefits.—

(1) In general.— Subsection (a) shall be applied by substituting "50 percent" for "20 percent" with respect to any employer reversion from a qualified plan unless—

(A) the employer establishes or maintains a qualified replacement plan, or

(B) the plan provides benefit increases meeting the requirements of paragraph (3).

(2) Qualified replacement plan.— For purposes of this subsection, the term "qualified replacement plan" means a qualified plan established or maintained by the employer in connection with a qualified plan termination (hereinafter referred to as the "replacement plan") with respect to which the following requirements are met:

(A) Participation requirement.— At least 95 percent of the active participants in the terminated plan who remain as employees of the employer after the termination are active participants in the replacement plan.

(B) Asset transfer requirement.—

(i) 25 percent cushion.— A direct transfer from the terminated plan to the replacement plan is made before any employer reversion, and the transfer is in an amount equal to the excess (if any) of—

(I) 25 percent of the maximum amount which the employer could receive as an employer reversion without regard to this subsection, over

(II) the amount determined under clause (ii).

(ii) Reduction for increase in benefits.— The amount determined under this clause is an amount equal to the present value of the aggregate increases in the accrued benefits under the terminated plan of any participants or beneficiaries pursuant to a plan amendment which—

(I) is adopted during the 60-day period ending on the date of termination of the qualified plan, and

(II) takes effect immediately on the termination date.

(iii) Treatment of amount transferred.—In the case of the transfer of any amount under clause (i)—

(I) such amount shall not be includible in the gross income of the employer,

(II) no deduction shall be allowable with respect to such transfer, and

(III) such transfer shall not be treated as an employer reversion for purposes of this section.

(C) Allocation requirements.—

(i) In general.— In the case of any defined contribution plan, the portion of the amount transferred to the replacement plan under subparagraph (B)(i) is—

(I) allocated under the plan to the accounts of participants in the plan year in which the transfer occurs, or

(II) credited to a suspense account and allocated from such account to accounts of participants no less rapidly than ratably over the 7-plan-year period beginning with the year of the transfer.

(ii) Coordination with section 415 limitation.— If, by reason of any limitation under section 415, any amount credited to a suspense account under clause (i)(II) may not be allocated to a participant before the close of the 7-year period under such clause—

(I) such amount shall be allocated to the accounts of other participants, and

(II) if any portion of such amount may not be allocated to other participants by reason of any such limitation, shall be allocated to the participant as provided in section 415.

(iii) Treatment of income.—Any income on any amount credited to a suspense account under clause (i)(II) shall be allocated to accounts of participants no less rapidly than ratably over the remainder of the period determined under such clause (after application of clause (ii)).

(iv) Unallocated amounts at termination.— If any amount credited to a suspense account under clause (i)(II) is not allocated as of the termination date of the replacement plan—

(I) such amount shall be allocated to the accounts of participants as of such date, except that any amount which may not be allocated by reason of any limitation under section 415 shall be allocated to the accounts of other participants, and

(II) if any portion of such amount may not be allocated to other participants under subclause (I) by reason of such limitation, such portion shall be treated as an employer reversion to which this section applies.

IRC Sec. 4980 (d)(2)(C)(iv)(II)

(3) Pro rata benefit increases.—

(A) In general.—The requirements of this paragraph are met if a plan amendment to the terminated plan is adopted in connection with the termination of the plan which provides pro rata increases in the accrued benefits of all qualified participants which—

(i) have an aggregate present value not less than 20 percent of the maximum amount which the employer could receive as an employer reversion without regard to this subsection, and

(ii) take effect immediately on the termination date.

(B) Pro rata increase.— For purposes of subparagraph (A), a pro rata increase is an increase in the present value of the accrued benefit of each qualified participant in an amount which bears the same ratio to the aggregate amount determined under subparagraph (A)(i) as—

(i) the present value of such participant's accrued benefit (determined without regard to this subsection), bears to

(ii) the aggregate present value of accrued benefits of the terminated plan (as so determined).

Notwithstanding the preceding sentence, the aggregate increases in the present value of the accrued benefits of qualified participants who are not active participants shall not exceed 40 percent of the aggregate amount determined under subparagraph (A)(i) by substituting "equal to" for "not less than".

(4) Coordination with other provisions.—

(A) Limitations.— A benefit may not be increased under paragraph (2)(B)(ii) or (3)(A), and an amount may not be allocated to a participant under paragraph (2)(C), if such increase or allocation would result in a failure to meet any requirement under section 401(a)(4) or 415.

(B) Treatment as employer contributions.— Any increase in benefits under paragraph (2)(B)(ii) or (3)(A), or any allocation of any amount (or income allocable thereto) to any account under paragraph (2)(C), shall be treated as an annual benefit or annual addition for purposes of section 415.

(C) 10-year participation requirement.— Except as provided by the Secretary, section 415(b)(5)(D) shall not apply to any increase in benefits by reason of this subsection to the extent that the application of this subparagraph does not discriminate in favor of highly compensated employees (as defined in section 414(q)).

(5) Definitions and special rules.— For purposes of this subsection—

(A) Qualified participant.—The term "qualified participant" means an individual who—

(i) is an active participant,

(ii) is a participant or beneficiary in pay status as of the termination date,

(iii) is a participant not described in clause (i) or (ii)—

(I) who has a nonforfeitable right to an accrued benefit under the terminated plan as of the termination date, and

(II) whose service, which was creditable under the terminated plan, terminated during the period beginning 3 years before the termination date and ending with the date on which the final distribution of assets occurs, or

(iv) is a beneficiary of a participant described in clause (iii)(II) and has a nonforfeitable right to an accrued benefit under the terminated plan as of the termination date.

(B) Present value.— Present value shall be determined as of the termination date and on the same basis as liabilities of the plan are determined on termination.

(C) Reallocation of increase.— Except as provided in paragraph (2)(C), if any benefit increase is reduced by reason of the last sentence of pargraph (3)(A)(ii) or paragraph (4), the amount of such reduction shall be allocated to the remaining participants on the same basis as other increases (and shall be treated as meeting any allocation requirements of this subsection).

(D) Plans taken into account.— For purposes of determining whether there is a qualified replacement plan under paragraph (2), the Secretary may provide that—

(i) 2 or more plans may be treated as 1 plan, or

(ii) a plan of a successor employer may be taken into account.

(E) Special rule for participation requirement.— For purposes of paragraph (2)(A), all employers treated as 1 employer under section 414(b), (c), (m), or (o) shall be treated as 1 employer.

(6) Subsection not to apply to employer in bankruptcy.— This subsection shall not apply to an employer who, as of the termination date of the qualified plan, is in bankruptcy liquidation under chapter 7 of title 11 of the United States Code or in similar proceedings under State law.

SEC. 4980A. TAX ON EXCESS DISTRIBUTIONS FROM QUALIFIED RETIREMENT PLANS.

(a) General Rule.— There is hereby imposed a tax equal to 15 percent of the excess distributions with respect to any individual during any calendar year.

(b) Liability for Tax.— The individual with respect to whom the excess distributions are made shall be liable for the tax imposed by subsection (a). The amount of the tax imposed by subsection (a) shall be reduced by the amount (if any) of the tax imposed by section 72(t) to the extent attributable to such excess distributions.

(c) Excess Distributions.— For purposes of this section

(1) In general.—The term ''excess distributions'' means the aggregate amount of the retirement distributions with respect to any individual during any calendar year to the extent such amount exceeds the greater of—

(A) $150,000, or

(B) $112,500 (adjusted at the same time and in the same manner as under section 415(d)).

(2) Exclusion of certain distributions.— The following distributions shall not be taken into account under paragraph (1):

(A) Any retirement distribution with respect to an individual made after the death of such individual.

(B) Any retirement distribution with respect to an individual payable to an alternate payee pursuant to a qualified domestic relations order (within the meaning of section 414(p)) if includible in income of the alternate payee.

(C) Any retirement distribution with respect to an individual which is attributable to the individual's investment in the contract (as defined in section 72(f)).

(D) Any retirement distribution to the extent not included in gross income by reason of a rollover contribution.

(E) Any retirement distribution with respect to an individual of an annuity contract the value of which is not includible in gross income at the time of the distribution (other than distributions under, or proceeds from the sale or exchange of, such contract).

(F) Any retirement distribution with respect to an individual of—

(i) excess deferrals (and income allocable thereto) under section 402(g)(2)(A)(ii), or

(ii) excess contributions (and income allocable thereto) under section 401(k)(8) or 408(d)(4) or excess aggregate contributions

IRC Sec. 4980A (c)(2)(F)(ii)

(and income allocable thereto) under section 401(m)(6).

Any distribution described in subparagraph (B) shall be treated as a retirement distribution to the person to whom paid for purposes of this section.

(3) Aggregation of payments.— If retirement distributions with respect to any individual during any calendar year are received by the individual and 1 or more other persons, all such distributions shall be aggregated for purposes of determining the amount of the excess distributions for the calendar year.

(4) Special rule where taxpayer elects income averaging.— If the retirement distributions with respect to any individual during any calendar year include a lump sum distribution to which an election under section 402(d)(4)(B) applies—

(A) paragraph (1) shall be applied separately with respect to such lump sum distribution and other retirement distributions, and

(B) the limitation under paragraph (1) with respect to such lump sum distribution shall be equal to 5 times the amount of such limitation determined without regard to this subparagraph.

(d) Increase in Estate Tax if Individual Dies With Excess Accumulation.—

(1) In general.—The tax imposed by chapter 11 with respect to the estate of any individual shall be increased by an amount equal to 15 percent of the individual's excess retirement accumulation.

(2) No credit allowable.— No credit shall be allowable under chapter 11 with respect to any portion of the tax imposed by chapter 11 attributable to the increase under paragraph (1).

(3) Excess retirement accumulation.— For purposes of paragraph (1), the term "excess retirement accumulation" means the excess (if any) of—

(A) the value of the individual's interests (other than as a beneficiary, determined after application of paragraph (5)) in qualified employer plans and individual retirement plans as of the date of the decedent's death (or, in the case of an election under section 2032, the applicable valuation date prescribed by such section), over

(B) the present value (as determined under rules prescribed by the Secretary as of the valuation date prescribed in subparagraph (A)) of a single life annuity with annual payments equal to the limitation of subsection (c) (as in effect for the year in which death occurs and as if the individual had not died).

(4) Rules for computing excess retirement accumulation.— The excess retirement accumulation of an individual shall be computed without regard to—

(A) any community property law,

(B) the value of—

(i) amounts payable to an alternate payee pursuant to a qualified domestic relations order (within the meaning of section 414(p)) if includible in income of the alternate payee, and

(ii) the individual's investment in the contract (as defined in section 72(f)), and

(C) the excess (if any) of—

(i) any interests which are payable immediately after death, over

(ii) the value of such interests immediately before death.

(5) Election by spouse to have excess distribution rule apply.—

(A) In general.—If the spouse of an individual is the beneficiary of all of the interests described in paragraph (3)(A), the spouse may elect—

(i) not to have this subsection apply, and

(ii) to have this section apply to such interests and any retirement distribution attributable to such interests as if such interests were the spouse's.

(B) De minimis exception.— If 1 or more persons other than the spouse are beneficiaries of a de minimis portion of the interests described in paragraph (3)(A)—

(i) the spouse shall not be treated as failing to meet the requirements of subparagraph (A), and

(ii) if the spouse makes the election under subparagraph (A), this section shall not apply to such portion or any retirement distribution attributable to such portion.

(e) Retirement Distributions.— For purposes of this section—

(1) In general.— The term ''retirement distribution'' means, with respect to any individual, the amount distributed during the taxable year under—

(A) any qualified employer plan with respect to which such individual is or was the employee, and

(B) any individual retirement plan.

(2) Qualified employer plan.— The term ''qualified employer plan'' means—

(A) any plan described in section 401(a) which includes a trust exempt from tax under section 501(a),

(B) an annuity plan described in section 403(a), or

(C) an annuity contract described in section 403(b).

Such term includes any plan or contract which, at any time, has been determined by the Secretary to be such a plan or contract.

(f) Exemptions of Accrued Benefits in Excess of $562,500 on August 1, 1986. — For purposes of this section—

(1) In general.—If an election is made with respect to an eligible individual to have this subsection apply, the individual's excess distributions and excess retirement accumulation shall be computed without regard to any distributions or interests attributable to the accrued benefit of the individual as of August 1, 1986.

(2) Reduction in amounts which may be received without tax.— If this subsection applies to any individual—

(A) Excess distributions.—Subsection (c)(1) shall be applied—

(i) without regard to subparagraph (A), and

(ii) by reducing (but not below zero) the amount determined under subparagraph (B) thereof by retirement distributions attributable (as determined under rules prescribed by the Secretary) to the individual's accrued benefit as of August 1, 1986.

(B) Excess retirement accumulation.— The amount determined under subsection (d)(3)(B) (without regard to subsection (c)(1)(A)) with respect to such individual shall be reduced (but not below zero) by the present value of the individual's accrued benefit as of August 1, 1986, which has not been distributed as of the date of death.

(3) Eligible individual.—For purposes of this subsection, the term ''eligible individual'' means any individual if, on August 1, 1986, the present value of such individual's interests in qualified employer plans and individual retirement plans exceeded $562,500.

(4) Certain amounts excluded. — In determining an indivudal's accrued benefit for purposes of this subsection, there shall not be taken into account any portion of the accrued benefit—

(A) payable to an alternate payee pursuant to a qualified domestic relations order (within the meaning of section 414(p)) if includible in income of the alternate payee, or

IRC Sec. 4980A (f)(4)(A)

(B) attributable to the individual's investment in the contract (as defined in section 72(f)).

(5) Election.— An election under paragraph (1) shall be made on an individual's return of tax imposed by chapter 1 or 11 for a taxable year beginning before January 1, 1989.

SEC. 4980B. FAILURE TO SATISFY CONTINUATION COVERAGE REQUIREMENTS OF GROUP HEALTH PLANS.

(a) General Rule.—There is hereby imposed a tax on the failure of a group health plan to meet the requirements of subsection (f) with respect to any qualified beneficiary.

(b) Amount of Tax.—

(1) In general.— The amount of the tax imposed by subsection (a) on any failure with respect to a qualified beneficiary shall be $100 for each day in the noncompliance period with respect to such failure.

(2) Noncompliance period.— For purposes of this section, the term "noncompliance period" means, with respect to any failure, the period—

(A) beginning on the date such failure first occurs, and

(B) ending on the earlier of—

(i) the date such failure is corrected, or

(ii) the date which is 6 months after the last day in the period applicable to the qualified beneficiary under subsection (f)(2)(B) (determined without regard to clause (iii) thereof).

If a person is liable for tax under subsection (e)(1)(B) by reason of subsection (e)(2)(B) with respect to any failure, the noncompliance period for such person with respect to such failure shall not begin before the 45th day after

the written request described in subsection (e)(2)(B) is provided to such person.

(3) Minimum tax for noncompliance period where failure discovered after notice of examination.— Notwithstanding paragraphs (1) and (2) of subsection (c)—

(A) In general.— In the case of 1 or more failures with respect to a qualified beneficiary—

(i) which are not corrected before the date a notice of examination of income tax liability is sent to the employer, and

(ii) which occurred or continued during the period under examination,

the amount of tax imposed by subsection (a) by reason of such failures with respect to such beneficiary shall not be less than the lesser of $2,500 or the amount of tax which would be imposed by subsection (a) without regard to such paragraphs.

(B) Higher minimum tax where violations are more than de minimis.— To the extent violations by the employer (or the plan in the case of a multiemployer plan) for any year are more than de minimis, subparagraph (A) shall be applied by substituting "$15,000" for "$2,500" with respect to the employer (or such plan).

(c) Limitations on Amount of Tax.—

(1) Tax not to apply where failure not discovered exercising reasonable diligence.— No tax shall be imposed by subsection (a) on any failure during any period for which it is established to the satisfaction of the Secretary that none of the persons referred to in subsection (e) knew, or exercising reasonable diligence would have known, that such failure existed.

(2) Tax not to apply to failures corrected within 30 days.— No tax shall be imposed by subsection (a) on any failure if—

(A) such failure was due to reasonable cause and not to willful neglect, and

(B) such failure is corrected during the 30-day period beginning on the 1st date any of the persons referred to in subsection (e) knew, or exercising reasonable diligence would have known, that such failure existed.

(3) $100 limit on amount of tax for failures on any day with respect to a qualified beneficiary.—

(A) In general.— Except as provided in subparagraph (B), the maximum amount of tax imposed by subsection (a) on failures on any day during the noncompliance period with respect to a qualified beneficiary shall be $100.

(B) Special rule where more than 1 qualified beneficiary.— If there is more than 1 qualified beneficiary with respect to the same qualifying event, the maximum amount of tax imposed by subsection (a) on all failures on any day during the noncompliance period with respect to such qualified beneficiaries shall be $200.

(4) Overall limitation for unintentional failures.— In the case of failures which are due to reasonable cause and not to willful neglect—

(A) Single employer plans.—

(i) In general.— In the case of failures with respect to plans other than multiemployer plans, the tax imposed by subsection (a) for failures during the taxable year of the employer shall not exceed the amount equal to the lesser of—

(I) 10 percent of the aggregate amount paid or incurred by the employer (or predecessor employer) during the preceding taxable year for group health plans, or

(II) $500,000.

(ii) Taxable years in the case of certain controlled groups.— For purposes of this subparagraph, if not all persons who are treated as a single employer for purposes of this section have the same taxable year, the taxable years taken into account shall be determined under principles similar to the principles of section 1561.

(B) Multiemployer plans.—

(i) In general.— In the case of failures with respect to a multiemployer plan, the tax imposed by subsection (a) for failures during the taxable year of the trust forming part of such plan shall not exceed the amount equal to the lesser of—

(I) 10 percent of the amount paid or incurred by such trust during such taxable year to provide medical care (as defined in section 213(d)) directly or through insurance, reimbursement, or otherwise, or

(II) $500,000.

For purposes of the preceding sentence, all plans of which the same trust forms a part shall be treated as 1 plan.

(ii) Special rule for employers required to pay tax.— If an employer is assessed a tax imposed by subsection (a) by reason of a failure with respect to a multiemployer plan, the limit shall be determined under subparagraph (A) (and not under this subparagraph) and as if such plan were not a multiemployer plan.

(C) Special rule for persons providing benefits.— In the case of a person described in subsection (e)(1)(B) (and not subsection (e)(1)(A)), the aggregate amount of tax imposed by subsection (a) for failures during a taxable year with respect to all plans shall not exceed $2,000,000.

(5) Waiver by Secretary.— In the case of a failure which is due to reasonable cause and not to willful neglect, the Secretary may waive part or all of the tax imposed by subsection (a) to the extent that the payment of such tax would be excessive relative to the failure involved.

IRC Sec. 4980B (c)(5)

(d) Tax Not To Apply To Certain Plans.— This section shall not apply to—

(1) any failure of a group health plan to meet the requirements of subsection (f) with respect to any qualified beneficiary if the qualifying event with respect to such beneficiary occurred during the calendar year immediately following a calendar year during which all employers maintaining such plan normally employed fewer than 20 employees on a typical business day.

(2) any governmental plan (within the meaning of section 414(d)), or

(3) any church plan (within the meaning of section 414(e)).

(e) Liability for Tax.—

(1) In general.— Except as otherwise provided in this subsection, the following shall be liable for the tax imposed by subsection (a) on a failure:

(A)(i) In the case of a plan other than a multiemployer plan, the employer.

(ii) In the case of a multiemployer plan, the plan.

(B) Each person who is responsible (other than in a capacity as an employee) for administering or providing benefits under the plan and whose act or failure to act caused (in whole or in part) the failure.

(2) Special rules for persons described in paragraph (1)(b).—

(A) No liability unless written agreement.— Except in the case of liability resulting from the application of subparagraph (B) of this paragraph, a person described in subparagraph (B) (and not in subparagraph (A)) of paragraph (1) shall be liable for the tax imposed by subsection (a) on any failure only if such person assumed (under a legally enforceable written agreement) responsibility for the performance of the act to which the failure relates.

(B) Failure to cover qualified bene-ficiaries where current employees are covered.— A person shall be treated as described in paragraph (1)(B) with respect to a qualified beneficiary if—

(i) such person provides coverage under a group health plan for any similarly situated beneficiary under the plan with respect to whom a qualifying event has not occurred, and

(ii) the—

(I) employer or plan administrator, or

(II) in the case of a qualifying event described in subparagraph (C) or (E) of subsection (f)(3) where the person described in clause (i) is the plan administrator, the qualified beneficiary,

submits to such person a written request that such person make available to such qualified beneficiary the same coverage which such person provides to the beneficiary referred to in clause (i).

(f) Continuation Coverage Requirements of Group Health Plans.—

(1) In general.— A group health plan meets the requirements of this subsection only if the coverage of the costs of pediatric vaccines (as defined under section 2162 of the Public Health Service Act) is not reduced below the coverage provided by the plan as of May 1, 1993, and only if each qualified beneficiary who would lose coverage under the plan as a result of a qualifying event is entitled to elect, within the election period, continuation coverage under the plan.

(2) Continuation coverage.— For purposes of paragraph (1), the term "continuation coverage" means coverage under the plan which meets the following requirements:

(A) Type of benefit coverage.— The coverage must consist of coverage which, as of the time the coverage is being provided, is identical to the coverage provided under the plan to similarly situated beneficiaries under the plan with respect to whom a qualifying event has not occurred. If coverage under the plan is modified for any group of similarly situated beneficiaries, the coverage shall also be modified in the same manner for all individuals who are qualified beneficiaries under the plan pursuant to this subsection in connection with such group.

(B) Period of coverage.— The coverage must extend for at least the period beginning on the date of the qualifying event and ending not earlier than the earliest of the following:

(i) Maximum required period.—

(I) General rule for terminations and reduced hours.—In the case of a qualifying event described in paragraph (3)(B), except as provided in subclause (II), the date which is 18 months after the date of the qualifying event.

(II) Special rule for multiple qualifying events.—If a qualifying event (other than a qualifying event described in paragraph (3)(F)) occurs during the 18 months after the date of a qualifying event described in paragraph (3)(B), the date which is 36 months after the date of the qualifying event described in paragraph (3)(B).

(III) Special rule for certain bankruptcy proceedings.—In the case of a qualifying event described in paragraph (3)(F) (relating to bankruptcy proceedings), the date of the death of the covered employee or qualified beneficiary (described in subsection (g)(1)(D)(iii)), or in the case of the surviving spouse or dependent children of the covered employee, 36 months after the date of the death of the covered employee.

(IV) General rule for other qualifying events.—In the case of a qualifying event not described in paragraph (3)(B) or (3)(F), the date which is 36 months after the date of the qualifying event.

(V) Qualifying event involving Medicare entitlement.—In the case of an event described in paragraph (3)(D) (without regard to whether such event is a qualifying event), the period of coverage for qualified beneficiaries other than the covered employee for such event or any subsequent qualifying event shall not terminate before the close of the 36-month period beginning on the date the covered employee becomes entitled to benefits under title XVIII of the Social Security Act.

In the case of a qualified beneficiary who is determined, under title II or XVI of the Social Security Act, to have been disabled at the time of a qualifying event described in paragraph (3)(B), any reference in subclause (I) or (II) to 18 months with respect to such event is deemed a reference to 29 months, but only if the qualified beneficiary has provided notice of such determination under paragraph (6)(C) before the end of such 18 months.

(ii) End of plan.—The date on which the employer ceases to provide any group health plan to any employee.

(iii) Failure to pay premium.— The date on which coverage ceases under the plan by reason of a failure to make timely payment of any premium required under the plan with respect to the qualified beneficiary. The payment of any premium (other than any payment referred to in the last sentence of subparagraph (C)) shall be considered to be timely if made within 30 days after the date due or within such longer period as applies to or under the plan.

(iv) Group health plan coverage or medicare entitlement.— The date which the qualified beneficiary first becomes, after the date of the election—

(I) covered under any other group health plan (as an employee or otherwise) which does not contain any exclusion or limitation with respect to any preexisting condition of such beneficiary), or

(II) in the case of a qualified beneficiary other than a qualified beneficiary described in subsection (g)(1)(D) entitled to benefits under title XVIII of the Social Security Act.

(v) Termination of extended coverage for disability.— In the case of a qualified beneficiary who is disabled at the time of a qualifying event described in paragraph (3)(B), the month that begins more than 30 days after the date of the final determination under title II or XVI of the Social Security Act that the qualified beneficiary is no longer disabled.

(C) Premium requirements.—The plan may require payment of a premium for any period of continuation coverage, except that such premium—

(i) shall not exceed 102 percent of the applicable premium for such period, and

(ii) may, at the election of the payor, be made in monthly installments.

In no event may the plan require the payment of any premium before the day which is 45 days after the day on which the qualified beneficiary made the initial election for continuation coverage.

(D) No requirement of insurability.— The coverage may not be conditioned upon, or discriminate on the basis of lack of, evidence of insurability.

(E) Conversion option.— In the case of a qualified beneficiary whose period of continuation coverage expires under subparagraph (B)(i), the plan must, during the 180-day period ending on such expiration date, provide to the qualified beneficiary the option of enrollment under a conversion health plan otherwise generally available under the plan.

(3) Qualifying event.— For purposes of this subsection, the term "qualifying event means, with respect to any covered employee, any of the following events which, but for the continuation coverage required under this subsection, would result in the loss of coverage of a qualified beneficiary—

(A) The death of the covered employee.

(B) The termination (other than by reason of such employee's gross misconduct), or reduction of hours, of the covered employee's employment.

(C) The divorce or legal separation of the covered employee from the employee's spouse.

(D) The covered employee becoming entitled to benefits under title XVIII of the Social Security Act.

(E) A dependent child ceasing to be a dependent child under the generally applicable requirements of the plan.

(F) A proceeding in a case under title 11, United States Code, commencing on or after July 1, 1986, with respect to the employer from whose employment the covered employee retired at any time.

In the case of an event described in subparagraph (F), a loss of coverage includes a substantial elimination of coverage with respect to a qualified beneficiary described in subsection (g)(1)(D) within one year before or after the date of commencement of the proceeding.

(4) Applicable premium.—For purposes of this subsection—

(A) In general.—The term "applicable premium" means, with respect to any period of continuation coverage of qualified beneficiaries, the cost to the plan for such period of the coverage for similarly situated beneficiaries with respect to whom a qualifying event has not occurred (without regard to whether such cost is paid by the employer or employee).

(B) Special rule for self-insured plans.— To the extent that a plan is a self-insured plan—

(i) In general.— Except as provided in clause (ii), the applicable premium for any period of continuation coverage of qualified beneficiaries shall be equal to a reasonable estimate of the cost of providing coverage for such period for similarly situated beneficiaries which—

(I) is determined on an actuarial basis, and

(II) takes into account such factors as the Secretary may prescribe in regulations.

(ii) Determination on basis of past cost.— If a plan administrator elects to have this clause apply, the applicable premium for any period of continuation coverage of qualified beneficiaries shall be equal to—

(I) the cost to the plan for similarly situated beneficiaries for the same period occurring during the preceding determination period under subparagraph (C), adjusted by

(II) the percentage increase or decrease in the implicit price deflator of the gross national product (calculated by the Department of Commerce and published in the Survey of Current Business) for the 12-month period ending on the last day of the sixth month of such preceding determination period.

(iii) Clause (ii) not to apply where significant change.— A plan administrator may not elect to have clause (ii) apply in any case in which there is any significant difference between the determination period and the preceding determination period, in coverage under, or in employees covered by, the plan. The determination under the preceding sentence for any determination period shall be made at the same time as the determination under subparagraph (C).

(C) Determination period.— The determination of any applicable premium shall be made for a period of 12 months and shall be made before the beginning of such period.

(5) Election.—For purposes of this subsection—

(A) Election period.— The term "election period" means the period which—

(i) begins not later than the date on which coverage terminates under the plan by reason of a qualifying event,

(ii) is of at least 60 days' duration, and

(iii) ends not earlier than 60 days after the later of—

(I) the date described in clause (i), or

(II) in the case of any qualified beneficiary who receives notice under paragraph (6)(D), the date of such notice.

(B) Effect of election on other beneficiaries.— Except as otherwise specified in an election, any election of continuation coverage by a qualified beneficiary described in subparagraph (A)(i) or (B) of subsection (g)(1) shall be deemed to include an election of continuation coverage on behalf of any other qualified beneficiary who would lose coverage under the plan by reason of the qualifying event. If there is a choice among types of coverage under the plan, each qualified beneficiary is entitled to make a separate selection among such types of coverage.

(6) Notice requirement.— In accordance with regulations prescribed by the Secretary—

(A) The group health plan shall provide, at the time of commencement of coverage under the plan, written notice to each covered employee and spouse of the employee (if any) of the rights provided under this subsection.

(B) The employer of an employee under a plan must notify the plan administrator of a qualifying event described in subparagraph (A), (B), (D), or (F) of paragraph (3) with respect to such employee within 30 days (or, in the case of a group health plan which is a multiemployer plan, such longer period of

IRC Sec. 4980B (f)(6)(B)

time as may be provided in the terms of the plan) of the date of the qualifying event.

(C) Each covered employee or qualified beneficiary is responsible for notifying the plan administrator of the occurrence of any qualifying event described in subparagraph (C) or (E) of paragraph (3) within 60 days after the date of the qualifying event and each qualified beneficiary who is determined, under title II or XVI of the Social Security Act, to have been disabled at the time of a qualifying event described in paragraph (3)(B) is responsible for notifying the plan administrator of such determination within 60 days after the date of the determination and for notifying the plan administrator within 30 days of the date of any final determination under such title or titles that the qualified beneficiary is no longer disabled.

(D) The plan administrator shall notify—

(i) in the case of a qualifying event described in subparagraph (A), (B), (D), or (F) of paragraph (3), any qualified beneficiary with respect to such event, and

(ii) in the case of a qualifying event described in subparagraph (C) or (E) of paragraph (3) where the covered employee notifies the plan administrator under subparagraph (C), any qualified beneficiary with respect to such event, of such beneficiary's rights under this subsection.

The requirements of subparagraph (B) shall be considered satisfied in the case of a multiemployer plan in connection with a qualifying event described in paragraph (3)(B) if the plan provides that the determination of the occurrence of such qualifying event will be made by the plan administrator. For purposes of subparagraph (D), any notification shall be made within 14 days (or, in the case of a group health plan which is a multiemployer plan, such longer period of time as may be provided in the terms of the plan) of the date on which the plan administrator is notified under subparagraph (B) or (C),

whichever is applicable, and any such notification to an individual who is a qualified beneficiary as the spouse of the covered employee shall be treated as notification to all other qualified beneficiaries residing with such spouse at the time such notification is made.

(7) Covered employee.— For purposes of this subsection, the term "covered employee" means an individual who is (or was) provided coverage under a group health plan by virtue of the performance of services by the individual for 1 or more persons maintaining the plan (including as an employee defined in section 401(c)(1)).

(8) Optional extension of required periods.— A group health plan shall not be treated as failing to meet the requirements of this subsection solely because the plan provides both—

(A) that the period of extended coverage referred to in paragraph (2)(B) commences with the date of the loss of coverage, and

(B) that the applicable notice period provided under paragraph (6)(B) commences with the date of the loss of coverage.

(g) Definitions.— For purposes of this section—

(1) Qualified beneficiary.—

(A) In general.— The term "qualified beneficiary" means, with respect to a covered employee under a group health plan, any other individual who, on the day before the qualifying event for that employee, is a beneficiary under the plan—

(i) as the spouse of the covered employee, or

(ii) as the dependent child of the employee.

(B) Special rule for terminations and reduced employment.— In the case of a qualifying event described in subsection (f)(3)(B), the term "qualified beneficiary" includes the covered employee.

(C) Exception for nonresident aliens.— Notwithstanding subparagraphs (A) and (B), the term "qualified beneficiary" does not include an individual whose status as a covered employee is attributable to a period in which such individual was a nonresident alien who received no earned income (within the meaning of section 911(d)(2)) from the employer which constituted income from sources within the United States (within the meaning of section 861(a)(3)). If an individual is not a qualified beneficiary pursuant to the previous sentence, a spouse or dependent child of such individual shall not be considered a qualified beneficiary by virtue of the relationship of the individual.

(D) Special rule for retirees and widows.— In the case of a qualifying event described in subsection (f)(3)(F), the term "qualified beneficiary" includes a covered employee who had retired on or before the date of substantial elimination of coverage and any other individual who, on the day before such qualifying event, is a beneficiary under the plan—

(i) as the spouse of the covered employee,

(ii) as the dependent child of the covered employee, or

(iii) as the surviving spouse of the covered employee.

(2) Group health plan.— The term "group health plan" has the meaning given such term by section 5000(b)(1).

(3) Plan administrator.— The term "plan administrator" has the meaning given the term "administrator" by section 3(16)(A) of the Employee Retirement Income Security Act of 1974.

(4) Correction.— A failure of a group health plan to meet the requirements of subsection (f) with respect to any qualified beneficiary shall be treated as corrected if—

(A) such failure is retroactively undone to the extent possible, and

(B) the qualified beneficiary is placed in a financial position which is as good as such beneficiary would have been in had such failure not occurred.

For purposes of applying subparagraph (B), the qualified beneficiary shall be treated as if he had elected the most favorable coverage in light of the expenses he incurred since the failure first occurred.

* * *

Chapter 47— Certain Group Health Plans

* * *

SEC. 5000. CERTAIN GROUP HEALTH PLANS.

(a) Imposition of Tax.— There is hereby imposed on any employer (including a self-employed person) or employee organization that contributes to a nonconforming group health plan a tax equal to 25 percent of the employer's or employee organization's expenses incurred during the calendar year for each group health plan to which the employer (including a self-employed person) or employee organization contributes.

(b) Group Health Plan and Large Group Health Plan.— For purposes of this section,—

(1) Group health plan.— The term "group health plan" means a plan (including a self-insured plan) of, or contributed to by, an employer (including a self-employed person) or employee organization to provide health care (directly or otherwise) to the employees, former employees, the employer, others associated with the employer in a business relationship, or their families.

(2) Large group health plan.— The term "large group health plan" means a plan of, or contributed to by, an employer or employee organization (including a self-insured plan) to provide health care (directly or otherwise) to the employees, former employees, the em-

ployer, others associated or formerly associated with the employer in a business relationship, or their families, that covers employees of at least one employer that normally employed at least 100 employees on a typical business day during the previous calendar year. For purposes of the preceding sentence—

(A) all employers treated as a single employer under subsection (a) or (b) of section 52 shall be treated as a single employer.

(B) all employees of the members of an affiliated service group (as defined in section 414(m)) shall be treated as employed by a single employer, and

(C) leased employees (as defined in section 414(n)(2)) shall be treated as employees of the person for whom they perform services to the extent they are so treated under section 414(n).

(c) Nonconforming Group Health Plan.— For purposes of this section, the term "nonconforming group health plan" means a group health plan or large group health plan that at any time during a calendar year does not comply with the requirements of subparagraphs (A) and (C) or subparagraph (B), respectively, of paragraph (1), or with the requirements of paragraph (2), of section 1862(b) of the Social Security Act.

(d) Government Entities.— For purposes of this section, the term "employer" does not include a Federal or other governmental entity.

* * *

Subtitle F— Procedure And Administration

* * *

Chapter 61— Information And Returns

* * *

Subchapter A— Returns And Records

* * *

Part III— Information Returns

* * *

Subpart B— Information Concerning Transactions With Other Persons

* * *

SEC. 6039D. RETURNS AND RECORDS WITH RESPECT TO CERTAIN FRINGE BENEFIT PLANS.

(a) In General.— Every employer maintaining a specified fringe benefit plan during any year beginning after December 31, 1984, for any portion of which the applicable exclusion applies, shall file a return (at such time and in such manner as the Secretary shall by regulations prescribe) with respect to such plan showing for such year—

(1) the number of employees of the employer,

(2) the number of employees of the employer eligible to participate under the plan,

(3) the number of employees participating under the plan,

(4) the total cost of the plan during the year,

(5) the name, address, and taxpayer identification number of the employer and the type of business in which the employer is engaged, and

(6) the number of highly compensated employees among the employees described in paragraphs (1), (2), and (3).

(b) Recordkeeping Requirement.— Each employer maintaining a specified fringe benefit plan during any year shall keep such records as may be necessary for purposes of determining whether the requirements of the applicable exclusion are met.

(c) Additional Information When Required by the Secretary.— Any employer—

(1) who maintains a specified fringe benefit plan during any year for which a return is required under subsection (a), and

(2) who is required by the Secretary to file an additional return for such year,

shall file such additional return. Such additional return shall be filed at such time and in such manner as the Secretary shall prescribe and shall contain such information as the Secretary shall prescribe.

The Secretary may require returns under this subsection only from a representative group of employers.

(d) Definitions and Special Rules.— For purposes of this section.—

(1) **Specified fringe benefit plan.**— The term "specified fringe benefit plan" means any plan under section 79, 105, 106, 120, 125, 127, or 129.

(2) **Applicable exclusion.**— The term "applicable exclusion" means, with respect to any specified fringe benefit plan, the section specified under paragraph (1) under which benefits under such plan are excludable from gross income.

(3) **Special rule for multiemployer plans.**— In the case of a multiemployer plan, the plan shall be required to provide any information required by this section which the Secretary determines, on the basis of the agreement between the plan and employer, is held by the plan (and not the employer).

SEC. 6047. INFORMATION RELATING TO CERTAIN TRUSTS AND ANNUITY PLANS.

(a) Trustees and Insurance Companies.— The trustee of a trust described in section 401(a) which is exempt from tax under section 501(a) to which contributions have been paid under a plan on behalf of any owner-employee (as defined in section 401(c)(3)), and each insurance company or other person which is the issuer of a contract purchased by such a trust, or purchased under a plan described in section 403(a), contributions for which have been paid on behalf of any owner-employee, shall file such returns (in such form and at such times), keep such records, make such identification of contracts and funds (and accounts within such funds), and supply such information, as the Secretary shall by forms or regulations prescribe.

(b) Owner-Employees.— Every individual on whose behalf contributions have been paid as an owner-employee (as defined in section 401(c)(3))—

(1) to a trust described in section 401(a) which is exempt from tax under section 501(a), or

(2) to an insurance company or other person under a plan described in section 403(a),

shall furnish the trustee, insurance company, or other person, as the case may be, such information at such times and in such form and manner as the Secretary shall prescribe by forms or regulations.

(c) Other Programs.— To the extent provided by regulations prescribed by the Secretary, the provisions of this section apply with respect to any payment described in section 219 and to transaction of any trust described in section 408(a) or under an individual retirement annuity described in section 408(b).

IRC Sec. 6047 (c)

(d) Reports by Employers, Plan Administrators, Etc.—

(1) In general.— The Secretary shall by forms or regulations require that—

(A) the employer maintaining, or the plan administrator (within the meaning of section 414(g)) of, a plan from which designated distributions (as defined in section 3405(e)(1)/section 3405(d)(3)) may be made, and

(B) any person issuing any contract under which designated distributions (as so defined) may be made,

make returns and reports regarding such plan (or contract) to the Secretary, to the participants and beneficiaries of such plan (or contract), and to such other persons as the Secretary may by regulations prescribe.

(2) Form, etc., of reports.— Such reports shall be in such form, made at such time, and contain such information as the Secretary may prescribe by forms or regulations.

(e) Employee Stock Ownership Plans.— The Secretary shall require—

(1) any employer maintaining, or the plan administrator (within the meaning of section 414(g)) of, an employee stock ownership plan—

(A) which acquired stock in a transaction to which section 133 applies, or

(B) which holds stock with respect to which section 404(k) applies to dividends paid on such stock,

(2) any person making or holding a loan to which section 133 applies, or

(3) both such employer or plan administrator and such person, to make returns and reports regarding such plan, transaction, or loan to the Secretary and to such other persons as the Secretary may prescribe. Such returns and reports shall be made in such form, shall be

made at such time, and shall contain such information as the Secretary may prescribe.

(f) Cross References.—

(1) For provisions relating to penalties for failure to file a return required by this section, see section 6652(e).

(2) For criminal penalty for furnishing fradulent information, see section 7207.

(3) For provisions relating to penalty for failure to comply with the provisions of subsection (d), see section 6704.

Subpart E— Registration of and Information Concerning Pension, Etc., Plans

SEC. 6057. ANNUAL REGISTRATION, ETC.

Editor's Note: Section 108(h)(5) of P.L. 103-296, the Social Security Administrative Reform Act of 1994, replaced the references to "Secretary of Health and Human Services" in §6057(d) and (f)(1) with a reference to the "Commissioner of Social Security," in accordance with the provisions of that act which established the Social Security Administration as a separate governmental agency. The change is effective March 31, 1995.

◊ ◊ ◊

(a) Annual Registration.—

(1) General rule.— Within such period after the end of a plan year as the Secretary may by regulations prescribe, the plan administrator (within the meaning of section 414(g)) of each plan to which the vesting standards of section 203 of part 2 of subtitle B of title I of the Employee Retirement Income Security Act of 1974 applies for such plan year shall file a registration statement with the Secretary.

(2) Contents.— The registration statement required by paragraph (1) shall set forth—

(A) the name of the plan,

(B) the name and address of the plan administrator,

(C) the name and taxpayer identifying number of each participant in the plan—

(i) who, during such plan year, separated from the service covered by the plan,

(ii) who is entitled to a deferred vested benefit under the plan as of the end of such plan year, and

(iii) with respect to whom retirement benefits were not paid under the plan during such plan year,

(D) the nature, amount and form of the deferred vested benefit to which such participant is entitled, and

(E) such other information as the Secretary may require.

At the time he files the registration statement under this subsection, the plan administrator shall furnish evidence satisfactory to the Secretary that he has complied with the requirement contained in subsection (e).

(b) Notification of Change in Status.—Any plan administrator required to register under subsection (a) shall also notify the Secretary, at such times as may be prescribed by regulations, of—

(1) any change in the name of the plan,

(2) any change in the name or address of the plan administrator,

(3) the termination of the plan, or

(4) the merger or consolidation of the plan with any other plan or its division into two or more plans.

(c) Voluntary Reports.—To the extent provided in regulations prescribed by the Secretary, the Secretary may receive from—

(1) any plan to which subsection (a) applies, and

(2) any other plan (including any governmental plan or church plan (within the meaning of section 414)),

such information (including information relating to plan years beginning before January 1, 1974) as the plan administrator may wish to file with respect to the deferred vested benefit rights of any participant separated from the service covered by the plan during any plan year.

(d) Transmission of Information to Secretary of Health and Human Services.— The Secretary shall transmit copies of any statements, notifications, reports, or other information obtained by him under this section to the *Commissioner of Social Security* [Secretary of Health and Human Services].

(e) Individual Statement to Participant.— Each plan administrator required to file a registration statement under subsection (a) shall, before the expiration of the time prescribed for the filing of such registration statement, also furnish to each participant described in subsection (a)(2)(C) an individual statement setting forth the information with respect to such participant required to be contained in such registration statement. Such statement shall also include a notice to the participant of any benefits which are forfeitable if the participant dies before a certain date.

(f) Regulations.—

(1) In general.— The Secretary, after consultation with the *Commissioner of Social Security* [Secretary of Health and Human Services], may prescribe such regulations as may be necessary to carry out the provisions of this section.

(2) Plans to which more than one employer contributes.—This section shall apply to any plan to which more than one employer is required to contribute only to the extent provided in regulations prescribed under this subsection.

IRC Sec. 6057 (f)(2)

(g) Cross References.—
For provisions relating to penalties for failure to register or furnish statements required by this section, see section 6652(d) and section 6690.

For coordination between Department of the Treasury and the Department of Labor with regard to administration of this section see section 3004 of the Employee Retirement Income Security Act of 1974.

SEC. 6058. INFORMATION REQUIRED IN CONNECTION WITH CERTAIN PLANS OF DEFERRED COMPENSATION.

(a) In General.—Every employer who maintains a pension, annuity, stock bonus, profit-sharing or other funded plan of deferred compensation described in part I of subchapter D of chapter 1, or the plan administrator (within the meaning of section 414(g)) of the plan, shall file an annual return stating such information as the Secretary may by regulations prescribe with respect to the qualification, financial condition, and operations of the plan; except that, in the discretion of the Secretary, the employer may be relieved from stating in its return any information which is reported in other returns.

(b) Actuarial Statement in Case of Mergers, Etc.—Not less than 30 days before a merger, consolidation, or transfer of assets or liabilities of a plan described in subsection (a) to another plan, the plan administrator (within the meaning of section 414(g)) shall file an actuarial statement of valuation evidencing compliance with the requirements of section 401(a)(12).

(c) Employer.—For purposes of this section, the term "employer" includes a person described in section 401(c)(4) and an individual who establishes an individual retirement plan.

(d) Coordination With Income Tax Returns, Etc.— An individual who establishes an individual retirement plan shall not be required to file a return under this section with respect to such plan for any taxable year for which there is—

(1) no special IRP tax, and

(2) no plan activity other than—

(A) the making of contributions (other than rollover contributions), and

(B) the making of distributions.

(e) Special IRP Tax Defined.— For purposes of this section, the term "special IRP tax" means a tax imposed by—

(1) section 408(f),

(2) section 4973, or

(3) section 4974.

(f) Cross References.—
For provisions relating to penalties for failure to file a return required by this section, see section 6652(e).

For coordination between the Department of the Treasury and the Department of Labor with respect to the information required under this section, see Section 3004 of title III of the Employee Retirement Income Security Act of 1974.

SEC. 6059. PERIODIC REPORT OF ACTUARY.

(a) General Rule.— The actuarial report described in subsection (b) shall be filed by the plan administrator (as defined in section 414(g)) of each defined benefit plan to which section 412 applies, for the first plan year for which section 412 applies to the plan and for each third plan year thereafter (or more frequently if the Secretary determines that more frequent reports are necessary).

(b) Actuarial Report.— The actuarial report of a plan required by subsection (a) shall be prepared and signed by an enrolled actuary (within the meaning of section 7701(a)(35)) and shall contain—

(1) a description of the funding method and actuarial assumptions used to determine costs under the plan,

(2) a certification of the contribution necessary to reduce the accumulated funding deficiency (as defined in section 412(a)) to zero,

(3) a statement—

(A) that to the best of his knowledge the report is complete and accurate, and

(B) the requirements of section 412(c) (relating to reasonable actuarial assumptions) have been complied with,

(4) such other information as may be necessary to fully and fairly disclose the actuarial position of the plan, and

(5) such other information regarding the plan as the Secretary may by regulations require.

(c) Time and Manner of Filing.— The actuarial report and statement required by this section shall be filed at the time and in the manner provided by regulations prescribed by the Secretary.

(d) Cross Reference.—

For coordination between the Department of the Treasury and the Department of Labor with respect to the report required to be filed under this section, see section 3004 of title III of the Employee Retirement Income Security Act of 1974.

* * *

Subchapter B— Miscellaneous Provisions

SEC. 6103. CONFIDENTIALITY AND DISCLOSURE OF RETURNS AND RETURN INFORMATION.

* * *

(2) Disclosure of returns and return information to the Department of Labor and Pension Benefit Guaranty Corporation.— The Secretary may, upon written request, fur-

nish returns and return information to the proper officers and employees of the Department of Labor and Pension Benefit Guaranty Corporation for purposes of, but only to the extent necessary in, the administration of titles I and IV of the Employee Retirement Income Security Act of 1974.

* * *

SEC. 6104. PUBLICITY OF INFORMATION REQUIRED FROM CERTAIN EXEMPT ORGANIZATIONS AND CERTAIN TRUSTS.

(a) Inspection of Applications for Tax Exemption.—

(1) Public Inspection.—

(A) Organizations described in section 501.— If an organization described in section 501(c) or (d) is exempt from taxation under section 501(a) for any taxable year, the application filed by the organization with respect to which the Secretary made his determination that such organization was entitled to exemption under section 501(a), together with any papers submitted in support of such application, and any letter or other document issued by the Internal Revenue Service with respect to such application shall be open to public inspection at the national office of the Internal Revenue Service. In the case of any application filed after the date of the enactment of this subparagraph, a copy of such application and such letter or document shall be open to public inspection at the appropriate field office of the Internal Revenue Service (determined under regulations prescribed by the Secretary). Any inspection under this subparagraph may be made at such times, and in such manner, as the Secretary shall by regulations prescribe. After the application of any organization has been opened to public inspection under this subparagraph, the Secretary shall, on the request of any person with respect to such organization, furnish a statement indicating the subsection and paragraph of section 501 which it has determined describes such organization.

(B) Pension, etc., plans.— The following shall be open to public inspection at such times and in such places as the Secretary may prescribe;

(i) any application filed with respect to the qualification of a pension, profit-sharing, or stock bonus plan under section 401(a) or 403(a), an individual retirement account described in section 408(a), or an individual retirement annuity described in section 408(b),

(ii) any application filed with respect to the exemption from tax under section 501(a) of an organization forming part of a plan or account referred to in clause (i),

(iii) any papers submitted in support of an application referred to in clause (i) or (ii), and

(iv) any letter or other document issued by the Internal Revenue Service and dealing with the qualification referred to in clause (i) or the exemption from tax referred to in clause (ii).

Except in the case of a plan participant, this subparagraph shall not apply to any plan referred to in clause (i) having not more than 25 participants.

(C) Certain names and compensation not to be opened to public inspection.—In the case of any application, document, or other papers, referred to in subparagraph (B), information from which the compensation (including deferred compensation) of any individual may be ascertained shall not be opened to public inspection under subparagraph (B).

(D) Withholding of certain other information.— Upon request of the organization submitting any supporting papers described in subparagraph (A) or (B), the Secretary shall withhold from public inspection any information contained therein which he de-

termines relates to any trade secret, patent, process, style of work, or apparatus, of the organization, if he determines that public disclosure of such information would adversely affect the organization. The Secretary shall withhold from public inspection any information contained in supporting papers described in subparagraph (A) or (B) the public disclosure of which he determines would adversely affect the national defense.

(2) Inspection by committee of Congress.— Section 6103(f) shall apply with respect to—

(A) the application for exemption of any organization described in section 501(c) or (d) which is exempt from taxation under section 501(a) for any taxable year, and any application referred to in subparagraph (B) of subsection (a)(1) of this section, and

(B) any other papers which are in the possession of the Secretary and which relate to such application,

as if such papers constituted returns.

(b) Inspection of Annual Information Returns.— The information required to be furnished by section 6033, 6034, and 6058, together with the names and addresses of such organizations and trusts, shall be made available to the public at such times and in such places as the Secretary may prescribe. Nothing in this subsection shall authorize the Secretary to disclose the name or address of any contributor to any organization or trust (other than a private foundation, as defined in section 509(a)) which is required to furnish such information.

(c) Publication to State Officials.—

(1) General rule.— In the case of any organization which is described in section 501(c)(3) and exempt from taxation under section 501(a), or has applied under section 508(a) for recognition as an organization described in section 501(c)(3), the Secretary at such times and in such manner as he may by regulations prescribe shall—

(A) notify the appropriate State officer of a refusal to recognize such organization as an organization described in section 501(c)(3), or of the operation of such organization in a manner which does not meet, or no longer meets, the requirements of its exemption,

(B) notify the appropriate State officer of the mailing of a notice of deficiency of tax imposed under section 507 or chapter 41 or 42, and

(C) at the request of such appropriate State officer, make available for inspection and copying such returns, filed statements, records, reports, and other information, relating to a determination under subparagraph (A) or (B) as are relevant to any determination under State law.

(2) Appropriate state officer.— For purposes of this subsection, the term "appropriate State officer" means the State attorney general, State tax officer, or any State official charged with overseeing organizations of the type described in section 501(c)(3).

(d) Public Inspection of Private Foundations' Annual Returns.— The annual return required to be filed under section 6033 (relating to returns by exempt organizations) by any organization which is a private foundation within the meaning of section 509(a) shall be made available by the foundation managers for inspection at the principal office of the foundation during the regular business hours by any citizen on request made within 180 days after the date of the publication of notice of its availability. Such notice shall be published, not later than the day prescribed for filing such annual return (determined with regard to any extension of time for filing), in a newspaper having general circulation in the county in which the principal office of the private foundation is located. The notice shall state that the annual return of the private foundation is available at its principal office for inspection during regular business hours by any citizen who requests it within 180 days after the date of such publication, and shall state the address and the telephone number of the private foun-

dation's principal office and the name of its principal manager.

(e) Public Inspection of Certain Annual Returns and Applications for Exemption.—

(1) Annual returns.—

(A) In general.— During the 3-year period beginning on the filing date, a copy of the annual return filed under section 6033 (relating to returns by exempt organizations) by any organization to which this paragraph applies shall be made available by such organization for inspection during regular business hours by any individual at the principal office of the organization and, if such organization regularly maintains 1 or more regional or district offices having 3 or more employees, at each such regional or district office.

(B) Organizations to which paragraph applies.—This paragraph shall apply to any organization which—

(i) is described in subsection (c) or (d) of section 501 and exempt from taxation under section 501(a), and

(ii) is not a private foundation (within the meaning of section 509(a)).

(C) Nondisclosure of contributors.— Subparagraph (A) shall not require the disclosure of the name or address of any contributor to the organization.

(D) Filing date.— For purposes of subparagraph (A), the term "filing date" means the last day prescribed for filing the return under section 6033 (determined with regard to any extension of time for filing).

(2) Application for exemption.—

(A) In general.—If—

(i) an organization described in subsection (c) or (d) of section 501 is exempt from taxation under section 501(a), and

(ii) such organization filed an application for recognition of exemption under section

IRC Sec. 6104 (e)(2)(A)(ii)

501, a copy of such application (together with a copy of any papers submitted in support of such application and any letter or other document issued by the Internal Revenue Service with respect to such application) shall be made available by the organization for inspection during regular business hours by any individual at the principal office of the organization and, if the organization regularly maintains 1 or more regional or district offices having 3 or more employees, at each such regional or district office.

(B) Nondisclosure of certain information.— Subparagraph (A) shall not require the disclosure of any information if the Secretary withheld such information from public inspection under subsection (a)(1)(D).

Chapter 68— Additions To The Tax, Additional Amounts, And Assessable Penalties

Subchapter A— Additions To The Tax And Additional Amounts

SEC. 6652. FAILURE TO FILE CERTAIN INFORMATION RETURNS, REGISTRATION STATEMENTS, ETC.

* * *

(d) Annual Registration and Other Notification by Pension Plan.—

(1) Registration.— In the case of any failure to file a registration statement required under section 6057(a) (relating to annual registration of certain plans) which includes all participants required to be included in such statement, on the date prescribed therefor (determined without regard to any extension of time for filing), unless it is shown that such failure is due to reasonable cause, there shall be paid (on notice and demand by the Secretary and in the same manner as tax) by the person failing so to file, an amount equal to $1 for each participant with respect to whom there is a failure to file, multiplied by the number of days during which such failure

continues, but the total amount imposed under this paragraph on any person for any failure to file with respect to any plan year shall not exceed $5,000.

(2) Notification of change of status.— In the case of failure to file a notification required under section 6057(b) (relating to notification of change of status) on the date prescribed therefor (determined without regard to any extension of time for filing), unless it is shown that such failure is due to reasonable cause, there shall be paid (on notice and demand by the Secretary in the same manner as tax) by the person failing so to file, $1 for each day during which such failure continues, but the total amounts imposed under this paragraph on any person for failure to file any notification shall not exceed $1,000.

(e) Information Required in Connection with Certain Plans of Deferred Compensation; Etc.— In the case of failure to file a return or statement required under section 6058 (relating to information required in connection with certain plans of deferred compensation), 6047 (relating to information relating to certain trusts and annuity and bond purchase plans), or 6039D (relating to returns and records with respect to certain fringe benefit plans) on the date and in the manner prescribed therefor (determined with regard to any extension of time for filing), unless it is shown that such failure is due to reasonable cause, there shall be paid (on notice and demand by the Secretary and in the same manner as tax) by the person failing so to file, $25 for each day during which such failure continues, but the total amount imposed under this subsection on any person for failure to file any return shall not exceed $15,000.

* * *

(g) Information Required in Connection with Deductible Employee Contributions.— In the case of failure to make a report required by section 219(f)(4) which contains the information required by such section on the date prescribed therefor (determined with regard to any extension of time for filing) there shall be paid (on notice and demand by the Secretary and in the same manner as tax) by the person failing so to file, an amount equal to $25 for each participant with respect to whom there was a failure to file such information, multiplied by the number of years during which such failure continues, but the total amount imposed under this subsection on any person for failure to file shall not exceed $10,000.

(h) Failure to Give Notice to Recipients of Certain Pension, Etc., Distributions.— In the case of each failure to provide a notice as required by section 3405(e)(10)(B), at the time prescribed therefor, unless it is shown that such failure is due to reasonable cause and not to willful neglect, there shall be paid, on notice and demand of the Secretary and in the same manner as tax, by the person failing to provide such notice, an amount equal to $10 for each such failure, but the total amount imposed on such person for all such failures during any calendar year shall not exceed $5,000.

(i) Failure to Give Written Explanation to Recipients of Certain Qualifying Rollover Distributions.— In the case of each failure to provide a written explanation as required by section 401(f), at the time prescribed therefor, unless it is shown that such failure is due to reasonable cause and not to willful neglect, there shall be paid, on notice and demand of the Secretary and in the same manner as tax, by the person failing to provide such written explanation, an amount equal to $10 for each such failure, but the total amount imposed on such person for all such failures during any calendar year shall not exceed $5,000.

* * *

SEC. 6659A. ADDITION TO TAX IN CASE OF OVERSTATEMENTS OF PENSION LIABILITIES. [Repealed]

* * *

SEC. 6662. IMPOSITION OF ACCURACY-RELATED PENALTY.

(a) Imposition of Penalty.— If this section applies to any portion of an underpayment of tax required to be shown on a return, there shall be added to the tax an amount equal to 20 percent of the portion of the underpayment to which this section applies.

(b) Portion of Underpayment to Which Section Applies.— This section shall apply to the portion of any underpayment which is attributable to 1 or more of the following:

(1) Negligence or disregard of rules or regulations.—

* * *

(4) Any substantial overstatement of pension liabilities.—This section shall not apply to any portion of an underpayment on which a penalty is imposed under section 6663.

(c) Negligence.— For purposes of this section, the term "negligence" includes any failure to make a reasonable attempt to comply with the provisions of this title, and the term "disregard" includes any careless, reckless, or intentional disregard.

* * *

(f) Substantial Overstatement of Pension Liabilities.—

(1) In general.— For purposes of this section, there is a substantial overstatement of pension liabilities if the actuarial determination of the liabilities taken into account for purposes of computing the deduction under paragraph (1) or (2) of section 404(a) is 200 percent or more of the amount determined to be the correct amount of such liabilities.

(2) Limitation.—No penalty shall be imposed by reason of subsection (b)(4) unless the portion of the underpayment for the taxable year attributable to substantial overstatements of pension liabilities exceeds $1,000.

* * *

SEC. 6663. IMPOSITION OF FRAUD PENALTY.

(a) Imposition of Penalty.— If any part of any underpayment of tax required to be shown on a return is due to fraud, there shall be added to the tax an amount equal to 75 percent of the portion of the underpayment which is attributable to fraud.

(b) Determination of Portion Attributable to Fraud.— If the Secretary establishes that any portion of an underpayment is attributable to fraud, the entire underpayment shall be treated as attributable to fraud, except with respect to any portion of the underpayment which the taxpayer establishes (by a preponderance of the evidence) is not attributable to fraud.

* * *

Subchapter B— Assessable Penalties

* * *

SEC. 6690. FRAUDULENT STATEMENT OR FAILURE TO FURNISH STATEMENT TO PLAN PARTICIPANT.

Any person required under section 6057(e) to furnish a statement to a participant who willfully furnishes a false or fraudulent statement, or who willfully fails to furnish a statement in the manner, at the time, and showing the information required under section 6057(e), or regulations prescribed thereunder, shall for each such act, or for each such failure, be subject to a penalty under this subchapter of $50, which shall be assessed and collected

in the same manner as the tax on employers imposed by section 3111.

SEC. 6692. FAILURE TO FILE ACTUARIAL REPORT.

The plan administrator (as defined in section 414(g)) of each defined benefit plan to which section 412 applies who fails to file the report required by section 6059 at the time and in the manner required by section 6059, shall pay a penalty of $1,000 for each such failure unless it is shown that such failure is due to reasonable cause.

SEC. 6693. FAILURE TO PROVIDE REPORTS ON INDIVIDUAL RETIREMENT ACCOUNTS OR ANNUITIES; PENALTIES RELATING TO DESIGNATED NONDEDUCTIBLE CONTRIBUTIONS.

(a) The person required by subsection (i) or (*l*) of section 408 to file a report regarding an individual retirement account or individual retirement annuity at the time and in the manner required by such subsection shall pay a penalty of $50 for each failure unless it is shown that such failure is due to reasonable cause.

(b) Penalties Relating to Nondeductible Contributions.—

(1) Overstatement of Designated Nondeductible Contributions.— Any individual who—

(A) is required to furnish information under section 408(o)(4) as to the amount of designated nondeductible contributions made for any taxable year, and

(B) overstates the amount of such contributions made for such taxable year, shall pay a penalty of $100 for each such overstatement unless it is shown that such overstatement is due to reasonable cause.

(2) Failure to File Form.—Any individual who fails to file a form required to be filed b the Secretary under section 408(o)(4) shall pay a penalty of $50 for each such failure unless it is shown that such failure is due to reasonable cause.

(c) Deficiency Procedures Not to Apply.— Subchapter B of chapter 63 (relating to deficiency procedures for income, estate, gift, and certain excise tax) does not apply to the assessment or collection of any penalty imposed by this section.

* * *

SEC. 6704. FAILURE TO KEEP RECORDS NECESSARY TO MEET REPORTING REQUIREMENTS UNDER SECTION 6047(d).

(a) Liability for Penalty.— Any person who—

(1) has a duty to report or may have a duty to report any information under section 6047(d), and

(2) fails to keep such records as may be required by regulations prescribed under section 6047(d) for the purpose of providing the necessary data base for either current reporting or future reporting,

shall pay a penalty for each calendar year for which there is any failure to keep such records.

(b) Amount of Penalty.—

(1) In general.— The penalty of any person for any calendar year shall be $50, multiplied by the number of individuals with respect to whom such failure occurs in such year.

(2) Maximum amount.— The penalty under this section of any person for any calendar year shall not exceed $50,000.

(c) Exceptions.—

(1) Reasonable cause.— No penalty shall be imposed by this section on any person for any failure which is shown to be due to reasonable cause and not to willful neglect.

(2) Inability to correct previous failure.— No penalty shall be imposed by this section on any failure by a person if such failure is attributable to a prior failure which has been penalized under this section and with respect to which the person has made all reasonable efforts to correct the failure.

(3) Pre-1983 failures.— No penalty shall be imposed by this section on any person for any failure which is attributable to a failure occurring before January 1, 1983, if the person has made all reasonable efforts to correct such pre-1983 failure.

* * *

Chapter 76—Judicial Proceedings
* * *

Subchapter B— Proceedings by Taxpayers and Third Parties
* * *

SEC. 7422. CIVIL ACTIONS FOR REFUND.

(a) No suit prior to filing claim for refund.—No suit or proceeding shall be maintained in any court for the recovery of any internal revenue tax alleged to have been erroneously or illegally assessed or collected, or of any penalty claimed to have been collected without authority, or of any sum alleged to have been excessive or in any manner wrongfully collected, until a claim for refund or credit has been duly filed with the Secretary, according to the provisions of law in that regard, and the regulations of the Secretary established in pursuance thereof.

(b) Protest or duress.— Such suit or proceeding may be maintained whether or not such tax, penalty, or sum has been paid under protest or duress.

(c) Suits against collection officer a bar.— A suit against any officer or employee of the United States (or former officer or employee) or his personal representative for the recovery of any internal revenue tax alleged to have been erroneously or illegally assessed or collected, or of any penalty claimed to have been collected without authority, or of any sum alleged to have been excessive or in any manner wrongfully collected shall be treated as if the United States had been a party to such suit in applying the doctrine of res judicata in all suits in respect of any internal revenue tax, and in all proceedings in the Tax Court and on review of decisions of the Tax Court.

(d) Credit treated as payment.— The credit of an overpayment of any tax in satisfaction of any tax liability shall, for the purpose of any suit for refund of such tax liability so satisfied, be deemed to be a payment in respect of such tax liability at the time such credit is allowed.

(e) Stay of proceedings.— If the Secretary prior to the hearing of a suit brought by a taxpayer in a district court or the United States Claims Court for the recovery of any income tax, estate tax, gift tax, or tax imposed by chapter 41, 42, 43, or 44 (or any penalty relating to such taxes) mails to the taxpayer a notice that a deficiency has been determined in respect of the tax which is the subject matter of taxpayer's suit, the proceedings in taxpayer's suit shall be stayed during the period of time in which the taxpayer may file a petition with the Tax Court for a redetermination of the asserted deficiency, and for 60 days thereafter. If the taxpayer files a petition with the Tax Court, the district court or the United States Claims Court, as the case may be, shall lose jurisdiction of taxpayer's suit to whatever extent jurisdiction is acquired by the Tax Court of the subject matter of taxpayer's suit for refund. If the taxpayer does not file a petition with the Tax Court for a redetermination of the asserted deficiency, the United States may counterclaim in the taxpayer's suit, or intervene in the event of a suit as described in subsection (c) (relating to suits against officers or employees of the United States), within the period of the stay of proceedings notwithstanding that the time for such pleading may have otherwise expired. The taxpayer shall have the burden of proof with respect to the issues raised by such counterclaim or intervention of the United States except as to the issue of whether the taxpayer has been guilty of fraud with intent to evade tax. This subsection shall not apply to a suit by a taxpayer which, prior to the date of enactment of this title, is commenced, instituted, or pending in a district court or the United States Claims Court for the recovery of any income tax, estate tax, or gift tax (or any penalty relating to such taxes).

(f) Limitation on right of action for refund.—

(1) General rule.— A suit or proceeding referred to in subsection (a) may be maintained only against the United States and not against any officer or employee of the United States (or former officer or employee) or his personal representative. Such suit or proceeding may be maintained against the United States notwithstanding the provisions of section 2502 of title 28 of the United States Code (relating to aliens' privilege to sue) and notwithstanding the provisions of section 1502 of such title 28 (relating to certain treaty cases).

(2) Misjoinder and change of venue.— If a suit or proceeding brought in a United States district court against an officer or employee of the United States (or former officer or employee) or his personal representative is improperly brought solely by virtue of paragraph (1), the court shall order, upon such terms as are just, that the pleadings be amended to substitute the United States as a party for such officer or employee as of the time such action commenced, upon proper service of process on the United States. Such suit or proceeding shall upon request by the United States be transferred to the district or division where it should have been brought if such action initially had been brought against the United States.

(g) Special rules for certain excise taxes imposed by chapter 42 or 43.—

(1) Right to bring actions.—

(A) In general.— With respect to any taxable event, payment of the full amount of the first tier tax shall constitute sufficient payment in order to maintain an action under this section with respect to the second tier tax.

IRC Sec. 7422 (d)

(B) Definitions.— For purposes of subparagraph (A), the terms "taxable event", "first tier tax", and "second tier tax" have the respective meanings given to such terms by section 4963.

(2) Limitation on suit for refund.— No suit may be maintained under this section for the credit or refund of any tax imposed under section 4941, 4942, 4943, 4944, 4945, 4951, 4952, 4955, 4971, or 4975 with respect to any act (or failure to act) giving rise to liability for tax under such sections, unless no other suit has been maintained for credit or refund of, and no petition has been filed in the Tax Court with respect to a deficiency in, any other tax imposed by such sections with respect to such act (or failure to act).

(3) Final determination of issues.— For purposes of this section, any suit for the credit or refund of any tax imposed under section 4941, 4942, 4943, 4944, 4945, 4951, 4952, 4955, 4971, or 4975 with respect to any act (or failure to act) giving rise to liability for tax under such sections, shall constitute a suit to determine all questions with respect to any other tax imposed with respect to such act (or failure to act) under such sections, and failure by the parties to such suit to bring any such question before the Court shall constitute a bar to such question.

(h) Special rule for actions with respect to partnership items.— No action may be brought for a refund attributable to partnership items (as defined in section 6231(a)(3)) except as provided in section 6228(b) or section 6230(c).

(i) Special rule for actions with respect to tax shelter promoter and understatement penalties.— No action or proceeding may be brought in the United States Claims Court for any refund or credit of a penalty imposed by section 6700 (relating to penalty for promoting abusive tax shelters, etc.) or section 6701 (relating to penalties for aiding and abetting understatement of tax liability).

(j) Cross references.—

(1) For provisions relating generally to claims for refund or credit, see chapter 65 (relating to abatements, credit, and refund) and chapter 66 (relating to limitations).

(2) For duty of United States attorneys to defend suits, see section 507 of Title 28 of the United States Code.

(3) For jurisdiction of United States district courts, see section 1346 of Title 28 of the United States Code.

(4) For payment by the Treasury of judgments against internal revenue officers or employees, upon certificate of probable cause, see section 2006 of Title 28 of the United States Code.

* * *

Subchapter C— The Tax Court

* * *

Part IV— Declaratory Judgments

SEC. 7476. DECLARATORY JUDGMENTS RELATING TO QUALIFICATION OF CERTAIN RETIREMENT PLANS.

(a) Creation of Remedy.— In the case of actual controversy involving—

(1) a determination by the Secretary with respect to the initial qualification or continuing qualification of a retirement plan under subchapter D of chapter 1, or

(2) a failure by the Secretary to make a determination with respect to—

(A) such initial qualification, or

(B) such continuing qualification if the controversy arises from a plan amendment or plan termination,

upon the filing of an appropriate pleading, the Tax Court may make a declaration with respect to such initial qualification or continuing qualification. Any such declaration shall have the force and effect of a decision of the Tax Court and shall be reviewable as such. For purposes of this section, a determination with respect to a continuing qualification includes any revocation of or other change in a qualification.

(b) Limitations.—

(1) Petitioner.— A pleading may be filed under this section only by a petitioner who is the employer, the plan administrator, an employee who has qualified under regulations prescribed by the Secretary as an interested party for purposes of pursuing administrative remedies within the Internal Revenue Service, or the Pension Benefit Guaranty Corporation.

(2) Notice.— For purposes of this section, the filing of a pleading by any petitioner may be held by the Tax Court to be premature, unless the petitioner establishes to the satisfaction of the court that he has complied with the requirements prescribed by regulations of the Secretary with respect to notice to other interested parties of the filing of the request for a determination referred to in subsection (a).

(3) Exhaustion of administrative remedies.— The Tax Court shall not issue a declaratory judgment or decree under this section in any proceeding unless it determines that the petitioner has exhausted administrative remedies available to him within the Internal Revenue Service. A petitioner shall not be deemed to have exhausted his administrative remedies with respect to failure by the Secretary to make a determination with respect to initial qualification or continuing qualification of a retirement plan before the expiration of 270 days after the request for such determination was made.

(4) Plan put into effect.— No proceeding may be maintained under this section unless the plan (and, in the case of a controversy involving the continuing qualification of the plan because of an amendment to the plan, the amendment) with respect to which a decision of the Tax Court is sought has been put into effect before the filing of the pleading. A plan

or amendment shall not be treated as not being in effect merely because under the plan the funds contributed to the plan may be refunded if the plan (or the plan as so amended) is found to be not qualified.

(5) Time for bringing action.— If the Secretary sends by certified or registered mail notice of his determination with respect to the qualification of the plan to the persons referred to in paragraph (1) (or, in the case of employees referred to in paragraph (1), to any individual designated under regulations prescribed by the Secretary as a representative of such employee), no proceeding may be initiated under this section by any person unless the pleading is filed before the ninety-first day after the day after such notice is mailed to such person (or to his designated representative, in the case of an employee).

(c) Retirement Plan.— For purposes of this section, the term "retirement plan" means—

(1) a pension, profit-sharing, or stock bonus plan described in section 401(a) or a trust which is part of such a plan, or

(2) an annuity plan described in section 403(a).

(d) Cross Reference.—For provisions concerning intervention by Pension Benefit Guaranty Corporation and Secretary of Labor in actions brought under this section and right of Pension Benefit Guaranty Corporation to bring action, see section 3001(c) of subtitle A of title III of the Employee Retirement Income Security Act of 1974.

* * *

Chapter 79— Definitions

SEC. 7701. DEFINITIONS.

(a) When used in this title, where not otherwise distinctly expressed or manifestly incompatible with the intent thereof—

* * *

(20) Employee.—For the purpose of applying the provisions of section 79 with respect to group-term life insurance purchased for employees, for the purpose of applying the provisions of sections 104, 105, and 106 with respect to accident and health insurance or accident and health plans, for the purpose of applying the provisions of section 101(b) with respect to employees' death benefits, and for the purpose of applying the provisions of subtitle A with respect to contributions to or under a stock bonus, pension, profit-sharing, or annuity plan, and with respect to distributions under such a plan, or by a trust forming part of such a plan, and for purposes of applying section 125 with respect to cafeteria plans, the term "employee" shall include a full time life insurance salesman who is considered an employee for the purpose of chapter 21, or in the case of services performed before January 1, 1951, who would be considered an employee if his services were performed during 1951.

* * *

(35) Enrolled actuary.— The term "enrolled actuary" means a person who is enrolled by the Joint Board for the Enrollment of Actuaries established under subtitle C of the title III of the Employee Retirement Income Security Act of 1974.

* * *

(37) Individual retirement plan.— The term "individual retirement plan" means—

(A) an individual retirement account described in section 408(a), and

(B) and individual retirement annuity described in section 408(b).

* * *

(46) Determination of whether there is a collective bargaining agreement.— In determining whether there is a collective bargaining agreement between employee representatives and 1 or more employers, the term "employee representatives" shall not include any organization more than one-half of the members of which are employees who are owners, officers, or executives of the employer. An agreement shall not be treated as a collective bargaining agreement unless it is a bona fide agreement between bona fide employee representatives and 1 or more employers.

* * *

(j) Tax Treatment of Federal Thrift Savings Fund.—

(1) In general.— For purposes of this title—

(A) the Thrift Savings Fund shall be treated as a trust described in section 401(a) which is exempt from taxation under section 501(a);

(B) any contribution to, or distribution from, the Thrift Savings Fund shall be treated in the same manner as contributions to or distributions from such a trust; and

(C) subject to section 401(k)(4)(B) and any dollar limitation on the application of section 402(e)(3), contributions to the Thrift Savings Fund shall not be treated as distributed or made available to an employee or Member nor as a contribution made to the Fund by an employee or Member merely because the employee or Member has, under the provisions of subchapter III of chapter 84 of title 5, United States Code, and section 8351 of such title 5, an election whether the contribution will be made to the Thrift Savings Fund or received by the employee or Member in cash.

(2) Nondiscrimination requirements.— Paragraph (1)(C) shall not apply to the Thrift Savings Fund unless the Fund meets the antidiscrimination requirements (other than any requirement relating to coverage) applicable to arrangements described in section 401(k) and to matching contributions. Rules similar to the rules of sections 401(k)(8) and 401(m)(8) (relating to no disqualification if excess contributions distributed) shall apply for purposes of the preceding sentence.

IRC Sec. 7701 (j)(2)

(3) Coordination with Social Security act.—Paragraph (1) shall not be construed to provide that any amount of the employee's or Member's basic pay which is contributed to the Thrift Savings Fund shall not be included in the term "wages" for purposes of section 209 of the Social Security Act or section 3121(a) of this title.

(4) Definitions.— For purposes of this subsection, the term "Member", "employee", and "Thrift Savings Fund" shall have the same respective meanings as when used in subchapter III of chapter 84 of title 5, United States Code.

(5) Coordination with other provisions of law.—No provision of law not contained in this title shall apply for purposes of determining the treatment under this title of the Thrift Savings Fund or any contribution to, or distribution from, such Fund.

* * *

Chapter 80— General Rules

Subchapter A— Application of Internal Revenue Laws

* * *

SEC. 7802. COMMISSIONER OF INTERNAL REVENUE; ASSISTANT COMMISSIONER (EMPLOYEE PLANS AND EXEMPT ORGANIZATIONS).

(a) Commissioner of Internal Revenue.— There shall be in the Department of the Treasury a Commissioner of Internal Revenue, who shall be appointed by the President, by and with the advice and consent of the Senate. The Commissioner of Internal Revenue shall have such duties and powers as may be prescribed by the Secretary of the Treasury.

(b) Assistant Commissioner for Employee Plans and Exempt Organizations.—

(1) Establishment of office.— There is established within the Internal Revenue Service an office to be known as the "Office of Employee Plans and Exempt Organizations" to be under the supervision and direction of an Assistant Commissioner of Internal Revenue. As head of the Office, the Assistant Commissioner shall be responsible for carrying out such functions as the Secretary or his delegate may prescribe with respect to organizations exempt from tax under section 501(a) and with respect to plans to which part I of subchapter D of chapter 1 applies (and with respect to organizations designed to be exempt under such section and plans designed to be plans to which such part applies).

(2) Authorization of appropriations.— There is authorized to be appropriated to the Department of the Treasury to carry out the functions of the Office an amount equal to the sum of—

(A) so much of the collections from taxes imposed under section 4940 (relating to excise tax based on investment income) as would have been collected if the rate of tax under such section was 2 percent during the second preceding fiscal year; and

(B) the greater of—

(i) an amount equal to the amount described in paragraph (A); or

(ii) $30,000,000.

* * *

Subtitle J— Coal Industry Health Benefits

* * *

Chapter 99— Coal Industry Health Benefits.

* * *

Subchapter A— Definitions of General Applicability

SEC. 9701. DEFINITIONS OF GENERAL APPLICABILITY.

(a) Plans and Funds.— For purposes of this chapter—

(1) UMWA benefit plan.—

(A) In general.— The term "UMWA Benefit Plan" means a plan—

(i) which is described in section 404(c), or a continuation thereof; and

(ii) which provides health benefits to retirees and beneficiaries of the industry which maintained the 1950 UMWA Pension Plan.

(B) 1950 UMWA benefit plan.— The term "1950 UMWA Benefit Plan" means a UMWA Benefit Plan, participation in which is substantially limited to individuals who retired before 1976.

(C) 1974 UMWA benefit plan.— The term "1974 UMWA Benefit Plan" means a UMWA Benefit Plan, participation in which is substantially limited to individuals who retired on or after January 1, 1976.

(2) 1950 UMWA pension plan.— The term "1950 UMWA Pension Plan" means a pension plan described in section 404(c) (or a continuation thereof), participation in which is substantially limited to individuals who retired before 1976.

(3) 1974 UMWA pension plan.— The term "1974 UMWA Pension Plan" means a pension plan described in section 404(c) (or a

continuation thereof), participation in which is substantially limited to individuals who retired in 1976 and thereafter.

(4) 1992 UMWA benefit plan.— The term "1992 UMWA Benefit Plan' means the plan referred to in section 9713A.

(5) Combined fund.— The term "Combined Fund" means the United Mine Workers of America Combined Benefit Fund established under section 9702.

(b) Agreements.— For purposes of this section—

(1) Coal wage agreement.— The term "coal wage agreement" means—

(A) the National Bituminous Coal Wage Agreement, or

(B) any other agreement entered into between an employer in the coal industry and the United Mine Workers of America that required or requires one or both of the following:

(i) the provision of health benefits to retirees of such employer, eligibility for which is based on years of service credited under a plan established by the settlors and described in section 404(c) or a continuation of such plan; or

(ii) contributions to the 1950 UMWA Benefit Plan or the 1974 UMWA Benefit Plan, or any predecessor thereof.

(2) Settlors.— The term "settlors" means the United Mine Workers of America and the Bituminous Coal Operators' Association, Inc. (referred to in this chapter as the "BCOA").

(3) National Bituminous Coal Wage Agreement.— The term "National Bituminous Coal Wage Agreement" means a collective bargaining agreement negotiated by the BCOA and the United Mine Workers of America.

(c) Terms Relating to Operators.— For purposes of this section—

(1) Signatory operator.— The term "signatory operator" means a person which is or was a signatory to a coal wage agreement.

(2) Related persons.—

(A) In general.— A person shall be considered to be a related person to a signatory operator if that person is—

(i) a member of the controlled group of corporations (within the meaning of section 52(a)) which includes such signatory operator;

(ii) a trade or business which is under common control (as determined under section 52(b)) with such signatory operator; or

(iii) any other person who is identified as having a partnership interest or joint venture with a signatory operator in a business within the coal industry, but only if such business employed eligible beneficiaries, except that this clause shall not apply to a person whose only interest is as a limited partner.

A related person shall also include a successor in interest of any person described in clause (i), (ii), or (iii).

(B) Time for determination.— The relationships described in clauses (i), (ii), and (iii) of subparagraph (A) shall be determined as of July 20, 1992, except that if, on July 20, 1992, a signatory operator is no longer in business, the relationships shall be determined as of the time immediately before such operator ceased to be in business.

(3) 1988 agreement operator.— The term "1988 agreement operator" means—

(A) a signatory operator which was a signatory to the 1988 National Bituminous Coal Wage Agreement,

(B) an employer in the coal industry which was a signatory to an agreement containing pension and health care contribution and benefit provisions which are the same as those contained in the 1988 National Bituminous Coal Wage Agreement, or

(C) an employer from which contributions were actually received after 1987 and before July 20, 1992, by the 1950 UMWA Benefit Plan or the 1974 UMWA Benefit Plan in connection with employment in the coal industry during the period covered by the 1988 National Bituminous Coal Wage Agreement.

(4) Last signatory operator.— The term "last signatory operator" means, with respect to a coal industry retiree, a signatory operator which was the most recent coal industry employer of such retiree.

(5) Assigned operator.— The term "assigned operator" means, with respect to an eligible beneficiary defined in section 9703(f), the signatory operator to which liability under subchapter B with respect to the beneficiary is assigned under section 9706.

(6) Operators of dependent beneficiaries.— For purposes of this chapter, the signatory operator, last signatory operator, or assigned operator of any eligible beneficiary under this chapter who is a coal industry retiree shall be considered to be the signatory operator, last signatory operator, or assigned operator with respect to any other individual who is an eligible beneficiary under this chapter by reason of a relationship to the retiree.

(7) Business.— For purposes of this chapter, a person shall be considered to be in business if such person conducts or derives revenue from any business activity, whether or not in the coal industry.

(d) Enactment Date.— For purposes of this chapter, the term "enactment date" means the date of the enactment of this chapter.

Subchapter B— Combined Benefit Fund

* * *

Part I— Establishment and Benefits

SEC. 9702. ESTABLISHMENT OF THE UNITED MINE WORKERS OF AMERICA COMBINED BENEFIT FUND.

(a) Establishment.—

(1) In general.— As soon as practicable (but not later than 60 days) after the enactment date, the persons described in subsection (b) shall designate the individuals to serve as trustees. Such trustees shall create a new private plan to be known as the United Mine Workers of America Combined Benefit Fund.

(2) Merger of retiree benefit plans.— As of February 1, 1993, the settlors of the 1950 UMWA Benefit Plan and the 1974 UMWA Benefit Plan shall cause such plans to be merged into the Combined Fund, and such merger shall not be treated as an employer withdrawal for purposes of any 1988 coal wage agreement.

(3) Treatment of plan.— The Combined Fund shall be—

(A) a plan described in section 302(c)(5) of the Labor Management Relations Act, 1947 (29 U.S.C. 186(c)(5)),

(B) an employee welfare benefit plan within the meaning of section 3(1) of the Employee Retirement Income Security Act of 1974 (29 U.S.C. 1002(1)), and

(C) a multiemployer plan within the meaning of section 3(37) of such Act (29 U.S.C. 1002(37)).

(4) Tax treatment.— For purposes of this title, the Combined Fund and any related trust shall be treated as an organization exempt from tax under section 501(a).

(b) Board of Trustees.—

(1) In general.— For purposes of subsection (a), the board of trustees for the Combined Fund shall be appointed as follows:

(A) one individual who represents employers in the coal mining industry shall be designated by the BCOA;

(B) one individual shall be designated by the three employers, other than 1988 agreement operators, who have been assigned the greatest number of eligible beneficiaries under section 9706;

(C) two individuals designated by the United Mine Workers of America; and

(D) three persons selected by the persons appointed under subparagraphs (A), (B), and (C).

(2) Successor trustees.— Any successor trustee shall be appointed in the same manner as the trustee being succeeded. The plan establishing the Combined Fund shall provide for the removal of trustees.

(3) Special rules.—

(A) BCOA.— If the BCOA ceases to exist, any trustee or successor under paragraph (1)(A) shall be designated by the 3 employers who were members of the BCOA on the enactment date and who have been assigned the greatest number of eligible beneficiaries under section 9706.

(B) Former signatories.— The initial trustee under paragraph (1)(B) shall be designated by the 3 employers, other than 1988 agreement operators, which the records of the 1950 UMWA Benefit Plan and 1974 UMWA Benefit Plan indicate have the greatest number of eligible beneficiaries as of the enactment date, and such trustee and any successor shall serve until November 1, 1993.

(c) Plan Year.— The first plan year of the Combined Fund shall begin February 1, 1993, and end September 30, 1993. Each succeeding plan year shall begin on October 1 of each calendar year.

SEC. 9703. PLAN BENEFITS.

(a) In General.— Each eligible beneficiary of the Combined Fund shall receive—

(1) health benefits described in subsection (b), and

(2) in the case of an eligible beneficiary described in subsection (f)(1), death benefits coverage described in subsection (c).

(b) Health Benefits.—

(1) In general.— The trustees of the Combined Fund shall provide health care benefits to each eligible beneficiary by enrolling the beneficiary in a health care services plan which undertakes to provide such benefits on a prepaid risk basis. The trustees shall utilize all available plan resources to ensure that, consistent with paragraph (2), coverage under the managed care system shall to the maximum extent feasible be substantially the same as (and subject to the same limitations of) coverage provided under the 1950 UMWA Benefit Plan and the 1974 UMWA Benefit Plan as of January 1, 1992.

(2) Plan payment rates.—

(A) In general.— The trustees of the Combined Fund shall negotiate payment rates with the health care services plans described in paragraph (1) for each plan year which are in amounts which—

(i) vary as necessary to ensure that beneficiaries in different geographic areas have access to a uniform level of health benefits; and

(ii) result in aggregate payments for such plan year from the Combined Fund which do not exceed the total premium payments required to be paid to the Combined Fund under section 9704(a) for the plan year, adjusted as provided in subparagraphs (B) and (C).

(B) Reductions.— The amount determined under subparagraph (A)(ii) for any plan year shall be reduced—

(i) by the aggregate death benefit premiums determined under section 9704(c) for the plan year, and

(ii) by the amount reserved for plan administration under subsection (d).

(C) Increases.— The amount determined under subparagraph (A)(ii) shall be increased—

(i) by any reduction in the total premium payments required to be paid under section 9704(a) by reason of transfers described in section 9705,

(ii) by any carryover to the plan year from any preceding plan year which—

(I) is derived from amounts described in section 9704(e)(3)(B)(i), and

(II) the trustees elect to use to pay benefits for the current plan year, and

(iii) any interest earned by the Combined Fund which the trustees elect to use to pay benefits for the current plan year.

(3) Qualified providers.— The trustees of the Combined Fund shall not enter into an agreement under paragraph (1) with any provider of services which is of a type which is required to be certified by the Secretary of Health and Human Services when providing services under title XVIII of the Social Security Act unless the provider is so certified.

(4) Effective date.— Benefits shall be provided under paragraph (1) on and after February 1, 1993.

(c) Death Benefits Coverage.—

(1) In general.— The trustees of the Combined Fund shall provide death benefits coverage to each eligible beneficiary described in subsection (f)(1) which is identical to the benefits provided under the 1950 UMWA Pension Plan or 1974 UMWA Pension Plan whichever is applicable, on July 20, 1992. Such coverage shall be provided on and after February 1, 1993.

(2) Termination of coverage.— The 1950 UMWA Pension Plan and the 1974 UMWA Pension Plan shall each be amended to provide that death benefits coverage shall not be provided to eligible beneficiaries on and after February 1, 1993. This paragraph shall not prohibit such plans from subsequently providing death benefits not described in paragraph (1).

(d) Reserves for Administration.— The trustees of the Combined Fund may reserve for each plan year, for use in payment of the administrative costs of the Combined Fund, an amount not to exceed 5 percent of the premiums to be paid to the Combined Fund under section 9704(a) during the plan year.

(e) Limitation on Enrollment.— The Combined Fund shall not enroll any individual who is not receiving benefits under the 1950 UMWA Benefit Plan or the 1974 UMWA Benefit Plan as of July 20, 1992.

(f) Eligible Beneficiary.— For purposes of this subchapter, the term "eligible beneficiary" means an individual who—

(1) is a coal industry retiree who, on July 20, 1992, was eligible to receive, and receiving, benefits from the 1950 UMWA Benefit Plan or the 1974 UMWA Benefit Plan, or

(2) on such date was eligible to receive, and receiving, benefits in either such plan by reason of a relationship to such retiree.

Part II— Financing

SEC. 9704. LIABILITY OF ASSIGNED OPERATORS.

◊ ◊ ◊

Editor's Note: Section 108(h)(9)(A) of P.L. 103-296, the Social Security Administrative Reform Act of 1994, replaced the references in §9704(b)(2) and (h) to the "Secretary of Health and Human Services," with references to the "Commissioner of Social Security," in accordance with the provisions of that act which established the Social Security Administration as a separate governmental agency. The change is effective March 31, 1995.

◊ ◊ ◊

(a) Annual Premiums.— Each assigned operator shall pay to the Combined Fund for each plan year beginning on or after February 1, 1993, an annual premium equal to the sum of the following three premiums—

(1) the health benefit premium determined under subsection (b) for such plan year, plus

(2) the death benefit premium determined under subsection (c) for such plan year, plus

(3) the unassigned beneficiaries premium determined under subsection (d) for such plan year.

Any related person with respect to an assigned operator shall be jointly and severally liable for any premium required to be paid by such operator.

(b) Health Benefit Premium.— For purposes of this chapter—

(1) In general.— The health benefit premium for any plan year for any assigned operator shall be an amount equal to the product of the per beneficiary premium for the plan year multiplied by the number of eligible beneficiaries assigned to such operator under section 9706.

(2) Per beneficiary premium.— The *Comissioner of Social Security* [Secretary of Health and Human Services] shall calculate a per beneficiary premium for each plan year beginning on or after February 1, 1993, which is equal to the sum of—

(A) the amount determined by dividing—

(i) the aggregate amount of payments from the 1950 UMWA Benefit Plan and the 1974 UMWA Benefit Plan for health benefits (less reimbursements but including administrative costs) for the plan year beginning July 1, 1991, for all individuals covered under such plans for such plan year, by

(ii) the number of such individuals, plus

(B) the amount determined under subparagraph (A) multiplied by the percentage (if any) by which the medical component of the Consumer Price Index for the calendar year in which the plan year begins exceeds such component for 1992.

(3) Adjustments for Medicare reductions.— If, by reason of a reduction in benefits under title XVIII of the Social Security Act, the level of health benefits under the Combined Fund would be reduced, the trustees of the Combined Fund shall increase the per beneficiary premium for the plan year in which the reduction occurs and each subsequent plan year by the amount necessary to maintain the level of health benefits which would have been provided without such reduction.

(c) Death Benefit Premium.— The death benefit premium for any plan year for any assigned operator shall be equal to the applicable percentage of the amount, actuarially determined, which the Combined Fund will be required to pay during the plan year for death benefits coverage described in section 9703(c).

(d) Unassigned Beneficiaries Premium.— The unassigned beneficiaries premium for any plan year for any assigned operator shall be equal to the applicable percentage of the product of the per beneficiary premium for the plan year multiplied by the number of eligible beneficiaries who are not assigned under section 9706 to any person for such plan year.

(e) Premium Accounts; Adjustments.—

(1) Accounts.— The trustees of the Combined Fund shall establish and maintain 3 separate accounts for each of the premiums described in subsections (b), (c), and (d). Such accounts shall be credited with the premiums received and debited with expenditures allocable to such premiums.

(2) Allocations.—

(A) Administrative expenses.— Administrative costs for any plan year shall be allocated to premium accounts under paragraph (1) on the basis of expenditures (other than administrative costs) from such accounts during the preceding plan year.

(B) Interest.— Interest shall be allocated to the account established for health benefit premiums.

(3) Shortfalls and surpluses.—

(A) In general.— Except as provided in subparagraph (B), if, for any plan year, there is a shortfall or surplus in any premium account, the premium for the following plan year for each assigned operator shall be proportionately reduced or increased, whichever is applicable, by the amount of such shortfall or surplus.

(B) Exception.— Subparagraph (A) shall not apply to any surplus in the health benefit premium account or the unassigned beneficiaries premium account which is attributable to—

(i) the excess of the premiums credited to such account for a plan year over the benefits (and administrative costs) debited to such account for the plan year, but such excess shall only be available for purposes of the carryover described in section 9703(b)(2)(C)(ii) (relating to carryovers of premiums not used to provide benefits), or

(ii) interest credited under paragraph (2)(B) for the plan year or any preceding plan year.

(C) No authority for increased payments.— Nothing in this paragraph shall be construed to allow expenditures for health care benefits for any plan year in excess of the limit under section 9703(b)(2).

(f) Applicable Percentage.— For purposes of this section—

(1) In general.— The term "applicable percentage" means, with respect to any assigned operator, the percentage determined by dividing the number of eligible beneficiaries assigned under section 9706 to such operator by the total number of eligible beneficiaries assigned under section 9706 to all such operators (determined on the basis of assignments as of October 1, 1993).

(2) Annual adjustments.— In the case of any plan year beginning on or after October 1, 1994, the applicable percentage for any assigned operator shall be redetermined under paragraph (1) by making the following changes to the assignments as of October 1, 1993:

(A) Such assignments shall be modified to reflect any changes during the period beginning October 1, 1993, and ending on the last day of the preceding plan year pursuant to the appeals process under section 9706(f).

(B) The total number of assigned eligible beneficiaries shall be reduced by the eligible beneficiaries of assigned operators which (and all related persons with respect to which) had ceased business (within the meaning of section 9701(c)(6)) during the period described in subparagraph (A).

(g) Payment of Premiums.—

(1) In general.— The annual premium under subsection (a) for any plan year shall be payable in 12 equal monthly installments, due on the twenty-fifth day of each calendar month in the plan year. In the case of the plan year beginning February 1, 1993, the annual premium under subsection (a) shall be added to such premium for the plan year beginning October 1, 1993.

(2) Deductibility.— Any premium required by this section shall be deductible without regard to any limitation on deductibility based on the prefunding of health benefits.

(h) Information.— The trustees of the Combined Fund shall, not later than 60 days after the enactment date, furnish to the *Commissioner of Social Security* [Secretary of Health and Human Services] information as to the benefits and covered beneficiaries under the fund, and such other information as the Secretary may require to compute any premium under this section.

(i) Transition Rules.—

(1) 1988 agreement operators.—

(A) 1st year costs.—During the plan year of the Combined Fund beginning February 1, 1993, the 1988 agreement operators shall make contributions to the Combined Fund in amounts necessary to pay benefits and administrative costs of the Combined Fund incurred during such year, reduced by the amount transferred to the Combined Fund under section 9705(a) on February 1, 1993.

(B) Deficits from merged plans.— During the period beginning February 1, 1993, and ending September 30, 1994, the 1988 agreement operators shall make contributions to the Combined Fund as are necessary to pay off the expenses accrued (and remaining unpaid) by the 1950 UMWA Benefit Plan and the 1974 UMWA Benefit Plan as of February 1, 1993, reduced by the assets of such plans as of such date.

IRC Sec. 9704 (i)(1)(B)

(C) Failure.—If any 1988 agreement operator fails to meet any obligation under this paragraph, any contributions of such operator to the Combined Fund or any other plan described in section 404(c) shall not be deductible under this title until such time as the failure is corrected.

(D) Premium reductions.—

(i) 1st year payments.—In the case of a 1988 agreement operator making contributions under subparagraph (A), the premium of such operator under subsection (a) shall be reduced by the amount paid under subparagraph (A) by such operator for the plan year beginning February 1, 1993.

(ii) Deficit payments.—In the case a 1988 agreement operator making contributions under subparagraph (B), the premium of such operator under subsection (a) shall be reduced by the amounts which are paid to the Combined Fund by reason of claims arising in connection with the 1950 UMWA Benefit Plan and the 1974 UMWA Benefit Plan as of February 1, 1993, including claims based on the "evergreen clause" found in the language of the 1950 UMWA Benefit Plan and the 1974 UMWA Benefit Plan, and which are allocated to such operator under subparagraph (E).

(iii) Limitation.—Clause (ii) shall not apply to the extent the amounts paid exceed the contributions.

(iv) Plan years.—Premiums under subsection (a) shall be reduced for the first plan year for which amounts described in clause (i) or (ii) are available and for any succeeding plan year until such amounts are exhausted.

(E) Allocations of contributions and refunds.—Contributions under subparagraphs (A) and (B), and premium reductions under subparagraph (D)(ii), shall be made ratably on the basis of aggregate contributions made by such operators under the applicable 1988 coal wage agreements as of January 31, 1993.

(2) 1st plan year.—In the case of the plan year of the Combined Fund beginning February 1, 1993—

(A) the premiums under subsections (a)(1) and (a)(3) shall be 67 percent of such premiums without regard to this paragraph, and

(B) the premiums under subsection (a) shall be paid as provided in subsection (g).

(3) Startup costs.—The 1950 UMWA Benefit Plan and the 1974 UMWA Benefit Plan shall pay the costs of the Combined Fund incurred before February 1, 1993. For purposes of this section, such costs shall be treated as administrative expenses incurred for the plan year beginning February 1, 1993.

SEC. 9705. TRANSFERS.

(a) Transfer of Assets From 1950 UMWA Pension Plan.—

(1) In general.—From the funds reserved under paragraph (2), the board of trustees of the 1950 UMWA Pension Plan shall transfer to the Combined Fund—

(A) $70,000,000 on February 1, 1993,

(B) $70,000,000 on October 1, 1993, and

(C) $70,000,000 on October 1, 1994.

(2) Reservation.—Immediately upon the enactment date, the board of trustees of the 1950 UMWA Pension Plan shall segregate $210,000,000 from the general assets of the plan. Such funds shall be held in the plan until disbursed pursuant to paragraph (1). Any interest on such funds shall be deposited into the general assets of the 1950 UMWA Pension Plan.

(3) Use of funds.—Amounts transferred to the Combined Fund under paragraph (1) shall—

(A) in the case of the transfer on February 1, 1993, be used to proportionately reduce the premium of each assigned operator under section 9704(a) for the plan year of the Fund beginning February 1, 1993, and

(B) in the case of any other such transfer, be used to proportionately reduce the unassigned beneficiary premium under section 9704(a)(3) and the death benefit premium under section 9704(a)(2) of each assigned operator for the plan year in which transferred and for any subsequent plan year in which such funds remain available.

Such funds may not be used to pay any amounts required to be paid by the 1988 agreement operators under section 9704(i)(1)(B).

(4) Tax treatment; validity of transfer.—

(A) No deduction.—No deduction shall be allowed under this title with respect to any transfer pursuant to paragraph (1), but such transfer shall not adversely affect the deductibility (under applicable provisions of this title) of contributions previously made by employers, or amounts hereafter contributed by employers, to the 1950 UMWA Pension Plan, the 1950 UMWA Benefit Plan, the 1974 UMWA Pension Plan, the 1974 UMWA Benefit Plan, the 1992 UMWA Benefit Plan, or the Combined Fund.

(B) Other tax provisions.— Any transfer pursuant to paragraph (1)—

(i) shall not be treated as an employer reversion from a qualified plan for purposes of section 4980, and

(ii) shall not be includible in the gross income of any employer maintaining the 1950 UMWA Pension Plan.

(5) Treatment of transfer.— Any transfer pursuant to paragraph (1) shall not be deemed to violate, or to be prohibited by, any provision of law, or to cause the settlors, joint board of trustees, employers or any related person to incur or be subject to liability, taxes, fines, or penalties of any kind whatsoever.

(b) Transfers From Abandoned Mine Reclamation Fund.—

(1) In general.— The Combined Fund shall include any amount transferred to the Fund under section 402(h) of the Surface Mining Control and Reclamation Act of 1977 (30 U.S.C. 1232(h)).

(2) Use of funds.— Any amount transferred under paragraph (1) for any fiscal year shall be used to proportionately reduce the unassigned beneficiary premium under section 9704(a)(3) of each assigned operator for the plan year in which transferred.

SEC. 9706. ASSIGNMENT OF ELIGIBLE BENEFICIARIES.

◊ ◊ ◊

Editor's Note: Section 108(h)(9)(B)(i)(iii) of P.L. 103-296, the Social Security Administrative Reform Act of 1994, replaced all of the references in §9706 the ''Secretary of Health and Human Services,'' with references to the ''Commissioner of Social Security,'' and made related conforming changes in accordance with the provisions of that act which established the Social Security Administration as a separate governmental agency. The change is effective March 31, 1995.

◊ ◊ ◊

(a) In General.— For purposes of this chapter, the *Commissioner of Social Security* [Secretary of Health and Human Services] shall, before October 1, 1993, assign each coal industry retiree who is an eligible beneficiary to a signatory operator which (or any related person with respect to which) remains in business in the following order:

(1) First, to the signatory operator which—

(A) was a signatory to the 1978 coal wage agreement or any subsequent coal wage agreement, and

(B) was the most recent signatory operator to employ the coal industry retiree in the coal industry for at least 2 years.

(2) Second, if the retiree is not assigned under paragraph (1), to the signatory operator which—

(A) was a signatory to the 1978 coal wage agreement or any subsequent coal wage agreement, and

(B) was the most recent signatory operator to employ the coal industry retiree in the coal industry.

(3) Third, if the retiree is not assigned under paragraph (1) or (2), to the signatory operator which employed the coal industry retiree in the coal industry for a longer period of time than any other signatory operator prior to the effective date of the 1978 coal wage agreement.

(b) Rules Relating to Employment and Reassignment Upon Purchase.— For purposes of subsection (a)—

(1) Aggregation rules.—

(A) Related person.— Any employment of a coal industry retiree in the coal industry by a signatory operator shall be treated as employment by any related persons to such operator.

(B) Certain employment disregarded.— Employment with—

(i) a person which is (and all related persons with respect to which are) no longer in business, or

(ii) a person during a period during which such person was not a signatory to a coal wage agreement,

shall not be taken into account.

(2) Reassignment upon purchase.— If a person becomes a successor of an assigned operator after the enactment date, the assigned operator may transfer the assignment of an eligible beneficiary under subsection (a) to such successor, and such successor shall be treated as the assigned operator with respect to such eligible beneficiary for purposes of this chapter. Notwithstanding the preceding sentence, the assigned operator transferring such assignment (and any related person) shall remain the guarantor of the benefits provided to the eligible beneficiary under this chapter. An assigned operator shall notify the trustees of the Combined Fund of any transfer described in this paragraph.

(c) Identification of Eligible Bene-ficiaries.— The 1950 UMWA Benefit Plan and the 1974 UMWA Benefit Plan shall, by the later of October 1, 1992, or the twentieth day after the enactment date, provide to the *Commissioner of Social Security* [Secretary of Health and Human Services] a list of the names and social security account numbers of each eligible beneficiary, including each deceased eligible beneficiary if any other individual is an eligible beneficiary by reason of a relationship to such deceased eligible beneficiary. In addition, the plans shall provide, where ascertainable from plan records, the names of all persons described in subsection (a) with respect to any eligible beneficiary or deceased eligible beneficiary.

(d) Cooperation by Other Agencies and Persons.—

(1) Cooperation.— The head of any department, agency, or instrumentality of the United States shall cooperate fully and promptly with the *Commissioner of Social Security* [Secretary of Health and Human Services] in providing information which will enable the *Commissioner* [Secretary] to carry out his responsibilities under this section.

(2) Providing of information.—

(A) In general.— Notwithstanding any other provision of law, including section 6103, the head of any other agency, department, or instrumentality shall, upon receiving a written request from the *Commissioner of Social Security* [Secretary of Health and Human Services] in connection with this section, cause a search to be made of the files and records maintained by such agency, department, or instrumentality with a view to determining whether the information requested is contained in such files or records. The *Commissioner* [Secretary] shall be advised whether the search disclosed the information requested, and, if so, such information shall be promptly transmitted to the *Commissioner* [Secretary], except that if the disclosure of any requested information would contravene national policy or security interests of the United States, or the confidentiality of census data, the information shall not be transmitted and the *Commissioner* [Secretary] shall be so advised.

(B) Limitation.—Any information provided under subparagraph (A) shall be limited to information necessary for the *Commissioner* [Secretary] to carry out his duties under this section.

(3) **Trustees.**— The trustees of the Combined Fund, the 1950 UMWA Benefit Plan, the 1974 UMWA Benefit Plan, the 1950 UMWA Pension Plan, and the 1974 UMWA Pension Plan shall fully and promptly cooperate with the *Commissioner* [Secretary] in furnishing, or assisting the *Commissioner* [Secretary] to obtain, any information the *Commissioner* [Secretary] needs to carry out the *Commissioner's* [Secretary's] responsibilities under this section.

(e) **Notice by *Commissioner* [Secretary].**—

(1) **Notice to fund.**— The *Commissioner of Social Security* [Secretary of Health and Human Services] shall advise the trustees of the Combined Fund of the name of each person identified under this section as an assigned operator, and the names and social security account numbers of eligible beneficiaries with respect to whom he is identified.

(2) **Other notice.**— The *Commissioner of Social Security* [Secretary of Health and Human Services] shall notify each assigned operator of the names and social security account numbers of eligible beneficiaries who have been assigned to such person under this section and a brief summary of the facts related to the basis for such assignments.

(f) **Reconsideration by *Commissioner* [Secretary].**—

(1) **In general.**— Any assigned operator receiving a notice under subsection (e)(2) with respect to an eligible beneficiary may, within 30 days of receipt of such notice, request from the *Commissioner of Social Security* [Secretary of Health and Human Services] detailed information as to the work history of the beneficiary and the basis of the assignment.

(2) **Review.**— An assigned operator may, within 30 days of receipt of the information under paragraph (1), request review of the assignment. The *Commissioner of Social Security* [Secretary of Health and Human Services] shall conduct such review if the *Commissioner* [Secretary] finds the operator provided evidence with the request constituting a prima facie case of error.

(3) **Results of review.**—

(A) Error.— If the *Commissioner of Social Security* [Secretary of Health and Human Services] determines under a review under paragraph (2) that an assignment was in error—

(i) the *Commissioner* [Secretary] shall notify the assigned operator and the trustees of the Combined Fund and the trustees shall reduce the premiums of the operator under section 9704 by (or if there are no such premiums, repay) all premiums paid under section 9704 with respect to the eligible beneficiary, and

(ii) the *Commissioner* [Secretary] shall review the beneficiary's record for reassignment under subsection (a).

IRC Sec. 9706 (f)(3)(A)(ii)

(B) No error.— If the *Commissioner of Social Security* [Secretary of Health and Human Services] determines under a review conducted under paragraph (2) that no error occurred, the *Commissioner* [Secretary] shall notify the assigned operator.

(4) Determinations.— Any determination by the *Commissioner of Social Security* [Secretary of Health and Human Services] under paragraph (2) or (3) shall be final.

(5) Payment pending review.— An assigned operator shall pay the premiums under section 9704 pending review by the *Commissioner of Social Security* [Secretary of Health and Human Services] or by a court under this subsection.

(6) Private actions.— Nothing in this section shall preclude the right of any person to bring a separate civil action against another person for responsibility for assigned premiums, notwithstanding any prior decision by the *Commissioner* [Secretary].

(g) Confidentiality of Information.— Any person to which information is provided by the *Commissioner of Social Security* [Secretary of Health and Human Services] under this section shall not disclose such information except in any proceedings related to this section. Any civil or criminal penalty which is applicable to an unauthorized disclosure under section 6103 shall apply to any unauthorized disclosure under this section.

Part III— Enforcement

* * *

SEC. 9707. FAILURE TO PAY PREMIUM.

(a) General Rule.—There is hereby imposed a penalty on the failure of any assigned operator to pay any premium required to be paid under section 9704 with respect to any eligible beneficiary.

(b) Amount of Penalty.— The amount of the penalty imposed by subsection (a) on any

failure with respect to any eligible beneficiary shall be $100 per day in the noncompliance period with respect to any such failure.

(c) Noncompliance Period.— For purposes of this section, the term "noncompliance period" means, with respect to any failure to pay any premium or installment thereof, the period—

(1) beginning on the due date for such premium or installment, and

(2) ending on the date of payment of such premium or installment.

(d) Limitations on Amount of Penalty.—

(1) In general.— No penalty shall be imposed by subsection (a) on any failure during any period for which it is established to the satisfaction of the Secretary of the Treasury that none of the persons responsible for such failure knew, or exercising reasonable diligence, would have known, that such failure existed.

(2) Corrections.— No penalty shall be imposed by subsection (a) on any failure if—

(A) such failure was due to reasonable cause and not to willful neglect, and

(B) such failure is corrected during the 30-day period beginning on the 1st date that any of the persons responsible for such failure knew, or exercising reasonable diligence would have known, that such failure existed.

(3) Waiver.— In the case of a failure that is due to reasonable cause and not to willful neglect, the Secretary of the Treasury may waive all or part of the penalty imposed by subsection (a) for failures to the extent that the Secretary determines, in his sole discretion, that the payment of such penalty would be excessive relative to the failure involved.

(e) Liability for Penalty.— The person failing to meet the requirements of section 9704 shall be liable for the penalty imposed by subsection (a).

(f) Treatment.— For purposes of this title, the penalty imposed by this section shall be treated in the same manner as the tax imposed by section 4980B.

Part IV— Other Provisions

* * *

SEC. 9708. EFFECT ON PENDING CLAIMS OR OBLIGATIONS.

All liability for contributions to the Combined Fund that arises on and after February 1, 1993, shall be determined exclusively under this chapter, including all liability for contributions to the 1950 UMWA Benefit Plan and the 1974 UMWA Benefit Plan for coal production on and after February 1, 1993. However, nothing in this chapter is intended to have any effect on any claims or obligations arising in connection with the 1950 UMWA Benefit Plan and the 1974 UMWA Benefit Plan as of February 1, 1993, including claims or obligations based on the ''evergreen'' clause found in the language of the 1950 UMWA Benefit Plan and the 1974 UMWA Benefit Plan. This chapter shall not be construed to affect any rights of subrogation of any 1988 agreement operator with respect to contributions due to the 1950 UMWA Benefit Plan or the 1974 UMWA Benefit Plan as of February 1, 1993.

Subchapter C— Health Benefits of Certain Miners

Part I— Individual Employer Plans

SEC. 9711. CONTINUED OBLIGA-TIONS OF INDIVIDUAL EMPLOYER PLANS.

(a) Coverage of Current Recipients.— The last signatory operator of any individual who, as of February 1, 1993, is receiving retiree health benefits from an individual employer plan maintained pursuant to a 1978 or subsequent coal wage agreement shall continue to provide health benefits coverage to such individual and the individual's eligible bene-ficiaries which is substantially the same as (and subject to all the limitations of) the coverage provided by such plan as of January 1, 1992. Such coverage shall continue to be provided for as long as the last signatory operator (and any related person) remains in business.

(b) Coverage of Eligible Recipients.—

(1) In general.— The last signatory operator of any individual who, as of February 1, 1993, is not receiving retiree health benefits under the individual employer plan maintained by the last signatory operator pursuant to a 1978 or subsequent coal wage agreement, but has met the age and service requirements for eligibility to receive benefits under such plan as of such date, shall, at such time as such individual becomes eligible to receive benefits under such plan, provide health benefits coverage to such individual and the individual's eligible beneficiaries which is described in paragraph (2). This paragraph shall not apply to any individual who retired from the coal industry after September 30, 1994, or any eligible beneficiary of such individual.

(2) Coverage.— Subject to the pro-visions of subsection (d), health benefits coverage is described in this paragraph if it is substantially the same as (and subject to all the limitations of) the coverage provided by the individual employer plan as of January 1, 1992. Such coverage shall continue for as long as the last signatory operator (and any related person) remains in business.

(c) Joint and Several Liability of Related Persons.— Each related person of a last signatory operator to which subsection (a) or (b) applies shall be jointly and severally liable with the last signatory operator for the provision of health care coverage described in subsection (a) or (b).

(d) Managed Care and Cost Containment.— The last signatory operator shall not be treated as failing to meet the requirements of subsection (a) or (b) if benefits are provided to eligible beneficiaries under managed care and cost containment rules and procedures described in section 9712(c) or agreed to by the last signatory operator and the United Mine Workers of America.

(e) Treatment of Noncovered Employees.— The existence, level, and duration of benefits provided to former employees of a last signatory operator (and their eligible beneficiaries) who are not otherwise covered by this chapter and who are (or were) covered by a coal wage agreement shall only be determined by, and shall be subject to, collective bargaining, lawful unilateral action, or other applicable law.

(f) Eligible Beneficiary.— For purposes of this section, the term "eligible beneficiary" means any individual who is eligible for health benefits under a plan described in subsection (a) or (b) by reason of the individual's relationship with the retiree described in such subsection (or to an individual who, based on service and employment history at the time of death, would have been so described but for such death).

(g) Rules Applicable to This Part and Part II.— For purposes of this part and part II—

(1) Successor.— The term "last signatory operator" shall include a successor in interest of such operator.

(2) Reassignment upon purchase.— If a person becomes a successor of a last signatory operator after the enactment date, the last signatory operator may transfer any liability of such operator under this chapter with respect to an eligible beneficiary to such successor, and such successor shall be treated as the last signatory operator with respect to such eligible beneficiary for purposes of this chapter. Notwithstanding the preceding sentence, the last signatory operator transferring such assignment (and any related person) shall remain the guarantor of the benefits provided to the eligible beneficiary under this chapter. A last signatory operator shall notify the trustees of the 1992 UMWA Benefit Plan of any transfer described in this paragraph.

Part II— 1992 UMWA Benefit Plan

* * *

SEC. 9712. ESTABLISHMENT AND COVERAGE OF 1992 UMWA BENEFIT PLAN.

(a) Creation of Plan.—

(1) In general.— As soon as practicable after the enactment date, the settlors shall create a separate private plan which shall be known as the United Mine Workers of America 1992 Benefit Plan. For purposes of this title, the 1992 UMWA Benefit Plan shall be treated as an organization exempt from taxation under section 501(a). The settlors shall be responsible for designing the structure, administration and terms of the 1992 UMWA Benefit Plan, and for appointment and removal of the members of the board of trustees. The board of trustees shall initially consist of five members and shall thereafter be the number set by the settlors.

(2) Treatment of plan.— The 1992 UMWA Benefit Plan shall be—

(A) a plan described in section 302(c)(5) of the Labor Management Relations Act, 1947 (29 U.S.C. 186(c)(5)),

(B) an employee welfare benefit plan within the meaning of section 3(1) of the Employee Retirement Income Security Act of 1974 (29 U.S.C. 1002(1)), and

(C) a multiemployer plan within the meaning of section 3(37) of such Act (29 U.S.C. 1002(37)).

(b) Coverage Requirement.—

(1) In general.— The 1992 UMWA Benefit Plan shall only provide health benefits coverage to any eligible beneficiary who is not eligible for benefits under the Combined Fund and shall not provide such coverage to any other individual.

(2) Eligible beneficiary.—For purposes of this section, the term "eligible beneficiary"' means an individual who—

(A) but for the enactment of this chapter, would be eligible to receive benefits from the 1950 UMWA Benefit Plan or the 1974 UMWA Benefit Plan, based upon age and service earned as of February 1, 1993; or

(B) with respect to whom coverage is required to be provided under section 9711, but who does not receive such coverage from the applicable last signatory operator or any related person,

and any individual who is eligible for benefits by reason of a relationship to an individual described in subparagraph (A) or (B). In no event shall the 1992 UMWA Benefit Plan provide health benefits coverage to any eligible beneficiary who is a coal industry retiree who retired from the coal industry after September 30, 1994, or any beneficiary of such individual.

(c) Health Benefits.—

(1) In general.—The 1992 UMWA Benefit Plan shall provide health care benefits coverage to each eligible beneficiary which is substantially the same as (and subject to all the limitations of) coverage provided under the 1950 UMWA Benefit Plan and the 1974 UMWA Benefit Plan as of January 1, 1992.

(2) Managed care.— The 1992 UMWA Benefit Plan shall develop managed care and cost containment rules which shall be applicable to the payment of benefits under this subsection. Application of such rules shall not cause the plan to be treated as failing to meet the requirements of this subsection. Such rules shall preserve freedom of choice while reinforcing managed care network use by allowing a point of service decision as to whether a network medical provider will be used. Major elements of such rules may include, but are not limited to, elements described in paragraph (3).

(3) Major elements of rules.—Elements described in this paragraph are—

(A) implementing formulary for drugs and subjecting the prescription program to a rigorous review of appropriate use,

(B) obtaining a unit price discount in exchange for patient volume and preferred provider status with the amount of the potential discount varying by geographic region,

(C) limiting benefit payments to physicians to the allowable charge under title XVIII of the Social Security Act, while protecting beneficiaries from balance billing by providers,

(D) utilizing, in the claims payment function "appropriateness of service" protocols under title XVIII of the Social Security Act if more stringent,

(E) creating mandatory utilization review (UR) procedures, but placing the responsibility to follow such procedures on the physician or hospital, not the beneficiaries,

(F) selecting the most efficient physicians and state-of-the-art utilization management techniques, including ambulatory care techniques, for medical services delivered by the managed care network, and

(G) utilizing a managed care network provider system, as practiced in the health care industry, at the time medical services are needed (point-of-service) in order to receive maximum benefits available under this subsection.

(4) Last signatory operators.—The board of trustees of the 1992 UMWA Benefit Plan shall permit any last signatory operator required to maintain an individual employer plan under section 9711 to utilize the managed care and cost containment rules and programs developed under this subsection if the operator elects to do so.

(5) Standards of quality.— Any managed care system or cost containment adopted by the board of trustees of the 1992 UMWA Benefit Plan or by a last signatory operator may not be implemented unless it is approved by, and meets the standards of quality adopted by, a medical peer review panel, which has been established—

(A) by the settlors, or

(B) by the United Mine Workers of America and a last signatory operator or group of operators.

Standards of quality shall include accessibility to medical care, taking into account that accessibility requirements may differ depending on the nature of the medical need.

(d) Guarantee of Benefits.—

(1) In general.— All 1988 last signatory operators shall be responsible for financing the benefits described in subsection (c), in accordance with contribution requirements established in the 1992 UMWA Benefit Plan. Such contribution requirements, which shall be applied uniformly to each 1988 last signatory operator, on the basis of the number of eligible and potentially eligible beneficiaries attributable to each operator, shall include:

(A) the payment of an annual prefunding premium for all eligible and potentially eligible beneficiaries attributable to a 1988 last signatory operator,

(B) the payment of a monthly per beneficiary premium by each 1988 last signatory operator for each eligible beneficiary of such operator who is described in subsection (b)(2) and who is receiving benefits under the 1992 UMWA Benefit Plan, and

(C) the provision of security (in the form of a bond, letter of credit or cash escrow) in an amount equal to a portion of the projected future cost to the 1992 UMWA Benefit Plan of providing health benefits for eligible and potentially eligible beneficiaries attributable to the 1988 last signatory operator. If a 1988 last signatory operator is unable to provide the security required, the 1992 UMWA

Benefit Plan shall require the operator to pay an annual prefunding premium that is greater than the premium otherwise applicable.

(2) Adjustments.— The 1992 UMWA Benefit Plan shall provide for—

(A) annual adjustments of the per beneficiary premium to cover changes in the cost of providing benefits to eligible beneficiaries, and

(B) adjustments as necessary to the annual prefunding premium to reflect changes in the cost of providing benefits to eligible beneficiaries for whom per beneficiary premiums are not paid.

(3) Additional liability.— Any last signatory operator who is not a 1988 last signatory operator shall pay the monthly per beneficiary premium under paragraph (1)(B) for each eligible beneficiary described in such paragraph attributable to that operator.

(4) Joint and several liability.— A 1988 last signatory operator or last signatory operator described in paragraph (3), and any related person to any such operator, shall be jointly and severally liable with such operator for any amount required to be paid by such operator under this section.

(5) Deductibility.— Any premium required by this section shall be deductible without regard to any limitation on deductibility based on the prefunding of health benefits.

(6) 1988 last signatory operator.— For purposes of this section, the term "1988 last signatory operator" means a last signatory operator which is a 1988 agreement operator.

Subchapter D—Other Provisions

SEC. 9721. CIVIL ENFORCEMENT.

The provisions of section 4301 of the Employee Retirement Income Security Act of 1974 shall apply to any claim arising out of an obligation to pay any amount required to be paid by this chapter in the same manner as any claim arising out of an obligation to pay withdrawal liability under subtitle E of title IV of such Act. For purposes of the preceding sentence, a signatory operator and related persons shall be treated in the same manner as employers.

SEC. 9722. SHAM TRANSACTIONS.

If a principal purpose of any transaction is to evade or avoid liability under this chapter, this chapter shall be applied (and such liability shall be imposed) without regard to such transaction.

Part 4

Index

	Law		Regulations	
	ERISA	IRC	26 CFR (Treas. Reg.)	29 CFR (DOL, PBGC, EEOC)

-A-

Note: Regulation references are included for researching convenience. Text of regulations can be found in *ERISA Regulations* (BNA Books, 1994). The prefix **p** indicates a proposed regulation.

Note: Regulation references are included for researching convenience. Text of regulations can be found in *ERISA Regulations* (BNA Books, 1994). The prefix **p** indicates a proposed regulation.

	Law		Regulations	
	ERISA	**IRC**	**26 CFR** **(Treas. Reg.)**	**29 CFR** (DOL, PBGC, EEOC)

Note: Regulation references are included for researching convenience. Text of regulations can be found in *ERISA Regulations* (BNA Books, 1994). The prefix **p** indicates a proposed regulation.

	Law		Regulations	
	ERISA	**IRC**	**26 CFR** **(Treas. Reg.)**	**29 CFR** **(DOL, PBGC, EEOC)**

Auto salesmen, fringe benefits | | 132 (i)(3) | 1.132-5(o)
1.132-5T(o) |

-B-

Bank
  Common or collective trust
    (*see* Common or Collective Trust)
  Definition | | 408 (n) | 1. 408-1(b)(2)(i)
  ESOP distribution | | 409 (h)(3)
  Investment manager | 3 (38)(B)(ii)
  Prohibited transaction
    exemptions
    Ancillary services | 408 (b)(6) | 4975 (d)(6) | | 2550. 408b-6
    Common or collective trust | 408 (b)(8) | 4975 (d)(8)
    Deposits | 408 (b)(4) | 4975 (d)(4) | | 2550. 408b-4
  Reports by | 103 (a)(2) | | | 2520. 103-3, -5
  | 103 (b)(3)(G) | | | 2520. 103-9

Bankruptcy
  Funding lien | 302 (f) | 412 (n)
  PBGC lien priority | 4068 (c)(2)-(4)
  Retiree health continuation | 602 (2)(A) | 4980 B(f)(2)(B)(i)
  | 603 (6) | 4980 B(f)(3)(F)
  | 607 (3)(C) | 4980 B(g)(1)(D)
"Basic benefits" | 4001 (a)(6)
  (*see also* Guaranteed benefits (PBGC))
"Beneficiary" | 3 (8)
Benefit liabilities
  Amount of unfunded | 4001 (a)(18)
  Definition | 4001 (a)(16)
  Outstanding amount of | 4001 (a)(19)
Benefit statement | 105
"Bingo game" | | 513 (f) | 1.513-5
Bonding of plan officials | 412 | | | 2509. 75-5
  | | | | 2550. 412-1
  | | | | 2580. 412-1 to -36
  | | | | p2580. 412-33
Bonds, value of | 302 (c)(2)(B) | 412 (c)(2)(B)
"Break in service" | | | | 2530. 200b-4
  Amendment of rules
    Eligibility | | | 1. 410(a)-6
    Vesting | | | 1. 411(a)-9

Note: Regulation references are included for researching convenience. Text of regulations can be found in *ERISA Regulations* (BNA Books, 1994). The prefix **p** indicates a proposed regulation.

	Law		Regulations	
	ERISA	IRC	26 CFR (Treas. Reg.)	29 CFR (DOL, PBGC, EEOC)

"Charitable gift annuity"		502 (m)(5)		
Church plan				
Definition	3 (33)	414 (e)	1.414(e)-1	
Elective deferral limit		402 (g)(2)		
Exclusion from ERISA	4 (b)(2)			
Election to be ERISA plan		410 (d)	1. 410(d)-1	
Health plan continuation,				
exclusion	601 (b)	4980 B(d)(3)		
Life insurance, group-term		79 (d)(7)		
Qualified plans				
Contribution limit		415 (c)(7)		
Correction period for		414 (e)(4)		
Domestic relations orders		414 (p)(9), (11)		
Funding		412 (h)(4)		
Participation		410 (c)(1)(B)	1. 410(d)-1	
Required beginning date		401 (a)(9)(C)		
Survivor annuities				
(last sentence)		401 (a)		
Vesting		411 (e)		
Retirement income accounts		403 (b)(9)		
Section 457 exclusion		457 (e)(13)		
Civil enforcement				
Title I		502		
Annual report, failure to file	502 (c)(2)			2560. 502c-2
				2570. 60 to .88
DOL enforcement request	502(b)(1)(B)			2560. 502-1
Medicare/Medicaid Coverage				
Data Bank information	502(a)(7), (c)(4)			
Prohibited transaction				
penalty (welfare plans)	502 (i)			2560. 502i-1
				2570. 1 to .12
Title IV				
Multiemployer plans	4301			
Single-employer plans	4070			
Claims procedure	503			2560. 503-1
Class-year plan vesting	203 (a)(3)(D)(iv)			411 (a)(3)(D)(iv)
COBRA continuation (*see* Health				
benefits, Continuation of)				
Co-fiduciary liability	405			2509.75-5
Collectible, investment by IRA				
prohibited		408 (m)	p1. 408-10	
Collective bargaining agreement		7701 (a)(46)	301.7701-17T	
Collectively bargained plans				
Accident or health plan				
(self-insured)		105 (h)(3)(B)(iv)	1. 1051(c)(2)(iii)(D)	

Note: Regulation references are included for researching convenience. Text of regulations can be found in *ERISA Regulations* (BNA Books, 1994). The prefix **p** indicates a proposed regulation.

	Law		Regulations	
	ERISA	**IRC**	**26 CFR** **(Treas. Reg.)**	**29 CFR** **(DOL, PBGC, EEOC)**

Compensation—*cont'd*
Limit on
   Deductible remuneration

	ERISA	**IRC**	**26 CFR (Treas. Reg.)**	**29 CFR (DOL, PBGC, EEOC)**
above $1 million		162(m)	p1.162-27	
Qualified plan		401 (a)(17)	1.401(a)(17)-1	
Deductions		404 (l)		
VEBAS		505 (b)(7)		
Property transferred for services		83	1.83-1 to -8	
Self-employed		414 (s)(2)	1.414(s)-1 (f)(1)	

Consultant, plan

	ERISA	**IRC**	**26 CFR**	**29 CFR**
Definition	411 (c)(2)			
Felon prohibited as	411			
"Contributing sponsor"	4001 (a)(13)			
"Contribution base unit"	4001 (a)(11)			

Contributions (*see also*
   Funding standard)
Deduction for (*see* Deductions)

	ERISA	**IRC**	**26 CFR**	**29 CFR**
Discontinuance of		411 (d)(3)		

Employee (*see*
   Employee contributions)
Multiemployer plan (*see also*
   Multiemployer plan, Funding)

	ERISA	**IRC**	**26 CFR**	**29 CFR**
Collection actions	502 (g)(2)			
Obligation to pay	515			

Refund of (*see* Refunds)
Single-employer plans

	ERISA	**IRC**	**26 CFR**	**29 CFR**
Annual payment	302 (c)(10)	412 (c)(10)		
Lien for failure to make	302 (f)	412 (c)(11)		
Quarterly payments	302 (e)	412 (m)		
Timing of	302 (c)(10) 4001 (b)(2)(A)	412 (c)(10)		

Control group
(*see* Controlled group)
Controlled group
Change in
   (*see also* Sale of assets)

	ERISA	**IRC**	**26 CFR**	**29 CFR**
Cash or deferred arrangement		401 (k)(10)	1.401(k)-1(d)(4)	
Qualified plans		401 (a)(26)(F) 410 (b)(6)(C)	1.410(b)-2(f)	
Reportable event (PBGC)				2615.19
Single-employer plan	4069 (b)			
Withdrawal liability	4218 (1)			
Collective net worth	4062 (d)(1)			2622. 4 to .6
Compensation			1.415-2(d)(6)	

Note: Regulation references are included for researching convenience. Text of regulations can be found in *ERISA Regulations* (BNA Books, 1994). The prefix **p** indicates a proposed regulation.

Note: Regulation references are included for researching convenience. Text of regulations can be found in *ERISA Regulations* (BNA Books, 1994). The prefix **p** indicates a proposed regulation.

	Law		Regulations	
	ERISA	**IRC**	**26 CFR** **(Treas. Reg.)**	**29 CFR** **(DOL, PBGC, EEOC)**
"Deficit reduction contribution"	302 (d)(2)	412 (l)(2)		
"Defined benefit plan"	3 (35)	414 (j)		
		415 (k)		
Separate account within		414 (k)		
"Defined contribution plan"	3 (34)	414 (i)		
(*see also* Individual account plan)		415 (k)		
Department store		132 (i)(2)		
Dependent care				
Credit			1. 44A-1 to -4	
"Dependent"		152		
Dependent care assistance programs				
Discrimination		129 (d)(3), (8)		
Exclusion from income		129		
Determination letters (IRS)				
Declaratory judgment		7476		
Disqualifications	3002			
Notice to employees	3001 (a)			
Procedure	3001			
Direct rollover				
(*see* Rollover of distributions)				
Disability insurance				
ERISA exclusion	4 (b)(3)			
"Disabled"		72 (m)(7)		
Disclosure				
(*see also* Reports and returns)				
Alternative compliance	110			
Participants and beneficiaries	101 (a)			2520. 101-1
Benefit statement	105			
	209			
Failure to furnish	502 (c)(1)(B)	6690		
Summary annual report	104 (b)(3)			2520. 104b-10, -12
Summary plan description	102			2520. 102-1 to -5
Written request from	104 (b)(4)			2520. 104b-1, -30
Public				
By DOL	106			
By IRS		6103		
		6104		
Qualification application				
To PBGC		6103 (l)(2)		
To public		6104 (a)(1)(B)		
Discrimination				
Age (*see* Age discrimination)				
Cafeteria plan		125 (b), (c), (g)		p1. 125-1, Q-9 to Q-13

Note: Regulation references are included for researching convenience. Text of regulations can be found in *ERISA Regulations* (BNA Books, 1994). The prefix **p** indicates a proposed regulation.

	Law		**Regulations**	
	ERISA	**IRC**	**26 CFR** **(Treas. Reg.)**	**29 CFR** **(DOL, PBGC, EEOC)**

Disqualified person
  (*see* Party in interest)
Distribution of benefits

Cash or deferred arrangements		401 (k)(2)(B)	1.401(k)-1(d)	
Early distribution, tax on				
Annuity		72 (q)		
Excess deferrals		402 (g)(2)(C)	1. 401(g)-1(e)(8)	
IRA		72 (t)		
Modified endowment contract		72 (v)		
Qualified plan		72 (t)		
Excess distributions, tax on		4980 A		
Lump sums, mandatory	203 (e)	411 (a)(11)		
	204 (d)	411 (a)(7)(B)		
	204 (e)	411 (a)(7)(B)		
Required distributions				
Annuities		72 (s)		
Failure to make		4974	54.4974-1	
			p54.4974-1(d)	
			p54.4974-2	
IRA		408 (a)(6)	p1. 408-8	
		408 (b)(3)		
Qualified plan		401 (a)(9)	p1. 401(a)(9)-1 to -2	
	206	401 (a)(14)		
Section 457 plan		457 (d)		
Tax-deferred annuities		403 (b)(10)-(11)	p1. 403(b)-2	
Spouse's benefits	205 (g)			
Taxation of				
(*see* Taxation of distributions)				
Diversification	404 (a)(1)(C)			2550.404a-(b)(2)(i)
Divorce (*see also* Qualified				
domestic relations order)				
Transfer of options		425 (c)(4)		

-E-

"Earliest retirement age"		417 (f)(3)		
Early retirement subsidies				
Accrual	204 (b)(1)(H)(iv)	411 (b)(1)(H)(iv)		
Reduction of	204 (h)(2)	411 (d)(6)(B)		
"Earned income"				
(self-employed)		401 (c)(2)		
Economically targeted				
investments				2509.94-1
Education or training		127(c)(1)		

Note: Regulation references are included for researching convenience. Text of regulations can be found in *ERISA Regulations* (BNA Books, 1994). The prefix **p** indicates a proposed regulation.

Note: Regulation references are included for researching convenience. Text of regulations can be found in *ERISA Regulations* (BNA Books, 1994). The prefix **p** indicates a proposed regulation.

	Law		Regulations	
	ERISA	**IRC**	**26 CFR** (Treas. Reg.)	**29 CFR** (DOL, PBGC, EEOC)

Employee Stock Ownership Plan (ESOP)—*cont'd*

Interest exclusion, ESOP loan		133	1. 133-1T	
Disposition of stock		4978		
		4978 B		
Reports		6047 (e)		
Leveraged ESOP	408 (b)(3)	4975 (d)(3)		2550. 408b-3
Maximum allocations		415 (c)(6)		
Prohibited transaction				
exemptions	408 (b)(3)	4975 (d)(3)		2550. 408b-3
	408 (e)	4975 (d)(13)		2550. 408c-2
Put option		409 (h)		
		4975 (e)(7)		
Reports		6047 (e)		
Reversion transferred to		4980 (c)(3)		
Disposition by ESOP		4978		
		4978 B		
Sale of stock to				
Nonrecognition of gain		1042		
Spouse's survivor benefits	205 (b)(2)	401 (a)(11)(C)		
Tax credit ESOP				
Cash distribution option		401 (a)(23)		
		409 (h)(2)		
Contribution allocation		409 (b)	1. 46-8(d)(6)	
Deduction for unused credit		404 (i)		
Definition		409 (a)	1. 46-8(b)	
Eligibility/coverage			1. 46-8(e)(3)	
		410 (b)(2)	1.410(b)-7(c)(2)	
Gain or loss on contributed				
securities		409 (m)		
Holding period (84 months)		409 (d)	1. 46-8(d)(9)	
Vesting		409 (c)		
Voting rights			1. 46-8(d)(8)	
Voting rights		133 (b)(7)		
		401 (a)(22)		
		409 (e)		
		4975 (e)(7)		
"Employee welfare benefit plan"	3 (1)			2510. 3-1
(*see also* Welfare benefit plan)				
Employees' beneficiary				
association	3 (4)			
(*see also* Voluntary employees'				
beneficiary association)				
Employer				
(*see also* Controlled group)				
Definition	3 (5)			

Note: Regulation references are included for researching convenience. Text of regulations can be found in *ERISA Regulations* (BNA Books, 1994). The prefix **p** indicates a proposed regulation.

	Law		Regulations	
	ERISA	**IRC**	**26 CFR** **(Treas. Reg.)**	**29 CFR** **(DOL, PBGC, EEOC)**

Excess contributions, tax on		4979	54.4979-1	
Excess deferrals, refund of		401 (k)(8)	1.401(k)-1(f)(4)	
(*see also* Elective deferrals)		402 (g)(2)	1. 402 (g)-1(e)	
			1.415-6(b)(1)(i)	
		4980 A (c)(2)(F)		
Excess distributions, tax on		4981		
Excess retirement accumulations		4980 A (d)		
Exclusive purpose/benefit	404 (a)(1)(A)	401 (a)		
		401 (a)(2)		
Exculpatory provisions	410 (a)			
Exempt organizations				
Agricultural		501 (c)(5)		
		501 (g)		
Amateur sports		501 (c)(3)		
		501 (j)		
Black Lung trust		501 (c)(21)	1.501(c)(21)-1	
Business leagues		501 (c)(6)		
Cemetery companies		501 (c)(13)		
Charity		501 (c)(3)		
Child care		501 (k)		
Civic leagues		501 (c)(4)		
Credit unions		501 (c)(14)		
		501 (l)		
Crop associations		501 (c)(16)		
Educational		501 (c)(3)		
		501 (f)		
Exemption application,				
disclosure of		6104 (a), (c)		
Football league		501 (c)(6)		
Fraternal societies		501 (c)(8)		
		501 (c)(10)		
Group legal services (*see*		501 (c)(20)	**p**1.501(c)(20)-2	
Group legal services plan)				
Holding company		501 (c)(2)		
Real estate		501 (c)(25)		
Hospital service organization		501 (e)		
Insurance associations				
Armed Forces veterans		501 (c)(23)		
Benevolent		501 (c)(12)(A)		
Small		501 (c)(15)		
Insurance provided by		501 (m)		
Labor organizations		501 (c)(5)		
Literary		501 (c)(3)		
Lobbying by		501 (h)		
Mutual telephone companies		501 (c)(12)(B)		

Note: Regulation references are included for researching convenience. Text of regulations can be found in *ERISA Regulations* (BNA Books, 1994). The prefix **p** indicates a proposed regulation.

Note: Regulation references are included for researching convenience. Text of regulations can be found in *ERISA Regulations* (BNA Books, 1994). The prefix **p** indicates a proposed regulation.

	Law		Regulations	
	ERISA	**IRC**	**26 CFR** **(Treas. Reg.)**	**29 CFR** **(DOL, PBGC, EEOC)**

Funding standard

Agency coordination	3002			
Alternative minimum funding standard	305	412 (g)	p1. 412(g)	
Anticipation of benefit increases payable in the future	302(c)(12)	412(c)(12)		
Due date for contributions				
Annual	302 (c)(10)	412 (c)(10)		
Quarterly	302 (e)(3)	412 (m)(3)		
Failure to meet				
Excise tax		4971	54. 4971-1 p54. 4971-1	
Lien	302 (f)	412 (n)		
Notice to participants	101 (d)			
Notice to PBGC	302 (f)(4)	412 (n)(4)		2615.31
Full funding limit				
Deduction limit		404 (a)(1)		
Definition	302 (c)(7)	412 (c)(7)		
Effect on funding	302 (c)(6)	412 (c)(6)		
Multiemployer plan	302 (b)(7)(E)	412 (b)(7)(E)		
Funding standard account	302 (b)	412 (b)		
Interest rates	302 (b)(5)	412 (b)(5)		
Liquidity requirement	302(e)(5)	412((m)(5)		
Required installments (quarterly)	302 (e)	412 (m)		
"Unfunded current liability"	302 (d)(8)(A)	412 (l)(8)(A)		
"Unfunded mortality increase amount"	302(d)(10)	412(l)10)		
Waivers and variances (*see also* Waived funding deficiency)				
Application for, due date of	303 (d)(1)	412 (d)(4)		
Benefit increases	304 (b)	412 (f)		
Extension of amortization periods	304	412 (e)		
Grant of waiver	303	412 (d)		
Interest on	303 (a)(1)	412 (d)(1)		
Notice of	303 (e) 304 (c)	412 (f)(4)		
Security for	306	412 (f)(3)		

	Law		Regulations	
	ERISA	IRC	26 CFR (Treas. Reg.)	29 CFR (DOL, PBGC, EEOC)

-G-

	Law ERISA	IRC	26 CFR (Treas. Reg.)	29 CFR (DOL, PBGC, EEOC)
Garnishment, qualified domestic relations order not	206 (d)(3)(M)			
Golden parachute payments		280G		
Coordination with remuneration limit		162(m)(f)		
Government contracts, study on	3032			
Governmental plan				
Congressional study of	3031			
Definition	3 (32)	414 (d)		
Exclusion of				
Title I	4 (b)(1)			
Title IV	4021 (b)(2)			
Group trust, participation in		401 (a)(24)		
Health plan continuation, tax exclusion		4980 B (d)(2)		
Qualified plans				
Domestic relations order		414 (p)(9), (11)		
Funding		412 (h)(3)		
Participation		410 (c)(1)(A)		
Pick-up of employee contributions		414 (h)(2)		
Police and firefighter plans (*see* Police and firefighter plans)				
Required beginning date		401 (a)(9)(C)		
Survivor annuity (last sentence)		401 (a)		
Top-heavy exception		401 (a)(10)(B)		
Vesting		411 (e)		
"Gross income"	4022 (b)(4)(B)	61	1.61-2 to -21	
"Group health plan"	607 (1)	5000 (b)(1)		
(*see also* Health benefits)				
"Large group health plan"		5000 (b)(2)		
"Nonconforming group health plan"		5000 (c)		
Group legal services plan				
Annual report (IRS)		6039 D		
Discrimination		120 (c) 505	p1. 120-2(c)	
Exclusion from income		120		
Exemption for trust		501 (c)(20)	p1.501(c)(20)-2	
Application required		505 (c)		

Note: Regulation references are included for researching convenience. Text of regulations can be found in *ERISA Regulations* (BNA Books, 1994). The prefix **p** indicates a proposed regulation.

	Law		Regulations	
	ERISA	**IRC**	**26 CFR** **(Treas. Reg.)**	**29 CFR** **(DOL, PBGC, EEOC)**
Group legal services plan—*cont'd*				
"Highly compensated employee"		505 (b)(5)		
Notice to IRS		505 (c)	1. 120-3	
Unrelated business taxable income		512 (a)(3)	1.512(a)-5T	
Written plan requirement		120 (b)	p1. 120-2(b)	
Group-term life insurance				
(*see* Life insurance, group)				
Group trust		401 (a)(24)		
"Guaranteed benefit policy"	401 (b)(2)(B)			
Guaranteed benefits (PBGC)				
Aggregate limit	4022 B			
Multiemployer plans				
Benefit amendments	4022 A(b)			
Insolvent plans	4022 A(a)			
Monthly limit	4022 A(c)			
Nonbasic benefits	4022 A(d)			
Supplemental guarantee	4022 A(g)(2)			
Single-employer plans				Parts 2613, 2621
Benefit amendments	4022 (b)(1)			2621. 5
	4022 (b)(7)			2621. 6 , .7
Disqualified plan	4022 (b)(6)			2621. 8
Monthly limit	4022 (b)(3)			2621. 3, .4, Appendix A
Nonbasic benefits	4022 (c)			
Qualified preretirement survivor annuity	4022 (e)			
Substantial owner	4022 (b)(5)			2621. 7
Gym or athletic facility		132 (i)(4)		

-H-

Hawaii Prepaid Health Care Act	514 (b)(5)			
Health benefits (*see also*				
Welfare benefit plan)				
Account in pension plan (*see*				
also Retiree health account)			1.401(a)(4)-1(c)(14)	
		401 (h)	1.401-14(b)(2)	
Adopted children, coverage required	609(c)			
Cafeteria plan		125 (g)(2)	1. 125-2T p1. 125-1, Q-17	

Note: Regulation references are included for researching convenience. Text of regulations can be found in *ERISA Regulations* (BNA Books, 1994). The prefix **p** indicates a proposed regulation.

	Law		Regulations	
	ERISA	**IRC**	**26 CFR** **(Treas. Reg.)**	**29 CFR** (DOL, PBGC, EEOC)

Health Benefits—*cont'd*
 Medicaid (*see* Medicaid)
 Medicare (*see* Medicare)

New York inpatient care charge		162(n)		
S corporation shareholder		162 (l)(5)		
Self-employed individual		162 (l)		

Highly compensated employee
 Definition

Cafeteria plan		125 (d)		
Cash or deferred arrangement		401 (k)(5)	1.401(k)-1(g)(8)	
Fringe benefits		132 (i)(6)		
Group legal services		505 (b)(5)		
Qualified plans		414 (q)	1.414(q)-1T	
			1.414(q)-1T	
VEBA		505 (b)(5)		

 Discrimination in favor of
  (*see* Discrimination)

Loans to	408 (b)(1)	4975 (d)(1)		2550. 408b-1

"Highly compensated individual"
 Cafeteria plan

Cafeteria plan		125 (e)(2)		
Health benefits (self-insured)		105 (h)(5)	1. 105-11(d)	

"Highly compensated participants"

		125 (e)(1)	p1. 125-1, Q-13	

Hospital services

		513 (e)	1.513-6	

"Hours of service"

	202 (a)(3)(C)	410 (a)(3)(C)		2530. 200b-2, -3

-I-

"Immediate annuity"

		72 (u)(4)		

Incentive stock option
 (*see* Stock option, Incentive)

"Income on the contract"

		72 (u)(2)(A)		

"Independent appraiser"

		401 (a)(28)(C)		

Independent contractors

Deferred compensation, deduction		404 (d)	1. 404(d)-1T	
Nonprofit organizations		457 (e)(12)		

Indicia of ownership outside U.S.

	404 (b)			2550. 404b-1

Individual account plan

Definition	3 (34)	414 (i)		
	4021 (c)(1)			

 Eligible individual account plan

Definition	407 (d)(3)			
Diversification	404 (a)(2)			2550. 404a-1(b)(2)(i)
	407 (a)(2)			
Employer securities	408 (e)			2550. 408e

Note: Regulation references are included for researching convenience. Text of regulations can be found in *ERISA Regulations* (BNA Books, 1994). The prefix **p** indicates a proposed regulation.

	Law		Regulations	
	ERISA	**IRC**	**26 CFR** (Treas. Reg.)	**29 CFR** (DOL, PBGC, EEOC)
"Industry or activity affecting commerce"	3 (12)			
Insurance company				
Guaranteed benefit policy	401 (b)(2)(B)			
Investment manager	3 (38)(B)(iii)			
Plan assets	401 (b)(2)			
Prohibited transaction exemptions				
Insurance company plan	408 (b)(5)	4975 (d)(5)		
Pooled investment fund	408 (b)(8)	4975 (d)(8)		
Report	103 (a)(2)			2520. 103-2, -5
	103 (b)(3)(G)			2520. 103-4, -9
	103 (e)			
Separate account				
Definition	3 (17)			
Plan assets	401 (b)(2)(B)			
Report	103 (a)(2), (b)(3)			2520. 103-4
Insurance contract plan	301 (b)	412 (i)		
Insurance salesman, as employee		7701 (a)(20)		
"Insurer"	401 (b)(2)(A)			
Integration with Social Security (*see* Social Security integration)				
Interference				
Coercive interference	511			
Rights protected by ERISA	510			
Inurement of plan assets	403 (c)	401 (a)(2)		
Investigative authority, DOL	504			
Investment company, registered				
Definition	3 (38)(B)(i)			
Fiduciary status	3 (21)(B)			
Plan assets	401 (b)(1)			
Investment manager				
Appointment	402 (c)(3)			2509.75-5
	403 (a)(2)			2550. 403a-(c)(2)
	405 (d)(1)			
Definition	3 (38)			2509.75-5
Investment policy				2509.94-2
Liability of other fiduciary	405 (d)			2509.75-8
Proxy voting guidelines				2509.94-2

-J-

	Law		Regulations	
Joint and survivor annuity (*see* Spouse's benefits)				
Joint Board for the Enrollment of Actuaries	3041			

	Law		Regulations	
	ERISA	**IRC**	**26 CFR** **(Treas. Reg.)**	**29 CFR** **(DOL, PBGC, EEOC)**

Note: Regulation references are included for researching convenience. Text of regulations can be found in *ERISA Regulations* (BNA Books, 1994). The prefix **p** indicates a proposed regulation.

Note: Regulation references are included for researching convenience. Text of regulations can be found in *ERISA Regulations* (BNA Books, 1994). The prefix **p** indicates a proposed regulation.

Note: Regulation references are included for researching convenience. Text of regulations can be found in *ERISA Regulations* (BNA Books, 1994). The prefix **p** indicates a proposed regulation.

	Law		Regulations	
	ERISA	**IRC**	**26 CFR** **(Treas. Reg.)**	**29 CFR** **(DOL, PBGC, EEOC)**
Multiple employer plan				
Participation, vesting, funding	210 (b)	413 (c)		2530. 210-210
Substantial employer				
Liability of	4063			
Notice of	4066			
Withdrawal of	4063			
Termination of	4064			
Multiple employer trust				
(*see* Multiple employer welfare				
arrangement)				
Multiple employer welfare				
arrangement				
Definition	3 (40)			
Preemption, exception from	514 (b)(6)			
Mutual fund (*see* Investment				
company, registered)				

-N-

	Law		Regulations	
"Named fiduciary"	402 (a)(2)			2509.75-5
Net operating loss deduction,				
employee contributions		72 (b)(3)		
"Net premiums"		72 (u)(2)(B)		
Net unrealized appreciation				
(*see* Employer securities,				
Net unrealized appreciaiton)				
"No-additional-cost service"		132 (b)		
"Non-basic benefits" (*see also*				
Guaranteed benefits (PBGC)	4001 (a)(7)			
"Nonconforming group health plan"			5000 (c)	
Nondeductible contributions		408 (o)		
		4972		
		6693 (b)(1)		
"Nonforfeitable"				
(*see also* Vesting)	3 (19)			
"Nonforfeitable benefit"	4001 (a)(8)			
"Non-key employee"		416 (i)(2)		
Nonresident aliens				
(*see* Aliens, nonresident)				
"Nonvested participant"				
Participation break in service	202 (b)(4)	410 (a)(5)(D)	1. 410 (a)-5(c)(4)	
Vesting break in service	203 (b)(3)(D)	411 (a)(6)(D)		2530. 203-2(d)

Note: Regulation references are included for researching convenience. Text of regulations can be found in *ERISA Regulations* (BNA Books, 1994). The prefix **p** indicates a proposed regulation.

	Law		Regulations	
	ERISA	**IRC**	**26 CFR** **(Treas. Reg.)**	**29 CFR** **(DOL, PBGC, EEOC)**

Note: Regulation references are included for researching convenience. Text of regulations can be found in *ERISA Regulations* (BNA Books, 1994). The prefix **p** indicates a proposed regulation.

Note: Regulation references are included for researching convenience. Text of regulations can be found in *ERISA Regulations* (BNA Books, 1994). The prefix **p** indicates a proposed regulation.

-Q-

Note: Regulation references are included for researching convenience. Text of regulations can be found in *ERISA Regulations* (BNA Books, 1994). The prefix **p** indicates a proposed regulation.

	Law		Regulations	
	ERISA	IRC	26 CFR (Treas. Reg.)	29 CFR (DOL, PBGC, EEOC)

	Law		**Regulations**	
	ERISA	**IRC**	**26 CFR** **(Treas. Reg.)**	**29 CFR** **(DOL, PBGC, EEOC)**

Note: Regulation references are included for researching convenience. Text of regulations can be found in *ERISA Regulations* (BNA Books, 1994). The prefix **p** indicates a proposed regulation.

	Law		Regulations	
	ERISA	**IRC**	**26 CFR** **(Treas. Reg.)**	**29 CFR** **(DOL, PBGC, EEOC)**

Reports and returns to—*cont'd*
IRS—*cont'd*

Multiemployer welfare plan		6039 D (d)(3)		
Nondeductible IRA contribution		408 (o)(4)		
		6923 (b)		
Owner-employee,				
plan covering		6047		
		6704		
Participant				
IRA		219 (f)(4)		
		6652 (g)		
Rollover		402 (f)	1. 402 (f)-1	
		6652 (i)		
Separated participant		6057 (e)		
		6690		
Pension Benefit Guaranty Corp.				
Annual report	4065			Part 2611
Failure to make contributions	302 (f)(4)			
Penalty, failure to file	4071			
Reportable events	4043			Part 2615
"Required beginning date"		401 (a)(9)(C)		
Retiree health account		401 (h)	1.401-14(b)(2)	
Reserve limits		419 A(e)		
Transfer of pension assets to		420		
Notice of	101 (e)			
Penalty for failure				
to give notice	502 (c)(1), (3)			
Prohibited transaction				
exemption	408 (b)(13)	4975 (d)(13)		
"Qualified transfer"		420 (b)		
Reversion tax, exemption		420 (a)(3)		
Retiree medical or life benefits				
Reserve limits		419 A(e)		
UMWA plans		9701 -9722		
Retirement bonds [repealed]			1. 409-1	
			p1. 409-1	
Retroactive plan amendments		401 (b)		
Reduction of benefits	204 (g)	411 (d)(6)		
	302 (c)(8)	412 (c)(8)		
Reversion of surplus assets				
(*see also* Retiree health account,				
Transfer of pension assets to)				
Excise tax on		4980		

-S-

Note: Regulation references are included for researching convenience. Text of regulations can be found in *ERISA Regulations* (BNA Books, 1994). The prefix **p** indicates a proposed regulation.

	Law		Regulations	
	ERISA	**IRC**	**26 CFR** **(Treas. Reg.)**	**29 CFR** (DOL, PBGC, EEOC)

Sale of assets—*cont'd*

Withdrawal liability	4204			2640. 5
				Part 2643
	4225 (a)			

Scholarships (*see also*
   Education or training)

Taxation		117	1.117-1 to -5	
Seasonal industry				
Guidelines withdrawn				2509.76-2, -3
Service for participation	202 (a)(3)(B)	410 (a)(3)(B)		
Service for vesting	203 (b)(2)(C)	411 (a)(5)(C)	1. 410 (a)-5(b)	
Year of participation	204 (b)(3)(D)	411 (b)(4)(D)		
"Secretary" (Title I)	3 (13)			
"Secretary of Treasury"	4001 (b)(2)(B)			
"Securities acquisition loan"		133 (b)		
Securities loans				
Exclusion from acquisition				
indebtedness		514 (c)(8)	1.514(c)-1	
Exclusion from UBTI		512 (b)	1.512(b)-1	
Payments with respect to, defined		512 (a)(5)		
"Security"	3 (20)			
Self-employed individuals				
(*see also* Owner-employees)				
Cash or deferred arrangements,				
partnership			1.401(k)-1(a)(6)	
Compensation		414 (s)(2)		
Custodial accounts	403 (b)(3)	401 (f)		2550. 403b-1(a)(3)(i)
Deduction limits				
Health insurance		162 (l)		
Qualified plan		404 (a)(8)	1. 404(a)(8)-1T	
		404 (e)	1. 404(e)-1, -1A	
Definition		401 (c)(1)(B)		
Dependent care assistance		129 (e)(3)		
Earned income of		401 (c)(2)		
		404 (a)(8)(B)	1. 404(e)-1(h)(3)	
			1. 404(e)-1A(i)(3)	
		416 (i)(3)(B)		
Educational assistance program		127 (c)(2)		
Fishermen		401 (c)(6)		
Group legal services plan		120 (d)(1)	p1. 120-2(f)(2)(ii)	
			p1. 120-2(i)(1)(iii)	
Health benefits				
COBRA continuation	607 (2)	4980 B (f)(7)		
Deduction		162 (l)		
Nonemployee status		105 (g)		

Note: Regulation references are included for researching convenience. Text of regulations can be found in *ERISA Regulations* (BNA Books, 1994). The prefix **p** indicates a proposed regulation.

	Law		Regulations	
	ERISA	**IRC**	**26 CFR** **(Treas. Reg.)**	**29 CFR** **(DOL, PBGC, EEOC)**

Note: Regulation references are included for researching convenience. Text of regulations can be found in *ERISA Regulations* (BNA Books, 1994). The prefix **p** indicates a proposed regulation.

Note: Regulation references are included for researching convenience. Text of regulations can be found in *ERISA Regulations* (BNA Books, 1994). The prefix **p** indicates a proposed regulation.

	Law		Regulations	
	ERISA	**IRC**	**26 CFR** **(Treas. Reg.)**	**29 CFR** **(DOL, PBGC, EEOC)**

Termination —pension plan

Allocation of assets	403 (d)			
	4044 (a)			Part 2618, 2619
Annuity contracts, purchase of	502(a)(9)			
Cessation of operations	4062(e)			
Discrimination	4044 (b)(4)			2618. 17(d)
Civil actions				
Multiemployer plan	4301			
Single-employer plan	4070			
Multiemployer plan				
Amendment ceasing accruals	4041 A(a)(1)			
Benefit reductions	4281			
Conversion to defined contribution plan	4041 A(a)(3)			
Date of	4041 A(b)			
	4048 (b)			
Definition of termination	4041 A			
Financial assistance (PBGC)	301 (d)	412 (k)		
	4261			
	4281 (d)			
Funding	301 (c)	412 (j)		
	4041 A(e)			
Lump sum distributions from	4041 A(f)(1)			
Mass withdrawal	4041 A(a)(2)			
Payment of benefits after	4041 A(c), (f)			
Multiple employer plan	4064			
Partial termination	4062 (e)	411 (d)(3)		
Recapture of benefit payments	4045			
Single-employer plan				
Collectively bargained	4041 (a)(3)			
Conversion to defined contribution plan	4041 (e)			
Date of	4048 (a)			
Distress termination	4041 (c)			Part 2616
Early termination (high-25)	203 (c)(2)	411 (d)(2)	1.401(a)(4)-5(b)	
Funding waivers or deficiencies	4062 (c)			
Involuntary (by PBGC)	4042			
Liability to PBGC	4062 (b)			Part 2617
Missing paricipants	4050			

Notices (*see* Notices, Distress
    termination; and Notices,
    Standard termination)				

Qualified replacement plan	404 (d)(1)	4980 (d)		
Recoupment of overpayments				Part 2623

Note: Regulation references are included for researching convenience. Text of regulations can be found in *ERISA Regulations* (BNA Books, 1994). The prefix **p** indicates a proposed regulation.

	Law		Regulations	
	ERISA	**IRC**	**26 CFR** **(Treas. Reg.)**	**29 CFR** **(DOL, PBGC, EEOC)**
"Unfunded guaranteed benefits"	4001 (a)(17)			
"Unfunded new liability amount"	302 (d)(4)	412 (l)(4)		
"Unfunded old liability amount"	302 (d)(3)	412 (l)(3)		
"Unfunded vested benefits"				
PBGC variable rate premium				2610.23
				p2610.23
Withdrawal liability	4213(c)			2640.4
Mass Withdrawal				2640.7
Uniformed Services Retirement				
Pay, Reduced		122		
United Mine Workers Fund				
Deduction for contribution to		404 (c)	1. 404(c)-1	
Health benefits		9701-9722		
Survivor benefits, 1950 Fund	205 (b)(3)	401 (a)(11)(E)		
Withdrawal from (*see* Withdrawal				
—multiemployer plan)				
"Unpredictable contingent event				
amount"**	302 (d)(5)	412 (l)(5)		
"Unpredictable contingent event				
benefit"**	302 (d)(7)(B)(ii)		412 (l)(7)(B)(ii)	
"Unrecovered investment"		72 (b)(4)		
Unrelated business taxable income				
Debt-financed income		512 (b)(4)		
		514	1.514(a)-(e)	
Definition of		512	1.512(a)-1	
Exclusions from		512 (b)	1.512(b)-1	
Partnerships				
Allocations		514 (c)(9)(E)	1.514(e)-1	
Debt-financed real property		514 (c)(9)(B)(vi)		
Income of		512 (c)	1.512(c)-1	
Publicly traded partnerships		512 (c)(2)		
Tax on		501 (b)		
		511	1.511-1 to -4	
"Unrelated trade or business"		513	1.513-1 to -2	
Unrelated party				
Definition	4204 (d)			
Sale of assets to	4204			
	4225 (a)			
"Unrelated trade or business"		513	1.513-1 to -2	
(*see also* Unrelated business				
taxable income)				

Note: Regulation references are included for researching convenience. Text of regulations can be found in *ERISA Regulations* (BNA Books, 1994). The prefix **p** indicates a proposed regulation.

| | Law | | Regulations | |
	ERISA	IRC	26 CFR (Treas. Reg.)	29 CFR (DOL, PBGC, EEOC)

Vesting—*cont'd*

| | Law | | Regulations | |
	ERISA	IRC	26 CFR (Treas. Reg.)	29 CFR (DOL, PBGC, EEOC)
Tax-credit ESOP		409 (c)		
Termination of plan		411 (d)(3)		
Top-heavy		416 (b)		
Variance from, temporary	207 1012			
"Year of service"	203 (b)(2)	411 (a)(5)		
Veterans' organization				
Exemption of		501 (c)(19), (23)		
Unrelated business taxable income		512 (a)(4)	1.512(a)-4	
Voluntary employees' beneficiary association (VEBA) (*see also* Welfare benefit plan, Funded)				
Discrimination		505 (b)		
Employee-pay-all plan		419 A(f)(5)		
Exemption from tax		501 (c)(9)	1.501(c)(9)-1 to -8	
Application required		505 (c)		
Geographic locale restriction			p1.501(c)(9)-2(d)	
Requirements for		505		
Notice to IRS		505 (c)		
Unrelated business taxable income		512 (a)(3)	1.512(a)-5T	

- W -

| | Law | | Regulations | |
	ERISA	IRC	26 CFR (Treas. Reg.)	29 CFR (DOL, PBGC, EEOC)
"Wages"		3121 (a)		
Waived funding deficiency (*see also* Funding standard)				
Amortization	302 (b)(2)(C)	412 (b)(2)(C)		
Credit for	302 (b)(3)(C)	412 (b)(3)(C)		
Definition	303 (c)	412 (d)(3)		
Security for	306	412 (f)(3)		
Welfare and Pension Plans Disclosure Act, repeal of	111			
"Welfare benefit"		419 (e)(2)		
"Welfare benefit fund"		419 (e)(1)		
"Fund"		419 (e)(3)		
Welfare benefit plan				
Controlled group		414 (t)		
Definition	3 (1)			2510.3-1
Exceptions				2510.3-1(b)-(k)
Financial statement	103 (b)			2520.103-1, -2

| | Law | | Regulations | |
	ERISA	IRC	26 CFR (Treas. Reg.)	29 CFR (DOL, PBGC, EEOC)

Funded (*see also*
  Voluntary employees'
  beneficiary association)				

Actuarial certification		419 A(c)(5)		
Collectively bargained		419 A(f)(5)		
Deduction limit		419 (b)		
Discrimination		505 (b)		
Independent contractors		419 (g)		
Limitation on additions to		419 A		
Method having effect of plan		419 (f)		
Qualified asset account		419 A		
Tax on disqualified benefits		4976		
Unrelated business tax		419 A(g)		
Multiple employer (*see* Multiple employer welfare arrangement)				
Payroll practices exception				2510.3-1(b)
Reports (*see* Reports and returns)				
Termination of	403 (d)(2)			
Withdrawal—multiemployer plan				
Amendments relating to				
Notice to employers	4214 (b)			
PBGC approval of	4220			Part 2677
Retroactive effect	4214 (a)			
Arbitration of disputes	4221			2640. 3 Part 2641
Building, construction industry				
Complete withdrawal	4203 (b)			
Free look rule	4210 (b)(1)			
Partial withdrawal	4208 (d)(1)			
Cessation before effective date	4217			
Complete withdrawal	4203			
Abatement	4207			2640. 6 Part 2647 pPart 2647
Building and construction	4203 (b)			
Date of	4203 (e)			
Entertainment industry	4203 (c)			
Resumption of operations	4207			2640. 6 Part 2647
Sale of assets	4204			2640. 5 Part 2643
Special rules, PBGC approval	4203 (f)			Part 2645
Trucking industry	4203 (d)			
Corporate reorganization	4218 (1)			
Default	4219 (c)(5)			2644. 2(b)

Note: Regulation references are included for researching convenience. Text of regulations can be found in *ERISA Regulations* (BNA Books, 1994). The prefix **p** indicates a proposed regulation.

| | Law | | Regulations | |
	ERISA	IRC	26 CFR (Treas. Reg.)	29 CFR (DOL, PBGC, EEOC)

Withdrawal—multiemployer plan—*cont'd*

De minimis reduction	4209			
United Mineworkers Fund	4211 (d)(2)			
Disputes, arbitration of	4221			2640. 3
				Part 2641
Free look rule	4210			
Labor dispute	4218 (2)			
Liability				
Actuarial assumptions	4213			
Allocation methods	4211			2640. 4
				Part 2642
Calculation of	4201 (b)			
Civil actions	4301			
Collection of	4202			
	4219			Part 2644
Deduction for		404 (g)	1. 404(g)-1	
De minimis reduction	4209			
Evade or avoid	4212 (c)			
Information, request for	4221 (e)			
Insolvency	4225 (b), (d)			
Merged plans, withdrawal from				2642.21-.27
Notice of	4202			
	4219			Part 2644
Outstanding claim for	4001 (a)(12)			
Partial withdrawal	4206			
Payment of	4001 (b)(2)(A)			
	4219 (c)			Part 2644
	4221 (d)			
Payments as contributions	302 (b)(7)	412 (b)(7)		
Penalty, failure to give notice	4302			
Refunds (*see* Refunds)				
Sale of assets	4204			2640. 5
				Part 2643
	4225 (a)			
Sole proprietor	4225 (c)			
Mass withdrawal				
Benefit reductions	4041 A (d)			
	4281			
Building and construction	4203 (b)(3)			
De minimis reduction	4209 (c)-(d)			2640. 7
				Part 2648
Redetermination of liability	4219 (c)(1)(D)			2640. 7
				Part 2648
Termination	4041 A (a)(2)			
United Mineworkers Fund	4216 (a)(2)			

	Law		Regulations	
	ERISA	**IRC**	**26 CFR** **(Treas. Reg.)**	**29 CFR** **(DOL, PBGC, EEOC)**
Notification of significant withdrawals	4215			
"Obligation to contribute"	4212 (a)			
Partial withdrawal				
Abatement	4208			Part 2646
Building and construction	4208 (d)(1)			
Definition of	4205			
Liability, adjustment for	4206			
Reduction of	4208			Part 2646
Retail food industry	4205 (c)			
Subsequent withdrawal				Part 2649
United Mineworkers Fund	4205 (d)			
Prohibited transaction exemption	408 (b)(10) 4219 (d)	4975 (d)(14)		
Sale of assets				
Limitation on liability	4225 (a) 4225 (e)			
Purchaser's liability	4204 (b)(1)			
Seller's secondary liability	4204 (a)(1)(C) 4204 (a)(2)			
United Mine Workers Fund	4211 (d)(2)			
"Unrelated party"	4204 (d)			
Variances, PBGC	4204 (c)		2640. 5 Part 2643	
Withdrawal as result of	4204 (a)			
Service of process	4301 (d)			
Statute of limitations	4301 (f)			
Succesor employer	4218			
Uncollectible withdrawal liability supplemental program	4222			
United Mine Workers Fund				
Allocation of liability	4211 (d)(1)			
De minimis reduction	4211 (d)(2)			
Mass withdrawal	4216 (a)(2)			
Payment schedule	4216 (a)			
Sale of assets	4211 (d)(2)			
20-year cap	4211 (d)(2)			
Withdrawal liability payment fund	4223			
Deduction		194 A		
Exemption		501 (c)(22)		
Withdrawal from **multiple employer plan**	4063			

Note: Regulation references are included for researching convenience. Text of regulations can be found in *ERISA Regulations* (BNA Books, 1994). The prefix **p** indicates a proposed regulation.

	Law		Regulations	
	ERISA	IRC	26 CFR (Treas. Reg.)	29 CFR (DOL, PBGC, EEOC)

Withdrawal of
 employee contributions 206 (c)   401 (a)(19)
                          203 (a)(3)(D) 411 (a)(3)(D)

Withholding
 Eligible rollover distributions   3405   31.3405(c)-1T
 Pension payments   3405
"Working condition fringe"   132 (d)
Workmen's compensation
 Coverage execption, Title I   4 (b)(3)
 Exclusion from income   104(a)(1)
Written plan
 Compliance with   404 (a)(1)(D)
 Required
  Cafeteria plans   125 (d)(1)   p1. 125-1, Q-3
  Dependent care assistance plan   129 (d)(1)
  Educational assistance program   127 (b)(1)
  Employee benefit plans   402 (a)(1)

-Y-

	ERISA	IRC	26 CFR	29 CFR
"Year of credited service"	4022 A(c)(4)			
"Year of participation"	204 (b)(4)	411 (b)(4)		2530. 204-1, -4
"Year of service"				2530. 200b-1
Eligibility to participate	202 (a)(3)	410 (a)(3)	1. 410(a)-5(a)	2530. 202 -2
Equivalencies				2530. 200b-3(c)-(f)
Tax-deferred annuity		403 (b)(4)	1. 403(b)-1(f)	
Vesting	203 (b)(2)	411 (a)(5)	1. 411(a)-6(a)	2530. 203-2